W9-BWG-921

International Encyclopedia of the SOCIAL SCIENCES

International Encyclopedia of the SOCIAL SCIENCES

DAVID L. SILLS EDITOR

VOLUME 7

The Macmillan Company & The Free Press

LIBRARY OF CONGRESS CATALOG NUMBER 68–10023

MANUFACTURED IN THE UNITED STATES OF AMERICA

International Encyclopedia of the SOCIAL SCIENCES

[CONTINUED]

HUMOR

Few behavioral phenomena present as many paradoxical contrasts as does humor. To one person a joke may be explosively funny while to another it may be disgusting or even horrifying. Understanding a joke is an intellectual achievement, yet reflective thought destroys the humor. A joke may be nonsensical and yet contain a profound truth. A witty remark or laughter can express either friendliness and affection or derision and hostility. Indeed, unrestrained laughter may signify either madness or good mental health. Perhaps the most dramatic of the contrasts are the attitudes of thoughtful men concerning humor: for some, like Freud (1905) and Grotjahn (1957), humor is liberating, ennobling, and a creative force, whereas for others, like Plato (*Philebus*), humor brings out the ugly and the destructive, degrading art, religion, and morals, and therefore should be avoided by civilized man.

Modern theory. Partly because of these protean qualities, humor has been a favorite topic of discourse among philosophers and writers, but it has evoked little serious attention from behavioral scientists as an area worthy of research or theory. There are undoubtedly numerous reasons for this lack of scientific interest in humor, but they are unrelated to its significance in human affairs and its possible contribution to general behavior theory. Behavioral theorists until recently have paid little attention to activities like humor and play, which are not clearly goal directed and which do not fit easily into the usual motivational models of drive reduction or need deprivation. Although this narrow view of motivation is now considered by many as untenable, emphasis on the negative or deprival motives for behavior persists.

White (1963) has attempted to take a more positive position toward motivation by postulating a primary drive: the striving for competence or mastery. This drive, which he calls "effectance," motivates the organism to explore, manipulate, be curious, play, and enjoy humor. Such a view is consistent with the many theories of humor that emphasize superiority, triumph, self-glory, mastery, and release of surplus energy. Whether or not this broad concept of effectance will prove useful remains to be seen. There is some danger that it is too inclusive in its attempt to place many diverse activities under a single rubric. However, it is clear that a further delineation of a motivational basis for self-rewarding activities continues to be needed.

The work of Berlyne (1960) typifies the attempt to apply a modified and more sophisticated version of drive reduction theory to activities like curiosity, exploration, play, and humor. He proposes that humor springs from an "arousal jag" that arises with the experience of threat, discomfort, uncertainty, or surprise, and then is followed by an event that indicates safety, readjustment, clarification, or release. To Berlyne the arousal involved in humor is not a psychological state but a neurophysiological one, denoting preparatory behaviors in the nervous system. While the language is different, the view is a familiar one, best expressed by Immanuel Kant (1790), who defined humor as "an affection arising from a strained expectation being suddenly reduced to nothing." Thus to Berlyne and Kant, sudden relief from tension is the key to all humor.

There is little question that laughter will erupt

in situations in which there is a sudden relief from anxiety or tension or when the individual aroused in preparation for threat suddenly finds he can relax. But must all situations evoking laughter be fit into this schema? We find, for example, experimental demonstration in the studies of Milgram (1963) that laughter will occur as anxiety is elevated, not reduced. He found that smiling and laughter with occasional convulsive outbursts regularly occurred under conditions of extreme tension in which normal subjects were ordered to administer what they thought was increasingly severe punishment to a supposed victim in the context of a learning experiment. As long as we do not fully understand the essential relationships between the various aspects of humor, for example, anxiety, aggression, surprise, and incongruity, neobehavioral models, even if couched in neurophysiological terms, will be of little help.

The protean character of humor. Humor remains a paradox only so long as one sees it as a simple behavioral process having a single meaning or function, involving a unitary class of stimuli which evoke a linear intensity scale of responses ranging from a faint smile to convulsive laughter. Phenomenologically, we know that this is not so. We know that smiling and laughing may have many meanings. Humor plays a myriad of roles and functions. We also know that the same joke may be enjoyed for different reasons, some of which may be minimally related to the joke's intent. Studies have found repeatedly that although the intended point of a cartoon was missed, subjects thought the cartoon was funny and attributed the funniness to some tangential detail. Psychotic patients often reacted in this manner; a severely schizophrenic young man laughed at a cartoon by Steinberg portraying a man aiming a gun at an apple on top of his head and remarked, "The guy's nuts. Why does he have to pop a perfectly good apple? I guess it's a McIntosh and he should eat it" (Redlich et al. 1951). In a recent study, children in grades two through five were often unable to comprehend the joke in a cartoon but they would focus on some detail and react as though this detail made the cartoon funny.

The importance of cognition. The fact that the schizophrenic patient missed the allusion to William Tell shows the importance of cognitive processes in the appreciation of humor. Appreciating a joke means that we are able to master the symbolic properties with their multiple figurative and allegorical referents; it is not unlike solving a complex problem. It is the sudden discovery achieved by the reshuffling of these symbols into a surprisingly new relationship which contributes to the pleasure in the joke, a fact thoroughly analyzed by Freud (1905). Part of the mild fun in the *double-entendre* ("gland: the only thing secretive about a woman" or "man refuses to give up biting dog") lies in grasping the two meanings. Man enjoys using his mental powers by solving puzzles or problems, inventing things, appreciating jokes, or decoding mysteries.

But the pleasure in humor is more than the exercise of cognitive functions, although there are philosophers who insist that the essence of comic laughter lies in man's use of his logical powers (Swabey 1961). Actually, an allusion or a double meaning is not the only way of making a joke, but it is plainly one of a number of techniques which can contribute to its structure. Other devices like incongruity, nonsense, condensation, plays on words, and exaggeration are all cognitive functions which make up the joke façade. As Freud (1905) pointed out, these same techniques make up dreams as well as jokes and are characteristic of the primitive modes of childhood thinking.

Regression in the service of the ego. Humor, then, like dreams, may be seen as a regression to infantile forms of thinking and acting, and it is partly the momentary freedom from the restraints of logical and realistic thinking that is gratifying. Freud concluded that humor involves a partial regression which is controlled by the ego and is in its service for pleasure rather than for defense. Kris (1952) has elaborated on this notion of "regression in the service of the ego," applying it particularly to the creative process. Recent interest in creativity has further pointed up this relationship with regression. The likelihood that the creative process utilizes more primitive and unregulated forms of thinking has been suggested by a number of investigators. Barron (1957), for example, has shown in a number of studies of the creative personality that originality is associated with the ability to regress. Wild (1962) found that a group of creative art students was able to shift more easily into primitive and unregulated modes of thought than other groups and derived more pleasure from this shift. The notion of adaptive regression as a basic condition in humor and the creative process is proving fruitful to theory and research.

Freud saw the regression in humor, as in dreams, play, and in literature, as a functionally adaptive mode of withdrawal from reality into a self-made world. The importance to adaptive ego functioning of the capacity to withdraw voluntarily from reality into an imaginary world can be seen in such eagerly pursued pleasures as play, sports, humor, sleep, intoxicated states, and literature. Psychodynamically, neuroses and psychoses represent similar regressive detachment from reality, but they are pathological and involuntary: they do not function for ego gratification but are attempts to cope with conflict and anxiety.

The humor illusion. One can conceptualize the enjoyment of humor as resting on the participation in the humor illusion, where the rules of logic, time, place, reality, and proper conduct are suspended. The make-believe world of the humor illusion is analogous to that found in art—the aesthetic illusion (Kris 1952)—in play, games, and literature, where the metacommunication "this is for fun" gives license to share in the disregard for reality and propriety. Aggression, obscenity, and nonsense are for the moment permissible. From the clumsy pratfalls and antics of the clown to the comedy on television, the sharing of the comic illusion liberates the audience from the procrustean demands of reality [*see* AESTHETICS; FANTASY].

By the achievement of these self-controlled illusions, man is able to soar with his imagination far beyond the confines of reality, whether in the form of a comedy, a novel, a poem, a dream, a painting, or a sculpture. These expressions of imagination may all be based upon common motivational forces and universal fantasies, but, as Freud postulated, their form and language are different.

The psychoanalytic theory. From the psychoanalytic viewpoint, then, humor gives pleasure in two independent ways:

(1) Joke *techniques* "aim at deriving pleasure from mental processes" and permit regression to infantile modes of thinking, feeling, and acting. The momentary relief from the need to be logical, rational, moral, and realistic is gratifying. Freud ingeniously demonstrated this source of pleasure by translating jokes into everyday language, thereby destroying the humor.

(2) The hostile or sexual *purpose* of humorous stimuli is gratifying because prohibited wishes originating in the unconscious are momentarily permitted release. The anxiety which normally accompanies the expression of these impulses is reduced or made superfluous by the structural characteristics of the joke that disguise or mitigate the impulse. Humor is consummately a social process and as a shared experience originating with someone else facilitates the regression and further alleviates the anxiety.

Thus, the joke serves as a disguise for the forbidden wish that slips through with little critical scrutiny. In fact, reflection penetrates the disguise and destroys the humor: explaining a joke spoils it. There appears to be some experimental evidence which suggests that during the appreciation of a joke or a cartoon critical judgment and realistic thinking are weakened. In a recent study it was found that college students judged aggressive humor significantly less aggressive while they were enjoying it as humor than when they judged it some time later for aggressive content.

The psychogenesis of humor. It should not be inferred that cognition is assumed to be inherently antithetical to humor, for clearly cognition not only is the mediator of this complex psychological process but also contributes to the pleasure. Understanding a joke is a challenge, and "solving" it is a source of satisfaction. Thus, when jokes are too obvious, they lose their punch. It has been found that as children developed intellectually, their enjoyment of humor depended upon increasingly more difficult jokes. Cartoons which made fewer cognitive demands were considered to be less funny than those which were more of a challenge to comprehension. With cognitive and language growth new and more complex modes of humor expression appear, particularly as symbols and words are elaborated and extended. There is thus an apparent error in conceptualizing sophisticated comedy and satire in the same manner as the stimuli that evoke the baby's first smiles. Indeed, little has been done to trace the development of humor from the earliest manifestations to the extremely complex social phenomena we encounter in adulthood.

Smiling and its development. As one of the earliest recognizable responses of the newborn infant, the smile has been identified as being in the beginning an innate reaction to pleasurable tactile and organic stimulation. Although the course of humor development has been a much-neglected area, the investigation of the baby's smile has been most intensively pursued. This great interest in these first expressions of pleasure no doubt springs from the recognition that they usher in the social development of the child and demonstrate the fundamental principles and processes of man's psychological growth. Spitz considers the appearance of the smiling response as the beginning of the organization of the ego, with the inception of thinking, reality testing, and object relations (Spitz 1959; Spitz & Wolf 1946). The adequate stimulus and the expressive meaning of the early smiling responses have challenged many investigators, no doubt because they are the harbingers of all the sociopsychological processes and affects that characterize the adult.

If scientists are in a quandary about the meaning of the baby's first smile, most mothers are not and attribute the smile to the child's sociability. Notwithstanding mothers' protests, however, the very first smiles may well be, as Schneirla (see Conference . . . 1955) maintains, nonspecific facial responses to low intensity introceptive stimulation, e.g., gas. However, the importance of the configuration of the human face as the adequate stimulus for the early smile has been amply shown by many investigators (for example, Spitz 1959). After the fifth month only familiar faces are adequate. There is consensus that the development of smiling is a paradigm of the social development of the child. The emotional contact and interaction inherent in the smile is an intrinsic and vital factor in all communication [*see* INFANCY].

Laughter and its development. The ontogenesis of laughter differs from that of smiling, most notably because laughter retains some characteristics of a partially involuntary convulsive reaction. That laughter never becomes fully controllable is evidenced by the fact that deliberate effort to restrain it only enhances the disposition to laugh. Furthermore, laughter is most easily evoked when ego control is impaired, as in intoxicated states, and when the brain has been damaged. Cases of pathological involuntary or forced laughing under the slightest stimulation are numerous in the neurological literature. Initially, the infant laughs in response to rhythmic and unexpected movement, later to tickling, and eventually to teasing situations like the game of peekaboo. According to Jacobson (1946), where the laughter-producing stimulus is most simple and primitive, the laughter is more expressive only of "pure uncontrolled motor pleasure." With growth, laughter becomes a social response integrated into the dialect of affective communication. But the sudden relief from great tension remains capable of eliciting laughter. Laughter differs from smiling not only in the intensity of the pleasurable affect expressed by much of the body but as a social response as well. Generally, the individual, by laughing, shows that he is caught up emotionally in the social situation, whereas, with a smile, he communicates a greater detachment and ego control. Cultural and social factors, too, seem to play a more significant role in the expressive style of laughter.

Humor as affective communication. But it is to be noted that both smiling and laughter, in all their expressive variety, transcend cultures and ontogenetic development as affective communication. These two types of expression are among the most primitive and basic interactions between people. Furthermore, we see that affects, including humor, are more effectively communicated by expressive movements, facial expression, and gestures than by language.

It is as humor that smiling and laughing not only communicate many diverse emotions but contribute to their mastery as well. But this mastery is not always successful, as is evidenced by ubiquitous experiences of displeasure and disgust to some humor. Kris (1952) has called this quality of humor its "double-edged" character. Responses to humor of displeasure and anxiety rather than of pleasure are most readily seen in psychiatric patients, who seem to be particularly vulnerable to the disturbing qualities of humor, especially when they are too thinly disguised (Levine & Redlich 1955; Levine & Abelson 1959; 1960).

The development of a sense of humor. We know little about how the child's sense of humor develops in conjunction with psychological and social growth. In the absence of systematic studies, we can only conjecture from anecdotal observations about the changes in humor behavior in relation to cognitive and emotional development. Humor, arising out of the play situation, clearly offers the growing child, while he is subjected to increasing demands and prohibitions, indirect outlets for the expression of his angry and sexual feelings and anxieties. By claiming "this is a joke" or "this is play," he can be naughty, talk bathroom talk, tease, and poke fun. Wolfenstein (1954) maintains that indirectness of expression is associated with developmental phases of the joke façade; impulses must be gratified but the child seeks to disclaim responsibility for them. As an illustration of this process, Wolfenstein describes a sequence of dirty jokes of children from 4 to 11 to demonstrate the increasing complication of the joke façade. Excretory activities are primary themes. Wolfenstein considers the development of aggression in children's humor as following a somewhat different course from sex and excretion. Wolfenstein's observations point up the fact that the development of humor seems to follow the course of the normal physical, intellectual, and emotional development of the child. The humor a child enjoys is related to the level and phase of its growth and is intimately associated with its mastery of activities. As Kris (1952, p. 213) aptly put it, "What was feared yesterday is fated to appear funny when seen today." The enormous importance of play and humor to children is sufficient proof of the need for understanding of their psychogenesis from simple undifferentiated behavior patterns to complex psychological processes.

Phylogenetic roots. When we talk about humor we usually think of it as an adult activity which emerges fully developed in man. We tend to disregard the biological and phylogenetic roots from which humor arises. In man, we overlook the primitive origins of humor as simple reflexlike reactions to specific stimuli. The phylogenetic gap betweeen man and the animals in respect to humor is apparently so great and unbridgeable that humor in man is viewed as an emergent phenomenon. Behavioral scientists acknowledge the validity of the most fundamental principle in biology, evolution, but completely ignore it in humor theory and research. Actually, the evidence, unsystematic and naturalistic as it is, strongly indicates that animals do possess primordial signs of a sense of humor, with the capacity to communicate pleasure by facial and bodily expressions which seem to be precursors of smiling and laughing (Darwin 1872; Yerkes & Yerkes 1929; Köhler 1917). Many of the higher animals are tireless in their teasing and their playing of mischievous pranks, being keenly aware of the importance both of surprise and of catching their victims unawares. Monkeys love to engage in clowning and funny posturing for the appreciative laughter of their human audience. The assumption of the humor illusion discussed above is clearly demonstrated in these antics, and the license of the mischief they undertake and the fun they have doing it attest to it.

Aggression and humor. It is out of these forms of teasing, pranks, and poking fun that children also develop their sense of humor. In the course of this development, aggression is an important component of the humor process, whether it is expressed as tickling, teasing, kidding, poking fun, being witty, or making wisecracks. Since aggression is such an important factor in humor, it has perhaps been more extensively studied than any other. A number of studies have shown convincingly that people who are generally aggressive or are easily aroused to anger tend to prefer hostile humor (for example, see Murray 1935; Byrne 1956; 1961; Strickland 1959). Attempts to demonstrate quantitatively that the greater the aggressive feelings the more hostile humor is appreciated have led to contradictory findings (Strickland 1959, Byrne 1956; 1961). Most studies relating humor and aggression are derived from psychoanalytic theory and are based upon the assumption that an increase in aggression which typically must be repressed leads to increased appreciation of humor as an outlet.

Perhaps a more important implication derived from psychoanalytic theory is that the enjoyment of aggressive humor leads to a cathartic reduction in the intensity of the aggressive feelings. Porr (1961) was not able to demonstrate a cathartic effect with sexual humor following sexual arousal, although Strickland (1959) found increased appreciation of sexual cartoons following sexual arousal. Singer (1964) was able to demonstrate that the enjoyment of aggressive humor led to a cathartic decrease in aggressive feelings. This experiment was conducted with Negroes during the summer of 1963 when the race conflict was of national concern. Singer first aroused strong aggressive feelings in Negro subjects by playing tape recordings which described the cruel treatment of integrationists in the South as well as a speech by a militant segregationist justifying segregation on the grounds that Negroes are genetically inferior. The subjects were then exposed to hostile antisegregationist humor and neutral humor from segments of recorded performances by a well-known Negro comedian. He found that the arousal communication in fact did evoke strong aggressive feelings as well as anxiety. There was a significant reduction in aggressive feelings and anxiety following the hostile humor. The neutral humor had no effect [*see* AGGRESSION, *article on* PSYCHOLOGICAL ASPECTS].

Humor as a social process. The study mentioned above suggests the potential fruitfulness of research on the role of humor in relation to social issues. The importance of humor as a molding force in all societies seems to be appreciated mainly by those who apply it in advertising and entertainment. Several historical examples may serve as illustrations. Many have noted that Cervantes with his classic Don Quixote was able to laugh out of existence the ridiculous posturing of medieval chivalry. Thomas Nast, in 1871, with just a few cartoons singlehandedly brought about the downfall of the notorious Tweed ring (Becker 1959, pp. 299–300). During the blitz of World War II the morale of the English was greatly strengthened by the sudden eruption of joking at the time of peril. Perhaps the most dramatic example of humor shaping history was reported by Franklin D. Roosevelt; at the Teheran meeting in 1943, he was able to melt the icy suspiciousness of Stalin and win him over by cracking jokes at Churchill's expense (Perkins 1946, p. 84).

Humor not only taps basic personality variables, as evidenced by the numerous studies with humor tests, but the popular humor of a people often expresses most clearly many of its concerns, conflicts, and aspirations (Hes & Levine 1962). Yet we know little that is fundamental about national and ethnic differences in humor behavior, although striking contrasts in patterns and ease of joking and laughter are familiar. While these differences are largely socially determined, there are archetypes of affective communication, laughter and joking, that transcend cultures and epochs. This fact is illustrated by the hilarious laughter evoked by Charlie Chaplin among the most primitive tribes of Africa. Completely in pantomime, he was able to convey the humor of certain family relationships which the tribesmen understood immediately (Grotjahn 1957).

The sharing of a humor experience by a group represents a pact between the participants to suspend for the moment the ordinary rules of conduct, logic, and speech. As Freud put it ([1905] 1960, p. 149), humor "is an invitation to common aggression and common regression."

Although the normal demands of propriety are given up, the social situation in humor creates its own rules of interaction based upon status, intimacy, and purpose. Goodrich, Henry, and Goodrich (1954) studied systematically the joking and laughter of a psychiatric staff conference. They found that laughter and joking served a variety of important social functions, such as promoting solidarity, freeing individuals to disparage others, reducing felt anxiety, and acting as a safety valve for divisive tensions. They concluded that the investigation of humor is just as valuable for an understanding of social processes as it is for an understanding of attitudes and feelings. In two comparable studies, Coser (1959; 1960) investigated the joking and laughter of patients and staff in a mental hospital. She also found that humor allowed its participants a number of functions, including mutual reinterpretation of their experiences, entertainment, reassurance, and communication; it also served to convey their interest in one another, to pull the group together, and to strengthen its structure.

Institutional humor. Since humor serves so many social functions, nearly every society has developed institutional forms of humor, primarily to serve as methods of social release and regulation. For example, in a study of ritual clowning Levine (1961) has shown that among many of our American Indians, like the Hopi, who are normally very reserved and proper, the ritual clown is a highly respected individual, yet in his grotesque comic antics he is permitted to violate nearly every social taboo, including incest. By the assumption of the illusion of humor, the clown and the participants in his rituals are able to throw off ego restraints and regress to the most archaic and infantile levels without undue consequences. This socially approved gratification is an example of regression in the service of the ego and occurs without anxiety or guilt.

The joking relationships of many primitive cultures have long been recognized by anthropologists as performing a crucial function in defining and maintaining certain kinship relationships. Brandt (1948) confirmed the generally held hypothesis that these relationships are expressions of some potential sexual relationships within kinships. Levine has shown that this form of institutionalized humor is typical in reducing the tensions of interpersonal relations (unpublished). The joking relationships were seen as one of the means used by the culture to provide external controls for the sexual and aggressive urges that are most likely to seek expression in the violation of social taboos. By the formalized joking behavior, these tabooed wishes are channeled and relieved in acceptable ways. Again, by the assumption of the humor illusion, taunting and poking fun are treated as a joke, whereas under reality conditions such ridicule could lead to suicide or homicide. Antithetically, when the humor illusion is not present, many anthropological examples exist of the extreme reactions of shame and disgrace suffered by individuals who are publicly laughed at.

Ridicule and satire are also forms of humor which often become institutionalized. Elliott (1960) studied the extraordinary powers of satire in many cultures, particularly "shame" cultures where the worst possible experience is to be laughed at publicly and where suicide is even considered to be appropriate under such circumstances. Elliott showed how great magical powers were attributed to the fool or the satirist who could be very frightening and how extreme measures to appease him often were taken. A dramatic example of such an institutional form of humor is shown among the Greenland Eskimos, where quarrels are resolved by a duel with laughter. Each contestant, armed only with a drum which he uses as an accompaniment, recites humorous insults and obscene jokes ridiculing his opponent. The duelist who wins the most laughter from the audience is the victor. The loser is profoundly humiliated, often going into exile.

It is clear that society, by tradition and experience, knows the powers of humor in shaping human affairs. But humor is inextricably bound to both an inner and an outer freedom, and the view that humor gives license hardly does justice to its potential as a liberating force. As Worcester expressed it, "The intellectual, critical spirit that attacks pretense and acts as the watchdog of society is the comic spirit" ([1940] 1960, p. 7). Where cultures fear freedom of expression and rigidly demand conformity, humor is repressed, and the role of the humorist is dangerous. But, nonetheless, humor provides some immunity and permits freedoms otherwise proscribed. Many have perceived this fact. For example, Freud stated, "In every epoch of history those who have had something to say but could not say it without peril have eagerly assumed a fool's cap. The audience at whom their forbidden speech was aimed tolerated it more easily if they could at the same time laugh and flatter themselves with the reflection that the unwelcome words were clearly nonsensical" ([1900] 1953, p. 444).

JACOB LEVINE

[*Other relevant material may be found in* DEVELOPMENTAL PSYCHOLOGY; LITERATURE, *article on* THE PSYCHOLOGY OF LITERATURE; PSYCHOANALYSIS.]

BIBLIOGRAPHY

BARRON, FRANK 1957 Originality in Relation to Personality and Intellect. *Journal of Personality* 25:730–742.

BECKER, STEPHAN D. 1959 *Comic Art in America*. New York: Simon & Schuster.

BERLYNE, D. E. 1960 *Conflict, Arousal, and Curiosity*. New York: McGraw-Hill.

BRANDT, CHARLES S. 1948 On Joking Relationships. *American Anthropologist* New Series 50:160–162.

BYRNE, DONN 1956 The Relationship Between Humor and the Expression of Hostility. *Journal of Abnormal and Social Psychology* 53:84–89.

BYRNE, DONN 1961 Some Inconsistencies in the Effect of Motivation Arousal on Humor Preferences. *Journal of Abnormal and Social Psychology* 62:158–160.

CONFERENCE ON GROUP PROCESSES, ITHACA, N.Y., *1954* 1955 *Group Processes: Transactions*. New York: Macy Foundation.

COSER, ROSE L. 1959 Some Social Functions of Laughter: A Study of Humor in a Hospital Setting. *Human Relations* 12:171–182.

COSER, ROSE L. 1960 Laughter Among Colleagues. *Psychiatry* 23:81–89.

DARWIN, CHARLES (1872) 1965 *The Expression of the Emotions in Man and Animals*. Edited by Francis Darwin. Univ. of Chicago Press.

ELLIOTT, ROBERT C. 1960 *The Power of Satire*. Princeton Univ. Press.

FLUGEL, J. C. 1954 Humor and Laughter. Volume 2, pages 709–734 in Gardner Lindzey (editor), *Handbook of Social Psychology*. Cambridge, Mass.: Addison-Wesley.

FREUD, SIGMUND (1900) 1953 *The Standard Edition of the Complete Psychological Works of Sigmund Freud*. Volumes 4 and 5: The Interpretation of Dreams. New York: Macmillan; London: Hogarth.

FREUD, SIGMUND (1905) 1960 *The Standard Edition of the Complete Psychological Works of Sigmund Freud*. Volume 8: Jokes and Their Relation to the Unconscious. London: Hogarth; New York: Macmillan.

GOODRICH, ANNE; HENRY, JULES; and GOODRICH, D. WELLS 1954 Laughter in Psychiatric Staff Conferences: A Sociopsychiatric Analysis. *American Journal of Orthopsychiatry* 24:175–184.

GROTJAHN, MARTIN 1957 *Beyond Laughter*. New York: McGraw-Hill.

HES, JOZEF; and LEVINE, JACOB 1962 Kibbuts Humor. *Journal of Nervous and Mental Diseases* 135:327–331.

JACOBSON, EDITH 1946 The Child's Laughter. Volume 2, pages 39–60 in *The Psychoanalytic Study of the Child*. New York: International Universities Press.

KANT, IMMANUEL (1790) 1951 *Critique of Judgment*. New York: Hafner. → First published as *Kritik der Urtheilskraft*.

KÖHLER, WOLFGANG (1917) 1956 *The Mentality of Apes*. 2d ed., rev. London: Routledge. → First published in German. A paperback edition was published in 1959 by Random House.

KRIS, ERNST 1952 *Psychoanalytic Explorations in Art*. New York: International Universities Press.

LEVINE, JACOB 1961 Regression in Primitive Clowning. *Psychoanalytic Quarterly* 30:72–83.

LEVINE, JACOB 1964 The Joking Relationship as Institutional Humor. Unpublished manuscript.

LEVINE, JACOB; and ABELSON, ROBERT 1959 Humor as a Disturbing Stimulus. *Journal of Genetic Psychology* 60:191–200.

LEVINE, JACOB; and REDLICH, FREDRICK C. 1955 Failure to Understand Humor. *Psychoanalytic Quarterly* 24:560–572.

LEVINE, JACOB; and REDLICH, FREDRICK C. 1960 Intellectual and Emotional Factors in the Appreciation of Humor. *Journal of Genetic Psychology* 62:25–35.

MILGRAM, STANLEY 1963 Behavioral Study of Obedience. *Journal of Abnormal and Social Psychology* 67: 371–378.

MURRAY, HENRY 1935 The Psychology of Humor. *Journal of Abnormal and Social Psychology* 29:66–81.

PERKINS, FRANCES [Wilson] 1946 *The Roosevelt I Knew*. New York: Viking Press.

PLATO *Philebus*. Jowett's translation, 3d ed. London and New York: Macmillan, 1892.

PORR, R. 1961 An Experimental Investigation of the Function of Sexual Impulses and Anxiety in Humor. Unpublished manuscript.

REDLICH, FREDRICK C.; LEVINE, JACOB; and SOHLER, THEODORE P. 1951 A Mirth Response Test: Preliminary Report on a Psychodiagnostic Technique Utilizing Dynamics of Humor. *American Journal of Orthopsychiatry* 21:717–734.

SINGER, D. 1964 The Cathartic Function of Humor. Unpublished manuscript.

SPITZ, RENÉ 1959 *A Genetic Field Theory of Ego Formation*. New York: International Universities Press.

SPITZ, RENÉ; and WOLF, K. M. 1946 The Smiling Responses: A Contribution to the Ontogenesis of Social Relations. *Genetic Psychology Monographs* 34:57–125.

STRICKLAND, JOHN F. 1959 The Effect of Motivational Arousal on Humor Preferences. *Journal of Abnormal and Social Psychology* 59:278–281.

SWABEY, MARIE C. 1961 *Comic Laughter*. New Haven: Yale Univ. Press.

WHITE, ROBERT W. 1963 Ego and Reality in Psychoanalytic Theory. *Psychological Issues* 3, no. 3, monograph 11.

WILD, CYNTHIA 1962 Adaptive Regression in Art Students, Teachers and Schizophrenics. Ph.D. dissertation, Yale Univ.

WILD, CYNTHIA 1965 Creativity and Adaptive Regression. *Journal of Personality and Social Psychology* 2:161–169.

WOLFENSTEIN, MARTHA 1954 *Children's Humor: A Psychological Analysis.* Glencoe, Ill.: Free Press.

WORCESTER, DAVID (1940) 1960 *The Art of Satire.* New York: Russell & Russell.

YERKES, ROBERT M.; and YERKES, ADA W. (1929) 1945 *The Great Apes: A Study of Anthropoid Life.* New Haven: Yale Univ. Press.

HUNTER, WALTER S.

Walter Samuel Hunter (1889–1954), American psychologist, was born in Decatur, Illinois. He went to public schools in Texas and graduated in 1910 from the University of Texas. He received the PH.D. in psychology from the University of Chicago in 1912, and taught at the universities of Texas and Kansas before becoming the G. Stanley Hall professor of genetic psychology at Clark University in 1925. He accepted the chairmanship of the psychology department at Brown University in 1936, holding that position until 1954.

Hunter was a liberal member of the behaviorist group in psychology. His doctoral thesis was directed by Harvey Carr, whom he credited with instilling in him a love of careful experimentation. The thesis was published as a monograph entitled *Delayed Reaction in Animals and Children* (1913). Its importance lay partly in the fact that the delayed reaction was a new technique which Hunter diligently exploited for the comparative study of human and infrahuman behavior. Perhaps more significant, however, was the theoretical approach, later to be more fully developed by Hunter, that clearly had its origins in this early study. The essential feature of the delayed reaction technique is that the animal must respond on the basis of a stimulus that is no longer present at the time when the response is made. In the original experiments, rats and dogs were found to be capable of correct responses only if they oriented themselves toward the stimulus while it was present and maintained their bodily orientation during the entire interval of delay between stimulus and response. Raccoons and children, on the other hand, could respond correctly even when longer delays were imposed and when specific orienting responses were interrupted before the response could be made. Hunter, therefore, inferred the existence in higher mammals of a "symbolic process," defined as a substitute for an overt stimulus situation leading to a selective response.

Later research by Hunter and many others revealed that behavior based on symbolic processes is, in fact, present even in lower mammals, but that it reaches successively higher levels of complexity in dogs, raccoons, monkeys, and children. In adult human behavior, symbolic processes presumably play a dominant role and underlie much of the activity that psychologists had traditionally subsumed under the topics of consciousness, language, insight, and intelligence.

In the 1920s Hunter addressed himself to the problems of consciousness, introspection, and instinct. In a series of theoretical papers he stressed the main theme of the behaviorists, namely, that the business of psychology is to observe the behavior of organisms. His approach was not as narrow or contentious as that of John B. Watson; Hunter freely admitted the central importance of the phenomena of conscious experience that traditional psychologists had claimed to study by the method of introspection. His concern was rather to point out that the term "introspection" had in fact been used to describe verbal responses under specified stimulus conditions; thus he gave introspection the same objective status as all other scientific observations. He attempted to introduce a new name, "anthroponomy," for the objective observation of behavior; but long usage had too firmly established the word "psychology," and it has survived in spite of its mentalist connotations. Although the word "psychology" resisted change during Hunter's lifetime, he could note with satisfaction that its meaning was shifting away from a study of subjective experience and toward a science of objective behavior.

The breadth of Hunter's experimental work can be seen from a listing of a few of his research topics: the aftereffect of visual motion; the reliability of the maze; the auditory sensitivity of the white rat; the behavior of the rat on inclined planes; voluntary activity from the standpoint of behaviorism; the span of visual discrimination as a function of duration and intensity of stimulation; and double alternation in young children.

Hunter served as editor of the *Psychological Index*, *Psychological Abstracts*, and *Comparative Psychology Monographs.* He was elected to membership in the American Academy of Arts and Sciences, the American Philosophical Society, and the National Academy of Sciences. He served as president of the American Psychological Association and of the Eastern Psychological Association and chairman of the applied psychology panel of the National Defense Research Committee. His success in the administration of that panel was recognized by President Truman, who awarded him the Medal for Merit in 1948. Hunter was active as a member of several other military advisory groups during and after World War II. Four years after his death a new building at Brown University was named the Walter S. Hunter Psychological Laboratory.

In summary, Hunter's main theoretical contribution was to help establish psychology as a science of behavior rather than as a study of experience. He developed and exploited new techniques of experimentation on human and animal behavior. Above all, he played an important role in establishing the stature of American psychology as a science and as a profession.

LORRIN A. RIGGS

[*See also* LEARNING, *especially the article on* REINFORCEMENT; *and the biography of* WATSON.]

WORKS BY HUNTER

1913 *Delayed Reaction in Animals and Children.* New York: Holt. → Also published as Volume 2, No. 1 of *Behavior Monographs.*

1915 Retinal Factors in Visual After-movement. *Psychological Review* 22:479–489.

(1919*a*) 1923 *General Psychology.* Rev. ed. Univ. of Chicago Press.

(1919*b*) 1928 *Human Behavior.* 3d ed., rev. Univ. of Chicago Press.

1924*a* The Problem of Consciousness. *Psychological Review* 31:1–31.

1924*b* The Symbolic Process. *Psychological Review* 31: 478–497.

1927 The Behavior of the White Rat on Inclined Planes. *Pedagogical Seminary and Journal of Genetic Psychology* 34:299–332. → Now called *Journal of Genetic Psychology.*

(1929) 1934 Experimental Studies of Learning. Pages 497–570 in Carl Murchison (editor), *Handbook of General Experimental Psychology.* Worcester, Mass.: Clark Univ. Press.

1930 Anthroponomy and Psychology. Pages 281–300 in *Psychologies of 1930.* Edited by Carl Murchison. Worcester, Mass.: Clark Univ. Press.

1940 HUNTER, WALTER S.; and SIGLER, M. The Span of Visual Discrimination as a Function of Time and Intensity of Stimulation. *Journal of Experimental Psychology* 26:160–179.

1946 Psychology in the War. *American Psychologist* 1: 479–492.

1952*a* Autobiography. Volume 4, pages 163–187 in *History of Psychology in Autobiography.* Worcester, Mass.: Clark Univ. Press.

(1952*b*) 1959 Behaviourism. Volume 3, pages 327–329 in *Encyclopaedia Britannica.* Chicago: Benton.

SUPPLEMENTARY BIBLIOGRAPHY

GRAHAM, CLARENCE H. 1958 Walter Samuel Hunter: March 22, 1889–August 3, 1954. Volume 31, pages 127–155 in National Academy of Sciences, *Biographical Memoirs.* Washington: The Academy. → Contains a bibliography.

HUNTING AND GATHERING

I
OLD WORLD PREHISTORIC SOCIETIES

The Paleolithic, or Old Stone Age, covers all but 1/200 of human history. The study of paleolithic society is, therefore, not only that of man's emerging technical ability and broadening cultural horizons, but also of his physiological and intellectual evolution. It includes examination of the effects of the climatic and physiographic changes that shaped the environments in which man lived and to which his cultural skills enabled him to adapt with increasing efficiency.

Paleolithic man was a hunter and gatherer, and the Paleolithic is divided into three substages—lower, middle, and upper. The lower Paleolithic is a stage of unspecialized hunting and gathering populations; the middle Paleolithic saw the beginnings of regional specialization; and the upper Paleolithic was a time of advanced hunting and collecting activities.

The Paleolithic appeared first in Africa during the later Villafranchian or Lower Pleistocene, some 1.75 million to 2 million years ago. The Villafranchian was a time of climatic change and significantly lowered temperature in higher latitudes coincident with the onset of the Quaternary Ice Age or glacial epoch. At the same period, the first true elephants, horses, and bovids appear in the fossil record. By the beginning of the Middle Pleistocene, probably about one million years ago, toolmaking had spread to Europe and Asia. This paleolithic stage of culture continued up to the end of the Pleistocene.

The world-wide termination of the Pleistocene period, approximately 10,000 years ago, was coincident with the end of the last glaciation in the Northern Hemisphere and of the last "pluvial" in the tropical and subtropical belts.

The close of the Pleistocene was marked by climatic amelioration—the recession of the ice sheets in northern Europe and Asia and the reafforestation of regions previously glaciated or covered only by tundra. It appears to have been a time of population increase, of movement into hitherto unoccupied country, and of a much more intensive use of environmental resources. The economy still consisted of hunting and gathering but at a more advanced level. This post-Pleistocene period is called the Mesolithic by some European prehistorians; in the Mediterranean Basin it is often referred to as the "epi-Paleolithic" while in sub-Saharan Africa it is known as the "Later Stone Age."

The Mesolithic ended first in the Levant, where by the eighth millennium B.C. incipient grain cultivation and domestication of sheep and goats initiated the beginnings of food production and thus the Neolithic or New Stone Age. By the seventh millennium B.C. (e.g., at Nea Nikomedeia, Macedonia) the new economy had spread to eastern Europe, and by the third millennium it had spread up the Danube to the Atlantic coast and Britain. [*See* DOMESTICATION.]

The initial spread of this new economy to the Nile Valley, India, and southeast Asia appears to have begun in the fifth millennium B.C., but its diffusion was retarded as it came into contact with the rich tropical savannas and forests of southern and eastern Asia and sub-Saharan Africa. Indeed, south of the Sahara the bulk of the population remained Later Stone Age hunters and food collectors until the introduction of metallurgy during the first millennium B.C.

Chronological basis of cultural succession. One of the prehistorian's chief concerns is establishing a chronology into which to fit his various cultural assemblages. In fact, it was the necessity felt by the eighteenth and nineteenth century antiquarians to prove the existence of "man before Adam"—as evidenced by the stone implements being found in direct association with fossil remains of extinct animals in ancient geological strata—that began the close collaboration of archeologist, paleontologist, and geologist, which still remains the basis for establishing the chronology of early man.

In Europe, culture history is based on the relationship of the different industrial stages to the deposits of the Pleistocene glacial advances and interglacial epochs. These are also correlated with periods of fluctuating sea level; the level was low when water was locked up in the ice sheets, and high during the interglacials, when much of the water was released as the ice melted. This geomorphological evidence can now be checked by studies of deep-sea cores. Each epoch supported a distinctive land fauna, while studies of pollen from interglacial deposits show that the general vegetation patterns also differed with each interglacial.

In Africa, geologists and archeologists have established a succession of pluvial and interpluvial oscillations, which they have sought to correlate with the glacials and interglacials of northern latitudes. Caution is needed, however, since in east Africa, which is the type region, tectonic movements cannot be discounted as factors in bringing about the fluctuation of lake levels on which the "pluvial hypothesis" is largely based. However, morphological studies of river systems and closed basins in areas where tectonic movement is absent show that climatic changes did indeed take place during Pleistocene times in Africa and, one may say, in the tropics generally. Except for the last pluvial and the post-Pleistocene episodes, their intensity and precise correlation with the glacial chronology is, however, as yet unknown. But there can be no doubt that the last pluvial is synchronous with the last glaciation in Europe.

Stratigraphy of glacial deposits, river terraces, changing sea and lake levels, and faunal and pollen stages provides a basis for a relative chronology of human cultural evolution. In recent years, however, the archeologist has had available several methods developed by natural scientists that provide an absolute chronology or age in terms of years obtained from organic and mineral samples found in association with the cultural material. These methods are still subject to refinement and elimination of error, but their use has introduced an over-all precision into Stone Age chronology never before possible. The most important are the radiocarbon method (Libby 1952) which, with the enrichment process, provides dates back to 75,000 years and the potassium–argon method (Evernden & Curtis 1965), which can be used to date volcanic rocks that are rich in potassium and provides dates for all but the most recent of such rocks.

These chronometric methods have the great advantage of providing the basis for accurate age determinations of cultural successions and fossil assemblages in widely separated regions independent of any factors on which the relative chronology is based.

Recovery and interpretation. Before World War II prehistorians were chiefly concerned with the classification of stone and bone artifacts, which were usually all that remained of the culture being studied. These artifacts were preserved in caves, where they were systematically excavated, as well as in gravel and ballast pits and similar commercial excavations. The recognition of regularly recurring artifact classes led to the establishment of industrial patterns, and where these were found to have consistent chronological and regional distribution they determined the existence of "cultures."

Thus it was largely the surviving lithic and bone elements of the material culture and their inferred function within the framework of the habitat that prehistorians drew on for their reconstruction of the paleolithic and mesolithic way of life. Since

World War II, however, improved field techniques have greatly increased the evidence an excavation can yield. Not only is the distribution of tools, waste, and food debris on an occupation surface studied in relation to special features such as hearths, stone concentrations, walls and other constructional features, and natural features of the site, but quantitative analysis is now used to demonstrate the relative importance of the different types and classes of tools. When the tool content of several successive occupation layers is examined, the way the industrial patterns change is studied in relation to such other significant differences as may be indicated by the pollen diagram or the animals that provided the main source of meat. Another complete dimension has thus been added from which to reconstruct the paleolithic hunting way of life.

A growing awareness of the possibility of reconstructing prehistoric society through the combined use of environmental, biological, and cultural evidence, and the perfection of the methods used are likely to result in a much wider understanding of paleolithic culture over the next few years.

Already, studies of the behavior and social organization of primates such as baboons, chimpanzees, and gorillas and the patterns of land use, settlement, and behavior of present-day hunting and gathering populations are valuable in demonstrating how social and economic organization might have made best use of the environmental resources at the Australopithecine and early mid-Pleistocene levels. Examination of the fossil evidence of primate and hominid evolution as seen in the changing nature of skeletal remains sometimes associated with the cultural record shows the limitations imposed by physiological factors. [*See* EVOLUTION, *articles on* HUMAN EVOLUTION *and* PRIMATE EVOLUTION.]

The lower Paleolithic

The earliest tool-makers. During the later Tertiary, groups of apes occupying tropical and equatorial savanna in northeastern Africa and southwestern Asia became fully bipedal simultaneously with the specialization of the hands for tool-using.

This selective adaptation probably was largely induced by the aridity of the tropics during the Pliocene and the consequent destruction of the natural environments of these hitherto unspecialized apelike forms. It appears to have taken some ten to twelve million years for these animals to evolve from *Ramapithecus* (in Africa *Kenyapithecus*) into the genus of man-apes known as the Australopithecines (Simons 1963).

Authorities are divided concerning the classification of the various Lower Pleistocene hominid fossils, but the majority are agreed that the Australopithecines are divisible into a small, gracile species —*Australopithecus africanus*—and a much heavier form—*A. robustus*—previously known as *Paranthropus*. The fossil *Homo habilis* (man having ability), described in 1964 (Tobias 1964; Leakey & Leakey 1964; Leakey et al. 1964) as representing a separate *Homo* ancestral stock distinct from the Australopithecines, is also classified by some investigators as a third form of Australopithecine *A. habilis* (Oakley 1964).

The Australopithecines are known from cave breccias in the Transvaal and northern Cape, Republic of South Africa (Sterkfontein, Swartkrans, Kromdraai and Taungs); from lake beds in east Africa (Laetolil, Olduvai, Peninj at Natron); and from Chad (Yayo). From fluviatile sediments in Java comes the closely related *Meganthropus*, often classified as an Australopithecine.

The earliest tools—Lower Pleistocene culture. Stone tools first appear in Lower Pleistocene context at the base of Bed I at the Olduvai Gorge. In South Africa they are found in early mid-Pleistocene breccias at Sterkfontein and Swartkrans. So far, however, it is only at Olduvai that the hominid fossils are unquestionably associated with faunal remains on living sites.

The problem arises as to which hominid made the tools; as yet, the evidence is inconclusive. It appears most likely, however, that tools were first made by a form akin to *A. africanus*, which, because of the selective advantages conferred by toolmaking, developed during the early part of the mid-Pleistocene into *Homo erectus* by way of the *H. habilis* form. The evidence of the Peninj jaw, found in 1964 near Lake Natron, makes it likely that *A. robustus*, while he *used* tools, did not make them (see Leakey & Leakey 1964; Isaac 1965).

The manufacture of stone tools was a development of the greatest importance, considerably facilitating the consumption of meat. The tools could also be used for pounding and for sharpening stakes for digging, thus increasing the sources of vegetable foods. Sometimes bone was also used. Natural stones were intensively collected at the habitation sites and must have been used as aids to hunting and protection. Indeed, since fire-making was unknown, such stones must have been one of man's chief means of keeping other scavengers away from his larder.

The tools themselves are of the simplest kind. Besides the natural stones showing little or no modification, others have been unifacially or bifacially flaked to form simple chopping implements. Various polyhedral stones attest to their use for bashing or pounding, and a number of flakes show minimal retouch or utilization for skinning and scraping. Artifact assemblages of this kind belong to the Oldowan culture. The living floors seem to have been temporary occupation surfaces on the edge of a brackish Olduvai lake. Tools are scattered over a comparatively confined area; in one instance, a roughly circular concentration of stone and broken bones about 15 feet in diameter leaves no doubt that the artifacts had been used to dismember and break up the bones of the small or young animals that formed part of the diet of these not very efficient hunters. At another site are two roughly semicircular concentrations of stones thought to have been the wall of some kind of windbreak or hide. Juvenile Australopithecines were dependent on their parents for a longer time than are the young of present-day pongids (Dart 1948); this fact and fear of predators were probably major reasons for the establishment of camps or home bases in the open savanna by these comparatively defenseless hominids. They did not live in caves, although they visited those in the Transvaal limestones—perhaps to find water or to trap game.

Thus, the picture that emerges of Lower Pleistocene tool-makers is of small family groups of gracile, swift-running hominids, within or very close to the Australopithecine pattern, living in open savanna country close to water and gallery forest. They were unspecialized, not very efficient hunters who supplemented their meat supply largely by scavenging and obtained most of their food from vegetable sources.

Middle Pleistocene culture. The beginning of the Middle Pleistocene witnessed the spread of tool-making to Europe and Asia. In Europe the oldest tools of this stage are abraded hand axes found in the 45-meter terrace of the Somme River in France and now believed to date to an early interstadial of the Mindel glaciation. Contemporary with these tools is the flake and chopper industry (Clactonian) from Vertesszollos on the Danube in Hungary, where the main source of meat was small animals—mice, voles, and other rodents (Kretzoi & Vértes 1964).

In the Middle East crude hand axes and chopping tools, associated with a rich, early mid-Pleistocene fauna and some hominid teeth and skull fragments, come from faulted lake beds at Ubeidiya in the Jordan Valley (Stekelis 1963), while in the Far East current excavations in the Lower Trinil beds at Sangiran, whence came the remains of *Pithecanthropus* (now *H. erectus*), are reported to be yielding stone implements *in situ* (Jacob 1964). In China, at Choukoutien, near Peking, *H. erectus* fossils are associated with a simple chopper and flake industry, much animal food debris, and hearths (Teilhard & Pei 1932). In Africa several occupation floors are known from Olduvai Bed II but are as yet not fully described.

The association of culture with large animals is a regular feature of the living sites of mid-Pleistocene man. At the base of Bed II at Olduvai the complete remains of a Dinotherium were found with simple chopping tools. At BKII, near the top of the bed, large, now-extinct species appear to have been driven into a swamp, butchered, and eaten (Leakey 1958). At Torralba and Ambrona in Spain the remains of over 45 straight-tusked elephants (*E. antiquus*) were found; the animals had been dismembered and eaten (Howell et al. 1962, pp. 28–29).

In Africa, a number of living sites from the later part of this period (Olduvai Bed IV, Kariandusi, Olorgesailie, Isimila, Kalambo Falls, Cave of Hearths) have now been excavated so as to recover all or part of the distribution or scatter pattern of artifacts, fauna, or associated objects on the occupation surfaces, from which a clearer picture is gained of the behavior and abilities of mid-Pleistocene man.

Sites at this time seem to have been occupied for longer periods of time and, it would seem, were sometimes revisited. At Latamne, in Syria, occupation debris is associated with a scatter of large limestone blocks, which may have formed some kind of structure (J. D. Clark 1964).

Living sites and butchery places are still close to water, indicating inadequate water-carrying and storage equipment. Artifact scatters cover wider areas than those of the Lower Pleistocene hominids, suggesting that the population was distributed in larger groupings—probably resulting from the improved technique developed for hunting large animals. Fire was first used in the periglacial north (such as Choukoutien, Torralba), only later spreading to the tropics.

Artifacts now begin to show specialization of function: There are cleavers, hand axes, choppers, small and large scrapers, points, polyhedrals, etc. Probably environmental adaptation dictated the concentration of chopping and flake tools found, on the one hand, in regions adjacent to the ice sheets and, on the other, in the tropical forest areas of southeast Asia as well as the composition of the "hand ax/cleaver" industries in the open, temperate forests and the savannas and grasslands of the tropics.

No tool at this time is exclusive to any one region, the different activity patterns being reflected in the varying proportions of artifacts in the tool kit.

The hominids. In the Far East and Africa the earlier mid-Pleistocene cultures are associated with the *Pithecanthropus* stock, in which slender and more robust forms are distinguishable. Later, however, greatly expanded cranial capacity led to the appearance of early sapient-like forms (Swanscombe, Steinheim, Fontechevade, Kanjera), and it is apparent that selectively adaptive characteristics distinguish both the hominids and their cultures in the various regions.

The middle Paleolithic

By the early Upper Pleistocene (beginning with the Riss Glaciation) more specialized industries point to distinct activity patterns, suggesting that groups now split up into small units for specific purposes. This specialization of activity is best seen in the Mousterian industries of the early Last Glacial (Würm), where distinct "traditions" are found interphasing in the caves and rock shelters which now formed regular homes for bands of hunters (Bordes 1961).

In Africa, the beginning of the last pluvial was a time of population explosion and movement into the previously unoccupied forests of Equatoria where regionally specialized cultures developed. This was made possible by the use of large woodworking tools and undoubtedly by the regular use of fire.

Much experimentation must have gone on, and this period saw the beginnings of deliberate burial, belief in an afterlife, and magical ritual. Populations were now emancipated from waterside sites, and the structural alteration of cave dwellings was begun. Hunting began to be selective; tools were hafted; and more functionally specialized implements were manufactured. Wooden spears and throwing and digging sticks are known, and the regular use of bone and antler first began at some localities (e.g., Salzgitter-Lebenstedt in northern Germany (Tode et al. 1953).

In Europe and Asia the makers of the Mousterian culture were the genetically overspecialized Neanderthals. Related types are known also from southeast Asia (*H. soloensis*) and Africa (*H. rhodesiensis*). Their disappearance when faced with competition from *Homo sapiens* is usually explained as due to genetic drift caused by isolation of small populations.

The upper Paleolithic

Homo sapiens first appeared in Europe, Africa, and the Near East at much the same time—about 35,000 years ago—and rapidly replaced the Neanderthals. In southeast Asia, a *H. sapiens* fossil from the Great Cave at Niah (Sarawak) is dated somewhat earlier—nearly 40,000 years ago.

In Europe and western and northern Asia *H. sapiens* was the bearer of the upper paleolithic blade and burin cultures. However, in Africa, India, and elsewhere in the tropics, no doubt for environmental reasons, the regional expressions retained to varying degree technical features of the middle paleolithic tradition.

The upper Paleolithic was a time of fundamental advances in technology. The hunting populations rapidly became regionally specialized and modified their social and economic behavior, making more extensive use of a wider variety of raw materials and more intensive use of some of these by the introduction of ever more efficient ways of food-getting.

The fish resources of rivers and lakes were exploited as never before, and man made use of sea foods for the first time. Hunting was often geared to the seasonal killing of one or two species (mammoth or reindeer in Eurasia; wildebeest, zebra, or pig in Africa). Some investigators regard the men of this time as partly responsible for the extinction of some of the more archaic Pleistocene animal species and, indeed, the upper paleolithic bands of Europe and northern Asia attained a degree of hunting efficiency unsurpassed by even such advanced specialists as the Eskimo or some of the North American Indians.

The technology was much more varied: there were knife blades; projectile points of stone, bone, and antler for spears and darts; spearthrowers; harpoons; fishhooks; and needles, chisels, and boring tools for engraving, for working antler and bone, or for making skins into clothing and covering for dwellings (Sonneville-Bordes 1963). By the end of the Paleolithic the bow and arrow were present in northern Germany (Ahrensburgian culture; Rust 1943, pp. 189–192) and probably somewhat earlier in Spain and north Africa also. To this tool list can be added throwing sticks and clubs; sometimes in Africa the clubs had a stone head enclosed in a greenhide sleeve.

This was again a time of population explosion and occupation of new territory, and man spread into the steppes of northern Russia to Siberia and across the Bering Strait into the New World. In southeast Asia he moved down the Malay peninsula and over the Sunda shelf to Australia.

Seasonal or semipermanent settlements are known from the loess country of central Europe, Russia, and Siberia, where the populations were largely mammoth hunters. They (Eastern Gravettians) built large communal summer structures, each with several hearths, as well as small, circular, tentlike dwellings with mammoth bone and ivory supports, covered probably with skins (e.g., the sites of Pavlov and Dolne Vistonice in Czechoslovakia). More elaborate winter tents also occur near Hamburg where they are found with a Magdalenian culture, while in European Russia and Siberia partly or fully subterranean earth houses are found, again with several hearths and occupied by several family groups in the winter.

Less is known about cave-site occupation, but excavations at the Abri Pataud in the Dordogne (Movius 1964) are showing that the nature of hearths, cooking methods, and lithic equipment underwent considerable modification during the earlier half of the upper Paleolithic.

The size of communities does not seem to have been any larger than hitherto, but the greatly superior technology permitted populations to spread more thickly and to occupy previously unfavorable territory—not only periarctic regions but also deserts such as the Namib in South West Africa and the Libyan Sand Sea.

The rich *art mobilier* and cave art of upper paleolithic man attests to both his high artistic ability and to a widespread code of magico–religious beliefs, which may be likened to those of the bison hunters of the North American Great Plains, the Australians, and the Bushmen.

Post-paleolithic hunting societies

In the northern hemisphere, the end of the Ice Age brought about the breakdown of the specialized hunting organizations of paleolithic man; the animals on which he depended moved away, and forests grew again on the tundra of northern Europe and Asia.

In the tropics, readjustment to the higher temperatures and spread of lowland forest and thicket occasioned a redistribution of population, necessitating a basic alteration in the livelihood pattern. The widespread diffusion of the bow and arrow—probably associated with the use of poison—and the general development of composite tools gave new impetus to hunting techniques. The individual hunter, or the small group, now acquired an efficiency previously the prerogative only of the community hunting in concert.

Seafood and the fish and other food resources of large rivers were now widely exploited—assisted by the use of rafts and boats—and there is no doubt that greater population density now led to increasingly intensive use of the natural resources of the environment.

Whereas upper paleolithic man had specialized often in the hunting of a single species of animal, the success of the mesolithic hunter was his ability to use a wide range of food sources, both animal and vegetable. A good example is the early Maglemosian settlement of Star Carr in Yorkshire (±7600 B.C.). It covered some two hundred square meters and was probably seasonally occupied, from October to April, for 12 to 15 years by some 16 to 25 individuals, of whom five were adult males able to hunt large game (J. G. D. Clark 1954). The community fished and collected food on the coast in the summer and hunted game and wildfowl in the winter.

The Later Stone Age populations of the south African coasts steadily increased their concentration on seafoods, correspondingly disregarding land animals and thus becoming more sedentary. Some coastal caves contained middens about 30 feet thick and are traditionally said to have been permanently occupied.

In southwest Asia the post-paleolithic Natufian populations achieved a settled way of life that differed little from that of the first food producers. The richness and rapid altitudinal range of the environments from the Jordan Rift over the mountains to the coast—a distance of not more than fifty miles—rendered these populations largely independent of the need to make seasonal moves.

Ruled by chiefs, they lived by hunting, fishing, and reaping wild grasses. They inhabited circular huts, burying their dead beneath the floor. They were an artistic people, and a shrinelike structure in the Natufian occupation at the base of the Jericho mound attests to the presence of organized magico–religious belief and ritual (Kenyon 1960, pp. 36–43).

It was the self-sufficiency of the Natufian economy that formed the basis for the development of cereal cultivation and animal domestication, perhaps in response to a temporary climatic swing toward greater aridity between 8000 and 7000 B.C.

J. DESMOND CLARK

[*See also* ARCHEOLOGY; DOMESTICATION; *and the biography of* BREUIL.]

BIBLIOGRAPHY

BORDES, FRANÇOIS 1961 Mousterian Cultures in France. *Science* 134:803–810.

BUTZER, KARL W. 1964 *Environment and Archaeology: An Introduction to Pleistocene Geography.* Chicago: Aldine.

CLARK, J. DESMOND 1959 *The Prehistory of Southern Africa.* Harmondsworth (England): Penguin.

CLARK, J. DESMOND 1964 Acheulian Occupation Sites in Syria and Africa: A Study in Cultural Variability. Unpublished manuscript. → Paper read at the Detroit meetings of the American Anthropological Association.

CLARK, J. G. D. 1954 *Excavations at Star Carr: An Early Mesolithic Site at Seamer Near Scarborough, Yorkshire.* Cambridge Univ. Press.

COLE, SONIA (1954) 1964 *The Prehistory of East Africa.* London: Weidenfeld & Nicolson.

DART, RAYMOND A. 1948 The Infancy of Australopithecus. Pages 143–152 in Royal Society of South Africa, Cape Town, *Robert Broom Commemorative Volume.* Edited by Alex. L. Du Toit. Cape Town: The Society.

EVERNDEN, J. F.; and CURTIS, G. H. 1965 The Potassium–Argon Dating of Late Cenozoic Rocks in East Africa and Italy. *Current Anthropology* 6:343–385. → Includes "Comments."

HOWELL, FRANCIS C.; and BOURLIÈRE, FRANÇOIS (editors) 1963 *African Ecology and Human Evolution.* Viking Fund Publications in Anthropology, No. 36. Chicago: Aldine.

HOWELL, FRANCIS C. et al. 1962 *Excavaciones en Torralba (Soria).* Servicio Nacional de Excavaciones Arqueológicas en España, No. 10. Madrid: Ministerio de Educación Nacional.

ISAAC, G. LL. 1965 The Stratigraphy of the Peninj Beds and the Provenance of the Natron Australopithecine Mandible. *Quaternaria* 7:101–130.

JACOB, TEUKU 1964 A New Hominid Skull Cap From Pleistocene Sangiran. *Anthropologica* New Series 6: 97–104.

KENYON, KATHLEEN M. 1960 *Archaeology in the Holy Land.* New York: Praeger.

KRETZOI, M.; and VÉRTES, L. 1964 Die Ausgräbungen der minderzeitlichen (Biharien-) Urmenschensiedlung in Vértesszöllös. *Acta geologica Academiae Scientiarum Hungaricae* (Budapest) 8, no. 1/4:313–317.

LEAKEY, L. S. B. 1958 Recent Discoveries at Olduvai Gorge, Tanganyika. *Nature* 181:1099–1103.

LEAKEY, L. S. B.; and LEAKEY, M. D. 1964 Recent Discoveries of Fossil Hominids in Tanganyika: At Olduvai and Near Lake Natron. *Nature* 202:5–7.

LEAKEY, L. S. B.; TOBIAS, P. V.; and NAPIER, J. R. 1964 A New Species of the Genus Homo From Olduvai Gorge. *Nature* 203:7–9.

LIBBY, WILLARD F. (1952) 1955 *Radiocarbon Dating.* 2d ed. Univ. of Chicago Press.

MOVIUS, H. L. JR. 1964 Upper Perigordian and Aurignacian Hearths at the Abri Pataud, Les Eyzies, Dordogne. Unpublished manuscript. → Paper read at the Detroit meetings of the American Anthropological Association.

OAKLEY, KENNETH P. (1949) 1956 *Man the Tool-maker.* 3d ed. London: British Museum. → A paperback edition was published in 1957 by the Univ. of Chicago Press.

OAKLEY, KENNETH P. 1964 The Evolution of Man. *Discovery: The Magazine of Scientific Progress* (Norwich, England) 25: 49 only. → A letter to the editor.

RUST, ALFRED (editor) 1943 *Die alt- und mittelsteinzeitlichen Funde von Stellmoor.* Neumünster (Germany): Wachholtz.

SIMONS, ELWYN L. 1963 Some Fallacies in the Study of Hominid Phylogeny. *Science* 141:879–889.

SONNEVILLE-BORDES, DENISE DE 1963 Upper Palaeolithic Cultures in Western Europe. *Science* 142:347–355.

STEKELIS, M. 1963 Recent Discoveries in the Jordan Valley. *South African Journal of Science* 59, no. 3: 77–80.

TEILHARD DE CHARDIN, PIERRE; and PEI, W. C. 1932 The Lithic Industry of the Sinanthropus Deposits in Choukoutien. Geological Society of China, *Bulletin* 11, no. 4:315–358.

TOBIAS, P. V. 1964 The Olduvai Bed I. Hominine With Special Reference to Its Cranial Capacity. *Nature* 203:3–4.

TODE, A. et al. 1953 Die Untersuchung der palaeolithischen Freilandstation von Salzgitter-Lebenstedt. *Eiszeitalter und Gegenwart* 3:144-220.

WASHBURN, SHERWOOD L. (editor) 1961 *Social Life of Early Man.* Viking Fund Publications in Anthropology, No. 31. Chicago: Aldine.

II
NEW WORLD PREHISTORIC SOCIETIES

Early European explorers coming to the New World encountered hundreds of different American Indian cultures, ranging in levels of development from the indigenous civilizations of Nuclear America to the simplest food-collecting groups of the arid deserts. There was virtually no area with moisture and vegetation sufficient to sustain human life that had not been occupied. The long period of development represented by this diverse and complex assemblage of cultures has been outlined with varying degrees of clarity by archeological studies. It is now clear that hunting and gathering cultures occupied most of the New World in the earlier phases of its prehistory and that in many areas cultures of this type persisted into the historic period. It is also important to note that in most areas outside the urban centers of civilization hunting and gathering continued to significantly supplement the produce of primitive cultivation.

Terminal Pleistocene big-game hunters

The date of man's first entry into the New World is still largely a matter of conjecture. Our best evidence concerning this problem is derived from archeological sites in which material of unquestionable cultural derivation is linked to reliable chronological estimates, such as those yielded by carbon-14 dating.

The earliest of these sites (as of 1965) is Muaco, Venezuela, where stone tools have been found associated with the bones of now extinct Pleistocene mammals, which had been charred, engraved, and split, presumably by human beings (Rouse & Cruxent 1963, pp. 34–36). A date of about 12,500 B.C. is likely for this material on the basis of carbon-14 evidence. By 10,000–9000 B.C. the human occupation of North America was fairly widespread, and by 8000 B.C. man had reached the southern tip of South America (Rubin & Berthold 1961, p. 96; Delibrias et al. 1964, p. 244). On the basis of the sum of this chronological evidence, the biological characteristics of the American Indian, the formal relationships among New World cultural industries, and our knowledge of cultures of the late Pleistocene in northern Asia, it would appear that man entered the New World via the Bering Strait land bridge about 17,500 B.C. Our knowledge of the environment of this arctic area during the Würm-Wisconsin glaciation (Hopkins 1959, p. 1527) indicates that the most likely means of survival for these men would have been the hunting of large mammals, such as mammoths.

This type of hunting appears to have continued as an important part of the subsistence pattern of the paleo-Indian cultures of terminal Pleistocene age. It is well demonstrated by sites in the western United States, such as the Clovis gravel pit in eastern New Mexico (Sellards 1952, pp. 29–31) and the Lehner site in southeastern Arizona (Haury et al. 1959), both dated to 10,000–9000 B.C., where the abundant remains of mammoth, bison, and other now extinct animals are found associated with distinctive Clovis fluted projectile points and other stone and bone tools. Later, in the same area, people using Folsom fluted points (8000 B.C.) and unfluted lanceolate points (8000–5000 B.C.) hunted several now extinct species of bison. While a somewhat similar evolution of distinctive projectile points is found in eastern North America (apparently during the same time period), no direct evidence has yet appeared associating these tools and weapons with the remains of large Pleistocene mammals. It is possible that the large-game hunting tradition continued where extensive herds existed, from the arctic to the western plains, while the temperate woodlands of the east, inhabited only by relatively solitary herbivores, supported different subsistence patterns.

Post-Pleistocene cultural diversity

In succeeding time periods it appears that economic patterns based on a greater diversity of resources began earliest in areas in which large herds were absent. By 6000–5000 B.C. the Early Archaic cultures of eastern North America were clearly utilizing a wide variety of forest resources, and, on the basis of notched in addition to lanceolate projectile points, they were using hunting techniques that differed from those of the paleo-Indian (see, for example, Fowler 1959).

During the same period in the arid regions of western North America, an adaptation to sparse resources had been made by the small bands of hunters and gatherers of the Desert Culture, who developed seasonal cycles of utilization of the most fruitful areas of their limited environment (see Jennings 1964, pp. 152–153). And, in the great river valleys of the northwest, Indians had apparently begun to utilize the abundant resources of annual salmon runs as a basic food source (Borden 1962, pp. 10–11). Thus, by the sixth millennium B.C., there appear to have been several distinct culture types in North America, each adjusted to the resources of a particular natural area. That a similar diversity was true of Middle and South America is suggested by archeological evidence found in Tamaulipas (MacNeish 1958), Tehuacán (MacNeish 1964*a*), and recent discoveries in the coastal desert and mountains of Peru (Lanning & Hammel 1961), where several specific adaptations suggest similar specialization in areas as yet unexplored.

The first New World appearance of food production occurs in northeastern and central Mexico during this period (MacNeish 1958; 1964*b*). However, because of diverse local environments and arid climatic conditions, it was several thousand years before the effects of this innovation radically influenced the development of the prehistoric cultures of Nuclear America. The trend from widespread cultural uniformity to increasing local diversity reflects the specialization of cultural adjustments and the increasing utilization of the most favorable resources of each specific habitat. This trend can be seen in the prehistoric cultural sequence in much of the New World from about 5000 B.C. to the period of the introduction of cultivation in each area. Only in the extremely arid regions is there little evidence of significant change following 5000 B.C. Here, in general, successful and near-optimal cultural adjustments had been made in earlier periods.

The Arctic. Where natural conditions were unsuited to primitive cultivation, increasing refinements of hunting and gathering techniques continued virtually up to the period of historic contact. Perhaps the most outstanding example of such a sequence is found in the arctic region. The earliest well-known cultural tradition began about 4000 B.C., represented in the western Arctic by the Denbigh phase (Giddings 1964, pp. 191–243), and spread eastward to the northern and eastern shores of Greenland by about 2000 B.C. (Knuth 1954). This tradition was characterized by the use of microlithic tools similar to and undoubtedly derived from the mesolithic industries of northern Eurasia. The eastward spread of this culture appears to coincide with the Altithermal, a climatic interval somewhat milder than present conditions, from about 5000 to 2500 B.C., when a generalized adaptation to arctic resources was probably sufficient for survival. Although much of the material culture was perishable, enough remains to indicate that certain basic elements of specifically arctic culture were already common; these include stone lamps, permanent semisubterranean houses, toggle-head harpoons, tailored clothing, and watercraft. The stone industry included many microlithic tools similar to those of mesolithic cultures in northern Eurasia, but it also includes distinctive bifacially flaked end-blades and side-blades, which were used for projectile points or harpoon points. The extensive finds of burins and burinlike tools probably reflect a substantial bone industry which is little known to prehistorians because of poor preservation. In the eastern Arctic, the Sarqaq and similar "arctic small-tool tradition" cultures appear to have given rise *in situ* and without extensive outside influence to the primitive Eskimo-like Dorset culture (Taylor 1959). By the last half of the first millennium B.C., these people, who were apparently similar to the historic Eskimo in physical appearance, had spread widely along the coastal areas of the eastern Arctic. The Dorset culture retained several features of the earlier traditions, such as microlithic tools, and lacked certain cultural techniques later developed by the Eskimo, such as the use of dog sleds, ceramics, and the bow drill. The Dorset people did not venture into open seas in pursuit of whales, although other large sea mammals were hunted. Near the end of the first millennium A.D., the Dorset culture appears to have been replaced by the intrusive and fully-Eskimo Thule culture (Collins 1954, pp. 87–93), which had developed in the western Arctic from an ancestry similar to that of Dorset but with the continued stimulus of contact with northeastern Asia. It was from Asia that a knowledge of ceramic techniques was probably received by about 1000 B.C. In general, the prehistoric cultures of the western Arctic indicate somewhat more interest in the resources of the interior (especially the caribou) than do those of the eastern Arctic.

Northwest coast. Our knowledge of the prehistoric hunting and gathering cultures of the boreal forest to the south of the Arctic is still poor; this area remains one of the least explored archeological territories in the New World. The northwest coast of North America, on the other hand, has yielded sufficient material to indicate that the spectacular marine-oriented cultures of the historic period were part of a long sequence of local development. Evidences of the distinctive Northwest Coast art style have been found in the Marpole cultural phase of the Fraser River delta area in the first millennium B.C. along with numerous artifacts similar to those employed by the historic Northwest Coast Indians (Borden 1962, pp. 12–13). It now seems likely that this culture owes its origin more to local innovation among peoples adjusted to the riverine resources of salmon and seal than to the southward diffusion of Eskimo technology, as was formerly believed. Cressman (1960) has demonstrated in sites at the Dalles, Oregon, that the riverine-oriented cultures of the northwest plateau area underwent a marked change in artifact inventory about 5000 B.C. Several technological features, such as microblades, burins, a particular type of projectile point, and bolas (presumably for snaring birds), disappeared at that time, and succeeding horizons are characterized by a wide variety of projectile points, end scrapers, mortars and pestles, etc., which suggests a more diversified utilization of resources, perhaps in response to the less favorable conditions of the warmer Altithermal period between 5000 and 2500 B.C. However, this hypothesis is difficult to confirm, since animal bone and other food refuse have as yet been found only in the earlier levels of the sequence.

Great Basin. To the south of the plateau, the 9,000-year-old hunting and gathering tradition of the Desert Culture continued almost unchanged into the historic period. The Great Basin Indians collected virtually every digestible substance to be found in the environment. This early utilization of diverse resources included the intensive use of plant fibers for implements and equipment such as sandals and clothing. In areas where game was more abundant or moisture required the use of more lasting materials, many of these items would have been made of animal hide. The arid conditions of the Great Basin throughout the post-Pleistocene period have resulted in the remarkable preservation of almost all material remains of this culture, leaving us with a much more complete picture of the technology than we have for any group of comparable age. In addition to these objects of normally perishable materials, the Desert Culture peoples made frequent use of milling stones and heavy chipped stone "pulper-planers," as well as a wide variety of small projectile points and scrapers of chipped stone.

California. Whether the early cultures of California originated out of the Desert Culture is still a matter of debate. While these early California cultures do not show evidence of a strong link with the paleo-Indian hunting traditions they seem also to lack many characteristic Desert Culture items. Some of these items, such as milling stones, would have been useful in processing a wide variety of edible plant foods in California. The prehistoric record in California indicates an increasingly dense population in areas of relatively abundant resources after about 2000 B.C. (Heizer 1964, pp. 122–131). It appears that the essential specialization in the utilization of acorns as food in the southern coastal and interior valley areas had taken place by this time. Acorns, supplemented by game and various other local resources, were sufficient to support villages of over one thousand persons in the early historic period. The increase in population in California appears to have been accompanied by increasing warfare or conflict and individual accumulation of wealth, two features frequently observed in the historic cultures of that area.

The Southwest. The Desert Culture of the southwestern United States is still relatively little known in comparison to the succeeding village–farming period. In the cultures of the Cochise tradition (Sayles & Antevs 1941) an adaptation similar to that of the Great Basin peoples seems to have been basic, encouraged by somewhat more abundant resources. By about 1000 B.C. gathering activities were supplemented by maize, squash, and bean cultivation, undoubtedly derived from Mexico.

To the east of the Desert Culture, other small groups of hunters and gatherers populated the Rocky Mountains, as, for example, the culture of the McKean phase (Mulloy 1954).

Great Plains. On the Great Plains hunting patterns seem to have persisted as the chief source of subsistence until the end of the first millennium B.C., when the earliest techniques of cultivation were introduced from the eastern woodlands. The lowest level of deposits of the Signal Butte site in western Nebraska (Strong 1935, pp. 224–239) yielded the small lanceolate points that perhaps persisted from earlier paleo-Indian traditions until about 2500 B.C.; these were accompanied and followed by a sequence of notched projectile points, which elsewhere are more typical of this time-horizon. The fauna represented in the lowest deposits of this site is similar to that of the historic period, including bison, deer, elk, and antelope.

Eastern woodlands. In the eastern United States in the late Archaic period (2500 B.C.), hunting and gathering cultures followed two major patterns of adjustment to local resources—a northern lacustrine-oriented way of life and a southern riverine-oriented pattern. Several less widespread adaptations also occurred, including utilization of the Atlantic coastal region. The northern lacustrine-oriented cultures apparently maintained a balance in subsistence between hunting, fishing, and plant collection. One interesting variant of this tradition, the Old Copper culture of the Michigan–Wisconsin area, made extensive use of the deposits of native copper in the vicinity of Lake Superior for the manufacture of a wide variety of implements, including knives, spear and arrow points, and woodworking tools (axes, adzes, etc.). The copper was worked by cold-hammering, or heated and hammered, but it was not smelted or cast. Implements made from copper, which came from the Lake Superior area, are frequently encountered in Archaic cultures of other Great Lakes areas and occasionally as far away as the southeastern United States. This implies widespread patterns of barter and exchange in eastern North America as early as 2000 B.C. Other items whose distribution yields evidence of extensive late Archaic trade patterns in this area are chipped implements of a distinctive gray hornstone deriving from southern Indiana and Illinois and modified fragments of large conch shells probably imported from the Gulf and Atlantic coasts of the southeast.

The occupation sites of southeast riverine-oriented food collectors are characterized archeologically by extensive accumulations of river mussels. This debris is obvious evidence for heavy reliance on mussels as a source of food, supplemented chiefly by deer, waterfowl, and collected plants, including large quantities of nuts. While the settlements of late Archaic food collectors in the southeast were larger than those of the northeast, there is no good evidence for more complex social patterns or status differentiation in the south. In burial practice, for example, there are no individual differences in the concentration of wealth represented by grave goods sufficient to postulate marked social differentiation. At about 1000 B.C. techniques of cultivation derived from Middle America began to contribute to the diet of the food collectors of eastern North America. During the next 500 years this pattern spread through most river valleys west of the Appalachians and south of the present limits of the 140-day growing season. In a scattering of less favorable habitats cultivation probably contributed a smaller portion of the diet, and hunting and gathering, which everywhere retained some importance in the subsistence pattern, was the major source of food.

Middle America. The early food-collecting cultures of Middle America are still little known. The few sites thus far explored in Mexico reveal an early stratum similar to the Desert Culture of the western United States at about 8000–7000 B.C. (MacNeish 1964*b*). The increasingly arid conditions of the Altithermal throughout most of Mexico produced an increasing intensity of collection of wild plants and the early cultivation of domestic forms, while hunting declined in importance. However, it was probably not until about 1500 B.C. that cultivation provided the major portion of food in any area of Middle America.

Central America. A single site in Central America, Cerro Mangote (5000 B.C.), on the west coast of Panama, is representative of a nonfood-producing horizon in this area (McGimsey 1956). The food refuse and stone tools suggest an economy largely dependent upon marine resources such as mollusks, fish, and crabs but supplemented by the hunting of deer and other land mammals and the use of plants (as evidenced by grindstones). The persistence of this pattern is seen at the nearby site of Monagrillo (Willey & McGimsey 1954), dated nearly three thousand years later, where a similar assemblage of tools, with the addition of pottery, has been reported. It has been suggested that this site represents the initial horizon of cultivation in Panama (Rouse & Cruxent 1963, p. 41). Cultures similar to that of Cerro Mangote were also characteristic of the food-collecting horizon in the Antilles, apparently depending on a similar group of resources. They differ from Cerro Mangote chiefly because of their more extensive use of large shells for implements and less frequent use of stone. That the Antillean cultures are roughly contemporary with those of Panama is indicated by a nonceramic site of this type in the Dominican Republic that is dated somewhat earlier than 2000 B.C. (Tamers et al. 1964, p. 158). They appear to have been gradually replaced in the late first millennium B.C. by peoples bringing a knowledge of cultivation north out of Venezuela. In a few peripheral areas, such as western Cuba, food-collecting cultures survived until the early historic period (Rouse 1964).

South America. In many areas of South America, as in North America, food collection persisted until the historic period, and hunting and gathering continued to supplement primitive cultivation except in the nuclear area of Andean civilization. Our most extensive knowledge of these cultures in South America comes from coastal settlements where the collection of marine animals supplemented land resources. The Cubagua phase of Venezuela, which is probably related to the early Antillean cultures, is represented by sites of this type (Rouse & Cruxent 1963, pp. 44–46). Farther to the south, along the Atlantic coast of Brazil, the *sambaquís*, or shell mounds, are frequently many feet thick; besides providing evidence of the extensive use of shellfish as early as 6000 B.C., these mounds also contain abundant remains of fish, land mammals, and birds (Hurt 1964). The cultural industries show a development from purely lithic assemblages containing relatively crudely chipped stone tools (Sambaquí de Maratuá) to a much more varied later assemblage (Torres Site), including ceramics, a wide variety of ground stone tools, and abundant bone and shell implements (Serrano 1946; Silva & Meggers 1963, pp. 124–125).

Along the Pacific coast, the Valdivia phase of Ecuador exhibits a primarily shellfish-gathering and fishing subsistence base (Estrada & Evans 1963, pp. 79–80). The presence of a well-developed ceramic industry in this phase, dated to about 3000 B.C., has led to a hypothesis of transpacific contact with the Jomon culture of Japan in which similar ceramics were being manufactured during this period. An external source is suggested, since these ceramics are the earliest known in the New World, and chronological evidence suggests a dispersal northward and southward from this area. The only alternative would seem to lie in a yet undiscovered ceramic tradition in the Amazon Basin, which could have been carried across the Andes into coastal Ecuador.

In coastal Peru the successors of the early hunting tradition appear to have migrated seasonally, spending winters in the vicinity of fog meadows along the coasts where grazing deer and guanaco were available as well as many wild plants (Lanning 1963). Resources of the nearby ocean were utilized to a lesser extent than in the previously mentioned cultures, although sea shells and fish bones both occur at most sites. Seasonal migration seems to have occurred: summers were probably spent in the highlands hunting and collecting different types of wild plants. Early in the third millennium B.C. a shift in the coastal currents off Peru resulted in the desiccation of the winter fog meadows and an increase in marine animal life. This, coupled with the beginning of cultivation of cotton and gourds, led to the establishment of permanent settlements along the coasts, ancestral to the civilizations of several thousand years later. The earliest well-known cultures of coastal Chile are characterized by assemblages which include varied types of fish hooks, harpoons for sea mammal hunting, and grindstones, presumably for plant food (Bird 1946*a*). While there is no firm chronology for these cultures, a date of 2000 B.C. does not seem unlikely. The long cultural sequence at Tierra del Fuego indicates that a cultural pattern similar to that of the historic Indians of that area persisted over a considerable time period: various types of projectile points, bolas stones, end scrapers, and bone awls are present in all but the earliest cultural levels (Bird 1946*b*).

Thus, throughout the New World we see a trend indicating a relatively rapid diversification of food-collecting cultures adjusting to local resources, following the period of relative cultural uniformity of the terminal Pleistocene. While general patterns of utilization of wild foods were established early, specific patterns of artifact design, reflecting relatively minor technological innovations, continued to change throughout the prehistoric sequence of these hunting and gathering cultures. In areas outside the centers of civilization, the gathering of wild plants and animals continued to be a major factor in the economies of most peoples who practiced cultivation. It was only in the Nuclear areas of Middle America and the Andes that the hunting and gathering of wild foods had lost importance by the time of European contact.

ARTHUR J. JELINEK

[*Directly related are the entries* ARCHEOLOGY; INDIANS, NORTH AMERICAN; *and the biographies of* GIFFORD; KROEBER; STRONG.]

BIBLIOGRAPHY

BIRD, JUNIUS (1946*a*) 1963 The Cultural Sequence of the North Chilean Coast. Volume 2, pages 587–594 in Julian H. Steward (editor), *Handbook of South American Indians.* New York: Cooper Square.

BIRD, JUNIUS (1946*b*) 1963 The Archeology of Patagonia. Volume 1, pages 17–24 in Julian H. Steward (editor), *Handbook of South American Indians.* New York: Cooper Square.

BORDEN, CHARLES E. 1962 West Coast Crossties With Alaska. Pages 9–19 in John M. Campbell (editor), *Prehistoric Cultural Relations Between the Arctic and Temperate Zones of North America.* Montreal: The Institute.

COLLINS, HENRY B. 1954 *Arctic Area: Indigenous Period.* Publication No. 60. Mexico City: Instituto Panamericano de Geografía é Historia.

CRESSMAN, L. S. 1960 Cultural Sequences at The Dalles, Oregon: A Contribution to Pacific Northwest Prehistory. American Philosophical Society, *Transactions* New Series 50:1–108.

DELIBRIAS, G.; GUILLIER, M. T.; and LABEYRIE, J. 1964 Saclay Natural Radiocarbon Measurements I. *Radiocarbon* 6:233–250.

ESTRADA, EMILIO; and EVANS, CLIFFORD 1963 *Cultural Development in Ecuador.* Pages 77–88 in Betty J. Meggars and Clifford Evans (editors), *Aboriginal Cultural Development in Latin America.* Washington: Smithsonian Institution.

FOWLER, MELVIN L. 1959 *Summary Report of Modoc Rock Shelter, 1952, 1953, 1955, 1956.* Illinois, State Museum of, Report of Investigations No. 8. Springfield: The Museum.

GIDDINGS, JAMES L. 1964 *The Archaeology of Cape Denbigh.* Providence, R.I.: Brown Univ. Press.

HAURY, EMIL W.; SAYLES, E. B.; and WASLEY, WILLIAM B. 1959 The Lehner Mammoth Site, Southeastern Arizona. *American Antiquity* 25:2–30.

HEIZER, R. F. 1964 The Western Coast of North America. Pages 117–148 in William Marsh Rice University, Houston, Texas, *Prehistoric Man in the New World.* Edited by Jesse D. Jennings and Edward Norbeck. Univ. of Chicago Press.

HOPKINS, DAVID M. 1959 Cenozoic History of the Bering Land Bridge. *Science* 129:1519–1528.

HURT, WESLEY R. 1964 Recent Radiocarbon Dates for Central and Southern Brazil. *American Antiquity* 30: 25–33.

JENNINGS, JESSE D. 1964 The Desert West. Pages 149–174 in William Marsh Rice University, Houston, Texas, *Prehistoric Man in the New World.* Univ. of Chicago Press.

KNUTH, EIGIL 1954 The Paleo-Eskimo Culture of Northeast Greenland Elucidated by Three New Sites. *American Antiquity* 19:367–381.

LANNING, EDWARD P. 1963 A Pre-agricultural Occupation on the Central Coast of Peru. *American Antiquity* 28:360–371.

LANNING, EDWARD P.; and HAMMEL, EUGENE A. 1961 Early Lithic Industries of Western South America. *American Antiquity* 27:139–154.

McGIMSEY, CHARLES R. 1956 Cerro Mangote: A Preceramic Site in Panama. *American Antiquity* 22:151–161.

MACNEISH, RICHARD S. 1958 Preliminary Archaeological Investigations in the Sierra de Tamaulipas, Mexico. American Philosophical Society, *Transactions* New Series 48, no. 6.

MACNEISH, RICHARD S. 1964*a* Ancient Mesoamerican Civilization. *Science* 143:531–537.

MACNEISH, RICHARD S. 1964*b* The Food-gathering and Incipient Agriculture Stage of Prehistoric Middle America. Volume 1, pages 413–426 in Robert Wauchope (editor), *Handbook of Middle American Indians.* Austin: Univ. of Texas Press.

MULLOY, WILLIAM 1954 The McKean Site in Northeastern Wyoming. *Southwestern Journal of Anthropology* 10:432–460.

ROUSE, IRVING 1964 Prehistory of the West Indies. *Science* 144:499–513.

ROUSE, IRVING; and CRUXENT, J. M. 1963 *Venezuelan Archaeology.* New Haven: Yale Univ. Press.

RUBIN, MEYER; and BERTHOLD, SARAH M. 1961 U.S. Geological Survey Radiocarbon Dates VI. *Radiocarbon* 3:86–98.

SAYLES, EDWIN B.; and ANTEVS, ERNEST 1941 *The Cochise Culture.* Medallion Papers, No. 29. Globe, Ariz.: Privately printed for Gila Pueblo.

SELLARDS, ELIAS H. 1952 *Early Man in America: A Study in Prehistory.* Austin: Univ. of Texas Press.

SERRANO, ANTONIO (1946) 1963 The Sambaquis of the Brazilian Coast. Volume 1, pages 401–407 in Julian H. Steward (editor), *Handbook of South American Indians.* New York: Cooper Square.

SILVA, FERNANDO A.; and MEGGERS, BETTY J. 1963 *Cultural Development in Brazil.* Pages 119–129 in Betty J. Meggars and Clifford Evans (editors), *Aboriginal Cultural Development in Latin America.* Washington: Smithsonian Institution.

STRONG, WILLIAM D. 1935 *An Introduction to Nebraska Archaeology*. Smithsonian Institution, Smithsonian Miscellaneous Collections, Vol. 93, No. 10. Washington: The Institution.

TAMERS, M. A.; PEARSON, F. J. JR.; and DAVIS, E. MOTT 1964 University of Texas Radiocarbon Dates II. *Radiocarbon* 6:138–159.

TAYLOR, WILLIAM E. 1959 Review and Assessment of the Dorset Problem. *Anthropologica* New Series 1: 24–46.

WILLEY, GORDON R.; and MCGIMSEY, CHARLES R. 1954 The Monagrillo Culture of Panama. Peabody Museum of Archaeology and Ethnology, Harvard University, *Papers* 49, no. 2:8–137.

III
CONTEMPORARY SOCIETIES

There are few hunting and gathering peoples left in the world today, and fewer still who maintain this type of economy in its purest form, without knowledge of agriculture, without domestication of animals, and without the use of imported foods obtainable through barter, trade, service, or any other means. There are not many parts of the world left where it is possible to maintain the kind of isolation that is vital to the continuation of a hunting and gathering tradition.

In order to live by hunting and gathering, a community must exist in a generous environment that supplies all its needs or, if it exists in less advantageous circumstances, either must be isolated from all contact with other food-producing economies or has to possess an ancient, powerful, and vital tradition that enables it to resist foreign influences. If the environment is bountiful, the community is able to maintain its economic independence with ease and with conviction in the face of outside influence. With eminent good sense, such people can see no point in abandoning their simple but fully satisfactory way of life in favor of the dubious advantages of a more "advanced" way, particularly if that new way involves working in the fields or, indeed, working anywhere in a place and at a time not of their own choosing. The most striking example of such a people is the group of Mbuti pygmies, of the central African rain forest. Another example is the gypsy, who in a sense is a hunter and gatherer and whose situation and organization carry many parallels.

Usually, however, where the environment is kindly, it becomes the object of attention of peoples who believe that they can make better use of it than can the indigenous inhabitants; with their advanced skills and technology they wittingly or unwittingly destroy the delicate balance that makes hunting and gathering possible. In such circumstances the hunters and gatherers, ill equipped for resistance, are either obliterated or absorbed.

If the environment falls short of abundance, either by its gradual impoverishment or through the arrival of newcomers who make additional and different demands upon its resources, then the indigenous hunters and gatherers usually seek a new way of life. They may adopt a new form of economy (generally cultivation), or they may become dependent upon the more successful newcomers.

But even under the harshest circumstances—and Africa again provides a classic example in the Bushmen of the Kalahari—hunters and gatherers do sometimes survive. If their tradition is ancient and powerful enough, and as long as there is someplace, however inhospitable, where they can be free from interference, a hunting people may well choose to retain their independence at the expense of all material comfort and ease.

An alternative response to a contact situation, one in which hunters and gatherers preserve their integrity to a great extent, is for both groups to accept the contact as inevitable but to erect a barrier between their two worlds, keeping physical contact at a minimum. In such cases trade may exist between hunters and gatherers and their farmer neighbors. Such trade may be no more than a matter of mutual economic convenience or a way of formalizing the relationship. But where ideological barriers exist, and where the environment is capable of supporting both hunters and farmers (or other "outsiders"), the traditional hunting and gathering way of life may survive, remarkably intact, while apparently a close, sometimes symbiotic relationship with foreign cultivators is maintained. Again the Mbuti of Africa are an example.

For the purposes of anthropological research and theoretical analysis, we need not look only for groups that subsist wholly by hunting and gathering. We may find many or all the essential elements of a hunting and gathering society among a people who make use of cultivated foods or who even practice a limited amount of cultivation themselves. Essentially, there should be *potential* total economic independence; the bulk of subsistence should come from hunting and gathering.

There are a number of such peoples in the New World—the Eskimo, the Indians of the Pacific Northwest Coast and the Great Plains, the Siriono of Bolivia, and other South American tribes, particularly the Yamana, often called Yahgan. In Africa the Mbuti pygmies and the Bushmen of the Kalahari desert offer two striking examples, and there are several smaller groups. In Australia the aborigines maintain their hunting and gathering economy under some of the most difficult conditions imaginable, and in India and southeast Asia there are a number of Negrito and other groups, of which the Birhor and the Andaman Islanders are probably the best known.

Environmental considerations

The most cursory survey of the abbreviated list given above indicates at once the enormously wide variety of environments in which hunting and gathering can persist: arctic, equatorial, tropical, subtropical, and continental. Hunters and gatherers are found inland and on seacoasts, in forests and on deserts, from sea level to 10,000 feet or more. It is also plain that there are few instances in which the environment can actually be said to favor hunting and gathering to the extent that it does, say, in the case of the African pygmies. In most cases the hunters suffer from extremes of temperature, from an uncertain supply of game and vegetable foods, or from the necessity of an arduous and often dangerous daily quest.

In a study of any hunting and gathering community, the environment is of paramount importance. It not only affects and often determines the exact nature of hunting and gathering activities, including the technology involved, but it also has a profound effect upon the social organization, the political system, and the religious beliefs of the people. Ultimately it may even be responsible for determining the nature of intergroup relationships, that is, relationships between hunters and gatherers and others who occupy the same environmental region. Each instance should first be studied on its own, without a search for an easy application of universal laws supposedly resulting from a superficial similarity of economy. The intimate relationship between hunters and gatherers and the world around them is perhaps the most important and certain common factor, and from it stem many, if not all, other similarities.

Theory of social evolution. There has been much fruitless generalization about hunting and gathering because of its self-evident simplicity, or perhaps "directness" is a better word. It has also attracted the attention of those concerned with social evolution. It was certainly one of the earliest forms of social life known to man, but it is neither helpful nor perceptive to regard it as a stage, or a level, through which the form and structure of society has evolved, any more than it is intelligent to suppose that peoples who still hunt and gather must necessarily be backward because they have not "advanced."

It is necessary to avoid generalizations about the social structure of these people. The alleged patrilineal bias of hunters and gatherers is one such dangerous assumption, although Elman R. Service (1962) has made a notable contribution by conducting very specific research into the structure of both contemporary and early bands of hunters and gatherers and has at least made available a great deal of data hitherto inaccessible. There is a remarkable dearth of factual monographs resulting from field work in this area.

With these warnings in mind, it is instructive to look at the hunting and gathering economy, as maintained under diverse environmental conditions, and to observe its effect on the over-all structure of the society.

Nomadic way of life

Hunting and gathering impose on a people, regardless of their environment, a certain degree of nomadism. When the game moves, or becomes hunted out, and when the vegetable foods are exhausted, there is no alternative but for the people to follow the game and to search for fresh vegetable supplies. The need for mobility immediately limits the extent of material culture, the entire possessions of a family having to be transportable, in some cases on a single back.

There is a continuum of nomadism that ranges from the daily wanderings of the jungle (Uthlu) Birhor of India and some Kalahari Bushmen, through the monthly change of hunting camps among the Congo pygmies, the quarterly movements of the Blackfoot Indians, and the biannual movements of Canadian coastal Eskimo, to the sedentary lives of the Pacific Northwest Coast Indians. The last, who depend mainly on fishing, are able to settle in villages and have an exceptionally rich and complex material culture. Nonetheless, they are forced to make temporary seasonal encampments following the migration of salmon.

The material culture of the Congo pygmies, whose environment is most abundant, is probably the most minimal and is comparable with that of the Andaman Islanders and other hunters who live in similar rain forests. The bow and arrow or spear (blowguns are not found in Africa) is the only necessary equipment, although nets are used by some pygmies. The carrying basket and the hammer for pounding out barkcloth are the only other items in general use. There is virtually no visual art other than decoration of the body. Among the Eskimo, on the other hand, whose environment makes rigorous demands, the technology is infinitely more complex, and much wider use is made of all available materials for artistic as well as practical purposes.

The Yamana of South America appear to offer a different picture, for their technology is slight although their environment is harsh. The notion that the Yamana are mentally backward because they do not know how to clothe themselves against the damp and cold is particularly absurd. It rests on the assumption that the relative values of hot and cold must be the same for the Yamana as for everyone else, but it ignores other factors. The Yamana use oil and grease against the cold and may well prefer to be unhampered by clothes when sailing the fragile canoes in which most of their life is spent. The canoe is probably their major technological response to the environment, serving not only as a means of pursuing their game but also as a home and a shelter. In all cases the technology of the hunters and gatherers is obviously adequate for survival. The degree of nomadism demanded by a successful adaptation to local conditions guides the particular form the technology will take and affects the sociopolitical organization of the group.

Social structure. In an examination of the different aspects of social structure of all hunters and gatherers, the only truly common element that emerges at the moment is the uniformly dominant and pervasive environmental factor. Otherwise the picture is one of great diversity; the range in material culture has already been cited, and a similar range exists in social organization at the family level. Steward (1955) and Service (1962) argue cogently for the hypothesis that hunting and gathering bands are by nature patrilineal, but this is by no means true of all contemporary societies. Except in the cases of the Birhor and the Australian aborigines, the constant movement of the group leads to a very fluid band composition, which is neither clearly patrilineal nor patrilocal.

Where hunting, primarily a male occupation, is the dominant activity, there is a tendency for such bands to be grouped around the men and for men who have grown up together and who know one another's ways (that is, "brothers") to form nuclear hunting units. This gives the appearance of patrilocality and patrilineality, but apart from the two cases cited above there is nowhere a clear reflection of any unilineal descent system in the over-all social structure. Even the kinship terminology does not reflect it, such terminology frequently being generational and thus having greater economic than lineal significance.

The size of the bands necessarily fluctuates according to the nature of food supply, and among nearly all hunting bands there seems to be a constant process of fission and fusion, for economic reasons, that again militates against any effective, corporate unilineal descent system.

It is not clearly established that hunting is always the major subsistence activity (see, e.g., Service 1966). Even when it has more economic importance, which is by no means in all cases, it does not necessarily carry greater prestige than gathering. It can probably be said that in most hunting and gathering societies the woman occupies a position of prestige equal to that of the man and is recognized as being equally important in domestic and economic life. It would indeed be impossible to find a convincing argument showing the advantage of patrilineality and patrilocality over any other descent system or residence pattern that would apply to all hunters and gatherers.

Marriage practices among hunters and gatherers do not reveal any singleness of mind or purpose with respect to line or residence. In most cases marriage is to a person outside one's own economic unit, but among the Canadian Eskimo the preference seems to be to marry within that unit. The incest restrictions are variously and often vaguely stated, being most formalized among the aborigines and the Birhor. The Birhor residential unit, or *tanda*, cuts directly across clan lines, however.

The extent to which the nuclear family maintains regular residential association with related families varies considerably. Even among the Canadian Eskimo, who with the Pacific Northwest Coast Indians and the Jaghi Birhor are probably the most settled of hunters and gatherers, there are continuous fluctuations in the composition of each settlement.

Economic organization. Although it might be said that the nuclear family is the primary economic unit among all hunters and gatherers, the degree to which such families group together for economic activities varies considerably. Among the Congo pygmies, those who hunt with bow and arrow spend most of the year in small units of three nuclear families, coming together as a larger band only once or twice. In the same rain forest, those who use a hunting net spend most of the year in bands of fifteen or twenty (up to thirty and no less than seven) nuclear families, splitting up for the two months of the honey season. In both cases the technology determines the most advantageous size of the economic unit.

Generally the size of the economic unit also varies according to local conditions of abundance or scarcity. The grouping process described above can be seen, for example, among the Blackfoot and the Washo Indians, who are forced to combine once a year for vital seasonal economic activity, but who spend the rest of the year in small, semi-isolated bands.

Preservation of food. Although there is knowledge of preservation of food among some groups, the major characteristic of a hunting and gathering economy is its diurnal nature. Even the Jaghi Birhor, who live in semipermanent villages and engage in trade, have no agriculture and hunt every day. Many hunters do not preserve meat for their own use but may do so for trade. The Eskimo and many North American Indians, however, preserve and store food against seasonal shortage or emergency.

Division of labor. Hunting is generally the province of men and gathering that of women and children, but for the most part hunting and gathering are jointly cooperative activities. Women may actually help their menfolk on the hunt, as among the Yamana and the Mbuti, or they may hunt smaller game on their own when opportunity provides. Where hunting is particularly arduous, as among some Eskimo, the women may restrict their activities to gathering and to looking after the household. But whether or not specific activities are shared, the economy undeniably depends on close cooperation between men and women. Even the aged and infirm are sometimes found a place in the economy, being left to guard the camp and look after young children or given tasks such as the manufacture of baskets, twine, and cloth.

Distribution. Although the distribution of produce does not always follow set lines, there appears always to be a stated obligation to share food within the same residential unit, related or otherwise. It is particularly striking that among wealth-producing hunters, such as the Blackfoot and the Kwakiutl, there are institutionalized means of distributing the wealth.

The cooperative nature of the economy and the egalitarian distribution of produce are perhaps a response to the basic insecurity of a diurnal economy. This also militates against the formation of exclusive groups, kinship or otherwise. In fact, a great deal of the fluctuation that takes place among hunting bands effectively acts as a means of establishing reciprocal rights and obligations to be called upon in times of need.

Political organization. The diurnal and immediate nature of the economy, correlated with cooperativeness and egalitarianism, is reflected in the political system. In the same way that the environment plays a large part in determining the nature of the economy and technology, so does it affect the political structure. Territoriality is determined to a large extent by natural barriers, such as hills, rivers, and ravines, but also by the migratory habits of the game. It is in the nature of a band to be self-sufficient, and in regions where the game and vegetable supply is abundant, as in the African rain forest, there is no need for trespass and each band remains happily distinct from its neighbors.

Authority. Except for the Pacific Northwest Coast Indians and the Birhor, there are no recognizable systems of chieftainship. With the Birhor such leadership is ritually based, and not necessarily hereditary, and it exists only at a local, not a tribal, level. There is an annual holiday at which the various neighboring clan groups unite for a joint hunt, but this temporary amalgamation has no single leader. Among the Indians of the Great Plains, similarly, local leadership is not necessarily hereditary but largely charismatic, resting on personal attributes. The Washo provide an example of hunters who have specific leaders for specific communal hunts, such as the rabbit hunt or the antelope hunt. The Siriono also boast chiefs. But nowhere do we find a clear-cut secular authority backed by power.

With the nuclear family as an effective economic unit in itself, there is no band leadership of anything but a charismatic and therefore temporary nature. Hunting issues tend to be decided by the younger men, who are the most active hunters. When hunting is combined with gathering the women also have a voice in determining where and how the hunt should take place. Older men and women are sometimes called upon to settle disputes and are usually relied on to determine the suitability of proposed marriages because of their knowledge of family and individual relationships.

Law and government. There are no true legal systems among hunters and gatherers, any more than there is true government. Sometimes, however, religious societies act as overseers of the law. Each issue is more usually settled as it arises by all who are concerned and who are present at the time. Ridicule and ostracism are the usual "punishments" among most contemporary hunters and gatherers. In exceptional cases, where personal property is of more significance, systems of fines have been introduced by rational administrators. The purpose of the fines is still not retributive but rather restorative. The prime concern of all sanctions is the maintenance of the delicate equilibrium that enables a hunting and gathering band to pursue its essentially cooperative, egalitarian economy.

Formal government would destroy the egalitarian nature of the society, and, lacking egalitarianism, the cooperative effort would collapse. The terms "cooperative effort" and "egalitarianism" are not intended to imply value judgments; they are merely necessities. It would be rare to meet a hunter who did not try to keep the best part of his catch for himself, but it would be far more rare to find a hunter who refused to share with one who had nothing. There is often an acute awareness among hunters that one day they themselves might need assistance, and old age is an ever-present reminder of the dependence of one human being upon another.

In such a society, individual authority and individual responsibility are unwanted and avoided in secular affairs. The so-called chief, or leader, generally is totally without individual power. At most he merely represents the commonly accepted tradition of behavior—the power lies in the tradition, not in the chief.

Religious life. In the absence of formal government, religious belief helps support a sense of law and order. It also helps provide a feeling of unity that stretches far beyond the only really effective unit, the hunting band, and within that band it heightens the already strong sense of economic dependence.

A religious sense, then, is generally highly developed among hunters and gatherers, but ritual performance again varies widely. At one extreme are the elaborate totemic rites of the Australian aborigines and the complex ceremonies of some American Indians, and at the other are the simple community songs of the Mbuti or the Yamana. Where curers or shamans exist they are not associated with a formal church but are believed to be able to divine the future through their dreams and thus avert evil. They are, in a sense, mere functionaries performing a task for which they have shown themselves to be fitted.

Religious thought is concerned primarily with the presence of spiritual powers over which the living have no direct control and secondarily with the problem of life after death. Depending as immediately as they do upon the environment, which supplies them with the necessities of life, hunters and gatherers tend to identify themselves closely with it. When ritual dances and songs exist, they express this identification. A good example of this relationship is apparent in the Mbuti, who address and refer to the forest as both "mother" and "father."

Values. As a result of their close dependence upon and intimate ritual relationship with the environment, hunters and gatherers must be profoundly influenced in their attitude to others by the relationship those others establish with the same environment. Hence the enormous latent hostility between the hunting Mbuti and the village cultivators who live in the same forest; hence also the sharp division the Lele (Congo) make between their lives as hunters and their lives as farmers. It is certainly this sense of identity, grown out of generations of close daily contact with the world around them, that persuades the Kalahari Bushmen to pursue their nomadic existence in the face of extraordinary hardships rather than throw their lot in with a people obviously not in tune with their world. Cultivation itself, in that it physically assaults the land, can become an act of desecration and profanity in the eyes of a hunter.

Religious life, then, is closely associated with all other aspects of the life of the hunter and gatherer and supplies the order that would otherwise have to be provided by formal institutions. And it is in his religious life that he expresses his widest sense of identity. The spectacular giraffe dances of the Bushmen, the Eskimo poetry to Sedna, goddess of the sea, and the Mbuti songs to the god of the forest all convey something of the amazing strength of unity that can exist in these loosely organized societies. Their very survival is sufficient testimony to the effectiveness of their informal structure and the directness of their response to the environment in which they have to live.

COLIN M. TURNBULL

[*Directly related is the entry* SOCIAL STRUCTURE.]

BIBLIOGRAPHY

BIRKET-SMITH, KAJ (1927) 1959 *The Eskimos.* Rev. & enl. ed. London: Methuen. → First published in Danish.

DOUGLAS, MARY 1954 The Lele of Kasai. Pages 1–26 in International African Institute, *African Worlds: Studies in the Cosmological Ideas and Social Values of African Peoples.* Edited by Daryll Forde. Oxford Univ. Press.

DRUCKER, PHILIP 1955 *Indians of the Northwest Coast.* American Museum of Natural History, Handbook No. 10. New York: McGraw-Hill.

EWERS, JOHN C. 1955 *The Horse in Blackfoot Culture: With Comparative Material From Other Western Tribes.* U.S. Bureau of American Ethnology, Bulletin No. 159. Washington: Smithsonian Institution.

GUSINDE, MARTIN (1937) 1961 *The Yamana: The Life and Thought of the Water Nomads of Cape Horn.* 5 vols. New Haven: Human Relations Area Files. → First published in German in 1937 as Volume 2 of *Die Feuerland Indianer.*

HOBHOUSE, LEONARD T.; WHEELER, GERALD C.; and GINSBERG, MORRIS (1915) 1930 *The Material Culture and Social Institutions of the Simpler Peoples: An Essay in Correlation.* London School of Economics and Political Science Monographs on Sociology, No. 3. London: Chapman.

HOLMBERG, ALLAN R. 1950 *Nomads of the Long Bow: The Siriono of Eastern Bolivia.* Institute of Social Anthropology, Publication No. 10. Washington: Smithsonian Institution. → Prepared in cooperation with the U.S. Department of State as a project of the Interdepartmental Committee on Scientific and Cultural Cooperation.

LOWIE, ROBERT H. 1939 Ethnographic Notes on the Washo. Volume 36, pages 301–352 in California, University of, *Publications in American Archaeology and Ethnology.* Berkeley: Univ. of California Press.

LOWIE, ROBERT H. 1954 *Indians of the Plains.* American Museum of Natural History, Anthropological Handbook No. 1. New York: McGraw-Hill.

MAN, EDWARD H. (1883) 1932 *On the Aboriginal Inhabitants of the Andaman Islands.* 2d printing. London: Royal Anthropological Institute.

RADCLIFFE-BROWN, A. R. (1922) 1948 *The Andaman Islanders.* Glencoe, Ill.: Free Press.

RADCLIFFE-BROWN, A. R. 1931 *The Social Organization of Australian Tribes.* Melbourne: Macmillan.

ROY, SARAT CHANDRA 1925 *The Birhors: A Little-known Jungle Tribe of Chota Nagpur.* Ranchi (India).

SERVICE, ELMAN R. 1958 *A Profile of Primitive Culture.* New York: Harper.

SERVICE, ELMAN R. 1962 *Primitive Social Organization: An Evolutionary Perspective.* New York: Random House.

SERVICE, ELMAN R. 1966 *The Hunters.* Englewood Cliffs, N.J.: Prentice-Hall.

SPENCER, BALDWIN; and GILLEN, F. J. 1899 *The Native Tribes of Central Australia.* London: Macmillan.

SPENCER, BALDWIN; and GILLEN, F. J. 1927 *The Arunta: A Study of a Stone Age People.* 2 vols. London: Macmillan.

STEWARD, JULIAN H. (1946–1959) 1963 *Handbook of South American Indians.* 7 vols. U.S. Bureau of American Ethnology, Bulletin No. 143. New York: Cooper Square.

STEWARD, JULIAN H. 1955 *Theory of Culture Change: The Methodology of Multilinear Evolution.* Urbana: Univ. of Illinois Press.

TURNBULL, COLIN M. 1960*a* The Elima: A Pre-marital Festival Among the Bambuti Pygmies. *Zaïre: Belgian African Review* 14:175–192.

TURNBULL, COLIN M. 1960*b* The Molimo: A Men's Religious Association Among the Ituri Bambuti. *Zaïre: Belgian African Review* 14:307–340.

TURNBULL, COLIN M. 1961 *The Forest People.* New York: Simon & Schuster.

TURNBULL, COLIN M. 1965 *Wayward Servants: The Two Worlds of the African Pygmies.* New York: Natural History Press.

WEYER, EDWARD M. (1932) 1962 *The Eskimos: Their Environment and Folkways.* Hamden, Conn.: Shoe String Press.

WISSLER, CLARK 1910 *Material Culture of the Blackfoot Indians.* Anthropological Papers of the American Museum of Natural History, Vol. 5, part 1. New York: The Museum.

WISSLER, CLARK 1912 *Social Organization and Ritualistic Ceremonies of the Blackfoot Indians.* Anthropological Papers of the American Museum of Natural History, Vol. 7. New York: The Museum. → Part 1 of this book was first published in 1911 as *Social Life of the Blackfoot Indians.*

HUNTINGTON, ELLSWORTH

Ellsworth Huntington (1876–1947), American geographer, was the most notable exponent of environmentalism in the English-speaking world in the twentieth century, rivaled only by the Australian geographer Thomas Griffith Taylor. Trained as a geologist, Huntington took a post in 1897 at a small college in Turkey; after two years at Harvard, 1901–1903, he was attached to the Pumpelly expedition for geographic and archeological explorations in Turkestan and Iran. This experience, and further travels in India, Tibet, and Siberia, inspired his first major work, *The Pulse of Asia* (1907), in which he stressed the role of climatic change, especially desiccation, in initiating chain reactions of nomadic movements that culminated in such upheavals as the Mongol, Mogul, and Manchu invasions. From 1907 until his death Huntington was associated with Yale University; he traveled extensively in all continents except Antarctica.

Although Huntington is best known for his stress on the climatic factor in historical causation, he was by no means neglectful of other factors, including cultural ones. In particular, he gave considerable weight to heredity, to selective migration and survival, and to the persistence of traits through endogamy: the last, indeed, is the theme of *The Character of Races* (1924). As a member, and sometime president, of the Eugenics Society, Huntington had a strong interest in biology, reflected in *Season of Birth* (1938). However, these aspects of his work should not be overstressed, since he ascribed the formation of group attributes and aptitudes primarily to environmental factors, especially climate.

Considerations of climate inform all Huntington's work but are perhaps most formally displayed in *Civilization and Climate* (1915). Here he followed up older ideas of a progressive shift of civilization from origins in the Afro–Asian riverine environments to the cooler and more varied climates of northwest Europe, and in a sense he sought to clinch this line of argument by the famous, or notorious, maps that compare regions climatically optimal for human energy with those of high civilization. These maps show a high degree of correlation between climate conducive to energy and civilization—north-central Europe, the United States, and southeast Australia have the highest ranking on both maps.

It is evident that Huntington's criteria in making his maps were highly subjective: for a man who had so much knowledge of Asia, he was extremely Eurocentric. Although, to be sure, Huntington himself did not claim that the map of climatic efficiency indicated the "cause of civilization," his uncritical acceptance of undifferentiated activism as a criterion of civilization opened the way to such misinterpretations. Moreover, his assessment of civilization and ethical value was often amazingly naive. He implied, for example, that Bulgaria, having more cars per head of population, was somehow more civilized than China; and he attempted to rank religions both by latitude and by ethical value (the order turned out to be the same!). Yet easy as it is to laugh at his belief in progress as mechanics, it may be asked what else is at the bottom of the welfare state and the endeavors to develop the undeveloped world.

These illustrations come from Huntington's culminating work, *Mainsprings of Civilization* (1945). This book, along with much fallacy, contains much sound observation drawn from an immense variety of phenomena, and also much penetrating argument. It repeats and often elaborates his main themes: the importance of climatic oscillations, whether short-term (such as sunspot cycles) or secular, and of noncyclical climatic changes, and the influence of these weather variations on human activity and the historic process; these he contrasted with the enduring significance of inherited physical and psychological attributes, which initially may have been environmentally determined. Huntington also tried to do justice, although his treatment is inadequate, to more purely institutional and cultural factors. It seems likely that at least some residuum of the argument in *Mainsprings* will have continuing value.

Environmentalism is today under a cloud, and the full position of Huntington and Taylor cannot possibly be sustained. But Huntington did put environmentalism on a new footing, especially by his detailed and, in general, well-documented stress on climatic factors. Many of his ideas reflect too faithfully a *simpliste* common-sense view of progress and of the effects of weather and climate on human life, and this has damaged his academic reputation. But although these factors cannot be allowed the altogether determinative character which Huntington (despite disclaimers) tended to ascribe to them, neither can it be assumed that they have no significant effects on human metabolism; and on a macroscale some, at least, of these effects may well carry over into social attitudes and, hence, into historical processes. With more finesse and sophistication and without Huntington's overbold generalizations about social and historical causation, a good deal of current research on human ecology and medical geography actually carries on the tradition of Huntington's thinking.

O. H. K. SPATE

[*See also* ENVIRONMENTALISM *and* GEOGRAPHY.]

WORKS BY HUNTINGTON

(1907) 1919 *The Pulse of Asia: A Journey in Central Asia Illustrating the Geographic Basis of History.* New ed. Boston: Houghton Mifflin.

(1915) 1924 *Civilization and Climate.* 3d ed., rev. New Haven: Yale Univ. Press.

1922 HUNTINGTON, ELLSWORTH; and VISHER, STEPHEN S. *Climatic Changes: Their Nature and Causes.* New Haven: Yale Univ. Press.

1924 *The Character of Races as Influenced by Physical Environment, Natural Selection and Historical Development.* New York: Scribner.

1938 *Season of Birth: Its Relation to Human Abilities.* New York: Wiley.

1945 *Mainsprings of Civilization.* New York: Wiley; London: Chapman.

SUPPLEMENTARY BIBLIOGRAPHY

SPATE, O. H. K. 1952 Toynbee and Huntington: A Study in Determinism. *Geographical Journal* 118:406–428. → Includes four pages of discussion.

VISHER, S. S. 1948 Memoir to Ellsworth Huntington: 1876–1947. Association of American Geographers, *Annals* 38:39–50. → Contains a bibliography.

HURGRONJE, CHRISTIAAN SNOUCK

See SNOUCK HURGRONJE, CHRISTIAAN.

HUSSERL, EDMUND

Edmund Gustav Albrecht Husserl (1859–1938), German philosopher, was born in Austrian Moravia (now part of Czechoslovakia), the son of a prosperous Jewish merchant. Husserl was a competent but not distinguished student, apparently introspective and slow to mature, and interested almost exclusively in mathematics and astronomy.

Following his secondary education in Vienna, he studied mathematics and science from 1876 to 1878 at the University of Leipzig, where he attended lectures by Wilhelm Wundt. He then went to Berlin to study mathematics and there developed his first scholarly interest in the philosophy of mathematics and in philosophy more generally. Returning to Vienna, he took his doctorate in 1882, with a dissertation entitled "Beiträge zur Variationsrechnung" ("Contributions to the Theory of the Calculus of Variations").

He served for a short time as assistant to the mathematician Weierstrass at Berlin, and then he returned again to Vienna, where he came under the most important influence of his career, that of the philosopher–psychologist–priest Franz Brentano. Husserl's phenomenology is descended from Brentano's "psychognosy," which is based on the concept of intentionality and on the classification of "psychical phenomena." In 1887 Husserl went as *Privatdozent* to the University of Halle—he had studied there earlier under the psychologist Carl Stumpf—and stayed there until 1901. He then became a professor at the University of Göttingen, and finally, from 1916 until his retirement in 1929, he taught at the University of Freiburg. He continued to live in Freiburg, teaching informally and writing, until his death. Although as a young man he had been converted to Protestantism, the Nazi regime defined him as a Jew; he was deprived of most honors and recognition in his final years, and only the heroic efforts of the Franciscan monk Hermann van Breda made it possible to save many thousands of manuscript pages written by Husserl in a private shorthand. These writings have since become the property of the Husserl Archives at the University of Louvain in Belgium.

Early philosophical works

Husserl's turn from mathematics to philosophy came as a result of the combined influences of Brentano and the logician Bernard Bolzano. His first work, *Philosophie der Arithmetik* (1891), which he dedicated to Brentano, contains his independent discovery of the concept of form-quality (*Gestaltqualität*), commonly associated with gestalt theory, but, more important for Husserl's development, it represents his first attempt at probing the foundations of his discipline. However, as the mathematician Gottlob Frege showed, Husserl's argument was mere "psychologism," and as a consequence of this critique Husserl undertook the first of the fundamental re-examinations that were to characterize his subsequent intellectual career.

In 1900 and 1901 he published the two volumes of his *Logische Untersuchungen*, which contain a brilliant extension of two concepts he owed to Brentano: the idea of intentionality—that it is characteristic of psychic activity to be directed toward an object—and the idea of the self-evident and therefore infallible character of psychic data. Husserl asserted that both poles of the intentional act, its intending as well as its object, must be conceived as aspects of consciousness. He put aside the question of an object's reality as not of legitimate concern—a philosophical tactic to which he gave the name "reduction." Thus in one fundamental move he eliminated the question of whether the object of the act of consciousness is "real" and revealed consciousness itself as a source of objectively valid data on which universal philosophical principles can be based. This Husserl proceeded to demonstrate in the field of logic.

The transcendental reduction. Having stated the major theses of his program for developing a pure phenomenology as the science of all sciences, Husserl took the further step, in his 1904–1905 lectures, *The Phenomenology of Internal Time-consciousness* (1928), of attempting a formal account of the fundamental structures of consciousness. [*See* TIME, *article on* PSYCHOLOGICAL ASPECTS.] The first phenomenological reduction had involved a suspension of the "natural attitude" toward the object of consciousness. In addition, Husserl now proposed a transcendental reduction that would "suspend" or "bracket" (*einklammern*) psychological experiences themselves. In this way he hoped to discover elemental structures that would resemble the abstract entities of mathematics, but with a transcendental rather than an empirical ego as nuclear principle. In another series of five lectures, delivered in 1907, *Die Idee der Phänomenologie* (see *Husserliana*, vol. 2), Husserl further systematized his method for achieving apodictic knowledge by claiming that intuition permits the immediate grasp of general essences. The latter, as objects of consciousness, are constituted in and by the transcendental ego, which thus becomes the source and agent of meanings in one's world. Thus sense data construct appearances, appearances construct things, and perception and imagination construct identities.

Program for phenomenology. In a manifesto and program, issued in 1911 as an essay entitled "Philosophy as Rigorous Science," Husserl argued that the merely contingent and factual data of the empirical sciences have to be replaced by essential structures which are revealed by the phenomenological reduction. Only by building from below in this manner can the sciences be provided with an absolute and objective basis. In the same year, on the urging of his students, Husserl began to plan a phenomenological journal, and when the inaugural volume of the *Jahrbuch für Philosophie und phänomenologische Forschung* appeared in 1913, it contained what was to become the first volume of his *Ideen zu einer reinen Phänomenologie und phänomenologischen Philosophie* (see *Husserliana*, vols. 3–5). This was the closest to a systematic exposition of his thought that he ever produced, but of the three volumes only the first appeared in his lifetime. Its translation, *Ideas* (see [1913] 1952), was for many years the only rendering of his work in English, with the exception of a brief article in the *Encyclopaedia Britannica* (14th ed., 1929). In *Ideas* there is presented a full statement of the phenomenological reduction, here called by the Skeptics' term *epoché*, as well as extended analyses of reality, idealism, essences, and the structure of consciousness.

Later works

Husserl published no further large-scale work until 1929, when, under the title *Formale und transzendentale Logik*, he put together a full exposition of intentional, or structural, analysis, finally identifying his own metaphysical position as idealism. The problem inherent in this position—which he attempted, with unsatisfactory results, to resolve in his *Cartesian Meditations* (1931), based on lectures delivered at the Sorbonne—was to account, within idealist suppositions, for other, independent egos. By another name, this is the problem of intersubjectivity, to which Husserl may have been drawn through the influence of his leading pupil and chosen successor, Martin Heidegger; or it may have been the events of a strident age that impelled Husserl to accommodate his thought to humanly significant issues.

The crisis of modern knowledge. Although he insisted that whatever is revealed of the "formations" of the world must be governed by necessities founded on essential structures of consciousness—as opposed to requirements dictated by empirical and contingent facts—he did during these years begin to develop an existentialist theme that was finally expressed in *Die Krisis der europäischen Wissenschaften und die transzendentale Phänomenologie* (see *Husserliana*, vol. 6), essays that were published posthumously. The "crisis" of the title refers to the tragically widening gulf between modern science, which grows ever more abstract and technical, and the *Lebenswelt*, or lived-world, that realm which stands as the all-encompassing horizon of our collective and individual life-worlds and in which science itself must be founded. Husserl thus appears to have come full circle in his thinking, from an initial absolutism and formalism, in which the absolutely given has its source in pure subjectivity, that "wonder of all wonders," to a plea for founding the concerns of philosophy in man's experience of his fellows. No resolution of the tension between these positions is to be found in Husserl's writings, and so the concept of the *Lebenswelt* remains ambiguous, leaning on both transcendentalist and existentialist theses. Various solutions have since been offered by students of Husserl, notably by Heidegger in his conception of *Dasein* as ontologically conceived human existence, by Jean-Paul Sartre in his definition of consciousness as nothing else but the very acts of a human individual, and by Maurice Merleau-Ponty in his notion of consciousness as totally "engaged" through the meaning-bestowing acts of a "body-subject."

Influence

Impact on philosophy. Husserl was not able to keep followers, and in the field of philosophy his legacy is an influence rather than a school. Heidegger, who succeeded Husserl at Freiburg (and then became rector of the university and consorted for a time with the Nazis), has moved steadily toward original ontological investigations and independent fame. In Heidegger's work, as in that of some of the other major intellectual descendants of Husserl, one finds Husserl's thought essentially transformed. Thus, Heidegger has become the fountainhead of a new therapeutic orientation known as existential analysis, largely through the interpretation of his work by the Swiss psychiatrist Ludwig Binswanger; Sartre has adapted the phenomenological method to his own purposes, as in his works on imagination, emotion, and "existential psychoanalysis"; and Merleau-Ponty, who was explicitly and empirically a psychologist of behavior, of language, of perception, of child development, and of the lived body as epicenter of meaning, viewed phenomenology as an approach and a style rather than as an apodictic science.

At Göttingen in 1907, Husserl strongly influenced the Munich circle, but their taste was primarily for what he called "picture book phenomenology." Of this group, Adolf Reinach, who was killed in World War I, made brilliant contributions toward showing the extent to which civil law is founded on natural law. Max Scheler, the most remarkable of the Munich circle and a friend rather than a pupil of Husserl, was perhaps the closest to psychology: even before the "existential" trend, he emphasized the person rather than consciousness, and he wrote on many topics of relevance to the social sciences—feelings and values, war, religion, social action, and interpersonal bonds.

In the United States, Husserl's intellectual descendants also have departed from his philosophical position. Marvin Farber, a key figure both as expositor of Husserl and as editor of the quarterly *Philosophy and Phenomenological Research*, now espouses naturalism rather than phenomenology; Alfred Schutz, never actually a pupil of Husserl's, was often at theoretical odds with him as he himself made original contributions to a phenomenologically oriented social science; and Herbert Spiegelberg, author of the definitive historical survey *The Phenomenological Movement* (1960), has restricted himself to essentially scholarly pursuits and to effecting a *rapprochement* between phenomenological philosophy and psychological theory. Aron Gurwitsch has perhaps remained closest to Husserl, as in his book *The Field of Consciousness* (1957).

Phenomenology and sociology. Husserl's influence on the social sciences seems to have been indirect, even diffuse, in part because of the programmatic nature of so much of his writing. He proposed to look for essences, directly given, which would be revealed in each discipline by methods unique to that discipline. In history, for example, intelligible unities were to be apprehended within an intuitively apprehended flow of world events.

Although any direct influence should be ruled out, interesting parallels may be demonstrated between Husserl and sociologists in the French tradition, such as Durkheim, who have chosen to study society with man left in, as it were; or between Husserl and Max Weber, even though Husserl showed little of Weber's broad interest in history; or even between Husserl and Howard Becker, particularly in the latter's "interpretive sociology" of ideal types as true social structures from which predictions can be made. Husserl's thinking is also consonant with that of George Herbert Mead, R. M. MacIver, and Florian Znaniecki, yet such relationships have not often been recognized; in Znaniecki's *Social Actions* (1936), for example, a program that sounds quite Husserlian is expounded with no reference to phenomenology. The journal literature of the social sciences contains a number of studies that can be classed as descriptive phenomenology—or as intentional psychology, to use Scheler's term. Such studies usually take the form of intuitive and impressionistic analyses of social structures. Husserl would have regarded these as essential. But in general it can hardly be said that the social sciences have found any important place for phenomenology as such.

Phenomenology and psychology. In psychology Husserl's influence may be traced in a broad range of writings, both in theory and in research. In an often striking parallel to the phenomenology of Merleau-Ponty, although developed independently of it, Jean Piaget's work stresses the significance for childhood development of the adaptive and assimilative processes of cognition. Alfred Adler's marked similarity in method and attitude to the phenomenologists is now widely recognized, but there is no evidence that Husserl ever influenced him directly. [*See* ADLER; INDIVIDUAL PSYCHOLOGY; DEVELOPMENTAL PSYCHOLOGY, *article on* A THEORY OF DEVELOPMENT.] Erwin W. Straus, both as a psychiatrist and as a phenomenological psychologist, has elaborated his own eidetic phenomenology and critique of contemporary scientific methodology. Phenomenological conceptions, sometimes considerably transformed, may also be detected in the school of thought known as existential psychology. [*See* PSYCHOLOGY, *article on* EXISTENTIAL PSYCHOLOGY.]

The most direct and specific of Husserl's effects on psychology, as may be expected, occurred in Europe. A notable instance is David Katz, whose investigations of the perception of color and of touch derived at least in part from contact with Husserl when both were at Göttingen. Of the important group who were at the University of Berlin just before World War I, and from whose joint efforts came the school of gestalt psychology, Max Wertheimer and Karl Duncker were apparently deeply influenced by phenomenology. During this time Kurt Goldstein, the neurologist, came under the influence of Husserl's thinking, as is quite evident in his later writings on organismic biology and psychopathology, as well as in his collaborative work with Martin Scheerer on the analysis of a structure of consciousness which they called the "abstract attitude." William Stern, also in the Berlin group, was later influential in espousing a "personalistic" psychology, and still another member, Kurt Lewin, based a productive career on phenomenological methods and conceptions: for example, his concept of an individual's "life space," his use of topology as a mathematics specific to psychological data, and his intuitive apprehension of "group" as an intelligible unity, an approach that gave rise to the area of research and study now known as group dynamics. Fritz Heider, in an early paper on "thing" and "medium," analyzed fundamental unities of space and action, and later contributed significantly to the exploration of phenomenal causality and to the problem of the "naïve" analysis of social action; and his influence, in turn, may be seen in recent investigations in "psychological ecology" by Roger Barker and Herbert F. Wright.

Shifting again from Europe to America, the school which follows Carl R. Rogers is, like its founder, not inconsistent in its approach with a phenomenological orientation, although admittedly by virtue of related attitudes toward science rather than because of any strict adherence to Husserl's thought. [*See* MENTAL DISORDERS, TREATMENT OF, *article on* CLIENT-CENTERED COUNSELING.] Robert MacLeod is probably the psychologist most clearly identified with Husserl, because of his proposals—unique in American psychology—for the application of a phenomenological approach in theoretical and social psychology. Finally, contemporary psychology in Germany and the Netherlands owes much to Husserl's influence—for example, Linschoten's studies of William James (1961), C. F. Graumann's investigations of perspective and of early behavioristic theory (1960), and the important work of F. J. J. Buytendijk on pain, on the psychology of women, and on human movement (1932; 1943; 1951; 1957).

This roster, although only partial, suggests that Husserl's influence on the empirical sciences has been far-reaching, but neither as pervasive nor as profound as it might have been, considering that he was at the forefront of what may turn out to have been an epistemological revolution. One reason for the relative neglect of his work—until recently, this neglect in the United States has been of shocking proportions—may be that by temperament as well as by the nature of his philosophic task, he was condemned to a never-ending search for "the beginning of the beginning." The current phase of his influence, indeed, appears to rest primarily on the later Husserl, the "engaged" thinker of the *Lebenswelt* doctrine, who helped to establish the philosophical basis for a basic science of man considered as a social creature. But because he conceived phenomenology not as a system but as a continuing and vital means of breaking new ground, his thought has served as a general inspiration and influence rather than as an inventory of specific problems. Recent work by Husserlian scholars, however, suggests that his work is now being read more carefully; noteworthy, for example, is Stephan Strasser's *Phenomenology and the Human Sciences* (1963). The Swiss philosopher Pierre Thevenaz, in his brilliant essay *What Is Phenomenology?* (1962), suggested that, in the perspective of history, Husserl stands between classical idealism and twentieth-century existentialism. To others, Husserl has seemed the central figure, perhaps even the source, of broadly based convergence of old and new philosophical traditions—a convergence marked by new styles of analysis for old problems and a bold critique of the excessive claims of scientific empiricism. In any case, whether as chief navigator of a main current or as a beacon to steer by, Husserl surely has a unique position in the history of Western thought.

JOSEPH LYONS

[*Other relevant material may be found in* FIELD THEORY; GESTALT THEORY; PHENOMENOLOGY; PSYCHOLOGY, *article on* EXISTENTIAL PSYCHOLOGY; *and in the biographies of* GOLDSTEIN; KATZ; LEWIN; SCHELER; SCHUTZ; STERN; WERTHEIMER.]

WORKS BY HUSSERL

1882 Beiträge zur Variationsrechnung. Dissertation, Univ. of Vienna.

1891 *Philosophie der Arithmetik: Psychologische und logische Untersuchungen.* Vol. 1. Halle (Germany): Pfeffer.

(1900–1901) 1913–1921 *Logische Untersuchungen.* 2d ed., 2 vols. Halle (Germany): Niemeyer. → Volume 1: *Prolegomena zur reinen Logik.* Volume 2: *Untersuchungen zur Phänomenologie und Theorie der Erkenntnis.* A French translation of the 2d German edition was published in 1959–1963 by Presses Universitaires de France.

(1911) 1965 Philosophy as Rigorous Science. Pages 71–147 in Edmund Husserl, *Phenomenology and the Crisis of Philosophy.* New York: Harper. → First published in German in Volume 1 of *Logos* as "Philosophie als strenge Wissenschaft."

(1913) 1952 *Ideas: General Introduction to Pure Phenomenology.* New York: Macmillan. → Translation of Volume 1 of *Ideen zu einer reinen Phänomenologie und phänomenologischen Philosophie.*

(1928) 1964 *The Phenomenology of Internal Time-consciousness.* Bloomington: Indiana Univ. Press. → First published as *Vorlesungen zur Phänomenologie des innern Zeitbewusstseins.*

1929 *Formale und transzendentale Logik: Versuch einer Kritik der logischen Vernunft.* Halle (Germany): Niemeyer. → A French translation was published in 1957 by Presses Universitaires de France.

(1931) 1960 *Cartesian Meditations: An Introduction to Phenomenology.* The Hague: Nijhoff. → Written in German and first published in French.

Husserliana: Edmund Husserl, Gesammelte Werke. 9 vols. The Hague: Nijhoff, 1950–1962. → Volume 1: *Cartesianische Meditationen und Pariser Vorträge*, 1950. Volume 2: *Die Idee der Phänomenologie: Fünf Vorlesungen*, 1950. Volumes 3–5: *Ideen zu einer reinen Phänomenologie und phänomenologischen Philosophie*, 3 vols. 1950–1952. Volume 6: *Die Krisis der europäischen Wissenschaften und die transzendentale Phänomenologie: Eine Einleitung in die phänomenologische Philosophie*, 1954. Volume 7–8: *Erste Philosophie (1923/1924)*, 2 vols., 1956–1959. Volume 9: *Phänomenologische Psychologie*, 1962.

SUPPLEMENTARY BIBLIOGRAPHY

BUYTENDIJK, F. J. J. (1932) 1936 *The Mind of the Dog.* Boston: Houghton Mifflin. → First published in Dutch.

BUYTENDIJK, F. J. J. (1943) 1962 *Pain, Its Modes and Functions.* Univ. of Chicago Press. → First published in Dutch.

BUYTENDIJK, F. J. J. (1951) 1953 *Die Frau.* Cologne (Germany): Bachem Verlag.

BUYTENDIJK, F. J. J. 1957 *Attitudes et mouvements.* Paris: Desclée de Brouwer. → Published simultaneously in Dutch.

GRAUMANN, CARL F. 1960 *Grundlagen einer Phänomenologie und Psychologie der Perspektivität.* Berlin: de Gruyter.

GURWITSCH, ARON (1957) 1965 *The Field of Consciousness.* Pittsburgh: Duquesne Univ. Press. → First published in French.

LINSCHOTEN, JOHANNES 1961 *Auf dem Wege zu einer phänomenologischen Psychologie: Die Psychologie von William James.* Berlin: de Gruyter.

SPIEGELBERG, HERBERT (1960) 1965 *The Phenomenological Movement: A Historical Introduction.* 2d ed., 2 vols. Phaenomenologica, Vols. 5–6. The Hague: Nijhoff.

STRASSER, STEPHAN 1963 *Phenomenology and the Human Sciences: A Contribution to a New and Scientific Ideal.* Pittsburgh: Duquesne Univ. Press.

THEVENAZ, PIERRE 1962 *What Is Phenomenology? And Other Essays.* Chicago: Quadrangle.

ZNANIECKI, FLORIAN 1936 *Social Actions.* New York: Farrar & Rinehart.

HUXLEY, JULIAN

Julian Sorell Huxley (born 1887), English biologist, writer, and publicist, is the grandson of Thomas Henry Huxley, the son of Leonard Huxley, biographer, poet, and editor, and of Julia Francis, the founder of Priors Field School for Girls, and the older brother of Aldous Huxley. Huxley was King's scholar at Eton and Brakenbury scholar at Balliol. At Oxford he studied zoology, taking a First in it in 1909. He was also much interested in poetry; in 1908 he won the Newdigate prize for English verse, and in 1932 he published a volume of poems, *The Captive Shrew*.

Huxley taught at Oxford from 1910 to 1912; at Rice University, Houston, Texas, from 1912 to 1916; at Oxford again from 1919 to 1925; and at King's College in the University of London from 1925 to 1927. In 1927 he resigned his professorship to devote all of his time to research, writing, lecturing, and public causes. In 1938 he was elected a fellow of the Royal Society and in 1953 received the society's Darwin medal. In 1958 he was knighted.

Huxley's first book, *The Individual in the Animal Kingdom,* was published in 1912. Since that time he has produced over forty books and innumerable articles in scientific and popular journals. Huxley has produced a number of fundamental works that have had a stimulating influence on the development of modern biology. Most notable among these are *Problems of Relative Growth* (1932*a*), *The Elements of Experimental Embryology,* with G. R. de Beer (1934), *Evolution: The Modern Synthesis* (1942), and a series of papers on bird courtship and display. In these and other works Huxley has made enduring contributions to our understanding of growth and development, animal behavior, sexual selection, systematics, and evolutionary processes and theory.

Through his popular writings on evolution, usually first published in periodicals and then in collected form in separate volumes, Huxley has greatly influenced the intellectual climate of his time. His able exposition of the fact of man's having uniquely moved into a new phase of adaptation—cultural or psychosocial adaptation—was developed in large part independently of the anthropologists and exercised no little effect upon their thinking. Hence, he has been much welcomed in anthropological circles and widely read by social scientists.

Since man has supplanted natural selection by a new method of evolution, the development of culture, this puts mind into the process of evolution. What, therefore, man does through the agency of his mind will determine his future. Huxley argues that in man's case natural selection is virtually suspended, that by the conscious selection of ideas and aims he is now in a position to control his own evolution. In the psychosocial phase, evolution is mainly cultural, not genetic. The focus is no longer solely on survival but increasingly directed toward fulfillment in quality of achievement. Such views have led Huxley to the development of an evolutionary humanism that he claims is capable of becoming a new religion, not necessarily supplanting existing religions but supplementing them.

Huxley's critiques of the concept of "race" as applied to man have greatly contributed to the continuing re-evaluation of that concept. His major contributions have been in the demonstration of the complete arbitrariness and formalism that have characterized the approach to the study of the variety of man, as well as in the repeated demolition of the social or popular notion of "race." Because the term "race" has become so encumbered by false meaning and political misuse, Huxley has suggested that it be dropped altogether from the vocabulary of the scientist and that the noncommittal term "ethnic group" be preferred. This suggestion has made more of an impression in England than it has in the United States, even though every use of the concept of "race" has come increasingly under attack in recent years in the latter country.

For many years Huxley's has been a powerful voice in population control, planned parenthood movements, and eugenics. Here his influence has largely been through the leadership he has provided in organizations, writings, and lecturing. For his work in this field he received the Lasker award in 1950. He is a past president of the Eugenics Society.

Huxley has traveled widely in five continents and has recorded his impressions in several books, notably *Africa View* (1931*a*), the long postscript to his wife's *Wild Lives of Africa* (1963), a *Scientist Among the Soviets* (1932*b*), *From an Antique Land* (1954), on past and present in the Middle East, and *TVA: Adventure in Planning* (1943*b*). *TVA* exemplifies Huxley's long-standing interest in planning and conservation. He was one of the founders of the influential private planning group P.E.P. (Political and Economic Planning) in London in 1932 and in 1961 produced a report to UNESCO on *The Conservation of Wild Life and Natural Habitats in Central and East Africa.*

He took part in the first British university expedition, that of Oxford, to Spitsbergen in 1921, and was one of the founders of the Society for Experimental Biology, the Association for the Study of Animal Behaviour, and the Association for the Study of Systematics, as well as of the Association of Scientific Workers; he was president of the three last-named.

ASHLEY MONTAGU

[*For the historical context of Huxley's works, see* EUGENICS; EVOLUTION; RACE.]

WORKS BY HUXLEY

1912 *The Individual in the Animal Kingdom.* New York: Putnam.
1923 *Essays of a Biologist.* New York: Knopf.
1926 *Essays in Popular Science.* London: Chatto & Windus.
1927*a* *Religion Without Revelation.* New York: Harper.
1927*b* *The Stream of Life.* New York: Harper.
1927 HALDANE, JOHN B. S.; and HUXLEY, JULIAN *Animal Biology.* Oxford: Clarendon.
1930*a* *Ants.* New York. Cape & Smith.
1930*b* *Bird Watching and Bird Behaviour.* London: Chatto & Windus.
1931*a* *Africa View.* New York: Harper.
1931*b* *What Dare I Think?* New York: Harper.
1931 HUXLEY, JULIAN; WELLS, HERBERT G.; and WELLS, G. P. *The Science of Life.* Garden City, N.Y.: Doubleday.
1932*a* *Problems of Relative Growth.* New York: Dial.
1932*b* *Scientist Among the Soviets.* New York: Harper.
(1932c) 1933 *The Captive Shrew and Other Poems.* New York: Harper.
1932–1935 ANDRADE, E. N. DA C.; and HUXLEY, JULIAN *An Introduction to Science.* Oxford: Blackwell. → Published in seven parts.
1934*a* *If I Were Dictator.* New York: Harper.
1934*b* *Scientific Research and Social Needs.* London: Watts.
1934 HUXLEY, JULIAN; and DE BEER, G. R. *The Elements of Experimental Embryology.* Cambridge Univ. Press.
1936 *At the Zoo.* London: Allen & Unwin.
1936 HUXLEY, JULIAN; and HADDON, ALFRED CORT *We Europeans: A Survey of "Racial"* Problems. New York and London: Harper.
1939 DARWIN, CHARLES *The Living Thoughts of Darwin.* Edited by Julian Huxley. London: Longmans.
1941*a* *Democracy Marches.* New York: Harper.
1941*b* *The Uniqueness of Man.* London: Chatto & Windus.
1942 *Evolution: The Modern Synthesis.* New York and London: Harper.
1943*a* *Evolutionary Ethics.* Oxford Univ. Press.
1943*b* *TVA: Adventure in Planning.* London: Architectural Press.
1944 *On Living in a Revolution.* New York: Harper.
1947 *Man in the Modern World.* London: Chatto & Windus.
1947 HUXLEY, THOMAS H.; and HUXLEY, JULIAN *Touchstone for Ethics: 1893–1943.* New York: Harper.
1949 *Soviet Genetics and World Science.* London: Chatto & Windus.
1953 *Evolution in Action.* New York: Harper.
1954 *From an Antique Land.* New York: Crown.
1956 *Kingdom of the Beasts.* London: Thames & Hudson.
1957 *New Bottles for New Wine.* New York: Harper; London: Chatto & Windus.
1958 *Biological Aspects of Cancer.* New York: Harcourt.
1961*a* *The Conservation of Wild Life and Natural Habitats in Central and East Africa: Report on a Mission Accomplished for UNESCO, July–September, 1960.* Paris: UNESCO.
1961*b* HUXLEY, JULIAN (editor) *The Humanist Frame.* New York: Harper; London: Allen & Unwin.
1963 Postscript. Pages 241–255 in Juliette Huxley, *Wild Lives of Africa.* New York: Harper. → An Introduction by Julian Huxley appears on pages 5–8.
1964 *Essays of a Humanist.* London: Chatto & Windus.
1965 HUXLEY, JULIAN (editor) *Aldous Huxley, 1894–1963: A Memorial Volume.* New York: Harper; London: Chatto & Windus.

HYPNOSIS

Hypnosis is a term frequently used to refer to any trance state and probably equally frequently to any condition in which an unusual degree of suggestibility is found. The term was originally introduced by James Braid in 1841 specifically to denote a sleeplike state presumably brought about in an individual by his intense and protracted visual fixation on a bright spot of light placed in a specific position relative to him. Subsequently the term came to refer to a group of presumably related conditions brought about in an individual by well-specified physical procedures. At a still later date, on the assumption that these various conditions were suggested artifacts, hypnosis once more was applied to a single condition that can best be described as *an altered state of awareness characteristically accompanied by increased suggestibility, which is brought about in some individuals, the subjects, through the use of certain procedures by another person, the hypnotist.* Characteristically this hypersuggestibility is initially selective, that is, the subject responds only to the hypnotist until told to do otherwise. By and large this has become the most widely accepted popular and scientific meaning of the term "hypnosis" as a concept.

By extension the term with the added qualification of "animal" has been used to denote a variety of conditions of abnormal immobility of varying durations and characteristics which can be brought about in animals by means of a number of physical procedures, including optical fixation. This so-called animal hypnosis covers such conditions as have also been variously termed cataplexy, catalepsy, death feint, hypertonicity, tonic immobility, inhibitory state, and other names, which may or may not all refer to one and the same thing.

The term "hypnosis," like its associated terms "suggestion" and "trance," has been greatly abused, overused, and misused by both laymen and professionals and has at times been given such a broad denotation as to render it meaningless. In particular there has been and still is extensive confounding between matters of definition, observation, theory, and plain belief. Because of the impossibility of clearly separating purely hypnotic from purely suggestive phenomena in many instances, it seems best to use the expression "hypno–suggestive" in such cases.

History

"Hypnotism" was the term originally used by James Braid to denote that which he otherwise called "nervous sleep" and which is today known as "hypnosis," the term hypnotism now having supplanted the term "Braidism" at first employed to denote the study and use of hypnosis. Hypnotism proper then began with Braid in 1841 as a consequence of his attempts to elucidate the true nature of mesmeric phenomena (after Franz Anton Mesmer). It is generally agreed today that mesmeric phenomena most probably were a combination of hypno–suggestive and psychopathological manifestations mistakenly ascribed to the effects of a vital fluid called animal magnetism. It is reasonable to assume that hypno–suggestive phenomena have a wide cultural and temporal distribution; nevertheless, much of what has been written in this regard is a matter of sheer speculation. This is the case, for instance, in regard to claims such as the ones that Moses induced mass hypnotic hallucinations in the Egyptians, that Christ healed, and that witches hexed through the "power" of suggestion, or that the dancing mania of the Middle Ages was the result of mass suggestion or mass hypnosis. Braid's chief scientific contribution was the isolation from mesmeric phenomena of that component which he named "hypnotism." About forty years later, Jean Martin Charcot introduced the next important development. He asserted that hypnosis was not a single entity but consisted of a group of three distinct nervous states which he named catalepsy, lethargy, and somnambulism. Each was capable of being separately induced by specific physical means. To these Paul Brémaud added a fourth state, fascination. Two other important claims of Charcot were that these states had a somatic neurological basis and that they could be elicited only in individuals suffering from *grande hystérie*, of which it was symptomatic, a notion that was to be carried into Pierre Janet's basic work on hysteria. About 1884, however, Charcot's position began to be openly and vigorously challenged with increasing success by Hippolyte Bernheim, who had followed up some ideas proposed somewhat earlier by A. A. Liébeault. Bernheim maintained that hypnosis and all of its attendant phenomena were not pathological manifestations and were entirely the result of suggestion. He did not claim, however, as he is often misinterpreted to have done, that hypnosis as a mental state does not exist; but he did firmly believe that it was functional in nature and brought about through the effects of suggestion, as were all other hypnotic manifestations. For the sake of historical accuracy it should also be noted that the idea of suggestion playing a major, if not essential, role in mesmeric and hypnotic phenomena was recognized and pointed out not only by Braid himself but even earlier by Alexandre Bertrand, a leading authority on mesmerism, and quite emphatically by the French royal commission that investigated Mesmer's claims in 1784. No doubt the experiments performed by Bernheim to support his thesis had some influence in establishing his views, but Braid and the royal commission too had reported clear-cut experiments in support of their views on suggestion. One must suspect that forty years of progress in the development of the scientific method and the temper of the respective times were probably of considerable influence in assuring the success of Bernheim's suggestion theory. [*See* CHARCOT.]

Although the notion that hypnotic or suggested phenomena represent a continuum and may be scaled had been discussed earlier by others, our modern scales of hypnotic depth, hypnotic susceptibility, and suggestibility are most directly derived from scales proposed first by Liébeault and later by Bernheim. The years between about 1885 and 1905 represent maximal interest and activity in hypnotism, mainly in France and Germany, not to be equaled again until the 1950s.

By 1910 scientific and medical interest in hypnotism had about completely died down. It has frequently been asserted that Freud and psychoanalysis were responsible for this loss of interest. It has also been said that the decline of interest was caused by the widespread use of hypnotism by charlatans and vaudeville artists. A careful examination of the existing records shows little support for either hypothesis. The increasingly obvious and disappointingly limited success of hypnosis and suggestion as then used was bound to give way to any other more promising psychiatric and medical technique and certainly to lead to a search in other directions. Furthermore, besides the fact that most of the past research had been done by medical men whose interest was then being redirected, the cultural and social forces which were inevitably to lead to behaviorism, operationism, and logical positivism were very likely a strong influence in the temporary abandonment of hypnotism as a topic for research. Then, too, it may well be that after more than half a century of intensive study of its phenomena, culminating in the widespread acceptance of Bernheim's view, it may have seemed to most investigators that there was little else to be found or said. Be that as it may, sporadic research went on during the next thirty years or so, with a temporary and limited renewal of interest in the psychiatric uses of hypnosis during World War I. The beginning of the next and current widespread interest in hypnotism appears to be in the early 1930s. Under the tutelage of Clark L. Hull a relatively sophisticated scientific and broad attack upon hypnotic phenomena was instigated. It came to an abrupt end following legal complications, but not before sufficient data had been collected to allow the publication of a book that may be considered as opening the way to current research on hypnotism (Hull 1933). In retrospect it cannot be said that the work of Hull, who essentially followed in the footsteps of Bernheim, threw much more light upon what hypnosis is. It did, however, show that hypno-suggestive phenomena are fit material for scientific study and that they can be studied alongside of other psychological phenomena. It also threw considerable light upon the limitations of suggestion. In spite of Hull's work, active interest in hypnotism remained at a relatively low ebb for the next twelve years or so. Since World War II, however, there has been a renewal of intense research activity in this field, at first primarily in the United States and then in other parts of the world. Here again it is doubtful that the work of any single man, such as Hull, was responsible for the current revival of interest. It appears more likely to be due to the same social forces that once again have made the study of subjective phenomena and the problems of consciousness acceptable topics for scientific investigation. In spite of this upsurge of interest remarkably few advances over those attained as of 1910 have thus far been made toward answering fundamental questions in the field.

Common conceptions of hypnotic phenomena

Typically, an individual, the *subject*, is asked by another person, the *hypnotist*, to gaze intensely at a small, bright object held in front of, at some distance from, and somewhat above his eyes. While the subject does this, the hypnotist tells him in a repetitious manner that he is becoming relaxed and drowsy; that his eyes are getting heavy and closing; that he is falling asleep; and, eventually, that he *is* asleep. An onlooker usually sees, especially if the subject is sitting, clear evidence of increasing relaxation; and eventually the subject does appear to fall asleep. However, in contrast to a person who is normally asleep, the subject seems to be *selectively* in sensory contact with the hypnotist and with him alone, and in general to be selectively and unusually able and willing to carry out all commands, requests, or suggestions of the hypnotist, no matter how unusual and even outlandish these may be. In consequence the subject is said to be in a selective *rapport* with and *selectively hypersuggestible* to the hypnotist. The subject's behavior most closely resembles that of the sleepwalker or *somnambule*, hence the alternate designation of artificial or induced somnambulism which has been given to hypnosis as thus conceived. The popular picture of the hypnotized person is one of an individual without volition who will not only believe, experience, and do whatever the hypnotist wishes along these lines but who is also capable of producing on demand behavior and phenomena out of the ordinary and bordering on the miraculous or supranormal. All of his physical and intellectual faculties and capacities are often said to be remarkably enhanced; and new ones such as psi-faculties (extrasensory perception, clairvoyance, etc.) are even said to appear. Spontaneously occurring unawareness during hypnosis and posthypnotic amnesia are also among the classical symptoms of hypnosis. In the common conception of hypnotic behavior there is no clear-cut distinction between suggestion proper and requests or commands. For all intents and purposes they are one and the same for the hypnotized subject. On the other hand, a clear separation is made between hypnosis and suggestion, hypnosis being considered as a state induced by the procedures outlined above and responsible for a remarkable enhancement of suggestibility, which in turn makes all other phenomena possible. Suggestibility, however, is also seen as existing separately from hypnosis, with the consequence that one distinguishes between hypnotic and waking suggestions, the latter sometimes being associated with a presumed condition inappropriately called walking hypnosis. Modern research (since about 1930) has aimed mainly at determining answers to the following questions: (1) Is there a state of hypnosis distinct from suggestibility and what are its criteria? (2) What procedures and conditions promote and enhance hypnosis and/or suggestibility? (3) What are the properties and nature of hypnosis and/or suggestibility? (4) What kind of effects can be brought about through hypnosis and/or suggestions, and what is their nature? Since, as will be seen in a moment, hypnosis as a state has remained a very illusive entity, research falling in the last three areas has primarily been about suggestion and suggestibility and about effects induced by suggestions.

The scientific facts

Somewhere close to ten thousand articles and about one thousand books have been published to date on the subject matter. In spite of this the sum total of our knowledge about the phenomena in question remains remarkably meager.

Hypnosis versus suggestion. Is there a condition of the individual different from the normal waking state which is associated with and/or responsible for so-called hypnotic phenomena? To date, physiological and psychological tests have been unable to detect any difference between individuals who are in a state of normal wakefulness and those who have been hypnotized and are overtly responding to suggestions. It has also been clearly demonstrated that the suggestion and exhibition of sleeplike characteristics are quite unnecessary for the production of hypnotic behavior. However, since hypnosis is defined as a state associated with the subject's ability to carry out essentially the same kinds of activities as a normal and fully awake individual, such findings are not particularly surprising and cannot be considered satisfactory evidence that hypnosis as an altered state of awareness does not exist. The bases currently available for believing that there is a condition which may be called hypnosis are the following: (1) After submitting to procedures aimed at producing hypnosis, certain individuals show an appreciable increase in suggestibility. (2) Their behavior and self-report consistently indicate the presence of an altered awareness. (3) Certain labile observable characteristics are frequently and consistently seen *immediately* following the presumed appearance of hypnosis. Among the more obvious one may list a tonic immobility including a characteristic fixity of stare ("trance stare"); an economy of movement when movement is induced; and a lack of motor, affective, and ideational spontaneity. Admittedly the last two groups of signs could be the result of implicit and unwitting suggestions or of self-suggestions and thus remain equivocal. On the whole the appearance of hypersuggestibility remains the one and only clear-cut criterion.

Suggestion. In any event, whether or not hypnosis exists as a distinct state of consciousness, it is generally agreed that suggestion and suggestibility, the capacity for responding to suggestions, are the all-important elements in both the production of the presumed state as well as of the associated phenomena. Suggestion itself has been a poorly defined and controversial concept often confounded with suggestibility. A careful examination of the various existing examples of suggestion seems to show one common characteristic: conceptually speaking they can all be described as ideas which produce a response on the part of an individual that does not appear to be initiated or mediated by all or any of the *ego processes* normally operative in *voluntary* or *intentional* behavior. As such the resulting behavior belongs to the class of automatisms. Suggestions (and suggestibility) have been variously categorized based on their linguistic and grammatical features, their source of origin, the nature of the stimulus used, the shape of the distribution curves of the responses to them, the context in which they are given, and on factor analysis. The typical suggestion used in connection with hypnotic phenomena has been variously and accordingly called a "personal," "direct," "prestige," or "primary" suggestion. Response to this type of suggestion is essentially unrelated to response to other types. In particular social suggestion, that is, the indirect influence by a group over an individual, is unrelated to it.

Suggestion has also been classified as heterosuggestion and autosuggestion (self-suggestion) depending on whether the suggestor is a person other than the suggestee or is the suggestee himself. A hypnotic suggestion given so as to be carried out after the subject is no longer hypnotized is called a posthypnotic suggestion. Finally, suggestions given to a group of people rather than to one individual are called mass (group) suggestions. [*See* SUGGESTION.]

Suggested phenomena—real or pretended? Bernheim raised the question whether hypnosis as a syndrome existed independently of suggestion. Some modern investigators have gone one step further and asked whether there even is such a thing as suggested behavior in the sense of an *automatism.* Stated another way, they propose that all hypno–suggestive behavior is voluntary or intentional activity fully initiated and mediated by the ego processes and that basically the subject is knowingly "pretending," "simulating," "play acting," or "role playing (taking)." That some subjects pretend or role play some suggested behavior, and sometimes all, is not to be questioned. That *all* subjects simulate *all* suggested behavior is anything but well demonstrated. It is in fact extremely difficult, for one thing, to consider as instances of mere role playing the many well-attested cases of individuals undergoing major surgery under hypnoanesthesia alone. In any case one of the most common arguments for the above view, namely, that all suggested phenomena, including unawareness of pain, can be exhibited by some individuals in the absence of suggestions or hypnosis is anything but conclusive. For not only must one ask whether suggestions can produce phenomena that completely transcend *all known human potentialities* but also whether suggestions can make it possible *for a given individual* to behave in a manner or at a level that transcends *his own* best output when presumably in a nonhypnotic, normal wakeful state. It appears that this last question can be answered positively, although in a much more limited way than was once believed. In any event, those who uphold the notion of role taking as the answer seem blatantly to ignore the fact that the situation surrounding such role playing appears to have an unusual power to selectively elicit role playing of an unusual kind in certain individuals. If role playing it is, it appears to stand out in a particular subcategory all its own among the totality of possible role-playing behaviors. In particular it would still appear true that having role-played becoming hypnotized as a result of submitting to certain procedures, some individuals become able to act as if they were in possession of an often remarkably greater ability to role play, whereas others do not. In the final analysis there does not seem as yet to be much gained, if anything, by substituting "elicited role playing" for "suggested behavior." To speak of role-taking ability in place of speaking of suggestibility with respect to certain kinds of instruction in no way makes the behavior any more understandable. [*See* ROLE, *article on* PSYCHOLOGICAL ASPECTS.]

Suggestibility and hypnotizability. Who can be hypnotized? What makes a person suggestible? Much time and effort has gone into an attempt to find answers to these questions, with very little success thus far. Various scales purporting to measure suggestibility as well as susceptibility to hypnosis have been devised. They are all based upon sampling a person's responsiveness to various test suggestions. If the subject is tested without the prior use of a procedure aimed at inducing hypnosis, the scale is considered to measure his *suggestibility*. If he has submitted to an induction of hypnosis prior to its administration the scale is considered to measure the *depth of hypnosis* attained. If such a test is considered as a predictive sampling of his behavior with regard to future inductions of hypnosis, it is considered a measure of *hypnotic susceptibility* or *hypnotizability*. Since none of these scales possesses an independent criterion for establishing whether or not the induction procedure had any effect at all, there is an obvious confounding of suggestibility with hypnosis. It has, however, been shown that following such an induction procedure some individuals do exhibit a definite increase in suggestibility as measured by these scales. At least such individuals are presumably hypnotized.

Results obtained with these scales and simpler tests indicate that, on the whole, children are more suggestible (and probably more hypnotizable) than adults. Women and girls are probably slightly more suggestible (and hypnotizable) than men and boys. Neurotics, as a whole, are also more suggestible (and hypnotizable) than normal individuals. Contrary to a common belief, psychotics are probably as suggestible (and hypnotizable) as normal individuals, and hysterics are neither more nor less suggestible (and hypnotizable) than other neurotics. Finally, there appears to be a slight positive correlation between suggestibility or hypnotizability and intelligence. Attempts to establish a relationship between suggestibility or hypnotizability and personality factors have generally been unsuccessful. Attitude, motivation, expectation, and emotions can enter as factors but are clearly not essential determinants of suggestibility or hypnotizability. Little is known regarding race and cultural differences. Depressants of the central nervous system, such as the barbiturates, can increase suggestibility (and hypnotizability) provided the subject is already suggestible. Satisfactory data regarding the effects of hallucinogenic drugs and the effects of stimulants are as yet unavailable. In general there does not appear to be any proven drug or device which by itself—that is, entirely through a physical action—can bring about an outstanding state of hypersuggestibility.

It needs to be remarked that the answers to many questions with regard to hypnotizability or hypnotic susceptibility are very much dependent upon (*a*) the criterion used to establish that a person is hypnotized, and (*b*) the "degree" or "depth" of hypnosis one has in mind. One of the main weaknesses in all of the studies reported by Hull, for instance, consists in the fact that closing of the eyes following suggestions to this effect is taken by him as a criterion of being hypnotized, this apparently being an all-or-none affair. There are, however, good reasons for questioning just how many subjects thus closing their eyes are really hypnotized—suggestible, yes; but whether hypnotized or not remains a moot question. To say, for instance, that 40 per cent, 2 per cent, and so on of individuals can or cannot be hypnotized is quite meaningless unless these figures are related to a clear criterion of what being hypnotized consists of. According to modern views hypnosis is on a linear continuum assumed to be isomorphic if not identical with a continuum of suggestibility. The questions "how hypnotized" or "how hypnotizable" can therefore be answered only in relation to a specified point on this continuum. A great many writers, particularly medical men, are willing to consider any sign of suggestibility, no matter how small, as a sign of hypnotizability. By this token just about everyone is hypnotizable. Others, like Braid and Charcot, insist on a full-scale manifestation of suggestibility before they consider a person hypnotizable. By this criterion only a very small percentage of individuals are susceptible to hypnosis. The majority of investigators, like Bernheim, prefer, however, to think of individuals as falling within ranges or intervals on the suggestibility continuum and speak of individuals as being insusceptible (5–30 per cent), light (33–50 per cent), medium (12–35 per cent), and deep or somnambulistic (5–29 per cent) subjects. Whether any of these are, however, actually hypnotized at the time they are ranked remains a difficult question to answer.

The effectiveness of suggestions. If it exists as a state, whatever other properties hypnosis may have were long ago pushed far into the background by the presumed hypersuggestibility that accompanies its presence. Although there may be some question whether exactly the same processes underlie the action of both waking and hypnotic suggestions, in their outward manifestations both seem to lie on the same continuum, there simply being more or less suggestibility. On the basis of the observed behavior and the reports of subjects, suggestions are apparently extremely effective in the cognitive domain. The most outstanding of these effects are hallucinations, delusions, anesthesias, paresthesias, amnesias, and paramnesias. These are *functional* effects that can be said to have the same kind of reality as similar functional manifestations associated with various psychopathologies. Suggestions appear to be able to bring about appreciable affective changes, particularly when these are indirectly brought about in association with hallucinations and delusions. On the other hand the power of suggestions to bring about improved sensory, motor, and intellectual performance is quite limited. Such enhanced performance as is usually observed appears to be most readily obtained as side effects of other suggested effects. The same is true of suggestions aimed at affecting the vegetative functions. Excluding improved performance, suggestions appear to be able to affect appreciably and directly all voluntary behavior, particularly at the motor level. On the whole, suggestions appear to be much more limited in their effectiveness than is commonly believed.

Regression and somatic effects. One of the more widely advertised suggested phenomena is *hypnotic regression*, whereby an individual is presumably caused to re-experience past events vividly, especially those of his childhood, and in the process is made to produce appropriate behavioral and even somatic manifestations. Individuals have been said by reliable sources to have thus "returned" to the first weeks of life. The matter remains controversial. Unquestionably in many cases much role playing is present, and in many instances one is dealing at best with some hypermnesia often mixed with confabulation. However, there do appear to be cases that seem to indicate the reliving of past experiences in a much more complete sense than that of a hypermnesia. By and large the matter remains unsettled.

Can somatic tissue changes, such as heat blisters, be brought about by suggestion? There are indications that this is probably possible but not readily so and perhaps only in individuals with special diatheses. The question of control of bleeding and removal of warts by suggestion remains on the whole unsettled.

Hypnosis and volition. Two perennial questions with regard to hypnosis are whether an individual can be hypnotized against his will and whether a hypnotized person can be made to act in certain ways against his will. No one can give an *absolute* negative answer to either question. In a general way the answer is negative, and if these effects are at all possible, they would be so only under rather unusual circumstances. It must be clearly understood that this assertion is made on the assumption that the subject is fully aware that efforts are being made to hypnotize him or that the act is one he cannot abide. There is evidence that if the situation in question can be so structured as to prevent the subject from being aware of the true nature of the acts involved, a person who otherwise would not want to be hypnotized can be hypnotized, and a hypnotized person who otherwise would not agree to perform a certain act will perform it. *Thus in this sense it would appear possible, in a manner of speaking, to bring about through hypno–suggestive procedures effects that are against the will of the person.* It might be added that for rather obvious ethical reasons, if for no others, a decisive experimental test of the matter is not likely to be done.

Moreover, and contrary to popular misconception, a hypnotized individual usually is not unconscious or bereft of all intellectual faculties. On the contrary, he is capable of perceiving, evaluating, reasoning, deciding, and carrying out his decisions; but he does appear to be limited in these respects by the nature of the suggestions he has been given.

Hypnosis and hypnosislike states

Whether or not it has a reality of its own, hypnosis as it has been popularly and scientifically conceived is a presumed state that appears to fall into a much larger class of altered states of awareness best subsumed under the heading *trance states*. The term "hypnosis" is best reserved to denote only those trance states that are associated with an initially selective hypersuggestibility and that are intentionally brought about in one individual by means of specific psychological and physical procedures and agents used by another individual. Such a definition appears overrestrictive to some writers for it tends to exclude from the class of hypnotic phenomena such occurrences as have been called "animal hypnosis," "spontaneous (or accidental) hypnosis," and "self-hypnosis." The facts, however, are that, at best, known cases of animal hypnosis could probably be identified with Charcot's induced human catalepsy when brought about by sudden stimulation. They have never been shown to have any but a very limited resemblance to the most generally accepted conception of heterohypnosis with which, incidentally, of Charcot's three syndromes, only his "somnambulism" can be identified. Additionally, there is some evidence that animal hypnosis, better referred to as an induced state of immobilization, is physiologically distinguishable from the usual form taken by hypnosis in humans. Finally, a study of the literature shows that the coining of the expression "animal hypnosis" has come entirely out of an unwarranted generalization of the term "hypnosis" under the influence of theoretical speculations. The same is largely true of "spontaneous (accidental) hypnosis," a phenomenon largely theorized but never clearly demonstrated to exist. The most recent abuse of the term "hypnosis" along this line is to be found in so-called "highway hypnosis," a highly speculative notion behind which there exists but the vaguest of factual evidence. As for "self-hypnosis," its existence has been obfuscated by the fact that "self" can be used in this case to refer to a number of different processes. The two most common and only practical so-called techniques of self-hypnosis *are basically cases of heterohypnosis*. In one the subject listens to a recording specially prepared by a hypnotist, and in the other he makes use of posthypnotic suggestions given to him at a previous time by a hypnotist. As for hypnosis induced without such aids by an individual acting as both hypnotist and subject and using solely a recognized technique equivalent to one used for the induction of heterohypnosis, no clear-cut cases of it have been reported. Such reported cases as those presumably seen among Tibetan monks, Hindu yogis, and Balinese dancers, to name only a few, have not been satisfactorily demonstrated to meet all the essential criteria of hypnosis previously mentioned. Considerable evidence exists showing that even in these instances the reported condition is brought about only after the individual involved has gone through specific and often intensive training with at least one teacher; hence there is a serious question of how free of hetero-influences these situations really are. Thus the exclusion of such rather nebulous and largely speculative entities by the definition that has been given does not present any real problem. This is not to say that some individuals probably do not spontaneously enter states of altered awareness under various conditions, as, for instance, when concentrating intensely upon a problem. It is essentially a foregone conclusion that they do. But is it hypnosis? It is clearly so only if one essentially defines hypnosis as *any* state of altered awareness. If, however, one retains the historical and popular meaning of the term, there does not as yet appear to be any justification for calling such conditions "spontaneous (accidental) hypnosis" or, even less, "self-hypnosis."

ANDRÉ M. WEITZENHOFFER

[*Directly related are the entries* PERSUASION *and* SUGGESTION. *Other relevant material may be found in* ATTENTION; ATTITUDES, *article on* ATTITUDE CHANGE; PAIN; ROLE, *article on* PSYCHOLOGICAL ASPECTS; SLEEP; *and in the biographies of* HULL *and* MESMER.]

BIBLIOGRAPHY

American Journal of Clinical Hypnosis. → Published since 1958.

BEAUNIS, HENRI 1896 *Le somnambulisme provoqué.* Paris: Baillière.

BERNHEIM, HIPPOLYTE 1891 *Hypnotisme; suggestion; psycho-thérapie.* Paris: Octave Doin.

BINET, ALFRED; and FÉRÉ, CHARLES (1887) 1892 *Animal Magnetism.* New York: Appleton. → First published in French.

BRAID, JAMES (1843) 1899 *Neurypnology: Or the Rationale of Nervous Sleep, Considered in Relation With Animal Magnetism.* 2d ed. London: Redway.

BRAMWELL, JOHN M. (1903) 1956 *Hypnotism: Its History, Practice and Theory.* New York: Julian Press.

Bulletin de l'École de Psychologie et de la Société de Psychothérapie. → Published since 1887. First published as *Revue de l'hypnotisme.*

CROCQ, JEAN (1896) 1900 *L'hypnotisme scientifique.* 2d ed. Paris: Société d'Éditions Scientifiques.

DESPINE, PROSPER 1880 *Étude scientifique sur le somnambulisme.* Paris: Savy.

HULL, CLARK L. 1933 *Hypnosis and Suggestibility: An Experimental Approach.* New York: Appleton.

JANET, PIERRE 1889 *L'automatisme psychologique.* Paris: Alcan.

Journal für Psychologie und Neurologie. → Published since 1892. First published as *Zeitschrift für Hypnotismus.*

Journal of Clinical and Experimental Hypnosis. → Published since 1953.

MOLL, ALBERT (1889) 1909 *Hypnotism.* New York: Scribner. → First published in German.

RICHER, PAUL (1885) 1891 *La grande hystérie.* 2d ed. Paris: Delahaye & Lecrosnier.

SCHNECK, JEROME M. (1953) 1963 *Hypnosis in Modern Medicine.* 3d ed. Springfield, Ill.: Thomas.

STOLL, OTTO (1894) 1904 *Suggestion und Hypnotismus in der Völkerpsychologie.* 2d ed. Leipzig: Veit.

VÖLGYESI, FRANZ 1938 *Menschen und Tierhypnose.* Zurich: Füssli.

WEITZENHOFFER, ANDRÉ M. (1953) 1963 *Hypnotism: An Objective Study in Suggestibility.* New York: Wiley.

HYPOTHESIS TESTING

The formulation of hypotheses and their testing through observation are essential steps in the scientific process. A detailed discussion of their role in the development of scientific theories is given by Popper (1934). On the basis of observational evidence, a hypothesis is either accepted for the time being (until further evidence suggests modification) or rejected as untenable. (In the latter case, it is frequently desirable to indicate also the direction and size of the departure from the hypothesis.)

It is sometimes possible to obtain unequivocal evidence regarding the validity of a hypothesis. More typically, the observations are subject to chance variations, such as measurement or sampling errors, and the same observations could have occurred whether the hypothesis is true or not, although they are more likely in one case than in the other. It then becomes necessary to assess the strength of the evidence and, in particular, to decide whether the deviations of the observations from what ideally would be expected under the hypothesis are too large to be attributed to chance. This article deals with methods for making such decisions: the *testing of statistical hypotheses*.

Probability models. A quantitative evaluation of the observational material is possible only on the basis of quantitative assumptions regarding the errors and other uncertainties to which the observations are subject. Such assumptions are conveniently formulated in terms of a probability model for the observations. In such a model, the observations appear as the values of random variables, and the hypothesis becomes a statement concerning the distribution of these variables [*see* PROBABILITY, *article on* FORMAL PROBABILITY].

The following are examples of some simple basic classes of probability models. Some of the most important applications of these models are to samples drawn at random from large populations and possibly subject to measurement errors.

Example 1—binomial model. If X is the number of successes in n independent dichotomous trials with constant probability p of "success," then X has a binomial distribution. This model is applicable to large (nominally infinite) populations whose members are of two types (voters favoring one of two candidates, inmates of mental institutions who are or are not released within one year) of which one is conventionally called "success" and the other "failure." The trials are the drawings of the n members of the population to be included in the sample. This model is realistic only if the population is large enough so that the n drawings are essentially independent.

Example 2—binomial two-sample model. To compare two proportions referring to two different (large) populations (voters favoring candidate A in two different districts, mental patients in two different institutions), a sample is drawn from each population. If the sample sizes are m and n, the observed proportions in the samples are X/m and Y/n, and the proportions in the populations are p_1 and p_2, then the model may assume that X and Y have independent binomial distributions. The same model may also be applicable when two samples are drawn from the same large population and subjected to different treatments.

Example 3—multinomial model. If a sample of size n is drawn from a (large) population whose members are classified into k types and the number of members in the sample belonging to each type is $X_1, \cdots, X_k$, respectively, then an appropriate model may assign to $(X_1, \cdots, X_k)$ a multinomial distribution.

Example 4—normal model. If $Z_1, \cdots, Z_n$ are measurements of the same characteristic taken on the n members of a sample (for example, test scores on a psychological test for n subjects or skull width for n skulls), an appropriate model may assume that $Z_1, \cdots, Z_n$ are independently and normally distributed with common mean μ and variance σ^2.

Example 5—normal two-sample model. To study the effect of a treatment (for example, the effect of training or of a drug on a test score) two independent samples may be obtained, of which the first serves as control (is not treated) and the second receives the treatment. If the measurements of the untreated subjects are $X_1, \cdots, X_m$ and those of the treated subjects are $Y_1, \cdots, Y_n$, it may be reasonable to assume that $X_1, \cdots, X_m; Y_1, \cdots, Y_n$ are all independently normally distributed—the X's with mean μ_X and variance σ_X^2, the Y's with mean μ_Y and variance σ_Y^2. Frequently it may be realistic to make the additional assumption that $\sigma_Y^2 = \sigma_X^2$, that the variance of the measurements is not affected by the treatment.

Example 6—nonparametric one-sample model. If the normality assumption in example 4 cannot be justified, it may instead be assumed only that $Z_1, \cdots, Z_n$ are independently distributed, each according to the same continuous distribution, F, about which no other assumption is made.

Example 7—nonparametric two-sample model. If the normality assumption in example 5 cannot be justified, it may instead be assumed only that $X_1, \cdots, X_m; Y_1, \cdots, Y_n$ are independently distributed, the X's according to a continuous distribution F, the Y's according to G. It may be realistic to suppose that the treatment has no effect on the shape or spread of the distribution but only on its location.

In a testing problem the model is never completely specified, for if there were no unknown element in the model, it would be known whether the hypothesis is true or false. One is thus dealing not with a single model but rather with a class of models, say Ω. For example, in a problem for which the models of example 1 are appropriate, Ω may consist of all binomial models corresponding to n trials and with p having any value between 0 and 1. If the model is specified except for certain parameters (the probabilities $p_1, \cdots, p_k$ in example 3, the mean, μ, and the variance, σ^2, in example 4), the class Ω is called *parametric;* otherwise, as in examples 6 and 7, it is *nonparametric* [*see* NONPARAMETRIC STATISTICS].

Statistical hypotheses. A hypothesis, when expressed in terms of a class of probability models, becomes a statement imposing additional restrictions on the class of models or on the distributions specified by the models.

Example 8. The hypothesis that the probability p_2 of a cure with a new treatment is no higher than the probability p_1 of a cure with the standard treatment, in the model of example 2, states that the parameters p_1, p_2 satisfy $H: p_2 \leqslant p_1$.

Example 9. Consider the hypothesis that the rate at which a rat learns to run a maze is unaffected by its having previously learned to run a different maze. If $X_1, \cdots, X_m$ denote the learning times required by m control rats who have not previously run a maze and $Y_1, \cdots, Y_n$ denote the learning times of n rats with previous experience on another maze, and if the model of example 7 is assumed, then the hypothesis of no effect states that the distributions F and G satisfy $H: G = F$. (Since, as in the present example, hypotheses frequently state the absence of an effect, a hypothesis under test is sometimes referred to as the *null hypothesis.*)

Hypotheses about a single parameter. Hypotheses in parametric classes of models frequently concern only a single parameter, such as μ in example 4 or $\mu_Y - \mu_X$ in example 5, the remaining parameters being "nuisance parameters." The most common hypotheses concerning a single parameter θ either (a) completely specify the value of the parameter, for example, state that $p = \frac{1}{2}$ in example 1, that $\mu = 0$ in example 4, or that $\mu_Y - \mu_X = 0$ in example 5—in general, such a hypothesis states that $\theta = \theta_0$ where θ_0 is the specified value; or (b) state that the parameter does not exceed (or does not fall short of) a specified value, for example, the hypothesis $p \leqslant \frac{1}{2}$ in example 1 or $\mu_X - \mu_Y \leqslant 0$ in example 5—the general form of such a hypothesis is $H_1: \theta \leqslant \theta_0$ (or $H_2: \theta \geqslant \theta_0$).

Two other important, although not quite so common, hypotheses state (c) that the parameter θ does not differ from a specified value θ_0 more than a given amount Δ: $|\theta - \theta_0| \leqslant \Delta$ or, equivalently, that θ lies in some specified interval $a \leqslant \theta \leqslant b$; or ($d$) that the parameter θ lies outside some specified interval.

Hypotheses about several parameters. In a parametric model involving several parameters, the hypothesis may of course concern more than one parameter. Thus, in example 3, one may wish to test the hypothesis that all the probabilities $p_1, \cdots, p_k$ have specified values. In example 5, the hypothesis might state that the point (μ_X, μ_Y) lies in a rectangle H: $a_1 \leqslant \mu_X \leqslant a_2$, $b_1 \leqslant \mu_Y \leqslant b_2$, or that it lies in a circle H: $(\mu_X - \mu_X^0)^2 + (\mu_Y - \mu_Y^0)^2 \leqslant c$, etc.

Hypotheses in nonparametric models. The variety of hypotheses that may arise in nonparametric models is illustrated by the following hypotheses, which have often been considered in connection with examples 6 and 7. In example 6, (1) F is the normal distribution with zero mean and unit variance; (2) F is a normal distribution (mean and variance unspecified); and (3) F is symmetric about the origin. In example 7, (1) $G = F$; (2) $G(x) \leqslant F(x)$ for all x; and (3) for no x do $G(x)$ and $F(x)$ differ by more than a specified value Δ.

Simple and composite hypotheses. A hypothesis, by imposing restrictions on the original class Ω of models, defines the subclass Ω_H of those models of Ω that satisfy the restrictions. If the hypothesis H completely specifies the model, so that Ω_H contains only a single model, then H is called *simple;* otherwise it is *composite.* Examples of simple hypotheses are the hypothesis $p = \frac{1}{2}$ in example 1 and the hypothesis that F is the normal distribution with zero mean and unit variance in example 6. Examples of composite hypotheses are the hypothesis $p_2 \leqslant p_1$ in example 2, the hypothesis $\mu = 0$ in example 4 when σ^2 is unknown, and the hypothesis that F is a normal distribution (mean and variance unspecified) in example 6.

Tests of hypotheses. A test of a hypothesis H is a rule that specifies for each possible set of values of the observations whether to accept or reject H, should these particular values be observed. It is therefore a division of all possible sets of values (the so-called sample space) into two groups:

those for which the (null) hypothesis will be accepted (the *acceptance region*) and those for which it will be rejected (the *rejection region* or *critical region*).

Tests are typically defined in terms of a test statistic T, extreme values of which are highly unlikely to occur if H is true but are not surprising if H is false. To be specific, suppose that large values of T (and no others) are surprising if H is true but are not surprising if it is false. It is then natural to reject H when T is sufficiently large, say when

$$(1) \qquad T \geqslant c,$$

where c is a suitable constant, called the *critical value*.

The above argument shows that the choice of an appropriate test does not depend only on the hypothesis. The choice also depends on the ways in which the hypothesis can be false, that is, on the models of Ω not satisfying H (not belonging to Ω_H); these are called the *alternatives* (or *alternative hypotheses*) to H. Thus, in example 8, the alternatives consist of the models of example 2 satisfying $p_2 > p_1$; in example 9, they consist of the models of example 7 satisfying $G \neq F$.

The following two examples illustrate how the choice of the values of T for which H is rejected and the choice of T itself depend on the class of alternatives.

Example 10. Consider in example 1 the hypothesis H: $p = \frac{1}{2}$ and the three different sets of alternatives: p is less than $\frac{1}{2}$, p is greater than $\frac{1}{2}$, or p is different from (either less or greater than) $\frac{1}{2}$. Since one expects the proportion X/n of successes to be close to p, it is natural to reject H against the alternative $p < \frac{1}{2}$ if X/n is too small. (Very small values of X/n would be surprising under H but not under the alternatives.) Similarly, one would reject H against the alternative $p > \frac{1}{2}$ if X/n is too large. Finally, H would be rejected against the alternative $p \neq \frac{1}{2}$ if X/n is either too large or too small, for example, if $|(X/n) - \frac{1}{2}| > c$.

Alternatives of the first two types of this example and the associated tests are called *one-sided;* those corresponding to the third type are called *two-sided.*

Example 11. In example 7, consider the hypothesis H: $G = F$ that the Y's and X's have the same distribution against the alternatives that the Y's tend to be larger than the X's. A standard test for this problem is based on the Wilcoxon statistic, W, which counts the number among the mn pairs (X_i, Y_j) for which Y_j exceeds X_i. The hypothesis is rejected if W is too large [*see* NONPARAMETRIC STATISTICS].

Suppose instead that the alternatives to H state that the Y's are more spread out than the X's, or only that G and F are unequal without specifying how they differ. Then W is no longer an appropriate test statistic, since very large (or small) values of W are not necessarily more likely to occur under such alternatives than under the hypothesis.

Significance. To specify the test (1) completely, it is still necessary to select a critical value. This selection is customarily made on the basis of the following consideration. The values $T \geqslant c$, for which the hypothesis will be rejected, could occur even if the hypothesis H were true; they would then, however, be very unlikely and hence very surprising. A measure of how surprising such values are under H is the probability of observing them when H is true. This probability, $P_H(T \geqslant c)$, is called the *significance level* (or *size*) of the test. The traditional specification of a critical value is in terms of significance level. A value α (typically a small value such as .01 or .05) of this level is prescribed, and the critical value c is determined by the equation

$$(2) \qquad P_H(T \geqslant c) = \alpha.$$

Values of T that are greater than or equal to c, and for which the hypothesis is therefore rejected, are said to be (statistically) *significant* at level α. This expresses the fact that although such extreme values could have occurred under H, this event is too unlikely (its probability being only α) to be reasonably explained by random fluctuations under H.

Tests and hypotheses suggested by data. In stating that the test determined by (1) and (2) rejects the hypothesis H with probability α when H is true, it is assumed that H and the rejection region (1) were determined before the observations were taken. If, instead, either the hypothesis or the test was suggested by the data, the actual significance level of the test will be greater than α, since then other sets of observations would also have led to rejection. In such cases, the prescribed significance levels can be obtained by carrying out the test on a fresh set of data. There also exist certain multiple-decision procedures that permit the testing, at a prescribed level, of hypotheses suggested by the data [*see* LINEAR HYPOTHESES, *article on* MULTIPLE COMPARISONS].

Determination of critical value. The actual determination of c from equation (2) for a given value of α is simple if there exists a table of the distribution of T under H. In cases where a complete table is not available, selected percentage points of the distribution, that is, the values of c corresponding to selected values of α, may have been published. If, instead, c has to be computed, it is frequently convenient to proceed as follows.

Let t be the observed value of the test statistic T. Then the probability $\hat{\alpha}$ of obtaining a value at least as extreme as that observed is called the *significance probability* (also *P-value, sample significance level,* and *descriptive level of significance*) of the observed value t and is given by

$$(3) \qquad P_H(T \geqslant t) = \hat{\alpha}.$$

For the observed value t, the hypothesis is rejected if $t \geqslant c$ (and hence if $\hat{\alpha} \leqslant \alpha$) and is otherwise accepted. By computing $\hat{\alpha}$, one can therefore tell whether H should be rejected or accepted at any given significance level α from the rule

$$(4) \qquad \text{reject } H \text{ if } \hat{\alpha} \leqslant \alpha; \text{ accept } H \text{ if } \hat{\alpha} > \alpha.$$

This rule, which is equivalent to the test defined by (1) and (2), requires only the computation of the probability (3); this is sometimes more convenient than determining c from (2).

When publishing the result of a statistical test, it is good practice to state not only whether the hypothesis was accepted or rejected at the chosen significance level (particularly since the choice of level is typically rather arbitrary) but also to publish the significance probability. This enables others to perform the test at the level of their choice by applying (4). It also provides a basis for combining the results of the test with those of other independent tests that may be performed at other times. (Various methods for combining a number of independent significance probabilities are discussed by Birnbaum 1954.) If no tables are available for the distribution of T but the critical values c of (2) are tabled for a number of different levels α, it is desirable at least to give the largest tabled value α at which the observations are nonsignificant and the smallest level at which they are significant, for example, "significant at 5 per cent, nonsignificant at 1 per cent." Actually, whenever possible, some of the basic data should be published so as to permit others to carry the statistical analysis further (for example, to estimate the size of an effect, to check the adequacy of the model, etc.).

In addition to the above uses, the significance probability—by measuring the degree of surprise at getting a value of T as extreme as or more extreme than the observed value t—gives some indication of the strength of the evidence against H. The smaller $\hat{\alpha}$ is, the more surprising it is to get this extreme a value under H and, therefore, the stronger the evidence against H.

The use of equation (2) for determining c from α involves two possible difficulties:

(*a*) If H is composite, the left-hand side of (2) may have different values for different distributions of Ω_H. In this case, equation (2) is replaced by

$$(5) \qquad \max_H P_H(T \geqslant c) = \alpha;$$

that is, the significance level or size is defined as the maximum probability of rejection under H. As an illustration, let T be Student's t-statistic for testing H: $\mu_Y \leqslant \mu_X$ in example 5 [*see* LINEAR HYPOTHESES, *article on* ANALYSIS OF VARIANCE]. Here the maximum probability of rejection under H occurs when $\mu_Y = \mu_X$, so that c is determined by the condition $P_{\mu_Y=\mu_X}(T \geqslant c) = \alpha$. This example illustrates the fact that $P_H(T \geqslant c)$ typically takes on its maximum on the boundary between the hypothesis and the alternatives.

(*b*) If the distribution of T is discrete, there may not exist a value c for which (2) or (5) holds. In practice, it is then usual to replace the originally intended significance level by the closest smaller (or larger) value that is attainable. In theoretical comparisons of tests, it is sometimes preferable instead to get the exact value α through randomization—namely, to reject H if $T > c$, to accept H if $T < c$, and if $T = c$ to reject or accept with probability ρ and $1 - \rho$ respectively, where ρ is determined by the equation $P_H(T > c) + \rho P_H(T = c) = \alpha$.

Power and choice of level. Suppose that a drug is being tested for possible beneficial effect on schizophrenic patients, with the hypothesis H stating that the drug has no such effect. Then a small significance level, by controlling the probability of falsely rejecting H when it is true, gives good protection against the possibility of falsely concluding that the drug is beneficial when in fact it is not. The test may, however, be quite unsatisfactory in its ability to detect a beneficial effect when one exists. This ability is measured by the probability of rejecting H when it is false, that is, by the probability P_A(rejecting H), where A indicates an alternative to H (in the example, an average effect of a given size). This probability, which for tests of the form (1) is equal to $P_A(T \geqslant c)$, is called the *power* of the test against the alternative A. The probability of rejecting H and the complementary probability of accepting H, as functions of the model or of the parameters specifying the model, are called respectively the *power function* and the *operating characteristic* of the test. Either of these functions describes the performance of the test against the totality of models of Ω.

Unfortunately, the requirements of high power and small level are in conflict, since the smaller the significance level, the larger is c and the smaller, therefore, is the power of the test. When choosing a significance level (and hence c), it is necessary to take into account the power of the resulting test against the alternatives of interest. If this power is too low to be satisfactory, it may be necessary to permit a somewhat larger significance level in order to provide for an increase in power. To increase power without increasing significance level, it is necessary to find a better test statistic or to improve the basic structure of the procedure, for example, by increasing sample size.

The problem of achieving a balance between significance level and power may usefully be considered from a slightly different point of view. A test, by deciding to reject or to accept H, may come to an erroneous decision in two different ways: by rejecting when H is true (error of the first kind) or by accepting when H is false (error of the second kind). The probabilities of these two kinds of errors are

$$P(\text{error of first kind}) = P_H(\text{false rejection}) = \alpha \tag{6}$$

and

$$P(\text{error of second kind}) = P_A(\text{false acceptance}) = 1 - \text{power}. \tag{7}$$

It is desirable to keep both the first probability and the second probability low, and these two requirements are usually in conflict. Any rule for balancing them must involve, at least implicitly, a weighing of the seriousness of the two kinds of error.

Choice of test. The constant c determines the size of the test (1) not only in the technical sense of (2) or (5) but also in the ordinary sense of the word, since the larger c is, the smaller is the rejection region. In the same sense, the test statistic T determines the shape of the test, that is, of the rejection region. The problem of selecting T is one of the main concerns of the theory of hypothesis testing.

A basis for making this selection is provided by the fact that of two tests of the same size, the one that has the higher power is typically more desirable, for with the same control of the probability of an error of the first kind, it gives better protection against errors of the second kind. The most satisfactory level α test against a particular alternative A is therefore the test that, subject to (5), maximizes the power against A: the *most powerful* level α test against A.

The fundamental result underlying all derivations of optimum tests is the Neyman–Pearson lemma, which states that for testing a simple hypothesis against a particular alternative A, the statistic T of the most powerful test is given for each possible set x of the observations by

$$T = \frac{P_A(x)}{P_H(x)} \tag{8}$$

(or by any monotone function of T), where P_A and P_H denote the probabilities (or probability densities) of x under A and H respectively.

In most problems there are many alternatives to H. For example, if the hypothesis specifies that a treatment has no effect and the alternatives specify that it has a beneficial effect, a different alternative will correspond to each possible size of this effect. If it happens that the same test is simultaneously most powerful against all possible alternatives, this test is said to be *uniformly most powerful* (UMP). However, except for one-tailed tests (and for tests of the hypothesis that the parameter lies outside a specified interval) in the simplest one-parameter models, a UMP test typically does not exist; instead, different tests are most powerful against different alternatives.

If a UMP test does not exist, tests may be sought with somewhat weaker optimum properties. One may try, for example, to find a test that is UMP among all tests possessing certain desirable symmetry properties or among all *unbiased* tests, a test being unbiased if its power never falls below the level of significance. Many standard tests have one or the other of these properties.

A general method of test construction that frequently leads to satisfactory results is the *likelihood ratio* method, which in analogy to (8) defines T by

$$T = \frac{\max_{\Omega} P(x)}{\max_{\Omega_H} P(x)}. \tag{9}$$

Here the denominator is the maximum probability of x when H is true, while the numerator is the over-all maximum of this probability. If the numerator is sufficiently larger than the denominator, this indicates that x has a much higher probability under one of the alternatives than under H, and it then seems reasonable to reject H when x is observed. The distribution of the test statistic (9) under H has a simple approximation when the sample sizes are large, and in this case the likelihood ratio test also has certain approximate optimum properties (Kendall & Stuart 1961, vol. 2, p. 230; Lehmann 1959, p. 310).

The specification problem. For many standard testing problems, tests with various optimum properties have been worked out and can be found in the textbooks. As a result, the principal difficulty, in practice, is typically not the choice of α or T but the problem of *specification*, that is, of selecting a class Ω of models that will adequately represent the process generating the observations. Suppose, for example, that one is contemplating the model of example 5. Then the following questions, among others, must be considered: (*a*) May the experimental subjects reasonably be viewed as randomly chosen from the population of interest? (*b*) Are the populations large enough so that the X's and Y's may be assumed to be independent? (*c*) Does the normal shape provide an adequate approximation for the distribution of the observations or of some function of the observations? (*d*) Is it realistic to suppose that $\sigma_X = \sigma_Y$? The answers to such questions, and hence the choice of model, require considerable experience both with statistics and with the subject matter in which the problem arises. (Protection against some of the possible failures of the model of example 5 in particular may be obtained through the method of randomization discussed below.)

Problems of robustness. The difficulty of the specification problem naturally raises the question of how strongly the performance of a test depends on the particular class of models from which it is derived. There are two aspects to this question, namely robustness (insensitivity to departures from assumption) of the size of the test and robustness of its power [*see* ERRORS, *article on* EFFECTS OF ERRORS IN STATISTICAL ASSUMPTIONS].

Two typical results concerning robustness of size of a test are the following: (*a*) In example 5, assuming $\sigma_Y = \sigma_X$, the size of Student's *t*-test for testing H: $\mu_Y = \mu_X$ is fairly robust against nonnormality except for very small sample sizes. (*b*) In example 5, the *F*-test for testing $\sigma_Y = \sigma_X$ is very nonrobust against nonnormality.

The second aspect, the influence of the model on power, may again be illustrated by the case of Student's *t*-test for testing H: $\mu_Y = \mu_X$ in example 5. It unfortunately turns out—and this result is typical—that the power of the test is not robust against distributions with heavy tails (distributions that assign relatively high probability to very large positive and negative values), for example, if normality is disturbed by the presence of gross errors. This difficulty can be avoided by the use of nonparametric tests such as the Wilcoxon test defined in example 11, which give only limited weight to extreme observations. The Wilcoxon test, at the expense of a very slight efficiency loss (about 5 per cent) in the case of normality, gives much better protection against gross errors. In addition, its size is completely independent of the assumption of normality, so that it is in fact a test of the hypothesis $G = F$ in the nonparametric model of example 7.

Design. Analysis of data, through performance of an appropriate test, is not the only aspect of a testing problem to which statistical considerations are relevant. At least of equal importance is the question of what observations should be taken or what type of experiment should be performed. The following are illustrations of some of the statistical problems relating to the proper *design* of an investigation [*see* EXPERIMENTAL DESIGN].

Sample size. Once it has been decided in principle what kind of observations to take, for example, what type of sampling to use, it is necessary to determine the number of observations required. This can be done by fixing, in addition to the significance level α, the minimum power β that one wishes to achieve against the alternatives of interest. When the sample size is not fixed in advance, a compromise in the values of α and β is no longer necessary, since both can now be controlled. Instead, the problem may arise of balancing the desired error control against the cost of sampling. If the sample size n required to achieve a desired α and β is too large, a compromise between n and the values of α and β becomes necessary.

Sequential designs. Instead of using a fixed sample size, it may be more advantageous to take the observations one at a time, or in batches, and to let the decision of when to stop depend on the observations. (The stopping rule, which states for each possible sequence of observations when to stop, must of course be specified before any observations are taken.) With such a *sequential* design, one would stop early when the particular values observed happen to give a strong indication of the correct decision and continue longer when this is not the case. In this way, it is usually possible to achieve the same control of significance level and power with a (random) number of observations, which on the average is smaller than that required by the corresponding test of fixed sample size. When using a sequential test, account must be taken of the stopping rule to avoid distortion of the significance level [*see* SEQUENTIAL ANALYSIS].

Grouping for homogeneity. The power of tests of the hypothesis $\mu_Y = \mu_X$ in example 5 depends not only on the size of the difference $\mu_Y - \mu_X$ but also on the inherent variability of the subjects, as measured by σ_X and σ_Y. Frequently, the power can be increased by subdividing the subjects into more homogeneous groups and restricting the comparison between treatment and control to subjects within the same group [*see* EXPERIMENTAL DESIGN, *article on* THE DESIGN OF EXPERIMENTS].

An illustration of such a design is the method of *paired comparisons*, where each group consists of only two subjects (for example, twins) chosen for their likeness, one of which receives the treatment and the other serves as control. If a sample of n such pairs is drawn and the difference of the measurements in the treated and control subjects of the ith pair is $Z_i = Y_i - X_i$, then $Z_1, \cdots, Z_n$ are distributed as in example 4. The appropriate test is Student's one-sample *t*-test, which is now, however, based on fewer degrees of freedom than for the design of example 5. To determine in any specific case whether the design of example 5, the paired-comparison design, or some intermediate design with group size larger than two is best, it is necessary to balance the reduction of variability due to grouping against the loss in degrees of freedom in the resulting *t*-test.

Randomization. When testing the effect of a treatment by comparing the results on n treated subjects with those on m controls, it may not be possible to obtain the subjects as a random sample from the population of interest. A probabilistic basis for inference and, at the same time, protection against various biases can be achieved by assigning the subjects to treatment and control not on a systematic or haphazard basis but *at random*, that is, in such a way that all possible such assignments are equally likely. Randomization is possible also in a paired-comparisons situation where within each pair one of the two possible assignments of treatment and control to the two subjects is chosen, for example, by tossing a coin. In the model resulting from such randomization, it is possible to carry out a test of the hypothesis of no treatment effect without any further assumptions.

Relation to other statistical procedures. The formulation of a problem as one of hypothesis testing may present a serious oversimplification if, in case of rejection, it is important to know which alternative or type of alternative is indicated. The following two situations provide typical and important examples.

(a) Suppose a two-sided test of the hypothesis $H: \theta = \theta_0$ rejects H when a test statistic T is either too small or too large. In case of rejection, it is usually not enough to conclude that θ differs from θ_0; one would wish to know in addition whether θ is less than or greater than θ_0. Here a three-decision procedure of the following form is called for:

conclude that $\theta < \theta_0$	if $T \leqslant c_1$
conclude that $\theta > \theta_0$	if $T \geqslant c_2$,
accept H	if $c_1 < T < c_2$.

The constants c_1, c_2 can be determined by specifying the two error probabilities $\alpha_1 = P_{\theta_0}(T \leqslant c_1)$ and $\alpha_2 = P_{\theta_0}(T \geqslant c_2)$, whose sum is equal to the error probability, α, of the two-sided test that rejects for $T \leqslant c_1$ and $T \geqslant c_2$. How the total error probability, α, is divided between α_1 and α_2 would depend on the relative seriousness of the two kinds of error involved and on the relative importance of detecting when θ is in fact less than or greater than θ_0. If concern is about equal between values of $\theta > \theta_0$ and values of $\theta < \theta_0$, the procedure with $\alpha_1 = \alpha_2 = \frac{1}{2}\alpha$ may be reasonable. It is interesting to note that this three-decision procedure may be interpreted as the simultaneous application of two tests: namely $T \leqslant c_1$ as a test of the hypothesis $H_1: \theta \geqslant \theta_0$ at level α_1 and $T \geqslant c_2$ as a test of $H_2: \theta \leqslant \theta_0$ at level α_2.

(b) If $\theta_1, \cdots, \theta_c$ denote the (average) effects of c treatments, one may wish to test the hypothesis $H: \theta_1 = \cdots = \theta_c$ to see if there are any appreciable differences. In case of rejection, one might wish to determine which of the θ's is largest, or to single out those θ's that are substantially larger than the rest, or to obtain a complete ranking of the θ's, or to divide the θ's into roughly comparable groups, etc.

Under suitable normality assumptions, the last of these objectives can be achieved by applying a *t*-test to each of the hypotheses $H_{ij}: \theta_i = \theta_j$, or rather by applying to each the three-decision procedure based on *t*-tests of the type discussed in (a). Combining the conclusions ($\theta_i < \theta_j$, $\theta_i = \theta_j$, or $\theta_i > \theta_j$) obtained in this way leads to a grouping of the kind desired. In determining the significance level, say α', at which the individual *t*-test should be performed, one must of course relate it to the significance level α that one wishes to achieve for the original hypothesis H. (For further details and references regarding this procedure, see Lehmann 1959, p. 275; Mosteller & Bush 1954, p. 304.)

These two examples illustrate how a procedure involving several choices may sometimes be built up by the simultaneous consideration of a number of situations involving only two choices, that is, a number of testing problems. A similar approach also leads to the method of estimation by confidence sets [*see* ESTIMATION, *article on* CONFIDENCE INTERVALS AND REGIONS].

The simultaneous consideration of a number of different tests also arises in other contexts. Frequently, investigators wish to explore a number of different aspects of the same data and for this purpose carry out multiple tests. This raises serious difficulties, since the stated significance levels relate to a single test without relation to others. Essentially the same difficulties arise when testing hypotheses *suggested by the data*, since this may be viewed as testing a (possibly large) number of potential hypotheses but reporting only the most significant outcome. This, of course, again invalidates the stated significance level. [*Methods for dealing with such problems are discussed in* LINEAR HYPOTHESES, *article on* MULTIPLE COMPARISONS.]

History. Isolated examples of tests, as statements of (statistical) significance or nonsignificance of a set of observations, occurred throughout the eighteenth and nineteenth centuries. A systematic use of hypothesis testing, but without explicit mention of alternatives to the hypothesis being tested, began with the work of Karl Pearson (1900) and owes much of its further development to R. A. Fisher (1925; 1935). That the choice of an appropriate test must depend on the alternatives as well as on the hypothesis was first explicitly recognized by Neyman and Pearson (1928; 1933), who introduced the concept of power and made it the cornerstone of the theory of hypothesis testing described here. Two other approaches to the subject, based on concepts of probability other than that of long-run frequency, which has been implicitly assumed here, are the Bayesian approach and that of Jeffreys [1939; *see also* BAYESIAN INFERENCE].

E. L. LEHMANN

[*See also* ESTIMATION; LINEAR HYPOTHESES; SIGNIFICANCE, TESTS OF.]

BIBLIOGRAPHY

BIRNBAUM, ALLAN 1954 Combining Independent Tests of Significance. *Journal of the American Statistical Association* 49:559–574.

FISHER, R. A. (1925) 1958 *Statistical Methods for Research Workers.* 13th ed. New York: Hafner. → Previous editions were also published by Oliver & Boyd.

FISHER, R. A. (1935) 1960 *The Design of Experiments.* 7th ed. New York: Hafner. → Previous editions were also published by Oliver & Boyd.

HODGES, JOSEPH L. JR.; and LEHMANN, E. L. 1964 *Basic Concepts of Probability and Statistics.* San Francisco: Holden-Day. → Contains a more leisurely exposition of the basic concepts of hypothesis testing.

JEFFREYS, HAROLD (1939) 1961 *Theory of Probability.* 3d ed. Oxford: Clarendon.

KENDALL, MAURICE G.; and STUART, ALAN 1961 *The Advanced Theory of Statistics.* New ed. Volume 2: Inference and Relationship. New York: Hafner; London: Griffin. → The first edition, published in 1946, was written by M. G. Kendall.

LEHMANN, ERICH L. 1959 *Testing Statistical Hypotheses.* New York: Wiley.

MOSTELLER, FREDERICK; and BUSH, ROBERT R. (1954) 1959 Selected Quantitative Techniques. Volume 1, pages 289–334 in Gardner Lindzey (editor), *Handbook of Social Psychology.* Cambridge, Mass.: Addison-Wesley.

NEYMAN, J.; and PEARSON, E. S. 1928 On the Use and Interpretation of Certain Test Criteria for Purposes of Statistical Inference. *Biometrika* 20A:175–240, 263–294.

NEYMAN, J.; and PEARSON, E. S. 1933 On the Problem of the Most Efficient Tests of Statistical Hypotheses. Royal Society of London, *Philosophical Transactions* Series A 231:289–337.

PEARSON, KARL 1900 On the Criterion That a Given System of Deviations From the Probable in the Case of a Correlated System of Variables Is Such That It Can Be Reasonably Supposed to Have Arisen From Random Sampling. *Philosophical Magazine* Fifth Series 50:157–175.

POPPER, KARL R. (1934) 1959 *The Logic of Scientific Discovery.* New York: Basic Books. → First published as *Logik der Forschung.* A paperback edition was published by Harper in 1965.

HYSTERIA

In contemporary usage, the name *hysteria* is given to a form of mental illness characterized by the exhibition of bodily signs such as paralysis or spasmodic movements and by complaints about the body, such as anesthesia or pain. The terms *conversion hysteria* and *dissociative reaction* are other names given to these phenomena. Bodily communications indistinguishable from those typical of hysteria may also be present in individuals diagnosed as hypochondriacal, neurasthenic, or schizophrenic, and sometimes in so-called normal persons as well.

Historical overview of the problem. The group of phenomena we now call hysteria and regard as a type of mental disease has been known since antiquity. Its many interpretations, during different historical periods, reflect the varied cultural concepts for explaining bodily illness and social deviance.

The term *hysteria* comes from the Greek word *hystera*, which means the womb or uterus. Hippocrates thought that the uterus was a free, peregrinating organ and that its wandering about the woman's body caused hysteria. Although he considered it a distinct, organic disease, he may have sensed its relation to the sexual passions, for he recommended marriage as the best remedy. The notion that hysteria was a condition limited to women was thus firmly established and was not seriously challenged until the latter half of the nineteenth century by Charcot (Zilboorg 1941).

During the first ten centuries of Christianity, with medical thought stagnating under the authoritarian influence of Galenic concepts, most cases of hysteria were probably mistaken for various bodily diseases. During the Middle Ages, as the attitude toward sickness changed from naturalistic to demonotheologic, many cases of hysteria, and undoubtedly of organic disease too, were interpreted as manifestations of witchcraft.

With the flowering of empiricism and science during the Renaissance, hysteria was again rediscovered as a disease. It is interesting that in the eighteenth century its main cause was attributed to emotions, passions, and human suggestibility, and in the early nineteenth, to organic dysfunction. It fell to Charcot, Janet, and Freud to clarify the distinction between neurological illness and hysteria. They showed that hysteria is a condition resembling physical disease that occurs in persons with healthy bodies. If this was hysteria, it is evident why it had to be distinguished from malingering. In theory, this was accomplished by defining hysteria as the unconscious imitation of illness, and malingering as the conscious imitation of it. In practice, the distinction was less easy to make.

It is only a small step from the psychoanalytic view of hysteria, which regards it as a form of illness, albeit without physical causation, to the communicational view of hysteria, which regards it as a form of communication—specifically, as the language of illness. The implications of the various concepts of hysteria for its epidemiology and therapy will be discussed later.

Phenomenology and explanations of hysteria

What is hysteria? What kind of "thing" is it? The most popular view today is that hysteria is a disease. Some consider it an organic disease; others, a mental disease.

Organic theory. The idea that hysteria is an organic disease has the merit of being logical. After all, the hysteric acts sick and looks sick; he is manifestly disabled; and he says he is ill. Supporters of this view argue that people have been disabled by many conditions—for example, diabetes and neurosyphilis—that were not understood as diseases with specifiable physicochemical causes and disturbances until recent times. They claim that hysteria is another such disease: we understand only its "mental symptoms," but in time will discover its physicochemical cause (Szasz 1961, pp. 91–93).

Thus, according to the organic theory of hysteria, the condition is basically similar to diseases of the central nervous system, such as multiple sclerosis. In this frame of reference, hysteria is a disease that happens to a person: he suffers from it and may be cured of it. Logically, this is a sound position. Factually, I consider it false.

Psychopathological theory. Few behavioral scientists accept the theory of the organic causation of hysteria. Those who consider hysteria an illness usually qualify it as a mental illness. Its pathology, therefore, is sought not in the patient's brain or body but in his psyche; hence we have various hypotheses about the so-called psychopathology of hysteria. The specific content of these hypotheses varies with the theories of particular schools of psychodynamics. There is general agreement, however, that hysterical bodily signs represent an unconscious conversion of repressed ideas, feelings, or conflicts into symptoms.

Thus, the psychopathological theory of hysteria also regards this condition as a disease, but with psychological causes rather than physiological. This explanation is weak logically (Ryle 1949) and is not adequately testable.

Communicational theory. Finally, there is the communicational theory of hysteria. It is based on the proposition that not all types of disability should be classified as illness; and, further, that so-called hysterical symptoms are a form of communication and game playing. Hysteria is a game with a theme of helplessness and helpfulness. The hysteric *acts* disabled and sick: however, his illness is not real, but is merely an imitation of a bodily illness. Because the hysteric impersonates the sick role, the result is genuine disability. But if we call this condition an *illness*, we use this term metaphorically, whether or not we realize it (Szasz 1961, pp. 259–279).

Thus, according to the communicational approach to hysteria, the phenomena that the patient presents are examined and interpreted not only in the context of his past, but in the context of his total human situation. Through body language, the hysteric communicates with himself and others —but especially with those who are willing, and often eager, to assume the role of being protective and controlling. This explanation is logically sound and testable. To date, I consider it our most adequate theory of hysteria.

Incidence

It is appropriate to raise certain questions now, such as: Is hysteria the same as it has always been or has it changed during the past fifty to eighty years? Is it more, or less, common today than it was in the past? Our answers will depend, in part, on our concept of hysteria.

It has been widely suggested (for example, by Chodoff 1954; Wheelis 1958; and others) that hysteria was more common in Austria toward the end of the last century than it is in America today. The evidence for this view is unconvincing. What has changed, without any doubt, is the sociology of medical practice. Thus, in the Paris or Vienna of the 1880s, persons with bodily complaints were seen by general practitioners or neurologists. The doctor's main task was to make a differential diagnosis between organic disease and conversion hysteria (and malingering). Today, such patients still seek the help of the general practitioner and the medical specialist. In the meantime, however, there developed a new medical specialty: psychiatry. Because hysterical patients consider themselves medically, not mentally, ill, they do not usually consult psychiatrists.

As psychiatry became a separate discipline, hysteria (and other mental disorders) became a specifically psychiatric diagnosis (much as, for example, myelogenous leukemia is a specifically hematologic diagnosis). It is expected, therefore, that this diagnosis will be attached to so-called psychiatric patients. However, persons who consult psychiatrists voluntarily or who are committed to their care involuntarily rarely suffer from what appears to be bodily illness; more often, they feel anguished or they annoy others. Thus, it is true that among the contemporary psychiatrist's patients hysteria is not a conspicuous complaint. But this does not mean that the incidence of hysteria in the population at large has decreased. I believe it has not.

The evidence suggests that hysteria is as common as ever, and perhaps more so. To be sure, as we have noted, persons who imitate illness, or who communicate with others in the language of illness, do not crowd the psychoanalyst's private office. Instead they go where—to paraphrase the signs that announce *Aquí se habla español* or *Ici on parle français*—the sign proclaims, We speak the language of illness. Where are such signs displayed? In the offices of general practitioners, internists, dermatologists, neurologists, and so forth; in medical clinics, and especially in famous diagnostic centers; in clinics where compensation for illness is awarded, such as those operated by the Veterans Administration; and in the offices of lawyers and in courts, where money damages may be sought and obtained for illness, both organic and mental, real and counterfeit.

Because of these radical changes during the past half century in the sociology of medical and psychiatric practice, I consider it misleading to speak simply of the incidence of hysteria. We must specify the particular situation, with respect to the social identity of both the observer and the observed, in which the incidence of the disorder is to be established.

Psychoanalytic theory of hysteria

Working as a physician, Freud developed his theory of hysteria to account for, and to help him cope with, some of the practical problems that faced him. What were these problems? Here is a typical example of one from Breuer and Freud's classic work, *Studies on Hysteria*:

> In the autumn of 1892, I was asked by a doctor I knew to examine a young lady who had been suffering for more than two years from pains in her legs and who had difficulties in walking. . . . All that was apparent was that she complained of great pain in walking and of being quickly overcome by fatigue both in walking and . . . standing, and that after a short time she had to rest, which lessened the pains but did not do away with them altogether. . . . I did not find it easy to arrive at a diagnosis, but I decided for two reasons to assent to the one proposed by my colleague, viz. that it was a case of hysteria. (Breuer & Freud [1893–1895] 1955, pp. 135–136)

What was wrong with this young woman? Because of the absence of neurological and other medical illness, and for certain other reasons as well, Freud concluded that she suffered from the disease called hysteria. How is this disease brought into being? This was Freud's explanation:

> According to the view suggested by the conversion theory what happened may be described as follows: She repressed her erotic idea from consciousness and transformed the amount of its affect into physical sensations of pain.—We may ask: What is it that turns into physical pain here? A cautious reply would be: Something that might have become, and should have become, mental pain. If we venture a little further and try to represent the ideational mechanism into a kind of algebraical picture, we may attribute a certain quota

of affect to the ideational complex of these erotic feelings which remained unconscious, and say that this quantity (the quota of affect) is what was converted. (Breuer & Freud [1893–1895] 1955, p. 166)

Etiology. The mechanism of the pathogenesis of hysteria was subsequently elaborated and refined by Freud and other psychoanalysts and came to include certain other features. According to Glover (1939, pp. 140–149), the following etiological factors are responsible for the occurrence and specific content of conversion symptoms:

(1) Somatic compliance. Symptoms are localized in accordance with the distribution and fixation of body libido; body parts or organs, overlibidinized by previous organic disease or continuous hyperfunction, become the media of expression.

(2) Frustration, introversion, and regression. If there is frustration of instinctual drives in adult life, the libido tends to turn from reality to fantasy. Fantasy is subject to the laws of regression.

(3) Reactivation of the Oedipus situation. Infantile fantasies, especially those associated with the Oedipus complex, are reactivated through regression.

(4) Breakdown of repression. Repression, faulty to begin with, cannot cope with the additional charge of the reactivated infantile fantasies. The defense crumbles and the repressed content breaks through: the return of the repressed.

(5) Symptom formation through displacement and symbolization. The specific form of conversion symptoms is determined partly by the degree of genital symbolization of various parts (that is, to what extent, for any particular person, parts of his body resemble the genital organs); and partly by the extent of the person's unconscious identification with his incestuous objects (that is, parents or siblings).

The result is an inhibition or exaggeration of bodily functions, giving rise to crippling or painful symptoms. These constitute a somatic dramatization of unconscious fantasies.

Hysteria as communication

The psychoanalytic theory of hysteria contains rudimentary suggestions for a communicational approach to this phenomenon. However, a systematic account of hysteria as language or communication was not developed until recently (Szasz 1961, pp. 115–163). To understand this view requires acquaintance with certain technical concepts, which I shall summarize here.

Anything in nature may or may not be a sign, depending on a person's attitude toward it. A physical thing—a chalk mark, a dark cloud, a paralyzed arm—is a sign when it appears as a substitute for the object for which it stands, with respect to the sign user. The three-part relation of sign, object, and sign user is called the relation of denotation.

Classes of signs. Three classes of signs may be distinguished: *indexical, iconic,* and *symbolic,* or *conventional,* signs.

In the indexical class belong signs that acquire their sign function through a causal connection. For example, smoke is a sign of fire and fever a sign of infectious disease.

In the iconic class belong signs that acquire their sign function through similarity. For example, a photograph is a sign of the person in the picture; a map is a sign of the territory it represents.

In the third class, symbolic, or conventional, signs, belong signs that acquire their sign function through arbitrary convention and common agreement—for example, words and mathematical symbols. Symbols do not usually exist in isolation, but are coordinated with each other by a set of rules called the rules of language. The entire package, consisting of symbols, language rules, and social customs of language use, is sometimes referred to as the *language game.* [*See* SEMANTICS AND SEMIOTICS.]

Hysteria and the language of illness. Communicational situations may comprise one, two, three, or a multitude of people. A semiotic and game-playing view of hysteria (Szasz 1961, pp. 115–293) does not imply a purely social approach and hence a neglect of the intrapersonal dimension of the problem.

For example, hysteria (and other so-called mental illnesses) may occur in a one-person situation. An individual who feels pain in his abdomen and concludes, falsely, that he suffers from acute appendicitis illustrates this phenomenon. Such a person fools himself, not others. He plays a game by disguising his personal problem as a medical disease. The advantage derived from such a one-person game corresponds closely to the psychoanalytic idea of primary gain.

However, since people generally do not live in isolation, the interpersonal and social aspects of hysterical (hypochondriacal, neurasthenic, etc.) communications are of great importance. Indeed, it is the complexity of communications among people that accounts for much of the complexity of hysteria as a so-called clinical syndrome (Szasz 1957).

Thus, if a person complains to his physician of abdominal pain and insists that it is due to an inflamed appendix, even though there is no other evidence to support this view, first his interpretation will be discredited, and then he himself will be discredited. The more he enlarges the social situation where he makes this claim, the more he risks being seriously discredited (for example, by being labeled schizophrenic and committed to a mental hospital). In a sense, such a person plays a game of fooling others. To the extent that he succeeds and is accepted as sick, he derives an advantage from his strategy. This advantage corresponds closely to the psychoanalytic idea of secondary gain.

From a communicational point of view, the traditional problem of differentiating hysteria from organic disease becomes one of distinguishing iconic signs from indexical ones. The physician and psychotherapist observe signs, not diseases—the latter being inferences drawn from the former. Thus, an analysis based on sign discrimination is likely to be more testable, as well as more serviceable, than one based on disease differentiation.

How, then, do we distinguish indexical signs from iconic signs? This is done by ascertaining whether the sign is "given" by a person or "given off" by him. Iconic signs resemble conventional ones because both are manufactured, more or less deliberately, by a person; indexical signs are passively given off, rather than actively emitted, by the signaling organism.

Thus, if a person complains of abdominal pain, our question is not, Is he suffering from acute appendicitis or from hysteria? but rather, Is the pain an indexical sign of an inflamed appendix or an iconic sign of it? Obviously, it could be both at once. It is therefore never possible to make a "diagnosis" of hysteria by ruling out organic illness, nor a diagnosis of organic illness by ruling out hysteria. Instead, in doubtful cases, both patient and physician must decide whether to approach the sign as though it were indexical, signaling a disease of the body, or as though it were iconic, signaling a complaint about the self and others. The former approach requires adequate medical investigation, the latter, meaningful communication.

Implications of a communicative view. I shall now list the major implications of a communicative view of hysteria:

First, hysteria is a particular type of forgery—namely, impersonation of the sick role.

Second, hysteria is a particular dialect of the language of sickness and health. It is a form of communication especially appropriate to the medical, or related, situation in which a person defines himself and is accepted as sick or disabled; those about him are then defined complementarily as physicians or healers.

Third, the language of hysteria is composed of iconic signs, is nondiscursive (Langer 1942), and hence ambiguous. The meaning the sender intends to convey is easily misunderstood or misinterpreted by the receiver. This may be useful to the sender, the receiver, or both.

Fourth, the language of hysteria cannot convey information accurately, but can induce feeling and promote action in others. It is thus a type of rhetoric, that is, a method of persuasion or coercion.

Rhetoric of hysteria. It is useful to distinguish between two types of communication—dialectical and rhetorical. The former term refers to attempts to explain something; the latter refers to efforts to convince someone.

I have suggested that hysteria is a form of rhetoric. I now wish to substantiate this view.

What does the hysteric do? Why is he called by this name? He complains of pain and suffering; he exhibits bodily signs suggesting that he is sick; and, finally, he adopts a general style of communication that enables him to arouse and alarm those about him. He does this by confronting them with desperate situations that seem to require immediate intervention.

Why does the hysteric do this? Freud and other psychoanalysts have suggested the main answers. However, I think there are two additional reasons. One is that the subject knows that he has no legitimate ground for making demands on others: he therefore resorts to the language of illness. The other is that he knows that the language of hysteria is more effective as a rhetorical device than everyday speech. The reason for this is simple.

To identify a person, we use his photograph or fingerprint, not a verbal description of his appearance. The hysteric uses an analogous principle. If one person seeks the attention, interest, or help of another individual, he can achieve these aims best by a dramatic display of messages that say, in effect, "I am sick! I am helpless! You must help me!" This can be accomplished more effectively by displaying the image or the icon of illness—an apparently sick body—than by asserting, calmly and in everyday language, the suspicion that one feels ill and perhaps ought to see a doctor. If one picture is worth a thousand words, one hysterical symptom is worth two thousand. Herein lies the rhetoric of hysteria.

Therapy of hysteria

Only in organic medicine can we speak meaningfully of treatment: a disease can be cured; a person can only be changed.

Does the hysteric want to be changed? Often

he does not. Instead, he wants to change others, so that they will comply with his wishes more readily. This insight, poorly understood and even more poorly articulated, led many physicians to conclude that such patients were "social parasites" who "would . . . steal anything conveniently within reach, lie, cheat, make work and trouble for others . . ." (Rogues de Fursac 1903, p. 317 in 1920 edition.).

Because hysteria is a form of rhetoric, it often evokes counter-rhetoric in response. The patient tries to coerce through symptoms; the physician tries to coerce through hypnosis. The result is often a mutually antagonistic, coercive relationship; sometimes the patient dominates, sometimes the doctor, and often the contest ends in a draw.

It is also possible for the physician, knowingly or unwittingly, to treat the hysteric as if he (or she) were ill. Such a physician accepts the patient's communications couched in the language of illness and replies in the same idiom. In the past, this took the form of mythical diagnoses, like uterine retroflexion or focal infection, and of surgical treatments whose value lay not in correcting abnormal bodily function but in symbolically legitimating the patient's sick role.

Today, this type of conversation between patient and doctor, employing the language of illness, can be carried on with greater ease than ever, since modern tranquilizing drugs constitute a socially accepted form of medical treatment for nonexistent medical illnesses. By prescribing such drugs, the physician acts as if he accepts the hysteric as genuinely sick; at the same time, he tries to repress (alter) the symptoms. This may be expedient for the therapist and acceptable to the patient.

Why, then, should we not rejoice in this modern approach to the "treatment" of hysteria (and other mental disorders)? Because we must remember that every "mental" symptom is a veiled outcry of anguish. Against what? Against oppression, or what the patient experiences as oppression. The oppressed speak in a million tongues—the myriad symptoms of hysteria (and mental illness). They make use of all the well-tried languages of illness and suffering and constantly add tongues newly created for special occasions. They need these marvelously complicated linguistic devices, for, at a single stroke, they must reveal and conceal themselves.

What of the psychiatrist or of others who wish to help such a person? Should they amplify the dissent and help the oppressed shout it aloud? Or should they strangle the cry and reoppress the fugitive slave? This is the psychiatric therapist's moral dilemma (Szasz 1964).

It is such considerations that led Freud to develop the psychoanalytic method and others to refine it. The psychoanalytic therapy of hysteria was thus a moral, rather than a purely medical, breakthrough in psychiatry.

Because hysteria is a form of rhetoric, it tends to evoke one of two responses: acceptance or rejection of the idea (and action) that the patient seeks to impose on the doctor. Either course leads to subsequent difficulties: the first to the doctor's inability to treat the patient, the second to an antagonistic relationship between patient and physician. Psychoanalysis seeks to avoid this interpersonal impasse by offering the patient another level of discourse. It substitutes dialectic for rhetoric and discursive language for nondiscursive.

THOMAS S. SZASZ

[*See also* PSYCHOSOMATIC ILLNESS. *Other relevant material may be found in* PSYCHOANALYSIS; *and the biographies of* CHARCOT; JANET.]

BIBLIOGRAPHY

ABSE, D. WILFRED 1959 Hysteria. Volume 1, pages 272–292 in *American Handbook of Psychiatry.* Edited by Silvano Arieti. New York: Basic Books. → A useful general work on hysteria.

BREUER, JOSEF; and FREUD, SIGMUND (1893–1895) 1955 *The Standard Edition of the Complete Psychological Works of Sigmund Freud.* Volume 2: Studies on Hysteria. London: Hogarth; New York: Macmillan. → First published in German.

CHODOFF, PAUL 1954 A Re-examination of Some Aspects of Conversion Hysteria. *Psychiatry* 17:75–81.

GLOVER, EDWARD (1939) 1949 *Psycho-analysis: A Handbook for Medical Practitioners and Students of Comparative Psychology.* London: Staples.

LANGER, SUSANNE K. (1942) 1961 *Philosophy in a New Key: A Study in the Symbolism of Reason, Rite, and Art.* New York: New American Library.

ROGUES DE FURSAC, JOSEPH (1903) 1938 *Manual of Psychiatry and Mental Hygiene.* 7th ed., rev. & enl. New York: Wiley. → First published as *Manuel de psychiatrie.*

RYLE, GILBERT (1949) 1962 *The Concept of Mind.* London: Hutchinson's University Library.

SZASZ, THOMAS S. 1957 *Pain and Pleasure: A Study of Bodily Feelings.* New York: Basic Books.

SZASZ, THOMAS S. 1961 *The Myth of Mental Illness: Foundations of a Theory of Personal Conduct.* New York: Harper.

SZASZ, THOMAS S. 1964 The Moral Dilemma of Psychiatry: Autonomy or Heteronomy? *American Journal of Psychiatry* 121:521–528.

WHEELIS, ALLEN 1958 *The Quest for Identity.* New York: Norton.

ZILBOORG, GREGORY 1941 *A History of Medical Psychology.* New York: Norton.

I

IBN KHALDŪN

Ibn Khaldūn (1332–1406), an Arab historian, statesman, and judge, was born in Tunis. His family traced its origin to a south Arabian tribe that entered Spain in the early years of the Muslim conquest. Toward the end of the ninth century, the family became known for leadership of revolutionary activities in Seville; some of its members were prominent in the administration of the city, and one of them distinguished himself in the first half of the eleventh century as a mathematician and astronomer. About the middle of the thirteenth century, when Seville was threatened by the Christians, the family left for north Africa and eventually settled in Tunis, the capital of the Ḥafṣid kingdom. The family was granted land holdings, its members held administrative posts, and one of them wrote a handbook on administration for government officials. Perhaps because misfortune beset the Ḥafṣids, Ibn Khaldūn's grandfather and father retired to lead quiet lives as scholars and members of a local mystic order.

Economically well-to-do and still patronized by the rulers of Tunis, the household in which Ibn Khaldūn grew up was frequented by the political and intellectual leaders of Muslim Spain and the Maghreb. His early education included the religious disciplines (the Koran, the collection of traditions approved by the Malikite school of law which prevailed in Western Islam, dialectical theology, jurisprudence, and mysticism), the philosophic disciplines (logic, mathematics, natural philosophy, metaphysics, and politics, including ethics and rhetoric), and practical training for government service, such as the art of writing official court correspondence and handling administrative affairs. The teacher he admired most during this period was the mathematician and philosopher Muḥammad Ibn Ibrāhīm al-Ābilī (1282/3–1356), whom he considered the most proficient of his contemporaries in the philosophic disciplines. His studies with Ābilī extended over five years, from 1347 to 1352. They began with mathematics and logic and then branched out to include various other philosophic disciplines. Ābilī introduced him to the major works of Avicenna and Averroës and acquainted him with the more recent philosophic and theological writings of the heterodox Shī'ites in Eastern Islam. Ibn Khaldūn's early work (1351) provides direct evidence for his philosophic interest and ideas during this period. His other early philosophic works, including treatises on logic and mathematics and a number of paraphrases of Averroës' works, have not been recovered as yet.

His involvement in the political affairs of the Maghreb and Muslim Spain began in Fez (the center of political power and cultural life in a region that, on the whole, lacked political stability) at the court of the Marīnid ruler Abū 'Inān. He was suspected of plotting against the ruler and was imprisoned in 1357. Shortly afterward he helped to overthrow Abū 'Inān's son and supported the latter's uncle Abū Sālim; but he failed to consolidate his position under the new ruler. In 1362 he moved to Granada, the capital of a more cultured and peaceful kingdom which suffered, however, from the military pressure of the Christians to the north and the political pressure of the Marīnids to the south. He was welcomed by the young ruler and his vizier, the celebrated writer Lisān al-Dīn Ibn al-Khaṭīb, to whom we owe the revealing characterization of Ibn Khaldūn as a man who commanded respect and was able, unruly, strong-willed, and ambitious to climb to the highest position of leadership. In 1364 he was sent on an embassy to Pedro el Cruel, king of Castile and Léon, to conclude a peace treaty between him and the ruler of Muslim Spain. He took advantage of his position at the court and attempted to instruct the young ruler, with the help of his early philosophic and religious works, to which he probably added his views on practical politics. Ibn al-Khaṭīb resented this and forced Ibn Khaldūn to leave Granada.

He proceeded to Bougie, where his friend, the Ḥafṣid prince Abū 'Abd Allāh, had gained control. This was Ibn Khaldūn's third and last venture in practical politics. He was in charge of the city's affairs for a little over a year, from 1365 to 1366, and attempted desperately to consolidate his friend's rule. But Abū 'Abd Allāh's severity, insolence, and political impotence, the dissensions among the city's inhabitants, and the ambitions of the rulers of the neighboring cities of Constantine and Tlemcen combined to thwart Ibn Khaldūn. Abū 'Abd Allāh was defeated by his cousin, losing his life in the battle.

Ibn Khaldūn spent the following decade occupied for the most part with research and teaching in Baskara and Fez; we have a work on mysticism which he wrote during this period (c. 1373–1375). He was frequently asked by various local rulers to perform special assignments for them, especially in connection with their dealings with the nomadic and seminomadic tribes of the region, while he on his part preferred to dedicate himself to study and avoid political activity. While on one of these assignments he decided to withdraw to the castle of Ibn Salāma (in the province of Oran), where he spent about four years (1374–1377) oblivious of the outside world. The previous twenty years had been spent in active participation in the political affairs of the Maghreb and Muslim Spain. He had personally experienced many of the important events of this region and had had access to the official documents relating to them. His official duties had brought him in contact with many important persons—ambassadors, officials, rulers, tribal chiefs, and scholars—from whom he had acquired information about events in which they had taken part and about others they had known by virtue of their official or social positions. He intended to record this experience and information in the form of a contemporary regional history of Western Islam.

After leaving his retreat in the castle of Ibn Salāma, Ibn Khaldūn spent four years in Tunis but found it difficult to avoid entanglement in political affairs and to devote himself to study and writing. In 1382 he left for Egypt, where he spent the last 25 years of his life. Here he could observe a mature and settled society, sophisticated social manners, and the effects of deep-rooted traditions and of economic prosperity—all of which presented sharp contrasts to the semibarbarous and confused conditions in the Maghreb. He taught at the al-Azhar and other schools in Cairo, was received by the ruler and remained active as a courtier, and was appointed six times as grand judge of the Malikite legal school. But for the most part he devoted himself to research and writing. He consulted new books and archival materials not available to him in north Africa, traveled and observed the topography of Egypt, western Arabia, and Syria (where he met Tamerlane in 1401), met learned men from many parts of Eastern Islam, and kept revising and completing his chief work, especially Book 2, which deals with the east. He also continued to add to his long "Autobiography," one of the most extensive in Arabic literature, which is complete up to a few months before his death (1377–1406).

Historical work

He began to write a short "Introduction" (*Muqaddimah*) to such a regional history, in which he spoke of the practical lessons of history and of its "external" and "internal" aspects. He related the projected work to earlier universal histories and to regional histories dealing with Eastern Islam. While he was writing this "Introduction," he became aware of a basic problem that made the plan of a regional history unfeasible: to understand the nature and causes of historical events, it is necessary to have correct information; but to be able to distinguish correct information from false it is necessary to know the nature and causes of these events. Ibn Khaldūn conducted a critical investigation of the works of previous Muslim historians and found that they had not possessed such knowledge or else they had not formulated it. He surveyed disciplines other than historiography, especially rhetoric, political science, and jurisprudence, and found that they too did not present a coherent account of the nature and causes of historical events. He himself had to create a new "science" to deal specifically with the "internal" aspect of history and to define its principles, method, subject matter, and purpose. Therefore he abandoned the early draft of the "Introduction," a portion of which can still be recognized in the final version that we have today ([1377*a*] 1858, vol. 1, pp. 51–52).

The new science was to be based on a comprehensive study of the data furnished by the history of the world from its intelligible beginnings to his own time. In its final form, the "History" (*Kitāb al-'Ibar* 1377–1382*a*) is divided into a Preface, an Introduction, and Books 1, 2, and 3. The Introduction deals with the problem of history in general; it was written in 1377, with a few revisions and additions made later when Ibn Khaldūn was in Egypt. Book 1 contains the new science; it was written in 1377 but underwent numerous revisions and changes throughout the rest of Ibn Khaldūn's life. The Preface, the Introduction, and Book 1 came to be known as the "Introduction" (*Muqaddimah*). Book 2 contains a universal history down to Ibn Khaldūn's own time; a skeleton of this book was written in Tunis between 1377 and 1382 and then extensively expanded and rewritten in Egypt (1377–1382*a*). Book 3, the originally planned history of Western Islam, was written in Tunis between 1377 and 1382, with some additions made in Egypt (1377–1382*b*).

Although in its final form Ibn Khaldūn's "History" was expanded to include the new science of culture (Book 1) and a universal history (Book 2), the chief interest of the work as a whole continues to center on the history of the contemporary Maghreb, in which the "History" culminates and which is Ibn Khaldūn's main contribution to historical scholarship. Ibn Khaldūn conceived of his own time and region as having a crucial place in world history. He divided world history into four major epochs or ages, each dominated by a group of nations and having its own characteristic conditions: political organizations, arts, languages, habits, conventions, and so forth ([1377*a*] 1858, vol. 1, pp. 44–45, 51–53). The third epoch started in the seventh century with the rise of Islam and of the Arabs; in the eleventh century the rule of the Arabs was challenged by the Turks in the east, the Berbers in the Maghreb, and the Christian Franks in the north, and by the fourteenth century this third epoch had come to a close and a new and fourth epoch had begun. Eastern Islam was deep-rooted in cultural traditions and resisted the changes leading to the end of the third epoch. In the Maghreb, where cultural traditions were more superficial, the end of the third epoch came sooner; by the middle of the fourteenth century the conditions characteristic of the third epoch had disappeared completely and a new epoch had already begun, which would eventually have radically new cultural characteristics. But because the new epoch was then still in its infancy, Ibn Khaldūn could not easily describe it in a manner that would take all its potentialities into account. This difficulty, which seems to have directed his attention to the necessity of undertaking a comprehensive study of the beginnings of earlier epochs and their subsequent developments, in turn led him to the discovery of the new science of culture or the comparative and descriptive account of the rise and decline of cultures in general. However, his chief purpose remained that of describing and making intelligible the beginnings of the new epoch. This led him to place special emphasis on historical beginnings in general and to pay particular attention to the physical conditions that surround and influence the emergence of culture.

Science of culture

Ibn Khaldūn's major contribution to the history of social thought is his new science of culture (*'umrān*). The genesis of this science can be traced in the Preface, the Introduction, and Book 1 ([1377*a*] 1858, vol. 1, pp. 1–8, 8–55, and 56–68, respectively), which present a systematic critique of Islamic historiography and of the Islamic legal–religious disciplines that provided traditional religious Islamic historiography with its principles and method. The aim of this critique is to show that to write history properly one must have knowledge of the nature and causes of historical events, their permanence and change, and their homogeneity and heterogeneity; this knowledge should provide the basis for the examination of reported information. While errors are inherent in historical accounts for a number of reasons (i.e., partisanship, overconfidence in the sources, failure to understand the intention of the reports, unfounded credulousness, failure to understand the events in their proper context, and interest in gaining favor with the powerful and the influential), the most significant cause of error is "ignorance of the nature and modes of culture" ([1377*a*] 1858, vol. 1, p. 57). In a carefully structured dialectical argument and through the examination of carefully chosen historical examples, Ibn Khaldūn showed the need for a systematically organized body of rational knowledge about the nature and causes of historical events in general and about human culture—the sum of all conventionalized social habits, institutions, and arts. He found two rational disciplines that dealt with problems similar to those of the new science: rhetoric and political science. But while the final end of rhetoric is to sway the multitude and that of political science is to order the city, the new science would be concerned primarily with understanding the nature and causes of actual historical events, and it would serve as a tool for rectifying reports about such events. Since history is a practical art useful to the statesman, the final end of the science of culture is to help produce the kind of history needed for excellence in the art of ruling; thus, the science of culture would contribute to the final end of political science.

Ibn Khaldūn proceeded next to expound the principles upon which he intended to construct the new science. In section 1 of Book 1 ([1377*a*] 1858, vol. 1, pp. 69–220), entitled "On Human Culture in General," he presented six such principles: (1) man's need for association (the evidence for this proposition is drawn from the investigations of animal and human nature conducted in natural philosophy); (2) the distribution of culture on earth; (3) the physical–geographical basis of culture: the temperate and intemperate zones and the influence of the climate on the physical characteristics of human beings; (4) the influence of the climate on man's moral habits; (5) the effects of the abundance and scarcity of food on men's bodies and habits (in points 2 to 5 Ibn Khaldūn simply restated the conclusions of the various branches that make up traditional natural philosophy, including geography and medicine); and (6) the classes of men who perceive the unseen by natural disposition or by effort: Ibn Khaldūn's own explanation of prophecy, soothsaying, dream vision, divination, magic, and so on, in this discussion is based on the natural properties of the human soul. All the principles of Ibn Khaldūn's science of culture are derived from traditional natural philosophy. His claim that the conclusions of the new science were natural, demonstrative, and necessary was to a large measure based on the fact that he considered all the principles of the new science to have these characteristics. He consciously avoided principles that were mere guesses, opinions, or generally accepted notions.

While Ibn Khaldūn admitted that the final end of the new science—that is, the rectification of historical reports—was not particularly noble, he asserted that "the problems it treats are noble in themselves and within their proper sphere" ([1377*a*] 1858, vol. 1, p. 63). He divided the subject matter of the new science into five major problems, which are discussed in sections 2–6 of Book 1, starting from what is prior or necessary and natural: (1) primitive culture and its transition to civilized culture; (2) the state; (3) the city; (4) practical arts and crafts; and (5) the sciences. These problems are treated genetically, analytically, and teleologically: the "efficient cause" of culture is social solidarity (*ʿaṣabiyya*); the organizing principle or "form" of culture is the state; and the "ends" of the state are the good of the ruler in this world, the good of the ruled in this world, and the good of the ruled in the world to come. He placed emphasis on the typical movement from primitive to civilized culture, which in turn declines and reverts to primitive culture—a cycle of birth, growth, and old age analogous to the life of individual human beings. He saw this "natural" cycle most clearly in those regions of north Africa and the Near East which are situated between the desert and settled culture, and he was aware that it does not obtain universally or at all times. In isolated regions in the intemperate zones, primitive cultures may persist over long periods without developing into civilized cultures. In the temperate zone, on the other hand, the establishment of cities, the development of the arts, and the formation of a social solidarity conducive to peaceful cooperation enable a society to develop and maintain civilized culture over thousands of years without serious interruptions.

As a partisan of nature and reason, Ibn Khaldūn belonged to a small but potent group in the Islamic community. This group was encouraged and protected by some intelligent rulers, and it was able to perpetuate itself and make its impact felt even in the religious disciplines. Ibn Khaldūn was the only representative of this group who made a frontal and massive attack on history, one of the fortresses of traditional religious learning. He trained a small number of students in Egypt, including the great historian al-Maqrīzī (1364–1442). In later times his works influenced the study of politics and history by scholars in the Maghreb, Egypt, and Turkey; in the eighteenth century he was discovered by Western orientalists and, through them, by a wider public that saw in him the father, or one of the fathers, of modern cultural history and social science.

MUHSIN MAHDI

[*For the historical context of Ibn Khaldūn's work, see* HISTORIOGRAPHY, *especially the articles on* AFRICAN HISTORIOGRAPHY *and* ISLAMIC HISTORIOGRAPHY; ISLAM. *See also* AFRICAN SOCIETY, *article on* NORTH AFRICA.]

WORKS BY IBN KHALDŪN

(1351) 1952 *Lubāb al-Muḥaṣṣal fī Uṣūl al-Dīn* (Gist of the Compendium on the Principles of Religion). Tetuán (Morocco): Editora Marroqui.

(c. 1373–1375) 1957–1958 *Shifāʾ al-Sāʾil li-Tahdhīb al-Masāʾil* (A Guide For Those Who Try to Clarify Problems). Istanbul: Osman Yalcin Matbaasi.

(1377*a*) 1858 *Muqaddimah Ibn Khaldūn* (Prolégomènes d'Ibn-Khaldoun). 3 vols. Paris: Imprimerie Nationale.

(1377*b*) 1934–1938 *Les prolégomènes d'Ibn Khaldoun.* 3 vols. Paris: Geuthner. → The French translation of Ibn Khaldūn 1377*a* and of the earlier portions of Ibn Khaldūn 1377–1406.

(1377c) 1950 *An Arab Philosophy of History: Selections From the* Prolegomena *of Ibn Khaldun of Tunis.* London: Murray. → Selections from Ibn Khaldūn 1377*a* in English translation.
(1377*d*) 1958 *The Muqaddimah: An Introduction to History.* 3 vols. New York: Pantheon. → An English translation of Ibn Khaldūn 1377*a*. Contains a bibliography.
(1377–1382*a*) 1867 *Kitāb al-'Ibar* (History). 7 vols. Bulak (Egypt): al-Maṭba'a al-Miṣriyya.
(1377–1382*b*) 1847–1851 *Kitāb al-Duwal al-Islāmiyya bi-l-Maghrib* (Histoire des Berbères et des dynasties musulmanes de l'Afrique septentrionale). 2 vols. Algiers (Algeria): Imprimerie du Gouvernement.
(1377–1382c) 1925–1956 *Histoire des Berbères et des dynasties musulmanes de l'Afrique septentrionale.* 4 vols. Paris: Geuthner. → A French translation of Ibn Khaldūn 1377–1382*b*.
(1377–1406) 1951 *al-Ta'rīf* (Autobiography). Cairo: Lajnat al-Ta'līf.

SUPPLEMENTARY BIBLIOGRAPHY

AYAD, MOHAMMED K. 1930 *Die Geschichts- und Gesellschaftslehre Ibn Haldūns.* Stuttgart and Berlin: Cotta.
FISCHEL, WALTER J. 1952 *Ibn Khaldūn and Tamerlane.* Berkeley: Univ. of California Press. → Pages 29–48 contain a translation of the last portion of the "Autobiography."
FISCHEL, WALTER J. 1967 *Ibn Khaldūn in Egypt; His Public Functions and His Historical Research (1382–1406): An Essay in Islamic Historiography.* Berkeley: Univ. of California Press.
MAHDI, MUHSIN (1957) 1964 *Ibn Khaldūn's Philosophy of History.* Univ. of Chicago Press.
SCHMIDT, NATHANIEL 1930 *Ibn Khaldūn: Historian, Sociologist and Philosopher.* Columbia Univ. Press. → Mainly of bibliographical interest.
SIMON, HENRICH 1959 *Ibn Khalduns Wissenschaft von der menschlichen Kultur.* Leipzig: Harrassowitz.

ID
See PSYCHOANALYSIS.

IDEAL TYPES
See COMMUNITY–SOCIETY CONTINUA; TYPOLOGIES; *and the biography of* WEBER, MAX.

IDENTIFIABILITY, STATISTICAL
See STATISTICAL IDENTIFIABILITY.

IDENTIFICATION, POLITICAL

Of the psychological processes directly relevant to political behavior, perhaps none is more pervasive than a person's identification with a group, regardless of whether the group is ostensibly political or not. Examples are an individual's identification with a nation, an ideological movement, a political party, a social class, a racial or ethnic group, a farm, labor, or veterans' association, a religious faith, and so on. In its most general sense, then, political identification means a person's sense of belonging to a group, if that identification influences his political behavior.

An early suggestion of the process, which did not, however, use the term "identification," was Marx's observation that the operation of the capitalist system would develop "class consciousness" among workers when they were situated where they could communicate with one another about their common deprivation, as in cities (Bendix & Lipset 1953). Wallas ([1908] 1962, p. 103) recognized, but did not define, party identification when he observed that a political party is "something which can be loved and trusted and which can be recognized at successive elections. . . ."

The term "identification," in its modern, group sense, was first elaborated by Freud (1921). It had long been observed that people in crowds tend to be irrational, impatient, uninhibited, and credulous, but Freud felt that the part played by group leaders as the object of emotional ties for the members of a group had been underestimated, and he sought to account for the origin of these emotions in the individual personality.

To Freud identification was "the earliest expression of an emotional tie with another person" (1921, p. 105). A boy identifies with his father as an "ego ideal"—someone he would like to *be*, rather than something or someone he would like to *have* (a sexual object). Identification may be ambivalent, as when the boy is jealous of the father's place in the mother's affections. After infancy the propensity to identify is carried over into new situations and "may arise with any new perception of a common quality shared with some other person who is not an object of the sexual instinct" (p. 108), hence its relevance to group behavior. Identification is partial, at times limited to a single characteristic of the ideal, and thus applicable to multiple identifications in a pluralist society. It is variable in force. Freud analyzed, as examples, the army, where the soldier takes the commander as his ideal but identifies with other soldiers, and the church, where Christ is the ideal. "Many equals, who can identify themselves with one another, and a single person superior to them all—that is the situation that we find realized in groups which are capable of subsisting" (p. 121).

Freud thus explained the need and ability of individuals to affiliate and the strength of the emotional ties involved—as essential for the genesis of man as a social animal. The infantile origins of the process of identification account for its operation below the conscious level, for its strength as a motivating factor, and for its sometimes irrational or regressive manifestations.

The ambivalent character of the Freudian concept of identification poses problems for scientific analysis: when will the positive action occur? when the negative reaction? which will predominate numerically? The usual tactic is to ignore negative identification, leaving it in the residual category of unexplained variance. In nonstatistical, after-the-fact accounts, it is recognized as "projection"—the tendency of an in-group to attribute to others their own "wicked" desires. For example, Davies (1963, pp. 39–45) thus accounts for the belief of Populist farmers that the cities were centers of greed and depravity.

Regressive identification is typified by the anti-Semitism of the Nazis, the Bolshevik theory of "capitalist encirclement," the sixteenth-century French religious wars, and nativist movements in the United States. These occur in periods of tension and anxiety (Neumann 1954). Some are Caesaristic, but a single, dramatic leader is not required; for example, the Ku Klux Klan leadership has been diffuse, disorganized, and incompetent. There is also a nonaffective, "libido-free" identification, less regressive and more transferable, as when modern bureaucratic groups are joined for the sake of material interests, and loyalty to them subsequently develops. Thus, the term is stripped of its Freudian overtones.

Class identification. Class identification presents a potent empirical test of the explanatory power of identification. This is because one may compile external, "objective" indices of a person's class (such as occupation, income, education, or the judgment of the interviewer), which are independent of the person's own "class identification." The latter is ascertained by asking him what class he belongs to. Identification was found to be relevant to voting behavior in a 1940 election study (Lazarsfeld et al. 1944), and its effect was found to be independent of actual socioeconomic status. Centers (1949) found identification had less effect than status on voting in the 1944 presidential election in the United States, and this was confirmed for later American elections by Eulau (1962). British studies (which do not often use the term "identification") show that class identification has an effect roughly equal to that of objective class, which itself has more impact on voting in Great Britain than on voting in the United States (Alford 1963; Milne & MacKenzie 1954, p. 43; Bonham 1954, p. 180).

National comparisons are difficult. There is variation in the degree to which identification and objective class coincide. The point on the status continuum that divides "middle class" from "working class" must be arbitrarily determined. Understandably, persons on the borderline may identify with either class, and identification exerts a strong effect on them (Degras et al. 1956).

Seeking to trace the effect of identification through intervening variables, such as the elector's perception of voting patterns in his own and the opposing party or his clear recognition of politically relevant class interests, has shown that identifiers are not sharply conscious of class differences in England and the United States. (Eulau 1962, chapter 5; Degras et al. 1956, pp. 114–122), but that class interests are readily perceived in a partisan frame of reference. Correlations between identification and corresponding political and social attitudes are low (Centers 1949, p. 202). Eulau found that those whose identification departed from their objective class diverged most from their status groups in their political attitudes and perceptions, somewhat less in their beliefs about the political process (such as whether one should participate), and least of all in their reported behavior—reading about, voting in, or working in the election. Apparently identification influences ideas, but the class in which one was actually socialized is likelier to influence behavior. Thus, he concluded that identification constitutes only "role potential" (Eulau 1962, p. 85).

As a process, class identification is usually completed by adolescence. It is more closely related to parental status than are political attitudes and vote preference, which may be absorbed from peers (Hyman 1959, p. 65; Berelson et al. 1954, p. 135). Residence in metropolitan areas and other circumstances that diminish contact between classes heighten class polarization. Middle-class persons are more likely than are workers to be aware of class-relevant issues and to vote in accordance with their perceptions (Michigan, University of . . . 1960, chapter 13); and they are more likely than are workers to identify with both nation and class (Buchanan & Cantril 1953). The effect of class identification varies considerably from election to election.

Party identification. Party identification is a concept developed in the United States, where there are no membership cards, few party rosters, varying legal definitions of party membership from state to state, and widespread ticket splitting (Key 1942, p. 390). The operational definition of a Republican is, therefore, "one who says he 'thinks of,' 'considers,' or 'regards' himself as a Republican."

Such questions had been asked by polls since 1937, but the term "party identification" was not widely used until after the 1948 election, when Truman's victory demonstrated the strength of partisanship. The delay in recognizing the importance of party identification was probably due to the excessive rationalism of popular political thought in the United States, where voters have been taught that their choices should be based upon deliberate assessment of issues and candidates. Identification was explicitly conceptualized as an independent variable motivating voting behavior and was analyzed along with candidate choice and issue orientation after the 1952 election (Campbell et al. 1954).

The genesis of party identification is in socialization within the family. American children begin to identify themselves as Republicans or Democrats at age seven or eight, before they know what a political party is. They adopt their party as they do their family name and religion (Easton & Hess 1962). In contrast, French children do not hear their parents talk politics, and their identifications are infrequent, weak, and unstable (Converse & Dupeux 1962). American children adopt their parents' party identification more completely than they assimilate their parents' opinions or even vote preference. An individual socialized into a party does not need to work out a set of attitudes to provide him with cues for political action; he may refer directly to his party's stand (Hyman 1959, p. 74). Most voters continue to vote in line with their original identification, and few change identifications during their lifetime. Strength of party identification increases with age (Michigan, University of . . . 1960). Party identification appears to influence behavior directly, although it may also influence attitudes toward government policy and perceptions of candidates. Thus, its effect is difficult to isolate.

The proportion of the American population identified with each major party has been remarkably stable for a quarter of a century. A variety of sampling methods and question wordings used from 1937 to 1952 found that the proportion of Democratic identifiers was from 36 to 50 per cent; the proportion of Republican identifiers, from 28 to 40 per cent (tabulations in *Public Opinion Quarterly, passim*). From 1952 through 1960, the Survey Research Center at the University of Michigan, using the same question and a tighter sampling scheme, found Democrats ranged from 43 to 47 per cent, Republicans from 26 to 32 per cent. Independents vary from 20 to 25 per cent, but most of them incline toward one party or the other. The data suggest that gross change in the balance of identification has been negligible since 1937. Contrasted with this partisan stability, election margins have varied substantially, and the popularity of party leaders, especially of incumbent presidents, has dipped and soared wildly. This is further confirmation that identification with a leader is not a necessary condition for the operation of the identifying process.

What produces governmental change, of course, is the shifting of marginal voters, including independents and weak identifiers. About 95 per cent of Republican identifiers, according to a Gallup poll, voted for the Republican presidential candidate in 1952, 1956, and 1960; and about 85 per cent of Democratic identifiers voted for the Democratic candidate in 1956, 1960, and 1964. Eisenhower won in 1952, when there was a shift of Democratic identifiers to him (23 per cent), and a similar shift on the part of Republicans (20 per cent) brought Johnson a landslide victory in 1964.

Although party identification is normally quite stable, it has been found, from the recollection of respondents (Michigan, University of . . . 1960, pp. 152–167), and confirmed by analysis of voting data (Key 1942, p. 535), that a large number of erstwhile Republican identifiers became Democrats early in the depression. Other realignments apparently occurred in the economic and political crises of 1860 and 1896. Between such critical periods there is a small drift out of the ranks of each party into the independent category and occasionally across to the opposition. There is also an intergenerational drift, caused sometimes by social mobility (Hyman 1959, p. 109), sometimes by politically irrelevant family quarrels (McClosky & Dahlgren 1959), sometimes by marriage between individuals who identify with opposing parties.

Although identification is a reality in most Western nations (Rokkan 1955), its significance varies with the political culture and structure. Comparatively few persons in France claim identification, and these identifications are vague and rather unstable. French parties provide a wide range of subtle cues for decision, but the variety apparently confuses the public (Converse & Dupeux 1962). Norwegian parties draw from distinct occupational, class, and religious groups, and these other identifications reinforce the political one, in contrast to the United States, where identification with the party *itself* provides a basis for choice relatively independent of other group associations (Campbell & Valen 1961).

The two schools of voting research in the United

States differ in their appraisal of partisan identification. Campbell and others at Michigan give it a central position, while the Columbia group (Berelson, Lazarsfeld) virtually ignore it, although they deal extensively with class identification. Some voting studies still use the phrase "party preference," which may apply either to identification or actual vote.

Religious identification. Religion affects political behavior by definition where there is a link between church and state or a church-affiliated party, e.g., in Italy, where the sacraments were denied Catholics who voted Left (Almond & Verba 1963, p. 137). But religious identification has an impact on voting in cases where there is no nominal relation between church and party, no difference in the faith of the candidates, and in fact, no religious issues involved in the campaign. Since 1936 American Catholics have tended to vote Democratic, and this effect is independent of either socioeconomic status or ethnic identification (Lipset 1964). Of course, the presence of a Catholic on the ticket increases the tendency, as in 1960, when many Catholic Republicans voted for, and Protestant Democrats against, Kennedy. Issues of ethical, moral, or doctrinal concern to certain faiths, such as social welfare, war, prohibition, gambling, and contraception, heighten the effect of religious identification on political behavior.

Research problems. Investigation through the survey method has been complicated by different operational definitions for each kind of identification. First, there is nominal membership, as when one is born into an ethnic group, baptized into a faith, or, later, chooses an occupation or joins a union. The respondent's answers to questions about these characteristics are accepted as factual data. With class, a second question is asked, to determine "subjective" identification, a distinction that is impossible or pointless in the case of party. Studies of class, religious, and ethnic identification go further, to ascertain whether the respondent perceives a relation between his group affiliation and the election—a measure of "salience." This latter technique demands a conscious verbal association as evidence of the link between identification and behavior, a demand not often clearly satisfied. With party identification, correlation with vote is taken as evidence of perhaps unconscious influence; i.e., the identification is conscious, but the connection with vote is not recognized. The evidence that party identification precedes political consciousness in the socialization of the child makes the supposition of an unconscious influence theoretically reasonable. Survey technique cannot yet cope with the level-of-consciousness problem.

WILLIAM BUCHANAN

[*See also* GENERATIONS; IDENTITY, PSYCHOSOCIAL; POLITICAL BEHAVIOR; SOCIALIZATION.]

BIBLIOGRAPHY

ALFORD, ROBERT R. 1963 *Party and Society: The Anglo–American Democracies.* Chicago: Rand McNally.

ALMOND, GABRIEL A.; and VERBA, SIDNEY 1963 *The Civic Culture: Political Attitudes and Democracy in Five Nations.* Princeton Univ. Press.

BENDIX, REINHARD; and LIPSET, SEYMOUR M. (1953) 1966 Karl Marx's Theory of Social Classes. Pages 6–11 in Reinhard Bendix and Seymour M. Lipset (editors), *Class, Status, and Power: Social Stratification in Comparative Perspective.* 2d ed. New York: Fress Press.

BERELSON, BERNARD; LAZARSFELD, PAUL F.; and MCPHEE, WILLIAM N. 1954 *Voting: A Study of Opinion Formation in a Presidential Campaign.* Univ. of Chicago Press.

BONHAM, JOHN 1954 *The Middle Class Vote.* London: Faber.

BUCHANAN, WILLIAM; and CANTRIL, HADLEY 1953 *How Nations See Each Other: A Study in Public Opinion.* Urbana: Univ. of Illinois Press.

CAMPBELL, ANGUS; GURIN, GERALD; and MILLER, WARREN E. 1954 *The Voter Decides.* Evanston, Ill.: Row, Peterson.

CAMPBELL, ANGUS; and VALEN, HENRY 1961 Party Identification in Norway and the United States. *Public Opinion Quarterly* 25:505–525.

CENTERS, RICHARD (1949) 1961 *The Psychology of Social Classes: A Study of Class Consciousness.* New York: Russell.

CONVERSE, PHILIP E.; and DUPEUX, GEORGES 1962 Politicization of the Electorate in France and the United States. *Public Opinion Quarterly* 26:1–23.

DAVIES, JAMES C. 1963 *Human Nature in Politics: The Dynamics of Political Behavior.* New York: Wiley.

[DEGRAS, HARRY E.]; GRAY, A. P.; and PEAR, R. H. 1956 *How People Vote: A Study of Electoral Behaviour in Greenwich,* by Mark Benney [pseud.]. . . . London: Routledge. → Mark Benney is the pseudonym of Harry E. Degras.

EASTON, DAVID; and HESS, ROBERT D. 1962 The Child's Political World. *Midwest Journal of Political Science* 6:229–246.

EULAU, HEINZ 1962 *Class and Party in the Eisenhower Years: Class Roles and Perspectives in the 1952 and 1956 Elections.* New York: Free Press.

FREUD, SIGMUND (1921) 1955 Group Psychology and the Analysis of the Ego. Volume 18, pages 67–143 in *The Standard Edition of the Complete Psychological Works of Sigmund Freud.* London: Hogarth. → First published in German.

HYMAN, HERBERT H. 1959 *Political Socialization: A Study in the Psychology of Political Behavior.* Glencoe, Ill.: Free Press.

KEY, VALDIMER O. (1942) 1964 *Politics, Parties, and Pressure Groups.* 5th ed. New York: Crowell.

LAZARSFELD, PAUL F.; BERELSON, BERNARD; and GAUDET, HAZEL (1944) 1960 *The People's Choice: How the*

Voter Makes Up His Mind in a Presidential Campaign. 2d ed. New York: Columbia Univ. Press.
LIPSET, SEYMOUR M. 1964 Religion and Politics in the American Past and Present. Pages 69–126 in Robert Lee and Martin E. Marty (editors), *Religion and Social Conflict.* New York: Oxford Univ. Press.
McCLOSKY, HERBERT; and DAHLGREN, HAROLD E. 1959 Primary Group Influence on Party Loyalty. *American Political Science Review* 53:757–776.
MICHIGAN, UNIVERSITY OF, SURVEY RESEARCH CENTER 1960 *The American Voter,* by Angus Campbell et al. New York: Wiley.
MILNE, R. S.; and MACKENZIE, H. C. 1954 *Straight Fight: A Study of Voting Behaviour in the Constituency of Bristol North-east at the General Election of 1951.* London: Hansard Society.
NEUMANN, FRANZ (1954) 1960 Anxiety and Politics. Pages 269–290 in Maurice R. Steiner, Arthur J. Vidich, and David M. White (editors), *Identity and Anxiety: Survival of the Person in Mass Society.* Glencoe, Ill.: Free Press.
ROKKAN, STEIN 1955 Party Preferences and Opinion Patterns in Western Europe: A Comparative Analysis. *International Social Science Bulletin* 7:575–596.
WALLAS, GRAHAM (1908) 1962 *Human Nature in Politics.* 4th ed. Gloucester, Mass.: Smith.

IDENTITY, PSYCHOSOCIAL

When we wish to establish a person's *identity,* we ask what his name is and what station he occupies in his community. *Personal identity* means more; it includes a subjective sense of continuous existence and a coherent memory. *Psychosocial identity* has even more elusive characteristics, at once subjective and objective, individual and social.

A subjective sense of identity is a sense of sameness and continuity as an individual—but with a special quality probably best described by William James. A man's character, he wrote in a letter, is discernible in the "mental or moral attitude in which, when it came upon him, he felt himself most deeply and intensely active and alive. At such moments there is a voice inside which speaks and says: '*This* is the real me!'" Such experience always includes "an element of active tension, of holding my own, as it were, and trusting outward things to perform their part so as to make it a full harmony, but without any guaranty that they will" (1920, vol. 1, p. 199). Thus may a mature person come to the astonished or exuberant awareness of his identity.

What underlies such a subjective sense, however, can be recognized by others, even when it is not especially conscious or, indeed, self-conscious: thus, one can observe a youngster "become himself" at the very moment when he can be said to be "losing himself" in work, play, or company. He suddenly seems to be "at home in his body," to "know where he is going," and so on.

The social aspects of identity formation were touched upon by Freud when in an address he spoke of an "inner identity" that he shared with the tradition of Jewry and which still was at the core of his personality, namely, the capacity to live and think in isolation from the "compact majority" ([1926] 1959, p. 273). The gradual development of a mature psychosocial identity, then, presupposes a community of people whose traditional values become significant to the growing person even as his growth assumes relevance for them. Mere "roles" that can be "played" interchangeably are obviously not sufficient for the social aspect of the equation. Only a hierarchical integration of roles that foster the vitality of individual growth as they represent a vital trend in the existing or developing social order can support identities. Psychosocial identity thus depends on a complementarity of an inner (ego) synthesis in the individual and of role integration in his group [*see* ROLE; *see also* Erikson 1959].

In individual development, psychosocial identity is not feasible before and is indispensable after the end of adolescence, when the grown-up body grows together, when matured sexuality seeks partners, and when the fully developed mind begins to envisage a historical perspective and seeks new loyalties—all developments which must fuse with each other in a new sense of sameness and continuity. Here, persistent (but sometimes mutually contradictory) infantile identifications are brought in line with urgent (and yet often tentative) new self-definitions and irreversible (and yet often unclear) role choices. There ensues what we call the *identity crisis.*

Historical processes in turn seem vitally related to the demand for identity in each new generation; for to remain vital, societies must have at their disposal the energies and loyalties that emerge from the adolescent process: as positive identities are "confirmed," societies are regenerated. Where this process fails in too many individuals, a *historical crisis* becomes apparent. Psychosocial identity, therefore, can also be studied from the point of view of a complementarity of life history and history (Erikson 1958; 1964, chapter 5).

In its individual and collective aspects, psychosocial identity strives for ideological unity; but it is also always defined by that past which is to be lived down and by that potential future which is to be prevented. Identity formation thus involves a continuous conflict with powerful negative identity elements. In times of aggravated crises these come to the fore to arouse in man a murderous hate of "otherness," which he judges as evil in strangers—and in himself. The study of psychosocial identity thus calls also for an assessment of the hierarchy of positive and negative identity elements present in an individual's stage of life and in his historical era.

These are dimensions which will prove indispensable to the study of identity in the variety of disciplines now to be listed. In the meantime, I hope to have disposed of the faddish contemporary "definition" of identity as the question, "Who am I?"

Interests and approaches

Psychiatry and social psychiatry. Intricate life processes often reveal themselves first in epidemiological states of dysfunction. Thus, in our time the significance of the identity process first became apparent to psychopathologists who recognized psychosocial factors in severe disturbances of the individual sense of identity (alienation, identity confusion, depersonalization) and to diagnosticians of social upheavals who found psychosocial phenomena at work (role conflict, anomie).

As the theoretical focus of psychoanalysis shifted from "instincts" to "ego," from defensive to adaptive mechanisms, and from infantile conflict to later stages of life, states of acute ego impairment were recognized and treated. A syndrome called *identity confusion* ("identity diffusion" proved a somewhat ambiguous term) was recognized as characterizing neurotic disturbances resulting from traumatic events, such as war, internment, and migration (Erikson [1950] 1964, pp. 38–45). But it also proved to be a dominant feature in developmental disturbances in adolescence (Erikson 1959, pp. 122–146). Identity crises aggravated by social and maturational changes can evoke neurotic or psychotic syndromes but are found to be diagnosable and treatable as transitory disturbances (Blaine & McArthur 1961). Identity confusion, furthermore, can also be recognized in pervert–delinquent and bizarre–extremist behavior, which can assume epidemiological proportions as a result of technological changes and population shifts (Witmer & Kotinsky 1956). Thus theory, therapy, and prevention are seen to lack the proper leverage if the need for psychosocial identity is not understood, and especially if instead the young deviant or patient is "confirmed" as a born criminal or a lifelong patient by correctional or therapeutic agencies (Erikson & Erikson 1957; K. T. Erikson 1957).

Child development and anthropology. The study of a variety of dysfunctions thus threw light on identity formation as the very criterion of psychosocial functioning at, and after, the conclusion of one critical stage of development: adolescence. Identity, to be sure, does not originate (and does not end) in adolescence: from birth onward the child learns what counts in his culture's space time and life plan by the community's differential responses to his maturing behavior. He learns to identify with ideal prototypes and to develop away from evil ones. But identity formation comes to a decisive crisis in youth—a crisis met, alleviated, or aggravated by different societies in different ways (Lichtenstein 1961; Erikson 1950).

History and sociology. Historical considerations lead back into man's prehistory and evolution. Only gradually emerging as one mankind conscious of itself and responsible to and for itself, man has been divided into pseudospecies (tribes and nations, castes and classes), each with its own overdefined identity and each reinforced by mortal prejudice against its images of other pseudospecies.

In history, identifications and identities are bound to shift with changing technologies, cultures, and political systems. Existing or changing roles thus must be reassimilated in the psychosocial identity of the most dominant and most numerous members of an organization. Large-scale irreconcilabilities in this ongoing assimilation result in *identity panic* that, in turn, aggravates irrational aversions and prejudices and can lead to erratic violence on a large scale or to widespread self-damaging malaise (Stein et al. 1960; Wheelis 1958).

The fact that the remnants of "tribalism" in an armed and industrialized species can contribute to conditions of utmost danger to the survival of the species itself is leading to a new consciousness of man's position in his own ongoing history.

Religion and philosophy. While projecting evil otherness on enemies and devils, man has habitually assigned a supreme "identity" to deities who guarantee, under revealed conditions, his chances for individual immortality or rebirth. This tendency is a proper subject for psychoanalytic and psychosocial investigation only insofar as it reveals the psychological and cultural variations of man's projection of his own striving for omnipotent identity on the "Beyond" (Erikson 1958).

Finally, man's psychosocial identity has been related philosophically to his striving to attain and to transcend *the pure "I"* that remains each individual's existential enigma. Old and new wisdom would suggest that man can transcend only what he has affirmed in a lifetime and a generation. Here, clinical and social science will concern themselves with the demonstrable, and philosophy with the thinkable (Lichtenstein 1963).

Out of this multiplicity of approaches we will now select a few converging themes for more coherent presentation.

A theory of psychosocial identity

The identity crisis. In some young people, in some classes, at some periods in history, the identity crisis will be noiseless; in other people, classes, and periods, the crisis will be clearly marked off as a critical period, a kind of "second birth," either deliberately intensified by collective ritual and indoctrination or spontaneously aggravated by individual conflict.

In this day of psychiatric overconcern, it must be emphasized that crisis here does not mean a fatal turn but rather (as it does in drama and in medicine) a crucial time or an inescapable turning point for better *or* for worse. "Better" here means a confluence of the constructive energies of individual and society, as witnessed by physical grace, mental alertness, emotional directness, and social "actualness." "Worse" means prolonged identity confusion in the young individual as well as in the society which is forfeiting the devoted application of the energies of youth. But worse can ultimately lead to better: extraordinary individuals, in repeated crises, create the identity elements of the future (Erikson 1958).

Identity closure and "ideology." In the individual, the normative identity crisis is brought about by contemporaneous and indivisible developments that have received uneven attention in various fields of inquiry. The "growing together" of late adolescence results in increasingly irreversible configurations of physical and sexual type, of cognitive and emotional style, and of social role. Sexual maturation drives the individual toward more or less regressive, furtive, or indiscriminate contact; yet the fatefulness of a narrowing choice of more permanent partners becomes inescapable. All of this is strongly related to maturing patterns of cognition and judgment. Inhelder's and Piaget's studies (1955) suggest that only in adolescence can man "reverse" in his mind a sequence of events in such a way that it becomes clear why what *did* happen *had* to happen. Thus, the irreversibility of consequences (more or less intended, more or less "deserved") becomes painfully apparent. With such cognitive orientation, then, the young person must make or "make his own" a series of personal, occupational, and ideological choices.

At the same time, an unconscious integration of all earlier identifications must take place. Children have the nucleus of a separate identity early in life; often they are seen to defend it with precocious self-determination against pressures which would make them overidentify with one or both of their parents. In fact, what clinical literature describes as identification is usually neurotic overidentification. The postadolescent identity must rely, to be sure, on all those earlier identifications that have contributed to a gradual alignment of the individual's instinctual make-up with his developing endowment and the tangible promise of future opportunities. But the wholeness of identity is more than the sum of all earlier identifications and must be supported by a communal orientation which we will call ideological. A living ideology is a systematized set of ideas and ideals which unifies the striving for psychosocial identity in the coming generation, and it remains a stratum in every man's imagery, whether it remains a "way of life" or becomes a militant "official" ideology [*see* IDEOLOGY]. An ideological world view may be transmitted in dogmatic form by special rites, inductions, or confirmations; or society may allow youth to experiment for specified periods (I have called them *psychosocial moratoria*) under special conditions (*Wanderschaft*, frontier, colonies, service, college, etc.).

Fidelity. Sooner or later, the young individual and the functioning society must join forces in that combination of loyalty and competence which may best be termed *fidelity* (Erikson 1963). This may be realized by the involvement of youth as beneficiaries and renewers of tradition, workers and innovators in technology, critics and rejuvenators of style and logic, and rebels bent on the destruction of hollow form in such experience as reveals the essence of the era. For contemporaries, it is often difficult to discern the vital promise of a new and more inclusive identity or to assess the specific alienation inherent in a historical period: there are prophetic voices in all eras which make a profession of ascribing man's existential self-estrangement to the sins of the time [*see* ALIENATION].

Obviously, an era's identity crisis is least severe in that segment of youth which is able to invest its fidelity in an expanding technology and thus evolves new and competent types and roles. Today, this includes the young people in all countries who can fit into and take active charge of technical and scientific development, learning thereby to identify with a life-style of invention and production. Youth which is eager for such experience but unable to find access to it will feel estranged from society until technology and nontechnical intelligence have come to a certain convergence.

Male and female identity. Do male and female identities differ? The "mechanisms" of identity formation are, of course, the same. But since identity is always anchored both in physiological "givens" and in social roles, the sex endowed with an "inner-bodily space" capable of bearing offspring lives in a different total configuration of identity elements than does the fathering sex (Erikson 1965). Obviously also, the childhood identifications to be integrated differ in the two sexes. But the realization of woman's optimal psychosocial identity (which in our day would include individuality, workmanship, and citizenship, as well as motherhood) is beset with ancient problems. The "depth," both concretely physical and emotional, of woman's involvement in the cycle of sexual attraction, conception, gestation, lactation, and child care has been exploited by the builders of ideologies and societies to relegate women to all manner of lifelong "confinements" and confining roles. Psychoanalysis has shown feminine identity formation to be prejudiced by what a woman cannot be and cannot have rather than by what she is, has been, and may yet become. Thus the struggle for legal and political equality is apt to be accompanied by strenuous attempts to base woman's identity on the proof that she is (almost) as good as man in activities and schedules fashioned by and for men. However, the flamboyant brinkmanship of technological and political men in matters now of vital concern to the whole species has revived the vision of a new identity of womanhood, one in which the maternal orientation is not at odds with work and citizenship but gives new meaning to both. But here as elsewhere new inventions will not suffice as long as deep-seated negative identities prevail [*see* INDIVIDUAL DIFFERENCES, *article on* SEX DIFFERENCES].

Negative identity and totalism. As pointed out, a negative identity remains an unruly part of the total identity. In addition, man tends to "make his own" the negative image of himself imposed on him by superiors and exploiters (Erikson 1959, pp. 31–38). To cite a contemporary issue, a colored child's identity may have gained strength from his parent's melodious speech, and yet he may come to suspect this speech as the mark of submission and begin to aspire to the harsh traits of a superiority from which the "master race" tries by every means to exclude him. A fanatical segregationist, in turn, may have learned to reinforce regional identity with the repudiation of everything colored and yet may have experienced early associations with colored people for which he remains nostalgic. He will, therefore, protect his superiority with a narrow-mindedness so defensive that it fails to provide a reliable identity in an enlightened society.

Two phenomena further complicate these inner rifts. For one, negative images become tightly associated with one another in the individual's imagery. The reinforced defense against a negative identity may make a pronounced he-man despise in himself and others everything reminiscent of female sentimentality, colored passivity, or Jewish braininess and at the same time make him fear that what is thus held in contempt may take over his world. This kind of reaction is the source of much human hate. In the event of aggravated crises, furthermore, an individual (or a group) may despair of his or its ability to contain these negative elements in a positive identity. This can lead to a sudden surrender to total doctrines and dogmas (Lifton 1961) in which the negative identity becomes the dominant one. Many a young German, once sensitive to foreign criticism, became a ruthless Nazi on the rebound from the love for a *Kultur* which in post-Versailles Germany seemed at odds with a German identity. His new identity, however, was based on a totalism marked by the radical exclusion of dangerous otherness and on the failure to integrate historically given identity elements also alive in every German. What differentiates such totalism from conversions promising a more inclusive wholeness is the specific rage that is aroused wherever identity development loses the promise of a traditionally assured wholeness. This latent rage is easily exploited by fanatic and psychopathic leaders. It can explode in the arbitrary destructiveness of mobs, and it can serve the efficient violence of organized machines of destruction.

Historical considerations

As predicted, developmental considerations have led us to examine historical processes, for identity and ideology seem to be two aspects of the same psychosocial process. But identity and ideology are only way stations on the route to further individual and collective maturation; new crises work toward those higher forms of social identification in which identities are joined, fused, renewed, and transcended.

There are, however, periods in history which are relative identity vacuums and in which three forms of human apprehension aggravate each other: fears aroused by discoveries and inventions (including weapons) which radically expand and change the whole world image, anxieties aggravated by the decay of institutions which had been the historical anchor of an existing ideology, and the dread of an existential vacuum devoid of spiritual meaning. In the past, ideological innovators evolved vital new identity ingredients out of their own prolonged and repeated adolescent conflicts (Erikson 1958; 1964, pp. 201–208). Today, however, the ideology of progress has made unpredictable and unlimited change itself the "wave of the future." In all parts of the world, therefore, the struggle now is for anticipatory and more inclusive identities. Revolutionary doctrines promise the new identity of "peasant-and-worker" to the youth of countries which must overcome their tribal, feudal, or colonial orientation. At the same time, new nations attempt to absorb regions, and new markets attempt to absorb nations; the world space is extended to include outer space as the proper locale for a universal technological identity.

Functioning societies can reconfirm their principles, and true leaders can create significant new solidarities only by supporting the development of more inclusive identities; for only a new and enlightened ethics can successfully replace dying moralisms. Nehru said that Gandhi had given India an identity; and, indeed, by perfecting an active mode of nonviolence, Gandhi had transformed a divisive and negative identity (the "passive" Indian) into an inclusive and militant claim on unified nationhood. In other parts of the world, youth itself has shown that when trusted to do so, it can provide patterns for new elites. One thinks here of Israel's "kibbutzniks," the U.S. Peace Corps, and the American students committed to the dislodgement of racial prejudice. In such developments, young men and women can be seen to develop new forms of solidarity and new ethics.

In conclusion, however, we must remind ourselves that the complementarity and relativity of individual identity and collective ideology (which no doubt has emerged as part of man's sociogenetic evolution) also bestows on man a most dangerous potential, namely, a lastingly immature perspective on history. Ideologies and identities, it is true, strive to overcome the tyranny of old moralisms and dogmatisms; yet, they often revert to these, seduced by the righteousness by which otherness is repudiated when the conditions supporting a sense of identity seem in danger. Old ideologists equipped with modern weaponry could well become mankind's executioners. But a trend toward an all-inclusive human identity, and with it a universal ethics, is equally discernible in the development of man, and it may not be too utopian to assume that new and world-wide systems of technology and communication may serve to make this universality more manifest.

ERIK H. ERIKSON

[*Directly related are the entries* PERSONALITY; PSYCHOANALYSIS, *article on* EGO PSYCHOLOGY; SELF CONCEPT. *Other relevant material may be found in* ADOLESCENCE; ANTHROPOLOGY, *article on* CULTURAL ANTHROPOLOGY; DEVELOPMENTAL PSYCHOLOGY; INFANCY; LIFE CYCLE; SOCIALIZATION.]

BIBLIOGRAPHY

BLAINE, GRAHAM B.; and MCARTHUR, CHARLES (editors) 1961 *Emotional Problems of the Student*. New York: Appleton.

ERIKSON, ERIK H. (1950) 1964 *Childhood and Society*. 2d ed., rev. & enl. New York: Norton.

ERIKSON, ERIK H. (1958) 1962 *Young Man Luther*. New York: Norton.

ERIKSON, ERIK H. 1959 Identity and the Life Cycle. *Psychological Issues* 1, no. 1.

ERIKSON, ERIK H. (editor) 1963 *Youth: Change and Challenge*. New York: Basic Books.

ERIKSON, ERIK H. 1964 *Insight and Responsibility*. New York: Norton.

ERIKSON, ERIK H. 1965 Inner and Outer Space: Reflections on Womanhood. Pages 1–26 in Robert Lifton, *The Woman in America*. New York: Houghton Mifflin.

ERIKSON, ERIK H. 1966 The Concept of Identity in Race Relations: Notes and Queries. *Dædalus* 95:145–171.

ERIKSON, ERIK H.; and ERIKSON, KAI T. 1957 The Confirmation of the Delinquent. *Chicago Review* 10:15–23.

ERIKSON, KAI T. 1957 Patient Role and Social Uncertainty. *Psychiatry* 20:263–274.

FREUD, SIGMUND (1926) 1959 Address to the Society of B'nai B'rith. Volume 20, pages 272–274 in Sigmund Freud, *The Standard Edition of the Complete Psychological Works*. London: Hogarth.

INHELDER, BÄRBEL; and PIAGET, JEAN (1955) 1958 *The Growth of Logical Thinking From Childhood to Adolescence*. New York: Basic Books. → First published as *De la logique de l'enfant à la logique de l'adolescent*.

JAMES, WILLIAM 1920 *Letters*. Volume 1. Boston: Atlantic Monthly Press.

LICHTENSTEIN, HEINZ 1961 Identity and Sexuality: A Study of Their Interrelationship in Man. *Journal of the American Psychoanalytic Association* 9:179–260.

LICHTENSTEIN, HEINZ 1963 The Dilemma of Human Identity. *Journal of the American Psychoanalytic Association* 11:173–223.

LIFTON, ROBERT J. 1961 *Thought Reform and the Psychology of Totalism: A Study of "Brainwashing" in China*. New York: Norton.

STEIN, MAURICE R.; VIDICH, ARTHUR; and WHITE, DAVID M. (editors) 1960 *Identity and Anxiety*. New York: Free Press.

WHEELIS, ALLEN 1958 *The Quest for Identity*. New York: Norton.

WITMER, HELEN L.; and KOTINSKY, RUTH (editors) 1956 *New Perspectives for Research on Juvenile Delinquency*. Washington: U.S. Children's Bureau.

IDEOLOGY

I
THE CONCEPT AND FUNCTION OF IDEOLOGY

Ideology is one variant form of those comprehensive patterns of cognitive and moral beliefs about man, society, and the universe in relation to man and society, which flourish in human societies. Outlooks and creeds, systems and movements of thought, and programs are among the other types of comprehensive patterns which are to be distinguished from ideology.

These comprehensive patterns differ from each other in their degree of (*a*) explicitness of formulation; (*b*) intended systemic integration around a particular moral or cognitive belief; (*c*) acknowledged affinity with other past and contemporaneous patterns; (*d*) closure to novel elements or variations; (*e*) imperativeness of manifestation in conduct; (*f*) accompanying affect; (*g*) consensus demanded of those who accept them; (*h*) authoritativeness of promulgation; and (*i*) association with a corporate body intended to realize the pattern of beliefs.

Ideologies are characterized by a high degree of explicitness of formulation over a very wide range of the objects with which they deal; for their adherents there is an authoritative and explicit promulgation. As compared with other patterns of beliefs, ideologies are relatively highly systematized or integrated around one or a few pre-eminent values, such as salvation, equality, or ethnic purity. They are more insistent on their distinctiveness from, and unconnectedness with, the outlooks, creeds, and other ideologies existing in the same society; they are more resistant to innovations in their beliefs and deny the existence or the significance of those which do occur. Their acceptance and promulgation are accompanied by highly affective overtones. Complete individual subservience to the ideology is demanded of those who accept it, and it is regarded as essential and imperative that their conduct be completely permeated by it. Consensus among all those who affirm their adherence is likewise demanded; all adherents of the ideology are urgently expected to be in complete agreement with each other. A corporate collective form is regarded as the mode of organization of adherents appropriate for maintaining discipline among those already committed and for winning over or dominating others.

Outlooks tend to lack one authoritative and explicit promulgation. They are pluralistic in their internal structure and are not systematically integrated. Lacking an authoritative promulgation, outlooks are more open to the entry and inclusion of elements from other outlooks and alien creeds than are ideologies or even creeds. Outlooks contain within themselves a variety of *creeds*, which differ from each other by divergent emphasis on different elements in the outlook; creeds tend, therefore, to be in conflict with each other on particular issues, while in many respects they accept the prevailing encompassing outlook of the society in which they exist. The vagueness and diffuseness of outlooks and—to a lesser extent—creeds are paralleled by the unevenness of the pressure for their observance in action. In expression, outlooks are relatively unaffective. They are also less demanding of consensus among their bearers than ideologies are.

Ideologies, especially in their incipient stage, are not usually espoused by the incumbents and custodians of the central institutional and value systems. In contrast, outlooks and their subsidiary creeds are the characteristic patterns of belief in those sections of the society which affirm or accept the existing order of society. Rulers and those elites associated with them in the conduct of the central institutional systems tend to espouse the outlook and one or several of the creeds which seek to give a more definite promulgation to certain elements of the prevailing outlook. Creeds which become alienated from the central institutional system tend to acquire the formal properties of ideologies. Whereas outlooks (e.g., Buddhism, Protestantism) bear only a very loose relationship with conduct, creeds (e.g., Quakerism, Roman Catholicism) aspire to a fuller influence on the conduct of those who espouse them.

Creeds often shade off into ideologies, but because they do not tend to take as sharply bounded a corporate form and because they have much less orthodoxy, they cannot command the concerted intellectual power of ideologies. Actual subscription to them tends, therefore, to be partial, fragmentary, and occasional. Unless a creed is taken in hand by a school of thought, it does not undergo systematic elaboration and its scope is not broadened to a point of universal comprehensiveness. Its founder or inspiring genius might have created a coherent system of moral, social, and political philosophy, which in its comprehensiveness, elaborateness, and explictness might be equivalent to the intellectual core of an ideology. However, if the founder forms neither a school of thought nor an ideological primary group, his influence, however great, will be carried by the winds. Each will take from this creed what he wants: it will become a pervasive influence, but it will lose the unity and the force which it needed to become an ideology. If, furthermore, the great thinker is neither far-reachingly alienated from the central value and institutional systems of his society nor unqualifiedly insistent on the complete realization of his doctrine in the conduct of his followers, there is little chance that an ideology will flow from his intellectual construction.

Systems and movements of thought are more or less explicit and systematic intellectual patterns developed in the course of generally undirected intellectual collaboration and division of labor (e.g., existentialism, Hegelian idealism, pragmatism). Like ideologies and unlike outlooks, they are elaborate and internally integrated. However, insofar as they do not insist on total observance in behavior, on a complete consensus among their adherents, and on closure vis-à-vis other intellectual constructions, they do not become ideologies.

A *program* is a specification of a particular limited objective (e.g., civil rights or electoral reform movements); thus, it represents the narrowing of a focus of interest that is implicit in an outlook and made more explicit or compelling in a creed or a movement of thought. Depending on the pattern from which a program originates, its relationship to more general cognitive and moral principles will be more or less elaborate and explicit. Since its major feature is the limited range of its objectives, it is less likely to be immediately ideological in its origin and association.

Like ideology, movements of thought and programs tend to be in disagreement with contemporaneous outlooks and dominant creeds and the practices through which they operate institutionally. But ideology differs from "dissensual" movements of thought and programs in the intensity of the affect which accompanies its dissent, in the completeness of its corporate self-separation, in its degree of intellectual closure, and in the range of its aspiration to encompass (cognitively, evaluatively, and in practice) all available objects and events.

Ideologies and those who espouse them allege that they speak for a transcendent entity—a stratum, a society, a species, or an ideal value—which is broader than the particular corporate body of those who believe in the ideology. Corporate carriers of the ideologies, whatever their actual practice, claim to act on behalf of an "ideal," the beneficiaries of which include more than members of the ideological group. Since the ideal always diverges from the existent, the ideology contends for the realization of a state of affairs which, its proponents allege, either never existed previously or existed in the past but exists no longer. (Karl Mannheim [1929–1931] designated the former type of ideals as utopias, the latter as ideologies. Moreover, within the category of ideology, he included sets of beliefs which affirm the existing order—that is, the patterns which I have designated as outlooks and creeds, schools of thought, and programs. Neither his terminology nor his classifications are adhered to in this analysis of patterns of belief.)

Ideology and central value systems

As compared with the prevailing outlook and its constituent and overlapping creeds, an ideology characteristically contends more strenuously for a purer, fuller, or more ideal realization of particular cognitive and moral values than exist in the society in which the ideology obtains currency. Ideologies are more insistent on an actual and continuous contact with sacred symbols and with a fuller manifestation of the sacred in the existent. Whereas outlooks and creeds connected with the central institutional system demand, in their programmatic promulgations, segmental changes or changes which do not diverge profoundly from what already exists, ideologies impel their proponents to insist on the realization of the ideal, which is contained in the sacred, through a "total transformation" of society. They seek this completeness either through total conquest (including conversion) or by total withdrawal so that the purer, ideal form of value can be cultivated in isolation from the contaminating influence of the environing society. Whereas the bearers of each of the several creeds of a prevailing outlook accept some measure of community with other creeds, the exponents of an ideology, being set against other ideologies and particularly against the dominant outlook and creeds, stress the differences between their ideology and the other outlooks and ideologies within the society and disavow the identities and affinities.

Nonetheless, every ideology—however great the originality of its creators—arises in the midst of an ongoing culture. However passionate its reaction against that culture, it cannot entirely divest itself of important elements of that culture. Ideologies are responses to insufficient regard for some particular element in the dominant outlook and are attempts to place that neglected element in a more central position and to bring it into fulfillment. There are, therefore, always marked substantive affinities between the moral and cognitive orientations of any particular ideology and those of the outlooks and creeds which prevail in the environing society and which affirm or accept the central institutional and value systems.

However, in their formal structure such outlooks are constellations of very loosely integrated and ambiguous moral and cognitive propositions and attitudes toward a variety of particular, often relatively concrete, objects and situations. In the minds of most of those who share an outlook, it does not form a consistent system focused on one central theme, principle, value, or symbol. In contrast, an ideology involves an intensification and generalization of certain central propositions and attitudes, a reduced emphasis on others and their subordination to the proposition (or propositions), which is raised to a position of predominance. An ideology differs, therefore, from a prevailing outlook and its creeds through its greater *explicitness*, its greater *internal integration* or *systematization*, its greater *comprehensiveness*, the greater *urgency* of its application, and its much higher *intensity of concentration* focused on certain central propositions or evaluations.

All ideologies—whether progressive or traditionalistic, revolutionary or reactionary—entail an aggressive alienation from the existing society: they recommend the transformation of the lives of their exponents in accordance with specific principles; they insist on consistency and thoroughgoingness in their exponents' application of principles; and they recommend either their adherents' complete dominion over the societies in which they live or their total, self-protective withdrawal from these societies. Even where the exponents of an ideology have been successful in attaining the key positions from which power is exercised in the central institutional system, they continue to be alienated from the outlook and creeds of the society over which they exercise power.

Ideologies passionately oppose the productions of the cultural institutions of the central institutional system. They claim that these institutions distort the truth about "serious" things and that they do so to maintain a system of injustice in the earthly order. Ideologies insist on the realization of principles in conduct; this is one of their grounds for accusing central value and institutional systems of hypocrisy, the compromise of principles, and corruption by power. Thus, ideologies and their exponents—whether out of power or in central positions of power over society—are relentlessly critical of the inconsistencies and shortcomings of conduct, evaluated with respect to rigorous principles of right and justice, in sectors of society over which they do not have complete control. Ideologies demand an intense and continuous observance of their imperatives in the conduct of their exponents.

Whereas the various component elements of an outlook may be unevenly distributed among those who share the outlook, an ideology insists on a greater completeness of possession by each of those who are committed to sharing in it. In other words, a "division of labor" in attachment to the diverse elements of ideological belief is less supportable to the most fervent exponents of ideology than a comparable division of attachment is to the exponents of an outlook, a creed, or a movement of thought.

Ideological politics

Ideologies are always concerned with authority, transcendent and earthly, and they cannot, therefore, avoid being political except by the extreme reaction-formation of complete withdrawal from society. Even in ages which saw no public politics permitted, ideological groups forced themselves into the political arena. Since the seventeenth century, every ideology has had its views on politics. Indeed, since the nineteenth century, most ideologies have come to be preponderantly political.

This appearance of thinking of nothing but politics is not identical with the attitude of the professional politician, who lives for politics to the exclusion of everything else. Ideologies which concentrate on politics do so because for them politics embraces everything else. The evaluation of authority is the center of the ideological outlook, and around it are integrated all other objects and their evaluations. Thus, no sphere has any intrinsic value of its own. There is no privacy, no autonomous spheres of art, religion, economic activity, or science. Each, in this view, is to be understood politically. (This is true of Marxism, despite the fact that it is reputed to have made everything dependent on economic relationships. In Marxist ideology the relations of production are property relations—i.e., relationships of authority, supported by the power of the state.)

Ideology, whether nominally religious or antireligious, is concerned with the sacred. Ideology seeks to sanctify existence by bringing every part of it under the dominion of the ultimately right principles. The sacred and the sacrilegious reside in authority, the former in the authority acknowledged by ideology, the latter in that which prevails in the "wicked world," against which ideology contends. From the viewpoint of an ideology, ordinary politics are the kingdom of darkness, whereas ideological politics are the struggle of light against darkness.

Participation in the routine life of the civil political order is alien to the ideological spirit. In fact, however, there are many adulterations of this ideological purity, and purely ideological politics are marginal and exceptional. The need to build a machine strong enough to acquire power in the state, even by conspiracy and subversion, enforces compromises with, and concessions to, the ongoing political order and the less than complete ideological orientation of potential and desired supporters. Failure, too, damages the purity of ideological politics. The pressure of competition enforces alliances and the adoption of procedures which are alien to their nature. Nonetheless, ideological politics, in splinters of rancorous purity or in attenuation, often penetrate into civil politics, and conversely, civil politics often force their way into ideological politics.

Among intellectuals there are many who have inherited an ideological tradition and to whom ideological politics appeal as the only right politics. Even where intellectuals often appear to be convinced of the inefficacy of ideological politics, the categories in which ideologies view the world, as well as the techniques and the heroes of ideological politics, often stir and master their imaginations.

The emergence of ideologies

An ideology is the product of man's need for imposing intellectual order on the world. The need for an ideology is an intensification of the need for a cognitive and moral map of the universe, which in a less intense and more intermittent form is a fundamental, although unequally distributed, disposition of man.

Ideologies arise in conditions of crisis and in sectors of society to whom the hitherto prevailing outlook has become unacceptable. An ideology arises because there are strongly felt needs, which are not satisfied by the prevailing outlook, for an explanation of important experiences, for the firm guidance of conduct, and for a fundamental vindication or legitimation of the value and dignity of the persons who feel these needs. Mere rejection of the existing society and the prevailing outlook of the elites of that society is not sufficient. For an ideology to exist, there must also be an attendant vision of a positive alternative to the existing pattern of society and its culture and an intellectual capacity to articulate that vision as part of the cosmic order. Ideologies are the creations of charismatic persons who possess powerful, expansive, and simplified visions of the world, as well as high intellectual and imaginative powers. By placing at its very center certain cosmically and ethically fundamental propositions, an ideology brings to those who accept it the belief that they are in possession of, and in contact with, what is ultimately right and true.

Some personalities are ideological by constitution. Such persons continuously feel a need for a clearly ordered picture of the universe and of their own place in it. They need clear and unambiguous criteria as to what is right and wrong in every situation. They must be able to explain whatever happens by a clear and readily applicable proposition, itself derived from a central proposition. Other persons become ideological under conditions of private and public crisis, which accentuate the need for meaningful moral and cognitive order; when the crisis abates, such persons become less ideological.

An ideology cannot come into existence without the prior existence of a general pattern of moral and cognitive judgments—an outlook and its subsidiary creeds—against which it is a reaction and of which it is a variant. It requires, in other words, a cultural tradition from which to deviate and from which to draw the elements which it intensifies and raises to centrality. An intellectualized religion provides the ideal precondition for the emergence of ideology, since the former contains explicit propositions about the nature of the sacred and its cultivation, which is what ideologies are about. The fact that an ideology already exists serves both to form an ideological tradition and to provide a medium in which ideological dispositions can be precipitated by emulation and self-differentiation.

Ideologies and ideological orientations have existed in all high cultures. They have, however, been especially frequent in Western culture. The continuous working of the prophetic tradition of the Old Testament and the salvationary tradition of the mystery religions and of early Christianity have provided a set of cultural dispositions which have been recurrently activated in the course of the Christian era in the West. The secularization of the modern age has not changed this. Indeed, the growth of literacy and of the educated classes and the "intellectualization" of politics have widened receptivity to ideological beliefs. The spread of Western ideas to Asia and Africa has involved, among many other things, the diffusion of a culture full of ideological potentiality.

The bearers of ideology

The disposition toward ideological construction is one of the fundamental characteristics of the human race once it reaches a certain stage of intellectual development. It is, however, a disposition which is usually latent. It finds its fullest expression in a charismatic ideologist, a person with an overwhelmingly powerful intellectual and moral drive to be in contact with the sacred and to promulgate that contact in comprehensive and coherent terms. The charismatic ideologist cannot, however, construct an ideology in isolation from a collectivity on behalf of which he speaks and with which he must share that ideology. An ideology-like intellectual construction produced in isolation from a political or religious sect would be no more than a rigorous system of religious, moral, social, and political thought based on fundamental propositions about the cosmos and history. It becomes more than that only when it is shared by a community constituted on the basis of the acceptance of that outlook.

The characteristic and primal bearer of an ideology is an *ideological primary group* (what Herman Schmalenbach [1922] called a *Bund*). The bond which unites the members of the ideological primary group to each other is the attachment to each other as sharers in the ideological system of beliefs; the members perceive each other as being in possession of, or being possessed by, the sacredness inherent in the acceptance of the ideology. Personal, primordial, and civil qualities are attenuated or suppressed in favor of the quality of "ideological possession." A comrade is a comrade by virtue of his beliefs, which are perceived as his most significant qualities. A fully developed ideological primary group is separated by sharply defined boundaries from the "world" from which it seeks to protect itself or over which it seeks to triumph. Stringent discipline over conduct and belief is a feature of ideological primary groups; intense solidarity and unwavering loyalty are demanded (as in revolutionary cells and in separatist religious sects).

In reality, of course, the ideological quality never completely supplants all other qualities, and the fully developed ideological primary group is never completely realized. Thus, the ideological primary group is subject to recurrent strains, not only because of the strains inherent within the ideology as an intellectual system, but also because the other qualities become, in various measures for many of the members of the group, significant qualities, on the bases of which supplementary and often alternative and contradictory attachments are formed. Even the most disciplined ideological primary group is under the strain of divergent beliefs among members, as well as the pull of their various attachments to the "world." All these anti-ideological tendencies within ideological primary groups are greatly aggravated in modern societies in which large parties are organized and in which large-scale bureaucratic administrations are necessary. Both of these generate many nonideological tendencies and place further strain on ideological purity and its cognate solidarity.

Nevertheless, ideologies have a self-reproductive power. They are often partially espoused by more loosely integrated circles, particularly when the ideology itself has moved into a condition of disintegration. Echoes and fragments of ideologies go on after their primal bearers have died or dissolved in defeat or disillusionment. Thus, ideologies sometimes turn into movements of thought. Moreover, fragments of ideology may become transformed into creeds and re-enter the outlooks from whence they once came and which they now change.

On the social origins of the bearers of ideology, little can be said. It was Max Weber's view that they came from the strata of traders and handicraftsmen and from sections of society which are shaken by a disruption in their conventional mode of life. There is some plausibility in this hypothesis. However, they also appear to come from educated circles as well and from ethnic "outsiders," whose prior alienation makes them receptive to ideological beliefs.

Endogenous and exogenous changes

Proponents of ideologies obdurately resist the explicit introduction of revision of their articles of belief. Ideologies aspire to, and pretend to, systematic completeness, and they do not appear to their proponents to be in need of improvement. Nonetheless, ideologies are never completely consistent or completely adequate to the facts of experience which they claim to interpret and dominate. Even the most systematically elaborated ideology, like all systems of belief, scientific and nonscientific, contains inconsistencies, ambiguities, and gaps. These tend to result in disputes among the adherents of the ideology who espouse divergent ways of filling the gaps and clarifying the ambiguities, each claiming that his way represents the "correct" interpretation of the unchanged and unchangeable fundamentals. Inconsistencies and ambiguities may be perceived on purely intellectual grounds, and the efforts to repair them may be motivated primarily by a concern for intellectual clarity and harmony. Such efforts are likely to arouse antagonism from the more orthodox exponents of the ideology—that is, those who adhere to the previously dominant interpretation. In this way, either through the triumph of the innovators or the triumph of the orthodox, the previous formulation of the ideology undergoes a change.

In addition to these more intellectual sources of changes in ideologies, further endogenous changes occur in consequence of conflicts among the proponents of divergent policies which appear to be equally sanctioned by the ideology. As a result of the triumph of one of the contending groups over the other, new emphases and developments occur within the ideology. These very properties which are sources of instability in ideologies and in the groups which support them are also prerequisites for their further development in the face of new situations and for their adaptation and compromise with the intractability of reality as an object of exhaustive cognition and control.

Ideologies also change because of the pressure of external reality. The "world" does not easily accommodate itself to the requirements of ideologies. The "facts" of life do not fit their categories; those who live their lives among these facts do not yield to the exhortations and offensives of the ideologists. The proponents of ideologies are often defeated in their campaigns for total transformation. Defeat is a shock, a pressing occasion for revision of the ideology to make it fit the "facts" which have imposed themselves. Despite resistance, the ideology is retouched, at first superficially, later more deeply. Fissures among the ideologists accompany this struggle to cope with the impregnability of the "world."

Another external factor which places a strain on ideology is the diminution of the crisis which gave rise to it and the consequent dissipation of ideological orientation. Those whom crisis has inflamed into an ideological state of mind either withdraw from, or loosen their connections with, the ideological primary group; if they are influential enough, they modify and adapt it to the demands of life in the environing society, into which they once more become assimilated. Under these conditions, the sharply defined boundaries of the group become eroded, and the members cease to define themselves exclusively by their ideological qualities. The specific modifications which the ideology introduced to differentiate it from the predominant outlook in the central institutional and value systems become less disjunctive, and its distinctive ideological elements fade into a ceremonially asserted formula. Under these conditions ideologies sometimes dissolve into creeds and programs or fall away into systems of thought. Quite frequently some elements of the ideology turn into accentuated and intensified forms of certain features of the prevailing outlook or creeds which had previously existed in a blurred and unemphasized state.

Quasi-ideological phenomena. The potentialities of ideological orientations relatively seldom come to realization. Quite apart from the tenacious hold of the central institutional and value systems on many persons who are simultaneously ideologically disposed, ideological orientations often do not eventuate in fully developed ideologies or ideological primary groups because the ideological needs of those who come under their influence are not sufficiently intense, comprehensive, and persistent. Without a powerful ideological personality, powerful in intelligence and imagination, ideological propensities in the more ordinary human vessels of ideological needs do not attain fulfillment.

Furthermore, once the ties binding an ideological primary group weaken, the ideology persists in a somewhat disaggregated form among the late members of the group. In that form, too, it continues to find adherents who, without the discipline of an ideological primary group, select certain congenial elements of the ideology for application and development. These elements constitute an ideological tradition which is available to subsequent ideologists and ideological primary groups.

Sometimes certain of these elements become a *program* of aggressive demands and criticism against the central institutional and value systems. Programs, like ideologies, are also emergents from prevailing outlooks and creeds; they "take seriously" some particular element in the outlook and seek to bring it to fulfillment *within* the existing order. A program accepts much of the prevailing institutional and value systems, although it fervently rejects one sector. Thus, a program stands midway between an ideology and a prevailing outlook or a creed; it can be reached from either direction (and testifies thereby to the affinities between ideologies and outlooks and creeds).

The programmatic forms of ideological orientation are sometimes concentrated on particular and segmented objects—for example, the abolition of slavery or the promotion of the rights of a particular sector of the population, such as an ethnic group or a social stratum. They do not expand to the point where they embrace the whole society as the objects of the sought-for transformation. The attachment of such programs to the central institutional or value systems may be so strong that it survives an intense but segmental alienation with respect to particular institutional practices or particular beliefs. This is characteristic of certain modern "reform movements," such as the abolitionist movements in Great Britain in the early eighteenth century and in the United States in the period up to the Civil War. These movements have focused their attention and efforts on specific segments of the central institutional system, demanding the conformity of conduct with moral principles that can neither be yielded nor compromised. Although such programs and the movements which are their structural counterparts do not insist on the complete transformation of the whole society, they are uncompromisingly insistent on the attainment of their particular ideally prescribed ends. Often these movements have been borne by a small circle of persons organized into a *quasi-ideological primary group*. To some extent this type of group draws boundaries around itself and regards itself as disjunctively separated from its enemies, who are not, however, as in more fully developed ideological primary groups, regarded as identical with the totality of the environing society.

Proto-ideological phenomena. Another variant of ideological phenomena is to be seen in those collectivities—such as adolescent gangs and military and paramilitary units—which, although "sodality-like" in structure, do not have the intellectual patterns which are here designated as ideological. Such collectivities are alienated from the prevailing outlook associated with the central institutional and value systems and draw sharply defined boundaries around themselves. Moreover, they insist on a concentration of loyalty to the group and on stringent discipline to the standards of the group and have simplistic criteria of partisanship and enmity. They do not, however, develop or espouse a coherent moral and intellectual doctrine. Such *proto-ideological primary groups* have no well-developed and principled view of the contemporary society which surrounds them; no less important, they have no image of a comprehensive order that would permanently replace the order from which they are alienated. The "world" is the enemy with which they are at war, but they have no interest in taking it over and refashioning it in the name of a cosmically significant principle. In this respect, this type of group approximates the "withdrawn" ideological primary group; however, unlike the latter, the proto-ideological group is aggressively at war with an enemy and lacks an intellectual doctrine.

The failure of the proto-ideological primary group to develop an ideology might be attributed to the insufficient intellectual endowment of its members and, above all, to the absence of a charismatic ideological personality, that is, a founder who is sufficiently educated or sufficiently creative to provide them with a more complex system of beliefs. Such groups lack sufficient contact with both the central value system and the tradition of ideological orientation. They are "rebels without a cause." (The boys' gangs of the great cities of the Western world are typical of these proto-ideological formations; as such, they contrast with the more ideological youth groups which flourished in Germany from the last years of the nineteenth century to the coming of World War II.)

The functions of ideologies

Ideologies are often accepted by persons who, by temperament or by culture, are ideologically predisposed. Such persons might be inclined to express their views with aggressive affect, might feel a strong need to distinguish between comrades and enemies, or might have been raised in a salvationary, apocalyptic culture. There are, however, persons who do not have this predisposition but who nevertheless come under the influence of ideology because of fortuitous circumstances or through the strain of crisis. In such persons ideologies can, up to a point and for a limited time, exert a powerful influence. By making them believe they are in contact with the ultimate powers of existence, ideology will greatly reinforce their motivation to act. They will gain courage from perceiving themselves as part of a cosmic scheme; actions that they would not dare to envisage before will now have the legitimacy which proximity to the sacred provides.

Ideologies intend either the disruption of the central institutional and value systems by conflict with them or the denial of the claims of these systems by withdrawal from them. In the former case, ideologies aim at "total" replacement. However, they do not succeed in this, even where their bearers are successful in the acquisition of power in the larger society. Where an ideological primary group succeeds in overcoming existing elites and comes to rule over the society, it is incapable of completely and enduringly suppressing the previously predominant outlook. It is unsuccessful on a number of grounds. First, the ideology has to contend with strong attachments to the previously prevailing central value systems or outlook among the population at large, and the resources available to the ideological elites are not adequate for suppressing these attachments; too much remains outside the scope of their control or surveillance. Then, as time passes, some elements (although never all) of the previously prevailing outlook reassert themselves. This process is assisted by the fact that the members of the ideological primary group themselves, in the course of time, fall away from their zealous espousal of the ideology and fall back toward one of the outlooks from which the ideology sprang. As the ideological primary group continues in power, the obstacles to the realization of their goals, the multiplicity of alternative paths of action, and other circumstances cause some of the members of the group, especially newly recruited ones, to have recourse to ideas which fall outside the once-adhered-to system of thought.

Ideological primary groups, whether or not they succeed in their aspiration to rule, inevitably fail in the fulfillment of their global aspirations. The "normal" pattern of value orientations, which they have sought to overcome, either persists or reasserts itself. However, some change does occur: these groups leave behind adherents who survive despite failure and in the face of restoration. Where routinization occurs, as in the case of an ideological elite which is not expelled from authority, the new routine is never quite the same as the one which it replaced, however much it diverges from the stringent demands of the ideology in the name of which it was originally established.

Once the ideological orientation comes to be passed on to the next generation, by tradition as well as by systematic teaching, it encounters the resistance which is characteristic of intergenerational relationships, and this in its turn introduces modifications in the direction of compromise and adaptation to primordial and personal needs, as well as to civil exigencies. However, the ideological orientation has not lived in vain. Those who appear to have rejected it or to have become more indifferent to it live under a tradition which has absorbed at least some of the heightened accents which the ideology has brought to the configuration of elements taken over from the prevailing outlook or creeds.

When an expansive ideological primary group does not succeed in attaining dominance, yet endures for a substantial period and impinges on the awareness of the custodians of the central institutional and value systems, it precipitates a partial reorientation of the previously dominant outlook, bringing about a new emphasis within the framework of the older outlook. It renews sensibilities and heightens consciousness of the demands of moral and cognitive orientations which have slipped into a state of partial ineffectiveness. The old order, against which it contended, is never the same because the old order has adapted itself to the challenge and assimilated into itself some of the emphases of the ideology.

Truth and ideology

The question of the relationship between truth and ideology has been raised by the tradition of European thought which culminated in Marxism and in the sociology of knowledge developed by Mannheim [*see the biography of* MANNHEIM]. According to this view, ideology is by its nature untruthful, since it entails a "masking" or "veiling" of unavowed and unperceived motives or "interests." These interests impel the deception of antagonists and the transfiguration of narrow sectional ends and interests by means of an ostensible universalization. They distort reality for the ideologists and for their antagonists. Thus, in this view, ideology is a manifestation of a "false consciousness."

Viewed from a more dispassionate standpoint, which is less involved in a particular historical metaphysic and less involved in proving everyone else wrong and itself incontestably and cosmically right, the question of the compatibility of scientific or scholarly truth with ideology does not admit of a single, unequivocal answer. Ideologies, like all complex cognitive patterns, contain many propositions; even though ideologists strive for, and claim to possess, systematic integration, they are never completely successful in this regard. Hence, true propositions can coexist alongside false ones. Ideologies hostile to the prevailing outlook and the central institutional system of a society have not infrequently contained truthful propositions about important particular features of the existing order, and have drawn attention to particular variables which were either not perceived or not acknowledged by scholars and thinkers who took a more affirmative, or at least a less alienated, attitude toward the existing order. On the other hand, ideologies have no less frequently been in fundamental error about very important aspects of social structure, especially about the working of the central institutional system, about which they have had so many hostile fantasies.

With reference to the cognitive truthfulness of ideologies, it should be pointed out that no great ideology has ever regarded the disciplined pursuit of truth—by scientific procedures and in the mood characteristic of modern science—as part of its obligations. The very conception of an autonomous sphere and an autonomous tradition of disciplined intellectual activity is alien to the totalistic demands of the ideological orientation. Indeed, ideologies do not accredit the independent cognitive powers and strivings of man.

This view is also expressed in the proposition that ideologies must necessarily be distortions of reality because they are impelled by considerations of prospective advantage or of interest. Like the ideological orientation, the view which asserts the inevitability of false consciousness assumes that cognitive motives and standards play little part in the determination of success or failure in the assessment of reality. It assumes that training in observation and discrimination and discipline in their exercise, rational criticism, and an intellectual tradition are of little importance in the formation of propositions about reality. For example, Mannheim conceived of the *freischwebende Intelligenz*, an intellectual stratum which would be able to free itself from the deformations of the ideological orientation in consequence of its "socially unattached" and therefore class-disinterested character, but he never considered that detachment could be a product of moral and intellectual training and discipline. This view is obviously incorrect in principle, even though in reality, evaluative (and therewith ideological) orientations have often hampered the free exercise of the powers of reason, observation, and judgment. Its incorrectness must be acknowledged as such by those who assert that all knowledge is ideological and that truth cannot be discerned because interests and passions interfere—at least if they believe in the truthfulness of their own assertion.

The ideological culture—in the sense described earlier—does in fact often interfere with the attainment of truth. This is, however, a result of the closure of the ideological disposition to new evidence and its distrust of all who do not share the same ideological disposition. The chief source of tension between ideology and truth lies, therefore, in the concurrent demands of the exponents of ideologies for unity of belief and disciplined adherence on the part of their fellow believers. Both of these features of the ideological orientation make for dogmatic inflexibility and unwillingness to allow new experience to contribute to the growth of truth. This applies particularly to the social sciences, the subject matter of which overlaps so considerably with that of ideology and which is therefore so often the object of ideological and quasi-ideological judgments. The tension is less pronounced with respect to the natural sciences; however, there, too, ideologies tend to inhibit the growth of understanding, because of their concern with man's nature and the nature of the universe and because of their insistence on the unity of knowledge. Thus, however great the insight contained in an ideology, the potentialities for the further development of understanding within the context of the ideology or by the efforts of the ideologists are hampered and distorted, especially where the proponents succeed in establishing control over the central institutional system (particularly the central cultural institutional system).

A related question, which has often been discussed, is whether all forms of scientific knowledge in the natural and social sciences are parts of ideologies. In the sense in which ideology has been defined and used in the foregoing analysis, this proposition must be rejected. The great advances in scientific knowledge have been influenced here and there by fragments of ideologies or quasi ideologies, just as they have been influenced, to a greater extent, by prevailing outlooks and creeds. (Outlooks and even creeds, by virtue of their inherent pluralism, allow more freedom for the uninhibited exercise of the cognitive powers of man.) But science is not and never has been an integral part of an ideological culture. Indeed, the spirit in which science works is alien to ideology. Marxism is the only great ideology which has had a substantial scientific content, and the social sciences have benefited from it in certain respects. Nonetheless, the modern social sciences have not grown up in the context of ideologies, and their progress has carried with it an erosion of ideology. It is true that the social sciences have absorbed and domesticated bits of ideologies and have formed parts of the prevailing outlooks, creeds, and movements of thought of the educated classes of various modern societies. As such they have often been opposed to, and critical of, various aspects of the existing social and cultural systems, but they themselves have seldom been ideological. Insofar as the social sciences have been genuinely intellectual pursuits, which have their own rules of observation and judgment and are open to criticism and revision, they are antipathetic to ideology. That they have come increasingly to contribute to the prevailing outlooks, movements of thought, and programs of their respective societies is not, and cannot be, relevant to any judgment concerning their truthfulness.

Although scientific activities and outlooks—in terms of both procedure and substance—are parts of a general culture or a prevailing outlook, they are very loosely integrated parts of those cultures or outlooks (just as the various parts of science are not completely integrated with each other). As explained above, it is characteristic of prevailing outlooks to be loosely integrated internally and to have no single element that predominates exclusively over the others. In a great variety of ways, the scientific and the nonscientific parts of prevailing outlooks, creeds, and movements of thought influence each other, and at the same time, each part possesses considerable autonomy. It is likely that this relationship will become more intense in the future and that scientific knowledge, although never becoming exclusively dominant, will have an even greater influence on prevailing outlooks, creeds, and movements of thought than it has had. For all these reasons, assertions to the effect that "science is an ideology" or that "the social sciences are as ideological as the ideologies they criticize" must be rejected.

The end of ideology?

In the 1950s, with the beginning of the "thaw" in the communist countries and the growing disillusionment about the realization of Marxist ideology in the advanced countries, reference was frequently made to an "end of ideology." Those who propounded this conception originally intended it to refer only to the situation existing at that time. However, antagonists of the idea took it to imply that ideologies (in the sense used in this article) could never again exist. Moreover, they also took it to mean that ideals, ethical standards, and general or comprehensive social views and policies were no longer either relevant or possible in human society. This was a misunderstanding engendered to some extent by the failure of both proponents and critics of the concept of the end of ideology to distinguish between ideology and outlook and between ideology and program. Since a better understanding of these distinctions might obviate much of the contention, I will attempt to clarify some of the issues involved.

In the first place, it is obvious that no society can exist without a cognitive, moral, and expressive culture. Standards of truth, beauty, and goodness are inherent in the structure of human action. The culture which is generated from cognitive, moral, and expressive needs and which is transmitted and sustained by tradition is part of the very constitution of society. Thus, since every society has a culture, each will have a complex set of orientations toward man, society, and the universe in which ethical and metaphysical propositions, aesthetic judgments, and scientific knowledge will be present. These will form the outlooks and creeds of the society. Thus, there can never be an "end" of outlooks and creeds. Similarly, there can never be an "end" of movements of thought and programs. The contention arose from the failure to distinguish these and ideology in the sense here understood.

However, the theoretical conception implicit in the idea of the end of ideology goes further than this. The concept implies not only that any culture is capable of being in a state of loose integration (with much autonomy of its different parts) but also that the ongoing culture of any society which has attained a considerable degree of differentiation is loosely integrated most of the time and therefore cannot be completely supplanted by an ideology. It follows that this theory regards an ideological state, which is characterized by a high degree of integration among the elements of a culture, as inherently marginal and highly unstable. According to the proponents of the end of ideology, the ideological state is one which is incapable of enduring extension to an entire society. The exponents of the end of ideology were taking note of the recession of the titanic attempts in Europe to extend the ideologies of fascism and communism to entire societies, as well as the diminution of the belief among Western intellectuals that such extensions were enduringly possible or desirable.

Moreover, those who spoke of the end of ideology did not assert or imply that the human race had reached a condition or a stage of development in and after which ideologies could no longer occur. On the contrary, the potentiality for ideology seems to be a permanent part of the human constitution. As we have seen, in conditions of crisis, when hitherto prevailing elites fail and are discredited and when the central institutions and culture with which they associate themselves seem unable to find the right course of action, ideological propensities are heightened. The need for direct contact with the sources or powers of creativity and legitimacy and for a comprehensive organization of life permeated by those powers is an intermittent and occasional need in most human beings and an overwhelming and continuous need in a few. The confluence of the aroused need in the former with the presence of the latter generates and intensifies ideological orientations.

As long as human societies are afflicted by crises and as long as man has a need to be in direct contact with the sacred, ideologies will recur. As long as there is a discrepancy between the ideal and the actual, a strong impetus for ideologies will exist. The strongly ideological potentialities of the tradition of the modern Western outlook are almost a guarantee of the persistent recurrence of ideology. The idea of the end of ideology was only an assertion that the potentiality for ideology need not always be realized and that in the 1950s this potentiality was receding in the West. It asserted that this was coming to be recognized and that both the facts and their recognition were desirable for the good ordering of society and man's well-being.

EDWARD SHILS

[*See also* KNOWLEDGE, SOCIOLOGY OF; SOCIAL MOVEMENTS. *For specific examples of ideologies, see* DEMOCRACY; FASCISM; INTERNATIONAL RELATIONS, *article on* IDEOLOGICAL ASPECTS; MARXISM; TOTALITARIANISM. *Other relevant material may be found in* ALIENATION; CONSENSUS; POLITICAL THEORY; *and in the guide to the reader under* RELIGION.]

BIBLIOGRAPHY

ARON, RAYMOND (1955) 1957 *The Opium of the Intellectuals.* Garden City, N.Y.: Doubleday. → First published in French. A paperback edition was published in 1962 by Norton. See especially pages 305–324 on "The End of the Ideological Age?"

ARON, RAYMOND 1965 Société industrielle, idéologies, philosophie. Parts 1, 2, and 3. *Preuves* no. 167:3–13; no. 168:12–24; no. 169:23–41.

BARTH, HANS (1945) 1961 *Wahrheit und Ideologie.* 2d ed., enl. Zurich: Rentsch.

BELL, DANIEL (1960) 1962 *The End of Ideology: On the Exhaustion of Political Ideas in the Fifties.* 2d ed., rev. New York: Collier. → See especially pages 21–38 on "America as a Mass Society: A Critique."

BENDIX, REINHARD 1964 The Age of Ideology: Persistent and Changing. Pages 294–327 in David E. Apter (editor), *Ideology and Discontent.* New York: Free Press.

BERGMANN, GUSTAV 1951 Ideology. *Ethics* 61:205–218.

GEERTZ, CLIFFORD 1964 Ideology as a Cultural System. Pages 47–76 in David E. Apter (editor), *Ideology and Discontent.* New York: Free Press.

JORDAN, PASCUAL 1955 Das Ende der Ideologien. *Neue deutsche Hefte* 2:581–594.

LENK, KURT (editor) (1961) 1964 *Ideologie: Ideologiekritik und Wissenssoziologie.* Neuwied (Germany): Luchterhand.

LICHTHEIM, GEORGE 1965 The Concept of Ideology. *History and Theory* 4:164–195.

LIPSET, SEYMOUR M. 1960 *Political Man: The Social Bases of Politics.* Garden City, N.Y.; Doubleday. → See especially pages 439–456 on "The End of Ideology." A paperback edition was published in 1963.

MANNHEIM, KARL (1929–1931) 1954 *Ideology and Utopia: An Introduction to the Sociology of Knowledge.* New York: Harcourt; London: Routledge. → First published in German. A paperback edition was published in 1955 by Harcourt.

OAKESHOTT, MICHAEL J. 1962 *Rationalism in Politics, and Other Essays.* New York: Basic Books. → See especially pages 1–36.

SCHMALENBACH, HERMAN 1922 Die soziologische Kategorie des Bundes. *Dioskuren* 1:35–105.

SHILS, EDWARD 1955 The End of Ideology? *Encounter* 5, no. 5:52–58.

SHILS, EDWARD 1958 Ideology and Civility: On the Politics of the Intellectual. *Sewanee Review* 66:450–480.

WEBER, MAX (1922) 1956 Umbildung des Charisma. Volume 1, pages 758–778 in Max Weber, *Wirtschaft und Gesellschaft: Grundriss der verstehenden Soziologie.* 4th ed. Tübingen (Germany): Mohr.

II
IDEOLOGY AND THE SOCIAL SYSTEM

The word "ideology" was first used, in the late eighteenth century, to mean "the study of ideas," but it soon came to refer to ideas about society, with the connotation that these ideas were distorted or unduly selective from a rational, objective point of view. It will be useful, however, to distinguish four meanings of "ideology."

(1) One of the most common uses of the term is defined as follows in *Webster's Third New International Dictionary:* "the integrated assertions, theories, and aims that constitute a sociopolitical program." Note that in this meaning an ideology embraces both normative and allegedly factual elements and that the allegedly factual elements are not *necessarily* distorted. Only slightly departing from this conception is the following definition: "*Ideology* is a pattern of beliefs and concepts (both factual and normative) which purport to explain complex social phenomena with a view to directing and simplifying sociopolitical choices facing individuals and groups" (Gould 1964, p. 315). This definition suggests the almost universal tendency of sociopolitical programs, in a polemical context, to simplify (that is, to distort) to some extent. Many writers, however, would reject the (perhaps unintended) implication that such distortion is necessarily conscious. The ideologist himself frequently distorts unwittingly; and the success of ideology, in the sense of its acceptance by a public, of course depends upon the public's being unaware on the whole that the ideas are distorted. Geertz (1964) thinks that a practical complex of ideas, values, and aims should mainly be viewed as a "schematic image of social order" in situations that are inadequately defined in traditional terms, and that the presence of distortion and selectivity should be regarded as secondary and as an empirical question in each case. "A schematic image of social order" is a possible definition of the "neutral" sense of "ideology." Not all writers who use the term "ideology" in the neutral sense, however, would confine it to ideas developed only in periods of change—but perhaps Geertz himself would not either; he happened to be writing about so-called developing countries or new nations.

(2) Another common meaning of the term "ideology" is defined in *Webster's Third New International* as follows: "an extremist sociopolitical program or philosophy constructed wholly or in part on factitious or hypothetical ideational bases." An ideology in this sense may be of the "left" or of the "right" (whatever these terms may mean in the specific sociopolitical context). An extremist ideology may be a comprehensive, closed system of ideas. It is this pretentious kind of ideology that Daniel Bell had in mind when he "defined an ideological writer as one who runs down the street crying 'I've got an answer, who's got a question?'" (see Gilroy 1966).

(3) Karl Marx, who gave prominence to the term "ideology," used it for distorted or selected ideas in defense of the *status quo* of a social system. Marxists today often use the term with this

connotation, as when they speak of "capitalist ideology"; but the various communist parties have more or less official ideologists, and they of course are not officially defined as distorters. Their task is to provide justification and apparent continuity for party policy by trying to show that particular policies and decisions are in line with the values and ideas of Marx (or Lenin, or Stalin, or Mao Tse-tung, etc.). Karl Mannheim also used the term "ideology" to refer to conservative ideas. Like Marx, he tended to imply that conservative ideas are always distorted; but, again like Marx, he was not consistent on this point. He gradually and unevenly worked away from his early view, inconsistently expressed, that all ideas are determined by their holders' position or positions in the social system and are necessarily distorted, to the more tenable view, previously expressed by Max Weber, among others, that although one's ideas may to some extent be related in various possible ways to one's social position, these ideas may or may not be distorted in the sense of being unscientific, and that the same criteria of truth and validity apply regardless of the social origin of ideas. The relevant works and aspects of Marx, Mannheim, and Weber are considered in the critical exposition and commentary by Merton ([1949] 1957, pp. 456–508).

(4) The definition of ideology adopted for the rest of this article is both broader and narrower than the foregoing definitions. Ideology consists of selected or distorted ideas about a social system or a class of social systems when these ideas purport to be factual, and also carry a more or less explicit evaluation of the "facts." This definition is narrow in that ideology consists *only* of those parts or aspects of a system of social ideas which are distorted or unduly selective from a scientific point of view. *An* ideology is a more or less coherent system of ideas in which ideological distortion is important. (Strictly speaking, the expression "ideological distortion" is pleonastic, but I shall use it nevertheless, since this technical meaning of "ideology" is not universally established.) This fourth definition of ideology is broader than some of the previous ones in that it does not restrict ideology to the conservative type. I shall return to this point below.

Since social life is complex and most people are not careful students of it, distorted ideas about social systems are extremely common. By simplifying complex situations, these ideas help many diverse people to cooperate toward the same goals. They define the situation and justify a particular course of action. Depending upon one's values and the particular circumstances, one can say, therefore, that ideology sometimes helps in achieving desirable social change, sometimes facilitates undesirable social change, and at other times facilitates desirable or undesirable resistance to social pressure for change.

Ideology and social values. Ideological distortion is either an exaggeration or an underrepresentation of the extent to which one or more social values are or can be institutionalized in the social systems in question (Parsons 1959). The precise meaning of "institutionalization" will be given below; but, briefly, the distortion in ideology has to do with the extent to which social values are actually realized or carried out in all the transactions of the system of social interaction. *Social values* are conceptions of what the social system would be like in its ideal form—conceptions, moreover, that people are committed to realizing. How many people, how deeply committed—these are variables.

This conception of ideology implies that we carefully distinguish between ideology, on the one hand, and, on the other, (1) social values themselves, (2) social science, (3) valid facts about particular social systems, and (4) nonempirical beliefs (e.g., religious ideas). The reasons for making these distinctions will appear below.

Social values. The reference to a social value system need not be direct. For example, racists in the United States (who are in a minority) believe that Negroes are biologically inferior to whites, that they are incapable of producing higher civilization, and that the attempt to integrate them with whites, or even to extend to them the right to vote (where they do not already have it), will, by encouraging eventual racial amalgamation, debase the biological conditions of civilization itself and thus destroy the American way of life. Thus, by denying, in effect, that Negroes are full human beings, these racists are denying that segregation and other forms of discrimination are really contrary to American social values. Since the racist belief is erroneous, it may be regarded as an ideology that exaggerates the extent to which certain social values are already realized in the social system of the United States. Strengthened by this ideology, these racists feel justified in resisting social reforms that the vast majority of the population favor to a varying extent.

Social science. Social science, of course, is abstract and general and consists of systematic statements about uniformities of process in social systems. Ideology, however, refers to particular social systems or classes of historical systems. Therefore, social science is not the *direct* criterion by which we judge whether or not particular ideas are ideological. The direct criterion is what Parsons (1959) calls a "value–science integrate." The ideas to be judged purport to describe a particular social system or some of its aspects. The corresponding value–science integrate is an objective description of the same social system, a description made with reference to the conceptual schemes of social science but showing to what extent in fact the cultural value system of that particular social system is carried out or realized in the various levels of its structure. If the ideas to be judged depart from this value–science integrate, the departures are said to be ideological.

This test is no doubt difficult to apply in some cases, but to deny the possibility of such a test is in effect to deny the possibility of social science. Some writers come close to doing exactly this. In the present article, however, I shall assume that there are objective and applicable criteria of validity for social science and that social science, despite its imperfections, does in fact exist and is being extended.

Note that the social values involved in a value–science integrate are empirical *data:* they are not necessarily the values of the social scientist; they are the values of the social system in question. Thus, the concept of a value–science integrate depends upon the theory, well established since the work of Durkheim, Weber, and Parsons, that the structure of a social system is fundamentally cultural and fundamentally normative, even though that structure may, of course, be stabilized in part by vested interests and even by ideology. Values are the highest level of the normative structure of a social system.

From these statements, it follows that a value–science integrate is not, in principle, either a defense of or an attack upon the social system to which it refers. To be adequate, it must show, for example, the respects in which the value system is *not* carried out, as well as the respects in which it is. In its essential neutrality, the value–science integrate differs, of course, from ideology, the function of which in a social system is always essentially polemical.

Valid facts. We do not ordinarily regard the acceptance of valid ideas as a phenomenon that requires special explanation. Many ideas that people have about the social systems in which they participate are, of course, accurate enough even from a social science point of view. But a great many popular ideas are distorted or selective and loaded with strained evaluations; and these ideas might well be the object of special investigation. Thus, the distinction between social science and valid descriptive statements, on the one hand, and ideology, on the other, is a desirable one.

Nonempirical beliefs. By definition, the conception of cognitive distortion and selectivity requires that a distinction be made between ideology and "religious" ideas (more precisely, nonempirical existential ideas). These latter are also likely, however, to be connected with ultimate social values. As was noted in passing, the stability of a *status quo* may depend, in part, upon ideology; but a given value system may be compatible with more than one set of cognitive ideas, and these need not be ideological. Therefore, it is scientifically desirable, as noted above, to distinguish between a value system itself and ideology.

Needless to say, however, all these distinctions are analytical. A particular set of ideas may contain, as elements, social values, nonempirical references, various empirical facts, and some ideological distortions.

Concept of institutionalization. The concept of institutionalization involves distinguishing four levels of social structure: values, norms, collectivities with more or less specialized goals, and status-roles. These four levels are increasingly specific in the double sense that they provide increasingly specific guidance to units in the social system and have increasingly specific reference to the situations in which these units act. All the levels are normative in a broad sense of the term. Values, norms, goals, and task-oriented roles all imply directionality and an effort to realize something desirable (from the point of view of the actor, of course).

The four levels compose a hierarchy of normative control in the sense that the more general levels are sources of legitimation for the more specific levels, provide directional guidance for the content of the more specific levels, and are sources of corrective pressure if the more specific levels depart from them. A fully institutionalized value system would be carried out ("specified," as Parsons puts it) through all the ramifications of the lower levels. This would mean that all aspects of social structure would be legitimate in the sociological sense, would be internalized in the personalities of the participants to whom they applied, would be the normative basis of operative complementary expectations in the entire interaction system, would be supported by positive and negative social sanctions, and would be the basis of legitimacy of vested interests in the system.

In fact, of course, no societal value system is fully institutionalized in this sense. Nevertheless, in any social system there is a "strain toward consistency," in the sense that the hierarchy of normative control operates as a dynamic factor to maintain pattern consistency, to correct inconsistencies, or to extend the implications of the value pattern. A social system with conflicting hierarchies of normative control that are approximately equal in power is in extreme disequilibrium. It has a grave problem of social control; it may well undergo far-reaching structural change; and, especially if it is a subsocietal system, it may be in danger of dissolution. Short of this extreme state of affairs, most social systems, although integrated to a greater extent, still are *imperfectly* integrated. Any hierarchy of control in operation encounters situational obstacles; and more or less stabilized accommodations between the situation and the value system (or one or more of its specifications) are more or less common. Various kinds and amounts of alienation and deviant behavior also occur. The normative integration of a social system is a variable matter of degree. Since social malintegration tends to generate ideology, the latter may be regarded, in many cases, as a symptom of malintegration.

Sources of ideology. This section will distinguish five fairly general interrelated sources of ideological distortion and selectivity: (1) social strain, (2) vested interests and prospective gains, (3) bitterness about social change that has already occurred, (4) limited perspective due to social position, and (5) the persistence of outmoded traditions of thought.

Social strain. One of the most general sources of distortion is the presence of strain in the social system. Strain is dissatisfaction with some aspect of the functioning of the system—with, for example, the level of goal attainment or with the distribution of rewards, opportunities, authority, or facilities. Dissatisfaction with the functioning of the system is ultimately the dissatisfaction of persons in status-roles, but the extent of strain will depend upon how many status-roles are affected and how deep the dissatisfaction is. Dissatisfaction with the value system, for instance, would necessarily mean dissatisfaction with all the levels of social structure below the value level.

Even if a social system were in perfect equilibrium, with all levels of social structure securely institutionalized, strain might well arise from some change in the environment. This does not mean, of course, that the stability of social structure requires an unchanging environment; but changes in the environment do tend to pose problems and to lead to distorted views.

Probably the most important external source of strain is cultural change. Changes in religion, science, or technology may have a profound impact on people's conceptions of what is possible and what is tolerable. Culture as an action system is, of course, interdependent with the social system, but analytically it is an independent system also, so that the impact of scientific change is technically an impact from outside the social system. The current controversy over the potential effects of automation (a result of scientific and technological change) illustrates both strain and ideological distortion. Even expert opinion ranges from the view that automation tends to increase employment opportunities to the view that, especially in the short run and in the very long run, automation threatens us with widespread unemployment and that our value system itself may have to change. It seems likely that the views being expressed cannot all be correct and that some of them express distorted conceptions even of the present society: in short, considerable ideology is involved in the discussion.

Another external source of strain and ideology is difficulty in the external relations of the social system. Frustration on a large scale is likely to be expressed, in part, in scapegoating, a particularly prominent kind of ideological distortion.

Large-scale immigration is a special case of strain arising from the environment. Persons socialized in a different social system, especially if they are numerous enough and concentrated enough to preserve a group identity and culture, may give rise to anxiety and distorted ideas. Anticipating this source of strain, an enlightened government will regulate the flow of immigration and will then take steps to forestall ideological distortion as much as possible.

Actually, of course, social systems always have some degree of malintegration, so that there are virtually always internal sources of strain. Of these, two are particularly important. First is perceived inconsistency at any level of social structure or between a higher level and a lower level or levels. An earlier section touched upon racist ideology in the United States. This ideology is in part a reaction to social pressure arising from the correction function of the hierarchy of control: Discriminatory patterns are manifestly inconsistent with the social values of equality of opportunity and equal protection of the laws, and many persons imbued with these values (whites as well as Negroes) are pressing to eliminate discrimination. This pressure and resistance to it are, of course, also connected with another source of ideology (or another aspect of the same source), vested interests and prospective gains. This point will be discussed again later.

The second internal source of strain is anomie: inadequacy of the cultural patterning of social interaction, as manifested in uncertainty and anxiety about rights and obligations and about the functioning of the social system as it affects particular social groups, categories, and persons-in-roles. In one sense of "inadequacy," the other internal source of strain (inconsistency between levels of social structure) is similar to anomie: the program implicit in the value system has been inadequately carried out. As distinguished from anomie in a narrow sense, however, the *inconsistent* patterns of expectation at a lower level or levels may be definite enough but are unacceptable because they are not fully legitimate in the sociological sense. Anomie, on the other hand (in the narrow sense intended here), is connected with two possible states of affairs.

The first is an aspect of a source of strain already mentioned—the impact of the situation upon the social system. For example, a sudden rise in unemployment or a sudden threat from another social system may produce confusion about what should be done. There may be agreement that *something* should be done, but until the political processes have had a chance to produce binding decisions and effective measures, there is likely to be considerable confusion, manifested in distorted ideas about the causes of the situation, the extent of its seriousness, and the rights and obligations of various participants in the system.

The second general cause of anomie in the narrow sense is the fact that adjustments to social change take time. Since it is characteristic of a system that its parts are interdependent, a change in one part of the system will tend to produce a kind of transitional strain until other parts of the system have caught up with the first change. During this transitional period, which may last a long time, there will be a certain amount of anomie—that is, lack of clarity in expectations. This strain is likely to be expressed in ideology as well as in other ways.

Vested interests. Closely connected with some of the above kinds of strain is concern for vested interests or prospective gains. By "vested interests" are meant all kinds of advantages, tangible and intangible, that enjoy some measure of legitimacy and protection from the *status quo* at any given time. Since the value system is seldom or never perfectly institutionalized, some vested interests are more secure than others in that they are more consistent with the value system and therefore are less likely to be successfully attacked so long as the value system itself is dominant. Any proposal for social change at the second or third level of social structure will, if successful, affect some vested interests adversely and will also bring prospective gains. In other words, social change involves a new definition of legitimate interests. The greatest redefinition of legitimate interests will occur, of course, if the value system itself is overthrown and a new one is put in its place.

The likelihood that groups and individuals who have vested interests will defend them by means of distorted arguments is too well known to require extended comment. If anything, many people exaggerate the relative importance of concern for vested interests as a source of ideology.

Those who stand to gain from a proposed social change are also, of course, likely to be less than objective in their appraisal of the *status quo* and of the general merit of the proposed change.

Bitterness. Social change usually takes place only against opposition, and even if it is successful, those who have lost something as a result of it are, of course, likely to be embittered. Thus an important source of ideology is the bitter feeling of groups, social categories, or individuals who have lost social prestige, wealth, income, or authority. They may think they see a far-reaching conspiracy against them and perceive the value system as decaying when more objective observers may feel that it has been invigorated by the social changes in question. The loss or reduction of prestige and influence can be rather subtle. For example, *cultural* differentiation in recent times has meant, in part, the growing distinctiveness of the various social sciences vis-à-vis the older humane disciplines, such as history and literature. The rise of sociology has meant the relative decline, *in certain fields of judgment*, of the influence of older literary experts. To some extent, the widespread, rather indiscriminate hostility to technical jargon expresses the status insecurity of the undifferentiated sage, who displaces his feelings by charging that dehumanization has occurred.

Limited social perspective. It may be presumed that a very general cause of distortion is the fact that everyone occupies a limited number of social positions and therefore does not have an opportunity to acquire firsthand knowledge of most of the system. Since whites in the United States have been segregated to a considerable extent from Negroes, they have also been insulated to some extent against detailed knowledge of the relative deprivation that many Negroes suffer. Consequently, many whites can innocently imagine that the value system is better realized than it actually is. This, of course, is ideology.

Outmoded science. The foregoing discussion has presented perhaps the main general sources of ideology. It is necessary to add another point. Ideology is often equated with rationalization in the psychological sense. This equation perhaps arises from the widespread and partly correct theory that ideology is essentially a defense of vested interests. Actually, however, people may have ideological ideas that are even contrary to their interests or that are related to their interests in so complex a way that experts would hesitate to attempt to calculate the net effect. Sutton and his associates (1956) pointed out this fact concerning widely held erroneous economic theories. Many people, for example, although fewer than formerly, believe that national bankruptcy is likely to occur if the national debt is allowed to get any bigger. This belief is due to misunderstanding of scientific theory or to the persistence, in popular thought, of outmoded theory. This particular belief must be regarded as ideological to the extent that it causes people to accept as inevitable problems that might be sharply reduced by appropriate government spending. In effect, these people are exaggerating the extent to which social values *have* been realized, by underestimating the extent to which they *could* be realized. Such ideology, however, is not necessarily a rationalization, for rationalization assumes that unconsciously the truth is known but cannot be faced at the conscious level.

Types of ideology. Ideologies fall fairly readily into four types: conservative, counter-, reform, and revolutionary (Parsons 1959). (We must keep in mind that the term "ideologies" means systems of doctrine that include a fairly large amount of ideology.) The four types strongly suggest the basic function of ideology, which is to define a particular program of social action as legitimate and worthy of support.

A conservative ideology cannot be identified by the content of the values it supports or advocates. It is conservative in that it is in effect an apology for the *status quo* in one or more of its aspects. A reform ideology favors reform; a revolutionary ideology favors change in the value system of the *status quo* (i.e., in the highest level of social structure); and a counterideology is an ideology that somehow by distortion or selection makes some kind of deviant behavior appear justified. A common form of counterideology is to exaggerate the extent of the deviant behavior in question and to claim that respectable people, if one only knew, practice the deviant behavior themselves but are hypocritical about it.

Perhaps it should be emphasized once more that not every conservative, reform, revolutionary, or counterdoctrine need contain a large amount of ideology. Ideology, properly speaking, is a variable element in such doctrines.

Focuses of ideology. Distorted or selective ideas tend to develop around focuses—that is, points that are crucial to the functioning of a social system. Of these, five can be usefully distinguished: (1) causes of strain, (2) extent of strain, (3) goals of social action, (4) other social systems (with which the system of reference is compared), and (5) the nature of the dominant value system and its implications.

Causes of strain. As has been noted, scapegoating is probably the most common form of ideology focused on the causes of strain. Scapegoating is the displacement of blame for frustration from the true cause onto a person or persons, a group or groups, who have little or nothing to do with the frustration. For scapegoating to occur, some at least of the scapegoaters must be unaware of the irrationality and injustice of what they are thinking and doing. They, as well as the scapegoat, must be the victims of ideology. These victims—the scapegoaters themselves—may or may not also be the victims of propagandists who are deliberately deceiving them in order to mobilize or to divert their energies. Some writers focus attention mainly on the deliberate ideologists—manufacturers, as it were, of "big lies"—but in every case one should also seek to understand both the susceptibility of the audience to the distorted ideas and the vulnerability of the scapegoat. These are related. The selection of a scapegoat is not determined by its weakness alone; the scapegoat is always *symbolically* connected with the frustrations of the scapegoaters (Parsons 1942*a*; 1942*b*).

A separate question, worthy of analysis in each case, is the effects of an episode of scapegoating upon the social system in which it occurs. Aside from the suffering of the scapegoat, which is common, an episode of scapegoating has other consequences for the social system, including the scapegoaters themselves, and these consequences vary according to circumstances. Since each case is likely to be rather complex, the reader is referred to some cases that have been well analyzed. (See Parsons 1942*a*; 1942*b*; Bell 1955; Woodward [1955] 1966, pp. 31–109.)

The causes of strain may of course be the focus of ideology in which scapegoating is only one component. Outmoded scientific ideas and slanted ideas due to limited social perspective may or may not involve scapegoating.

Extent of strain. The second focus of ideology, the extent of strain, is tantamount to a focus on grievances or alleged grievances in the social system, although strain also occurs over goal attainment. Those who are opposed to change will tend to play down or underestimate the extent of legitimate grievance; those who favor change will tend to exaggerate grievances. This does not mean, of course, either that there are never any real grievances or that grievances are always exaggerated.

Goals of social action. Closely connected with ideas about the sources and extent of strain are ideas about how the strain might be removed. Thus, reform and revolutionary movements crystallize goals for social action. At this point also there is room for ideology. In particular, reform movements may have an exaggerated or unrealistic idea of the benefits to expect if the reforms they propose are carried through. As for revolutionary movements, their tendency to foster utopian hopes is well known.

Other social systems. An ideology often refers to other social systems. According to Myrdal (1966), many people in Europe, envying the prosperity and progress of Sweden, think that the Swedes are bored and unhappy; as evidence, these envious critics like to refer to the allegedly high suicide rate in Sweden. Myrdal suggests, however, that there is little objective evidence that the Swedes are less happy than other peoples; certainly they do not have to struggle to have enough to eat, a decent place to live in, adequate medical care, and both the time and the means for recreation. As for the suicide rate, that of Sweden is actually lower than the rates in several other countries and shows no sign of becoming higher as Sweden's prosperity increases. Moreover, there are reasons for believing, even so, that the suicide rates in other countries may actually be higher than official statistics indicate, for in most countries suicide is a sin and a crime, and people cover up some suicides by reporting other causes of death; but in Sweden suicide is viewed as an individual right and a personal matter, and the ethical code of the country forbids newspapers to give publicity to suicides. Misrepresentation of Sweden in the United States is probably not due to envy, or not to envy alone. One aspect of American individualism is a playing down of problems of the nation as a whole, in the sense of playing down the need for coordinated cooperation of the whole nation toward attaining collective goals; there has even been a strong tradition of distrust of government, especially of the central government. One may speculate, therefore, that many Americans are disposed to think that the welfare state, as exemplified by Sweden, must destroy people's moral fiber and individual initiative. Many foreigners are much impressed by the relative backwardness of the United States in social welfare, the more so since the United States is the richest country in the world but has enormous urban and rural slums. Speculating further, it is probable that many Americans are unaware that private enterprise in Sweden is both highly developed and highly valued.

Ideology is extremely common in international relations, probably because of relatively poor communication and mutual distrust, rivalry, or outright hostility. According to Chinese propagandists on the mainland, the so-called proletariat in the United States is waiting to be rescued from its capitalist, imperialist oppressors. Some Chinese in Taiwan, and a few people in the United States, imagine that the totalitarian government of mainland China has little or no popular support.

In a sense, the goals of a revolutionary movement are an example of focus upon another society —an imaginary society of the future. Conservative and anomic ideologies tend to romanticize the past —that is, to present a distorted favorable conception of a type of society alleged to have existed, in which people recognized truths and values now allegedly lost or being lost.

Value system. The fifth possible focus of ideology is the value system, the chief source of legitimation. Given the hierarchy of control that operates in social systems, the legitimation of social action, whether conservative or radical, is always a matter of concern. A value system is involved in the personalities of actors, and therefore in their motivation.

A radical ideology tends to exaggerate the failure of the social system to realize the dominant values. The dominant value system is declared to be a sham; those who profess the values are said to be hypocrites. The value system is pictured as a set of fake promises, issued to forestall needed social change. This negative picture of the value system of the *status quo* is the obverse of the utopianism involved in the picture of the ideal future society, to be realized under the guidance of a new or partly new value system. Revolutionary leaders claim legitimacy on the basis of the rightness of this new value system and their commitment to it.

Examples of conservative distortion of the value system of the *status quo* are likely to be more subtle. Thus, people who resist extending civil rights to Negroes in the United States have distorted the value system by ignoring its implications. A good example was the attempt, some years ago, to deny Negroes the right to vote in some southern states by claiming that the Democratic party was a private association and could make its own rules for participation in its primaries. (The Supreme Court ruled that the parties are so intimately involved in the electoral process that to exclude qualified voters from the primaries was in effect to disfranchise them, thus denying them equal rights.) Less subtle is the distortion by conservatives of the value system of the revolutionary movement or movements to which they are opposed. This distortion may be as great as the revolutionaries' distortion of the value system of the *status quo*.

Importance of ideology. The fact that ideology is distorted or selective does not necessarily prevent it from having positive effects. Ideology may help a social system to achieve greater integration or greater adaptation or adaptive capacity. In this sense, it may be functional. For one thing, an ideology is likely to be a relatively simple definition of a complex situation—too simple, perhaps, by scientific standards, but for that very reason able to "explain" difficulties for a large number of people and able to activate them according to a common definition of the situation and a common plan. Even irrational hopes, if they are not so unrealistic as to cause grave disillusionment and greater strain, may help people to overcome their fear or their routine responses. The effects of earlier socialization, now inappropriate, may have to be neutralized. Participation in a movement for change may require loosening oneself to some extent from old loyalties and forming new ones. A certain kind of distortion connected with partisanship in general is usually considered to be an indicator of good morale, of identification with the group and loyalty to it. One would not wish one's wife to be perfectly objective about the merits of her husband.

Ideology also, however, makes it easier, at times, for people to resist desirable change blindly. No judgment about functional consequences can be made without analysis of the system in which they occur and of its situation.

Since ideology is a symbol system, it may be viewed, to some extent, as if it were a work of art; and an analyst, equipped with the proper scientific perspective, might be able to infer from it a great deal about the total orientation of those who created it or to whom it appealed successfully. Like some works of art or other products of the creative imagination—dreams, for example—an ideology may reveal, to a qualified analyst, aspects of motivation that are latent or only dimly understood by the ideologist himself. Thus, the technical analysis of ideology can be a tool for the diagnosis, so to speak, of some aspects of the functioning (or malfunctioning) of the social system. The *concept* of ideology plays a part in the sociological theory of social stability and social change.

The analysis of ideology may also have practical value. No doubt the selection of this or that body of ideas for analysis may be determined, in part, by the social scientist's own values. No matter: even if this is so, it does not necessarily mean that the analysis itself will be unscientific. In both domestic and international relations, *rational* action requires that each group expose, examine, and seek to understand dispassionately its own distortions and those of other groups. "Understanding" ideology is more than grasping the fact that distortion exists. It involves explaining *why* distortion exists, and why this particular distortion. For instance, in dealing with an adversary's distortions, it is not enough to spread "the" correct facts; it is desirable (for greater effectiveness) to take into account the particular sources of the adversary's ideology.

Control of ideology. Despite the fact that ideology may have positive functions for a social system, it is not necessary to emphasize that ignorance and error are not, generally speaking, a solid basis for the functioning of either a social system or a personality. If ideology builds up like an oyster's secretion around strain, then anything that reduces strain will tend to limit the spread of ideology. Thus, all social mechanisms for the orderly expression and redress of grievances probably tend in the long run to reduce both strain and ideology.

Parsons believes that the professions can help to limit ideology, since they link the systematic sciences and studies, on the one hand, with the broad public, on the other. In limiting ideology, social science and law are perhaps especially important; but, since selection and distortion are the defining characteristics of ideology, probably the professionalizing of journalism, with higher educational requirements, more specialization, greater professional pride and independence, and higher standards of accuracy in analyzing, reporting, and anticipating the news, also operates to limit the spread of ideology.

Ideology, values, and evaluations. Popular thinkers, including ideologists, do not explicitly and habitually think in terms of a hierarchy of normative control comprising four levels of social structure. Therefore, the relevance of Parsons' definition of ideology is not always evident at first glance. At the same time, careful analysis of popular ideas for their implicit ideological content in Parsons' sense, plus the attempt to *explain* distortion and selectivity in sociological terms, can make valuable contributions both to sociology and to practical life.

Geertz has suggested that it is hardly scientific to define ideology as distortion and selectivity. It is a fact, however, that distorted and selective ideas about social reality are extremely common, and there can be no valid objection to trying to explain why. Whether one wishes to call such ideas "ideological" is merely a matter of definition, but there is nothing unscientific about this usage. Geertz himself acknowledges that distortion does exist in social life when he attacks Edward Shils in the following way: "Shils's tack of invoking the extreme pathologies of ideological thought—Nazism, Bolshevism, or whatever—as its paradigmatic forms is reminiscent of the tradition in which the Inquisition, the personal depravity of Renaissance popes, the savagery of Reformation wars, or the primitiveness of Bible-belt fundamentalism is offered as an archetype of religious belief and behavior" (Geertz 1964, p. 51). Neither Parsons nor Shils, however, has said that political doctrines and programs are composed entirely of ideology, or even that ideology is part of every political doctrine. In their sense, ideology is an *element*, present in highly variable degree, in popular ideas (and also in ideas that purport to be scientific).

Geertz also reminds us of the symbolic and often metaphorical character of polemical doctrines. They are not always intended or understood in a literal sense. Evaluative language does not necessarily involve cognitive distortion. (For an excellent analysis of the symbolic character of an ideology, see Parsons 1942*a*; 1942*b*.)

It remains scientifically and practically interesting, however, to know what Chairman Mao Tse-tung, for example, actually believes about the United States, and why, even when one makes due allowance for the fact that some of the things he and Marshal Lin Piao say contain purely rhetorical exaggerations.

It is extremely important to keep in mind Parsons' distinction between values and cognitive conceptions. White, for example, is not to be taken as a defender of mass culture and mass-produced personalities because he showed that distortion is involved in some commentaries on contemporary American society (1961). What White and Parsons have questioned is the assumption, which many writers make, that individuality and individual initiative are less strong now in the United States than they have been in the past (Parsons & White 1961). They show that not a little ideological distortion is involved in much recent criticism of mass culture, the other-directed personality, the organization man, conformity, and the like. According to them, the progressive differentiation of contemporary society has produced more individuality, not less. This differentiation, however, with its accompanying variety of personalities, has intensified the problem of coordination and organizational integration; there is an intensified need for psychological sensitivity, and more sophistication is expected in interpersonal relations. As for the supposed disastrous decline in popular culture, Parsons and White are not out to praise comic strips and TV shows, but they do point out, as other social scientists have also done, that in times past a far larger proportion of the population could not even read, that the sources of information and entertainment were far more meager than those available today, and that far more people spent so much time in drudgery that they could hardly have cultivated their minds to any notable extent. (See, for instance, Bell 1960, chapter 1, and Bell's footnote references.)

These are matters of fact, however difficult an exact determination of the facts may be. The work of Parsons and White in analyzing certain ideological distortions common among intellectuals of the "sage" type has added considerably to Durkheim's theoretical insights concerning the important processes of social differentiation and cultural differentiation.

Several writers have noted "the end of ideology" in relatively advanced societies, whose social institutions permit a constant process of orderly self-revision. Among the characteristics of what might be called a "self-revising" society are the following: a high degree of consensus with respect to societal values (the first level of social structure); a relatively clear-cut distinction between values and norms, so that attacking norms (i.e., institutions, at the societal level) does not necessarily mean attacking the values and thus proposing a new hierarchy of control (see Smelser [1962] 1963, pp. 280–281); relative absence of the cleavage causing segments of the population to be in conflict over several important issues and keeping them from being bound by compensating common interests; a stable institutional pattern for the legislative process; and effective institutionalized channels for the expression of grievance and for obtaining redress. Such writers as, for example, Shils (1955), Lipset (1960), and Bell (1960) are not only speaking for themselves; they are also reporting and commenting upon a broad trend among Western intellectuals generally. For example, there is no longer a widespread tendency to regard capitalism and socialism as necessarily radically different in social aims. "The end of ideology" certainly does not mean that ideology in the sense of this article is disappearing in the world at large, in democratic societies generally, or even in the work of professional social scientists. What is meant is that in certain advanced societies there is, or may be, a tendency for intellectuals to be less attracted to grandiose social doctrines, doctrines that contain a few simple principles purporting to explain any and all social events, doctrines that favor drastic revolution in pursuit of utopian goals. The "end of ideology" writers cannot by any means fairly be said to be opposed to social change in general or even to revolution in general.

There may well be some truth in their contention. That some such development is likely is suggested by two broad facts. First, some societies have indeed evolved social institutions that facilitate relatively orderly social change and make violent revolution less necessary and less attractive. Second, the development of social science in these same countries has revealed the intellectual inadequacy of extremist "explanations" of complex social phenomena and has also made social scientists more aware, perhaps, of the enormous social cost of revolution and of the presence, in most revolutionary thinking, of utopian elements. For these general reasons, there may be less inclination to romanticize the idea of revolution.

Among sociologists and others, however, there is not, of course, complete agreement on these points. Whatever may be said about the decline of extremist thinking among intellectuals in self-revising societies, we may certainly continue to expect a great deal of controversy over the interpretation of particular social phenomena. Ideology by its very nature does not readily yield to scientific criticism.

HARRY M. JOHNSON

[*Other relevant material may be found in* ALIENATION; INTELLECTUALS; NORMS; SYSTEMS ANALYSIS, *article on* SOCIAL SYSTEMS; VALUES; *and in the biographies of* MANNHEIM; MARX; WEBER, MAX.]

BIBLIOGRAPHY

BELL, DANIEL (editor) (1955) 1963 *The Radical Right: The New American Right Expanded and Updated.* Garden City, N.Y.: Doubleday. → A paperback edition was published in 1964.

BELL, DANIEL (1960) 1962 *The End of Ideology: On the Exhaustion of Political Ideas in the Fifties.* 2d ed., rev. New York: Collier.

BIRNBAUM, NORMAN 1962 *The Sociological Study of Ideology, 1940–60: A Trend Report and Bibliography.* Prepared for the International Sociological Association, with the support of UNESCO. Oxford: Blackwell.

GEERTZ, CLIFFORD 1964 Ideology as a Cultural System. Pages 47–76 in David E. Apter (editor), *Ideology and Discontent.* New York: Free Press.

GILROY, HARRY 1966 Ideologies Stir P.E.N. Delegates. *New York Times* June 18: p. 29, col. 4.

GOULD, JULIUS 1964 Ideology. Pages 315–317 in Julius Gould and William L. Kolb (editors), *A Dictionary of the Social Sciences.* New York: Free Press.

LIPSET, SEYMOUR M. 1960 *Political Man: The Social Bases of Politics.* Garden City, N.Y.: Doubleday. → See especially Chapter 13.

MERTON, ROBERT K. (1949) 1957 *Social Theory and Social Structure.* Rev. & enl. ed. Glencoe, Ill.: Free Press.

MYRDAL, GUNNAR 1966 The Swedish Way to Happiness. *New York Times Magazine* January 30: pp. 14–15, 17–18, 20, 22.

PARSONS, TALCOTT 1942*a* The Sociology of Modern Anti-Semitism. Pages 101–122 in Jacques Graeber and Steuart H. Britt (editors), *Jews in a Gentile World: The Problem of Anti-Semitism.* New York: Macmillan.

PARSONS, TALCOTT 1942*b* Some Sociological Aspects of the Fascist Movements. *Social Forces* 21:138–147.

PARSONS, TALCOTT 1959 An Approach to the Sociology of Knowledge. Volume 4, pages 25–49 in World Congress of Sociology, Fourth, Milan and Stresa, 1959, *Transactions.* Louvain (Belgium): International Sociological Association.

PARSONS, TALCOTT; and WHITE, WINSTON 1961 The Link Between Character and Society. Pages 89–135 in Seymour M. Lipset and Leo Lowenthal (editors), *Culture and Social Character: The Work of David Riesman Reviewed.* New York: Free Press.

SHILS, EDWARD 1955 The End of Ideology? *Encounter* 5, no. 5:52–58.

SMELSER, NEIL J. (1962) 1963 *Theory of Collective Behavior.* London: Routledge; New York: Free Press.

SUTTON, FRANCIS X. et al. 1956 *The American Business Creed.* Cambridge, Mass.: Harvard Univ. Press.

WHITE, WINSTON 1961 *Beyond Conformity.* New York: Free Press.

WOODWARD, C. VANN (1955) 1966 *The Strange Career of Jim Crow.* 2d rev. ed. New York: Oxford Univ. Press.

ILLEGITIMACY

The term "illegitimacy" is derived from the Latin *illegitimus*, meaning "not in accordance with the law." An illegitimate child is one conceived and born outside of the regulatory sanctions of marriage. Although illegitimacy is a universal phenomenon, all societies prefer procreation only within marriage. This preference is reinforced by laws and customs that provide for a socially recognized and regulated relationship between the sexes serving to legitimize coition as well as births and to denote some responsibility for the rearing of children. Although the customs and laws regulating marriage vary considerably among different societies, they reflect an almost universal disapproval of births out of wedlock. The form and degree of this disapproval, however, vary from society to society as well as from time to time and among different groups within the same society.

There are three basic measures of illegitimacy: number, ratio, and rate. The number of illegitimate births indicates the total volume of illegitimacy and is used to compute the ratio and rate. The *illegitimacy ratio* is the number of illegitimate births per 1,000 live births. This measure indicates the proportion of all reproduction occurring outside of marriage and is used to show whether illegitimacy is increasing or decreasing in a specific population. The *illegitimacy rate*, in the technical sense of the term, is the number of illegitimate births per 1,000 unmarried females of childbearing ages; it indicates whether illegitimacy is increasing or decreasing in relation to the opportunities for it. The term "rate of illegitimacy" is used frequently in a less technical sense to denote the illegitimacy ratio as a percentage of 100, in which case a "4 per cent rate of illegitimacy" indicates a ratio of 40 illegitimate births per 1,000 live births.

Extent and variation of illegitimacy

The foregoing definition and measures of illegitimacy provide at best only a very general guide for comparing the occurrence of illegitimacy in different countries. Wide variations exist among countries in the statutes and cultural traditions regulating marriage, coition, and reproduction, and it is these statutes and customs that define which births are "not in accordance with the law." Comparisons among countries, as well as among different socioeconomic groups within a given country, are further complicated by differences in the completeness of birth registration, by the extent of misrepresentation on birth records to conceal illegitimate births, and by variations in the methods used to measure illegitimacy. In some countries illegitimacy rates are based on births to women between the ages of 15–24, and the term "unmarried women" is defined strictly as those who have never married; however, in other countries the rate is based on the entire range of childbearing ages from 10 to 49 and may include adulterine births, as well as children born to widowed or divorced women as a result of extramarital unions.

A few examples based on data for the mid-1950s will illustrate that illegitimacy is understandable only within the context of its entire sociological and historical setting and therefore cannot be viewed as a cross-cultural index of sexual morality. World illegitimacy ratios in 1958 ranged from a low of 4 in Israel to a high of 739 in Panama (*Demographic Yearbook 1959*, table 10). In a number of Central American countries and Caribbean political units where illegitimacy ratios exceed 500, there are sizable indigenous populations that adhere to tribal and religious marital rites and remain indifferent to the concept of legal marriage. Consequently, a very high illegitimacy ratio based on the concept of legal marriage would include most of the births the parents view as having been legitimized by long-standing tribal and religious rites. An illustrative case is Mauritius, where the illegitimacy ratio decreased from 498 in 1954 to 11 in 1955, when infants born of marriages performed by religious authority but not registered or performed by civil authorities were no longer considered illegitimate (*Demographic Yearbook 1954; 1955*).

Comparisons among countries also need to take into account such factors as abortions, marriages preceded by conceptions, and the average age at marriage. For example, in the mid-1950s Panama's illegitimacy ratio was almost fifty times higher than Japan's (*Demographic Yearbook 1959*), but in Japan legalized abortions annually exceeded one million—a total approximately equal to the number of all live births (Taeuber 1958). Jamaica's illegitimacy ratio in the mid-1950s was about fifteen times that of the United States, but the average age at marriage was ten years older in Jamaica than in the United States. In 1957 Denmark's ratio of 69 was considerably lower than that of Honduras (645), Venezuela (566), Paraguay (455), Ecuador (351), Iceland (250), and Mexico (236); however, in Denmark about one-third of all marital first births occurred within the first six months of marriage (*Demographic Yearbook 1959*).

Gross historical trends. In highly industrialized countries, illegitimacy generally decreases or is relatively low during periods of economic depression and the early years of a major war. On the other hand, it increases or is relatively high during periods of economic prosperity and the immediate postwar years and is generally highest when prosperity and an immediate postwar period coincide. In many of the industrialized countries of western Europe and North America, illegitimacy ratios in the late 1950s had declined from the high ratios in the postwar period of the late 1940s but were still considerably higher than in the economic depression years of the 1930s. The very limited data available for the World War I period show that illegitimacy ratios followed a pattern similar to that for World War II (see Vincent 1961, chapter 1).

For countries in the early stages of industrialization, the illegitimacy ratio usually increases very rapidly at first and then fluctuates quite unpredictably. This may be the result of changes in traditional familial patterns and sexual mores and even of more far-reaching changes in basic demographic conditions. Interpretation of such gross trends is subject to many exceptions and limitations of data, some of which may be illustrated with specific reference to the United States.

Illegitimacy in the United States. In the United States during the period 1938–1958, the estimated number of illegitimate births increased from 87,900 to 208,700; the estimated number of illegitimate births per 1,000 live births (the *illegitimacy ratio*) from 38.4 to 49.6; and the estimated number of illegitimate births per 1,000 unmarried females of childbearing age (the *illegitimacy rate*) from 7.0 to 21.0 (Vincent 1961, p. 1; for more recent information see U.S. National Vital Statistics Division . . . , annual issues). The limitations of such data, however, made it difficult to establish whether there had been a true increase in illegitimacy during this period. The number of illegitimate births, on which ratios and rates were based, reflected a marked increase in total live births, and there was also a substantial increase in the number of states not recording illegitimacy status on birth records (from 5 in 1940 to 15 in 1960). The estimates of nonrecording states not only complicated national estimates but also may have affected the figures from recording states. For example, the state of Utah had one of the lowest ratios and rates of any recording state during this period; however, Utah is almost encircled by nonrecording states, and it is known that a considerable proportion of unmarried mothers in the United States migrate temporarily from their home states during pregnancy (see, for instance, Vincent 1961, pp. 208–209).

A further complication in assessing the nature and amount of increase in illegitimacy in the United States involves the far greater increase in the number of illegitimate births to nonwhite mothers than to white mothers—an increase of from 46,700 to 147,500 for nonwhites as contrasted with an increase from 41,200 to 93,500 for whites, the years compared being 1938 and 1962 (Vincent 1964, table 2, p. 515). However, during this same period there was also a considerable increase in the proportion of all nonwhite live births taking place in hospitals or attended by physicians elsewhere (50.8 per cent in 1940, compared with 89.1 per cent in 1961); the increase in the proportion of white live births so attended was less than one tenth as great (*ibid.*, table 3). If it is assumed that an illicit birth is more likely to be reported as such when attended by a member of the medical profession than when attended by a midwife, relative, or friend (especially at home), much of the apparent increase in Negro illegitimacy may have represented only a more complete and accurate counting.

In the late 1950s, a greater awareness of such data limitations resulted in increased questioning of the racial, age, socioeconomic, and rural–urban differences in illegitimacy that had been emphasized in the 1930s and 1940s. There was also increased recognition that the focuses of public concern about illegitimacy were not always reliable guides for research. The considerable public concern focused upon the increasing number of very young unmarried mothers in the late 1950s and early 1960s, for example, did not take into account either the marked increase in the total population of young teen-agers or the fact that between 1938 and 1957 the illegitimacy *rate* had increased least among females aged 15–19 (108 per cent) and most among females aged 25–29 (453 per cent) (adapted from Schachter & McCarthy 1960, tables D and F). During the more recent period of 1957–1962, the illegitimacy rate for females between 15 and 19 years old actually decreased by 4 per cent; for the same period, the rate increases for each five-year grouping of those aged 20 and older ranged from 3 per cent for the 30–34 age group to 23 per cent for the 25–29 age group (Vincent 1964, table 1, p. 514). In 1962 the illegitimacy rate was only 15 per cent for those aged 15–19, whereas it ranged between 27 per cent and 46 per cent for each five-year grouping of those aged 20–34 (*ibid.*).

Causes of illegitimacy

Prior to about 1960, explanations of illegitimacy in western Europe and the United States were limited primarily to descriptions of social, familial, and psychological factors found to be associated with selected groups of unmarried mothers. These descriptions reflected historical trends in the choice of etiological scapegoats. In the 1920s the descriptions of unmarried mothers found in rescue homes and other charitable institutions were consistent with the contemporary emphasis upon immorality and mental deficiency as causes of illegitimacy. In the 1930s the official records of unmarried mothers found in domestic court files and homes for wayward girls reinforced the popular emphasis upon broken homes, poverty, and disorganized neighborhoods as "causes" of illegitimacy. In the 1940s and early 1950s the histories of unmarried mothers studied by psychiatric social caseworkers and psychotherapists appeared to support the fashionable emphasis on emotional disturbances. However, such descriptions, although applicable to the groups studied, did not explain why the majority of all females who fitted the descriptions did not become unwed mothers. In the late 1950s studies of unmarried mothers made from multiple sample sources at last provided tentative evidence that within given age and social groups such mothers were fairly representative of the general population of unmarried females with respect to education, intelligence, and socioeconomic status (Vincent 1961).

In the early 1960s research on illegitimacy showed a definite trend toward a more comprehensive focus. Improvements in vital statistics as well as their availability from an increasing number of countries were beginning to stimulate cross-culture analyses (see especially Goode 1960; 1961). These studies were guided by more sophisticated, sociocultural theories of illegitimacy and indicated modifications of Malinowski's "principle of legitimacy." This principle involved what Malinowski interpreted to be a universal social rule, that "no child should be brought into the world without a man—and one man at that—assuming the role of sociological father, that is, guardian and protector, the male link between the child and the rest of the community" (1930, p. 137). Goode's analysis of attitudes and social practices in a number of Caribbean political units—where illegitimacy rates exceed 50 per cent and where there exists differential status placement for legitimate and illegitimate children, as well as for illegitimates of different social strata—underlies his modifications of Malinowski's principle. According to Goode, the principle of legitimacy rests primarily upon the function of status placement rather than upon that of locating a father as "protector"; and he argues that Malinowski's interpretation does not take into account the differences in norm commitment among different strata.

Additional evidences of the trend toward more comprehensive research include the long-neglected study of males who have impregnated unmarried mothers; longitudinal studies of young, unmarried, and never pregnant females to ascertain factors associated with those who subsequently become unmarried mothers; follow-up studies of mothers who keep their illegitimate children and of recidivistic unmarried mothers; and studies of the more inclusive category of unwanted pregnancies, legitimate as well as illegitimate. Studies are now in progress in each of these areas.

Social attitudes and public policy

One gross historical trend in social attitudes and public policy concerning illegitimacy has been the gradual change from the child to the mother (and quite recently to the father) as the target of censure. In the Middle Ages, the common law of England was ruthless in its denial of rights to illegitimate children. The bastard was scorned, derided, and punished to such an extent that in retrospect it would almost appear that he was held responsible for the circumstances of his own birth. The English Poor Law Act of 1576 made the mother and putative father responsible for the child's maintenance; bastardy was not an offense against the criminal laws, but bearing an illegitimate child who might become a public charge became an offense against the poor laws. The purpose of the Poor Law Act, as well as that of the legislation on the support of bastards enacted early in the history of the United States, was to prevent the child from becoming dependent on the community. Under early Germanic law, bastards had to be cared for and supported by the mother under the kinship group. In France, prior to the early 1800s, the illegitimate child had the right to support by the father; however, from the adoption of the Code Napoléon until 1912, the investigation of paternity was expressly forbidden, and neither the unmarried mother nor the illegitimate child had any legal recourse (Brinton 1936).

Modern developments. During the second decade of the twentieth century, however, a new philosophy began to make itself felt. A Norwegian law of 1915 pioneered in making the state, rather than the mother, responsible for establishing paternity and for fixing maintenance, and the Scandinavian countries led the industrialized societies in establishing statutes by which the state sought to provide greater equality of rights for the illegitimate child. In the U.S.S.R. the elimination of illegitimacy by fiat in the Family Code of 1918, which recognized no legal or social distinction between a child born in and one born out of wedlock, was consistent with other familial and social changes following the 1917 revolution. U.S.S.R. family law now provides financial gratuities and honorific titles for unwed as well as married mothers who bear three or more children and gives the state responsibility for rearing all children of unwed and married mothers unable to do so. However, article 19 of the 1944 Family Decree provides that only registered marriages create legal obligations and rights. Thus, if the mother remains unmarried, she can either receive a small monthly stipend to assist in rearing her child or she can place the child in a special government institution established for this purpose; but the child cannot claim either the father's property or his name (Field 1955). This denial of inheritance, with its resulting differential status placement for legitimate and illegitimate children, is consistent with the observations by David and Vera Mace (1963, pp. 240–244) that there is a trend toward harsher attitudes concerning the unmarried mother and her child in the U.S.S.R.

There was an apparent temporary reversal of the liberal trend in attitudes toward illegitimacy in Japan, Germany, and England during the immediate post-World War II period, but this reversal was selective in that it involved far greater censure of illegitimacy resulting from the presence of United States troops than of indigenous illegitimacy and was probably more indicative of feelings among the respective countries than of Western attitudes in general. Increasingly in the twentieth century the legislation formerly concerned with protecting citizens from having to support illegitimate children has now turned to emphasizing the enforcement of parental responsibility for them; to this end, public funds have been appropriated to help in assuring the rights and well-being of illegitimate children.

United States. In the United States the liberal trend became apparent between 1930 and 1960. There were increased efforts to accord to illegitimate children the same care and legal and social rights accorded to other children; for example, an increasing number of states no longer recorded illegitimacy status on birth records. The number of illegitimates in the United States was estimated in 1960 at seven million. By that time more than 150 maternity homes had been developed under private auspices to care for unmarried mothers, and federal social security benefits under the Aid to Dependent Children (ADC) program had been made available for illegitimate children.

There were a few exceptions to this liberal trend in the United States in the early 1960s, including considerable criticism of low-income Negro females who had repeated illegitimate births. Two southern states (North Carolina and Louisiana) attempted to legislate provisions for the sterilization of females having more than one illicit pregnancy, although repeated illegitimate births had been condoned if not encouraged as a subcultural pattern in the South at an earlier time, when economic practices placed a higher value on Negro females as reproducers (in or out of wedlock) of future plantation workers than as wives to their husbands. In the early 1960s there was also increased criticism that the ADC program was providing an indirect subsidy of illegitimacy, and some states considered excluding illegitimate children of recidivistic unwed mothers from ADC benefits, although evidence indicated that less than 10 per cent of all illegitimate children received such benefits (U.S. Bureau of Family Services 1960).

Future world trends. The apparent world-wide liberal trend in social policy concerning illegitimacy during the first six decades of the twentieth century faced some opposition at the beginning of the 1960s. The demand for adoptable infants exceeded the supply during the late 1940s and early 1950s, when the higher birth rates for many countries were viewed initially as compensating for the population losses of World War II and the low birth rates of the 1930s. During the postwar period this demand minimized the censure of unwed mothers, who provided childless couples with adoptable infants, and stimulated at the international level a variety of laws and activities concerned with the adoption and rights of illegitimate children. Beginning in the late 1950s and early 1960s, however, a marked decrease in the demand for adoptable infants and a growing concern about the "population explosion" have had the potential to reverse this liberal trend of social policy.

CLARK E. VINCENT

[*See also* ADOPTION; FERTILITY CONTROL; POPULATION, *article on* POPULATION POLICIES.]

BIBLIOGRAPHY

BRINTON, CRANE 1936 *French Revolutionary Legislation on Illegitimacy: 1789–1804.* Cambridge, Mass.: Harvard Univ. Press.

DAVIS, KINGSLEY 1939 Illegitimacy and the Social Structure. *American Journal of Sociology* 45:215–233.

Demographic Yearbook. → Issued annually by the United Nations since 1948. See especially the yearbooks covering 1954, 1955, and 1959.

FIELD, MARK G. 1955 Social Services for the Family in the Soviet Union. *Marriage and Family Living* 17: 244–249.

GOODE, WILLIAM J. 1960 Illegitimacy in the Caribbean Social Structure. *American Sociological Review* 25: 21–30.

GOODE, WILLIAM J. 1961 Illegitimacy, Anomie, and Cultural Penetration. *American Sociological Review* 26: 910–925.

MACE, DAVID R.; and MACE, VERA 1963 *The Soviet Family.* Garden City, N.Y.: Doubleday.

MALINOWSKI, BRONISLAW 1930 Parenthood: The Basis of Social Structure. Pages 113–168 in Victor F. Calverton and Samuel D. Schmalhausen (editors), *The New Generation: The Intimate Problems of Modern Parents and Children.* New York: Macaulay.

REED, RUTH 1934 *The Illegitimate Family in New York City: Its Treatment by Social and Health Agencies.* New York: Columbia Univ. Press. → Contains an annotated bibliography of 384 references published between 1912 and 1933.

SCHACHTER, JOSEPH; and MCCARTHY, MARY 1960 *Illegitimate Births: United States, 1938–1957.* Washington: Government Printing Office.

SHAPIRO, SAM 1950 Illegitimate Births: 1938–1947. U.S. National Office of Vital Statistics, *Vital Statistics—Special Reports* 33:69–106.

TAEUBER, IRENE B. 1958 *The Population of Japan.* Princeton Univ. Press.

U.S. Bureau of Family Services 1960 *Illegitimacy and Its Impact on the Aid to Dependent Children Program.* Washington: Government Printing Office.

U.S. National Vital Statistics Division 1939— *Vital Statistics of the United States.* Washington: Government Printing Office. → Published since 1939; the 1939 issue covers the year 1937.

Vincent, Clark E. 1961 *Unmarried Mothers.* New York: Free Press. → Contains a bibliography of 191 items.

Vincent, Clark E. 1964 Illegitimacy in the Next Decade: Trends and Implications. *Child Welfare* [1964]: 513–520.

ILLITERACY

See Literacy; Reading disabilities.

ILLNESS

In non-Western, relatively nonindustrialized and nonurbanized societies, illness is characteristically perceived, defined, experienced, and treated as a condition that is not only biological, psychosomatic, and metaphysical, but also "sociosomatic" in nature. That is, illness is viewed as a physical, spiritual, and psychological state that is significantly influenced and can even be caused by such social and cultural factors as the social status an individual occupies and the reactions it evokes in him and in others; the quality of his relations with the members of his family and with other persons important to him or to his kin; and the strength of his commitment and the degree of his conformity to the norms and taboos of his society.

Although this insight is also a part of Western medical thought and tradition, for many centuries in Western societies it was overshadowed by a preoccupation with the "natural," physical causes of disease, their detection, and their mastery through the media of science and technology. It was not until the mid-nineteenth century in European and American societies that an appreciation of the role of social and cultural factors in health and illness became salient and organized enough to lead to the contention that "medicine is a social science" and to the expression of that conviction in a series of public health, social hygiene, and social medicine measures and movements (Rosen 1963). In the mid-twentieth century the attempt to understand the interrelationships between physical and emotional illness, on the one hand, and social and cultural forces, on the other hand, has become sufficiently analytic and systematic for the emergence of a scientific subfield that might appropriately be called the "sociology of illness." This empirical area of inquiry is not a domain exclusive to sociology. Rather, it has developed out of the convergent and collaborative investigations of internists, psychiatrists, psychologists, and cultural anthropologists, as well as sociologists. In this regard, it reflects a trend larger than itself—a progressive tendency for interdisciplinary work in the behavioral sciences.

Illness as a social role. Perhaps the most important theoretical contribution to the sociology of illness has been made by Talcott Parsons in his conception of illness as a social role characterized by certain patterned exemptions, rights, and obligations that are shaped by the society of which the sick person is a member (T. Parsons 1948; 1951; 1958; 1964; T. Parsons & Fox 1952). Parsons has defined the attributes of the sick role in contemporary Western society, and particularly in present-day American society, in the following way. First, the sick person is exonerated from certain kinds of responsibility for his illness: he is not held morally accountable for having gotten sick, nor is he expected to make himself better. He is also considered to have some impairment in his capacity to carry out normal role and task obligations, and thus, according to the nature and degree of his illness, the sick person is exempted from some of his usual activities and responsibilities. Moreover, because of these rights and exemptions, which are not normally accorded to persons in the society, the sick person may be said to be cast in a type of deviant role. This is a deviant role that is partially and conditionally legitimated—one that is contingent on certain obligations to which the sick person is subject. Thus the sick person is expected to define the state of being ill as undesirable and to do everything possible to try to get well. Above all, he is enjoined to seek technically competent advice and help, preferably from a qualified physician. In so doing, he enters the role of patient, who is expected to facilitate his recovery by cooperating with a doctor. In modern Western society this includes willingness to submit to the techniques and facilities of medical science, to the ministrations of other designated medical personnel, and to hospitalization if it is deemed necessary.

Definitions of illness. Once designated as ill by socially authorized medical agents, the individual gains access to certain rights and becomes subject to certain duties. What he presents as a potential illness to a medical practitioner, and what the practitioner in turn diagnoses, certifies, and treats as illness, is determined as much by social and cultural factors as by biological considerations. The extent to which the definition of illness and treatment is contingent on the state of society's knowledge, its prevalent value system, and its institutional structure was insightfully satirized by Samuel

Butler in his novel *Erewhon*, written in 1872. In Erewhon (the fictitious country that Butler created by imagining late nineteenth- and early twentieth-century England stood on its head), persons afflicted with what physicians would call tuberculosis are found guilty in a court of law and sentenced to life imprisonment, whereas persons who forge checks, set houses on fire, steal, and commit acts of violence are diagnosed as "suffering from a severe fit of immorality" and are cared for at public expense in hospitals. Indeed, it is a historical fact that over the past few centuries in western European and American societies, partly as a consequence of certain far-reaching social and cultural changes, we have seen a progressive process by which persons with psychological disorders, who in an earlier era would have been adjudged "wicked," "possessed by the devil," or "criminal," have come to be regarded as mentally or emotionally ill and treated accordingly [*see* SOCIAL CONTROL].

This close and sensitive interrelationship between social and cultural forces, on the one hand, and the attitudes, sentiments, and behaviors defined as illness in a society or group at a given time, on the other hand, has been amply documented in medical and social scientific literature. Numerous studies demonstrate that what constitutes an illness or disability in one society or in a particular subgroup of a society is not necessarily regarded as such in other societies or groups. For example, the Navajo Indians of the southwestern United States do not view a congenital dislocation of the hip as a disease or handicap (McDermott et al. 1960, pp. 280–281). In "Regionville," a town in upper New York State, members of the highest socioeconomic class generally report a persistent backache to a physician as a medical symptom, whereas members of the lowest socioeconomic class regard it as an inevitable and innocuous part of life and thus as inappropriate for referral to a doctor (Koos 1954).

The anthropological and social psychiatric literature also contains descriptions of patterned beliefs and behaviors that would be considered manifestations of emotional illness in modern Western societies, but which in traditional tribal or folk milieus are part of the culturally accepted and sanctioned magicoreligious system. In rural villages of the western region of Nigeria, for instance, *elére* or *elegebe* are alternative terms applied to a child who is believed to have invisible little people three feet high as playmates. The parents of such a child respond in the culturally indicated way by providing small feasts for these miniature beings in order to invoke their benevolence and protection (Cornell–Aro . . . 1963, pp. 36, 80, 146–147). Finally, anthropological field workers have reported certain symptoms, apparently sociopsychosomatic in nature, that seem to be unique to a particular society or subculture—for example, *coléra*, a culturally patterned attack of rage that occurs among the populations of Indian villages in Guatemala (Paul 1953), and *empacho*, a stress-induced digestive condition that affects Mexican-Americans in Texas (Rubel 1960).

The experience of illness. In modern Western society, an individual who is defined as ill and cast in the sick role is regarded as being in a state attributable to causes that fall outside the realm of both his personal control and his moral responsibility. However, it would seem, as Bronislaw Malinowski has eloquently suggested (1925), that illness is an emotional and an existential experience of such magnitude for human beings that they generally find it difficult to think of their illness in purely nonmetaphysical and nonmoral terms, even when the society of which they are members encourages them to do so. There is a paradoxical sense in which a society or a group that insists upon an exclusively logico-rational explanation of sickness, thus precluding religious, moral, or magical considerations, may augment rather than decrease the "problems of meaning" with which persons in that society feel themselves confronted when they become ill. At any rate, such empirical studies as we have of the deeper emotional reactions of gravely ill, hospitalized patients in present-day American society reveal them as grappling with the "whys" of their illness in moral, religious, and cosmic, as well as medical terms; they do not have the easily available, legitimate recourse to the transcendent explanations provided by most non-Western, less science-oriented societies (Fox 1959, pp. 132–135).

The experience of illness as an event that is more than natural may be universal. But the particularities and nuances of the emotional meaning of an illness to an individual and the nature of his affective response to his state and symptoms are profoundly influenced by his social and cultural background as well as by his personality traits. For example, it has been observed that people in Japan like to go to bed with mild illnesses not only because they receive attention for small aches and pains but also because illness provides the patient and family members who care for him with a culturally approved way of living out and nonverbally communicating the sorts of deep, tender feelings of love and concern that are not ordinarily expressed in even the most intimate of relations between Japanese (Caudill 1961).

Whereas the emotional atmosphere around illness in Japan tends to be "peaceful," intensive case studies of southern Italian women hospitalized for schizophrenia reveal that a striking number of these patients feel and act in a "jealous, capricious" pattern that is apparently related to some of the competitive, aggressive, emotionally charged, and labile ways of reacting and behaving that are characteristic of socialization and family life in southern Italy (A. Parsons 1960). Emotionality and volatile behavior in the face of both physical and psychological illness have been observed to be characteristic not only of patients of southern Italian background but also of Jewish patients. This is in part a consequence of the fact that the expression of strong feelings is socioculturally permitted, expected, and favored in the Jewish and Italian families from which these patients come; in these particular groups, crying out in the face of illness is felt to be a way of helping to get the sickness "out of one's system," along with the emotions it engenders, as well as a way of mobilizing the intensive concern and support of one's family (Mechanic 1963; Zborowski 1952).

The degree to which this highly affective way of responding to illness is contingent on social and cultural factors is supported by the finding that patients from other social groups with socialization and family patterns that discourage the exhibition of certain kinds of strong feelings show a consistent tendency to behave in a quite different characteristic fashion. For example, patients of Anglo-Saxon Protestant origins who are afflicted with pain-accompanied conditions have been noted to be controlled, forbearing, and almost clinically detached in their attitudes and behaviors (Zborowski 1952), whereas seriously ill Irish-American patients have been reported as engaging in counterphobic, gallows humor and joking behavior as one of their shared ways of coping with the physical and emotional stresses of their situation (Fox 1959, pp. 175–177, 190).

Not only do the basic emotional meanings of illness and patterned ways of reacting to it vary systematically in certain ways from one group to another, but also in illness, as in health, society and culture penetrate so deeply into the unconscious layers of the individual's psyche that they even influence the inner imagery he experiences. This is most clearly seen in connection with emotional illness, where social and cultural factors are among the most important determinants of the extent to which patients have delusions and fantasies, how rich and elaborate they are, and precisely what form they take (Cornell–Aro . . . 1963; Opler 1959; A. Parsons 1961; Paul 1953).

Illness, deviance, and social control

In virtually all societies the person who is ill is regarded as being in an exceptional and implicitly deviant role. Manifestly, as in modern Western society, illness may be defined as "not the fault" either of the person beset by it or of those with whom he is interrelated. In certain historical eras and in particular religious and moral contexts, illness may even be looked upon as an indicator of a special state of grace. For example, in traditional Christian thought disease is regarded as a form of suffering that purifies the soul of man and brings him closer to God (Sigerist 1960), and throughout most of the nineteenth century in western European society there was a romantic tendency to associate tuberculosis with intellectual and artistic genius (Dubos & Dubos 1952, pp. 44–66). But inherent in even such sympathetic and glorifying cultural attitudes toward illness is the conception that sickness is a state that is not, and ideally should not be, the collective and continuing fate of many persons; that is, it is a condition out of which one should graduate if possible, through a combination of will, effort, good fortune, and the help of others.

If one begins to reflect on what would be the consequences for a society if a large proportion of its population were to secede from normal social tasks and obligations, invoking illness as their legitimate reason for doing so, it becomes apparent why illness is usually socially defined as a kind of deviance and why, in every society, the right to certify illness as bona fide is assigned only to certain persons in certain roles. The effect of great numbers of persons in a society taking to their beds could, in its passive way, be as disruptive of the usual functioning of that social system as an insurgent refusal on the part of those same individuals to tend to their daily activities and responsibilities. The exemption, withdrawal, and dependence that illness characteristically entails is an especially strategic and threatening form of deviance in certain kinds of societies—for example, in the United States, with its high cultural emphasis on responsibility, activity, achievement, and independence (T. Parsons & Fox 1952), or in Soviet Russia, where, in the name of the collective industrial and agricultural development of the society, maximum effort, work, and productivity are expected of all citizens at all times (Field 1957, pp. 146–180).

In modern Western societies, the agent who screens signs and symptoms, makes a professional judgment as to whether or not they constitute illness as the society he represents defines it, and formally certifies an ill person as legitimately meriting certain dispensations is the physician. In so doing, he performs several latent social control functions. He sorts out "malingerers"—those who unconsciously or consciously feign or simulate illness—from those who are authentically ill, according to the medical and scientific criteria recognized and institutionalized in the society (Szasz 1956). In principle, he refuses to acknowledge the conditions of malingerers as real and legitimate illnesses and denies them the exonerations of sickness. With respect to those individuals whom the physician certifies as ill, he sets into motion a therapeutic process, which is composed of sociopsychological as well as physical elements and which is designed to return the patient to full-scale participation in his society. In modern Western society the focal site of this process has become the hospital.

The functions of hospitalization. The prevalence of hospitalization is associated with the specialized personnel and facilities that scientific medicine can now bring to bear on the diagnosis and treatment of illness. In the hospital trained professionals, technical apparatus, and medicaments are coordinated and mobilized in a way that could scarcely be replicated in a physician's private office or in a sick person's home. Reinforcing these manifest technological and administrative reasons for the widespread hospitalization of the ill in modern Western society are latent sociopsychological factors.

As Parsons and Fox have pointed out (1952), the small, conjugal, relatively isolated, close-knit, emotionally intense family unit characteristic of such an urbanized and industrialized society, with its focus on the formation and integration of the personalities of its members and its emphasis upon achievement, is prone to certain difficulties in dealing with illness. The sick role, comprising as it does a semilegitimate channel of withdrawal from adult responsibilities and a basis of eligibility for care by others, is inviting to various family members in patterned, often unconsciously motivated ways. To the wife–mother of the modern urban family it offers an institutionalized way of reacting to her heavy affective–expressive responsibilities in the family and a compulsively feministic way of reacting to her exclusion from certain prerogatives and opportunities open to the man. For the husband–father, illness legitimizes respite from the discipline, effort, and dualistic demands of interdependence and autonomy that his occupation demands of him. For the child, being moved by the process of socialization along the tension-ridden path toward adulthood, illness provides an escape from increasingly exacting obligations to behave as a mature person. And for the elderly individual, retired from the occupational system, widowed, and with no traditionally assured place in the families established by his children, illness may serve as an opportunity to solicit forcibly their concern and care.

Not only are the members of the modern urban family prone to illness in these sociopsychologically influenced ways, but they are also likely to be emotionally threatened by the illness of a person in their small, tightly knit, affectively toned family unit with its particular kinds of strains. Under these circumstances there is a high probability that the family will overreact to the illness of one of its members with either excessive sympathy or excessive severity. Such responses can impede the full and rapid recovery of the ill person.

In the light of these family vulnerabilities, it would seem that one of the important latent functions of hospitalizing the sick person is to insure the more effective social control of illness. Hospitalization places the patient in an extrafamilial setting, where he is less likely to be emotionally reinforced in illness and where professional objectivity and dispassion in the attitudes and behavior of the medical staff provide leverage to move him out of the sick role. At the same time, isolating the sick person from members of his family mitigates their emotional strain and thus helps them resist the contagious temptation to take to their beds in response to the situation.

The hospital as a social system. However, life in the ward of a hospital is accompanied by its own particular stresses and potential seductions. A small but steadily growing number of studies of (largely American) psychiatric and general hospitals as social systems has yielded some insights into what it is like, sociologically and psychologically, to be a hospitalized patient (Belknap 1956; Caudill 1958; Coser 1962; Davis 1964; Fox 1959; Goffman 1961; Greenblatt et al. 1957; Stanton & Schwartz 1954). The physical and psychological symptoms of illness and the attributes of the sick role that the individual enters once he is diagnosed as ill subject him to certain tensions, regardless of whether or not he is hospitalized. These include incapacity and inactivity; uncertainty as to the prognosis and eventual outcome of the illness; in some cases, the objective prospect of nonrecovery and the imminence of death; problems of meaning; isolation from the world of the normal and healthy; submission to the authority of medical science, the physician, and other medically trained personnel (Merton & Barber 1963, pp. 111–113). Entering the hospital as a patient, however, increases the extent to which the ill person is removed, psychically and socially as well as physically, from the universe of the healthy. It subjects him totally to the care, control, and technology of modern medicine and the complex team that administers it. Under certain conditions it makes him a potential object of medical experimentation and research (Fox 1959). And it introduces him into a new "small society," which demands that he become an adjusted and cooperative member. [*See* DEATH.]

Every one of the studies made of the hospital as a social system describes it as an elaborately structured, rigidly stratified, tightly disciplined bureaucratic organization. These characteristics are viewed as functionally related to the fact that the hospital staff must survey and regulate virtually all the activities of a large number of patients and to the fact that the staff must be geared to respond to medical exigencies, dangers, and emergencies with the synchrony of a precise, resolute, swift-moving team. These characteristics of the hospital have at least two significant consequences for the attitudes and conduct of patients.

Patients who are hospitalized for a long time may become so habituated to a predictable round of daily activities and a clearly delineated set of duties, rights, and privileges that any alteration in them may be experienced as disturbing. In the case of children, this routinized compliance to an impersonal institutional authority may have dysfunctional consequences for their psychosocial development. It may cause them to regress, at least temporarily, to an earlier stage of socialization where they depend more on external than on internal superego type controls (Davis 1964, pp. 120–123).

Another effect that the social organizational properties of the hospital can have on patients is best demonstrated by Stanton and Schwartz's microanalysis of the social and psychological dynamics of pathological excitement and collective disturbances of patients in the wards of a mental hospital (Stanton & Schwartz 1954, pp. 342–365; 378–400). In every case that they examined, they found that a high level of continuing, covert tension and conflict between staff members in charge of patients was the major etiological factor involved. What this illustrates is how intricately entwined are the relations between staff and patients in a hospital. Structurally and functionally, the interdependence within and between each group is so close-webbed that even latent tension in one part of the social system may significantly affect its other parts. The impact of such tension on patients is augmented by the magnitude of physical and psychological dependence on hospital staff that being ill entails and by the heightened perception of the attitudes and feelings of staff members that this degree of dependency may foster.

It would seem, then, that although the hospital may help insulate patients from the sorts of emotional reactions on the part of family members that might complicate or impede their recovery, it may generate structural strains of its own that can have similar nontherapeutic or antitherapeutic consequences. A basic social science insight related to this phenomenon lies at the heart of a method of therapy and rehabilitation that has come into vogue in psychiatric hospitals since the 1950s. The insight is that, even outside the formally defined treatment situation, the affective quality and content of interaction between hospital staff and patients have a significant effect on the progress of the patient. The method is what has come to be known as the "therapeutic community" approach—a planned attempt to create a hospital milieu in which the therapeutic potentialities in all relationships within the hospital are maximized and utilized for the benefit of the patient (Jones 1952; Rapoport et al. 1961).

Studies on the hospital as a social system indicate that the patterned ways in which patients adjust to illness and hospitalization are influenced as much by fellow patients as by members of the medical staff. Patients grouped together for any time in the hospital wards constitute close-knit communities, with shared ideas and norms about how one ought to think, feel, and act in the face of the common predicament of illness and hospitalization; moreover, they develop their own systems of socialization, social support, and social control for effectively transmitting and enforcing these conceptions. Despite the considerable variation in the types and composition of the wards studied (male, female, and children's wards; general medical, surgical, and psychiatric wards; wards devoted to a particular disease; research wards, etc.), in every case the patients exhibit certain ways of coping with illness in the hospital. These include organization of the patient subculture in the form of a club with a name, charter of purposes, list of rules, and roster of offices; the cultivation by patients of medical expertise, particularly in connection with their own disorders; and the expression of potentially threatening basic emotions in counterphobic humor. There is evidence that the sources of such mechanisms do not lie only in the personality characteristics of individual patients or the experience of illness per se. They are also influenced by the social system properties of a hospital, by more general characteristics of the larger society into which the hospital fits, and, above and beyond these, by transsituational, cross-cultural, and perhaps even universal tendencies in the ways that human beings deal with major life stresses.

The optimally "good" and "successful" patient, by sociological definition, is the one who progresses steadily toward recovery, leaves the world of the hospital behind him, psychically and physically, and returns to full participation in his normal societal roles. In crucial ways, compliance with the norms of the sick role and those of the hospital as a social system contributes to this process. The paradox that many of the studies in the sociology of illness point up is that it is also true that the better a person becomes adjusted to the sick role, and the better his integration to the small society of the hospital is, the harder it is for him to make the sociopsychological journey back to health.

Illness confronts the sick person with psychological challenges, and it also brings him the kinds of gratifications that Freud termed "secondary gains." It removes him from the universe of the healthy and enmeshes him in that of the hospitalized sick. By virtue of these experiences, illness may significantly alter his attitudes, values, beliefs, and behavior. This being the case, his recovery from sickness and re-entry into the world of the healthy may involve him, the members of his family, his friends, and the professional associates to whom he returns in still another process of adjustment and resocialization.

RENÉE C. FOX

[*See also* HEALTH; MEDICAL CARE, *article on* ETHNOMEDICINE; MENTAL DISORDERS, TREATMENT OF, *article on* THE THERAPEUTIC COMMUNITY; MENTAL HEALTH; PUBLIC HEALTH.]

BIBLIOGRAPHY

BELKNAP, IVAN 1956 *The Human Problems of a State Mental Hospital.* New York: McGraw-Hill.

CAUDILL, WILLIAM 1958 *The Psychiatric Hospital as a Small Society.* Cambridge, Mass.: Harvard Univ. Press.

CAUDILL, WILLIAM 1961 Patterns of Emotions in Modern Japan. Unpublished manuscript.

CORNELL-ARO MENTAL HEALTH RESEARCH PROJECT IN THE WESTERN REGION, NIGERIA 1963 *Psychiatric Disorder Among the Yoruba: A Report,* by Alexander H. Leighton, T. Adeoye Lambo et al. Ithaca, N.Y.: Cornell Univ. Press.

COSER, ROSE L. 1962 *Life in the Ward.* East Lansing: Michigan State Univ. Press.

DAVIS, FRED 1964 *Passage Through Crisis: Polio Victims and Their Families.* Indianapolis: Bobbs-Merrill.

DUBOS, RENÉ; and DUBOS, JEAN 1952 *The White Plague: Tuberculosis, Man and Society.* Boston: Little.

FIELD, MARK G. 1957 *Doctor and Patient in Soviet Russia.* Cambridge, Mass.: Harvard Univ. Press.

FOX, RENÉE C. 1959 *Experiment Perilous: Physicians and Patients Facing the Unknown.* Glencoe, Ill.: Free Press.

GOFFMAN, ERVING (1961) 1962 *Asylums: Essays on the Social Situation of Mental Patients and Other Inmates.* Chicago: Aldine.

GREENBLATT, MILTON et al. (editors) 1957 *The Patient and the Mental Hospital: Contributions of Research in the Science of Social Behavior.* Glencoe, Ill.: Free Press.

HENDERSON, LAWRENCE J. 1935 Physician and Patient as a Social System. *New England Journal of Medicine* 212:819–823. → A now classic, pioneering essay in the field of the sociology of medicine, which was the direct inspiration for Talcott Parsons' conception of the sick role.

JONES, MAXWELL (1952) 1953 *The Therapeutic Community: A New Treatment Method in Psychiatry.* New York: Basic Books. → First published as *Social Psychiatry.*

KOOS, EARL L. 1954 *The Health of Regionville: What the People Thought and Did About It.* New York: Columbia Univ. Press.

MCDERMOTT, WALSH et al. 1960 Introducing Modern Medicine in a Navajo Community. Parts 1–2. *Science* 131:197–205, 280–287.

MALINOWSKI, BRONISLAW (1925) 1948 Magic, Science and Religion. Pages 1–71 in Bronislaw Malinowski, *Magic, Science and Religion, and Other Essays.* Glencoe, Ill.: Free Press.

MECHANIC, DAVID 1963 Religion, Religiosity, and Illness Behavior: The Special Case of the Jews. *Human Organization* 22:202–208.

MERTON, ROBERT K.; and BARBER, ELINOR G. 1963 Sociological Ambivalence. Pages 91–120 in Edward A. Tiryakian (editor), *Sociological Theory, Values and Social Change: Essays in Honor of Pitirim A. Sorokin.* New York: Free Press.

OPLER, MARVIN K. 1959 Cultural Differences in Mental Disorders: An Italian and Irish Contrast in the Schizophrenias—U.S.A. Pages 425–442 in Marvin K. Opler (editor), *Culture and Mental Health: Cross-cultural Studies.* New York: Macmillan.

PARSONS, ANNE 1960 Family Dynamics in South Italian Schizophrenics. *Archives of General Psychiatry* 3: 507–518.

PARSONS, ANNE 1961 A Schizophrenic Episode in a Neapolitan Slum. *Psychiatry* 24:109–121.

PARSONS, TALCOTT (1948) 1953 Illness and the Role of the Physician. Pages 609–617 in Clyde Kluckhohn and Henry A. Murray (editors), *Personality in Nature, Society, and Culture.* 2d ed., rev. New York: Knopf.

PARSONS, TALCOTT 1951 *The Social System.* Glencoe, Ill.: Free Press. → See especially pages 428–479 on "Social Structure and Dynamic Process."

PARSONS, TALCOTT 1958 Definitions of Health and Illness in the Light of American Values and Social Structure. Pages 165–187 in E. Gartly Jaco (editor), *Patients, Physicians and Illness: Sourcebook in Behavioral Science and Medicine.* Glencoe, Ill.: Free Press.

PARSONS, TALCOTT 1964 *Social Structure and Personality.* New York: Free Press. → See especially pages 325–358 on "Some Theoretical Considerations Bearing on the Field of Medical Sociology."

PARSONS, TALCOTT; and FOX, RENÉE C. (1952) 1958 Illness, Therapy, and the Modern Urban American Family. Pages 234–245 in E. Gartly Jaco (editor), *Patients, Physicians and Illness: Sourcebook in Behavioral Science and Medicine.* Glencoe, Ill.: Free Press. → First published in Volume 8 of the *Journal of Social Issues.*

PAUL, BENJAMIN D. 1953 Mental Disorder and Self-regulating Processes in Culture: A Guatemalan Illustration. Pages 51–68 in Milbank Memorial Fund, *Interrelations Between the Social Environment and*

Psychiatric Disorders. Proceedings, No. 29. New York: The Fund.

RAPOPORT, ROBERT N. et al. 1961 *Community as Doctor: New Perspectives on a Therapeutic Community.* Springfield, Ill.: Thomas.

ROSEN, GEORGE 1963 The Evolution of Social Medicine. Pages 17–61 in Howard E. Freeman, Sol Levine, and Leo G. Reeder (editors), *Handbook of Medical Sociology.* Englewood Cliffs, N.J.: Prentice-Hall.

RUBEL, ARTHUR J. 1960 Concepts of Disease in Mexican-American Culture. *American Anthropologist* New Series 62:795–814.

SIGERIST, HENRY E. 1960 *On the Sociology of Medicine.* New York: MD Publications. → See especially pages 9–22 on "The Special Position of the Sick."

STANTON, ALFRED H.; and SCHWARTZ, M. S. 1954 *The Mental Hospital: A Study of Institutional Participation in Psychiatric Illness and Treatment.* New York: Basic Books.

SZASZ, THOMAS S. 1956 Malingering: "Diagnosis" or Social Condemnation? Analysis of the Meaning of "Diagnosis" in the Light of the Interrelations of Social Structure, Value Judgment and the Physician's Role. *AMA Archives of Neurology and Psychiatry* 76:432–443.

ZBOROWSKI, MARK 1952 Cultural Components in Responses to Pain. *Journal of Social Issues* 8:16–30.

ILLUSIONS

See under PERCEPTION.

IMITATION

Learning by vicarious experience has historically been referred to as "imitation," although in the contemporary social science literature essentially the same phenomenon is subsumed under other terms, such as "observational learning," "social facilitation," "vicarious learning," "contagion," and "identification."

Accounts of the acquisition and modification of social behavior are frequently limited to descriptions of behavioral change based on principles of trial and error or instrumental conditioning. Although the efficacy of direct conditioning procedures has been well documented by laboratory studies, it is doubtful if many of the responses that almost all members of a society exhibit would ever be acquired if social learning proceeded entirely by these methods.

Informal observation and experimental analyses of the social-learning process reveal that a person can rapidly acquire new responses and that his existing behavioral repertoire can be considerably modified, solely as a function of his observing the behavior of others without performing any overt responses himself. The provision of models not only serves to short-circuit and accelerate the learning process but also, in cases where errors are dangerous or costly, becomes an indispensable means of transmitting and modifying social response patterns.

Theories of imitation

The concept of imitation in psychological theory has had a long history, dating back to Tarde (1890) and McDougall (1908), who regarded imitativeness as an innate or instinctive propensity.

Association and classical conditioning. As the instinct doctrine fell into disrepute, a number of psychologists, notably Humphrey (1921), Allport (1924), and Holt (1931), attempted to account for imitative behavior in terms of associative, or Pavlovian, conditioning principles. According to Holt, for example, when an adult copies a response made by a child, the child tends to repeat the behavior; and as this circular sequence continues, the adult's matching behavior becomes an increasingly effective stimulus for the child's response. If, during this spontaneous mutual imitation, the adult performs a response that is novel to the child, the child will copy it. Piaget (1945) is a more recent exponent of essentially the same point of view.

Although the classical conditioning theories accounted adequately for the imitator's repetition of his own behavior, they failed to explain the psychological mechanisms governing the emergence of *novel* responses during the model–observer interaction sequence. Moreover, demonstrations of observational learning in animals and humans do not ordinarily commence with a model's matching a semi-irrelevant response of the learner. Thus, in utilizing modeling procedures to teach a bird to talk, the trainer does not engage initially in the circular process of imitating crowing behavior; instead, he begins by emitting verbal responses that do not exist in the bird's behavioral repertoire.

Instrumental conditioning theories. As theoretical explanations of learning shifted the emphasis from classical conditioning to instrumental learning based on rewarding and punishing response consequences, theories of imitation similarly assumed that the occurrence of observational learning is contingent on the administration of reinforcing stimuli either to the model or to the observer. This point of view was most clearly expounded by Miller and Dollard in the classic publication *Social Learning and Imitation* (1941). According to this theory, the necessary conditions for learning through imitation include a motivated subject who is positively reinforced for matching the correct responses of a model during a series of initially random trial-and-error responses.

The experiments reported by Miller and Dollard in the monograph cited above involved a series of two-choice discrimination problems in which a trained leader responded to environmental stimuli of which the subject was unaware; consequently, the subject's own responses were totally dependent upon the cues provided by the leader's behavior. The leader's choices were consistently rewarded, and the observing subject was similarly reinforced whenever he matched the choice responses of the imitatee. This form of imitation was labeled by the authors as "matched-dependent behavior" because the subjects relied on the leader for relevant cues and matched his responses. Based on this paradigm, it was demonstrated that both rats and children readily learn to follow their respective models and generalize imitative responses to new stimulus situations, new models, and different motivational states.

Although these experiments have been widely accepted as demonstrations of learning by imitation, they in fact represent only the special case of discrimination place learning, in which the behavior of others provides discriminative stimuli for responses that already exist in the subject's behavioral repertoire. Had the relevant environmental cues been made more distinctive, the behavior of the models would have been quite irrelevant, and perhaps even a hindrance, to the acquisition process. In contrast, most forms of imitation involve *response* rather than *place* learning, in which subjects acquire new ways of behaving as a function of exposure to models. Moreover, since this conceptualization of observational learning requires that the subject perform the imitative response before he can learn it, the theory propounded by Miller and Dollard evidently accounts more adequately for the emission of previously learned matching responses than for their acquisition. Continuing with our example of language learning, in order for a myna bird to learn the word "encyclopedia" imitatively, it would first have to emit the word "encyclopedia" in the course of random vocalization, match it accidentally with the trainer's verbal response, and secure a positive reinforcement. It is evident from the foregoing discussion that the conditions assumed by Miller and Dollard to be necessary for learning by imitation place severe limitations on the types of behavioral changes that can be attributed to the influence of social models.

Sensory feedback theory. Mowrer's proprioceptive feedback theory (1960) similarly highlights the role of reinforcement, but unlike Miller and Dollard, who reduce imitation to a special case of instrumental learning, Mowrer emphasizes the classical conditioning of positive and negative emotions to matching response-correlated stimuli. Mowrer distinguishes between two forms of imitative learning in terms of whether the observer is reinforced directly or vicariously. In the former case, the model makes a response and at the same time rewards the observer. Through the repeated contiguity of the model's behavior with rewarding experiences, these responses gradually take on positive value for the observer. On the basis of stimulus generalization, the observer can produce self-rewarding feedback experience simply by reproducing as closely as possible the model's positively valenced behavior.

In the second, or "empathetic," form of imitative learning, the model not only exhibits the responses but also experiences the reinforcing consequences himself. It is assumed that the observer, in turn, experiences empathetically the sensory concomitants of the model's behavior and also intuits the model's satisfactions or dissatisfactions. As a result of this higher-order vicarious conditioning, the observer will be predisposed to reproduce the matching responses for the attendant positive sensory feedback.

There is some research evidence that imitative behavior is enhanced by an increase in the rewarding qualities of a model (Bandura & Huston 1961), and by positive reinforcers administered to a model (Bandura et al. 1963; Walters et al. 1963). However, the reinforcement theories of imitation fail to explain the learning of matching responses when the observer does not perform the model's behavior during the acquisition process and for which reinforcers are not dispensed either to the model or to the observer (Bandura & Walters 1963).

Stimulus contiguity and mediation. The acquisition of imitative responses under the conditions described above appears to be accounted for more adequately by recent theories of observational learning (Bandura 1962; 1965*b*; Sheffield 1961) that emphasize stimulus contiguity and mediational symbolic responses. According to Sheffield, when an observer witnesses a model exhibiting a sequence of responses, the observer learns, through contiguity of sensory events, perceptual and symbolic responses that are capable of eliciting, at some time after observation, overt responses corresponding to those that had been modeled.

Bandura's conceptualization of the imitative process similarly assumes that as a function of observing a model's behavior, the subject acquires cue-producing symbolic responses that subsequently can be translated into their motoric equivalents. Additionally, it is assumed that the *acquisition* of matching responses takes place primarily through stimulus contiguity, whereas reinforcements administered to the model or the subject exert their major influence on the *performance* of imitatively learned responses. The importance of distinguishing between learning and performance in discussing the necessary conditions for the occurrence of imitation is illustrated by findings from an experiment (Bandura 1965*a*) that proceeded in the following manner.

Children observed a film-mediated model perform a set of novel physical and verbal responses. In one condition the model was severely punished, and in a second the model was generously rewarded, whereas the third condition presented no response consequences to the model. A postexposure test of imitation revealed that differential reinforcement had produced differential amounts of imitative behavior. Children in the model-rewarded and the no-consequences groups spontaneously performed a significantly larger number of imitative responses than did subjects in the model-punished condition. Following the performance test, children in all three groups were offered highly attractive incentives contingent on their reproducing the model's responses, in order to activate performance of what the children had learned through observation. The introduction of rewards completely wiped out the previously observed performance differences, revealing an equivalent amount of learning among the children in the model-rewarded, model-punished, and no-consequences conditions. Thus, reinforcement was seen to be related to performance rather than to learning.

It is also evident from the results of this experiment that mere exposure to modeling stimuli does not provide sufficient conditions for imitative or observational learning. The fact that most of the children failed to reproduce the entire repertoire of behavior exhibited by the model, even under positive-incentive conditions designed to disinhibit and to elicit matching responses, indicates that other variables combine with contiguous stimulation in governing the process of imitative response acquisition. Clearly, an observer does not function like a passive video tape recorder, registering indiscriminately and storing all behavioral events that he happens to encounter in his daily experiences.

Factors affecting imitation. Exposing a person to a complex sequence of stimulation does not guarantee that he will attend to the entire range of cues, that he will necessarily select from a total stimulus complex only the most relevant stimuli, or that he will even perceive accurately the cues to which his attention is directed. Motivational variables, prior training in discriminative observation, and the induction of incentive-oriented sets may be highly influential in channeling, augmenting, or reducing the observation of responses, which is a necessary conditioning for imitative learning.

In addition to attention-directing variables, the rate, amount, and complexity of modeling stimuli presented to the observer may partly determine the degree of imitative learning. The acquisition of matching responses through observation of a lengthy, uninterrupted sequence of behavior is also likely to be governed by principles of associative learning, such as frequency and recency, serial order effects, and other multiple sources of associative interference.

Social responses are generally composed of a large number of different behavioral units combined in a particular manner. Responses of higher-order complexity are produced from combinations of previously learned components that may, in themselves, represent relatively complicated behavioral patterns. Consequently, the rate of acquisition of intricate matching responses through observation may be partly determined by the number of necessary components that are contained in the observer's repertoire.

Data on most of the variables mentioned in the foregoing discussion are lacking; consequently, considerably more research is needed to determine the manner in which motivational and other attention-directing variables combine with stimulus contiguity to facilitate or impede observational learning.

Although imitation has received considerable attention in psychological theorizing, and the influential role of vicarious experiences in social learning has been widely acknowledged, surprisingly little research designed to elucidate this important, but poorly understood, process has been conducted. There has been a substantial increase in the past few years, however, in the amount of research devoted to systematic experimental analyses of vicarious learning phenomena. A number of evaluative reviews of the major theoretical issues, research strategies, and findings pertaining to observational learning in both human and animal subjects have been recently published (Bandura 1965*b*; Bandura & Walters 1963; Hall 1963). Some of the main empirical findings are summarized in the remainder of this article.

Three effects of the observation of models

Exposure to the behavior of models may have three rather different behavioral effects on an observer's subsequent behavior.

Modeling effect. A subject may acquire patterned responses that did not previously exist in his behavioral repertoire by observing the behavior of another person. In demonstrating this modeling effect experimentally, the model exhibits responses that the observer has not yet learned to make and must later reproduce in substantially identical form.

For example, in an experiment (Bandura 1962) designed to study the social transmission of aggression, young children witnessed an adult model who exhibited highly novel physical and verbal aggressive responses. In order to compare the relative efficacy of real-life and symbolic models, one group of children observed real-life models, a second group viewed the same models presented on film, while children in a third group were shown a film in which a cartoon character displayed the same pattern of behavior. Two control groups of children were also included, one observing no models and the other witnessing the adult displaying inhibited and nonaggressive behavior. After exposure to the models, all children were mildly frustrated, and measures were obtained of the amount of imitative and nonimitative aggression they exhibited in a new setting with the model absent.

The children who had observed the aggressive models displayed a great number of precisely imitative aggressive responses, whereas such responses rarely occurred in either the nonaggressive-model group or the control group. In addition, the results indicated that filmed displays are essentially as effective as real-life models in transmitting novel response patterns.

Inhibitory and disinhibitory effects. Exposure to the behavior of others may also strengthen or weaken inhibitory responses in the observer. In the experiment to which reference has just been made, children who witnessed the aggressive models, regardless of whether they were presented in real-life or symbolic form, subsequently displayed approximately twice as much aggression as subjects in the control group or those who observed behaviorally inhibited models.

A series of experiments by Blake and his associates (1958) demonstrates the influence of models in reducing inhibitions to social deviation. In these studies, accomplices of the experimenter violated traffic signals or signs prohibiting certain types of behavior. Subjects who observed the deviating models more readily performed the transgressions than subjects who observed conforming models.

The occurrence of inhibitory and disinhibitory effects is significantly influenced by whether the model experiences reward or punishment as a consequence of his behavior. These consequences may either occur immediately after the model's responses or be inferred from certain discriminative symbols, attributes, and skills possessed by the model that tend to be regularly correlated with differential reinforcements.

The manner in which these consequences of the model's behavior enhance or inhibit imitation is demonstrated in an experiment (Bandura et al. 1963) in which children observed an adult model being either rewarded or punished following displays of aggression. Subjects who witnessed the aggressive model being rewarded showed more imitative behavior and more preference for emulating the successful aggressor, even though they disapproved of his actions, than children who observed the aggressive model being punished, who both failed to reproduce his behavior and rejected him as a model for emulation. Thus, the rewarding consequences of the model's behavior outweighed the acquired value systems of the observers.

In an experiment conducted by Walters, Leat, and Mezei (1963), kindergarten children were first shown an assortment of attractive toys with which they were forbidden to play. Children who later saw a film in which a child was rewarded after playing with the forbidden toys subsequently deviated more readily than subjects who saw the film-mediated model being punished, whereas control children showed an intermediate degree of resistance to deviation.

Inhibition or disinhibition of social behavior is frequently mediated by conditioned fear responses. A series of experiments by Berger (1962) demonstrates how emotional responses may be acquired vicariously without the observer's receiving any direct aversive stimulation. In each study one person, the performer or model, participated in a classical conditioning procedure in which a buzzer was sounded and, shortly thereafter, an electric shock was supposedly administered to the model, who feigned pain reactions by jerking his arm away from the source of the "shock" and wincing. The observers who witnessed the performer undergoing the conditioning trials exhibited conditioned psychogalvanic skin responses to the buzzer alone, although they had not experienced the electric shock directly.

Although vicarious conditioning by this procedure has been clearly demonstrated, wide individual differences in the rate and magnitude of vicariously acquired emotional responses have been noted. Further research is needed, therefore, to identify the variables that contribute to this learning process.

Response-facilitating effects. In addition to transmitting new response patterns and strengthening or weakening inhibition of existing repertoires, the behavior of models may serve as eliciting stimuli for previously learned responses that match precisely or resemble closely those exhibited by the model. Response facilitation effects can be distinguished from disinhibition when the behavior in question is not likely to have incurred punishment and any observed increase in responsivity is therefore not attributable to the reduction of inhibitory responses.

Determinants of imitative phenomena

The initial laboratory investigations of imitation were primarily concerned with isolating the different behavioral effects of exposure to models on observers. Current research in this area is directed primarily toward identifying the variables that govern the occurrence and magnitude of imitative behavior.

Characteristics of the model. Evidence is accumulating to indicate that the characteristics of the model partly determine the extent to which matching responses will be exhibited by observers. A model's social power, competence, tendency to reward, and esteemed position in an age-grade or prestige hierarchy tend to be positively associated with imitation. As mentioned earlier, the characteristics of the consequences of the model's responses are also highly influential in promoting response matching.

Mode of model presentation. It is often mistakenly assumed that imitative learning phenomena are largely confined to younger age groups and to stimulus situations in which real-life models exhibit, intentionally or unwittingly, particular social response patterns. Once a person has developed an adequate verbal repertoire, increasing reliance is placed on *symbolic* models. Pictorial stimuli and verbal statements that describe the appropriate responses and their sequencing constitute prevalent means of providing symbolic models. Indeed, without the response guidance furnished by instructional manuals and social codes of behavior, members of a society would be forced to engage in exceedingly tedious and often hazardous trial-and-error experimentation. Studies concerned with the relationship between imitation and mode of model presentation suggest that the imitative process is essentially the same regardless of whether the model's behavior is exhibited through demonstration, pictorial presentation, or verbal description.

Characteristics of the observer. Characteristics of the observers, deriving from their previous social-learning histories, also influence the degree to which imitative behavior occurs. Persons who are dependent, are emotionally aroused, lack self-esteem, or believe themselves to be similar to the model in some attributes are especially prone to imitate successful models. Once imitative responses have been acquired, their maintenance, persistence, and generalization can be effectively controlled by reinforcers administered directly to the observer.

Since attending behavior is a necessary prerequisite to imitative learning, a systematic analysis of motivational and incentive variables that facilitate, impede, or channel observing responses would throw considerable light on this particular mode of response acquisition. Continued exploration of these factors, as well as of the learning parameters mentioned earlier, promises to provide the type of data that will eventually permit adequate explanation, prediction, and control of the vicarious psychological processes commonly subsumed under the general term "social imitation."

ALBERT BANDURA

[*See also* IDENTITY, PSYCHOSOCIAL; IMPRINTING. *Other relevant material may be found in* LEARNING; SELF CONCEPT; SOCIALIZATION.]

BIBLIOGRAPHY

ALLPORT, FLOYD H. 1924 *Social Psychology.* Boston: Houghton Mifflin.

BANDURA, ALBERT 1962 Social Learning Through Imitation. Volume 10, pages 211–269 in *Nebraska Symposium on Motivation.* Edited by Marshall R. Jones. Lincoln: Univ. of Nebraska Press.

BANDURA, ALBERT 1965*a* Behavioral Modifications Through Modeling Procedures. Pages 310–340 in Leonard Krasner and Leonard P. Ullmann (editors), *Research in Behavior Modification.* New York: Holt.

BANDURA, ALBERT 1965*b* Vicarious Processes: A Case of No-trial Learning. Volume 2, pages 1–55 in Leonard Berkowitz (editor), *Advances in Experimental Social Psychology.* New York: Academic Press.

BANDURA, ALBERT; and HUSTON, ALETHA C. 1961 Identification as a Process of Incidental Learning. *Journal of Abnormal and Social Psychology* 63:311–318.

BANDURA, ALBERT; ROSS, DOROTHEA; and ROSS, SHEILA A. 1963 Vicarious Reinforcement and Imitative Learning. *Journal of Abnormal and Social Psychology* 67: 601–607.

BANDURA, ALBERT; and WALTERS, R. H. 1963 *Social Learning and Personality Development.* New York: Holt.

BERGER, SEYMOUR M. 1962 Conditioning Through Vicarious Instigation. *Psychological Review* 69:450–466.

BLAKE, ROBERT R. 1958 The Other Person in the Situation. Pages 229–242 in Renato Tagiuri and Luigi Petrullo (editors), *Person Perception and Interpersonal Behavior.* Stanford (Calif.) Univ. Press.

HALL, K. R. L. 1963 Observational Learning in Monkeys and Apes. *British Journal of Psychology* 54:201–226.

HOLT, E. B. 1931 *Animal Drive and the Learning Process*. Vol. 1. New York: Holt.

HUMPHREY, GEORGE 1921 Imitation and the Conditioned Reflex. *Pedagogical Seminary and Journal of Genetic Psychology* 28:1–21. → Now called the *Journal of Genetic Psychology*.

McDOUGALL, WILLIAM (1908) 1950 *An Introduction to Social Psychology*. 30th ed., enl. London: Methuen. → A paperback edition was published in 1960 by Barnes and Noble.

MILLER, NEAL E.; and DOLLARD, JOHN 1941 *Social Learning and Imitation*. New Haven: Yale Univ. Press.

MOWRER, ORVAL H. 1960 *Learning Theory and the Symbolic Processes*. New York: Wiley.

PIAGET, JEAN (1945) 1951 *Play, Dreams, and Imitation in Childhood*. New York: Norton; London: Heinemann. → First published as *La formation du symbole chez l'enfant*.

SHEFFIELD, F. D. 1961 Theoretical Considerations in the Learning of Complex Sequential Tasks From Demonstration and Practice. Pages 13–32 in Arthur A. Lumsdaine (editor), *Student Responses in Programmed Instructions: A Symposium on Experimental Studies of Cue and Response Factors in Group and Individual Learning From Instructional Media*. National Research Council Publication No. 943. Washington: National Academy of Sciences–National Research Council.

TARDE, GABRIEL (1890) 1903 *The Laws of Imitation*. New York: Holt. → Translated from the second French edition of 1895.

WALTERS, RICHARD H.; LEAT, MARION; and MEZEI, LOUIS 1963 Inhibition and Disinhibition of Responses Through Empathetic Learning. *Canadian Journal of Psychology* 17:235–243.

IMMIGRATION

See MIGRATION *and* REFUGEES.

IMPERIALISM

The word "imperialism" is widely used as an emotive—and more rarely as a theoretical—term to denote specific forms of aggressive behavior on the part of certain states against others; the concept refers primarily to attempts to establish or retain formal sovereignty over subordinate political societies, but it is also often equated with the exercise of *any* form of political control or influence by one political community over another.

The word *impérialiste* was originally coined in France in the 1830s to denote a partisan of the one-time Napoleonic empire (Koebner & Schmidt 1964). "Imperialism" soon developed into a term of abuse employed before 1848 to castigate the Caesaristic pretensions of Louis Napoleon. It was later used in a similar way both by French opponents of Napoleon III and by British adversaries of French rule and expansionism. In the 1870s British antagonists of Disraeli began to use the word as a domestic invective. But other British writers and politicians sought to rehabilitate the term. They applied it first to the policy of establishing a "Greater Britain" (Dilke 1869), through "the expansion of England" (Seeley 1883) into an "imperial federation" of Britain, its overseas settlements, and India. The acquisition of a large colonial empire in Asia and Africa led to the view that it was the "white man's burden" (Kipling) to assume a "dual mandate" (Lugard 1922) for offering civilization to "backward" peoples and for opening their territories for the benefit of the world. Thus the term became increasingly identified with British colonialism.

The need for colonies was often argued in economic terms, both by British advocates of colonial expansion, who saw in an enlarged empire a means of preserving markets in an increasingly protectionist world, and by writers on the European continent who ascribed Britain's wealth to her possession of colonies and hence demanded colonies to increase their nations' wealth. While some identified "imperialism" with British world politics, others used the term to include the widespread desire for expansion on the part of European states generally.

Developments in China first, and later the Boer War, which was popularly regarded on the European continent as "la guerre de la Bourse contre les Boers," initiated a powerful anti-imperialist current, eloquently articulated in J. A. Hobson's study *Imperialism* (1902). Hobson (an economic heretic of radical-liberal persuasion) sought to explain European expansionism as based on the underconsumptionist tendencies of modern capitalism and the particular manipulations of groups of profiteering capitalists. Such views were systematized into a more elaborate theory by a number of Marxist writers in Germany and Austria (Bauer 1907; Hilferding 1910; Luxemburg 1913; Sternberg 1926; Grossmann 1929) and in Russia (chiefly Lenin 1917 and Bukharin 1918), by English radical writers (e.g., Brailsford 1914; Woolf 1920; Dobb 1937; and, in a much revised form, Strachey 1959), by the American economists Sweezy and Baran (see Sweezy 1942; Sweezy & Baran 1966), and by numerous historians who have increasingly influenced textbooks the world over.

In the interwar period such views achieved a massive political influence, mainly through Lenin's *Imperialism: The Highest Stage of Capitalism* (see Lenin 1917), but also through the propaganda efforts of such ill-matched groups as pacifists and isolationists, who agreed in ascribing wars to the insidious influence of armaments manufacturers, and National Socialists, who lashed out at Anglo-Saxon-cum-Jewish plutocracy.

Since World War II, the frequent identification of capitalism, colonialism, and imperialism has become rarer in the Western world; the aggressive policies of Germany, Italy, and Japan have made many observers aware of the unwarranted optimism in the theory that imperialist aggression was simply the product of a passing social system, like capitalism, or of particularly evil men, like capitalists. While after 1945 western Europe witnessed the demise of practically the whole of its colonial system, communism did not seem to lessen the expansionist policies of Russia and China.

"Imperialism" has now become part of a propaganda battle. In communist parlance the word remains restricted to the policies of the West, in particular the United States, whose Wall Street imperialism is thought to supplant that of the older European colonial powers. Western authors have, for their part, sought to identify communist policies with "the new imperialism" (Seton-Watson 1961; Kolarz 1964). Writers in the emerging countries have practically made the word interchangeable with "neocolonialism," defined by Nkrumah (1965, p. ix) as a situation in which "the state . . . is, in theory, independent and has all the outward trappings of international sovereignty" but where "its economic system and thus its political system is directed from outside." Others have extended the term to refer to the economic, political, and military policies of all industrialized states, including the Soviet Union, or of the white race as such, or even of any unsympathetic foreign state. The word has thus become one of the most powerful slogans of our time, used indiscriminately against any state, or even any group, regarded as inimical to a speaker's interest.

From this development, some have concluded with Lenin that the phenomenon of imperialism represents the most important problem of our times. Others have regarded it as a "pseudo-concept which sets out to make everything clear and ends by making everything muddled . . . a word for the illiterates of social science" (Hancock 1950, p. 17). Whereas many historians reserve the term by preference for the period of European expansion after 1870, others regard this modern imperialism only as one example of an age-old phenomenon, defined by Schumpeter as "the objectless disposition on the part of a state to unlimited forcible expansion" ([1919–1927] 1951, p. 7) and specified by Langer as "simply the rule or control, political or economic, direct or indirect, of one state, nation or people over other similar groups, or . . . the disposition, urge or striving to establish such rule" (1935, p. 67).

Marxist theories of imperialism

The Marxist theories of imperialism still represent the most elaborate and influential attempt to explain the alleged propensity of capitalist states to engage in imperialist expansion.

Marxist authors (building on the non-Marxist Hobson) have agreed in finding the causes of European and American expansion in the latter part of the nineteenth century and early twentieth in changes which took place within a maturing capitalist system, but they have differed about particular causes. Some theorists have regarded imperialism as a necessary condition for capitalist growth, whether because of the impossibility of continued accumulation of capital unless an effective demand is found among noncapitalist groups and societies (Luxemburg 1913), or because of the desire to acquire investment opportunities (Hobson 1902), or because of the need to offset the periodic depressions which were a characteristic of capitalist economies. Others explained imperialism mainly as a particularly profitable (though not inevitable) policy of powerful capitalist groups, like the attempt of "finance capitalists" to overcome the alleged secular tendency of profits to fall, or to find profitable uses for idle capital resulting from the increasing tendency toward monopolies, or to achieve the largest possible protected market which trusts and cartels could exploit and use as a basis for their further struggle for the world market (Bauer 1907, Hilferding 1910). While some authors have concentrated mainly on negative domestic factors which *pushed* capitalist economies into imperialist policies, others have given greater weight to positive colonial assets that *pulled* capitalists into foreign lands: cheap labor, raw materials, enforceability of favorable terms of trade, job opportunities, and new lands suitable for exploitation or settlement.

The various theories were formed mainly to account, *post factum*, for the scramble for Africa. But they served a more revolutionary purpose, since at least Luxemburg and Lenin used imperialism to explain the inevitability of world wars, once the world was fully brought under the control of rival capitalist states. Using his theory, Lenin explained the role of part of the working class (the "labor-aristocracy," or social-democrat "lackeys of imperialism") who supported their governments in 1914. Against them he called on true socialists to convert the war into a revolution at home. He also fashioned the explosive formula that the nationalist bourgeoisie in the colonial countries and the communists in the more advanced countries should combine their forces for a joint onslaught on the citadels of capitalism. Theories of imperialism still serve Marxists to explain the survival of capitalist economies, and the persistence of great inequalities in economic development levels between the onetime colonial powers and their former subject colonies. They also claim to provide a definite criterion by which to distinguish progressive from reactionary, historical from antihistorical, wars. But disputes have arisen among communist theoreticians over the question whether imperialism will inevitably lead to the holocaust of a new world war (as Chinese doctrine states) or whether the suicidal nature of modern armaments, coupled with the increased strength of the peace-loving forces in the world of the mid-1960s, may enable socialist and capitalist states to coexist more or less peacefully (as is argued with some hesitation in the Soviet Union).

Criticism of the Marxist theories. There has been a barrage of criticism of the Marxist theories which has taken three forms (in order of decreasing generality): (*a*) a rejection of the premise that wars are fought primarily for economic reasons; (*b*) a denial that capitalism is especially likely to foster imperialist tendencies; and (*c*) a critique of the attempt to explain late nineteenth-century colonialism as the result of capitalist forces exclusively.

Economic causation of war. Numerous authors (e.g., Robbins 1939; Wright 1942; Morgenthau 1948) have questioned the view that modern war has been waged primarily for economic motives. Norman Angell documented the unprofitability of war before World War I in *The Great Illusion* (1910). L. F. Richardson (1960) found that only 29 per cent of the wars from 1820 to 1929 can be directly attributed to economic factors. No serious historian would today subscribe to the prejudice, widespread in the 1920s and 1930s, that World War I was the direct result of the nefarious activities of armaments manufacturers, and few would hold that the entry of the Soviet Union into World War II in 1941 suddenly transformed a war of capitalist economic imperialism into one of patriotic idealism.

Capitalism and imperialist tendencies. Critics of the Leninist theory have pointed to the frequency of war and imperial conquest long before capitalism, and to the expansionist record of postcapitalist Russia, to deny any special relationship between capitalism and imperialist policies. On the contrary, many theorists have held with Adam Smith, Herbert Spencer, and Richard Cobden that capitalism per se is likely to foster international understanding and peaceful tendencies. Even the Marxist Karl Kautsky envisaged (1915) the possible disappearance of intercapitalist wars through the establishment of an ultraimperialism in which international finance capital would exploit the world. Criticizing Marxist theories, Schumpeter (1919–1927) held, in line with Auguste Comte and Thorstein Veblen (cf. Aron 1958), that capitalism was inherently a democratizing, individualizing, and rationalizing force which channeled potentially aggressive energies in entrepreneurial, and hence relatively peaceful, directions. He regarded imperialism as mainly the result of atavistic drives of a precapitalist era and believed popular imperialism in modern states to be a logical impossibility. He later retracted this view, subscribing to Karl Renner's doctrine of social imperialism (Renner 1917; see also Schumpeter 1939, vol. 2, p. 696), but continued to regard the forces behind imperialism as fundamentally irrational (Winslow 1948, p. 235). Hannah Arendt (1951) has attributed imperialism to an alliance between mob and capital, which ultimately destroyed capitalism.

Capitalism and colonialism. The virtual identification of imperialism, capitalism, and colonialism has also come in for considerable criticism from historians.

First, economic historians have questioned the assumption that the new colonies acquired by European powers in the latter part of the nineteenth century played an important role in capitalist development. By far the greater part of European investments after the 1870s flowed not to the colonies but to independent states in Europe (which had absorbed more than half the French and German foreign investments by 1914), to North and South America (which accounted for more than half the British foreign investments by 1914), and to South Africa and Australasia (Staley 1935; see Hobson 1914; Feis 1930; Cairncross 1953; Imlah 1958; Segal & Simon 1961). Trade with the colonial dependencies was generally only a small fraction of all British and French foreign trade, and an infinitesimal share for Italy, Germany, and Japan. Noncolonial countries had generally easy access to markets of colonies of other states, and these colonies in turn traded more with foreign lands than with their imperial masters (Clark 1936). Raw materials were important in the case of some colonial acquisitions, but their share in the raw material market as a whole was relatively slight. Advanced states did not lack access to raw materials in peacetime, and in wartime strategic and military, rather than economic, factors were decisive. Similarly, the terms of trade were not particularly favorable to Europe during the high tide of imperialism; indeed, they were less favorable than they are in the present period of large-scale "dis-imperialism" (Strachey 1959). There was almost no emigration to the new colonies, while most emigrants even from colonial nations went to other lands.

Second, the alleged identity of imperialism with colonialism and capitalism is also proved false by the circumstance that many nonimperialist states (like Switzerland and the Scandinavian countries) found little difficulty in attaining a high level of growth, foreign trade, and foreign investments, while capital-importing states with underdeveloped economies, notably Italy and tsarist Russia, followed starkly expansionist policies.

Third, historians have disproved the universality of the correlation between monopoly capitalism and imperialism (Feis 1930; Langer 1935; Hancock 1950). This viewpoint originated mainly in Germany, where there was indeed a relatively close connection between banks, heavy industry, and militarist and colonialist circles, though even in Germany colonial conquest predated somewhat the strong cartelization drive. In England and France, on the other hand, monopolies were hardly present at the time of strong imperialist expansion, and relations existing between the ordinary banking and industrial world and the investment brokers dealing in foreign loans were far from close. In the United States the situation was again different. The growth of trusts and cartels long preceded any strong overt inclination toward imperial conquests. In some countries the money market was relatively open to all, and in others (e.g., France and Germany) political interests manipulated foreign investments, rather than the reverse. Studies of the types of foreign loans issued in the heyday of colonial expansion reveal that much the greater part were in fixed-interest government securities; that the profitability of foreign investments was only marginally higher, if not lower, than that of domestic investments; and that in the end many European investors lost their money through defaults (see Feis 1930; Cairncross 1953; Blaug 1961).

Finally, the specific attribution of colonial policies to small groups of profiteering capitalists has also been challenged. Special interests have often pressed for colonial conquest and have frequently profited from them. But actual study of the entire record (Staley 1935) reveals that traders and investors have often been used as instruments by rulers and governments set on imperialist expansion for other reasons; private interests usually proved ineffective when such other concerns were absent.

The idea of a monolithic capitalism fully bent on imperialist conquest is, therefore, a myth. Many capitalist interests have opposed imperialist policies, while others have cheered them on. But in that case the real problem is not to identify the role of particular capitalist interests in certain imperialist exploits, but to indicate other factors which explain why, in particular instances, capitalist forces pressing for imperialism could be stronger than those that did not or those that actively resisted particular imperialist policies.

Other explanations of European expansion

If neither monopoly capital, nor domestic underconsumption, nor the need of markets for goods, or capital, or sources of raw materials was the special factor accounting for changes in European expansionist policies, what were the relevant factors?

Some Marxist writers have attempted to save economic determinism by insisting that annexations of areas of little economic importance were really "strategic," "protective," or "anticipatory" (Sweezy 1942). But this goes far to destroy the causal link between economics and politics on which the Marxist theory really rests.

A review of modern historical writing on European expansionism (see Langer 1935; Hallgarten 1951; Brunschwig 1960; Fieldhouse 1966) shows three predominant trends: (*a*) greater stress on noneconomic, and especially on purely political, determinants; (*b*) more attention to the considerable differences in the causes of particular imperialist incidents; and (*c*) increasing emphasis on the need to regard events after 1870 in a much longer time perspective than that usually called the period of "modern imperialism."

Newer historians have thus found the mainspring of the movement of European expansion less in the expanding industrial economy and more in the political area of world strategies and ideologies of competing expansive nations. They have strongly emphasized (*a*) the unification of Germany and Italy, which fanned a new assertive nationalism in these countries; (*b*) the effects of the Franco-Prussian War of 1870, which tempted France into colonial adventures in order to regain a sense of glory and grandeur, to give employment and experience to the country's military cadres, and to expand its potential manpower reservoir for possible *revanche;* (*c*) the continued expansion of Russia toward Constantinople, Persia, India, and the Far East, which increasingly threatened long-established British imperial interests; (*d*) the fact that Britain could not remain aloof from formal annexations when others threatened to move in, thus threatening the foundations of splendid isolation and of traditional balancing policies; or, more generally, (*e*) the search for compensation and for diplomatic advantage outside Europe, since the powers were deadlocked on the Continent itself. But the spread of European rivalries changed the pattern of international politics. As extra-European powers such as Japan, the United States, and China became increasingly involved, European dominance gave way to world politics in the true sense of the term.

Others have explained European imperialism less in terms of intra-European conflict than as a culmination of a great number of local conflicts. Detailed historical research of particular imperialist adventures has revealed the operation of a great variety of forces in each instance. Sheer power play, diplomatic maneuvering, strategic and geopolitical concerns, humanitarian interests and racial ideologies, economic drives and cultural expansionism have often intermingled without a priori dominance of any single factor. Frequently, particular conflicts resulted merely from the exploits of "private imperialists," whether traders, explorers, concession hunters, or missionaries. Outside powers got entangled in indigenous warfare and disputes, while the inevitable instability of unsettled borders and the feared action by rival groups and governments often led to improvised interventions. Hence, new imperialist actions often resulted from past imperial commitments (India being a prime example). In this view, local rivalries slowly developed into imperialist policies on a world scale, to be interpreted only afterward and anachronistically as deliberate and planned expansion on the part of particular "imperial powers."

At the same time, other writers have continued searching for more determinist explanations than either intra-European rivalry or localized imperial exploits provide. They have focused on longer-term technological, political, and social developments. Some have thus singled out the effects of the great changes in world communications which started when improved weaponry and navigation technology basically altered the relations of power between Europe and the rest of the world. To explain the upsurge of imperial expansion in the nineteenth century, they have stressed the impact of the change from wooden ships to steamers, which revolutionized the entire scale of international trade, affected the traditional dominance of the British navy, and led to a demand for coaling stations and for safeguards and control over international arteries like the Bosporus, the Suez Canal, and the Panama Canal. This view logically extends to the later strategic concern with oil supplies. Railways posed similar strategic issues and facilitated the penetration of hitherto practically untouched inland areas. The advent of the telegraph immeasurably speeded the flow of information and held out the tempting prospect of direct rule over outlying lands, but again demanded safeguards for cables and cable stations. Of even greater influence was the simultaneous growth of a world press, which, coupled with the growing literacy rate in Europe and the United States, created mass publics that were often violently jingoistic.

Certain authors (e.g., Gallagher & Robinson 1953; Robinson & Gallagher 1961; 1962) have underscored this trend by emphasizing in particular the sociological effect of European expansionist policies on political regimes outside Europe. Rejecting the conventional view that there was a sharp break between the older mercantilist imperialism of the fifteenth through eighteenth centuries and the new high tide of imperial expansion in the late nineteenth century, they have spoken of the intervening period as one of "the imperialism of free trade." In this period European power and commerce were extended mainly through diplomatic and economic leverage, not by direct colonial rule. But while this was to a large extent feasible and successful in the Americas, in the Ottoman Empire, in north Africa, and in China—and could even be accompanied by a withdrawal of imperial controls in Canada, Australasia, and South Africa—it broke down increasingly in Afro–Asia after 1870 through the corrosive political and commercial effects that European policies had upon key African and Asian governments. The political and financial collapse of these governments brought European interests into play and led to a process of direct competitive annexations. European imperialism, in this view, is therefore a long-standing process in which, in Afro–Asia at least, extending imperialist activity was the result of the preceding activities of informal penetration and the protonational reactions that they eventually provoked.

Thus, on the one hand European expansion after 1870 is regarded as part of an almost self-evident process through which European power, enterprise, and culture spread over land and sea by formal as well as informal methods. On the other hand, exact study of this process leads to increasingly complex interpretations of the forces behind actual events and incidents.

The wider meanings of imperialism

The view of imperialism as a general and age-old phenomenon which predates and postdates the period of European overseas expansion (whether dated from the fifteenth or from the nineteenth century) poses new theoretical complications.

On the one hand, there is a tendency to regard as imperialism any form of more or less sustained aggressive action of one political system toward another. Thus defined, the term gets easily lost in vague generalities. Theoretical interpretation loses contact with concrete social and historical situations and is inevitably reduced to overgeneral explanations, attributing the phenomenon to postulated universal behavior traits of man (i.e., to psychological mechanisms) or of men (i.e., to group interaction). Imperialism has thus been explained by such presumably universal human emotions as fear, the will to power, pride, prestige, pugnacity, predacity, etc.

On the other hand, the attempt to narrow the definition of imperialism so as to make it suitable for more specific analyses has led other theorists into a tautological trap. They have found only those factors significant in the explanation of imperialism which their own definition has already singled out as determining or important. Thus some authors have spoken of imperialism only in the case of expansion by certain countries, or by states with a specific social system, or by particular groups within states. Some have restricted the word to specific types of aggressive policies, reserving the term for cases of overseas expansion but not for extension of power over contiguous land areas, or regarding as imperialism only the annexation of tropical or agrarian countries or territories with particular raw materials. Others have restricted the word to certain expansionist goals, e.g., economic exploitation, racial domination, cultural messianism. Still others have thought of imperialism only when certain conditions are fulfilled as to methods and duration of control, demanding as a criterion direct occupation but not indirect mechanisms like bribery, economic intervention, or military threats. Finally, certain authors have limited imperialism to attempts by states to reverse an existing *status quo;* imperialist policies are those which aim at acquiring new power (dynamic imperialism to others), but not those which seek to maintain an existing empire (which others call static imperialism). Such restrictive definitions often prejudge explanations of actual power relations and may be motivated by the political desire to defend or attack the policies of particular states.

These complications, which are the immediate result of the complexity of the numerous phenomena that have been subsumed under the term "imperialism," make it doubtful whether a satisfactory theory of imperialism can ever be evolved. Many theorists of international relations have therefore dropped the term, as useless for theoretical analysis. Other authors have preferred to speak of imperialisms (in the plural) following Schumpeter (1919–1927). This suggests the phenomenon of "imperialism" must at least be broken down into a number of subtypes, which could be classified according to (*a*) goals pursued, (*b*) methods used, and (*c*) activating forces.

Imperialist goals. Expansionist political systems have historically pursued one or more of the following goals.

Economic gain. Throughout history forceful appropriation of material benefits has been a powerful factor in imperialist policies. Gains have consisted both of booty (e.g., precious objects, crops) acquired in single raids and of labor and products of populations subjected to enduring servitude and often forced to suffer a drastic overhaul of property relations and production systems.

Political power. Conquest of foreign lands was often motivated by the desire to augment political power. This could be in a direct sense, for instance, when foreign manpower was used to reinforce the armed strength of the imperialist nations, or when strategic raw materials were monopolized, or when areas of a strategic nature were occupied. It could also be indirect, as when foreign dominion brought added prestige and increased bargaining power for the imperialist state or for leading persons and groups within it.

Ideology. Frequently imperialist ideologies have been merely convenient cloaks to cover other drives. But throughout human history certain political, religious, or cultural beliefs have sometimes waxed so strong as to force states independently into "missionary" activities, to spread "civilization," or the "true" gospel, or a particular national culture or dominant political creed.

Diversion of domestic unrest. Aggressive action abroad has often been believed capable of deflecting domestic tension. Once set in motion, however, this mechanism has frequently gone beyond its original purpose. In Schumpeter's words, ". . . created by wars that required it, the machine now created the wars it required" ([1919–1927] 1951, p. 33). Other writers have suggested that totalitarian regimes are particularly prone to expansionist policies. Since internal rule cannot be maintained unless the system is insulated from foreign influences, totalitarian countries tend to show the twin reactions of isolation and expansion in order to avoid or destroy threatening foreign forces (Feierabend 1962).

Methods of control. Imperial relationships may be further classified according to the way control is exercised over subject peoples.

Types of pressure exerted. Pressure can range from relatively peaceful practices (normal financial and economic transactions, cultural activities, diplomatic argument) through more forceful measures (bribery, economic sanctions, military intimidation) to outright violence (varying from a temporary show of arms to actual conquest and permanent repression).

Legal instruments. International law contains a great variety of instruments that can be used to exercise control: leases, concessions, capitulations, suzerainty, protectorates, mandates, trusteeships, forced alliances, temporary occupations, permanent annexations, etc.

Actual political relations. Following Hans Kohn (1958, p. 4), one may distinguish five types of imperial relationships, according to whether (1) a subject people has full autonomy within an imperial framework; (2) individual subjects enjoy full citizenship in the imperial state but are denied the expression of separate nationhood; (3) subject peoples are reduced to permanently inferior status; (4) subject peoples are physically exterminated; or (5) one nation establishes and maintains political domination over a geographically external political unit inhabited by people of any race and at any state of cultural development. Kohn reserves the term "colonialism" for the last of these categories.

Activating forces. Different kinds of imperialism, as well as theories about imperialism, may be distinguished according to whether particular individuals, special social groups, a particular condition of nations, or the general characteristics of the international system are thought to constitute the core of imperialist action.

Individuals as the main agents of imperialism. Imperialist policies can stem mainly from the special ambitions of, or the particular psychological pressures working on, people in positions of effective political influence. This influence can result either from their formal or informal political roles at home or from their strategic importance in connection with particular diplomatic constellations abroad (e.g., Cecil Rhodes and other "private imperialists"). This category would also include those theories which attribute imperialism to the parallel but individual psychological reactions of people which sustain group aggression. Usually, however, both the role and the reactions of individuals can be explained satisfactorily only on the basis of particular social conditions and relationships.

Social groups as the carriers of imperialism. Nearly every kind of social group has been held responsible for imperialist actions: ruling dynasties, out for glory, wealth, and dominion; aristocratic warrior castes, depending on wars for status and income; military officers and civilian officials, whose loyalties are swayed by their exclusive identification with the interests of the state they serve; the middle classes as the natural supporters of national states; religious and intellectual ideologizers who extol a particular political system or culture; the peasantry, sensitive to traditional love for the fatherland and easily persuaded of the value of gaining new land through foreign conquest; the urban proletariat, likely to cheer foreign adventures in compensation for their own downtrodden existence, etc. But closer analysis usually reveals the inadequacy of single-group explanations, partly because their postulated unity is proved false by detailed historical inquiry and partly because the special importance of certain groups can itself be accounted for only by other factors.

Imperialism as an extension of nationalism. Whereas older sociologists saw the roots of imperialism in racial struggle, more modern thinkers have pointed particularly to the forces behind assertive nationalism. These, in turn, they have explained as the inevitable outcome of particular communication processes which constantly reinforce nationalist cohesion at the expense of international interaction; as a deflection of widespread insecurity (itself a product of manifold social changes) toward alleged enemies at home and abroad; as the inevitable result of the distortions or stereotypes in the perception of other groups and nations; or as the product of new ideologies that ascribe to particular nations special rights in the assumed international struggle for survival. Such theories have the merit of wide applicability, but they fail to account for the lack of expansionist policies on the part of some nations, as well as for the occurrence of imperialism long before nationalism developed as a dominant factor in world politics.

Imperialism as the natural consequence of international power relations. Many observers have held imperialism to be the inevitable result of the simultaneous existence of independent sovereign states. Some have started from the assumption that a balance of power situation leads automatically to attempts by rivals on either side to strengthen their positions at the expense of weaker states and territories; this then initiates a vicious circle of fear, distrust, and armaments which strengthens aggressive tendencies. Others have laid more stress on the objective instability of power relations, as each war sows the seeds of a new one through the continued expansionist spirit of the victor or revanchist desires on the part of the loser. Seemingly stable power relations can, moreover, become unstable through changes of will or modifications in power variables which stir up new fears and new hopes for conquest. Others have regarded the relations between stronger and weaker states as unstable by definition.

As is clear from these and similar models, the explanation of imperialism shades into a general theory of international relations. The term loses its historical connotation and becomes a purely theoretical concept, differently defined in the context of specific theoretical systems.

The word "imperialism" is, therefore, entirely at the mercy of its user. It has been corroded by overfrequent, emotional usage, but if overuse has blunted it as an intellectual tool, the resulting vagueness has certainly not diminished its potency as a political slogan.

HANS DAALDER

[*See also* COLONIALISM; FOREIGN AID; MODERNIZATION; NATIONALISM; PAN MOVEMENTS; TRUSTEESHIP. *Other relevant material may be found in* ECONOMIC GROWTH; EMPIRES; INTERNATIONAL RELATIONS; SOCIAL MOVEMENTS; *and in the biographies of* FANON; HOBSON; KAUTSKY; LENIN; LUXEMBURG; SCHUMPETER.]

BIBLIOGRAPHY

ANGELL, NORMAN (1910) 1913 *The Great Illusion: A Study of the Relation of Military Power to National Advantage.* 4th ed. New York: Putnam.

ARENDT, HANNAH (1951) 1958 *The Origins of Totalitarianism.* 2d ed., enl. New York: Meridian.

ARON, RAYMOND 1951 The Leninist Myth of Imperialism. *Partisan Review* 18:646–662.

ARON, RAYMOND (1951) 1954 *The Century of Total War.* Garden City, N.Y.; Doubleday. → First published in French. A paperback edition was published in 1955 by Beacon.

ARON, RAYMOND 1958 *War and Industrial Society.* Oxford Univ. Press.

BAUER, OTTO (1907) 1924 *Die Nationalitätenfrage und die Sozialdemokratie.* 2 vols. Vienna: Wiener Volksbuchhandlung.

BLAUG, MARK 1961 Economic Imperialism Re-visited. *Yale Review* 50:335–349.

BRAILSFORD, HENRY N. (1914) 1917 *The War of Steel and Gold: A Study of the Armed Peace.* 8th ed. London: Bell.

BRUNSCHWIG, HENRI (1960) 1966 *French Colonialism, 1871–1914: Myth and Realities.* New York: Praeger. → First published in French.

BUKHARIN, NIKOLAI I. (1918) 1929 *Imperialism and World Economy.* New York: International Publishers. → First published in Russian.

CAIRNCROSS, ALEXANDER K. 1953 *Home and Foreign Investment, 1870–1913: Studies in Capital Accumulation.* Cambridge Univ. Press.

CLARK, GROVER 1936 *The Balance Sheets of Imperialism: Facts and Figures on Colonies.* New York: Columbia Univ. Press.

DAALDER, HANS 1962 Capitalism, Colonialism and the Underdeveloped Areas: The Political Economy of (Anti-)Imperialism. Pages 133–165 in Egbert de Vries (editor), *Essays on Unbalanced Growth: A Century of Disparity and Convergence.* The Hague: Mouton.

DILKE, SIR CHARLES W. (1868) 1885 *Greater Britain: A Record of Travel in English-speaking Countries During 1866 and 1867.* 8th ed. London: Macmillan.

DOBB, MAURICE (1937) 1940 *Political Economy and Capitalism: Some Essays in Economic Tradition.* Rev. ed. New York: International Publishers.

EMERSON, RUPERT 1960 *From Empire to Nation: The Rise to Self-assertion of Asian and African Peoples.* Cambridge, Mass.: Harvard Univ. Press. → A paperback edition was published in 1962 by Beacon.

FEIERABEND, IVO K. 1962 Expansionist and Isolationist Tendencies of Totalitarian Political Systems: A Theoretical Note. *Journal of Politics* 24:733–742.

FEIS, HERBERT (1930) 1961 *Europe, the World's Banker, 1870–1914.* New York: Kelley.

FIELDHOUSE, D. K. 1961 Imperialism: An Historiographical Revision. *Economic History Review* Second Series 14:187–209.

FIELDHOUSE, D. K. 1966 *The Colonial Empires.* London: Weidenfeld & Nicolson.

FREYMOND, JACQUES 1951 *Lénine et l'impérialisme.* Lausanne (Switzerland): Payot.

GALLAGHER, JOHN; and ROBINSON, RONALD E. 1953 The Imperialism of Free Trade. *Economic History Review* Second Series 6:1–15.

GROSSMANN, HENRYK 1929 *Das Akkumulations- und Zusammenbruchsgesetz des kapitalistischen Systems (Zugleich eine Krisentheorie).* Leipzig: Hirschfeld.

HALLGARTEN, GEORGE W. F. (1951) 1963 *Imperialismus vor 1914.* 2d ed., enl. 2 vols. Munich: Beck.

HANCOCK, WILLIAM K. 1950 *Wealth of Colonies.* Cambridge Univ. Press.

HILFERDING, RUDOLF (1910) 1955 *Das Finanzkapital: Eine Studie über die jüngste Entwicklung des Kapitalismus.* New ed. Berlin: Dietz.

HOBSON, CHARLES K. 1914 *The Export of Capital.* London: Constable.

HOBSON, JOHN A. (1902) 1948 *Imperialism: A Study.* 3d ed. London: Allen & Unwin.

IMLAH, ALBERT H. 1958 *Economic Elements in the Pax Britannica: Studies in British Foreign Trade in the Nineteenth Century.* Cambridge, Mass.: Harvard Univ. Press.

KAUTSKY, KARL 1915 *Die Internationalität und der Krieg.* Berlin: Vorwärts.

KOEBNER, RICHARD; and SCHMIDT, HELMUT D. 1964 *Imperialism: The Story and Significance of a Political Word, 1840–1960.* Cambridge Univ. Press.

KOHN, HANS 1958 Reflections on Colonialism. Pages 2–16 in Robert Strausz-Hupé and Harry Hazard (editors), *The Idea of Colonialism.* New York: Praeger.

KOLARZ, WALTER 1964 *Communism and Colonialism: Essays.* Edited by George Gretton. New York: St. Martins.

LANDES, DAVID S. 1961 Some Thoughts on the Nature of Economic Imperialism. *Journal of Economic History* 21:496–512.

LANGER, WILLIAM L. (1935) 1951 *The Diplomacy of Imperialism: 1890–1902.* 2d ed. 2 vols. New York: Knopf.

LENIN, VLADIMIR I. (1917) 1947 *Imperialism: The Highest Stage of Capitalism.* Moscow: Foreign Languages Publishing House.

LENIN, VLADIMIR I. 1939 *New Data for V. I. Lenin's* Imperialism: The Highest Stage of Capitalism. Edited by E. Varga and L. Mendelsohn. New York: International Publishers. → Posthumously published materials originally intended for Lenin's *Imperialism.*

LUGARD, FREDERICK J. D. (1922) 1965 *The Dual Mandate in British Tropical Africa.* 5th ed. London: Cass.

LUXEMBURG, ROSA (1913) 1964 *The Accumulation of Capital.* New York: Monthly Review Press. → First published in German.

MORGENTHAU, HANS J. (1948) 1960 *Politics Among Nations: The Struggle for Power and Peace.* 3d ed., rev. New York: Knopf.

NADEL, GEORGE H.; and CURTIS, PERRY (editors) 1964 *Imperialism and Colonialism.* New York: Macmillan.

NEISSER, HANS 1960 Economic Imperialism Reconsidered. *Social Research* 27:63–82.

NKRUMAH, KWAME (1965) 1966 *Neo-colonialism: The Last Stage of Imperialism.* New York: International Publishers.

RENNER, KARL (1917) 1918 *Marxismus, Krieg und Internationale.* 2d enl. ed. Stuttgart (Germany): Dietz.

RICHARDSON, LEWIS F. 1960 *Statistics of Deadly Quarrels.* Pittsburgh: Boxwood Press.

ROBBINS, LIONEL 1939 *The Economic Causes of War.* London: Cape.

ROBINSON, RONALD E.; and GALLAGHER, JOHN 1961 *Africa and the Victorians: The Official Mind of Imperialism.* London: Macmillan; New York: St. Martins.

ROBINSON, RONALD E.; and GALLAGHER, JOHN 1962 The Partition of Africa. Volume 11, pages 593–640 in *The New Cambridge Modern History.* Cambridge Univ. Press.

SCHUMPETER, JOSEPH A. (1919–1927) 1951 *Imperialism and Social Classes.* With an introduction by Bert F. Hoselitz. New York: Kelley. → First published as *Zur Soziologie der Imperialismen,* 1919, and *Die socialen Klassen im ethnisch homogenen Milieu,* 1927. A paperback edition was published in 1955 by Meridian.

SCHUMPETER, JOSEPH A. 1939 *Business Cycles: A Theoretical, Historical, and Statistical Analysis of the Capitalist Process.* 2 vols. New York: McGraw-Hill. → An abridged version was published in 1964.

SEELEY, JOHN R. (1883) 1931 *The Expansion of England: Two Courses of Lectures.* London: Macmillan.

SEGAL, HARVEY H.; and SIMON, MATTHEW 1961 British Foreign Capital Issues: 1865–1894. *Journal of Economic History* 21:566–581.

SEMMEL, BERNARD 1960 *Imperialism and Social Reform: English Social–Imperial Thought, 1895–1914.* Cambridge, Mass.: Harvard Univ. Press.

SETON-WATSON, HUGH 1961 *The New Imperialism.* London: Bodley Head.

SNYDER, LOUIS L. (editor) 1962 *The Imperialism Reader: Documents and Readings on Modern Expansion.* Princeton, N.J.: Van Nostrand.

STALEY, EUGENE 1935 *War and the Private Investor: A Study in the Relations of International Politics and International Private Investment.* Garden City, N.Y.: Doubleday.

STERNBERG, FRITZ 1926 *Der Imperialismus.* Berlin: Malik.

STRACHEY, JOHN 1959 *The End of Empire.* London: Gollancz.

SWEEZY, PAUL M. (1942) 1956 *The Theory of Capitalist Development: Principles of Marxian Political Economy.* New York: Monthly Review Press.

SWEEZY, PAUL M.; and BARAN, PAUL A. 1966 *Monopoly Capital: An Essay on the American Economic and Social Order.* New York: Monthly Review Press.

THORNTON, ARCHIBALD P. 1959 *The Imperial Idea and Its Enemies: A Study in British Power.* New York: St. Martins.

THORNTON, ARCHIBALD P. 1965 *Doctrines of Imperialism.* New York: Wiley.

VINER, JACOB (1924–1949) 1951 *International Economics: Studies.* Glencoe, Ill.: Free Press.

WINSLOW, EARLE M. 1948 *The Pattern of Imperialism: A Study in the Theories of Power.* New York: Columbia Univ. Press.

WOOLF, LEONARD S. 1920 *Economic Imperialism.* London: Swarthmore.

WRIGHT, HARRISON M. (editor) 1961 *The "New Imperialism": Analysis of Late Nineteenth-century Expansion.* Boston: Heath.

WRIGHT, QUINCY (1942) 1965 *A Study of War.* 2d ed. Univ. of Chicago Press.

IMPORTS

See INTERNATIONAL TRADE.

IMPRINTING

The term "imprinting" refers to the rapid acquisition by young animals of the primary social bond to their parents during a limited period very early in life. This imprinting phenomenon can be most clearly seen in precocial bird species, whose young are hatched at a relatively advanced stage of development and are able to move about independently rather soon after hatching. Such species include ducks and other waterfowl, as well as chickens and turkeys. Imprinting also appears to exist in some precocial mammal species, such as the guinea pig (Hess 1959*a*; Shipley 1963). In all of these cases the attachment of the young to the mother is evident when he follows her about. As Morgan (1896) remarked, there is evidently an innate tendency to follow but there is no requirement that the object to be followed be the biological mother. After the infantile following behavior has been outgrown, the attachment continues to exist and forms the basis of later social preferences (Lorenz 1935).

It also appears that the primary socialization processes in other social animals contain features highly similar to those of imprinting. It is now well known that early life experiences play a decisive role in the formation of an animal's or a person's affectional system (e.g., Bowlby 1951; Harlow 1958; Harlow & Harlow 1962). Under normal conditions the first social experiences are with the parents and, in many species, often also with siblings. It is through these early social experiences that individuals become attached to members of their own species. On the other hand, under unusual circumstances, produced either experimentally in a laboratory or accidentally, social attachments to members of an alien species or even to inanimate objects can be formed during the earliest life period.

Primary socialization is of extreme importance not only in determining the cohesiveness of animal groups, important for immediate survival, but also in the continuation of the species, for it often influences the nature of sexual behavior, in particular with respect to the object chosen or accepted (Lorenz 1935). Precocial species provide the clearest instances of imprinting. In the case of species that are not precocial, primary socialization may have different grades of similarity with the classical imprinting phenomenon. One of the most important differences is that the time period involved is not so dramatically short as it is in imprinting and may extend throughout the period of association between young and parents (e.g., Klinghammer 1962; Klinghammer & Hess 1964). But in all cases the primary socialization occurs during the first life period.

History. The importance of a relatively limited period in early life for the formation of social bonds has been well noted. Pliny the Elder, for example, told the tale of a goose that followed Lacydes faithfully (*Naturalis historia*, x). Both D. A. Spalding (1873) and C. L. Morgan (1896) reported that when they hand-reared chicks away from the mother, the chicks completely refused to have anything to do with her when they finally met. C. O. Whitman (Craig 1908) turned this phenomenon to a practical use with nonprecocial, or altricial, species: whenever he wanted to cross two species of pigeons, he would rear the young of one species with foster parents of the other species. When fully grown, pigeons reared with foster parents of a different species preferred to mate with members of that species rather than of their own. Later, Heinroth and Heinroth (1924–1928) hand-reared the young of almost every species of European bird, and noted that many of the social responses of these birds were transferred to their human caretaker. Indeed, interspecies sexual fixation has been observed in other birds, some fishes, and two mammals, the alpaca and vicuña (Goodwin 1948; Baerends & Baerends-van Roon 1950; Hodge 1946).

It was Konrad Lorenz, the eminent European zoologist, who first looked at the phenomenon of imprinting scientifically and postulated some laws governing its occurrence. In a classic paper in 1935, Lorenz described it and gave it its name (in German, *Prägung*). Lorenz pointed out for the first time that if imprinting is to occur, the young animal must be exposed to its object during a *critical period* early in its life. He postulated that the first object to elicit a social response on the part of a young animal later released not only that response but also related ones, such as sexual behavior.

The first systematic investigations on imprinting were published in 1951. The independent work of Ramsay (1951) in the United States and of Fabricius (1951*a*; 1951*b*) in Europe gave the first indications of some of the important factors in imprinting. Most of Ramsay's experiments dealt with exchange of parents and young, although he also imprinted some waterfowl with such objects as a football or a green box. He worked with several species of ducks and a variety of chicken breeds. He noted the importance of auditory stimulation in imprinting and the effect of changes in coloring on recognition of the young by the parents, as well as of the parents by the young. His findings indicated that color is an essential element in recognition, while size or form seemed to be of less importance. Fabricius studied several species of ducks, including tufted ducks, eider ducks, and shovellers. He observed that newly hatched ducklings have a very strong tendency to follow the first moving objects with which they come in contact, for when they were exposed to older ducklings of a different species, they followed them persistently even though they were rewarded only with harassment and violent nipping. Fabricius found that there was a sensitive period during which imprinting occurred most easily: it had its peak at the age of 12 hours and then decreased until, after the age of 24 hours, imprinting was more or less impossible, for the animals became increasingly fearful of new objects. Movement was discovered to be a great influence in eliciting imprinting, as also were rhythmic calls.

Ramsay and Hess (1954) reported a method of studying imprinting in the laboratory, using a runway and a model fitted with a loudspeaker. Later the apparatus was modified as seen in Figure 1. Then Hinde (1955), using moorhens and coots, confirmed the importance of motion in eliciting imprinting responses. He also reported that follow-

Typical apparatus used in imprinting studies, showing a duckling following a decoy around a circular runway. Usually a curtain or screen prevents the animal from seeing the experimenter.

Figure 1

Source: Hess 1959a.

ing was most easily elicited during the first day after hatching; older birds usually fled from the model he presented to them, thus showing the role of fear in ending the sensitive period for imprinting. Furthermore, he noted that if birds were exposed to different models, persistent following took place only with a familiar model.

Since then there have been an increasing number of experimenters who have attempted to assay the imprinting phenomenon, and their work has brought about an increasing understanding of the imprinting process and of the socialization process in general.

The critical period. The most salient feature of the imprinting phenomenon is that it occurs so early in life. Very soon after hatching, chicks and ducklings can follow mother objects and, in fact, show a strong desire to do so. At the very outset, Lorenz (1935) postulated that imprinting could "only take place within a brief critical period in the life of an individual," which was "a very specific physiological state in the young animal's development." He noted that Greylag geese were imprinted during the first few hours after hatching and suggested that imprinting could occur as early as the first few minutes after hatching. He also recorded his observation that some partridges he happened to come across in a field when they were only a few hours old had obviously already been imprinted to their parents and could not be induced to approach him. Other researchers have noted that the readiness to follow an object wanes with increasing age (Alley & Boyd 1950; Hinde 1955; Hinde et al. 1956; Fabricius 1951*b*; Fabricius & Boyd 1954).

However, it was Ramsay and Hess (1954) who determined in the laboratory that there is indeed a rather limited age period during which mallard ducklings can be well imprinted, and that *maximum* imprinting occurs consistently only in ducklings imprinted at the age of 13 to 16 hours. The existence of an optimum developmental stage for imprinting has also been confirmed by Gottlieb (1961*a*), who used special procedures in order to pinpoint the age of his ducklings in days and hours from the very beginning of their embryonic development. It was determined that the age of 27 to 27½ days from the beginning of incubation was indisputably the most sensitive time for imprinting, and that by the age of 28½ days very little imprinting could take place.

Fear has been suggested by many writers as the factor that ends the period of imprintability, and Fabricius (1951*a*) has suggested that the initial inability of birds to locomote could account for the first rise in imprintability. Hess (1959*b*) actually plotted locomotor ability and fearfulness of chicks as a function of age and found that the emergence of fearfulness coincided exactly with the limits of the critical period for imprinting. However, initial imprintability is higher than increasing locomotor skill would suggest.

Interspecies and intraspecies differences. Species and breed differences are emerging as an increasingly important factor in assessing the various parameters of the imprinting phenomenon. According to Hess (1959*a*), some species and breeds, such as wild mallard ducks, show an extremely high degree of imprintability and usually respond quite vigorously to the first imprinting object they meet. They also retain the effects of the experience quite firmly. Leghorn chicks, in comparison with Vantress broiler chicks, may not show as much responsiveness in a laboratory imprinting situation, and even when they have had relatively extensive exposure to an imprinting object, this experience may not be as effective. In spite of the fact that chicks and ducklings have the same critical-period ages for imprinting, the peak of the strength-of-imprinting curve is much lower for chicks than it is for ducklings, as is the general curve itself. There are probably also differences among different species in the type of object that is adequate to arouse imprinting. Other differences between species and between breeds will be brought up as the topic is further pursued. It is, therefore, well to remember that while the socialization processes in different animals may resemble imprinting, generalization between, and even within, species must be cautious and limited.

Prior social and sensory experiences. Many researchers have found that housing chicks communally prior to the imprinting experience decreases imprintability or responsiveness (Guiton 1958; 1959; Sluckin & Salzen 1961; Hess 1962; 1964). It appears that under these circumstances they become imprinted to each other, and that this prior imprinting hinders the formation of imprinting toward a new object. The inhibition of imprinting to a new object when imprinting has already occurred appears to be a basic characteristic of the imprinting phenomenon and has been confirmed by Hess (1959*a*), who found that ducklings imprinted more strongly to models to which they had been first exposed than to a model they met immediately afterward.

Under natural conditions it does appear that imprinting to siblings can occur either simultaneously with or immediately after imprinting to the mother; this might account for "flocking" behavior. The nature of the effect of exposure to siblings before the laboratory imprinting experience has been found to be related both to species membership and to age at exposure to the imprinting experience (Hess 1964). In chicks and ducklings the effect of prior socialization was found to lower imprintability to the model. However, in the case of chicks the amount of following of the model was increased as a result of the socialization experience, especially when these chicks were well past the critical-period age, 36 hours. With ducklings, however, socialization decreased the amount of following as well as of imprintability.

Moltz and Stettner (1961) varied the visual stimulation of some ducklings with hoods that permitted them only diffuse light stimulation. When subjects were tested for imprintability, those that had experienced diffuse light were found to show greater imprintability when first exposed to the imprinting model at the ages of 12, 24, and 48 hours than did those that had lived in normal light conditions. The animals raised in diffuse light were most responsive at the age of 24 hours, while the normal animals were most responsive at the age of 12 hours and responded very little at the age of 48 hours, when the diffuse-light subjects still showed strong responsiveness. Hess (1964), however, has reported somewhat different results with chickens. Dark-reared chicks (like dark-reared ducklings) have maximum responsiveness at the age of 13 to 16 hours after hatching. However, socially isolated chicks exposed for two hours to patterned light stimulation prior to the imprinting experience behaved no differently from completely dark-reared animals if they were placed in the imprinting situation at the age of 16 hours; but if they were exposed to imprinting at the age of 48 hours, they followed somewhat better than the dark-reared ones. This difference, nevertheless, is much less than that resulting from prior social experience.

Experimental variables. Hess (1957) has postulated a law of effort in imprinting, which states that the more effort a young chick or duckling expends while following or attempting to be with the imprinting model, the more strongly it will be imprinted, as shown by later preference behavior when both the imprinting model and an unfamiliar one are offered. Imprinting-strength scores were obtained for 12- to 17-hour-old ducklings, who were made to follow an imprinting model for different distances in a ten-minute period. The greater the distance the ducklings had to follow, the better they were imprinted. This held true up to 50 feet, after which further distances did not materially increase imprinting strength. Moreover, when ducklings were allowed different amounts of time to follow the model for the same distance, the imprinting-strength scores for the same following distances were essentially identical. Evidently time in itself has no effect on the strength of imprinting.

Furthermore, muscle relaxation prevents imprinting, as shown by the failure of chicks and ducks that had been imprinted while under the influence of either meprobamate or carisoprodol to show any effect of the experience when tested later. If animals are imprinted normally but tested under drug conditions, there is no effect of the drug (Hess 1957; Hess et al. 1959). This, together with the fact that socialized chicks follow well but do not imprint well when an attempt is made to imprint them after the critical period, demonstrates that the law of effort applies only to socially naive normal animals exposed to the imprinting situation at the critical-age period.

It also appears, on the basis of several experiments (Hess 1957; 1959*a*; 1959*c*), that some of the research that has attempted to assess the law of effort by preventing animals from following the imprinting model have failed to take into account the effort expended by subjects struggling to escape restraint or approach the model. The effectiveness of struggle when animals cannot move is shown by the fact that chicks and ducklings have a greater imprintability in the first few hours after hatching than their locomotor skill would seem to indicate. Furthermore, Gottlieb (1961*b*) has shown that equal imprinting strength in two different duck varieties does not necessarily reflect the same amount of following; thus, if the amount of following is to be taken as a valid indicator of probable imprinting strength, any comparisons must be between animals of the same variety.

The effect of painful stimulation during the imprinting experience is also an important factor. Fabricius (1951*a*) early reported the fact that his ducklings persisted in following older ducklings who maltreated them vigorously. Hess (1959*c*) observed that when ducklings were being imprinted to a human being who carelessly stepped on their toes, they did not run away in fear but stayed even closer. Kovach and Hess (1963) have demonstrated experimentally that during the critical-age period the administration of painful electric shocks enhances the amount of following during the imprinting experience, while after the critical age electric shocks depress following. These results emphasize the importance of the critical-age period; during it imprinting is enhanced by punishment, while after it imprinting is hindered, suggesting that the processes occurring after the critical period conform far more closely to the laws of conventional association learning than do the processes occurring during the critical period.

Other variables. While a perusal of the research literature shows that young birds can respond to an amazingly wide variety of different objects in the same way in which they would respond to their own mother, there are also indications that some characteristics of a potential imprinting object are more effective in eliciting imprinting than are others. Ramsay (1951), for example, indicated early that color was important, while size and shape appeared to be less so. Others (Lorenz 1935; Fabricius 1951*a*) have shown that rhythmic sounds are more effective than other types of sounds, that low-pitched ones arouse imprinting more than high-pitched ones (Collias & Collias 1956), and so forth. Schaefer and Hess (1959) have demonstrated that certain colors are more capable of eliciting imprinting, and that certain shapes are more potent than others in terms of both following behavior during imprinting and test scores when the chicks were confronted at a later age with the imprinting model and unfamiliar ones.

Food imprinting. Hess (1962; 1964) has suggested that imprinting, conceived of as the rapid acquisition of an object toward which an innate response could be directed, is not limited to the formation of social bonds but also applies to the learning of food objects by chicks at the third day of age. He carried out experiments in which chicks were given food reward for pecking at specific stimuli and were not rewarded for pecking at others. In the face of withdrawal of food, the effects of this experience were strongest when the rewarding had occurred during the third day of age; the greater the time interval between that age and the time of rewarding, the less was the effect of the experience. When the rewarding had occurred at the age of one day or at more than five days, there was no effect on the pecking behavior; but when the chicks had been rewarded at the age of three days, they continued to peck at the specific stimuli for at least ten days without any signs of decreasing intensity, even though there was no longer any food reward.

Furthermore, Hess (1962; 1964) found that if the food-reward experience took place while the three-day-old chicks were under the influence of either meprobamate or carisoprodol, when food reward was removed the chicks behaved essentially as if they had never had the reward experience. Hess therefore concluded that this phenomenon showed much more similarity to imprinting than to more common association-learning processes and must represent true imprinting of food objects. He did not, of course, claim food imprinting and social imprinting to be alike in all respects, for they are related to two very different vital functions—social cohesiveness, necessary for the survival of a social species, and ingestion of nutritious material, necessary for the survival of the individual.

Imprinting and learning. While in both imprinting and learning, a relationship or "connection" is established between an object and a response, there is a basic distinction between the two processes. In imprinting there is a critical period, developmentally timed, during which certain wide classes of stimuli act as releasers or unconditioned stimuli for certain types of innate responses; whereas, in ordinary association learning, the object in question does not act as an unconditional stimulus for the response but is initially neutral in its effect on the animal's behavior. There is no critical period for association learning, although cases have been found where learning ability *increases* with age, in contrast to the *decreasing* of imprintability as the animal grows older.

Association learning is more effective when practice trials are spaced than when they are massed, whereas in imprinting massed effort has been found to facilitate the formation of imprinted social bonds.

Furthermore, Hess (1962; 1964) has reported that meprobamate and carisoprodol do not at all hinder either the learning or the retention of ordinary visual-discrimination learning with food as a reward, whereas it impedes both social and food imprinting.

Finally, it is well established that in association

learning it is what has been most recently learned that is remembered the best. However, in imprinting, what has been learned first is the strongest, as shown by experiments in which ducklings were exposed to two different imprinting models during the critical-age period (Hess 1959*a*; 1959*b*; 1959*c*). The studies of the effects of socialization with siblings on imprintability to a parent model also demonstrate the importance of primacy in imprinting (Hess 1964).

It is of extreme importance to be aware of these differences between imprinting and association learning, because once the appropriate critical-age period has passed without imprinting's having occurred, for lack of exposure to a suitable object, it is possible to use any stimulus to which the animal could have responded earlier as a potential conditioned stimulus, to which it may be trained, through conventional means, to make conditioned responses. Here the animal can readily generalize to other objects, thus increasing the range to which it can make conditioned responses, in contrast to the fact that when an animal has actually been imprinted to an object during the critical period, only this particular object or ones very much like it will, from then on, act as unconditional stimuli, though the range to which the animal was first capable of responding was very broad. What is more, even if imprinting has already occurred during the critical period, the animal can still be trained, through association learning, to make conditioned responses to objects to which it has not been imprinted. In such a case the response to the imprinted object may seem, superficially, to be just like the conditioned responses that the animal has been trained to make to a conditioned stimulus. But these two categories of responses are completely different in terms of the conditions of their origins and also in terms of their long-range effects on the character of the animal's behavior.

Both social imprinting and food imprinting have counterparts in association learning. Taming is the association-learning counterpart of social imprinting; humans can tame an animal that has already been imprinted to its own species. But the two social bonds are not alike, for a tamed animal will court and attempt to mate with members of the opposite sex of its own species, not with human beings. Skinnerian experiments, in which birds are trained to peck at colored lights in order to obtain food or water, reflect the association-learning counterpart of food imprinting. But upon complete withdrawal of food reward, the bird's pecking response to a colored light will soon disappear, while chicks imprinted to certain food objects when three days old do not lose their acquired pecking habits, even after long experience with no food reward.

ECKHARD H. HESS

[*Other relevant material may be found in* ETHOLOGY; INSTINCT; LEARNING; PSYCHOLOGY, *article on* COMPARATIVE PSYCHOLOGY; SOCIALIZATION.]

BIBLIOGRAPHY

ALLEY, R.; and BOYD, H. 1950 Parent–Young Recognition in the Coot. *Ibis* 92:46–51.

BAERENDS, G. P.; and BAERENDS-VAN ROON, J. M. 1950 *An Introduction to the Study of the Ethology of Cichlid Fishes*. Behaviour Supplement no. 1. Leiden (Netherlands): Brill.

BOWLBY, JOHN 1951 *Maternal Care and Mental Health*. Geneva: World Health Organisation.

COLLIAS, NICHOLAS E.; and COLLIAS, ELSIE C. 1956 Some Mechanisms of Family Integration in Ducks. *Auk* 73: 378–400.

CRAIG, WALLACE 1908 The Voices of Pigeons Regarded as a Means of Social Control. *American Journal of Sociology* 14:86–100.

FABRICIUS, ERIC 1951*a* Zur Ethologie junger Anatiden. *Acta zoologica fennica* 68:1–178.

FABRICIUS, ERIC 1951*b* Some Experiments on Imprinting Phenomena in Ducks. Pages 375–379 in International Ornithological Congress, Tenth, Uppsala, 1950, *Proceedings*. Uppsala (Sweden): Almqvist & Wiksell.

FABRICIUS, ERIC; and BOYD, H. 1954 Experiments on the Following Reactions of Ducklings. Wildfowl Trust, *Annual Report* 6:84–89.

GOODWIN, D. 1948 Some Abnormal Sexual Fixations in Birds. *Ibis* 90:45–48.

GOTTLIEB, GILBERT 1961*a* Developmental Age as a Baseline for Determination of the Critical Period in Imprinting. *Journal of Comparative and Physiological Psychology* 54:422–427.

GOTTLIEB, GILBERT 1961*b* The Following-response and Imprinting in Wild and Domestic Ducklings of the Same Species. *Behaviour* 18:205–228.

GUITON, PHILIP 1958 The Effect of Isolation on the Following Response of Brown Leghorn Chicks. Royal Physics Society of Edinburgh, *Proceedings* 27:9–14.

GUITON, PHILIP 1959 Socialization and Imprinting in Brown Leghorn Chicks. *Animal Behavior* 7:26–34.

HARLOW, HARRY F. 1958 The Nature of Love. *American Psychologist* 13:673–685.

HARLOW, HARRY F.; and HARLOW, MARGARET K. 1962 Social Deprivation in Monkeys. *Scientific American* 207, Nov.:136–146.

HEINROTH, OSKAR; and HEINROTH, MAGDALENA 1924–1928 *Die Vögel Mitteleuropas*. 3 vols. Berlin: Bermühler.

HESS, ECKHARD H. 1957 Effects of Meprobamate on Imprinting in Waterfowl. New York Academy of Sciences, *Annals* 67:724–732.

HESS, ECKHARD H. 1959*a* Imprinting. *Science* 130:133–141.

HESS, ECKHARD H. 1959*b* The Relationship Between Imprinting and Motivation. Volume 7, pages 44–77 in *Nebraska Symposium on Motivation*. Edited by Marshall R. Jones. Lincoln: Univ. of Nebraska Press.

HESS, ECKHARD H. 1959*c* Two Conditions Limiting Critical Age for Imprinting. *Journal of Comparative and Physiological Psychology* 52:515–518.

HESS, ECKHARD H. 1962 Imprinting and the "Critical Period" Concept. Pages 254–263 in Eugene L. Bliss (editor), *Roots of Behavior.* New York: Harper.

HESS, ECKHARD H. 1964 Imprinting in Birds. *Science* 146:1128–1139.

HESS, ECKHARD H.; POLT, JAMES M.; and GOODWIN, ELIZABETH 1959 Effects of Carisoprodol on Early Experience and Learning. Pages 51–64 in James G. Miller (editor), *The Pharmacology and Clinical Usefulness of Carisoprodol.* Detroit, Mich.: Wayne State Univ. Press.

HINDE, R. A. 1955 The Following Response of Moorhens and Coots. *British Journal of Animal Behaviour* 3: 121–122.

HINDE, R. A.; THORPE, W. H.; and VINCE, M. A. 1956 The Following Response of Young Coots and Moorhens. *Behaviour* 9:214–242.

HODGE, W. H. 1946 Camels of the Clouds. *National Geographic Magazine* 89:641–656.

KLINGHAMMER, ERICH 1962 Imprinting in Altricial Birds: The Ring Dove *Streptopelia roseogrisia* and the Mourning Dove *Zenaidura macruora carolensis.* Ph.D. dissertation, Univ. of Chicago.

KLINGHAMMER, ERICH; and HESS, ECKHARD H. 1964 Imprinting in an Altricial Bird: The Blond Ring Dove *Streptopelia risoria. Science* 146:265–266.

KOVACH, JOSEPH; and HESS, ECKHARD H. 1963 Imprinting: Effects of Painful Stimulation on the Following Response. *Journal of Comparative and Physiological Psychology* 56:461–464.

LORENZ, K. Z. 1935 Der Kumpan in der Umwelt des Vogels. *Journal für Ornithologie* 83:137–213, 289–413

MOLTZ, HOWARD 1960 Imprinting: Empirical Basis and Theoretical Significance. *Psychological Bulletin* 57: 291–314.

MOLTZ, HOWARD; and STETTNER, L. JAY 1961 The Influence of Patterned-light Deprivation on the Critical Period for Imprinting. *Journal of Comparative and Physiological Psychology* 54:279–283.

MORGAN, C. LLOYD 1896 *Habit and Instinct.* London and New York: Arnold.

RAMSAY, A. O. 1951 Familial Recognition in Domestic Birds. *Auk* 68:1–16.

RAMSAY, A. O.; and HESS, E. H. 1954 A Laboratory Approach to the Study of Imprinting. *Wilson Bulletin* 66:196–206.

SCHAEFER, HALMUTH H.; and HESS, ECKHARD H. 1959 Color Preferences in Imprinting Objects. *Zeitschrift für Tierpsychologie* 16:161–172.

SHIPLEY, WILLIAM U. 1963 The Demonstration in the Domestic Guinea Pig of a Process Resembling Classical Imprinting. *Animal Behaviour* 11:470–474.

SLUCKIN, W. 1964 *Imprinting and Early Learning.* London: Methuen.

SLUCKIN, W.; and SALZEN, E. A. 1961 Imprinting and Perceptual Learning. *Quarterly Journal of Experimental Psychology* 13:65–77.

SPALDING, DOUGLAS A. (1873) 1954 Instinct, With Original Observations on Young Animals. *British Journal of Animal Behaviour* 2:2–11.

INCENTIVES

See ACHIEVEMENT MOTIVATION; DRIVES; INDUSTRIAL RELATIONS; MOTIVATION; SOCIAL CONTROL; STIMULATION DRIVES; WAGES.

INCEST

Incest is the infraction of the taboo upon sexual relations between any two members of the nuclear family except husband and wife, that is, between parents and children or any sibling pair. The taboo may be extended to include other specific relatives or categories of kin, whose relationship ties may be biological, affinal, classificatory, or fictive, and sexual relations between any two individuals so defined will be treated as incest. "Taboo" is a more appropriate term than "prohibition," for the incest interdiction, which often lacks any legal sanction, is typically accompanied by a special sense of intense horror. In its most stringent applications the taboo may preclude any overt expression of intimacy by, or interaction between, those affected by the interdiction. Although the incest taboo in some form occurs in every known society, there is great variation among societies not only with regard to the extensiveness of its application and the range of intensity of associated emotions but also in the occurrence of ceremonial and customary abrogations and in the relative frequency of specific types of infraction.

As the incest taboo serves to distinguish between those with whom sexual relations are forbidden and those with whom they are permitted, it provides a basis for more elaborate types of differentiation. Discrimination among more distant kin may take the form of a gradual modification of the taboo upon intimacy, so that, by small degrees, permitted overt expressions of affection, ribald joking, and minor courtship behavior shade into permitted intercourse, informal cohabitation, and fully recognized marriage. The incest taboo may also provide a basis for distinguishing those relatives with whom marriage is preferred or upon whom it is enjoined.

In effect the incest taboo establishes bounded groups in complementary relationship to each other. In most societies one finds a complementary relationship between the small, inner group of kin, whose members are forbidden to have sexual relations with or marry one another (except where, under special circumstances, the taboo is abrogated), and a larger social group, within which marriage is condoned, permitted, preferred, treated as a legal right (as when a man has a claim on his mother's brother's daughter as a potential wife), or, in the extreme case, enjoined. In some societies, very specific boundaries to this group are set, insofar as marriage may be enjoined upon members of moieties, within a lineage or a caste, or upon members of two castes (Davis 1941). A further extension would forbid sex relations or, more specifically, marriage with anyone not belonging to a particular lineage or caste or with anyone belonging to a different religious, ethnic, or racial group. In some societies the penalties for crossing this outer boundary may be no less stringent than the sanctions on incest within the small kin group, and infractions of the prohibition may evoke a similar feeling of "grisly horror" (Murdock 1949; see also Davis 1941; Merton 1941). In other societies, however, the sanctions on out-group marriage may be very mild, and the occurrence of such marriages may evoke only slight disapproval (Fox 1962; Goode 1963).

Functionally the incest taboo serves to establish a double set of boundaries, the dimensions of which are specific to each society. Observances of correct behavior within these boundaries confer certain benefits, such as solidarity within the family and the household (Malinowski 1927; also Parsons 1954; Seligman 1929); clarity of rules (Homans 1950; Parsons 1954); continuity of social ties, based on marriage within families, clans, communities, tribes, or political states (Fortune 1932); and clarity of definition of the larger group —the caste, the class, the cluster of lineages, the village, the tribe, the religious group, or the nation—within which marriage is permitted and outside of which ties based on marriage should not be formed.

Conventionally the term "incest" has been applied to all infractions of the taboo upon sex and marriage with those who belong to the innermost circle, that is, the set of primary biological kin and those categories of persons who, by cultural definition, are assimilated to close kin. A category of this kind may include all members of the opposite sex in one's own matrilineal or patrilineal group—a definition that provides the basis for the association frequently made between totemism and exogamy (Durkheim 1898; Frazer 1910)—or it may include all members of the opposite sex belonging to one's own half of a dual organization. Other categories of persons who may be so defined include step and foster kin, coresidents of a household, a spouse's close kin (as in England, where until recently marriage to a deceased wife's sister was prohibited), children of hereditary trade partners, godparent and godchild, physician and patient, and, occasionally, two persons who once were but no longer are betrothed or married to each other.

In most societies, however, certain differences are recognized between those who are close biological kin and those who are, in fact, classificatory kin or whose kinship is based on affinal or fictive ties. Outside the immediate family group the sense of horror, which is so pervasive and intense an element in attitudes toward incest between primary kin, is progressively diluted, and penalties for infractions become milder. This weakening of restraints is reflected in the existence of devices by which prohibitions against sex and marriage may be overcome or evaded. Among aboriginal Australians, for example, elopement followed by a period of ostracism was a necessary prelude to the recognition of certain marriages. In much the same way in the United States, prohibitions that prevent marriage between ineligible persons are often modified by certain devices. For example, the laws of some states forbid the marriage of a white person and a person of any known African ancestry to the third generation (Davis 1941), and in other states first-cousin marriage is prohibited (Weinberg 1955). In such instances, marriage may involve travel to a state where a legal ceremony can be performed.

In the study of primitive societies, anthropologists differentiate between the rules of exogamy, which define the inner circle within which marriage is forbidden, and the rules of endogamy, which define the boundaries within which marriage is enjoined. Today, in large, complex societies endogamous regulations have for the most part fallen into disuse, and in general, specific legal prohibitions against marriage are limited to those affecting members of the nuclear family. There are, however, certain exceptions. The various laws against interracial marriage in the southeastern United States, the apartheid laws in South Africa, the decrees forbidding the marriage of Jews and gentiles instituted by the Nazi regime in Germany, and the special form of morganatic marriage between royalty and commoner in Europe (a rare occurrence today) exemplify politically enforced endogamy. Endogamy also may be enjoined by regulations based, not on political, but on religious sanctions. Examples of this kind of interdiction against out-group marriage are the sanctions that seek to prevent an Orthodox Jew from marrying a gentile, a Balinese woman from marrying a man of a lower caste than her own, a Quaker from marrying out of meeting, or a Singhalese Bahai from marrying into any other sect. Although the state in some countries (for example, Italy, Greece, and Israel) gives legal support to religious sanctions against certain types of out-group marriage, this practice contravenes the tendency of modern states to recognize as a civil right the freedom of any citizen to marry any other citizen.

In contrast, in primitive and exotic societies the distinctions between legal and religiously or magically sanctioned prohibitions may be far less clearly marked. Those who enter into inappropriate sex relations or who attempt to override prohibitions against marriage may be punished by socially enforced penalties such as banishment or death. Alternatively, punishment may be left to the automatic operation of supernatural sanctions, such as those expressed in the beliefs that the child of an incestuous union will be deformed or will die or that the whole line will be cursed. Similarly taboos upon intercaste, interreligious, or interracial marriage may be heavily supported by legal penalties, or alternatively, their observance may be enforced mainly by fear of the sense of outrage, loathing, and horror that any infraction would evoke.

Balinese traditional culture illustrates very well the complexity of such a sanctioning system. Primary incest, which was treated both as a legal and as a religious offense, required the banishment of the offenders and a ritual cleansing of the land. A sexual relationship between a high-caste man and a lower-caste woman could be religiously regularized, but the reverse situation, in which a woman became sexually involved with a man belonging to a caste lower than hers, was classified with bestiality, and the offense was treated with the same severity as primary incest. The birth of twins of opposite sex to low-caste parents was also treated as primary incest, as it was assumed that brother and sister had committed incest in the womb. In contrast, twins of opposite sex born to a family of the *Kṣatriya* caste, from which rajas came, were enjoined to marry (Belo 1935). In these Balinese institutions, one finds both the expression of horror evoked by human behavior that is equated with the behavior of animals and inversions of a kind that occur in connection with the privileged breaking of taboos. Such contrasting forms of behavior are not genuine polar opposites; rather, they are aspects of different psychological categories and may have different historical antecedents.

Approaches to the study of incest

The most satisfactory hypotheses about the origins of the association of the incest taboo with the sanction of horror are those formulated by Émile Durkheim (1898) and Sigmund Freud (1913; 1919). Durkheim, in his analysis, emphasized the horror of shedding the blood of a "blood" relative, regardless of whether the bloodshed was occasioned by an act of murder or came about as a result of defloration and childbirth. Freud, in turn, emphasized the psychic ambivalence that characterizes attitudes toward close kin and related to this the sense of horror combined with the sense of the uncanny associated with the commission of acts that recall repressed forbidden impulses.

Historically, discussions of incest have suffered both from a failure to distinguish fully among the numerous themes with which incest prohibitions and infractions of the incest taboo have been associated and from a failure to distinguish fully among the various social contexts within which infractions have occurred. The explicit abrogation of the incest taboo in royal marriage (e.g., in Egypt and Hawaii, among the Inca of Peru and the Azande of west Africa); the treatment of incest as a sacred ritual act (as when a man copulates with his sister or daughter before some magically sanctioned undertaking); the practice of marrying or of taking a forbidden relative as a sexual object on the part of a tyrant, as a demonstration of his power; the appropriation of women of a lower caste or class by men in superordinate positions; the tyranny exercised by a father or an elder brother within some isolated social group; and the occurrence of incest within a socially stigmatized group—each of these is a different kind of event in a different type of social setting; each must be interpreted within the specific context of that larger whole of which the broken marriage regulation forms only a part. If, for example, the marriage of royal brother and sister is itself regarded, not as a privileged, but as a sacred act, there is a fusion of attitudes toward the "sacred and holy" and the "sacred and horrible."

Discussions of incest have suffered also from a failure to take into account the full range of relevant behaviors. Whereas some writers have focused primarily on the question of the origins of the incest taboo (Briffault 1927; Durkheim 1898; Frazer 1910; S. Freud 1913; Westermarck 1889), others have been concerned mainly with the problem of function—with the incest taboo as it serves to protect the integrity of the family (S. Freud 1930; Malinowski 1927; 1929; Parsons 1954; Seligman 1929), as it serves to prevent very close inbreeding, with its genetic implications (Aberle et al. 1963; Tylor 1888; Westermarck 1889), or, conversely, as it supports the social functions of exogamic rules (Fortune 1932; Lévi-Strauss 1949; White 1948).

A different approach to the problem has been taken by those who have raised questions about various aspects of the incest taboo. Discussions of this kind have been concerned, for example, with the differences between parent–child and brother–sister incest (Fox 1962); with the relative importance of prohibitions on each of the four types of first-cousin marriage (Ember 1966); with the relationship of incest regulations to attitudes of aversion toward the primary kin with whom the individual is reared (Westermarck 1889) or, conversely, with their relationship to feelings of attraction toward primary kin (S. Freud 1913); and with the conflict between society's demand for participation and the preference of pairs for withdrawal (P. E. Slater 1963). At different periods shifts in interest in specific aspects of behavior related to incest have been reflected in marked changes in emphasis in studies of the subject. While some years ago the problem of the relationship of incest taboos to totemism was a subject of major interest (Bergson 1932; Durkheim 1898; Frazer 1910), a contemporary analysis of totemism may omit any discussion of the problem of the association between the incest taboo and a kin group taboo on a plant or an animal (Lévi-Strauss 1962).

Although several attempts have been made to treat incest inclusively (e.g., Lowie 1948; Murdock 1949), these tend to be very schematic, in the sense of including under one rubric an extremely wide variety of human institutions that are concerned with the prohibition of sex relationships. Moreover, the prevailing emphasis on incest taboos as they are related to the regulation of marriage has resulted in an almost total neglect of homosexual incest, except for Parsons' role speculations (1954). Goode (1963) has demonstrated that Western ethnocentrism has affected adversely the ability of research workers to discern forms of incest found in non-Western societies. Recently, Cohen (1964) has attempted to relate methods of inculcating the primary incest taboos on other features of social organization. His analysis indicates that the early extrusion of children from the parental home is systematically associated with the assignment of teaching and training roles to specified kin and with the juridical interchangeability of members of a kin group. In contrast, in those societies in which children remain within the parental home until adolescence, they are taught sometimes by parents and sometimes by strangers and there is individual responsibility before the law. Although Cohen's study has opened up a new line of inquiry, it is compromised by the invocation of still another psychological single-origin hypothesis, namely, the idea that incest regulation is based on the individual's need for privacy.

The fragmentation and the discontinuities that have characterized discussion of the incest complex have resulted in a vast proliferation of empty polemics. One source of the difficulty has been the undifferentiated use of a single, ethnocentrically loaded word to refer to historically and cross-culturally diverse forms of behavior (Goody 1956). But the development of an integrated theory based on a full consideration of available data also has been hindered by the accidents of the division of labor among the social sciences and by social scientists' peculiar preference for originality—rather than progression—as the criterion for a "new" theoretical formulation.

In general, sociologists have been concerned with incest as it reflects social or familial disorganization (Weinberg 1955) or as it has been useful in the development of role theory or of formal models of social structure (Davis 1941; Homans 1950; Merton 1941; Parsons 1954). Dynamically oriented psychologists and psychiatrists have focused their attention mainly on the existence of impulses toward incest and on the psychological defenses against the expression of these impulses (Bettelheim 1954; S. Freud 1913; Róheim 1934). Anthropologists, who have obtained most of their data through studies of primitive peoples and kin-based social systems, have concentrated on the description and analysis of the basic forms of the incest taboo and its extensions. At times, however, as a result of undisciplined excursions into other disciplines (Devons & Gluckman 1964), they have attempted the formulation of various physiologically or biologically based theories of the origins of these taboos in imputed human emotions or cognitive capacities (Crawley 1902; Frazer 1910; Seligman 1950; Tylor 1888; Westermarck 1889).

Other factors, also, have contributed to the discontinuity of discussion and the lack of theoretical integration. Chief among these is the problem of inclusiveness. More recent attempts to make a comprehensive analysis (e.g., Cohen 1964; Davis 1941; Goody 1956; Merton 1941; Middleton 1962; Parsons 1954) underline the difficulties that are inherent in any attempt to treat within the limits of a single article or small book the ramifications of the subject of forbidden, permitted, and enjoined sexual relationships on a world-wide basis. This problem was foreshadowed long ago in Frazer's massive four-volume study, *Totemism and Exogamy* (1910). Invariably, the effort to achieve conciseness has resulted not only in an overemphasis on some aspects at the expense of others but also in the neglect of much of the comparative evidence. For example, we are lacking a careful examination of the sanctions on near-kin marriage among commoners in Egypt and possibly also in Iran (Middleton 1962). In addition, these partial studies have tended to emphasize discontinuous, as opposed to cumulative, theory building.

Recently, fresh approaches to the subject have been stimulated by research findings in a wider range of disciplines. The rapid expansion of knowledge about the conditions of pre-Homo-sapiens life has led to a re-examination of earlier premises about the institutional origins of incest taboos (Aberle et al. 1963; M. K. Slater 1959, based on Krzywicki 1934; Wallis 1950). Recent research on human genetics has been followed by new work on the dysgenic effects of endogamy as well as on the eugenic effects of specific types of marriage regulation (Aberle et al. 1963; Ember 1966; Stern 1949). Following on Sigmund Freud's work, which was based on studies of adult patients, a more detailed examination, through child analysis, has been made of the involvement of individuals in various phases of development, specifically in respect to incest (Erikson 1950; A. Freud 1965). Psychoanalytic insights also have given a new impetus to the study of myth and fantasy as they express themes related to incest and incest prohibitions (Herskovits & Herskovits 1958; Layard 1960; Lessa 1956). In the same period closer observational and experimental studies of the behavior of wild and domesticated animals (Allee 1938; Altmann 1961; Count 1958; Hutchinson 1959; Lorenz 1959) have made it possible to place the issues of early experience and the establishment of forms of mating and parental behavior within the context of behavior as an evolutionary mechanism (Roe & Simpson 1958). And finally, the adaption of methods developed in modern clinical studies to modern ethnological materials has opened the way to detailed examinations of contemporary familial structures, such as the delineation of the three-generation pattern in eastern European Jewish culture (Landes & Zborowski 1950) and the analysis of the modern institution of the honeymoon (P. E. Slater 1963).

Considered conjointly, these approaches—which have provided new material on familial structures; on childhood behavior based on direct observation; on adult fantasy as expressed in myth, dream, and free association; on the structure of hominid communities in terms of age, generational spread, and size of group; and on the operation of natural selection on predispositions that are genetically controlled—have led to a reassessment of previously held assumptions in anthropology. In particular, they have made possible a re-examination of older anthropological conclusions about the Oedipus complex (Kroeber 1939). Today, Oedipal conflict can be treated as a biological survival from an evolutionary stage in which hominid forms reached reproductive maturity without an intervening latency phase (Mead 1961*a*; 1963*a*; 1963*b*).

Examination of cases of incest that have occurred in situations in which even limited intrafamilial or community sanctions against incest were lacking (Barry & Johnson 1958; Rascovsky & Rascovsky 1950; Weinberg 1955; Wilson 1963) supports the hypothesis that incestuous behavior is a strong human potentiality. On the other hand, evidence to support the hypothesis presented by Westermarck (1889), namely, that familiarity and great permissiveness breed aversion, is provided by studies of children who have been reared as an age set in a fictive kinship setting, as, for example, in an Israeli kibbutz (Spiro 1958; see also Fox 1962).

Incest in contemporary societies

Problems of immediate social urgency have arisen from the specific conditions of modern urban life. In general, very rapid and world-wide industrialization, urbanization, and modernization have tended to strengthen the nuclear family, at the expense of larger household and kin groups. But there also have been countermovements, in which attempts have been made to weaken primary family ties through collective forms of living, as in the case of the historic Hutterite communities, the earlier forms of collectivization in the Soviet Union, the modern Israeli kibbutzim, and, most recently, the collective communities reported for China. For those who are reared within it, each type of social setting—the nuclear family, the joint or extended family, or the collectivity of children organized into age grades—has its special hazard. In the nuclear family, this may take the form of overdependence on childhood ties; in the extended family, a tendency to develop endogamous overspecialization; and in age-graded children's groups, an overdependence on the peer group. Within the context of industrialized urbanization the problems that are most prominent are those peculiar to the narrowly defined two-generation family.

At present in the United States, one finds associated with the institution of the two-generation family both very early, parentally stimulated sexual behavior and flaunted, exhibitionistic physical intimacy on the part of adolescents (Wolfenstein

1965). Early marriage and early parenthood are replacing economic independence as the most significant marks of the individual's break with his (or her) family of origin and of the resolution of childhood attachments to the parents (Mead 1959; 1961*b*).

In contemporary societies the phenomena of increased life expectancy, reduced hazards of childbearing, and frequent divorce have been accompanied by a widespread acceptance of a "scientific" explanation of the incest taboo as having no function other than the prevention of close inbreeding, with its assumed deleterious genetic effects. Where this explanation has been accepted as sufficient, it has meant a weakening of the sanctions that, in the past, protected the relations between adults and stepchildren or foster children, particularly between stepfathers and stepdaughters and between sons and fathers' young second wives. Where the more broadly based sanctioning system has broken down, the household may become a setting for cross-generational reciprocal seduction and exploitation, rather than fulfilling its historic role of protecting the immature and permitting the safe development of strong affectional ties in a context where sex relationships are limited to spouses. This development has coincided with and must be seen in relation to a world-wide reorganization of traditional attitudes toward caste, class, racial, and religious interrelationships. Incest itself has become a literary theme, a symbol for the expression of violence, social discord, alienation of feeling, and various beliefs about the transformation of man under new conditions produced by science. Today there are even arguments in favor of incest, on the grounds that the taboo was associated with a now outmoded period of history, when small groups required this form of protection (Masters 1963), and that new evidence suggests that, in the past, high cultures have been able to incorporate the marriage of very near kin (Middleton 1962).

Incest taboos, as one aspect of the regulation of sex and marriage, are integral to all known forms of social organization. Their form and function have varied extremely from one culture to another, in small and large societies, and in simple and complex societies. There seem to be no grounds for attributing the formation of this sanctioning system, by which an equilibrium is maintained between close and wide social ties, to any single set of innate human characteristics or to any specific set of historical circumstances. The universality of the occurrence of incest regulations, whatever form they may take or particular functions they may serve in a specific culture, suggests that they are part of a very complex system with deep biological roots, a system that is both a condition and a consequence of human evolution. Variations in the form and function of incest taboos suggest also that the formation of human character and the functioning of social systems are so intricately related to specific historical forms that changes within a social system are necessarily accompanied by some breakdown in the previously recognized patterning of personal relationships. Widespread failure to observe incest regulations is an index of the disruption of a sociocultural system that may be even more significant than the more usual indexes of crime, suicide, and homicide.

MARGARET MEAD

BIBLIOGRAPHY

ABERLE, DAVID F. et al. 1963 The Incest Taboo and the Mating Patterns of Animals. *American Anthropologist* New Series 65:253–265.

ADAMS, ROMANZO 1937 *Interracial Marriage in Hawaii.* New York: Macmillan.

ALDRIDGE, ALFRED O. 1951 The Meaning of Incest From Hutcheson to Gibbon. *Ethics* 61:309–313.

ALLEE, W. C. (1938) 1951 *Cooperation Among Animals, With Human Implications.* Rev. & enl. ed. New York: Schuman. → First published as *The Social Life of Animals.* A paperback edition was published in 1958 by Beacon.

ALPERT, HARRY 1958 Émile Durkheim: Enemy of Fixed Psychological Elements. *American Journal of Sociology* 63:662–665.

ALTMANN, MARGARET 1961 Sex Dynamics Within Kinships of Free Ranging, Wild Ungulates. Paper presented at the sixtieth annual meeting of the American Association for the Advancement of Science. Unpublished manuscript.

ARIETI, SILVANO 1955 *Interpretation of Schizophrenia.* New York: Brunner.

BARRY, MAURICE J. JR.; and JOHNSON, ADELAIDE M. 1958 The Incest Barrier. *Psychoanalytic Quarterly* 27:485–500.

BEALS, RALPH L.; and HOIJER, HARRY (1953) 1965 *An Introduction to Anthropology.* 3d ed. New York: Macmillan.

BELO, JANE 1935 A Study of Customs Pertaining to Twins in Bali. *Tijdschrift voor indische taal-, land- en volkenkunde* 75:483–549.

BERGSON, HENRI (1932) 1954 *The Two Sources of Morality and Religion.* Garden City, N.Y.: Doubleday. → First published in French.

BETTELHEIM, BRUNO 1954 *Symbolic Wounds: Puberty Rites and the Envious Male.* Glencoe, Ill.: Free Press.

BRIFFAULT, ROBERT 1927 *The Mothers: A Study of the Origins of Sentiments and Institutions.* 3 vols. London: Macmillan.

COHEN, YEHUDI A. 1964 *The Transition From Childhood to Adolescence: Cross-cultural Studies of Initiation Ceremonies, Legal Systems, and Incest Taboos.* Chicago: Aldine.

COULT, ALLAN D. 1963 Causality and Cross-sex Prohibitions. *American Anthropologist* New Series 65:266–277.

COUNT, EARL W. 1958 The Biological Basis of Human Sociality. *American Anthropologist* New Series 60: 1049–1085.

CRAWLEY, ERNEST (1902) 1932 *The Mystic Rose.* 4th ed., rev. 2 vols. London: Watts.

DAVIS, KINGSLEY 1941 Intermarriage in Caste Societies. *American Anthropologist* New Series 43:376–395.

DEVONS, ELY; and GLUCKMAN, MAX 1964 Conclusion: Modes and Consequences of Limiting a Field of Study. Pages 158–261 in Max Gluckman (editor), *Closed Systems and Open Minds.* Edinburgh: Oliver & Boyd.

DURKHEIM, ÉMILE (1898) 1963 *Incest: The Nature and Origin of the Taboo.* New York: Stewart. → First published in Volume 1 of *L'année sociologique.* The 1963 edition is bound together with *The Origins and the Development of the Incest Taboo,* by Albert Ellis.

EMBER, MELVIN 1966 The Evolution of Marriage. Unpublished manuscript.

ERIKSON, ERIK H. (1950) 1964 *Childhood and Society.* 2d ed., rev. & enl. New York: Norton.

FISCHER, H. T. 1950 The Concept of Incest in Sumatra. *American Anthropologist* New Series 52:219–224.

FORTUNE, REO 1932 Incest. Volume 7, pages 620–622 in *Encyclopaedia of the Social Sciences.* New York: Macmillan.

FOX, J. R. 1962 Sibling Incest. *British Journal of Sociology* 13:128–150.

FRAZER, JAMES G. 1910 *Totemism and Exogamy.* 4 vols. London: Macmillan. → First published in 1887.

FREUD, ANNA 1965 *Normality and Pathology in Childhood: Assessment of Development.* New York: International Universities Press.

FREUD, SIGMUND (1913) 1959 Totem and Taboo. Volume 13, pages ix–162 in Sigmund Freud, *The Standard Edition of the Complete Psychological Works of Sigmund Freud.* London: Hogarth; New York: Macmillan.

FREUD, SIGMUND (1919) 1955 The "Uncanny." Volume 17, pages 218–252 in Sigmund Freud, *The Standard Edition of the Complete Psychological Works of Sigmund Freud.* London: Hogarth; New York: Macmillan.

FREUD, SIGMUND (1930) 1961 Civilization and Its Discontents. Volume 22, pages 64–148 in Sigmund Freud, *The Standard Edition of the Complete Psychological Works of Sigmund Freud.* London: Hogarth; New York: Macmillan.

GOODE, WILLIAM J. 1963 *World Revolution and Family Patterns.* New York: Free Press.

GOODY, JACK R. 1956 A Comparative Approach to Incest and Adultery. *British Journal of Sociology* 7:286–305.

HERSKOVITS, MELVILLE J.; and HERSKOVITS, FRANCES 1958 Sibling Rivalry, the Oedipus Complex, and Myth. *Journal of American Folklore* 71:1–15.

HILLER, ERNEST T. 1933 *Principles of Sociology.* New York: Harper.

HOBHOUSE, L. T. (1906) 1951 *Morals in Evolution: A Study in Comparative Ethics.* With a new introduction by Morris Ginsberg. 7th ed. London: Chapman & Hall.

HOEBEL, E. ADAMSON 1953 An Eighteenth Century Culturological Explanation of the Incest Tabu. *American Anthropologist* New Series 55:280–281.

HOMANS, GEORGE C. 1950 *The Human Group.* New York: Harcourt.

HUTCHINSON, G. E. 1959 A Speculative Consideration of Certain Possible Forms of Sexual Selection in Man. *American Naturalist* 93:81–91.

KROEBER, ALFRED L. 1920 *Totem and Taboo:* An Ethnologic Psychoanalysis. *American Anthropologist* New Series 22:48–55.

KROEBER, ALFRED L. 1939 *Totem and Taboo* in Retrospect. *American Journal of Sociology* 45:446–451.

KRZYWICKI, LUDWIK 1934 *Primitive Society and Its Vital Statistics.* London: Macmillan.

LABARRE, WESTON 1954 *The Human Animal.* Univ. of Chicago Press.

LANDES, RUTH; and ZBOROWSKI, MARK 1950 Hypotheses Concerning the Eastern European Jewish Family. *Psychiatry* 13:447–464.

LAYARD, JOHN 1960 On Psychic Consciousness. *Eranos-Jahrbuch: 1959* 28:277–344.

LESSA, WILLIAM A. 1956 Oedipus-type Tales in Oceania. *Journal of American Folklore* 69:63–73.

LÉVI-STRAUSS, CLAUDE 1949 *Les structures élémentaires de la parenté.* Paris: Presses Universitaires de France.

LÉVI-STRAUSS, CLAUDE (1962) 1963 *Totemism.* Boston: Beacon. → First published as *Le totémisme aujourd'hui.*

LORENZ, KONRAD Z. 1959 The Role of Aggression in Group Formation. Pages 181–252 in Conference on Group Processes, Fourth, *Group Processes: Transactions.* Edited by Bertram Schaffner. New York: Josiah Macy Jr. Foundation.

LOWIE, ROBERT H. (1920) 1947 *Primitive Society.* New York: Liveright. → A paperback edition was published in 1961 by Harper.

LOWIE, ROBERT H. (1948) 1960 *Social Organization.* New York: Holt.

MCLENNAN, JOHN FERGUSON (1865–1876) 1886 *Studies in Ancient History.* New York: Macmillan. → Includes *Primitive Marriage: An Inquiry Into the Origin of the Form of Capture in Marriage Ceremonies* (1865).

MAINE, HENRY J. S. (1861) 1960 *Ancient Law: Its Connection With the Early History of Society, and Its Relations to Modern Ideas.* Rev. ed. New York: Dutton; London and Toronto: Dent. → A paperback edition was published in 1963 by Beacon.

MALINOWSKI, BRONISLAW (1927) 1953 *Sex and Repression in Savage Society.* London: Routledge; New York: Harcourt. → A paperback edition was published in 1955 by Meridian.

MALINOWSKI, BRONISLAW (1929) 1962 *The Sexual Life of Savages in North-western Melanesia: An Ethnographic Account of Courtship, Marriage, and Family Life Among the Natives of the Trobriand Islands, British New Guinea.* New York: Harcourt.

MASTERS, R. E. L. 1963 *Patterns of Incest: A Psycho–Social Study of Incest, Based on Clinical and Historical Data.* New York: Julian Press.

MEAD, MARGARET 1949 *Male and Female: A Study of the Sexes in a Changing World.* New York: Morrow.

MEAD, MARGARET 1959 Cultural Contexts of Puberty and Adolescence. Philadelphia Association for Psychoanalysis, *Bulletin* 9, no. 3:59–79.

MEAD, MARGARET 1961*a* Cultural Determinants of Sexual Behavior. Volume 2, pages 1433–1479 in William C. Young (editor), *Sex and Internal Secretions.* 3d ed. Baltimore: Williams & Wilkins.

MEAD, MARGARET 1961*b* The Young Adult. Pages 37–51 in Eli Ginzberg (editor), *Values and Ideals of American Youth.* New York: Columbia Univ. Press.

MEAD, MARGARET 1963*a* Some General Considerations. Pages 318–327 in Symposium on Expression of the Emotions in Man, New York, 1960, *Expression of the Emotions in Man.* Edited by Peter H. Knapp. New York: International Universities Press.

MEAD, MARGARET 1963b *Totem and Taboo* Reconsidered With Respect. Menninger Clinic, *Bulletin* 27:185–199.

MERTON, ROBERT K. 1941 Intermarriage and the Social Structure: Fact and Theory. *Psychiatry* 4:361–374.

MIDDLETON, RUSSELL 1962 Brother–Sister and Father–Daughter Marriage in Ancient Egypt. *American Sociological Review* 27:603–611.

MORTON, NEWTON E. 1961 Morbidity of Children From Consanguineous Marriages. *Progress in Medical Genetics* 1:261–291.

MURDOCK, GEORGE P. 1949 *Social Structure*. New York: Macmillan.

NAG, MONI 1962 *Factors Affecting Human Fertility in Non-industrial Societies: A Cross-cultural Study*. Yale University Publications in Anthropology, No. 66. New Haven: Yale Univ. Press.

PARSONS, TALCOTT 1954 The Incest Taboo in Relation to Social Structure and the Socialization of the Child. *British Journal of Sociology* 5:101–117.

PARSONS, TALCOTT; and BALES, ROBERT F. 1955 *Family, Socialization and Interaction Process*. Glencoe, Ill.: Free Press.

RANK, OTTO (1912) 1926 *Das Inzest-Motiv in Dichtung und Sage: Grundzüge einer Psychologie des dichterischen Schaffens*. Vienna and Leipzig: Deuticke.

RASCOVSKY, MATHILDE WENCELBLAT DE; and RASCOVSKY, ARNALDO DE 1950 On Consummated Incest. *International Journal of Psycho-analysis* 31:42–47.

ROE, ANNE; and SIMPSON, GEORGE G. (editors) 1958 *Behavior and Evolution*. New Haven: Yale Univ. Press.

RÓHEIM, GÉZA 1934 *The Riddle of the Sphinx: Or, Human Origins*. London: Hogarth.

ROSE, FREDERICK 1951 More on the Origin of Incest Rules. *American Anthropologist* New Series 53:139–141.

SAHLINS, MARSHALL D. 1959 The Social Life of Monkeys, Apes and Primitive Man. Pages 54–73 in Symposium on the Evolution of Man's Capacity for Culture, Chicago, 1957, *The Evolution of Man's Capacity for Culture: Six Essays*. Edited by J. N. Spuhler. Detroit, Mich.: Wayne State Univ. Press.

SCHNEIDER, DAVID M. 1964 Incest. Pages 322–323 in Julius Gould and William L. Kolb (editors), *A Dictionary of the Social Sciences*. New York: Free Press.

SELIGMAN, BRENDA Z. 1929 Incest and Descent: Their Influence on Social Organization. *Journal of the Royal Anthropological Institute of Great Britain and Ireland* 59:231–272.

SELIGMAN, BRENDA Z. 1950 The Problem of Incest and Exogamy: A Restatement. *American Anthropologist* New Series 52:305–316.

SLATER, MARIAM K. 1959 Ecological Factors in the Origin of Incest. *American Anthropologist* New Series 61:1042–1059.

SLATER, PHILIP E. 1963 On Social Regression. *American Sociological Review* 28:339–364.

SMITH, ALFRED G.; and KENNEDY, JOHN P. 1960 The Extension of Incest Taboos in the Woleai, Micronesia. *American Anthropologist* New Series 62:643–647.

SPIRO, MELFORD E. 1958 *Children of the Kibbutz*. Cambridge, Mass.: Harvard Univ. Press.

STERN, CURT (1949) 1960 *Principles of Human Genetics*. 2d ed. San Francisco: Freeman.

SULLIVAN, HARRY STACK 1948 The Meaning of Anxiety in Psychiatry and in Life. *Psychiatry* 11:1–13.

SZABO, DENNIS 1959 *L'inceste en milieu urbain*. Paris: Presses Universitaires de France.

TYLOR, EDWARD B. (1888) 1961 On a Method of Investigating the Development of Institutions: Applied to Laws of Marriage and Descent. Pages 1–28 in Frank W. Moore, editor, *Readings in Cross-cultural Methodology*. New Haven: Human Relations Area Files Press. → First published in Volume 18 of the *Journal of the Royal Anthropological Institute*.

VETTER, GEORGE B. 1928 The Incest Taboos. *Journal of Abnormal and Social Psychology* 23:232–240.

WALLIS, WILSON D. 1950 The Origin of Incest Rules. *American Anthropologist* New Series 52:277–279.

WEINBERG, S. KIRSON 1955 *Incest Behavior*. New York: Citadel Press.

WESTERMARCK, EDWARD A. (1889) 1922 *The History of Human Marriage*. 3 vols. 5th ed. New York: Allerton.

WHITE, LESLIE A. 1948 The Definition and Prohibition of Incest. *American Anthropologist* New Series 50:416–435.

WHITE, LESLIE A. 1959 *The Evolution of Culture: The Development of Civilization to the Fall of Rome*. New York: McGraw-Hill.

WILSON, PETER J. 1963 Incest: A Case Study. *Social and Economic Studies* 12:200–209.

WOLFENSTEIN, MARTHA 1965 Changing Patterns of Adolescence. Pages 195–215 in A. V. S. de Reuck and Ruth Porter (editors), *Transcultural Psychiatry*. London: Churchill.

YOUNG, WILLIAM C. (editor) (1932) 1961 *Sex and Internal Secretions*. 2 vols. 3d ed. Baltimore: Williams & Wilkins.

INCOME AND EMPLOYMENT THEORY

The modern theory of income and employment, for which we may thank the genius of J. M. Keynes (1936), is without question the most important advance in economic analysis in the twentieth century. Keynes taught us to understand the nature of depressions and radically changed our thinking about how to deal with them. Keynesian principles have been widely applied in the policies of most industrialized countries, and governmental responsibility for the maintenance of "full employment" is now generally accepted. In the United States the growing influence of the "new economics" led, in 1946, to the passage of the Employment Act, which created the Council of Economic Advisers and committed the federal government "to promote maximum employment, production, and purchasing power."

In addition to its profound influence on economic policy, the modern theory of income and employment has paved the way for important developments in many areas of economic analysis. The purpose of the present essay is to provide a broad, simple outline of the theory. Many subtleties and extensions have necessarily been glossed over or omitted completely. [*The interested reader is urged to consult the separate articles on topics treated only briefly in this article:* CONSUMPTION FUNCTION; EMPLOYMENT AND UNEMPLOYMENT; FISCAL POLICY; INFLATION AND DEFLATION; INTEREST; INVESTMENT; LIQUIDITY PREFERENCE; MONETARY POLICY; *and* MONEY.]

Meaning of unemployment. It is important at the outset to be clear about the meaning of unemployment. Full employment implies that all who wish to work at the existing level of wage rates are employed. There are, to be sure, potential workers who choose not to seek employment because wage rates are too low. But such persons are said to be voluntarily unemployed, and the theory of employment is not concerned with them; rather, it is concerned with *involuntary unemployment*—with a situation in which there are workers who would be willing to take employment at prevailing wages but cannot find it.

Pre-Keynesian economics generally held that involuntary unemployment could persist only as the result of market imperfections. The excess supply of labor implied by involuntary unemployment would cause wages to fall, and the combined effect of an increased demand for labor (owing to the fall in its cost) and the voluntary withdrawal of some workers from the labor market (owing to the lower wage rate) would be to clear the labor market and restore full employment, just as a fall in price in any market would eliminate excess supply. On the other hand, Keynes and his followers argued that a state of involuntary unemployment could persist and that many levels of employment could be thought of as equilibrium levels. The path to full employment, moreover, lay not in the direction of wage rate adjustments but rather in the direction of raising the total level of spending in the economy.

Structure of the theory

The theory of income and employment is an aggregative theory which lumps all markets for final goods and services into a single *product market*, all financial markets into a single *money market*, and all markets for labor services into a single *labor market*. Customarily the analysis proceeds with a description of the properties of the individual markets and then links them together into an overall picture.

Product market. The sum total of the production of *final* goods and services (defined as output that is not resold in any form during the accounting period) when valued at market prices is the *gross national product*. The deduction of a capital consumption allowance for the replacement of capital equipment that was used up during the course of producing current output reduces this total to the *net national product* (NNP). The figure that results when NNP is "deflated" by an index of prices of final products in order to obtain constant dollar values we call *real* NNP, which for present purposes we refer to simply as *income*, denoted by the symbol Y.

Income and employment analysis begins by breaking income down into several components. The typical approach is to divide the economy into sectors and to examine the determinants of spending and the income receipts of each sector. A complete analysis would include a household sector, a business sector, a government sector, and a foreign sector [*see* NATIONAL INCOME AND PRODUCT ACCOUNTS]. However, for present purposes it suffices to confine the analysis to the household and business sectors. The portion of production that is purchased by households is called *consumption*, C. The remainder of the nation's output accrues to the business sector in the form of capital goods (new plant and equipment) or of additions to the stocks of finished and unfinished goods. Denoting the product retained by the business sector as *net realized investment*, I_r, we have the basic definition

$$Y \equiv C + I_r.$$

Provided that the business sector retains no earnings, each dollar of expenditure will be received by households as income. Since households are free either to consume or to save their incomes, we also have

$$Y \equiv C + S,$$

where S is the level of *saving*. When we equate the two expressions we obtain the fundamental accounting identity

$$I_r \equiv S.$$

We proceed with the theory of income determination by considering the consumption component first. Although aggregate consumption spending is related to many variables, we confine ourselves to the original proposition of Keynes that consumption is an increasing function of the level of income. In Figure 1 the curve labeled C represents an imaginary aggregate consumption function. Consumption rises as income rises, but not by as much. In the hypothetical situation of Figure 1 a rise in income of 200 from an initial level of 200 is accompanied by an increase in consumption of 150 to a level of 350. The ratio of the rise in consumption to the rise in income, $\Delta C/\Delta Y$, is the *marginal*

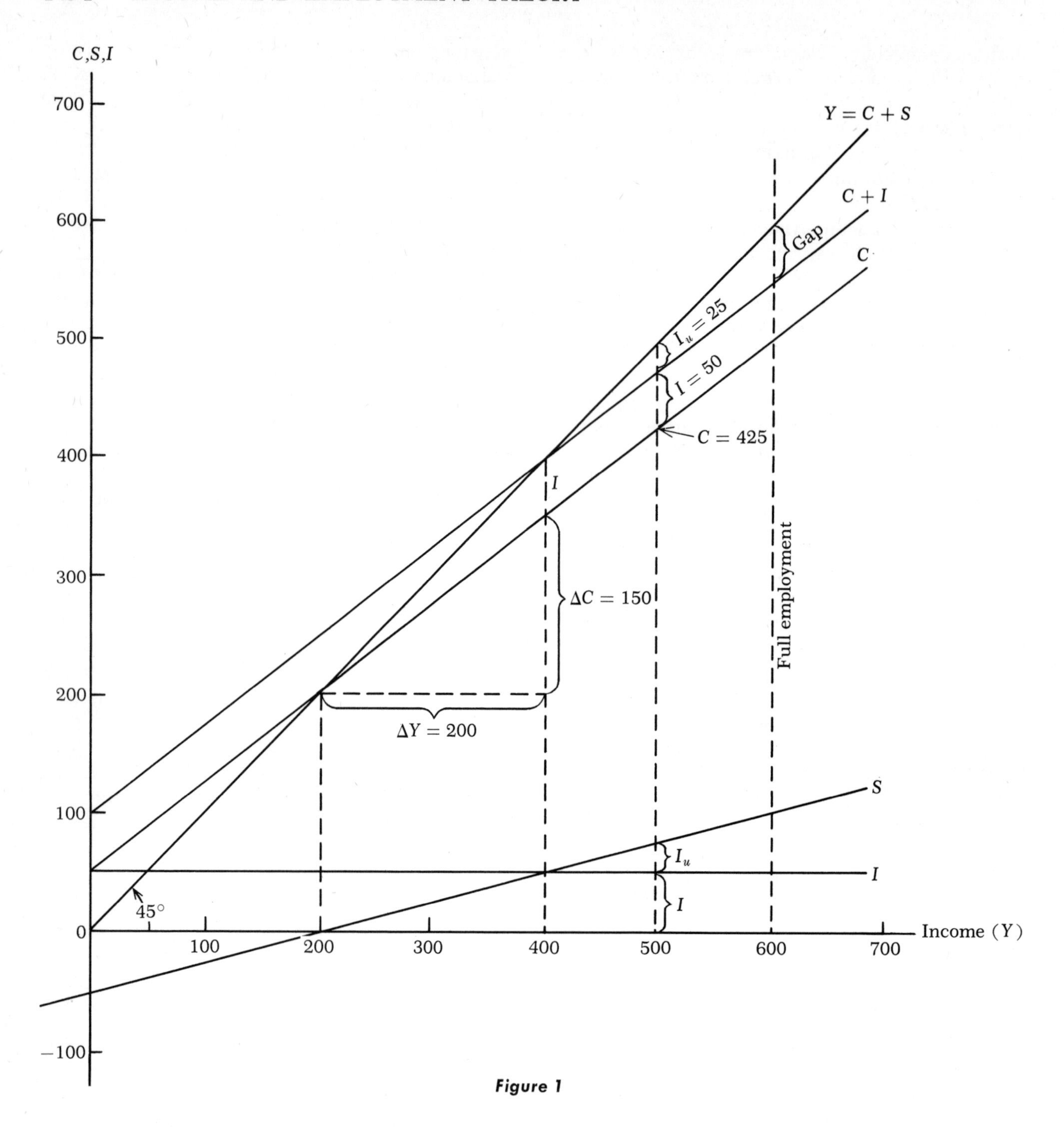

Figure 1

propensity to consume, which is simply the slope of the consumption function; in this example it has a value of $\frac{3}{4}$.

Because saving is the difference between income and consumption, the level of saving can be measured as the vertical distance between the 45° line and the consumption function, or the separate S curve of Figure 1. The ratio of the change in saving to the corresponding change in income is the *marginal propensity to save.* Since an extra dollar of income must be either spent or saved, the sum of the marginal propensity to consume and the marginal propensity to save must be 1.

The consumption function is a schedule of intentions. It indicates what the level of consumption spending will be at different levels of income. We may now introduce a schedule of business *intended investment* spending, which we may either plot separately or add to the consumption function in order to obtain the *aggregate demand*, $C + I$, schedule. The aggregate demand schedule shows the level of total spending that will be forthcoming at different levels of income. In the present example it is assumed that intended investment is 50 at all levels of income.

Care must be taken to distinguish between intended investment, I, and realized investment, I_r. Realized investment consists of all output that is retained by the business sector; intended investment is only that portion of output that the business sector actually intended to retain when production plans were formulated. Realized investment will exceed intended investment if business overestimates the level of potential sales and will fall short of intended investment if potential sales are underestimated. The amount of this discrepancy is *unintended investment*, I_u, so by definition

$$I_r \equiv I + I_u.$$

The presence of unintended investment implies that sales forecasts have been mistaken. In order to reduce unintended inventory accumulation, output will be cut back; in order to offset unintended inventory depletion (negative unintended investment) due to underestimation of potential sales, production will be increased. Intentions and realizations, then, will be equal only when unintended investment is absent. Since by definition

$$I_r \equiv I + I_u \equiv S,$$

and since equilibrium requires I_u to be zero, we infer that equilibrium requires intended investment to equal saving. Although realized investment must always equal saving, intended investment will equal saving only when the product market is in equilibrium.

A glance at Figure 1 confirms that $I = S$ at an income level of 400. This income level must necessarily also be where the aggregate demand schedule cuts the 45° line. Any other income level would be characterized by the presence of unintended investment. For example, if business produces $500 billion worth of output, consumption will be $425 billion and intended investment will be $50 billion. Total demand of $475 billion therefore falls short of production of $500 billion, with the consequence that unintended investment is $25 billion. Realized investment is $75 billion, and this does, to be sure, equal the level of saving, but undesired inventories will pile up as long as production is maintained at $500 billion and thus business must revise its sales estimates and reduce the level of output.

Multiplier. Any change that raises the aggregate demand schedule will raise the level of income. Moreover, the rise in the level of income will exceed the size of the shift in aggregate demand that brings it about. Referring again to Figure 1, we may suppose for a moment that intended investment is zero and observe that the equilibrium level of income is 200, since that is where saving is zero. Assume next that intended investment rises from zero to 50 and remains there. The equilibrium level of income jumps to 400—an increase not of 50 but of 200. This multiplied increase in income results from the fact that the increase in investment spending raises income, thereby inducing additional consumption spending. It can be seen from Figure 1 that the rise in income from 200 to 400 is composed of the increase in investment of 50 plus an increase in consumption of 150.

The ratio of the change in income to the change in investment, $\Delta Y/\Delta I$, is the *multiplier*, and its numerical value is the reciprocal of the marginal propensity to save. If intended investment rises by one dollar, equilibrium will not be restored until saving has also risen by one dollar. If the marginal propensity to save has a value of x, an income increase of $1/x$ dollars is required to raise saving by one dollar. In the present example, when income rises by one dollar saving rises by 25 cents. Since saving must rise by one dollar, the required increase in income is four dollars. [*For an alternative and more elaborate discussion of the multiplier, see* CONSUMPTION FUNCTION.]

The multiplier permits us to calculate the effect on the level of income of an upward shift in the aggregate demand schedule. The multiplier also tells us how much aggregate demand must be raised to reach an income level which will bring full employment. In Figure 1, if the equilibrium level of income is 400 and the *full-employment level of income* is 600, the required increase in income is 200. Since the multiplier is 4, a policy that shifts the aggregate demand schedule up by 50 will raise income to the full-employment level. The required shift in aggregate demand can also be found by measuring the *deflationary gap*, which is defined as the deficiency of aggregate demand measured at the full-employment level of income. Inspection of Figure 1 confirms that the magnitude of this gap is 50.

Before we add to this simplest of all models, it might be instructive to put the model into algebraic form. In linear form the consumption function can be written

$$C = a + bY = 50 + .75Y,$$

where a is the level of consumption associated with a zero level of income and b is the marginal propensity to consume. The saving function must be

$$S = Y - C = -a + (1-b)Y = -50 + .25Y,$$

where $1-b$ is the marginal propensity to save. Since the equilibrium condition is

$$I = S,$$

we have

$$I = -a + (1-b)Y,$$

or

$$50 = -50 + .25Y.$$

Thus, we can solve for Y and obtain

$$Y = \frac{a+I}{1-b} = \frac{50+50}{1-.75} = 400.$$

The multiplier is

$$\frac{\Delta Y}{\Delta I} = \frac{1}{1-b} = \frac{1}{1-.75} = 4.$$

The next step in constructing the theory of income and employment is to drop the assumption that intended investment is a constant somehow determined by factors outside the economic system. Although many alternative theories of investment behavior have been developed, we take note here only of the fact that ordinarily a business decides to borrow in order to expand its stock of productive capacity or its inventory holdings only when the expected rate of return on the new investment (the *marginal efficiency of capital*) is in excess of the cost of borrowing funds (the *rate of interest*). Alternatively, if funds are available without borrowing, the firm must determine whether it is more profitable to invest or to engage in some form of lending—for example, the purchase of government bonds. The higher the cost of borrowing (or the return on lending), the less inclined firms will be to engage in investment spending. For this reason the level of intended investment is usually regarded as a decreasing function of the rate of interest, i.

If the saving function is written in the general form

$$S = S(Y),$$

(read: saving is an increasing function of the level of income) and the investment demand function in the form

$$I = I(i),$$

(read: intended investment is a decreasing function of the rate of interest), and if we equate intended investment with saving, it becomes apparent that the equilibrium level of income depends upon the rate of interest. To put it differently, we now have two variables, i and Y, but only one equation,

$$I(i) = S(Y),$$

and we must therefore find out how the rate of interest is determined.

Money market and the rate of interest. The rate of interest is the return on lending or the cost of borrowing money. It can also be thought of as the return that wealth holders forgo when they hold money balances that could have been lent at interest, and it therefore constitutes the cost of holding money balances. Given the quantity of money held by wealth holders, the equilibrium rate of interest is that rate at which they feel no incentive to convert money into other financial assets or vice versa. Such a situation is denoted as *monetary equilibrium;* it obtains when the demand for money balances to hold equals the supply of money.

The simple theory of income and employment customarily treats the supply of money, usually defined as the currency and demand deposits held by the nonbank public, as a policy variable—i.e., its size is determined by the central monetary–fiscal authority. Under fractional reserve banking, however, money can, within limits, be created or destroyed by the commercial banking system. Money is created, for example, when banks convert excess reserves into earning assets, since this involves creation of additional deposits. Thus, the size of the money supply depends to some extent upon the degree to which banks are willing to make this conversion. The uncertainty that arises from the possibility of deposit withdrawal makes some holding of excess reserves desirable. However, banks forgo earnings when they hold excess reserves. Since a rise in the rate of interest increases this cost, such a rise is likely to be accompanied by an increase in bank lending and therefore in the money supply. For this reason many modern writers treat the supply of money as an increasing function of the rate of interest. A money supply function might be written in real terms as

$$M_s/p = \phi(R/p, i),$$

where R is the quantity of nominal bank reserves (determined by the monetary–fiscal authority), i is the rate of interest, M_s is the nominal stock of money, and p is the level of prices.

Keynes's theory of the demand for money was one of his most important contributions. He delineated three motives for holding money—the *transactions*, *precautionary*, and *speculative (liquidity preference)* motives. The transactions and precautionary demands were recognized by traditional theory. Keynes's great insight was to add the liquidity preference motive and to recognize the importance of the rate of interest in determining the demand for money.

The transactions demand for money arises from the necessity for economic units to hold certain levels of money balances because money receipts and disbursements are not perfectly synchronized in time. For example, an individual who receives $1,000 at the beginning of a month, makes disbursements at a uniform rate throughout the month, and ends the month with a zero money balance will have an average cash balance of $500. In the long run the magnitude of such average balances depends upon the nature of institutional payments-practices and upon the growth of income and wealth. In the short run the size of transactions balances depends upon the number and size of the transactions that the individual makes. Keynes and earlier writers therefore regarded the transactions demand for money as proportional to the level of income.

Precautionary balances are held in order to meet unforeseen contingencies and to take advantage of fortuitous opportunities. The magnitude of these balances was also viewed as proportional to the level of income.

Keynes held that the speculative demand for money arises out of fear that interest rates may rise in the future and that wealth holders will therefore suffer a capital loss if they hold bonds instead of money. The lower the rate of interest, the greater is the risk of such a capital loss and the lower is the return on bond holdings (the cost of holding money). Consequently, the quantity of speculative balances held is viewed as a decreasing function of the rate of interest.

The theory of liquidity preference has been attacked on a number of grounds (see Tobin 1958) which we need not go into except to note that money balances can usually be converted into riskless savings accounts. Nevertheless, empirical research (e.g., Tobin 1947) discloses a strong correlation between the rate of interest and the average length of time that money is held between transactions, a circumstance which seems to indicate that the demand for money is a decreasing function of the interest rate. This suggests that transactions and precautionary balances are also interest-elastic. Individuals who accumulate cash balances in anticipation of a large future outlay may convert these balances into short-term securities, which they liquidate when cash is needed. The greater the return on such securities relative to the transactions costs which their purchase and sale entails, the greater is the incentive to economize on money balances and the lower will be average transactions balance held (Baumol 1952; Tobin 1956).

The distinctions between the three motives for holding money are regarded as arbitrary by contemporary monetary theorists. Nevertheless, it is useful for expository purposes to maintain a distinction between transactions (active) balances and speculative (idle) balances. In any case it is clear that the demand for money is a function of both the rate of interest and the level of income, so we may ignore the separate motives and write quite generally

$$M_d/p = L(i, Y)$$

as the demand for money to hold in real terms.

Joint equilibrium of the two markets. It was seen earlier that product market equilibrium is established when intended investment equals savings—i.e., when

$$I(i) = S(Y). \quad (1)$$

Similarly, monetary equilibrium is established when the demand for and the supply of money are equal. Accordingly, we have

$$\phi(R/p, i) = L(i, Y) \quad (2)$$

as the condition for monetary equilibrium. If the real value of the stock of bank reserves is known, the two equations determine the equilibrium level of income and the rate of interest.

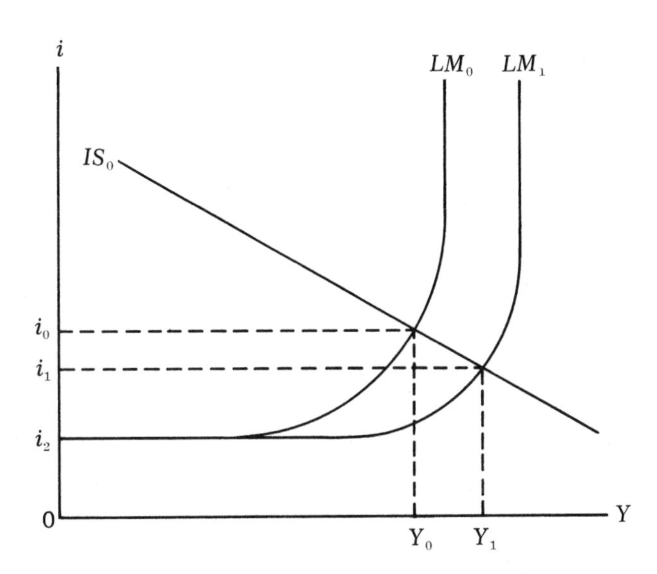

Figure 2 — **Income and employment theory**

In Figure 2 this general equilibrium solution is sketched out in a way originally presented by Hicks (1937). The curve labeled IS_0 is a diagrammatic representation of equation (1). It represents all combinations of interest rates and income levels that are consistent with equality of intended investment and saving. The curve has a negative slope because a decline in the rate of interest raises the level of investment and therefore also the level of saving and income.

The LM_0 curve depicts equation (2), representing all combinations of income levels and interest rates that yield monetary equilibrium. The curve ordinarily has a positive slope because a rise in the level of income raises the required quantity of transactions balances so that monetary equilibrium is usually obtainable only if the rate of interest rises. The point of intersection of IS_0 and LM_0 defines the equilibrium level of income, Y_0, and rate of interest, i_0—the values that are compatible with equilibrium in both markets simultaneously.

Monetary versus fiscal policy. An increase in the money supply brought about by a central bank purchase of securities on the open market shifts the *LM* curve to the right (for example, from LM_0 to LM_1 in Figure 2) because for any level of income, it is only at a lower rate of interest that wealth holders can be induced to hold the additional money balances. As can be seen from Figure 2, the size of the increase in income that this shift brings about depends upon the slope of the *LM* curve in the range in which it intersects the *IS* curve.

The vertical range of the *LM* curve represents the classical view that in a state of monetary equilibrium, money balances are never held except for transactions purposes. Thus, a rise in the money supply must cause the interest rate to fall and investment and income to rise until income rises by enough to absorb all of the additional money into transactions balances. If, therefore, the *IS* curve cuts the *LM* curve in the *classical* range, the level of income must rise in direct proportion to the increase in the money supply.

The horizontal portion of the *LM* curve represents Keynes's *liquidity trap.* Once the rate of interest falls to a critically low level (i_2 in Figure 2), wealth holders regard bonds and money as perfect substitutes, and banks simply allow excess reserves to pile up. Consequently, if the *IS* curve cuts the *LM* curve in the horizontal range, the open market purchase of securities by the central bank fails to lower the rate of interest, since all the added money balances are simply held as speculative balances. As a result the level of investment and the level of income fail to rise at all.

Whereas classical theory supports the effectiveness of monetary policy and Keynesian theory denies it, exactly the opposite views emerge with respect to fiscal policy. An increase in government purchases, for example, can be thought of as an upward shift in the investment demand schedule of Figure 1. The consequence of this increase in aggregate demand is that the *IS* schedule shifts to the right by an amount equal to the increase in government purchases times the multiplier. However, whether the actual increase in income also equals the multiplier again depends upon the slope of the *LM* curve.

The reader can visualize that a shift in the *IS* curve which cuts the *LM* curve in the liquidity trap range will yield a fully multiplied increase in income whereas an intersection in the classical range will yield no increase in income at all. In the classical case the attempt to increase total spending is frustrated because a rise in the rate of interest cannot bring about an increase in transactions balances. The rise in government purchases cannot generate a multiplier response, since any tendency for income to rise will drive up the demand for money and raise the interest rate until private investment is reduced by exactly the amount of the increase in government purchases. In the liquidity trap range, on the other hand, rising income merely activates idle money balances without affecting the rate of interest, and the level of private investment, therefore, does not decline.

In the classical view fiscal policy is incapable of raising the level of income, and fiscal changes merely have the effect of redistributing national output between the private and the public sectors; reliance is to be placed on monetary policy. In the Keynesian view, on the other hand, fiscal policy is the more certain (and in some cases the only) method of raising the level of income.

Labor market and automatic adjustment. In the Keynesian view the equilibrium level of income that is jointly determined by product market and money market equilibrium need not be the full-employment level. However, if an equilibrium level of income (for example, Y_0 in Figure 2) implies the presence of involuntary unemployment, will not competition for jobs among workers cause wage rates to fall, and will this not cause the level of employment and income to increase?

The theory of income and employment is a theory of the behavior of the economic system in the short run. It therefore presupposes that the stock of capital equipment is fixed and views labor as the only variable factor of production. From the theory of the competitive firm it can be deduced that labor will be hired up to the point where the value of its marginal product just equals the wage rate. Expressed in symbols, this condition is

$$w = MP \times p,$$

where w is the *money wage rate,* MP is the *marginal physical product of labor,* and p is the price of output. Dividing through by p, we obtain

$$w/p = MP,$$

where w/p is the *real wage rate.* According to the law of diminishing returns, an increase in employment will be accompanied by a decline in the marginal physical product of labor. A rise in employment, therefore, cannot take place unless the real wage is reduced. Since the demand for labor is a decreasing function of the real wage, we can write

$$N_d = D(w/p)$$

as the demand for labor function.

In the classical view the quantity of labor supplied is normally an increasing function of the real wage rate; it can be written

$$N_s = S(w/p).$$

If there exists a labor market clearing mechanism such that N_d tends to equality with N_s, these two expressions can be equated to yield the equilibrium level of employment. Since involuntary unemployment would be eliminated, this level of employment would be the full-employment level. The full-employment level of income can then be determined by substituting the level of employment into the *production function*,

$$Y = X(N),$$

which specifies the technical relation between factor inputs and the level of output.

Whether the level of income is determined by product market and money market equilibrium (the Keynesian view) or by competition in the labor market (the classical view) depends upon whether a labor market clearing mechanism operates so as to equate the demand for and the supply of labor. If involuntary unemployment exists, the supply of labor exceeds the demand, and the restoration of full employment requires that the real wage be reduced. Job competition among workers will reduce the money wage rate, but whether the real wage rate will also fall depends on what happens to the price level.

A fall in money wage rates leads business to expand the level of output and to increase the level of employment. However, since the marginal propensity to consume is less than unity, only a fraction of the additional output will be bought by consumers; unintended investment in inventories will therefore take place, and output will tend to return to its original level. In Figure 1 it is apparent that a rise in output of 100 from the original equilibrium level of 400 causes consumption to rise by 75, and the remaining additional output of 25 represents unintended investment. Unintended investment will not be eliminated until output falls back to 400. Since the equilibrium level of income will be the same as before the wage cut, the level of employment must also return to its original level, and this implies that the real wage will be restored to its original level as the result of a fall in the price level proportional to the original fall in the money wage rate. It is clear, then, that the equilibrium level of income cannot change unless the fall in money wage rates somehow succeeds in shifting the entire aggregate demand schedule upward.

We have seen that the fall in money wage rates will induce a fall in the price level. This means that the real value of the money supply, M_s/p, will increase, which in turn will cause the rate of interest to fall. As a consequence the level of intended investment will rise, and so also will the levels of income and employment. The argument can be visualized by reference to Figure 2. The increase in the real value of the money supply shifts the *LM* curve from LM_0 to LM_1, the rate of interest drops from i_0 to i_1, and the level of income rises from Y_0 to Y_1.

Underemployment equilibrium. There were two reasons, in Keynes's view, why this interest–investment mechanism might fail to work. First, there is the possibility of the liquidity trap, which, if present, would mean that the increase in the real value of the money supply could not lower the rate of interest. Second, there is the strong possibility that under depressed economic conditions investment would be insensitive to changes in the rate of interest. The first possibility can be visualized by further reference to Figure 2. If the *IS* curve cuts the *LM* curve in the horizontal (liquidity trap) range, the increase in the real value of the money supply would have no effect on the rate of interest or on the level of income. The second possibility can be visualized if we recognize that the *IS* curve would be vertical if investment were totally insensitive to changes in the rate of interest. If it is true, as is implied by the Keynesian analysis, that a fall in money wage rates will not raise the level of income, either because of the presence of the liquidity trap or because investment is interest-inelastic, then the labor market clearing mechanism fails to operate, and the existing level of income can be thought of as an equilibrium level.

The most elegant challenge to the Keynesian doctrine of *underemployment equilibrium* came from Pigou (1943), who suggested that if consumption were a function not only of the level of income but also of the level of wealth, a fall in the price level would increase the real value of the stock of currency and government debt held by the private sector, and this increase in wealth would cause the consumption function to shift upward. As long as the labor market remained uncleared, wages and prices would continue to fall, wealth would continue to increase, and the consumption function would continue to shift upward until the full-employment level of income was reached.

The theoretical issue cannot be said to have been resolved. A fall in wage rates may either raise or lower the level of income. The corrective *interest–investment* and *Pigou effect* mechanisms discussed above may, for example, be offset by the generation of adverse expectations. If wage reductions take place in a sluggish, piecemeal manner, entrepreneurs in industries where wages have not yet fallen will anticipate cost reductions by reducing output and employment and by selling from inventory. And if consumers expect the price level to fall, postponable consumption expenditures will be reduced. Moreover, a wage reduction will redistribute income in favor of profit earners, whose marginal propensities to consume may be lower than those of wage earners, and this could cause the aggregate consumption function to shift downward.

For practical purposes it is sufficient to recognize that in advanced economies wages and prices tend to be downwardly rigid. It would be difficult to implement a national wage reduction policy, and, as Keynes recognized, there is little that can be accomplished by such a policy that cannot also be accomplished by a relatively painless expansionary monetary policy. Output and employment cannot be raised without an increase in aggregate demand. Such an increase in demand might conceivably be brought about by wage reduction, but a policy of wage reduction would be inefficient and might not work at all. If it did work, the desired effects might take an intolerably long time to materialize. And the policy would certainly be inferior to a policy of direct demand expansion through monetary–fiscal measures.

Money illusion. In recognizing the institutional facts of life, Keynes broke away from the classical theory of labor supply. Instead of assuming that the supply of labor depends on the real wage, he assumed that labor is subject to *money illusion*—i.e., that the quantity of labor supplied responds to changes in money wage rates but not to changes in the price level and that the supply of labor is therefore a function of the money wage rate rather than of a real wage rate. In Figure 3, w_0 is the historically given money wage rate, and p_0 is the ruling price level. At money wage w_0 workers will offer anywhere from zero to N^* units of labor. Thus, at w_0/p_0 the labor supply curve is a horizontal line up to N^*. Although the money wage rate cannot be made to fall, it will rise when all who are willing to work at w_0 are employed and additional workers are desired. Consequently, the labor supply curve bends up sharply once N^* is reached. The labor

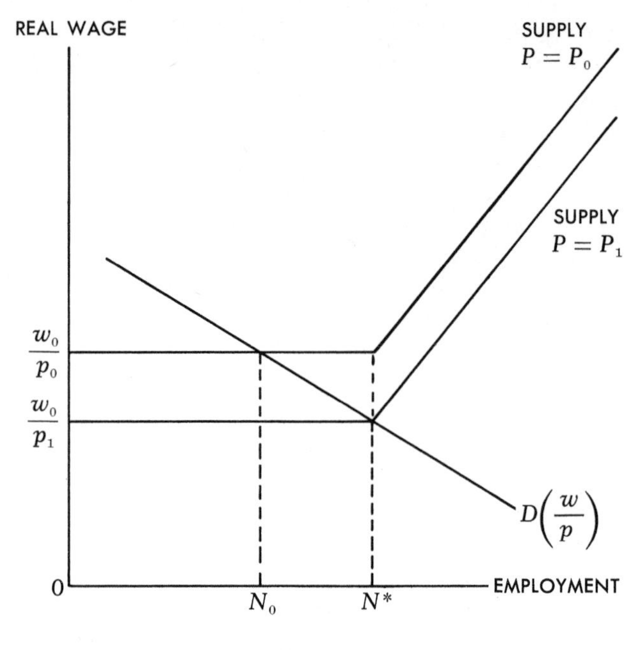

Figure 3

demand schedule cuts the supply schedule at N_0, and the distance N^*N_0 therefore measures involuntary unemployment.

Since the money wage rate is assumed to be rigid downward, full employment can be restored only through a fall in the real wage brought about by an increase in aggregate demand and a rise in the price level. If such a rise in the price level takes place, the entire labor supply schedule shifts downward, and involuntary unemployment is eliminated. Thus, at real wage w_0/p_1 the labor demand curve cuts the supply curve at N^*, where all who are willing to work at the new real wage are employed. Even though the real wage has fallen, the assumption of money illusion on the part of workers implies that the same quantity of labor will be supplied at the new real wage as at the old.

Synthesis of Keynesian and classical models

The Keynesian and classical models may now be sharply delineated. Although these models are static systems in which the equilibrium values of the variables are simultaneously determined, it is nevertheless instructive to think of the determination of the equilibrium values as running in a definite sequence.

In the Keynesian system, product market equilibrium can be written more generally as

$$I(i, Y) = S(i, Y)$$

to reflect the traditional view that a rise in the rate of interest induces individuals to increase the level of saving and to incorporate the notion that the level of investment depends upon the level of income as well as upon the rate of interest. When the monetary equilibrium condition,

$$\phi(R/p, i) = L(i, Y),$$

is added and the level of real bank reserves is assumed to be known, the two relations jointly determine the level of income and the rate of interest, as well as the levels of consumption, saving, and intended investment. The level of income being known, the production function,

$$Y = X(N),$$

defines the level of employment. The demand for labor, together with the historically given rigid money wage rate, w_0, provides the equation needed to determine the price level,

$$N = N_d = D(w_0/p).$$

In the classical system the sequence can be thought of as beginning with the labor market, where the real wage and the level of employment are determined by labor market equilibrium,

$$D(w/p) = S(w/p).$$

The full-employment level of employment, N^*, is now known, and the full-employment level of income follows from the production function; since the level of income is known, the product market equilibrium equation collapses to

$$I(i) = S(i),$$

which implies the classical proposition that the investment and saving functions serve only to determine the rate of interest and the way aggregate output is divided between consumption and investment. Finally, since both the level of income and the rate of interest are known, the monetary equilibrium condition can be collapsed to

$$R/p = \text{constant},$$

which implies that the price level is entirely determined by the nominal stock of bank reserves. In the absence of fractional reserve banking, the preceding expression can be replaced by the more familiar

$$M/p = \text{constant},$$

which reflects the traditional notion that given a fixed level of income, the level of prices must be directly proportional to the quantity of money.

The substantial differences between the ways in which the equilibrium values of the variables are determined rest upon whether the equilibrium level of income can differ from the full-employment level. This is illustrated in Figure 4, where it is assumed that the original LM curve is LM_0 and the full-employment level of income is Y^*. If the IS curve cuts LM in the horizontal range at less than full employment (curve IS_0), the rate of interest is the liquidity trap rate which cannot be changed by a shift in the IS curve within the horizontal range of the LM curve. The IS curve, in turn, determines the equilibrium level of income which cannot be affected by changes in the money market (shifts in the LM curve).

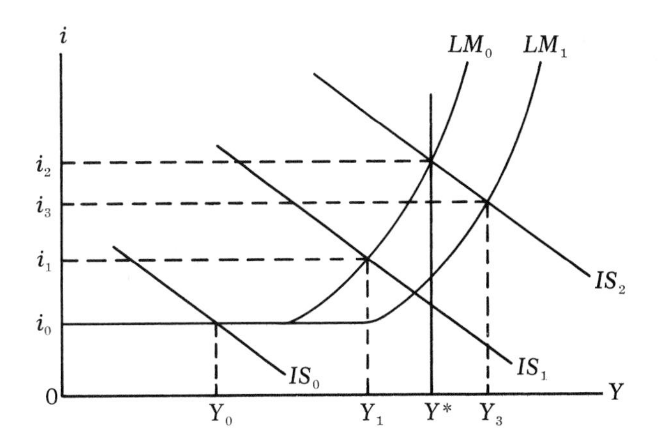

Figure 4

If the IS curve (curve IS_1) cuts the LM curve at less than full employment but in a range where the LM curve has a positive slope, the equilibrium level of income, Y_1, and rate of interest, i_1, are jointly determined by conditions in the product and money markets, and both can be affected by changes in either market.

Finally, suppose that the IS curve (curve IS_2) cuts the LM curve at the full-employment level of income and interest rate i_2. Suppose next that the money supply is increased and shifts the LM curve to LM_1. Joint product market and money market equilibrium would now obtain at interest rate i_3 and income level Y_3. But Y_3 is in excess of the full-employment level of income and is therefore not attainable. Excess demand for goods and services must now exist. As a consequence, the price level rises, and the real value of the money supply decreases—the LM curve shifts back to the left. Since the LM curve must shift back exactly to its original position if equilibrium is to be restored, the increase in the money supply only produces a proportional increase in the price level and leaves unaffected the other equilibrium values of the variables. The only possible equilibrium interest rate in this classical case is the *natural rate* of interest, i_2. It is found at the point of intersection of the IS curve and the vertical line at the full-employment level of income, and it exactly equates intended investment with the full-employment level of saving.

THOMAS DERNBURG

[*See also the biography of* KEYNES, JOHN MAYNARD.]

BIBLIOGRAPHY

WORKS CITED

BAUMOL, WILLIAM J. 1952 The Transactions Demand for Cash: An Inventory Theoretic Approach. *Quarterly Journal of Economics* 66:545–556.

HICKS, JOHN R. 1937 Mr. Keynes and the "Classics": A Suggested Interpretation. *Econometrica* 5:147–159.

KEYNES, JOHN MAYNARD 1936 *The General Theory of Employment, Interest and Money*. London: Macmillan. → A paperback edition was published in 1965 by Harcourt.

PIGOU, A. C. 1943 The Classical Stationary State. *Economic Journal* 53:343–351.

TOBIN, JAMES 1947 Liquidity Preference and Monetary Policy. *Review of Economics and Statistics* 29:124–131.

TOBIN, JAMES 1956 The Interest-elasticity of Transactions Demand for Cash. *Review of Economics and Statistics* 38:241–247.

TOBIN, JAMES 1958 Liquidity Preference as Behavior Towards Risk. *Review of Economic Studies* 25, no. 2:65–86.

STANDARD REFERENCES

ACKLEY, GARDNER 1961 *Macroeconomic Theory*. New York: Macmillan.

AMERICAN ECONOMIC ASSOCIATION 1955 *Readings in Fiscal Policy*. Homewood, Ill.: Irwin.

AMERICAN ECONOMIC ASSOCIATION 1965 *Readings in Business Cycles*. Homewood, Ill.: Irwin.

BAILEY, MARTIN J. 1962 *National Income and the Price Level: A Study in Macrotheory*. New York: Macmillan.

DERNBURG, THOMAS F.; and MCDOUGALL, DUNCAN M. (1960) 1963 *Macro-economics: The Measurement, Analysis, and Control of Aggregate Economic Activity*. 2d ed. New York: McGraw-Hill.

HANSEN, ALVIN H. 1949 *Monetary Theory and Fiscal Policy*. New York: McGraw-Hill.

HANSEN, ALVIN H. 1953 *A Guide to Keynes*. New York: McGraw-Hill.

HARRIS, SEYMOUR E. (editor) (1947) 1965 *The New Economics: Keynes' Influence on Theory and Public Policy*. New York: Kelley.

KLEIN, LAWRENCE R. 1947 *The Keynesian Revolution*. New York: Macmillan. → A paperback edition was published in 1961.

MUELLER, MAX G. (editor) 1966 *Readings in Macroeconomics*. New York: Holt.

SMITH, WARREN L.; and TEIGEN, RONALD L. (editors) 1965 *Readings in Money, National Income, and Stabilization Policy*. Homewood, Ill.: Irwin.

INCOME DISTRIBUTION

I. FUNCTIONAL SHARE	*Irving B. Kravis*
II. SIZE	*Stanley Lebergott*

I FUNCTIONAL SHARE

The distribution of income has been a focal point in the study of economics since the time of Adam Smith. At first, the emphasis was almost exclusively on the functional distribution—that is, the division of income among the factors of production. For Smith and many of his successors in the development of economic thought, including Ricardo and Marx, the distribution of income among the suppliers of labor, land, and capital was the key indicator of the relative welfare of different groups in society. Rents represented the income of agricultural proprietors; profits, the income of commercial and industrial entrepreneurs; wages, the income of laborers.

Even before the end of the nineteenth century, more attention began to be given to the distribution of income by size—in terms of individuals, families, or other consumer units. This was made more and more relevant by the blurring, particularly in the United States, of the sharp lines between various economic classes. Quantitative studies of the size distribution were encouraged by the growing availability of data from income tax returns and, subsequently, from modern sample surveys.

It is true, of course, that the direct identification of social groups with particular types of income can no longer be made so readily as in the past. In the United States in 1950, for example, over half the interest, dividends, and rents received by urban consumer units went to units headed by employees (Kravis 1962), and during the period between the two world wars the top 1 per cent of income receivers obtained about a third of their income in the form of employee compensation (Kuznets 1953). However, the significance of the dispersion of various types of income among all socioeconomic groups can easily be exaggerated. Income units headed by clerical, sales, and blue-collar workers received about 90 per cent of their incomes in the form of wages and salaries. The salaried-managerial group were the only employees for whom property incomes were important; in 1950, for example, they received about a fifth of their incomes in the form of rent, interest, and dividends. Property incomes are also important for the self-employed and the not-gainfully employed. Thus, it remains true that a given shift in the functional distribution is still likely to affect certain socioeconomic groups in the population favorably and others unfavorably.

Even if sources of income for individuals or families were more thoroughly mixed than in fact they are, an analysis of the functional distribution would still be an important step toward an explanation of the size distribution. This is true as long as the income of any individual or family depends, at least to a major extent, upon the supplies of the various factors that he or it is able to offer on the market and if the conditions underlying demand and supply differ from one factor of production to another.

However, our interest in the study of factor shares need not be limited to the implications for particular groups in society. We may be interested in measuring changes in the productivity of individual factors of production. Or we may wish to know how the division of returns to current effort and returns to accumulated assets has altered over time. In both instances, our understanding of the historical processes of the society would be enhanced even though every person might contribute some of each factor.

Finally, the historical trend of factor shares has sometimes been used in efforts to explain other significant aspects of the economy. For example, Kalecki (1954) has used the percentage of entrepreneurs' markup over direct cost as an index of the degree of monopoly, and Weintraub (1962) has used the entrepreneurs' markup over the compensation of employees as a basis for explaining and predicting changes in the level of prices.

The empirical study of income shares

The study of the trends in the functional distribution of income is handicapped by the fact that the nature of the components of income for which we have data has not been determined by the requirements of economic analysis but, rather, by the legal and institutional arangements of our society. Each factor share found in the national accounts, as maintained, for example, in the United States by the Department of Commerce, differs significantly from its corresponding theoretical concept. The "rent" of national accounting is the "rental income of persons" and does not represent a scarcity return either on the indestructible resources of nature or on specific factors temporarily fixed in quantity. A significant part of it may be regarded as a reward for entrepreneurial activity. It does not, however, include the net income on all leased property, but only the portion thereof received by persons; the net income on real estate owned by businesses is not counted as rent, but as part of corporate profits or unincorporated business income. Corporate profits also include explicit or computed interest received by firms, and the income of unincorporated enterprises contains not only rent and interest but also the return for the labor of the proprietor. Even employee compensation cannot be regarded as a pure return to current effort in a modern economy such as that of the United States, where substantial resources have been invested in the education and training of the labor force.

A threefold division of national income. Accepting for the moment the accounting framework used for national income purposes, a threefold division of income into employee compensation, entrepreneurial (unincorporated) income, and property income (rent, interest, and corporate profit) is perhaps most relevant to the study of functional shares. Data for the United States cast in these terms are set out in the form of average shares for overlapping decades in Table 1. Employee compensation rose in two long swings, from 55 per cent in 1900–1909 to 67 per cent in the 1930s, and then again to 70 per cent by the decade beginning in the mid-1950s. It is possible to view the record as a generally upward trend—interrupted only by the swelling of profits and the corresponding diminution of the wage share during the war prosperity of the second decade of the century, and more seriously, by the contraction of profits and the unusually large and temporary expansion in the wage share during the great depression of the 1930s. (For an analysis of cyclical changes which finds that the labor share is inversely correlated with changes in the level of economic activity, see Burkhead 1953.)

The bulk of the increase in the share of employee compensation came at the expense of entrepreneurial income, which declined from 24 per cent to 15 per cent, and then to 12 per cent. The upward trend in wages, or total employee compensation, and the decline in entrepreneurial income have their beginnings in the nineteenth century. E. C. Budd (1960) has estimated that the share of wages in private income rose from about 43 per cent in 1869–1870 to about 48 per cent in 1909–1910.

The long-run rise in the employee share and the decline in the entrepreneurial share of income reflect two other important and interrelated trends in the nation's economic structure—the change from an agricultural to an industrial country and the shift out of self-employment into wage and salary employment. The proportion of persons engaged in agriculture declined from more than half of the work force in 1870 to less than 40 per cent at the turn of the century, and to 7 per cent in the early 1960s, while the proportion of wage and salary employees rose from 58 per cent in 1870 to 64 per cent at the turn of the century, and to about 85 per cent in the 1960s (Budd 1960; *Survey of Current Business*, July 1963).

It should not be inferred that managerial employees were the main beneficiaries of the rise in employee compensation. On the contrary, the share of corporate officers dropped from around 4 per cent in the 1920s and 1930s to around 3 per cent

Table 1 — Distributive shares in U.S. national income, 1900–1963 (averages of percentage shares for individual years in overlapping decades)

	DISTRIBUTIVE SHARES							PROPERTY SHARE, VARIOUS CONCEPTS			
		Entrepreneurial income							Total property share[b]		
	Employee compensation	Farm	Nonfarm	Corporate profits	Interest	Rent	Total[a]	Interest, rent, and corporate profits	Asset basis	Labor basis	Proportionate basis
	(1)	(2)	(3)	(4)	(5)	(6)	(7)	(8)	(9)	(10)	(11)
1900–1909	55.0	11.6	12.1	6.8	5.5	9.0	100	21.3	30.6	32.2	32.1
1905–1914	55.2	11.4	11.6	6.9	5.8	9.1	100	21.8	31.2	32.8	32.9
1910–1919	53.6	11.7	12.1	9.1	5.4	8.1	100	22.6	32.6	35.8	34.8
1915–1924	56.9	9.7	11.5	8.9	5.3	7.7	100	21.9	31.0	32.4	31.8
1920–1929	60.8	7.2	10.3	7.8	6.2	7.7	100	21.7	29.2	28.5	28.8
1925–1934	64.5	6.1	9.3	5.0	8.7	6.4	100	20.1	26.6	26.4	25.3
1930–1939	67.5	6.0	8.8	4.0	8.7	5.0	100	17.7	22.9	19.8	21.4
1929–1938	66.6	6.2	9.3	4.3	8.9	4.6	100	17.8	22.6	19.8	22.0
1934–1943	65.1	6.6	9.9	9.1	6.0	3.3	100	18.4	23.6	23.5	22.9
1939–1948	64.6	6.9	10.3	11.9	3.1	3.3	100	18.3	23.5	25.6	24.0
1944–1953	65.6	6.4	10.0	12.5	2.1	3.4	100	18.0	23.1	24.7	23.6
1949–1958	67.3	4.5	9.3	12.5	2.9	3.4	100	18.8	23.0	22.7	23.2
1954–1963	69.9	3.2	8.7	11.2	4.0	3.0	100	18.2	c	20.6	21.8

a. Details may not add to total because of rounding.
b. Final stages of estimation carried out in terms of aggregates for decades.
c. Not available.

Sources: 1900–1909 to 1930–1939: Johnson 1954, p. 178. Johnson's estimates were based on data of U.S. Office of Business Economics, *National Income 1951*; Kuznets 1941; King 1930; National Industrial Conference Board 1939. 1929–1938 to 1949–1963: derived from U.S. Office of Business Economics, *National Income 1954*; U.S. Office . . . 1958a; *Survey of Current Business*, July issues for 1957–1964.

in the 1940s and 1950s (Kravis 1959, p. 920). Even allowing for a substantial understatement of the actual earnings of this group, it seems unlikely that its share has been expanding. It is, of course, possible that the income share of corporate managerial employees below the officer level has been rising.

The share of property income (interest, rent, and corporate profits) hovered around a level of 21 or 22 per cent until the depression decade of the 1930s. At that time the share dropped by three or four percentage points, and it has since remained around a level of 18 or 19 per cent. This relative stability of the property share has, however, been the result of offsetting shifts in its components, particularly interest and corporate profits. In 7 out of the 11 decade-to-decade changes in Table 1, the interest and corporate profits shares move in opposite directions, describing about one and one-half long cycles during the half century or more. (The interest and corporate profit shares move in the same direction in only 2 out of the 11 decade-to-decadal changes; in the other 2 instances, one of the shares remains unchanged.) There was a peak in the profits share and a trough in the interest share during the prosperity of World War I, a profits trough and interest peak in the depressed 1930s, and high profits and low interest shares in the prosperous 1940s and 1950s. This seesaw relationship between a return based on a fixed claim and one representing a residual share contrasts with the decline in the rent share from 9.0 per cent in 1900–1909 to around 3.3 per cent in 1934–1943 and ensuing periods. In a sense, this reduction in the rent share plays an important role in producing the relative stability of the property share. Compared with those of most previous decades, the recent levels of the profit share tend to be higher by a large number of percentage points than the interest share is lower, and were it not for the fact that the rent share has been only one-half or one-third of its former levels, the property share would have risen. (For a discussion of the decline of the rent share, see Kravis 1959, pp. 921–923.)

The growing importance of corporate profits in the composition of property incomes adds significance to the changes in the allocations of corporate profits to dividends, taxes, and retained earnings. Unlike the other property shares, allocations to taxes and undistributed profits may create a substantial gap between profits earned by corporations and income actually paid out by them to income receivers in the form of dividends. The record for the period since World War I is shown in Table 2.

Well over half of the relative rise in corporate profits from the 1920s and the 1930s has been

Table 2 — Percentage share of corporate profits in U.S. national income, 1919–1963

	TOTAL*				UNDIS-TRIBUTED
	Before tax	After tax	TAXES	DIVIDENDS	PROFITS*
1919–1928	8.4	6.7	1.7	5.3	1.4
1924–1933	5.9	4.7	1.2	6.4	−1.7
1929–1938	4.3	3.1	1.2	6.9	−3.8
1929–1938	4.3	2.8	1.5	6.0	−3.2
1934–1943	9.1	5.3	3.8	4.9	0.4
1939–1948	11.9	6.0	5.9	3.5	2.5
1944–1953	12.6	6.3	6.3	3.1	3.2
1949–1958	12.5	6.2	6.3	3.3	2.9
1954–1963	11.2	5.6	5.6	3.5	2.1

* Includes inventory valuation adjustment. It should be noted that the shares of corporate profits shown differ somewhat from those in Table 1, mainly because different sources and methods were used in deriving the figures.

Sources: 1919–1938: Kuznets' shares of corporate dividends and corporate saving (1959, p. 217) in national income, adjusted so as to include the federal corporate income and excess profits taxes as shown by Schuller (1953, p. 312). 1929–1963: U.S. Office of Business Economics, *National Income 1954*; U.S. Office . . . 1958a; *Survey of Current Business.*

accounted for by the increase in tax liability. The share of dividends in the national income has actually decreased. The implication is that property income has declined relative to labor income in terms of income actually paid to income recipients (personal income) even more than it has in terms of income earned (national income).

The employee share in individual sectors. When the behavior of shares in individual sectors and industries of the U.S. economy is examined, we find that the employee share tends to conform to the movement of the employee share in the economy as a whole (see Table 3). The typical pattern is an initial decline, with the trough most often coming in the 1940s, and then a swing upward, the share for the final period exceeding that for the initial one. There are, however, some important exceptions. The corporate sector as a whole and several industries, including manufacturing and mining, have higher employee shares at the beginning than at the end. The initial share in each of these cases is high because of the impact of the great depression; in some instances, periods of two or three years are found in the early 1930s when the employee share exceeded 100 per cent (that is, the compensation of employees was actually greater than the income originating, owing to negative profits). For the last four entries in the table, the U-shaped pattern of the share movements is inverted; there is a peak in the middle of the period, which falls most frequently in the 1944–1953 decade.

The trend in other countries. The available evidence for other countries seems to indicate that the broad pattern of the movement in shares is similar to that of the United States. (See Table 4.) At least from the second decade of the twentieth century the share of employee compensation has increased mainly, though not entirely, at the expense of the entrepreneurial share. The property share also has tended to decline, not only after World War II, as in the United States, but after

Table 3 — Shares of employee compensation in income originating in U.S. national economy and in various sectors, 1929–1963 (averages of percentages for individual years in overlapping decades)

	Per cent of income devoted to employee compensation					
	1929–1938	1934–1943	1939–1948	1944–1953	1949–1958	1954–1963
Entire economy	66.7	65.1	64.6	65.6	67.3	70.0
Private economy (exc. gov't.)	61.1	58.8	59.3	60.7	63.2	65.4
Private business (exc. gov't. and households)	62.6	60.0	58.8	60.3	63.3	66.0
Corporate business	85.9	78.9	75.7	72.2	76.6	80.2
Unincorporated business	38.2	35.9	36.0	38.5	42.1	45.1
Agriculture, forestry, and fisheries	18.4	16.8	16.3	16.6	18.5	20.3
Mining	86.3	75.6	75.3	75.3	73.8	76.1
Contract construction	72.0	71.7	72.7	72.0	73.2	75.5
Manufacturing	86.4	77.9	74.6	74.5	75.4	78.5
Wholesale and retail trade	76.9	66.3	59.6	62.6	69.6	73.8
Finance, insurance, real estate	31.8	32.0	29.0	28.6	29.8	32.3
Of which: Finance and insurance	(89.0)	(81.2)	(73.8)	(69.8)	(70.7)	(73.9)
Transportation	80.6	76.1	76.1	81.2	83.7	86.7
Communications	70.6	69.6	72.7	76.6	72.5	65.2
Public utilities	45.4	44.9	47.3	51.3	51.0	48.9
Services	58.4	58.2	59.4	60.4	59.4	59.4
Households and institutions	73.3	75.2	80.7	79.6	70.5	66.6

Sources: U.S. Office of Business Economics, *National Income 1954*; U.S. Office . . . 1958a; *Survey of Current Business.*

Table 4 — Factor shares in national income, selected countries and periods

	Employee compensation	Unincorporated business	Property income	Total*
United Kingdom				
1860–1869	47.4	16.7	35.9	100
1890–1899	49.8	17.5	32.7	100
1905–1914	47.2	16.2	36.6	100
1920–1929	59.7	14.6	25.7	100
1930–1939	62.2	13.7	24.1	100
1940–1949	68.8	12.9	18.3	100
1945–1954	71.6	12.2	16.2	100
France				
1913	44.6	33.1	22.4	100
1920–1929	50.4	29.1	20.5	100
1929–1938	56.2	23.7	20.1	100
1952–1956	59.0	31.3	9.6	100
Germany				
1913	47.8	32.7	19.5	100
1925–1929	64.4	26.2	9.4	100
1930–1934	67.7	22.9	9.4	100
1935–1938	62.9	26.0	11.1	100
Switzerland				
1938–1942	48.9	23.1	28.0	100
1943–1947	54.1	24.3	21.6	100
1948–1952	59.6	20.7	19.7	100
1952–1956	60.6	18.9	20.5	100
Australia				
1938–1939	56.0	20.2	23.8	100
1946–1950	50.6	28.4	20.9	100
1952–1956	58.5	23.0	18.5	100
Canada				
1926–1930	59.8	24.2	16.0	100
1954–1958	67.3	13.8	18.9	100

* Details may not add to total because of rounding.

Sources: Canada, Goldberg 1964, p. 205; other countries, Kuznets 1959.

World War I as well. Kuznets, upon whose work these generalizations are based (1959, p. 49), thinks it most likely that the property share tended to remain stable in most countries between the third quarter of the nineteenth century and World War I.

The influence of the accounting framework. The trends in shares analyzed in the preceding sections may be challenged both on statistical and on conceptual grounds. Statistically, the quality of the data becomes worse as we go back in time. For the United States, they are generally accepted as reasonably accurate for the period since 1929, somewhat less reliable for 1919 to 1929, and subject to wide margins of error for the first two decades of the century. The basic estimates for the two early decades were in some instances derived by estimating methods that make them unsatisfactory for the determination of relative shares; for some industries, for example, entrepreneurial earnings were extrapolated backward according to the movements of total wages (Lebergott 1964). Some of the errors that have been pointed out exaggerate the tendency toward a rising wage share and others to understate it, and it is difficult to judge their net effect. The figures in Table 1 relating to the first two decades must therefore be regarded with great reserve.

The share figures are affected not only by the methods of estimation but more fundamentally—at least for recent decades—by the accounting framework under which they were produced. While there is, on the whole, widespread agreement upon the methods of social accounting, some issues which may affect the income share estimates remain controversial (Conference on Research . . . 1958, especially the papers by G. Jaszi, R. T. Bowman and R. A. Easterlin, and E. C. Budd; Kravis 1957). In addition, even some of the conventional procedures that are followed may have won agreement more on the ground of statistical convenience than on that of conceptual adequacy. We are faced with the question, therefore, of whether the trend in shares that we have observed—particularly the rise in the wage share—would persist if the issues concerning accounting methods had been resolved in another way. The effects of some of these factors, such as the shift of certain activities from households to the market, the omission from the national accounts of the returns on certain types of property (namely, property owned by government and durable goods other than residences owned by consumers), and the exclusion from the estimates of interest on government debt and the inclusion of the compensation of government employees, have been discussed elsewhere (Kravis 1962). Effects of changes in tax laws and in regulations governing depreciation allowances and the practice of using historical rather than replacement-cost depreciation have also been studied (Brown 1963).

The outcome of these studies is that the factors commonly cited as limiting the usefulness of national accounts data for the study of income shares are not of sufficient quantitative importance to throw into question the major trends in the threefold division of income. The marked rise in the labor share and the decline in the entrepreneurial share are hardly affected. At worst, a little doubt is cast upon the persistence of the decline in the property share in the 1930s. If we impute returns to property owned by government, especially military property, or if we place the method of computing depreciation on a more consistent basis, much or all of the diminution in the property share is offset. On the other hand, if we exclude government completely, or if we use replacement-cost depreciation, the original result remains unaffected.

Table 5 — Distributive shares in U.S. personal income, 1909–1963 (averages of percentage shares for individual years in overlapping decades)

	NATIONAL BUREAU DATA					COMMERCE DEPARTMENT DATA					
	1909–18	1914–23	1919–28	1924–33	1929–38	1929–38	1934–43	1939–48	1944–53	1949–58	1954–63
Labor income[a]	51.9	56.3	61.4	64.1	67.3	65.2	67.4	69.5	71.5	73.4	74.9
Wages and salaries					64.4	61.5	63.8	65.6	66.4	67.6	68.0
Transfers					2.9	3.7	3.6	3.9	5.1	5.8	6.9
Entrepreneurial income	27.4	24.3	19.6	15.9	14.6	14.7	16.8	18.2	17.4	14.6	12.3
Property income	20.7	19.4	19.0	19.9	18.2	20.1	15.8	12.2	11.2	12.0	12.8
Rent	10.7	8.9	7.3	6.3	5.0	4.3	3.3	3.5	3.6	3.6	3.2
Interest	4.0	4.8	6.1	7.3	7.2	10.1	7.6	5.0	4.3	4.9	6.0
Dividends	6.0	5.7	5.6	6.3	6.0	5.7	4.9	3.7	3.3	3.5	3.6
Total[b]	100.0	100.0	100.0	100.0	100.0	100.0	100.0	100.0	100.0	100.0	100.0

a. For 1909–1918 to 1924–1933 includes government transfer payments. From 1929 on, personal contributions for social insurance were deducted from labor income. Division between wages, salaries, and transfers not available until 1929.

b. Details may not add to total because of rounding.

Sources: 1909–1938, derived from Creamer 1956, pp. 116–123; 1929–1963, derived from U.S. Office of Business Economics, *National Income 1954*; U.S. Office . . . 1958a; *Survey of Current Business.*

A threefold division of personal income. For some purposes it may be preferable to consider distributive shares in income received by households rather than in income produced by the nation —that is, shares in personal rather than national income. The U.S. data are set out in this manner in Table 5.

For the period preceding 1929, transfers and corporate taxes, which constitute the most important differences between national and personal income, were of smaller quantitative significance, and the shares in personal income were not far different in magnitude and direction of change from the shares in national income. After 1929, however, government policies brought about an expansion of both transfer payments and corporate taxes, and the share of property in personal income declined sharply, whereas its share in national income remained roughly constant. The relative importance of corporate profits in property income rose, while the share of corporate profits allocated to dividends (see Table 2)—the only part of corporate profits that enters into personal income—fell. The gap between the property share in earned income and in income actually paid out to income recipients was further widened by a rise in corporate saving; undistributed profits have amounted to 2 or 3 per cent of the national income in recent decades. (For a discussion of the impact of the accounting framework, see Kravis 1962.)

A twofold division of income. Although the threefold division into labor, entrepreneurial, and property shares is as far as the usual accounting records of the economy can carry us, it is necessary to attempt to divide entrepreneurial income into its labor and property components if we are to probe some questions that arise: Has the increase in the share of labor been attributable mainly to the shift from self-employment in the proprietorship form to employment under the corporate form of business organization? What has happened to the share of income representing returns to the current efforts of persons engaged in economic activity (i.e., what we shall call the "total labor" share) as compared with the share representing the return on past accumulations of wealth (i.e., what we shall call the "total property" share)?

Of course, if all or virtually all entrepreneurial income could be considered as a reward for the labor of the entrepreneur, the answer to these questions would be very simple. In that case, our findings would be that the relative shares of labor and property in the national income have remained almost constant for more than half a century, except for a shift in favor of labor in the years around 1930.

The difficulty with this view is that it implicitly assumes that the returns upon the assets of unincorporated enterprises have been zero or negligible. These assets form a substantial, albeit declining, share of total private wealth. In 1958, unincorporated businesses and farms accounted for 18 per cent of the nation's total tangible assets; in 1900, they accounted for 35 per cent (Goldsmith & Lipsey 1963, p. 43). Therefore, the assumption about the rate of return earned by these assets is critical to an evaluation of the property share in entrepreneurial income.

One possible assumption is that the rate of yield

on entrepreneurial property may be imputed from the rates observed in the market place for similar types of property. We have made some very rough calculations along these lines, distinguishing only between farm real property, farm nonreal property, and tangible assets of nonfarm unincorporated businesses. For farm real property, rents were estimated on the basis of rents on rented farm land. For farm nonreal property, the interest rates on farm mortgages were taken as the rate of return, and for unincorporated businesses the rate of return was taken to be the same as that for manufacturing corporations. (The methods followed are largely those used by Johnson 1948, with the aid of data from Brownlee & Conrad 1961; National . . . 1939; Stigler 1961; U.S. Bureau . . . 1960; U.S. Department of Agriculture, *Agricultural Statistics*.) When the entrepreneurial property shares calculated in this fashion are added to the other property shares (interest, rent, and corporate profits) to obtain what may be called the total property share, the results are as shown in column 9 of Table 1. This will be referred to as the "asset basis" for estimating the property share in entrepreneurial income.

The asset basis regards the return to entrepreneurial labor as the residual component of entrepreneurial income. It seems just as logical—and has the sanction of at least occasional practice—to calculate the labor component directly and to regard the property portion as the residual return. This can be done by assuming that the annual value of the labor of a proprietor is equal to the annual earnings of a hired worker. Since there are wide differences in annual earnings from one industry to another, the labor earnings of entrepreneurs in different industries should be estimated separately. In our rough estimates, however, only two "industries" are distinguished—farm and nonfarm. The figures produced by this approach, the "labor basis" for splitting up entrepreneurial income, are presented in column 10 of Table 1. (The sources are U.S. Office of Business Economics, *National Income* 1954; U.S. Office . . . 1958*a*; *Survey of Current Business*. For the years before 1929 they are Kuznets 1941; Creamer 1956; King 1930; National Industrial Conference Board 1939; Douglas 1930; U.S. Bureau of the Census 1960.)

The difficulty with both the asset basis and the labor basis is that they tend to concentrate the effects of fluctuations in the entrepreneurial share upon one or the other component. It may be more realistic to argue that when the entrepreneur commits his labor and capital to an enterprise, he is taking the risk that he will get much less than the market rates of return on both the labor and capital in the hope, of course, that he will get much more. Since the two types of input are jointly committed, both should be allowed to share in the ups and downs of entrepreneurial income. In this approach to the allocation of entrepreneurial income, the "labor" reward of entrepreneurs is computed as in the "labor" basis and the "property" reward as in the "asset" basis, and the two are adjusted proportionately so as to make their total conform to actual entrepreneurial income. We have labeled this the "proportionate" basis. In our actual computations entrepreneurial property returns were assumed to bear the same ratio to rent, interest, and corporate profit as entrepreneurial assets bear to all other tangible assets. The resulting total property share shown in column 11 of Table 1 differs in level but not in direction of movement from the share that is produced when the asset method is employed to derive the property component in the "proportionate" method calculations.

The calculations in the last four columns of Table 1 indicate that the general pattern of movement is similar for these four ways of measuring the property share. In the first decade or two of the century—the period for which the data are least reliable—there is a slight rise in the property share, *however* measured. There follows a decline that becomes more marked with the depressed 1930s; after the 1930s, however, little if any of this decline is recovered. The amplitude of the decline from the 1920s to the ensuing decades is, however, substantially greater for the *total* property share, regardless of the method by which it is estimated, than for the simple (interest, rent, and corporate profits) property share. This result would follow even from the addition of a constant percentage of the declining entrepreneurial share to the near-constant simple property share. For this not to be the outcome, the imputation would have to allocate a rapidly rising fraction of entrepreneurial income to property. As we have seen, in other business sectors, in recent decades at least, the property share has tended to fall rather than to rise.

All in all, the evidence thus points to an increase in the share of national income attributable to current human effort. This may either be the result of a structural shift brought about by, or at least coinciding with, the great depression, or it may be the result of longer-run tendencies. The latter view is plausible if we regard the property shares as having been artificially depressed by the great depression. Had it not been for the unprecedented collapse of incomes, the property share might have shown a smoother and more continuous decline from the second or third decade of the century to the most recent decade. Obviously, this is not a trend that can continue forever, but it requires explanation.

Reasons for decline in property share

The distribution of income among the factors of production is the net result of the operation of the whole intricate clockwork of the economy. Nothing less than a full set of equations setting out the general equilibrium of the system could be certain to include all the elements at work, and even in this approach it would be difficult, if not impossible, to take full account of shifts in resources, tastes, and technology, any of which may affect factor shares. The practical problem therefore becomes the familiar one of seeking to identify the key elements affecting the movement of relative shares. The literature on this subject, which has been growing apace in recent years, has in common only this tacit agreement on a search for the key variables. There has not even been agreement on what it is that has to be explained. Some writers, brushing aside the government and unincorporated business sectors, have found a striking constancy in relative shares and have sought to explain that. Others have found that it was an increase in the employee share that had to be explained. Nor has there been agreement, not even within either group, on the selection of the key variables that affect the constancy or movement of relative shares.

The explanations that have been advanced may be classified into three categories, according to the nature of the key variables selected: structural, factor-oriented, and aggregative.

Structural explanations. The structural approach attempts to explain the movement in over-all income shares in terms of changes in some basic characteristic of the economy, such as shifts in the relative importance of different industries, alterations in the bargaining power of labor and/or employers (monopoly power), and variations in the size of firms.

In general, any intersectoral shift which changes the relative importance of sectors with either very high or very low, or with rapidly rising or rapidly falling, employee shares will have an impact on the over-all share.

We have already had occasion to mention two such shifts that are often cited in attempts to probe the sources of the increase in the share of employee compensation in the national income—the growth in the importance of the government sector (with an employee share of 100 per cent) and the decline in the importance of unincorporated business (with a below-average employee share in the 35–45 per cent range). Sometimes one or both of these sectors are omitted from the analysis, but the conceptual simplicity thus obtained is purchased at a high price. The functioning of factor markets in determining relative shares can hardly be explained satisfactorily if employers of significant amounts of the factors are left out. In 1962, for example, nearly 20 per cent of total employee compensation was paid by the nonbusiness sector and nearly 40 per cent by the nonbusiness and noncorporate business sectors combined.

A number of writers have analyzed the effects upon relative shares of changes in the importance of different sectors of the economy. Kuznets (1941, pp. 241–250), Denison (1952), Johnson (1954), and Budd (1964), working with different periods during the past half century, have produced results which indicate that changes in the industrial composition of employment and income have tended somewhat to increase the share of labor. It seems clear, however, that the rise in the employee share cannot be explained away in terms of sectoral shifts. This conclusion holds even within each of the more restricted sectors of the economy (such as the private business and corporate sectors), which have sometimes been advanced as more appropriate for the study of relative shares (Budd 1964).

Solow (1958) has called attention to the possible operation of what might be termed a microeconomic share-stabilizing mechanism. This would exist if there were a tendency, when labor shares are rising, for industries with high labor shares to diminish in relative importance in originating national income and for those with low labor shares to increase in relative importance. However, Solow's findings concerning the existence of such a mechanism were generally negative.

Changes in the degree of monopoly power represent another type of structural shift that may significantly affect the employee share. The assumption of a significant and growing degree of monopoly was used by Kalecki as the basis for an explanation of relative shares which has been criticized elsewhere (Kaldor 1955–1956). It should be noted, however, that Kalecki's original formulation referred essentially to wage earners in manufacturing. (For another use of the markup idea, see Weintraub 1959.) In a firm enjoying a sheltered market position, both wage and nonwage incomes may be higher than under competitive conditions, but the nonwage incomes are apt to be more above the competitive level than are the wage incomes, since the firm is presumably hiring labor under market conditions that are more competitive than those under which it is selling its product. Therefore, the share of labor will vary inversely with the degree of monopoly exercised by firms, and if monopoly has had anything to do with the rise in the labor share, monopoly must have become less pervasive. Or, if the degree of monopoly in product markets has remained unchanged or even has increased somewhat, perhaps the rising role of unions has provided an offsetting source of monopoly power that has pushed the wage share up. However, there is no agreement among labor economists that unions have in fact succeeded in raising labor's share (Reder 1959, pp. 184–185).

Among other structural factors that may affect factor shares, mention may be made of changes in the price level, the size of firms (Goldberg 1964, p. 234), and the quality of labor. For rising prices to bring about a reduction in the property share, their adverse effect upon contractual property incomes (rent and interest) must outweigh their positive effect upon residual property incomes (profits). This differential effect of rising prices upon rent and profit may explain much of the fall in rent and rise in profits mentioned earlier (Brownlee & Conrad 1961).

Even if structural factors could be found which accounted for all of the changes observed in the labor share, a theory of factor shares would still be required to explain what mechanism tends to keep the shares constant in the absence of such structural changes. Our data suggest, however, that it is not constancy which requires explanation, but an expansion in the share of income accruing as a reward for current effort and a decline in the share arising as a return on accumulated assets. The shifts are small relative to the over-all growth in real income (more than a fivefold increase from 1900–1909 to 1954–1963) or to the rise in the capital–labor ratio (probably half again as high in 1954–1963 as in 1900–1909). (See Kravis 1959, pp. 936–938.) Nevertheless, the changes are real and significant, considering that limits on shifts in the distribution of income are imposed by the requirements of social stability.

Theories of relative shares

It is possible to formulate a variety of tautological relationships between the wage or the property share, on the one hand, and its various "determinants," on the other hand. In factor-oriented theories the independent variables are usually the prices and quantities of the factors of production. The marginal productivity theory of distribution, which occupies a commanding position in the literature, may be classified under this heading. For empirical purposes, marginal productivities are usually estimated from an aggregate production function, and shifts in factor shares are seen to depend upon the elasticity of substitution. [*See* PRODUCTION.]

In aggregative theories the independent variables usually include Keynesian aggregates, particularly savings and investment. For example, a simple kind of identity often employed is

$$(1) \qquad \frac{R}{Y} = \frac{R}{K} \times \frac{K}{Y},$$

where R is property income; Y, total income; and K, the capital stock. The property share may easily be related directly to savings and investment propensities, as shown in a formulation used by Kaldor:

$$(2) \qquad \frac{R}{Y} = \left(\frac{1}{s_r - s_w}\right)\left(\frac{I}{Y} - s_w\right),$$

where I is investment and s_r and s_w are the marginal propensities to save out of property and wage incomes, respectively (Kaldor 1955–1956; Kaldor's theory assumes full employment). If, as Kaldor seems to argue, the savings propensities tend to be constant, then the property share depends on the level of investment.

The line separating the factor-oriented and aggregative theories is not a sharp one. Indeed, if the explanation is pushed far enough, a factor-oriented theory reaches the aggregative variables, and the converse is also true. In addition, some aggregates, such as wages and income, are found in both groups of theories. However, where there is such overlap, the factor-oriented theories are more apt to concern themselves with explanations of the way in which the aggregates are built up from the individual factors or products than are the aggregative theories.

No effort will be made here to review these various approaches to a theory of relative shares, since several such surveys have recently appeared (for example, Reder 1959; Scitovsky 1964). What follows is an attempt at an explanation of the rise in the labor share in empirical terms, using a factor-oriented approach.

The relation of property to wage income can be regarded as the product of capital–labor quantity and price ratios:

$$(3) \qquad \frac{R}{W} = \frac{Q_k}{Q_l} \times \frac{P_k}{P_l},$$

where R = total property income, W = aggregate wages ($R + W$ = total income, Y), Q = quantity, P = price, k = capital, and l = labor.

Changes in relative shares thus result from

changes in the quantity and/or price ratios. (Once R/W is known, the property share in income, R/Y, can be calculated, since the sum of the wage and property shares must equal 1: $w + r = 1$, where $w = W/Y$ and $r = R/Y$; thus, $(r \div R/W) + r = 1$. The property share can be found by substituting the numerical value of R/W and solving for r.) Since the ratio of the percentage change in the quantity-ratio to the inverse of the percentage change in the price-ratio is equal to the elasticity of substitution, we are dealing with the familiar proposition that changes in relative shares depend upon the elasticity of substitution. [*See* ELASTICITY.]

Now, if we could assume that the price and quantity ratios would move in opposite directions, the opportunity for factor substitution would clearly serve as a built-in stabilizing mechanism limiting changes in relative shares. Where the opposite percentage changes in the quantity and price ratios are equal—i.e., where the elasticity of substitution is unity—relative shares will of course remain unchanged. Even with fairly large departures from unity, however, factor substitution may confine share shifts to fairly narrow limits. For example, with a 75–25 division of national income between labor and capital, a 20 per cent increase in the ratio of the price of labor to the price of capital would not cause the labor share to stray more than 3 or 4 percentage points from 75 were the elasticity of substitution as low as 0.25 or as high as 2.

In fact, there is reason to believe not only that the quantity and price ratios move in opposite directions, thus tending to limit the extent of the change in relative shares, but also that the elasticity of substitution is below 1. For example, the ratios for the United States at two periods, roughly a half century apart, are as shown in Table 6 (Kravis 1959, p. 940):

Table 6

	Q_k/Q_l	P_k/P_l
1900–1909	1.26	0.309
1949–1957	2.60	0.092

These figures yield a "historical" arc elasticity of substitution of 0.64. This compares with an arc elasticity of 0.62 computed by Kendrick for total manufacturing between 1953 and 1957 (1964, p. 141). Kendrick also made separate estimates for 20 two-digit manufacturing industries: 18 were between 0 and 1. Arrow and his colleagues (see Arrow et al. 1961) obtained elasticities ranging from 0.721 to 1.011 for 24 industries based on a cross section of 19 countries; the values fell between 0.800 and 0.899 for 11 of the 24 industries and between 0.900 and 0.999 for 8 industries. The last group of estimates are based on the assumption of an elasticity of substitution that is constant—but not, of course, necessarily unity, as the Cobb–Douglas production function posited.

The magnitude of the elasticity of substitution depends on the techniques of production, on other influences affecting the demand for the factors, and on the supply of the factors.

In the short run with fixed plant, the opportunities for factor substitution may be limited. In the long run, technological progress—especially to the extent that it consists of finding new ways to produce old products—may be viewed partly as a process in which the range of producers' choice among factor combinations is extended.

Among the other influences on demand are the share-stabilizing influence of responses in commodity markets to an increase in the relative price of a given factor, say labor. Consumers may be expected to respond to an increase in the relative price of labor-intensive commodities by shifting their purchases to other goods, thus bringing about a shift toward a greater utilization of capital in the economy as a whole even though there has been no change in the capital–labor ratio in any industry. Solow's investigation, reported upon under "Structural explanations," does not seem to suggest that this kind of mechanism has played a major role in the U.S. economy.

A hypothesis consistent with the facts is (1) that the behavior of the price and quantity ratios cited above is attributable to the differences between the supply conditions under which capital and labor are provided, and (2) that the demand conditions have been permissive rather than determining. This can be brought out by making a series of alternative assumptions about the relative impact of economic growth upon the demands for capital and labor respectively and determining what supply conditions for the two factors could have produced the historical changes in their price and quantity ratios that have been noted.

Let us first assume that the expansion in demand was neutral, in the sense that the relative marginal productivities were unchanged for any given ratio of capital to labor. (Geometrically, the isoquant drawn with capital on the vertical axis and labor on the horizontal axis merely shifts upward and to the right; its slope is unchanged at the point of intersection with any given gradient drawn from the origin indicating the capital–labor ratio.) If both capital and labor were perfectly elastic in supply, there would be proportionate increases in both, and no change in relative prices or shares in income would occur. If one were more elastic in supply than the other, the relative quantity of the more elastic factor would increase, and given imperfect substitutability between the factors, its relative price would fall. In the actual event, capital nearly tripled in quantity, with no secular increase in rate of return (Kravis 1959, p. 938), while the number of man-hours rose by less than 50 per cent despite a better than threefold rise in hourly compensation. Thus, if technical progress was neutral, the facts would fit the hypothesis.

Next consider the case in which economic growth is not neutral but increases the demand for capital relative to labor: For any given capital–labor ratio, the marginal productivity of capital has improved relative to that of labor. In Hicks's terminology, technical progress is labor-saving (1932, pp. 121–122 in 1935 edition). (The higher isoquant has a smaller slope than the lower one at the points of intersection with any given gradient from the origin.) But we are immediately confronted with the problem of explaining why the return on capital did not rise relative to that of labor. As in the previous case, the answer appears to turn on the supply conditions: additional supplies of capital were readily forthcoming, while the supply of labor was so inelastic that even the smaller increase in the demand for it resulted in large price increases.

Finally, there is the case in which innovations raise the marginal productivity of labor in relation to that of capital (Hicks's capital-saving category). If the supplies of both factors were perfectly elastic, there would be an increase in the relative quantity of labor. If, at the other extreme, the supplies of both factors were perfectly inelastic, the relative quantities would remain the same and the relative price of labor would rise. The only circumstances that would produce a *decrease* in the relative quantity of labor as well as an increase in its relative price, such as occurred in the history of the period, are those in which the supply of capital is more readily responsive to increased demand than is the supply of labor.

Whatever the nature of the demand influences, therefore, the increase in the capital–labor ratio and the relative increase in the price of labor are attributable to differences in supply conditions. However, we have explained only the direction of the movements of the quantity and price ratios; to account for the rise in the labor share, we have to explain why labor increased in relative price more than it decreased in relative quantity. The answer to this question depends not only upon the difference in the supply elasticities but also upon the marginal rate of substitution between capital and labor (MRS). If the MRS were constant from one equilibrium position to another, there could be no change in relative prices; only relative quantities would change. The fact that relative prices changed so much indicates not only that there was a great difference in the elasticities of supply but also that the substitutability of capital for labor diminished. Nevertheless, the impetus to the change came from the supply conditions for the factors; otherwise, with neutral innovations there would have been no change in the MRS, and with labor-saving innovations the change in the MRS would have been opposite to the observed direction. Only in the less likely case of capital-saving inventions would the MRS move in the right direction without aid from the supply side, and even in this case we have to invoke the supply conditions to explain the quantity changes.

We have thus far glided over the difficulties encountered in deriving supply and demand curves from historical data. Not the least of these is the familiar problem of distinguishing the supply effects from the demand effects in historical statistics. If we could assume that the supply schedule for labor had remained constant over the entire half century and that the observed prices and quantities reflect the upward shift of the demand for labor, then the arc elasticity of supply of man-hours could be easily calculated as 0.31 for the period covered by the price and quantity ratios given above. If the supply also shifted upward, though not as much as did the demand, the elasticity may well have been less than 0.31; if the number of man-hours offered at each real hourly wage actually tended to diminish, the elasticity would have been greater than 0.31. In any case, the tripling of real earnings per man-hour with an increase in man-hours worked of only 40 per cent is consistent with the hypothesis of inelastic supply or with the related hypothesis that the growth in demand was greater than the growth in supply.

Matters are much less clear-cut with respect to capital. Even if we assume that the actual rate of return represents a good stand-in for the expected rate of return, the rate which presumably governs the supply of capital, it is difficult to draw any generalizations (see Kravis 1959, p. 943). The periods spanning the years of the great depression had lower rates of return and smaller increments in the stock of capital than the more prosperous periods before and after. In the more prosperous periods, however, there was little association between changes in the rate of capital formation and changes in the actual rate of return from one overlapping decade to another. Perhaps the actual rate of return is a poor proxy for the expected rate, particularly since capital gains, which are excluded from the actual rate of return, may at certain times have been a more important motive to capital formation than was income in the sense used in the national accounts. Also, the rate of return that is relevant to new investment is the marginal rate rather than the average rate, which is the only rate available. Finally, and this is an important limitation for labor as well as capital, price might be a relatively minor influence in determining changes in available quantities.

Whatever the reason, then, under conditions of rapid expansion in production, labor was relatively inelastic in supply and rising rapidly in price, and capital was apparently either much more elastic or, at any rate, growing rapidly in supply. Thus entrepreneurs substituted capital for labor, or to put it more precisely, they increased their use of capital at a more rapid rate than they increased their use of labor. It is not clear in what degree the relatively expanded use of capital was possible by virtue of existing techniques—owing either to the adaptability of equipment in use or to the availability of stand-by techniques requiring more capital and less labor—or in what degree it was the result of newly created capital-using techniques whose development was stimulated by the growing relative scarcity and high price of labor. If the common conception of the rate of application of new knowledge to industrial processes has any validity, innovations must have played a major role in the change in the ratio.

A slightly different view of the same phenomena can be obtained by introducing the capital stock into equation (3). This involves decomposing the elements in (3) so as to express the property–labor income shares as the product of (a) output per man-hour, (b) the capital–output ratio, and (c) the ratio of the price of capital to the price of labor:

$$\frac{R}{W} = \frac{Y}{Q_l} \times \frac{Q_k}{Y} \times \frac{P_k}{P_l}. \tag{4}$$

One of the new terms (Y/Q_l) is a measure of the average productivity of labor, and the other (Q_k/Y), the capital–output ratio, is the reciprocal of the average productivity of capital. The capital–output ratio rose in the depressed 1930s, when capacity was not fully utilized; declined in the booming 1940s, when capacity was used to the hilt; and during the 1950s remained at a level corresponding to about 70 per cent of the 1900–1909 level; in terms of capital productivity, this amounts to an increase of less than 45 per cent between the opening and closing decades of the half century. Labor productivity, on the other hand, doubled within the same time span. (See Kravis 1959.) This relative economizing in the use of labor may seem to imply that innovations during the period must have been labor-saving, but the economizing may flow merely from a shift in factor proportions; the average productivity of labor necessarily rises relative to that of capital whenever the quantity of labor falls relative to that of capital, that is,

$$\frac{Y}{Q_l} \div \frac{Y}{Q_k} = \frac{Q_k}{Q_l},$$

whether the change in relative quantities is or is not due to changes in techniques. The presumption in favor of the hypothesis that adoption of labor-saving techniques accompanied the growth in capital relative to labor is supported by the further presumption that a rapidly rising relative wage rate created an inducement for innovations biased in this direction. (Probably the most common view is that inventions have been labor-saving. See Hicks 1932, p. 124 in 1935 edition. For an argument that inventions may have been neutral, see Solow 1957 and Reder 1959.)

Our discussion thus leads to the view that the impetus to the rise in the labor share came from sharp increases in real wages, owing to the lack of responsiveness in the supply of man-hours to the rising demand for labor attendant upon rapid economic growth. The use of relatively more capital was made possible by price-induced substitution and by price-induced capital-using (labor-saving) innovations.

It is possible that important pieces of the share puzzle lie within realms of the social mechanism other than the purely economic. Some of these are obvious and tangible, such as the dependence of changes in the size of the labor force upon the rate of population growth and labor force participation rates. Others, perhaps equally important, are much more difficult to establish. One source of the forces favoring the labor share may conceivably be found in the relative effects upon the supply prices of labor and capital of our society's acceptance of continuously rising incomes as a normal result of the economic process.

IRVING B. KRAVIS

BIBLIOGRAPHY

ARROW, KENNETH et al. 1961 Capital–Labor Substitution and Economic Efficiency. *Review of Economics and Statistics* 43:225–250.

BACH, GEORGE L.; and ANDO, ALBERT K. 1957 The Redistributional Effects of Inflation. *Review of Economics and Statistics* 39:1–13.

BROWN, MURRAY 1963 Depreciation and Corporate Profits. *Survey of Current Business* 43, no. 10:5–12.

BROWNLEE, OSWALD; and CONRAD, ALFRED 1961 Effects Upon the Distribution of Income of a Tight Money Policy. *American Economic Review* 51, no. 2:74–85.

BUDD, E. C. 1960 Factor Shares, 1850–1910. Volume 24, pages 365–406 in Conference on Research in Income and Wealth, *Studies in Income and Wealth.* Princeton Univ. Press.

BUDD, E. C. 1964 Comment on Goldberg's Paper. Volume 27, pages 276–285 in Conference on Research in Income and Wealth, *Studies in Income and Wealth.* Princeton Univ. Press. → Comment on Goldberg 1964.

BURKHEAD, JESSE V. 1953 Changes in the Functional Distribution of Income. *Journal of the American Statistical Association* 48:192–219.

Business Statistics. → Published since 1931 under various titles. Since 1951 issued by the U.S. Office of Business Economics. See especially the 1957 issue.

CONFERENCE ON RESEARCH IN INCOME AND WEALTH 1958 *A Critique of the United States Income and Product Accounts.* Studies in Income and Wealth, Vol. 22. Princeton Univ. Press.

CREAMER, DANIEL B. 1956 *Personal Income During Business Cycles.* National Bureau of Economic Research, Studies in Business Cycles, No. 6. Princeton Univ. Press.

DENISON, EDWARD F. 1952 Distribution of National Income: Pattern of Income Shares Since 1929. *Survey of Current Business* 32, no. 6:16–23.

DOUGLAS, PAUL H. 1930 *Real Wages in the United States, 1890–1926.* Pollack Foundation for Economic Research, Publications, No. 9. Boston: Houghton Mifflin.

FABRICANT, SOLOMON 1952 *The Trend of Government Activity in the United States Since 1900.* National Bureau of Economic Research, Publication No. 56. New York: The Bureau.

GOLDBERG, S. A. 1964 Long Run Changes in the Distribution of Income by Factor Shares in Canada. Volume 27, pages 189–237 in Conference on Research in Income and Wealth, *Studies in Income and Wealth.* Princeton Univ. Press.

GOLDSMITH, RAYMOND W. 1952 The Growth of Reproducible Wealth of the United States of America From 1805 to 1905. Pages 242–328 in International Association for Research in Income and Wealth, *Income and Wealth of the United States, Trends and Structure.* Income and Wealth, Series 2. Cambridge: Bowes.

GOLDSMITH, RAYMOND W. 1955–1956 *A Study of Saving in the United States.* 3 vols. Princeton Univ. Press. → Volume 1: *Introduction; Tables of Annual Estimates of Saving, 1897 to 1949.* Volume 2: *Nature and Derivation of Annual Estimates of Saving, 1897 to 1949.* Volume 3: *Special Studies*, by R. W. Goldsmith, Dorothy S. Brady, and Horst Mendershausen. See especially Volume 3.

GOLDSMITH, RAYMOND W. 1962 *The National Wealth of the United States in the Post War Period.* National Bureau of Economic Research, Studies in Capital Formation and Financing, Vol. 10. Princeton Univ. Press.

GOLDSMITH, RAYMOND W.; and LIPSEY, ROBERT E. 1963 *Studies in the National Balance Sheet of the United States.* 2 vols. National Bureau of Economic Research, Studies in Capital Formation and Financing, Vol. 11. Princeton Univ. Press. → See especially Volume 1.

HICKS, JOHN R. (1932) 1964 *The Theory of Wages.* New York: St. Martins.

JOHNSON, D. GALE 1948 Allocation of Agricultural Income. *Journal of Farm Economics* 30:724–749.

JOHNSON, D. GALE 1954 The Functional Distribution of Income in the United States, 1850–1952. *Review of Economics and Statistics* 36:175–182. → Published by Harvard University Press. Data in Table 1 reproduced by permission.

KALDOR, NICHOLAS 1955–1956 Alternative Theories of Distribution. *Review of Economic Studies* 23:83–100.

KALECKI, MICHAEL 1954 *Theory of Economic Dynamics: An Essay on Cyclical and Long-run Changes in Capitalist Economy.* New York: Rinehart.

KENDRICK, JOHN W. 1961 *Productivity Trends in the United States.* National Bureau of Economic Research, General Series, No. 71. Princeton Univ. Press.

KENDRICK, JOHN W. 1964 Comment on Solow's Paper. Volume 27, pages 140–142 in Conference on Research in Income and Wealth, *Studies in Income and Wealth.* Princeton Univ. Press.

KING, WILLFORD I. 1930 *The National Income and Its Purchasing Power.* National Bureau of Economic Research, Publication No. 15. New York: The Bureau.

KRAVIS, IRVING B. 1957 The Scope of Economic Activity in International Income Comparisons. Volume 20, pages 349–377 in Conference on Research in Income and Wealth, *Studies in Income and Wealth.* Princeton Univ. Press.

KRAVIS, IRVING B. 1959 Relative Income Shares in Fact and Theory. *American Economic Review* 49:917–949.

KRAVIS, IRVING B. 1962 *The Structure of Income: Some Quantitative Essays.* Philadelphia: Univ. of Pennsylvania Press.

KUZNETS, SIMON S. 1941 *National Income and Its Composition: 1919–1938.* 2 vols. National Bureau of Economic Research, Publication No. 40. New York: The Bureau.

KUZNETS, SIMON S. 1952 Long Term Changes in the National Income of the United States of America Since 1870. Pages 23–241 in International Association for Research in Income and Wealth, *Income and Wealth of the United States: Trends and Structure.* Income and Wealth, Series 2, Cambridge: Bowes.

KUZNETS, SIMON S. 1953 *Shares of Upper Income Groups in Income and Savings.* National Bureau of Economic Research, Publication No. 55. New York: The Bureau.

KUZNETS, SIMON S. 1959 Quantitative Aspects of the Economic Growth of Nations: IV. Distribution of National Income by Factor Shares. *Economic Development and Cultural Change* 7, no. 3, part 2.

KUZNETS, SIMON S. 1961 *Capital in the American Economy: Its Formation and Financing.* National Bureau of Economic Research, Studies in Capital Formation and Financing, No. 9. Princeton Univ. Press.

LEBERGOTT, STANLEY 1964 Factor Shares in the Long Term: Some Theoretical and Statistical Aspects. Volume 27, pages 53–86 in Conference on Research in Income and Wealth, *Studies in Income and Wealth.* Princeton Univ. Press.

NATIONAL INDUSTRIAL CONFERENCE BOARD 1939 *National Income in the United States, 1799–1938,* by Robert F. Martin. New York: The Board.

PESEK, BORIS P. 1960 A Comparison of the Distributional Effects of Inflation and Taxation. *American Economic Review* 50:147–153.

REDER, M. W. 1959 Alternative Theories of Labor's Share. Pages 180–206 in *The Allocation of Economic*

Resources: Essays in Honor of Bernard Francis Haley. Stanford Studies in History, Economics, and Political Science, No. 17. Stanford Univ. Press.

SCHULLER, G. J. 1953 The Secular Trend in Income Distribution by Type, 1869–1948: A Preliminary Estimate. *Review of Economics and Statistics* 35:302–324. → Published by Harvard University Press. Data in Table 2 reproduced by permission.

SCITOVSKY, T. 1964 A Survey of Some Theories of Income Distribution. Volume 27, pages 15–31 in Conference on Research in Income and Wealth, *Studies in Income and Wealth.* Princeton Univ. Press.

SOLOW, ROBERT M. 1957 Technical Change and the Aggregate Production Function. *Review of Economics and Statistics* 39:312–320.

SOLOW, ROBERT M. 1958 A Skeptical Note on the Constancy of Relative Shares. *American Economic Review* 48:618–631.

STIGLER, GEORGE J. 1961 Economic Problems in Measuring Changes in Productivity. Volume 25, pages 47–63 in Conference on Research in Income and Wealth, *Studies in Income and Wealth.* Princeton Univ. Press.

Survey of Current Business. → Published since 1948. See especially the July issues, 1957–1964.

U.S. BUREAU OF THE CENSUS 1958 *Statistical Abstract of the United States.* Washington: Government Printing Office. → Published since 1878.

U.S. BUREAU OF THE CENSUS 1960 *Historical Statistics of the United States; Colonial Times to 1957: A* Statistical Abstract *Supplement.* Washington: Government Printing Office.

U.S. DEPARTMENT OF AGRICULTURE *Agricultural Statistics.* → Published since 1936. See especially 1953–1962 editions.

U.S. OFFICE OF BUSINESS ECONOMICS *National Income.* → Published since 1934 under various titles. See especially 1951 and 1954 issues.

U.S. OFFICE OF BUSINESS ECONOMICS 1958*a* *U.S. Income and Output: A Supplement to the* Survey of Current Business. Washington: The Office.

U.S. OFFICE OF BUSINESS ECONOMICS 1958*b* New Estimates of National Income, 1946–1957. *Survey of Current Business* 38, no. 7:3–17.

WEINTRAUB, SIDNEY 1949 *Price Theory.* New York: Pitman.

WEINTRAUB, SIDNEY 1958 *An Approach to the Theory of Income Distribution.* Philadelphia: Chilton.

WEINTRAUB, SIDNEY 1959 *Forecasting the Price Level, Income Distribution and Economic Growth.* Philadelphia: Chilton. → A college edition was published simultaneously as *A General Theory of the Price Level, Output, Income Distribution and Economic Growth.*

WEINTRAUB, SIDNEY 1962 A Keynesian Model of the Price Level and the Constant Wage Share. *Kyklos* 15:701–719.

WOODEN, D. C.; and WASSON, R. C. 1956 Manufacturing Investment Since 1929 in Relation to Employment, Output, and Income. *Survey of Current Business* 36, no. 11:8–20.

II
SIZE

The distribution of power, prestige, and pelf has been a topic of durable concern to most societies. In distant eras, and in simple cultures, the distribution of economic power and advantage could be fairly closely measured in simple terms—e.g., the number of the flocks in ancient Israel, or the amount of land in the Domesday Book. But recent centuries have witnessed the notable rise of urban industry. They have also seen bewildering gains in geographic and social mobility: "Men become their own fathers," making their own status. However, the incentives that press the Rastignacs or Jim Bradys of the rising groups toward high consumption make their wealth only the coarsest measure of their economic advantage. Such forces have vitiated the use of data on landed wealth, or even total wealth, as a clear-cut measure of economic differences. Hence, interest in the distribution of wealth has largely given way, in our time, to interest in the distribution of income.

Uses of the data

Income size distributions may be used as measures both of economic productivity and of welfare.

Income as a measure of productivity. For measuring productivity, the relevant income distribution is that for individuals, more particularly those engaged in production for markets. In most economies, the income received by the typical worker, peasant, or businessman reflects chiefly the quantity and quality of the goods and services which he brings to market. Such an indication of the income recipient's "productivity" measures no inherent, inalienable set of personal talents and charms. Thus, the income that a farmer receives from marketing his crops necessarily reflects, in part, the accumulated knowledge he derives from society: he can raise more rice per acre of land than his father could because better varieties of seed have been developed and because the government provides better weather information. He receives more for each bushel he raises because an improved transportation network and futures market enable him to market his crop at a time, and in a condition, that make it command a better price. Similarly, today's worker may receive a higher wage per hour for his labor than his grandfather did because of the education that his parents and society have given him and because employment agencies, unions, and newspapers help to create an efficient labor market. To the extent to which the social order and private enterprisers apply new technologies, develop cheaper materials with which the worker can labor, provide capital at lower cost—to that extent the productivity of the worker will advance, and with it the amount of product with which he is compensated.

Two obvious considerations should be noted: All is not roses and fair shares in consequence. Just as inadequacies in the social order may reduce the absolute reward of everyone in it, so government and private restrictions on entry to an industry, a region, or an occupation will tend to affect relative shares. Effective monopolies or public incentives that favor one factor of production will increase the share of those who provide that factor.

The productivity being measured pertains only to the period covered, most commonly a year. Therefore the usual income distribution will reflect differences associated with age and period in life. Thus, it is fairly typical for individuals to have relatively low-value productivity in the years just after they enter the labor force full time and just before they leave it—reflecting a combination of part-time work and low or impaired skills. Perhaps more important is the displacement of income that occurs between years, and within a lifetime, depending on the nature of the work. For example, cyclical variations in the weather and predators that affect rubber or coffee crops will swing incomes in any given year well below or above a longer-term average. If an occupation requires a lengthy training period, with both costs of training and a loss of income during that period—e.g., a machinist's apprenticeship, a physician's period in medical school—very low or zero incomes will be recorded for the individual in his younger years, with compensating higher incomes later on. The national size distribution at any time will therefore reflect the proportion of persons in these industries, occupations, and age groups (Mincer 1958; Brady 1965).

We take these as so many givens when we speak of the productivity of the individual income earner. Nevertheless, it is that productivity—however derived—which is relevant in the actual state of the labor market, both in market economies and in state-operated ones.

Income as a measure of welfare. A second common use of income data relates to the measurement of welfare. Moralists have long had difficulty equating "goods" with "the Good." And economists have become notably wary of interpersonal utility comparisons. Not only do they lack any agreed basis for translating measured income into measurable welfare, but even when a fairly extensive set of axioms is stipulated (including an assumption of equal total output), they fail to agree on whether a more equal pattern of income distribution is preferable to a less equal one (Strotz, Fisher, & Rothenberg 1961).

For translating income into tests of welfare we must resort to a simpler proposition: In a free consumer market, differentials in income will indicate differentials in the command over goods and services. (Should the state or private sellers engage in rationing—e.g., by limiting the freedom to rent or purchase housing of certain types or in certain areas, to buy imported cars or the services of private clubs—even this premise is denied.)

As an indicator of the command over goods and services, the most informative distribution of income is that for families, not for individuals. The limitation of the latter measure is that in most societies the family acts as the primary agent for redistributing income. Children and housewives earn little or no income, but their command over goods is not equally trivial. Indeed, as the income of family heads has increased in many nations, the earnings of children have dwindled: instead of continuing to work full time in textile mills, children began to spend most of their days in school. As wives in lower-income families found their husbands' incomes rising, they left full-time work to earn zero (or at most pin money) levels of income. The facility with which family members can substitute leisure for income will increase as the income of the family head, and the family, increases. Therefore the income distribution of persons tells us too little about their changing command over goods and services, including leisure as a good.

Given the primitive communism that exists within the family structure, the distribution of family income is more serviceable than that of individual income for measuring the distribution of command over goods and services. But even this distribution has important limitations.

(1) If incomes are measured before taxes, the distribution will be substantially more skewed than on an after-tax basis. The precise intent of income taxation in many nations is, of course, to contribute to such leveling. The *corvée* in eighteenth-century France, road labor in nineteenth-century Africa, conscription in twentieth-century United States (given exemptions that are related to marital status and education)—each is likely to have had a differential impact by income. (Recent empirical studies for several countries appear in International Association . . . 1964.)

(2) Expenditure by the state will differentially benefit families in the different income groups. Whether defense and police protection aid the well-to-do disproportionately has been argued to conflicting conclusions. There is probably more agreement that such explicit payments as family allowances, unemployment insurance, or subsidies to farmers do vary by income level.

(3) Comparisons between more and less industrialized nations (or periods in the life of a nation) are substantially affected by the amount of income

received in nonmonetary form. Farm and mining families have frequently received significant amounts of their real income in the form of food and shelter, making no explicit payment for them. Urban residents who receive an identical volume of such goods and services command more of the economy's real resources: the costs of transport to the city, and of the distribution of goods within it, must be covered. But whether their perceived levels of well-being are greater *pari passu* is a matter admitting of "a wide answer."

(4) The more persons who share a given family income, the less the value of goods commanded by each—even assuming economies of scale in the consumption of housing, of works of art, etc. Hence the systematic attempts since Atwater and Ammon to adjust food consumption and total budgets to an "adult male equivalent" or other standardized basis. (For a recent example see Lamale 1965.) Such a scale can rest on a fairly objective basis so far as mere nutrient intake is concerned. But any allowance for food palatability or for the satisfactions from other budgeted items (clothing, amusements, etc.) tends (*a*) to embody the investigator's personal judgments, (*b*) only to report (somewhat indirectly) the actual consumption levels or elasticities of a particular society at a given stage in its history, or (*c*) both.

Possibly more important is the implicit assumption that because welfare will be affected by the number of persons in a family, income must be measured on a per person basis. Any such assumption applies only weakly to those religious groups and entire cultures which regard fecundity per se as a goal or a moral imperative. Since such groups prefer, in principle, more children to more material goods, a per capita income measure will bluntly conflict with one of their primary values.

(5) An equal amount of income does not translate into an equal command over goods and services at all income levels. Lower-income families frequently live in outlying districts, without cheap transportation. They are therefore confronted by few sellers of the goods and services they would buy. Discrimination because of caste (social, cultural, religious) may additionally restrict access to housing. Under such circumstances lower-income families are confronted by higher prices for an identical budget of goods and services than are upper-income families: their real incomes are therefore less than the current distribution of money incomes would indicate.

(6) Many nations seek to assure a per person minimum for particular goods and services (from zoos to well-baby clinics). These are provided without user charges, so that all persons (or all who pass a means, citizenship, and manners test) can have full access to presumably critical items. The list of such items has steadily expanded on every continent. Moreover, public social-welfare payments have increasingly replaced private charities. Thus, a number of the vexing impediments to the use of income distributions to mark the relevant differences in command over goods and services are readily disposed of in the context of actual problems. For given a specific, real world context, it may be possible to bound the impact of particular biases.

Because of the widespread receipt of assistance and income in kind—neither fully included in most income distributions—those concerned with economic welfare have found an analysis of the actual pattern of consumption a helpful supplement. Family budget surveys provide one such body of information. Data in the national accounts (on the constant dollar value of consumption) provide another such body of data. Together they remove any necessity for using the approximate statistics on income distribution to determine the extent of either grinding poverty or wealth beyond the dreams of avarice.

Other uses. Income distribution data have been tirelessly used as explanatory variables in studies by economists and political scientists. From the first systematic model developed by Tinbergen (1956), economists have tried to utilize distributional data to help explain variations in national saving, shifts in the factor shares of labor and capital, and short run changes in consumption patterns. Because of the lack of continuous estimates of size distribution in most nations until recent years these models have used proxy variables instead, e.g., the separate sums for wage and nonwage income (Klein et al. 1961). One may expect the actual distributions to be exploited more fully in the future.

There is perhaps no need to discuss more general inferences—e.g., that changes in income distribution determine the possibilities of revolutions and riot, land reform, or the development of a middle class (Davis 1941). Such speculations, however perceptive, have used data chiefly for decorative purposes. But the advent of more reliable data and more precise analysis may yet establish what contribution the study of changes in income and wealth size-distributions can make to the study of economic and political history.

Changes in income distribution

Central to much interest in income distribution data is one question: Does the inequality in income distribution increase or decrease through time? In principle, we would answer this question by comparing the income distributions of an identical set of income receivers in different periods. Such comparisons would indicate fairly directly whether the rich were getting richer, the poor getting poorer, etc.

In fact, most analyses simply compare distributions for all income receivers at two dates, whether or not the same recipients are included at both. But between these dates, forces are working to change the underlying population. Hence the reported income distribution will change even if no one receives lower hourly wages, or higher dividends, etc. Such forces include the following:

(1) The consequences of aging and mortality. Younger persons who work part time while in school report an increase in income when they leave school and begin full-time work. Older persons retire between one period and the next, shifting down from wage to pension income levels.

(2) The demographic and social consequences of a change in aggregate economic activity. When an economy shifts from underemployment to high employment, incomes will rise. Reported income inequality may rise in consequence. For example, the increase in U.S. incomes from the 1930s to the 1940s led elderly persons to move out of their children's homes into rooms and apartments of their own (Brady 1958). Presumably both the older persons and the families with growing children found that separate establishments provided a real advance in their welfare. Yet the usual income distribution data will report an increase in inequality: the number of "low-income families"—in the form of newly created "families" of older persons who had previously been included with their children—has increased.

Similarly, the stronger the labor market, the earlier young people find work and establish homes of their own. As a result, instead of one family being reported, with a combined income including the incomes of young persons and older persons, two families will be reported—each with a lower income.

(3) By widening the scope of income taxation, modern legislation has increased the incentives to receive income in forms other than current monetary receipts. It has thereby helped create a series of remarkable innovations whose consequences appear in the distribution of income. For upper-income groups the most significant of these innovations has probably been the conversion of ordinary income into the form of capital gains and gains from stock options. But these are typically excluded from the tabulations of income distribution. (It would indeed be difficult to decide how to include them.) Distorted results can therefore be produced by comparing income distributions between nations and between points in time when the incentives to convert income into capital gains differ (and the knowledge of techniques for doing so and the relevant legislative provisions also differ). The distribution only of ordinary income could under such circumstances offer a singularly inadequate indication of trends in income concentration.

Other innovations that affect income distribution include the contract for deferring payment until a future date and the multiplication of nontaxable trusts. The proliferation of business expense accounts since World War II suggests that resources devoted to the feeding and amusement of entrepreneurs, and their coadjutors, have also become increasingly potent substitutes for outright income payment. An executive may find a Picasso on his office wall to be a quite tolerable substitute for the million dollars (pounds, francs, etc.) of income that he would otherwise have to earn in order to enjoy the same painting on his living room wall for a few hours in the evening. The expansion of fringe benefits to workers—in the form of contributions to pension funds, subsidized lunches, etc.—similarly distorts comparisons of reported figures on income.

(4) The expanded role of the state as a taxing agency links to its expanded role as a redistributive mechanism. Public assistance payments and surplus foods add significantly to the resources of lower-income families, but are typically not reported in their incomes. Public guarantees of home loans and bank deposits provide middle-income families with lower interest rates, which may make the difference between owning and not owning their homes. But the saving of interest is never treated as income. The clearing of unsightly slums, the dredging of yacht harbors, and the selection of the best public school teachers for the best residential areas all benefit upper-income groups. The impact of this wandering pattern of taxation and benefit must be evaluated before simple comparisons of changes in income distributions through time can be taken to mean what they appear to mean.

(5) Finally, there are statistical problems of no mean magnitude. The amount of tax evasion is virtually unknown in most nations. Its effect in distorting reported income distributions is even more obscure. In the single publicly available report for the United States, for 1949, something like 23 per cent of taxable farm income was not re-

ported in tax returns (see Marius Farioletti's tables in Conference on Research . . .). Persons reporting $10,000 (or less) in adjusted gross income failed to report 4 per cent of that income, while persons owning businesses understated net profit by from 13 per cent (printing and publishing) to 37 per cent (hotels) and 87 per cent (amusement services). Reported income distribution figures are almost never adjusted for such evasion of taxes or understatement of income. In the very few instances in which they are adjusted (e.g., in the U.S. Department of Commerce figures), the adjustment is not differential by income level, there being no data upon which to base a reasonable differential adjustment. It is clearly captious to be concerned about the validity of data for those few nations which provide both distributions and information giving the user a fair chance to assess them. Nonetheless, intelligent use of income data must take these considerations into account.

Trends in dispersion. A long view of economic development suggests forces that would work toward and against greater inequality of the income distribution. Some theorists have argued that as societies become more developed, the contribution of each individual becomes more specific. This enables him to receive greater rent on his ability, thereby increasing inequality (Lachmann 1951). History does indeed suggest a trend toward concentration, to be surmised from periodic confiscations—the redistribution of the land under Solon, of monastic wealth under Henry VIII and the sans-culottes, and of property in land and slaves under Tsar Nicholas and Lincoln. But no less significant has been the long rise in prices generated by the discovery of silver in the Old World and of gold in the New World. This trend has, in Sir Josiah Stamp's phrase, brought the unseen robbery of generations. By eroding existing accumulations of wealth, it has offered later generations the fair prospect of more equal chances to earn and to accumulate income.

Kuznets' review of a mass of nineteenth- and twentieth-century data on income distribution in many nations concludes that there has been some long-run tendency toward leveling (1955). The expansion of public education, the opening of occupations to children of lower-class origin, the widening of credit facilities, the cheapening of transport (destroying local monopolies)—all these raised the income levels of the lower-income groups and thereby made for greater equality in the income distribution.

U.S. experience. Work initiated by Kneeland and others in the 1930s established a continuous series for U.S. income distribution (U.S. Bureau of the Census; U.S. Office of Business Economics). This work makes possible long-period comparisons for the United States, provided one is prepared to allow for, or ignore, the qualifications noted above on temporal comparisons. These estimates suggest that the distribution of income in the United States became substantially more equal after 1944 than it had been in 1935–1936—whether we measure the distribution of income among families or among consumer units—and even after allowance for capital gains (Goldsmith et al. 1954). Reductions in inequality since 1944, however, prove to be small compared with the change from 1935–1936 to 1944. The lowest fifth of American families received 4–5 per cent of family personal income in 1935–1936, in 1941, and in the years since 1946; the top fifth received 52 per cent in 1935–1936 and has received 45–46 per cent ever since 1946 (Goldsmith et al. 1954, p. 9; Fitzwilliams 1963, p. 18). The proportion of American families with incomes below $3,000 (in 1962 prices)—the rough poverty line suggested by the Council of Economic Advisers—averaged 32 per cent in 1947 and about 20 per cent in 1962 and 1963. Allowing for differential income requirements by family size would significantly cut the proportions below an adjusted poverty line. Doing so would, however, include enough more of the larger families so that poor families would include about the same number of persons (Orshansky 1965). Up to this point we have discussed the experience of poverty or riches associated with a single year. What of a more extended period? The data show that approximately three-fourths of the families with incomes below $3,000 in 1962 remained in that status in 1963 as well (U.S. President 1965, p. 165).

Redistributive taxation and expenditure have helped bring about the decline in the proportion of income received by the top fifth since the 1930s and the decline in the proportion of low-income families. However, the massive cut in unemployment appears to have been more directly responsible. One indication of this is that the major shifts between 1935 and 1963 took place from 1935 to 1944, when unemployment fell from one-fifth to one-twentieth of the labor force. Data for Great Britain are similar in this respect—the top 1 per cent got 15.2 per cent of income in 1938 and 10.5 per cent in 1949, with but little further change—e.g., to 9.1 per cent by 1957 (Lydall 1959). Another indication is the striking change in the characteristics of families in the low-income group. These had been fairly representative families in the

1930s, judged by demographic and personal characteristics. By the early 1960s the group had become a mixture of older persons, nonwhites, farm families, families with female heads, and others marginal in characteristics other than income.

The formation of income distributions

The mechanism that creates the distribution of income has been explained in ways that range from historical–sociological theories of great generality to hypotheses of sharply defined stochastic process. One hypothesis, first suggested many decades ago, was that the Gaussian normal distributions (which fit many human characteristics, such as height, weight, IQ) might apply to income as well. But records for many societies, despite their unreliability, agree in suggesting that this is not so. Broadly speaking, two types of explanation developed subsequently. One premises the normal distribution as a starting point, then seeks to explain how that distribution was truncated or otherwise forced so that the usual skewness of income distributions developed. The second category of explanations premises that the underlying distribution is lognormal, or Poisson. Some specialists have sought primarily to find a single function that could describe many existing distributions. Others have been more concerned with understanding what economic processes could reasonably produce the distributions and then have more or less systematically proceeded to fit various functions to data.

Among the analyses concerned with explaining how income distributions arise from the incentives and institutions of typical economies, many have emphasized the arithmetic normal distribution as the starting point. A substantial bias in that distribution may be assumed to result from the impact of property inheritance, from differentials in parental interest and ability to invest in training for their children, and from the consequences of inherited social position. High incomes are then explicable by the greater potential some persons have for earning income (given their advanced training and status) or for acquiring it (i.e., returns from inherited property). The impact of inheritance has been emphasized by Pigou and Dalton (see Dalton 1920). Marxist critics have focused also on status and sociological differentiations.

While the inheritance of property was a substantial element in the British experience, the present role of incomes from such inheritance in most Western nations is not such as to make it likely to be a significant factor per se in explaining the skewness of income distributions. On the other hand, the inequality of training and contacts among young persons beginning their work career is surely relevant, particularly given the recent literature that emphasizes private monetary returns to investment in education. To the extent that all this is simply an application of the Biblical stipulation "to him who hath shall be given," one would expect to see mounting inequality over time. Such a trend is not apparent, either in the West or in underdeveloped nations. (However, such a tendency could be masked by the consequences of concurrent attempts to redistribute income and to widen access to education, which often first take place in a nation during the very periods for which the first data become available, permitting comparison of its income distributions through time.)

It has recently been contended that abilities to earn income in fact form a truncated arithmetic normal distribution—whose apparent skewness in some societies reflects the fact that credit-granting agencies provide capital to persons with high money-making abilities (thus enabling them to compound these to attain very high incomes), whereas these agencies truncate the other end of the income distribution by denying credit to most large-scale speculators, whose skills would otherwise enable them to develop large risky enterprises that would lose large sums of money and generate large negative incomes (Lebergott 1959).

An important group of analysts stipulate that there are really two underlying distributions. Thus Tinbergen (1956) has suggested that persons who possess great ability for certain jobs (e.g., artists, craftsmen) will have a particularly strong desire to engage in them and will therefore lower their wage demands in order to enter them, whereas workers with lesser abilities will choose more widely, taking those jobs which command higher monetary returns. Friedman (1953) has emphasized not two classes of individuals but two classes of actions—more and less venturesome—in which individuals engage. Greater possibilities of very high incomes inhere in the more venturesome (job choices, investment choices, gambles). If a mechanism exists for redistributing the proceeds of quasi lotteries, one can generate some extremely high incomes without generating negative ones—since entry to the lottery requires only a small admission fee. The model is thus consistent with the usual skewed distributions. It will be noted that both models require some rather strong corollary assumptions for them to apply to recent periods or to modern nations—e.g., that highly skilled people are willing to take unusually low wages, that some widespread redistributive mechanism exists to take from the poor(er) to give to the rich(er). Neither assumption is descriptive of behavior in many labor markets or of the impact of the usual governmental taxing and redistributive mechanisms.

Another group of analysts has emphasized the contribution made to the shape of the over-all income distribution by its component distributions. Since Mill and Cairnes pointed to the presence of "noncompeting groups," it has been clear that the distribution of incomes for a peasant group, for a wage-earning group, and for the sons of the rich will each have a characteristic shape. If, then, all persons in a given country are taken together, the over-all distribution will reflect the symmetry or, more generally, the actual shape of the underlying distributions (Hayakawa 1951; Miller 1964). Such considerations are, of course, consistent with an over-all distribution ranging from the near-symmetrical to the wildly skewed.

Probably the most widely attempted explanations in recent years involve those which specify the income distribution as lognormal, with the logarithms of income normally distributed even though income itself is not. Originally sparked by Gibrat's pioneering study (1931), this distribution has received repeated attention in recent decades (see Kalecki 1945; Champernowne 1952; Aitchison & Brown 1957; Bjerke 1961; Mincer 1958). These writers assume that a Markov process is at work in which the incomes received, e.g., in a given year, will change by some percentage from that year to the subsequent year, the size of that percentage being independent of the income in the initial year. Given that the probabilities of such changes are independent, application of the central limit theorem enables us to conclude that as sufficient time passes the original shape of the distribution will no longer be significant. What we will then come to observe is the skewed lognormal distribution. The simpler models of this sort imply vast increases in income inequality, for each of the assumed random changes will add to the variance of the distribution (Kalecki). Such increasing inequality, however, does not appear in most sets of empirical data of reasonable validity. Various additional side conditions have been specified to prevent the model from leading to such a conclusion (Champernowne, Rutherford). One substantial difficulty with these amended models is that they fail to fit recent reliable income distributions. It is also to be noted that by premising random percentage increments, they stipulate a pattern of random reward in the income acquisition process that seems uncharacteristic of many societies. Most economies structure income receipt with respect to economic contribution (e.g., such as marginal productivity of labor), or social status, or some combination of known economic incentives and social restraints.

Measurement

Modern analysis of income distribution begins with Vilfredo Pareto. Somewhat earlier Quetelet, Leroy Baulieu, and others had given brief consideration to data then flowing from various taxing systems. But it was Pareto, one of the group of economists engaged in transforming a branch of natural philosophy into a rigorous system of analysis, who first observed how similar many income distributions were when evaluated in terms of what is still called the Pareto coefficient (Pareto 1896–1897, vol. 2, p. 305).

The Pareto coefficient. The Pareto coefficient is a in the equation $\log N = \log A - a \log x$, where N is the number of persons with incomes at least as large as x. Pareto's review of data for various countries suggested to him that the coefficient was approximately 1.5 in every instance, although in fact he reports data ranging from 1.24 to 1.79 (*ibid.*, p. 312). This putative fact led to the inference that a natural constant had been discovered: "A decrease in the inequality of incomes cannot come about . . . except when total income increases more rapidly than the population" (*ibid.*, p. 320). Following Pareto, even very modern writers, noting that the parameter ranges from 1.6 to 2.4, infer that such a narrow range, although referring to widely separated countries and occasions, would seem to indicate a common underlying mechanism. Massive differences between economies, centuries, and continents are submerged by this measure into a simple single coefficient, originally offered (and frequently taken) as a kind of ultimate social law.

The theoretical limitations of this measure were canvassed by Macaulay and Mitchell (1922), and others. One difficulty is that the formula will estimate an infinite number of recipients for incomes greater than a near-zero amount: it must therefore be used only to estimate the number above some level arbitrarily chosen to give sensible results. It is, at the very least, a signal difficulty that one function should hold above some income level picked by the analyst on an *ad hoc* basis, while another presumably explains the distribution below that arbitrary level. Another difficulty is that differences in the coefficient which appear small on casual inspection, and therefore lead to the assumption of its constancy, may not be small so far as any serious economic or political issue is concerned. (Thus the ratio of wives to husbands is fairly close to 1.0 in most Western nations. Yet one can be certain that any community in which the ratio was 1.01 would have an interesting basis for tea-time discussion and police action.) In this respect the position of Harold Davis, while extreme, was more reasonable when he declared that small variations in the coefficient made the difference between revolution and peace in many a historic situation (1941).

In fact, Pareto's equation does not fit distributions recorded in recent years at all well, and even his original fit was to a mixture in which data for both individuals and corporate bodies were included. It may be a more reasonable inference that the coefficient is simply insensitive to major differences in concentration if our criterion of stability in the coefficient is casual inspection. However, the coefficient is a convenient smoothing device and in recent years has frequently been used for computing income aggregates from distributions.

Pareto's premise, and that of some later writers, that the constancy of his a demonstrated that redistribution was impossible and that incomes could be improved only by an increase in total product, is an interesting example of a theorist drawing policy conclusions from an empirical observation—with no theory behind his speculation. It was pardonable that half a century of subsequent redistribution through progressive tax systems had not been revealed to him as demonstrating the contrary, but the lack of an analytic model stipulating why no shift was possible was less warranted.

Lorenz curve. Another measure widely used—in part because it is associated with a simple graphic presentation—is the Lorenz curve (Lorenz 1905). Total income is measured on one axis and total population on the other. For each percentile point the cumulated income and cumulated population are recorded. If all members of the distribution were to receive the same income, a simple diagonal would appear on the graph, running from the origin (southwest) to northeast. As it is, the Lorenz curve always reports that income is not distributed equally. This discovery is hardly one of unusual moment (1) because ocular standards rather than formal tests of significance are involved and (2) because the standard of perfect equality is used, rather than some actual reality, such as, say, the average distribution for several high employment years or that for a nation with an active policy of redistribution, etc. But the curves are most commonly used to demonstrate the degree to which the distribution has shifted toward or away from equality from one period to the next, or differs from equality from one nation to the next. Since the extent of movement may be considered trivial to one temperament and significant to another, the significance of a difference between two curves is best assessed by comparison with the difference between two other curves—e.g., is the change from period 1 to 2 greater than that from 2 to 3? In comparisons between nations it is, of course, essential that comparable populations be contrasted. A contrast between a distribution of income taxpayers in one nation and the total population in another, or between two tax-paying populations with different levels of exemption, may produce fierce findings of difference in the measures despite a total lack of difference in the actual distributions.

The Gini index. For the study of capital formation, class warfare, and related purposes, the index of concentration developed by Corrado Gini has been widely used. It is a straightforward measure based on the area of the triangle under the line of perfect equality: the area between the Lorenz curve and the diagonal of perfect equality is taken as a percentage of the total area in the triangle. It is computed from the equation $\log N = \delta \log Y - \log c$, where N measures the number of individuals with incomes above a given amount "z" and Y measures the aggregate of incomes above z (δ is commonly termed the Gini coefficient). Gini's N is a function of S, the total of incomes above z, whereas Pareto's N is a function of z itself. (Other measures, and computation formulas, appear in Yntema 1933 and Dalton [1920] 1949, appendix.)

In addition to such summary measures, considerable use has been made of such straightforward measures as the proportion of income received by the upper 1 per cent or 5 per cent of income recipients (Kuznets 1955; Lampman 1959) or the proportion of families with incomes below some income level. Since many policy proposals are related to a judgment that there are too many poor or too many wealthy families, the use of the full range of data proves to be more relevant than single summary measures such as the Pareto and Gini coefficients. It should be emphasized that all such measures focus on income received—almost always on money income alone. Since an essential aspect of income receipt in most societies (capitalist, communist, primitive) is that money incomes are complemented by nonmonetary factors (ease of work, short hours, income in kind, stability of employment, prestige, etc.), the income data report only the aspects that have been monetized. This limitation is a grave one for nations with substantial rural populations and is becoming a severe one for nations with taxes and regulations that increase incentives toward compensation in nonmonetary form.

STANLEY LEBERGOTT

[*See also* CONSUMERS, *article on* CONSUMPTION LEVELS AND STANDARDS; LABOR FORCE, *article on* PARTICIPATION; POVERTY; SIZE DISTRIBUTIONS IN ECONOMICS; *and the biographies of* GINI; PARETO.]

BIBLIOGRAPHY

AITCHISON, JOHN; and BROWN, J. A. C. 1957 *The Lognormal Distribution: With Special Reference to Its Uses in Economics.* Cambridge Univ. Press.

ANDERSON, W. H. L. 1964 Trickling Down: The Relationship Between Economic Growth and the Extent of Poverty Among American Families. *Quarterly Journal of Economics* 78:511–524.

BJERKE, KJELD 1961 Some Income and Wage Distribution Theories: Summary and Comments. *Weltwirtschaftliches Archiv* 86:46–66.

BRADY, DOROTHY S. 1958 Individual Incomes and the Structure of Consumer Units. *American Economic Review* 48, no. 2:269–278.

BRADY, DOROTHY S. 1965 *Age and the Income Distribution.* U.S. Department of Health, Education, and Welfare, Social Security Administration, Division of Research and Statistics, Research Report No. 8. Washington: The Department.

CHAMPERNOWNE, DAVID G. 1952 The Graduation of Income Distributions. *Econometrica* 20:591–615.

CONFERENCE ON RESEARCH IN INCOME AND WEALTH *Studies in Income and Wealth.* → See especially Volumes 3, 5, 13, 15, and 23. These volumes contain a sampling of studies by specialists on the meaning and limitations of distribution data. Tables 2 and 5, compiled by Marius Marioletti, in Volume 23 contain data indicating the role of tax evasion in distorting reported income distributions.

DALTON, HUGH (1920) 1949 *Some Aspects of the Inequality of Incomes in Modern Communities.* London: Routledge.

DAVIS, HAROLD T. 1941 *The Analysis of Economic Time Series.* Cowles Commission for Research in Economics, Monograph No. 6. Bloomington, Ind.: Principia Press.

FITZWILLIAMS, J. M. 1963 Size Distribution of Income in 1962. *Survey of Current Business* 43, no. 4:14–20.

FRIEDMAN, MILTON 1953 Choice, Chance and the Personal Distribution of Income. *Journal of Political Economy* 61:277–290.

GARVY, GEORGE 1954 Functional and Size Distributions of Income and Their Meaning. *American Economic Review* 44, no. 2:236–253.

GIBRAT, ROBERT 1931 *Les inégalités économiques.* Paris: Sirey.

GOLDSMITH, SELMA F. 1957 Changes in the Size Distribution of Income. *American Economic Review* 47, no. 2:504–518.

GOLDSMITH, SELMA F. et al. 1954 Size Distribution of Income Since the Mid-thirties. *Review of Economics and Statistics* 36:1–32.

HAYAKAWA, MIYOJI 1951 The Application of Pareto's Law of Income to Japanese Data. *Econometrica* 19: 174–183.

INTERNATIONAL ASSOCIATION FOR RESEARCH IN INCOME AND WEALTH 1957 *Income and Wealth.* Series 6. London: Bowes.

INTERNATIONAL ASSOCIATION FOR RESEARCH IN INCOME AND WEALTH 1964 *Income and Wealth.* Series 10. London: Bowes.

KALECKI, MICHAEL 1945 On the Gibrat Distribution. *Econometrica* 13:161–170.

KINGSTON, J. 1952 A designaldade na distribuição das rendas (Inequality of Income Distribution). *Revista brasileira de economía* 6:7–90.

KLEIN, LAWRENCE R. et al. 1961 *An Econometric Model of the United Kingdom.* Oxford: Blackwell.

KUZNETS, SIMON S. 1953 *Shares of Upper Income Groups in Income and Savings.* National Bureau of Economic Research, Publication No. 55. New York: The Bureau.

KUZNETS, SIMON S. 1955 Economic Growth and Income Inequality. *American Economic Review* 45:1–28.

LACHMANN, L. M. 1951 The Science of Human Action. *Economica* New Series 18:412–427.

LAMALE, HELEN 1965 Poverty: The Word and the Reality. U.S. Bureau of Labor Statistics, *Monthly Labor Review* 89:822–835.

LAMPMAN, ROBERT J. 1959 Changes in the Share of Wealth Held by Top Wealth Holders, 1922–1956. *Review of Economics and Statistics* 41:379–392.

LEBERGOTT, STANLEY 1959 The Shape of the Income Distribution. *American Economic Review* 49:328–347.

LORENZ, MAX O. 1905 Methods of Measuring the Concentration of Wealth. *Journal of the American Statistical Association* 9:209–219.

LYDALL, HAROLD F. 1959 The Long-term Trend in the Size Distribution of Income. *Journal of the Royal Statistical Society* 122, part 1:1–46.

MACAULAY, F.; and MITCHELL, W. (editors) 1922 The Personal Distribution of Income in the United States. Volume 2 in National Bureau of Economic Research, *Income in the United States: Its Amount and Distribution, 1909–1919.* New York: Harcourt.

MILLER, HERMAN P. 1963 *Trends in the Income of Families and Persons in the United States: 1947–1960.* U.S. Bureau of the Census, Technical Papers, No. 8. Washington: Government Printing Office. → Conveniently summarizes U.S. Bureau of the Census P-60 data for 1947–1960.

MILLER, HERMAN P. 1964 *Rich Man, Poor Man.* New York: Crowell.

MINCER, JACOB 1958 Investment in Human Capital and Personal Income Distribution. *Journal of Political Economy* 66:281–302.

MORGAN, J. N. et al. 1962 *Income and Welfare in the United States.* New York: McGraw-Hill.

MORGAN, THEODORE 1953 Distribution of Income in Ceylon, Puerto Rico, the United States and the United Kingdom. *Economic Journal* 63:821–834.

MUSGRAVE, RICHARD et al. 1956 The Incidence of the Tax Structure and Its Effects on Consumption. Pages 96–113 in U.S. Congress, Joint Committee on Economic Report, *Federal Tax Policy for Economic Growth and Stability.* Washington: Government Printing Office.

ORSHANSKY, MOLLIE 1965 Counting the Poor: Another Look at the Poverty Profile. *Social Security Bulletin* 28, no. 1:3–29.

PARETO, VILFREDO (1896–1897) 1927 *Cours d'économie politique professé à l'Université de Lausanne.* 2d ed. 2 vols. Paris: Giard & Brière.

SARGAN, JOHN D. 1957 The Distribution of Wealth. *Econometrica* 25:568–590.
SOLOW, ROBERT 1960 Income Inequality Since the War. Pages 93–138 in Ralph E. Freeman (editor), *Postwar Economic Trends in the United States.* New York: Harper.
STROTZ, ROBERT; FISHER, F.; and ROTHENBERG, J. 1961 How Income Ought to Be Distributed: Paradox Regained. *Journal of Political Economy* 69:162–180, 271–278.
Survey of Current Business. → Published since 1921. Since 1953 it has presented at intervals current data on income distribution derived by adjusting reports from the Bureau of the Census and the Internal Revenue Service. See U.S. Office of Business Economics entry below.
TINBERGEN, JAN 1956 On the Theory of Income Distribution. *Weltwirtschaftliches Archiv* 77, no. 2:155–173.
TSURU, SHIGETO 1961 *Has Capitalism Changed? An International Symposium on the Nature of Contemporary Capitalism.* Tokyo: Iwanami Shoten. → See especially pages 20–21, 86–87.
UNITED NATIONS ECONOMIC COMMISSION FOR EUROPE *Economic Survey of Europe.* → Published annually since 1947. Presents income distribution data at intervals.
U.S. BUREAU OF THE CENSUS *Current Population Reports: Consumer Income.* Series-P60. → Issued annually, the *Reports* provide detailed distribution data for persons and for families, classified in considerable detail.
U.S. OFFICE OF BUSINESS ECONOMICS *Income Distribution in the United States, by Size, 1944–1950.* → Issued in 1953 as a supplement to the *Survey of Current Business.* The basic Bureau of the Census and Internal Revenue Service data are combined and adjusted for error and incomparabilities by the Office of Business Economics. Estimates for subsequent years appear, at intervals, in the *Survey of Current Business* (e.g., April 1960; April 1962).
U.S. PRESIDENT 1965 *Economic Report of the President.* Washington: Government Printing Office. → Published annually since 1947.
YNTEMA, DWIGHT B. 1933 Measures of the Inequality in the Personal Distribution of Wealth or Income. *Journal of the American Statistical Association* 28: 423–433.

INCOME TAXES
See under TAXATION.

INDEPENDENCE MOVEMENTS
See COLONIALISM; INTERNAL WARFARE; NATIONALISM; PAN MOVEMENTS; *and the biography of* FANON. *Specific independence movements are discussed in* AFRICAN SOCIETY, *article on* NORTH AFRICA; ASIAN SOCIETY, *article on* SOUTHEAST ASIA; CARIBBEAN SOCIETY.

INDEX CONSTRUCTION
See INDEX NUMBERS; STRATIFICATION, SOCIAL, *article on* SOCIAL CLASS.

INDEX NUMBERS

I
THEORETICAL ASPECTS

An index number measures the magnitude of a variable relative to a specified value of the variable. For example, suppose that a certain type of apple sold at an average price of 10 cents last year but sells at an average price of 11 cents this year. If last year's price is chosen as a base and is arbitrarily set equal to 100 (to be thought of as a pure number or as 100 per cent), then the index number identified with this year's price would be 110 (that is, $[11/10] \times 100$), which indicates that this year's price is 10 per cent higher than last year's price. Rather than comparing the price at two different dates, we might wish to compare the current price of this type of apple in New York City with that in Chicago, in which case we would choose the price in one of those two cities as a base and express the price in the other city relative to the base. Thus, index numbers can be used to make comparisons over both time and space.

If index numbers were used only to compare such variables as the price of a *single* commodity at different dates or places, there would be little need for a special theory of index numbers. However, we might wish to compare, for example, the general price levels of commodities imported by the United States in two different years. The prices of some commodities will have risen, and the prices of others will have fallen. The problem that arises is how to combine the relative changes in the prices of the various commodities into a single number that can meaningfully be interpreted as a measure of the relative change in the general price level of imported commodities. This example illustrates perhaps the major problem dealt with in index number theory, and this article discusses primarily the various solutions that have been proposed.

Two approaches. The possibility of using an index number as an aggregate measure of the price change of several commodities seems to have been recognized in the eighteenth century, but deliberate theoretical discussions did not begin until the middle of the nineteenth century. Among the formulas suggested then were those of the German economists Étienne Laspeyres and Hermann Paasche, which are still used extensively. The choice of formula was made according to what was considered to be "fair." A major step forward in the development of criteria by which to judge the various formulas was the set of tests suggested by Irving Fisher (1922). From the 1920s on, however, greater care was taken to place the index in an economic context. Thinking mainly of cost-of-living comparisons, investigators defined the price index as the relative change in income necessary to maintain an unchanged standard of living.

The two lines of thought, the mainly statistical one and the economic one, still exist side by side. The economic approach starts with some economic considerations but does not arrive at a definite result. In contrast to this, the statistical approach starts with some subjectively chosen rules but arrives at formulas that may be used directly in practical work. Fortunately, the index formulas derived in these two ways are usually very similar. There is, however, still need of a more unified theory of index numbers.

The statistical theory

The pure statistical theory of index numbers is general in the sense that it could be applied to any index without regard to what the index represents. In order to avoid confusion, this discussion will refer mainly to price indexes and will revert to quantity indexes only when necessary for the development of the price index theory.

Consider the relations p_{i1}/p_{i0} $(i = 1, \cdots, n)$ between the prices of n commodities at two points of time, t_0 and t_1. These relations, called price ratios or price relatives, could be considered as elements having a certain distribution, the central measure of which is sought. Thus, it is natural to construct a weighted arithmetic, harmonic, or geometric average of the price ratios.

By choosing the weights in different ways it is possible to arrive at many types of indexes. Unweighted arithmetic averages were long used. However, by the first half of the nineteenth century, Arthur Young, Joseph Lowe, and G. Poulett Scrope, all of England, used weighted arithmetic averages of the price ratios. The weight w_i given to the price ratio p_{i1}/p_{i0} was

$$w_i = \frac{p_{i0}q_i}{\sum_{j=1}^{n} p_{j0}q_j},$$

where q_i is a quantity of commodity i showing its general importance in the list of commodities. If q_i is specified to be the quantity of commodity i traded during a period around t_0, so that $q_i = q_{i0}$, the resulting formula is the one suggested in 1864 by Laspeyres, namely,

$$P_{01}^{L} = \sum_{i=1}^{n} \frac{p_{i0}q_{i0}}{\sum_{j=1}^{n} p_{j0}q_{j0}} \cdot \frac{p_{i1}}{p_{i0}} = \frac{\sum_{i=1}^{n} p_{i1}q_{i0}}{\sum_{i=1}^{n} p_{i0}q_{i0}}.$$

The subscripts on P^L simply indicate that the index measures the price level at date t_1 relative to that at the base date t_0.

There is a complication here that does not seem to have attracted much attention. In practice, prices are observed at *points* of time, whereas quantities generally have to be taken as referring to *periods* of time. However, the denominator in Laspeyres's formula is usually interpreted as the actual value of transactions during the base *period* t_0. This implies either that prices have been constant within the period or that the p_i are to be interpreted as average prices. To avoid ambiguity it will be assumed in the following discussion that the periods are very short, so that the prices can be regarded as constant during each period.

A formula equivalent to Laspeyres's but using q_{i1} instead of q_{i0} in the weights naturally suggested itself and seemed equally justifiable. It was advocated in 1874 by Paasche.

Alfred Marshall suggested that instead of using quantities referring to one of the two points of time compared by the index, an average of the corresponding quantities should be used—that is,

$$P_{01}^{E} = \frac{\sum_{i=1}^{n} p_{i1}(q_{i0} + q_{i1})}{\sum_{i=1}^{n} p_{i0}(q_{i0} + q_{i1})}.$$

Because this index formula was strongly advocated by F. Y. Edgeworth, it is often called Edgeworth's formula. The use of a geometric average of the quantities associated with the two dates has also been suggested.

Fisher's tests. The various formulas gave results that were sometimes widely different, and it was evident that criteria for judging the quality of the formulas were needed. Fisher suggested a set of criteria that have remained the most extensive and widely used. Before describing Fisher's criteria, let us define P_{rs} as the index number given by formula P expressing the change in the general price level between dates r and s relative to the price level at date r; that is, date r is the base.

The *time reversal test* states that in comparing the prices at two dates, a formula should give the same result regardless of which of the two dates is chosen as the base. For example, if a formula indicates that the price level in 1965 was double that in 1964 when 1964 is taken as the base, then it should indicate that the price level in 1964 was one half that in 1965 when 1965 is taken as the base. Symbolically, the test requires that

$$P_{rs}P_{sr} = 1, \qquad \text{for all } r \text{ and } s.$$

The *circular test* requires that

$$P_{rs}P_{st} = P_{rt}, \qquad \text{for all } r,\ s, \text{ and } t;\ r \neq t.$$

For example, if a formula indicates that the price level doubled between 1963 and 1964 and then doubled again between 1964 and 1965, it should indicate that the price level in 1965 was four times that in 1963 when 1965 and 1963 are compared directly. Although this test has great intuitive appeal, Fisher argued that it is not an essential test and even suggested that a formula that satisfies it exactly should generally be rejected.

The *factor reversal test* presupposes that the weights used in the price index formula are functions of quantities. It states that if the price index P_{01} is multiplied by a corresponding quantity index Q_{01}, derived by interchanging p and q in the index formula, the result should equal the value ratio—that is,

$$P_{01}Q_{01} = \frac{\sum_{i=1}^{n} p_{i1}q_{i1}}{\sum_{i=1}^{n} p_{i0}q_{i0}}.$$

Fisher's tests have been found to be inconsistent with each other. However, Fisher classified all the formulas he tested according to which tests they fulfilled. He found only four formulas that deserved a "superlative" rating, all of which used quantities from both t_0 and t_1. They included Edgeworth's formula, noted above, and the corresponding formula with geometric instead of arithmetic means of quantities. Also "superlative" were the arithmetic and geometric means of Laspeyres's and Paasche's formulas. Fisher called the geometric mean of these formulas the "ideal" index.

Chain indexes. The discussion so far has dealt with a comparison of prices between only two points of time. In practice, however, indexes are calculated for many dates at regular intervals—for example, monthly or annually. Thus, the question that arises is how a series of index numbers should be calculated. For convenience, it is customary to use a fixed base, say t_0, and calculate successively $P_{01}, P_{02}, \cdots, P_{0k}$. This means that if Laspeyres's formula is used, a comparison of prices at t_{k-1} and t_k is in fact made using quantities that do not refer to either of these dates but refer instead to t_0.

Since very often the comparison of the prices of one date with those of the immediately preceding date is more important than the comparison with the base date, it may be useful to compute for every t_r an index $P_{r-1,r}$ and then define

$$P_{0k} = P_{01} \cdot P_{12} \cdot \cdots \cdot P_{k-1,k}.$$

This *chain index*, originally suggested by Marshall in 1887, satisfies the circular test for any $r < s < t$. In spite of Fisher's doubts, satisfaction of the circular test is a very attractive property, and chain indexes are often used. Any index formula could be applied for the index $P_{r-1,r}$ within the links.

The development of the chain index may be said to have originated in a desire to find an index with the properties expressed by Fisher's circular test. It is interesting to note that a somewhat similar result may be obtained by reasoning from the factor reversal test. Following Divisia (1925) and Törnqvist (1937), we start from the criterion

$$P_{0t}Q_{0t} = \frac{\sum_{i=1}^{n} p_{it}q_{it}}{\sum_{i=1}^{n} p_{i0}q_{i0}}.$$

Taking logarithms of both sides and differentiating with respect to t, we have

$$\frac{1}{P_{0t}} \cdot \frac{dP_{0t}}{dt} + \frac{1}{Q_{0t}} \cdot \frac{dQ_{0t}}{dt} = \frac{1}{\sum_{i=1}^{n} p_{it}q_{it}} \left(\sum_{i=1}^{n} q_{it}\frac{dp_{it}}{dt} + \sum_{i=1}^{n} p_{it}\frac{dq_{it}}{dt} \right).$$

To obtain symmetry between the price index and the quantity index, the terms may be equated pairwise—that is, the first term on the left-hand side of the equality sign may be set equal to the first term on the right-hand side of the equality sign, and similarly for the second terms.

Integrating the equations, we obtain for P_{01}

$$(1) \qquad \log P_{01} = \sum_{i=1}^{n} \int_{t_0}^{t_1} c_i(t)\, d\log p_{it},$$

where $c_i(t) = p_{it}q_{it} / \sum_{i=1}^{n} p_{it}q_{it}$. Thus, the value of P_{01} depends on the development of the $c_i(t)$ between t_0 and t_1, which are the proportions of the different commodities in the total budget. If an assumption is made about this development, the integral can be solved explicitly. Thus, if the $c_i(t)$ are assumed to be constant over time—that is, if all commodities are assumed to have a price elasticity of demand equal to one, we obtain the geometric index formula

$$P_{01} = \prod_{i=1}^{n} \left(\frac{p_{i1}}{p_{i0}}\right)^{c_i}.$$

If no assumptions are made about the c_i, the mean value theorem of the integral calculus may be applied to (1) to obtain

$$\log P_{01} = \sum_{i=1}^{n} \bar{c}_i (\log p_{i1} - \log p_{i0}), \quad (2)$$

where $\bar{c}_i$ is a weighted mean of the $c_i(t)$ over the period from t_0 to t_1. If this period is not too long, $\bar{c}_i$ may be approximated by the share of commodity i in the total expenditure during the period. The definite integral in (1) can be split up into a sum of several integrals, each covering a period short enough to make this approximation satisfactory. The resulting series of price indexes corresponds to a chain index composed of weighted geometric means of price changes.

Best linear indexes. A further development of the idea that an index does not compare only two points of time has been suggested by Theil (1960). He argues that in the calculation of an index the situation during all observed points of time should influence the result symmetrically.

In terms of the notation used above, Theil starts from an arithmetic mean index with fixed weights —that is,

$$P_{0t} = \sum_{i=1}^{n} w_i \frac{p_{it}}{p_{i0}}.$$

If $\alpha_i p_{i0} / \sum_{i=1}^{n} \alpha_i p_{i0}$ is substituted for w_i, this index may be written

$$P_{0t} = \frac{P_t}{P_0} = \frac{\sum_{i=1}^{n} \alpha_i p_{it}}{\sum_{i=1}^{n} \alpha_i p_{i0}}.$$

Here P_t and P_0 may be called absolute indexes to contrast with the relative index P_{0t}.

Using the absolute indexes, each individual price could be represented as

$$P_{it} = a_i P_t + v_{it},$$

where v_{it} is a disturbance or error term. If all prices moved proportionately, the v_{it} could be made zero. In general, however, this is not the case. But if the v_{it} cannot be made zero, the parameters a_i and α_i can be determined so that the v_{it} are minimized in some sense. If the parameters are determined in this way, the resulting index is called a best linear index.

If a quantity index is defined in a similar way, symmetric best linear price and quantity indexes with some interesting optimal properties can be derived. By a suitable choice of minimization procedure, the indexes could be made to minimize the sum of squares of "cross-value discrepancies," that is, they could be made to minimize

$$\sum_{r,s} (P_r Q_s - \sum_{i=1}^{n} p_{ir} q_{is})^2,$$

where r and s take on all observed values of t. This is a kind of generalization of the factor reversal test. The factor reversal test could be said to specify that

$$(P_0 Q_0 - \sum_{i=1}^{n} p_{i0} q_{i0})^2 + (P_1 Q_1 - \sum_{i=1}^{n} p_{i1} q_{i1})^2 = 0.$$

It has been found that the best linear index tends to be biased in the sense that the differences $(P_r Q_r - \sum_{i=1}^{n} p_{ir} q_{ir})$ are systematically positive. To construct a best linear unbiased index, Kloek and de Wit (1961) introduced the condition

$$\sum_{r} (P_r Q_r - \sum_{i=1}^{n} p_{ir} q_{ir}) = 0.$$

Fulfillment of this condition means that the factor reversal test is satisfied "on the average." As in the case of the best linear index, the weights are obtained by finding the largest latent root of a certain matrix.

The economic theory

The economic theory of index numbers is most often discussed in terms of a consumer price index. The object is to measure the changes in the cost of living of a person or of a group of persons who have identical tastes for goods. A utility, U (not necessarily a cardinal number), is associated with every combination of quantities of goods that is under consideration. The person is assumed to be well adapted to the prevailing price situation, so that given his income he chooses the set of quantities that gives him the highest level of utility. For each point of time t (defining a set of prices) there exists for each level of utility U an expenditure $\mu(t,U)$ which is the lowest possible expenditure to attain U.

The constant utility index. At the point of time t_0 the person's choice of quantities and his expenditure $\mu(t_0,U_0)$ are observed. The equivalent observations are made at t_1. If it can be stated that for the person observed $U_0 = U_1$, the price index for this level of utility is

$$P_{01}(U_0) = \frac{\mu(t_1,U_0)}{\mu(t_0,U_0)}.$$

This index, sometimes referred to as the "indifference defined index" or "the constant utility index," was first discussed by Konüs ([1924] 1939). It is to be noted that the price index is associated with a certain value of U—in this case U_0. For other values of U the price index may be different.

It is very seldom known whether U_0 is greater than, equal to, or less than U_1; that is, the value of $\mu(t_1,U_0)$ is generally not known. Thus, to estimate $\mu(t_1,U_0)$ it is necessary to make certain assumptions or approximations. Alternatively, it is possible to find an upper and/or a lower limit to the value of the constant utility index.

Upper and lower limits. It can be shown that a Laspeyres index gives an upper bound to P_{01}. The Laspeyres index shows the change in expenditure necessary to buy the same quantities of all goods at t_1 as those actually bought at t_0. However, this corresponding expenditure at t_1 may under the new price structure be disposed of differently so as to give a level of utility higher than U_0. The utility U_0 would then be attainable with a lower expenditure, and the indifference defined index for U_0 would be lower than the Laspeyres index.

In a similar way it is possible to show that a Paasche index gives a lower limit to a constant utility index for the utility level U_1. Thus,

$$P_{01}^L \geqslant P_{01}(U_0) \tag{3a}$$

and

$$P_{01}^P \leqslant P_{01}(U_1). \tag{3b}$$

However, since without further assumptions nothing is known about the relation between $P_{01}(U_0)$ and $P_{01}(U_1)$, these rules do not, contrary to what has sometimes been believed, give upper and lower limits for the same index.

Several attempts have been made to arrive at simultaneous upper and lower limits. Thus, Staehle (1935) tried to find a utility level U' such that the set of quantities corresponding to $\mu(t_1,U')$ would cost as much at t_0 prices as $\mu(t_0,U_0)$. Since clearly $U' \leqslant U_0$ (the budget was available at t_0 but was not chosen), $\mu(t_1,U') \leqslant \mu(t_1,U_0)$ and

$$\frac{\mu(t_1,U')}{\mu(t_0,U_0)} \leqslant \frac{\mu(t_1,U_0)}{\mu(t_0,U_0)} = P_{01}(U_0).$$

Thus, this index constitutes a lower limit to $P_{01}(U_0)$, and since P_{01}^L gives an upper limit, the desired result is obtained. There remains, however, the problem of determining $\mu(t_1,U')$. Under certain circumstances it can be determined from family budget data.

Ulmer (1949) took a quite different approach, which can be described as follows. Let D_u be the difference between $P_{01}(U_0)$ and $P_{01}(U_1)$. It could be positive or negative. The difference between the Laspeyres and Paasche indexes can then be written

$$\begin{aligned} P^L - P^P &= [P^L - P(U_0)] + [P(U_1) - P^P] + [P(U_0) - P(U_1)] \\ &= \quad D_L \quad + \quad D_P \quad + \quad D_u, \end{aligned}$$

where the subscript "01" on the P's has been dropped for convenience. Using this identity together with the inequalities (3a) and (3b), it can be shown that

$$P^L - D_L - D_P \leqslant P(U_0) \leqslant P^L$$

and that

$$P^P \leqslant P(U_1) \leqslant P^P + D_L + D_P.$$

Hence, both constant utility indexes are given upper and lower bounds.

Although $(D_L + D_P)$ is not directly observable, $(D_L + D_P + D_u) = (P^L - P^P)$ is, and Ulmer argued that it is usually reasonable to suppose that

$$\max_t (D_L + D_P) \leqslant \max_t (D_L + D_P + D_u)$$

and therefore that $\max_t (P^L - P^P)$ would be a conservative estimate of the difference between the upper and lower bounds on $P(U_0)$ or $P(U_1)$.

Point estimates. Several attempts have been made to arrive at a point estimate of a constant utility index by using family budget data. If such data were available for each period for which the index was to be calculated, criteria could be developed to find in each period a family or group of families with a given level of utility. By comparing their expenditures in different periods, an index could be calculated. These methods have not been used in practice.

An approximation to a constant utility index has been found by Theil (1965). Following Theil, it may be shown that

$$\frac{\partial \log \mu(t,U_0)}{\partial \log P_{it}} = c_i(t),$$

where $c_i(t)$ is, as before, the value share of commodity i in the total budget at time t. Using this relation and applying the Taylor expansion to $\log \mu(t,U_0)$ as a function of $\log p_{1t}$, $\log p_{2t}, \cdots,$ $\log p_{nt}$, we obtain (keeping terms up to the second degree) the relation

$$\log \mu(t,U_0) = \log \mu(t_0,U_0) + \frac{1}{2}\sum_{i=1}^{n} [c_i(t_0) + c_i(t)] \log \frac{p_{it}}{p_{i0}},$$

which gives, for example,

$$P_{01} = \frac{\mu(t_1, U_0)}{\mu(t_0, U_0)} = \prod_{i=1}^{n} \left(\frac{p_{i1}}{p_{i0}}\right)^{\frac{1}{2}[c_i(t_0) + c_i(t_1)]}$$

This is very similar to formula (2), which was obtained by purely statistical reasoning.

Thus, the economic and statistical lines of thought point to similar formulas. There is, however, still very little interaction between the two approaches.

ERIK RUIST

[*See also* AGGREGATION; UTILITY.]

BIBLIOGRAPHY

DIVISIA, FRANÇOIS 1925 L'indice monétaire et la théorie de la monnaie. *Revue d'économie politique* 39:842–861.

FISHER, IRVING (1922) 1927 *The Making of Index Numbers: A Study of Their Varieties, Tests, and Reliability.* 3d ed., rev. Boston: Houghton Mifflin.

FRISCH, RAGNAR 1936 Annual Survey of General Economic Theory: The Problem of Index Numbers. *Econometrica* 4:1–38.

INTERNATIONAL STATISTICAL INSTITUTE 1956 *Bibliographie sur les nombres indices; Bibliography on Index Numbers.* The Hague: Mouton.

KLOEK, T.; and DE WIT, G. M. 1961 Best Linear and Best Linear Unbiased Index Numbers. *Econometrica* 29:602–616.

KLOEK, T.; and THEIL, H. 1965 International Comparisons of Prices and Quantities Consumed. *Econometrica* 33:535–556.

KONÜS, A. A. (1924) 1939 The Problem of the True Index of the Cost of Living. *Econometrica* 7:10–29. → First published in Russian.

STAEHLE, H. 1935 A Development of the Economic Theory of Price Index Numbers. *Review of Economic Studies* 2:163–188.

THEIL, H. 1960 Best Linear Index Numbers of Prices and Quantities. *Econometrica* 28:464–480.

THEIL, H. 1965 The Information Approach to Demand Analysis. *Econometrica* 33:67–87.

TÖRNQVIST, LEO 1937 Finlands Banks konsumtionsprisindex. *Nordisk tidskrift for teknisk økonomi* 8:79–83.

ULMER, MELVILLE J. (1949) 1950 *The Economic Theory of Cost of Living Index Numbers.* New York: Columbia Univ. Press.

II
PRACTICAL APPLICATIONS

The search for a measure of the effect on the purchasing power of money of the influx of precious metals into Europe after the discovery of America resulted in the first index number of price changes, as far as we know today. In 1764 an Italian nobleman, Giovanni Rinaldo Carli, calculated the ratios of prices for three commodities—grain, wine, and oil—for dates close to 1500 and 1750. A simple average of these three ratios constituted his measure of the price change that had occurred over the 250-year period. This idea of isolating the effect of price changes in the measures of value changes in economic life has been a dominant and continuing theme in the development and use of index numbers.

Measures of changes in prices and changes in quantities have become a familiar and useful part of current economic life. In most countries of the world official agencies now issue regular reports on one or more of the following kinds of index numbers: wholesale prices, retail prices (often called cost-of-living), prices of goods in foreign trade, quantities of goods produced, and quantities of goods in foreign trade. These indexes are frequently supplemented with indexes for domestic trade and for specialized types of goods, such as agricultural commodities and raw materials.

In most cases these official indexes are designed as general-purpose indexes, and their availability leads to their use for many and varied purposes. "General-purpose" indexes are at variance with the first principle advocated by many serious students of the making of index numbers, stated by Wesley C. Mitchell as "defining the purpose for which the final results are to be used" ([1915] 1938, p. 23). Irving Fisher, who examined various methods of computing index numbers, disagreed with this principle and thought that ". . . from a practical standpoint, it is quite unnecessary to discuss the fanciful arguments for using 'one formula for one purpose and another for another,' in view of the great practical fact that all methods (if free of freakishness and bias) *agree!*" ([1922] 1927, p. 231). Melville Ulmer and others put forth the point of view, now generally accepted in principle by most economists, that the making of index numbers should be tied to economic concepts and that these concepts should be expressed in operational terms (Ulmer 1949, pp. 23–24). But despite the massive amount of discussion and the long history of index number practice, the empirical difficulties of closing the gap between theory and practice have not been overcome in many cases.

This article is concerned with some of the practical aspects of index number making—the general characteristics of indexes, the kinds of data employed, and the problems and difficulties encountered because we do not live in a static economy. It is intended as a nontechnical guide to those index number practices that an index user should review to help determine whether a specific index is the appropriate one for his purpose and is likely to be an adequate approximation for the use he intends (or more realistically, what limitations are likely to result from the use of the only index available). Although the discussion is oriented largely to price indexes, the major problems and procedures also apply to quantity indexes.

Index designations. Most of the indexes of prices labeled "wholesale" refer to the primary market level—the prices charged by manufacturers or producers to wholesalers and other buyers. In a few countries these indexes relate to the wholesale level of distribution.

Indexes of changes in retail prices are popularly referred to as cost-of-living indexes. However, the indexes in all countries are basically measures of price change (with minor variations), and official titles attempt to indicate this. In France the index is called the general retail price index; in the Federal Republic of Germany, the price index of living; in the United Kingdom, the index of retail prices. Although the name "cost-of-living index" is still retained by some countries, the most common name is "consumer price index." This name grew out of the controversy over the United States index during World War II, when it was an important factor in wage stabilization. "Consumer price index" was adopted to help clarify interpretation of what the index measured.

The names for other indexes may vary to a minor degree, but in general they are self-explanatory: e.g., index numbers of industrial production; index numbers of the volume of wholesale (or retail) trade; quantity and unit value of commodities in external trade.

Calculation formulas. In most countries, indexes of wholesale and retail prices are measures of price changes with "fixed" quantity weights as of some earlier period; that is, the calculation framework is that of a Laspeyres formula, (1) below, or some modification of it [*see* INDEX NUMBERS, *article on* THEORETICAL ASPECTS]. The use of this form for approximating changes in living costs is particularly controversial, although the practical difficulties of translating a "welfare" or "utility" concept into practice are generally recognized. The use of a consumer price index with fixed weights for the escalation of wages or for determining wage policy is an attempt to maintain the real purchasing power of the workers' dollar and might be interpreted as providing the income required to maintain the base-period utility level. However, the base-period utility level can be attained without keeping the kinds and quantities of goods fixed. When there are differential changes in prices among items, consumers are likely to buy a different collection of goods. If they increase their purchases of products whose relative prices have declined, escalation according to a fixed weight index will allow an increase in utility.

Whatever the limitations of a consumer price index on a conceptual basis, the present systems of index numbers do provide a measure of the average changes in prices for the quantities of the earlier year. The corresponding quantity indexes provide a measure of average changes in quantities at fixed prices, those of the base year. The relationships are

price ratio for the current period

$$= \frac{\text{current-period price} \times \text{base-period quantity}}{\text{base-period price} \times \text{base-period quantity}} = \frac{p_i \times q_0}{p_0 \times q_0}$$

and

quantity ratio for the current period

$$= \frac{\text{base-period price} \times \text{current-period quantity}}{\text{base-period price} \times \text{base-period quantity}} = \frac{p_0 \times q_i}{p_0 \times q_0}.$$

These simplified forms refer only to an individual commodity. When they are expressed for aggregations of commodities, the Greek capital sigma (Σ) is used to indicate the sums, and the formulas for the Laspeyres indexes become

Price index / Quantity index

$$(1) \qquad I_{pi} = \frac{\Sigma p_i q_0}{\Sigma p_0 q_0}, \qquad I_{qi} = \frac{\Sigma p_0 q_i}{\Sigma p_0 q_0}.$$

The denominator of both expressions is the total value in the base period of the aggregation of goods in the index. The numerator of the price index is the value of the base-period goods at current prices. The numerator of the quantity index is the value of current quantities at base-period prices.

The corresponding forms for Paasche indexes, which use current weights, are

Price index / Quantity index

$$(2) \qquad I_{pi} = \frac{\Sigma p_i q_i}{\Sigma p_0 q_i}, \qquad I_{qi} = \frac{\Sigma p_i q_i}{\Sigma p_i q_0}.$$

The numerator of these expressions is the total expenditure in the current period. Since it is unusual to have separate quantity data available to use in these formulas for every item in the index, an algebraic equivalent (which is in effect a weighted average of relatives, or price ratios) is generally employed, to permit the use of value data: e.g., the Laspeyres price index becomes

$$I_{pi} = \frac{\Sigma(p_i/p_0)(p_0 q_0)}{\Sigma(p_0 q_0)}.$$

Since it is also unusual for the values of consumption, production, or other variables to relate exactly to the period selected as a reference base for the index series, many indexes use the following form for a price index with fixed quantity weights:

$$I_{pi} = \frac{\sum(p_i/p_o)(p_a q_a)}{\sum(p_a q_a)},$$

where the subscript a refers to the date for which the values are available.

These formal calculation formulas are further modified in practice to accommodate changes in samples of items, sources of reports, incomplete data, and similar unpredictable problems of noncomparability. The usual procedure, called linking, is to calculate an index for each period, with the preceding period as a base, and multiply successive indexes together to obtain an index on a fixed base.

The reference-base period. Index numbers have two kinds of base dates: the date to which the consumption or production weights refer (date a in the preceding formula) and the date on which the price-change comparisons are based (date 0 in this formula). The former may be called the weight base, and the latter the reference base. It is customary to set the index equal to 100 at the reference-base date.

The initiation of index numbers and the deep interest in their fluctuations indicate that the needs for such economic measures were engendered by unusual periods of economic activity, such as inflations, depressions, and wars. This is probably the reason why there historically has been so much emphasis on the choice of a "normal" period for a reference base. Such a choice is extremely difficult because few, if any, periods can be said to be normal for all segments of the economy. The emphasis is perhaps justified to the extent that an index series is more meaningful when the weight base and the reference base are identical or not widely separated in time. In practice compromises must be made, and the two base dates seldom correspond exactly.

For the most part indexes are more reliable for short-period comparisons and, theoretically, more reliable for periods close to the weight base. But because of the extensive resources required to keep the weights continuously up to date and because in practice moderate weight changes have less influence on an index than have price changes, a common practice is to change the reference-base period more frequently than the weighting structure.

An index with a fixed reference base makes direct comparisons between the base selected and any one of the succeeding dates. Comparisons with any period other than the reference base require conversion to a new base. Such conversions, essentially, are made every time a percentage change is obtained, as shown in Table 1.

If the conversions are done correctly, percentage changes from one date to another will aways be the same for the original series and for the converted series (except for minor rounding differences, as shown in two instances in Table 1).

In about half the countries that maintain retail price indexes the practice has been to select a reference-base period reasonably close to the weight base and to change the reference base when the indexes are revised. This has the advantage of alerting the user to the fact that revisions have been made and of getting him to consider whether such revisions are so important that the indexes before and after the revision cannot be considered comparable. In Hungary the index is computed with the preceding year as base, and in the United Kingdom with January of each year as base. In the United States the present policy is to update the reference base about every ten years and to convert most economic index series to a uniform base to facilitate their use in economic analysis.

Uniform base periods for various economic series and for various components of the same index must be used with some discrimination, in order to present facts in proper perspective. Since there is seldom one period that can be considered "normal" for all segments of an economy, conversions of indexes to other periods for supplementary exposition is often required. For example, the change in

Table 1 — Example of the conversion of an index to a new reference base

	ORIGINAL BASE 1950 = 100		CONVERTED BASE 1955 = 100		CONVERTED BASE 1960 = 100	
Year	Index	Per cent change from preceding date	Index	Per cent change from preceding date	Index	Per cent change from preceding date
1950	100.0		90.9		87.0	
1955	110.0	10.0	100.0	10.1	95.7	10.0
1960	115.0	4.5	104.5	4.5	100.0	4.5
1965	120.0	4.3	109.1	4.4	104.3	4.3

the base period for United States indexes after World War II gave rise to complaints that the consumer price index gave a distorted picture. A postwar reference base (1947–1949 average) was substituted for a prewar base (1935–1939 average) at a time when the price rise for the commodity sector was leveling off but the rise for services, prices for which had remained fairly stable during the war, was beginning. The postwar base period thus highlighted a major price rise for medical care and other services throughout the 1950s. A fairer picture of the changes for commodities relative to services was afforded by comparisons with prewar prices. The rise from 1939 for services did not equal that for commodities until 1962.

Weights. The system of weights for price indexes relates to the level of distribution for which measures are desired.

For wholesale price indexes, censuses and similar surveys are utilized to derive the total value of sales, exclusive of taxes, for all commodities produced or processed by the private sector of the economy and sold in primary markets. In some cases both imports and exports are included. In some countries weights are limited to sales of goods for domestic consumption, thus including imports but not exports. Generally the principal exclusions from the "universe" covered by wholesale price indexes are business services, construction and real estate, sales by government, military production, securities, and goods produced and consumed within the same plant.

For consumer price indexes, weights representing the importance of individual goods and services are usually derived from special surveys of expenditures by the groups in the population for which price changes are measured, e.g., urban wage earners, farmers, low-income families, families of two or more, single consumers, etc. Generally the weights include all taxes directly associated with the purchase or ownership of specific goods and services, such as sales and excise taxes, property taxes, car registration fees, and the like. The principal exclusions are direct taxes, such as income taxes; expenditures for investments; contributions to churches and other organizations; and goods and services received without direct cash outlay, such as gifts received, home-produced foods, fringe benefits paid for by employers, and services supplied by government agencies without payment of a special tax or fee.

Indexes of industrial production generally use weights of the "census value-added" type; that is, the weights are usually proportional to value added at factor cost in different industries, as given by census data, and are derived by reducing values of gross output by costs of raw materials, fuels, containers, industrial services, etc. In a few countries weights represent gross value of production.

Price data. The sample of commodities and services priced regularly for the computation of price indexes is usually selected with considerable care, so that the items are well distributed among the major classification groups. The number of individual items priced varies considerably from country to country but in most cases is large enough to provide fairly reliable indexes, for groups and subgroups, of commodities and services.

Prices for the selected items in the wholesale price indexes are obtained from a sample of manufacturers or other producers and refer to the form in which the item enters commercial markets. Thus, as raw materials are processed into semifinished or finished goods, prices at each successive stage of processing may be included if the product is sold in primary markets in that form. Prices are usually reported for a precise specification, a specific class of buyer, and a specific level of distribution, quantity of purchase, and set of delivery terms. Prices are usually net of discounts, allowances, and excise taxes. Practices vary with regard to transportation costs; in the United Kingdom "delivered" prices are used for imported goods purchased by industry and "ex-works" prices for domestically produced goods; in the United States prices exclude delivery costs unless it is the normal custom to quote on a delivered basis.

Price data for consumer price indexes are usually obtained from a sample of stores and service establishments in a sample of communities that provides a good geographical coverage of the country. In a few cases the index is confined to one city or a few large cities. The prices quoted are generally cash prices for goods as offered for sale to the consumer. Usually all sales and other taxes applicable to the purchase of the specific item are added to the quoted price. In the United States and a few other countries, concessions and discounts are deducted.

The care with which data are gathered determines in large measure whether a price index for a particular period is good, bad, or indifferent. The essence of the collection process is to obtain "comparable" prices for successive periods, so that changes in the index refer to price changes only, not to a mixture of price, quality, and marketing changes. Comparability of outlets or producers is obtained by using a matched sample for each two successive time periods.

The description or specification of the individual

quality of the item for which data are requested plays a key role. The precision of the descriptions used by various countries differs in degree, but the principle of comparability is generally adhered to. For Ireland's consumer price index, for example, the requirement is that the item priced conform to a general commodity description and that it be in substantial demand in the area for which prices are being reported. Comparability is achieved by obtaining prices of the identical item in the same store for two successive periods. In most countries, however, detailed descriptions or specifications are developed to identify the quality of the item to be priced. These detailed descriptions define quality in terms of physical features, such as the kind and grade of materials, parts, construction and workmanship, size or capacity, strength, packaging, and similar factors or identification characteristics. The item is described as it enters into transactions in the market, and the assumption is made that the physical makeup determines performance characteristics.

The specifications adopted generally allow some latitude for minor variations in quality, in recognition of the many small differences from firm to firm or store to store. Within limits explicitly stated, all articles are considered comparable, and the price of the one specific item sold in largest volume each period is usually reported. Substitutions from time to time of items that fall outside the stated quality limits require special comparison procedures (as discussed for quality change below).

Major problems and limitations. There are many problems in the making of index numbers that materially affect the precision with which they can be applied. The unpredictable difficulties that occur as a regular part of the collection-and-comparison process were referred to briefly above. The major problems and limitations pervading most indexes are discussed in the following paragraphs.

Definition of "universe." One limitation that has relevance to the uses made of the indexes is the definition of the "universe" to which the indexes relate, that is, which segment of the population, which categories of business, etc. Retail or consumer price indexes for city families may be inappropriate for estimating the change in prices paid by farm families, not only because farm families may purchase their goods in different places but also because food and housing are a less important part of their expenditures than of the expenditures of city families. An index of wholesale prices of commodities, regardless of how good a measure it is, tells nothing about changes in other costs of doing business, such as wages and salaries, costs of printing, advertising, and other business services. Nor can it be assumed that wholesale prices in commercial markets are a good indicator of changes in prices paid by governments, because of special contract arrangements typical of government purchases. In such circumstances, when lack of an appropriate series forces the use of an index that is available, the user must evaluate its limitations for the specific purpose.

Sampling error. Sampling of some kind is a requirement for practically all indexes. Sampling, as opposed to complete coverage, introduces the familiar sampling error—a difficult factor to measure. In the absence of measures of sampling error, we can only judge precision intuitively, by knowing the composition of the sample. Although measurement of sampling error was being attempted in the United States for its consumer price index [*see* INDEX NUMBERS, *article on* SAMPLING], actual measures were still lacking. It is probable that understatements and overstatements of price change are quite small for the comprehensive "all-items" indexes in most countries but are larger at the group and subgroup levels.

Quality changes. The problems that occupy the greater part of the time and effort of those who compile indexes are the identification and measurement of the effect of quality changes in the items in the market, the introduction of new items and variations and disappearance of old, changes in the importance of various products and services from one time to another, changes in the types of establishments through which goods flow during the marketing process, and many of the other facets of change in an economy that is not standing still. The measurement instrument must seek to disentangle the changes in prices from the effects on price of all the other changes that take place.

The problems of eliminating the effect of quality changes are particularly difficult, and the extent to which adjustments are made for them varies considerably from country to country. Where they are taken into account, market price valuations for quality changes are generally obtained in one of three ways: (1) by assuming that the price difference is all due to quality change; (2) by estimating the value of the quality difference associated with changes in physical characteristics; or (3) by estimating the value of quality changes through operating characteristics.

When two varieties of an item are selling in volume simultaneously, the assumption that a difference in price between them is entirely due to a quality difference is realistic and reasonable. When two or more varieties do not sell simultaneously, it is uncertain whether a price difference results entirely from price change, entirely from quality change, or from a mixture of both. Thus, for automobiles and other highly complex products, the prices of new models are seldom compared directly with those of the old, since it is a common market practice to introduce price changes simultaneously with model changes. In these cases producers and sellers aid in identifying the changes made in the physical characteristics and provide production costs or estimated market prices, to permit the development of quality adjustment factors. In a few countries the adjustments for quality changes for some of the complex products are applied to one or more operating or use characteristics. For example, for turbines, in the Soviet Union the price or cost per unit of potential power is obtained. In Sweden the estimate of the relative worth of different automobile models is based on results of engineering, road, and other tests.

Considerable ingenuity and experimental work has been devoted to the quality problem in index numbers. But the very elusive nature of the quality concept, combined with the difficulties of detecting quality improvement and deterioration and of deriving objective values for these changes, means that considerable judgment and discrimination must be exercised. In some cases it is likely that the mechanics of the index make too large an adjustment for quality changes, and since most of the changes are labeled "improvement," some downward bias may be introduced. On the other hand, it is also probable that insufficient allowance has been made for quality improvement of other items. In any one monthly, quarterly, or annual interval, the total index will be made up largely of commodities and services that are unchanged in quality, and the effect of incomplete measurement for individual changes up and down is likely to be unimportant. For longer periods of time the influence may be greater, particularly for specific goods, where small quality changes cumulate from year to year and may not be detected. An evaluation of how much the factor of quality change may have influenced the movement of an index must be based on fairly detailed knowledge of both the timing and degree of quality change during the period under consideration and of the way in which they were accounted for in the index calculation.

New products. Closely related to the quality problem is the problem of timing the introduction of new products. Modifications or new varieties of older products are generally put into an index, when they have been in the market long enough to sell in substantial volume, by adjusting for quality change in the manner indicated above. But truly new products—those, such as television, that have no earlier counterpart—are generally introduced into an index only at major revisions, when new weights are available to reflect their impact throughout the weighting system. New products frequently enter the market in small volume at relatively high prices. As production and sales volume increase, price reductions are generally made. Some upward bias in an index can result if new items are introduced after major price reductions have occurred. However, the specific timing for introducing new items and the method of handling volume changes in the weights are still matters of some disagreement between index technicians.

Long-term comparisons and revision. Here the phrase "long-term comparisons" is used to mean comparisons over a period that encompasses a revision of an index. These present special problems. Theoretically, revisions in the conceptual structure, coverage, system of weights and/or operational aspects of index construction result in an index different from the previous one. If, however, an agency always presented a revised index as a new measure, individual users would have to provide some kind of a bridge from one index to the other to obtain a long-term perspective. Consequently, the issuing agencies usually "chain" the different indexes together to form a seemingly continuous series. This practice is common in most countries and provides many advantages. But users must also recognize, through a study of the changes in the makeup of the two or more separate indexes that have been chained together, the limitations involved in such comparisons.

The retail price index of the United Kingdom and the consumer price index of Sweden are examples of indexes with annual changes in weights. Technically speaking, the index for each year is different from the index for the preceding year because the weights represent a different level of living. Studies of the effect of changes in weights on the index indicate that year-to-year comparisons are so nearly the same with the old and the new weights that for all practical purposes the effect of the weight differences can be ignored for comparisons over two or three years. Over a period of five or ten years the differences may be more significant, since the continuous series includes the net effects of changes in the distribution of living expenditures over the longer period. In the United Kingdom it is felt that short-term comparisons are the most important to index users. In the United States, the importance of short-term comparisons is recognized but it is felt that the available resources should be devoted to maintaining the adequacy of current price data. The net effects of changes in living habits in the United States over approximately ten years are introduced at one time, during a major revision, rather than in smaller increments. Hence, the problems to be considered by users over periods of more than ten years are the same in both countries.

A more serious question would be raised if the conceptual structure of an index were changed. If a consumer price index were revised to measure the constant level of utility defined in economic theory or if weights at wholesale were changed from total value of shipments at each stage of processing to "value added" weights, such changes would have major influences on the index, and "long-term" comparisons would be practically meaningless.

A practical guide to users on the effect of changes made during revisions is usually provided by issuing agencies, in the form of concurrent indexes on both the old and new basis, either through continuation of the old after the new has been issued or (less frequently) through the recalculation retroactively of the preceding index.

ETHEL D. HOOVER

BIBLIOGRAPHY

CARLI, GIOVANNI (1760) 1785 Del valore e della proporzione de' metalli monetati con i generi in Italia prima delle scoperte dell' Indie, col confronto del valore e della proporzione de' tempi nostri. Volume 7, pages 1–190 in Giovanni Carli, *Delle opere*. Milan: Nell' Imperial Monistero di S. Ambrogio Maggiore.

Definitions and Explanatory Notes. 1964 United Nations, Statistical Office, *Monthly Bulletin of Statistics* [1963], no. 5 (Supplement). → This supplement is a good general reference for descriptions of the statistical series for the various countries of the world in the *Monthly Labor Bulletin*. The descriptions are necessarily brief but include the main features, as well as a reference to the various national publications, where greater detail may be found.

FISHER, IRVING (1922) 1927 *The Making of Index Numbers: A Study of Their Varieties, Tests, and Reliability*. 3d ed., rev. Boston: Houghton Mifflin.

GILBERT, MILTON 1961*a* Quality Changes and Index Numbers. *Economic Development and Cultural Change* 9:287–294.

GILBERT, MILTON 1961*b* The Problem of Quality Changes and Index Numbers. U.S. Bureau of Labor Statistics, *Monthly Labor Review* 84:992–997.

GILBERT, MILTON 1962 Quality Change and Index Numbers: The Reply. U.S. Bureau of Labor Statistics, *Monthly Labor Review* 85:544–545.

GRILICHES, ZVI 1962 Quality Change and Index Numbers: A Critique. U.S. Bureau of Labor Statistics, *Monthly Labor Review* 85:542–544.

HOFSTEN, ERLAND VON 1952 *Price Indexes and Quality Changes*. Stockholm: Forum.

HOOVER, ETHEL D. 1961 The CPI and Problems of Quality Change. U.S. Bureau of Labor Statistics, *Monthly Labor Review* 84:1175–1185.

INTERNATIONAL LABOR OFFICE 1962 *Computation of Consumer Price Indices: Special Problems*. Report No. 4. Geneva: The Office.

MITCHELL, WESLEY C. (1915) 1938 *The Making and Using of Index Numbers*. 3d ed. U.S. Bureau of Labor Statistics, Bulletin No. 656. Washington: Government Printing Office. → The preface contains a discussion of the 1915 and 1921 editions.

MUDGET, BRUCE D. 1951 *Index Numbers*. New York: Wiley.

ORGANIZATION FOR EUROPEAN ECONOMIC CO-OPERATION 1956 *Quantity and Price Indexes in National Accounts*, by Richard Stone. Paris: The Organization.

ULMER, MELVILLE J. 1949 *The Economic Theory of Cost of Living Index Numbers*. New York: Columbia Univ. Press.

UNITED NATIONS, ECONOMIC AND SOCIAL COUNCIL 1965 The Gathering and Compilation of Statistics of Prices. E/CN.3/328. Mimeographed.

U.S. BUREAU OF THE CENSUS 1960 *Historical Statistics of the United States, Colonial Times to 1957: A Statistical Abstract Supplement*. Washington: Government Printing Office.

U.S. BUREAU OF THE CENSUS 1965 *Historical Statistics of the United States, Colonial Times to 1957: Continuation to 1962 and Revisions*. Washington: Government Printing Office.

U.S. BUREAU OF LABOR STATISTICS 1964 *Computation of Cost-of-living Indexes in Developing Countries*. Bureau of Labor Statistics, Report No. 283. Washington: The Bureau.

U.S. CONGRESS, JOINT ECONOMIC COMMITTEE 1961 *Government Price Statistics*. 2 parts. Hearings before the Sub-committee on Economic Statistics. Washington: Government Printing Office. → Part 1 contains the report prepared by the Price Statistics Review Committee of the National Bureau of Economic Research, *The Price Statistics of the Federal Government: Review, Appraisal, and Recommendations*. Part 2 contains the comments of witnesses before the Joint Economic Committee on the contents of the report.

III
SAMPLING

No matter how one resolves the conceptual and practical problems described in the two accompanying articles, the actual construction of an index number will almost always be based on sampling. The quality of an index will, therefore, depend upon the nature of the sampling process. Although this dependence has long been recognized (see King 1930, for discussion and references to earlier work), the sampling aspects of index number construction have been relatively neglected.

This article emphasizes the following points: (1) most economic index numbers have a complex sampling structure; (2) the sampling precision of an index number can be defined, even though conceptual and practical problems are not fully solved; (3) estimates of sampling error are required both for the analytic use of index numbers and for reasonable allocation of resources in designing the data-gathering procedure on which the index number is based; and (4) most components of sampling error can be estimated only by use of replication.

In order to make the discussion specific, it is framed in terms of Laspeyres indexes of consumer prices, with special reference to the consumer price index of the United States Bureau of Labor Statistics. Nearly all the discussion, however, is readily applicable to other kinds of index numbers.

Sampling aspects of a price index. The various points at which sampling must be employed in order to provide data for constructing a consumer price index are easily identifiable.

A Laspeyres price index for an individual consumer can be viewed as a weighted average of price ratios for the commodities and services purchased by the individual, where the weights are proportions of total expenditures in the base period for the different items of the index. The weights may be called *base year value weights.* An index for a *group* of consumers, for example, those living in a particular city or geographic area, then involves the following major sampling problems: (1) average base year value weights must be estimated from a sample of consumers; (2) since it is impossible to price all of the goods and services purchased by all of the consuming units in the population, this list of goods and services must be sampled; and (3) an average price for any good or service, in either the base year or at a current point in time, must be estimated from a sample of outlets.

The foregoing sampling problems relate to the production of an index for a particular city or geographic region. If one wishes to construct an index that relates to a country, then it becomes necessary to select a sample of cities or regions and combine their individual results into an over-all index. Finally, prices must be collected at repeated points in time, and thus temporal sampling is involved.

Some general views on sampling

Although price indexes are based on highly complex sampling structures, measures of sampling precision are not available for any of the currently prepared indexes, although I understand that the Bureau of Labor Statistics is planning to provide such information about the consumer price index starting in early 1967 (see Wilkerson 1964). Three related arguments have been set forth to justify the absence of such reporting.

The Laspeyres index follows the prices of a sample of goods and services through time. Because the universe of goods and services available to the consumer is continually changing (some items change in quality, others disappear, and new items enter the universe), it is necessary to make a variety of adjustments in the sample items and in observed prices. Since there exists no "best" procedure for making these adjustments, the index is subject to a *procedural* error. It is then argued that the sampling error is probably small in relation to the procedural error and that it is therefore neither necessary nor desirable to attempt to estimate its magnitude.

Because of the complexity of the adjustment procedures, it is frequently stated that it is impossible to define and estimate that portion of the sampling variability of an index that arises from the sampling of commodities. Hence it is impossible to define or estimate the sampling precision of the index itself.

A third argument admits that it might be possible to employ probability sampling for all components of a price index. But the great complexity of the design and data-gathering operations are then stressed and the conclusion is reached that the attainment of this goal would require the use of more or less unlimited resources. These views have been expressed by Hofsten (1952, p. 42; 1959, p. 403) and Jaffe (1961), among others; and direct quotations from these articles are provided by McCarthy (1961, pp. 205–209).

Definition of sampling precision. The argument that it is impossible to discuss sampling precision because of the changing nature of the universe of commodities is clearly basic to a consideration of the other two arguments. Adelman (1958) seems to accept this view and, as a consequence, sets forth a method of index number construction that is more directly in line with modern sampling theory as described by Hansen, Hurwitz, and Madow (1953). She suggests periodic stratified resamplings of the changing commodity universe, together with the use of a chain index in place of the Laspeyres index. The meaningfulness of the Adelman approach to index number construction will not be argued here. Rather, it will be argued that it is quite reasonable to talk about the sampling precision of a Laspeyres index, provided (1) that a very general view of sampling precision, similar to that described by Stephan and McCarthy (1958, pp. 226–229), is adopted and (2) that one does not always expect to measure this precision by the application of standard formulas from the theory of sampling.

Replication to estimate sampling error. Assume the existence of a set of adjustment procedures that are used to follow a sample of goods and services through time, so that sampling variability arises only from the fact that a sample of items is selected at time zero. If one now thinks of drawing an indefinitely large number of independent samples in accordance with the same sampling procedure and of independently following each of these through to time t in accordance with the defined adjustment procedures, the resulting values of the index will define the sampling distribution of the index with respect to the sampling of items. The variance of this distribution is an acceptable measure of sampling precision for the index, and it includes a component for any inherent variability of the adjustment procedure. Furthermore, an estimate of this variance can easily be obtained by actually drawing two or more independent samples of items and independently following them through time, that is, through the use of replicated samples. It should be observed that the use of two independent samples, for example, does not mean that each sample must be as large as the desired over-all sample of commodities. Each sample may be only half as large as the over-all sample, and the published index would be the average of the two resulting indexes. Of course the reliability of the estimate of variance would improve as the number of independent samples increases. It should also be noted that in practice the independence of the samples would be difficult to preserve as time goes on.

Bias. The measure of sampling precision just defined is obviously taken about the mean of the sampling distribution of the index. If the population value of this index at time t is denoted by $R_P^{(t)}$, where $R_P^{(t)}$ would be obtained by applying the adjustment procedures to *all* commodities, then the difference between the expected value of the index and $R_P^{(t)}$ is the bias of the estimate arising from the sampling and estimation procedures. If the selection were based on expert judgment, then such bias might arise because all the experts might, consciously or unconsciously, not consider for selection items having a different form of price behavior from those items considered for selection. [*See* SAMPLE SURVEYS, *article on* NONPROBABILITY SAMPLING.]

Imperfection of adjustment procedures. In addition, one usually questions the adjustment procedures and therefore views $R_P^{(t)}$ as only an approximation to the index that would be obtained through the use of a "perfect" adjustment procedure.

Three components of total error. As a result of the foregoing, the total error in a single estimate can be viewed as the sum of three components. The first component represents the error of variability that arises from the use of sampling (plus possible contributions from variability in applying adjustment procedures); the second component represents the bias arising from the sampling and estimation procedures; and the third component represents the bias that arises through inherent imperfection in the adjustment procedures. Other errors may of course arise from interviewing, in clerical work, or from computations; but these will not be treated in this article. [*See* ERRORS, *article on* NONSAMPLING ERRORS.]

It would appear that at least some of the differences in opinion on sampling for index numbers can be traced to a failure to distinguish carefully among these three components of error, particularly between the first and third components. All writers agree that it is unlikely that anyone will ever be able to devise a "perfect" set of rules for treating quality changes and for introducing new items into the index, but this does not mean that it is impossible or unnecessary to estimate the values of all three components.

Importance of sampling error. Next consider the argument that this precision is dominated by the procedural error and can therefore be ignored. Some investigations reported by McCarthy (1961) suggest that the procedural error of current consumer price indexes may indeed dominate the sampling error, although empirical investigations of the over-all effect of procedural error are almost as lacking as those of sampling error. This does not necessarily mean that sampling error can be ignored. It remains important for several reasons, in particular:

(1) If the goal is to estimate the *level* of the "true" index at various points in time and if resources are fixed, then the most efficient way of improving the accuracy of these estimates would be to divert resources from the maintenance of a relatively large sample of commodities and to use these resources in basic research aimed at reducing the magnitude of the procedural error. It is clear that good estimates of sampling precision and of bounds on the procedural error are required in order to make judgments of this kind.

(2) If the goal is to estimate short-term *changes* in the level of the "true" index, then it appears likely that sampling error will be more important than procedural error and hence an estimate of sampling error becomes essential.

(3) The construction of a price index involves not only a set of adjustment procedures and the sampling of commodities but also the sampling of localities and the sampling of price reporters within these localities. There must be a balance between these errors and the sampling errors arising from the other parts of the design. Again it is im-

possible to discuss such a balancing operation unless some attempt is made to measure these components of error.

Reporting estimates of error. Estimates of error for the various components of a price index should also be available in published form to assist those who wish to use the indexes in a critical fashion. When one considers that small monthly changes in important indexes may lead to major policy decisions, and that these indexes are basic tools in much economic analysis, the necessity for having measures of error becomes apparent. Kruskal and Telser (1960) have emphasized the latter point.

Probability sampling for index numbers

In order to guard against nonmeasurable biases from sampling and estimation, it seems reasonable that some appropriate form of probability sampling should be utilized in the selection of each sample that enters an index design. The selection of a sample of consumers, from which to estimate the base year expenditure weights, and the selection of a sample of cities or regions, from which to obtain current price data, should cause no more difficulty than is encountered in the ordinary large-scale sample survey. The sampling of goods and services does, however, pose an especially difficult problem. Nevertheless, the following are some of the convincing reasons for attempting to use probability sampling methods in the original selection of items: (1) The replicated sample approach can provide an estimate of sampling precision for almost any type of sampling procedure, but it cannot even indicate the existence of bias. The only way to ensure that biases due to sampling and estimation are small or nonexistent is to use appropriate probability sampling methods. (2) A probability model will make clear the manner in which one can obtain two or more independent samples of goods and services. (3) Even the mere attempt to make the sampling of goods and services conform to some appropriate probability model will force one to make definite decisions about problems of definition and estimation that exist no matter how such a sample is chosen but that can too easily be ignored with judgment procedures.

Probability sampling of goods and services. Although probability sampling of goods and services has not been the practice in the past, the general format that possible procedures would probably follow can be indicated. Items of expenditure would be divided into major groups, then into subgroups, sub-subgroups, and so on. Ultimately this subdivision process leads to what may be termed specific items, for example, one item might be mattresses for single beds. These specific items could be grouped into strata, using any available information about substitutability, similarity of price movements, and other related variables. The first sampling operation would then consist of selecting one or more specific items out of each stratum.

Drawing a specific item into the sample usually draws an entire cluster of specified-in-detail items into the sample. One or more specified-in-detail items must be chosen from the cluster defined by each of the selected specific items, and this is the second sampling operation to be considered. For example, with the single-bed mattress item, one might specify number of coils; gauge of wire; type of cover; padding material; and so on. The chosen specified-in-detail items are the ones on which price quotations are to be obtained. At this second level of sampling, the problems become much more difficult than at the first level. Complete lists of specified-in-detail items will be difficult, if not impossible, to obtain; some specified-in-detail items may not be purchased by the consumer group to which the index is supposed to refer; and expenditure weights may not be available for many of the items. Possibly anything that one can do at this level (for example, using a restricted list of specified-in-detail items instead of a complete list or assuming equal base year expenditure weights when actual weights are unequal) is going to be only an approximation to what one would like to do; but at least this type of approach can be described accurately, and it should be possible to investigate the effects of some of the approximations that are used. The U.S. Bureau of Labor Statistics has experimented with this approach in connection with a recently completed revision of the U.S. consumer price index, and their experiences will be available as a guide to others in the future. Banerjee (1960) has written on this aspect of the sampling problem.

Probability sampling of outlets. It might also be observed that the probability sampling of outlets, from which to obtain current price reports, is a much more troublesome problem than might appear at first sight. Lists of outlets are difficult to obtain; many different commodities will ordinarily be priced in the same store and this introduces correlation among the price quotations; in addition, the maintenance of a panel of price reporters is complicated by the birth and death of firms.

The production of an index number obviously involves a highly complex network of samples. Even though probability sampling could be used for all components, it would be extremely difficult, or even impossible, to apply on a routine basis ordinary variance estimating procedures.

The difficulties involved in the determination of sampling variability for estimates derived from complex sample surveys are not unique to index number problems. The necessity for obtaining "simple" procedures for the routine estimation of sampling error has long been recognized and has been discussed by many authors under such titles as "interpenetrating samples," "replicated samples," "ultimate clusters," and "random groups" (Deming 1960; Hansen, Hurwitz, & Madow 1953, vol. 1, p. 440; Mahalanobis 1946; Stephan & McCarthy 1958, pp. 226–229). This matter was discussed briefly here in connection with the sampling of goods and services, but a more detailed treatment of the application of the principles of replication to sampling for index numbers has been given by McCarthy (1961).

PHILIP J. MCCARTHY

[*See also* SAMPLE SURVEYS.]

BIBLIOGRAPHY

ADELMAN, IRMA 1958 A New Approach to the Construction of Index Numbers. *Review of Economics and Statistics* 40:240–249.

BANERJEE, K. S. 1960 Calculation of Sampling Errors for Index Numbers. *Sankhyā* 22:119–130.

DEMING, W. EDWARDS 1960 *Sample Design in Business Research.* New York: Wiley.

HANSEN, MORRIS H.; HURWITZ, WILLIAM N.; and MADOW, WILLIAM G. (1953) 1956 *Sample Survey Methods and Theory.* Vol. 1. New York: Wiley.

HOFSTEN, ERLAND VON 1952 *Price Indexes and Quality Changes.* Stockholm: Bokförlaget Forum.

HOFSTEN, ERLAND VON 1959 Price Indexes and Sampling. *Sankhyā* 21:401–403.

JAFFE, SIDNEY A. 1961 The Consumer Price Index: Technical Questions and Practical Answers. Part 2, pages 603–611 in U.S. Congress, Joint Economic Committee, *Hearings: Government Price Statistics.* 87th Congress, 1st Session. Washington: Government Printing Office.

KING, WILLFORD I. 1930 *Index Numbers Elucidated.* New York: Longmans.

KRUSKAL, WILLIAM H.; and TELSER, LESTER G. 1960 Food Prices and the Bureau of Labor Statistics. *Journal of Business* 33:258–279.

MCCARTHY, PHILIP J. 1961 Sampling Considerations in the Construction of Price Indexes With Particular Reference to the United States Consumer Price Index. Part 1, pages 197–232 in U.S. Congress, Joint Economic Committee, *Hearings: Government Price Statistics.* 87th Congress, 1st Session. Washington: Government Printing Office.

MAHALANOBIS, P. C. 1946 Recent Experiments in Statistical Sampling in the Indian Statistical Institute. *Journal of the Royal Statistical Society* Series A 109: 326–378. → Contains eight pages of discussion.

STEPHAN, FREDERICK F.; and MCCARTHY, PHILIP J. (1958) 1963 *Sampling Opinions: An Analysis of Survey Procedure.* New York: Wiley.

WILKERSON, MARVIN 1964 Measurement of Sampling Error in the Consumer Price Index: First Results. American Statistical Association, Business and Economics Section, *Proceedings* [1964]:220–233.

INDIAN POLITICAL THOUGHT

Ancient thought

In the epoch that began with the philosophical movements which are expressed in the mystical texts known as Upaniṣads and culminated in the regime of the emperor Aśoka, whose rule extended over all but southernmost India, the dimensions of Indian social thought were established. During these formative centuries, roughly from the seventh to the middle of the third century B.C., new modes of economic production, the incorporation of indigenous peoples into the Aryan community, and other social changes rendered the old agencies of integration inadequate; with many of the certainties of life dissolving and new social relationships demanding new justifications, men were faced with the need to re-examine basic values and institutions. A variety of ideas about the nature and destiny of human life began to challenge traditional religious conceptions.

Cosmology. Discussion of a system of political beliefs and speculations requires a general understanding of the symbolic forms in terms of which reality is comprehended by a people. Men reveal reality to themselves through particular ways of seeing, which discriminate objects and events from the whole in which they are embedded. Observation is purposive behavior, and in the first stages of the development of human knowledge acts of discrimination and the assignment of meaning are closely bound together. Later, as thought becomes theoretical, the contents of experience are grouped and correlated, and in time strict definition becomes possible, as facts are subsumed under general ideas and conceptually grasped. When the subject of our investigation is the political thought of the last several centuries in Europe or America, the cosmology at the base of such ideas may be taken for granted. But the study of ancient civilizations cannot properly proceed without a consideration of symbolic and mythic materials, although such materials may be only indirectly related to political theory and although we may have to content ourselves with what is at best informed conjecture.

In this attempt to discover the different ways in which the world is viewed we discover that, except for the Greeks in the classical age, existence is rarely comprehended in terms of a rational order which lends itself to intellectualistic investigation. More frequently the imagery is dramatic: the world derives its meaning from its creator rather than from the logic of its structure, and knowledge takes the form of mystic apprehension (*gnosis*) instead of rational inquiry. Insight into the meaning of a world not yet completed depends on revelation and supernatural capacities: the emphasis is on encounter instead of examination. In one version of this latter world view the god–creator involves himself in the universe, assuming a variety of forms and disguises. Man's response to this sacred power may take the form of supplication or ritual, in which instance professionals are usually required to act as intermediaries between man and the holy. But sometimes the godhead is not seen as a deity possessing will and design, and the individual worshiper may seek through discipline and contemplation to merge himself in the cosmic process.

Ancient Indian political thought must be understood in the context of religious beliefs. In the earliest cosmology the political order was seen as analogous to the cosmos, its creation a repetition of the divine creation of the cosmic system. Vedic liturgy was essentially an effort to reproduce the cosmic order so as to ensure the effective functioning of society. By the later Vedic period the anthropomorphic gods of the heroic age had been eclipsed by more imposing and aloof deities, and the rituals had become a highly formalized religion with a complex ceremonialism. As religion came to be tied to technical expertise, the priests strengthened their position, isolating themselves from social controls. By the end of this period the Aryan invaders had extended their hegemony over the whole of the Gangetic plain.

The early texts. The most authoritative statement of the orthodox tradition exists in the venerable Ṛg Veda, which provides the earliest historical record of the Indo-Aryan peoples who invaded northwest India in the middle centuries of the second millennium B.C. The Vedic hymns themselves can be dated from at least the eleventh or twelfth century. When the interpretation of the Vedas required explanatory texts, a set of ritual manuals, the Brāhmaṇas, were appended to the hymns. The later Vedas, Brāhmaṇas, and the early Upaniṣads belong to the centuries 900–600 B.C. It is probable that the original versions of the epics Mahābhārata and Rāmāyaṇa were in existence shortly after the end of this period. The sources of heterodox doctrine are found in the pronouncements of great teachers who lived at this time. (It was not until the fourth century that the Pāli Buddhist canon was compiled.) Although the Ṛg Veda, the Brāhmaṇas, and other early texts contain much material relevant to the study of political thought, literature expressly devoted to legal and political questions is encountered only with the Dharma Sūtras (500–200 B.C.). The Arthaśāstra literature, which deals with the art of government and what is described as "the science of material gain," may date back to the sixth century, but the oldest treatise that remains is the work ascribed to Kauṭilya, which is usually believed to date from the early years of the Mauryan state (c. 300 B.C.), but which may be as late as the third or fourth century A.D. During the several centuries before and after the beginning of the Christian era, the Mahābhārata attained the form in which we have the work, and the major Dharma Śāstra treatise, the code of Manu, was compiled. The Dharma Śāstra and Arthaśāstra literature extends well into the medieval period of Indian history; some texts, however, are as recent as the ninth and tenth centuries A.D. It will be apparent to the reader by now that only the broadest chronological arrangement of these writings is possible. By the eighth century the Arabs had dominated the lower Indus valley; however, long before the Muslim conquests the creative period of Sanskrit theory was over. Not until the nationalist and reform movements of the nineteenth century was there a significant revival of Indian political speculation.

There is little evidence that Vedic kingship was considered a divine institution; few priestly functions were performed by the king. Sometimes the ruler is compared with certain of the gods—or it may be said that he has superhuman attributes, or that during the sacrifice he takes on aspects of divinity. There is no evidence that the early monarchy was elective in any modern sense of the word (although the texts often suggest that the king was chosen by the people), but there are indications that the ruler was dependent on the support of at least the aristocracy, and we may assume that "election" must be understood as approval or appointment. The authority of the assembly and the role of the people in the coronation ceremony point to a degree of popular participation that was never equaled in later times.

Brahmanism. When the tribal organization based on kinship relations was no longer adequate to meet the strains on social cohesion, the ruling nobility grew increasingly dependent on the *brāhmaṇ* priests to provide new principles of legitimation which could justify political authority. By the later Vedic age the priests had come to control the sacrifice and through the sacrifice the means of salvation. At this time the ideas of *karma* and transmigration began to assume a central importance. Every soul, according to this belief, has existed from eternity and journeys through a series of rebirths until it has earned eternal bliss. Each thought and action has consequences for the destiny of the soul and determines one's position and status in society. In the light of these doctrines it would be extremely difficult to reconcile religious interest with social reform. As Max Weber remarked, the sanction for traditionalism was as complete as any contrived by the mind of man. With the *brāhmaṇ* priest at the apex of the class structure and *karma* ideology as its foundation, we are confronted with a society so effectively integrated by religion that political institutions need play only a minor role in regulating conflict. And, indeed, throughout most of Indian history social coordination was accomplished through caste and village institutions.

The vitality and naive optimism of the Vedic age had succumbed to a more restrained philosophical and religious perspective. The Brāhmaṇic deities had become manifestations of an impersonal cosmic principle. Prajāpati, lord of creation, was exalted above the other gods: but he had himself become the harmonizing sacrifice. The figure of Prajāpati provides a link between earlier Indian religion and the varieties of mysticism that served to shift religious emphasis from ritualism to individual spiritual insight.

In the political speculation of this time, most of which is found in *brāhmaṇ* texts, we are not surprised to find that the authority of the *brāhmaṇs* is considered superior to that of the king and that the priests are independent of the secular power. Mitra, the old Vedic god who was taken to represent the priesthood, at one time stood apart from Varuṇa, who in this instance epitomized power. That is, mind was conceived to be independent of will. But just as will relies on intelligence, *regnum* (*kṣatra*) could not exist without *sacerdotium* (Brahmā). There are passages in the texts that qualify this characterization, but they are rare.

The first suggestion of an attempt to explain the origins of government occurs in the Aitareya Brāhmaṇa (I, 14). The gods, at first disunited, came to realize that victory over the titans could be theirs only if they yielded to Indra, the great warrior, and granted him their collective powers. The account of the royal coronation in this work (VIII, 15) contains a theory of kingship that is at least a primitive version of the European political philosophies which locate the basis of authority in a contract. For a closer approximation to the idea of the state's contractual basis we must turn to the later Buddhist legends. The functions of the royal authority were secularized to a degree uncommon in the ancient world, and the spheres of politics and religion were differentiated (as the *kṣatra*–Brahmā distinction indicates); yet there remained a religious dimension to kingship and an aura to the person of the king that impeded the development of a concept of contract between the king and his people. [*See* SOCIAL CONTRACT.]

The texts of this period argue that the primary obligation of the king is the preservation of *dharma*. This term, which defies any exact rendition, is used to describe the totality of rules and duties, the eternal and necessary moral law, truth, and justice. It is a category of theology, ethics, and law: The central importance of this concept in Indian political philosophy expands the boundaries of speculation to include aspects of human experience not generally associated with politics in Western thought on the subject. In this conception law is ultimately god-given. *Dharma* stood above the king, and the king's failure to preserve the sacred tradition must have disastrous consequences. It was the function of the power of sanction and coercion (*daṇḍa*) to ensure compliance with *dharma*, and the *rājadharma*, the *dharma* of the king, thus existed as guarantor of the whole social order with its hierarchy of privileges and duties. Behind this doctrine lies the belief that it is only the fear of punishment that makes men righteous in their conduct.

In the Dharma Sūtras, which are condensed technical prose works consisting of rules governing the broad area of human conduct, the individual is still not sharply distinguished from the group. Local custom and law are recognized as authorities in this age of transition from the tribal community to the territorial state. With the systematization of usage and tradition in the Sūtras, the legitimacy of royal power—formerly dependent on priestly proclamation—came to be based on the law codes. But this in itself did not mean that the king was becoming more independent of *brāhmaṇ* controls. Actually the powers of the king were more rigidly defined. Heretical religious beliefs were beginning to appear at this time, however, and since there was the possibility that competing ethical and religious movements would be successful in eliciting the support of the king, the prestige and power of the ruler continued to expand, and the position of the *brāhmaṇs* became increasingly vulnerable.

This was a turbulent period in Indian history, and the capacity to respond effectively to environmental challenge must have dictated an adaptability in the ideological superstructure of the nascent state—an allowance, so to speak, for the necessity of sin. Symbols of foundation were continually invoked. The concept of foundation implies the possibility of the "artificial" establishment of social aggregates. The heroic role thus came to be institutionalized: it was the assertive, transmoral role charged with the upholding of honor and the protection (by violence if need be) of the order of things. And it was kept within bounds by its subservience to the higher spiritual power. The harmony of the two complementary powers—the temporal, or *kṣatra*, and the spiritual, or Brahmā, ensured the harmony of the world. The former (whether represented by Romulus or Varuṇa) is that mysterious potency which is always in an equivocal relationship to society. In guarding the established order against hostile forces it may be necessary to take on characteristics not unlike those of the enemy. Authority is transformed into naked power. In India the amoral dimension of *kṣatra* found its fullest expression in the figure of the god Indra, who represented the warrior virtues, power as well as authority. Indra had the right to go above the sacred code when necessary for its protection. But purification and compensation were always required. This is one reason for the importance of the sacrifice in Aryan ideology.

The most characteristic feature of the sacred is its dangerous and proscriptive property. Intermediaries are needed to make possible communication between the realms of the sacred and the profane, since the forces unleashed in the contact between the two spheres are so powerful they might otherwise destroy each other. The *brāhmaṇ* priest acted as this intermediary in the conduct of the sacrifice. It must have been only a matter of time before the power to manipulate the gods began to seem superior to the gods themselves. This *brāhmaṇ* potency, projected into the pantheon, ultimately returned in the conception of Prajāpati (or Brahman). Some students of Indian philosophy insist that the monistic principle usually associated with the Upaniṣads had long been dominant in Brahmanism.

Political and legal treatises. Although in the Vedas an embryonic caste form is portrayed (the Puruṣa hymn names the four orders but does not directly indicate that status distinctions are intended; see Ṛg Veda x, 90, 11 ff.), by the end of the Vedic period the institution had become stereotyped, and it was fairly prevalent by the time of the Buddha. The *brāhmaṇ* was the referent whereby rank position was determined, and distinctions had come to be based on relative ritual purity. The two highest castes (*brāhmaṇ* priests and *kṣatriya* nobility) monopolized duties that required ritual purity. The *brāhmaṇs* possessed the right to study the scriptures, perform the sacrifice, pursue the ascetic life, and "receive gifts." By the later Vedic period they and the *kṣatriyas* had become virtually endogamous. The *kṣatriya* ideal that dominated the centuries of the Gangetic expansion—personal honor and military valor—was tamed with the establishment of the territorial state. Protection and regulation became the major responsibilities of the governing elite. The demand for specialists in the techniques of coordination and adaptation grew, and the influence of the minister began to challenge the traditional status of the knight. The needs of the settled community were bringing the *brāhmaṇ* more directly into political activity; he was often the person best qualified for the deliberative, advisory, and supervisory roles of the emergent state. But at the same time the governing nobility took unto itself offices and powers that had formerly been reserved for the various corporations of society and for religious functionaries. The *kṣatriya* role had become more specifically political—in that secular authorities, with bureaucratic instrumentalities at their disposal, regarded themselves as charged with mobilization of social resources for the achievement of collective purposes. Below these dominant classes were the agriculturalists and herdsmen, traders and artisans (collectively the *vaiśya* class), and the *śūdras*, who are described as the servants of the other classes of society and who were, for all practical purposes, beyond the pale of justice.

Before this class structure had hardened into a caste system, it was confronted by the indirect challenge of heterodox salvation religions, which themselves were part of an intellectual movement reaching back to the seventh century B.C. It is the theme of many of the Upaniṣads that knowledge alone—knowledge acquired through meditation—can transform the individual, raising him to union with the eternal One. In such an argument each member of society is equal to every other, in that all participate in the divine. By the time of the Buddha (c. 560–480 B.C.) there existed in India the better part of a hundred distinguishable doctrines, and they ran the gamut from idealism to bald materialism and nihilism. These new disciplines and schools, Buddhism included, were not reform philosophies intent on social change; they offered, rather, an alternate way of life, introspective and world-renouncing. Buddhism is not the expression of active brotherliness; it would be more accurate to say that the teaching calls for a retreat from intense involvement in social relationships. Although not a social philosophy, Buddhism, with its greater attention to ethical considerations and the role of human volition in determining social arrangements, opened new possibilities for political speculation. Induction and reason are of greater importance because less can be explained as the result of divine intervention. By way of Buddhist arguments, secularization could be carried further than had been possible in orthodox theory, and we find, for example, theories assuming the human origin of kingship that allow the unambiguous acceptance of the contract as the basis of obligation; taxes are payment to the king in return for protection. The Buddhist view of social evolution postulated an idyllic state of nature at the beginning of time. Gradual moral decline at length underscored the differences dividing men, and social institutions were introduced to cope with the problems that arose. To establish order the greatest among men was named king and received, in return, a portion of the produce.

As in the Brāhmaṇic literature, punishment (*daṇḍa*) is a duty of the king, but it no longer has the central position it had in earlier political thought. The Buddhist conception of *dhamma* connotes the supreme principle of righteousness. It is closer to Western concepts of virtue than is the Brahmanical *dharma*, which generally has a legalistic ring and is tied to the maintenance of caste prerogatives. Furthermore, Buddhism offers more in the theory and technique of organization than does Brahmanism. The coordination of missionary activities, the preservation of Buddhist tradition and *dhamma*, and the supervision of discipline were functions of the monastic community known as the Saṅgha. The only distinction recognized among the monks was seniority, and resolutions, to carry, had to have the consent of all present (on rare occasions the majority principle was employed). Although it was a self-governing and democratic body, the Saṅgha had no power to prescribe new laws that contradicted the precepts of the founder.

In searching for reasons to explain the growing influence of such heterodox systems as Buddhism and Jainism at this time, we may speculate that with the waning of tribal institutions and with the appearance of new forms of economic production and political organization, the salvation religions might be viewed as substitutes for the lost reservoir of psychic strength. It is not that a sense of loneliness or impotence was felt on a conscious level, for there is no precise moment when the kinship role is replaced by the occupational role. But before expectations, roles, and controls were integrated (caste was not yet sufficiently advanced to serve this function), the sharpened sense of guilt which accompanied the relaxing of clan and tribal authorities may have produced a tormenting uneasiness and "self-consciousness." It remained for the new religions to turn this estrangement to positive ends. Buddhism encouraged the internalization of controls, and this development in itself must have helped ease the transition from one type of external authority to another—preventing, if we are right in our speculation, a greater reliance on arbitrary force.

Also, in the absence of a "correspondence theory" which projects political events into the cosmic order, such activities are confined to the area of human relationships, and political innovation is less apt to be discouraged. Despite the explicit goals of Buddhism, a consequence of the radical shift in cosmological symbolization would conceivably be the justification of secular ends as legitimate in their own right. A clearly perceived tension between sacred and profane could produce either the spirit of world renunciation and asceticism or the frank acceptance of the contrary demands of the two levels of existence. And when salvation became more distinctly a private affair, the state was allowed a freer scope for its activities than was possible in the era of *brāhmaṇ* supremacy.

Perhaps most apparent is the opportunity that heterodoxy provided the ruling class to free itself of priestly influence. The Buddhist emperor Aśoka (c. 270–232 B.C.) interpreted *dhamma* broadly so that it provided the basis of a civic code that amounted to a rejection of the sacrificial cult of the *brāhmaṇs* and the inequities it justified. Although the policy pronouncements that remain in the form of rock and pillar inscriptions indicate that Aśoka was always careful to avoid antagonizing the priests directly, his heterodox sympathies threatened the traditional balance of power. When the state combined Brahmā and *kṣatra* in its own authority it approached a self-legitimating caesaropapism. Thus there existed the opportunity for religion to become the instrument of government. In the first "pillar edict" we learn that it was sometimes necessary for Aśoka's religious agents to "persuade" those who wandered from the true path.

Hindu thought

Portions of the great heroic epic the Mahābhārata were influenced by Sāṅkhya doctrine—perhaps the most important philosophical influence on the development of early Hinduism—before the epic was revised to conform with Vedānta teaching, a system more congenial to the priestly group. The atheistic and rationalist Sāṅkhya philosophic system, of ancient origin but outside the Vedic tradition, shares certain features with Buddhism, such as the belief in the "constant becoming" of the world and a conception of life as suffering. But the Sāṅkhya of the Mahābhārata embraces a concept of God, who is the expression of the highest excellence. Many of the incidents in the Mahābhārata refer back to the remote Vedic period, but the major *brāhmaṇ* modifications and additions probably date from the second and first centuries B.C. In the most famous section of the work, the Bhagavad Gītā, Krishna, the divine charioteer of the warrior–prince Arjuna, seeks to convince the *kṣatriya* of the need to fulfill his caste obligations. Arjuna, who had lost conviction in his motives for fighting, returns to the battle confident of the importance of upholding *dharma*. The Gītā offers an alternative to the world-renouncing ideal of the monk; worldly activity is valued as long as it is not motivated by selfish desire. Caste gains in religious significance in such a philosophy, while simultaneously the promise of salvation is offered to every man who leads a life of detachment and devotion to God. The *kṣatriya* was always more the hero than the achiever, and in this sense the ideal depicted in the philosophic poem is not a radical departure from the traditional figure of the knight. The knight has been civilized and his energies turned to the larger purposes of the community, but it remained for Kauṭilya and the Arthaśāstra theorists to emphasize achievement and to declare that *artha* (material gain) was a fundamental principle of society and essential to the building of an empire.

The Śānti Parvan, the twelfth book of the epic, is the major source of political commentary in the Mahābhārata. The subject of this didactic book is *nīti*, the science of worldly pursuit. We are told that at first *dharma* kept everything in its place, but the shadow of greed and lust eventually fell across the land. The resultant condition of anarchy (*mātsyanyāya*, the "law of the fishes"—what we might describe as the law of the jungle) is disorder of Hobbesian proportions. The account of the origin of kingship that follows contains justifications of authority in terms of function, heredity, subordination to the *brāhmaṇs*, and finally, divinity itself. The authority of the ruler is exalted in these passages, for "when the science of politics (chastisement) is neglected, the Vedas and all virtues decline." Taxes were considered the king's remuneration for protecting and furthering the interests of his people. But in taxing his subjects the king must resemble the subtle leech and the gentle cowherd, extracting the necessary revenue without destroying initiative.

The Arthaśāstra writings. The Mahābhārata mentions a number of schools of Arthaśāstra doctrine, and the names of previous writers (some as early as the fifth century B.C.) agree with those found in the Arthaśāstra of Kauṭilya. In the earlier stages of its history the science of politics was termed *rājadharma*, but when the study was broadened to include both politics and economics, it came to be called *arthaśāstra*. (In treatises which emphasize that fear of retribution is the real basis of order, the term *daṇḍanīti* is sometimes employed.) Most political thought assumed the existence of a monarchical form of government, and politics was accordingly defined as the science of kingship. The Arthaśāstra texts were intended as guides for the king and his ministers, and they included such subjects as public administration, economic regulation, foreign policy, techniques of warfare, and civil law. The most important of these works, and the earliest we have, is the treatise generally attributed to Kauṭilya, the minister of the first Mauryan emperor.

Kauṭilya is not primarily concerned with broad political speculation on the origin and nature of the state (India provides no philosophical text that can be compared with the major theoretical works of Europe), and his originality is not to be found in the realm of abstraction. The treatise is, as its author explains, a compendium and summary of earlier Arthaśāstra writings. Of the three ends of human life—virtue, wealth, and enjoyment—Kauṭilya assigns first importance to wealth, but he is always aware of the instrumental value of religion and ethical norms in preserving the structure of society. He allows the king to determine for himself what shall have the sanction of law, although the Vedas are accepted as sources of *dharma*, and statute law must be compatible with the sacred texts. Despite the significance he attaches to the role of the king, Kauṭilya is pragmatic in his approach and would give priority to that component of sovereignty which happens to be of most consequence at any particular time. In Indian theory sovereignty was usually thought to contain seven elements: the king, the ministers, the populace, the fort, the treasury, the army, and the ally. (The same catalogue may be found in the Kāmandakīya, the Śukranītisāra and the Manu-Smṛti.) The theory, in which diplomacy is made an integral part of politics, is intended to show the necessary conditions for the effective functioning of the state.

The Arthaśāstra leaves the reader with the impression that its author is little concerned with ethical considerations. Political expedience had been a characteristic of the Arthaśāstra tradition, and in such works as the Śānti Parvan right is equated with might in a world in which the stronger live upon the weaker. Kauṭilya usually recommends unscrupulous tactics only against those who would subvert the social order, and he is aware that power, if not restrained in its use, can be destructive of itself. The author of the Arthaśāstra was sensitive to the economic bases of power and opposed any decentralizing tendency that would weaken the control of the state over the economic life of society. Yet the state should not seek to eliminate the independent group life of the community. The caste structure was accepted as long as the general well-being was not prejudiced by narrow class prerogatives. The Arthaśāstra represents an important step in the direction of authority based on the interests of all. The king was advised to see no interest other than the interest of his subjects. However, Kauṭilya also makes clear that prosperity rests on the good will of the people and that the power of the state depends on wealth. This conception of authority must necessarily include many functions previously reserved to institutions that were not considered political. The scope of political authority, then, was markedly broadened, and in the literature of this period we begin to read such statements as "the king is maker of his age."

The Nītisāra of Kāmandaka, usually placed in the Gupta period (fourth or fifth century A.D.), is essentially an abridgment of the Arthaśāstra, although the later writer neglects a number of subjects that Kauṭilya obviously believed of great importance. Two-thirds of the Kāmandakīya Nītisāra relates to foreign policy and the conduct of hostilities.

All the literature that has been considered thus far was produced in northern India, and, except for Buddhist writings, in Sanskrit. The contributions of Tamil and other south Indian writers are now beginning to receive more attention. Perhaps the most important work produced in the south (broadly contemporaneous with the Nītisāra) was the Tīrukkuraḷ (Kuraḷ) of Tiruvaḷḷuvar, which also owes much to Kauṭilya. Several Jaina texts can be classed among the Arthaśāstra writings. Such authors as Hemacandra (twelfth century A.D.) were willing to allow the ethical standards of their religion to inform political life, but generally they can be contrasted with authors of Buddhist canonical works, who demanded the subordination of politics to ethics and held in contempt the "*kṣatriya* science."

The last great comprehensive political study of the ancient Hindus, the Śukranītisāra (probably ninth to thirteenth century A.D.), though a smaller work than the Arthaśāstra, is wider in scope. It is as much a moral treatise as it is a political one: the great attention to the moral norms necessary for regulating conduct prevents a sharp distinction between politics and ethics. Probably the dearth of comment regarding the origins of state and government must be taken to mean that the author of the text considered the state as having existed in some form from earliest time, being the product of human needs. Śukra, like Kauṭilya, is concerned with the actual mechanism of government, the organization of power, and the theory of empire. The usual seven components of sovereignty are elaborated, but Śukra introduces an analogy to the human body, which has led some students of the work to describe it as an organic theory of the state. The ministers have an important place in this theory; they were to be consulted on all questions of policy. Their recommendations must be accepted by the king. By the time of Śukra eight ministers constituted the standard council. With the possible exception of the minister of religion and the crown prince, the roster is not greatly different from modern cabinets. Public officials were to be chosen on the basis of character and accomplishment: circumstances of birth were of less importance to Śukra than to other theorists.

The Dharma Śāstra writings. Whereas the Arthaśāstra literature introduces inductive reasoning and a greater realism into political thought, the Dharma Śāstras are essentially deductive in nature. In the first centuries A.D. the prose Dharma Sūtra texts were reworked in verse form, and the social and religious regulations of the orthodox *brāhmaṇ* culture were systematized. These codes are accepted as authentic guides to law, custom, and duty. Through the centuries they achieved a stature comparable to that of the Vedic hymns, although it is not possible to say whether any of the law codes were deliberately employed as regulations backed by coercive sanctions. The Manu-Smṛti is the oldest and most famous of the Dharma Śāstras; it is usually regarded as the most authoritative work on Hindu law. In defining sacred law, the treatise includes, in addition to the sacred tradition, individual conscience and the example of virtuous men. Allowance must be made for local custom, and past usage must be considered in the settling of legal disputes. The king is understood to be divinely created and ordained to protect the people from a barbarous state of nature, but the absolutism of the European divine right argument is not found in the conception. The king embodies the virtues of eight deities; his authority is derived from the divine nature of his office and the significance of his crucial role in the preservation of the social order, as well as from the supernatural origin of his person. It goes without saying that such characterizations of kingship as we find in the Manu-Smṛti and the Mahābhārata are compatible only with hereditary kingship. Caste distinctions are also made the product of divine decree as well as the result of social necessity. *Brāhmaṇ* superiority is described and justified in the most extravagant terms. In the Manu-Smṛti and most of the law books, punishment increased in severity as social status diminished.

A basic tenet of Hindu political thought was the belief that the king must regard himself not as the creator of the law but only as its guardian. The Nārada-Smṛti is an exception. In this work the royal decree is regarded as legitimate in its own right. Perhaps the most authoritarian of Indian writers, Nārada demands that the king be obeyed whether right or wrong in his actions. However, from about the third century B.C. there seems to have developed a growing appreciation of the need to relate law and tradition to changing social conditions. This awareness can be seen in the Dharma Śāstra work attributed to Yājñavalkya. In that work and in the codes of other legal authorities it is argued that the edict must harmonize with customary and sacred law and that departures from the original *rājadharma* must be carefully controlled. Judicial offices were generally to be filled by *brāhmaṇs*, since no man could be judged by one who was not at least his social equal and since the sin involved in the crime must also be judged. The earliest court was likely the king's palace, but by the time of the Dharma Śāstras complexities of judicial administration necessitated formal institutions of a more specialized nature. There existed a regular procedure for appeal from lower to higher courts.

The political commentary of the Dharma Śāstras is similar to that of the Arthaśāstra writers and requires little further discussion here. Tax revenue was seen as the king's rightful due in return for the security he provided. Concern for social stability induced some of the legal theorists to elaborate rules of statecraft with Kauṭilyan candor, but usually (as in Yājñavalkya) military action was to conform to a code of conduct. The technique of the power balance was understood, and alliances were considered among the major assets of the state. In Hindu political theory, diplomacy is constructed on the interrelationships within a group of states, all neatly described in terms of their probable effect on the fortunes of the home state. This theory (*maṇḍala*) is based on the assumption that the king, by nature, aspires to conquest and that his neighbor is his enemy. The natural ally is the kingdom on the opposite frontier of the enemy.

The Purāṇas. The Purāṇas, compendia of ancient legends and lore covering a wide variety of topics, in their present form belong to the first seven or eight centuries A.D. Again we are reminded of the fundamental importance of punishment in preserving *dharma*. In these texts, as in others, there is no place for the right of resistance. The problem of individual rights as opposed to the right of the state does not arise in ancient Hindu theory—except, possibly, with reference to *brāhmaṇ* immunities. The king is advised to be neither mild nor harsh in dealing with his subjects and to exert his authority to bring about their full spiritual and material development. If he fulfills his duty he is entitled to a sixth part of the merit earned by his people.

Modern thought

There are Arthaśāstra works, including several Jaina commentaries, which belong to the period following the decline of the Gupta regime, but few writers go beyond apology and justification and, as was true also of earlier theory, there is little attention to defenses of the individual against the pressures of society. Nor did the centuries of the sultanate contribute much to the heritage of Indian political philosophy, except, perhaps, for the area of legal theory. In Islamic thought the law, which is based on revealed principles, is the arbiter of the struggle which rages in man's own soul and which constitutes a potential threat to the stability of society. The significance of the protective role of the monarch in this theory led certain theorists, Abu-l Fazl among them, to depict the king as the chosen instrument of God. Such an exaltation of royal authority left little place for popular participation in selecting rulers and determining policy.

The nationalist movement. With the attempts of the Marāthās and Sikhs in the seventeenth century to throw off the foreign power, political theory enjoyed a temporary revival, but it was not until the nationalist movement of the nineteenth century that political literature acquired more than a fragmentary form and political argument was organized around fundamental problems of obligation and the proper scope and ends of political power. The majority of the theorists who supported reform legislation or self-government based their positions on Western ideas, without wishing to abandon elements of the Indian tradition.

Rājā Rām Mohan Roy (d. 1833) believed that the ancient ideals of India could be restored by removing "the senseless accretions that had defiled [*dharma*] in later years."

G. K. Gokhale (d. 1915) located the roots of India's misfortunes not in foreign imperialism but in the traditional society; he described England's involvements in India as a "providential arrangement." England, he argued, possessed components of character—freedom and self-assertion—that complemented those of India. These were qualities necessary to training for eventual self-government within the empire. Toward this end he established, in 1905, the Servants of India Society, which worked to inspire a commitment to the nation (a goal implying the idea of one nationality), to organize the political education of the people, and to encourage economic development and the improvement of the condition of the depressed classes.

Gokhale and the moderates, who had dominated the Indian National Congress since its inception in 1885, confined their political agitation to constitutional methods, but Bal Gangadhar Tilak (d. 1920) and his followers proposed civil disobedience and insisted that political independence must precede reform. Although he provided no elaborate program of social reconstruction, it was Tilak more than any other figure who popularized the nationalist movement. This he accomplished through a frankly revivalist appeal, which directed religious sentiments into a movement with strong political ramifications. The restoration of Hindu orthodoxy, not liberal and democratic ideals, constituted his primary objective.

Gandhism. Mohandas K. Gandhi (d. 1948) is, of course, the towering figure of modern Indian history and of modern Indian political theory, although his thought is often the response to a practical need and does not assume the form of an elegantly constructed treatise. Gandhi employed traditional concepts and symbols but without hesitation introduced interpretations and ideas foreign to Indian culture that evince the importance of Western humanism in his approach. He opposed Western technology on the grounds that the machine civilization brought with it the exploitation of men and the concentration of power. Here he followed Tolstoi, whose writings, with those of Thoreau and others, he studied while in South Africa. He described his twenty years there as a time of experiment—the trying out of different modes of political action and different types of political program. The influence of Gokhale on his thought is readily apparent, as is the impact of the strand of Indian nationalist political thought represented by Tilak. These influences are seen in Gandhi's attempt to redirect religious individualism and his emphasis on native languages and the Swadeshi principle. Swadeshi puts first those duties nearest us in space and time: it is "that spirit in us which restricts us to the use and service of our immediate surroundings to the exclusion of the more remote." Humanity is served through service to our neighbor; our understanding of the world is only the understanding we have of those with whom we live.

This argument has major economic implications: those things produced at home are to be preferred. Its extension, the use of the boycott, is another legacy of Tilak. According to Gandhi, reconstruction begins at the local level, and the village is the basis of social planning. Village activity and an individual's effort and initiative are stressed in his writings and speeches. He invariably favored small-scale organization and the use of simple tools and materials at hand. His campaign for the use of only hand-spun and hand-woven cloth (*khādar*) was of central importance to the larger program, and it was the spinning wheel that Gandhi chose as the symbol of social freedom. His ideas on land reform were radical, but he did not call for the abolition of private property. He hoped, rather, that the propertied class could be persuaded to accept the ideal of economic equality: the idea of wealth held in trust for the poor would make expropriation by legislative enactment unnecessary. Gandhi argued that the accumulation of riches beyond a man's legitimate requirements is akin to theft. This additional wealth must be used for the welfare of the community. Gandhi also insisted on the importance of physical labor for everyone—what he called bread-labor. Constructive work, which he considered an essential part of civil disobedience and other political action, included also the removal of untouchability (which ranked with the spread of *khādar* as a goal of critical significance to the movement), communal unity (here he is closer to Gokhale than to Tilak), and basic education through the knowledge of a craft. In learning a necessary craft the young person not only acquires a skill but also intensifies his bonds with the community and thus comes to an understanding of purposes.

Gandhian philosophy postulates a universe very different from that governed by the law of the fish.

History is as much the record of harmonious adjustment as it is the story of conflict. The technique for adjusting and reconciling differences, a method on which Mahatma Gandhi's fame must ultimately rest, assumes the moral potential of the wrongdoer, the possibility of reasonableness in the adversary. In his political theory Gandhi concentrated on the means of achieving political ends to a degree uncommon in the history of Western thought. If there is a single theme in his philosophy it is that the character of the means determines that of the results. As one student of Gandhi has remarked, "It is only when means themselves are understood to be—and designed to be—more than instrumental, to be, in fine, *creative*, that the next step will be taken in the evolvement of a constructive philosophy of conflict" (Bondurant 1958, p. 232).

The crucial element of this theory is *ahiṃsā*—"action based on the refusal to do harm." *Ahiṃsā* is first mentioned in the Chāndogya Upaniṣad as one of the five ethical qualities, and it was later associated particularly with Jainism. In modern India Jainism is strongest in Gandhi's native Gujarāt. (In medieval India, it should be noted, the idea of nonviolence was influential but was never taken to mean the proscription of either war or capital punishment.) Not only is physical injury to be avoided, according to Gandhi, but one's tactics may not even seek to embarrass the adversary. The first step in resolving differences is to emphasize interests that the parties to the conflict share, or to formulate interests that they might conceivably share, and to attempt to establish cooperation on this basis. Issues must be made as simple as possible so that difficulties are not further aggravated by misunderstandings. Gandhi believed that there were always common purposes, but he did not believe that compromise—in which each side makes concessions so as to reach agreement—was the means for arriving at these purposes. Only when principles were not involved should compromise be employed as a technique. Instead of reducing demands, a program for resolving conflict should aim at bringing about a new and higher level of adjustment which would prove mutually satisfactory.

Satyagraha ("holding on to truth") envisages the possibility of conversion, the possibility that a sense of justice may be awakened in the opponent. *Satyagraha* moves from rational persuasion to the stage of suffering (which is intended to encourage an openness to rational argument) to the stage of what is sometimes called nonviolent coercion. This last form, which includes noncooperation and civil disobedience, is the final resort when the other forms have not succeeded. Civil disobedience, the most drastic phase, was understood by Gandhi as a higher obedience—obedience to a transcendent moral law. It can be a dangerous instrument and readily misused; Gandhi always advised great caution—as in the instance of the fast, which too drastically limits the alternatives available to the opponent and therefore should be undertaken only by those disciplined in the methods of *satyagraha*. He wished to distinguish nonviolent forms of resisting evil, which are usually forms of passive resistance (and often intent on harassment), from *satyagraha*, which forsakes the courting of injury. Fasting, he thought, may easily become a type of passive resistance. Yet in a choice between cowardice and slavery on the one hand and the use of violence on the other, Gandhi was unambiguous in recommending violence. [*See* CIVIL DISOBEDIENCE.]

Ahiṃsā is not the highest good: it is the necessary condition of truth. Truth is supreme among values. Truth is destroyed by violence, and our inability to know the truth with absolute certainty requires us to be tolerant of those who disagree with us. Gandhi has said that *satyagraha* does not permit the use of violence because the absolute truth cannot be known by man, and for this reason he is not competent to punish others. Here Gandhi spoke as a relativist, arguing that loyalty to truth rules out fixed modes of thought and action. But it can be said that the most sublime truth is the sacredness and unity of life.

Satyagraha has inspired the mass of the population as few ideas have been able to do. In the movement led by Khan Abdul Ghaffar Khan *satyagraha* acquired Muslim overtones, but its objective remained political independence and social reform. Gandhi was reluctant to speculate on the nature of a government based on nonviolence, but it is clear that the sense of community aroused in the people by *satyagraha* would be the basis of the new polity. Democracy, or self-government, meant independence of controls—whether those exercised by a foreign power or those of a centralized national government. The ideals of the anarchist could never be fully realized, Gandhi admitted, but state intervention in the conduct of human affairs could be considerably reduced if the democratic state were in actual fact a federation of village communities in which voluntary associations flourished, rights flowed from the fulfillment of obligations, and a high degree of self-sufficiency made possible the relative autonomy of each village.

More recently, Vinoba Bhave urged that the coercive power of the state be replaced by direct, voluntary action on the part of the people. The

Sarvodaya movement, under the leadership of Bhave, held that the good of one man is inseparable from the good of others; in his efforts to translate this idea into an economic reform program, Bhave invoked the Gandhian theory of the trusteeship of wealth. Millions of acres of land have been turned over to landless peasants, but the revolution has come "from above" and not as the consequence of direct efforts of the people to solve their own problems.

Bhave, like Gandhi before him, insisted that the only change that endures is that which rests on the conversion of men to principles of truth, selflessness, and nonviolence—principles which guard against the subordination of means to ends and which have their dramatic statement in the lives and aphorisms of the ancient teachers.

CHARLES DREKMEIER

[*See also* ASIAN SOCIETY, *article on* SOUTH ASIA; BUDDHISM; HINDUISM; *and the biography of* KAUṬILYA.]

BIBLIOGRAPHY

BASHAM, ARTHUR L. (1954) 1963 *The Wonder That Was India: A Study of the History and Culture of the Indian Sub-continent Before the Coming of the Muslims.* New ed., rev. New York: Hawthorn.

BHAVE, VINOBA 1953 *Bhoodan Yajna: Land-gifts Mission.* Ahmedabad (India): Navajivan.

BONDURANT, JOAN V. (1958) 1965 *Conquest of Violence: The Gandhian Philosophy of Conflict.* Rev. ed. Berkeley: Univ. of California Press.

DASGUPTA, SURENDRA N. 1922–1955 *A History of Indian Philosophy.* 5 vols. Cambridge Univ. Press.

DHAWAN, GOPI N. 1946 *The Political Philosophy of Mahatma Gandhi.* Bombay: Popular Book Depot.

DREKMEIER, CHARLES 1962 *Kingship and Community in Early India.* Stanford Univ. Press.

DUMÉZIL, GEORGES 1940 *Mitra-Varuna: Essai sur deux représentations indo-européennes de la souveraineté.* Paris: Leroux.

GANDHI, MOHANDAS K. (1924) 1954 *Autobiography: The Story of My Experiments With Truth.* Washington: Public Affairs Press. → First translated from Gujarati in 1927–1929. A paperback edition was published in 1962 by Beacon.

GANDHI, MOHANDAS K. 1942–1949 *Non-violence in Peace and War.* 2 vols. Ahmedabad (India): Navajivan.

GHOSHAL, UPENDRA N. 1959 *A History of Indian Political Ideas: The Ancient Period and the Period of Transition to the Middle Ages.* Oxford Univ. Press.

HOCART, ARTHUR M. (1938) 1950 *Caste: A Comparative Study.* London: Methuen. → First published in French as *Les castes.*

HOPKINS, EDWARD W. 1889 The Social and Military Position of the Ruling Caste in Ancient India as Represented by the Sanskrit Epic. *Journal of the American Oriental Society* 13:57–374.

HULTZSCH, EUGEN (editor) 1925 *Inscriptions of Aśoka.* Oxford: Clarendon.

HUTTON, JOHN H. (1946) 1964 *Caste in India: Its Nature, Function and Origins.* 4th ed. Oxford Univ. Press.

JOLLY, JULIUS E. (1896) 1928 *Hindu Law and Custom.* Calcutta (India): No publisher given. → First published as *Recht und Sitte.*

JOLLY, JULIUS E. (editor and translator) 1889 *The Minor Law-Books.* Part 1: Nārada [and] Brihaspati. The Sacred Books of the East, Vol. 33. Oxford: Clarendon.

KANE, P. V. 1930–1962 *History of Dharmaśāstra (Ancient and Mediaeval Religious and Civil Law).* Vols. 1–4. Poona (India): Bhandarkar Oriental Research Institute.

KAUṬILYA *Kauṭilya's* Arthaśāstra. 3d ed. Translated by Dr. R. Shamasastry with an introductory note by the late Dr. J. F. Fleet. Mysore (India): Wesleyan Mission Press, 1929.

KOSAMBI, DAMODAR D. 1956 *An Introduction to the Study of Indian History.* Bombay: Popular Book Depot.

MACDONELL, ARTHUR A.; and KEITH, ARTHUR B. 1912 *Vedic Index of Names and Subjects.* London: Murray.

MAHĀBHĀRATA *The Mahābhārata.* Critically edited by Vishnu S. Sukthankar et al. Vols. 1–19. Poona (India): Bhandarkar Oriental Research Institute, 1927–1964. → Volumes 13–16: *Sāntiparvan.*

MAHĀBHĀRATA *The Bhagavadgītā.* Sanskrit text, with an introductory essay, English translation, and notes by Sarvepalli Radhakrishnan. London: Allen & Unwin, 1948.

MAJUMDAR, RAMESH C. (editor) 1951–1963 *The History and Culture of the Indian People.* Vols. 1–4. London: Allen & Unwin.

MANU *The Laws of Manu.* Translated with extracts from seven commentaries by G. Bühler. The Sacred Books of the East, Vol. 25. Delhi: Motilal Banarsidass, 1964. → This edition was first published in 1886.

MÜHLMANN, WILHELM E. 1950 *Mahatma Gandhi: Eine Untersuchung zur Religionssoziologie und politischen Ethik.* Tübingen (Germany): Mohr.

NARAIN, JAYA PRAKASH 1946 *Towards Struggle: Selected Manifestoes, Speeches and Writings.* Bombay: Padma.

NEHRU, JAWAHARLAL (1941) 1958 *Toward Freedom: The Autobiography of Jawaharlal Nehru.* Boston: Beacon.

RAU, WILHELM 1957 *Staat und Gesellschaft im alten Indien, nach den Brāhamana-Texten dargestellt.* Wiesbaden (Germany): Harrassowitz.

RENOU, LOUIS 1953 *Religions of Ancient India.* London: Athlone.

ŚATAPATHA-BRÂHMANA *The Śatapatha-brâhmana.* According to the text of the Mâdhyandina School, translated by Julius Eggeling. 5 vols. The Sacred Books of the East, Vols. 12, 26, 41–44. Delhi (India): Motilal Banarsidass, 1963.

SHARMA, RAM S. 1959 *Aspects of Political Ideas and Institutions in Ancient India.* Delhi (India): Motilal Banarsidass.

SHRIDHARANI, KRISHNALAL J. 1939 *War Without Violence: The Sociology of Gandhi's Satyagraha.* New York: Harcourt.

THAPAR, ROMILA 1961 *Aśoka and the Decline of the Mauryas.* Oxford Univ. Press.

TILAK, BAL G. 1922 *Bal Gangadhar Tilak: His Writings and Speeches.* Madras: Ganesh.

UPANISHADS *The Thirteen Principal Upanishads.* 2d ed., rev. Oxford Univ. Press, 1962. → Translated from the Sanskrit, with an outline of the philosophy of the Upanishads and annotated bibliography by Robert Ernest Hume. This edition was first published in 1921.

VEDAS, ṚIGVEDA *Hymns From the Ṛigveda*. Selected and metrically translated by A. A. Macdonell. Calcutta (India): Association Press; Oxford Univ. Press, 1922. → The Introduction supplies a brief sketch of the form and contents of the *Ṛigveda*.

WEBER, MAX (1921) 1958 *The Religion of India: The Sociology of Hinduism and Buddhism*. Translated and edited by Hans H. Gerth and Don Martindale. Glencoe, Ill.: Free Press. → First published in German as *Hinduismus und Buddhismus*, Volume 2 of *Gesammelte Aufsätze zur Religionssoziologie*.

WOLPERT, STANLEY A. 1962 *Tilak and Gokhale: Revolution and Reform in the Making of Modern India*. Berkeley: Univ. of California Press.

YAJÑAVALKA *Yajñavalkya Smriti*. With the commentary of Vijnaneśvara, called the Mitaksara, and notes from the gloss of Bâlambhatta. Book 1: The Achâra Adhyâya. Translated by Śriśa C. Vidyârṇava. Allahabad (India): Pâninî Office, 1918.

ZIMMER, HEINRICH R. (1951) 1964 *Philosophies of India*. Cleveland: World Publishing.

INDIAN SOCIETY

See ASIAN SOCIETY, *article on* SOUTH ASIA; CASTE, *article on* THE INDIAN CASTE SYSTEM; HINDUISM; ISLAM; POLLUTION; *and the biography of* MAJUMDAR.

INDIANS, NORTH AMERICAN

Americanists of the early twentieth century were primarily interested in historical problems, and the classifications of culture types were designed to that end. Since the 1930s, however, there has been an increasing interest in structural and functional approaches to the understanding of American Indian societies and cultures and a more adequate comprehension of the role of ecological factors in their development. By combining historical and structural–functional methods, it has been possible to control our comparisons to a greater extent, both synchronically and over time, and to recognize certain of the processes involved in cultural continuity and social change. With the aid of new techniques of dating, such as the radiocarbon method and lexicostatistical estimates, and with complex techniques of inference in archeology and linguistics, it is possible to outline the framework for a more adequate reconstruction of the development of New World social and cultural forms. In this article we will be concerned primarily with the Indians of North America, north of Mexico.

The pioneer study of North American social systems was that of L. H. Morgan. In *Systems of Consanguinity and Affinity of the Human Family* (1871), he presented comparative data on kinship systems and clan organization for much of the region east of the Rocky Mountains, but the evolutionary framework in which he placed his data led to criticism and rejection of most of his contributions. Students of Boas, in the American historical "school," emphasized a more inductive approach and more cautious reconstructions, with Swanton (1905) and Goldenweiser (1915) presenting preliminary syntheses of North American social organization and Spier (1925) and Lowie (1929) developing empirical classifications of terminological systems of relationship. It was not until after World War II that a more comprehensive analysis and interpretation of the North American data was begun by Murdock (1949; 1955) and Eggan (1955; 1966).

During much of this period American anthropologists were concerned with the identification of the culture types in the New World and the delineation of the resulting culture areas. The work of Wissler (1917), Kroeber (1939), Driver (1961), and Spencer and his colleagues (1965) has contributed to this development, and we shall utilize the culture area as a convenient framework within which to describe social structure. Kroeber viewed the culture area as containing essentially a single growth of culture, or a regionally individualized type, but Boas and others have noted that social structures do not always conform to the culture area. We shall examine a number of such instances in the course of our survey. [*See* BOAS; GOLDENWEISER; KROEBER; LOWIE; SPIER; SWANTON; WISSLER.]

North America, north of Mexico, was inhabited in pre-Columbian times by approximately a million Indians, who spoke a variety of languages and dialects and who were organized into a large number of tribes, ranging from small bands to confederacies of considerable size. The Indians are all variants of a basic Mongoloid stock, and their ancestors entered the New World by way of the land bridge across the Bering Strait which was in existence during the last glacial period. While some migrants may have arrived earlier, there is clear evidence for Clovis projectile points associated with mammoth remains in the high Plains and the Southwest between 11,500 and 11,000 years ago, followed by Folsom and other points associated with the hunting of extinct forms of bison and other large game. There is evidence for a parallel development in western North America of an early gathering culture, known generally as the Desert Culture, which exploited wild plant resources and small game and which provided the basis for the later development of agriculture in Mexico and neighboring regions. In the eastern forest regions of North America, the early hunters turned in part to the exploitation of wild plants and forest products, as well as the utilization of mussels and fish, to develop a variety of Archaic cultures whose relationships are being worked out by the archeologists. [*See* HUNTING AND GATHERING, *article on* NEW WORLD PREHISTORIC SOCIETIES.]

The first scientific classification of North American Indian languages (Powell 1891) indicated some 53 language stocks north of Mexico, but subsequent research by Sapir (1929) reduced this number to 6, with further reductions in prospect. Until recently there was no clear evidence of genetic relationships with the languages of northeast Asia, but Eskimo–Aleut is now known to be related to Chukchee and Koryak on the Asiatic side of the Bering Strait. In general, there is greater linguistic diversity in western North America than in the East; aboriginal California shows the greatest variety.

Cultural differentiation and development have proceeded from a mesolithic base and have occurred as a result both of migration and of adaptation to differing ecological conditions. The discovery of plant domestication in the regions to the south and its gradual spread northward had a profound effect on many groups. Present evidence indicates that the domestication of corn, beans, squash, cotton, and other crops took place in the Tehuacán and other valleys in the central Mexican highlands between 5000–3500 B.C. and gradually diffused northward (as well as in other directions), reaching the Southwest around 1500 B.C. Here there was also a long developmental period; agriculture was not firmly established until around A.D. 1, by which time it had also reached other areas of North America.

Cultural anthropologists divide North America into some 10 to 12 culture areas, or geographical regions, occupied by societies with generally similar culture patterns. In certain culture areas, such as the Arctic, there is a close correlation between language, physical type, and cultural pattern, but in general, race, language, and culture are differently distributed. Some culture areas, such as the Great Basin, show considerable time depth, with little change in archeologically known artifact types. Other areas, such as the Plains, show evidence of recent migration, with cultural adaptation to a new environment and borrowing as important processes. [*See* CULTURE AREA.]

The dominant subsistence activities in northern North America centered on the hunting of large game—sea mammals in the Arctic area, caribou and moose in the Canadian Subarctic regions, bison and buffalo on the Plains; salmon was important on the Northwest Coast. In much of western North America, i.e., in the Plateau, California, and Great Basin areas, the gathering of plant foods—acorns, piñon nuts, and wild seeds and roots of various kinds—predominated, with hunting of small game and fishing being generally secondary. Horticulture was important in the Southwest and in the regions east of the Mississippi River, although the hunting of deer and other sedentary game, along with fishing and the gathering of wild fruits and nuts, furnished about half of the subsistence in the latter areas. The introduction of the horse by the Spaniards into the Southwest and its subsequent diffusion to the Plains tribes and their neighbors after A.D. 1600 led to a florescence of Plains culture, but the full utilization of the horse as a domestic animal was not achieved until the reservation period although some groups utilized the horse for food.

The aboriginal Indian population was unevenly distributed in North America. The greatest population densities for the major regions were found in California and the Northwest Coast, areas which were nonagricultural but where natural food resources were both relatively abundant and reliable. In the Southwest, the Pueblo Indians lived in towns with locally dense populations but surrounded by relatively empty semideserts. In the eastern regions there was a more uniform distribution of population. In general, there was a greater density along the coasts than in the interior, reflecting the greater variety and number of food resources. The range of population densities was from a little over 1 per 100 square kilometers (about 38 square miles) in the northern interior Subarctic regions to around 43 per 100 square kilometers in aboriginal California, with 28 per 100 square kilometers on the Northwest Coast, 11 per 100 square kilometers in the Southwest, and 7 per 100 square kilometers in the eastern areas. For North America as a whole the population density was around 5 persons per 100 square kilometers, or about 1 person per 7 square miles.

The social and political organization of the Indians of North America shows a surprising variety of forms but does not attain to the high level of organization reached in Middle America and the Andean regions, where large confederations and states developed in connection with urban life. The low level of technological development and limited resources of aboriginal North America combined to keep it a marginal area in terms of population concentration and social and political elaboration, despite the diffusion of agriculture and other practices from Mexico and some contacts with Asia across the Bering Strait and possibly by sea.

Everywhere in North America the local group

or band was important, although there was considerable variation in size and formal organization. In a few regions, such as the Great Basin and the northern regions, the bands were small and of varying structure, as related family groups combined for subsistence and social purposes. In more favorable regions the local groups might have permanent territories and a lineage organization based on unilineal descent and definite residence patterns, or develop into larger composite bands with a central political structure and a feeling of tribal unity. In the agricultural regions the tribal groups were often relatively sedentary, with a village or town organization and a social structure based on unilineal descent groups, or clans, and a more centralized and powerful religious and political structure. In a few regions in the east political confederations developed among related tribes as a means of survival or protection against pressures from the European colonists and alien groups.

Western North America, west of the Rocky Mountains, was generally a region of uncentralized societies with autonomous village communities or local groups. Sometimes, the village community was not a political unit, although usually it had a headman or local leader. This is true even of the more elaborately organized societies of the Northwest Coast, where warfare was common and social stratification well developed. Over much of the intermontane region, including the Plateau, the Great Basin, and the Pueblo portions of the Southwest, there was a generally peaceful ethos and a lack of social differentiation and stratification. Not until we reach the lower Colorado River, among the Yuman-speaking peoples and their neighbors, do we find strong tribal organization and fully developed warfare.

The region east of the Rocky Mountains, in contrast, was characterized by politically organized tribes with well-developed chieftainship, considerable social stratification, and an emphasis on war and raiding. There is some archeological evidence for more elaborate sociopolitical structures centering on platform mounds and earthworks, but their focus appears to be primarily religious in character, although the archeological remains give evidence of extensive trade networks. The Arctic and Subarctic regions lacked extensive political development and social stratification, but feuds were common, and there was general enmity between the Eskimos and adjacent Indian groups.

In almost all regions of North America there were seasonal movements relevant to the food quest that brought about new alignments of population and interaction with different groups. Frequently the local group inhabited a winter village and broke up into smaller family or multifamily units during the summer or at other seasons. In some regions the pattern was reversed, as in the high Plains, where bands wintered separately but aggregated in a camp circle during the summer months. In other areas there was a more complex seasonal round. Only the Pueblo (and to a lesser extent the southeastern tribes) and the Iroquois and their neighbors approximated a pattern of sedentary town dwelling. In almost all areas the geographical environment, coupled with a primitive technology, placed an effective population ceiling on the size of the local groups and affected their distribution and complexity. Only in a few places was the technology sufficiently advanced to free peoples from a primary dependence on environmental offerings and allow them to develop larger populations and more complex institutions.

The regional developments

With this brief introduction we might now consider North America region by region, with particular reference to the social and political institutions each has developed and with some attention to historical developments, so far as they are known at present.

The Arctic. The Arctic culture area, which extends from Alaska to Greenland across the northern tundra, is inhabited by a single group, the Eskimo. The Aleutian archipelago was formerly occupied by their linguistic and cultural relatives, the Aleuts, but relatively few of the latter have survived the processes of acculturation, and little is known about their aboriginal institutions. The Eskimo, however, are still flourishing and play an active role in new development programs in the north.

The archeological origins of Eskimo culture were long sought in northern Asia, but there is growing evidence for the culture's development from mesolithic complexes in the region of southwestern Alaska and the Bering Strait. Here Eskimo culture went through a number of stages, involving adaptation both to the resources of the sea and of the land. Around one thousand years ago a migration of a portion of the Eskimo took place across northern Canada to Greenland (Thule Eskimo), perhaps following the migrations of the whale, on which they largely depended. Later uplifts in the central regions forced them either to return or to adapt to the severe conditions of the tundra and the ice shelf. Those who remained were the forebears of the modern Central Eskimo, who hunt seal and walrus during the winter and move south during the brief summer to exploit the caribou migrations. More favorable conditions in Alaska and parts of Greenland led to greater specializations in subsistence and to more complex social institutions. However, despite a long history of adjustment to differing ecological conditions, there is a generic unity to Eskimo life and culture. The boundary between Eskimo and Indians, on the other hand, is relatively sharp and is maintained by differing patterns of ecological adjustment and by general enmity.

The distribution of the Eskimo–Aleut languages further supports the archeological record. The hypothesis that Eskimo–Aleut is genetically related to Chukchee–Koryak in Siberia suggests the development of Eskimo culture from local origins over a long time period. The major division into Aleut and Eskimo took place in southwestern Alaska several thousand years ago, and Eskimo later separated into Yupik, the language spoken in south Alaska and on both sides of the Bering Strait, and Inupik, the language spoken from Norton Sound to Greenland, the dialects of which are still mutually intelligible for the most part. The relative distinctiveness of the Eskimo physical type and its resemblances to northeast Asian forms further suggest that the Eskimo have developed from local populations. Whether they are the most recent migrants to the New World, as their geographic position would indicate, is not yet clear.

The Eskimo at the time of contact numbered about 60,000–75,000, with an estimated 10,000–15,000 Aleuts, who have since been reduced to a small fraction of this number. Today there are some 35,000–40,000 Eskimo, the bulk of them divided between Alaska and Greenland, with about 10,000 Eskimo in the central regions. A few, such as the Polar Eskimo, live above the Arctic Circle in Greenland, while other groups, such as the Pacific Eskimo and the South Greenlanders, are accustomed to open water and subarctic conditions. There is a further division between coastal and inland Eskimo, a few groups living primarily on caribou in the Canadian barrens or in Alaska and others exploiting both regions seasonally or through trading relationships.

The Eskimo refer to themselves as *inuit,* "men," and set themselves off from their Indian neighbors who occupy the forest zones in the interior. Tribal divisions exist only as geographical units of people linked by bonds of consanguinity and marriage, which are utilized to establish a complex network of relationships that facilitate movement and trade and maintain a common culture and language over wide areas.

Within the geographical divisions are local groups which are bilaterally organized around kin or family nuclei and which may break up or recombine, depending on the season and the available resources. In the central regions the local group generally formed a winter community under the leadership of some respected person who provided advice but had little authority. Certain hunting techniques, such as catching seal at their breathing holes, required a number of men for greater efficiency; and there were community patterns for the sharing of the catch.

Inside the local band the elementary or nuclear families were the basic units. The husband–wife relationship is the most important bond in most Eskimo regions, and the spouses have complementary roles and duties. In favorable areas, extended families might develop through polygamy; patrilocal residence, or attachment of siblings or affinal relatives to the group. The size of the local group might vary from twenty-five to thirty at a minimum to two hundred or more, but the actual family composition could change from year to year and from season to season.

Within such a community the chief bonds were those of kinship. Life expectancy was low, and both adoption and infanticide were practiced to provide for maintenance and survival of the group. The chief means of social control centered on feuding and revenge, with satirical sanctions playing an important role. As a last resort the community as a whole could take action against a nonconformist by arranging his execution. Along with kinship relations there were a number of quasi-kinship extensions, e.g., seal flipper associations, which involved the reciprocal distribution of food and the spouse-exchange institutions. In some regions strangers who could not establish kin relationships might be treated as enemies.

The kinship systems of the Eskimo, once thought to be similar to the modern American–European system, are now known to be considerably more complex and variable. Thus, instead of a single set of cousin terms, there is a great variety of combinations, some of which have been tentatively correlated with different ecological situations, perhaps relating to the density and distribution of local groups. Little is known with regard to the Greenland communities as yet, but in the Bering Strait region, on Nunivak and St. Lawrence Island, a more sedentary and denser population is associated with incipient patrilineages and a variant of the Iroquois–Dakota pattern of kinship terminology. A similar development apparently took place among the Aleut as well.

In northern Alaska and the Bering Strait region there was a greater development of voluntary associations related to whaling and to the performance of rituals and dances. Leadership was also more institutionalized, and it centered in part on the ownership of boats and ritual paraphernalia. In addition to the community leader, who was generally selected for his personal qualities and supported by his kin group, the shaman, or *angakok*, was also an important figure. He mediated between the community and the world of nature. In the central regions he might "visit" Sedna, the goddess of sea mammals, in times of crisis and persuade her to release her "children" for the welfare of the community. Where such crises were thought to be the result of transgressions, the shaman would obtain public confessions to placate the offended deities. The shaman was also responsible for the maintenance of the health of the community, and he utilized trance states and suggestion to that end.

The Eskimo techniques for survival in the Arctic regions are well known and do not need to be described in any detail. Within this environment a number of ecological adaptations are possible, and the Eskimo have exploited most of them. The central regions offer the severest limitations, and the Eskimo groupings here are minimal and subject to seasonal fluctuation. Incipient divisions into people born in summer and those born in winter existed in recent times for limited social and ritual purposes but never developed into effective dual organization. In the west, and possibly in Greenland, more elaborate social institutions developed. Here there was a greater amount of food available, and populations were larger and more sedentary. Such archeological sites as Ipiutak, at Point Hope, were both larger and culturally more complex than modern settlements in the same region.

This raises the question as to whether the modern Central Eskimo social organization is a simplified version of that developed in Alaska or the basic organization on which the latter has developed specialized social structures. In broadest historical perspective both processes have probably been operative. Early Eskimo–Aleut social structure must have been relatively simple, if we can judge from the situation among the Chukchee and Koryak of Siberia, but the greater elaboration of social organization in the Bering Strait region may well have taken place before the Thule migrations. The expansion of the Eskimo across Arctic America apparently was by small groups and was not conducive to the retention of more specialized forms of social structure. In more ecologically favorable localities more elaborate social systems were redeveloped as food resources permitted. Within Eskimo society there is considerable structural regularity, but it has a built-in flexibility which has enabled it to adapt to some of the severest ecological conditions under which man lives anywhere.

The Northwest Coast. The Northwest Coast culture area is a rich and complex region extending from southern Alaska to northwestern California. Like the Eskimo area, much of this region is oriented toward the sea. The topography is extremely rugged, and the coastal climate, as a result of the Japanese Current, is very wet and mild; a coniferous forest is characteristic of the whole region. Here, in addition to the sea mammals available, the annual runs of salmon offered a food supply comparable to that produced by agricultural technology and allowed in favorable regions both a higher population ceiling and the leisure time for the development of elaborate ceremonies and a unique art.

The Indians occupying the Northwest Coast spoke a variety of languages and had different historical backgrounds but shared to a considerable degree a common culture. In the north the Tlingit and Haida were linguistic relatives of the Athabaskan-speaking peoples of the interior, while the Tsimshian were Penutian speakers, a superstock with many divisions farther south. In the central region the Kwakiutl and Nootka, Wakashan speakers, were linguistically related to the neighboring Coastal Salish, who centered on Puget Sound and had close relatives in the adjacent Plateau area. The Oregon coastal tribes largely spoke languages related to Penutian, but there were Athabaskan-speaking enclaves along the coast as well. Despite this linguistic diversity, the whole region was characterized by similar cultural patterns, attitudes, and values. Even the northwest California tribes, the Hupa, Yurok, and Karok, were closer to the Northwest Coast in culture than to their central Californian neighbors.

The origins of the Northwest Coast peoples and the history of their cultural development are not as yet well known. The distribution of certain culture traits on both sides of the north Pacific suggests occasional contacts in earlier periods, and excavations along the lower Fraser River indicate certain early Eskimoan traits, suggesting a northern origin for the whaling activities of the Nootka and Makah. The initial development of Northwest Coast culture patterns is thought to have taken place in the central region, with later elaborations in the north. Travel in the area is difficult, except by water, and in later times there was much trading along the coast as well as raids for obtaining slaves and other purposes. We now know that much of the elaboration of art took place in the nineteenth century, after the acquisition of iron tools. The fur trade also brought prosperity to this region, modifying seriously the extensive ceremonial exchanges centering on the potlatch. But by the beginning of the twentieth century native life was rapidly disintegrating under the combined influence of missionaries, government agents, and the canning industry.

The population of the Northwest Coast at the time of contact with European explorers is estimated at around 130,000, with a concentration along the coasts and rivers, the hinterland being only sporadically utilized. The tribal groups were relatively large, but each "tribe" generally was divided into a number of smaller local groups, each of which occupied a village center during the winter period, with seasonal shifts in residence during the rest of the year in accordance with subsistence and other activities. Despite the common cultural patterns and values, there was considerable variation with regard to social structure. The northern tribes, the Tlingit, Haida, and Tsimshian, were organized in terms of matrilineal descent; the Kwakiutl and Nootka of the central region were essentially bilateral in descent; and the groups further south emphasized patrilineal affiliations. In all groups, also, there were social divisions: chiefs or nobles, commoners and slaves; but except for the slaves (who were usually captives taken in war), the individuals were ranked on a graded scale in terms of birth position and maintained their status with the aid of their kinsmen.

The Tlingit were divided into matrilineal exogamous moieties called Raven and Wolf (or Eagle), which held the whole society together through intermarriage. In addition, there were some 14 local groups, each with a general territory and a winter village, composed of a number of large permanent cedar-plank houses. Each house had its own name and crest and belonged to a local segment of one of the moieties. The two sets of houses exchanged services as well as wives and were the major units in the great public exchanges of property and feasting known as potlatches, which here centered on death and mourning. While descent was matrilineal, the house was owned and occupied by a group of men related through the female line: this was accomplished by sending boys to live with their mothers' brothers at about the age of eight. The houses on each side were ranked in importance and characterized by the ownership of various crests and privileges and by the control of rights to fishing places, berry patches, and trading activities. Each had a house chief, and the chiefs of the most important houses in each moiety served as community leaders. Neighboring communities were united in part by intermarriages and by local clan segments of the dual divisions, but they would fight with one another on occasion. Beyond the local group there was no formal political organization other than common language and the moiety organization.

Within the village the basic relationships were organized in terms of matrilineal kinship and cross-cousin marriage. The kinship system was a modified Crow type; a man's closest relationships were with his mother's brother and other lineage mates rather than with his father, who belonged to the other moiety segment and was treated as an affine. Through cross-cousin marriage the two sets of households were firmly tied together, and the social and ceremonial exchanges were mediated through the kinship system. Inheritance and succession to office were in the matrilineal line, as was authority. However, through avunculocal residence the men belonging to the matrilineage were enabled to live and work together as a unit and to maintain and operate the corporate assets of the household and local clan.

The Haida of Queen Charlotte Islands had a similar, although slightly simpler, social organization. The Tsimshian were more complexly organized, in that they had four matrilineal phratry groupings, each of which was represented in every village, and an Iroquois type of kinship system. A few groups to the south were also matrilineal in descent, but we have relatively little information about them.

Among the Kwakiutl the social structure was formally quite different. Here the village was the local unit, the southern Kwakiutl having some twenty such "tribelets," but within the village there were smaller bilateral units, called *numayma*, each of which in theory descended from a mythological ancestor. These units, averaging around one hundred members, occupied houses in one section of the village and consisted of related families bound together by strong social obligations. Originally each *numaym* may have been a separate village group, and most marriages were between different *numayma*, although occasionally marriages were arranged within the group to conserve wealth or enhance prestige.

Numaym structure is most easily understood as a set of status positions, each of which had a name, a seat, and a particular rank, as well as being a corporate group owning various types of property and privileges. When a "position" became vacant through the death or retirement of the holder, the *numaym* group could fill it in various ways. Primogeniture was the normal method, but if a woman should be in line her brother or husband might exercise the privileges of the position until her son was old enough.

While membership in the *numaym* was through bilateral descent, residence was generally patrilocal, so that the houses were occupied by related males with their wives, who came from other *numayma*. In such a system an individual might have claims to status positions in several *numayma*, and a man might go to live with his wife's group where advantageous. The early depopulation of the Kwakiutl through introduced diseases and the elaboration of the potlatch system as a result of the fur trade make it difficult to specify the actual operation of the social system under aboriginal conditions.

The ranking of the named positions determined the social ranking of the *numayma* in a particular locality, but changes in social position could be achieved through the potlatch system. The holder of the top position was generally the political leader in the region, and he maintained his position both by distributing surplus wealth to other *numaym* leaders as guests and by receiving gifts in return. If the *numaym* could not support the position, other groups might gradually assume the role through being given gifts first at potlatches. The great elaboration of the potlatch as an instrument of aggression in late nineteenth-century Kwakiutl life seems clearly related to the increased competition for status brought about by the concentration of formerly separate groups around the new trading centers. But the chiefs who engaged in these social conflicts were representatives of the *numaym* groups and required their support to maintain their positions. [*See* EXCHANGE AND DISPLAY.]

The Kwakiutl divided the year into a summer season, in which subsistence and secular activities were dominant, and a winter, or sacred, season, in which the spirit world was important. During the winter season the *numaym* organization gave way to a parallel organization of graded or ranked secret societies, which performed ceremonies and dances and initiated new members. There were some fourteen such societies organized into two sets, relating to land and water respectively, but we have detailed data only on the famous Cannibal Society. The position of members in the winter dance societies corresponded in general with their *numaym* positions, and initiation into the Cannibal Society was restricted to the sons of important chiefs. The rituals involved possession by spirits and their ultimate taming, but the right to be possessed was transferable and the participants in the initiation were repaid with potlatch gifts. Here shamanistic activities have been organized in terms of the Kwakiutl social system.

The Nootka of Vancouver Island, the Coastal Salish of the Gulf of Georgia and Puget Sound region, and the coastal tribes down to the Chinook at the mouth of the Columbia River participated to varying degrees in the social and cultural institutions just noted. The Nootka had an elaborate whaling technology, supported by rituals for the control of the whale and other sea mammals, and their main dancing society was concerned with wolf spirits. The local group structure showed greater stress on paternal relationships, and local groups were often allied by intermarriage. Among some of the Coastal Salish the whole community might live in a single dwelling, with patrilocal residence insuring male cooperation and solidarity. The Chinook took advantage of their strategic position to become traders, and the Chinook jargon became the trading language for much of the region.

Farther south along the Oregon coast there is little information available on the remnant tribes, but Northwest Coast cultural patterns are found among the Yurok, Karok, and Hupa, who live in the last region where the salmon runs are sufficient for supporting social life. Here the villages were small, and they were occupied by groups of kinsmen related in the male line. There were no headmen, but social control was strong and was embodied in a code of regulations which emphasized the relative status of individuals and families. Only the periodic construction of fish weirs and the holding of ceremonies involved larger units than the village.

These variations in social structure suggest that the peoples of the Northwest Coast have had a complex culture history, a suggestion that is reinforced by their linguistic complexity. However, looking at the household as a relatively permanent unit, it is clear that in each region it was occupied by a group of males who cooperated in subsistence and prestige activities and represented a corporate group of some type, regardless of the differences in formal descent. The local groupings also had a similar over-all character, so far as we know them. Only at the "tribal" level were there significant differences in social structure, but since these larger groupings did not operate as political units, they were not in active competition with one another.

Western interior areas. The western interior areas, such as the western Subarctic culture area, the Plateau, and the Great Basin, along with aboriginal California, were inhabited by a variety of culture types which were closely adjusted to ecological conditions but were also considerably influenced by interaction with their neighbors on the Northwest Coast and elsewhere. The basic subsistence patterns centered on hunting, gathering, and fishing, but the availability of food was such that the population densities were relatively low over most of these regions, with the exception of aboriginal California. The social systems were organized on the basis of the family and the band, for the most part, with seasonal movements and variations. Only in California and in a few other localities did more elaborate social structures develop. Political organization above the band level was relatively weakly developed, except among the Yuman-speaking tribes on the lower Colorado River and the eastern Shoshoneans after they adopted the horse.

Western Subarctic. The western Subarctic culture area, which encompasses the interior of Alaska and northwestern Canada, was occupied by groups of Indians speaking Athabaskan, who exploited the fish and game resources of the northern coniferous forest. They numbered less than 50,000, with an extremely low population density. The basic cultural division is between tribes in the Pacific drainage and tribes in the Mackenzie drainage, but there are many variations, particularly on the margins of these areas. The tribal names essentially refer to linguistic units, the local groups being amorphous bands composed of extended family units which might split up or recombine in varying ways, depending on seasonal availability of food and other resources. In the Mackenzie drainage the bands were relatively small and highly mobile. They usually operated under the leadership of an experienced hunter. The nuclear family was important; kinship was bilateral and not widely extended; and residence at marriage was generally matrilocal, the husband working for his wife's parents for a period. In a few of the groups there is some suggestion of preferential cross-cousin marriage, but this may be a relatively late development.

The tribes of the Pacific drainage were able to utilize the salmon runs to increase their food supply, and they also engaged in trading relationships with the adjacent Northwest Coast tribes and to some extent with the Eskimo. The utilization of the potlatch as the mechanism for trading led to the organization of several of the interior groups on the model of their Northwest Coast neighbors, so that they came to have a matrilineal moiety organization and intermarried to some extent with the Tlingit and related groups. In this process some Athabaskan groups were absorbed into Tlingit culture, and the matrilineal moiety patterns and cross-cousin marriage spread as far as the Kaska, east of the divide. But there is evidence that during much of the year these elaborations were in abeyance, as the various bands moved seasonally to exploit limited food resources. Nowhere in the interior were the salmon runs sufficient for sedentary life, and the only Athabaskan-speaking group to reach the sea, the Tanaina of Cook Inlet, shows a series of variations approaching the Tlingit pattern. On the southern margins, Athabaskan-speaking groups have broken off and entered the Plains and Southwestern regions, where they make up the various Apache and Navajo tribes; other such groups are found in Oregon and northwestern California, in such tribes as the Tolowa and the Hupa.

The Plateau. The Plateau culture area encompasses the territory between the Cascades and the Rocky Mountains, which is generally within the drainage systems of the Columbia and Fraser rivers. In this geographical region there is considerable ecological diversity, and the boundaries with neighboring regions are transitional rather than sharp. The population of this region, numbering around 50,000, showed considerable linguistic diversity, with Sahaptin- and Klamath-speaking tribes in the west and south and Interior Salish-speaking groups in the north and east, along with Kutenai-speaking groups, which are not clearly placed. Recent archeological investigations indicate that man has been living in this region for a long period, and lexicostatistical studies of the Salishan languages demonstrate a considerable period of development *in situ*.

The basic culture of the Plateau has been strongly influenced through interaction with Northwest Coast tribes and by the introduction of Plains horse culture, particularly in the nineteenth century. This basic culture type is found in clearest form among the Salish-speaking Sanpoil–Nespelem and their neighbors in the middle Columbia River region. These tribes, numbering only a few thousand, occupied a series of small villages along the Columbia River in open semidesert country. They depended on salmon fishing, gathering of camas roots, and hunting in the nearby mountains. The winter villages were composed of large semisubterranean earthlodges or mat-covered houses which held a number of families, but during the rest of the year the community often broke up into smaller family groups to exploit the root-gathering grounds or fishing and hunting sites.

Two features set off these central Plateau groups from their neighbors—their intense pacifism and their strong sense of individual equality and autonomy. Kinship was bilateral and there was a definite Salish type, but kinship was somewhat subordinated to community activities. Patrilocal residence was general and led to the grouping of related men in the extended households, a process which facilitated their cooperation in hunting and fishing. Root gathering, on the other hand, was the work of women.

The community had a village chief who served as leader and adviser and whose main role was to maintain peace, both between and within villages. He was selected by an assembly composed of all married adults, both men and women, and the assembly met informally at his house to discuss important problems and to achieve consensus. During the salmon-fishing season, a Salmon Chief, who was usually an important shaman, was given power to organize the activities relating to the construction of the fishing weirs and the First Salmon Ceremony, the most important group ceremony. He also supervised the actual fishing procedures, which were in the hands of the men, and the distribution of the catch to the village as a whole.

Beyond the village there was no formal political organization, but both rivalry and cooperation existed in salmon rituals and particularly in the Winter Spirit dances. Guardian-spirit vision quests were highly developed and participated in by both boys and girls. Shamanism depended on successful quests, and the resulting powers were used for both curing sicknesses and the protection of the community. The major expression of the guardian spirit cult came during the winter period, when each village in turn held initiation dances to which other villages came as guests. During these ceremonies the participants imitated their guardian spirits, particularly the bluejay and the owl, and had to be released from their power at the end of the dance.

In the north, the Salish-speaking Lillooet, Shuswap, and Thompson illustrate the results of long contact and interaction with their coastal neighbors. Here there was greater emphasis on chieftainship and status differences, and both warfare and trade were important. But the local organization and subsistence patterns were not essentially different. Other tribes, such as the Wishram, were trading specialists who utilized their strategic position at The Dalles on the Columbia to control down-river trade with the Chinook and other coastal groups. To the south the Klamath and Modoc illustrate the transition from Plateau life to native Californian culture patterns. Here the acquisition of wealth on a broad scale became important, and the "rich man" supplanted the peace chief as a dominant figure. But it was in the east that the major changes took place. The introduction of the horse via the eastern Shoshone around A.D. 1700 led to great changes in material culture and techniques of warfare, as well as in band organization and leadership, for both the Plateau and northern Great Basin tribes. Groups such as the Nez Perce and Flathead took over horse culture on a large scale, and horses were traded all the way to the coast.

One interesting development in the central Plateau region was the organization of intervillage and intertribal "task forces" for buffalo hunting and trading expeditions. Such "task forces" might involve a considerable number of families, and they would travel large distances to reach their objectives. Such activities required adequate leadership, organization, and discipline—characteristics which had been developed originally on a local community basis and expanded as a result of new opportunities.

The Great Basin. The Great Basin culture area, which encompasses the great semidesert and desert interior drainage areas lying between the Sierra Nevada and Rocky Mountains and south of the Plateau to the Colorado River, was occupied almost exclusively by Shoshonean-speaking groups—the Northern Paiute, the Shoshone, the Southern Paiute, and the Ute. This is a region of basins and hills, bordered by higher mountains, with relatively low rainfall except on the higher levels and varied but limited flora and fauna.

The aboriginal population is estimated at 25,000–30,000, giving an extremely low density for the region as a whole and reflecting the paucity of food resources. The poorest areas were in the center—here the Nevada Shoshone moved in small family groups or microbands from valley to range, the women gathering wild grass seeds and roots and the men hunting rabbits and other small game. Piñon nuts were the prized food, but the harvests were erratic and undependable. Rabbit drives and occasional antelope drives required cooperation of several groups and allowed for temporary interaction, including social dances, which were important in courtship, and shamanistic competitions.

The Great Basin has been occupied since the end of the Pleistocene and is one of the regions in which the Desert Culture was developed. Despite the continuity in archeological culture type, however, the modern Indian populations entered the region relatively late—around the beginning of the thirteenth century. In the central regions ecological conditions were so severe as to require a seminomadic existence, but on the margins of the Great Basin more favorable conditions existed, which enabled a more sedentary life and a denser population. Thus the Owens Valley Paiute had mountain streams and more concentrated food resources, which enabled them to live in larger communities, and the Northern Shoshone could exploit the salmon that came up the Snake River as well as larger game in the nearby mountains. In the south, limited horticulture in oasis sites enabled the Southern Paiute to supplement hunting and gathering. And the introduction of the horse, noted above, allowed the Ute and Eastern Shoshone to move out toward the plains and to hunt and raid more effectively. Within the central Great Basin there was a peaceful ethos, and there were no sharp boundaries between linguistic groups, although there was some conflict with neighboring groups along the edges of the area.

The social organization of the Great Basin is interesting, both in terms of its simplicity and in terms of its utilization of marriage to create a kinship network which spread across language lines and formed a communication mechanism that aided in survival. Kinship was bilateral and made considerable use of self-reciprocal terminology. The nuclear family could be self-sufficient on occasion, and the division of labor between men and women was roughly equal. But families were more often united in larger units through various marriage practices, particularly for the winter "villages," which were usually located in some sheltered place adjacent to wood and water.

Brother–sister exchange in marriage was widespread, and along with sororal polygyny and fraternal polyandry, as well as the sororate and levirate, provided new bonds for the enlargement and continuity of small family groups. In the poorer ecological regions, such groups might split up and assemble in different combinations seasonally, but in a few central localities resources were stable enough to allow cross-cousin marriage to develop sufficiently to influence the kinship terminology. Cross-cousin marriage, if practiced effectively, tends to break the kinship network with neighboring groups. The Northern Shoshone, under more favorable ecological conditions, apparently shifted from cross-cousin marriage to pseudo-cross-cousin marriage—that is, marriage with a step-cross-cousin—and thus maintained a wider integration.

Although residence patterns were variable, they were commonly matrilocal. In groups such as the Owens Valley Paiute, where the women came to "own" concentrations of wild food plants, matrilocal residence gave rise to matrilocal bands, a process which very possibly underlies the development of matrilineages among the Western Pueblos to the south. The introduction of the horse led to the development of larger, more amorphous bands, led by a chief, in the eastern portions of the area, but in the central part of the region the horse competed with the Shoshone for grass seeds and was generally killed for food rather than utilized for transport. The practice of horticulture had spread from the south as far as the Great Salt Lake but retreated in the thirteenth century in the face of unfavorable climatic changes. Southern Paiute bands were larger and more sedentary in areas where horticulture continued to be feasible.

The California culture area. Aboriginal California, centering on the great central valley drained by the Sacramento and San Joaquin rivers, but including the coastal ranges and the Sierra Nevada as well as the desert areas to the south, offered a great range of ecological environments, and at the time of contact was inhabited by approximately 130,000 Indians speaking a variety of languages and dialects. Food resources were variable but abundant, the acorn being the major staple, supplemented by fish, small game, roots, and marine resources. As a result, much of the population was sedentary or semisedentary, and the local groups claimed territories within which they exploited the resources and kept out trespassers.

The peoples of the central valley spoke mainly Penutian languages, while most of the groups to the north and west spoke variants of Hokan. In the southern regions the population was largely Shoshonean in speech, continuous with the Great Basin, while Yuman-speaking tribes dominated the lower Colorado River. (We have noted earlier the Athabaskan groups and other groups of northwestern California who are part of the Northwest Coast culture area.)

With the exception of the northwestern California groups and the Yuman-speaking peoples of the lower Colorado, who practiced floodwater agriculture and had a genuine tribal organization, the Californian groups did not differ greatly in subsistence level, social organization, or religious activity. The gathering, grinding, leaching, and storing of acorns and other plant products was time-consuming but relatively simple, and the crop, unlike the piñon nuts in the Great Basin, seldom failed.

The local group normally occupied a permanent winter village but occasionally moved around in its territory during the other seasons. The average size of the group was around one hundred persons, and patrilocal residence led to the families being related through the male line. In many regions the patrilineage became an important descent unit, controlling territory and exercising rights in common, providing a headman, regulating marriage, and owning ritual possessions.

In a few regions the patrilineal local groups were organized into larger moiety structures. Thus the Yokuts, in the central valley, were made up of approximately fifty local groups, each with its own name, dialect, and territory, and averaging about 250 persons to a group. There were two patrilineal exogamous divisions, the "upstream people" and the "downstream people," each symbolically associated with totemic animals. These two groups, represented in each village and family, engaged in rivalry and games and mourned for each other's dead. There were chiefs from each moiety who received presents from the community and were expected to give feasts and property to the people. This pattern extended to the Miwok and neighboring groups. Farther south, some of the Shoshonean-speaking tribes were also organized in terms of exogamous moieties, with animals such as the coyote and the wildcat symbolizing the opposing groups. A few groups, such as the Southern Pomo and the Wappo, apparently had matrilineal descent and a Crow type of kinship system, but most of the peoples in the central valley, including the Wintun, Miwok, and Yokut, had an Omaha type of kinship system, generally associated with patrilineal descent. Some of the Miwok practiced matrilateral cross-cousin marriage, but aboriginal marriage practices did not survive the breakdown of tribal cultures incident to missionization and the gold rush. The kinship systems of the southern California Shoshoneans are not known in any detail, but the lower Colorado Yuman tribes had patrilineal exogamous clans and a distinctive pattern of kinship. Here there are also political chiefs and a feeling of tribal solidarity evidenced in wars with the Pima and Papago to the east. The coastal tribes may have had a distinctive culture, particularly the Chumash who occupied the Channel Islands and utilized plank canoes, but little remains beyond the archeological record and early historical accounts.

Religion in California centered on a complex development of shamanism, but there was some development toward a priesthood in the activities of secret societies, such as the Kuksu cult in central California and the Toloache cult farther south. In the Sierra Nevada region and in southern California the annual mourning ceremony symbolically re-enacted the cremation rites as kinsmen threw goods and clothing on a large fire. In much of southern California the lineage headman acted as a religious leader, performing the rituals associated with a ceremonial bundle belonging to the group. Among the Yuman the song cycles were believed to be received via dreams.

Californian Indians can be viewed in larger perspective as having a specialized development of subsistence and other cultural practices characteristic of the intermontane regions we have been describing, and they also participated to a considerable extent in their peaceful ethos and their lack of social differentiation. The greater availability of food, once the technology had been established, led to more elaborate social systems and religious activities, but cultural achievements—except in basketry—never reached the level of the Northwest Coast or Pueblo neighbors. Even agriculture was never adopted, except in the lower Colorado, although the pattern of winter rainfall may have been the most important factor.

The Southwest. The Southwest culture area, comprising the Colorado plateau and lower desert regions of Arizona and New Mexico, and extending across the Mexican border, is an area of much greater cultural complexity than any of those we have so far surveyed. Here is found, in the well-known Pueblo culture, the highest cultural development north of Mesoamerica, but on the margins and interspersed between the Pueblo groups are hunting and gathering cultures, such as the Apache tribes and the Upland Yuman, some of whom, like the Navajo, have partly adopted agriculture or pastoral activities in more recent times.

The surviving Pueblo groups live in towns and depend primarily on agriculture for subsistence, supplemented by hunting and gathering and sheep-raising. Despite their essential unity as a cultural type they have different archeological backgrounds, speak a variety of languages, and show important differences in social structure. The Basket Maker-Pueblo (Anasazi) archeological tradition developed out of the Desert Culture, as did the Mogollon and Hohokam cultural traditions to the south. These latter cultures were influenced by contacts with Mexico, which gradually introduced agriculture and techniques of pottery making, along with irrigation techniques that made life in the desert practical. The fusion of these culture types in the thirteenth and fourteenth centuries gave rise to the Western Pueblo. The great drought of A.D. 1276–1299, which led to the withdrawal of Pueblo populations from the Mesa Verde and San Juan regions of Colorado and northern Arizona, resulted in migrations both to the western Pueblo regions and to the Rio Grande, where the people became the Eastern Pueblos.

The Upland Yuman-speaking tribes of Arizona, the Walapai, Havasupai, and Yavapai, are essentially gathering and hunting peoples who continue the Desert Culture of the Great Basin, although some groups, such as the Havasupai, have employed agriculture to a considerable extent. (The linguistically related River Yuman, who developed floodwater agriculture along the lower Colorado, have been noted in connection with aboriginal California.) The Athabaskan-speaking peoples of the Southwest, the various Apache tribes, and the Navajo are relatively late migrants from the north, arriving around six hundred years ago and gradually differentiating into the modern groups. The Chiricahua and Mescalero Apache remained hunters and gatherers for the most part, while the Navajo and Western Apache adopted agriculture from their Pueblo neighbors. Later the Navajo and Jicarilla also took over sheep raising and pastoral activities. Farther south, the Pima and Papago and their linguistic relatives in northern Mexico practiced irrigated agriculture and lived in villages along the streams, or in localities favorable for flash-flood farming. The Pima and Papago may be the descendants, in part, of the archeologically known Hohokam.

The aboriginal population of the American Southwest is estimated to be about 100,000 Indians, and today the Indian population is even greater, since the Navajo have increased about eightfold. This is the one region in North America where Indian populations were able to preserve considerable portions of native culture in certain areas, either by developing techniques of concealment or by living in isolated areas.

Pueblo social and ceremonial organization is well known and needs only brief description. Among the Western Pueblo, who speak several unrelated languages, descent is uniformly matrilineal and residence matrilocal. There is little political development, and the chiefs are primarily priests in small theocratic states. The matrilineal clan groups own agricultural land and houses and control ceremonial power. The women are responsible for the household, but the men do much of the agricultural work as well as carry out the ceremonial activities. The ceremonial calendar is organized in terms of a yearly cycle, and the ceremonies are performed by secret societies whose membership cuts across the clan system, although the "owning" clan provides the chief priest and cares for the ritual paraphernalia. Both rain-making and curing activities are important.

The Eastern Pueblo, particularly the Tanoan-speaking groups on the Rio Grande, utilize irrigation techniques and are not so dependent on rainfall. The Tewa villages, north of Santa Fe, are organized in terms of two patrilineal ceremonial divisions, the Summer People and the Winter People, who alternate in control of the community. The cacique is selected for life and with his assistants exercises strong political and ceremonial control; deviants are forced from the pueblo. There are no clans here, and kinship is essentially bilateral; the extended families are based on bilocal residence. While the Tewa are nominally Catholics, the native religious system is still maintained. There is considerable emphasis on curing, and the medicine societies are important, along with societies concerned with hunting, war, and clowning.

The Keresan-speaking Pueblo in part bridge these differences. The western Keresans are related to the Western Pueblo, but the eastern Keresans on the Rio Grande and its tributaries have moved in part toward the Tewa type of kinship pattern. Here a combination of ecological factors and historical factors, including forced migration and forced acculturation under the Spanish, has resulted in basic differences in social organization and social control, while other culture patterns have remained very similar, if not identical.

The various Apache tribes, along with the Navajo, show considerable variation in social structure and ceremonial organization. The Chiricahua and Mescalero were organized in large bands, under the control of headmen, some of whom became famous war leaders in the struggles against the U.S. Army. Each band was further divided into local groups composed of several matrilocal extended families under the leadership of a prominent man. The Navajo and Western Apache were organized in terms of matrilineal descent, and their clans were grouped into phratries. They had some control of agricultural lands. The Jicarilla Apache had dual ceremonial divisions that participated in races and games. Kinship was generally bilateral, although there was considerable variation in detail. The Apache ceremonial system centered on the girls' puberty rite, which was accompanied by the dancing of masked spirits. Among the Navajo these rituals were greatly elaborated in a series of ceremonial chants which combined myths, rituals, and sandpaintings to effect cures and harmony. Political centralization was not achieved among any of the southern Athabaskan tribes, although with the advent of the horse they became famous raiders and warriors until they were defeated and placed on reservations.

The Pima and the Papago, along with their neighbors and linguistic relatives to the south, occupy the deserts of southern Arizona and northern Mexico and subsist by irrigated farming and hunting and gathering. The two groups are closely related culturally and linguistically. Both were divided into patrilineal moieties which had ceremonial functions but did not regulate marriage. The Pima and Papago also had patrilineal clans, but in recent times these have had few functions. In the Spanish period the Pima had a tribal organization, with a head chief selected by the village chiefs, but the Papago village units were autonomous, with a headman assisted by a council of adult males. Harvest festivals were held periodically, and the Papago had a summer rain ceremony which centered on the drinking of saguaro cactus wine.

The development, under the stimulus of contacts from the south, of sedentary living in permanent villages was an important accomplishment, and Pueblo culture has shown a vitality even to the present. But it has been limited to areas where water was available and corn, beans, and squash could grow. Some communities have been in the same locality since before Spanish penetration. The advent of Athabaskan nomads from the north and other invaders disturbed the peaceful character of Pueblo life, but a portion of the Athabaskan-speaking groups, notably the Navajo and the Western Apache, became farmers and pastoralists and adapted Pueblo social structure and ceremony to their own needs and patterns. Today these groups are further adapting to Western ways but are still maintaining their individuality.

The Plains. The Great Plains were occupied by Indian tribes who had developed a distinctive culture, centered on large-scale bison hunting and warfare. The most typical tribes in the High Plains were seminomadic, but the tribal groups in the prairie Plains to the east divided their time between horticulture and hunting and resided in relatively permanent earthlodge villages along streams. The Plains culture area usually is extended to cover both of these regions, but the differences in social structure make it important to treat them as separate areas.

The High Plains were early occupied by post-Pleistocene large-game hunters, but, by the time of Coronado's expedition, 1540–1542, the area was only sparsely occupied by foot nomads who followed the bison herds and by sedentary populations who combined horticulture and hunting. The introduction of the horse via the Spanish settlements in New Mexico after A.D. 1600 greatly intensified cultural activities and drew marginal groups with a promise of greater rewards into the High Plains orbit. In this process tribes from both the east and west, as well as from the north, gave up their earlier cultural activities and became typical Plains tribes. Others attempted to exploit both ways of life, dividing their time between sedentary agricultural life and the excitement of buffalo hunting and plains raiding and warfare.

The High Plains. The High Plains were occupied by some dozen tribes who ranged the short grass steppe east of the Rocky Mountains from southern Canada to the Mexican border. They spoke a variety of languages but had come to participate in a common culture pattern centered on the communal hunting of bison, a tribal organization for war and raiding, and the annual performance of the Sun Dance and other tribal ceremonies. In the north and center were the Algonkian-speaking Blackfoot confederacy, and the Gros Ventre, Arapaho, and Cheyenne, as well as the Siouan-speaking Assiniboin, Crow, and Teton Dakota. In the south were the Kiowa and Kiowa–Apache, and the Shoshonean-speaking Comanche.

All of the typical tribes were divided into a series of bands which camped and hunted independently for much of the year but which came together during the late spring or summer in the form of a tribal camp circle. The bands ranged in size from 150 to 500 persons and varied in composition. Descent was bilateral, although rules of residence were often matrilocal, thus creating matrilocal extended family units within the bands. Change of band affiliation was possible. The tribal organization came into operation during the summer months. Each band had its position in the circle, and a political organization of selected chiefs set up its lodge within the circle. Warrior or military societies drew their membership from all the bands, and ritual bundles and their keepers had special positions. One warrior society was usually selected as the camp police, acting as the enforcement agency for the council of chiefs. Their main task was to organize and police the communal hunts, where violation of the rules might endanger the community food supply. On these occasions they might whip offenders and destroy their lodges and other property.

The oscillation between band and camp circle was closely related to the habits of the buffalo. During the fall and winter the large herds broke up into small groups and scattered widely, seeking shelter and forage. The Plains populations did likewise in order to survive the winter. With the coming of spring the buffalo came together in larger numbers for the mating season. The horse made communal hunting much more effective and enabled larger tribal aggregations during the summer.

The patterns of warfare and raiding in the Plains were also important factors in the size of the groups. Tribes had to maintain control over hunting areas in order to survive, and smaller groups often established symbiotic relations with larger groups, as when the Kiowa–Apache became a band in the Kiowa tribal camp circle, or the Sarsi joined the Blackfoot confederacy. Horses were essential to later life on the Plains and were normally secured by trade or by raiding. Status was acquired through successful raiding and personal combat.

Within the tribe and band, kinship was important and widely extended. The kinship terminology was bilateral and classificatory, with cousins being classed as siblings for the most part. The High Plains tribes were organized in terms of generations, and relatives, especially "brothers," had important responsibilities for aid and support. Marriages were contracted outside the range of known kinship and were generally arranged by the family groups. Although variable, residence was often taken up with the wife's parents or other relatives, since an extended family was more effective than a nuclear family in subsistence activities and protection from raids.

The unity of the tribe was represented by a set of sacred symbols and the performance of tribal rituals as well as in the political activities and the kinship network. The Cheyenne, for example, had four sacred medicine arrows, which were symbolically associated with the tribal welfare. A murder within the tribe polluted the arrows and they had to be cleansed and renewed by the keeper in a special ceremony. The Sun Dance ritual not only dramatized tribal values and activities but was also concerned with the fertility of the buffalo, on which so much depended.

The Prairie Plains. The Prairie Plains area (the Missouri River region and extending into Illinois, southern Wisconsin, and northern Indiana) was occupied by a number of semisedentary tribes who lived in permanent villages and depended primarily on horticulture, with hunting of secondary importance. These groups were organized in much more complex fashion than were the High Plains tribes. Thus the Central Siouans—the Omaha and their neighbors in the lower Missouri region—were organized in terms of patrilineal clans grouped into exogamous moieties. These clans had corporate functions in connection with political and ritual positions, and the dual divisions were symbolically associated with various aspects of nature. In addition, there were societies centering on war and curing, some of which were age-graded. All were involved in the calendric tribal ceremonies. The residence pattern in the earthlodge villages, however, was matrilocal. The women of the lodge cultivated gardens in the bottom lands. But after the planting season, the able-bodied members went on a communal hunt in which they utilized the camp circle, with each clan having a special position and the camp circle reflecting the moiety grouping through patrilocal residence.

Farther north, the Hidatsa and Mandan and the Caddoan-speaking Pawnee and Arikara were organized for the most part in terms of matrilineal descent and matrilocal residence. The Hidatsa and Mandan, Siouan-speaking groups, were also divided into dual divisions which were less well developed, and residence in the earthlodges was matrilocal. The Crow, in the northern High Plains, represents an offshoot from the Hidatsa villages in precontact times who became completely nomadic and gave up agriculture, except for the ceremonial planting of tobacco.

Farther east, the Central Algonkian-speaking tribes—the Fox, Sauk, Illinois, Potawatomi, Miami, Shawnee, and others—developed a social structure very similar to that of the Central Siouans, although not so highly elaborated. Here the populations were early disrupted by Iroquois raids and by the pressures of the fur trade, and life was less sedentary and secure.

The kinship systems of the Prairie Plains tribes were organized in terms of the lineage pattern, with the patrilineal groups having Omaha-type systems and the matrilineal groups having a Crow type. This type of system is consonant with unilineal descent and is related to the corporate character of the clan system, since groups of relatives are classed together in terms of the clan and have common duties and responsibilities.

This brief comparison indicates that the social structures of the two regions contrast at almost every point and reflect, in part at least, the ecological adjustments which have been made. The social structures of the Prairie Plains are more highly specialized and developed, and they are organized for stability and continuity over time. The High Plains tribes, on the other hand, have a much more flexible structure, based on generation rather than on descent, which is more adapted to the uncertain conditions of Plains life. We know that many of the High Plains groups are recent migrants into the area, and it is evident that tribes with different social structures have come to conform to a common type. In the case of groups such as the Crow, we find that they are halfway between their Hidatsa relatives and their High Plains neighbors, and they illustrate the way in which a specialized social structure is remodeled to meet the new social and ecological conditions which require greater flexibility for survival of the society. On the other hand, groups coming out of the Great Basin into the High Plains, such as the Comanche and the Wind River Shoshone, had to strengthen their tribal structure to maintain their positions among the tribes already there.

The eastern culture areas. The Indian tribes occupying the forested regions of eastern North America show considerable cultural variation, but much less than the variation noted for western North America. About half the aboriginal population resided in the east, if we include the Plains populations, and this is the region first colonized by the French and English. Three centuries and more of contact resulted in most of the Indians being killed off, driven out, or removed to western reservations, so that only remnants remain today in their original habitat.

Modern archeology shows the extension of Clovis and some other large-game hunting traditions into this region, following the melting of the ice sheets. This early period was followed by a long Archaic period, in which adaptation to the new forest conditions was established, including the utilization of acorns, wild plants, and mussels and fish. The introduction of agriculture was slow, but it led to an increase in population and archeological cultures, such as Adena, Hopewell, and Middle Mississippi, with elaborate earthworks and art styles reminiscent of Middle America.

The Indians of the region spoke a variety of languages—Algonkian in the north, Iroquoian in the central areas, and Muskogean and Siouan in the south and east, along with some groups not yet classified. Recent evidence that Algonkian is genetically related to Muskogean and the Gulf languages, along with the probability that Siouan and Iroquoian belong together and are distantly related to Muskogean, suggests a common linguistic basis for the general cultural unity of the whole region.

The eastern forest zone is conveniently divided into a number of culture areas, in part on the basis of whether or not agriculture is possible. The Eastern Subarctic encompasses the region north of the Great Lakes and St. Lawrence River and is inhabited by Algonkian-speaking groups who depended on hunting and fishing in much the same manner as their Athabaskan-speaking neighbors to the west. The Northeastern culture area includes the Iroquoian-speaking tribes of the eastern Great Lakes and their Algonkian neighbors. All or most of these groups practiced agriculture, some of them intensively, and social organization was much more elaborate than in the west. The Southeast culture area centered on the Muskogean-speaking tribes in the south and the Iroquoian, Cherokee, and Siouan Catawba in the east, along with marginal groups speaking other languages.

The Eastern Subarctic. The tribes of the Eastern Subarctic region are generally known as the Northeastern Algonkians, and include the Montagnais-Naskapi of the Labrador Peninsula and the closely related Cree to the west, as well as the Ojibwa and their neighbors, the Ottawa and Potawatomi, who resided near the northern Great Lakes and were later forced west and south under pressures from the fur trade and the Iroquois raids. The Northeastern Algonkians numbered about 60,000, the Ojibwa comprising half of this total, with the population density increasing from north to south in terms of the ecology.

All of these groups were organized in small bands which resided together during the summer but which often broke up into family groups during the winter. The Naskapi, on the edge of the Labrador barren grounds, hunted the migratory caribou during the summer and depended on small game and fish during the winter. The Montagnais to the south divided the forested region into "family hunting territories," each of which was utilized by two or three related families during the winter and guarded by rules of trespass and conservation. This system, earlier believed to be aboriginal, is now thought to be a reaction to the fur trade.

Within the small bands, which were under the leadership of a headman, kinship was bilateral and cross-cousin marriage was practiced, although in later times Catholic acculturation caused its partial abandonment in many groups. The kinship system is in accordance with these marriage practices, indicating a considerable period of development.

The northern Ojibwa show a similar kinship base and also practice cross-cousin marriage, but in addition they have developed a patrilineal clan–phratry organization which controls marriage and facilitates visiting but does not greatly affect community life. The southern Ojibwa who were forced west and south, however, have given up cross-cousin marriage and developed a more elaborate clan system, supported by more abundant food resources and a greater population density. The Potawatomi, close linguistic relatives, show a clear shift from this pattern to the Central Algonkian patterns, where the clans become corporate groups and an Omaha pattern of kinship develops, as noted in the Prairie Plains. On the other hand, the Ojibwa who moved onto the Plains developed a Plains pattern of social organization and kinship, giving up both the clan organization and cross-cousin marriage.

Political organization was little developed in this area, and the tribal chiefs were largely the creation of white administrators. Warfare was relatively rare and there is some evidence that the populations moved into this region as a result of raids by the Iroquois and other groups farther south. Religion was simple, being based on shamanism.

Animals were believed to be controlled by deities who had them in their charge and might withdraw them if taboos and customs were violated.

The Northeast. The tribes of the Iroquois confederacy, along with the Huron, Erie, and other Iroquoian groups, occupied the Lake Ontario region, thus separating the Central Algonkians who expanded southward from the western Great Lakes and the Eastern Algonkian tribes who occupied the coastal regions from the St. Lawrence River south to the Chesapeake Bay. The conflicts between the Iroquois and the Algonkians, aided and abetted by English and French rivalries, played an important role in New World politics and did not cease until after the colonies became independent in 1776.

The Iroquois proper—the Mohawk, Oneida, Onondaga, Cayuga, and Seneca—occupied the Finger Lakes region in upper New York State and are perhaps the best-known tribes of American Indians. When first discovered they were as far north as the St. Lawrence, but archeological research has demonstrated a long period of development in their historic homeland. The Iroquois never numbered more than a few thousand, but their skill in warfare and their abilities in political organization led to their control of the whole region south of the Great Lakes and north of the Ohio River.

The Iroquois were organized in matrilineal exogamous clans which were grouped into dual divisions for political and ceremonial purposes. In the early historic period each clan segment, or lineage, lived in a longhouse, with the husbands joining their wives at marriage. Women were responsible for most of the agricultural activities, while the men did the hunting and went on raids or to war. The villages were relatively small and moved periodically as the soil became exhausted.

Sometime around A.D. 1600 the Iroquois tribes established a confederation on the model of their tribal councils. The confederation operated with a council composed of fifty chiefs, or sachems, drawn unevenly from the five tribes, with each position being hereditary within a particular lineage. These chiefs were always male, but they were selected by the women of the controlling lineage and confirmed by the moiety and tribe before installation. The council of the League of the Iroquois was primarily concerned with external affairs, such as war and peace and treaties with the Europeans. Each tribe had its own council for internal affairs. The decisions of the council were arrived at by consensus, after much oratory and debate, since the League could act only when the members were unanimous. The confederation foundered when it was unable to agree on whether to support their British allies or the Americans in the Revolutionary War, and some fled to Canada after the British defeat, where they still reside.

The Iroquois held a number of major religious ceremonies which were calendrical and concerned with agriculture, various wild crops, the curing of illness, and thanksgiving for the new year. The organization of the League was not concerned with religious rituals, with the exception of the condolence ceremony on the death of a sachem, which was conducted by the opposite moiety, and the ritual of installation for a new member. In the period of disorganization following the Revolutionary War and the defeat of Iroquois forces, a new religious movement arose, called the Handsome Lake religion, after its founder. Today this is the longhouse religion of the pagan Iroquois, which is preserved on their various reservations and maintains Iroquois values in the face of general acculturation.

The tribes to the west of the Iroquois, including their linguistic relatives the Huron, were largely decimated in wars for control of the fur trade or forced to take refuge in areas beyond Lake Michigan. We have noted the Central Algonkian-speaking tribes in connection with the prairie Plains. All practiced some agriculture and were divided into patrilineal clans and ceremonial moieties, for the most part. There is some evidence, as for the Potawatomi, that several of these tribes once had a social organization similar to that of the northern Ojibwa, based on cross-cousin marriage and a simple clan system. The increased population brought about by better conditions for agriculture and the need for protection against raids led to the development of a more complex social structure based on corporate lineages and an Omaha kinship system, similar to that of their Central Siouan neighbors. Here there was considerable interaction and borrowing, but the two developments are partly independent.

The Eastern Algonkians had much in common, culturally, but they ranged from the Micmac, Penobscot, and Abnaki, who were primarily dependent upon hunting and fishing, through the Massachusetts and other southern New England tribes, who practiced maize agriculture to some extent, to the Delaware and Powhatan groups in the Chesapeake Bay region, who were intensive agriculturalists. The northern tribes had a social organization much like that of the Northeastern Algonkians, although the bands were somewhat larger and had a greater emphasis on patrilocality, particularly with regard to the family hunting territory groups. The southern New England tribes appear briefly in the early historic accounts, but were wiped out by newly introduced diseases before their social organization could be investigated. Farther south, the Delaware and Powhatan confederacy had matrilineal emphases, a reflection of their position on the margins of the Southeast, but they also had hunting territories.

The Southeast. The tribes of the Southeast occupied a solid block of territory east of the Mississippi and south of the Ohio. In general, they conformed to a single culture type, although the Calusa and other groups in Florida and the coastal tribes west of the Mississippi were nonagricultural and varied considerably from the central groups. The Choctaw, Chickasaw, Creek, and Seminole, along with the Natchez, spoke Muskogean, as probably did the now extinct Calusa, while the Cherokee and Tuscarora spoke Iroquoian, and the Yuchi and Tutelo spoke Siouan. The Muskogean-speaking tribes participated in the development of the middle Mississippi cultural tradition and expanded into the Southeast about a century or two before De Soto. Most of these tribes divided their subsistence activities between agriculture and hunting, and they had developed fairly large populations. Thus the Creeks numbered about 20,000, the Seminole 5,000, the Choctaw 15,000, the Chickasaw 5,000, and the Cherokee about 25,000, with smaller numbers for marginal groups.

The population of each tribe resided in "towns" organized around a ceremonial square. The households were scattered among the agricultural plots rather than being concentrated around the center. Each town had a civil chief and a war chief, and this pattern was repeated for the larger groupings into districts and tribes. In some tribes there was a further division of the towns into "red" towns, associated with war, and "white" towns, associated with peace. Each tribe had a system of social classes as well—chiefs, honored men, warriors, and commoners, the last not active in war.

The social structure of the major tribes conformed to a common pattern, based on matrilineal descent and matrilocal residence. Each tribe was composed of a number of matrilineal clans, usually named after animals or birds, which were further grouped into phratries or moieties. Thus the Choctaw originally had their clans grouped into two great matrilineal moieties, which were exogamous, and the Creek had an even more complicated system. The kinship systems were all of the matrilineal lineage, or Crow type, with extensions based on the clan. In each town the households were occupied by an extended family based on matrilocal residence, the husband coming to live in a residence adjacent to his wife's relatives. The women of the household cultivated gardens in common and gathered fruits and nuts, while the men hunted or went to war.

A number of marginal groups developed variant structures on this basic pattern. Thus the Yuchi had a division of the men into two patrilineal societies, "chiefs" and "warriors," which crosscut the clan system. These societies were symbolically associated with "peace" and "war" respectively, and they were important in both ceremonial and political life. The Natchez had developed a more complex pattern of social stratification and marriage, as well as a theocratic political system. However, few Natchez survived the French period, and we know little as to the details of how their social system actually worked. For the Calusa of southern Florida, a fairly large but nonagricultural group, there is evidence from the Spanish records of a stratified society with elaborate religious activities; this appears to have a different archeological history.

Everywhere there were similar ceremonial systems, centering on rituals in the town square and culminating in the harvest festival and beginning of the new year. In addition to a variety of shamanistic performers, there was a class of "fasting men," or doctors, who had regular instruction in schools and who both cured individuals and protected the community against witches and other supernatural dangers. In the town rituals the social position of the various classes and groups was symbolically expressed, and tribal welfare was emphasized.

There was a dual pattern of chieftainship, with a civil or peace chief who was generally chosen from the same clan as his predecessor, and a war chief, who might also come from a designated clan. Each had a staff of assistants. The civil chief was responsible for town affairs and the settlement of legal disputes, and the war chief was responsible for taking charge when war was decided by the council. War was carried out with much ritual, and captives were sometimes burned or enslaved.

Because of their location between the French, Spanish, and English colonies, the southeastern tribes were subject to intense pressures in the eighteenth century and were forced to organize more effectively or face extinction. Under the leadership of the Creek towns, a confederacy was formed which ultimately included every major tribe in the Southeast, and for a while it was able to act as a unit against the Europeans. But with the retirement of the French and Spaniards the newly established United States, under President Andrew Jackson, began the task of removing all the southeastern tribes to Indian Territory, beginning with the Choctaw in 1832.

In Indian Territory, the Five Civilized Tribes, as the Creek, Choctaw, Chickasaw, Cherokee, and Seminole were called, made remarkable progress under the guidance of Indian agents, missionaries, and army officers, despite all the difficulties and tragedies incident to removal and the later Civil War. Ultimately their lands were allotted, and they became citizens in the new state of Oklahoma. However, a few conservative groups still maintain their language and certain traditional customs, and different groups participate in the Pan-Indian movement, which centers on powwows and social dances.

Summary and conclusions

This brief survey of cultural patterns and social organization in various regions of North America indicates that their development is much more complex than is generally realized. It also suggests that modern social anthropology has developed methods which make possible a more adequate synthesis and interpretation of North American society and culture than we now possess. It has done so not by rejecting the work of earlier students interested in culture history and process but by combining their historical and processual interests with the structural–functional approach of modern social anthropology. Ultimately it should be possible to extend this type of analysis to the whole of the New World and present a reconstruction of culture history that will be satisfying to both historians and social scientists.

Lewis H. Morgan, the pioneer student of American Indian social organization, concluded that all Indians had similar social systems and were at the same stage of evolutionary development. But he was able to survey only the tribes east of the Rocky Mountains and thus had a very inadequate sample. Franz Boas and his students rejected Morgan's evolutionary stages and emphasized diffusion and borrowing as the major processes in culture building. But in doing so they broke culture into units, rather than treating it as a functional system, and the resulting reconstructions of culture history on the basis of trait distributions turned out to be too simple. [*See* BOAS; MORGAN, LEWIS HENRY.]

Over fifty years ago, Edward Sapir, in *Time Perspective in Aboriginal American Culture: A Study in Method* (1916), outlined the procedures for reconstructing culture history, but their implementation required both the collection of new data from archeology, ethnology, and linguistics and the development of new methods and techniques, as well as a more modern point of view. Social anthropology, by initially concentrating on social structures and their functions, and by looking at them as adaptive systems, has developed a more adequate basis for comparison, both synchronically and over time. This method of controlled comparison, as I have called it, utilizes the archeological record, the linguistic relationships, the historical accounts, and the ethnographic data to evaluate the similarities and differences which are found by comparison and to isolate the factors, ecological or social, which may be involved. As the frame of comparison becomes more precise, so do the conclusions. [*See* SAPIR.]

The summary account presented above includes mainly the ingredients for a new synthesis and interpretation of American Indian society and culture, but it also foreshadows some of the results. One important factor has been the growing recognition of the significance of the environment with regard to cultural development. American anthropologists, led by Boas, had rejected environmental determinism in its extreme forms and came to view the environment as essentially neutral, considering the coincidences of geographical area and culture type to be primarily the results of the cultural processes of diffusion and borrowing. The modern view of ecology, which presents society, technology, and the environment in dynamic interaction, has had important consequences for social anthropology in emphasizing the processes of social and cultural adaptation and in setting limits to population size and density. In almost every area we have surveyed, the ecological factors have played a significant role, both directly and through their effects on population. But it is also important to note that societies at different levels of cultural complexity have different relationships with the environment.

The Athabaskan-speaking peoples offer an opportunity to illustrate the possibilities of the methods of comparison and points of view we have been discussing. From their western Subarctic base in interior Alaska and northwestern Canada, which almost certainly represents their homeland in North America, they have migrated at determinable times to the adjacent Northwest Coast, to northwest California and the Oregon coast, to the High Plains, and to the Southwest. In each of these regions, including their homeland, they have developed new adaptations and have interacted with their neighbors to produce new social and cultural forms. Here we can compare peoples with similar social and cultural institutions going into different ecological conditions. Conversely, a close comparison of peoples moving into a relatively uniform ecological area, such as the High Plains, illustrates what happens when groups with different social systems and cultural patterns enter into interaction in a similar environment. In such situations we have some approximation of experimental conditions, and from them we can develop hypotheses to test elsewhere.

Our knowledge about social structures can also be further developed, both by seeing how they change under new conditions and by noting the degree to which variant types can achieve the same ends. Social structures have tasks to perform and they change in predictable ways. Unlike culture patterns, there seem to be a limited number of stable forms of social structure, although there may be considerable latitude in their operation. Here we can learn a great deal by studying what has happened to American Indian societies as they have been placed on reservations or have partially merged with white society. The great amount of documentary data available in the various archives of Canada and the United States is just beginning to be exploited and will ultimately result in the revision of our histories of Indian–white contacts. We can also see, as with the Five Civilized Tribes removed to Oklahoma, that similar changes in social structures have taken place under similar types of acculturation pressure. We can utilize what we learn about regularities of change and the relative effectiveness of different forms of social structure for different purposes in order to further interpret the archeological record. Here archeologists are reconstructing paleoenvironments through the utilization of pollen analysis and other techniques and are providing new data on settlement patterns and household activities. By means of cluster analysis techniques, utilizing computers to develop the various combinations, it is beginning to be possible to present hypotheses as to the nature of residence and descent patterns in prehistoric communities with a considerable degree of confidence and in favorable instances to note changes in such patterns over time. [*See* ARCHEOLOGY, *article on* RESEACH METHODS.]

These and other developments have revived the interest of anthropologists in social and cultural evolution. Morgan viewed the American Indians as essentially at the same stage of evolutionary development, although he had to reduce the Aztecs to an Iroquois-style confederacy to do so. He likewise thought that the stages of savagery, barbarism, and civilization were connected with one another "in a natural as well as necessary sequence of progress" and that this sequence was historically true as well. But he also made an important distinction between social evolution and cultural evolution, although they were interrelated in his grand scheme. Social evolution was concerned with domestic institutions that express the growth of certain ideas and passions and unfold in a certain order, whereas cultural evolution was concerned with the great sequence of inventions and discoveries that were cumulative and progressive, and ultimately led to modern civilization.

The summary data presented above confirms the views of most anthropologists that Morgan's conception of necessary sequences is erroneous. But anthropologists are more interested than ever in social and cultural development and its possible regularities. Archeologists find V. Gordon Childe's reformulation of archeological stages and cultural revolutions useful and stimulating, although the evidence from both Mexico and the Southwest indicating that the domestication of food plants took some 1,500 years to become effective does not sound particularly revolutionary.

The data do suggest, however, that social systems are quite sensitive to new conditions of various types and that it may be possible to generalize these changes in more satisfactory form. Thus G. P. Murdock, in a preliminary survey of "North American Social Organization," concluded that ". . . the North American Indians are basically characterized by social systems of bilateral type and have acquired unilinear systems only here and there, not through any single evolutionary process nor through successive waves of diffusion, but independently in widely separated regions in response to peculiarly favorable local conditions" (1955, p. 95). Edward Spicer and his collaborators, in *Perspectives in American Indian Culture Change* (see Interuniversity . . . 1961), have begun to deal with the complexities of culture-contact situations and the processes of change in terms of documentary and other records. My own view is that the situation is even more complex than Murdock envisages and that there has been an alternation between simple, flexible social systems and more complex and specialized social systems as the ecological social conditions that groups have to adapt to change or are modified. This is a working hypothesis that can be applied to the whole range of New World societies and that can be tested, in part at least, with the more sophisticated archeological methods now being developed; it emphasizes adaptation as a cultural process but suggests that there are recurring conditions which result in similar forms, as well as the obvious borrowings through interaction and contact. The resulting evolutionary sequences will be complex, but they will have an empirical historical base that Morgan did not provide.

FRED EGGAN

[*Other relevant material may be found in* ECOLOGY, *article on* CULTURAL ECOLOGY; ETHNOLOGY; KINSHIP; STATELESS SOCIETY; TRIBAL SOCIETY.]

BIBLIOGRAPHY

Anthropology in North America, by Franz Boas et al. 1915 New York: Stechert.

BENEDICT, RUTH (1934) 1959 *Patterns of Culture.* 2d ed. Boston: Houghton Mifflin. → A paperback edition was published in 1961.

BIRKET-SMITH, KAJ (1927) 1959 *The Eskimos.* Rev. & enl. ed. London: Methuen. → First published in Danish.

CALLENDER, CHARLES 1962 *Social Organization of the Central Algonkian Indians.* Milwaukee Public Museum Publications in Anthropology, No. 7. Milwaukee, Wis.: The Museum.

DOZIER, EDWARD P. 1954 *The Hopi–Tewa of Arizona.* Berkeley: Univ. of California Press.

DOZIER, EDWARD P. 1960 The Pueblos of the Southwestern United States. *Journal of the Royal Anthropological Institute of Great Britain and Ireland* 90: 146–160.

DRIVER, HAROLD E. 1961 *Indians of North America.* Univ. of Chicago Press.

DRUCKER, PHILIP 1955 *Indians of the Northwest Coast.* American Museum of Natural History, Anthropological Handbook No. 10. New York: McGraw-Hill.

EGGAN, FRED 1950 *Social Organization of the Western Pueblos.* Univ. of Chicago Press.

EGGAN, FRED 1952 The Ethnological Cultures and Their Archeological Backgrounds. Pages 35–45 in James B. Griffin (editor), *Archeology of the Eastern United States.* Univ. of Chicago Press.

EGGAN, FRED 1954 Social Anthropology and the Method of Controlled Comparison. *American Anthropologist* New Series 56:743–763.

EGGAN, FRED (1955) 1962 Social Anthropology: Methods and Results. Pages 485–551 in *Social Anthropology of North American Tribes.* 2d ed., enl. Edited by Fred Eggan. Univ. of Chicago Press.

EGGAN, FRED 1966 *The American Indian: Perspectives for the Study of Social Change.* Chicago: Aldine.

FENTON, WILLIAM N. 1940 Problems Arising From the Historic Northeastern Position of the Iroquois. Pages 159–251 in Smithsonian Institution, *Essays in Historical Anthropology of North America in Honor of John R. Swanton.* Smithsonian Miscellaneous Collections, Vol. 100. Washington: The Institution.

FOREMAN, GRANT 1934 *The Five Civilized Tribes.* Norman: Univ. of Oklahoma Press.

GOLDENWEISER, A. A. 1915 The Social Organization of the Indians of North America. Pages 350–378 in *Anthropology in North America,* by Franz Boas et al. New York: Stechert.

GRIFFIN, JAMES B. (editor) 1952 *Archeology of the Eastern United States.* Univ. of Chicago Press.

HALLOWELL, A. IRVING 1937 Cross-cousin Marriage in the Lake Winnipeg Area. Pages 95–110 in Philadelphia Anthropological Society, *Twenty-fifth Anniversary Studies.* Publications of the Philadelphia Anthropological Society, Vol. 1. Philadelphia: Univ. of Pennsylvania Press.

HAURY, EMIL (editor) 1954 The Southwest Issue. *American Anthropologist* New Series 56:529–731.

HAYNES, C. VANCE JR. 1964 Fluted Projectile Points: Their Age and Dispersion. *Science* New Series 145: 1408–1413.

INTERUNIVERSITY SUMMER RESEARCH SEMINAR, UNIVERSITY OF NEW MEXICO, *1956* 1961 *Perspectives in American Indian Culture Change.* Edited by Edward H. Spicer. Univ. of Chicago Press.

JOHNSON, FREDERICK (editor) 1946 *Man in Northeastern North America.* Papers of the Robert S. Peabody Foundation for Archaeology, Vol. 3. Andover, Mass.: The Foundation.

KROEBER, A. L. 1925 *Handbook of the Indians of California.* Smithsonian Institution, Bureau of American Ethnology, Bulletin No. 78. Washington: Government Printing Office.

KROEBER, A. L. 1939 Cultural and Natural Areas of Native North America. California, University of, *Publications in American Archaeology and Ethnology* 38: 1–242.

LONGACRE, WILLIAM A. 1964 Archeology as Anthropology: A Case Study. *Science* New Series 144:1454–1455.

LOWIE, ROBERT H. (1929) 1959 Relationship Terms. Volume 19, pages 84–90 in *Encyclopaedia Britannica.* 14th ed. Chicago: Benton.

LOWIE, ROBERT H. 1954 *Indians of the Plains.* American Museum of Natural History, Anthropological Handbook No. 1. New York: McGraw-Hill.

LOWIE, ROBERT H.; and EGGAN, FRED 1966 Kinship Terminology. Volume 13, pages 377–381 in *Encyclopaedia Britannica.* Chicago: Benton.

MACNEISH, RICHARD S. 1964 Ancient Mesoamerican Civilization. *Science* New Series 143:531–537.

MORGAN, LEWIS HENRY (1851) 1962 *The League of the Iroquois.* New York: Citadel. → First published as *The League of the Ho-dé-no-sau-nee, or Iroquois.*

MORGAN, LEWIS HENRY 1871 *Systems of Consanguinity and Affinity of the Human Family.* Smithsonian Contributions to Knowledge, Vol. 17, Publication No. 218. Washington: Smithsonian Institution.

MORGAN, LEWIS HENRY (1877) 1964 *Ancient Society.* Edited by Leslie A. White. Cambridge, Mass.: Belknap.

MURDOCK, GEORGE P. (1941) 1960 *Ethnographic Bibliography of North America.* 3d ed. New Haven: Human Relations Area Files Press.

MURDOCK, GEORGE P. 1949 *Social Structure.* New York: Macmillan. → A paperback edition was published in 1965 by the Free Press.

MURDOCK, GEORGE P. 1955 North American Social Organization. *Davidson Journal of Anthropology* (University of Washington) 1, no. 2:85–97.

OLIVER, SYMES C. 1962 *Ecology and Cultural Continuity as Contributing Factors in the Social Organization of the Plains Indians.* Berkeley: Univ. of California Press.

OSGOOD, CORNELIUS 1936 *The Distribution of Northern Athapaskan Indians.* Yale University Publications in Anthropology, Vol. 7. New Haven: Yale Univ. Press.

POWELL, J. W. 1891 *Indian Linguistic Families of America North of Mexico.* From the U.S. Bureau of

American Ethnology, Annual Report No. 7. Washington: Government Printing Office.

QUIMBY, GEORGE 1960 *Indian Life in the Upper Great Lakes: 11,000 B.C. to A.D. 1800.* Univ. of Chicago Press.

RAY, VERNE F. 1939 *Cultural Relations in the Plateau of Northwestern America.* F. W. Hodge Anniversary Fund, Vol. 3. Los Angeles: Southwest Museum.

SAPIR, EDWARD 1916 *Time Perspective in Aboriginal American Culture: A Study in Method.* Geological Survey, Anthropological Series, No. 13, Memoir 90. Ottawa: Government Printing Bureau.

SAPIR, EDWARD (1929) 1949 Central and North American Languages. Pages 169–178 in Edward Sapir, *Selected Writings in Language, Culture and Personality.* Berkeley: Univ. of California Press.

Social Anthropology of North American Tribes. Edited by Fred Eggan. 2d ed. (1937) 1955 Univ. of Chicago Press.

SPENCER, ROBERT et al. 1965 *The Native Americans: Prehistory and Ethnology of the North American Indians.* New York: Harper.

SPICER, EDWARD H. 1962 *Cycles of Conquest.* Tucson: Univ. of Arizona Press.

SPIER, LESLIE 1925 *The Distribution of Kinship Systems in North America.* University of Washington Publications in Anthropology, Vol. 1, No. 2. Seattle: Univ of Washington Press.

STEWARD, JULIAN H. 1938 *Basin–Plateau Aboriginal Sociopolitical Groups.* Smithsonian Institution, Bureau of American Ethnology, Bulletin No. 120. Washington: Government Printing Office.

STEWARD, JULIAN H. 1955 *Theory of Culture Change: The Methodology of Multilinear Evolution.* Urbana: Univ. of Illinois Press.

SWANTON, JOHN REED 1905 The Social Organization of American Tribes. *American Anthropologist* New Series 7:663–673.

SWANTON, JOHN REED 1946 *The Indians of the Southeastern United States.* U.S. Bureau of American Ethnology, Bulletin No. 137. Washington: Government Printing Office.

WEDEL, WALDO 1961 *Prehistoric Man on the Great Plains.* Norman: Univ. of Oklahoma Press.

WISSLER, CLARK (1917) 1957 *The American Indian: An Introduction to the Anthropology of the New World.* 3d ed. Gloucester, Mass.: Smith.

INDIFFERENCE ANALYSIS

See UTILITY.

INDIVIDUAL DIFFERENCES

I. OVERVIEW — *Anne Anastasi*
II. SEX DIFFERENCES — *Leona E. Tyler*

I OVERVIEW

The study of individual and group differences in psychological traits is the domain of differential psychology. The measurement of such differences has led to the accumulation of a vast array of descriptive data that is of direct scientific and practical interest. A more fundamental aim of differential psychology, however, is to provide one approach to an understanding of behavior. Differential psychology approaches this task through a comparative analysis of behavior under varying environmental and biological conditions. By relating observed behavioral differences to known concomitant circumstances, we are able to identify the relative contributions of different factors to behavior development. If we can discover why one individual reacts differently from another, we shall thereby advance our knowledge of what makes each behave as he does.

Individual differences in behavior are not limited to the human species; they occur throughout the animal scale. Investigations of animal behavior, from unicellular organisms to anthropoid apes, reveal wide individual differences in learning, motivation, emotionality, and other measurable traits. So large are these differences that the distributions of individual performance overlap, even when widely separated species are compared. When tested with the same learning problem, for example, the brightest rat in a given sample may excel the dullest monkey (see Anastasi 1958, pp. 48–53).

Interaction of heredity and environment

All traits are the result of innumerable and complex interactions between the individual's heredity and his environment. An individual's heredity consists of the genes he receives from each parent at conception. Genes are units of complex chemical substances that affect the course of the individual's development from the one-cell stage to the mature organism. If there is a chemical deficiency or imbalance in one of these genes, a seriously defective organism may result, with bodily anomalies as well as severely retarded intelligence. Certain rare forms of mental deficiency, such as that associated with phenylketonuria, have been traced to defective genes. In these cases, some of the minimum physical prerequisites for normal intellectual growth are lacking. Except for such pathological deviates, however, heredity sets very broad limits to behavior development. Within these limits, what the individual actually becomes depends upon his environment.

Environment includes the sum total of stimuli to which the individual responds from conception to death. It comprises a vast multiplicity of factors, ranging from air and food to the social and emotional climate of home and community and the beliefs and attitudes of one's associates. Environmental influences begin to operate before birth. Nutritional deficiencies, toxins, and other chemical or physical conditions of the prenatal environment may exert a profound and lasting effect upon both physical and mental development. Several varieties of mental deficiency, for example, result from abnormalities of prenatal environment. Such terms as "inborn," "innate," and "congenital" may be misleading because they suggest that all characteristics present at birth are hereditary, which is not the case. Another common confusion is that between organic and hereditary conditions. Mental deficiency resulting from early brain injury, for instance, may be properly said to have an organic but not a hereditary origin.

The research techniques employed to investigate the operation of hereditary and environmental factors in behavioral development may be classified under three major approaches, namely, selective breeding, experimental variation, and statistical studies of familial resemblance. [*See* GENETICS, *article on* GENETICS AND BEHAVIOR.]

Selective breeding for behavioral characteristics has been successfully applied to several species. From a single initial group of rats, for example, it proved possible to breed two strains comprising good and poor maze-learners, respectively (Tryon 1940). After seven generations during which good performers were mated only with good performers and poor performers only with poor performers, virtually no overlapping remained between the distributions of maze scores of the two strains. Later cross-breeding of good and poor performers yielded results indicating that a large number of genes influence maze performance in rats. That the two strains did not differ in general learning capacity, however, was demonstrated by the finding that both strains performed equally well in certain other learning problems (Searle 1949). Other data suggested that emotional and motivational factors may have played an important part in the maze performance of the two strains. There is also evidence that the two strains differed significantly in certain biochemical factors that affected the efficiency of brain action (Rosenzweig et al. 1960).

More recent selective breeding experiments have extended these procedures to other behavior functions and other types of organisms (see Fuller & Thompson 1960). Of particular significance was the development of techniques for measuring individual differences in behavior among such organisms as the fruit fly *Drosophila* (Hirsch 1962). It thus became possible to capitalize on the mass of available genetic knowledge regarding the morphology of *Drosophila*, as well as on such other advantages as the short time span between generations and the abundance of progeny. By these procedures, a strain of fruit flies has been bred that will fly toward a source of light and another that will fly away from it. Similarly, one strain has been developed that tends to fly upward, and another downward, when released in a vertical maze. [*See* EUGENICS.]

A second approach to the heredity–environment problem is concerned with the behavioral effects of systematic variations in experience. This method has frequently been used with animals to study a wide variety of activities, ranging from the swimming of tadpoles and the singing of birds to sexual behavior and care of the young (see, for example, Beach & Jaynes 1954). Many experiments have utilized artificial devices to reduce or cut off sensory stimulation or to eliminate opportunity for the exercise of specific motor functions, in order to discover how far a function will develop in the absence of appropriate experience. Others have followed the opposite approach, providing intensive controlled training in various activities. Significant effects of such prior experiences have been reported for nearly all aspects of behavior, including perceptual, motor, learning, emotional, and social reactions. Through such experiments, many activities formerly regarded as completely unlearned or "instinctive," such as nest building and care of the young by rats, have been shown to depend upon the animal's prior experiences (Beach & Jaynes 1954; Birch 1956). Even when the animal has no opportunity to learn the specific activity in question, his behavior may be influenced by the exercise of other, related functions. [*See* ETHOLOGY *and* INSTINCT.]

Of particular interest to differential psychology is a group of experiments on monkeys demonstrating the effect of prior experience upon learning ability itself (Harlow 1949). Through the formation of learning sets, the animals were able to learn the solution of complex problems because of their prior experience in solving simpler problems of a similar nature. By means of this problem-solving experience, the animal thus "learns how to learn." Other research has shown that animals exposed to a rich variety of perceptual experience during early life are better subsequent learners than those deprived of such experience.

In studies of infants and young children, one group of experiments has utilized the method of co-twin control. In these experiments, one member of a pair of identical twins is given intensive training in some activity, such as climbing stairs or manipulating objects, while the other is retained as a control subject and temporarily prevented from exercising the function under investigation.

The results generally show that, if training is introduced when the child is physically ready for it, progress will be faster than if training is given earlier. Another method is the comparative study of children reared in culturally deprived or psychologically limited environments, such as isolated mountain communities, gypsy caravans, houseboats, and orphanages. Considerable intellectual retardation has been found in all these situations, the retardation becoming more severe with increasing age. Some studies have demonstrated significant improvement in intellectual functioning as a result of preschool education on the part of orphanage children and other culturally deprived groups.

Among adults, it is well established that intelligence test scores correlate highly with the amount of schooling completed. Follow-up studies of groups retested after 10 to 30 years have revealed that individuals who continue their education longer show larger mean gains in intelligence test scores than do those with less intervening education (see Anastasi 1958, chapters 4 and 7).

The third major approach is based upon statistical analyses of familial resemblances and differences. Similarity of performance on both aptitude and personality tests has been investigated for parents and children, siblings, and twins (including both fraternal and identical pairs). In general, the closer the hereditary relation, the more similar the test scores will be. On most intelligence tests, for example, identical twin correlations are close to .90, being nearly as high as the correlations between test and retest scores of the same persons. Fraternal twin correlations cluster around .70; those between siblings cluster around .50, as do those between parents and children. It should be noted, however, that a family is a cultural as well as a biological unit and that a hierarchy of environmental similarity and mutual influence parallels the hierarchy of hereditary relationships. Special studies of foster children and of identical twins reared apart permit some isolation of hereditary and environmental influences, but various uncontrolled factors preclude definitive interpretation of results (see Anastasi 1958, chapter 9).

Physique and behavior

The term "physique" is herein used to refer collectively to all organic characteristics, including anatomical, physiological, and biochemical properties of the organism. The relationship between physique and behavior concerns the differential psychologist for both theoretical and practical reasons. Investigation of the role of physical factors in the development of psychological traits advances our understanding of the causes of individual differences in these traits. Insofar as heredity contributes to behavioral differences, moreover, identification of the physical bases of such differences is an important step in tracing the long and intricate path from gene to behavior. From a practical standpoint, interest in the relationship between physical and psychological traits stems from the possibility of assessing people and predicting behavior on the basis of physical characteristics.

In evaluating the results of any study of the relationship between physique and behavior, we must bear in mind that a significant correlation may mean that the physical condition influences the behavior in question, or that the behavior influences the physical condition, or that both result independently from the common influence of some third factor. [*See* PSYCHOLOGY, *article on* CONSTITUTIONAL PSYCHOLOGY.] The many ways in which physical factors influence behavior may be arranged along a continuum, ranging from relatively direct and rigidly limiting control to highly indirect and flexible relationships (see Anastasi 1958, chapter 5). The former extreme is illustrated by neurological, glandular, and metabolic disorders (of either hereditary or environmental origin) that lead to severe behavioral pathology. The abnormally small brain of the microcephalic, the underactive thyroid of the cretin, and the metabolic disorder of the phenylketonuric are examples of this mechanism. In all these instances, the individual lacks the minimum organic prerequisites for normal intellectual development. Unless the physical disorder can be corrected at an early developmental stage, behavioral deficiencies will result.

A more indirect influence of physique on behavior is illustrated by severe sensory or motor handicaps, such as blindness, deafness, or cerebral palsy, which reduce normal social intercourse and interfere with education. Unless special instructional techniques are employed, these physical handicaps may seriously retard intellectual development and affect personality in various ways. Depending upon concomitant circumstances, however, these physical conditions may lead to very dissimilar effects in different individuals.

At the other extreme of the continuum of indirectness is the operation of social stereotypes. Through this mechanism, the individual's visible physical characteristics serve as social stimuli, which elicit differential responses from his associates. They may thus affect the attitudes he encounters, the opportunities he receives, and the shaping of his own self concept. As a result, his behavior may gradually come to approximate that associated with the stereotype.

The reverse relation, in which behavior influences physique, is illustrated by the powerful shoulder muscles of the swimmer and by the scholar's stoop. Smiles and frowns, too, eventually leave their marks upon the human countenance. Of particular interest in this connection are psychosomatic disorders, that is, physical diseases in whose development psychological factors play at least a contributing part. From another angle, research on immigrant groups has demonstrated that such characteristics as stature and skull shape may be influenced by dietary habits, child-rearing practices, and other culturally determined behavior. Still another example is provided by comparative studies of schizophrenics and normals, in which organic differences may result from differences in emotional stress, degree of activity, nutritional state, and other behavioral variables associated either with the psychotic condition itself or with institutionalization.

The third type of causal relation between physique and behavior is that in which the correlation results from the common influence of a third factor, such as socioeconomic level. The child reared in a superior home, for example, has richer opportunities for intellectual development, as well as better diet, hygiene, and medical care, than does the child who grows up in a city slum or poor rural area. Consequently, some positive correlation will be found between intelligence and a number of physical conditions within a culturally heterogeneous population. The correlation usually disappears, however, when socioeconomic level is held constant (see Anastasi 1958, chapter 5).

Nature and distribution of intelligence

Intelligence has been commonly identified with the intelligence quotient (IQ) obtained on an intelligence test. Such tests do reflect, at least partly, the concept of intelligence current in the culture in which they were developed. Nevertheless, once an intelligence test has undergone the years of preparation and standardization required for its construction, it may tend to freeze a particular concept of intelligence and thereby retard change. Moreover, intelligence tests are designed to meet practical demands within specific settings. Hence they often represent a compromise between practical testing needs and the concept of intelligence that might have developed in the less restricted context of basic research. [*See* INTELLIGENCE AND INTELLIGENCE TESTING.]

Most intelligence tests measure chiefly scholastic aptitude, or that combination of abilities required for school achievement. Modern intelligence testing originated with Alfred Binet's development of a test to assess intellectual retardation among school children. Current intelligence tests have frequently been validated against such academic criteria as school grades, teachers' ratings of intelligence, promotion and graduation data, and amount of schooling completed. High positive correlations between test scores and these criterion measures are regarded as evidence that the test is a valid measure of intelligence.

With regard to content, most intelligence tests are heavily weighted with verbal aptitudes. To a lesser extent, they may also sample arithmetic skills, quantitative reasoning, and memory. Different intelligence tests, moreover, may cover somewhat different combinations of abilities. Nonlanguage and performance tests, for instance, often make much heavier demands upon spatial visualization, perceptual speed and accuracy, and abstract reasoning than do the usual verbal-type tests. It is largely for this reason that an IQ should always be accompanied by the name of the test from which it was derived. [*See* ACHIEVEMENT TESTING.]

Following the widespread application of intelligence tests, psychologists soon recognized that certain aptitudes remained largely unmeasured by these tests. The increasing participation of psychologists in vocational counseling and in the screening and classification of industrial and military personnel highlighted the need for tests of other aptitudes. As a result, so-called special aptitude tests were developed to supplement general intelligence tests in mechanical, clerical, musical, artistic, and other aptitude areas. [*See* APTITUDE TESTING *and* VOCATIONAL INTEREST TESTING.]

At the same time, clinical psychologists working intensively with individual cases were impressed with the large intraindividual differences often found from one intelligence test to another, or among different parts of the same intelligence test. Thus an individual might score consistently better on performance than on verbal tests; or within the same intelligence test, he might do well on numerical and poorly on verbal tasks.

Concurrently, basic research on the nature of intelligence was being conducted by the techniques of factor analysis. Essentially, these techniques involve statistical analysis of the intercorrelations among test scores in the effort to discover the smallest number of independent factors that can account for their interrelations. Among the aptitudes or "factors" thus identified are verbal comprehension, word fluency, arithmetic skills, quantitative reasoning, perceptual speed, spatial visualization, and mechanical comprehension. Through factor analysis, what had formerly been called intelligence could itself be subdivided into relatively independent aptitudes, and these aptitudes could be recombined with some of those underlying special aptitude tests to provide a more comprehensive picture of intelligence.

Later factor-analytic research has been extending the concept of intelligence in our culture to include creativity, originality, and divergent thinking, in contrast to the comprehension and retention skills emphasized in traditional intelligence tests (Guilford 1959). Several research projects concerned with creativity have been exploring new testing areas and developing new types of tests suitable for measuring divergent thinking in both children and adults. Although these new test materials have not been incorporated to any appreciable extent in commercially available intelligence tests, it is likely that they will be utilized increasingly in the intelligence tests of the future. [*See* FACTOR ANALYSIS.]

Recognizing that the IQ is a composite measure and that its nature shifts with changing concepts of intelligence, we may nevertheless inquire into its distribution in the population. In intelligence, as in all psychological traits, individuals do not fall into sharply separated categories or types. Instead they vary by degree along a continuous scale. Most psychological tests are constructed so as to conform with the bell-shaped normal probability curve, with the greatest clustering of persons near the center of the range and a gradual decrease in numbers as the extremes are approached. First derived by mathematicians in their study of probability, the normal curve is obtained whenever the variable measured is the result of a very large number of independent and equally weighted factors. In view of the extremely large number of genes and of environmental factors that contribute to the development of intelligence in the general population, the normal curve is generally accepted as the most appropriate model for the distribution of intelligence.

The mentally deficient and the gifted represent the lower and upper extremes of the distribution of intelligence. Because the distribution is continuous, there is no clearly defined separation between these groups and the normal. In terms of intelligence test performance, mental deficiency is customarily identified with IQ's below 70. About 2 to 3 per cent of the general population fall in this range. Decisions regarding the disposition and treatment of individual cases ought, of course, to take much more than an IQ in account. They should be based upon a comprehensive study of the individual's intellectual level, social competence, educational history, physical condition, familial situation, and other pertinent data. [*See* MENTAL RETARDATION.]

With regard to etiology, one distinction is that between unifactor and multifactor mental deficiency. Unifactor cases are extreme deviates; they manifest both organic pathology and intellectual defect, which are traceable to a single defective gene or to a major environmental disturbance. Multifactor defectives, on the other hand, represent merely the lower end of the normal distribution of intelligence. They exhibit varying degrees of deficiency, depending upon the particular combination of adverse hereditary and environmental factors in each case. Since the unifactor defectives are added to the multifactor defectives at the lower end of the distribution, the frequency of low IQ's should exceed that expected in a mathematically derived normal probability curve. Large-scale surveys of the distribution of IQ's in various populations do, in fact, reveal such a deviation from normality at the low end of the scale (Dingman & Tarjan 1960; Roberts 1952).

The intellectually gifted have been investigated by many techniques and from many points of view. In the monumental study conducted by Terman and his associates at Stanford University, approximately one thousand California school children with Stanford–Binet IQ's of 140 or higher were intensively examined and followed up through adulthood (Terman & Oden 1959). Slightly more than 1 per cent of the general population obtain IQ's at this level. The results of the Stanford study, which have been corroborated in other studies conducted elsewhere, revealed the gifted child as typically successful in school, healthy, emotionally well-adjusted, having wide interests, and excelling his average classmates in nearly every trait measured. Although there were individual exceptions, the group as a whole clearly dispelled the early stereotype of the intellectually gifted child as weak, sickly, timid, and narrowly specialized. As they grew into maturity, the California gifted children amply fulfilled their youthful promise in outstanding adult achievements. [*See* TERMAN; CREATIVITY, *article on* GENIUS AND ABILITY.]

Since the middle of the twentieth century, the most conspicuous development in the investigation of superior deviates is to be found in research on creativity with both adults and children (Golann 1963). Although such research is yielding a wealth of data with important practical and theoretical implications, we must guard against exaggerating the distinction between creativity and intelligence as traditionally measured. To be sure, neither a high IQ on current intelligence tests nor high academic achievement is identical with creativity. These qualifications do not ensure that an individual will make outstanding contributions. On the other hand, they do not preclude creativity, nor are they completely unrelated to it. Traditional intelligence tests show a moderate but significant positive correlation with measures of creativity. Rather than differentiating between intelligence and creativity, moreover, we need to broaden the concept of intelligence to include newly identified creative traits (Guilford 1959). [*See* CREATIVITY, *article on* PSYCHOLOGICAL ASPECTS.]

Sex differences

An important fact about all comparisons among human groups is that individual differences within each group are far greater than average differences between groups. As a result, the distributions of the groups overlap to a marked degree. Even when the means of two groups differ by a large and statistically significant amount, individuals can be found in the low-scoring group who surpass individuals in the high-scoring group. Hence an individual's membership in a particular group is a very unreliable indicator of his standing in most psychological traits. Group averages need to be evaluated with reference to some measure of overlap of total distributions, such as the proportion of one group that reaches or exceeds the median of the other.

Another methodological problem in group comparisons arises from the use of unrepresentative samples, in which selective factors may have operated differentially for the two populations. Insofar as more boys than girls drop out of school, for example, a comparison of the intelligence test performance of high school boys and girls will yield a mean sex difference in favor of boys. This difference would disappear, however, if we were to include drop outs, who tend to score near the low end of the distribution. A similar error in the opposite direction is illustrated by surveys of institutions for mental defectives, which generally show an excess of males. Although once regarded as evidence of the greater incidence of mental deficiency among males, these findings were later traced to selective admission policies. For a variety of social and economic reasons, mentally defective women are more likely to remain in the community than are males of the same intellectual levels.

The use of global scores on intelligence tests may also be misleading in the study of sex differences. In the construction of several intelligence tests, such as the Stanford–Binet, sex differences have been ruled out by omitting items that favored either sex. Even when this is not done, a composite score on a heterogeneous test may obscure genuine group differences in specific abilities.

Psychological test surveys in contemporary Western cultures have demonstrated significant mean differences between the sexes in a number of aptitudes and personality traits (see Anastasi 1958, chapter 14). Males as a group excel in speed and coordination of gross bodily movements, spatial orientation, mechanical comprehension, and arithmetic reasoning. Females excel in manual dexterity, perceptual speed and accuracy, memory, numerical computation, verbal fluency, and other tasks involving the mechanics of language. Among the principal personality differences found between the sexes are the greater aggressiveness, achievement drive, and emotional stability of the male and the stronger social orientation of the female.

Most investigations of sex differences yield only descriptive data about existing differences between men and women within a given culture. The origins of such differences must be sought in the complex interactions of cultural and biological factors. Although living in the same homes, boys and girls in most societies are reared in different subcultures. In countless ways, they receive differential treatment from parents, other adults, and age peers. They are dressed differently, given different toys, taught different games, and expected to behave differently in many situations. The personalities of mother and father are themselves important factors in the child's developing concept of sex roles, providing models of what is expected of each sex in the particular culture.

From a biological viewpoint, the different parts men and women play in the reproductive function undoubtedly contribute to sex differentiation in psychological development. Thus the long period of child bearing and child rearing, which falls biologically upon the female, has far-reaching implications for sex differences in interests, attitudes, emotional traits, vocational goals, and achievement. Sex differences in aggressiveness and dominance are associated with the greater body size, strength, and physical endurance of the male, as well as with the presence of male sex hormones.

Another significant sex difference is to be found in the developmental acceleration of girls. Not only do girls reach puberty earlier than boys, but throughout childhood they are further advanced toward their own adult status in all physical traits. The psychological effects of this sex difference in developmental rate probably vary widely from trait to trait. In infancy, the developmental acceleration of girls may be an important factor in their more rapid acquisition of language and may give them a head start in verbal development as a whole. These few examples suffice to illustrate the varied and intricate mechanisms whereby biological and cultural differences between the sexes interact to produce differences in aptitudes, interests, and other psychological traits.

Race and culture

The biological concept of race refers to populations that differ in the relative frequency of certain genes. Races are formed when a group becomes relatively isolated, for either geographic or social reasons, so that marriage among its members is more common than marriage with outsiders (see Dobzhansky 1962, chapter 10). The very isolation that leads biologically to race formation also fosters cultural differentiation. Hence the populations that have been compared in research on race differences have usually differed in their cultural environments as well. Under these conditions, any differences in aptitudes or personality traits found between racial groups cannot be unequivocally attributed to racial or genetic factors.

In an effort to circumvent cultural differences among groups, some investigators have utilized so-called culture-free tests (see Anastasi 1958, pp. 561–569; 1961, chapter 10). These tests have been especially developed for comparative studies of persons reared in different cultures. They not only undertake to eliminate language barriers, but they also employ content presumably common to all cultures. Parenthetically, it should be noted that the term "culture-free test" is a misnomer. Since a psychological test is only a standardized measure of a behavior sample, any condition that influences behavior will be reflected in test scores. It is theoretically possible to construct a test that presupposes only experiences *common* to different cultures, but not one that is *free* from cultural influences.

Even this theoretical goal, however, has not been attained by any available test; each test still favors certain cultural groups and handicaps others. Every psychological test inevitably draws most heavily upon the information, skills, work habits, and attitudes fostered by the culture in which it was developed. The difference between "culture-free" and other tests is merely one of degree. Even the use of paper and pencil or the presentation of abstract tasks having no immediate practical significance will tend to discriminate against some cultures or subcultures. Other cultural differences include intrinsic interest of test content, degree of familiarity with pictorial or diagrammatic representation, rapport with the examiner (especially one of a different race), motivation to perform well on a test, competitive desire to excel others, and previously developed problem-solving attitudes.

The analysis of population differences has also been approached through experimental designs that permit some isolation of biological and cultural influences. Test performance of hybrid, or racially mixed, groups, has been investigated for this purpose. It has been argued that, if one race is intellectually superior to another because of genetic factors, the hybrid offspring of both races should be intermediate in intelligence. Genetically, this hypothesis is questionable, since it assumes complete linkage between the genes determining skin color or other racial indices and the genes determining intelligence. With incomplete linkage, the correlation between racial characteristics and intelligence would disappear within a few generations of crossbreeding. The results are further complicated by the fact that race mixture is usually selective within either or both races, as well as by the tendency toward greater cultural assimilation of hybrids. In groups that are fairly homogeneous in their assimilation of the dominant culture, the correlation between test score and extent of race mixture is negligible (e.g., Rohrer 1942).

Another group of studies concerns changes in the comparative test performance of racial groups with age. Several investigations of American Negro infants and preschool children, for example, revealed little or no retardation in terms of white norms (Anastasi & D'Angelo 1952; Brown 1944; Gilliland 1951; Pasamanick 1946). Tests of school-age children conducted in the same areas and periods, on the other hand, showed significant mean retardation that increased with age. These findings are similar to those obtained with other culturally deprived groups. The age decrement has been ascribed to the cumulative effects of deficient environments and to the increasing inadequacy of such environments to meet the expanding intellectual needs of the growing child. From a broader viewpoint, such an age decrement in relation to test norms may be said to occur when a test demands intellectual functions not fostered in a particular culture or subculture (Levinson 1961).

A third approach is based upon a comparison of samples of the same race reared in different environments. In general, such studies have yielded larger differences in test performance among subgroups of a given race living in different milieus than among different racial groups living under more nearly similar conditions (see Anastasi 1958, pp. 584–592). That the regional differences found within a racial population are associated with cultural differences rather than with selective migration has been demonstrated in several studies. Of particular relevance are the results of a longitudinal investigation of American Negro children who had moved from an area with poorer school facilities to one with better school facilities (Lee 1951). Mean intelligence test scores of these children improved significantly with increasing length of residence in the educationally more favorable area.

Despite a mass of descriptive data on psychological differences among races, research on the origins of such differences is meager and beset with methodological difficulties. In the light of available knowledge, only a few conclusions can be drawn with confidence. First, no biological basis has as yet been identified for any existing psychological differences among races. Second, there is considerable evidence, both from racial studies and from other types of investigations in differential psychology, showing the part played by cultural factors in producing the sort of behavioral differences commonly found among racial groups. Finally, in all psychological traits, the range of individual differences within each race is far greater than mean differences between races.

ANNE ANASTASI

[*Other relevant material may be found in* DEVELOPMENTAL PSYCHOLOGY; INTELLECTUAL DEVELOPMENT; PERSONALITY, *article on* PERSONALITY DEVELOPMENT; TRAITS.]

BIBLIOGRAPHY

ANASTASI, ANNE 1958 *Differential Psychology: Individual and Group Differences in Behavior.* 3d ed. New York: Macmillan. → First published in 1937.

ANASTASI, ANNE 1961 *Psychological Testing.* 2d ed. New York: Macmillan. → First published in 1954.

ANASTASI, ANNE; and D'ANGELO, RITA Y. 1952 A Comparison of Negro and White Preschool Children in Language Development and Goodenough Draw-a-Man IQ. *Journal of Genetic Psychology* 81:147–165.

BEACH, FRANK A.; and JAYNES, JULIAN 1954 Effects of Early Experience Upon the Behavior of Animals. *Psychological Bulletin* 51:239–263.

BIRCH, HERBERT G. 1956 Sources of Order in the Maternal Behavior of Animals. *American Journal of Orthopsychiatry* 26:279–284.

BROWN, FRED 1944 An Experimental and Critical Study of the Intelligence of Negro and White Kindergarten Children. *Journal of Genetic Psychology* 65:161–175.

DINGMAN, HARVEY F.; and TARJAN, GEORGE 1960 Mental Retardation and the Normal Distribution Curve. *American Journal of Mental Deficiency* 64:991–994.

DOBZHANSKY, THEODOSIUS 1962 *Mankind Evolving: The Evolution of the Human Species.* New Haven: Yale Univ. Press.

FULLER, JOHN L.; and THOMPSON, W. ROBERT 1960 *Behavior Genetics.* New York: Wiley.

GILLILAND, ADAM R. 1951 Socioeconomic Status and Race as Factors in Infant Intelligence Test Scores. *Child Development* 22:271–273.

GOLANN, STUART E. 1963 Psychological Study of Creativity. *Psychological Bulletin* 60:548–565.

GUILFORD, J. P. 1959 Three Faces of Intellect. *American Psychologist* 14:469–479.

HARLOW, HARRY F. 1949 The Formation of Learning Sets. *Psychological Review* 56:51–65.

HIRSCH, JERRY 1962 Individual Differences in Behavior and Their Genetic Bases. Pages 3–23 in Eugene L. Bliss (editor), *Roots of Behavior: Genetics, Instinct, and Socialization in Animal Behavior.* New York: Harper.

LEE, EVERETT S. 1951 Negro Intelligence and Selective Migration: A Philadelphia Test of the Klineberg Hypothesis. *American Sociological Review* 16:227–233.

LEVINSON, BORIS M. 1961 Subcultural Values and IQ Stability. *Journal of Genetic Psychology* 98:69–82.

PASAMANICK, BENJAMIN 1946 A Comparative Study of the Behavioral Development of Negro Infants. *Journal of Genetic Psychology* 69:3–44.

ROBERTS, JOHN A. FRASER 1952 The Genetics of Mental Deficiency. *Eugenics Review* 44:71–83.

ROHRER, JOHN H. 1942 The Test Intelligence of Osage Indians. *Journal of Social Psychology* 16:99–105.

ROSENZWEIG, MARK R.; KRECH, DAVID; and BENNETT, EDWARD L. 1960 A Search for Relations Between Brain Chemistry and Behavior. *Psychological Bulletin* 57:476–492.

SEARLE, LLOYD V. 1949 The Organization of Hereditary Maze-brightness and Maze-dullness. *Genetic Psychology Monographs* 39:279–325.

TERMAN, LEWIS M.; and ODEN, MELITA 1959 *Genetic Studies of Genius.* Volume 5: The Gifted Group at Mid-life: Thirty-five Years' Follow-up of the Superior Child. Stanford Univ. Press.

TRYON, ROBERT C. 1940 Genetic Differences in Maze-learning Ability in Rats. Volume 1, part 1, pages 111–119 in National Society for the Study of Education, *39th Yearbook.* Bloomington, Ill.: Public School Publishing Company.

II
SEX DIFFERENCES

Since the beginning of the twentieth century, psychological sex differences have been the subject of continuous research. The objectives and orientation of this research, however, have shifted several times. At the beginning, the feminist movement generated interest in the question of whether the intelligence of women was or was not equal to that of men. What most investigators hoped to find was scientific evidence for the equality of the sexes.

As techniques for measuring aspects of personality as well as mental abilities were developed in the 1920s and 1930s, more and more comparisons of male and female groups on nonintellectual characteristics were reported. Psychoanalysis was becoming increasingly influential during this period, and personality theorists drew from the writings of Freud and his followers hypotheses about what sex differences should be explored through research. The social objectives were to prevent neurosis and improve relationships between the sexes through understanding the differing emotional needs and ways of expression in men and women. Some investigators also hoped during this period—roughly the second quarter of the century—to construct a scale for measuring *general* masculinity or femininity that would be accurate enough to differentiate between persons of the same sex. They thought that such a scale would have many practical uses, such as the assignment of individuals to suitable occupations and the diagnosis of homosexual trends.

During the 1950s the emphasis shifted once more. Investigators became very much aware of sex *roles*. Questions about when and how a young child learns what these roles are and develops preferences and patterns of behavior in accordance with them began to seem very important. The concept of *identification*, as interpreted in psychoanalytic writings and in other types of personality theory, became the focus of much research effort. The objectives of the research of this period were not just to understand sex differences for their own sake, but to utilize information about this highly visible aspect of personality development as a source of clues about the developmental processes through which many other aspects of personality may have come into existence.

One persistent question has stimulated research interest throughout all these periods: why have women's achievements failed to match those of men? Why are there so few outstanding female artists, scientists, or statesmen? As the processes of rapid social change have produced an occupational situation in which highly trained professional persons are in demand and unskilled workers are needed in fewer and fewer numbers, this problem has taken on a new urgency. Findings from all the main types of research on differences in abilities, personality traits, roles, and development have been brought to bear on this issue.

Sex differences in abilities

Intelligence. As sophistication in mental-testing procedures increased over the years, it became apparent that the question investigators first asked about the differences in intelligence between the sexes is unanswerable, at least by present methods of measurement. Hundreds of studies were made, most of them using students as subjects. Some reported male superiority, some female superiority, and some no significant differences. Analyzing these conflicting results, one could see that some of the discrepancies arose from selective factors in the groups tested. But, more important, discrepancies were related to the type of intelligence test the investigators happened to use. Some tests consistently gave girls a slight advantage; others favored boys.

From many sources, evidence was accumulating that intelligence tests of all varieties do not and cannot measure pure *native* capacity. Although genetic differences in intellectual potential undoubtedly exist, the only way we have to *test* a person is to ask him questions or give him problems to solve. His performance in such a situation always reflects the experience he has undergone as well as his native capacity. It is, therefore, only natural that males show superiority in dealing with some kinds of questions and tasks and that females show superiority in dealing with others. In order to produce intelligence tests that will be equally fair to members of both sexes, psychologists try to include approximately the same number of both kinds of items. McNemar (1942) has explained how this was done in developing the Terman–Merrill revision of the Stanford–Binet test. When this kind of test is given to samples of the population that are really representative, sex differences in over-all score or IQ turn out to be negligible. The two major surveys undertaken by the Scottish Council for Research in Education in 1939 and 1949, in which all children in the country who had been born on certain dates were tested, revealed almost identical mean IQ's the first time and a 4-point difference in favor of boys the second time. This 4-point difference, although statistically significant for this large number of cases, appears not to have much practical significance in view of the fact that the group test given in the same survey produced a 2-point difference in favor of girls. [*See* ACHIEVEMENT TESTING; INTELLIGENCE AND INTELLIGENCE TESTING.]

Verbal, mathematical, and spatial abilities. More meaningful than the question of whether one sex is more intelligent than the other is the question of what special abilities are related to sex. Much of the research on this problem is summarized by Terman and Tyler (1954). Females appear to excel in verbal ability, when this is defined as fluency—the *use* of words rather than the comprehension of verbal meanings. Females tend to talk more, to read faster, and to be less susceptible to reading and speech difficulties. They do not typically score higher than boys on vocabulary tests, and one study of a large and representative sample of English children from 5 to 15 years of age showed consistent although small differences in favor of boys on four oral vocabulary tests from leading intelligence scales (Dunsdon & Roberts 1957).

Males consistently score higher than females on mathematical ability, when this is defined as reasoning or problem solving rather than computational skill. There also is a large and significant difference in favor of males on tests of spatial visualization. These differences, especially the one in mathematics, partially explain why males tend to do better in science. In the annual science talent search carried on each year in the United States, high school male applicants score significantly higher on the achievement test than female applicants, despite the fact that the girls who apply are much more highly selected than the boys who apply (Edgerton & Britt 1947).

Vocational aptitudes. Vocational psychologists have found that on tests of aptitude for particular kinds of work, females score significantly higher for clerical aptitude and dexterity, males significantly higher for mechanical aptitude. Aptitude tests for art and music tend to give higher scores for females, but this may be because more girls than boys are exposed to art and music lessons as they grow up.

Two general findings must be kept in mind if misinterpretations of these differences in ability are to be avoided. One is that in all such comparisons there is a large amount of overlap between the distributions for the two sexes. In making any practical decision about job placement, admission to professional schools and training programs, and the like, one must judge on the basis of the individual's own ability rather than on the basis of sex. Individual differences far outweigh sex differences. The other general finding from comparisons of sex groups at different ages is that most of these varieties of differences in ability do not show up until the elementary school years or later. With regard to mathematical ability, for example, girls at the kindergarten and preschool levels do as well as boys in counting and identifying numbers. Sex differences become more apparent with increasing education, even when it is coeducation. [*See* APTITUDE TESTING.]

Cognitive style. One promising line of research has identified what may be important sex differences in *cognitive style.* Witkin and others (1954) discovered that females are less able than males to disregard the visual field in which a perceptual pattern they are trying to grasp is embedded. The difference was apparent on tests in which the subject was required to straighten a tilted chair in a tilted room and thus to separate kinesthetic cues from visual distractions; the difference was also apparent on the purely visual embedded-figures test. This tendency toward what Witkin labeled *field-dependence* was related to personality characteristics having to do with passive acceptance rather than active coping with one's environment. Sandström (1953) reported a somewhat similar phenomenon. Women are less accurate than men in pointing to a luminous spot of light in a completely darkened room and are more likely than men to show disoriented behavior. In problem-solving experiments, the difficulty females have been shown to experience in *restructuring* the problem situation would appear to involve this same factor of field-dependence.

Interests, motives, and personality

All of the evidence seems to point to a conclusion that the sexes differ far more in their general orientation to life than they do in abilities.

Interests and values. Strong (1943) has presented the most comprehensive findings with regard to interest differences, findings that are corroborated by other research on the topic. Males respond with a higher degree of preference than do females to interest items of the following kinds: (1) mechanical and scientific activities; (2) physically strenuous, adventuresome activities; (3) legal, political, and military occupations; (4) selling; (5) certain forms of entertainment, such as smokers, "roughhouse" initiations, and chess; (6) certain miscellaneous aspects of work, such as outdoor activity rather than indoor and self-employment rather than working for others. The distinctly feminine interests are seen in responses that indicate greater preference for the following kinds of items: (1) musical, artistic activities; (2) literary activities; (3) certain kinds of persons, especially the unfortunate and disagreeable; (4) certain forms of entertainment, such as fortunetelling, full-dress affairs, and social-problem movies; (5) clerical work; (6) teaching; (7) social work; (8) merchandise, that is, looking at shop windows, displaying merchandise, etc. Strong constructed a masculinity–femininity scale for the Vocational Interest Blank made up of these discriminating items.

Although representative groups of men and women reveal different patterns of scores on the occupational scales of the Strong and other interest tests, there is some evidence that highly selected groups of women in predominantly male occupations, such as medicine and life insurance selling, obtain interest scores very similar to those of their male colleagues. Women, in general, show a standard pattern of occupational interest scores.

The large majority of them receive their only high scores on the office worker, stenographer–secretary, and housewife scales of the Strong Vocational Interest Blank for women. [*See* VOCATIONAL INTEREST TESTING.]

When groups of men and women are compared on the Allport–Vernon (now Allport–Vernon–Lindzey) test of values, men obtain significantly higher scores on theoretical, economic, and political values; this indicates that they are more oriented than women toward abstract ideas, practical success, and power. Women receive higher scores on aesthetic, social, and religious values; this indicates that they are oriented more toward art, religion, and social welfare.

Studies of children. Numerous studies of children's interests using many observational and assessment techniques reveal marked interest differences even at any early age. Boys engage more in active games and vigorous physical activity and prefer tales of adventure and violent action in books and in radio and television programs. Girls are more likely to enjoy dolls, paper activities, and games calling for skillful movements and to prefer sentimental and domestic stories. Tyler's comparison of the responses of English and American children to questions on an interest inventory (1956) and Gaier and Collier's comparison of the reading interests of American and Finnish children (1960) both suggest that sex differences are greater than nationality differences, at least within Western culture.

Motivation. Another large-scale research program that has repeatedly revealed sex differences is the work of McClelland, Atkinson, and their associates on achievement motivation (McClelland et al. 1953). The projective method employed in these studies, the evaluation of stories written about achievement-oriented pictures for various indicators of achievement motivation, typically shows males to be much more oriented toward competitive effort than females are.

Males and females also differ in their propensity to take risks (Kogan & Wallach 1964). Generally speaking, women seem to be less given to taking risks than men, but the ingenious experiments these authors report show that the sex difference interacts in a complex way with variation in the nature of the task or situation and with the personality traits of anxiety and defensiveness.

Emotionality. There is considerable evidence from many sources that males and females differ in the strength of some of their emotional needs and the manner in which these are expressed. Some kinds of free responses in standardized situations suggest that these differences are related to body images and the differing requirements of sexual intercourse. Erikson (1951), for example, in the California guidance study asked the subjects to "construct an exciting movie scene" from materials provided. Boys typically produced high structures, ruins, and scenes suggesting sudden arrest of motion, whereas girls produced static, open enclosures, such as rooms. It is difficult to see how all of the differences reported in studies of this sort can be explained simply on the basis of differential treatment of boys and girls in home and community.

The emotional characteristic about which the largest amount of evidence has accumulated is aggression. Again and again, whether the subjects are preschool children, adult men and women, or any age group in between and whether the comparison is made on the basis of personality test scores, observations and ratings, or projective techniques, male groups score significantly higher on aggression than female groups. [*See* AGGRESSION.]

An equally consistent type of finding, although not resting on quite as substantial a body of research findings, is that females are more oriented toward other persons than males are. Sometimes this orientation toward people shows up as sensitivity and responsiveness, sometimes as passivity and dependence, sometimes as needs for succorance, nurturance, and affiliation. A finding that is perhaps related to these is that neuroticism seems to be more prevalent among females than among males, just as delinquency seems to be more prevalent among males than among females.

Summary of differences. Bennett and Cohen (1959), on the basis of a comprehensive study of their own, summarized the differences between the masculine and feminine approaches under five general principles. These fit in with most of the reported research on personality differences.

(1) Masculine thinking is of less intensity than feminine thinking.

(2) Masculine thinking is oriented more in terms of the self, whereas feminine thinking is oriented more in terms of the environment.

(3) Masculine thinking anticipates rewards and punishments determined more as a result of the adequacy or inadequacy of the self, whereas feminine thinking anticipates rewards and punishments determined more as a result of the friendship or hostility of the environment.

(4) Masculine thinking is associated more with desire for personal achievement, feminine thinking more with desire for social love or friendship.

(5) Masculine thinking finds value more in

malevolent and hostile actions against a competitive society, whereas feminine thinking finds value more in freedom from restraint in a friendly and pleasant environment.

It must always be remembered that these sex differences are only group trends and the distributions for males and females on measures of any of them overlap to a considerable extent. As in the ability domain, there are marked individual differences within each sex. But the evidence suggests that the *average* difference between sex groups is somewhat greater for temperamental qualities than for abilities.

Masculinity–femininity scales

Because consistent sex differences show up on many kinds of items used in personality tests and because there are differences within each sex group in the responses individuals give to these items, many psychologists found it feasible to construct empirical masculinity–femininity (*M–F*) scales made up entirely of items that had been shown to differentiate the sexes. It was hoped that such scales would be useful for diagnostic and counseling purposes, as masculinity–femininity would seem to be a fundamental aspect of an individual's personality.

The first and most comprehensive of these *M–F* scales was the Terman and Miles Attitude–Interest Analysis Blank (Terman & Miles 1936). The authors carried out an extensive research program using this test to determine how various special groups in the population distribute themselves with regard to the *M–F* variable. Among occupational groups, men who are athletes and engineers obtained the most masculine scores. Men who are journalists, artists, and clergymen were least masculine. Women who are domestic employees were most feminine; women who are athletes and doctors were least feminine. The age trends differed for the two sexes. Eighth-grade girls were the most feminine of all the groups tested, eleventh-grade boys the most masculine. With advancing age, males tended to become a little more feminine, females a little more masculine.

Since Terman and Miles began on this line of research, several other *M–F* scales have been constructed in the same manner. It is common practice for a multiscore test, like the Strong Vocational Interest Blank or the Minnesota Multiphasic Personality Inventory, to include an *M–F* key among the other scoring keys.

Critique of *M–F* scales. Although all of these scales have served a useful research purpose, they have not had as much practical value as had been expected. In general, they have not been of much use in diagnosing homosexuality. Terman and Miles in their original series of investigations showed that it was only the passive homosexuals (those who customarily played female roles in homosexual relationships) who made unusually feminine scores on the test, and since this effect was based to a large extent on the Interests subtest, on which persons like artists and clergymen also tend to make feminine scores, one must be very cautious about drawing diagnostic conclusions from test performance. The same difficulty arises in connection with the later *M–F* scales. There are various factors that tend to produce deviant scores, so that one cannot assume they point to homosexuality.

The hope has been largely abandoned that *M–F* scales might play a useful part in counseling situations to help individuals find work and living situations that would fit in with their basic temperamental qualities. The difficulty is that masculinity–femininity is not unidimensional. Two persons with identical *M–F* scores may have obtained them from a very different combination of item responses. The emotional qualities that characteristically differentiate males from females show little or no correlation with masculine or feminine interests. It is quite possible for either a man or a woman to deviate in the direction of the opposite sex on one type of item and not on another. Several studies have produced unambiguous evidence of this lack of unidimensionality. One of the most recent (Barrows & Zuckerman 1960) showed that the correlations between three commonly used *M–F* scales were only about .3.

The organization of personality

A kind of research evidence that is being increasingly emphasized as psychologists attempt to incorporate what they know about sex differences into some coherent theoretical system is the repeated finding that variables are related differently to one another in male and female samples. Often the difference in the pattern of correlations between variables appears more impressive than the mean differences on any one variable. Such differences in correlational pattern have been identified in many areas of personality research, and in most cases the reasons for their existence have not yet been made clear. It is possible only to summarize these areas and in some cases suggest tentative explanations.

Discrepant patterns for the two sexes have repeatedly turned up in factor-analytic research on abilities and on personality traits. The only general conclusion one might draw from a miscellany of such studies is that perhaps females are less differentiated than males. There is a tendency for fewer factors to emerge from the data of females than from those of males.

The predictive validity of scholastic aptitude and achievement tests seems to be greater for females than for males (Seashore 1962). However, in longitudinal studies in which personality status at adulthood is to be predicted from childhood measurements of a particular trait (Kagan & Moss 1962), females are more predictable in some areas, males in others. The fact that the stability coefficients are higher on aggression for males and on passivity-dependence for females suggests the reasonable hypothesis that traits characterizing either sex as a whole are more stable within that sex group than are traits characterizing the other sex as a whole.

Different personality variables show significant relationships to general adjustment and popularity in males and females. Correlations often even turn out to be of opposite sign. The only general summary one might hazard of a number of studies in this area is that characteristics related to conformity of behavior and attitude bring more social rewards for females and that those related to initiative and independence bring more social rewards for males. Many specific findings, however, cannot be classified under this one statement.

The developmental antecedents of some traits, especially aggression and underachievement in school, are different for the two sexes. The growth curves differ in shape for these and several other characteristics that have been studied.

It is this last type of finding that has generated what appears to be the most fruitful research ideas for dealing with the whole mass of diverse material. What they suggest is that the *development* of male and female individuals follows a different course. Thus developmental concepts would seem to offer the most promising theoretical formulations.

Sex role concepts and behavior

Much of the developmental research of the 1950s and 1960s has focused on the learning of *sex roles.* Sociologists are primarily responsible for the formulation of the role concept, but it fits in well with several varieties of psychological personality theory. Historical as well as biological factors enter into the formulation of what the sex roles are in any given culture, but once these roles exist, the shaping of masculine and feminine personalities in growing children requires that each person learn in detail what these roles are and at the same time learn to prefer for himself what is considered appropriate for his sex. The purpose of much developmental research is to determine when and how such learning occurs and what factors influence it, both positively and negatively.

Various experimental techniques for finding out what young children consider the proper sex roles to be and how they relate themselves to them have been devised. These techniques include standardized doll-play situations, the telling of stories about pictures, and the choice of toys or activities for a hypothetical boy or girl. Investigators find with considerable consistency that children as young as five understand what is considered appropriate behavior for each sex in much the same way as adults do. Some researchers have worked with children as young as three and have shown that the same sex role concepts, not quite so precisely formulated, can be identified even at this early age. When children are asked to make choices or state preferences, interesting age trends appear. In general, increasing age, from the preschool years on, brings an increasing degree of preference for the characteristics and activities of one's own sex, but there are irregularities and exceptions. Particularly at the early ages, girls show more preference for the activities of boys than boys show for those of girls (Brown 1956).

Identification. In trying to find out how such learning occurs, psychologists have made use of the concept of *identification.* It is difficult, if not impossible, to specify a precise meaning for this term, but most of the particular ways in which it has been used in research on sex differences have something to do with the way that an individual makes the standards and attitudes of his parents a part of himself. Some studies in this field have compared boys from families that are intact with boys from families in which the father is temporarily or permanently absent. Sex-typed behavior, such as aggression, develops at an earlier age in boys with fathers in the home than in boys from "father-absent" families; this suggests that sex roles are acquired through identification. The fact that most boys from "father-absent" homes eventually develop the sex-typed behavior, however, suggests that identification with the parent of the same sex is not the only way in which such roles can be acquired. Other studies have shown that preschool children are aware of what their parents expect of boys and girls and are influenced by these expectations. Father–son and mother–daughter similarities on tests of interests and values have been demonstrated.

In all of these types of investigation, many individual irregularities and exceptions to the prevailing trend of the evidence occur. The process through which a son learns from his father and a girl learns from her mother may not be identical. Most aspects of the mother's sex role can be directly observed and imitated by her daughter, whereas the son does not have the same opportunity to observe and imitate his father's actual behavior. Boys must thus proceed more on the basis of inference. Rapid social change complicates the problem of sex roles. What a child learns in his own home may not be completely appropriate to the situation that exists when he becomes an adult. These and many more considerations point to the conclusion that the learning of sex-appropriate behavior is an enormously complex process, as yet only incompletely understood.

General significance of research

As indicated in the introduction, the study of sex differences has been undertaken in order to answer important practical questions and in order to contribute to our knowledge of the ways in which many sorts of individual differences in personality come into existence. If the complicated interweaving of biological and social determiners can be unraveled from the fabric of sex differences in our culture, perhaps the pattern of other designs of still greater complexity can be traced. Both practical and theoretical purposes continue to influence the planning and conduct of research. In the middle 1960s, the theoretical purpose predominates. Research on sex differences is a strategic meeting ground for biologists, psychologists, anthropologists, and sociologists. An adequate theory, when one is achieved, must represent a synthesis of ideas from many sources.

LEONA E. TYLER

[*Other relevant material may be found in* IDENTITY, PSYCHOSOCIAL; ROLE; SEXUAL BEHAVIOR.]

BIBLIOGRAPHY

BARROWS, GORDON A.; and ZUCKERMAN, MARVIN 1960 Construct Validity of Three Masculinity–Femininity Tests. *Journal of Consulting Psychology* 24:441–445.

BENNETT, EDWARD M.; and COHEN, LARRY R. 1959 Men and Women: Personality Patterns and Contrasts. *Genetic Psychology Monographs* 59:101–155.

BROWN, DANIEL G. 1956 Sex-role Preference in Young Children. *Psychological Monographs* 70, no. 14.

DUNSDON, M. I.; and ROBERTS, J. A. F. 1957 A Study of the Performance of 2,000 Children on Four Vocabulary Tests. *British Journal of Statistical Psychology* 10:1–16.

EDGERTON, HAROLD A.; and BRITT, STEUART H. 1947 Technical Aspects of the Fourth Annual Science Talent Search. *Educational and Psychological Measurement* 7:3–21.

ERIKSON, E. H. 1951 Sex Differences in the Play Configurations of Preadolescents. *American Journal of Orthopsychiatry* 21:667–692.

GAIER, EUGENE L.; and COLLIER, MARY J. 1960 The Latency-stage Story Preferences of American and Finnish Children. *Child Development* 31:431–451.

KAGAN, JEROME; and MOSS, HOWARD A. 1962 *Birth to Maturity: A Study in Psychological Development.* New York: Wiley.

KOGAN, NATHAN; and WALLACH, MICHAEL A. 1964 *Risk Taking: A Study in Cognition and Personality.* New York: Holt.

MCCLELLAND, DAVID C. et al. 1953 *The Achievement Motive.* New York: Appleton.

MCNEMAR, QUINN 1942 *The Revision of the Stanford–Binet Scale.* New York: Houghton.

SANDSTRÖM, CARL I. 1953 Sex Differences in Localization and Orientation. *Acta Psychologica* 9:82–96.

SEASHORE, HAROLD G. 1962 Women Are More Predictable Than Men. *Journal of Counseling Psychology* 9: 261–270.

STRONG, EDWARD K. JR. 1943 *Vocational Interests of Men and Women.* Stanford (Calif.) Univ. Press.

TERMAN, LEWIS M.; and MILES, CATHERINE C. 1936 *Sex and Personality: Studies in Masculinity and Femininity.* New York: McGraw-Hill.

TERMAN, LEWIS M.; and TYLER, LEONA E. 1954 Psychological Sex Differences. Pages 1064–1114 in Leonard Carmichael (editor), *Manual of Child Psychology.* 2d ed. New York: Wiley.

TYLER, LEONA E. 1956 A Comparison of the Interests of English and American School Children. *Journal of Genetic Psychology* 88:175–181.

WITKIN, HERMAN A. et al. 1954 *Personality Through Perception.* New York: Harper.

INDIVIDUAL PSYCHOLOGY

Alfred Adler's individual psychology has rightfully been called the first psychological system that was developed in a social science direction. Adler considered man as an entity firmly embedded in society and unthinkable apart from his social relations—or their absence. In this respect, Adler is similar to such social theorists as James M. Baldwin, George H. Mead, and especially Charles H. Cooley.

The emphasis on the individual in his social setting was but one aspect of Adler's holistic, humanistic, organismic, and personalistic orientation. He considered the views of Eduard Spranger, Wolfgang Köhler, William Stern, Kurt Goldstein, and Jan Smuts close to his own.

Adler's main interest was the construction of a theory that would be serviceable for general human guidance in the school and the home, as well as in the psychiatrist's office. Consistent with this endeavor, he was in expressed sympathy with the pragmatism of William James and the transactionalism of John Dewey.

For Adler, the individual was not a mere product

determined by circumstances but was an active determiner of his own life. Every human being, with the exception of the feeble-minded, was considered endowed with such creative power. Adler quoted from Johann H. Pestalozzi: "The circumstances make man, but man makes the circumstances," a sentence that, incidentally, had been used also by Karl Marx in rejecting mechanistic materialism.

Seeing man as an active and creative, socially embedded whole, Adler held the unique self, or ego, to be the very center of psychology. He parted from Freud in 1911 precisely on this issue. The following represents the final development of Adler's work.

Methodology

Phenomenology. The great contribution of Freud was that he listened to his patients. In this respect he used the phenomenological method. But he devalued the patient's subjective accounts, his introspections, as mere signs, disguises, and screens for more objective underlying causes, which were supposedly deeply buried in the patient's past and his unconscious and by which behavior could be explained—hence, the designation "depth" psychology.

Adler took the patient's subjective accounts not as signs for something else but as samples of behavior of a self-consistently creative individual. From these accounts, an understanding of the person could be gained, provided they were seen in the context of other samples of behavior, subjective and objective, past and present, and provided it was assumed that the individual is oriented toward some goal of success. Adler's psychology is then not a depth psychology but what might be called a "context" psychology.

Far from reducing the subjective accounts of the patient to objective causes in the past, Adler took the beliefs, attitudes, and goals in the future as the ultimate causes of overt behavior. Not objective facts but a person's opinion of them, his subjective evaluation, will determine his behavior. Adlerian psychology is an attitudinal, cognitive, and relatively ahistorical psychology.

Operationism. Adler combined phenomenology with operationism by validating subjective data against overt action. "By their fruits ye shall know them."

His operationism derived from his conception of life as movement, and of human life as movement toward a subjectively conceived goal of success. Thereby, the subject matter receives a dimension in space, becomes transactional and open to inspection. One will not find in Adler terms or metaphors referring to inner, unobservable, and unreportable processes, such as repression, latent homosexuality, primary processes, and real self. Instead, his terms describe a movement with regard to a point outside, such as hesitating attitude, leaning, retreat, detour, distance.

Fictionalism. From the comparison of a person's overt actions with his subjective reports, Adler drew inferences regarding the person's purposes and goals beyond those expressed by the person. In doing so, Adler went emphatically beyond pure phenomenology—for example, as represented today by client-centered counseling—and beyond operationism.

But he did not mistake his inferences for "truths" that he had "discovered," perhaps in the "unconscious." Rather, he took the inferences as his inventions, as useful fictions, with the aid of which the patient would be able to reconstruct or reorganize his view of himself and the world.

Although Adler sometimes seemed to yield to the temptation of reifying the inference, he stated initially very clearly, for example, that a person's final goal was fictional. And again, at the end of his life, he wrote: "I, myself, as the inventor of the 'inferiority complex' have never thought of it as of a spirit, knowing that it has never been in the consciousness or unconsciousness of the patient but only in my own consciousness, and have used it rather for illumination so that the patient could see his attitude in the right coherence" (Adler 1937, p. 776).

This refinement in methodology can be traced to *The Philosophy of "As If"* of Hans Vaihinger, to whom Adler felt greatly indebted. Vaihinger is considered to have developed a German form of pragmatism.

Personality theory

Striving to overcome—goal of superiority. Adler conceived of human life as upward movement, consisting of activity, in social space. Life moves upward; it is growth. From this conception, Adler derived one master motive as required by a holistic theory of personality. He speaks variously of the upward striving, striving to overcome, or striving for superiority. This striving is "innate in the sense that it is part of life" (1956, p. 104). All other drives and motives are readily subsumed under this striving.

Subjectively, this striving is expressed in the individually conceived goal of superiority, perfection, or success. Here Adler often distinguished between the individual's concretized goal, corresponding to an actually conscious goal similar to Kurt Lewin's level of aspiration, and the individual's fictional goal. The latter may mean the ultimate goal of which the individual is only dimly aware or the psychologist's inference or hypothesis regarding the ultimate goal.

Superiority in itself does not mean superiority over others. This is the case only in the "failures in life," in mental disorder, where social interest is underdeveloped. In mental health it means superiority over the general difficulties of life, a goal of superiority not at the expense of others but in which the benefit of others is automatically included.

Inferiority feelings are the normal outcome and counterpart of the striving. "In comparison with unattainable ideal perfection, the individual is continuously filled by an inferiority feeling and motivated by it" (1956, p. 117). This is a reversal of Adler's earlier view, in which he saw the striving as a compensatory effort for primary inferiority feelings and which actually paralleled drive-reduction theory, which at best does justice only to deficit motivation, not to growth motivation. The later reformulation represents a great improvement in theory.

Activity—opinion of oneself. One factor, or dimension, of the striving process is activity, including the concepts of strength, temperament, and personal tempo. A uniform kind of activity, acquired in childhood, can always be observed, and is in constant supply, enduring throughout life.

Subjectively, degree of activity, an energy concept, would seem to have its counterpart in a person's appraisal of his physical and mental resources, his opinion of himself, his self-esteem. Adler had no doubt that "every individual conducts himself in life as if he had a definite idea of his power and his capacities" ([1933], p. 19 in 1938 edition). The more active people will probably have a greater feeling of strength and a lesser feeling of incompletion, insecurity, or inferiority.

Social interest—opinion of the world. Adler's most important concept, and most specific to him, is *Gemeinschaftsgefühl,* generally translated as "social interest." It represents the second dimension, with activity as the first, in a two-dimensional, dynamic theory of personality structure.

Adler rejected the view that man is by nature self-centered, let alone that his socialization depends on repression of an antisocial and partly destructive animal nature. Instead, man is viewed as having an innate readiness or aptitude for a positive social orientation, which, however, must be trained.

Objectively, social interest is expressed in the direction of the individual's striving. With adequate social interest, this striving will be on the socially useful side of life; without such interest, it will be on the useless side. Social interest includes making contact, cooperating, contributing to the common welfare, making spontaneous social efforts, and behaving as part of mankind.

Subjectively, social interest is a positive opinion of the world, including identification with others, empathy, feeling of belonging, feeling at home on this earth, in harmony with the universe. Lack of social interest correspondingly is a negative opinion, with feelings that one is in enemy country. Social interest is similar to Durkheim's sentiments of sympathy and solidarity; lack of social interest is similar to the psychological aspects assumed by concepts such as Durkheim's "anomie" and Marx's "alienation." [*See* ALIENATION; SYMPATHY AND EMPATHY; *and the biography of* DURKHEIM.]

Style of life. Individual psychology becomes outstandingly idiographic through the concept of the style of life, the individually unique totality of life. All general processes such as drives, feeling, thinking, and perception are at the command of the whole, the life style. A particular life style will include a particular schema of apperception.

"The child builds up his whole life, which we have called concretely style of life, at a time when he has neither adequate language nor adequate concepts. When he grows further in the sense [of his style of life], he grows into a movement which has never been formulated into words and therefore, unassailable to criticism, is also withdrawn from the criticism of experience" (1956, p. 191).

The life style, or style of living, is not something the individual *has.* It *is* the individual as an ongoing process, an individually unique way of living and goal-striving. It is very similar to what the existentialists have since named "mode-of-being-in-the-world."

Developmental factors. The life style is not the product of heredity and environment. These furnish only the bricks, so to speak, from which the individual creatively fashions his life style like a work of art. Nevertheless, Adler attributed great significance to organic and social factors as providing probabilities and allurements for the individual.

Organic factors. Adler's first monograph, on organ inferiorities, pointed to the importance of all aspects of the physique for the development of the life style. Sex, physiologically, is merely one of the organic factors, although, to be sure, very important.

Organ inferiorities will—with a certain probability—be compensated for, be responded to, unfavorably. Yet the relationship is not one of direct causation, so that in exceptional cases the outcome can be very positive.

Adler greatly appreciated the work of Ernst Kretschmer on *Physique and Character* and Walter B. Cannon's *The Wisdom of the Body.* In keeping with this tradition of taking physiology fully into account, Adlerian psychiatrists today are very receptive to the advances of drug therapy in conjunction with psychotherapy.

Social factors. A child's entire early social setting was considered by Adler of great importance for later development, although it is again the way in which the child responds to the situation that is crucial. Thus Adler would note the birth-order position and the interaction not only with the parents but especially also with siblings and other significant persons. Described sociometrically, Adler's concept of the child in the family is in the form of a network of interactions among all the group members. Freud, by contrast, in the so-called oedipal situation, emphasized the relationship of each child to his parents, the authority figures.

The importance of sex in the child's development rested for Adler, who referred every process to its larger, societal context, primarily in the sexual role into which the child learns to grow and in his conception of this role.

Psychotherapy

Mental disorder. In keeping with the simplicity of a unitary theory of motivation and a two-dimensional theory of personality structure, Adler presented a unitary theory of mental disorders. These are not considered different illnesses but the outcome of a mistaken way of living. They are all "failures in life"; however, each is unique as all individuals are.

The mistake consists in striving for exaggerated personal superiority, without enough social interest. It is the pampered life style, an immaturity in which a person expects everything while contributing nothing, leaning on, or exploiting others. It is the person's own creation, for which the parents are not wholly to be blamed and may be found in the absence of actual pampering and even in neglect. Except in very special circumstances, it will lead to failure because the important problems in life—occupation, friendship, and sex—are all social problems requiring cooperation for their successful solution.

Symptoms originate when such a person faces a problem that is too difficult for him because of his inadequate social interest. They serve as excuses to safeguard the self-esteem when the person is threatened with defeat and will persist as long as the problem does.

In a broader sense, neurotics, psychotics, criminals, alcoholics, problem children, perverts, and prostitutes are all failures in life because they are lacking in social interest.

Treatment. From interviews and observations, including the patient's early recollections, his dreams, his birth-order position, the therapist gains an understanding of the patient's unique life style, how it all started, and the self-consistency and constancy with which the patient continues to fashion his life in the manner that led to the present predicament.

One aspect of treatment is to get the patient to recognize the mistake in his life style, the striving for a self-centered fictive goal of superiority as the therapist has understood it. While this is in principle not a complicated process and relatively not lengthy, the difficulty lies in the patient's biased schema of apperception and private sense of reasoning, which prevent him from seeing his situation in a common-sense fashion. It therefore becomes necessary to use the material from further interviews to interpret to the patient again and again how all his expressions fit his life style.

But primarily, treatment is a training in cooperation and responsibility in which the patient is deficient. This begins by the therapist showing great social interest toward the patient in order to give him the opportunity for experiencing a trustworthy fellow man. Thereby the patient will be encouraged to develop his own potentiality for social interest. What are otherwise called "permissive atmosphere" and "transference" are, operationally, aspects of social interest. "Psychotherapy is an exercise in cooperation and a test of cooperation" (1956, p. 340). With this understanding, Adlerian therapists have from the start been active in all forms of group psychotherapy.

If the patient could originally be "seduced" by circumstances to develop a mistaken style of life, it is conceivable that the cure can also be accomplished without "insight." Different circumstances could seduce him toward the socially useful side. Thus Adlerian psychology has always been favorably disposed toward milieu therapy, the therapeutic community, and various forms of social psychiatry or community psychiatry.

Whatever the treatment, "As soon as he [the patient] can connect himself with his fellow men on an equal and cooperative footing, he is cured" (1956, p. 347).

Mental health. While the definition of positive mental health is today still an extensively discussed problem, Adler resorted to a pragmatic answer by making the criterion cooperation and social usefulness, i.e., a well-developed social interest.

Mental health in this sense does not mean conformity to any existing social group but a spontaneous social effort contributing toward a better society. This is likely to imply the changing of existing norms in the interest of a better community rather than conforming to them. Mere conformity "would be nothing other than an exploitation of the accomplishments of the striving of others" (1956, p. 107). It is rather a sign of neurosis than of mental health.

Relevance to social science

Adler's psychology is directly relevant to a number of concepts and areas in the social sciences. The relationship of the concepts of *anomie* and *alienation* to lack of social interest has already been mentioned. The concept of *status* is directly related to the striving for superiority and success. Some of the general areas are:

International relations. Adler saw no intrinsic motivation toward war, such as a death instinct. Wars are the outcome of a mistaken striving for power and can be abolished with the further development of social interest.

Prejudice. Prejudice is one form of the depreciation tendency, an expression of the striving for superiority at the expense of others. It is widespread because depreciation of others is an easy way to boost one's own self-esteem. Prejudice as scapegoating would be, in Adlerian terms, a way of providing excuses for one's own inadequacies.

Industrial morale. Assuming that the striving to overcome is basic, one would predict, everything else being equal, morale to be higher when a man is working than when he is idle. Studies during World War II in U.S. shipyards support this hypothesis, as do morale studies in the army.

Unemployment and old age. The mental hardship in both unemployment and old age is that one is prevented from contributing and thus feels useless. Older people should, as long as possible, be given an opportunity for working and striving.

Leadership and group morale. A main component of group morale is a common goal, and a main function of the leader is to formulate the goal and give the group a sense that it can be attained. Leadership requires, according to Adler, social interest, optimism, self-confidence, and quick action.

Religion. For Adler the idea of God is a concretization of a goal of perfection, greatness, and superiority in which an entire culture can share. Reversing Freud's characterization of religion as an illusion, Adler held the unpremised mechanistic position to be an illusion, because it lacks goal and direction without which a mentally healthy life is not possible. As for the ceremonial part of religion, Adler saw in it a sanctification of human relations in accordance with social interest.

HEINZ L. ANSBACHER AND
ROWENA R. ANSBACHER

[*See also the biography of* ADLER. *Other relevant material may be found in* PHENOMENOLOGY; POSITIVISM; PSYCHOANALYSIS.]

WORKS BY ADLER

(1909–1920) 1964 *The Practice and Theory of Individual Psychology.* Translated by Paul Radin. Rev. ed. New York: Harcourt. → First published in German. Contains 28 papers originally published in medical journals between 1909 and 1920.

(1927) 1946 *Understanding Human Nature.* New York: Greenberg. → First published as *Menschenkenntnis.* Based on lectures delivered in the 1920s before an adult-education audience. A paperback edition was published in 1965 by Premier Books.

(1928–1937) 1964 *Superiority and Social Interest: A Collection of Later Writings.* Edited by Heinz L. Ansbacher and Rowena R. Ansbacher. Evanston, Ill.: Northwestern Univ. Press. → Supplementing Adler 1956, this book contains 21 selections, including Adler's essay on religion and a biographical essay by Carl Furtmüller; introduction and commentaries by the editors; and a bibliography of over 300 items.

(1929) 1964 *Problems of Neurosis: A Book of Case Histories.* With an Introduction by Heinz L. Ansbacher. New York: Harper. → Contains 37 case histories interwoven with theoretical considerations. See especially the Introduction, which includes a summary of the theory.

(1930) 1963 *The Problem Child: The Life Style of the Difficult Child as Analyzed in Specific Cases.* With an Introduction by Kurt A. Adler. New York: Capricorn. → First published in German. Twenty case-study chapters of interviews with children, their parents, and their teachers in Adler's open-community child guidance center.

(1931) 1960 *What Life Should Mean to You.* London: Allen & Unwin. → A paperback edition was published in 1958 by Capricorn Books. Includes chapters on crime and its prevention, adolescence, school, love, and marriage.

(1933) 1939 *Social Interest: A Challenge to Mankind.* New York: Putnam. → Adler's last presentation of his views in book form. First published as *Der Sinn des Lebens.* A paperback edition was published in 1964 by Capricorn Books.

1937 Psychiatric Aspects Regarding Individual and Social

Disorganization. *American Journal of Sociology* 42: 773–780.

1956 *The Individual Psychology of Alfred Adler.* Edited by Heinz L. Ansbacher and Rowena R. Ansbacher. New York: Basic Books. → A systematic compendium of selections from all of Adler's writings, with commentary and bibliography. A paperback edition was published in 1964 by Harper.

SUPPLEMENTARY BIBLIOGRAPHY

ADLER, KURT A.; and DEUTSCH, DANICA (editors) 1959 *Essays in Individual Psychology: Contemporary Application of Alfred Adler's Theories.* New York: Grove Press. → Contributions by some fifty authors.

DREIKURS, RUDOLF 1957 *Psychology in the Classroom: A Manual for Teachers.* New York: Harper. → Based on Adlerian principles.

Journal of Individual Psychology. → Published since 1940; title varies.

OLIVER BRACHFELD, F. (1936) 1951 *Inferiority Feelings in the Individual and the Group.* New York: Grune. → Family, unemployment, race, nationality, etc., are discussed in this broadly based book. First published as *Los sentimientos de inferioridad.*

WAY, LEWIS 1950 *Adler's Place in Psychology.* New York: Macmillan. → A paperback edition was published in 1962 by Collier.

INDOCTRINATION

See BRAINWASHING; EDUCATION; EDUCATIONAL PSYCHOLOGY; PROPAGANDA; SOCIALIZATION.

INDUSTRIAL CONCENTRATION

Industrial concentration, influencing as it does the competitive nature of private enterprise, has been of interest as long as the market economy itself. The normal interest has been stimulated from time to time by ascendance of various theories of history predicting that economies based on private enterprise must contain an inherent drift toward increasing economic concentration. Marx, for example, saw not only universal monopoly but also extreme concentration of wealth and income as ultimate and inevitable results of capitalism. Similar theses have come forth from non-Marxist sources, particularly during the 1930s, when some observers discerned a steady "decline of competition" woven into the fabric of history and blamed it for many of the ills of the great depression.

The issue of economic concentration as it has emerged is essentially twofold in nature. On the one side, there is the question of industrial concentration, of the degree to which a few firms dominate the output of industries taken individually. On the other side, there is the question of inequality of wealth and income in the economy as a whole. [*See* INCOME DISTRIBUTION, *article on* SIZE; NATIONAL WEALTH, *article on* DISTRIBUTION.] We shall be concerned here only with concentration in the first sense.

Concentration indexes. The pattern of concentration in an industry is usually shown by a *concentration curve*, each point of which represents the *concentration ratio* (the percentage of total output, employment, or similar size variable) associated with the corresponding number of firms arrayed from largest to smallest, the firms being plotted on the horizontal axis (see Figure 1). By construction the curve will rise to the right at a nonincreasing rate and generally at a decreasing rate throughout. That is, it will generally be convex upward. The more unequal the firm sizes are over any range, the more convex the curve will be. Hence the shape of a particular curve is defined by two parameters—the degree of inequality in firm size and the number of firms.

Although it is not normal practice to do so, the

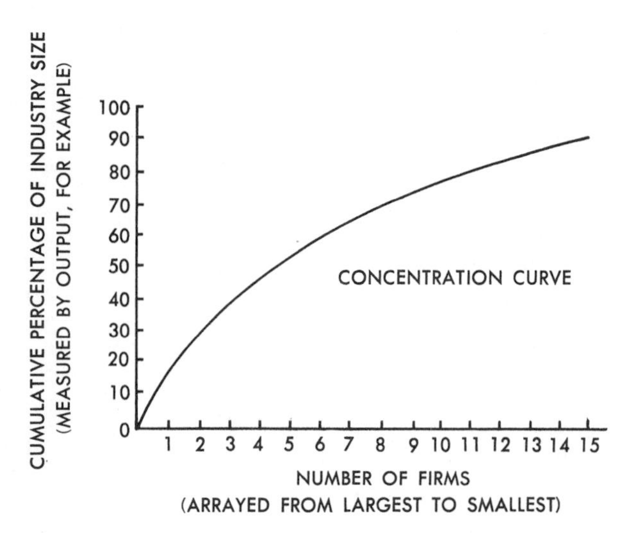

Figure 1

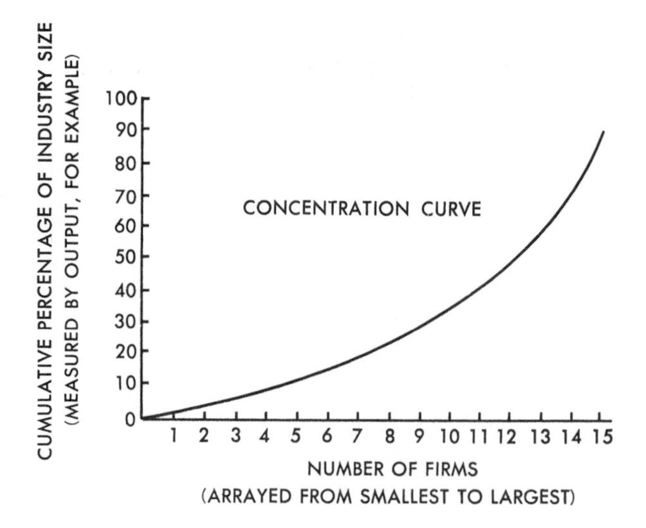

Figure 2

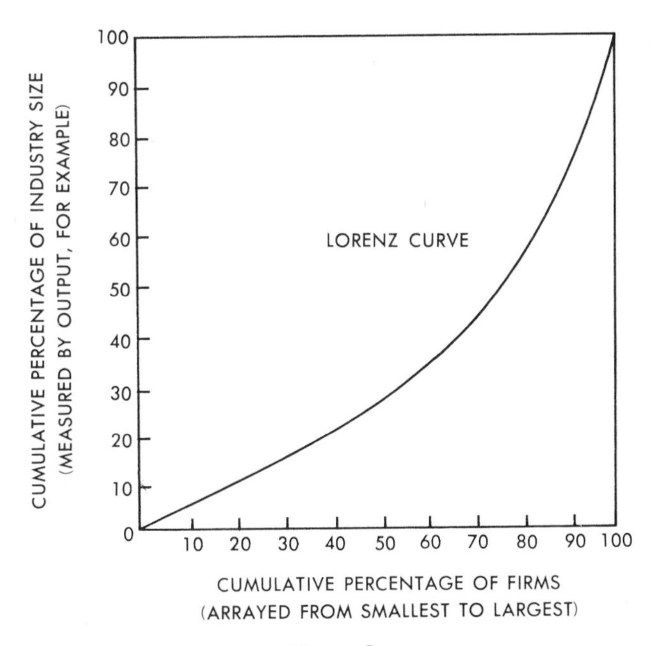

Figure 3

concentration curve could equally well be plotted against the number of firms arrayed from smallest to largest, in which case the curve would generally rise at an increasing rate (see Figure 2). Constructed in this way, the concentration curve is easily transformed into the well-known *Lorenz curve* by substituting relative for absolute numbers of firms on the horizontal axis—that is, by dividing the horizontal scale by the total number of firms (see Figure 3).

If the observed size distribution of firms in an industry fits well into a standard statistical distribution, a Lorenz curve is directly derived as the relation between the cumulative distribution function and first-moment distribution function of that cumulative distribution function. In such a case, the concentration curve can be reproduced if the parameters of the distribution function are known along with the total number of firms. Observed density distributions of firm size are almost always unimodal and skewed upward: firms are clustered about a relatively limited range of sizes with a longer taper toward the larger sizes than toward the smaller ones. It is reasonable to suppose that this characteristic shape results at least in part from a stochastic growth process, and some economists have therefore tried, with varying degrees of success, to approximate observed size distributions by lognormal, Yule, Pareto, and similar distributions that can be generated by stochastic processes (Hart & Prais 1956; Hymer & Pashigian 1962; Mansfield 1962; Quandt 1966; Shepherd 1964, pp. 208–209; Simon & Bonini 1958). Even if good fits could always be obtained, it would be prohibitively expensive, in terms of both collecting and processing data, to analyze an economy of any size in this way. Moreover, a collection of curves would mean little without some theoretical framework for interpreting them. Unfortunately, no systematic theory of industrial structure has yet emerged from studies of this type to command broad agreement among professional economists.

In the absence of such a theory, measures of industrial concentration are generally confined to descriptive indexes not amenable to formal statistical analysis. A standard comprehensive measure of this nature is the *Herfindahl index*—the summed squares of firm sizes, with the sizes expressed as proportions of the total industry size. In mathematical language,

$$H = \sum_{i=1}^{N} \left(\frac{s_i}{S}\right)^2$$
$$= \frac{1}{N^2\bar{s}^2}\left[\sum_{i=1}^{N} (s_i - \bar{s})^2 + N\bar{s}^2\right]$$
$$= \frac{1}{N}\left[\frac{\sigma^2}{\bar{s}^2} + 1\right],$$

where N is the number of firms, S is the total size of the industry (the summed sizes of the firms), s_i is the size of firm i, and $\bar{s}$ is the mean size of firm (S/N). In other words, the Herfindahl index is the squared coefficient of variation plus one, the sum divided by the number of firms. If all firms are of equal size ($\sigma^2 = 0$), the index is the reciprocal of the number of firms, reaching its maximum value of unity under monopoly. For any given number of firms greater than one, the index increases with the coefficient of variation. Since it is generally impractical to compile all the data needed for the comprehensive Herfindahl index, a partial index is normally computed from data for some fraction of the leading firms.

Restrictions on disclosure of information about individual firms, a normal condition for most statistics collected and published by Western governments, also place limits on the kinds of indexes of concentration that can be computed. The practice followed in official sources in the United States is not to reveal data for fewer than four firms at a time. In Canada and the United Kingdom, the minimum number is three. Points on concentration curves based on officially published statistics are therefore defined at best for only every third or fourth firm. Researchers may, of course, be given access to more detailed data, but any published results must conform to standard disclosure rules.

For the various reasons discussed, it has become

common practice to describe industrial concentration with a few simple indexes that summarize the concentration curve only in part. These include concentration ratios for specified numbers of firms in multiples of three or four, areas under portions of the concentration curve, partial Herfindahl indexes, and *occupancy counts*. The last is the inverse of a concentration ratio, giving the number of leading firms required to account for a specified concentration ratio. For example, the 80 per cent occupancy count is the number of firms, arrayed from largest to smallest, that together make up 80 per cent of the size of the industry. In studies of U.S. and Canadian manufacturing industries, it has been found that the various partial measures all yield about the same rank order of industries in terms of concentration (Universities–National Bureau Committee for Economic Research 1955, pp. 64–69).

Concentration and monopoly. Given the current state of economic theory and leaving aside problems of identifying industries, one should not expect any simple correlation between pricing behavior and degree of concentration as reflected by the described indexes, except in extreme cases. Perhaps the most that can be said is that the higher the concentration, the more likely an industry will behave monopolistically, and the lower the concentration, the more likely it will behave competitively.

There are difficulties even with this broad conclusion, depending on the index being used to measure concentration. For example, suppose two industries show the same high concentration ratio for the four leading firms but industry B has twice as many firms as industry A. The Herfindahl index may not be smaller for B than for A, since differences in inequality of firm size may counterbalance differences in number of firms. Put the other way around, even though two industries have the same Herfindahl index, the numbers of firms, partial concentration ratios, and inequalities of firm size may differ in many possible ways.

The meaning and significance of concentration indexes are affected by practical as well as conceptual problems. Foremost is the difficulty of identifying industries so that they will be relevant for economic analysis and consistent with available data. In the first place, systematic and comprehensive statistics on industrial structure are limited primarily to the areas of manufacturing, mining, and public utilities. Most studies of concentration therefore deal only with these areas and, in fact, almost exclusively with manufacturing.

In the second place, the systems of industrial classification used in basic statistical sources, especially in census-type materials, are not designed primarily for analysis of pricing behavior. Establishments and products are grouped together mainly on the basis of technological, not economic, characteristics. Moreover, the accuracy of data aside, special technical difficulties in analyzing data may arise because of the way in which data are classified into industrial categories. For example, an industry may be defined on an establishment or on a product basis, or on the first basis for some purposes and the second for others. If defined on an establishment basis, value of output and similar data represent the total for all commodities produced by establishments assigned to the industry, assignment being based on the commodity of principal value in the establishment in question. If defined on a product basis, value of output represents the value of those commodities assigned to the industry, no matter where producing establishments are assigned. For analysis of industrial concentration, statistics should generally be compiled on a product basis, but this is not always possible. A final problem exists in matching firms with industries, a procedure that normally requires access to unpublished data.

In the third place, the scope of industrial categories usually affects the height of concentration indexes. The more narrowly industries are defined, the higher concentration indexes are likely to be. Concentration indexes should not, therefore, be interpreted without regard to the general scope of industrial categories. Although elaborate industrial classification systems have been evolved in many Western countries, a given level of classification (for example, the four-digit level) need not mean a comparable scope for all included categories. Indeed, it is not at all clear what is meant by a "comparable scope," even though the desirability of some such standardization is apparent.

In the fourth place, statistics are usually compiled on a national basis, whereas relevant market areas are sometimes smaller or larger, differing from one industry to another [*see* MARKETS AND INDUSTRIES]. Concentration indexes computed on a national basis may or may not be meaningful from the point of view of pricing policy, depending on the circumstances for particular industries.

For all these reasons, one must take care in attributing specific degrees of monopoly, whatever that might mean, to specific concentration indexes. At the same time, both very low and very high indexes, applied to relevantly defined industries, convey useful information on likely pricing behavior. Similarly, significant differences in levels of concentration for the same industries over time or among countries at the same time provide important evidence on likely differences in pricing behavior.

Comparative levels of concentration. A number of important studies of industrial concentration have been conducted over the last three decades, covering the United States, the United Kingdom, Canada, and Japan; less extensive studies have been made for Sweden, France, Italy, and India (see bibliography and Bain 1966, pp. 183–200). These studies have focused primarily on manufacturing, measuring and analyzing concentration in a variety of ways. The findings cannot be adequately summarized here, but a few broad generalizations can be drawn from them.

In recent years, between 14 and 18 per cent of national income in the United States has originated in highly concentrated industries, high concentration being defined in general by a four-firm concentration ratio of 50 per cent or more for industries at the four-digit level of classification (Einhorn 1964, p. 13). In manufacturing alone, the fraction of income originating in highly concentrated industries is 32 to 35 per cent (*ibid.*, p. 26). For roughly the same years and for the sector of manufacturing alone, a greater extent of concentration is clearly shown by the evidence for Canada (Rosenbluth 1957, pp. 75–93), less clearly by the evidence for the United Kingdom (Universities–National Bureau Committee for Economic Research 1955, pp. 70–77; Shepherd 1961). In the case of Japan, the degree of concentration is now generally higher than in the United States for manufacturing industries that can be matched with U.S. counterparts, but the extent of concentration is roughly the same as in the United States in both manufacturing and the economy as a whole (Rotwein 1964, pp. 275–276).

In studies of manufacturing, concentration has been found to be inversely related to size of industry: larger industries generally have smaller concentration indexes and vice versa. This relation being taken into account, concentration also shows a significant direct relation to average firm size but no significant relation one way or the other to inequality of firm size within an industry.

Trends in concentration. Although there has been considerable interest in the question of industrial concentration for many years, systematic evidence on trends in concentration has been collected and analyzed only over relatively recent years. So far, it has been possible to study long trends only in the case of the United States. Changes in concentration in British manufacturing between 1935 and 1951, a short period for most purposes, have also been examined with inconclusive results.

The safest conclusion to draw from the studies of the United States is that there has been no pronounced trend in concentration either way. When due allowance is made for all the infirmities and incomparabilities of the measurements, there appears to be a rough stability in the fraction of national income originating in highly concentrated industries throughout the economy over the period from 1899 to 1958 (Nutter 1951; Einhorn 1964; Shepherd 1964). The same conclusion holds for the manufacturing sector taken alone.

Beneath the stability lies a rapid turnover, displacement, and replacement of industries. While some industries are becoming more highly concentrated, others are becoming less highly concentrated in roughly equal measure. Stability results because young and rapidly growing industries tend to become less and less concentrated while old and slowly growing (or declining) industries tend to become more and more concentrated. Why the two forces have managed to come so close to balancing themselves is another of the many unexplained mysteries of history.

Causes of concentration. Evidence collected so far would seem to assign an important role to technological factors, determined within the existing regime of patents and similar constraints, as causes of industrial concentration. For instance, comparison of U.S. and Canadian manufacturing shows a similar ranking of industries by both degree of concentration and number of firms, indicating similar technological conditions. But Canadian industries are generally more concentrated than their U.S. counterparts, despite the fact that they are characterized by less inequality in firm size. The greater concentration, therefore, seems attributable in general to a smaller number of firms in each industry, the result of smaller markets under the given technological conditions (Rosenbluth 1957, pp. 75–93).

The dominant role of technology is further shown by the normally high negative correlation within a country between concentration and size of industry, and the normally low correlation between concentration and inequality of firm size. Moreover, when concentration in an industry is high (or low) in terms of firms, it is ordinarily also high (or low) in terms of plants.

Other factors are no doubt important in explaining industrial concentration, but they have not been clearly isolated by statistical analysis. Some suggested causal factors have been rejected: the durability of commodities and the nature of purchasers (whether businesses or households) do not have a systematic relation to degree of concentration in an industry. While it seems reasonable to suppose that legal constraints such as antitrust laws have an important effect on concentration and its trend, we do not yet have quantitative estimates of that importance.

G. WARREN NUTTER

[*See also* ANTITRUST LEGISLATION; ECONOMIES OF SCALE; OLIGOPOLY.]

BIBLIOGRAPHY

ADELMAN, M. A. 1951 The Measurement of Industrial Concentration. *Review of Economics and Statistics* 33:269–296.

BAIN, JOE S. 1966 *International Differences in Industrial Structure: Eight Nations in the 1950's.* New Haven: Yale Univ. Press.

BLAIR, JOHN M. 1956 Statistical Measures of Concentration in Business: Problems of Compiling and Interpretation. Oxford University, Institute of Statistics, *Bulletin* 18:351–372.

BURNS, ARTHUR R. 1936 *The Decline of Competition: A Study of the Evolution of American Industry.* New York and London: McGraw-Hill.

EINHORN, HENRY A. 1964 Enterprise Monopoly and the Concentration of Domestic Industrial Output: 1939–1958. Ph.D. dissertation, Columbia Univ.

EVELY, RICHARD W.; and LITTLE, I. M. D. 1960 *Concentration in British Industry: An Empirical Study of the Structure of Industrial Production, 1935–1951.* National Institute of Economic and Social Research, Economic and Social Studies, No. 16. Cambridge Univ. Press.

GORT, MICHAEL 1962 *Diversification and Integration in American Industry.* National Bureau of Economic Research, General Series, No. 77. Princeton Univ. Press.

HART, P. E.; and PRAIS, S. J. 1956 The Analysis of Business Concentration: A Statistical Approach. *Journal of the Royal Statistical Society* Series A 119:150–191.

HYMER, STEPHEN; and PASHIGIAN, PETER 1962 Firm Size and Rate of Growth. *Journal of Political Economy* 70:556–569.

LEAK, H.; and MAIZELS, A. 1945 The Structure of British Industry. *Journal of the Royal Statistical Society* Series A 108:142–207.

LEWIS, W. ARTHUR 1945 *Monopoly in British Industry.* London: Fabian.

MANSFIELD, EDWIN 1962 Entry, Gibrat's Law, Innovation, and the Growth of Firms. *American Economic Review* 52:1023–1051.

NELSON, RALPH L. 1963 *Concentration in the Manufacturing Industries of the United States: A Midcentury Report.* Economic Census Studies, No. 2. New Haven: Yale Univ. Press.

NUTTER, G. WARREN 1951 *The Extent of Enterprise Monopoly in the United States, 1899–1939: A Quantitative Study of Some Aspects of Monopoly.* Univ. of Chicago Press.

QUANDT, RICHARD E. 1966 On the Size Distribution of Firms. *American Economic Review* 56:416–432.

ROSENBLUTH, GIDEON 1957 *Concentration in Canadian Manufacturing Industries.* National Bureau of Economic Research, General Series, No. 61. Princeton Univ. Press.

ROTWEIN, EUGENE 1964 Economic Concentration and Monopoly in Japan. *Journal of Political Economy* 72: 262–277.

SHEPHERD, W. GEOFFREY 1961 A Comparison of Industrial Concentration in the United States and Britain. *Review of Economics and Statistics* 43:70–75.

SHEPHERD, W. GEOFFREY 1964 Trends of Concentration in American Manufacturing Industries: 1947–1958. *Review of Economics and Statistics* 46:200–212.

SIMON, HERBERT A.; and BONINI, CHARLES P. 1958 The Size Distribution of Business Firms. *American Economic Review* 48:607–617.

THORP, WILLARD L.; and CROWDER, WALTER F. 1941 *The Structure of Industry.* U.S. Temporary National Economic Committee, Investigation of Concentration of Economic Power, Monograph No. 27. Washington: Government Printing Office.

UNIVERSITIES–NATIONAL BUREAU COMMITTEE FOR ECONOMIC RESEARCH 1955 *Business Concentration and Price Policy.* National Bureau of Economic Research, Special Conference Series, No. 5. Princeton Univ. Press.

WILCOX, CLAIR 1940 *Competition and Monopoly in American Industry.* U.S. Temporary National Economic Committee, Investigation of Concentration of Economic Power, Monograph No. 21. Washington: Government Printing Office.

INDUSTRIAL DEMOCRACY

See DEMOCRACY; LABOR RELATIONS; LABOR UNIONS.

INDUSTRIAL ORGANIZATION

For the theoretical aspects of industrial organization, see the articles dealing with forms of market organization: COMPETITION; MONOPOLY; OLIGOPOLY; *and the more general articles* FIRM, THEORY OF THE; MARKETS AND INDUSTRIES. *More specific topics in industrial organization are treated under* CARTELS AND TRADE ASSOCIATIONS; ECONOMIES OF SCALE; INDUSTRIAL CONCENTRATION; MERGERS; PRICES, *article on* PRICING POLICIES. *For particular sectors of the economy, see* HOUSING, *article on* ECONOMIC ASPECTS; INTERNAL TRADE; MEDICAL CARE, *article on* ECONOMIC ASPECTS; TRANSPORTATION, *article on* ECONOMIC ASPECTS. *For government regulation of economic activity, see* ANTITRUST LEGISLATION; LICENSING, OCCUPATIONAL; PATENTS; PRICES, *article on* PRICE CONTROL AND RATIONING; REGULATION OF INDUSTRY; RESALE PRICE MAINTENANCE.

INDUSTRIAL RELATIONS

I
INDUSTRIAL AND BUSINESS PSYCHOLOGY

Industrial psychology is rapidly becoming multidisciplinary, international, and accepted as an essential ingredient for decision making by the new managers of the business world. Problems related to industrial psychology cover a wide range, from the communication aspects of international road signs (Krampen 1961) to the cross-cultural studies of the attitudes of managers (Haire et al. 1963). Not only has industry become a place to apply the findings of experimental, clinical, and social psychology; it also provides the office, the plant, and the laboratories of research and development for the study of the needs and achievements of human beings (Gilmer 1961; Marcus-Steiff 1961).

Who is the industrial psychologist? Traditionally, he has been a person trained in experimental psychology who worked with business enterprises; but as his roles have expanded, it is becoming harder to distinguish him from the clinician, the sociologist, or, in some respects, the industrial engineer. He may be thought of as that behavioral scientist who attempts to bring into focus the classical problems of the personnel man, the social aspects of human relations, and the new and difficult human problems caused by the inescapable confrontation of men and machines.

What does the psychologist in industry do? As a researcher, he designs and validates selection tests, studies the relationships between individual personalities and organizational climates, and works on an interdisciplinary team in analyzing the human factors in systems (Forehand & Gilmer 1964; Gagné 1962). As a staff specialist, he advises the industrial relations department on the company's pending contract negotiations with the union or designs a study to determine the buying habits of the suburban housewife. During one hour, the industrial psychologist may be discussing learning theory with the training director who has become interested in teaching machines; during the next hour, he may be participating in a conference on a morale survey to be conducted in an out-of-town plant. And the staff psychologist may finish the day conferring with the company psychiatrist and the safety director on accident prevention.

The development of industrial psychology

Industrial psychology began in the early 1900s, in the United States (Ferguson 1963—) with research and application on selection, training, and vocational guidance, and in England (Farmer 1958) on what soon became known as occupational psychology. A new era of industrial social psychology started around 1925, and during and following World War II industrial psychology became international in scope as the emphasis shifted to the study of people in groups and to the way in which culture is related to individual differences. Whereas the former concentration was on the efficiency of the worker, emphasis now began to be placed on studies of leadership and communication and on the human problems involved in man–machine systems. By 1960, industrial mental-health programs began to open up to the psychologist.

At the close of World War II, international lists of psychologists indicated that only a few were employed in industry. Two decades later, full-time industrial psychologists number several thousand, and many more of them function in part-time or full-time consulting capacities. One index of the present scope of industrial psychology can be seen by the attendance of professionals from several continents at the meetings of the International Congress of Applied Psychology. Papers presented include problems of absenteeism, marketing, evaluation, counseling, and work efficiency; problems of criteria, equipment design, and incentive schemes; and a host of problems related to communication and leadership.

Industrial psychologists' changing roles. Traditional organizational theory, which described the layout of jobs and how workers should perform their tasks, largely ignored man's psychological life. The early "scientific managers" made the erroneous assumptions that people on the job try to satisfy only physical and economic needs, that there is automatically a similarity of goals among members of the organization, and that people try rationally to seek the best solution to a problem.

With the beginning of mass production, the assembly worker began to lose whatever independence he had had. He was told what his work was, and how and when to do it. Gradually, as industrial organizations moved toward participative management, the worker had someone else to plan for him. With the coming of information technology in the late 1950s, and the many aspects of automation in general, it appears that the man in middle management may himself be pushed down in importance, separating the production worker still further from the rest of the organization. Even the top executive is being forced by automation to do more "systems thinking." Such technological advancements, epitomized by the high-speed computer, are bringing on new types of human problems and offering new horizons for behavioral science research (Green 1963).

With a growing acceleration in technology—it is estimated that of all of the scientists and engineers who have lived since the beginning of time, most are working today—human problems are expanding. New ideas are coming from mathematicians, engineers, and a host of social scientists, dealing with problems of operations analysis, social environments, informal organizations, work groups, communication, and decision making. They involve problems of methodology, power structure, and innovation and change. Thus, to the traditional areas of personnel and industrial social psychology is being added a new dimension called organizational psychology (Leavitt & Bass 1964). The new industrial psychology is concerned with four relationships of man as he functions in industry: between person and person, between person and group, between person and object, and between man and his inner self.

This discussion will continue with a view of organizational environments, followed by the more classical areas of personnel psychology. There is a section that deals with men and machines, including physical environments, performance appraisal, accidents, engineering psychology, and the place of the human factors analyst. Another section deals with the problems of individual adjustments to work situations. The final section discusses the trends of industrial psychology, which is becoming more international in scope.

Organizational environments

For the most part, we can consider that the anatomy of the modern company is made up of both physical and psychological structures. Although there is no typical industry and no cultural pattern is common to all business enterprises, most companies can be described in terms of variations of line and staff organizations, hierarchies of responsibility, and size. Labor unions as physical structures do not differ very much from management organizations, but in power structure and goals they differ extensively. Although the physical structures of organizations are closely related to psychological structure, the descriptions here will be confined to the psychological structure. The modern corporation has become more than an efficient form of organizing large-scale production and distribution; it has become a community within the community, manifesting a genuine social structure of its own.

The informal organizations. The informal organization of the modern company has been called various names: the setup, the system, the ropes, or our way of doing things. It may result from friendships, car pools, nearness of work places, community interests, union associations, personality likes and dislikes, or even the association of those who have only the single bond of self-defense. Basically, it is a tissue of relationships that are never static; these are revealed through symbols, subtle permissions, and even taboos. The corporate image so carefully cultivated by public relations may be vastly different from the power and status structure as seen from within. Decision control may formally be specified in terms of hierarchical structure.

The industrial psychologist is distinguished from his colleagues in other branches of the discipline by the setting in which he works. Since the industrial psychologist is concerned with the interaction between the individual and his environment, he is close to the theories and techniques employed by other social scientists.

The sociogram has proved to be a practical instrument for taking a graphic look at informal communication in terms of leadership structure, helping the industrial psychologist to identify cliques, isolates, and mutual admiration societies [*see* SOCIOMETRY]. To a large extent, the many studies of informal organizations have as a common denominator the problem of ego identification. Many employees in industry are being deprived of the sense of doing interesting, significant work. Increasing supervisory pressure to maintain production often creates resistance. Out of studies on worry, work maladjustments, and the other unanticipated behaviors there have come planned programs of counseling, job enlargement, and job rotation for the worker, as well as better selection and training of the foreman and a restructuring of his job. Attention is also being given to the adjustment of the man in middle management, the executive, and the professional staff man of the industrial organization. It is at these higher levels that industrial psychologists are beginning to do research related to climates within organizations.

Psychological climates. As Gellerman (1960) pointed out, the personalities of companies cannot be neatly categorized; each one is unique. This orientation has given modern emphasis to an old problem described by philosophers, playwrights, and novelists and now recognized by modern-day managers who speak of environmental factors, leadership climates, and the "shadow of the organization."

The range of climate studies includes diverse organizations. For example, one study concludes that hotel environments vary along such dimensions as size, local culture, economic competition, sensitivity to criticism, sophistication of clients, attitude toward tourists, and the current pattern of acceptability. University climates have been described as manifesting differing "cultures"—collegiate, vocational, academic, and nonconformist.

Military and governmental organizations, as well as business firms, are being studied along such scales as autocratic–permissive and conservative–liberal. Many of these analyses have been informal and descriptive, but an increasing number of studies attempt to measure organizational climate and its effects (Forehand & Gilmer 1964).

Some researches focus on how companies vary in size, structure, systems complexity, leadership patterns, and goal directions. They lead to hypotheses concerning personality groupings within the organization. Within the same company, one department in which the important individuals are "people-oriented" may differ greatly from another in which influence is from those who are "system-oriented." Although one may not wish to place people into rigid categories, their behaviors do differ, and some types of people fit into a given organization better than others. For example, the large organization provides a more sympathetic work place for the upward-mobile person (who is less critical of some of the values that lead to success) than for the type of individual who wishes to escape through indifference or for the person who contests the *status quo* (who wants change for the sake of change).

The marketing influence. Three factors have contributed to the growth of the modern industrial complex: mass production, research and development, and marketing. The following sections will discuss the human factors related to production, research, and development, including a brief discussion of the human aspects of marketing and distribution.

One world-wide corporation made a study to determine in detail the structures of high-level policy decisions and concluded that in terms of influence, if not control, sales held a ranking position. The psychologist in the marketing area is a member of a team involved in several diverse but interdependent activities—advertising, selling, sales promotion, customer service, public relations, and market research. Special attention is being given to consumer attitudes and to various aspects of economic psychology.

A review of the role of the psychologist in marketing concludes that his problems are expanding (Guest 1962). Psychologists continue to occupy important staff positions in marketing departments in business organizations, in consumer research companies and advertising agencies, and as private consultants. They contribute knowledge of method in sampling, in experimental and correlational designs, and in questionnaire construction; and they have been the originators and major proponents in the uses of projective and other techniques for exploration of the substrata of human motives. They are giving increasing attention to perceptual, cognitive, and learning factors in advertising and selling.

Personnel psychology

Psychologists in industry, although often dealing with a wide range of personnel problems, have tended to cluster into specialties, such as selection and training. The industrial psychologist, whether he is concerned with general problems or plays the role of critic and of problem solver in some specific work situation, usually works within restricted limits. These limits may be prescribed by budget, management policy, or union practices. Occasionally, he may have the time, energy, facility, and support to perform experiments. He is often called upon to give advice based on his knowledge of general principles of psychology or on personal observations and wisdom. Let us consider some of his specialties.

Selection. The development of psychological tests, and the consequent quantitative investigation of relationships between human abilities and various criteria for behavior, represents one of the outstanding achievements of the social sciences to date. Problems in selection and classification range widely, from the comparatively simple determination of the potential abilities of a lathe operator to the multidimensional problem of predicting executive success. Personnel selection may utilize tests of intelligence, special aptitudes, achievement, or personality and usually includes the use of application blanks, references, biographical and interpersonal data, and interviews.

It is common to use short intelligence tests, developed specifically for screening industrial personnel, to predict performance in training, job proficiency, job turnover, and promotion potential. At higher levels, more extensive tests are used in the selection of creative talent. Custom-made tests designed for a particular job may be used in the measurement of special aptitudes, such as mechanical comprehension, clerical aptitude, and motor skills. Achievement tests are used as measures of current proficiency related to some experience or training or as predictors of subsequent performance. Personality tests used in personnel selection include measures of interest, personality inventories, projective techniques, and situational tests closely approximating actual work samples. Psychological measurement has developed extensively in recent years and, despite the opinions of some critics, is providing the most useful tools available in developing adequate solutions to the selection problem.

By its very nature, research with personnel-selection devices is almost always actuarial. Practicing psychologists are now finding that the sophisticated industrialist realizes that selection is a continuing process. Selection not only takes place when a person is first hired but whenever he is promoted, transferred, or reassigned. The precision of selection procedures, whether for initial hiring or for training programs, is influenced by the adequacy of manpower supply (Guion 1965).

Training and education. "Training," in the industrial context, means the teaching of specific skills, such as instruction given to an operator in the running of a grinding machine. "Education" refers to a broader type of teaching in which knowledge is related to future situations, such as instructions given in business schools to executive trainees. Industry is now in the process of upgrading training departments to include both. At the supervisory level, for example, it is necessary to combine training in the specifics of handling problems in safety, discipline, and cost control with education that would involve thinking ahead and broadening the base for individual learning.

Psychologists are becoming more involved in training. Technological advancement means that men must be trained not only for an immediate job but also for possible conversion to other or future jobs. Special attention must be given to automated plants in which one error may be too many. Not only can psychologists offer learning theory to industry, but they can also offer much in the way of practical findings from military situations. For example, the Human Resources Research Office of George Washington University has a number of prototype training "packages" for tank crews, for missile operations, and for high-level leadership. This involves analysis of a given system and of a given job, and the development of proficiency tests to determine what skills and knowledge are needed to perform a task. These are transformed into training objectives, which are supplemented by appropriate materials and finally evaluated in the practical setting.

There are many ways in which the psychologist can be of aid to the training director—in waste reduction, conference leadership, and evaluation, to name a few. He is also of help in providing the director, the supervisor, and top management with generalized information on behavior, which is so vital to the understanding of human problems in general and learning problems specifically—problems of criteria and performance appraisal, how goals are related to learning, massed versus spaced practice, reinforcement, and programmed learning. And he helps structure the appropriate climate to motivate learning.

Motivation and work. Industry has made much progress in helping both the worker and the manager satisfy some economic and physical needs. Progress, however, has been slower in other respects, such as in helping the man feel that he belongs, that he has the opportunity to measure up to his own ambitions. There are two main reasons for this retardation: (1) with the growth in the size of many organizations, people are finding it increasingly difficult to get individual satisfaction from the work situation, and (2) what a man needs from his job changes with time and circumstances. In youth, men look more for opportunity; they want and expect challenge, for herein lies the path to recognition. In older men, change is often unwelcome, even resisted, and competition is shunned because few have the stamina to keep up the pace. Even the successful middle-aged man has his problems of need satisfaction, often displaying aggression toward his job and his family as he examines success and failure in terms of previous goals.

That the industrial psychologist has long been aware of the problems of job satisfaction is witnessed by the fact that over two thousand research publications have dealt with the problems of industrial morale, job-factor comparisons, attitudes and productivity, and need variations within individuals and across groups. To some, these problems are near the heart of industrial psychology.

In a book-length summary (Vroom 1964), an attempt was made to reduce the gap between applied and basic research. Vroom has explored the seldom-treated conceptual and theoretical underpinnings of industrial psychology and has analyzed such diverse problems as occupational choice, the determinants of job satisfaction, the relationship between these and performance, and the role of ability and motivation in work performance in terms of a conceptual model of human behavior. The book contains an extensive review of the literature of studies from the laboratory and from within industrial settings.

Supervision and leadership. The emphasis on human relations in industry became most pronounced following World War II and centered primarily on the first-line supervisor. Research in the area had its beginnings some two decades earlier with the classical Hawthorne studies (Roethlisberger & Dickson 1939). Information on the nature of good supervisory practice has come in recent years from many sources and adds up to several generalizations. The more secure the foreman feels with his superiors, the greater is group productivity. More productivity comes from work groups in which (1) the supervisor assumes a leadership role, (2) there is a combination of emphasis on productivity and employee consideration, and (3) recognition for effort is given. In a series of studies, it was found that there was more efficient production when the supervisor could influence his superiors and used this power to help the workers achieve their goals. Good supervisory practices must be the concern at all levels of the organization, and the organizational climate is of prime importance. Leadership behavior is not a thing apart but is imbedded in a social setting. Human relations in supervision has become a focal point for many of the social aspects of the applications of psychology in industry (Kay & Palmer 1961).

Until recently, little research attention was devoted to executive leadership and development, but along with the upgrading of schools of business administration and the rise to power of the better-educated upward-mobile type of manager, psychologists and sociologists are finding their studies of the executive accepted.

From a variety of studies come the descriptions of successful high-level leadership as involving strong mobility drives, company orientation, and ability to make decisions, to organize, and to act independently. From studies of the motivations, goals, and attitudes of managers in a variety of countries, it was found that managers want the opportunity to use their talents, to realize themselves as individuals (Haire et al. 1963). Not unexpectedly, these researchers found the effects of cultural differences. The goals of Japanese and Norwegian managers, for example, may not be the same, but self-realization and autonomy are universally more important to managers than prestige, social satisfactions, and even security.

In giving a description of the executive, Ghiselli (1963) concluded that the individual with managerial talent is a gifted person and an unusual one. He has pointed out that this individual might well be ill fitted for other kinds of activity, such as science, medicine, or politics. It has been shown that even the scientist may differ in his responses to organizational climates. The academic scientist is more likely to be professionally oriented, whereas the industrial scientist is organizationally oriented.

What is the "right environment" for leadership success? In studies made on an international basis in an oil corporation, a conclusion was reached that the same behaviors that lead to the firing of one manager may lead to a vice presidency in another climate. Research in industrial leadership is beginning to look at the characteristics of individuals and the way they relate to the characteristics of organizations in terms of group interactions, goals, inputs, outputs, function among members, hierarchies of structure, and reward systems.

Special groups. Whether or not the older person likes being classified as a "golden ager" or the blind employee wishes he could be treated like his sighted co-workers, people do find themselves falling into special groups, and industry must deal with them as such.

On the basis of studies made in many countries, there appears to be an almost universal prejudice against women in industry, from both labor and management points of view. The multiple roles played by women in our culture affect problems related to work, and industrial psychologists are becoming concerned with these problems. As research findings are helping to belie old myths, women are slowly being given more opportunity in industry. Even more progress is being made with the acceptance of the handicapped worker now that studies show that through adequate job analysis, measurement, training, and job orientation, most physically handicapped workers are economic assets, motivation being an important variable.

Automation is adding emphasis to another special group—the unemployed and the unemployables. From studies by industrial psychiatrists, sociologists, and psychologists have come data showing that the degree to which unemployment affects the individual depends upon past experience, individual aspirations, socioeconomic class, community associations, age, sex, education, status, attitudes, resistance to change, personality, and the length of unemployment. Experience is also beginning to show that even the best programs of retraining may lead only to training for oblivion when technological advancement moves very rapidly.

A special group, increasing in numbers and influence, is currently receiving attention from both labor and management—the aging worker and manager. Industrial psychology is learning to answer certain questions: When does the man become unproductive? Have we been making the correct assumptions about age and creativity? How is personality related to retirement success? When should job decompression begin?

Findings from many studies of the aging person, reviewing his career development, are giving a new emphasis to the problems of mental health in industry, with consideration of the importance of the individual.

Men and machines

The problems of work efficiency, physical working conditions, evaluation of job performance, boredom, fatigue, and safety—long the traditional subject matter of industrial psychology—are now becoming organized within a framework of men and machines. The experimental psychologist has joined with the engineer in developing new machine systems. What is a system? How does man fit into it? How are the roles of the psychologist changing with automation? What can be done about the changing context of our human problems of work? These questions have only partial answers but are important to the new general industrial psychology.

The work environment. The principal contributions of psychologists in dealing with the problems of working efficiency have been methodological. Through their emphasis on experimental designs that control the effects of such factors as suggestion and attitude changes, it has been possible to develop at least some optimum levels of illumination, atmospheric conditions, noise control, and, more recently, weightlessness, confinement, and other factors related to space travel. Particular attention is being focused on the effects of certain extreme environmental conditions upon human performance. Psychologists have stimulated the investigation of individual differences in the effects of environmental variables (Anastasi 1964).

The industrial psychologist is interested in a wide range of problems at both the physical and mental levels: such physiological measures as blood pressure, oxygen consumption, and muscular responses, and such psychological indexes as fatigue, tiredness, boredom, and the effects of rest. The reader may appreciate the complexity of these "simple problems" by trying to determine what criteria can be used in devising a "comfort index" for clothing, a problem so far unsolved.

Performance appraisal. The analysis of the work of a typist, for example, may be thought of in terms of the typist's job itself, or in terms of the typed letter as an end product, or in terms of what the person does in typing the letter. Whether an analysis of the job, product, or man is involved, the psychologist is interested in helping to make evaluations, because they impinge upon so many things—personnel requirements, training content, job efficiency, wage rates, ratings for promotion, and production control. Evaluation, then, is being given increasing attention, whether at the level of time and motion study, merit rating, or the appraisal of executive decision making. Evaluation in industry is a problem as difficult, in some respects, as the measurement of "good teaching," and it sometimes carries with it the same emotional impact and resistance of those concerned.

Accidents and safety. Accident prevention, long looked upon as an engineering problem to be solved through the proper design of mechanical safety devices, is finally receiving attention as a behavior problem. The psychologist is interested in the interaction between unsafe acts and unsafe conditions, and in the relation of accidents to time of day, to job operation, and to cause-and-effect information. He has obtained data that question the assumptions that intelligence is related to accident occurrence and that injury is the result of accident proneness. There are researches that deal with problems of sensory defects and muscular coordination, motor and perceptual speed, fatigue, adjustment to stress, physical working conditions, and the effects of experience on accidents. Personality factors are being studied, and more recently the psychological climate of the workplace has been given attention. Complementary theories are beginning to emerge that should assist industry not only to escape the defeatism caused by an oversimplification of the problem but also to develop programs of accident prevention and to devise better techniques in motivating safety.

Engineering psychology and systems. The coming of age of a systematic conception of the application of psychological principles to the invention, development, and use of complex man–machine systems can be dated as the early 1960s (Gagné 1962). The driver and his horse and buggy constitute a system, as does the Bell Telephone Company, but in the context here the systems concept can be considered as a way of putting the man and the machine on even terms, no matter how complicated their relationship may be. The system is bigger than the sum of the elements that compose it, involving "inputs," "control," and "outputs."

The psychologist here has an interest in the human operator—how he perceives, interprets, and acts. He is interested in the channels of communication and how they can become overloaded, in the part redundancy plays in conveying information, and how information gets processed into perceptions, judgments, and decisions. He is also interested in the study of motor skills and reaction times in the interpretation of errors, as well as in the problems of automation.

For the industrial psychologist the problems are expanding, and in the role of the "human factors specialist" he must work with others, sometimes on a team with members as diverse as engineers, mathematicians, production specialists, and accountants. In research or development, the psychologist who follows the "systems approach" may become engaged in a wide variety of problems ranging from equipment design to the mapping of a human factors subsystem for the establishment of a new processing plant or organizational change. The systems psychologist must be creative and must have the ability to deal effectively with interrelationships between people and work environments and the processes whereby they interact.

The individual

Industrial psychology deals with the individual—how he behaves in small and in large groups, how he reacts to change, and how he responds in general to the organizational climate. Concern is given to personal aspirations and to the conflicts that arise when the work situation is not conducive to the satisfaction of individual needs, as well as to the ways in which organizations help or fail to help an individual to know how anxieties may improve or distort his perception of the company.

In studying the basis for career planning, industrial psychologists have considered generalizations about people and jobs, ranging from adolescent identifications that play a part in shaping vocational interests to what is involved in self-development. It also involves problems of criteria of success, upward mobility, technical obsolescence, and job change, as well as the ways in which levels of aspiration are related to abilities and to individual stress levels. Both the cognitive and the feeling approaches are important for understanding alternatives in personal aspirations, in the development of personal skills, and in the patterns of career survival.

Mental health in industry involves studies of absenteeism, alcoholism, grievances, and emotional disorders; dissatisfaction caused by pressure, frustration, and conflict; the defensive behaviors of individuals, which result in aggressive reactions, withdrawal reactions, and compromise reactions; and other behaviors commonly found among people in general. The industrial psychologist is concerned with providing some understanding of why people behave as they do, but he has no nostrums, panaceas, or gimmicks to offer an industrial society.

Trends

Researches in the area of general industrial psychology are published in several places: some in the professional journals of business, education, and sociology; a few in publications devoted mainly to engineering and medicine; but most in psychology journals, about two dozen of them North American, the remaining few world-wide. Textbooks in the field reflect a trend away from technology and toward more general coverage; most are published in English, some through translation. Although in volume most articles in the general area of industrial psychology are found in U.S. publications, many of the researches have come from world-wide sources.

In research, there appear to be trends toward intercultural studies and toward investigations of the interrelations between situational variables and personal characteristics; in addition, economic psychology is beginning to emerge, taking its place beside the new organizational psychology. No doubt the computer specialists, interested in decision-making processes and systems, will help expand the influence of psychology to higher levels of management. Some writers predict that industrial psychology, which began when the businessman asked for help from the academic psychologist and has remained to answer all kinds of practical problems, may venture forth with suggestions and proposals for new organizational theories. Human problems in industry will receive more attention as technological advancements and the increasing size of organizations give renewed emphasis to the needs of the individual. As industrial psychology approaches its seventh decade, the trend continues—*people are important.*

B. VON HALLER GILMER

[*Other relevant material may be found in* AUTOMATION; ENGINEERING PSYCHOLOGY; LEADERSHIP; ORGANIZATIONS; SOCIOMETRY.]

BIBLIOGRAPHY

The classical areas are covered by the Journal of Applied Psychology; Industrial Psychology; Personnel; *Centre d'Études et Recherches Psychologiques,* Bulletin; Occupational Psychology; *South African Council for Scientific and Industrial Research, National Institute for Personnel Research,* Journal; *and* Personnel Psychology. *Human relations trends can be traced through such journals as* Human Organization *and* Journal of Social Issues. *Articles on human factors in systems may be found in the* Journal of Experimental Psychology, *in* Ergonomics, *and in the* Hitotsubashi Journal of Commerce and Management. *Organizational psychology is discussed in* Management Science; Behavioral Science; Management International; Harvard Business Review; *and other business school journals. General trends are reviewed in the* American Psychologist; *yearly reviews of materials on industrial psychology appear in the* Annual Review of Psychology.

American Psychologist. → Published since 1946 by the American Psychological Association.

ANASTASI, ANNE 1964 *Fields of Applied Psychology.* New York: McGraw-Hill.

Annual Review of Psychology. → Published since 1950.

Behavioral Science. → Published quarterly since 1956 by the Mental Health Research Institute, University of Michigan.

CENTRE D'ÉTUDES ET RECHERCHES PSYCHOLOGIQUES *Bulletin.* → Published since 1951.

Ergonomics. → Published since 1957 by the Ergonomics Research Society.

Farmer, Eric 1958 Early Days in Industrial Psychology: An Autobiographical Note. *Occupational Psychology* 32:264–267.

Ferguson, Leonard W. 1963— *The Heritage of Industrial Psychology.* Hartford, Conn.: Finlay. → A multivolume series in progress.

Forehand, G. A.; and Gilmer, B. von Haller 1964 Environmental Variation in Studies of Organizational Behavior. *Psychological Bulletin* 62:361–382.

Gagné, Robert M. (editor) 1962 *Psychological Principles in System Development.* New York: Holt.

Gellerman, Saul W. 1960 *People, Problems and Profits.* New York: McGraw-Hill.

Ghiselli, Edwin E. 1963 Managerial Talent. *American Psychologist* 18:631–642.

Gilmer, B. von Haller (1961) 1966 *Industrial Psychology.* 2d ed. New York: McGraw-Hill.

Green, Bert F. Jr. 1963 *Digital Computers in Research? An Introduction for Behavioral and Social Scientists.* New York: McGraw-Hill.

Guest, Lester 1962 Consumer Analysis. *Annual Review of Psychology* 13:315–344.

Guion, Robert M. 1965 *Personnel Testing.* New York: McGraw-Hill.

Haire, Mason; Ghiselli, E. E.; and Porter, L. W. 1963 Cultural Patterns in the Role of the Manager. *Industrial Relations* 2, no. 2:95–117.

Harvard Business Review. → Published since 1922 by the Graduate School of Business Administration, Harvard University.

Hitotsubashi Journal of Commerce and Management. → Published since 1961 by Hitotsubashi University.

Human Organization. → Published since 1941 by the Society for Applied Anthropology.

Journal of Applied Psychology. → Published since 1917 by the American Psychological Association.

Journal of Experimental Psychology. → Published since 1916 by the American Psychological Association.

Journal of Social Issues. → Published since 1945 by the Society for the Psychological Study of Social Issues.

Kay, Brian R.; and Palmer, Stuart 1961 *The Challenge of Supervision.* New York: McGraw-Hill.

Krampen, M. 1961 Storia dei segnali stradali. *Stile industria* (Milan) 32:23–34.

Leavitt, Harold J. 1962 Management According to Task: Organizational Differentiation. *Management International* 2, no. 1:13–22.

Leavitt, Harold J.; and Bass, Bernard 1964 Organizational Psychology. *Annual Review of Psychology* 15: 371–398.

Management International. → Published since 1961.

Management Science. → Published since 1954 by the Institute of Management Sciences.

Marcus-Steiff, Joachim 1961 *Les études de motivation.* Paris: Hermann.

Occupational Psychology. → Published since 1922 by the National Institute of Industrial Psychology.

Personnel. → Published since 1919 by the American Management Association.

Personnel Psychology. → Published since 1948.

Roethlisberger, Fritz J.; and Dickson, William J. (1939) 1961 *Management and the Worker: An Account of a Research Program Conducted by the Western Electric Company, Hawthorne Works, Chicago.* Cambridge, Mass.: Harvard Univ. Press. → A paperback edition was published in 1964 by Wiley.

South African Council for Scientific and Industrial Research *Journal.* → Published irregularly from 1948 to 1961.

Vroom, Victor H. 1964 *Work and Motivation.* New York: Wiley.

II

THE SOCIOLOGY OF WORK

Sociology has a long tradition behind it, but as a science it is of recent origin. In the course of establishing its scientific credentials it has continually improved its methodology and refined its conceptual apparatus; this process has inevitably confronted it with new areas for study. In particular, sociological research has applied itself to the phenomenon of work and to the various aspects of industrial society or society in process of industrialization. The result has been the emergence of the sociology of work (*sociologie du travail*)—a designation which, as used by French sociologists, has a rather broader application than the Anglo–American "industrial sociology."

No formal definition could do justice to the great variety of concerns that are usually listed under this head. A systematic account of the sociology of work, one that would outline its main dimensions and demonstrate its connections with neighboring fields, would require a theoretical framework that sociology does not yet possess, although some progress has been made in this direction. Thus Etzioni (1958), using a Parsonian frame of reference, has defined industrial sociology as a branch of organizational sociology; but this definition seems too restrictive in view of the range of problems usually dealt with by the sociology of work. For lack of a general theoretical framework we are forced to fall back on a rule-of-thumb definition: the sociology of work is the study, in all its varied aspects, of work as a human activity and of all the social institutions that arise for its sake (Friedmann & Naville 1961–1962). Such a definition has the advantage of highlighting the complex nature of work and of showing how its different manifestations are bound up with each other. On the other hand, it is not a definition that leads to a systematic or intuitively satisfying classification of the problems actually studied. Other definitions of the sociology of work, such as those of Miller and Form (1951) and Schneider (1957), are still broader in scope, and it will be noted that their authors organize their coverage of the topic in ways quite different from that attempted here.

What is work? But what does "work" really signify? One long-standing tradition of inquiry seeks to define work in terms of the dynamic relationship between man and nature. Marx, for instance, saw work as being essentially man's transformation, through technology, of his natural environment, which reacts in turn by modifying man's own nature. Against this, one can argue that the activity of man in industrial society no longer has much in common with that of the earlier *Homo faber*, since it is no longer bound to be either rural or industrial. This is because, with the development of the so-called tertiary sector of the economy, and the accompanying increase in managerial and administrative tasks, work often means the action of man upon man (or upon groups, or even the larger society) instead of upon a nonhuman environment.

Other writers have sought to formulate a definition of work based on the economic necessities that underlie it. They argue that the function of work was originally the satisfaction of elementary human needs; in industrial society, however, men work in order to obtain the wherewithal to satisfy a range of needs that is constantly expanding. Since the reward of work is no longer the direct satisfaction of needs, but the financial means by which they may be satisfied, to work implies a certain economic dependence which, since its nature varies, offers a basis for distinguishing between work activities according to whether they are wage-earning, self-employed, etc. The problems of social justice generated by industrialization—problems that have been, and continue to be, the focus of much controversy—impelled many social philosophers to take up the related problem of work. The stream of thought that resulted has been responsible in large part for the emergence of the sociology of work.

This is not the place to pursue these definitions of work in greater detail. It should, however, be noted that a word of caution is in order when dealing with general definitions that lack any base in history, sociology, ethnography, or economics. Definitions of work that take into account neither the variety of concrete forms it may assume in different societies, cultures, and civilizations nor the various ways in which it forms part of the life and experience of those who perform it cannot help but lead to a scientific dead end.

In actual fact, work undergoes the same evolutions and transformations that societies do; it is therefore hardly surprising that the sociology of work, which is concerned with depicting this process, should undergo corresponding changes in both scope and content. To be more specific, technological transformations such as the mechanization of agriculture, the introduction of computers for administrative and commercial purposes, the various advances in transportation, and so forth, have all combined to give a new and rapidly expanding meaning to the very concept of industry. The term "industrial sociology" reflects these developments, as does the somewhat forced extension of its meaning by which it has come to include studies of nonindustrial institutions or even of industrial civilization in general. From this perspective, the "sociology of work" is a much clearer expression. But, from a different point of view, it embraces a wider field, for it cannot be denied that hospitals, schools, and universities—to name only a few examples—contain permanent work forces. It may be asked whether these are really work institutions (*collectivités de travail*). But the conclusion seems unavoidable that they are, even if the functions of these organizations are not purely economic. The industrial sociologist holds no monopoly on the study of such institutions; his way of approaching a problem is different from but compatible with that of the educational sociologist, for example, or the sociologist of organizations. Here, the fluid boundaries of the sociology of work can no longer be explained by the changing nature of society but, rather, by the development of sociology itself, the provisional quality of its conceptual tools, and the newness of the territory that it explores. Because sociology lacks a theoretical framework to divide it into specific fields, encroachment of one sociological specialty upon the domain of another is unavoidable. But we should not take alarm at this: from a relativistic point of view, encroachment of this kind is perfectly legitimate.

Accordingly, it seems that the best way of giving an intelligible account of the sociology of work is to review the main questions with which it has been concerned and the results that it has obtained. But first a brief historical account of its development will be necessary.

Origins of the sociology of work

It is now generally admitted that the origins of the sociology of work can be traced to the monumental series of experiments conducted by Elton Mayo and his Harvard colleagues at the Hawthorne Works of the Western Electric Company (for a description of the state of research, both psychological and physiological, into the work process at the time when Mayo began his experiments, see Friedman 1946; Madge 1962, pp. 162–166 in 1963 edition).

In 1927 the management of this important factory invited Mayo to come and study the variations in its workers' output. The management had already begun to study the effect on output of lighting workshops at different levels of intensity and had obtained some results that it found itself quite unable to explain. Mayo's study took over five years (for an account, see Roethlisberger & Dickson 1939). The first stage was taken up with scrupulous measurement of the output of five female operatives engaged in the assembly of telephone relays. The operatives' consent to this measurement was obtained, and their working conditions were the same as those in the main workshop, except that they were in a room apart from the other workers. During this whole period, Mayo systematically varied the working conditions of these five operatives in such respects as the number and duration of their rest periods and coffee breaks, as well as their total hours of work.

The results were disconcerting: there was definitely a steady increase in output, but there were also fluctuations in output that appeared to have no connection with the variations in the environment or in working conditions. Even the abolition of certain privileges these operatives had been granted did not cause a decline in their level of production. On the contrary, the more production increased, the more positive became the girls' attitude toward their work.

Mayo and his co-workers interpreted these results in terms of the group relations that had been established both among the workers themselves and between the workers and their supervisors. They believed that relations of trust and friendship had been established with these young workers to such a degree that, practically speaking, there was no longer any need to supervise them. In other words, the morale of these workers had improved as soon as they were no longer coerced or interrupted, and, at the same time, they had begun to produce more. The way was now open for the study of morale, supervision, and productivity.

The second stage of Mayo's inquiry took the form of a series of nondirective interviews, the results of which confirmed his earlier conclusions. These interviews highlighted the importance of subjective factors but also brought out the fact that the workers' participation in various groups outside the factory could have an adverse effect on productivity and morale inside the factory.

Nevertheless, these results encouraged Mayo to complete his study by a number of on-the-spot observations of groups inside the factory. During this third stage observers were placed in a workshop where the usual working conditions of the factory were in force, with a view to studying, on a day-to-day basis, both the individual workers and their relations with each other. Thus the earlier interviews were complemented by direct observation of behavior. The observers very soon discovered the existence of various restrictive practices and curbs on production, even though the workers were paid according to how much they produced (restriction of output has since been much studied—see, for example, Roy 1952; Durand 1959*a*; a general discussion of the role of financial incentives can be found in Whyte et al. 1955). Each worker's level of production was informally determined by the group, which turned out to have a life of its own, complete with customs, norms, and a system of social control that was most effective in exacting conformity to its rules. This "informal organization" of the group could therefore set itself up in tacit opposition to managerial expectations; it protected the workers against outside interference as well as against indiscretion within their own ranks.

Accordingly, this series of experiments led to the "discovery" of the importance of the work group and of social relations in factory life. Although it may be conceded that, compared with developments in sociological theory during the same period, the Hawthorne experiments did not amount to any genuine scientific discovery, they did afford a scientific demonstration, *in vivo*, of the role of social groups.

Mayo's inquiries stimulated much comment, as well as some violent criticism (see especially Kerr & Fisher 1957). But this criticism was directed more against the general philosophy of Mayo and his followers than against his empirical methods and results. Mayo did indeed believe that one of the tasks to which industry had been called in the modern world was to integrate the isolated, anomic individual into society by providing him with a harmonious social order in which it would be possible for him to find happiness (see, for instance, Mayo 1933; 1945). He thought that thanks to the social skills of management, such integration and harmony could be achieved and that, as a result, conflicts of interest would disappear (a savage criticism of the personnel policies inspired by this philosophy can be found in Wilensky & Wilensky 1951).

This ideology was able to emerge because of the Hawthorne study's main shortcoming: it allowed the company to remain as if in a social vacuum and gave no information whatsoever about the factory's environment and the various economic and social bases of its existence (Friedmann 1946, pp. 301–323 in 1954 edition). It cannot be denied that the economic, social, and cultural environment of the factory had a certain influence on the behavior of its employees, but the authors of the study were far more interested in what was going on inside the factory.

Criticism of this kind should not make us forget

the considerable stir created by the Hawthorne study. For instance, Madge (1962, pp. 208–209 in 1963 edition) is of the opinion that the study resulted in a number of methodological innovations that were very advanced by the standards of the time; among these he numbers the nondirective interview, content analysis, experimental design, and observation in a factory with the cooperation of both management and workers. The conclusions of Mayo and his co-workers completely upset the commonly held notions of how workers react to authority and how production can be stimulated. Instead, a social model of the worker was put forward to oppose the mechanistic, economic, and even psychological models then current. This social model installed the logic of human emotions side by side with the logic of costs or efficiency. After the Hawthorne experiments it had to be granted that an informal structure of social relations did exist behind the formal organizational structure and that numerous phenomena could not be explained on any other grounds.

The work of Kurt Lewin on group behavior ran parallel to that of Mayo and his school, although Lewin's findings owed nothing to Mayo. In a famous experiment (Lewin et al. 1939) he demonstrated that in a boys' club a democratic style of leadership was more effective in increasing both group productivity and satisfaction with work than either an authoritarian or a laissez-faire style. Lewin's general approach is not far removed from Mayo's: one finds the same sort of emphasis on the group and on interpersonal relations that is such a prominent feature of American culture in general. The meeting of these two currents of research, together with the sociocultural preoccupations of the wartime and postwar periods that followed, gave considerable impetus to research in the United States and elsewhere, and made possible the study of new problems [*see* LEADERSHIP]. It is to this research in new areas and its results that we must now turn.

Work groups and supervision

The literature on morale and productivity stems directly from the work of Mayo and his associates and represents by far the largest body of data on any topic in the field. But the importance of the results obtained is not proportionate to the number of studies published; indeed, the research too often merely confirms earlier work without adding anything to it.

The usual strategy of this type of research is to treat group supervision and styles of leadership as independent variables, mainly with a view to explaining rates of productivity and absenteeism. Other frequent objects of interest are turnover of personnel, industrial accidents, communication networks, union membership, work disputes, and the "go-slow" (i.e., voluntary restriction of output). Morale is seen as an intervening variable that mediates between these two classes of phenomena; it is an ambiguous concept, best described as a kind of sum total of all the satisfactions afforded to an individual by his belonging to an organization (see, for instance, Morse 1953). The meaning of "morale" is never defined systematically; it is a blanket term for all sorts of emotional states that should be specified in detail. Some attempts have been made to isolate its main dimensions, and it has become clear that the relations of a group of workers with each other and with their supervisors reflect only one aspect of work satisfactions.

It is known that morale varies with different styles of leadership; a work group that has a boss who allows his workers some autonomy, is careful of their feelings, and so on, will display higher work satisfaction, at least in the United States. Such leadership will also result in greater group cohesion, another source of work satisfaction (Kahn & Katz 1953; Seashore 1955), and will make it easier to introduce technological innovations (Coch & French 1948).

At first it was thought that a high level of morale always involves a high level of productivity, and conversely. However, even though this relation is the one most frequently encountered, later and more sophisticated research has shown that low morale can coexist with healthy productivity or high morale with impaired productivity. There is no lack of explanations that purport to account for such correlations: in the former case it may be that the group has been stimulated to produce by fear of punishment or of authoritarian leadership, while in the latter it may be that the group is a cohesive one, with goals of its own that interfere with production.

For those in search of a formula, these results are somewhat disappointing. Recent studies have served only to complicate the situation by specifying the conditions under which the relationship between morale (or its various dimensions) and productivity is positive or negative. Such studies, as we shall see, have been especially concerned with organizational structure—an emphasis that has arisen partly from the failure of, and consequent attempt to evaluate, company training programs in "human relations." It is now realized that the individual work group does not exist in isolation: the organization of which it forms part *is* its environment and cannot be overlooked. Thus, it has been found that a manager is not likely to follow a style of supervision that differs from the one used by his immediate superior—and so on, throughout the entire organizational hierarchy (Fleishman 1951; Mann 1951). Again, a foreman who runs his shop "by the book" will inspire high morale only if he has influence with management (Pelz 1952).

The sociology of organizations

Earlier sections of this article have shown how, in order to understand the behavior of workers, it is necessary to grasp the importance of certain social phenomena at the level of the work group and of the social relations implied by the group. But the business firm as a whole constitutes no less of a setting for the actions of its members; it is a social system in itself, with its own characteristics and requirements. It is along these lines that research into business firms and work institutions, qua organizations, has made rapid progress, so that it has now become one of the established approaches to the sociology of work. Each of the many studies undertaken in this direction has provided a springboard for further studies, until the field now known as the "sociology of organizations" has taken shape. Moreover, researchers in this field have been tempted into going beyond the traditional boundaries of the sociology of work and have carried their observations to noneconomic institutions such as prisons, churches, hospitals, universities, and voluntary associations. Thus a source of progress in this area has been the juxtaposition of data drawn from different types of institutions.

At this point it is probably best to digress briefly in order to define what is meant by "organization." Research seems to show that organizations have five salient features: a *network of statuses*, circumscribed and defined within a whole, that are filled by replaceable individuals; an attitude of *responsible role commitment* on the part of the individuals who fill those statuses; *specific goals* toward which all the members of the organization are supposed to work; a stable and coordinated system of relations between statuses—in other words, a *structure;* and one or more *centers of power* for controlling the organization's activities and guiding it toward the realization of its goals. In brief, although an organization chart may summarize organizational structure, it does not give an exhaustive description of an organization. It is also clear that unless a firm or institution assumes fairly considerable dimensions, it is not usually called an organization at all [*see* ORGANIZATIONS, *article on* THEORIES OF ORGANIZATIONS].

One trend in the study of organizations is closely derived from the work of Mayo and the human relations school. This is the contrast that is often made between formal and informal organizational structure. By informal structure is meant the social relations that develop both parallel to and outside the relations laid down by the organization chart. Formal organization imposes constraints on individuals and groups through its distribution of statuses and authority. The most effective organization will be the one that can give most satisfaction to its members, since, by making the workers "happy" and by responding to their needs through giving them opportunities for participation in decision making (and other appropriate techniques of management and communication), it will make them both identify with and cooperate in fulfilling the organizational goals.

Somewhat in reaction to this school of thought, several authors have drawn attention to the formal structure of organizations (see Merton et al. 1952; Blau 1956; Blau & Scott 1962; Selznick 1957). In the tradition of Frederick Winslow Taylor and, above all, Max Weber, they have specified the conditions for the effectiveness of a rational, bureaucratic organization: perfect adaptation of means to ends, and the use of abstract and universal rules. In short, they provide a timely reminder that an organization must give priority to reaching the goals it has set itself (the supporters of Mayo and his school had indeed tended to neglect this limiting factor in their search for industrial harmony). This new emphasis on goals has given rise to much empirical analysis of organizational structure. For instance, the effects of centralization and decentralization on organizational effectiveness have been studied by Tannenbaum (1956*a*), who distinguishes two aspects of control—total amount and distribution—and then relates them to the effectiveness of organizations in attaining their goals.

But the ideal of bureaucratic organization is seldom realized because of interference from the human factor, which introduces an element of irrationality that shows itself in bureaucratic routine, inertia, and ritualism. Every new regulation or extension of authority designed to remove these sources of inefficiency only tends to aggravate the problem, and the organization continues to deviate from its original goals.

Some more recent studies (see, for instance, Foundation for Research . . . 1959; Etzioni 1961*a*;

1961*b*; Crozier 1961; 1963) have attempted to combine formal and informal organization, or normal and dysfunctional behavior, within a single conceptual scheme. Contemporary theories of organization claim, in effect, to explain at the same time both conformity and nonconformity to the norms of rationality. But these norms do not guarantee organizational effectiveness. Neither individually conceived courses of action nor interpersonal relationships are necessarily alien or deviant when judged in terms of the formal organizational framework. Sometimes they may increase efficiency by making official relationships, such as that between superior and subordinate, both more flexible and less remote. They can also depend on more formal exchanges and make them more harmonious (see, for example, Gouldner 1954; Gross 1953).

For a long time, organizations were considered to be stable, closed systems; the question of organizational change was not raised at all. Increasingly, however, various authors are taking into consideration conflict that arises within the organization itself. The possible mechanisms of change are no longer confined to external stimuli; they are also to be found in the individual and collective strategies of members who seek power or who form centers of hard-core opposition to present policy (Crozier 1963).

The social morphology of work

Sociological interest in the relations between technology and social patterns is of long standing. Authors such as Karl Marx and Max Weber have made contributions in this area, but only at the level of generalities about whole societies and cultures. More recently, other authors have studied the effects of technological change on individual cities and industries (Warner & Low 1947; Walker 1950; 1957).

Contemporary sociology has developed two major concerns in this field. The first of these is the study of how changes in the technical and organizational aspects of work have an impact on skill levels, on the structure of work groups, and on occupational socialization. Most of the research in this area is of European, especially French, origin (Friedmann 1946; 1956; Touraine 1955; Durand 1959*b*; Verry 1955). On the one hand, the course of technological progress can be traced from the versatile type of machine that, like a tool, serves to prolong certain operations performable by human beings, to automatic machinery that performs tasks beyond human reach, with the specialized, single-operation machine representing an intermediate stage. On the other hand, the progress made in the organization of production has resulted in a coordination of multistage tasks that is increasingly complex, precise, and deliberate. These two trends, which have run parallel, have eliminated the craftsman with his slowly acquired knowledge of product, raw materials, and tools. Instead, a multitude of jobs have been created in which one or several fragmented operations designed by management are repeated ad infinitum by workers who are never called upon to exercise any initiative. Thus the worker becomes more and more dependent, until he loses all vestige of autonomy. In an automated setting, work becomes a matter of keeping alert, of watching instrument panels and interpreting the symbols on them (Naville 1958).

Also symptomatic of these changes are the trends, apparent from labor statistics, in the relative numbers of unskilled, skilled, and professional workers. The work group, too, is in process of transformation. At one time it had a steep, continuous hierarchy based on differences in knowledge; experience made it possible to climb from one level of the hierarchy to another. Mechanization made the hierarchy discontinuous: the specialized worker did not depend on his co-workers; the foreman was no longer omnicompetent; promotion by experience ceased to exist. Automation, however, appears to have made workers more dependent on each other (Mann & Hoffman 1960).

The second major concern in the social morphology of work is analysis of workers' interaction and attitudes, and of group structure—that is, of the strategies open to workers, given the technical conditions of the work setting (see, for example, Whyte 1951*a*; Sayles 1958). In particular several authors have demonstrated that there is a close relationship between the technical characteristics of the work setting and the status or prestige system of the work group. This relationship becomes especially obvious when technological change upsets informal group structure and causes unrest among the employees so affected; for instance, workers' resistance to innovation can sometimes be explained in this way. Here there is a convergence of interests with certain members of the human relations school.

Industrial relations and trade unionism

Much has been written about trade unions, trade unionism, and the relations between unions and employers. But this literature, though plentiful, is disappointing, since little progress has been made in the sociological analysis of problems in this field. All these studies tend to have a parochial character because they hardly ever contain any integrating concepts. All too often an author is content merely to describe how unions work; studies of the labor movement that succeed in integrating or transcending the historical and legal levels are extremely rare. As a result, findings based on one situation usually cannot be applied to others, and it is very difficult to compare different findings or draw general conclusions from them. Moreover, it seems likely that the ideological component historically associated with trade unionism has stood in the way of impartial scientific observation. In spite of this handicap and the reservations already mentioned, it can be said that enough genuine sociological analysis has been done in this area to raise a whole series of questions.

The first group of these questions relates to the reasons for becoming a union member and for participating in union activities. Various partial explanations of these phenomena have been obtained from comparison of active members, passive members, and nonmembers (Tannenbaum & Kahn 1958; Tagliacozzo & Seidmann 1956; Benoit 1962; see Lipset & Gordon in Bendix & Lipset 1953). In the special cultural setting of the United States, active union members are characterized by longer job tenure (which means that they have more of a stake in the situation) and by less social mobility than other workers; they are not necessarily more hostile to management—in fact, they are sometimes more friendly (Stagner 1954). However, it seems likely that these findings apply mainly to trade unions of a definite type. It is not at all clear that union members in a different kind of context—a revolutionary one, for instance—would have the same kinds of reasons for joining or taking part.

A second and more important group of questions centers on the relations between union and management at the factory level. What type of union is responsive to what type of management? In what ways do union and management influence each other, and what mutual transformations do they effect? Which conditions encourage conflict, and which ones cooperation? Some authors have ventured to construct typologies of union–management relations (see, for instance, Illinois, University of . . . 1954). Another promising approach is the study of union and management behavior over time. Indeed, if we follow Whyte (1951*b*) in believing that what a union wants at the factory level is to be the initiator of any interaction with management (which is itself a form of power), then it is clear that if opportunities to initiate interaction were more equitably distributed, a more harmonious form of coexistence between union and management would result. Here again the concern of American sociologists has been to guarantee industrial peace. Nevertheless, at least one American author has argued that industrial conflict, since it can be organized as an adaptive force, may have certain positive functions (Dubin 1960). The more it is assumed that trade unions, as far as management is concerned, constitute a kind of countervailing power, the more it will appear that conflicts of interest between union and management, while inevitable, are not necessarily to be deplored [*see* LABOR UNIONS, *article on* THEORIES OF THE LABOR MOVEMENT].

These considerations have led to a view of the union as a complex organization. The internal functioning of unions has been studied with the aid of the admittedly crude methodology originally developed for the study of industrial organizations. Because trade unionism is one of the mainstays of democratic ideology, the distribution of power in unions poses a number of particularly acute problems. In fact, democracy in trade unions is the exception, not the rule, as Lipset and his colleagues have shown (1956). A more original study (Tannenbaum 1956*b*) has dealt with the relations between democracy and effectiveness in the dealings of unions with employers; the important variable is neither union democracy nor the sharing of power between all levels of union organization but, rather, the total amount of power at the union's disposal.

The fourth group of questions stems from the problems of society as a whole. Here mention should be made of those theories of the labor movement which tend to explain variations in union behavior by pointing to national differences in degree or rate of industrialization or (since the labor movement is part of a nation's political life) in political stability (Touraine 1960).

The study of industrial conflict, especially of strikes, which represent the most violent form taken by such conflict, constitutes a fifth problem area that involves industrial relations at all four of the analytical levels distinguished above. At the social-psychological or motivational level, there is the question of how strikers differ from nonstrikers. At the level of industrial relations in the factory itself, it is necessary to inquire into the nature of the factors that trigger a strike. At the level of union organization a whole series of questions presents itself. How do unions decide to go on strike? What functions do strikes fulfill? How are unauthorized strikes to be evaluated? At the societal level, it has been demonstrated that the number, length, and intensity of strikes are closely related to the institutional framework of industrial relations (Ross & Hartman 1960). At the same level, the fact that some industries are more prone to strikes than others has been attributed to the physical and social isolation of the majority of workers in these industries, most of which are located far from the central cities and therefore offer little opportunity for social mobility. If workers in these industries, it is argued, were integrated with the rest of society, they would be less likely to resort to violence [Kerr & Siegel 1954; *see also* LABOR RELATIONS, *article on* STRIKES].

A sixth and final group of questions deals with worker participation in factory management (the so-called workers' councils). This is an essentially European phenomenon, and a very controversial one (Delamotte 1959; Clegg 1960). The truth seems to be that worker participation, when it really takes place, is always closely bound up with the existing machinery for settling disputes at the factory level. There is no solid evidence that workers' councils radically alter the balance of power in a factory, and it does not seem likely that any better results will be obtained from them in future. According to Sturmthal (1961), programs for worker participation in factory management represent an essentially ideological approach to the problem of worker control. The administrative bodies set up for the purpose of worker participation tend, in Poland at least, to reduce union activity to a low level rather than to keep the factory running smoothly.

Work and industrial civilization

The sociology of work is not exclusively concerned with problems that arise in the actual work setting. Many of these problems carry over into life outside the place of work. A truly comprehensive study of work phenomena necessarily implies study of nonwork phenomena, because both classes of phenomena are linked in a mutually causal relationship which in itself constitutes an area largely unexplored by social scientists.

A case in point is the study of occupational careers, which can be approached from two different points of view. In the first of these, the focus of interest is not on the place of work but on the individual's entire working life. What are the stages of the working career, from the first entry into regular employment up to the point of retirement? How do these stages vary under different technological and social conditions? What attitudes and aspirations are associated with the different types of careers and their various stages? Studies of occupational and social mobility have provided us with dynamic models of careers and career-related attitudes (see especially Lipset & Bendix 1952). We know, for instance, that downwardly mobile individuals do not exhibit the same patterns of behavior as those who are upwardly mobile or those who have retained their position in the social hierarchy (Lipset & Gordon in Bendix & Lipset 1953; Wilensky & Edwards 1959). Thus the sociological significance of an individual's career is held to consist in the amount and type of social mobility that he achieves.

The second point of view is one that considers the working career in terms of relations with peer groups. "Professionalization" is the name sociologists have given to the way in which the span of working life tends to follow the pattern of a more or less regulated career over which occupational peers have an increasing amount of control at the expense of formal superiors, so that the occupation acquires a more or less recognized social status (Foote 1956). As such, professionalization is a recent phenomenon. "Professionalized" groups model themselves on the liberal professions. They are, to a large extent, self-regulating. They confer on their members, who are employed by organizations, a certain measure of autonomy that is not based wholly on expertise. Under these circumstances, relations between the occupation and the general labor market become less close and less determined by purely economic factors [*see* OCCUPATIONS AND CAREERS].

Other studies have sought to understand the role of different occupational groups, especially workers, engineers and technicians, and the managerial elite, both in the factory and in the larger society. The development of these social groups throws light on the development of society and its equilibrium. Thus the sociology of work becomes the study of industrial society.

There is no doubt that residential patterns, family life, and leisure in many respects both influence and are influenced by the complex of phenomena that we call work. The sociology of work is not concerned with these areas external to work except insofar as reciprocal influences of this kind can be said to exist. But research on this whole topic is a difficult undertaking because the leading issues have not yet been clearly defined.

General contribution of the field

The sociology of knowledge has laid bare the dependence of scientific research—the problems it selects and the manner in which it approaches them—on economic, social, and cultural conditions. The sociology of work is no exception to this rule of dependence. It has already been shown how closely the very definition of work is bound up with the problems of society. The same applies to all the areas dealt with by this branch of sociology. If this discussion were taken up again from its beginning, it would be easy to demonstrate how for each group of sociological problems there has always been a corresponding group of social problems on which researchers have sought to throw light. Every question posed by researchers is the product of a unique moment in the history of the topic, a moment associated with the emergence of a particular social problem. Thus the theory of organizations, although it had some forerunners, reached its full development only during a period in which there was a rising public consciousness of the way in which large corporations and public bureaucracies were extending their control over the centers of power and the lives of individuals.

The sociology of work has been much criticized for combining sociological research with the study of social problems. It has been argued that the field can never be more than an applied science concerned with strictly practical problems; the studies it has produced have been called "piecemeal and repetitious," and therefore of no use to the development of sociological theory. But even if it is true that the theoretical contributions of the sociology of work have been relatively weak, considering the impressively large output of studies, it should nevertheless be concluded that these criticisms are exaggerated. The positive contribution of the sociology of work should be abundantly clear from the studies cited in this article; at the least, this contribution consists in the perspective afforded by a scientific consideration of the facts, as opposed to philosophical and ideological speculation on social matters.

Future trends

At the present time, one of the most pressing of all social problems is the economic and social development of the "third world." The subject has claimed the attention of many researchers already well known for their contributions to the sociology of work. But it is hardly possible to treat the problems of work in the countries of the third world in the same way as the problems of countries that have long since been industrialized. The need is beginning to be felt for a more diachronic approach, with greater emphasis on whole societies and on cultural variation between societies (Moore 1963).

Every section of this article could be reviewed in terms of the new perspectives opened up by the study of problems in countries that are undergoing industrialization. For instance, how can the norms of a traditional culture be reconciled with the norms of an industrial organization, and vice versa? The question of the relations between formal and informal organization also arises in the developing countries, but in a quite different form. Study of the trade union movement in these countries is far more concerned with the movement's links to the centers of political power and to economic development in general than with union activity at the local level (Galenson 1959; Touraine 1960).

In the same way, study of the effects of the technological revolution is being broadened; it is no longer confined to changes at the job or factory level, but includes the entire process of technological change (Moore 1963). Technological change, moreover, is no longer treated as a *fait accompli* with effects that are studied only after the event. Instead, attempts are being made to discover the conditions capable of producing technological change. For this reason a special interest attaches to any factors associated with change or innovation. It does indeed appear that most of the developing countries, unlike nineteenth-century Europe, have a strong desire for and willingness to accept economic development. This trend has inspired Harbison and Myers (see Princeton University . . . 1959) to undertake research on the role of different elites in the process of industrialization. This new orientation of the sociology of work has had, like its predecessors, a beneficial effect on approaches to the problems that came before it. On the one hand, it has helped researchers to place more emphasis on the internal preconditions for change, whereas formerly the social system was regarded as tending naturally toward stability and equilibrium, with change coming only from outside. On the other hand, it has abandoned determinism in favor of a view of human action that is more voluntaristic and teleological.

ODILE BENOIT-GUILBOT

[*Directly related are the entries* AUTOMATION; BUSINESS MANAGEMENT; INDUSTRIALIZATION; LABOR FORCE; LABOR RELATIONS; LABOR UNIONS; ORGANIZATIONS; TECHNOLOGY; WORKERS. *Other relevant material may be found in* GROUPS; INDUSTRY, SMALL; LEADERSHIP; MODERNIZATION; OCCUPATIONS

AND CAREERS; PROFESSIONS; SOCIAL MOBILITY; *and in the biographies of* BARNARD; LEWIN; MAYO.]

BIBLIOGRAPHY

Wilensky 1954 *is a comprehensive bibliography for the period before 1950; for the period 1951–1962 see* Tréanton & Reynaud 1963–1964.

BENDIX, REINHARD; and LIPSET, SEYMOUR M. (editors) 1953 *Class, Status and Power: A Reader in Social Stratification.* Glencoe, Ill.: Free Press. → See especially the article by Seymour M. Lipset and J. Gordon, "Mobility and Trade-union Membership."

BENOIT, ODILE 1962 Statut dans l'enterprise et attitudes syndicales des ouvriers. *Sociologie du travail* 4:230–242.

BLAU, PETER M. 1956 *Bureaucracy in Modern Society.* New York: Random House.

BLAU, PETER M.; and SCOTT, W. RICHARD 1962 *Formal Organizations: A Comparative Approach.* San Francisco: Chandler.

CLEGG, HUGH A. 1960 *A New Approach to Industrial Democracy.* Oxford: Blackwell.

COCH, LESTER; and FRENCH, JOHN R. P. JR. 1948 Overcoming Resistance to Change. *Human Relations* 1: 512–532.

CROZIER, MICHEL 1961 De la bureaucratie comme système d'organisation. *Archives européennes de sociologie* 2, no. 1:18–50.

CROZIER, MICHEL (1963) 1964 *The Bureaucratic Phenomenon.* Univ. of Chicago Press. → First published as *Le phénomène bureaucratique.*

DELAMOTTE, YVES 1959 Conflit industriel et participation ouvrière. *Sociologie du travail* 1:12–23.

DUBIN, ROBERT 1960 A Theory of Conflict and Power in Union–Management Relations. *Industrial and Labor Relations Review* 13:501–518.

DURAND, CLAUDE 1959*a* Rémunération au rendement et motivations ouvrières. *Sociologie du travail* 1:46–57.

DURAND, CLAUDE 1959*b* L'évolution du travail dans les laminoirs. *Revue française du travail* 13, no. 1:3–18.

ETZIONI, AMITAI (1958) 1961 Industrial Sociology: The Study of Economic Organizations. Pages 130–141 in Amitai Etzioni (editor), *Complex Organizations: A Sociological Reader.* New York: Holt.

ETZIONI, AMITAI 1961*a* *A Comparative Analysis of Complex Organizations: On Power, Involvement, and Their Correlates.* New York: Free Press.

ETZIONI, AMITAI (editor) 1961*b* *Complex Organizations: A Sociological Reader.* New York: Holt.

FLEISHMAN, E. A. 1951 Leadership Climate and Supervisory Behavior: A Study of the Leadership Role of the Foreman in an Industrial Situation. Unpublished manuscript, Ohio State Univ., Personnel Research Board.

FOOTE, NELSON N. 1956 The Movement From Jobs to Careers in American Industry. World Congress of Sociology, 3rd, *Transactions* 2:30–40.

FOUNDATION FOR RESEARCH ON HUMAN BEHAVIOR 1959 *Modern Organization Theory: A Symposium.* Edited by Mason Haire. New York: Wiley.

FRIEDMANN, GEORGES (1946) 1955 *Industrial Society: The Emergence of the Human Problems of Automation.* Glencoe, Ill.: Free Press. → First published as *Problèmes humains du machinisme industriel.* See especially pages 301–323.

FRIEDMANN, GEORGES 1956 *Le travail en miettes: Specialisation et loisirs.* Paris: Gallimard.

FRIEDMANN, GEORGES; and NAVILLE, PIERRE 1961–1962 *Traité de sociologie du travail.* 2 vols. Paris: Colin.

GALENSON, WALTER (editor) 1959 *Labor and Economic Development.* New York: Wiley.

GOULDNER, ALVIN W. 1954 *Patterns of Industrial Bureaucracy.* Glencoe, Ill.: Free Press.

GROSS, E. 1953 Some Functional Consequences of Primary Control in Formal Work Organizations. *American Sociological Review* 18:368–373.

ILLINOIS, UNIVERSITY OF, INSTITUTE OF LABOR AND INDUSTRIAL RELATIONS 1954 *Labor–Management Relations in Illini City.* Volume 2: Exploration in Comparative Analysis. Champaign, Ill.: The Institute.

KAHN, ROBERT L.; and KATZ, DANIEL (1953) 1960 Leadership Practices in Relation to Productivity and Morale. Pages 554–570 in Dorwin Cartwright and Alvin F. Zander (editors), *Group Dynamics: Research and Theory.* 2d ed. Evanston, Ill.: Row, Peterson.

KERR, CLARK; and FISHER, LLOYD H. 1957 Plant Sociology: The Elites and the Aborigines. Pages 281–309 in Mirra Komarovsky (editor), *Common Frontiers of the Social Sciences.* Glencoe, Ill.: Free Press.

KERR, CLARK; and SIEGEL, A. 1954 The Interindustry Propensity to Strike: An International Comparison. Pages 189–212 in Arthur W. Kornhauser, Robert Dubin, and Arthur M. Ross (editors), *Industrial Conflict.* New York: McGraw-Hill.

LEWIN, KURT; LIPPITT, R.; and WHITE, R. K. 1939 Patterns of Aggressive Behavior in Experimentally Created "Social Climates." *Journal of Social Psychology* 10:271–299.

LIPSET, SEYMOUR M.; and BENDIX, REINHARD 1952 Social Mobility and Occupational Career Patterns. *American Journal of Sociology* 57:366–374, 494–504.

LIPSET, SEYMOUR M.; TROW, MARTIN A.; and COLEMAN, JAMES S. 1956 *Union Democracy: The Internal Politics of the International Typographical Union.* Glencoe, Ill.: Free Press. → A paperback edition was published in 1962 by Doubleday.

MADGE, JOHN H. (1962) 1964 *The Origins of Scientific Sociology.* New York: Free Press.

MANN, FLOYD C. 1951 Changing Superior–Subordinate Relationships. *Journal of Social Issues* 7, no. 3:56–63.

MANN, FLOYD C.; and HOFFMAN, L. RICHARD 1960 *Automation and the Worker: A Study of Social Change in Power Plants.* New York: Holt.

MAYO, ELTON (1933) 1946 *The Human Problems of an Industrial Civilization.* 2d ed. Boston: Harvard Univ., Graduate School of Business Administration, Division of Research. → A paperback edition was published in 1960 by Viking.

MAYO, ELTON 1945 *The Social Problems of an Industrial Civilization.* Boston: Harvard Univ., Graduate School of Business Administration.

MERTON, ROBERT K. et al. (editors) 1952 *Reader in Bureaucracy.* Glencoe, Ill.: Free Press.

MILLER, DELBERT C.; and FORM, WILLIAM H. (1951) 1964 *Industrial Sociology.* 2d ed. New York: Harper.

MOORE, WILBERT E. 1963 Industrialization and Social Change. Pages 299–370 in North American Conference on the Social Implications of Industrialization and Technological Change, Chicago, 1960, *Industrialization and Society.* Edited by Bert F. Hoselitz and Wilbert E. Moore. Paris: UNESCO.

MORSE, NANCY C. 1953 *Satisfactions in the White Collar Job.* Ann Arbor: Univ. of Michigan, Institute for Social Research, Survey Research Center.

NAVILLE, PIERRE 1958 Vues préliminaires sur les conséquences du développement de l'automation pour la main-d'oeuvre industrielle. *Cahiers d'étude de l'automation* No. 2:3–25.

PELZ, DONALD C. 1952 Influence: A Key to Effective Leadership in the First-line Supervisor. *Personnel* 29: 209–217.

PRINCETON UNIVERSITY, INDUSTRIAL RELATIONS SECTION 1959 *Management in the Industrial World: An International Analysis.* New York: McGraw-Hill.

ROETHLISBERGER, FRITZ J.; and DICKSON, WILLIAM J. (1939) 1961 *Management and the Worker: An Account of a Research Program Conducted by the Western Electric Company, Hawthorne Works, Chicago.* Cambridge, Mass.: Harvard Univ. Press. → A paperback edition was published in 1964 by Wiley.

ROSS, ARTHUR M.; and HARTMAN, PAUL T. 1960 *Changing Patterns of Industrial Conflict.* New York: Wiley.

ROY, DONALD 1952 Quota Restriction and Goldbricking in a Machine Shop. *American Journal of Sociology* 57: 427–442.

SAYLES, LEONARD R. 1958 *Behavior of Industrial Work Groups: Prediction and Control.* New York: Wiley.

SCHNEIDER, EUGENE V. 1957 *Industrial Sociology: The Social Relations of Industry and the Community.* New York: McGraw-Hill.

SEASHORE, STANLEY E. 1955 *Group Cohesiveness in the Industrial Work Group.* Ann Arbor: Univ. of Michigan, Institute for Social Research, Survey Research Center.

SELZNICK, PHILIP 1957 *Leadership in Administration: A Sociological Interpretation.* Evanston, Ill.: Row, Peterson.

STAGNER, R. 1954 Dual Allegiance as a Problem in Modern Society. *Personnel Psychology* 7:41–47.

STURMTHAL, ADOLF 1961 The Workers' Councils in Poland. *Industrial and Labor Relations Review* 14:379–396.

TAGLIACOZZO, D. L.; and SEIDMAN, J. 1956 A Typology of Rank-and-file Union Members. *American Journal of Sociology* 61:546–553.

TANNENBAUM, ARNOLD S. 1956*a* The Concept of Organizational Control. *Journal of Social Issues* 12, no. 2: 50–60.

TANNENBAUM, ARNOLD S. 1956*b* Control Structure and Union Functions. *American Journal of Sociology* 61: 536–545.

TANNENBAUM, ARNOLD S.; and KAHN, ROBERT L. 1958 *Participation in Union Locals.* Evanston, Ill.: Row, Peterson.

TOURAINE, ALAIN 1955 *L'évolution du travail ouvrier aux usines Renault.* Paris: Centre National de la Recherche Scientifique.

TOURAINE, ALAIN 1960 Contribution à la sociologie du mouvement ouvrier: Le syndicalisme de contrôle. *Cahiers internationales de sociologie* 28:57–88.

TRÉANTON, JEAN-RENÉ; and REYNAUD, JEAN-DANIEL 1963–1964 Industrial Sociology, 1951–1952: A Trend Report and Bibliography. *Current Sociology* 12, no. 2.

VERRY, MAURICE 1955 *Les laminoirs ardennais: Déclin d'une aristocratie professionnelle.* Paris: Presses Universitaires de France.

WALKER, CHARLES R. 1950 *Steeltown: An Industrial Case History of the Conflict Between Progress and Security.* New York: Harper.

WALKER, CHARLES R. 1957 *Toward the Automatic Factory: A Case Study of Men and Machines.* New Haven: Yale Univ. Press.

WARNER, W. LLOYD; and LOW, J. O. 1947 *The Social System of the Modern Factory.* New Haven: Yale Univ. Press; Oxford Univ. Press.

WHYTE, WILLIAM F. (1951*a*) 1962 Social Structure of the Whole Organization: The Restaurant. Pages 104–111 in Robert Dubin (editor), *Human Relations in Administration.* 2d ed. Englewood Cliffs, N.J.: Prentice-Hall.

WHYTE, WILLIAM F. 1951*b* *Pattern for Industrial Peace.* New York: Harper.

WHYTE, WILLIAM F. et al. 1955 *Money and Motivation: An Analysis of Incentives in Industry.* New York: Harper.

WILENSKY, HAROLD L. 1954 *Syllabus of Industrial Relations: A Guide to Reading and Research.* Univ. of Chicago Press.

WILENSKY, HAROLD L.; and EDWARDS, H. 1959 The Skidder: Ideological Adjustments of Downward Mobile Workers. *American Sociological Review* 24:215–231.

WILENSKY, JEANNE L.; and WILENSKY, HAROLD L. 1951 Personnel Counseling: The Hawthorne Case. *American Journal of Sociology* 57:265–280.

III
HUMAN RELATIONS

In the twenty-year period starting in the late 1930s and extending through the late 1950s, the term "human relations in industry" was applied widely to a variety of cross-disciplinary research studies and commentaries on the social organization of economic institutions. The most characteristic feature of the human relations approach was a shift away from the tradition of "scientific management," with its narrowly logical methods of layout and job design and its uncritical emphasis on payment-by-result incentive plans, to an interest in the effects on employees of informal group membership and supervisory practices. At the same time, sociologists, social psychologists, and social anthropologists began to interest themselves in the nature of industrial society as a complex social phenomenon.

Historical overview

The human relations movement, as it came to be called, has been the subject of broad controversy, and the term "human relations" itself is not without unfavorable connotation (though perhaps more in the United States than in western Europe and Asia). At least three sources of conflict can readily be identified. (1) Competition among the three social science disciplines noted above and with economists who had long worked alone in the field of industrial and business administration produced arguments over methodology and conceptual apparatus. (2) The enormous interest and enthusiasm generated by the subject brought popularizers into the field, and a host of marginal academic people were attracted by the widespread public acceptance of human relations "findings." (3) The subject matter itself touched on such areas of significant social conflict as the relative power of business and its leaders and the balance of power between managers and employees, whether organized or unorganized. It could be argued that the principal significance of the human relations movement in industry (and of its counterpart, human relations in the family and the community) was that it represented the coming of age of social science, in the sense that the findings of social science were now accepted as having relevance to everyday problems outside the university, the consulting room, or the laboratory. For the businessman, in particular, the study of human relations seemed to offer enormous benefits in terms of increased productivity and diminished industrial strife. Many students (and would-be students) were attracted by the glamour and excitement of a field that promised findings of relevance to the world of affairs as well as to the world of scholarship.

The subject matter of the field can best be defined by reviewing the major concepts; their relationship to larger social science theory will be considered below. The most widely used concepts are leadership, informal group, morale, role and status, equilibrium, resistance to change, and motivation.

The Western Electric studies. There is surprising unanimity that "human relations in industry," as a field of interest, achieved momentum with the Western Electric studies. These were a series of field investigations conducted at the Hawthorne Works of the Western Electric Company in Chicago between 1927 and 1932 (Roethlisberger & Dickson 1939). The research itself stemmed from the joint interests of the Western Electric Company and the investigators—headed by Elton Mayo—in the effects of monotony on workers. The Western Electric Company's own researches had produced startling findings. Beginning with a rather mechanical view of fatigue and productivity, the engineers had endeavored to study the effect of the quantity and quality of illumination on efficiency. They had discovered that decreased illumination as well as increased illumination could produce increases in output.

Mayo and his colleagues later argued that such unusual findings could be explained by changes in human relations that transcended the purely physical changes prescribed by "scientific management." But this conclusion is more clearly illustrated in the first major component of the primary Western Electric researches—the Relay Assembly Test Room (RATR) experiment.

A group of five girls doing light assembly work was isolated in a separate factory location. A series of experimental changes were then made in their working conditions, including the addition of rest periods, refreshments, and a shortened work day. In the famous twelfth experimental period all the physical changes that had presumably improved conditions of work were withdrawn. Up to this time output had been gradually rising, and now it went up once again, somewhat as it had done during the illumination experiments when the physical conditions of work were made increasingly adverse.

Three types of explanations have been proposed for this remarkable series of output increases. The first emphasizes perception and cognition: the girls observed that management was concerned with their welfare; they had been singled out for a great deal of attention by both management and researchers, and they were appreciative of their newfound importance. This reaction has come to be widely known as the Hawthorne effect—a confounding variable in field experiments of this type.

Observers placed in the room noted, and interviews confirmed, an increased amount of on-the-job and off-the-job interaction among the girls, the emergence of an informal leader, and a sense of team membership. While the girls were not told to increase their output or that there was any such objective in the study, through their group they committed themselves to this objective while feeling no sense of urgency or pressure. The functional relationship implied here is that increased group cohesiveness leads to increased productivity. In the literature of human relations, managers were urged to be concerned with providing mutually compatible groups and the opportunity for group interactions. Later work by Seashore (1955) and Sayles (1958) has suggested that this relationship was oversimplified. Cohesiveness could lead to output restriction and effective opposition to management goals as well as to work efficiencies. However, still unchallenged is one of the other conclusions implicit in the RATR study: cohesiveness in the small group reduces turnover in the larger organization. Mayo and Lombard (1944), studying the burgeoning aircraft industry, noted that workers attached to stabilized groups or to informal leaders would be less likely to quit [*see* COHESION, SOCIAL].

The third explanation has its roots in the field

of applied anthropology and the work of Arensberg (1951), Chapple (1940), and Homans (1950). These researchers observed the dependency of attitudes on interaction. In the RATR, the girls were placed in the position of initiating interaction with the experimenters, of being consulted, of having an opportunity to disagree with and even to veto proposals for modifications of working conditions. In the regular factory they had no such opportunities for up-the-line initiations but were passive recipients of originations down the line from management (Arensberg 1951, pp. 347–351). Further, the test room gave them the opportunity for highly increased "horizontal" contacts or free communication. This major change in the structure of supervisory patterns and interaction increased productivity.

All three explanations emphasize improved "morale," which is defined simply as the will to work, as distinct from skill or the capacity to work. However, the most complete analysis, which emphasizes dynamic processual concepts, is provided by Arensberg.

> The process [of change in the RATR] took the form of this definite order of developments: (1) an increase of managerial initiative, (2) followed by an increase of inter-worker communication, (3) followed by an increase of redressive up-the-line action of the workers upon foremen or spokesmen, (4) which resulted in further changes of rewarding sort in managerial action, (5) changing individual attitudes, (6) reaching expression as new group attitudes or morale [the "norms" of Homans], (7) which won informal sanction by the workers on one another, (8) and stimulated further releases of individual output productivity [*sic*]. (Arensberg & Tootell 1957, p. 316)

It is worth noting the increase in sophistication provided by this "processual" analysis which goes beyond simple correlations to provide a total situational assessment.

Following the RATR studies, with their emphasis on social-psychological experimentation, the research moved into its second major phase. The Bank Wiring Room experiment was designed like an anthropological field study to permit consecutive observations of a typical industrial work group *in situ*. Fourteen men in three interdependent jobs had their work stations shifted to a room suitable for careful observation of who contacted whom, when, where, and how frequently. While interviewing had provided the major data to interpret productivity changes in the RATR, in the Bank Wiring Room it was subordinated to precise, detailed observation.

Careful analysis of the data again revealed the importance of the social group in providing an outlet for the individual and in controlling his output. Here output restriction was the dominant norm, although there were slight differences between the two distinct cliques in the room. Company rules were violated and the supervisor subjected to carefully contrived pressures in order to maintain the social equilibrium and economic interests of the group. While informal group elaborations and leadership influence could explain some of the observed behavior, a good deal of the variance could be attributed to the patterns of relationships that had been implicitly prescribed by the division of labor—that is, the separate tasks that required interaction and coordination to complete (Homans 1950, pp. 54–73).

In the years following the Western Electric studies, this last point tended to be forgotten as human relations emphasized the power and autonomy of the informal group. Management often sought to coopt the group without recognizing that the behavior of the group was attributable to prescribed constraints such as technology.

Human relations research

In a study of the restaurant industry, Whyte (1948) combined a number of intensive case studies to show how organizational growth, increasing specialization, and the distinctive work flow problems of a restaurant produce distinctive interactional pressures. He showed that different personalities and various supervisory skills are more or less effective, depending on the predictable stress being experienced by job holders. Harbison and Dubin (1947) studied General Motors and Studebaker collective bargaining relationships and learned that the behavior of the participants and their perceptions were a function of the pressures associated with being in a "power center" and "pattern setting" position. Company politics and internal union politics have also been analyzed in terms of situational pressures such as cost-saving campaigns and intergroup competition. There has been a continuing interest in economic incentives for higher productivity (Whyte et al. 1955).

Rensis Likert and others have studied the impact of differential supervisory styles on employee morale. Their work is in the tradition of Kurt Lewin's studies of democratic leadership in small groups. One of the best-known studies to use the Lewinian concepts of quasi-stationary equilibria and democratic leadership is one that analyzes how a discussion leader, by means of participative techniques, induced a group of textile workers to accept voluntarily changes in methods that groups dealt with in more traditional supervisory styles had resisted (Likert 1961).

Human relations research on motivation has generally argued that employees are more productive when satisfactions come directly from the work itself, rather than from present or deferred economic rewards or fears of punishment (McGregor 1966). McGregor (1960) has sought ways to adjust managerial control techniques to provide the same incentives for executives. Bavelas and Leavitt, in a series of laboratory experiments, have controlled access to communication linkages, showing the differential effect of various types of communication networks on speed and accuracy in problem solving by small groups (Leavitt [1958] 1964, pp. 228–241).

Interest in developing greater awareness among managers of the impact of their actions on subordinate perceptions and on opportunities for "self-actualization" has characterized some recent research on human relations. Argyris (1957) has synthesized a vast quantity of human relations research to argue that modern organizations inspire rather little effective motivation because jobs are not challenging (because of poor delegation and the extreme division of labor) and supervisors are authoritarian. Employee and managerial reactions to mass production, particularly in automobile assembly plants and in integrated steel mills, have also been investigated. It has been found that workers are frustrated with small, inconsequential jobs and that foremen are torn between the demands of multiple staff and line groups (Walker & Guest 1952; Walker et al. 1956). A landmark study of an International Business Machines Company manufacturing plant by Richardson and Walker (1948) identified morale and productivity concomitants of a reduction in the number of managerial levels in the organization and a shift from batch production to continuous work flows.

The effects of technological change on industrial management have been investigated by Lawrence and his associates, who have shown how attitudinal changes may follow interactional changes (Ronken & Lawrence 1952) and how changes in the structure of relationships among managers were in one instance dependent upon the adoption of new interaction patterns (Lawrence 1958).

Critique of human relations

In its most naive form, human relations has meant an emphasis on nonscientific management variables. For example, it has been argued that managers tend to regard employees in physical, machinelike terms. According to human relations theorists, managers believe that decreasing the load or frictions (by making jobs easier, lighter, etc.) increases worker output. On the other side, by increasing the energy that would be expended or the "pull" (by providing economic incentives through piecework plans), it is thought that employees can be made to work harder, just as a machine will go faster if the power is turned up. Advocates of the human relations approach made the simple observation that employees are not machines and do not respond in these mechanical terms.

While not profound from a social science theory point of view, doubtless there have been significant contributions to both economic productivity and social welfare through the wide dissemination of "human relations" findings. In particular, the post-World War II teams composed of management and trade union representatives from western European nations were impressed with the contribution made to U.S. managerial success by human relations training. Such training, while showing little effect on gross behavioral patterns, has concentrated on dispelling simplistic views concerning employees. Supervisors learn that individual hedonism is not the sole or even the primary motivation; work does not get accomplished simply by threats or reprimand; clear communication can be distorted; employees elaborate an impressive and significant social structure that cannot be ignored in management decision making.

While it is futile to dispute the truism that employees are human beings, some of the more extreme expressions of this "philosophy" are less legitimate: employees are not rational; managers are rational; employees respond emotionally and thus ignore their own true interests (e.g., fail to earn available bonuses or foolishly restrict output).

Recent studies of employee response to incentive plans show substantial rationality as workers seek to obtain "looser" rates, protect jobs, de-emphasize tight-rated jobs, and manipulate job elements such as "down time" and "tooling-up" to increase their "paper" output (Whyte et al. 1955). On the other hand, research on management groups (which has been late in developing) shows the same types of output restriction, informal group leadership and norms, and resistance to authority (Dalton 1959).

Traditional human relations dealt with a relatively small number of variables and a simple social system. Leaders (or supervisors) gain additional control by dealing with groups of subordinates rather than just individuals and by identifying their leaders and group norms. They also reduce turnover by encouraging the formation of informal groups and permitting catharsis either by developing their own skills of nondirective counseling or by utilizing trained outsiders as interviewers or staff counselors. Leaders can effectuate change by using participatory techniques, "feeding back" startling morale scores to the supervisors involved, and endeavoring to fit the change into the social system.

There was mounting criticism that such techniques were manipulative, helped create an administrative elite, and served to increase the power of the employer relative to the employee and/or his unions (Barkin 1950). *Ammunition*, the monthly magazine of the United Automobile Workers, has frequently referred to human relations as "cow psychology," presumably because it is felt that the purpose of human relations is to induce compliant behavior. A partial response to these criticisms was the application of human relations to the study of unions (Sayles & Strauss 1953) and to conflict-laden union–management relations (Whyte 1951). Further, Solomon Barkin, research director of the Textile Workers Union and one of the most vehement critics of human relations, began to adapt its techniques to the study of problems of organizing the unorganized workers in the South.

More profound criticism dealt with human relations as an ideology: it ignored conflict, equated loyalty (or security) with freedom, protected the *status quo*, and glorified a closed, static society with fixed statuses and tight, all-embracing controls that served to preserve a monolithic structure (Kerr & Fisher 1957).

Interestingly, the liberal economist's critical view that the mores and traditions of employees should be none of the concern of managers (who should focus on price–quantity decisions) is transmuted when the scene shifts to less developed countries. In this context, the critics of human relations in fully industrialized countries appear to encourage sociological and anthropological assessments, and do not see them as violations of pluralism or separations of economic from social analysis (Kerr et al. 1960).

Sociologists like Blumer (1947) have accused human relations of ignoring institutional forces and of failing to come to grips with power differences and the quest for power. At an earlier period, economists, too, criticized human relations for its failure to consider institutional forces and its overemphasis on interpersonal relationships. More particularly, it was argued that market forces, the business cycle, and profitability had an enormous effect on human relationships. Dunlop and Whyte (1950) and others countered by showing the value of following through the impact of economic forces on the attitudes and behavior of the participants in the economic process.

It has been suggested that these critics based their vehemence on interpretations of Mayo's personal views (as distinct from his research findings) and the potential uses of these views by management. But there is no evidence that employees can be fooled into thinking that they are participating in important decisions when, in fact, they are being masterminded, or that they will accept psychological satisfactions in exchange for economic and social objectives. Neither status nor job satisfaction can be created by words. Both are dependent on the actual pattern of relationships, of give and take in the organization. Status and satisfaction are positively correlated with the availability of increased initiative, the ability to control the environment, and the opportunity to be relatively autonomous and free from excessive pressures and controls. (Sayles 1964). Thus managers who wish to increase pride and job attachment have to make real changes in the interactional structure of the organization, not just in supervision. Also, there is no simple functional relationship between employee happiness and productivity. Naive employers who think that good supervision and recognition of the importance of social relations can be substituted for financial rewards will be disappointed.

It has also been argued that human relations ignored the community and larger social and economic forces. However, Hart (1949) very early traced the changing relationships of church, social agencies, managers, and unions. Lloyd Warner, who had been a consultant on the Western Electric studies, designed some parts of his Yankee City research to be a continuation of the earlier work. Here the loss of status of skilled employees and the resulting industrial conflict are traced to changes in economic factors: the structure of the shoe industry, technological changes, the locus of ownership, and changes in the social system of the community (Warner & Low 1947).

Scientific, as distinct from ideological, criticisms of human relations have emphasized the neglect of structural factors in favor of primary group relationships and interpersonal skills. Although a careful review of Mayo's research has exonerated it of the easy assumption that supervisors are free to adopt a variety of leadership styles independent of larger organizational forces, the study of the organization as an organization has begun rather recently (Landsberger 1958).

The contentiousness surrounding the human relations field has also involved the area of research methodology. There are some strange ironies here. The earlier human relations studies, such as the one of the Relay Assembly Test Room, utilized naive models drawn from the experimental psychology of the time. These models have been shown to be inadequate for comprehending more complex social organizations in which a multiplicity of variables, including the role of experimenter, economic conditions, and an evolving social structure, reacted with one another. The Bank Wiring Room experiment lent support to the idea that the techniques of anthropological field work were of use to sociologists when the total situation could be observed over time in its natural setting. Disparate pathways have led from this. One direction was taken by Chapple (1940). Homans (1950), Whyte (1948), Bales (1950), Lawrence (1958), and Sayles (1958) have also emphasized the measurement of interaction: who does what with whom, when, where, and how often. Operationalism has been emphasized by interaction measures that can be recorded in fractions of a second by the interaction chronograph (Chapple 1949) or in somewhat larger units by trained observers (Bales 1950).

Simultaneously, others have emphasized unique case studies combining observation and interviews and their quantification. Thus a study by Zaleznik and others (1958) sought to predict the interrelationship between status, satisfaction, and performance in several work groups in an organization.

Present state of the field

In the 1960s the term "human relations" has been less commonly used, which is symbolic of the disputes the field has engendered. Even American management (although not European and Asian management) has learned to be less than totally enthusiastic about human relations. Management has been told that human relations means a deemphasis on production in favor of satisfaction. Academicians have come to prefer such terminology as "organizational behavior" and "human resources." However, research and teaching continue to be focused on the relationship problems of organization members.

Two sharply demarcated trends are evident. One has its source in psychology. A number of scholars have sought to identify those factors in the work situation which provide "higher-level" need satisfactions, particularly "self-fulfillment" or "self-actualization." These needs presumably become more important once physical and social needs have been satisfied. Such studies stress job enlargement, participative supervision, and "sensitivity training." Argyris (1964) has prepared a good summary of this position. Sensitivity training, like role playing, got its start with the sponsorship of a number of disciples of Kurt Lewin associated with the National Training Laboratories (Bethel, Maine). It is designed not as a research tool but as a training technique, giving participants the opportunity to see themselves as others see them through unstructured discussions of one another's personality traits (Schein & Bennis 1965).

The other trend is in the direction of more empirical investigation of the impact of organization structure, controls, and technology on behavior. Since about 1950, the Tavistock Institute in London has been a pioneer in such researches, also breaking new ground in the adaptation of sophisticated statistical techniques to the analysis of human relations data (Trist et al. 1963). The institute has also emphasized the significance of industrial economic and market structures on managerial behavior—an "open system" approach to the study of organizations (Rice 1963). Also in Britain, Paterson (1960) has sought to relate structure to behavior, and Woodward (1965) has shown with quantitative significance that small-batch production, mass production, and continuous-process production involve predictably different types of human relations problems as well as predictably distinctive organization structures.

In the United States there has been a search for a conceptual apparatus to study the interrelationships and negotiations among managers and specialists—"lateral" relationships with ambiguous power and deference patterns (Sayles 1964; Dubin 1962). The application of systems theory to these more complex networks in which simplistic notions of maximization and authority do not apply is in its infancy.

For the most part, the applied anthropologists and those who draw their research methods and conceptual apparatus from them stress structural change as the primary method of introducing change in institutions. Their various researches emphasize that behavioral change precedes attitudinal change and that the former can best be accomplished by dealing with the division of labor, layout, controls, and reporting relationships. On the other hand, those with strong psychological leanings, whose primary interests are in satisfaction and motivation, see change as flowing from new insights, greater awareness, and better understanding. Thus sensitivity training, feedback of morale surveys to key decision makers, and validating perceptions become key variables. These two positions are not easily reconciled. If attitudes stem from position within a structure, it would appear fruitless to engage in prolonged therapeutic techniques to affect perception. On the other hand, administrative skill obviously has some role to play in maintaining organizational stability and adaptability.

In retrospect, two of the most important contributions of human relations have been its emphasis on the problems of introducing change in social institutions and the vitality it has provided to social science. As Gouldner (1956) suggests, many of the theoretical propositions of traditional social science have proved inadequate to deal with the problems of change. Further, although human relations has utilized concepts drawn from traditional social science, it has repaid this debt by a substantial reverse contribution of empirical research that has enriched theory.

LEONARD R. SAYLES

[*Directly related are the entries* GROUPS, *article on* THE STUDY OF GROUPS; INTERACTION, *article on* INTERACTION PROCESS ANALYSIS; LABOR RELATIONS; LEADERSHIP; ORGANIZATIONS, *article on* EFFECTIVENESS AND PLANNING OF CHANGE; *and the biographies of* LEWIN; MAYO.]

BIBLIOGRAPHY

ARENSBERG, CONRAD M. 1951 Behavior and Organization: Industrial Studies. Pages 324–352 in Conference on Social Psychology at Crossroads, Univ. of Oklahoma 1950, *Social Psychology at the Crossroads*. Edited by John H. Rohrer and Muzafer Sherif. New York: Harper.

ARENSBERG, CONRAD M.; and TOOTELL, GEOFFREY 1957 Plant Sociology: Real Discoveries and New Problems. Pages 310–337 in Mirra Komarovsky (editor), *Common Frontiers of the Social Sciences*. Glencoe, Ill.: Free Press.

ARGYRIS, CHRIS 1953 *Executive Leadership: An Appraisal of a Manager in Action*. New York: Harper.

ARGYRIS, CHRIS 1957 *Personality and Organization: The Conflict Between System and the Individual*. New York: Harper.

ARGYRIS, CHRIS 1962 *Interpersonal Competence and Organizational Effectiveness*. London: Tavistock; Homewood, Ill.: Dorsey.

ARGYRIS, CHRIS 1964 *Integrating the Individual and the Organization*. New York: Wiley.

BAKKE, E. WIGHT (1946) 1947 *Mutual Survival: The Goals of Unions and Management*. New York: Harper.

BALES, ROBERT F. 1950 *Interaction Process Analysis: A Method for the Study of Small Groups*. Reading, Mass.: Addison-Wesley.

BARKIN, SOLOMON 1950 A Trade Unionist Appraises Management Personnel Philosophy. *Harvard Business Review* 28, no. 5:59–64.

BENNIS, WARREN et al. (editors) 1961 *The Planning of Change: Readings in the Applied Behavioral Sciences*. New York: Holt.

BLUMER, HERBERT 1947 Sociological Theory in Industrial Relations. *American Sociological Review* 12:271–278.

BURLING, TEMPLE; LENTZ, EDITH M.; and WILSON, ROBERT N. 1956 *The Give and Take in Hospitals: A Study of Human Organization in Hospitals*. New York: Putnam.

CHAPPLE, ELIOT D. 1940 Measuring Human Relations: An Introduction to the Study of Interaction of Individuals. *Genetic Psychology Monographs* 22:3–147.

CHAPPLE, ELIOT D. 1949 The Interaction Chronograph: Its Evolution and Present Application. *Personnel* 25: 295–307.

DALTON, MELVILLE 1959 *Men Who Manage: Fusions of Feeling and Theory in Administration*. New York: Wiley.

DUBIN, ROBERT 1962 Business Behavior Behaviorally Viewed. Pages 11–55 in George B. Strother (editor), *Social Science Approaches to Business Behavior*. Homewood, Ill.: Dorsey.

DUNLOP, JOHN T.; and WHYTE, WILLIAM F. 1950 Framework for the Analysis of Industrial Relations: Two Views. *Industrial and Labor Relations Review* 3:383–401.

GOULDNER, ALVIN W. 1956 Explorations in Applied Social Science. *Social Problems* 3:169–181.

HARBISON, FREDERICK; and DUBIN, ROBERT 1947 *Patterns of Union–Management Relations: United Automobile Workers (CIO), General Motors, Studebaker*. Chicago: Science Research Associates.

HART, CHARLES W. M. 1949 Industrial Relations Research and Social Theory. *Canadian Journal of Economics and Political Science* 15:53–73.

HOMANS, GEORGE C. 1950 *The Human Group*. New York: Harcourt.

KERR, CLARK; and FISHER, LLOYD H. 1957 Plant Sociology: The Elite and the Aborigines. Pages 281–309 in Mirra Komarovsky (editor), *Common Frontiers of the Social Sciences*. Glencoe, Ill.: Free Press.

KERR, CLARK et al. 1960 *Industrialism and Industrial Man: The Problems of Labor and Management in Economic Growth*. Cambridge, Mass.: Harvard Univ. Press. → A second edition was published in paperback in 1964 by Oxford University Press.

LANDSBERGER, HENRY A. 1958 *Hawthorne Revisited:* Management and the Worker; *Its Critics, and Developments in Human Relations in Industry*. Ithaca, N.Y.: Cornell Univ. Press.

LAWRENCE, PAUL 1958 *The Changing of Organizational Behavior Patterns: A Case Study of Decentralization*. Boston: Harvard Univ., Graduate School of Business Administration.

LEAVITT, HAROLD J. (1958) 1964 *Managerial Psychology: An Introduction to Individuals, Pairs, and Groups in Organizations*. 2d ed. Univ. of Chicago Press. → See especially pages 228–241, "Communication Nets in Groups: Designs for Getting the Word Around."

LEIGHTON, ALEXANDER H. (1945) 1964 *The Governing of Men: General Principles and Recommendations Based on Experience at a Japanese Relocation Camp*. New York: Octagon.

LIKERT, RENSIS 1961 *New Patterns of Management*. New York: McGraw-Hill.

LIVERPOOL, UNIVERSITY OF, SOCIAL SCIENCE DEPARTMENT 1954 *The Dock Worker: An Analysis of Conditions of Employment in the Port of Manchester*. Univ. Press of Liverpool.

MCGREGOR, DOUGLAS 1960 *The Human Side of Enterprise*. New York: McGraw-Hill.

McGregor, Douglas 1966 *Leadership and Motivation: Essays of Douglas McGregor.* Edited by Warren C. Bennis, Edgar H. Schein, and Caroline McGregor. Cambridge, Mass.: M.I.T. Press.

Mayo, Elton (1933) 1946 *The Human Problems of an Industrial Civilization.* 2d ed. Boston: Harvard Univ., Graduate School of Business Administration, Division of Research. → A paperback edition was published in 1960 by Viking.

Mayo, Elton; and Lombard, George F. F. 1944 *Team Work and Labor Turnover in the Aircraft Industry of Southern California.* Boston: Harvard Univ., Graduate School of Business Administration, Bureau of Business Research.

Paterson, Thomas T. 1960 *Glasgow Limited: A Case-study in Industrial War and Peace.* Cambridge Univ. Press.

Rice, A. Kenneth 1963 *The Enterprise and Its Environment: A System Theory of Management Organization.* London: Tavistock.

Richardson, Frederick L. W. Jr.; and Walker, Charles R. 1948 *Human Relations in an Expanding Company: A Study of the Manufacturing Departments in the Endicott Plant of the International Business Machines Corporation.* New Haven: Yale Univ., Labor and Management Center.

Roethlisberger, Fritz J.; and Dickson, William J. (1939) 1961 *Management and the Worker: An Account of a Research Program Conducted by the Western Electric Company, Hawthorne Works, Chicago.* Cambridge, Mass.: Harvard Univ. Press. → A paperback edition was published in 1964 by Wiley.

Rogers, Carl R. 1942 *Counseling and Psychotherapy: Newer Concepts in Practice.* Boston: Houghton Mifflin.

Ronken, Harriet O.; and Lawrence, Paul R. 1952 *Administering Changes: A Case Study of Human Relations in a Factory.* Boston: Harvard Univ., Graduate School of Business Administration, Division of Research.

Sayles, Leonard R. 1958 *Behavior of Industrial Work Groups: Prediction and Control.* New York: Wiley.

Sayles, Leonard R. 1964 *Managerial Behavior: Administration in Complex Organizations.* New York: McGraw-Hill.

Sayles, Leonard R.; and Strauss, George 1953 *The Local Union: Its Place in the Industrial Plant.* New York: Harper.

Seashore, Stanley E. 1955 *Group Cohesiveness in the Industrial Work Group.* Ann Arbor, Mich.: Univ. of Michigan, Institute for Social Research, Survey Research Center.

Schein, Edgar H.; and Bennis, Warren G. 1965 *Personal and Organizational Change Through Group Methods: The Laboratory Approach.* New York: Wiley.

Touraine, Alain 1965 *Workers' Attitudes to Technical Change: An Integrated Survey of Research.* Paris: Organisation for Economic Co-operation and Development.

Trist, Eric L. et al. 1963 *Organizational Choice: Capabilities of Groups at the Coal Face Under Changing Technologies: The Loss, Re-discovery and Transformation of a Work Tradition.* London: Tavistock.

Walker, Charles R.; and Guest, Robert H. 1952 *The Man on the Assembly Line.* Cambridge, Mass.: Harvard Univ. Press.

Walker, Charles R.; Guest, Robert H.; and Turner, Arthur N. 1956 *The Foreman on the Assembly Line.* Cambridge, Mass.: Harvard Univ. Press.

Warner, W. Lloyd; and Low, J. O. 1947 *The Social System of the Modern Factory.* New Haven: Yale Univ. Press; Oxford Univ. Press.

Whitehead, Thomas N. 1938 *The Industrial Worker: A Statistical Study of Human Relations in a Group of Manual Workers.* 2 vols. Cambridge, Mass.: Harvard Univ. Press.

Whyte, William F. 1948 *Human Relations in the Restaurant Industry.* New York: McGraw-Hill.

Whyte, William F. 1951 *Pattern for Industrial Peace.* New York: Harper.

Whyte, William F. 1961 *Men at Work.* Homewood, Ill.: Dorsey. → One of the best summaries of the current status of the human relations field; includes a brief survey of major empirical research.

Whyte, William F. et al. 1955 *Money and Motivation: An Analysis of Incentives in Industry.* New York: Harper.

Woodward, Joan 1965 *Industrial Organization: Theory and Practice.* Oxford Univ. Press.

Zaleznik, Abraham; Christensen, Carl; and Roethlisberger, Fritz J. 1958 *The Motivation, Productivity and Satisfaction of Workers: A Prediction Study.* Boston: Harvard Univ., Graduate School of Business Administration, Division of Research.

IV
REWARD SYSTEMS AND INCENTIVES

Owners and managers of industrial enterprises have used various methods of increasing the human effort upon which their output is seen to depend; but by far the commonest practice is to provide an increment of reward proportional to each increment of effort. The reward is commonly money, both in the form of cash wages (at least enough to assure subsistence) and as fringe benefits. From a sociological point of view, the latter form of reward has special interest, since any "benefit" other than a direct increase in the purchasing power of the worker must reflect some aspect of the society's general value system. Thus a company may be said to dispense prestige (in the form of promotion to a better position), security (by means of insurance, pensions, or opportunities to purchase company stock), or leisure (as when it gives the employee extra time off, perhaps in its own vacation resort). However, the relationship between effort and reward must be calculated in monetary terms if the reward system is to be applied to substantial numbers of employees with any degree of economic rationality. Most reward systems, therefore, employ a monetary base; and it is only with systems so based that the present discussion is concerned.

Reward systems may be classified into three types, according to whether they are applied to motivation at the individual level, the group level, or the collective level. Of course, a given system may be designed to affect all three levels; and some systems contain features that can be adapted to apply at more than one level. This classification is useful, however, in stressing the fact that management may regard the worker as an isolated individual, as a member of a face-to-face work group, or as a unit in the collectivity of all the employees.

Individual incentive systems. Individual systems are of three main types: "piecework and standard time," "shared gains," and "variable return." Under the first, the individual receives an identical and predictable amount for each unit of output; under the second, he receives a proportion of the value of his output beyond a standard amount (as in the Halsey, Rowan, and Bedaux systems); under the third, he receives amounts per unit which differ according to his level of output (as in the Taylor and Emerson systems). "Commissions" may be regarded as more complicated variants of piecework plans. In all individual systems, the work is usually guaranteed a minimum amount (or "base pay") to compensate him for time when, through no fault of his own (because of machinery breakdown, for example, or supply failure), he cannot work. There may also be other special conditions—usually as a result of union demands—when a minimum wage is guaranteed.

Group incentive systems. Under the group system, the earnings of a group of men, such as a work crew, are pooled, and each receives a proportion of the value of any output beyond a standard amount. Occasionally the group includes all or most of the employees (as in the Rucker and Scanlon plans); more usually, it is a group of men who interact in the course of their normal duties. Payoff occurs as a proportion of labor saved or of costs reduced.

Collective systems. Collective arrangements include profit sharing, deferred compensation bonuses, stock purchase options, and the like. Those systems shade off into fringe benefits, such as pension plans, insurance, surgical plans, and other benefits or services such as vacations, credit unions, athletic facilities, lunchrooms, and parking facilities. The incentive impact of most collective arrangements seems to be tenuous, owing to the relatively remote connection between them and the effort expended by the individual employee. Profits are pleasant to receive; but the worker can scarcely feel (and certainly not predict) that extra effort on his part will result in a proportional profit return—an upturn in the market may return him far more. Measures such as these are more properly regarded (especially in the United States) as devices to secure tax advantages and as general measures to reduce worker turnover and raise morale. Some of them may be required by law or even (as in the case of social security) be provided by the government itself.

History of reward systems

Although Karl Marx characterized piece rates as "the form of wages most in harmony with the capitalist mode of production" ([1867–1879] 1925–1926, p. 608), their use antedates modern capitalism by at least two thousand years. Incentive systems are recorded as having been used as early as 400 B.C. by the Chaldeans and probably by the Romans in the first century A.D. Such systems are also quite common among agricultural and peasant peoples in many places. They began to be used widely in the West with the breakdown of the guild system and the coming of the putting-out system: the merchant provided materials for domestic work, paying for products by the piece—a form of subcontracting that was not long in turning into employment under piecework. The spirit of such a relationship is being drawn on by the present-day employer who speaks of his piecework employees as being "in business for themselves."

The factory system of the nineteenth century made wide use of incentive systems, mostly of the individual type. Their appeal was mainly as an approach to reducing labor costs: employers could cut piecework rates to keep workers' income at a definite level while total output increased. This fact, together with the lack of objective means for determining production norms, led to the profound hostility of workers to incentive plans (such plans even being blamed for economic depressions) which is widespread even now, although it is decreasing. Around the turn of the century, a method for establishing appropriate production norms by analysis of the individual job (rather than by looking to the experience of the worker) was devised by Frederick W. Taylor and his followers (see Marriott 1957, chapter 1). The assumption by this group that motivation was largely an individual matter, and their arrogation of the title "scientific management" to their method, resulted in powerful and resentful opposition. At present it is widely recognized that job analysis and measurement, however carefully executed, involve subjective judgments and that solutions to measurement problems often reflect little more than the relative strength of union and management or the social norms. Indeed, it was recognition of the difficulty of setting minimum or average production levels that helped to lead to the development of the Halsey and Rowan plans, both of which, in allowing a level to be set too low, discouraged management from rate-cutting because it shared in the gains when the level was exceeded (Marriott 1957, p. 52).

Present distribution. The extent to which incentive systems are used today is difficult to measure because of lack of data. Labor unions, especially in the United States, claim that their use is declining; but such objective studies as are available do not bear this out. As of 1963, from 25 per cent to 30 per cent of workers in U.S. industry (mostly in manufacturing) were estimated to be covered by incentives, a figure which appears to have remained stable since the end of World War II (Belcher [1955] 1962, pp. 381 ff.). It appears that this stability is not due to a balancing of the firms that abandon incentive systems by an equivalent number of firms that adopt them for the first time but rather by the expansion of coverage in firms already using them (Mangum 1962, pp. 93–94).

Comparing European figures with figures for the United States is made difficult by the European practice of using "piece rate" as synonymous with the broader "incentive system"; this may have inflated the European figures. However this may be, the proportion of the working force in Europe that is covered by some kind of reward system is in general higher than in the United States. In the United Kingdom, 42 per cent of wage earners in 1961 were on "payment by results," an increase of 8 per cent over the figure for 1938. In 1949, of all hours worked in industry, the proportion at piece rate was 37 per cent in West Germany, 41 per cent in Denmark, close to 60 per cent in Norway and Sweden, and 70 per cent in Hungary (Marriott 1957, pp. 43 ff.; Mangum 1962, pp. 93 ff.). Piecework is, apparently, as much "in harmony" with the communist as with the capitalist mode of production.

Future prospects. Increasing automation has led some forecasters to see the complete abandonment of incentive payments since, it is claimed, the output level of self-operating, decision-making machinery cannot be attributed to the effort of the man who watches the dials or subjects it to periodic maintenance checks [*see* AUTOMATION]. Available data, although spotty, give little support to this expectation; on the contrary, the use of "equipment utilization incentives" (incentives for keeping the machines running or for not slowing down) seems to be growing (Mangum 1962, pp. 87 ff.). But perhaps the best insurance that incentive systems will continue to be utilized for a long time is the lack of effective methods of evaluating them in operation. The number of firms abandoning them for the wrong reasons will surely be offset by the number extending or adopting them for different, although equally wrong reasons.

Current theory and research

The field of industrial relations is one in which a greater gap than is usual in science exists between researcher and practitioner. Students of industrial sociology, industrial psychology, and management have been critical of all incentive systems, but managers of firms and personnel administrators install them notwithstanding, out of a belief, widespread in industry, that they "work." Laboratory experiments, although offering the advantage of control of variables, have been inconclusive; comparisons of performance by subjects "alone" and "together," although they have been carried out at least since the late nineteenth century, offer inconsistent results. For manual tasks, individual productivity has usually been shown to be superior to group productivity; but the structure of the group is of major significance (Gross 1958, chapter 14). The need for specialization and supervision, or the effects of interpersonal compatibility, may be critical. On the other hand, the superiority claimed for group work arrangements over the individual often proves illusory when results are calculated in number of man-minutes required to reach a solution (Hare 1962, pp. 354 ff.; Dunnette et al. 1963).

Yet even were the results of such experiments to point uniformly in the same direction, they would bear little on industrial incentive systems. Not only are laboratory controls lacking under actual factory conditions, but confounding variables make a truly scientific evaluation almost impossible. The installation of an incentive system requires the establishment of performance standards. If an incentive system is to motivate behavior, it must be possible for an average worker to make a bonus over his base pay. Hence one must measure the output of an average worker; but the very making of such measurements almost always leads to discoveries that the job can be simplified or improved. Also, since the workers can make a bonus only if supplies are continually forthcoming, management will take special pains to be sure there is a continual flow. Through such job and supply improvement, costs may indeed go down, whether one has the incentive system or not. Evaluation would require separating out the effects of these various changes.

Incentive systems in operation

Many incentive systems fail to motivate because their designers ignore the social nature of work. Appeals to the isolated worker ("*You* work harder and *you* will get more") ignore his relationship to his fellows and, in fact, operate to reduce the motivation to cooperate with work-crew members or even with management itself. Further, incentive system designers often assume the worker is a lazy organism that in the absence of incentive will do nothing at all, or as little as possible. He must be continually jogged: hence the incentive system. Such a pessimistic view of man is itself largely responsible for the state of affairs that it deplores.

The social nature of work makes itself felt in a variety of ways relevant to the operation of an incentive system. In the case, for example, of a group incentive system, workers are supposed to be motivated to cooperate. This they may indeed do; but they will rigidly limit this cooperation to their own work crew, excluding both other work crews and management itself. For example, they will refuse to accept trainees or apprentices, who pull down the group's average output. Management will therefore have to undertake the training of these persons separately.

It is often claimed that piece-rate systems reduce the need for close supervision, since labor costs are self-policing: if workers slow down on the job, they themselves will suffer for it. In reality, supervisors are likely to be judged by the bonus earned by the work group. It is felt that if a group is earning a respectable bonus it is doing a good job and must be satisfied; conversely, if it is not earning a bonus, its morale must be low and its work inefficient. In either case, the results may be attributed to the supervisor. Hence supervisors find themselves spending far more time supervising such a group than they would if they were on time earnings. Supervisors may even reach the point of colluding with their men in the securing of loose incentive rates that make it difficult for the group to avoid earning a substantial bonus.

Incentive systems often result in group conflict. Under individual job evaluation, it is assumed that since job A requires more education, involves more responsibility, or requires greater concentration than job B, therefore job A should be rated at, say, $1.50 per hour while job B is rated at $1.25 per hour. But job B is on incentive, and it is soon discovered that workers on job B are earning $1.60 per hour. Management is then puzzled when a worker in job B refuses a "promotion" to job A. It may also be that maintenance men, who service the machines on which incentive workers earn bonuses, demand a share of those earnings, since they feel that they are partly responsible for the high output.

Restriction of output

It is impossible to understand restriction of output unless one recognizes that it is not an individual but a group phenomenon. If the individual worker were to restrict consistently, then he would simply be discharged, for his low productivity in comparison to others would be patent. Restriction is not simply a matter of one worker holding back but of an entire group holding to an *agreed* rate: only then can the individual avoid sanctions for restriction, since management judges his performance relative to that of his work group.

There appear to be at least six main reasons for restriction (Gross 1958, chapter 14): (1) deliberate slowdowns may compel management to give favorable piece rates; (2) management, it is feared, may cut the rates if earnings get too high; (3) the worker may feel (often justifiably) that he needs more time to relax on the job; (4) avoidance of the sanctions suffered by the rate buster, who will at best be ostracized, thus acquiring a reputation with management for being hard to get along with, and will at worst be physically attacked by his workmates; (5) the general desire to give personal meaning to a job by performing it in an individualistic manner; (6) a difference in the structure of the aspirations of middle-class managers on the one hand and working-class persons on the other.

This last point deserves expansion. Middle-class people, as research has repeatedly confirmed, aim at success and advancement through achievement and are brought up to defer gratifications that might impede the pursuit of these ends (see Straus 1962). Working-class people, by contrast, habitually aim at no more than holding on to their jobs, raising their children so that they, too, can hold jobs and avoid "trouble," and enjoying the company of their families and circle of friends. It seems clear that individual incentive plans appeal far more to middle-class than to working-class values. In any case, the real chance that a working-class person can appreciably raise his wage (base pay) by his own effort is not large (the range for his job is usually narrow, and he reaches the top very early in his career); his chances of promotion (as a reward for effort) are even smaller. Hence, after a few years, perhaps, of trying to live up to middle-class standards of "success," he is likely to turn to other values, perhaps leaving to a union or a political party the task of keeping his earnings proportional to the cost of living.

These six factors are obviously potent and will hardly disappear because an incentive scheme offers the chance to earn an extra 10 per cent per hour. Where incentive systems work best it will be found that they have been tied to the workers' values. Examples include their relatively successful use in the commission system for salesmen, in bonuses for management, in the favorable response of rate busters (who, although a small group, do have values which are more like those of management than those of their fellows), and in situations where effort bears a relation to strongly sensed societal goals. Productivity goes up in wartime or when workers feel a relationship between what they do and national values they hold dear (as in incentive systems in some totalitarian countries or utopian communities), or if their work is seen by them as a sign of grace or means to heaven.

The individual reward system that seems to come closest to tying incentives to worker values is the Scanlon plan. Its main feature is a structure which provides for labor–management cooperation and consultation in labor-saving and in adoption of worker suggestions. Restriction of output seems to be low under this plan (Lesieur 1958).

Incentives, industry, and society

The success of incentive systems is also related to the market or community in which the industry must operate. If the incentive system results in increased production, then demand for the product must be elastic, or else inventories will pile up. Indeed, the fear that this may happen (and workers be laid off) motivates workers to keep production down. In some industries—the needle trades of New York City provide an excellent example—the piecework system is universal. This is because of the very stiff competition among the many small firms, because of tradition, and because of the acceptance of piecework by the unions, who are largely responsible for the stability of the industry.

Incentive systems have many latent effects. They put pressure on management to evaluate jobs more carefully, to supervise with greater rationality, to provide for a more dependable flow of supplies, to inspect products more closely, and to seek out and train specialists in job evaluation, wage and salary administration, time and motion study, accounting, and other such functions. However well or poorly a given incentive system works, management may thus be doing a more efficient job as a result of adopting it. At the same time, the personnel department becomes a more significant element in the organization; and incentive systems are often also an attractive feature in recruiting new workers. Whether these last two considerations justify incentive systems is a moot question.

The data do not permit us to conclude whether the use of industrial reward systems, on a worldwide scale, is increasing or decreasing, or whether they will necessarily increase productivity or lower costs. Pieceworkers usually out-produce those paid on a straight-time basis, other variables being rarely controlled (Mangum 1962, p. 87); but such gains are at least partly offset by the costs of installation and administration of the system. Time study, extra inspections for quality, job evaluation —all these direct labor-saving measures have to be paid for. Clearly more research is needed, both under laboratory conditions and in field situations. Yet the questions of policy and societal values to which we have referred suggest that the merits of industrial reward systems cannot be decided on any purely scientific grounds; the subject still requires public discussion and solutions founded on intuition and imagination.

EDWARD GROSS

[*See also* WAGES, *article on* SYSTEMS OF PAYMENT; *and the biography of* MAYO.]

BIBLIOGRAPHY

Data on the distribution of incentive systems, both in particular industries and in whole countries, are available in Belcher 1955; International Labor Office 1951; Marriott 1957. *The details of particular incentive systems may be found in* Abruzzi 1956; Belcher 1955; Lesieur 1958; Louden & Deegan 1944; Marriott 1957; Wolf 1957. *A good summary and critical review of small group experiments on productivity may be found in* Hare 1962 (*chapters* 12 *and* 13).

ABRUZZI, ADAM 1956 *Work, Workers, and Work Measurement.* New York: Columbia Univ. Press. → A critical evaluation of attempts to measure work movements.

BELCHER, DAVID W. (1955) 1962 *Wage and Salary Administration.* 2d ed. Englewood Cliffs, N.J.: Prentice-Hall. → A thorough treatment which places the subject of wage incentives in the context of money payments in general.

DUNNETTE, MARVIN D.; CAMPBELL, JOHN; and JAASTAD, KAY 1963 The Effect of Group Participation on Brainstorming Effectiveness for Two Industrial Samples. *Journal of Applied Psychology* 47:30–37.

GROSS, EDWARD 1958 *Work and Society.* New York: Crowell. → Work motivation from a sociological viewpoint.

HARE, A. PAUL 1962 *Handbook of Small Group Research.* New York: Free Press. → A careful, comprehensive examination of research on small groups, with particular emphasis on productivity under laboratory conditions.

HERZBERG, FREDERICK; MAUSNER, BERNARD; and SNYDERMAN, BARBARA BLOCH (1957) 1959 *The Motivation to Work*. 2d ed. New York: Wiley. → A psychological approach to work motivation.

INTERNATIONAL LABOR OFFICE 1951 *Payment by Results*. Studies and Reports, New Series, No. 27. Geneva: International Labor Office. → An international survey.

KENNEDY, VAN DUSEN 1945 *Union Policy and Incentive Wage Methods*. New York: Columbia Univ. Press.

LESIEUR, FREDERICK G. (editor) 1958 *The Scanlon Plan: A Frontier in Labor–Management Co-operation*. Cambridge, Mass.: M.I.T. Press.

LOUDEN, J. KEITH; and DEEGAN, J. WAYNE (1944) 1959 *Wage Incentives*. 2d ed. New York: Wiley. → A detailed description of wage incentive systems.

MANGUM, GARTH L. 1962 Are Wage Incentives Becoming Obsolete? *Industrial Relations* 2, no. 1:73–96.

MARRIOTT, R. 1957 *Incentive Payment Systems: A Review of Research and Opinion*. London: Staples. → A critical examination of incentive systems, with particular attention to laboratory studies and with extensive materials on the European experience.

MARX, KARL (1867–1879) 1925–1926 *Capital: A Critique of Political Economy*. 3 vols. Chicago: Kerr. → Volume 1: *The Process of Capitalist Production*. Volume 2: *The Process of Circulation of Capital*. Volume 3: *The Process of Capitalist Production as a Whole*. Volume 1 was published in 1867. The manuscripts of Volumes 2 and 3 were written between 1867 and 1879. They were first published posthumously in German in 1885 and 1894.

STRAUS, MURRAY A. 1962 Deferred Gratification, Social Class, and the Achievement Syndrome. *American Sociological Review* 27:326–335. → A review of the theoretical and research literature.

VITELES, MORRIS S. 1953 *Motivation and Morale in Industry*. New York: Norton. → A psychological approach.

VROOM, VICTOR H. 1964 *Work and Motivation*. New York: Wiley.

WHYTE, WILLIAM F. et al. 1955 *Money and Motivation: An Analysis of Incentives in Industry*. New York: Harper.

WOLF, WILLIAM B. 1957 *Wage Incentives as a Managerial Tool*. New York: Columbia Univ. Press.

INDUSTRIAL REVOLUTION

See ECONOMIC GROWTH; ECONOMY AND SOCIETY; INDUSTRIALIZATION; MODERNIZATION.

INDUSTRIALIZATION

I. ECONOMIC ASPECTS — *J. R. T. Hughes*
II. SOCIAL ASPECTS — *Wilbert E. Moore*

I ECONOMIC ASPECTS

Industrialization is the system of production that has arisen from the steady development, study, and use of scientific knowledge. It is based on the division of labor and on specialization and uses mechanical, chemical, and power-driven, as well as organizational and intellectual, aids in production. The primary objective of this method of organizing economic life, which had its genesis in the mid-eighteenth century, has been to reduce the real cost, per unit, of producing goods and services. The resulting increases in output per man-hour have been so large as to stagger the imagination. The average American worker today produces as much in half an hour as his British counterpart did in a whole working day a century ago, and that American worker has ten times as much industrial capital behind him as he would have had a century ago (Slichter 1961).

This revolutionary rise in available output and supply of economic resources has been associated primarily with the development of industrial economies in, for the most part, a limited number of countries (League of Nations . . . 1945; Kuznets 1959; Maizels 1963). By far the larger part of the dramatic rise in man-hour productivity is fairly recent—most of it occuring since the turn of the twentieth century—and apparently is still continuing powerfully in those economically advanced countries where the application of modern science to output continues to develop. Even so, the origins of modern industrialism can be found in the distant past. Industrialization is the outcome of a long and complex historical development, and it obviously has not yet run its full course as a long-range historical phenomenon. Judging from the record of the past, modern industry may be only a crude beginning of what is to come. It is not just the volume of output that measures the general economic impact of industrial development. The phrase "industrial society" has come to encompass a whole way of economic organization in which the social structure, from industrial management to the fine arts, utilizes the economies of standardization and specialization in basic human activities to produce, paradoxically, an ever more varied set of final products. Change in the structure of final output is ceaseless.

The history of economic change in the two hundred-odd years since the classical industrial revolution in England is varied and would have been difficult to predict. The ever-changing tides of technology, and the society that produces technical change, are manifestations of continuing growth of complexity in human specialization in all matters relating to economic life. Hence, by the 1960s two-thirds of the labor force in the United States worked in areas *not* concerned directly with the production of food and manufactured goods, compared with only 16 per cent of the labor force thus employed in 1820. European and Japanese industrial growth shows the same result in the occupational distribution of the labor force over time. Occupational diversity in nonmanufacturing life seems to be a product of industrialization wherever human society is free to respond to its own potentials as efficiency in economic life permits labor to go beyond direct production. What begins as mastery of basic mechanical technique ends by creating both the demands and the resources for a revolution in mass education and in science—a change in the "quality" of the labor force. Historical support for these general observations may be seen in the development and general characteristics of industrial society.

History

The phrase "industrial revolution" has long been used to identify the period roughly from 1750 to 1825, during which the accelerated application of mechanical principles, including steam power, to manufacturing in Great Britain produced an identifiable change in economic structure and growth. Workers were grouped together in factories using concentrations of capital equipment greater in cost and more efficient in operation than the capital equipment known in Britain earlier. These factories utilized a few mechanical innovations, primarily in textiles and iron manufacturing, which, with the application of the steam engine, made factory-sized scale the most economic size for the production unit. The proximity of others engaged in such manufacturing activities became a further cost-reducing factor of great importance, resulting in "external economies" that encouraged the grouping together of manufacturing enterprises and, hence, the growth of new urban aggregations. [*See* EXTERNAL ECONOMIES AND DISECONOMIES.] The result was that Britain rapidly became the first urbanized industrial state.

There is now little agreement among scholars about the origins of the industrial revolution in Britain. Recent work even questions the uniqueness of the classical period of the industrial revolution in the long-term evolution of the industrial structure of the British economy (Deane & Cole 1962). The older view that the agricultural improvements of the late seventeenth century and early eighteenth century, together with the rise of foreign trade, made a manufacturing sector with a rapidly increasing population possible in Britain has also been questioned. These ultimate problems of economic historiography concerning the industrial revolution in Britain cannot be resolved here.

The pattern of industrialization in other countries after 1800 has been broadly similar in many respects to that experienced by Britain, although, of course, the permutations were never the same in any two countries (Maizels 1963). "Textiles first" (along with food processing) has been almost the rule in industrialization, followed by transportation development, heavy industry, and more sophisticated enterprises, such as metalworking, chemicals, and electronics. In most cases, substantial advances in agricultural output, or increased foreign trade, or both, have been concomitants of industrial development. These have been essential since, as in eighteenth-century Britain, industrialization has been accompanied by two ubiquitous demographic phenomena: a rapid increase in the size of the total population and its aggregation in urban areas.

There has been some confusion concerning the lessons of this history. Since World War II, certain economists interested in promoting the development of industrially backward nations have urged the adoption of "balanced growth" planning. According to this proposal, the developing economy should supply its own market outlets and production inputs, with all sectors growing "simultaneously" (Lewis 1955, p. 283). The history of successful industrial growth shows no evidence of such growth in the past (Hughes 1958). Instead, industrialization has been the product of certain industries or groups of industries—"leading sectors" and "dominant industries" (Rostow 1952; Hoffmann 1931) —pushing ahead of others as technological breakthroughs occurred and new markets opened. Retardation in the rate of growth and even absolute decline of particular industries have also characterized industrial development, the lag in over-all growth being compensated for by new industrial ventures that come into existence and push toward their maximum growth rates, thus carrying the economy with them (Kuznets [1953] 1954, pp. 253–277; Burns 1934). No given set of industries making up a given industrial structure in any country has been responsible for industrial development, because change has been continuous.

Preconditions. Since industry cannot grow without markets and sources of capital, similarities in the economic "preconditions" for industrial development have been identified. These bases for the development of an industrial sector include an available labor force, markets for finished production, access to raw materials (whether at home or through foreign trade), a source of investment funds (whether from the wealth and savings of the private sector, from the accumulations of the public sector, or from abroad), and, finally, access to technology. The last has in every case necessitated the extensive development of mass education, because access to technology on a large scale means, ultimately, access to science. In the long run, successful industrialization has been achieved in those nations which not only realized the preconditions but also were able to adapt to changes in technology which required extensive organizational flexibility on all levels. Examples of such necessary flexibility are antitrust laws, internal population migrations, and changes in representational balance due to shifts in the franchise.

Although some countries, notably the United Kingdom and the United States, experienced their industrial development under conditions of political and economic freedom that were based upon rational and calculable law, the experiences of Germany, Russia, and Japan in the nineteenth and twentieth centuries indicate that the basic economic preconditions for industrialization are to some extent independent of political framework. The same can be said of commercial policy—successful industrial development has occurred under regimes ranging all the way from free trade to state barter. It is true that the industrial nations with highest income per capita are those which have Western-style political democracy and basically free markets for labor, food, and commodities. But it is also clear that rising per capita income, the *sine qua non* of economic development, comes primarily from industry, *however organized.* There are few "poor" nations with extensive industry. There are poor democracies as well as poor dictatorships of all varieties. The question of the political preconditions for industrialization has no clear answer except for the evidence of the past, and even this furnishes no clear "lesson of history," since, in terms of *rates* of growth, the communist dictatorships have ranked near the top in recent times.

The spread. The time path of world industrial development is marked by the slow spread of the "industry state" from Britain to the United States, to northwest and central Europe, Russia, and Japan, and then to other parts of the world. There are now industrial complexes in nearly all parts of the world except the polar regions. Counting mining and oil production, industry has spread to deserts and jungle alike, yet until the 1950s there was no significant industrial power, except Japan, which was not a European country or an overseas offshoot of Europe.

In modern times the international permeation of technology stemming initially from the advances of the British industrialization has been a slow and stubborn process, with all countries being borrowers as well as originators of invention. The United States developed a large-scale industry and an extensive internal transportation sector before 1860. Then, in the period extending roughly from 1870 to 1910, the United States experienced an accelerated development of heavy industry and surpassed all other nations to become, and remain, the leading industrial power. Conditions were favorable for industrialization in Belgium, parts of Germany, parts of France, and to some extent in Scandinavia and Russia by the end of the Napoleonic Wars. For several reasons (about which there has been abundant academic dispute), including lack of resources, an unnecessarily restrictive commercial policy, and inappropriate social organization, industrialization in France was constrained in the nineteenth century. But Frenchmen and French capital participated widely in the industrialization and economic development of other parts of the world (Cameron 1961; Landes 1958). Belgium had an iron industry early in the nineteenth century as a result of available raw materials and English *émigrés* (Henderson 1954). Although parts of Germany, including the Rhineland, Saxony, and Silesia, had long histories of industry, especially textiles, great industrial development came only after unification in 1871 (Sombart 1903).

Under the tsars, Russia was unable, despite abundant raw materials, to achieve the other preconditions for industrial development on a scale anywhere near its obvious potential, and by 1914 it trailed Britain, Germany, and France as an industrial power but was fourth in the world behind the United States, Britain, and Germany as a textile manufacturer. After the emancipation of the serfs in 1861, great efforts were made by the Russian government to achieve industrial growth, and after the 1880s considerable development occurred, especially in railroad construction. Under the Soviet government after 1917, and especially since the adoption of the first Five-Year Plan in 1928, the Soviet Union has become the leading European industrial power—although still a poor country on the basis of per capita income—and is second only to the United States in many areas of industrial development.

Japan is a remarkable phenomenon in the history of world industrialization. Through the great efforts of the government (Rosovsky 1961) and a cohesive ruling class, Japan went from being a backward, Oriental feudal state to becoming a substantial industrial power in the years between 1859 and 1910, overcoming a lack of raw materials and despite social customs which needed drastic adaptation to meet the needs of industrial growth. In spite of vastly wasteful military efforts in the twentieth century and a catastrophic military defeat, by the 1960s the Japanese had achieved a near-European level of output per head of population and a structure of industry developing along Western patterns, that is, textiles and other light manufacturers being displaced by the growth of engineering and chemical industries (Maizels 1963). Japan is the only non-European country, or country not of European origin, to achieve such a measure of economic growth based upon industrialization up to the mid-twentieth century. Other Asian countries, especially India and China, have mounted major long-term industrialization campaigns.

The experience of substantial economic growth—rising output per capita—based upon industrial development is still not widespread even in the 1960s, in spite of great efforts to achieve industrial growth among the more economically backward countries. By the mid-twentieth century perhaps two-thirds of mankind had not achieved these fruits of industrialization (Maizels 1963). The industrial economies, on the other hand, being the chief places where productivity has risen, have become the nodal points of economic progress. The rest of mankind has participated in economic progress almost solely through contact with that portion of humanity which has developed industry.

Over the course of industrial development since the industrial revolution, the interaction between the industrially developing economies has been widespread and intense, including not only great advances in trade in commodities but in people and capital as well. Thus, the Atlantic migration of the nineteenth and early twentieth centuries was by far the largest human migration in history. It transferred needed labor power from the surplus area (Europe) to the deficit areas (the United States, Canada, Latin America) and, to a lesser extent, to other areas of overseas European settlement like Australia, New Zealand, and South Africa. Accompanying this migration were capital flows of great magnitude which financed industrial growth throughout the world in advance of the possibilities of local wealth and savings in the receiving countries. In the past, industrialization has in a very real sense been an "international" affair, and it still is. However, in recent years privately financed capital flows have been exceeded by government transfers from the United States, western Europe, the Soviet Union, and even Communist China.

Comparative development

As might be expected, the industrial nations are generally far richer in output per capita than the nonindustrial nations. In fact, at the extremities of the international scale of income distribution the differences are incredible. In 1961 the mean income per capita in the United States was $2,790. In India the figure was $70, less than 3 per cent of the American figure.

Cross-sectional. The extremes indicated for the year 1961 in the cases of the United States and India (China, with a quarter of the world's population, is apparently slightly better off than India—the UN estimate for 1961 was $85 per capita) largely reflect the general results Kuznets (1959) found in his study of world income distribution for 1956. Scaling incomes of some 58 nations into seven classes by income relatives (Class VII = 100; VI = 200; V = 270; IV = 400; III = 650; II = 1,000; I = 1,700), Kuznets showed that, with the exception of the richest nations and those in Class IV, the higher the per capita income, the higher the proportion of the total generated by manufacturing industry (and, with no exceptions, the higher the proportion derived from agriculture, the lower the income per capita). These results are shown graphically in Figure 1, to which further reference will be made. All exceptions to the above rule can be covered by rephrasing the statement: In neither of the two richest (aggregated) categories of countries is the proportion of income derived from manufacturing less than 34 per cent of the total, nor is the proportion from agriculture more than 24 per cent. In neither of the two poorest categories is the proportion derived from manufacturing as high as 18 per cent, nor is the proportion derived from agriculture less than 42 per cent. We leave aside for the moment the question of the quality of agriculture and manufacturing in the rich as opposed to the poor countries. In the cases of individual nations there are of course several exceptions, but these scarcely negate the importance of the general results. Yugoslavia, for example, with some 42 per cent of its income in 1961 derived from manufacturing and mining, against 27 per cent derived from agriculture, forestry, and fishing, is one of the poorest (per capita) nations in Europe—although by no means poor compared with most Asian nations or those of Latin America and Africa. Similarly, Japan, with 30 per cent of its income derived from manufacturing in 1960, compared with 15 per cent from agriculture, forestry, and fishing, has a lower income per capita than all but the poorest European nations yet is the richest nation, by this measure, in Asia. In the case of New Zealand, which had the sixth highest level of income per capita in the world in 1961, income derived from agriculture and industry was nearly balanced (it was 22 per cent each in 1954), but it was a scientific agriculture, and New Zealand, with its preferences for food imports from the United Kingdom, is a very special case indeed. In the United States, manufacturing, strictly defined, accounted for only 28 per cent of national income by

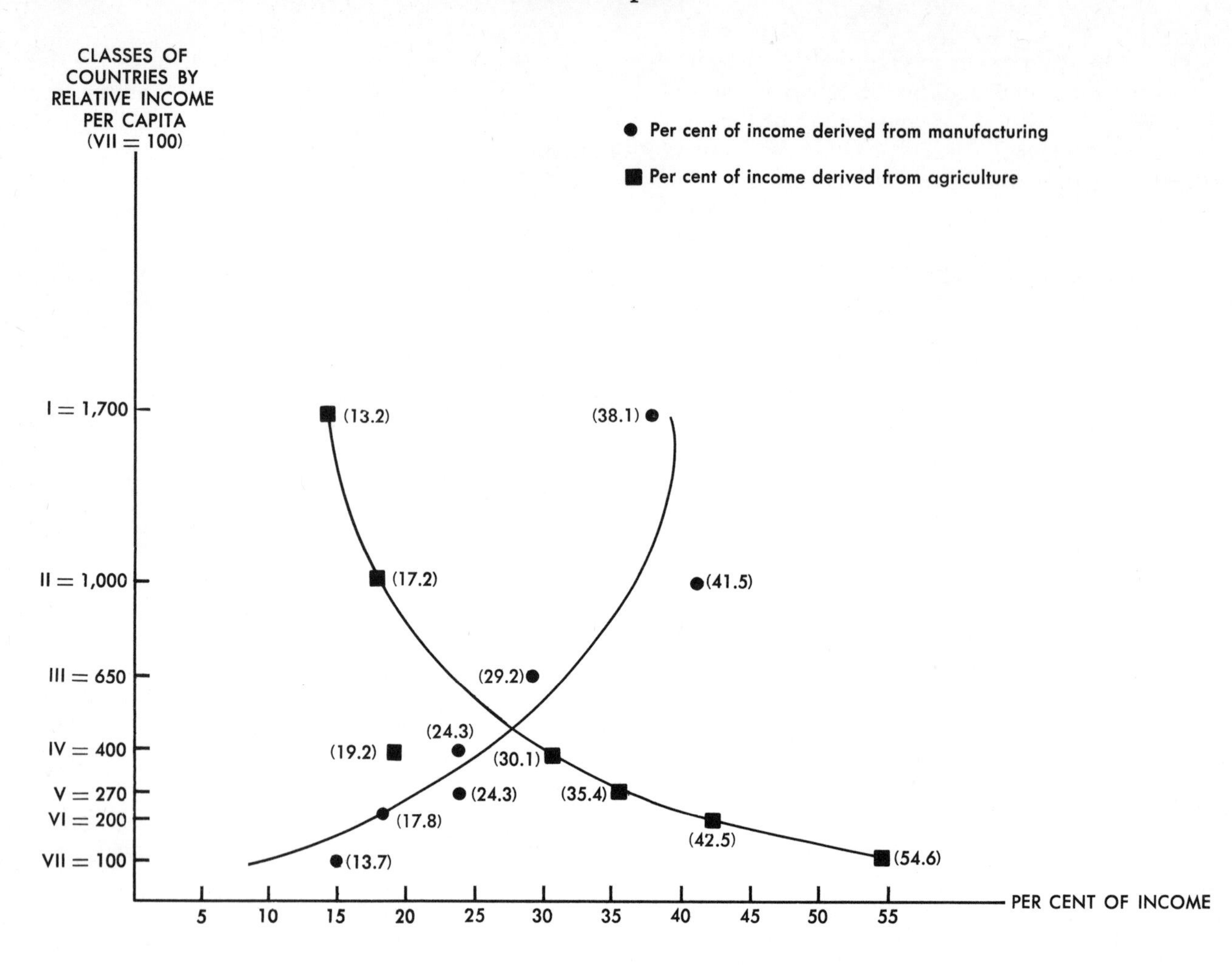

Figure 1 — Sectoral income distribution by country class

Source: Kuznets 1959. © 1959, The Free Press, a Corporation.

1961—some 65 per cent being attributable to commerce, services, and the professions.

Bearing such special cases in mind, the main conclusion holds despite the great differences internationally in agricultural and industrial technique: The proportion of national income derived from manufacturing is a rough indicator of the amount of income generated per head—greater utilization of industry exists in the richer than in the poorer nations. The rule is made more general if the proportion of income derived from industry is related to that proportion derived from agriculture. The anomaly of the richest countries and of those in Class IV disappears, and it is simply the case that the higher this ratio, the higher the income per capita. Thus, dividing the percentage of income derived from manufacturing by the percentage derived from agriculture yields the following: I = 2.89; II = 2.41; III = 1.52; IV = 0.81; V = 0.69; VI = 0.42; VII = 0.25.

Historical. The general outcome shown in the cross section of the present-day world economy reflects the level of productive technique employed. Interestingly enough, the world cross section roughly approximates the history of industrialization in this regard. At first, as industrialization progressed, the proportional contribution of manufacturing increased rapidly while that of agriculture fell. But then the proportional contribution of manufacturing grew less rapidly, agriculture continued to decline, and the proportion arising from commerce, services, the professions, etc., rose. British income estimates (Deane & Cole 1962), for example, show that about 45 per cent of income was generated from agriculture in 1770, while 32 per cent was derived from agriculture, forestry, and fishing in 1801; the rate then fell to about 18 per cent by 1861, just over 6 per cent in 1901, and only about 4 per cent in 1961. At first the proportion of income derived from industrial pursuits (unhappily, mining and building are included with the estimate for manufacturing) rose strongly, from 23 per cent of the total in 1801 to 36 per cent fifty years later. In the next fifty years the proportion grew only slowly, from 40 per cent in 1901 to 45 per cent by 1961. The figures for the United States (U.S. Bureau of the Census 1960; *Statistical Abstract*) show the same pattern, with agriculture declining as a proportion of national income from about 20 per cent in the period 1869–1879 to just over 9 per cent in 1939–1948 and down to 4 per cent by 1961. Income generated in the manufacturing sector rose from about 14 per cent of the total in 1869–1879 to 27 per cent in 1939–1948 and was still about 28 per cent of the total in 1961. (The United States manufacturing sector figure for 1961 comparable with the British figure of 45 per cent, which includes mining and building, was 36 per cent.)

Relative maturity. It is virtually a truism in economic development that, where an agricultural society has previously existed, a massive transfer of labor to industry must be made possible if industry is to grow. In both Britain and the United States industrial development was accompanied by this transfer of labor until the industrial sector reached a certain degree of maturity (a marked slowing down in the rate of increase of industry's proportion of GNP); then the transfer no longer appeared as a shift to industrial employment but, rather, to trade, services, professions, and the like. The last movement seems to be a characteristic of industrial maturity as we know it thus far in the development of industrial economies (Maizels 1963). It is a logical progression, since the more sophisticated uses of the human brain in science, scholarship, finance, etc., can be widely achieved only after basic needs in food and goods are achieved. In Britain in 1801, 35.9 per cent of the labor force was in agriculture and 29.7 per cent was in manufacturing and mining, leaving 34.4 per cent in all other occupations. The industrial sector had more or less stabilized at 46.3 per cent of the labor force as early as 1901, but with agriculture still declining proportionately and employing only 8.7 per cent of the labor force, some 45 per cent of the labor force was "released" from direct production of goods and food. In 1951, with industry employing 49.1 per cent of the labor force and agriculture a mere 5 per cent, 45.9 per cent of the labor force was thus released for services, professions, etc.

This particular structural transformation was much more pronounced in the history of industrialization in the United States. There, both agriculture and manufacturing experienced higher man-hour productivity than in Britain, and, with easier access to general education (elementary and secondary), a more pronounced movement away from the direct output of goods and food was experienced than in Britain. Also, the movement was more dramatic than in Britain because the industrial revolution found the United States more agricultural in terms of labor distribution than was Britain, where a considerable movement into skilled trades, hand manufacturing, and so forth had taken place before the inventions of the classical industrial revolution appeared. In 1820, when 71.8 per cent of American "gainful workers" were employed in agriculture and 12.2 per cent in "manufacturing and trades," a mere 16 per cent did not produce either food or goods. Agriculture then declined in importance as an employer while the industrial sector expanded. By 1900, 36.8 per cent of gainful workers were in agriculture, 21.8 per cent were in industry, and 41.4 per cent had been freed from direct production for trades and services. By 1940, with 16.9 per cent in agriculture and 22.4 per cent in industry, 60.7 per cent of the gainfully employed did not directly produce goods and food. In 1963, with 5.8 per cent of the "civilian labor force" in agriculture and 28.4 per cent in manufacturing, 65.8 per cent of the labor force had been released for commerce, services, professions, etc.

Obviously, the productivity growth of agriculture and industry in the United States has been very great, and one cannot foresee the limits of the release of labor from direct production of food and goods. The process of developing "sophisticated," or tertiary, uses of labor resources seems to be characteristic of industrial development. The classical Marxist industrial "proletariat" does not grow apace with industrial development but, rather, its growth in proportion to total employment slows down.

Two paradoxical results of the Kuznets data are illuminated by the foregoing history of structural change in income and labor distribution. As can be seen in Figure 1, those countries with highest income, Class I, derive a slightly smaller proportion of their income from manufacturing than do those in Class II, the next most productive class. This is apparently due to the rising importance of services and professions of all sorts as industrialization so raises productivity as to release men and resources from direct production of food and goods. "Services" in Class I countries occupy 45.3 per cent of the labor force, compared with 41.7 per cent in Class II. Services in Class I countries generate 48.7 per cent of income, compared with 41.2 per cent in Class II countries. The structural impact of industrial development sheds light on another paradox in the Kuznets findings depicted in Figure 1. Class I countries, the most productive per head of population and generally the most "advanced" countries industrially, derive a smaller proportion of their incomes from the sum of agriculture and manufacturing than do the poorest and generally least industrialized nations. The sums of percentages of income derived from agriculture and from manufacturing, in descending order of income per head, are as follows: I = 51.3; II = 58.7; III = 48.4; IV = 54.4; V = 59.7; VI = 60.3; VII = 68.3. In the poorest nations, Classes VI and VII, where agriculture forms the greatest part of income-producing activity, one finds the highest proportions of the populations directly engaged in producing goods and services. In the middle ranges, III and IV, there are no apparent uniformities in this regard. The extent of the "liberation" of labor from direct production of goods and services in the richest countries bears witness to the efficiency of their economic activities and underscores the point made by Jacob Viner that "the real problem in poor countries is not agriculture as such, but poverty and backwardness, poor agriculture and poor manufacturing" ([1952] 1953, p. 52).

Role of education. In the most productive nations the possibilities of continuously improving the "quality" of the labor force by education, and thus of creating ever more productive societies, are very great (Maizels 1963) and are apparently proceeding apace. Historical statistics on educational achievement in the United States (U.S. Bureau of the Census 1960) show a tremendous change in the attainment of formal education by the labor force in the twentieth century. As late as 1900 only 6.4 per cent of American youths aged 17 had graduated from high school. By 1956 this number had reached the extraordinary level of 62.3 per cent. In 1900 only 4 per cent of American youths between the ages of 18 and 21 were enrolled in institutions of higher learning; by 1956 the figure was 29.9 per cent, and by 1964 the figure was apparently in the neighborhood of 33 per cent. If American society is prototypical of the world industrial society of the future, one result of industrialization is a vast improvement in the quality of the labor force (so far as that can be effected by formal education) and, hence, of productive potential. [*See* CAPITAL, HUMAN.]

Other characteristics

Urbanization. Another economic consequence of industrial development is urbanization. Cities have existed since antiquity as trade, financial, and administrative centers. But until the industrial revolution urban size was characterized by substantial stability—enough, for example, to make the medieval city wall a practical undertaking. With the industrial revolution the relatively stable relationship between town and country vanished, and the industrial conurbation began to spread. Because of the internal economies of the division of work based upon the prime mover and managerial centralization, the system of factories developed rapidly after the introduction of steam engines as prime movers in the 1780s. Factories based upon water power had existed earlier; but they were necessarily placed near fast-moving water, as was the case with John Lombe's spinning factory, which was operating as early as 1718. Factories brought people together, and the external economies of proximity brought factories together; it paid to be near a labor force, skilled mechanics, sources of parts for machinery, and so forth. Where transportation could bring raw materials together with markets for the eventual products, new cities and factory districts grew up, changing the demographic maps of each area to which industrial growth came.

In Britain new centers—the Midlands around Birmingham and Wolverhampton, the textile districts from York and Leeds southwestward to Liverpool on the Irish Sea, and Newcastle and Stockton in the northeast—displaced older centers of population like Oxford, Norwich, the old market towns of the south, and the home counties, except, of course, London itself. For this change in the distribution of English population to have occurred in so short a time was itself "revolutionary." It created social problems and upheaval on a scale unknown in Britain since Tudor times and resulted in fundamental changes in the English constitution.

In American development, there was roughly the same experience. Cincinnati, Pittsburgh, Columbus, Indianapolis; such Great Lake ports as Chicago, Cleveland, and Toledo; and so forth were cities of the American industrial revolution, not products of the earlier trade and finance which underpinned the population centers on the East and the Gulf coasts.

From the north of France across the Rhine estuary, central Europe, Russia, then in Japan (and now China), industrial conurbations grew rapidly in the nineteenth and twentieth centuries as manufacturing techniques spread. In most respects, industrial society became urban society.

A few figures from American data underscore the point. In 1840 nonfarm population in the

United States was 10.5 per cent of the total; in 1960 it was 92.6 per cent of the total, of which 69.4 per cent lived in urban areas. In the United States, population classed as "rural" has fallen some since the 1940s, while that classed as "farm" has fallen sharply, from 30.5 million in 1940 to 14.3 million by 1962. The number of farms has also declined sharply. In Britain, on the other hand, the agricultural population declined, but the decline represented more a reduction in the number of hired laborers than any reduction in the number of farmers. In both countries, though, a decline of farm population reflected the growth of cities as the population grew. The experience of other nations in industry has been similar—urban population growing while rural population shrinks; in recent times the Soviet Union has provided an additional dramatic example.

Population growth. Until recently it was generally accepted that the great expansion of total population which accompanied the growth of industry and urbanization was a product of industrialization. The effective agent was thought to have been reduction of the death rate, especially infant mortality. The advances in real income, including more varied diets, better sanitation, heating, and housing generally, had contributed to the elimination of plague, to the building of resistance to communicable diseases of all sorts, and, generally, to a more healthful population (a view condemned by those whose argument it is that, until 1848 at least, industrialization impoverished and debilitated the population in spite of the explosive increase in numbers). This plausible view seemed to account satisfactorily enough for the prodigious increases in total population that came to the British Isles in the early nineteenth century, spread across Europe eastward and southward with the proliferation of the techniques and income effects of industrial development, and supplied millions of immigrants to the New World and other areas of overseas European settlement by 1914 while, at the same time, raising European population from 192 million to more than 450 million.

However, this view of population growth, which emphasizes a causal link with industrialization, has recently been questioned to some extent by those scholars who, by studying British records, have discerned an increase in birth rates in the United Kingdom *before* the industrial revolution took hold (before, say, 1780). The revisionist view (Deane & Cole 1962) holds essentially that the process of industrialization, by contributing to a fall in death rates, helped to accelerate a population growth already in process as a result of rising birth rates. Even more recently the revisionist view itself has been questioned (Tucker 1963). It is noted that alternate estimates of population in the sixteenth century could eliminate much of the forcefulness of the evidence of a dramatic rise in population growth in Britain before the industrial revolution. At present these problems are not resolved. All parties agree, of course, that industrialization and urbanization were associated with a gigantic population increase. The line of causation is, however, not clear.

International trade. Probably no part of the history of industrialization has been subject to more controversy than that relating to international trade. Thanks to customs controls, a vast amount of national information exists, but because of problems of valuation the information has been, and still is, remarkably inconsistent. There is no doubt that industrialization has been a powerful stimulus to the growth of international trade. What has been a subject of considerable controversy is the extent to which the argument is reversible: To what extent has international trade been a stimulus to industrialization?

Since rising productivity creates markets, and rising productivity has been the hallmark of world industrialization, the connection between the great increase in world trade which followed the industrial revolution (and the Napoleonic Wars) and the rise of industry has never been doubted. The industrial nations not only became great importers of raw materials, thus drawing the nonindustrial nations into the vortex of the international economy, but they also became, by virtue of their high incomes, the primary importers of manufactured goods. In 1959 the industrial countries accounted for 55 per cent of world imports of manufactured goods, most of the world's imports of primary commodities, and most of the growth of total world imports since World War II (Maizels 1963). In every industrial country, however, the pattern of exports and imports has changed considerably over time in continuous reaction to domestic technological change, thus creating difficulties for primary producers whose product flexibility is more narrowly limited.

Widening markets are a stimulus to industrial investment, but since exports of manufactures are usually less than domestic sales, it is not at all clear to what extent exports have been a necessary (although no doubt a helpful) ingredient of industrial growth. Those extractive industries in the primary producing countries which have no important domestic markets—for example, Saudi Arabian oil —are an exception. Indeed, it is believed by some economists that no important *manufacturing* specialty in international trade can be developed where a successful domestic market has not been achieved. (This is a matter of practical economics, not of theoretical necessity.) In this qualitative sense, trade in manufactured goods has been viewed as a product of industrial development, but the argument is not reversible.

In the cases where foreign investment has been complementary to exports, international trade has been viewed by some as partly inimical to domestic industrial growth. Great Britain at the beginning of the twentieth century is the major example; it is held by some that Britain's backwardness in industrial technique by 1913 was due to the lure of foreign investment. In the previous half century foreign investment had grown more rapidly than domestic investment. Indeed, by 1913 British foreign investment apparently was half as large as domestic investment, and by far the greater part of new issues in the London capital market were for foreign accounts (Cairncross 1953). On the other hand, it has also been argued that foreign investment, by stimulating growth of export industries which led the way in domestic economic expansions, acted as a fillip to the growth of income generally at home and abroad (Thomas 1954). Both views have been extensively developed, at least since the work of John Hobson and Lenin, and the differences in conclusions cannot be reconciled here.

By 1914 a remarkable system of world trade and payments, centering on the industrial nations, provided for total currency convertibility—the gold standard. The system had developed apace with the spread of industrialization, and it was adopted by country after country as multilateralism in payments displaced various bilateral and triangular trading systems. By 1900, when the United States adopted the gold standard, that system reached its apex. The world's payment system was still centered on London as late as the 1870s, but as international financial power spread with industrial growth and the convertibility of currencies, many centers of financial settlement appeared. By 1914 the now almost legendary gold standard was the accepted system of trade and payments among the commercial nations.

> By 1914 a large part of multilateral trade was based, not upon this series of disconnected patterns mainly centered around Britain . . . but upon a complex network of activity embracing whole continents or subcontinents, derived from a new world-wide division of economic functions. . . . The rapidly industrializing countries of Europe and North America expanded their purchases of raw materials and foodstuffs from the primary producers, and all, with the significant exception of Britain, ran up heavy deficits in their balances with those countries. (Saul 1960, pp. 44–45)

The connection that developed between industrialization and trade was striking. By 1913 the United States produced 35.8 per cent of the world's manufactured goods, and the United States, Germany (15.7 per cent), the United Kingdom (14 per cent), France (6.4 per cent), and Russia (5.5 per cent) between them produced 77.4 per cent of the world's total manufactures and occupied the center of world trade. By 1936–1938 the same five nations still carried on 75.1 per cent of world manufacturing and, with Japan, Sweden, Belgium, and a handful of other nations, accounted for some 89 per cent of world imports and exports. Only 11 per cent of world trade originated between the two-thirds of mankind that was bereft of industry. By 1959 the underdeveloped nations of Latin America, Africa, and Asia produced only 10 per cent of world manufactures (excluding the Soviet bloc). By 1926–1929 two-thirds of the earth's population had a supply of manufactured goods equal to $7 per head, a third of mankind averaged $104 per head, the United States averaged $254 per head, and the United Kingdom averaged $112 per head. Like the income statistics noted earlier for the 1960s, manufacturing supplies were most unevenly available to mankind by the time industrialization had reached fruition in the (primarily Western) countries of its origin. By 1959 the major industrial countries, containing 28 per cent of mankind, consumed 82 per cent of the world's manufactures. [*See* INTERNATIONAL TRADE, *article on* PATTERNS OF TRADE.]

World War II and its aftermath of course added further disruptions to world industrial development. The international flow of capital, so much a feature of the old gold standard and choked off by the 1929 financial debacle, has only begun to make a comeback since the mid-1950s. Currency convertibility was still incomplete by the early 1960s, after nearly two decades of international cooperation in that area, and the world's trade was badly split by the cold war and by the inability of the underdeveloped nations to earn foreign exchange. In 1961, for example, three-fourths of the known supply of world monetary gold ($41,000 million) was held by the usual industrial nations: the United States, the members of the European Economic Community, the United Kingdom, and Switzerland (a country which attracts foreign exchange by unique inducements—security from taxes, wars, confiscations, etc.). The wide inequalities of income resulting from success and failure in industrial growth show no signs of being reduced. There are no logical reasons why these inequalities would be reduced by international trade alone. Indeed, some economists have argued that trade has a tendency to make matters worse in this regard—to result in the rich countries' exploitation of the poor—a view which has not been accepted on the basis of its formal merits (United Nations . . . 1950; Prebisch 1959; Flanders 1964).

International migration. In addition to present-day problems of trade and capital flows, which many believe to be barriers to a wider dissemination of industrial development, the flow of persons in international economic life has been constrained. In the theory of international trade, factor price equalization is held to be, under highly restrictive conditions, a consequence of trade in commodities alone. Equalization of incomes is not implied by that logic because of unequal "factor endowments" (a phrase which includes, of course, the quality of "human capital"). But the international flow of persons and capital before 1914 assuaged to some extent the impact of differing rates of productivity growth and of unequal natural endowments. The poor could at least migrate to higher-income countries. All of the industrial nations benefited from the migration of skilled persons, and the so-called countries of European overseas settlement received a massive direct input of labor in the great nineteenth-century migration. The United States alone received 35 million immigrants between 1820 and 1914. Such labor contributions were accompanied by large-scale capital transfers. At least for those who left low-income countries to go to high-income countries, migration brought some "equalization" of the growing income resulting from industrial development and foreign trade. The migrations themselves were subject to the rhythms of long-term economic growth. [*See* MIGRATION, *article on* ECONOMIC ASPECTS; *see also* Thomas 1954.]

Because of the nationalistic restrictions placed on immigration in modern times, especially since the 1920s, and because of the cold war, migration of persons is not a possible solution to international income inequalities (apart from particular situations such as that existing between the United States and Canada or between members of the EEC); neither the permanent migration on a large scale of skilled persons nor the movement of mass labor to areas of highest marginal returns is feasible. Migration, in any case, does nothing for income per capita in the low-income countries unless the migrants are the unemployed and other nonproductive persons who are charges on national income. To solve these problems, foreign aid schemes and the temporary loan of thousands of technicians by the advanced and industrialized countries on both sides of the iron curtain have been tried. However, these measures have not been notably successful thus far in spreading industrial development. [*See* FOREIGN AID, *article on* ECONOMIC ASPECTS; TECHNICAL ASSISTANCE.]

Theoretical generalizations

Finally, we might ask: Are there any observable "laws" in the economics of industrial development? As national economies have changed in their internal structures and in their economic relations with each other under the impact of industrial change, some apparent uniformities in their histories have given rise to attempts to generalize the "process" of industrial development on the basis of observed facts. The intractability of the facts has hindered those interested in so-called theories of economic development, and those facing the known facts have found more success in classification than in explanation. The "stage" systems, in which industrialization is cut into chronological segments, are the results of inductive methods, and however weak they may be as examples of theoretical virtuosity, they are useful in viewing a world of factual information which has rarely yielded to rigorous testing of theories of economic growth.

The attempt to establish stages is a natural course of thought when economic logic is confronted with a mass of facts representing primarily economic change. The American data on income and employment structure presented earlier fall easily into three stages: the present is greatly changed from the earliest days, and somewhere in-between is demonstrably different from early times or the present. The characteristics of Stage I are most prominent in the data around 1860, when a growing industrial sector was still overshadowed by agriculture and foreign trade was characterized by sale of raw materials and food to the world in return for manufactures. These characteristics faded into those of Stage II. In Stage II, with its high point somewhere between the two world wars, manufacturing industry dominated income and employment, agriculture was overshadowed, imports consisted mostly of food and raw materials (the apparent outcome of the whole history of American industrialization), and exports consisted mainly of manufactures. In Stage III, the period since 1945, the sum of income and labor in manufacturing is less than that in employment not directly concerned with the creation of food and goods, and imports of finished manufactures are rising as a proportion of the total (thus reversing the apparent outcome of American industrial development), representing more diversified consumer tastes and larger consumer incomes. The most rapidly growing sectors are not in industry but in finance, professions, commerce, services, and the like.

This simple stage-system corresponds roughly in time periods to a more formal one developed by Sumner Slichter on the basis of data relating to productivity (1961). In Slichter's Stage I, from earliest times until 1880–1900, there was a rise in capital–output ratios, since capital grew faster than income as the nation built its basic industrial plant. In Stage II, from 1880–1900 to 1929, the "sensational" increase in the uses of energy in electrical and internal-combustion engines caused income to grow faster than the stock of capital. The basic industrial plant was being rationalized and refined through technological progress. Since 1929 or so, Stage III, the technological revolution in managerial practices and industrial research, has raised productivity more through brain power than through applications of more capital and more powerful physical energy units. Thus, productivity has risen while the capital–output ratio has fallen.

Obviously, any industrial system with a considerable history is subject to such analysis. The two stage-schemes outlined above are based upon changes in given statistical evidence over time for the United States only. Of particular interest are two stage-systems which purport to be of more general applicability, those of W. W. Rostow and Walther Hoffmann. Rostow's system (1960) faintly resembles the so-called classical stage-system, wherein any economy develops from agriculture and mining through industrialization, with an increasing part of the labor force employed in secondary and tertiary activities. In Rostow's five-part system, development begins in a traditional economy, which gradually finds resources for investment until a critical proportion is reached wherein growth of income per capita accelerates, providing for self-sustained growth. This is the "take-off." After that, the society moves forward toward maturity and high mass consumption. A further stage is suggested in which the marginal utility of real income diminishes. The problem in such a stage would obviously be to make leisure creative in some nonmaterial sense. According to Rostow, most industrial nations are now in Stage V, high mass consumption, and the Soviet Union is rapidly approaching it. Other societies are trailing on this time map all the way back to primitive traditionalism.

An interesting system adapted from formal theorizing about economic development is that developed by Walther Hoffmann (1931). The relevant theory comes from the work of the Austrian economist Eugen von Böhm-Bawerk, who held that "capital" in an economy is the indirectness or "degree of round-aboutness" in production [*see* BÖHM-BAWERK]. It follows that the more developed an economy is, the greater that part of its industrial production devoted to the creation of producers', as opposed to consumers', goods. Measuring the world's industrial activity against Böhm-Bawerk's propositions, Hoffmann developed a four-stage system into which the major industrial economies are fitted historically. At first the highest proportion of industrial output is in consumers' goods. As a nation becomes more advanced, the ratios of output of goods and inputs of labor in consumers' goods industries fall relative to producers' goods industries. Hoffmann's system is much more narrowly defined than Rostow's, since it embraces only the manufacturing sector of the economy. Also, the logical extension of Böhm-Bawerk's theory is that the degree of round-aboutness would find expression in "human capital" as science became more sophisticated. But since Hoffmann does not extend his analysis beyond the manufacturing data, he does not detect the phenomenon noted earlier, namely, that the more advanced an industrial country becomes, the greater the proportion of its labor force liberated from the production of goods and food—once a critical level of industrial development is reached.

Other stage systems might be mentioned, for example, Lewis Mumford's gigantic system based upon technological development or Douglass North's special system for the analysis of regional growth. All of these are methods for simplifying the massive and nearly chaotic evidence relating to industrial development. Their usefulness is to some extent mitigated by a millenarian tendency which characterizes too much thinking about the worldwide industrial development that followed the industrial revolution. A survey of the history and modern characteristics of industrialism and its economic effects ought to be sufficient to deter the wise from making predictions, except, perhaps, to note that economic change has come relentlessly on the heels of technological change.

J. R. T. HUGHES

[*See also* ECONOMIC GROWTH; ECONOMY, DUAL.]

BIBLIOGRAPHY

ASHTON, THOMAS S. (1948) 1964 *The Industrial Revolution: 1760–1830.* Rev. ed. Oxford Univ. Press.

BURNS, ARTHUR F. 1934 *Production Trends in the United States Since 1870.* New York: National Bureau of Economic Research.

CAIRNCROSS, ALEXANDER K. 1953 *Home and Foreign Investment: 1870–1913.* Cambridge Univ. Press.

CAMERON, RONDO 1961 *France and the Economic Development of Europe, 1800–1914: Conquests of Peace and Seeds of War.* Princeton Univ. Press.

DEANE, PHYLLIS; and COLE, W. A. 1962 *British Economic Growth, 1688–1959: Trends and Structure.* Cambridge Univ. Press.

FLANDERS, M. JUNE 1964 Prebisch on Protectionism: An Evaluation. *Economic Journal* 74:305–326.

HABAKKUK, H. J. 1953 English Population in the Eighteenth Century. *Economic History Review* Second Series 6:117–133.

HENDERSON, W. O. 1954 *Britain and Industrial Europe, 1750–1870: Studies in British Influence on the Industrial Revolution in Western Europe.* Liverpool Univ. Press.

HOFFMANN, WALTHER G. (1931) 1958 *The Growth of Industrial Economies.* Rev. & enl. Manchester Univ. Press. → First published as *Stadien und Typen der Industrialisierung.*

HUGHES, J. R. T. 1958 Foreign Trade and Balanced Growth: The Historical Framework. *American Economic Review* 49, no. 2:330–337.

KINDLEBERGER, C. P. 1961 Foreign Trade and Economic Growth: Lessons From Britain and France, 1850 to 1913. *Economic History Review* Second Series 14:289–305.

KRAUSE, J. T. 1958 Changes in English Fertility and Mortality: 1781–1850. *Economic History Review* Second Series 11:52–70.

KUZNETS, SIMON S. (1953) 1954 *Economic Change: Selected Essays in Business Cycles, National Income, and Economic Growth.* London: Heinemann.

KUZNETS, SIMON S. (1959) 1961 *Six Lectures on Economic Growth.* New York: Free Press.

LANDES, DAVID S. 1958 *Bankers and Pashas: International Finance and Economic Imperialism in Egypt.* Cambridge, Mass.: Harvard Univ. Press.

LEAGUE OF NATIONS, SECRETARIAT, FINANCIAL SECTION AND ECONOMIC INTELLIGENCE SERVICE 1942 *The Network of World Trade.* Geneva: The League.

LEAGUE OF NATIONS, SECRETARIAT, FINANCIAL SECTION AND ECONOMIC INTELLIGENCE SERVICE 1945 *Industrialization and Foreign Trade.* Geneva: The League.

LEWIS, W. ARTHUR 1955 *The Theory of Economic Growth.* Homewood, Ill.: Irwin.

MAIZELS, ALFRED 1963 *Industrial Growth and World Trade: An Empirical Study of Trends.* Cambridge Univ. Press.

MANTOUX, PAUL (1906) 1962 *The Industrial Revolution in the Eighteenth Century.* London: Cape. → First published in French. A paperback edition was published in 1965 by Harper.

NURKSE, RAGNAR (1953) 1962 *Problems of Capital Formation in Under-developed Countries.* New York: Oxford Univ. Press.

PREBISCH, RAÚL 1959 Commercial Policy in the Underdeveloped Countries. *American Economic Review* 49, no. 2:251–273.

ROSOVSKY, HENRY 1961 *Capital Formation in Japan, 1868–1940.* New York: Free Press.

ROSTOW, WALT W. (1952) 1960 *The Process of Economic Growth.* Rev. ed. New York: Norton.

ROSTOW, WALT W. (1960) 1963 *The Stages of Economic Growth: A Non-Communist Manifesto.* Cambridge Univ. Press.

SAUL, S. B. 1960 *Studies in British Overseas Trade, 1870–1914.* Liverpool Univ. Press.

SLICHTER, SUMNER H. 1961 *Economic Growth in the United States: Its History, Problems and Prospects.* Baton Rouge: Louisiana State Univ. Press.

SOMBART, WERNER (1903) 1927 *Die deutsche Volkswirtschaft im neunzehnten Jahrhundert und im Anfang des 20. Jahrhunderts: Eine Einführung in die Nationalökonomie.* 7th ed. Berlin: Bondi.

THOMAS, BRINLEY 1954 *Migration and Economic Growth: A Study of Great Britain and the Atlantic Economy.* National Institute of Economic and Social Research, Economic and Social Studies, No. 12. Cambridge Univ. Press.

TUCKER, G. S. L. 1963 English Pre-industrial Population Trends. *Economic History Review* Second Series 16:205–218.

UNITED NATIONS, ECONOMIC COMMISSION FOR LATIN AMERICA 1950 *The Economic Development of Latin America and Its Principal Problems.* Lake Success, N.Y.: United Nations, Department of Economic Affairs.

U.S. BUREAU OF THE CENSUS 1960 *Historical Statistics of the United States; Colonial Times to 1957: A Statistical Abstract Supplement.* Washington: Government Printing Office.

U.S. BUREAU OF THE CENSUS *Statistical Abstract of the United States.* → Published since 1878.

VINER, JACOB (1921–1951) 1958 *The Long View and the Short: Studies in Economic Theory and Policy.* Glencoe, Ill.: Free Press. → See especially pages 277–305, "Power Versus Plenty as Objectives of Foreign Policy in the Seventeenth and Eighteenth Centuries."

VINER, JACOB (1952) 1953 *International Trade and Economic Development: Lectures at the National University of Brazil.* Oxford: Clarendon.

II
SOCIAL ASPECTS

Industrialization, in the strict sense of the term, entails the extensive use of inanimate sources of power in the production of economic goods and services. Even so restrictive a definition does not limit the concept solely to manufacturing, as agriculture is also subject to mechanization (as well as other modes of technical rationalization), and so are services such as transportation and communication. It is true, of course, that manufacturing is an essential ingredient, as the machines and instruments used in the production of raw materials or services are likely to be factory-produced.

The use of an initially technological criterion of industrialization does not imply a kind of technological determinism. On the contrary, there are clearly institutional and organizational preconditions and counterparts of large-scale and efficient utilization of power. Extensive industrialization (in the strict sense) is quite unlikely in the absence of a highly specialized and coordinated labor force, monetary exchange and rationalized accounting systems, the technology of precise measurement and production control, and so on. Furthermore, technology itself is properly viewed not as a kind of inanimate force but rather as a body of practical knowledge and skills; it is a social product having social consequences.

The term "industrialization" is often used in a broader sense as equivalent to any form of economic modernization. There is some justification for this looser usage, since there is no example of sustained economic growth (measured, say, by real income per head) without the extensive practice of manufacturing or the use of its products. Making industrialization equivalent to economic development runs some risks, however, particularly for somewhat fine-grained analysis of the components of economic growth. The risk is comparable to that displayed in Marxist theory, which attaches structural and dynamic primacy to "the economic factor" but then includes "dependent" variables in the independent one, so that the determination is by definition, or, worse, includes several elements and components that are independently variable, so that these variations are suppressed or defined away. Even if the structural integration of economic systems were greater than can be empirically confirmed, the order and rate of change of one or another component in a wide range of "economic factors" would still have significant consequences. The risk is minimized by its recognition, however, and industrialization will be used here in its broader sense except where finer distinctions are necessary and appropriate.

Theoretical and methodological issues

The conceptual models of complex social systems, including societies, used by most social scientists involve assumptions about structural determinateness and congruity that need careful scrutiny. In extreme form, these models assume such a close interdependence of elements in social systems that a substantial autonomous (or, more likely, exogenous) change in one component would lead to definite and congruent changes in others. This would be particularly true of such a crucial aspect of social organization as the system of economic production. If this degree of integration could be used with predictive reliability, the "system requirements" of industrialism could be worked out theoretically and checked against a single established case for empirical confirmation. The actual situation is more complex, however, as the variety in extant industrial societies makes evident. A theoretical approach involving a "system" concept is empirically warranted, but must focus on the *degree* of determination of the structural correlates and the consequences of economic transformation and continuing change.

The appropriate cautions in interpretation may be made explicit. First, structural congruities may apply between classes and ranges of structural forms rather than between specific features. For example, a strictly hereditary mode of occupational placement is clearly inconsistent with the recruitment of an industrial labor force in the broad sense, if for no other reason than the changing proportions of occupational categories and the appearance and disappearance of occupations from the "market mix." Second, incongruities are probable. Persistent ones—for example, as between labor mobility and employer identification—may be kept within tolerable limits by various tension-management devices, but perfect solutions are unlikely and may be impossible. The low probability of absolutely synchronic change implies incongruities arising from leads and lags. Third, even empirical uniformity is not conclusive proof of theoretical *necessity;* structural alternatives simply may not have been tried. For example, the bureaucratic form of authoritative coordination of specialized workers in large productive units seems almost, if not completely, universal as the standard form of industrial organization. However, from direct and indirect evidence at hand, it cannot be determined whether this is a structural necessity, and if so, within what limits of variation, and if not, what are equally or more viable alternatives. The replication of a standard form of organization may derive from mere imitation, abetted by an untested theory of functional necessity, rather than from successive independent developments based upon experimentation with alternatives. These cautions do not imply chaos or random variability of social and economic structures; however, they do bespeak a stance of skeptical inquiry with respect to the theory and the available evidence.

Correlational and sequential analysis. In addition to doubts about the determinateness of functional or structural necessities, an important problem of *time* presents itself. When are these structural changes associated with industrialization to appear—immediately or in the "long run"? Can anything be said about the order of their appearance? These are questions that the integration models of society are plainly unsuited to answer. It is distressing to note how often this kind of analysis fails to make explicit the "change model" on which it relies. But even when the model is made explicit, it is clearly unacceptable. Although it has been characterized as a three-stage model, only the middle, transitional stage of it has been seriously studied; its preindustrial and postindustrial stages are usually assumed to be static and "integrated" (for these and other criticisms see Feldman & Moore 1962). Change in preindustrial societies may be relatively slow or infrequent, but this assumption of stasis runs counter to evidence that all societies are subject to change from intrinsic sources and to the clear historic fact that most of the "newly developing" areas have had political, economic, and often religious contact with the Western world for periods ranging from decades to centuries. The assumption of postindustrial stability could only be an implication of scholarly neglect, for it is absurd when made explicit.

The extensive, empirically based generalizations about the social aspects of industrialization are, paradoxically, mainly consistent with this contrary-to-fact change model and with an exaggerated equilibrium or integration model as applied to the stages not directly examined. The fact is that, within limits, common origins and common destinations can be assumed. However, the errors of the theoretical structure appear when more detail is sought concerning routes and trajectories of change and the varieties of (temporary) destinations, or when attention is turned to the continuing dynamics of industrial societies.

Before-and-after comparisons abound in the descriptive and analytical literature. They gain their validity from the reality of structural constraints on social organization imposed by any of the variant forms of an industrial economy. What is clearly missing in the current state of knowledge, however, is any precision in the sequence and timing of structural changes. Moreover, since these factors are no more likely to be invariant than the antecedent conditions or the character of industrial societies, a change-model typology is also missing. The notion that each case is unique, though obviously true in some details, would defeat both generalization and prediction, and it is a prematurely pessimistic position. Generalization is indeed possible, as will be indicated in this article, but the day of "easy" generalizations is past.

Of course, cross-sectional data are still needed for establishing the range of conditions and the correlates of various forms and degrees of industrialization. There is an even more critical need for repeated observations through time, including quantitative trends. As social statistics become more widely available, at least through decennial censuses, the recent course of change in newly developing areas may be compared with the older historic record, which also awaits systematic quantitative analysis. It may be confidently expected that since trends in one or another measurable aspect of economic and social structure are not truly autonomous, somewhat complex "stochastic" models will be needed for analysis of temporal patterns.

Conditions for industrialization

A review of the circumstances under which industrialization and broader economic development can take place may appropriately start with those most clearly economic in character. It should be noted at once, however, that the distinction between the economic and noneconomic components of social systems is not as sharp as is often assumed for analytic convenience. Industrialization involves, for example, extensive remobilization of the "factors of production," including new supplies of capital, new power sources, "embodied technology" in capital goods and equipment, and workers with skills that are different from those required in the preindustrial economy. But lying just behind these economic inputs (or comprising the same requirements in different semantic guise) are the organization of capital markets or the investment decisions of the state, a network of relationships between suppliers and manufacturers, an external or internal training system for workers, and so on.

Just how much formal education is a requisite "capital investment" for economic growth is a matter of some conjecture and scholarly dispute. Moreover, given limited investment resources and urgently competing demands on them, there is also uncertainty as between an "elitist" policy, which concentrates attention on training professional, technical, and managerial personnel, and a kind of "populist" policy, which emphasizes the economic as well as social values of widespread education as a mechanism of attitudinal development along with cognitive learning. The historic record of the industrialized countries is poorly known and barely analyzed, and in any event it might or might not yield precise and applicable answers for countries with largely illiterate populations and extremely short historical backgrounds in the cultivation of the professions and other intellectual occupations.

It is a truism that underdeveloped areas suffer from a shortage of capital and, generally, a surplus of labor. Domestic capital resources may exist to some degree, however, and the problem becomes one of tapping unproductive savings, providing means and motives for diversion of capital from traditional to novel investments, or perhaps establishing a system of "forced saving" through the taxation system and fiscal policies of the state. Labor supplies are likely to represent underemployment in agriculture, but the actual diversion of labor to industrial employment is likely to require a reorganization of agriculture. Improved efficiency of labor in agriculture and some actual increase in farm output are needed to supply the needs for food and fiber of those who will not be engaged in primary production. The supplies of workers for industry, although numerically ample, are quite unlikely to have the necessary skills—to say nothing of attitudes and habits—for industrial work (Moore 1951). Thus some investment in training will be a requisite for new productive systems.

The historic cases of successful industrialization have involved countries that were either rich in territory and resources or else engaged in extensive international trade in capital, raw materials, and products. In contrast, many of the new nations are both poor and small, and they are not likely to be economically viable without the formation of international trading organizations or actual economic unification across political boundaries.

Institutional structures. As to the requisite organizational and institutional structure, we may note some further normative conditions for industrialization. Property rights must be transferable if land, raw materials, and other material factors of production are to be converted to new uses and passed, say, from supplier to manufacturer to consumer. Nominal ownership by the state changes this condition only in detail, as transfers of power over and responsibility for the materials of production are still necessary. Labor, too, must be transferable; short of reliance on the police power of a totalitarian state, this normally means the establishment of a "labor market" and a system of financial and other rewards to induce workers to move from one economic sector to another, one employer to another, one skill level to another, and so on. At the very least, fixed hereditary assignment of economic roles must somehow be broken down. Eventually, a whole new structure of social placement and relative status must be established; however, this structure may be viewed as a consequence rather than a condition of economic modernization.

Even exchange relationships, though nominally contractual and perhaps predicated on individual self-interest, are necessarily based on norms of propriety and fair dealing, compliance with promises for future performance, and restraints on competitive strategies that would destroy the system. The classic formulation by Durkheim (1893) of the "non-contractual elements in contracts" is in point here. The actual organization of monetary exchange relationships must be established where it does not exist. Industry, in particular, commonly involves assembling the factors of production over considerable distances (often crossing political boundaries) and over considerable periods of time. Systems of credit, stabilization of currency and its rates of exchange, and state fiscal policies of some reliability are thus necessary.

Since rules are not always self-enforcing or organizational arrangements self-policing, a modicum of stable political power is essential. The noninterference of the state in the development of "laissez-faire capitalism" was systematically and hypocritically exaggerated by ideologists for private businesses that generally benefited from direct and indirect governmental assistance. In the contemporary world of the newly developing areas, the state is likely to play a prominent, overt, and often dominant part in developmental policies and their concrete implementation. This comes about in part because only the state can muster the necessary capital from domestic and foreign sources and make the other necessary changes in social organization and the legal embodiment of normative codes.

Motives and values. It is also true that industrialization and other measures of economic development have become instruments of national policy in virtually the entire world; this fact brings us to questions of motives and values. Classical economic analysis operated with a very simple set of motivational assumptions: that individuals would act rationally in ways designed to maximize their own material self-interests. Just what those interests were, beyond health, food, clothing, and shelter, was left vague, or the question was simply neglected. Yet, despite this neglect, these motivational assumptions appear sounder than the rather exaggerated "value relativism" advanced by anthropological and sociological critics of economic theory. Once some knowledge of the possibility of economic betterment became fairly widespread, discontent with poverty also became widespread. At this level, the motivational requisites appear to be satisfied. But as usual the problem is somewhat more complex. New employments and styles of life are not always better than old ones, and they are never unmixed blessings. A simple quest for improvement does not automatically yield the means for its achievement.

Economists have long identified the functions of "entrepreneurship" as requisites for the development of the capital investment and extensive organizational and technical innovations that are necessary for economic modernization. Their faith was often a little magical and somewhat restricted to a free-market economy. Hagen (1962) has restated and broadened the case for the importance of creative or innovative personality types. Yet, in any case, leadership is not independent of the motives of those who are led. To balance this exclusive emphasis on the innovators or managers, other scholars have argued for the importance of labor commitment—not only performance but also acceptance of the relevant norms—and for the importance of some participation in decisions and actions for the appearance of commitment (Moore & Feldman 1960).

The motives of the ordinary individual participant in economic activities are not necessarily the same as the values espoused by national planners and their spokesmen. Short of terroristic totalitarianism, the two presumably have some congruence, but it need not be perfect. Industrialization and other developmental measures are always instrumental goals—but for which more ultimate values are they instrumental? Mere widespread improvement of present economic conditions would presumably best satisfy the aspirations of most participants. But maximizing present returns is likely to be at the cost of sustained future growth, which requires substantial savings and capital accumulation. The long-term view is likely to have little appeal to those who are faring least well in their present situations. The older solution to this problem, in terms of profits available for reinvestment, rested on the institutionalization of a particular property system; and, as for all forms of socially legitimized power, the foundations of that power were values and thus nonrational. In societies now just beginning to foster rapid economic development, the proprietary solution has been generally mixed with or superseded by an appeal to national interest and power. Those values are also nonrational, but they provide an ideological rationale for present sacrifice or forbearance and an appeal to collective rather than purely selfish interests.

It is perhaps premature to list nationalism as a precondition for industrialization, but for the reasons just given it would have a high priority among the values preceding major economic change. Nationalism serves another, correlative function, in providing a sense of identity and meaning for populations that are physically and socially uprooted. For the economic rewards, even if paid, have social costs, and those too merit attention.

Concomitants and consequences

The array of necessary and probable effects of economic modernization is extensive. It seems appropriate to start with the structural features of society that are primarily economic in form or function, then to proceed to the demographic and ecological characteristics of populations rearranged by economic development, and finally to attend to certain outstanding features of social organization.

A monetary basis of exchange is essentially a prior condition for any substantial industrialization; even remote, small, and isolated manufacturing establishments must either pay wages to their workers or set up a commissary. The extension of "custodial" arrangements has early limits, including the problem of finding external sources of supply. As economic modernization continues, the "economic calculus" tends to grow in importance. The variety of producers' and consumers' goods makes money the necessary medium for their acquisition and transfer. Perhaps even more significant for the transformation of traditional social forms is the movement of both new and old services and reciprocities through the market. Mutual aid among family members and neighbors either gives way to more specialized, hired services or, if it persists, tends to be given a market evaluation. The ubiquity of financial transactions and market evaluation becomes almost total: it affects clubs, religious orders, families, and welfare associations, as well as governments, banks, and retail shops.

Change in occupational structures. One of the more ridiculous conventions of traditional economic analysis was to treat labor as an aggregate of interchangeable units, its availability being governed over the short run by a market price translated into a wage rate. Even in the earliest stages of industrialization, a quotient of more skilled manpower is necessary, and this demand for differentiated services increases with time. Several interrelated and continuing processes of change in occupational structures can be traced to industrialization.

The first is that of "sectoral relocation": the transfer of producers out of agriculture and other preindustrial pursuits into industrial and commercial employments. In a limited sense this process is true by definition, but the process is a continuing and probably an accelerating one. It is in fact often a mixture of two analytically separable changes: first, the formation of a labor force in the technical sense, by setting monetary values on productive performance, and second, the relocation of constructive effort from less productive to more productive economic sectors.

Specialization is a second characteristic process of occupational change. A few traditional positions are successively subdivided as larger units provide the organizational mechanism for division of labor. At least equally important is the creation of demand for new skills associated with changes in the technology of products and processes and the steady expansion of services that are ancillary to the productive process or provide information and technique for the problems and aspirations of increasingly sophisticated consumers.

The subdivision of traditional craft skills and the partial substitution of mechanical for human effort in production have given rise to the criticism that industrialization is essentially degrading to the workmen. Ample evidence for this effect can be found historically, and there is little doubt that it will happen again and again. Yet, the initial effect of industrialization is to create demands for a new range of skills, and those new demands tend to require steadily higher levels of education and experience. On balance, and without denying the human costs and wastage involved, the long-term consequence of industrialization is an upgrading of occupational structures.

A final process of occupational change is that of bureaucratization: that is, the employment of specialized workers in large administrative organizations, which provide coordination by means of hierarchical authority rather than through the medium of contractual exchange in a market. Whether this rather authoritarian ordering of the work force is a necessary consequence of industrialization has not been fully examined, as noted above. It appears probable, for example, that the steady upgrading of the labor force reduces both the necessity and the efficacy of bureaucratic organization, which assumes the superior wisdom (and commitment) of the managers as compared with those managed. The loosening and decentralization of administrative controls may gradually supersede the rigidly hierarchical coordination of specialized producers.

Demographic and ecological effects. By very indirect and largely unintentional means, industrialization tends to create part of its own labor supply. This comes about by mortality reductions deriving from the whole range of public health, medical, and food-producing technologies. Birth rates, however, are not so immediately affected; they may in fact increase slightly, owing to better health and nutrition. The historic record indicates that after a variable period of rapid transitional growth, fertility also gradually comes under a measure of rational control. The interpretations of declining fertility vary and remain in dispute. That lower birth rates result from deliberate family limitation can scarcely be doubted, but the explanation of the attitudinal and behavioral change is by no means settled. In any event, the immediate effect of rapid population growth may be dampening to rates of economic growth, though not in any simple way, since rapid growth also produces an expanding labor force and, given other favorable conditions, expanded consumer demand. It seems highly probable that fertility declines will eventually happen in newly developing areas; and the combination of official concern and new contraceptive techniques may speed the process, as compared with past experience, just as death rates can now be reduced more rapidly than was historically true [*see* FERTILITY].

To population growth as a consequence of industrialization must be added a major spatial redistribution. The historic association between industrialization and urbanization was close but not perfect; large commercial and political centers antedated the industrial era, and, here and there, manufacturing establishments can be operated without large urban agglomerations. Even now, the rate of urbanization in newly developing areas commonly exceeds the rate of industrialization, as measured by employment in manufacturing. The urbanization rate displays attitudinal dissatisfaction with present conditions in conspicuous and troublesome ways; the "flight from the land" is an unmistakable "vote with the feet" for better opportunities. The cities of the world, even if not important manufacturing centers, are not "independent" of industrialization. The metropolitan complex vends the products of manufacturing and depends upon industrial products for communication, transportation, water, sewerage, public health measures, and public and private construction. The rate of urbanization is probably increasing everywhere, and it is likely to continue wherever there remain substantial residues of marginal agricultural producers [*see* POPULATION, *article on* DISTRIBUTION].

Social structural changes. The consequences of industrialization are also evident in the principal features of social structure. Most conspicuous and far-reaching, perhaps, is the impact of industry on kinship and the family, for in many nondustrial societies the constellation of kinsmen constitutes the major source of social position and personal identification. The required geographical and social mobility of an industrialized economy clearly weakens or breaks up the multigenerational and laterally extended "corporate" kin group. The destruction is unlikely to be total, however, which is contrary to certain interpretations that saw the functional utility of the "nuclear" family in an industrial society but did not comprehend the importance of the close bonds between generations and among siblings even in the small-family system. Intergenerational tensions are in fact likely to be sharpest in the very early stages of industrialization, as youths are the likeliest recruits to new occupations and styles of life. After a few generations, intergenerational disparities are less distinct, since they are within the "modernized" social system, rather than between radically different systems.

At the very time that traditional kinship ties are weakened or broken, the network of other essentially informal relationships is also likely to disappear for the urban industrial recruit. Village or tribal identities may be transferred to the cities temporarily, but they rarely survive in important measure among the first urban-born generation. For many of those displaced, there is little social framework between the immediate family and the (possibly remote) state. If either of these links to society fails, and especially if both do, apathy, alienation, and amoral or criminal conduct are likely to ensue. This is a persistent problem of industrial societies, despite the gradual growth or deliberate creation of new formal associations and forms of political participation.

The institutionalization of rationality—that is, an emphasis on problem-solving and impersonal relationships—often leads to a kind of "instrumentalism" and lack of fundamental value orientations. The family retains its importance in these circumstances as an affectional and personal set of relationships, permitting legitimate individuality and emotionality. On the larger scale, nationalism and religion compete, uneasily, for nonrational adherence. Both are threatened by secularization; in response to skeptical questioning of received doctrine, each attempts to provide answers to the intrinsic doubts and uncertainties of human existence. Nationalism rarely offers a sufficiently personal meaning to death and misfortune to supersede entirely the richer theology of traditional religions.

For social differentiation and stratification, the consequences of industrialization are, to say the least, complex. The invariant and probably inevitable initial effect of industrialization is a polarization of social status *within the modernized sector*. The managers and the managed, the innovators and the reluctant followers, are likely to represent radical differences in education, income, and power. This polarization may lead to apathy and discontent on the part of the lower orders, but only rarely to revolutionary disturbances. By the time the modernized sector has incorporated a substantial portion of the population, its status system has become far more complex. Multiple status gradations, including a disproportionate expansion of "middle positions," are further complicated by multiple criteria of differential valuation and relative position—a "lateral" extension of differentiation.

Marx correctly observed the polarities in early industrialization and almost correctly predicted (with some exaggeration) the disappearance of preindustrial strata. Although Marx was categorically wrong in his expectation of increasing polarization in Western societies, his theory does possess a certain validity in predicting the characteristics of early industrialization in the areas that are now beginning the process of economic modernization. The disparity between the great speed of "ideological" incorporation of impoverished populations into the common aspirations of the modern world and the slower pace of actual structural transformations may well increase the revolutionary potential in newly developing areas.

It is quite clear by now that rapid industrialization is consistent with a rather wide range of political regimes, although not all. Political centralization and substantial stability are clearly requisite for continuing growth, but democracy is not. In fact, in the contemporary world the state more nearly shapes the industrial structure than conversely; moreover, various alternative forms of the state, as well as various unprecedented combinations of technology and economic strategies, may be constructed eclectically from a world-wide pool of precedents. Any modern state is likely to hit upon forms of popular political participation as a mode of tension management under conditions of strain and rapid change. However, manipulative and essentially totalitarian management of such participation appears to be a viable alternative to genuine democracy. Though the ministries of political administration are likely to look pretty much alike in one capital or another, their ultimate accountabilities are likely to differ widely.

Continuities

The variability of political structures associated with industrialization highlights a weakness in the assumption that industrialization leads to a common social destination. The structural congruities are real enough, but they fall short of indicating structural determinism. Some persistent differences will be matters of detail and not very consequential at a generalized level of analysis. Others cannot be dismissed so lightly; they bear witness to a measure of systemic "openness."

Industrial societies of course have no stable, final destination, and this is part of the problem in predicting the exact consequences of industrialization in areas now beginning the process. Some underlying processes, such as continuous specialization and functional differentiation, are likely to provide sounder bases of generalization than the finer features of social structure at any particular time. Similarly, the substitution of machines for men is likely to be ubiquitous and continuous, with correlative positive consequences for occupational upgrading, ambiguous implications for the use of leisure, and negative consequences for those displaced or for those unable to fit such standardized selective mechanisms as the school.

Predicting the future of industrial societies has excited remarkably little scholarly, as opposed to literary, attention. That enterprise cannot seriously engage us here, except for one additional point. Paradoxically, and despite political diversity and exceptionally dangerous international tensions, there is a lesson of theoretical importance in worldwide industrialization. The contemporary form of industrialization is not autonomous and "autarchic," country by country, and indeed it never was. But now the new arrivals benefit from accumulated technological and organizational experience. The resulting "eclecticism" has at least two theoretical implications: novel combinations of structural elements may be expected, some of them viable; and, in many instances, the society (approximately equated with the national state) will no longer be the most useful comprehensive system for analytic purposes. In other words, in seeking to understand present and future large-scale, dynamic processes, we will have to view the world as a single system.

WILBERT E. MOORE

[*Directly related are the entries* ECONOMIC GROWTH; ECONOMY AND SOCIETY; MODERNIZATION. *Other relevant material may be found in* AUTOMATION; ENTREPRENEURSHIP; LABOR FORCE, *article on* DEFINITIONS AND MEASUREMENT; WORKERS; *and in the biographies of* MARX *and* WEBER, MAX.]

BIBLIOGRAPHY

BRAIBANTI, RALPH; and SPENGLER, JOSEPH J. (editors) 1961 *Tradition, Values, and Socio-economic Development.* Durham, N.C.: Duke Univ. Press.

DE VRIES, EGBERT; and MEDINA ECHAVARRÍA, JOSÉ (editors) 1963 *Social Aspects of Economic Development in Latin America.* 2 vols. Paris: UNESCO.

DURKHEIM, ÉMILE (1893) 1960 *The Division of Labor in Society.* Glencoe, Ill.: Free Press. → First published as *De la division du travail social.*

Economic Development and Cultural Change. → Published since 1952. Especially valuable for theoretical and empirical studies of industrialization.

FELDMAN, ARNOLD S.; and MOORE, WILBERT E. 1962 Industrialization and Industrialism: Convergence and Differentiation. Volume 2, pages 151–169 in World Congress of Sociology, Fifth, *Transactions.* London: International Sociological Association.

HAGEN, EVERETT E. 1962 *On the Theory of Social Change.* Homewood, Ill.: Dorsey.

INTERNATIONAL SOCIAL SCIENCE COUNCIL 1958 *Social, Economic, and Technological Change: A Theoretical Approach.* Paris: The Council.

INTERNATIONAL SOCIAL SCIENCE COUNCIL 1962 *Social Implications of Technological Change.* Paris: The Council.

MARX, KARL (1867–1879) 1925–1926 *Capital: A Critique of Political Economy.* 3 vols. Chicago: Kerr.

MOORE, WILBERT E. 1951 *Industrialization and Labor: Social Aspects of Economic Development.* Ithaca, N.Y.: Cornell Univ. Press.

MOORE, WILBERT E. 1963 *Social Change.* Englewood Cliffs, N.J.: Prentice-Hall. → See especially pages 89–112 on "Modernization."

MOORE, WILBERT E. 1965 *The Impact of Industry.* Englewood Cliffs, N.J.: Prentice-Hall.

MOORE, WILBERT E.; and FELDMAN, ARNOLD S. (editors) 1960 *Labor Commitment and Social Change in Developing Areas.* New York: Social Science Research Council.

NORTH AMERICAN CONFERENCE ON THE SOCIAL IMPLICATIONS OF INDUSTRIALIZATION AND TECHNOLOGICAL CHANGE, CHICAGO, *1960* 1963 *Industrialization and Society: Proceedings.* Edited by Bert F. Hoselitz and Wilbert E. Moore. Paris: UNESCO.

WEBER, MAX (1904–1905) 1930 *The Protestant Ethic and the Spirit of Capitalism.* Translated by Talcott Parsons, with a foreword by R. H. Tawney. London: Allen & Unwin; New York: Scribner. → First published in German. The 1930 edition has been reprinted frequently.

WEBER, MAX (1922) 1957 *The Theory of Social and Economic Organization.* Edited by Talcott Parsons. Glencoe, Ill.: Free Press. → First published as Part 1 of *Wirtschaft und Gesellschaft.*

INDUSTRIES, REGULATED

See REGULATION OF INDUSTRY.

INDUSTRY

See MARKETS AND INDUSTRIES.

INDUSTRY, SMALL

"Small industry" means manufacturing carried on in relatively small establishments. Several quite different forms of organization come within this definition (see Table 1), and few generalizations

Table 1 — Forms of manufacturing organization

Family-use system	*Artisan system*	*Putting-out or dispersed factory system*	*Factory system*
1. Manufacture for own use	2. Artisan homework	4. Industrial homework (wage-paid)	6. Small factory
	3. Artisan workshop	5. Dependent or quasi-independent small shops	7. Medium factory
			8. Large factory

Small industry: 1, 2, 3, 4, 5, 6
Small factory: 6
Nonfactory industry: 1, 2, 3, 4, 5
Artisan industry: 2, 3, overlapping with 4, 5
Household industry: 1, 2, 4, sometimes 5

are valid for all. In traditional economies that have not experienced the industrial revolution, small industry (indeed, all manufacturing) is predominantly of the nonfactory type. In modern industrialized economies, the predominant form of small industry is the small factory. In transitional economies—that is, economies in the process of development from traditional to modern—all forms of small industry usually exist, some on the way down, some, particularly the small but modern factory, on the way up.

Functional and statistical classification. Nonfactory forms of manufacture are nearly always carried on in quite small establishments; therefore, the problem of defining an upper boundary to small industry hardly arises for them. But it does arise when we talk about the small factory. Beyond what point is a factory no longer small? Any such specification must be more or less arbitrary. It is like defining hot water. Just as the concept of hot water depends on whether one is thinking of shaving or of running a steam turbine, so the boundary of small industry can reasonably be set differently for different purposes and for countries at different stages of development. The main reason for distinguishing small industry from large is that the two have characteristics and problems sufficiently diverse that different developmental approaches and methods are necessary. Therefore, before suggesting any quantitative line of demarcation, let us first note some of these *functional* differences.

The following are characteristics of small industry that justify separate analysis of its role in development and require special developmental techniques.

(1) Relatively little specialization in management. With some overstatement, we may say that small industry is characterized by "one-man management." The small firm cannot afford, as can large firms, vice presidents or staff specialists for production, sales, finance, or research. Therefore, the needs of small industry for advice, aid, and management training are rather different from the needs of large industry.

(2) Close personal contacts. The manager is personally in touch with production workers, customers, suppliers, and owners (ownership is often identical with management). If the manager is a good one, this characteristic of small industry gives a quality of human concern and a flexibility in daily operations—for example, in meeting a customer's special requirements—that may in properly chosen lines mean a competitive advantage over large industry.

(3) Handicaps in obtaining capital and credit. The small industrial firm cannot raise capital in the organized securities market, and—owing to greater unit costs of small transactions, greater risks, the habits and social connections of people with wealth, and other factors—it often finds difficulty in getting loans and credits from banks or other financing institutions. This characteristic, of course, also suggests needs for special types of developmental aids.

(4) Sheer numbers of small industry units. It is often impractical, or at any rate uneconomic, to apply to thousands of small units the same developmental techniques (e.g., individual feasibility studies) that can be applied to tens of large units. Group techniques must be devised for small industry development that are analogous to the extension methods used in agriculture to reach small farmers.

It is known that no statistical classification can coincide perfectly with these important functional distinctions and that different classifications (both administrative and statistical) are appropriate in differing environments; nevertheless, it is desirable to achieve a greater degree of consistency in use of terms than exists today, at least for international comparisons. For example, a United Nations report (*The Development of Manufacturing Industry in Egypt, Israel, and Turkey* 1958) referred to manufacturing establishments employing 10 or more persons as "medium-scale and large-scale," whereas, at the other extreme, small business in the United States is officially defined to include manufacturing establishments with 250, 500, or even as many as 1,000 employees, depending on the industry. Another difficulty is that no single measure of the size of an industrial establishment is satisfactory by itself. Possible measures include the number of persons employed, capital investment, various measures of output, amount of energy used, and relative position in the industry. All are relevant in any complete characterization. The number of persons employed is, however, the most widely available, the most convenient, and the most readily comparable internationally, because it is unaffected by vagaries of prices and exchange rates. On the whole, it is probably the least objectionable for general purposes.

It is suggested, therefore, that the term "small industry" normally be understood to mean, especially in international comparisons, manufacturing establishments employing up to 100 persons. Nearly all industrial censuses break at 100; otherwise a somewhat lower figure, say 75, might be better. But somewhere in this size range, according to observations in many countries, specialization within management and the other functional differences that distinguish large from small industry usually become fairly significant, although it must be emphasized that this varies with the industry and with factors in the economic environment.

It is also desirable to differentiate in industrial censuses between factory and nonfactory producers. This is done now in some countries, especially the industrially advanced ones. But in the newly industrializing countries it is often not possible to obtain separate data on artisan and household units for special study of their developmental trends. Nor is it possible to study small factories without finding the data confused by the inclusion of an unknown number of nonfactory units.

Developmental prospects. As a country moves through the transitional stage from a predominantly traditional to a more and more modernized economy, the character of its small industry changes. Somewhat oversimplified, the outlook is for traditional artisan industry to be *transformed*, for household cottage industry to be largely *replaced*, and for small but modern factories to be *developed*.

In newly industrializing countries, the competition of factory-made goods, both imported and locally produced, makes obsolete large segments of traditional artisan activity, often with devastating effect on such old-line craftsmen as weavers, potters, blacksmiths, and shoemakers. At the same time, many new, distinctly modern artisan activities arise. These are not so much in manufacturing as in services: automobile repairing, radio and television servicing, installation and repair of electrical appliances and plumbing fixtures, and photographic work. Some old-line crafts continue and even expand in modernized form. Rural blacksmiths, for instance, instead of making farm tools by hand become repairmen and dealers in agricultural implements and machinery, while carpenters turn to new products and methods. The rise of new crafts and the modernization of old ones have belied predictions that were common in the late nineteenth century in the then industrializing countries of Europe that factory competition would lead to the disappearance of the artisan. The highly industrialized, modern economies of today seem, on the contrary, to be using increasing numbers of new types of artisans whose functions have undergone a transformation from the making of manufactured goods to their installation, servicing, and repair. The modern artisan, instead of competing with the factory, supplements it.

Household industry, on the other hand, seems destined to be gradually replaced as countries modernize. Household industry is almost always technologically unprogressive and subject to grave social abuses. However, in the poorer and more densely populated countries the process of replacement may be a very long and gradual one. In certain special situations, there is a good economic and social case for preserving and even promoting household industry—for example, as a part-time supplement to the incomes of farmers and mountain dwellers—but experience suggests that this had better be done under careful regulation and preferably with the help of an organization that will function as a benevolent intermediary between the homeworkers and the pressures of the market.

The role of the small modern factory. The small but modern factory is the segment of small industry with greatest developmental potential in newly industrializing countries. It has too often been overlooked and neglected by development planners and the makers of industrialization programs.

Historically, small factories preceded large ones. But today, in countries that are importing the industrial revolution, the sequence is often reversed. Nowadays newly industrializing countries do not have to evolve their factories gradually, inventing each new device as they go along. Instead, they take over many industrial ideas and techniques from more developed countries. While traditional industry continues in most of the economy, modern industry is built up in port cities or other key centers. This modern industry is likely to appear in large units—oil refineries, textile mills, sugar mills, cement plants. Later come other fairly large-scale units that produce or assemble products for which the market has been prepared by the import trade.

Thus, modern large factories develop ahead of modern small factories. For some time the middle range of small but modern-type manufacturing is likely to be less well represented in a newly industrializing country than in the highly industrialized countries. There tends to be a hollow area in the industrial size structure, an "excluded middle," until local enterprise turns to modern-type manufacturing and fills in the relatively neglected sector of the small but modern factory. Until this happens, the efficiency of the whole industrial complex suffers.

At the middle stages of industrial development, if local entrepreneurs become proficient in modern factory-type industry, the role of the small factory is likely to increase rapidly. In many countries at this middle stage, small factories can be expected to gain a larger relative role than in the highly industrialized countries. This follows from the smaller total demands associated with lower income levels, from markets segmented more by inadequate transport and communications, from less experience and expertise in the kinds of organization and management required to make large enterprises efficient, and from other factors. Thus, the relative role of small factories in newly industrializing countries may now start very low, subsequently rise quite high, then gradually decline and level off as the country moves toward industrial maturity.

Even at a high level of industrial maturity, small factories will by no means disappear. This is the experience of the most industrialized countries. The available statistical evidence appears to refute the belief that, in a given country, the relative role of small manufacturing establishments must continue to fall indefinitely. In fact, the relative share of small factories in manufacturing employment has shown a surprising stability in industrialized countries since World War I. In the United States, 91 per cent of all manufacturing establishments as of 1958 had fewer than 100 employees. These establishments employed 27 per cent of all manufacturing employees and produced 23 per cent of the total value added by manufacture. The relative importance of small manufacturers in other industrialized countries is as great or greater (Staley & Morse 1965, chapter 1).

Competitive ability. In view of the well-known economies of scale, why is it that small factories manage to compete as well as they do? Some of the reasons follow.

(1) Economies of scale are less important in some lines of production than in others. In the case of blast furnaces and cement kilns there are great engineering advantages and cost advantages from the use of big pieces of equipment to handle large amounts of materials; these are not undertakings suitable for small units. But in the manufacture of garments or certain kinds of machine tools the advantages of scale are much less significant, and a moderate-sized plant may be just as efficient as, or even more efficient than, a large one.

(2) Small units have an advantage where shipping costs are high or the product is perishable. Thus, bricks and tiles and freshly baked goods can be produced more economically by relatively small, local establishments than by great central factories.

(3) Small manufacturing establishments have an advantage in meeting highly specialized or individualized demands or in catering to a small-volume market or one requiring frequent quick readjustments because of style changes or for other reasons. They compete very well in certain kinds of precision instruments, some types of specialized machinery, some types of surgical equipment, women's wear, and so on. Here the flexibility of the small firm stands it in good stead. Large enterprises are handicapped by their bureaucratic procedures and their relatively large overhead expenses. It does not pay for them to produce short "runs" of a nonstandard item, but the small factory can often do so at a profit. It can "fill the cracks" between the large-volume, standardized outputs of large factories. For example, a successful small cycle manufacturer near Madras, India, produces junior-sized bicycles, also tricycles and tricycle-mounted delivery carts, thus supplementing rather than competing with a major bicycle factory in his immediate vicinity.

(4) Where labor and social laws are applied more stringently to large than to small plants, as is often the case in newly industrializing countries, this may be a factor (whether or not a desirable one) in the competitive ability of small plants.

(5) The small factory can produce components and supplies for large factories. Much of Japanese small industry works on contract for large industry. One of the reasons for the efficiency of industry in the United States and Europe is that large plants characteristically buy many specialized parts from hundreds or even thousands of other plants, both large and small. A small enterprise supplying a specialized item to several large firms may have greater economies of scale on that item than any of the large firms could obtain. Also, small industry often performs job shop operations for large industry.

(6) The small factory often serves to initiate new products and sometimes grows large with growth of the market for the product. Henry Ford and other pioneer automobile manufacturers started on a very small scale. The electronics in-

dustry today is bursting with small firms, as well as large ones, hopefully exploiting new ideas. In countries where industrial diversification is at an early stage, small-scale manufacturers often discover opportunities to introduce products that are new to the country though not necessary new in the world.

Small factories in development strategy. There are several kinds of benefits that a newly industrializing country may gain by intelligent promotion of its small factory sector. Progressive small firms serve as a nursery for entrepreneurial talent, and they grow in some cases into large industry. Small manufacturers are usually local entrepreneurs; thus, healthy growth of their firms helps to balance the importation of foreign capital and to prevent domination by foreign-owned enterprises. Small factories can be important in local and regional development and in promoting a more decentralized pattern of industrial growth. Vigorous small industry helps to create a tradition of independent initiative by alert individuals and a strong middle class, which in turn is an important underpinning of political democracy.

Also, vigorous small factories help to check monopoly, improving prices and services to consumers. Alert small entrepreneurs in intimate contact with market needs and possessing practical technical competence may be important sources of product innovation and adaptation. Also, they tap sources of capital (especially from family savings and, if the enterprise is successful, from plowed-back profits) that would not otherwise contribute to capital formation. The limited size of the home market in many newly industrializing countries makes production unfeasible on the scale that is usual in the major industrialized countries; smaller plants may be able to produce the smaller quantities required at reasonable cost if provided with appropriate kinds of information, encouragement, and services.

Implications for development policy. For those concerned with development programs in newly industrializing countries, the following policy implications of the preceding analysis may be stressed:

First, development planners will do well to give attention to the constructive possibilities in modernization and growth of the small industry sector.

Second, in the development of a modern small industry sector there will be, over the long run, a declining place for household industry. Traditional artisan industry will give way to modern service trades, which supplement rather than compete directly with factories. The small factory will rise in importance, taking its place as a complement of the large factory in a diversified industrial structure.

Third, in encouraging development of small factories, careful selection of suitable product lines is essential. The suitability of a given product for small-scale manufacture varies from country to country, from one part to another of the same country, and from time to time as a country develops. Because so many technical and economic factors are involved, provision for continuing analysis of specific situations is advisable in development programs for small industry.

Specific methods that have been found useful in newly industrializing countries for practical development of modern small industry include industrial advisory or counseling services, industrial training services, industrial research services, measures to improve small industry financing, industrial estates or industrial parks, marketing aids, aids in the procurement of materials and equipment, and the fostering of interfirm assistance and self-help by industrial associations.

EUGENE STALEY

BIBLIOGRAPHY

INTERNATIONAL LABOR OFFICE 1961 *Services for Small-scale Industry.* Studies and Reports, New Series, No. 61. Geneva: The Office.

NANJUNDAN, S.; ROBISON, H. E.; and STALEY, EUGENE 1962 *Economic Research for Small Industry Development, Illustrated by India's Experience.* Bombay: Asia Publishing House.

STALEY, EUGENE; and MORSE, RICHARD M. 1965 *Modern Small Industry for Newly Developing Countries.* New York: McGraw-Hill.

STANFORD RESEARCH INSTITUTE, INTERNATIONAL DEVELOPMENT CENTER 1960*a* *Small Industry: An International Annotated Bibliography.* Compiled by Marian C. Alexander-Frutschi. Glencoe, Ill.: Free Press.

STANFORD RESEARCH INSTITUTE, INTERNATIONAL DEVELOPMENT CENTER 1960*b* *Small Industry Advisory Services: An International Study,* by Joseph E. Stepanek. Glencoe, Ill.: Free Press.

UNITED NATIONS, DEPARTMENT OF ECONOMIC AND SOCIAL AFFAIRS 1958 *The Development of Manufacturing Industry in Egypt, Israel, and Turkey.* New York: United Nations.

INFANCY

I
INFANT DEVELOPMENT

Infancy is the period of time that begins with the organism's emergence into the world as a separate being and ends with the organism's achieving a measure of independence. Because the organism is immature and environmental stimulation is new, infancy is the simplest and clearest arena in which the controversy of nature and nurture has been waged. This controversy is one main issue in the study of the origins of behavior. Another main issue is the effect of early experience upon later behavior. A study of the origins of behavior, however, can transcend these issues: the processes by which an infant organism comes to learn the nature of the world into which it is born and to adapt its behavior to the physical and social properties of that world merit scrutiny in their own right. That the infant changes so rapidly in structure and function, in physical growth and behavioral achievement, does not render the study impossible. Rather, these characteristics of the immature organism contribute to the challenge: to discover even in infancy the principles governing behavior.

The facts and theories concerning the origins of behavior in infancy can be organized in many ways. Change with age constitutes one way. The development of different classes of behavior—sensory, motor, social, and language—constitutes another. A historical account of methods employed in the study of infancy, from the anecdotal to the experimental, constitutes a third. These are traditional ways and may be found in textbooks of child and developmental psychology. The contributions of different theoretical schools—for example, psychoanalytic theory, behavior and learning theory, and the theories of Piaget—to developmental psychology would also provide an interesting system of organization.

The present account uses still a different system of organization. Here, the facts and theories concerning the origins of behavior in infancy will be organized under four main principles: (1) the infant is responsive to stimulation; (2) the infant is an active organism; (3) the infant's behavior is modifiable; and (4) the infant modifies the environment, particularly the social environment.

This organization possesses the advantage of carrying the account to the advancing margin of developmental psychology and of starting with the intact organism, whole, living, and already behaving. It also bypasses old controversies. Furthermore, since the principles apply to the behavior of older as well as younger organisms, they will serve to establish continuity between the infant, child, and adult. And, since they apply to the behavior of all living organisms, they will serve to establish continuity between man and animal.

The principles challenge the notion, still extant, that the infant is insensitive to environmental stimulation, that his behavior is random and uncoordinated, that he is passive rather than active, that sleep and ingestion are his most important activities, that his behavior patterns are innate and fixed, and that he has no power to affect his environment. Yet, it would be inaccurate to assert, as do some in protest to the older notions, that the infant is competent. Although he is responsive, active, and profits by experience, although he becomes increasingly competent in handling his environment, he is nevertheless still deficient in skills, limited in experience, and wanting in language.

The period of time covering infancy requires a word of definition. Birth marks its beginning, to be sure, but what of its end? The end differs with the species; in general, the more intelligent the species, the longer its period of infancy. Still, the end of infancy is a matter of opinion. To set the end for the human infant by the calendar does not allow for varying rates of development. To set the end by developmental stage is more reasonable, but there is no agreement on the criteria. Here, for the human infant the criterion of speech is proposed, that is, speech adequate to obtain simple wants. It is an arbitrary criterion, to be sure, but it does correspond to the beginning of what Pavlov termed the "second signal system." For the infant "reality is signalized almost exclusively by stimulations . . . which come directly to the special cells of the visual, auditory, or other receptors of the organism" ([1934] 1955, p. 262). The infant is a nonverbal organism; he vocalizes, but he does not speak; he communicates but not with words.

Behavior, then, is the topic of this account of infancy. The physiological and neurological substrates of behavior are largely ignored, although their relevance is plain. The behavior of the *human* infant, furthermore, is the topic of discussion. Behavior in infancy regardless of species is another topic; a comparative psychology of infancy lies beyond the scope of this article. And, even then, behavior in the first few months of life will receive more attention than that in later months.

The infant is responsive

The first principle is that the human infant is responsive to a wide range of external stimulation. At birth, or shortly after, every sense of the neonate is functioning, although it must be conceded that the neonate's sensitivity is not commensurate with that of later life (Peiper [1949] 1963, p. 92). Furthermore, from birth the infant possesses almost all the sensory systems of the adult human. In this respect he differs from such mammals as, for example, the rat, dog, and cat, whose young are born blind and deaf. As a consequence, the human infant from the beginning lives in a broad environment.

The nature of the environmental stimuli to which an organism responds tells us not only which sensory systems are functioning but also which experiences can affect its behavior. Stimuli are called upon to serve several functions in any theory of behavior: they elicit behavior, they reinforce behavior, and they serve as discriminative stimuli for behavior (i.e., they signal whether the behavior will be reinforced). Thus, if we wish to study the effects of early experience on later behavior, we must know the stimuli to which the infant organism is responsive.

Although motor responses, such as eye movements or changes in bodily activity, have been most frequently used as indicator responses, physiological responses, such as changes in respiration and heartbeat, and neurological responses, such as the electroretinogram and the electroencephalogram, have also been employed. Conditioned-response studies of the classical type can also supply information on the infant's sensitivity to particular stimuli and his ability to discriminate between two similar stimuli. Instrumental, in distinction to classical, conditioning could supply similar information by the manipulation of reinforcing and discriminative stimuli, although it has not yet been so employed. The methods of demonstrating sensitivity, therefore, are varied, but the indicator response is always a change in behavior or function in relation to a stimulus.

In the following partial account of the infant's sensitivities, attention will be paid to method as well as to results. Munn (1955), Peiper (1949), and Riesen (1960) offer more complete accounts and also wrestle with the difficulties encountered in measuring the sensitivities of so response-limited an organism as the human infant.

The skin senses. Although there is no clear evidence of pain sensitivity at birth, most infants react to cutaneous irritation by the end of the first week of life. Sensitivity to pain increases rapidly, however, and by the end of the first year the infant localizes the site of stimulation and deliberately withdraws a stimulated extremity. The face is the most sensitive area. Pinpricks are the common experimental stimuli, and the measures are crying, changes in general activity, widening of the eyes, and turning of the face, limb, or body away from the stimulus, often accompanied by a visual search for the spot being irritated.

The infant is also responsive to tactile stimulation, especially about the mouth and face. He turns his head toward a touch near his mouth; this has been called the rooting or search reflex and is especially prominent when he is hungry. The infant is also responsive to the stimulation provided by a nipple within his mouth; to such stimulation he responds by sucking.

The infant is sensitive to heat and cold, to the lowering or elevating of ambient temperature, and to warm and cold stimuli in the mouth, on the skin, or close to the skin. Locally circumscribed temperature stimulation evokes turning of the stimulated body part toward or away from the stimulus, as well as such general responses as restlessness, grimacing, and crying [*see* SKIN SENSES AND KINESTHESIS].

Taste sensitivity. The newborn can clearly distinguish sweet from salty, bitter, and sour substances, but, according to Peiper (1949), there is no evidence that he can differentiate between salty, bitter, and sour substances. Measures used by different investigators are sucking and changes in fontanel pulse, respiration, body movement, and facial expression. Reported results in this area, as well as in many others, are often sketchy and sometimes contradictory. Several factors contribute to such a state of affairs: the condition of the infant at the time of testing; whether it is awake or asleep, quiet or disturbed; the number of trials; the order of stimuli and interactions based on the order; the variability of the response; and the extended latency period characteristic of the immature organism. On the basis of clinical observation, Peiper feels that the taste sense of the infant is far more delicate than the experimental evidence indicates.

Olfactory sensitivity. The determination of the infant's sensitivity to smell has presented the methodological problem of ensuring that only olfactory receptors and not those of taste and pain are being stimulated. The indicator responses often include facial and bodily signs of aversion or pleasure. Studies carried out in the early 1960s (e.g., Engen et al. 1963) employing changes in leg motion, general bodily activity, respiration, and heart rate showed that newborn infants responded to the smell of acetic acid, asafetida, phenylethyl alcohol, and anise oil and that thresholds of sensitivity appeared to decrease during the first four days of life. These, along with older studies (see Munn 1955), demonstrate the infant's sensitivity to olfactory stimuli [*see* TASTE AND SMELL].

Vision. The eyes of the infant are relatively large for his size, compared with the eye of the adult, and are anatomically functional at birth. From the beginning, the pupils react to light. The infant's eyes also fixate on light and track it briefly, although not always with conjugate movements.

He responds to bright light with the eye–neck reflex (throwing the head back), with a decrease in bodily activity, and with changes in respiration, showing thereby that he discriminates different intensities of illumination.

Movement. Visual pursuit of moving objects is not fully developed at birth, but by 10 to 15 days of age infants do follow moving objects briefly after some lag (Kistiakovskaia 1959). At 3 to 4 weeks of age, pursuit is smooth, and the head, as well as the eyes, turn. At this age, infants will look from one object in the environment to another, and at 2 to 3 months of age they will follow the transit of a dangling ring moved in arcs from right to left and from head to foot.

Patterns, objects, depth. From the first month of life the infant can see equally well at distances of 5, 10, and 20 inches; he can also see black and white stripes as narrow as 1/8 inch at a 10 inch distance, acuity corresponding to a visual angle of a little less than one degree. The infant, from the first days of life, also discriminates patterns, looking longer at simple black and white drawings than at plain colored surfaces. In the first few months of life, furthermore, the infant looks longer at complex patterns than at simple ones and longer at a solid sphere than a flat circle (Fantz 1961). These data were obtained by the *stimulus preference* method: a longer duration of regard for one of two simultaneously presented visual patterns was assumed to indicate a preference and hence the ability to discriminate. A variation of the method, contrasting regard of familiar and novel stimuli, yielded similar results for patterns (Saayman et al. 1964) and for objects of different shapes (Venger 1962). The *discrimination* method in which the subject is rewarded for selecting one of two (or more) stimuli would probably constitute a more convincing test of the ability to differentiate; it is, however, a more difficult and time-consuming method, requiring training over many trials. Ling (1941) employed this method in training infants six months of age to discriminate a circle from other forms by making the circle sweet to the taste and movable. Thus, all the evidence suggests that from a very early age the infant prefers patterned to nonpatterned visual stimuli and that shortly thereafter he discriminates the form and shape of objects.

By the time the infant can locomote on his own, he perceives a drop-off (the visual cliff) and tends to avoid it (Walk & Gibson 1961); his tendency to avoid the drop-off increases as the depth increases, further evidence that the infant is sensitive to visual differences in surface texture.

Color. There is considerable evidence to suggest that infants also perceive color. At three and four months of age they look longer at colored than at gray stimuli (Spears 1964). Older children reach more often for colored than gray objects and select red and yellow more often than green and blue. Munn (1955) discusses the methodological problems in equating the brightness of different hues for the infant eye; this reservation aside, it seems likely that the infant perceives color [*see* PERCEPTION, *articles on* PERCEPTUAL DEVELOPMENT *and* DEPTH PERCEPTION; VISION].

Hearing. There is no doubt that the infant is sensitive to sound. From birth he responds to sound, especially to loud noises, by blinking and starting, by changes in respiration and general bodily activity, or, occasionally, by turning head and eyes to the source of sound. He responds to sounds of lower intensity, too; an absolute threshold between 38 and 48 decibels of a tone of 1,000 cycles per second has been found by measuring cardiac acceleration (Bartoshuk 1964). During the first month of life, according to normative studies (Bayley 1933), the infant responds to the click of a telegraph snapper by blinking, frowning, starting, increasing or decreasing activity, or crying; during the second month he responds to the speaking voice by head turning, vocalizing, or a ceasing of activity; and in the fourth month he will turn his head toward a sound made at his right or left side [*see* HEARING].

Summary. This account of the infant's sensitivities to stimulation summarizes what is presently known as the result of controlled investigations. It is obvious that it would be unwise to declare that the neonate lacks this or that sensitivity, for the statement is always dependent upon the method. Careful probing with improved techniques almost always yields evidence of keener sensitivity than had been suspected.

In general, sensitivity to certain stimuli means not only that these stimuli can elicit behavior but also that they can reinforce behavior and serve as discriminative cues. It is these additional functions of stimuli which are important for the third principle, that the infant's behavior is modifiable; the evidence suggests that stimuli in all the sense modalities can affect the infant's behavior.

The infant is an active organism

The chief characteristic of a young organism, in distinction to an older one, is its almost constant physical activity when awake, often in the absence of observable stimulation. This characteristic makes its appearance very early in the life of the human infant. His awake periods lengthen rapidly, and during them he may be observed to look, to move his body, to touch, reach, and grasp; even the newborn turns his head and eyes, raises and lowers his arms, opens and closes his hands, flexes and stretches his legs, makes sucking movements, vocalizes, and cries—and this is only a partial inventory of his activities. More important still, this activity leads him into contact with his environment and thereby increases the amount of stimulation to which he is exposed [*see* STIMULATION DRIVES].

Of his many activities, attention will be paid here to only a few: visual exploration, postural and locomotor behavior, manipulating and reaching toward objects, vocalizing and smiling, and distress responses. For each it will be shown how contact with the environment is effected and how his own stimulation is thereby increased. The possibility of modification of behavior by feedback from the contact, the third principle in this account, will be anticipated.

Visual exploration. By the end of the first month, the infant looks at the world around him and is quiet as he looks. He looks at near and far objects, at the play of light, at bright and shiny things, at everything that moves within his scope. Patterned objects hold his gaze. Chief among these are people; they offer not only patterned visual stimuli that move, but also complex auditory and tactile stimuli. The infant moves his eyes and his head as he visually explores one part of his environment after another. Now he looks intently at one constellation of stimuli, moves on to another, and returns to the first. As he grows older, he may become quiet for a moment as he looks, only in the next moment to become physically active, to kick and vocalize; what he sees apparently excites him. During his waking hours he is constantly observing, attending, investigating. Before the infant can move himself to any object, before he can reach out to anything, his eyes have made contact with it, he has explored it visually, and he has come to know its dimensions. Because he is so physically limited, vision plays an important role in his life.

Posture and locomotion. The general physical activity of the infant soon takes specific form. He raises his head, arches his back, rolls over, pivots, sits up, crawls, creeps, and then walks, a progression of achievements easily listed but arduously won. To be sure, he learns by trial and error, with no tuition, obeying no command, and unaware of the goal striven for. What is important here, however, is not so much the achievement as the persistence and energy with which the achievement is attained. Failures do not deter him, neither do hurts and bruises. The result of this tireless and sustained activity is physical contact with the world seen and, not least, a measure of independence from his caretakers.

Manipulation and reaching. In the meantime, his hands have not been idle. At first they closed on what they chanced to touch: breast, bottle, clothes, the bars of his crib, his own hands, or a toy. Now he holds, releases, scratches, fingers, but still does not look at what his hands manipulate. At 3 months of age his hands begin to make waving movements on the appearance of an interesting object; at 4 months the hands definitely approach the object (Gesell & Thompson 1934). During these months the infant is also clasping his own hands and observing them with interest. Before long the infant brings objects to his mouth, transfers them from hand to hand, waves and shakes them, hits and bangs them. In reaching toward an object, his glance shifts from his own hand to the object (Piaget 1936). At 4½ to 5 months of age, the hand opens in anticipation of contact, and grasping has been achieved (White et al. 1964). Finally, the infant brings two objects together, drops a pellet into a bottle, hits a spoon against a cup, places one block on top of another. Except for his first holdings and fingerings, he looks at what he touches, the eye guiding the hand.

Each object grasped supplies information about its physical nature; at the same time, each supplies additional stimulation. By the coordinated use of eye and hand he builds up his acquaintance with the world. As with visual exploration and locomotion, his grasping and manipulating of objects occur without tuition or encouragement. The object is the stimulus, but only in part; the repeated striving for it and the endless manipulations and inventive combinations stem from him alone.

Vocalizations. The infant, when in a state of comfort, vocalizes from the first day of life. At first he utters soft, low sounds, but day by day they become louder, more vigorous, and more frequent. He coos, sustaining the vowel sounds, and now and then introduces a consonant. Separate syllables are heard, and several are strung together. The syllables become linked into two-part chains, the second repeating the first; by six months of age he is saying the sounds, but not yet the words, "mama" and "dada." By now he has already made all the sounds he will need for later speech. Before a year of age he has at least three words in his vocabulary, including "mama" and "dada." At the same time he "speaks" his other sounds with the inflection of the language he hears (see McCarthy 1954 for a review of the development of language).

The stimuli for his vocalizing are not always patent. He vocalizes in response to the sight of people and things and to their sounds. As early as three months of age, he not only initiates a "conversation" but engages in one. Often, though, he appears to vocalize to himself alone, to make sounds for their own sake. He plays with sound, experimenting with new combinations, now in low, now in loud tones. The infant appears in fact to enjoy vocalizing; thus, these sounds have often been called pleasure sounds to differentiate them from distress sounds.

The investigator of the infant's behavior would like to discover the dimensions of auditory and visual stimuli which evoke his vocalizations (although it seems likely that they will not account for all his vocalizations) and to discover the role of the response which people make to his vocalizing (although he often vocalizes in the absence of such a response). These interesting topics notwithstanding, the vocalizing of the infant by itself is a convincing illustration of his active nature. He experiments with sound; he practices like a virtuoso; he explores the effect of his vocalizations upon himself and others. By any count, vocal behavior is prominent.

Smiling. The infant's smiles, like his vocalizations, are attractive to the beholder and are usually greeted with a smile in return. The first smile, especially, is eagerly awaited and signals for the parent the beginning of the infant's human quality: social responsiveness is now mutual. The infant smiles often, first coaxed by a varied display of stimuli from the adult, including talking, looking, smiling, and light stroking of the chin or cheek; later, at three months of age, he smiles at just the appearance of the adult. In fact, the adult need now only present himself, with sober face and without speech, to evoke in the infant the full smiling response, a sequence of behaviors composed of, in order, intent regard (associated with decreased activity), brightening of the face, smiling, bursts of activity, and vocalizing. Smiles are almost always accompanied by vocalizations; vocalizations, in contrast, may occur in the absence of smiles.

Although the sight of another human being is the stimulus for the infant's smile, so also is the sight of some inanimate objects and even geometric patterns (Preyer 1881; Piaget 1936). When the responses to people and rattles were contrasted, it was found that the infants smiled and vocalized to both people and rattles, but more often to people (Rheingold 1961).

Crying. The infant produces yet another class of vocalizations, those made when he is in a state of discomfort. They may be called distress vocalizations and include not only crying but also the precursors of crying: protests and fusses. Crying, to take the most prominent of the distress vocalizations, has been inhibited in the newborn by playing a tape recording of a normal heartbeat (Salk 1962) and by giving the infant an empty nipple to suck (Kessen & Leutzendorff 1963). Although crying characterizes infancy, it may be so common a behavior that, these studies aside, it has generally tended to escape notice as a topic for scientific investigation. It is, furthermore, unpleasant to the hearer, and for this, or other culturally derived reasons, we hold the conviction that the infant should not cry. Whatever the reasons, we tend to overlook the significance of crying as a means of vocal communication between infant and caretaker. Crying, however, does effect contact with the social environment: it brings to the infant's side people who not only minister to his primary biologic needs but also supply stimulation. Often the infant's cries are terminated by just the appearance or voice of a person or by being picked up. Only imperceptiveness to the intelligence of the infant could permit us to label such behavior "being spoiled." Distress vocalizations may be viewed, then, as a mode of dealing with the environment.

Summary. The main purpose of this section has been to show by means of a few representative response classes that the infant is an active organism. He not only responds to external stimuli, but he often seems to be active in the absence of definable external stimulation. These activities carry him into contact with the environment. At the same time, they also increase the amount of stimulation to which he is exposed. By means of them, as we shall see next, he tests, weighs, assesses, examines, and discovers the nature of the world in which he lives.

The infant's behavior is modifiable

The third principle is that the infant's behavior is modifiable by experience; he is capable of learning. From the beginning, he is learning the nature of things and of people, their look and feel, the response they give to his overtures (which may be called the contingencies of his environment), and the regularity with which they respond (which may be called the schedules).

Controversy has arisen in the past over the extent to which behavior in the immature organism is fixed and stimulus-bound and the extent to which it is flexible and modifiable: maturation was set in opposition to learning, nature to nurture, heredity to environment. The lively issues of the past are well set forth by McGraw (1946). Although the issues possess theoretical importance, the processes of maturation and learning are no longer set in opposition. It is understood now that any behavior, no matter how simple or how early, is already the result of an interaction of genetic material and environmental conditions. To claim that the infant's behavior is modifiable claims nothing about the origin of the behavior, whether innate or learned, for it is always possible to begin the study of learning with any response or behavior the organism already possesses. The advantage of this premise is that it permits the formulation of questions more accessible to experiment. Thus, we now ask what behaviors can be modified by what kinds and amounts of experiences occurring at what ages in the life of the organism. In short, we seek to analyze the processes of learning.

Experimental studies of learning. Although the evidence for the modifiability of the infant's behavior is everywhere to be seen by even the casual observer, the process of learning can best be studied under controlled conditions. It is to such studies rather than to anecdote that we turn our attention. By now, many principles governing the learning of older humans and animal subjects are known. Do the same principles govern the learning of the immature organism? What qualifications need we make to extend these principles to the human infant and to the infants of other species?

The human infant is certainly not the easiest subject for experimental study. His physical characteristics change rapidly; he is alert only briefly; he has few responses suitable for objective measurement. What responses he has cannot be called forth by verbal explanation, as with older human subjects, or by deprivation, as with infrahuman subjects. For extraneous stimulation to be controlled, the infant must be brought to the laboratory for study, a procedure which not only makes demands on his mother but, because of the strangeness of the laboratory, often suppresses the behavior of interest. Conducting research in the familiar environment, the home, reduces some of these difficulties but introduces others. Each difficulty poses a problem to be solved, and, in various ways, investigators have solved some of the problems and have succeeded in demonstrating that the infant's behavior is modifiable.

Excellent reviews of laboratory studies of infant learning are presented by Munn (1954) and Lipsitt (1963). Only a few studies will be presented here. Some are so recent that they have not yet found their way into reviews. Others possess especial interest because they illustrate how early in life behavior may be modified, how various are the behaviors and the reinforcers, or how different are the experimental procedures.

Sucking. That the nature of the first feeding of an infant at the breast may affect subsequent feedings was reported by Gunther (1961). If the nipple did not stimulate the back of the infant's mouth, the infant did not suck; instead he showed an "apathy" which reappeared at subsequent feedings. Or, if at the first nursing the infant's upper lip or the mother's breast covered his nostrils, obstructing respiration, the infant cried and "fought" with his fists. On the second or third experience of the same conditions, he cried whenever he was turned toward the mother. Thus, the consequences of the infant's behavior modified his subsequent behavior, an example of instrumental conditioning (although Gunther viewed the nipple as a releasing stimulus and cast her observations into an ethological framework).

Sucking in infants three and four days of age was experimentally modified by Lipsitt and Kaye (1964). In the classical conditioning procedure of pairing an auditory stimulus with insertion of a rubber nipple into the baby's mouth, the infant came to suck to the sound alone after only 20 pairings. It should be noted that the infant sucked an empty nipple; there is no question here of milk as a reinforcer. Milk as a reinforcer, however, was used in a study (Stanley et al. 1963) of neonatal puppies that with only slight modification could be adapted to the human infant. Sucking was increased by pairing insertion of a nipple in the mouth with milk given from an eye dropper and decreased by pairing insertion of the nipple with a solution of quinine and water. Classical conditioning with elements of instrumental conditioning was therefore demonstrated. Incidentally, studies of this nature, as noted earlier, also supply information on the sensitivity of the young organism. Here, the results demonstrate not only learning but also the gustatory sensitivity of the newborn pup: it can discriminate between milk and quinine.

Head turning. Other responses besides sucking can be modified. The infant's turning of his head was brought under experimental control by Papousek (1961). As early as the second week of life, after ten trials a day during the first week of life, infants turned their heads to the left at the sound of a bell. By the beginning of the second month, the conditioned response was well established. At three months of age, the infant learned to turn his head to the right at the sound of a buzzer and to the left at the sound of a bell; response differentiation was effected. In the fourth month, infants learned to reverse the differentiation, now turning their heads to the left at the sound of the buzzer and to the right at the sound of the bell. The learning may be classified as classical conditioning, because the auditory stimulus was paired with milk; it may also be classified as instrumental conditioning, because head turning was followed by food. One sees here, in the modification of a simple and elementary response, the first steps in the development of adaptive behavior.

Orienting behaviors. Visual stimulation can also modify the infant's behavior. On an auditory signal, infants learned to turn the head and eyes toward a light appearing at the side of their cribs (Karlova 1959). Six-month-old infants not only looked but also reached for the light and smiled at it. Karlova labeled these responses "unconditioned orienting reflexes." Later on, infants learned to look for the light after only a few pairings with an auditory signal. The response was retained for several days and then was quickly extinguished when the light did not follow the auditory signal. These results are interesting on two counts: learning, even in the first year of life, can occur very quickly, and stimuli other than food can modify the infant's behavior [*see* ATTENTION].

Vocalization and smiling. Other classes of behavior besides sucking and head turning have also been experimentally modified. The number of vocalizations uttered by a three-month-old infant in the presence of the experimenter was increased when the experimenter responded to each vocalization by simultaneously smiling, saying "tsk, tsk, tsk," and touching the infant's abdomen (Rheingold et al. 1959). Similarly, the rate of smiling in infants four months of age was increased by an adult's picking the child up and talking to him following each smile (Brackbill 1958). Both are examples of instrumental conditioning.

Summary. These are illustrative studies, selected to show the varieties of responses, reinforcers, and techniques used in recent studies. It can be predicted with confidence that many other responses of the infant will also yield to experimental modification. The rich accounts given by Piaget (1936) of the moment-by-moment learning of his own children supply models for experiments of the greatest variety. Such experiments will demonstrate under controlled conditions the processes by which the infant learns the nature of the environment in which he lives and discovers the different physical properties of things and people, the ways in which they respond to his own behavior, and the regularity or variability with which they respond.

Social attachments. In the first few months of life, the human infant gives positive responses to almost all social objects. By three months of age, he gives some signs of discriminating the strange person, not by negative or withdrawing responses, but by sobering, staring, and cessation of movement. By six months of age, negative and withdrawing responses appear in some infants. From an early age, then, the infant organism can differentiate between the familiar and the novel. To acquire this differentiation he had to be exposed to some set of stimuli sufficiently long for it to become familiar. In this sense, then, experience modifies his behavior, and the ability to discriminate between the strange and the familiar offers yet another example that his behavior is modifiable.

Although, in general, any organism tends to prefer what he has become accustomed to, the process is especially clear in the case of social attachments. In fact, it is a basic requirement; attachments *are* built up by familiarity. The institutionalized infant, if cared for by many different caretakers, smiles to all. The home infant, with fewer caretakers, in time smiles more to those he knows, less or not at all to strangers, from whom, indeed, he may withdraw; he shows a narrower, discriminated attachment.

Although some degree of familiarity is a basic factor in the genesis of social attachments (Scott 1963), it alone may not be sufficient; other attributes of the social object may also be required. Opinion (Bowlby 1958) and research on human infants (Schaffer & Emerson 1964) suggest that, in addition to the satisfying of primary biologic needs, the providing of "interesting" auditory and visual stimulation may be an important factor in the formation of social attachments.

Maternal behavior. Which experiences will become familiar to the infant, what the nature of his accustomed environment will be, and who the people will be with whom he has contact depend almost entirely on the caretaker, his mother. Observations of maternal behavior in homes (Rheingold 1960) revealed striking variations even among first-born infants within a homogeneous socioeconomic group. Differences appeared in the number and kinds of toys, the extent of quiet and isolation for naps, the amount of auditory stimulation provided by radio, television, or phonograph, the number and nature of contacts with other people, the amount of time left alone, and the number and nature of excursions outside the home. These are only the simplest and most obvious measures of environmental stimulation to which an infant is exposed. More important still are the responses of the caretaker to such behaviors of the infant as his smiling, vocalizing, and crying. The environmental events supplied by the caretaker become the infant's accustomed environment; only departures from the accustomed are strange.

Maternal deprivation. Familiarity and strangeness constitute poles of but one of the important dimensions of the stimulation provided by the caretaker. Other dimensions are, at the simplest level, sheer amounts of stimulation and, at a more complex level, the kinds of stimulation. We can look to rearing practices, to maternal behavior—if maternal is taken in its generic sense and is meant to include any other member of the family or group who has commerce with the infant—for information on these dimensions. Although at the present we do not know the effects of different kinds of stimulation upon infant behavior, there is evidence on the effects of amounts of stimulation, more specifically, on the effects of less than average stimulation. The evidence comes from studies of what is called "maternal deprivation."

Placing maternal deprivation in the category of stimulation which may modify the infant's behavior serves three purposes. First, it establishes theoretical links with the work in general behavior theory on the effects of sensory deprivation; second, it structures maternal deprivation in terms which can lead to experimental operations; and third, it opposes enrichment to deprivation.

Massive deprivation as an experimental procedure is not to be entertained in human research. Certain short-term deprivations might be feasible but have not been experimentally employed. To date, knowledge about the effect of deprivation has come from descriptive studies of life situations in which infants were deprived of normal stimulation by force of circumstance. As scientific evidence, much of the inference on the damaging effects of institutionalization and other forms of maternal deprivation is open to criticism (Casler 1961; Yarrow 1961): the subjects were not assigned to treatments at random, and factors responsible for placement were unknown and unmeasured. The extent to which these factors affected the findings cannot be assessed. Furthermore, neither institutionalization nor maternal deprivation is a unitary variable, although each has so been considered. It is not now possible to ascribe the reported deleterious effects specifically to reduced stimulation, delayed relief of distress, or multiple caretakers, to mention a few likely factors.

Enriched stimulation. Informative as deprivation studies might be, a more attractive alternative and one that is possible of experimental analysis is investigating the effects of increased environmental stimulation. Such studies can best be carried out in environments which now offer less than adequate stimulation; actually they can be carried out in any environment that the experimenter can control for even short periods of time. The study of long-term effects of complex variables upon complex behavior is still the goal of many investigators and must, of course, be the ultimate objective of a science of behavior. But at present, the study of the short-term effects of unitary and, hence, simpler variables upon unitary and simpler behaviors stands a better chance of providing useful data. Parenthetically, a theoretical question remains: Can studies of increased stimulation provide the same information on the process of learning as studies of stimulus deprivation? Until more data from controlled studies are available, we cannot specify the dimensions of adequate stimulation, to say nothing of optimal stimulation.

So far we have been considering only the amount and nature of stimulation. It is possible, however, that the timing of stimulation is also important. The learning of different skills does appear to proceed more rapidly at some ages than at others. That events occurring at these periods have lasting inhibitive or facilitative effects (the "critical period" hypothesis) has not yet been demonstrated in the human infant. A lively discussion of the implications of the hypothesis for one class of infant behavior, the formation of attachments, has been presented by Caldwell (1962).

The questions asked in research on the effects of enriched stimulation will depend in part on the temper of the times and the social values of the community; the nature of adequate or optimal stimulation will depend on what the culture dictates the desirable characteristics of its members shall be. That at the present time a large proportion of the population is not receiving adequate stimulation during infancy and childhood may be surmised from the poor academic performance of many children when first exposed to formal education.

Summary. We have presented an account of the kinds of behavior which have been modified, of the environmental events which modify, and of the processes by which modification occurs. The evidence indicates that learning begins early. The environment, social no less than physical, exerts its pressures. As a consequence, the infant learns the dimensions of his universe, guides his behavior to achieve his own ends, and behaves in an adaptive—and yes, an intelligent and socialized—fashion. The laws by which his behavior is modified, it is proposed, are the same as those by which the behavior of all organisms is modified.

The infant modifies the environment

The fourth general principle is that the infant modifies the environment in which he lives, in particular, that he modifies his social environment. It is, of course, obvious that each organism has an effect upon some part of the environment. Still, one so young and helpless as the human infant might be thought incapable of affecting his environment. It is especially these characteristics, however, which confer upon him extraordinary powers. He must, of course, be cared for. But even more, so great is his attractiveness that all members of his group pay him attention. He is small, lively, and responsive; his babyish ways charm caretakers and onlookers alike. Many small and immature creatures appeal to man; the small and immature of his own species appeal even more. Man is not alone in this respect; other mammals, especially the primates (Jay 1963; DeVore 1963), also find their young attractive. Who can say that a father does not look forward each evening to the welcome he receives from his young? Thus, not only does the infant affect the behavior of others, he may well have been one of the social forces responsible for the formation of the family.

Infants modify their social environments in still another way. Just as the people around him provide the environmental events that shape his behavior—by the stimulation they provide and the rewards they distribute—so, too, the infant shapes the behavior of his caretakers. His smiles produce an even greater display in the adult of the behavior that evoked the smile in the first place. His cries command a response. It follows, then, that the infant arouses and reinforces nurturant behavior in his parents; of men and women he makes fathers and mothers. An obvious statement? Yes, but the evidence is wanting in humans; animal studies (e.g., Harlow et al. 1963; Rosenblatt & Lehrman 1963) do show the contribution of the young to the "maternal condition."

As is the case in any social interaction, so it is too in the interaction between child and parent; the response of one to the other may be inappropriate in nature or faulty in timing. Such insensitivity between partners often arises because of preconceived notions on the part of one about how the other ought to behave. Much of the literature on parent–child relationships explores the preconceptions of the parent about his role as parent. The more fixed his notions the less sensitive he may be to the behavior of the child. But it is time now to investigate also the other side, child–parent relationships. Infants, too, may be insensitive to the demands of their caretakers; at any rate, they are partners to the interaction and affect its nature.

That the infant modifies the behavior of others seems clear; the process, however, still awaits analysis.

In this account, the active and responsive nature of the human infant has been emphasized. Much that is customarily included in accounts of this topic has been omitted. There is, for example, no discussion of habit training, maternal attitudes, individual differences, or the effects of breast versus bottle feeding. These and other topics are deliberate omissions. The goal here is to formulate what is known about the behavior of the infant in such a way that it can be integrated with the larger body of knowledge about the principles governing the behavior of all organisms, both humans more mature than the infant and other species. Such a formulation should reveal more clearly the questions still awaiting answers and the research procedures most likely to supply the answers. The gain, one may anticipate, will be in the contribution of knowledge about the *origins* of behavior to the *science* of behavior.

HARRIET L. RHEINGOLD

[*Directly related is the entry* DEVELOPMENTAL PSYCHOLOGY. *Other relevant material may be found in* AFFECTION; INTELLECTUAL DEVELOPMENT; LEARNING, *article on* LEARNING IN CHILDREN; MENTAL DISORDERS, *article on* CHILDHOOD MENTAL DISORDERS; SENSORY AND MOTOR DEVELOPMENT; SOCIALIZATION.]

BIBLIOGRAPHY

BARTOSHUK, ALEXANDER K. 1964 Human Neonatal Cardiac Responses to Sound: A Power Function. *Psychonomic Science* 1:151–152.

BAYLEY, NANCY 1933 *The California First-year Mental Scale.* Berkeley: Univ. of California Press.

BOWLBY, JOHN 1958 The Nature of the Child's Tie to His Mother. *International Journal of Psycho-analysis* 39:350–373.

BRACKBILL, YVONNE 1958 Extinction of the Smiling Response in Infants as a Function of Reinforcement Schedule. *Child Development* 29:115–124.

CALDWELL, BETTYE M. 1962 The Usefulness of the Critical Period Hypothesis in the Study of Filiative Behavior. *Merrill–Palmer Quarterly of Behavior and Development* 8:229–242.

CASLER, LAWRENCE 1961 Maternal Deprivation: A Critical Review of the Literature. Society for Research in Child Development, *Monographs* 26, no. 2.

DEVORE, I. 1963 Mother–Infant Relations in Free-ranging Baboons. Pages 305–335 in Harriet L. Rheingold (editor), *Maternal Behavior in Mammals.* New York: Wiley.

ENGEN, TRYGG; LIPSITT, LEWIS P.; and KAYE, HERBERT 1963 Olfactory Responses and Adaptation in the Human Neonate. *Journal of Comparative and Physiological Psychology* 56:73–77.

FANTZ, ROBERT L. 1961 The Origin of Form Perception. *Scientific American* 204, no. 5:66–72.

GESELL, ARNOLD; and THOMPSON, HELEN 1934 *Infant Behavior: Its Genesis and Growth.* New York: McGraw-Hill.

GUNTHER, MAVIS 1961 Infant Behaviour at the Breast. Pages 37–39 in Tavistock Study Group on Mother–Infant Interaction, London, 1959, *Determinants of Infant Behaviour.* Edited by Brian M. Foss. London: Methuen.

HARLOW, H. F.; HARLOW, M. K.; and HANSEN, E. W. 1963 The Maternal Affectional System of Rhesus Monkeys. Pages 254–281 in Harriet L. Rheingold (editor), *Maternal Behavior in Mammals.* New York: Wiley.

JAY, P. 1963 Mother–Infant Relations in Langurs. Pages 282–304 in Harriet L. Rheingold (editor), *Maternal Behavior in Mammals.* New York: Wiley.

KARLOVA, A. N. 1959 Orientirovochnye refleksy u detei rannego vozrasta (Orienting Reflexes in Young Children). *Zhurnal vysshei nervnoi deiatel'nosti* 9:37–44.

KESSEN, WILLIAM; and LEUTZENDORFF, ANNE-MARIE 1963 The Effect of Nonnutritive Sucking on Movement in the Human Newborn. *Journal of Comparative and Physiological Psychology* 56:69–72.

KISTIAKOVSKAIA, M. YU. 1959 Ob ustoichivosti zritel'nykh reaktsii u detei pervykh mesiatsev zhizni (Stability of Visual Reactions in Infants During the First Months of Life). *Voprosy psikhologii* 5, no. 5:124–133.

LING, BING-CHUNG 1941 Form Discrimination as a Learning Cue in Infants. *Comparative Psychology Monographs* 17, no. 2.

LIPSITT, LEWIS P. 1963 Learning in the First Year of Life. Volume 1, pages 147–195 in Lewis P. Lipsitt and Charles C. Spiker (editors), *Advances in Child Development and Behavior.* New York: Academic Press.

LIPSITT, LEWIS P.; and KAYE, HERBERT 1964 Conditioned Sucking in the Human Newborn. *Psychonomic Science* 1:29–30.

MCCARTHY, DOROTHEA 1954 Language Development in Children. Pages 492–630 in Leonard Carmichael (editor), *Manual of Child Psychology.* 2d ed. New York: Wiley.

MCGRAW, MYRTLE B. 1946 Maturation of Behavior. Pages 332–369 in Leonard Carmichael (editor), *Manual of Child Psychology.* New York: Wiley.

MUNN, NORMAN L. 1954 Learning in Children. Pages 374–458 in Leonard Carmichael (editor), *Manual of Child Psychology.* 2d ed. New York: Wiley.

MUNN, NORMAN L. 1955 *The Evolution and Growth of Human Behavior.* Boston: Houghton Mifflin.

PAPOUSEK, H. 1961 Conditioned Head Rotation Reflexes in Infants in the First Months of Life. *Acta paediatrica* 50:565–576.

PAVLOV, IVAN P. (1934) 1955 The Conditioned Reflex. Pages 245–270 in Ivan P. Pavlov, *Selected Works.* Moscow: Foreign Languages Publishing House. → First published in Russian.

PEIPER, ALBRECHT (1949) 1963 *Cerebral Function in Infancy and Childhood.* New York: Consultants Bureau. → First published as *Die Eigenart der kindlichen Hirntätigkeit.*

PIAGET, JEAN (1936) 1952 *The Origins of Intelligence in Children.* New York: International Universities Press. → First published in French. A paperback edition was published in 1963 by Norton.

PREYER, WILLIAM (1881) 1919 *The Mind of the Child.* Volume 1: The Senses and the Will. New York: Appleton. → First published in German.

RHEINGOLD, HARRIET L. 1960 The Measurement of Maternal Care. *Child Development* 31:565–575.

RHEINGOLD, HARRIET L. 1961 The Effect of Environmental Stimulation Upon Social and Exploratory Behaviour in the Human Infant. Pages 143–171 in Tavistock Study Group on Mother–Infant Interaction, London, 1959, *Determinants of Infant Behaviour.* Edited by Brian M. Foss. London: Methuen.

RHEINGOLD, HARRIET L. (editor) 1963 *Maternal Behavior in Mammals.* New York: Wiley.

RHEINGOLD, HARRIET L.; GEWIRTZ, JACOB L.; and ROSS, HELEN W. 1959 Social Conditioning of Vocalizations in the Infant. *Journal of Comparative and Physiological Psychology* 52:68–73.

RIESEN, AUSTIN H. 1960 Receptor Functions. Pages 284–307 in Paul H. Mussen (editor), *Handbook of Research Methods in Child Development.* New York: Wiley.

ROSENBLATT, J. S.; and LEHRMAN, D. S. 1963 Maternal Behavior of the Laboratory Rat. Pages 8–57 in Harriet L. Rheingold (editor), *Maternal Behavior in Mammals.* New York: Wiley.

SAAYMAN, G.; AMES, E. W.; and MOFFETT, A. 1964 Response to Novelty as an Indicator of Visual Discrimination in the Human Infant. *Journal of Experimental Child Psychology* 1:189–198.

SALK, LEE 1962 Mothers' Heartbeat as an Imprinting Stimulus. New York Academy of Sciences, *Transactions* 24:753–763.

SCHAFFER, H. RUDOLPH; and EMERSON, PEGGY E. 1964 The Development of Social Attachments in Infancy. Society for Research in Child Development, *Monographs* 29, no. 3.

SCOTT, J. P. 1963 The Process of Primary Socialization in Canine and Human Infants. Society for Research in Child Development, *Monographs* 28, no. 1.

SPEARS, WILLIAM C. 1964 Assessment of Visual Preference and Discrimination in the Four-month-old Infant. *Journal of Comparative and Physiological Psychology* 57:381–386.

STANLEY, WALTER C. et al. 1963 Conditioning in the Neonatal Puppy. *Journal of Comparative and Physiological Psychology* 56:211–214.

VENGER, L. A. 1962 Razlichenie formy predmetov det'mi rannego vozrasta (Discrimination of Form of Objects by Children of Early Age). Akademiia Pedagogicheskikh Nauk RSFSR, *Doklady* 2:75–80.

WALK, RICHARD D.; and GIBSON, ELEANOR J. 1961 A Comparative and Analytical Study of Visual Depth Perception. *Psychological Monographs* 75, no. 15:1–44.

WHITE, BURTON L.; CASTLE, PETER; and HELD, RICHARD 1964 Observations on the Development of Visually-directed Reaching. *Child Development* 35:349–364.

YARROW, LEON J. 1961 Maternal Deprivation: Toward an Empirical and Conceptual Reevaluation. *Psychological Bulletin* 58:459–490.

II
THE EFFECTS OF EARLY EXPERIENCE

The damaging effects of early institutional care on the human infant, particularly in the first six months of life, have been well established (Bowlby 1951). The viability of institutionalized infants is reduced: they are less resistant to disease, and their physical development is hampered. In later life their capacity for affective relationships and their capacity for abstract thinking appear to have been damaged by this experience of early institutionalization.

Maternal deprivation. Perhaps the most striking of the studies dealing with institutionalization was carried out by Spitz (1946). He compared two institutions, a prison nursery and a foundling home, equated for level of medical care. In the former, delinquent mothers cared for their own babies. In the latter, there was one nurse available for every seven infants after they had been weaned. The mortality rate in the prison nursery, over a three-and-a-half-year period, with 122 cases each year, was zero. The mortality rate in the foundling home during a two-year period was 37 per cent.

The immediate social consequence of these observations was early placement of institutionalized infants in foster homes, to minimize the amount of institutional experience. The question remains, however, what neural and physiological mechanisms could have mediated these effects. We shall consider here experimental work undertaken since about 1950. We shall further consider recent discoveries about brain function that may constitute a framework in which both experimental evidence and observations on maternal deprivation can be incorporated.

Early experience and stress. Weininger showed (1954) that postweaning handling of the infant laboratory rat by the experimenter for a few minutes a day increased the adult rat's resistance to heart damage and stomach ulceration when it was subjected to the severe stress of 48 hours of immobilization. In a subsequent experiment, Long (1955) showed that handled rats survived starvation an average of 53.8 hours longer than comparable unhandled rats of the same weight.

Weininger also found that the handling of the rat was related to increased skeletal growth and body weight. The studies of Ruegamer, Bernstein, and Benjamin (1954) showed that these gains were due to superior assimilation of food by the handled animal, rather than to a greater food intake.

Together with other results, these findings suggested that postweaning handling altered the balance of hormonal output from the anterior pituitary, decreasing the output of adrenocorticotrophic hormone (ACTH) under chronic stress and increasing the normal output of somatotropic (growth) hormone. Such an alteration of hormonal output from the pituitary could be mediated by the hypothalamus, which is the final common pathway for neural influence on the pituitary (Harris 1960).

It should be noted here that a wide variety of noxious stimuli, ranging from solar radiation at the beach to examinations in medical school, have been shown to have the nonspecific effect of inducing a higher than normal release of ACTH from the anterior pituitary into the blood stream, thereby stimulating the release of adrenal cortical hormones, such as hydrocortisone in humans and dogs and corticosterone in rats, from the adrenal cortex. The end effect of this reaction, first discovered by Selye in 1936 (Selye 1950), is protein catabolism; protein reserves are converted into glucose for the short-term energy requirements of the organism.

At the same time, the sympathetic division of the autonomic nervous system stimulates release of epinephrine and norepinephrine (adrenaline and noradrenaline) from the adrenal medulla, through the action of the great splanchnic nerve. These powerful hormones further aid in the emergency reaction. The twin arms of the response to stress, i.e., the pituitary–adrenal response and the sympatheticoadrenal medullary response, occur together and are mediated by the posterior and medial hypothalamic zone.

The response to stress is therefore an expenditure of metabolic reserves to prepare the organism for an emergency situation. In the case of physical stress, such as extreme cold, this preparation is essential, and without the adrenal cortex the animal will quickly die. In the case of psychological stress, however, such as a medical examination or an international crisis, where a more differentiated response may be required, the stress reaction has no obvious value. Indeed, if prolonged it may lead to cardiovascular and renal damage and eventually to the death of the animal (Selye 1950).

In the case of emotional or psychological stress the organism may be said to be responding to psychological assault as if it were actually physical assault (Wolff 1953). The terms "psychological" and "emotional," as used here, refer to the fact that in such stress the noxious stimulus must necessarily be mediated by the central nervous system—that without such neural mediation, the stress response will not occur. In general, psychological stress may be thought of as a noxious stimulus that does not threaten immediate tissue damage to the organism, for example, an insult or social rejection by a group. Psychological rather than physical stress may be considered to predominate in an industrialized and urban environment.

Extending the work of Weininger and others, Levine (1962) and others have since shown that preweaning stimulation of the infant rat can have marked physiological consequences in the adult, including a reduced plasma corticosterone response to chronic stress. Even noxious stimulation (for example, electric shock) appears to have this effect, which Levine believes is related to the earlier maturation of the pituitary–adrenal axis in the early-stimulated animal. Nowhere, however, have there been any results to indicate that early shock *increases* resistance to starvation or other forms of severe physical stress.

The mechanism operating in Weininger's and Levine's studies appears, on the whole, to be an alteration in the threshold of response to stress in the early-handled or early-stimulated animal. In general, the early-stimulated animal is less responsive to environmental change that does not involve tissue damage, such as being moved about in the laboratory, and on these grounds as well as others could be termed less reactive emotionally. Levine was able to show, however, that the early-stimulated animal responds more sharply (measured in terms of plasma corticosterone levels) to acute forms of stress, such as electric shock applied to the soles of the feet.

One can therefore conclude from these experimental studies that in all likelihood the experience of preweaning stimulation (usually removal from the nest for a few minutes) and postweaning handling have the common effect of raising the rat's threshold of response to chronic environmental stress. As evidence of this, Weininger showed that adrenal weights of handled rats following 48 hours of immobilization were lower than those of unhandled rats undergoing the same stress.

Other studies (Yates et al. 1961) have shown that a hypothalamic homeostatic mechanism presets the pituitary–adrenal response, measured in terms of plasma corticosterone, to any given noxious stimulus, such as laparotomy (incision through the abdominal wall), for the rat. If the amount of corticosterone normally produced under such stress is injected into the blood stream *before* the stress, no further increase in plasma corticosterone level will occur in response to the actual stress.

A simple hypothesis to explain the results of a majority of studies is, therefore, that early handling and stimulation have set the hypothalamic "homeostat" for chronic stressors at a higher level, thus producing a higher threshold for stress. This could be accounted for by inhibition of the posterior hypothalamic zone, which mediates the response to stress, and by increased activity of the anterior zone.

Population density and stress. What consequences of an increased or decreased pituitary–adrenal response to stress would result respectively from depression or from elevation of the stress threshold? The results of an increased pituitary–adrenal response to environmental change can be most clearly seen in studies on population density and stress at the Philadelphia zoo and in the field (Christian & Lemunyan 1958; Christian & Davis 1964).

Christian has shown that as the density of a given animal population increases, two mechanisms come into play to inhibit further population growth: (*a*) an inhibition of sexual maturation, apparently due to inhibition of gonadotropin output from the anterior pituitary, and (*b*) a decrease in female lactation after birth of the young and hence a reduced survival rate among litters. Both of these effects are apparently related to increased pituitary–adrenal activity resulting from crowding, the second of the two mechanisms apparently being an extra-adrenal effect of ACTH.

A remarkable finding of Christian and his associates has been, however, that if the animal population being investigated has received tranquilizing drugs, such as reserpine or chlorpromazine, increasing population density has no effect on mortality—the two inhibitory mechanisms limiting population growth are silent. Further, these inhibitory mechanisms do not work with placid animal populations, no matter how crowded the individuals are. Finally, Christian has shown an inverse relation between social dominance and adrenal weight—the more dominant the animal in a competitive species, the less pituitary–adrenal activity results from crowding and competition.

The effects of population density on mortality and the consequent self-limitation in population growth are therefore due to competition and aggression among members of the species and the resultant increase in pituitary–adrenal activity. Christian was able to show that increasing population density causes renal disease in woodchucks, an effect that could be replicated by administering exogenous doses of ACTH to these animals.

These dramatic studies show the consequences of increased pituitary–adrenal activity (among them, lowered resistance to infection) in an animal population and further suggest that these effects depend on hypothalamic mediation of the noxious stimuli. If the hypothalamic response is inhibited, as through the action of tranquilizing drugs or the effects of early handling, then it can be presumed that the noxious effects of increasing population density will be reduced.

These considerations would imply, for the human species, a relation between early experience and survival in conditions of increasing population density and competition.

Early stress and life span. The work of Hardin Jones (1956) has suggested that early stress experience reduces the individual's life span, whether this stress is in the form of childhood disease in humans or radiation in animals. Early stress appears to have a multiplicative effect—stress damage increases exponentially with a linear increase in time. Jones's work has established a clear-cut relation in human populations between amount of childhood disease and life span. His figures show that reduction of childhood disease in Scandinavian populations has resulted in a significantly long life span for these populations in comparison with Americans. It would seem possible that the amount of early emotional stress experienced by the individual may be also related to life span and that those individuals with higher stress thresholds would be relatively more protected from emotional stress and would live longer, but this point remains to be demonstrated experimentally.

Threshold for stress. The work we have been considering here suggests that a reduced pituitary–adrenal response to emotional or psychological stress has protective consequences for the organism and may increase its resistance to severe physical stress. We may consider here that the organism is endowed with a fixed initial amount of "adaptation energy" (Selye 1950), or negentropy, for its lifetime. If these metabolic resources are used up early in the individual's life span through excessive response to environmental change, leaking across a low threshold for stress, then one may expect that these reserves will be depleted when severe life-threatening stress is encountered at a later date.

For this reason the threshold for stress is crucial in any individual animal or person. If the threshold is set too low in an environment such as ours, where psychological rather than physical stress predominates—and where a pituitary–adrenal response and consequent expenditure of protein reserves may be considered inappropriate—then one can expect impairment of viability. Too high a setting in a physically stressful environment, as would be the case for a tame laboratory rat released in the natural habitat of the wild rat, would be equally fatal.

The actual threshold for stress may be considered to be set by a combination of genetic and experiential factors, the latter including the amount of prenatal stress experienced by the pregnant female. One mechanism by means of which early experience of the organism influences the threshold for stress may involve a direct effect on brain cells of blood plasma corticosterone (mouse) or hydrocortisone (dog, monkey, man) induced by early stress. Howard (1965) has shown that exogenous corticosterone in mice inhibits brain as well as body growth in the first few days of life, and completely prevents the normal increase in forebrain deoxyribonucleic acid (DNA) found in untreated animals.

Neural mechanisms. Recent studies of brain stimulation in human (Sem-Jacobsen & Torkildsen 1960) and animal (Lilly 1960; Olds 1960; Howard 1965) subjects have revealed the existence of two great neural systems, closely related anatomically, running from the anterior end of the brain to the brain stem. The first, or positive, system, when stimulated electrically, elicits in animal subjects behavior (bar-pressing) that will continue the stimulation and elicits pleasant feelings in human subjects, according to reports from patients who experienced this stimulation as part of neurosurgical procedure. The second, or negative, system, when stimulated electrically, elicits in the rat or monkey behavior that will stop the stimulation and, when stimulated accidentally in the human patient, elicits highly unpleasant feelings.

These two great systems converge on the hypothalamus, their final common pathway for influence on the endocrine system and the autonomic nervous system (Bovard 1961). The positive system is represented in the anterior and lateral hypothalamus, and neural activity in this region has parasympathetic autonomic and, in general, protein anabolic consequences, such as promotion of digestion. The negative system is represented in the posterior and medial hypothalamus, and neural activity in this region has sympathetic autonomic and, in general, protein catabolic consequences, such as breakdown of protein into glucose. This negative system mediates the response to stress.

The interesting point about these two great brain systems of opposite function is that from available evidence they appear to be reciprocally inhibitory—activity in one automatically inhibits activity in the other (Bovard 1962). In terms of their operation, we can now account for the effects of maternal deprivation (Bowlby 1951).

Brain mechanisms in maternal deprivation. In comparison with the normal infant, the absence of handling and affection for the institutionalized infant in Bowlby's studies would mean an absence of stimulation of the positive system in the first few months of life, and hence relative dominance of the negative, or stress-mediating, system. This would result in a low threshold for stress in the institutionalized infant and, therefore, in an excessive pituitary–adrenal response to environmental change. The resultant depletion of metabolic reserves could be expected to lead to the reduced resistance to disease and physical stress found by Spitz (1946). Evidence from studies of animals (Eells 1961) and of humans suggests that noxious stimulation may be better than none at all, but that positive stimulation is preferable to noxious stimulation.

But as we have noted, the negative and positive systems are reciprocally inhibitory. Relative dominance of the negative system would therefore inhibit activity of the positive, or rewarding, system. This will result in a higher threshold for reinforcing stimuli, and hence such maternally deprived individuals would show a reduced capacity for responses to such positively reinforcing stimulation as affection and social approval. It would be more difficult to reach them by these means.

Finally, emotional stress appears to interfere with abstract thinking by polarizing thought around the noxious stimulus, thus restricting the normal range and sweep of ideas. What the mechanism is here has not been established, but it may involve a functional reduction in the number of neurons available for thinking. If this is the case, the individual with a low threshold for stress could be expected to have difficulty thinking abstractly. The relative impairment of abstract thinking found by Goldfarb (1947) in children institutionalized before six months may be related to such a functional reduction of cortical activity resulting from a low stress threshold.

It is of interest in this connection that handled rats, with a higher threshold for stress, have been found to learn mazes faster and with fewer errors than unhandled controls (Bernstein 1957). The reason for this is apparently that handling dampens the fear response, which has been shown to inhibit exploratory behavior. The handled rat simply explores his environment more, and therefore learns more about it—including how to open the wire-mesh covers of the maze runways with paws and nose, which unhandled rats never learn.

These studies suggest that exploratory responses, in behavior or thought, are inhibited by emotional stress. A low stress threshold set by early experience could therefore inhibit the development of abstract thinking and would most probably limit innovations in thinking.

We have now considered the evidence linking the effects of early experience on viability to neuroendocrine mechanisms, in particular the axis of the hypothalamus, the anterior pituitary, and the adrenal cortex. It is by means of this axis that the external environment influences the internal metabolic dispositions of the organism in the direction of either protein anabolism or protein catabolism. A crucial function of this neuroendocrine system is to set the threshold for the pituitary–adrenal axis's response to stress, a setting apparently made in part on the basis of the organism's experience of an early sample of what life is like. This setting in large measure determines the rate of expenditure of metabolic reserves in response to environmental change.

EVERETT W. BOVARD

[*Other relevant material may be found in* DEVELOPMENTAL PSYCHOLOGY; DRUGS, *article on* PSYCHOPHARMACOLOGY; NERVOUS SYSTEM; SENSORY AND MOTOR DEVELOPMENT; STRESS.]

BIBLIOGRAPHY

BERNSTEIN, LEWIS 1957 The Effects of Variations in Handling Upon Learning and Retention. *Journal of Comparative and Physiological Psychology* 50:162–167.

BOVARD, EVERETT W. 1958 The Effects of Early Handling on Viability of the Albino Rat. *Psychological Review* 65:257–271.

BOVARD, EVERETT W. 1961 A Concept of Hypothalamic Functioning. *Perspectives in Biology and Medicine* 5:52–60.

BOVARD, EVERETT W. 1962 The Balance Between Negative and Positive Brain System Activity. *Perspectives in Biology and Medicine* 6:116–127.

BOWLBY, JOHN 1951 *Maternal Care and Mental Health.* Geneva: World Health Organization.

CHRISTIAN, JOHN J.; and DAVIS, DAVID E. 1964 Endocrines, Behavior and Population. *Science* 146:1550–1560.

CHRISTIAN, JOHN J.; and LEMUNYAN, COBERT D. 1958 Adverse Effects of Crowding on Lactation and Reproduction of Mice and Two Generations of Their Progeny. *Endocrinology* 63:517–529.

DENENBERG, V. H. 1962 The Effects of Early Experience. Pages 109–138 in E. S. E. Hafez (editor), *The Behaviour of Domestic Animals.* London: Baillière.

EELLS, JANET F. 1961 Inconsistency of Early Handling and Its Effect Upon Emotionality in the Rat. *Journal of Comparative and Physiological Psychology* 54:690–693.

GOLDFARB, WILLIAM 1947 Variations in Adolescent Adjustment of Institutionally-reared Children. *American Journal of Orthopsychiatry* 17:449–457.

HARRIS, G. W. 1960 Central Control of Pituitary Secretion. Volume 2, pages 1007–1038 in John Field (editor), *Handbook of Physiology.* Section 1: Neurophysiology. Washington: American Physiological Society.

HOWARD, EVELYN 1965 Effects of Corticosterone and Food Restriction on Growth and on DNA, RNA and Cholesterol Contents of the Brain and Liver in Infant Mice. *Journal of Neurochemistry* 12:181–191.

JONES, HARDIN B. 1956 A Special Consideration of the Aging Process, Disease, and Life Expectancy. Pages 281–337 in John H. Lawrence and Cornelius A. Tobias (editors), *Advances in Biological and Medical Physics.* New York: Academic Press.

LEVINE, SEYMOUR 1962 Psychophysiological Effects of Infantile Stimulation. Pages 246–253 in Eugene L. Bliss (editor), *Roots of Behavior.* New York: Harper.

LILLY, JOHN C. 1960 Learning Motivated by Subcortical Stimulation: The "Start" and the "Stop" Patterns of Behavior. Pages 78–103 in Estelle R. Ramey and Desmond S. O'Doherty (editors), *Electrical Studies on the Unanesthetized Brain.* New York: Hoeber.

LONG, H. G. 1955 Differential Survival Under Food and Water Deprivation as a Function of Early Handling. M.A. thesis, Univ. of Toronto.

OLDS, JAMES 1960 Differentiation of Reward Systems in the Brain by Self-stimulation Technics. Pages 17–49 in Estelle R. Ramey and Desmond S. O'Doherty (editors), *Electrical Studies on the Unanesthetized Brain.* New York: Hoeber.

RUEGAMER, WILLIAM R.; BERNSTEIN, LEWIS; and BENJAMIN, JOHN D. 1954 Growth, Food Utilization, and Thyroid Activity in the Albino Rat as a Function of Extra Handling. *Science* 120:184–185.

SELYE, HANS 1950 *The Physiology and Pathology of Exposure to Stress: A Treatise Based on the Concepts of the General-adaptation-syndrome and the Diseases of Adaptation.* Montreal: Acta.

SEM-JACOBSEN, CARL W.; and TORKILDSEN, ARNE 1960 Depth Recording and Electrical Stimulation in the Human Brain. Pages 275–290 in Estelle R. Ramey and Desmond S. O'Doherty (editors), *Electrical Studies on the Unanesthetized Brain.* New York: Hoeber.

SPITZ, RENÉ A. 1946 Hospitalism: A Follow-up Report. *Psychoanalytic Study of the Child* 2:113–117.

WEININGER, OTTO 1954 Physiological Damage Under Emotional Stress as a Function of Early Experience. *Science* 119:285–286.

WOLFF, HAROLD G. 1953 *Stress and Disease.* Springfield, Ill.: Thomas.

YATES, F. E. et al. 1961 The Interaction Between Plasma Corticosterone Concentration and Adrenocorticotropin-releasing Stimuli in the Rat: Evidence for the Reset of an Endocrine Feedback Control. *Endocrinology* 69: 67–80.

INFANT MORTALITY

See MORTALITY *and* PUBLIC HEALTH.

INFERENCE, STATISTICAL

See STATISTICS.

INFLATION AND DEFLATION

Inflation is a fall and deflation is a rise in the purchasing power of money, as measured ordinarily by an index number of prices. When the price index rises, economists speak of the purchasing power of money falling—of inflationary conditions—and the converse when this index falls. Associated expressions relating to the external purchasing power of money (that is, its purchasing power in terms of foreign exchange) are *devaluation* and *upward revaluation* (or sometimes *up-valuation*). When a currency loses purchasing power in terms of foreign currency, by reason of inflation at home or deflation abroad, it is effectively devalued; and again, the converse. The order of events may also be reversed, with devaluation leading to inflation through rises in the import components of the domestic price level; upward revaluation may have deflationary consequences through declines in the import components.

On the side of inflation, particularly, it has become customary to speak of creeping, trotting, galloping, and runaway inflation (also called hyperinflation). Clear distinctions are lacking. However, a general price increase of less than 1 per cent per quarter (approximately 4 per cent per year) is often considered a creeping inflation, despite its eventual consequences if unchecked. At the other extreme, Phillip Cagan's definition of hyperinflation as a price rise of 50 per cent a month has received wide acceptance (1956).

Despite substantial agreement in principle as to the definitions of inflation and deflation, there remains disagreement in detail, a disagreement symptomatic of some confusion in the general theory of the subject. We list some issues often slurred over by the elementary definitions:

(1) Which of an infinite number of possible price levels is used to measure the purchasing power of money? Much recent literature (since World War II) has tended to use a national income or gross national product (GNP) "deflator," whereas earlier literature often relied on wholesale price indexes. In many cases price indexes will show widely differing rates of inflation or deflation, and the differences may become political issues. When wages, for example, are rising more rapidly than wholesale prices, the income deflators and consumer price indexes will also rise more rapidly.

(2) How are index numbers to be computed? In particular, what allowance should be made for the tendency of buyers to shift their purchases in the direction of those products that have fallen most or risen least in price from one period to the next;

and what adjustment should be made for possible upward biases in price indexes, reflecting increases in living standards? These problems are often solved in practice by using so-called Laspeyres price indexes, in which price quotations are "weighted" by consumption in the "base" period. An upward bias results, which is reduced by revising base periods relatively frequently. [*See* INDEX NUMBERS.]

(3) What allowance should be made for new products, quality improvements, product availabilities, and so on? In the United States an AFL–CIO task force emphasized these factors during World War II, alleging that the official indexes understated the magnitude of wartime inflation. In the late 1950s a National Bureau of Economic Research (1961) task force headed by George Stigler argued that the indexes overstated the rate of American inflation after the Korean War by confusing product improvement with inflation.

(4) When price controls are in effect, should the indexes be based on black market as well as on official prices? The terms *repressed inflation* and *suppressed inflation* are used for cases in which only official prices are used, as distinguished from open inflation, when controls are not in effect or when black market prices are used to compute price index numbers. An unsettled issue is whether repressed inflation and suppressed inflation are most usefully considered as types of inflation or as alternatives thereto.

(5) When commodity taxes, sales taxes, and subsidies are used widely, should prices be taken gross or net of such taxes and subsidies? Suppose also that, as in France before 1959, such taxes and subsidies are influenced by price index considerations, with commodities in the official indexes treated differently from others. How reliable are price indexes under this sort of sampling bias?

(6) Following destruction and disruption due to war, flood, earthquake, or other calamity, there are often sharp rises in prices. Is such a result to be called inflationary when no change in monetary or fiscal policy has occurred? Does it make any difference, in answering the last question, whether the same destruction and disruption simultaneously create unemployment?

(7) For any of a number of reasons, including income redistribution and "money illusion," a rise in the price level may lead to at least a short-run increase in real output, in employment, and in economic growth [*see* INCOME AND EMPLOYMENT THEORY]. Is such a price increase really inflationary, or should the term be limited to cases in which no significant increases in output or employment occur?

(8) During the 1920s technical progress in western Europe and North America brought about widespread reduction in production costs with no corresponding reduction in prices (in most countries). The resulting increases in money wages and profits were later called inflationary by Friedrich Hayek and other adherents (primarily Austrian) of the "neutral money" school. Is this a defensible position?

Our answers to these and related questions are often affected by extraneous issues, such as whether we consider inflation or commodity taxes or price controls to be a "good thing" or not. If one considers inflation, for example, a "bad thing," it is difficult to avoid a question-begging definition that will render "good results" somehow noninflationary even when accompanied by price level increases.

For those who cannot accept the evidence of price indexes alone, a number of alternative definitions of inflation and deflation are available. We cite four, but the list is not exhaustive.

(1) Inflation is a condition of generalized excess demand for stocks of goods and flows of real income, in which "too much money chases too few goods." Conversely, deflation is a condition of generalized excess demand for stocks and flows of money, in which "too many goods chase too little money."

(2) Inflation is a rise of the money stock or money income in a society, either total or per capita. Conversely, deflation is a fall in one or more of these magnitudes. These definitions are favored by the apostles of monetary neutrality.

(3) Inflation (deflation) is a rise (fall) in price levels with a number of additional characteristics or conditions: it does not increase real output and employment; it leads (through cost changes) to further price movements; it is faster than some "safe" rate; it arises "from the side of money"; it is measured by prices net of commodity taxes and subsidies; it has been imperfectly anticipated.

(4) Ralph Turvey (1949) has formulated a comprehensive definition of inflation, which has no obvious counterpart on the deflationary side. To Turvey inflation is the process resulting from competition in attempting to maintain total real income, total real expenditure, and/or total output at a level which has become physically impossible or attempting to increase any of them to a level which is physically impossible.

Historical record. During the century preceding World War I, periods of inflation and deflation largely canceled each other in the Western world. It became customary to consider price levels as stable in the long run, to assume that "what goes up must come down," and to employ accounting conventions based on the principle that "a dollar is a dollar." These views, and plans based upon them, embody what has come to be known as the "money illusion."

There have in fact been relatively few periods of equally protracted balance between inflationary and deflationary forces. Currency debasement, gold and silver discoveries, fractional reserve banking, and, more recently, the appeal of "full employment at whatever cost" have more than outweighed periods of strict adherence to inflexible metallic standards. The secular trend of prices has been upward, perhaps as a social rebuttal to the mathematical force of compound interest. This has led Murray Rothbard, presenting "The Case for a 100 Per Cent Gold Dollar," to state: *"The natural tendency of the state is inflation"* (1962, p. 109). This may be an exaggeration, but consider the pound sterling (originally a pound of silver, at 90.5 cents per fine ounce), currently pegged at $2.80; the French franc (formerly "livre," meaning "pound"), currently worth slightly more than 20 cents after a nominal hundredfold upward revaluation; and the Italian lira (with the same meaning), currently 625 to the dollar. Or consider the evaporation into the infinitesimal of such values as the British farthing, the Italian *centesimo*, the Japanese *rin* and *sen*, etc. Developments from 1939 to 1951 have been summarized on a close to world-wide basis by Arthur J. Brown in *The Great Inflation* (1955), while Lester Chandler has treated American developments in *Inflation in the United States, 1940–1948* (1951). Studies of many past hyperinflations are also available, a notable one being Constantino Bresciani-Turroni's *Economics of Inflation* (1931). The principal interruptions of the inflationary trend since 1945 have occurred in centrally planned economies, such as the Soviet Union and the People's Republic of China. These countries have held official prices down, and often lowered them, by rationing and by heavy commodity taxes (not included in the price quotations). It is with particular respect to these countries that the question whether a suppressed inflation is a form of inflation or an alternative thereto is most significant.

In discussing the theory of price level changes, we shall therefore follow contemporary practice and concentrate on inflationary cases.

Theoretical aspects

We may classify economic theories of price level movement into three principal types:

(1) Demand theories.
- (a) Demand for nonmonetary assets: the quantity theory of money.
- (b) Demand for real income.

(2) Cost theories.
- (a) Wage–price spiral.
- (b) Administrative inflation.
- (c) Sectoral inflation.

(3) Structural theories.
- (a) Resource disproportionality.
- (b) Economic growth.
- (c) Income distribution.

Demand theories. The quantity theory of money may be classified as a demand theory—the demand for nonmonetary assets.

Quantity theory of money. Prior to 1929 the dominant explanation of price level movements was the quantity theory of money [*see* MONEY]. If, in the so-called equation (identity) of exchange devised by Irving Fisher, we let M represent the quantity of money, including bank deposits and (sometimes) time deposits; V the number of times per period a unit of money, including bank deposits, changes hands; P the price level; Y the level of real income; and T the volume of real transactions, we have

$$MV_y = P_yY \quad \text{and} \quad MV_t = P_tT,$$

where the subscripts y and t relate to income and transactions respectively. (For example, transactions involving the purchase of existing securities and houses are taken into account in V_t and P_t but not in V_y and P_y.) To return to the quantity theory: if we suppose V, P, and T approximately constant, we then have, for any periods 1 and 2, $(P_2/P_1) = (M_2/M_1)$. Over short periods, this involves some difficulty because velocity rises in periods of prosperity and falls in periods of depression, and over long periods there is difficulty because of secular growth in Y and T, not to mention a possible secular fall in velocity. Nevertheless, the quantity theory usually yields accurate forecasts of price level changes, both in this elementary form and in the more advanced one (developed in Friedman 1956), in which other variables, principally wealth, interest rates, and the proportion of "human" to nonhuman wealth, are introduced explicitly. The implication of the quantity theory is that price level movements can be controlled by varying M, but it does not in itself explain why M varies as it does. One common criticism, in fact, interprets the level of prices as an active factor and the volume of money as a passive one, adjusting to meet the so-called needs of trade as prices change.

The quantity theory of money is classified as a demand theory because of the psychology underlying its operation: As the nominal amount of money expands (in the inflationary case), people who hold the increased stock of money desire to exchange some part of the increase for other assets,

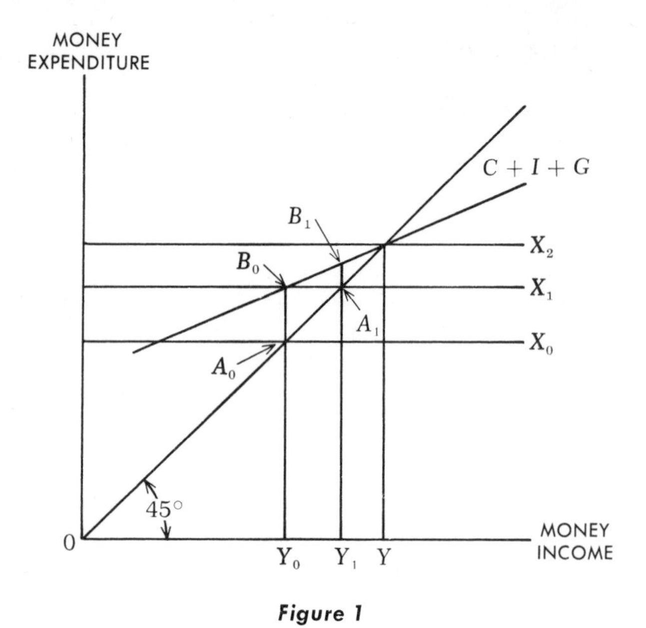

Figure 1

meaning consumer goods, investment goods, and securities. Their attempts to "balance their portfolios" increase the demand for these alternatives; the prices of consumer and investment goods rise, and the yields (interest rates) on securities fall.

Demand for real income. The exposition in this article of the quantity theory approach to inflation and deflation has been based on the work of Fisher and Friedman. In the same way, the income theory approach, embodying the notions of inflationary and deflationary gaps, is due to John Maynard Keynes (1940) and his disciples in the decade 1936 to 1946.

In Figure 1 money income is measured along the horizontal axis and money expenditures along the vertical axis. The resulting expenditure function is called $(C + I + G)$, since it represents the vertical sum of three principal components: personal consumption (C), private domestic investment (I), and government expenditures for goods and services (G). The equilibrium money income level is Y, since only at Y does aggregate income equal aggregate expenditures in money terms. (The 45-degree line through the origin 0 indicates this equality.) Suppose, however, that the capacity of the economy at full employment were only X_0, measured in the prices of the preceding period. At the full employment income level, Y_0, there is an inflationary gap, A_0B_0, with aggregate expenditures exceeding aggregate capacity. This gap causes a rise in prices. If the initial price increase raises nominal capacity (measured in new prices) to X_1, full employment money income becomes Y_1 and the inflationary gap falls to A_1B_1. The process continues until nominal capacity rises to X_2, full employment income rises to Y_2 $(= Y)$, and the inflationary gap is eliminated.

A difficulty with this analysis is that the expenditure function $(C + I + G)$ does not seem to be a stable function of money income. It tends, in most cases, to rise as money income rises; a representative consumer, with a fixed \$5,000 income, who spent \$4,000 at a price level of 100, for example, may spend \$4,500 in an effort to maintain his accustomed living standard when the level rises to 120; \$5,000 when it rises to 150; and \$5,500 (dipping into capital) when it rises to 200. When we make allowance for the instability of the expenditure function in money terms, it is not at all clear that the inflationary gap is in fact reduced by price increases or that any equilibrium price level exists.

A more sophisticated variant of the income theory is represented by Figure 2. Here the income measured along the horizontal axis is *real* income, deflated for price changes; and the vertical axis represents "the" price level. If the quantity of money is held constant, the demand for income (D_0, D_1) slopes downward. This means that more is demanded at lower prices than at higher prices. One rationalization of this result is that aggregate demand depends on wealth as well as income and that wealth moves with "real cash balances," that is, with the constant nominal amount of money deflated by the price level. At the same time, with constant money wage rates, the aggregate supply curve, S, slopes upward with the price level until a capacity ceiling is reached (a vertical line on

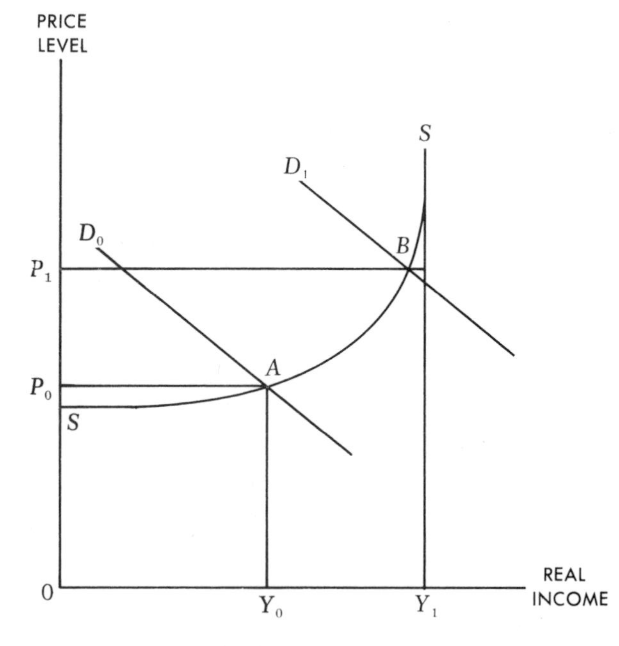

Figure 2

Figure 2). The argument runs here that an increase in prices increases profits and thence the demand for productive resources, particularly labor. The upward slope of *S* is generally slight until the point *A* is reached, christened by A. P. Lerner "low full employment." Subsequently it increases more rapidly, becoming almost vertical at *B*, which corresponds to Lerner's "high full employment" (1951).

The policy implication of income theory is that major emphasis should be placed on fiscal policy, particularly public expenditures and taxation, in controlling price level movements by shifting the aggregate demand curve *D* to the right or left, as the case may be.

Cost theories. While the two positions we have just examined consider price level movements as resulting from shifts in demand for assets and incomes, respectively, the view has gathered strength since the end of the Korean War (particularly from the persistence of price level increases in periods of mild recession) that the Western world is faced with a "new inflation," whose motive force comes primarily from the cost or supply side.

Wage–price spiral. The most general form of cost-inflation argument is known by a number of titles, "cost-push," "wage–price spiral," and so on. The argument is that organized economic pressure groups raise prices in excess of any rise in productivity, particularly when full employment is approached, and leave the government with the responsibility of preventing any fall in real output and in employment that might normally result. In many forms of this argument one particular pressure group, the trade unions, is assigned major responsibility for inflation, since its objective is considered a dynamic one (maximum wage increase per period) rather than a static maximization of income or profits. Sidney Weintraub (1959) represents this position most straightforwardly, on the basis of statistics showing net sales (gross sales minus purchases) to be a near-constant multiple of payrolls.

Figure 3 illustrates this position graphically. It is similar to Figure 2, except that the supply function shifts upward as shown. Starting at P_0, the price level rises to P_1 and P_2, if real income is maintained at Y_0, by increases in aggregate demand from D_0 to D_1 and D_2. If aggregate demand is held at D_0, real income falls from Y_0 to Y_1 and Y_2, and employment likewise falls; the price rise, while reduced, is not eliminated. A compromise path, denoted by *abcde*, shows alternations of recession and recovery as a country's attention shifts back and forth between inflation and unemployment situations.

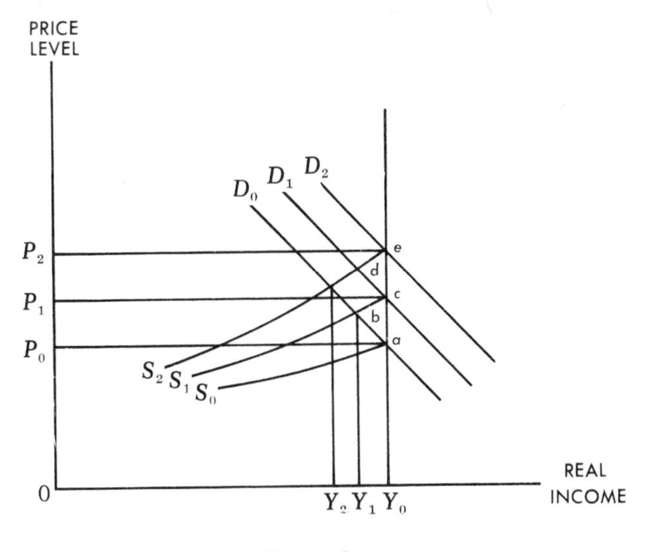

Figure 3

Cost-push theories suggest that inflation in a pressure-group economy at high employment is difficult to control without direct regulation of prices and/or wages. The London *Economist* has spoken of "The Uneasy Triangle" (1952) of full employment, strong labor organizations, and stable prices, of which no more than two are obtainable simultaneously. Comparing the rates of change of money wage rates with the rates of unemployment in the prior year, A. W. Phillips (1958) has led in the development of "Phillips curves," of which Figure 4 is an idealized version. If the vertical line *A* is a maximum politically acceptable rate of unemployment (possibly 4 per cent) and the horizontal line *B* is the maximum economically possible rate of noninflationary wage increase (in the absence of drastic redistribution of personal incomes), the Phillips curves for most countries (including the

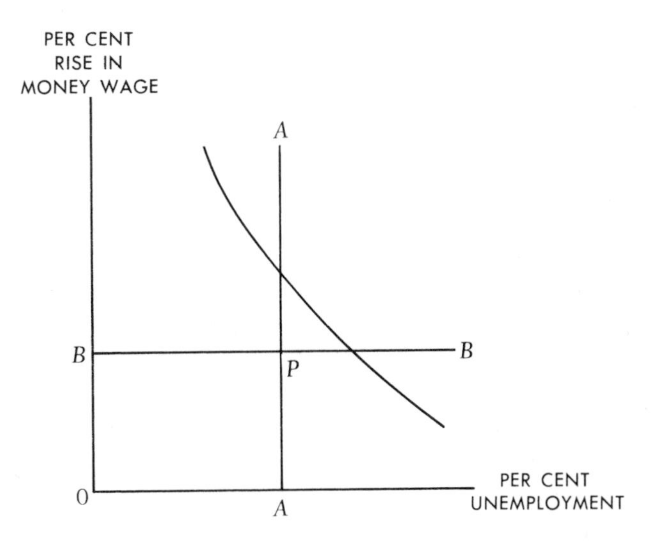

Figure 4

United States but apparently not Great Britain) pass outside their intersection at *P*. This, like the *Economist*'s uneasy triangle, illustrates the dilemma of the anti-inflation policy maker in a parliamentary democracy and in a basically free economy.

Administrative and sectoral inflation. The anti-union animus of many, if not most, of the views summarized in the last section has not gone unanswered. Gardiner C. Means (1962) believes he has evidence of "administered inflation," as industry inches a bit at a time toward a maximum profit position by raising prices in prosperity and maintaining them in recession. Labor, in this view, has merely protected its real wage and traditional income share.

A neutral variant, "blaming" neither labor nor capital, is the sectoral-inflation theory of Charles Schultze (1959). Imagine an economy producing two goods, *a* and *b*, whose prices are both rigid downward. Suppose that demand shifts from sector *b* to sector *a*. The price of *a* rises in response to the demand shift. The price of *b* remains constant despite the demand shift. An index number combining the prices of *a* and *b* must rise. If higher profits in *a* induce wage demands there that are won in collective bargaining, similar increases may also be won in *b*, forcing prices to rise there as well.

Structural theories. Structural theories of inflation have resulted from doubts about the efficacy of policies based on either demand-inflation or cost-inflation views. Of the three examples presented, one stresses factor disproportionality, one income distribution, and one the economic growth rate. There are many other forms, since "structuralism"

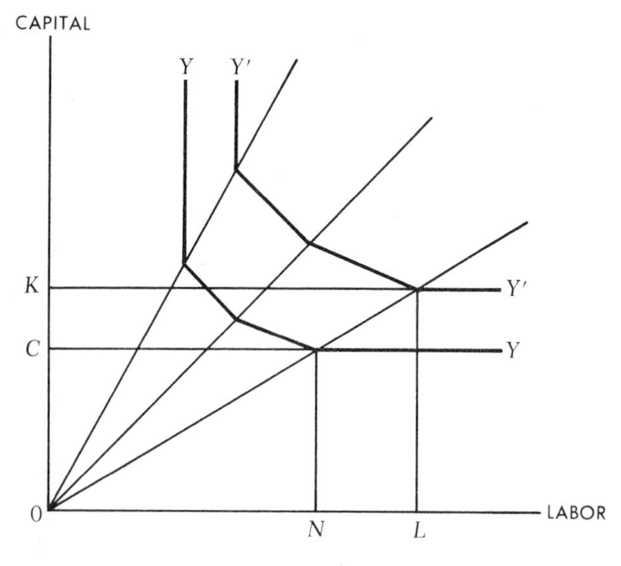

Figure 5

is seldom defined and covers a wide variety of economic phenomena, particularly in Latin America but also in other underdeveloped areas.

Resource disproportionality. Within the structuralist camp (in Spanish, *estructuralismo* or *cepalismo*) one variant is the disproportionality theory. In our simplified picture of this theory (Figure 5), there are only two productive resources, homogeneous capital goods and homogeneous labor. A number of industries use capital and labor, each in fixed proportions. In the bundle of rays through the origin in Figure 5, each ray depicts a different industry. There is a labor force of *L* workers and a capital stock of *C* machines. Of the *L* workers, at least *NL* are in open or disguised unemployment, since their marginal productivity is zero. A capital stock of *K* is required to employ all *L* workers. In this situation, inflation can impose forced abstinence upon the community by concentrating credit in capital goods industries. These can drive the capital stock toward *K* from *C*, raise warranted employment above *N*, and increase the national income above Y.

Economic growth. A principal argument of structuralists, exemplified by Raúl Prebisch of the Economic Commission for Latin America, is that monetary or fiscal controls on inflation in developing economies check precisely those structural changes that bring about sustainable growth. Many structuralists dislike static diagrammatic and mathematical treatment of their dynamic problems; it is difficult to formalize their views.

Consider, however, Figure 6, and turn to the right-hand panel. Structuralists believe that increases in the nominal amount of money increase both aggregate supply and aggregate demand functions when these relate to *domestic* output *currently* produced. A rise in money and prices is a partial expropriation of *rentiers*, who prefer capital export and land speculation to domestic production as investment outlets. It subsidizes the active elements who both produce and purchase current domestic output, since these are the initial recipients of easy money and credit. On the diagram the (vertical) shift in the aggregate supply function from S_0 through S_1 to S_2 reflects higher money wages and other costs. The (horizontal) shift in the aggregate demand function from D_0 through D_1 to D_2 reflects increased money incomes. A curve labeled Q passes through the intersections (Q_0, Q_1, Q_2). Its positive slope in the range from Q_0 to *R* should not be confused with the slopes of true supply functions. This slope illustrates the structuralist opinion that aggregate output and employment vary in the same direction as the price level (at least up to

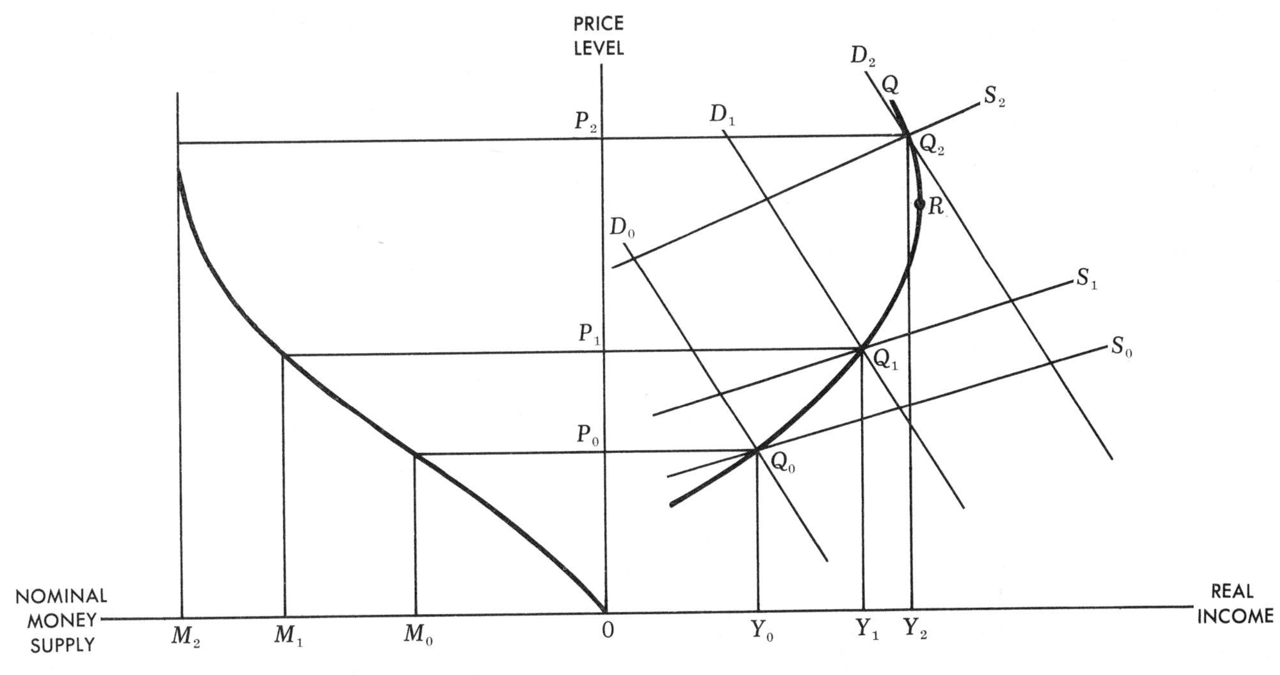

Figure 6

a point). If this is the case, premature application of indirect controls slows down the growth rates of output and employment.

According to the left-hand panel, an increase in the nominal money supply raises prices from P_0 to P_1, but the real output rises from Y_0 to Y_1. A further increase in the money supply raises real output further, to Y_2, but it raises prices by a larger proportionate amount, to P_2. The policy implication is that the first increase is desirable; the second increase, if it is in the range beyond R, may not be.

Income distribution. The issues of income and wealth distribution are brought into the foreground of the inflation discussion by another structuralist group, the "sociological school" of economists, centered in France. These writers view inflation in terms of conflicting money-income demands by rival social classes. The fixed-income receivers (salariat, *rentiers*, etc.) have a claim to F units of money income (see Figure 7, based upon Reder 1948). The variable-income receivers (wage earners and entrepreneurs) claim varying amounts of money income (V) as the price level rises. The total of income claims (demands), related to the price level, is plotted as $F + V$ in Figure 7. Let the (given) total of real income be a ray through the origin, 0 —the higher the real income, the steeper the slope of the ray. As prices rise, the total of income claims rises more slowly, up to a point; the fixed-income element provides a stabilizer. In fact (P_1, Y_1) in Figure 7 is a stable-equilibrium price and income level. If prices rise further, however, the total of income claims eventually rises faster than the price level. Some fixed claims are "escalated," and others include in their demands protection against the inflation they foresee in the short run. On the diagram, the $(F + V)$ function becomes concave upward and the second equilibrium level (P_2, Y_2) becomes unstable. A price level 10 per cent above P_2, for example, generates income claims 15 per cent above Y_2; if granted, these spiral, in turn, to further price increases.

The implication of this picture (Figure 7) is disturbing. Once P_1 is well behind, stable equilibrium at a stable price level is hard to restore, even though real income increases, without refusing the

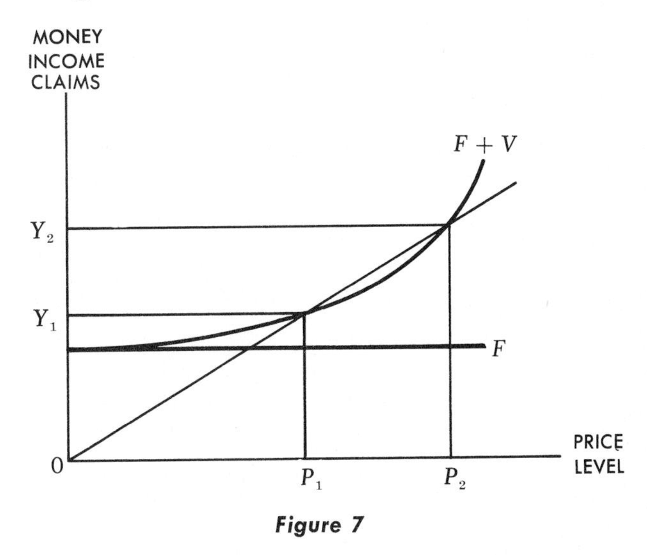

Figure 7

income claims of one or more variable-income classes—workers or entrepreneurs. This, in turn, is difficult to do without some form of major social disturbance.

Empirical aspects

Statistical testing. While the foregoing theories of inflation are not mutually exclusive, there is room for substantial disagreement as to their relative importance. The theoretical dispute has called forth a substantial volume of statistical research designed to illuminate this issue of relative importance, but the results have not been accepted unequivocally.

Much of the statistical research since World War II has been carried on by advocates of the sophisticated "modern" version of the quantity theory of money, in attempted refutation of one or another of the rival views presented above. The nature of a few selected studies may be indicated briefly:

(1) Studies of historical changes in the quantity of money, the velocity of circulation, the price level, and the level of real income have tended to show that monetary changes come first—the others come later (with relatively long and variable lags)—and that income can be forecast as well from monetary changes as from changes in the income theory's "autonomous" variables (investment, government spending, and the constant term in the consumption function). In addition to Friedman himself (see Friedman & Meiselman 1963), outstanding work along this line has been done by Clark Warburton (1951).

(2) Studies of hyperinflation tend to show that, in addition to the quantity of money, an index of expected future price changes (extrapolated from the recent past) is all that is needed for satisfactory explanation and prediction. Here the work of Cagan (1956) has blazed the trail, at least on the statistical side.

(3) Correlation studies at the microeconomic level, between individual price and quantity changes, have cast some doubt on cost theories of inflation, since the observed correlations have been large and positive. Edmund Phelps (1961) and Richard Selden (1959) have worked along these lines.

(4) Studies of inflation and economic growth attempt to locate and estimate within broad limits an optimum rate of inflation (from the viewpoint of growth). Results here are much in doubt because of the impinging of so many additional variables, not to mention the suppression of inflation.

(5) The number and variety of Phillips-curve studies, involving a number of countries, periods, and additional variables has already been mentioned. It remains open to question, however, whether the Phillips curve is independent of monetary and fiscal policy. That is to say, a higher degree of unemployment may well be required, to avoid inflationary wage increases, when the monetary authorities have a long record of validating such increases by expansionary policies than when they have not.

(6) An interesting recent variant of ordinary functional relations between M (the money supply) and P (the price level) is provided by A. C. Harberger's study of Chilean monetary history (1963). Given a high statistical correlation between P_t (dependent variable) and the lagged money supply (M_{t-1}, M_{t-2}), Harberger inquires: By how much could this correlation be increased by including such additional dependent variables as an index of wage rates, representing cost-push effects, and the force of inflationary acceleration ($P_{t-1} - P_{t-2}$), representing an inflationary or deflationary economic structure? Harberger's initial results for Chile suggest that the additional correlation is very small.

(7) For the United States, the National Bureau of Economic Research (1961) task force headed by George Stigler has supported the thesis that published price indexes exaggerate the degree of inflation and understate the degree of deflation, by reason of a number of defects, the most significant being the omission of new products and quality changes and the use of quoted, rather than actual, prices. The last-named point also bears upon the validity of Means's thesis (1962) of inflationary price administration.

Speed, duration, and extent of inflation. Let us agree that an inflationary process occurs when active claims for shares in real national income or expenditure exceed the amount that can be produced in time to satisfy them. Inflation then continues until the conflicting claims are somehow reconciled or modified. The speed of the inflation that follows an initial inflationary shock depends upon the reactions of various income and spending groups. If there are few reactions and these are delayed and/or mild, the pace of inflation will be slow and will not go far beyond the initial shock. However, if the successive reactions are numerous, rapid, and vigorous, the resulting inflation may be explosive (hyperinflation). The properties of the inflation, given an inflationary shock of specific size, will then depend on a number of factors:

Effects on expenditure demands. Rising prices do not, in the aggregate, necessarily imply increases in the quantity of goods and services supplied or reductions in the quantity demanded, as in the case of individual commodities. At least, they do not do so if the nominal quantity of money and the money wage rate are both free to vary. This is because rising prices and wages are incomes to some groups, as well as costs to others. While it is therefore possible for an inflation to continue forever, this seldom happens, because the inflationary process reduces the level of real expenditures in one or more of the following ways: (*a*) "money illusion" on the part of spenders who plan their purchases in money rather than real terms; (*b*) a change in the distribution of income away from *rentiers*, pensioners, aged persons, and others with high marginal-spending propensities; (*c*) a rise in the marginal tax rate of progressive income and profits taxes; (*d*) real balance effects, as represented in Figure 3, if prices rise more rapidly than the quantity of money; (*e*) rising real interest rates, sometimes reinforced by credit rationing; (*f*) balance of payments difficulties if the country is inflating more rapidly than its trading partners.

Effects on income claims. The process of inflation will affect the ability of different economic groups to push for higher incomes. In a demand inflation, for example, there may be an initial fall in the level of unemployment and an initial rise in the rate of profit. Inflation then accelerates as labor achieves large wage increases that lead, in turn, to higher prices. In a cost inflation unemployment tends to increase. This reduces subsequent cost pushes until the inflation comes to an eventual halt. This process is thwarted, of course, to whatever extent the government's full-employment policy "validates" wage and price increases that would otherwise raise the level of unemployment.

Lags. Lags influence strongly the character of inflationary movements. Without them, an inflation would run its course almost instantaneously. Their existence is largely responsible for the manageable rates of inflation in most Western nations since 1950. Perhaps the most important lag is the wage lag, which results from the fact that collective bargaining is seldom initiated more frequently than once a year and that negotiations may drag on for weeks or months. The process is also slowed by the fact that some months usually elapse before price changes are reflected in published index numbers. The wage lag is usually even greater for the so-called passive, or fixed income, groups. The greater the size of these elements, with their frequently anti-inflationary political views, the slower and smaller the rise in prices.

In industries that administer prices on the basis of cost changes, the lag between cost and price changes is probably less than the lag of wage rates behind changes in the cost of living. (On the other hand, such prices may be insensitive to demand changes in a demand inflation.) In the public sector, there are lags in both receipts and expenditures. Increases in tax receipts, induced by inflation, are not received immediately in the Treasury. Government expenditures often lag behind appropriations. In both legislative and administrative processes of inflation control, furthermore, there are "inside" lags delaying the application of whatever controls are decided upon and "outside" lags delaying their effectiveness. These public-sector lags are probably the principal exceptions to our generalization that long lags mean slow inflations and vice versa.

Escalation. Escalated increases in income are no different in principle from wage increases or farm prices negotiated directly. When escalated wage increases, for example, are no greater than warranted by the excess demand for labor, they can be considered on a par with wage increases on the open market. When wages are forced up by escalation, despite deficient demand for labor, the results are analogous to a cost push. In general, when escalated increases substitute for increases that would otherwise have been attained through other means, the institutional arrangements of escalation cannot be considered to have contributed to the inflationary process.

The impact of escalation will depend, in addition, upon the rate and frequency of adjustment as well as the percentage of population covered. If the total income-earning population were covered, with incomes escalated both immediately and proportionately to changes in a cost-of-living index, a crucial stabilizing lag would be eliminated from the system. Typically, these conditions are not met in full and the lag is preserved in part.

Statistical studies summarized by Franklyn D. Holzman (1964) suggest, surprisingly enough, that formal wage escalation has had no discernible influence on the speed of inflation in the United States, Great Britain, or Denmark. The results suggest that escalation in these countries has served primarily as a substitute for, rather than an addition to, other income increases and that its extent has been determined largely by market forces.

Consumer expectations. It is well known that expectations play a major role in accelerating inflation, once price increases are already rapid. Hyperinflations, in particular, are characterized by a so-called flight from cash, which Cagan explains statistically as a consequence of an index of expected price changes.

In less rapid inflations, however, the public seems willing to pay a high price for the convenience of holding its customary stock of cash balances. In the first place, people differ in their perceptions of past price trends, so that in creeping inflations not everyone realizes what has gone on. In the second place, recognition that prices have risen need not lead to anticipations of future increases. In the third place, even expectations of future increases do not necessarily lead to an acceleration of purchases. In the United States, high and rising prices in both 1951 and 1957 led to a drop, rather than a rise, in expenditures for a wide range of consumer durable items. Interview data suggest that this occurred because consumers resented the high level of prices and went on a buyers' strike. This attitude was more widespread than any incentive to "buy early and beat the price rise." And finally, increases in expenditures based on expected price increases are more likely to cause "once-and-for-all" increases in expenditures than are the continuous increases that accelerate inflation. As long as people are willing to hold cash balances at a sacrifice of real income, continuous inflationary shifts in demand from money to goods require an increasing certainty about the upward price trend or an increase in the supply of cash or credit, or (more usually) both, as in the hyperinflationary cases.

Redistributive effects of inflation

Inflation alters the distributions of both income and wealth, partly in a random and partly in a systematic manner. Prices of different goods and services, different productive resources, and different monetary assets, real assets, and liabilities are not equally flexible and respond differently to inflationary pressure. Furthermore, when inflation and deflation change the real value of cash balances, supply and demand functions for other goods and services change in different degrees, depending on their complementarities with cash balance holdings. Purely monetary assets and liabilities (cash, insurance policies, bonds) are completely inflexible unless escalated. Their nominal market values are independent of price level changes. Most monetary rent and interest incomes in America and western Europe are fixed contractually for long periods and so react slowly to price increases. In underdeveloped countries, on the other hand, rent and interest obligations *in kind* are favorite inflation hedges. The values of physical assets held for use, rather than sale, adjust more or less proportionately to the price level. Most other prices move with the price level but at different rates. The prices of durables tend to rise faster than the price of food; the wages of government workers and professionals usually lag behind those of industrial workers; and common stock and real estate prices usually overadjust to changes in commodity price levels. (For this reason, these assets are often used as inflation hedges, along with precious metals, jewelry, art objects, and stable foreign currencies, whose prices have also shown overadjusting tendencies.)

Assessment of the redistributive impact of inflation requires consideration of the relative impact on individuals and sectors of all these elements of inflation sensitivity. It is also difficult to separate the effects of general price movements on relative prices from the effects of other changes, including general economic growth.

In general, the differential impact of inflation on individuals and groups is a function of two factors: their ability to forecast the course of inflation and their ability to adjust their economic behavior to take account of what they foresee. If everyone had equal abilities along these lines, inflation and deflation would have little or no redistributive effects. There are, in fact, great differences on both accounts. These differences are responsible for the "inequities" of inflation. It should also be remembered, on the other hand, that the larger the number of people who anticipate price changes correctly and adjust to them promptly, the more rapid the changes are likely to be.

Two related hypotheses on the redistributive effects of inflation on income have been accepted for many years but have only recently been analyzed with care. The first of these hypotheses is that in inflation money wages lag behind prices, so that there is a shift away from wages and in favor of profits. The second hypothesis states that business firms gain through inflation at the expense of households and public bodies, and vice versa for deflation.

The wage-lag hypothesis has been argued in a number of historical studies. Earl J. Hamilton (1952) used it as an explanation of the financing of western European industrialization following the discovery of Mexican and Peruvian gold and silver deposits. Similiar studies cover the periods of the American Civil War and of the inflations that followed World War I. Their conclusions have, however, been challenged, particularly by Armen Alchian and Reuben Kessel (1959). These and other critics ascribe the orthodox results to an arbitrary choice of beginning and ending years and to other factors, such as population growth and migration to the cities, that would have presumably caused wage lags regardless of the course of general prices. Alchian and Kessel conclude their study by considering the United States after World War II, when labor organization had achieved substantial strength. They argue that, if the wage-lag hypothesis is valid, firms with large annual wage bills (relative to equity) would show proportionately higher profit increases. The opposite seems to have been in fact the case.

Several American studies have examined the changes in the functional distribution of income since 1945, in attempts to test the wage-lag hypothesis more aggregatively. With regard to wages and profits, the picture is mixed. Some periods, such as 1946 to 1948, apparently conform to the wage-lag hypothesis whereas others, such as 1949 to 1953 and 1955 to 1958, do not. Phelps (1961) has suggested that a demand inflation conforms to the hypothesis more closely than does a cost inflation. The studies of labor share, moreover, include both the effects of wage-rate changes and the effects of changes in factor proportions—as capital is (or is not) substituted for labor, as technical improvements occur, and as wage rates rise. It is, in any case, agreed that "active elements" (wages and profits) gain relatively to "passive elements" (interest and rent) whenever prices rise, and vice versa, so that the wage-lag controversy reduces to the question of *which* active elements gain most from the partial expropriation of the passive ones. Harold M. Levinson (1960) approached this by dividing the private economy of the United States into two sectors, one in which trade unions are strong (manufacturing, mining, transportation, and utilities) and one in which they are weak (commerce, finance, trade, services, and agriculture). His results indicate that the wage-lag hypothesis is confirmed in the "nonunion" group but not confirmed in the "union" one.

The other conclusion—that business, or the corporate sector, gains through inflation and loses through deflation—involves two assumptions. If it is true that wages lag behind prices, it would follow that corporate profits tend to rise during inflations. A more common assumption, associated with both Fisher and Keynes, asserts that business is a net debtor and gains during inflation by the opportunity to pay debts in cheaper money. A corollary is the proposition that banks, being particularly large debtors (with an unusually large ratio of debt to equity), should gain disproportionately in inflation. (This does not seem to be the case, perhaps because bank investments are concentrated in fixed money claims.)

The several studies by Alchian and Kessel confirm the Keynes–Fisher assertion of the importance of the debtor–creditor status in inflation. They take issue, however, with the assertion that business firms are net debtors. This assumption was true before World War I in the United States, but the Alchian–Kessel samples (1959) for the period after World War II found business firms distributed evenly between net debtors and net creditors. The stock prices of debtor companies rose by larger percentages than those of creditor companies, but even this aspect of conventional wisdom was questioned in another study, by G. L. Bach and Albert Ando (1957), covering the period 1939 to 1954. Bach and Ando found the debtor–creditor position often overbalanced by the effects of a number of other factors, most importantly the volume of sales.

Turning from income to *wealth*, Bach and Ando studied the redistributive effect of inflation in terms largely of the net *monetary* (fixed price) asset or liability positions of different population groups. The aggregative figures show that in the United States over the decade 1939 to 1949 the household sector became a large net creditor and the government sector a large net debtor. Unincorporated business, nonfinancial corporations, and financial corporations were all nearly neutral. More revealing was the percentage of net assets held in monetary form by income groups classified by income size. Except for the lowest income group, this percentage was approximately constant at from 13 per cent to 15 per cent of total assets. Calculations suggest that, as compared with personal income taxes particularly, losses on net monetary account from inflation are regressive.

The real locus of the burden of holding monetary assets in inflation is revealed by making similar calculations for different occupational and age groups. By far the highest concentration of monetary assets is found among the retired. High proportions are also indicated for professional and semiprofessional workers and for unskilled workers. Farm operators and managers, on the other hand, suffer only minimally. The high figure for retired people is emphasized by the age-group breakdown, which records a higher proportion of monetary assets in the oldest age group (55 years old and over) than in any other. Finally, renters tend to lose relatively to homeowners when prices are rising. Since most members of the lower income groups cannot afford their own homes, this aspect of the cost of inflation weighs most heavily upon them.

M. BRONFENBRENNER

[*See also* BUSINESS CYCLES.]

BIBLIOGRAPHY

ACKLEY, GARDNER 1961 *Macroeconomic Theory.* New York: Macmillan. → A useful textbook presentation of the problems of inflation and deflation. See especially Chapter 16, "The Theory of Inflation."

ALCHIAN, ARMEN A.; and KESSEL, REUBEN A. 1959 Redistribution of Wealth Through Inflation. *Science* 130:535–539. → A summary of the authors' several studies.

BACH, G. L.; and ANDO, ALBERT 1957 The Redistributional Effects of Inflation. *Review of Economics and Statistics* 39:1–13.

BALL, R. J. 1964 *Inflation and the Theory of Money.* Chicago: Aldine.

BIACABE, PIERRE 1962 *Analyses contemporaines de l'inflation.* Paris: Sirey. → A sympathetic presentation of structural and allied theories.

BRESCIANI-TURRONI, CONSTANTINO (1931) 1937 *The Economics of Inflation: A Study of Currency Depreciation in Post-war Germany.* London: Allen & Unwin. → First published as *Le vicende del marco tedesco.*

BRONFENBRENNER, MARTIN; and HOLZMAN, FRANKLYN D. 1963 Survey of Inflation Theory. *American Economic Review* 53:593–661. → A parallel discussion of many of the points in this article.

BROWN, ARTHUR J. 1955 *The Great Inflation: 1939–1951.* Oxford Univ. Press. → Contains theoretical as well as historical material.

CAGAN, PHILLIP 1956 The Monetary Dynamics of Hyperinflation. Pages 25–117 in Milton Friedman (editor), *Studies in the Quantity Theory of Money.* Univ. of Chicago Press.

CHANDLER, LESTER V. 1951 *Inflation in the United States: 1940–1948.* New York: Harper. → Contains theoretical as well as historical material.

CONFERENCE ON INFLATION, HELSINGØR, DENMARK, *1959* 1962 *Inflation: Proceedings of a Conference Held by the International Economic Association.* Edited by Douglas Hague. New York: St. Martins. → Valuable as a confrontation of rival theories.

DE PODWIN, HORACE J.; and SELDEN, RICHARD T. 1963 Business Pricing Policies and Inflation. *Journal of Political Economy* 71:116–127.

DERNBURG, THOMAS F.; and MCDOUGALL, DUNCAN M. (1960) 1963 *Macro-economics: The Measurement, Analysis, and Control of Aggregate Economic Activity.* 2d ed. New York: McGraw-Hill. → A good textbook presentation of the topic. See especially pages 203–218, "Fundamentals of Growth Economics."

FRIEDMAN, MILTON (editor) 1956 *Studies in the Quantity Theory of Money.* Univ. of Chicago Press. → See especially pages 5–21 on "The Quantity Theory of Money: A Restatement," by Milton Friedman.

FRIEDMAN, MILTON; and MEISELMAN, DAVID 1964 The Relative Stability of Monetary Velocity and the Investment Multiplier in the United States, 1897–1958. Pages 165–268 in *Stabilization Policies: A Series of Research Studies Prepared for the Commission on Money and Credit.* Englewood Cliffs, N.J.: Prentice-Hall.

HAMILTON, EARL J. 1952 Prices as a Factor in Business Growth: Prices and Progress. *Journal of Economic History* 12, no. 4:325–349.

HANSEN, BENT 1951 *A Study in the Theory of Inflation.* London: Allen & Unwin.

HARBERGER, ARNOLD C. 1963 The Dynamics of Inflation in Chile. Pages 219–250 in *Measurement in Economics: Studies in Mathematical Economics and Econometrics in Memory of Yehuda Grunfeld,* by Carl F. Christ et al. Stanford Univ. Press.

HOLZMAN, FRANKLYN D. 1950 Income Determination in Open Inflation. *Review of Economics and Statistics* 32:150–158.

HOLZMAN, FRANKLYN D. 1964 Escalation and Its Use to Mitigate the Inequities of Inflation. Pages 177–229 in *Inflation, Growth and Employment: A Series of Research Studies Prepared for the Commission on Money and Credit.* Englewood Cliffs, N.J.: Prentice-Hall.

KEYNES, JOHN M. 1940 *How to Pay for the War: A Radical Plan for the Chancellor of the Exchequer.* New York: Harcourt. → The standard presentation of income theory in relation to price level changes.

KOOPMANS, TJALLING 1942 The Dynamics of Inflation. *Review of Economics and Statistics* 24:53–65. → A comment by A. Smithies and a reply by Koopmans appear on pages 189–190.

LERNER, ABBA P. 1951 *Economics of Employment.* New York: McGraw-Hill. → See especially pages 191–241 on "Full Employment and Inflation."

LEVINSON, HAROLD M. 1954 Collective Bargaining and Income Distribution. *American Economic Review* 44, no. 2:308–316.

LEVINSON, HAROLD M. 1960 *Postwar Movement of Prices and Wages in Manufacturing Industries.* Supplementary Technical Material to the Staff Report, by George W. Bleile and Thomas A. Wilson. U.S. Congress, Joint Economic Committee, Study Paper No. 21. Washington: Government Printing Office. → Material prepared in connection with the study of employment, growth, and price levels.

MEANS, GARDINER C. 1962 *Pricing Power and the Public Interest.* New York: Harper.

NATIONAL BUREAU OF ECONOMIC RESEARCH, PRICE STATISTICS REVIEW COMMITTEE 1961 *The Price Statistics of the Federal Government: Review, Appraisal, and Recommendations.* Edited by George J. Stigler. New York: The Bureau.

PHELPS, EDMUND S. 1961 A Test for the Presence of Cost Inflation in the United States: 1955–1957. *Yale Economic Essays* 1:28–69.

PHILLIPS, A. W. 1958 The Relation Between Unemployment and the Rate of Change of Money Wage Rates in the United Kingdom: 1861–1957. *Economica* New Series 25:283–299. → Statistical test of compatibility between full employment and price level stability.

REDER, MELVIN W. 1948 The Theoretical Problems of a National Wage–Price Policy. *Canadian Journal of Economics and Political Science* 14:46–61.

ROTHBARD, MURRAY N. 1962 The Case for a 100 Per Cent Gold Dollar. Pages 94–136 in Leland B. Yeager (editor), *In Search of a Monetary Constitution.* Cambridge, Mass.: Harvard Univ. Press.

Schultze, Charles L. 1959 *Recent Inflation in the United States.* U.S. Congress, Joint Economic Committee, Study Paper No. 1. Washington: Government Printing Office. → Discusses cost theories.

Seers, Dudley 1962 A Theory of Inflation and Growth in Under-developed Economies Based on the Experience of Latin America. *Oxford Economic Papers* New Series 14, no. 2:173–195. → A sympathetic presentation of structural and allied theories.

Selden, Richard T. 1959 Cost-push Versus Demand-pull Inflation: 1955–1957. *Journal of Political Economy* 67:1–20. → A good empirical study.

Smithies, Arthur 1943 The Behavior of Money National Income Under Inflationary Conditions. *Quarterly Journal of Economics* 57:113–128.

Thorp, Willard L.; and Quandt, Richard E. 1959 *The New Inflation.* New York: McGraw-Hill. → Discusses cost theories.

Turvey, Ralph 1949 Period Analysis and Inflation. *Economica* New Series 16:218–227.

The Uneasy Triangle. 1952 *Economist* 164:322–323, 376–378, 434–435.

Warburton, Clark 1951 The Misplaced Emphasis in Contemporary Business-fluctuation theory. Pages 284–318 in American Economic Association, *Readings in Monetary Theory.* Homewood, Ill.: Irwin; Philadelphia: Blakiston.

Weintraub, Sidney 1959 *Forecasting the Price Level, Income Distribution, and Economic Growth.* Philadelphia: Chilton. → A college edition was published simultaneously as *A General Theory of Price Level, Output, Income Distribution, and Economic Growth.*

INFLUENCE

See Authority; Diffusion, *article on* interpersonal influence; Interest groups; Lobbying; Persuasion; Power; Propaganda; Public relations; Suggestion.

INFORMATION STORAGE AND RETRIEVAL

I
THE FIELD

The major determinants behind current information storage and retrieval efforts are the great volume of data pouring from our printing presses and our inability to locate much of it after it has appeared.

Responsibility for storage and retrieval of printed information has traditionally rested with the librarian. Early libraries concentrated on arranging books in some prescribed order on shelves. As the number of books increased, a complex organization became necessary in order to make the contents of a library collection more readily accessible. To provide such organization, librarians developed subject-classification schemes, the card catalogue, and other tools. These bibliographic devices now constitute the basic structure for control of library collections and are the fundamental finding aids that researchers employ.

Although conventional library tools today make location of a particular title among miles and miles of shelving a routine and simple task, they are not designed to provide more than a rough-cut approach to the subjects covered. For the users of general libraries this may be all that is needed, but when the same subject-classification techniques are applied to highly specialized collections of nonbook, technically detailed data, the imprecision of such methods of content retrieval becomes apparent. Because all knowledge and language are dynamic, constantly changing processes, any subject classification becomes obsolete almost from the moment of its creation. Furthermore, as one moves into increasingly specialized areas of knowledge, research becomes more complex. As new ideas generate new facts and new terminology, the task of organizing them and establishing their proper relationship to one another becomes ever more difficult.

An important distinction has been made between systems that locate documents and systems that produce information. Yehoshua Bar-Hillel has emphasized the difference between "literature searching" and "information retrieval," pointing out that the problems of storing and retrieving documents should be considered apart from problems concerning information. Literature searching, he contends, involves determining which documents or books are relevant to a chosen topic. Information retrieval is the act of obtaining answers to questions about a selected subject (1957).

Emphasis has thus been placed on finding new ways and means of codifying or indexing data so that they will lend themselves to correlation at time of searching. The trend has been to achieve greater depth of content analysis. Not only have new analytical methods been devised but investigations have also been made of the feasibility of employing electronic machines for analysis, storage, and retrieval of information. Because of the great mass of data involved, new storage and handling techniques may have to be invented; these techniques must be more advanced than those customarily used for manually shelving books and filing documents. The emergence of information storage and retrieval as a new field reflects an awareness among librarians and others that the selection and manipulation of fragments of information, rather than of entire documents, will require unconventional tools.

A critical need for more advanced information systems has evolved because of the steady growth of publishing and the complex ways in which information has come in recent years to pervade decision-making processes in business, science, and government. References to the effects of expanded publishing were made by Fremont Rider (1944) and Vannevar Bush (1945). Shortly thereafter, the implications of the "information explosion" in science and technology were discussed at the first international conference on the subject, held in London by the Royal Society (1948). At that time, it was already clear that the publishing rate in science and technology was increasing exponentially and that specialization in individual sciences and the development of interdisciplinary research were generating multiple uses for the same information. Although interest in information storage and retrieval thus received its start in the world of science, it soon spread to other areas, particularly business, industry, and government and, notably, to institutions like the U.S. Library of Congress (King 1963).

Another factor responsible for the independent development of the field of information storage and retrieval has been the impact of technology. Research and development in the computer sciences, the photographic industry, and signal communication promise to provide powerful new methods and techniques for information storage and retrieval. Modern data-processing equipment has already been successfully applied to the numerical areas of scientific computation and business operations. The prospect of being able to use computers to solve nonnumerical problems that involve natural language has been a major impetus encouraging the evolution of advanced information storage and retrieval techniques. The appearance in 1948 of Shannon's theoretical foundation for a general theory of information stimulated researchers to investigate the possibility of applying the principles of mathematics to the problems of information communication, by means of computers (Shannon & Weaver 1949).

The field of information storage and retrieval involves librarians, documentalists, mathematicians, system designers, linguists, equipment manufacturers, operations researchers, and computer programmers, among others. All are concerned with methods of expediting the prompt retrieval of information in such diverse areas as libraries, business and industry, military command and control, and scientific research. Because the field is interdisciplinary, considerable confusion regarding the boundaries of the effort has existed. A comprehensive bibliography covering the broad spectrum of interest appeared in 1958 (Bourne 1958–1962), and an introductory textbook on the subject was published in 1963 (Becker & Hayes 1963).

Classification of subjects in documents. Several specialists have devoted themselves to research into the problems of information organization. Among them is Mortimer Taube, who is identified with the concept of *coordinate indexing,* which provides a method of coordinating index terms as combinations rather than permutations. Taube called his index terms *uniterms,* and a coordinate index consists of a set of uniterm cards on which appear the identification numbers of the documents relevant to each uniterm. Searching is accomplished by selecting those uniterm cards pertinent to a request and correlating their document numbers. Matching numbers represent those documents for which the uniterms are simultaneously relevant (Taube et al. 1953–1957).

Calvin Mooers, one of the earliest proponents of coordinate indexing, proposed a concept of storing in one fixed place the codes for the subjects in a document, one code being *superimposed* on another. This technique is particularly applicable where coding space is at a premium, such as on edge-notched cards. Mooers also conducted extensive research into the mathematical structure of coding (Mooers 1951).

James W. Perry and Allen Kent have advanced the idea of the so-called *telegraphic abstract,* in which a *phrase* represents the logical unit of thought in a document, *subphrases* represent the individual words and concepts, and *role-indicators* describe the role that a particular word plays in the *phrase.* By using this method it is possible to describe a document in an artificial language or system that has more meaning than the sum of separately assigned subjects (Perry et al. 1956). *Faceted classification,* still another technique for organizing concepts expressed in documents, has been examined by S. R. Ranganathan and Brian C. Vickery (see Vickery 1958).

Computer analysis of natural language. A number of experiments have been conducted, and corresponding computer programs have been written, on the possibility of using computers to perform quasi-intellectual functions. Within the past few years, increasing emphasis has been placed on machine analysis of the syntax and semantics of natural language. This has led to the development of computer programs for such functions as language data-processing, machine translation, automatic indexing, automatic abstracting, concordance building, and text condensation. Still other computer programs have been written for the preparation of permuted title indexes as well as conventional printed indexes (Edmundson & Wyllys 1961). Several researchers have produced computer programs that embody sophisticated mathematical principles for searching natural language. Research work has explored ways of extracting meaning from a text by means of word association, syntactical analysis, and even contextual analysis. M. E. Maron and J. L. Kuhns have applied the calculus of probability to automatic indexing in an attempt to establish a theory of relevance (Maron & Kuhns 1960).

Converting text to machine readable form. The ability to convert original data automatically from the printed page to an input form usable by machines is fundamental if electronic computers are to be employed in work involving information. Until this becomes possible the use of computers cannot be considered economical. In the absence of automatic conversion equipment it is necessary either to type or keypunch the data over again. These processes are expensive, slow, and unreliable. For these reasons, efforts are continuing to produce *character-recognition* machines (Symposium . . . 1962). These are devices engineered to scan automatically the letters, words, and sentences of a text and to convert them directly into discrete digital representations.

The goal is to "read" rapidly large quantities of printed information, so that further processing of the data can be performed by a computer. Optical scanning and magnetic-ink reading are the two most common character recognition techniques in use. Thus far, only alphanumeric data in a prescribed type font are readable by machine. Research in auditory recognition is also under way to determine whether a machine can automatically discriminate phonetic sounds and, in so doing, produce a satisfactory digital code for input to a computer.

Compact storage of source material. Microfilm is, at present, the most effective means of storing original documents and of thereby controlling their volume. An impressive array of different cameras and a multiplicity of microfilm media are available commercially. Roll film, aperture cards, film in cartridges, microfiche, sheet film, and microcards are but a few of the examples of common microforms at present in use in information installations.

New dry processes have been introduced to overcome the disadvantages of wet chemical development, which is normally associated with the silver-halide film process. Diazo, for example, is a film which is exposed with ultraviolet light and developed in gaseous ammonia. Kalvar, another film, is exposed with ultraviolet light but is developed with heat at a temperature equivalent to that of a warm iron. The latest dry process is photochromics, which claims data-compression ratios of up to 400:1 with practically no loss of resolution. Photochromic film is exposed with ultraviolet light and can be erased, if necessary, with white light.

Printed material that is compressed into a microform calls for auxiliary equipment—inspection viewers, service viewers, and printing equipment for individual page copying. Equipment available on the market makes it possible to view any microform and to obtain a copy of an entire page or part of a page in seconds. Devices that fall into this category provide push-button copying, frame by frame, using manual, semiautomatic, or fully automatic auxiliary means.

Ever since Vannevar Bush proposed a Memex machine in 1945, much equipment has been designed to combine the dense-storage capability of film with the searching speed of electronics. The Rapid Selector, the first such device to be built, recorded frames of abstracts and corresponding digital codes on a 2,000-foot reel of 35-mm. film.

Following the Rapid Selector, other equipment appeared, such as Minicard, Media, Flip, Filesearch, Lodestar, Verac, and Walnut. Originally, each of these devices was designed to satisfy the needs of highly specialized information-system customers, but all of them represent technical progress toward combined use of electronic and photographic media for many purposes.

Minicard and Media are systems which store digital and graphic information on chips of film. Flip, Filesearch, and Lodestar, on the other hand, require the stored information to be contained in sequence on reels of film. Verac and Walnut are slightly different. The former uses a store of glass plates on which a matrix of images is recorded; the latter, strips of Diazo film for recording. Both, like all the others, have electronic-searching capabilities.

None of the techniques mentioned above was designed for book storage; in adapting them for this purpose, greatest attention has been focused on recording articles in technical journals or in special multipage reports. Since all these techniques are basically photographic, storage is not limited to the printed text alone, for all forms of graphic material can be stored by use of the same treatment (Becker & Hayes 1963, pp. 193–218).

Communication of information. No discussion of the technologies pertinent to the field of information storage and retrieval would be complete without consideration of the role of communication.

In the early 1950s, RCA conducted a demonstration of Ultrafax at the Library of Congress. A film copy of *Gone With the Wind* was sent over communication lines to a receiving point in a distant city. This facsimile transmission heralded the use of communication facilities for the transfer of visual data from one point to another. Video recording and transmission provide still another medium for sending graphic information over great distances.

Retrieval at a distance of digital and graphic information presupposes the availability of an interconnected communications network. On this assumption, research has been conducted to explore the relationship between man and machine in order to define more clearly the division of tasks between them. This in turn has led to further research of on-line systems, which establish direct communication between the man at an input–output console and the computer. The Massachusetts Institute of Technology has led the research effort to place at a user's fingertips the communications equipment needed to interrogate a large store of information under the control of a computer while numerous other users are simultaneously using it (Kessler 1965).

From the above review of machine research-and-development activities pertinent to the field of information storage and retrieval several desiderata emerge: to find automatic means of converting printed data to machine language; to achieve more compact storage of source material; to enhance intellectual access to information; and to display or provide information rapidly in a form suitable for individual use. Microphotography, the evolution of unconventional subject-classification systems, the application of computers, and the use of communications techniques, among other things, represent various stages in the historical development of information storage and retrieval.

JOSEPH BECKER

[*Other relevant material may be found in* CONTENT ANALYSIS *and* INFORMATION THEORY.]

BIBLIOGRAPHY

BAR-HILLEL, YEHOSHUA 1957 A Logician's Reaction to Recent Theorizing on Information Search Systems. *American Documentation* 8:103–122.

BECKER, JOSEPH 1964 Demonstrating Remote Retrieval by Computer at Library U.S.A. American Library Association, *Bulletin* 58:822–824.

BECKER, JOSEPH; and HAYES, ROBERT M. 1963 *Information Storage and Retrieval.* New York: Wiley.

BOURNE, CHARLES P. 1958–1962 *Bibliography on the Mechanization of Information Retrieval.* With supplements 1–4. Menlo Park, Calif.: Stanford Research Institute.

BUSH, VANNEVAR 1945 As We May Think. *Atlantic Monthly* 176, July: 101–108.

EDMUNDSON, H. P.; and WYLLYS, R. E. 1961 Automatic Abstracting and Indexing: Survey and Recommendations. Association for Computing Machinery, *Communications* 4, no. 5:226–234.

KESSLER, M. M. 1965 The MIT Technical Information Project. *Physics Today* 18, no. 3:28–36.

KING, GILBERT W. 1963 *Automation and the Library of Congress.* Washington: Government Printing Office.

MCMURTRIE, DOUGLAS C. (1927) 1943 *The Book: The Story of Printing and Bookmaking.* 7th ed. New York: Oxford Univ. Press. → First published as *The Golden Book.*

MARON, M. E.; and KUHNS, J. L. 1960 On Relevance, Probabilistic Indexing and Information Retrieval. *Journal of the Association for Computing Machinery,* 7, no. 3:216–244.

MOOERS, CALVIN N. 1951 Zatocoding Applied to Mechanical Organization of Knowledge. *American Documentation* 2, no. 1:20–32.

PERRY, JAMES W.; KENT, ALLEN; and BERRY, MADELINE M. 1956 *Machine Literature Searching.* New York: Interscience.

RIDER, FREMONT 1944 *The Scholar and the Future of the Research Library.* New York: Hadham.

ROYAL SOCIETY OF LONDON, SCIENTIFIC INFORMATION CONFERENCE 1948 *Report and Papers Submitted.* London: The Society.

SHANNON, CLAUDE E.; and WEAVER, WARREN (1949) 1959 *The Mathematical Theory of Communication.* Urbana: Univ. of Illinois. → The first paper is reprinted from the July and October 1948 issues of the *Bell System Technical Journal.*

SYMPOSIUM ON OPTICAL CHARACTER RECOGNITION, WASHINGTON, D.C. 1962 *Optical Character Recognition.* Edited by George L. Fischer et al. Washington: Spartan Books.

TAUBE, MORTIMER et al. 1953–1957 *Studies in Coordinate Indexing.* Vols. 1–4. Washington: Documentation Incorporated.

VICKERY, BRIAN C. (1958) 1959 *Classification and Indexing in Science.* 2d ed. London: Butterworth; New York: Academic Press.

II
INFORMATION SERVICES

Among the more important information services available to scientists have been abstracting services and data archives. In response to the developing information crisis in the social sciences, they are now being adapted to the special needs of these disciplines. Abstracting services prepare and distribute succinct synopses and summaries of the growing volume of publications and research activities, whereas archives acquire, process, and make available existing social science data.

Neither of these services has been fully able to accomplish the purposes for which it was established. This relative failure is partly due to the inadequate facilities available for solving an overwhelming challenge. It is also explained in part by the lack of concern with and knowledge about information problems, needs, and solutions in the social sciences. The dimensions of the information crisis are only now being isolated, and the tools for its resolution are still in an early stage of development. This article will outline the scope of the information crisis in the social sciences, the range of responses designed to resolve the crisis, the contributions and limitations of abstracting and archive services, and the relation of the operations and concerns of these services to broader theoretical developments in the social sciences.

The information crisis

The contemporary information crisis in the social sciences has several salient features that create special difficulties for the social science information services. First, with the increase in the size and heterogeneity of the social science community, opposing demands are often placed on information services. For example, some scholars value brief, descriptive reviews of a wide range of published articles, whereas others prefer longer, evaluative analyses of a limited range of current publications. Second, with the growth of social science research and writing, it is becoming extremely difficult to locate and report on developments and materials relevant to the social sciences. The expansion of the social sciences around the world, together with the extensive amount of classified research conducted by governments and other groups, further adds to this difficulty. Third, research in the social sciences is perhaps more erratic in quality than that in other sciences. As a consequence, a great volume of irrelevant and harmful materials clogs the social science communication channels, consuming valuable resources and detracting from the cumulative development of the field.

Considerable attention has been given to the consequences of the information crisis, both upon individual scientists and upon science viewed as a system (Menzel 1964). Individual scholars find it increasingly difficult, if not impossible, to keep abreast of new concepts, methods, theories, and findings, even in their narrow field of specialization, let alone in adjacent, relevant fields. This difficulty does not refer solely to the scholar's lack of time to read all the relevant literature or to his inability to remember what is relevant in what he reads. It also refers to the absence of information facilities that are capable of locating, organizing, and retrieving the relevant material.

This maldistribution of information manifests itself in costly duplication of research efforts and in a failure to build upon prior scientific work. In an exploratory study of bibliographic needs of economists, psychologists, and anthropologists, approximately 60 per cent of each discipline reported that "they sometimes or often have failed to learn in time about some relevant prior work that would have made a difference in their research or teaching" (Appel & Gurr 1964). Clearly, the expansion of information is creating a major crisis for the future development of science. Unless new methods are perfected to help locate and preserve available information, it will be extremely difficult to maintain the cumulative effect of research. Abstracting services and data archives are only two of many methods that have been developed to retrieve, process, and distribute information in a more rational and effective manner.

Responses to the information crisis

Efforts to cope with the information challenge can be described from three different perspectives: first, overarching, multifaceted programs that focus on the entire information system; second, specific devices such as abstracting services and archives developed to meet particular needs; and third, issues and problems related to the organization and performance of specific kinds of information services.

National information programs. An increasing number of countries are formulating national information policies involving a wide range of specific programs designed to rationalize the nation's scientific information system. There are a number of motivations behind these developments, not the least of which relate to national security interests. For example, the United States government, especially the military sector, is a major source of research and development funds for many scientific disciplines. In order to plan and manage their programs, these sponsors need information as to who is engaged in what problems, how great the scope of the effort is, who is supporting the work, what additional work is being planned, what the time schedule is, etc. However, "resources information" is only one element in planning scientific programs. In addition, the scientists engaged in the work also need information programs.

A major milestone in the American government's development of a national information policy occurred with the passage of the National Defense Education Act of 1958, an act empowering the National Science Foundation to establish a science information center that would support and encourage work related to indexing, abstracting, translating, and the development of mechanized systems for retrieving, storing, and disseminating information. A number of government and private groups have made their own studies of the information crisis, and these contributed to the creation in 1958 of the National Federation of Science Abstracting and Indexing Services, a group fostering greater cooperation and coordination between its members; these efforts also contributed, partly through the encouragement of the National Science Foundation, to the creation in 1964 of the National Council of Social Science Data Archives, a cooperative venture encouraging the coordination and development of the activities of its members (Mitchell 1964). These various developments have also helped to make individual scholarly associations more conscious of their own information problems. For example, the American Psychological Association has conducted a series of studies on a wide range of information problems experienced in that field.

These American programs have major implications for social science communication in other countries, because the American services are increasing their coverage of information produced in other countries, because the American scientific output looms so large in the over-all international perspective, and because the information services in many countries are relatively weak or do not exist.

However, many countries have especially strong information programs in the physical, natural, and medical sciences, as well as in technology. Most noteworthy is the All-Union Institute of Scientific and Technical Information (Vsesoyuznyi Institut Nauchnoi i Tekhnecheskoi Informatsii, usually abbreviated VINITI), originally created by the Soviet Union's Academy of Sciences in 1952; a somewhat comparable group exists in Poland; both Uruguay and Argentina, as well as the state of São Paulo in Brazil, have established research councils that perform various information functions; and through the encouragement of the American government, research and information services have been established by several other countries, including Turkey and Thailand.

International information programs have also been initiated. Of special significance to the social sciences are the activities of the United Nations Educational, Scientific and Cultural Organization (UNESCO), the International Committee for Social Sciences Documentation, and the International Social Science Council. These groups encourage coordinated, international efforts in standardizing information procedures and in exchanging information; they also produce various abstracts, indexes, and bibliographies.

Range of specific information services. The varied nature of the information crisis suggests the need for a wide range of information services. Furthermore, no single service is fully capable of meeting all the needs for which its genre of services is designed. For example, an abstracting service will probably not be able to facilitate casual "browsing" and also provide the detailed information that some scholars may need. However, recent developments in mechanized information-storage-and-retrieval techniques are likely to increase the variety and quality of services that any information facility will be able to offer.

There are several ways to categorize information services—by the techniques they use; by the way they are organized and financed; by their subject-matter specialization. For present purposes they will be arbitrarily classified according to the quality and (for lack of a better word) completeness of the information they provide. At one extreme are various services that simply help locate references to larger bodies of information, which may or may not have the relevant information a scholar requests. Midway are services that help locate information and also provide a capsule description of the information; some services also evaluate the materials. At the other extreme are services that locate, evaluate, and provide the information in a form the user requests.

Bibliographies, indexes, directories, and library card catalogues are examples of services that typically present limited information; they help the user locate materials that might be relevant to his interests. These services differ in the completeness and organization of their files. Some attempt to refer to all publications relevant to a particular topic (such as the annual bibliographical issue of the *Journal of Asian Studies*); others refer only to published books, thereby excluding the large volume of periodical literature. Some organize their information by broad subject topics; others alphabetize by authors, topics, or key words. Relatively few give any detailed information about the contents of an article, although library catalogue cards typically provide some information about chapter or section headings. These simple locator devices are perhaps most helpful to users interested in very broad topics. Primary consideration in evaluating such services would include the completeness of listings, the general categories used in organizing the files, and the degree to which the lists of titles accurately indicate the content of the materials.

Information services that provide more than locator references but less than a complete copy of the entire information, fully evaluated, can be classified according to whether they emphasize descriptions or evaluations. Annotated bibliographies, abstracts, and clearing houses tend to emphasize the descriptive dimensions. Abstracts will be discussed in greater detail later in this article. Annotated bibliographies often present less information than abstracts do, and several of the more useful ones have tended to focus on fairly specific topics, such as juvenile delinquency or the relationships between education and national development (e.g., Stanford Research Institute's *Human Resources and Economic Growth*). Several clearing houses have been established to assist scholars. These facilities—such as the Science Information Exchange of the Smithsonian Institution—provide, on request, copies of abstracts reporting on research related to the kinds of information desired. The primary concern is helping the user to contact sources and people who might be able to provide him with more complete answers to his questions.

Other information services go beyond mere description; they attempt to place current publications in some larger context, and they attempt to evaluate in various ways the quality and contribution of current scholarly output. Annual reviews, encyclopedias, guides to literature, textbooks, and state-of-the-art reviews (such as *Sociology Today,* edited by Robert K. Merton, Leonard Broom, and Leonard S. Cottrell, Jr., and *Anthropology Today*, edited by A. L. Kroeber) represent attempts to place current research in some larger perspectives; the present encyclopedia, for example, is a major effort to take stock of social science developments over the last three decades at the conceptual, methodological, and theoretical level.

Although these evaluation services perform invaluable functions, they have well-known limitations. For example, they typically review only books, not articles. (Some abstracts, such as those in *The American Behavioral Scientist,* cover both. Some publications, such as *Current Sociology*, combine an evaluative state-of-the-art review with an appended annotated bibliography.) Book reviews do not cover as many books as abstracts cover; they do not give equal treatment to all parts of the book; they are subject to the biases of the reviewer; and reasons of space tend to limit the review to a relatively few, cursory comments. Some social science publications attempt to emphasize quality and thoroughness of their reviews by inviting rather extensive analytical reviews of selected publications; "regular-length" reviews receive smaller space, and "book-notice" reviews are given only a few paragraphs.

Information services of the final category to be mentioned are those that not only evaluate materials but also provide all the information the user might need. In some instances this evaluation results in discarding poor-quality and outmoded materials; in other instances the service provides all available information but also evaluates its strengths, weaknesses, possibilities, and limitations. Specialized libraries, data archives, and information centers are major examples of these kinds of services, although none is a perfect example. These services are becoming increasingly important.

Abstracting services

Most of the general issues relevant to the activities of any information service have already been mentioned. Four of these will serve as focuses for the following brief discussion of abstracting services: coverage, currency, quality of the abstract, and organization of the abstracting services' files or cataloguing systems. In addition, several evolving trends and likely developments will be discussed. Technical and administrative aspects of abstract operations, however, will not be considered.

Coverage. The rapid expansion in the volume of social science research, in combination with the spread of the social sciences into more and more countries, continually increases the burden of the overtaxed abstracting services. Several comparative statistics suggest that none of the social science abstracting services is likely to reach the scope of operations currently found in some of the physical and natural sciences. In the social sciences, *Sociological Abstracts* in 1964 published 3,114 abstracts from about 115 journals, published in approximately twenty countries and in eleven languages. American and other English-language journals are by far the most important sources abstracted. *Psychological Abstracts* in 1964 published 10,500 abstracts from about 450 journals, published in approximately a dozen languages and in two dozen countries. On the other hand, *Chemical Abstracts* published approximately 165,000 abstracts in 1962. It abstracted materials from some 8,000 journals, in more than fifty languages, from approximately 85 countries. In 1960, the Russian abstracting service VINITI was processing approximately 15,000 periodicals, published in 65 different countries. One of the largest American abstracting services in this same year had a staff of 500 and an annual budget of $5 million.

By these standards the total output of all social science abstracting services is relatively small. The country coverage of most services is rather limited and, usually, only includes several of the major producers. Coverage is least in eastern Europe and in some of the developing countries—areas where the social sciences themselves are least developed, where there are relatively few social scientists, and where the language problem is an obstacle to abstracting services.

Since some of the new periodicals being established in the developing countries (e.g., *America latina*) append summaries in one or more Western languages, geographical coverage in the social sciences may become less of a problem in the future. Problems of geographical coverage are also being handled by the establishment of regional social science documentation centers. For example, UNESCO has established such a center in Rio de Janeiro, Brazil, and one in New Delhi, India. (The latter, however, is scheduled to terminate its existence before 1970.) The creation and strengthening of abstracting services in individual developing countries will also serve to facilitate efforts of scholars to locate relevant materials from other countries.

Even the best social science abstracting services tend to focus almost exclusively on major periodicals. Their coverage is limited, leaving out the growing number of fugitive documents, government reports, reprints, master's theses, doctoral dissertations, and conference papers. This situation is likely to improve as abstracting services coordinate their efforts more closely and publish abstracts prepared by other services and as there are technological advances in computer-produced abstracts.

If these developments rapidly increase the volume of published abstracts, other technical innovations, now in the developmental stage, will probably be adopted. For example, new kinds of abstracting publications—such as science newspapers—will be produced, and new mechanical document-switching centers, similar to the Defense Documentation Center of the American government, will be created to send out abstracts or documents on request.

Currency. Time is another dimension of coverage. That is, coverage decreases with an increase in the interval between the appearance of an article and the appearance of its abstract. Since the financial and human resources of abstracting services rarely keep pace with the growth of scientific literature, the currency problem is likely to become more serious. It is already a serious problem in some fields. For example, a study of the information situation among psychologists discovered that articles in psychological journals were based on work initiated, on the average, between 30 and 36 months prior to publication. It takes approximately another 15 months before the article is abstracted in *Psychological Abstracts*. Between the initiation of a research project and final abstracting of the article, the project directors report on their work at professional meetings, various drafts or preprints are distributed to a select audience, and about nine months pass between the submission of an article to a journal and its eventual publication. Similar delays occur in other fields. For example, articles submitted to some Russian scientific journals in 1952 were not published until 1955. In today's rapidly developing scientific world such time lags can be very costly. A number of scholars may be working on problems already solved and spending funds that could be better used to advance, rather than to replicate, scientific findings.

Two developments are likely to help reduce the time-lag problem. First, there are a number of information services that report on research in progress. In the United States, clearing houses such as the State Department's Office of External Research, together with the Smithsonian Institution's Science Information Exchange, perform this function. Annual reports of foundations, as well as directories of current research, also provide information on research in progress. The second development—automated, or computer-produced, abstracts—has yet to be perfected, although various groups have been working on this technique. Since many abstracting services rely on authors of articles to provide their own abstracts, and since this procedure helps to retard the publication of abstracts, any program that reduces the abstract's reliance on authors would help to solve the currency problem.

Quality. Social science abstracting services face peculiar problems in insuring the completeness, accuracy, and general quality of their abstract entries. For one thing, it is generally recognized that a relatively high proportion of social science writings have serious defects: data are questionable, samples are limited, methods are inadequate, findings are trite, and conclusions are not well supported. Such literature may not be worth abstracting; furthermore, to treat it seriously is likely to be a disservice to the future development of a scientific discipline. In short, the quality problem refers in large part to the general quality of social science work, and the eventual solution to this problem will depend in large part on the greater selectivity of journals and publishers, as well as on the general maturing of the social sciences.

The quality problem is one reason evaluative reviews and state-of-the-art summaries are so valuable to some scholars. However, abstracting services have to consider the variety of needs scholars have, and therefore they cannot afford to be too selective. Some users may value "browsability" more than depth and critical judgment, exhaustiveness more than selectivity, hard facts more than syntheses, and methods more than concepts. These contradictory demands on information services have contributed to a growth in research concerning the kinds of information needs scientists have. (It is generally recognized that the needs of science as a system may not coincide with the felt needs of individual scientists; the individual may limit his concern to his own narrow specialization, whereas the development of science may depend on the blending of developments from two or more specialties.)

Quite aside from the quality of research publications and the kinds of abstracts needed, there is the separate issue of the quality and accuracy of the abstract itself. Since a high proportion of the abstracts are prepared by the authors of the abstracted article, the problem of quality is related to the general problem of the quality of social science work. It is very likely that experiments will be conducted to compare the usefulness of abstracts prepared by authors with that of abstracts prepared by professional abstractors and, eventually, by computers.

Organization of the files. A major purpose of abstracts is to help scholars locate materials they might want to investigate in greater detail. To serve this purpose, the abstract must briefly and accurately cover the relevant portions of the larger manuscript. Furthermore, the abstract journal must be indexed so that the user can locate all the relevant materials quickly, with the assurance that he is not missing anything because of the searching procedure forced on him by the abstract's index or filing system. Also, the abstract's filing system must avoid providing the user with too much information: that is, it should ideally provide him only with materials directly pertinent to his initiating question. (If he is only browsing, this may be an irrelevant consideration.) The organization of an abstract's filing or cataloguing system is an important determinant of how much the abstract can contribute to the advancement of a science.

Implied in the last statement is an assumption that abstracts are used only for research related to the advancement of science; but, of course, they are used for teaching and other purposes as well. Even researchers will differ in the demands they make of an abstract, so a catalogue system suitable to one group of scholars may be useless and annoying to another. Some abstract users are interested primarily in very general topics, such as legislative systems; others are seeking information about research methods; others wish to see how a single concept has been used in various contexts; still others will be primarily interested in specific variables or in empirical relationships between specified kinds of variables. Not only are the initiating concerns different, but so are the complexities of the request. For example, a cataloguing system will be organized one way if most of its requests are for general topics and another way if most of its requests refer to information on multivariate relations between such items as liquidity preference, religiousness, and political involvement.

Social science abstracting journals tend to be organized around traditional subject-matter topics rather than around variables, concepts, and findings. Even the topics tend to be gross in content. For example, in 1964 *Sociological Abstracts* organized its materials into approximately fifty categories, including "public opinion," "political sociology," and "sociology of the family." On the other hand, *Psychological Abstracts* has more than three times this number of categories, and it publishes a very detailed and extensive supplementary subject index.

Most of the shortcomings mentioned above can be attributed to a lack of resources available to abstracting services and to the precomputer creation of their organizing principles. With the maturing of the social sciences, the recognition of new methods of organizing materials, and the pressure from an accumulating mass of literature, a new view of abstracting problems and services is slowly appearing. Studies of information needs will help determine the most appropriate organization of a catalogue; the development of natural language systems for storing, organizing, and retrieving information may change the perspective on cataloguing systems (Gardin 1965; Scheuch & Stone 1964); and the success of computerized information services, such as the Defense Documentation Center, may alter the concept of what services an information center can provide.

Emergent trends. Reference has already been made to several developments that have the possibility of profoundly improving the information services that to this time abstracts have provided. The extent and speed of these improvements will depend on financial considerations, the development of a national information policy, the future course of the social sciences, and the progress other scientific fields make in solving their information problems. Many of these developments cannot be clearly seen, because information specialists are only now discovering the potentialities provided by modern computer technology. Computer-produced translations can expand the amount of materials that can be considered for abstracting; computer-produced abstracts can increase the number of abstracts that can be prepared, and they can also reduce the lag between publication and abstract; by means of "interest profiles"—a list of words indicating a person's interests—computers can facilitate a more aggressive dissemination of information; and by means of computer-based systems for information storage and retrieval, abstracts can be more than document-switching services; they can become invaluable research tools.

The last point deserves special mention, since it may involve a radical departure in traditional conceptions of abstracting services. At the present time abstracts are considered devices to alert scholars to materials they might wish to explore more fully. However, exploratory work in developing systems for information storage and retrieval in social science data archives indicates that such systems can be used to retrieve and organize specific kinds of information, such as "findings" on the relationship between family structure and educational achievement. Therefore, rather than merely providing references to existing information, abstracting services could develop into facilities that actually create new information. That is, they can serve as sources of data.

Information banks will be of primary interest to those who are seeking results of studies rather than to those who are concerned more with the methods by which the information was collected and analyzed. In the physical sciences and in engineering, specialized "mission-oriented" groups have been created to service requests for data, results, methods, and analytical procedures. In the United States, groups such as the Defense Metals Information Center and the Thermophysical Properties Research Center are prepared to winnow out irrelevant and poorly performed research; they provide state-of-the-art summaries, information on the latest findings and techniques, and references to who is doing what in the field. These and other similar groups provide specific, evaluated answers to questions, not just information on whom to see or what to read in order to answer the question.

There are indications that these same kinds of information centers will develop within the social sciences. For example, in 1964 Michigan State University began to create a diffusion documents center, a facility designed to provide bibliographic references, existing data, and other information related to the adoption of various new farming and other techniques and practices. Also, the Special Operations Research Office of the American University has created CINFAC, a service that responds to requests for information, materials, and analyses of the human factors involved in insurgency and counterinsurgency situations in specific geographical areas. There are also a variety of local and national centers that have a heavy applied or policy orientation, being concerned with intergroup relations, community planning, and various economic matters.

Data archives

Whereas abstracting services report on published literature and research in progress, social science data archives acquire, store, process, and distribute basic social science data produced by various research and administrative groups. These data, primarily materials that are in a form for machine processing, together with their accompanying study designs, code books, research reports, etc., are used by researchers for purposes of secondary analysis and by teachers for purposes of training. ("Secondary analysis" refers to the use of materials for purposes unrelated to those for which they were originally collected.)

Such secondary materials have played a key role in the development of the social sciences, although the contribution differs in accordance with the attention different disciplines give to quantitative social research and with the standards of evidence and inference upheld in the various fields. At one extreme, economics and demography have been heavily quantitative in orientation. While there are certainly major exceptions, in large part the materials used in these fields result from the normal bookkeeping operations of various government and private administrative operations. At the other extreme, anthropology has been largely a descriptive discipline, concerned primarily with "qualitative" materials, or, more properly, information collected by observation of one sort or another. Sociology and, more recently, political science fall between these two poles. In the past, pathbreakers such as Quetelet, Durkheim, and Sorokin based some of their most significant research on existing published statistical data, whereas more recently, beginning in large part with the *American Soldier* volumes, there has been an increasing research interest in working with the punched cards produced by research projects that have terminated their activities.

With the advent of modern data-processing equipment, social scientists are able to utilize new techniques on new bodies of data. This in turn has contributed to new concepts, theories, and methodologies and to demands for still more data. The change in research orientation can be seen in the history of the concern with existing materials, especially with public-opinion data. Recognizing the significance of these materials very early, *Public Opinion Quarterly* began in July 1938 to publish the poll results released by the American Institute of Public Opinion; the American and overseas coverage of releases was increased until 1951, when this regular feature was discontinued. However, it was reinstituted some ten years later. In the meantime, the *International Journal of Opinion and Attitude Research*, published from 1947 to 1951, ran a major feature called "World Opinion." Between 1943 and 1948 the National Opinion Research Center published eleven issues of *Opinion News*, which included releases from polling groups in the United States, as well as other countries. In 1951 Cantril and Strunk compiled their book *Public Opinion 1935–1946*, which included opinion-poll materials from sixteen countries. In 1960 Cole and Nakanishi edited *Japanese Polls With Socio–Political Significance, 1947–1957*, and comparable volumes of German, Swedish, and Italian materials have been published. In 1965 the Steinmetz Institute of Amsterdam assumed the editorial responsibilities for *Polls*, an international journal reporting the research results obtained by about seventy organizations from more than twenty countries.

With the further development of survey methodology, research interests, and data-processing equipment, scholars became increasingly aware of the limitations of these published volumes of research findings. Only a small portion of all the findings and materials was reported; and the materials that did appear in print were at most simple marginal distributions, although two-variable tabulations were sometimes given. In no sense were these materials being adequately exploited. Since large quantities of the basic materials were being destroyed, it appeared that these invaluable research resources would be lost forever.

Although public-minded commercial research agencies, both in America and in Germany, had expressed an early interest in having their materials preserved and made available to scholars, it was not until 1955 that steps were taken to provide an over-all solution to the problem of archiving these data. In 1957 York Lucci and Stein Rokkan reported on their two-year investigation of archive prospects in the United States and Europe. Among other suggestions, the authors proposed the creation in the United States of a central national archive containing survey materials collected from around the world. It was felt that the level of research practices and sophistication among Europeans required that the creation of European archives be accompanied by training programs in the use of survey materials, as well as methodological studies of problems involved in the use of such data. Prior to 1957 individual university research centers maintained archive operations for their own materials, making them available primarily to graduate students for their dissertations. After 1957 a number of specialized archives were created. Although a study in the United States in 1963 discovered that there were, on the average, three or four archives per state (Ferguson & Lazarsfeld 1964), most of these were repositories of materials that were not made readily available to the academic community. But by 1965 approximately fifteen university archives were in existence or in the process of being created in the United States. Other archives were being created in Norway, Finland, the Netherlands, France, England, Germany, and Argentina. This proliferation in turn led to the creation in 1964 of the Council of Social Science Data Archives, an American group, and to the beginnings of an international coordinating network.

Most of these archives were created in response to the research needs of local faculties. Because of this, the archives differ considerably in their scope of concerns, the services they offer, and the data they collect. Some archives have focused primarily on one kind of data—survey materials or aggregative statistics. (The Yale Political Data Program is concerned with national aggregative statistics; an archive at Indiana University is concerned with the more qualitative aspects of nation-states.) Some are concerned with particular regions of the world. (The International Data Library and Reference Service of the Survey Research Center of the University of California at Berkeley specializes in materials from the developing nations; Steinmetz Stichting, a University of Amsterdam archive, focuses on materials from the Netherlands; and the Zentralarchive für Empirische Sozialforschung at the University of Cologne is devoted primarily to German materials.) Others are concerned with materials pertaining to limited substantive research interests. (The Inter-university Consortium for Political Research, an American group with offices at the University of Michigan, focuses primarily on politically relevant American materials.) Still others are primarily concerned with materials provided by particular kinds of data suppliers. (The Roper Public Opinion Research Center has relied primarily on commercial polling agencies for the materials it distributes.)

In the course of their development, archives have found it necessary to prepare their materials for machine processing, sometimes to evaluate them, and increasingly, to store information that will help to locate the materials which users request.

Archives in the beginning were concerned almost exclusively with sample survey data, since these included the attitudinal materials of central concern to many of the social sciences. Such materials are being produced at an extremely rapid rate. Information presented at the Second Conference on Data Archives in the Social Sciences indicated that more than two thousand surveys, representing approximately two million interviews, were conducted in Britain from 1963 to 1964. Between four and five thousand surveys were conducted in continental Europe in 1963. An estimated fifteen hundred of these studies could be made available in one form or another to scholars for purposes of secondary analysis. The American production of survey materials is even greater; and since survey research methods are being adopted in almost all the developing countries, a truly vast sea of materials is potentially available for research purposes. Add to these materials all the court decisions, police department records, manpower-and-income data, social security records, educational statistics, and the quantities of materials produced by the "knowledge industry" around the world, and it seems that scholars have a wealth of data to work with if these data can be made readily and inexpensively available.

In addition to survey-research materials, other kinds of materials have also been collected in the archives. For example, the aggregative or ecological materials organized by the Yale Political Data Program include averages, events, rates, percentages, measures of dispersion or variance, traditions, developmental patterns, and the like. Information is collected on daily newspaper circulation, cinema attendance, extent of urbanization, military expenditures, election results, immigration, the distribution of agricultural land, and many more variables. The quantitative data, which typically refer to a defined geographical or administrative unit, are reported in raw numbers, as well as in rank orders.

Along somewhat different lines, ethnographic materials from a large sample of world societies have been collected and organized by the Human Relations Area Files into an elaborate classification scheme (Yale University 1938). Although these materials, unlike the others that have been mentioned, are not in a machine-manipulative form, there have been pilot projects designed to facilitate their use by means of computers. In the early 1960s attention was also given to machine manipulation of other kinds of quantitative data, including Rorschach tests and materials on the relationship between culture and personality.

Two major arguments—one referring to economic efficiency and the other to theoretical significance—have been used to justify the creation of these various data services. From the economic perspective it has been noted that collecting primary data entails considerable costs; large field staffs are needed; competences that many scholars do not have are required; and a full-time commitment on the part of the scholar is necessary. The cost, personnel, competence, and time obstacles prevent scholars from pursuing their research interests. Balanced against these obstacles is the existence of vast quantities of already collected materials on a wide variety of topics from many different countries. These materials, which can be obtained for only a fraction of their original costs, have typically never been analyzed or reported in depth.

For example, the International Data Library and Reference Service of the Survey Research Center of the University of California at Berkeley describes its data as referring to political attitudes and behavior, attitudes toward foreign nations and international relations, patterns of stratification and mobility, family structure and family planning, personal and public ethics, religious beliefs and practices, standards of living, material needs and economic outlook, and many other topics of interest to social scientists. Its materials have been used in studies of political attitudes and behavior in Latin America, North America, Europe, and Asia; of anti-Semitism in Europe and America; of religion and politics in the United States and France; of social class and voting in Great Britain, Australia, Canada, and the United States; of student politics in Asia, Africa, and Latin America, etc. In many instances the same questions are asked in the same country at different periods, permitting trend analysis, or in several different countries, permitting cross-cultural, international comparisons.

The major theoretical significance of the files lies in the increasing use of existing materials for purposes of secondary analysis and for student training. This has not occurred without methodological criticisms and research difficulties. However, the very availability of such data has encouraged scholars to develop and systematize the logic underlying secondary analysis. Some of the university-based archives, especially those concerned with data collected outside the United States and data that are to be used for purposes of international comparative analysis, have taken an active concern with evaluating the materials they acquire and with specifying the various substantive and methodological limits to which their data could be used.

In part the evaluation issue arises because archives use different standards in deciding what materials to acquire. Some archives accept whatever their suppliers offer them; others feel that quality is more important than sheer inclusiveness. In fact, some scholars argue that inclusiveness of coverage, in the sense referred to in the discussion of abstracting services, can be detrimental to the social sciences, for it is necessary to exclude materials that are trivial, insignificant, and of poor quality. Poor data may be worse than no data at all, and good data are preferable to poor data.

Until such time as archives establish standards for determining what is substantively relevant and methodologically adequate, archives will contain large volumes of relatively unimportant, low-use data. Some groups have argued that archives would probably perform a greater service than they do now if they concentrated more of their resources on obtaining, evaluating, and servicing a smaller body of materials.

Evaluation and methodological issues raised with regard to survey materials collected by social science data archives have equal relevance to the collection and use of primary materials. Therefore, the research and methodological efforts encouraged by the development of archives benefit a wide range of social science research concerns. By the very fact of raising these issues, a general distinction can be drawn between the two topics discussed in this review—abstracting services and social science data archives. On the one hand, abstracting services facilitate the research and teaching efforts of scholars by providing them with descriptive information on what scholars have done and are doing. On the other hand, while sharing many of the same organizational problems encountered by abstracting services, social science data archives provide more than information on what has been done: they actually provide the basic raw materials used by other researchers. Because they are concerned with data rather than with information only, they must often concern themselves with an entirely different range of issues, namely, how these materials can be used, what their limitations are, and what contributions they might make to the development of a social science based on firm empirical foundations.

ROBERT E. MITCHELL

BIBLIOGRAPHY

APPEL, JOHN S.; and GURR, TED 1964 Bibliographic Needs of Social and Behavioral Scientists: Report on a Pilot Survey. *American Behavioral Scientist* 7, no. 10:51–54.

BANKS, ARTHUR S.; and TEXTOR, ROBERT B. 1963 *A Cross-polity Survey.* Cambridge, Mass.: M.I.T. Press.

BISCO, RALPH L. 1966 Social Science Data Archives: A Review of Developments. *American Political Science Review* 60, no. 1:93–109.

BORKO, HAROLD; and DOYLE, LAUREN B. 1964 The Changing Horizon of Information Storage and Retrieval. *American Behavioral Scientist* 7, no. 10:3–8.

Data in Comparative Research. 1964 *International Social Science Journal* 16:7–97. → Consists of nine articles.

FERGUSON, JACK; and LAZARSFELD, PAUL F. 1964 Social Science Information Services: Progress Report on a Survey. *American Behavioral Scientist* 7, no. 10:20–22.

GARDIN, JEAN C. 1965 *SYNTOL.* Rutgers Series on Systems for the Intellectual Organization of Information, Vol. 2. New Brunswick, N.J.: Rutgers Univ., Graduate School of Library Service.

HYMAN, HERBERT H. 1955 *Survey Design and Analysis: Principles, Cases, and Procedures.* Glencoe, Ill.: Free Press.

LUCCI, YORK; and ROKKAN, STEIN 1957 A Library Center of Survey Research Data. Unpublished manuscript, Columbia Univ., School of Library Service.

MACHLUP, FRITZ 1962 *The Production and Distribution of Knowledge in the United States.* Princeton Univ. Press.

MENZEL, HERBERT 1964 The Information Needs of Current Scientific Research. *Library Quarterly* 34:4–19.

MITCHELL, ROBERT E. 1964 Discussion Draft of Proposals for an Inter-university Social Science Data Archive Network. Unpublished manuscript, Univ. of California, Survey Research Center.

MITCHELL, ROBERT E. 1965*a* A Social Science Data Archive for Asia, Africa and Latin America. International Social Science Council, *Social Sciences Information* 4, no. 3:85–103.

MITCHELL, ROBERT E. 1965*b* Survey Materials Collected in the Developing Countries: Sampling, Measurement, and Interviewing Obstacles to Intra- and Inter-national Comparisons. *International Social Science Journal* 17, no. 4:665–685.

POOL, ITHIEL DE SOLA; and ABELSON, ROBERT P. 1961 The Simulmatics Project. *Public Opinion Quarterly* 25:167–183.

ROKKAN, STEIN 1963 International Conference on the Use of Quantitative Political, Social and Cultural Data in Cross-national Comparisons. International Social Science Council, *Social Sciences Information* 2, no. 4: 89–103.

ROKKAN, STEIN 1964 Introduction: The Use of Sample Surveys in Comparative Research. *International Social Science Journal* 16:7–18.

RUSSETT, BRUCE et al. 1964 *World Handbook of Political and Social Indicators.* New Haven: Yale Univ. Press.

SCHEUCH, ERWIN K.; and STONE, PHILIP J. 1964 The General Inquirer Approach to an International Retrieval System for Survey Archives. *American Behavioral Scientist* 7, no. 10:23–28.

U.S. CONGRESS, HOUSE, COMMITTEE ON EDUCATION AND LABOR 1963 *National Information Center: Hearings Before the Ad Hoc Subcommittee on a National Re-*

search Data Processing and Information Retrieval Center. 2 vols. Washington: Government Printing Office.

U.S. NATIONAL REFERRAL CENTER FOR SCIENCE AND TECHNOLOGY 1965 *A Directory of Information Resources in the United States: Social Sciences.* Washington: The Center.

YALE UNIVERSITY, INSTITUTE OF HUMAN RELATIONS (1938) 1961 *Outline of Cultural Materials.* 4th ed., rev. New Haven: Human Relations Area Files.

III
LIBRARIES

The library has been from its beginnings, as they are known to us, a social instrument, the constantly revised invention of men working together in an organized society. The clay tablets of Ashurbanipal's royal library at Nineveh, the papyrus rolls at Alexandria, the parchment and vellum codices at Pergamum, were all brought together, organized, and preserved because these societies needed recorded information for the maintenance of the state, the preservation and communication of religious belief, the transaction of commerce, the education of youth, the bequeathing of the culture to subsequent generations.

It is undoubtedly true that a society stagnates unless it makes constant provision for the injection and absorption of new knowledge. A society is a duality of action and thought, bound together by a communication system that itself is a duality of mechanism and message—that which is transmitted, as well as the manner of its transmission. In a given society or culture in which language is the medium and the graphic record one of the instrumentalities, libraries of every kind constitute a network within the total communication system, a subsystem whose effectiveness depends upon the librarian's understanding of the nature of knowledge and its importance to both the individual and society. The library can be socially effective only if its operations derive from and are harmonized with an understanding of the ways in which knowledge is generated and flows through the communication channels of a constantly evolving social and intellectual organization; and it is this changing social structure that in large measure determines how knowledge is translated into action.

The librarian's professional resources must include an understanding of the processes of intellectual differentiation and the interrelationships of knowledge within a complex social organization. He must recognize not only that intellectual forces shape social structures but also that cultures and their symbol systems shape thought; for example, such concepts as freedom and democracy are both culturally and linguistically delimited. Since libraries are agencies for the diffusion of cultural products, the theory and practice of librarianship must be founded upon what I call *social epistemology*—the study of social knowledge, the means whereby society as a whole achieves a perceptive relation to its total environment, the totality of the stimuli that act upon a society, nation, or culture, with specific reference to the production, flow, integration, and consumption of all forms of communicated thought through the entire social fabric. Social epistemology is of particular importance to the librarian, because he stands at the point where recorded knowledge and social action meet and his concern is with what Kenneth Boulding has called the *transcript* (whether written or not) of the culture and the impact of that transcript upon—again to borrow Boulding's term—the *image*, that which man believes to be true, which largely determines and directs his individual and group behavior.

Every society or culture produces a transcript of its collective thought, a record in more or less permanent form that can be passed from person to person and generation to generation and can thus, at least in a limited way, transcend both space and time. In primitive, nonliterate societies, this transcript usually takes the form of verbally communicated ritual, ceremony, myth, legend, song, even law. The transmission of the store of common knowledge, information, and belief becomes one of the principal concerns of the group, exerts upon it a cohesive force, affects and may even dominate the thinking and actions of individuals, and can become a powerful brake upon innovation and change. The invention of written communication marked the beginning of a substantial degree of dissociation of communicator from receptor. It expanded the potential audience for the communicated message by transcending the bounds of human memory, made possible a virtually unlimited accumulation of knowledge by a society or a culture, and gave rise to the need for a social agency to preserve the written record. As the art of writing increased the intellectual resources of the individual by bringing to him the thought and experiences of people whom he had never seen, so the accumulation and organization of written records in libraries expanded the intellectual resources of societies. Thus, the epistemological pattern became increasingly linear and cumulative as the communication system, of which libraries constitute a subsystem, grew in carrying capacity and absorptive (or storage) power. Not only could individuals build upon the experience of other individuals, but societies, also, could profit from the experience of other societies. These capabilities were immeasurably extended by the invention of printing with movable type, and among the consequences of this invention was a social revolution that eventually made possible the concept of libraries for all the people.

The structure and communication of knowledge form an open system, which changes as the functions and needs of the individual and society shift. But the library is more than a link in the communication chain; as an operational system it is part of the total knowledge process—or of the knowledge situation at any given point in time. The knowledge process itself is a unity of *subject*, *vehicle*, and *object*. The subject is the self, the perceiver in the act of awareness (the library user); the vehicle is the instrumentality or mechanism through which the subject approaches the object (the library's bibliographical apparatus); and the object is the ultimate goal or referent, knowledge itself (obtained from the library's store).

There is no direct relationship between any collectivity and its cultural manifestations. Since the objective of the librarian should be to maximize the social utility of graphic records, his bibliographic and information systems must be structured to conform as closely as possible to the patterns of man's use of those records and the transmission of knowledge within society. His procedures and techniques, which for centuries have been derived from *ad hoc* assumptions, modified by trial and error, about man's need for and use of recorded knowledge, must be examined within the context of the cognitive and communication processes in society. The librarian dare not assume that his tools and methods for the control of his collections reflect permanent or even relatively permanent relationships between user and printed word. He must be prepared constantly to revise the configuration of the classification schemes, subject-heading lists, indexes, and other devices at his command for the efficient management of his bibliographic store, to reconcile them with the changing demands of his society.

The communication process in contemporary society has become increasingly complicated by the growth of specialization. The present structure of education, as well as society's system of economic rewards, tends to direct students of the highest intellectual promise into graduate study and professional schools. Such "educational hybridism" (as Whitehead has characterized it) has resulted in unprecedented progress in certain areas but has also tended to break down generalized communication and understanding among specialists and with the public. Only recently has the academic world begun to recognize the validity of an interdisciplinary approach to education and the social importance of interdisciplinary communication. Even more recently the librarian has increased his appreciation of the fact that he can play a significant social role as a mediator between specialists if he will prepare himself to be a comprehensivist, or highly educated generalist, and develop for librarianship a discipline, analogous to Buckminster Fuller's "comprehensive-design science," based on a general-systems theory applied to the organization and use of bibliographic materials.

Like any other social institution, the library, through the centuries, has responded to social needs, and alterations and modifications in its morphology have taken place under the impact of social change. Librarians in ancient Alexandria were scholars who worked in seclusion over the manuscripts in their custody. The monastic libraries of the Middle Ages were presided over by recluses who devoted their lives to the production and preservation of religious writings. With the dawn of the age of science and the coming of the Enlightenment, the library became the focal point for man's inquiry into the physical and social phenomena of his environment. The rise of universal elementary education in the United States during the first half of the nineteenth century prepared the way for the public library, which Horace Mann saw as "the crowning glory of our public schools." The industrial and technological revolution in society has been reflected, during the present century, in the growth of "special" libraries to serve a wide variety of managerial and research needs.

Between 1930 and 1945, two influences threatened to change completely the intellectual, social, and professional orientation of American librarianship. The first was the coming of the great depression. Not only were library budgets sharply curtailed, but the use of libraries—particularly public libraries—assumed new patterns. People turned to the free libraries for nonrecreational and cultural materials to improve their educational qualifications and skills, in the hope of achieving economic security. It was in direct response to such demands that the American Library Association began publishing its "Reading With a Purpose" series. It was no accident that at this time Alvin Johnson described the public library as "the people's university."

The second major influence changing the character of American librarianship was World War II, during which—for the first time—information was discovered to be an important strategic weapon. In feeding the insatiable appetite for military intelligence of a nation engaged in a struggle for survival, librarians found themselves very much in the midst of the world of action and were recognized by that world as providing services that were significantly more than a cultural adornment. Never before had librarians been called upon to help fight a war in a capacity other than that of citizen soldier, and the demands that were made of them demonstrated to the profession and the public alike the crucial importance to the national economy of the ready availability of recorded knowledge.

Concurrently with this demand for rapid access to precise and accurate information came the technological revolution of automation. An enormous increase in research activity was forcing upon business, industry, and government a new appreciation for the value of information in almost every area of human activity. But existing channels for the dissemination of recorded knowledge were no longer adequate to the burden that was being placed upon them, and the use of computers, with their ability to manipulate large masses of data at high rates of speed, seemed to promise an escape from the growing morass of print. In due course the very capabilities of the machines had a direct effect upon both professional and lay thought concerning the library's role in society, and the dramatic flight of the first Sputnik gave a new impetus to the librarian's participation in the affairs of science. Scientists, as well as humanists, found a place in librarianship, and to the technical jargon of the profession was added a whole new vocabulary derived from electronics, communications, systems engineering, and information theory; e.g., *noise*, *malfunction*, *programming*, *on-line*, *mathematical model*, *lattice*, *PERT*. Furthermore, the librarians' ranks are being invaded by engineers, data processors, and systems designers, who have brought into the field a new terminology for established library concepts; for instance, reference work has become *information retrieval* or *information transfer;* subject headings, *descriptors;* collections of library materials, the *store;* the library, an *information center;* and the librarian himself, an *information specialist.*

To this invasion of their once comfortable domain, and to the threat of technological unemployment, librarians are reacting as did the palace scribes, the Luddites, the locomotive firemen, and any number of other challenged groups. Some are ignoring the invaders as being either inconsequential or irrelevant to the librarian's responsibilities and sphere of activity. Others are combative and argue vigorously that the new technology is not appropriate to library operations. Some deny the existence of the crisis, while others seek a common bond of understanding, in the hope of enriching librarianship with whatever values the innovations possess. Whatever the ultimate resolution of this conflict, it should provide an interesting case study of the dynamics of a profession confronted by the necessity for drastic change.

But distressing as the present disorientation of the profession is to its members, the ultimate values may be great. Because of the emerging "science of information," librarianship is, for the first time in its long history, being compelled to formulate self-consciously its role in society, to examine critically its intellectual foundations, and to view itself holistically, as an integrated system that serves man, both as an individual and as a member of society, throughout his life. Despite the obvious relationship of librarianship to its coeval culture, the library has been recognized as a sociological entity only within the last half century. The rise of the public library in the United States coincided with important new developments in sociological theory, and the beginnings of a search for status encouraged all lines of inquiry that might help to establish the librarian's claim to being "professional."

During the 1920s a group of distinguished social scientists at the University of Chicago created an environment for the study of all aspects of the science of society. Perhaps as a result, when the Graduate Library School was established there its faculty included a number of scholars trained in disciplines other than librarianship, who brought to bear upon library theory the new tools and techniques of sociological research. Douglas Waples began to explore the social effects of reading and the impact of the public library upon mass social behavior. Louis Round Wilson, dean of the school during the 1930s, focused his attention upon what he called "the geography of reading," by which he meant the effects of sociogeographical factors upon the library as a social instrumentality; his work was strongly influenced by studies in cultural regionalism and the work of Howard Odum, Lloyd V. Ballard, and President Hoover's Committee on Recent Social Trends. Carleton B. Joeckel (1935) prepared his classic study of the relation of the public library to local and state government. Pierce Butler (1933) wrote the prolegomena to an incipient library *science*, which sought to harmonize the humanistic and scientific foundations of librarianship, and encouraged his students to pursue inquiries into intellectual history (which he called the history of scholarship) and its relation to the library. From this one school, in a period of scarcely a decade, came a small band of unusually articulate disciples, who gradually assumed positions of professional influence and carried the social philosophy of their teachers to the rest of the world.

Western society is so heavily dependent upon the printed word that in a very real sense it can be characterized as a paper culture; projecting past and present library demands into an unpredictable future, librarians are directing their educated judgment toward increasing their professional capacity for efficient service. The small, the large, and the highly specialized libraries are all being affected by the changing information requirements of society, and the institutional pattern of library service is being reshaped. Plans are being laid for the establishment of information networks that will link the resources of many libraries in a variety of fields, and the time is certainly not far distant when the unique resources of any library in the country will be available on immediate call and at minimal cost to any individual who may have a need for them. There is a trend toward the creation of larger units of service, through formal cooperation between political entities too small to support independent libraries. Throughout the library profession there is developing a steadily increasing concern with the improvement of both the economic and the program efficiency of libraries, as analyzed and measured by the methods of social science. In a number of urban centers public libraries are turning to city planning, community analysis, and other techniques of municipal government and public administration for guidance in the allocation and utilization of their resources, especially with reference to the structuring of branch systems and other facilities for the extension of library service to meet changing economic, social, and population patterns of city and suburban life. The public librarian is improving his skill in working effectively with other educational and social agencies in his service area, and for the first time he is being called upon to participate in large-scale community programs for nonreaders, the functionally illiterate, the undereducated, the culturally deprived. In recent decades, and especially within the past few years, the public library has broadened and strengthened its role in the thinking and decision making of the community. In no way do these "auxiliary" functions diminish the library's independence, initiative, or social prestige.

Programs for the professional education of the librarian have reflected changes in educational philosophy as well as in the theory of librarianship. Originally, apprentice training of the most elementary kind was followed by formal public-library training classes, which slowly gave way at the turn of the century to undergraduate programs in a few colleges and technical schools. C. C. Williamson's influential report on library education (1923), prepared at the request of the Carnegie Corporation of New York, encouraged the development of graduate programs, and the Graduate Library School, established in 1926 at the University of Chicago, offered the first doctoral degree. Today all of the library schools accredited by the American Library Association award master's degrees, and some half dozen have programs leading to the doctorate; several require study in a cognate subject area for the doctorate. A sound general education with a good undergraduate major in a subject field is essential to the librarian, and he should pursue his subject specialty as far as his resources permit. No longer must he come to his profession by way of the humanities; today his province is the whole spectrum of human knowledge.

JESSE H. SHERA

BIBLIOGRAPHY

BERELSON, BERNARD 1949 *The Library's Public.* New York: Columbia Univ. Press.

BORDEN, ARNOLD K. 1931 The Sociological Beginnings of the Library Movement in America. *Library Quarterly* 1:278–282.

BOULDING, KENNETH E. 1956 *The Image: Knowledge in Life and Society.* Ann Arbor: Univ. of Michigan Press.

BUTLER, PIERCE 1933 *An Introduction to Library Science.* Univ. of Chicago Press.

EGAN, MARGARET E. 1955 The Library and Social Structure. *Library Quarterly* 25:15–22.

HARBISON, FREDERICK; and MYERS, CHARLES A. 1964 *Education, Manpower, and Economic Growth.* New York: McGraw-Hill.

JOECKEL, CARLETON B. 1935 *The Government of the American Public Library.* Univ. of Chicago Press.

MACHLUP, FRITZ 1962 *The Production and Distribution of Knowledge in the United States.* Princeton Univ. Press.

MARTIN, LOWELL A. 1937 The American Public Library as a Social Institution. *Library Quarterly* 7:546–563.

SHERA, JESSE H. (1949) 1965 *Foundations of the Public Library.* Hamden, Conn.: Shoe String Press.

SHERA, JESSE H. 1965*a* Emergence of a New Institutional Structure for the Dissemination of Specialized Information. Pages 34–50 in Jesse H. Shera, *Libraries and the Organization of Knowledge.* London: Lockwood.

SHERA, JESSE H. 1965*b* The Library as an Agency of Social Communication. *Journal of Documentation* 21: 241–243.

SHERA, JESSE H. 1965*c* Social Epistemology, General Semantics, and Librarianship. Pages 12–17 in Jesse H. Shera, *Libraries and the Organization of Knowledge.* London: Lockwood.

SHERA, JESSE H. 1966 *Documentation and the Organization of Knowledge.* Hamden, Conn.: Shoe String Press.

WAPLES, DOUGLAS; BERELSON, BERNARD; and BRADSHAW, FRANKLYN R. 1940 *What Reading Does to People.* Univ. of Chicago Press.

WILLIAMSON, CHARLES C. 1923 *Training for Library Service.* New York: Carnegie Corporation.

WILSON, LOUIS R. 1938 *The Geography of Reading: A Study of the Distribution and Status of Libraries in the United States.* Univ. of Chicago Press.

WOOD, LEDGER (1940) 1941 *The Analysis of Knowledge.* Princeton Univ. Press.

IV
REFERENCE MATERIALS AND BOOKS

The development of social scientific thought is often based on information available in libraries. Marx did not do field research; he relied upon the factory reports available to all users of the British Museum. Frederick J. Turner's thesis presented in *The Frontier in American History* rested on the published reports of United States censuses of population. The Brandeis Brief, the celebrated sociological argument made in the U.S. Supreme Court in 1908, was written chiefly from European government reports located in the Astor Library. The 1965 report by Daniel Moynihan, *The Negro Family,* published by the U.S. Department of Labor, exploits population data from the United States census. Like these famous studies, much journeyman social science rests on facts drawn from reference books. "Even the craggiest, most stonily factual reference book, when a little mellowed by time, becomes a quarry from which some perceptive scholar can extract handsome building materials, as John Stuart Mill did from the venerable *Annual Register,* and James Ford Rhodes from the *Tribune Almanac*" (Nevins 1958, pp. 7–8).

Social science materials may be presented in many forms, depending on the editorial purpose they subserve and the type of publication. Encyclopedias, dictionaries, and atlases, general and specialized, represent three classic types of reference books of fundamental importance. Reference materials proliferate and necessitate reference books galore: periodicals lead to periodical indexes and to abstracts; court reports to citators and to digests; statutes to legal codes; decades of census publications to a single-volume abstract; books to card catalogues, national library catalogues, and bibliographies; bibliographies to bibliographies on bibliographies! The establishment of archives has led to a need for guides to them and to their contents. The development of libraries has brought interlibrary loans and the publication of reference books like library directories and union lists of serials. The publication of manuscripts on microfilm and reproduction through methods like xerography have done away with distinctions like that between primary and secondary sources. The electronic computer, working directly from data on magnetic tape, permits researchers to omit printed statistical reference books such as census reports. Taking account of these magnificent changes in the storage and communication of information, this article will stress the major traits of reference materials and reference books encountered by social scientists.

The importance of reference works to social science has scarcely been matched by scholarly inquiry into this subject. Critical reviews and notes are rarely found in professional journals. Perhaps more notice is given reference works in the book reviews and quarterlies of general circulation. The attention won by reference works has simply not yet grown to be a subject in itself in any of the disciplines. As a result, the appraisals of reference books are fugitive pieces, fragments lacking theme or tradition. This article draws on these fragments to summarize the traits shown by reference materials and books in the social sciences.

When a social scientist assesses the nature and quality of reference works, he inescapably sees them as subjective parts of the discipline that they appear to serve with objectivity. The data of reference volumes are collected by editors with social predilections and published under auspices, whether commercial or governmental, with political preferences. Taken with the foibles men are prone to, these tendencies contribute to the production and dissemination of reference works containing errors of fact and slanting interpretations that are seldom signaled.

The librarians have generally played a neutral role in regard to reference materials. Speaking of the bibliographic and indexing services, a leading librarian has declared that "except in a few exceptional instances, the library and the library world exercise practically no control over the conditions which affect the compilation and publication of this apparatus" (Clapp 1964, p. 83).

Dependence on librarians who are not themselves social scientists has wrought rather arid definitions of reference books, like the following:

> From the point of view of use, books may be divided into two groups: those which are meant to be read through for either information or enjoyment, and those which are meant to be consulted or referred to for some definite piece of information. Books of this second class are called reference books, and are usually comprehensive in scope, condensed in treatment

and arranged on some special plan to facilitate the ready and accurate finding of information. This special arrangement may be alphabetic, as in the case of most dictionaries or encyclopedias; chronological, as in historical outlines and similar compends; tabular, as in the case of statistical abstracts; regional, as in atlases; classified or systematic, as in the case of some bibliographies, technical handbooks, etc. (Mudge as quoted in Winchell 1951, p. xvi)

Libraries themselves have changed so drastically since the 1930s, in making whole collections readily available to users, that earlier distinctions between types of books have been blurred. Social scientists, like today's scholars in the humanities and the physical sciences, seldom take the necessary classifications in a library collection as boundaries to their work. In the diverting and instructive book *The Modern Researcher*, Barzun and Graff (1957, p. 74) group reference books into nine types: encyclopedias, biographical dictionaries, indexes to periodicals, dictionaries of quotations and concordances, atlases, chronologies, language dictionaries, handbooks and source books, and bibliographies. Jack Alden Clarke's useful short guide, *Research Materials in the Social Sciences* (1959, p. 3), includes only titles of interest to students of two or more of the social sciences. An impressive review article by Kister (1966), in covering a grand variety of sources, praises *Sources of Information in the Social Sciences* (White et al. 1964) as "indispensable."

Most commentators see three great divisions among the materials in a modern library: (1) reference materials which are the undigested records of institutions and individuals; (2) reference books which are the collated and organized summaries of knowledge ordinarily presented as objective summaries; and (3) interpretive books, general or monographic, clearly standing for man's effort to describe, explain, and interpret social phenomena. In the present article, we are especially interested in the first two kinds of publications.

Reference materials

Government publications. Reference materials include government serials like *Hansard's Parliamentary Debates* and the newspapers, journals, and reports issued commercially. These materials standing alone are often largely unindexed, and so reference books have been created either to digest this raw data or to provide a key to unlock the information contained there. The need for keys to the vast storehouse of accumulating reference materials has resulted in ever more reference books. The voluminous judicial and administrative reports of rulings in the United States have led to the creation of commercially published digests and topical reporters to pinpoint the important for lawyers and students of law. These reference books are almost entirely products of the twentieth century (Price & Bitner 1953).

The publication and dissemination of reference materials by governments—local, regional, national, and international—is a remarkable development in the whole conception of government, which has, at the same time, amply fed the thirst for knowledge about society. In England there was a long battle over the right of government to keep its proceedings secret, and, at first, reporting of debates of Parliament was controlled. Both initiative and courage were needed in the development of a commercial system of publishing the proceedings of Parliament. This pattern has been followed in most democratic nations: legislative reports, the orders of administrative agencies, and the decisions of courts were kept so private by government that private printers, and later large commercial publishers, grasped the opportunity to sell the available information to the public. In democratic countries a claim of the public's right to know coincided with the development of bureaucracies that were willing and able to offer the same information through government printing facilities. Thus, in the United States the Government Printing Office was formed in 1862. It took over the publication of reports of Supreme Court cases from private hands in 1872 and also the debates of the national legislature with the initiation of the *Congressional Record* in the same year (Schmeckebier & Eastin [1936] 1961, p. 124). In England, the publication of *Hansard's Parliamentary Debates* was assumed by Her Majesty's Stationery Office in 1909 (see Wilding & Laundy 1958, p. 258).

Government publications have mushroomed. The *Monthly Catalog of United States Government Publications* lists some 25,000 items annually, compared with about 17,000 commercially published titles in the United States each year. Practically the whole list of government titles falls into the category of reference materials, a smaller number are reference books and periodicals, and just a few are interpretive monographs.

Government reference materials are sold at cost plus 50 per cent, but with only direct-mail advertising and displays in antiseptic government bookstores or offices. The designation of established libraries as depositories for government publications has made these materials easily available to a wide audience (in the United States there are some 550 depository libraries, only 125 of which are full depositories; see Murphey 1958, pp. 184–188). This idea has been adopted in most countries and by the United Nations as well.

The chief distortion in government publications arises from their being political documents. Remarks made in floor debate may be altered after utterance but before publication in the *Congressional Record* (Mantel 1959). Years pass before diplomatic papers of most nations are published, and to this time lag may be added the possibility of deletions and distortions in the text. Government publications often serve the regime, the ideology, the men in command. Social scientists in a specialized field ordinarily possess considerable awareness of existing distortions, but the fact that such distortions exist is hardly made obvious by these publications. Nor are governmental publications, in contrast with similar materials published commercially, regularly subjected to critical review. This may be explained in part by the fact that government publications are shunted to one side as reference materials and hence are not reviewable, or by the fact that these publications are never advertised in the reviewing media or in scholarly journals.

Historical editing. Whitehead once cautioned against taking "the official documents of an epoch at their full value" by omitting reflection on "the emotional atmosphere which activated its people and the general ideas under whose sway they lived" (Whitehead as quoted in Cappon 1966, p. 56). Since World War II this challenge has largely been met, in an era of "comprehensive editing," by the historical editor who is "a knowledgeable scholar concerned with the meaning of the sources at his command" (Cappon 1966, p. 75). Historical editing in the United States has existed only since the 1890s, but in this time standards have been broadened and raised. Current editorial projects include the publication of the papers of Jefferson, Calhoun, Franklin, Clay, Adams, Hamilton, and Madison, begun between 1944 and 1956 and expected to total 289 volumes when complete. Professional editing today rests on this rationale: "The historical editor of source materials is a historian whose responsibility consists, first, in transmitting authentic and accurate texts of all extant documents within a rational frame of reference, with due respect for archival principles, and, second, in making these texts more intelligible" (*ibid.*, p. 57). Archivists editing current public papers of the presidents of the United States follow similar canons (Reid 1962, p. 438).

Contemporary historical editing, because of its scale and scope (not because of the internal editorial standards used), has been condemned as the documentary, objective, professional, organized, or official *style* in the academic study of the American past (Marx 1961, p. 48). The whole field of historical editing is "a remarkable program and, as Emerson would say, a sign of the times—affluent, conservative, and nationalistic times" (*ibid.*). Some critics of the field argue that so much energy, foundation support, and praise for documentation is making historical editing an end in itself rather than leading scholars to use "these splendid volumes" to create "a richer, and by that I mean a more imaginatively relevant, historical literature" (*ibid.*, p. 51). Although it is true that intellectual resources may thus be misapplied, on the other hand, the condemnation of a concern for accuracy as a tragic expression of pop culture is simply fearful exaggeration (see Macdonald 1952).

Social scientists often enough perform both the feat of documentation and that of interpretation. For example, at the University of Wisconsin after the turn of the century, John R. Commons and his associates first collected and edited, in ten volumes, *A Documentary History of American Industrial Society*, published in 1910 and 1911, and then wrote a four-volume *History of Labour in the United States*, published from 1918 to 1935. Other monographs spun off from this body of work, including Perlman's *A Theory of the Labor Movement*, which appeared in 1928. It took 25 years to complete this entire body of work.

Newspapers, magazines, and journals. As reference materials, newspapers, magazines, and journals constitute a major resource for social scientists. Beginners approach these sources with such innocence that some critical word is appropriate. The newspaper, as a record of unfolding events, is rife with defects. One critic, summarizing Liebling (1961), has questioned, in terms of general semantics, the reliability of the modern newspaper: "Newspapers like to think they print 'all' the 'news' in an 'objective' way. Actually, of course, they merely abstract a few events out of the current scene and make news stories describing these happenings. The decision as to which events to abstract is the heart of the criticism of newspapers" (Wanderer 1963, p. 491). The abundant criticism of newspapers and magazines of general circulation has been absorbed by the intellectual community, and students are alerted to handle these materials with care.

This is known to be as true of great newspapers of record like *The Times* of London and the *New*

York Times as of the tabloid press (on the latter, see Friedrich 1959, p. 467). The *New York Times* has become a frequent target of criticism in recent years. The charges include inaccurate reporting of the collectivization of agriculture in the Soviet Union in the 1930s (Muggeridge 1961, p. 87), failure to perceive abiding changes in French politics in the 1950s (Kempton 1961, p. 91), and inadequate coverage of European economic and political events in the 1930s (Lichtheim 1965). A sweeping criticism of American newspapers in general and the *New York Times* in particular stressed the amateur quality of its news gathering and news reporting methods—"the American press as an institution is comparable to the medical schools of fifty years ago" (Kristol 1967, p. 52). Attacks like these and the many defenses of the *New York Times* as being an extraordinary journalistic achievement (see Manchester 1959) would fill a book.

Indexes. The *Index to the Times* (London) and the *New York Times Index* are significant reference books which are exclusive keys to the relevant reference materials of the respective newspaper files. They are perhaps the contemporary reference works most heavily used by students of social, economic, and political developments. Typically, though, newspapers and their indexes have rarely been scrutinized by social scientists for accuracy, completeness, and quality of interpretation. Most needed is a call for verification of editorial generalization on many social science subjects. Still, the newspapers of record with indexes remain important combinations of reference materials and reference works.

If indexes to newspapers reflect limitations in the contents they key, the available periodical indexes and abstracts in libraries have strengths and weaknesses of their own. There is no master index to the vast periodical literature in, and of relevance to, social science. Most disciplines have, since World War II, developed separate indexes and abstracts through their respective national and international associations. However, the number of periodicals published in the world far outreaches the number to be found in general indexes to this material. Thus, a leading commercial publisher of periodical indexes has succinctly shown "that there is a 'vanishing point' beyond which it is neither practical or feasible to have published indexing at today's high cost, and that there are literally thousands of specialized periodicals which are so sparsely held by libraries that the few holding libraries could not support published indexing of them" (Haycraft 1962, p. 129). Haycraft reported that in 1960 the New York Public Library maintained subscriptions to 25,568 periodicals. The Wilson periodical indexes covered a total of about 1,250 periodicals; other indexes and abstracts covered at most about 3,000 periodicals. He concluded that "of 25,568 periodicals received, more than 22,000 are *not* indexed in any published index and probably never will be" (*ibid.*, p. 129). As crucially important reference books, then, the periodical indexes are blunt instruments for identifying a vast range of periodical articles. Within a discipline the articles of the leading national and regional association journals and the more specialized reviews are ordinarily well indexed. But in the larger world, where the disciplines intersect with each other and with periodicals of other sorts, the nature of existing reference materials is highly unsatisfactory. This is the conclusion reached by one expert: "The variations from one bibliographic service to another—in scope, coverage, arrangement, periodicity, format, etc.—are so great that they create a confusing welter rather than a perspicuous guide to published information" (Clapp 1964, p. 84).

Reference books

Reference books are, in a sense, codifications of the larger world of knowledge—especially that contained in reference materials in libraries. It is extraordinarily difficult to condense knowledge and organize and publish it in the seemingly objective forms presented by reference books.

A touchstone is needed to judge the achievements of reference books. In addition to certain specialized requirements, a number of scholarly standards come into play. Editorial whimsicality should be low; explicit assumptions, a clearly stated range of coverage, and a strong awareness of measures of inclusion and exclusion are needed. A fairly selected, apt title should be sought, although it is difficult to achieve. Classification and indexing in a reference book must be intrinsically wise and connected with traditional practices in a given field of knowledge, if these two goals can be reconciled. The information should be consistent in its completeness. If it is not, the work should be representative of a larger range of facts. Consistent usage, especially in serials, and the continuity of data presented in tabular form are also valued.

Encyclopedias. The encyclopedia is the reference book as code of knowledge, par excellence. Standing above the touchstone of scholarly standards named here is one giant obstacle to the development of an entirely satisfactory encyclopedia. This is the editorial difficulty of resolving the inevitable conflicts of values concerning a range of topics. Questions where nationalism, ideology, race, and religion arise have always posed almost insuperable difficulties for encyclopedia makers.

For example, early editions of the *Encyclopaedia Britannica*, expressing the intellectual traditions of Edinburgh, drew strong criticism for their independent analysis of various religions, particularly Roman Catholicism and Christian Science (Einbinder 1964, p. 66). Recent editions have offered the imperfect solution of simply publishing clerical apologetics, statements on religious matters by officials of various churches (*ibid.*, pp. 189–193).

The problem of race is just as difficult as that of religion. Reviewing the five-volume *Dictionary of American History*, Nevins wrote (1941, p. 4): "Perhaps the most unsatisfactory of the general articles are the two on Race Elements in America and the Race Problem. In the former the term 'race' is used in a sense that ethnologists would not approve, and in the latter there is too much pessimism about the subject." The single-volume *American Negro Reference Book*, published in 1965, is one corrective, and the establishment of a separate branch of the New York Public Library for works on Negro history (the Schomberg Collection) is another. Single reference books may be limited, but a collection of them can overcome individual deficiencies.

Encyclopedias have often promoted nationalism or other ideological positions. Indeed, the *Enciclopedia italiana di scienze, lettere ed arti*, consisting of 36 volumes published from 1929 to 1939, aimed to provide "an inventory of Italian knowledge," and it did so in accord with the views of the Fascist regime of the time. The decree of the Soviet Union's Council of Ministers in 1949, which established the second edition of the *Bol'shaia sovetskaia entsiklopediia*, declared that it "should elucidate broadly the world-historical victories of Socialism in our country. . . . With exhaustive completeness it must show the superiority of Socialist culture over the culture of the capitalist world" (as quoted in Benton 1958, p. 553). More recently, many of the new nations of the world have initiated encyclopedias with explicit national biases. But all of this is in the grand tradition, and the wonder is that encyclopedias have ever developed which have disowned such biases. One that was a great success in this regard was the *Encyclopaedia of the Social Sciences*, published from 1930 to 1935, whose pages, according to Sidney Hook's review (1935), "showed the fruits of the best type of international intellectual cooperation." Hook praised the absence of a "synthetic, positive social philosophy" and the presence of contributors "of every school of thought—conservatives, liberals, radicals of every hue and shade." He concluded that "the emphasis upon the interrelations between the various disciplines, honored in the observance as well as in the program, the treatment of the social implications of material drawn from the arts and sciences make of these fifteen volumes a kind of universal encyclopedia of knowledge." This is all the more an achievement when it is realized that similar, though less ambitious, projects, such as the *Cyclopedia of American Government* published in 1914, were accorded strong contemporaneous condemnation for slipshod editing, weak conceptualization, and erroneous information.

A contemporary test of whether severely diverse approaches can be held within the covers of a single reference book is seen in the dispute over editorial policy for an international encyclopedia of comparative law being undertaken by the International Association of Legal Science. The issue is "whether topics in the law of Marxian socialist countries can be integrated with the law of other legal systems under appropriate subject headings" or whether "such topics must be treated separately from the law of non-Marxist countries by placing them in a separate volume devoted solely to their various East European and Asian forms" (Hazard 1965, p. 278). The Marxist view makes universalism the aim; but if unification cannot be achieved, then comparison has no purpose. In contrast, Hazard argues (1965, p. 286) that the aim of the editorial committee is to foster "peaceful co-existence between differing social and economic systems" and stresses the educational value of topical comparison for students of law in all societies. He then cites the law of property and contracts as proof that his approach is feasible (*ibid.*, pp. 287–302).

Multivolume encyclopedias running through many editions have developed "continuous revision" as the most suitable method of change. If ten per cent of the articles are revised annually, the whole would change completely in ten years. But Einbinder (1964) has shown that in the case of the *Encyclopaedia Britannica*, several hundred articles have been reprinted intact from editions fifty or more years old; also, articles are disturbed by cuts when they are alphabetically proximate to freshly developed subjects. In the Soviet Union, when Beria fell from power the publishers of the *Bol'shaia sovetskaia entsiklopediia* ("Great Soviet Encyclopedia") removed the entry for Beria and made available to its 250,000 subscribers in the Soviet Union a special replacement section containing expanded entries on the eighteenth-century courtier F. W. Bergholz, on the Bering Sea, and on Bishop Berkeley (Benton 1958, p. 567).

Biographical reference books. Personal vanity, weak editorial hands, and poorly developed concepts of impartial analysis have been factors in the production of inadequate biographical reference books. In the first edition of *Who's Who in American Education*, which was published in 1928, "thousands of obscure public school teachers of all grades, and of all ages from the early twenties up, are listed, while hundreds of distinguished educators are not" (Vance 1961, p. 323). But this has been shown to be only one of hundreds of "who's who" projects, exclusive of the carefully prepared Marquis volumes and some others, which "simply capitalize upon human vanity and gullibility. Purchase becomes the price for being listed. And the work of the editor-promoter is relatively easy. All he needs is names—several thousands of them. The less important the people invited to be listed, the more readily they will pay" (*ibid.*, pp. 326–327). Contributors to *Appleton's Cyclopedia of American Biography*, published from 1887 to 1889, could suggest names for inclusion and submit articles which were published untouched by the editors, and were paid space rates. These considerations seem to account for the presence in the *Cyclopedia* of some fifty articles on nonexistent botanists or completely trumped-up accounts of real scientists from South America (Schindler 1936, p. 687). Entirely different points are made in a critique of a ten-year supplement to the *Dictionary of National Biography (1941–1950)*. The review acknowledges the merits of the *DNB* as an Oxford-edited book of the British Establishment but complains that the editors' values led to serious exclusions of matter: "I examined the lives of three known homosexuals, and found the fact mentioned in none; of three persons who died insane, and found the fact omitted in two and only hinted at in the third; of two persons who died by their own hands, and found the fact omitted in one, but squarely faced in the other (Lord David Cecil's model account of Virginia Woolf)" (Corke 1959, p. 77).

The multivolume, national biographical reference set has nonetheless been a great achievement, and its vitality is testified to in the announcement, in 1966, that the *Dictionary of National Biography*, first published from 1890 to 1910, is to be entirely revised and rewritten at Oxford during the next decade. The *Dictionary of American Biography*, published from 1929 to 1934, has already been shown to be dated by its almost complete neglect of Negroes. And the first volume of the projected 20 volumes of the *Dictionary of Canadian Biography* appeared in 1966, arranged chronologically rather than alphabetically. By covering a specific period of history, each volume stands on its own as published and affords a balanced view of individuals included. This dictionary also departs from tradition by including introductory essays to set the historical stage for the biographies. The slow-paced publication of the distinguished French national biographical dictionary, *Dictionnaire de biographie française* (begun in 1933 but with the volumes up to the letter D completed only in 1966), suggests the chronological to be superior to the alphabetical arrangement, at least during the long years of publication.

Dictionaries. It remains to note that controversy and criticism have surrounded two other types of reference books: the monolingual dictionary and the geographical atlas. *Webster's Third New International Dictionary*, published in 1961, was achieved after some 25 years of compiling a word list, recording definitions in usage, and noting pronunciations under an editorial mandate to apply the science of structural linguistics to lexicography. Philip Gove, the editor, has said that the new dictionary was deeply affected by the work of Leonard Bloomfield, who wrote the charter of contemporary descriptive linguistics. According to Gove, "the fundamental step in setting down postulates for descriptive linguistics is observing precisely what happens when native speakers speak" (Sledd & Ebbitt 1962, p. 66). *Webster's Third New International Dictionary* was built empirically, from research into the spoken American language of today. The editorial view was that a dictionary should have no traffic with "artificial notions of correctness and superiority. It must be descriptive and not prescriptive" (Gove in Sledd & Ebbitt 1962, p. 74). In the reception of *Webster's Third* this point was central to most critics, who believed that linguistics was a pseudo science that would turn over the language to the mobocracy, that standards of correctness had to be imposed by educated authority, and that the dictionary should be and, in any event, inevitably was, prescriptive (these criticisms are collected in Sledd & Ebbitt 1962).

Considering that a critical storm was begun by a dictionary rooted in modern linguistics and executed by an expert staff at enormous expense, it is clear that the many glossaries prepared by social scientists for student and popular use deserve the kind of scrutiny that they rarely receive. One handbook, *A Dictionary of Politics*, published in 1957, treated words like Bolshevism, capitalism, and collectivism so arbitrarily and carelessly that one reviewer declared the book "a fraud and a brazen manipulation of facts" (Schlamm 1957). Many specialized dictionaries, such as the *Dictionary of the Social Sciences*, published in 1964 under UNESCO auspices, are useful, though they are written by authorities rather than built empirically from usage in context.

Atlases. The atlas, as perhaps the most technically complex reference book, presents the greatest challenge and the best chance for things to go wrong. In trenchant essays, Richard Edes Harrison has named *scope*, *design*, and *execution* as the major criteria in the evaluation of atlases. In regard to scope, or breadth of coverage, he notes that most American "world atlases" shortchange the rest of the world. States and countries may each gain a page regardless of size; Rhode Island and Texas, Switzerland and the Soviet Union, are treated alike. "Such enormous disparities in scale can only lead to erroneous and confused conceptions of geography" (Harrison 1961*a*, p. 6). Harrison believes that maps are central and require papers, inks, and procedures that should make extraneous statistics, gazetteers, and photographs unwelcome. Design, the second element, "deals with the title page and all other type matter, with the maps and their myriad detail, with page layouts, the treatment of borders, scales, map titles, keys, selection of places, categorization of towns, the generalization of geographical detail, indication of topography, etc." (*ibid.*). The criterion of execution "deals with the beauty and accuracy of the drawing, engraving and printing." Harrison's best advice is "that a good atlas is always explicit about its methods and content." On these grounds Harrison condemned the giant *Life Pictorial Atlas of the World*, published in 1961, as a pretentious, careless, and superficial book.

Technological developments

Typography and format in reference books, often questioned by uneasy but helpless critics, have attracted some attention because of McLuhan's interpretations of communication media (1962) and through the development of alternative methods of information storage and retrieval. Harrison (1961*b*, p. 40), in his criticism of the *Life Pictorial Atlas*, complained of captions set in neat blocks of sans-serif type: "It is a pity that such artificial and immaterial considerations are allowed to take precedence over the business of communicating with the reader." Carl P. Rollins had earlier (1929) condemned both the *Encyclopaedia Britannica* and the *Dictionary of American Biography* as being "dull and insipid typographically." McLuhan (1964, chapter 2) views the very form of communication as inseparable from content, his watchword being that "the medium is the message." He argues that "the 'message' of any medium or technology is the change of scale or pace or pattern that it introduces into human affairs" (McLuhan 1964, p. 8).

Since Gutenberg, Western intellectual assumptions have been forged by the typographic principles of uniformity, continuity, and linability (McLuhan 1962). This repeatability, and the distribution of the end product, has made the conveyance of information through reference materials and reference books possible. Now, in the mid-twentieth century, a host of intertwined technological developments makes possible further and fuller collection of information and facilitates its duplication, distribution, and use. Clapp (1964) has shown that even with high-ratio photoreproduction, full cataloguing, complete data processing, and related information storage and retrieval, no single library, however well endowed, can hope to come close to embracing all the world's sources. Thus, to overcome this problem, a carefully developed system of cooperation among libraries is essential. Clapp's premise is that "the general research library of the future will increasingly be required to make available to its users the informational records of mankind" (1964, p. 53).

Social statistics. Changing technologies will not by themselves overcome the many obstacles to amassing coherent social statistics. The periodic government census of population and of other subjects such as housing, agriculture, and business has become a standard program of most central governments. In contrast, the vital and health records of most countries are decentralized, and the development of national record keeping and publication has been slow. Spiegelman (1963) has explained that problems of definition arise at every stage—for example, definitions of date of birth, nature of illness, cause of divorce, cause of death—so that the development of reliable vital and health statistics is an awesome task. Criminal statistics present similar difficulties; and while the records of Britain and Wales are outstanding, the *Uniform Crime Reports* of the U.S. Federal Bureau of Investigation have come under frequent criticism since their beginning in 1929 (see Pittman & Handy 1962). Another area where more accurate statistics are needed is that of religious affiliation. In the United States it is difficult to assess the claims of churches to membership growth because of the problems of defining religious affiliation and the impossibility of making the subject a part of the regular U.S. census of population. The result is that each church takes its own count; since there is a lack of uniform rules, reliability is poor (see Lipset 1959). Automobile accidents are another subject where central, uniform statistics are lacking. One critic has blamed this state of affairs on the pressure of car manufacturers to suppress facts about traffic safety (Nader 1965, p. 284).

These weaknesses in the web of information, these disparagements of reference sources, and these criticisms of reference books should not override the very considerable achievements that are everywhere in evidence in the research library. The collection of economic data and their use in constructing economic indicators have definitely contributed to the wise and timely application of government power to national economies. Documentation of the official acts of government is increasingly complete and current. The list of standard reference books which are indispensable itself fills a book (see Winchell 1951). References like the *Union List of Serials*, Hamer's *Guide to Archives and Manuscripts in the United States*, published in 1961, and the *Research Centers Directory* help to bring the resources of all research collections to the desk of any library. If constructive criticism of reference books prepared by and used by social scientists can be further developed, the quality of information at our disposal can be vastly improved.

CLEMENT E. VOSE

[*See also the guide to related articles under* GOVERNMENT STATISTICS.]

BIBLIOGRAPHY

The reference materials and books described in this article are, for the most part, not included in the bibliography. The works listed below are primarily guides to and criticisms of them.

AMERICAN COUNCIL OF LEARNED SOCIETIES DEVOTED TO HUMANISTIC STUDIES 1962 *The Social Studies and the Social Sciences.* New York: Harcourt.

BARZUN, JACQUES; and GRAFF, HENRY F. 1957 *The Modern Researcher.* New York: Harcourt.

BENTON, WILLIAM 1958 The Great Soviet Encyclopedia. *Yale Review* New Series 47:552–568.

BUTLER, PIERCE (1933) 1961 *An Introduction to Library Science.* Univ. of Chicago Press.

CAPPON, LESTER J. 1966 A Rationale for Historical Editing, Past and Present. *William and Mary Quarterly* Third Series 23:56–75.

CLAPP, VERNER W. 1964 *The Future of the Research Library.* Urbana: Univ. of Illinois Press.

CLARKE, JACK A. 1959 *Research Materials in the Social Sciences.* Madison: Univ. of Wisconsin Press.

COLLISON, ROBERT L. W. 1964 *Encyclopaedias: Their History Throughout the Ages; a Bibliographical Guide With Extensive Historical Notes to the General Encyclopaedias Issued Throughout the World From 350 B.C. to the Present Day.* New York: Hafner.

CORKE, HILARY 1959 Praising Famous Men. *Encounter* 13, no. 2:74–77.

EINBINDER, HARVEY 1964 *The Myth of the Britannica.* New York: Grove.

FRIEDRICH, OTTO 1959 A Vivacious Blonde Was Fatally Shot Today: Or, How to Read a Tabloid. *American Scholar* 28:467–473.

HARRISON, RICHARD E. 1961*a* Sound Advice for Atlas Buyers. *New York Herald Tribune Books* November 26, p. 6.

HARRISON, RICHARD E. 1961*b* A Worldly Perspective [Book Review] *New York Times Book Review Section* October 22, pp. 6, 40.

HARVARD UNIVERSITY (1949) 1964 *The Harvard List of Books in Psychology.* 3d ed. Cambridge, Mass.: Harvard Univ. Press.

HAYCRAFT, HOWARD 1962 Problems of Selecting Periodicals for Wilson Indexes. *Special Libraries* 53:127–129.

HAZARD, JOHN N. 1965 Socialist Law and the International Encyclopedia. *Harvard Law Review* 79:278–302.

HOOK, SIDNEY 1935 A Triumph of Scholarship. *Saturday Review of Literature* 13, December 7:38, 42.

HOSELITZ, BERT F. (editor) 1960 *A Reader's Guide to the Social Sciences.* Glencoe, Ill.: Free Press.

JACOBSTEIN, J. MYRON 1962 Legal Periodicals. *Library Trends* 10:374–380.

KEMPTON, MURRAY 1961 Letter From New York. *Encounter* 16, no. 6:90–92.

KISTER, KENNETH F. 1966 The Literature of the Social and Behavioral Sciences. *Choice: Books for College Libraries* 3:99–102.

KRISTOL, IRVING 1967 The Underdeveloped Profession. *Public Interest* no. 6:36–52.

LICHTHEIM, GEORGE 1965 "All the News That's Fit to Print": Reflections on the *New York Times. Commentary* 40, September: 33–46.

LIEBLING, A. J. 1961 *The Press.* New York: Ballantine. → Much of this material appeared originally in the *New Yorker* (1946–1961).

LIPSET, SEYMOUR M. 1959 Religion in America: What Religious Revival? *Columbia University Forum* 2, no. 2:17–21.

MACDONALD, DWIGHT 1952 Book-of-the-Millennium Club. [Review of *The Great Ideas: A Syntopicon of Great Books of the Western World*] *New Yorker* 28, November 29: 171–188.

MCLUHAN, MARSHALL 1962 *The Gutenberg Galaxy: The Making of Typographic Man.* Univ. of Toronto Press.

MCLUHAN, MARSHALL 1964 *Understanding Media: The Extensions of Man.* New York: McGraw-Hill. → A paperback edition was published in 1965.

MANCHESTER, WILLIAM 1959 *The Times:* The World's Greatest Newspaper. *Holiday* 26, October: 34–46.

MANDELBAUM, DAVID G. et al. (editors) 1963 *Resources for the Teaching of Anthropology.* Berkeley: Univ. of California Press.

MANTEL, HOWARD N. 1959 The *Congressional Record*: Fact or Fiction of the Legislative Process. *Western Political Quarterly* 12:981–995.

MARKE, JULIUS J. 1963 Legal Literature. *Library Trends* 11:244–258.

MARX, LEO 1961 The American Scholar Today. *Commentary* 32:48–53.

MUGGERIDGE, MALCOLM 1961 The Eye-witness Fallacy. *Encounter* 16, no. 5:86–89.

MURPHEY, ROBERT W. 1958 *How and Where to Look It Up: A Guide to Standard Sources of Information.* New York: McGraw-Hill.

NADER, RALPH 1965 *Unsafe at Any Speed: The Designed-in Dangers of the American Automobile.* New York: Grossman.

NEVINS, ALLAN 1941 [A Book Review of] *Dictionary of American History,* James Truslow Adams, Editor in Chief. *New York Times* December 7, p. 4 only.

NEVINS, ALLAN 1958 A New Horizon for *Who's Who:* A Proposal. *Who's Who in America* 30:7–8.

PITTMAN, DAVID J.; and HANDY, W. F. 1962 Uniform Crime Reporting: Suggested Improvements. *Sociology and Social Research* 46:135–143.

PRICE, MILES O.; and BITNER, HARRY (1953) 1962 *Effective Legal Research.* Student ed., rev. Boston: Little.

REID, WARREN R. 1962 Public Papers of the Presidents. *American Archivist* 25:435–439.

ROLLINS, CARL PURINGTON 1929 Some Recent Cyclopedias. *Saturday Review of Literature* 6, October 19: 304 only.

SCHINDLER, MARGARET C. 1936 Fictitious Biography. *American Historical Review* 42:680–690.

SCHLAMM, WILLIAM S. 1957 A Book to Burn. [Review of *A Dictionary of Politics,* by Elliott and Summerskill] *National Review* 3:425–427.

SCHMECKEBIER, LAURENCE F.; and EASTIN, ROY B. (1936) 1961 *Government Publications and Their Use.* Rev. ed. Washington: Brookings Institution.

SLEDD, JAMES; and EBBITT, WILMA R. (editors) 1962 *Dictionaries and That Dictionary: A Casebook on the Aims of Lexicographers and the Targets of Reviewers.* Chicago: Scott.

SPIEGELMAN, MORTIMER 1963 The Realm of Vital and Health Statistics. *American Behavioral Scientist* 6, no. 9:18–23.

VANCE, WILLIAM S. 1961 "Who's Who" Publications: Who Are the Elect? *South Atlantic Quarterly* 60:321–331.

WANDERER, BOB 1963 The Decline in News Reporting. *ETC: A Review of General Semantics* 20:490–494.

WHITE, CARL M. et al. 1964 *Sources of Information in the Social Sciences: A Guide to the Literature.* Totowa, N.J.: Bedminster Press.

WILDING, NORMAN; and LAUNDY, PHILIP 1958 *An Encyclopaedia of Parliament.* New York: Praeger; London: Cassell.

WINCHELL, CONSTANCE M. 1951 *Guide to Reference Books.* 7th ed. Chicago: American Library Association. → Based on the sixth edition, by Isadore Gilbert Mudge.

YONGE, ENA L. 1962 World and Thematic Atlases: A Summary Survey. *Geographical Review* 52:583–596.

V
BIBLIOGRAPHIC ISSUES IN THE BEHAVIORAL SCIENCES

During the 1950s scholars from various fields of specialization began the process of defining the new scientific development called the behavioral sciences. Implicit in their writings was a conception of the behavioral sciences as "a multidisciplinary pursuit of knowledge" about the roots and manifestations of behavior "in man and animals, in individuals, groups, and cultures, and in all conditions, normal, exceptional, and pathological" (Editorial 1960, p. 701). The literature that has resulted from the effort to unify this evolving knowledge creates unusual bibliographic problems which call for new solutions.

This literature is international in scope; in the world's bibliographic and library systems, however, it is not presented as literature of the behavioral sciences. Research in a special subject area may be as diversified as the behavioral sciences as a whole, as shown in the literature on psychopharmacology, where topics range from chemistry to creativity, from anthropology to addiction, from medicine to mysticism, memory, and "control of the mind," and involve legal and social issues. Yet the customary bibliographic categories cannot reflect this significant variety of aspects in the study of human behavior. Moreover, progress in the behavioral sciences has strengthened the conviction of many that ethical considerations must be an integral part of a science of human behavior. Literature in which scientific data relate to ethical concerns raises entirely new bibliographic issues.

Current interpretations of the concept "behavioral sciences" vary (Bry & Afflerbach 1965, p. v). According to some definitions, the behavioral sciences are a part of the social sciences and include various new fields such as game theory and value inquiry (Handy & Kurtz 1964). If the literature of the behavioral sciences were confined to the literature of the social sciences, even to that of the "behavioral social sciences"—cultural anthropology, sociology, and social psychology—important bibliographic problems would arise (see Foskett 1963).

Bibliographic issues typical of the behavioral sciences begin when the literature of disciplines outside the social sciences must be included, particularly that of psychology and psychiatry. Psychology appears by tradition under "philosophy," but the psychological literature is increasingly scattered through other fields, especially the social sciences, education, and physiology. Traditionally, psychiatric literature has been organized under "medicine." Partly as a result of social conditions of the past, the bibliographic and library resources for medicine are often separated physically from those of the other fields. In a reversal of earlier trends, the biomedical, behavioral, and environmental health sciences are now being brought together in programs that develop new scientific and social perspectives (Pearsall 1963). MacKenzie and Bloomquist, who interpret the behavioral sciences as "a synthesis of disciplines in the biological and social sciences and in the humanities" (1964, p. 220), have demonstrated the impact of the behavioral sciences upon bibliographic issues in such programs.

A special bibliographic system is needed to reflect the content and to show the progress of the behavioral sciences. It can become generally effective only if it is designed to supplement, not replace, the basic systems of internationally organized bibliography. The methods of identifying and selecting this new literature, however, would have to be derived from developments in the behavioral sciences.

Dilemmas of bibliographic identification. Bibliographic and library systems based on the nineteenth-century disciplinary organization of the sciences started with the assumption that the content of a scientific publication would be confined to its discipline—for example, that journals in the field of geology would deal with geology alone. When psychology first became a discipline at the end of the nineteenth century, this rule no longer applied. The scholars who compiled the annual psychological bibliographies in France, Germany, and the United States had to search through journals in philosophy, physics, medicine, anthropology, and other fields in order to draw together the literature of psychology (Bayne & Bry 1954). The same difficulty developed in another form for psychoanalysis. Freud's prepsychoanalytic publications had appeared in the medical and neurological literature, but his psychoanalytic writings from 1900 on did not fit the existing bibliographic structure. He was thus led to believe that his early psychoanalytic books and papers had been deliberately ignored, when they had actually gained unusual attention in journals of a wide variety of disciplines such as psychology, criminal anthropology, and sexology (Bry & Rifkin 1962).

In principle, the same problems arise again in the literature of the behavioral sciences, although now they are far more complicated. This literature becomes an organic whole only through the unity of the scientific purpose of the behavioral sciences. There is no single disciplinary structure that could hold it together. In the behavioral sciences there are, however, many elements that belong to a structure. Human and animal behavior can only be studied in a concrete situation or in a setting such as a kindergarten, a medical school, or a space laboratory. And the behavior studied is not that of a man or animal in the abstract; it is behavior of birds, artists, or people living in a particular society. When specialists participate in interdisciplinary projects, their functional relationships do not change the basic pattern in which their disciplines are separately organized; although psychiatrists join sociologists, for example, in studies of mental health in a community, psychiatry and sociology remain separate disciplines, while social psychiatry is developing as a specialized field. The behavioral sciences thus superimpose a unitary function—the study of human and animal behavior—upon a pluralistic structure. The resulting literature appears under a vast variety of auspices, often those provided by the disciplines or settings involved in a given project. The actual publications are distributed according to their immediate function, and they may be found wherever they appear to be most useful—in educational, medical, general, or other libraries. A special bibliographic system is needed to identify the publications that serve the unity of function of the behavioral sciences, and this system should itself be functionally organized.

An "anthropotropic" organizing principle. The encyclopedic systems of knowledge that most strongly influenced the organization of libraries and general bibliographies in the late nineteenth century were anthropocentric, in the sense that they saw man in the center of the world he explores. An organizing principle for the literature of the behavioral sciences, however, should be "anthropotropic" (Bry & Afflerbach 1965) in order to reflect the "turning toward man" in man's search for knowledge about himself. The idea is not new. During the romantic period around 1800, the "anthropological sciences," "human sciences," or "sciences of man" included the study of man's body and mind and of man as a whole, as an individual and in social relationships. A hundred years later, a similar view was expressed by the French philosopher Edmond Goblot in the form of an interdisciplinary concept, "*bio–psycho–sociologie*." During the twentieth century, the term "human behavior" began to be used to distinguish the scientific approach from the philosophical approach to knowledge about man. Around 1950, the phrase "behavioral sciences" was introduced in the United States as a unifying term for the study of human and animal behavior in the psychological, biological, and social sciences.

The search for a clearly defined, internationally acceptable term for this scientific development continues. In England and France, "human sciences" and "*sciences humaines*" seem to be preferred. In German publications, "*Verhalten*" corresponds to "behavior" in the several meanings of this word in the American technical literature. At present, *Verhaltensforschung* in German usage refers chiefly to studies of animal behavior; its literal translation, "behavioral research," refers in current American usage to studies of human and animal behavior. It is essential to identify international contributions to the behavioral sciences on the basis of their actual scientific content, regardless of terminology.

In terms of the anthropocentric schemes for organizing the literature, "man as a whole" has been dismembered and does not appear as a uniform object of knowledge at all. National bibliographies in whatever country—Canada, Peru, Russia, or India—impose upon the literature of the behavioral sciences schemes which use the very divisions that the behavioral sciences must transcend. Therefore, an organizing principle that can reflect the anthropotropic orientation has been proposed for the literature of the behavioral sciences (Bry & Afflerbach 1965). In applying such a principle, it appears useful to place the literature of the psychological sciences—psychology, psychiatry, and psychoanalysis—in the center of a bibliographic scheme, including fields already merged with the psychological sciences, such as psychopharmacology or social psychiatry. Publications from other fields—for example, genetics, economics, or religion—would take an "orbital" position, depending on the extent to which they convey knowledge to, or draw knowledge from, the psychological sciences. As new relationships among various fields develop, such a scheme could form a basis for the increasingly necessary cross references. It would reflect the intellectual integration that is being achieved by the scholars from formerly separate fields of specialization. So organized, a functional and dynamic bibliographic system for the behavioral sciences could remain open to new developments, and it could also be superimposed upon the existing bibliographic structure without destroying it.

Indirect methods of selection. If the literature of the behavioral sciences is to be confined to significant publications that are distinctly relevant to the behavioral sciences (Mental Health . . . 1963), the question of methods of selection arises. Traditionally, scholarly bibliographies apply a direct method of selection, which is based on the bibliographers' own judgments. The monthly *The American Behavioral Scientist* published an annotated guide to recent publications in the social and behavioral sciences (The American . . . 1965), which uses the direct method: the compilers of this bibliography make their own selection from journals and books, including many publications that have appeared outside the United States.

As the behavioral sciences develop in new directions and the literature is published in an increasing number of languages, it becomes necessary to design indirect methods of selection which utilize the competent judgments already made by behavioral scientists as part of their scholarly activities. One attempt to develop such a method was made by the Psychoanalytic Collections Conference of New York City, 1950–1956, a cooperative project of librarians who undertook a bibliographic pilot study of publications "which seemed to bear . . . upon human behavior and human relations." After identifying monographic series in the psychological sciences published on an international scale since the late nineteenth century, this group stated the principle of indirect methods of selection in terms of that particular study: when a series is edited by an authority on the subject, the editor's selection of the monographs assures their relevance and significance to the purpose of the series (Bayne & Bry 1954). The editor's choice is especially important in the monographic series of newly developing fields, as illustrated by the early psychoanalytic monographic series under the editorship of Freud (Bry et al. 1953). A collection of serially published monographs identifies the pertinent topics, the editors responsible for the series, and the authors who have been invited to contribute the monographs. Their names, in turn, provide a key to other pertinent books by the same writers.

Book reviews have also been used as research material for developing an indirect method of selection (*Mental Health* . . .). The selection of books reviewed in scientific journals involves several stages. Publishers, authors, and journal editors participate in varying degrees in the selection of books sent to the journals for review. The editors then select the books that are actually to be reviewed and the specialists who are to review them (Kinney, Franck, & Bry 1955). The citations of book reviews in journals relating to the behavioral sciences have been cumulated in a pilot study by the Mental Health Book Review Index, a project based on that of the Psychoanalytic Collections Conference but broadened through the cooperation of behavioral scientists and of librarians in leading libraries in many parts of the United States. The cumulation reveals different patterns in the alignment of reviews. Certain books may be reviewed in many journals from different disciplines over a period of years. In some instances, the editors of the reviewing journals themselves as well as other authorities in the field review the same book. This process of collective evaluation selects significant books relevant to the behavioral sciences and can thus be used for an indirect method of selection based on competent judgments already made (Editorial 1961, p. vi; 1962). But the strengths and weaknesses of the whole process of book evaluation across national and disciplinary borders remain to be studied by social science and general systems research (Bry & Afflerbach 1964).

Various indirect methods of selection would have to be combined in order to overcome the limitations of any single one. An index of selected bibliographies of subjects important to the behavioral sciences would be particularly useful. It should include not only the bibliographies that are separately published but also those that appear as journal articles or parts of books. Contributions made by behavioral scientists to a special bibliographic system need not themselves be of a bibliographic nature. The proceedings of pertinent conferences and symposia, for example, may serve as guideposts indicating the direction the literature of the behavioral sciences may take in the future. *Festschriften* (Mental Health . . . 1963, p. 242) may also forecast later developments, when they project a scholar's influence and interests into the history of ideas. The position the behavioral sciences occupy in the total advance of knowledge might be traced in broad lines through endowed lectures in which leading scientists and scholars interpret progress in their respective fields. The basic themes of many long-established lectureships have religious or humanistic implications, and behavioral scientists invited to deliver such lectures appear to use this medium to clarify also the social and ethical implications of their scientific work. If these and other developments that can contribute to a bibliographic system for the behavioral sciences could be brought into focus, a system that can integrate the relevant data would offer a basis for a valid selection of the significant literature.

"Sociobibliography." The behavioral sciences and the field of bibliography have other problems in common, which could be studied by a new subdiscipline—perhaps to be called "sociobibliography" —through combining the approaches of social research with research in bibliography. A few examples may suggest the type of problems to which sociobibliographic research could be applied.

An analysis of data about twenty thousand book reviews published during the years 1955 to 1961 in 150 journals—in the English language but international in origin—relating to the behavioral sciences showed that about one-third of the reviews were concentrated in a relatively small number of older journals, many of which represented the disciplinary tradition, while about two-thirds of the reviews were scattered through some 130 journals, many of which were recent and reflected newer scientific perspectives. The established journals, which contained only a portion of the reviews, are available in many more libraries and are more widely recorded and indexed than the new ones (Editorial 1961, pp. iii–v). Sociobibliographic research could develop methods that would either extend the advantages of international bibliographic and library cooperation to the more recent literature of the behavioral sciences or compensate for the lack of these advantages through other means.

There is a need for studying the literature and bibliography of the behavioral sciences as part of the intellectual, social, and cultural history of the past hundred years (Bayne & Bry 1954; *Journal of the History* . . .). Historical bibliographic data may throw light on cultural differences that influenced progress in fields relating to the behavioral sciences. For example, by the 1880s changes in psychiatric theory had led, in France and various other countries, to a substantial literature on hysteria in men. In spite of Germany's important position in psychiatry, scarcely any articles on this subject had then been published in that country. It appears from pertinent nineteenth-century sources that the national self-image had inhibited the diagnosis and study of male hysteria in Germany at that time (Bry & Rifkin 1962). Sociobibliographic research could lead to an understanding of cultural differences that influence contemporary developments in the behavioral sciences. [*See* KNOWLEDGE, SOCIOLOGY OF.]

Another contemporary problem belongs in the context of culture change. International bibliographic codes, such as subject headings and classification numbers, may continue to reflect the attitudes and social conditions on which they were based, but which have been or are being changed. There is an urgent task for sociobibliography to analyze obsolete social and behavioral implications of bibliographic categories and symbols before the programming of computers for library use proceeds beyond trial stages (Bry & Afflerbach 1964). The presentation of the literature of the social and behavioral sciences should be consistent with the content that this literature is intended to communicate. The cultural implications of bibliographic categories are particularly significant in subject areas where attitudes and social change are an integral part of the subject under discussion—

for example, in the literature on population problems, race relations, new nations, or international understanding.

Values and visibility. In a pioneer study, Albert and Kluckhohn (1959) offered a retrospective inventory of values that were the subject of discussion in the literature they had surveyed. Although there is as yet no science of values (Handy & Kurtz 1964, pp. 131–136), behavioral scientists often identify, debate, and clarify the issues involving values—philosophical, cultural, social, psychological—that arise in the course of their work. Positions taken on such issues are being further clarified in the course of evaluating the literature of the behavioral sciences; so are the values embodied in theories and in the concepts that organize the facts.

Since values implicit in the work of behavioral scientists and in various schools of thought enter into the evaluation, the entire process of evaluation is becoming increasingly visible in the literature itself. In the pertinent journals, the trend has been to give as much information about book reviewers as about other contributors, to establish prizes for papers and monographs, and to identify those who bestow honors, tributes, or awards as fully as those who receive them. The evaluating process that leads to scholarly recognition should also be visible in the bibliographic record. The current standard bibliographic presentation, however, includes little information that would indicate the scholarly significance of important and influential works.

A bibliographic system for the behavioral sciences could begin to make values visible by providing a continuous record of the topics in the pertinent literature that are explicitly concerned with values. Furthermore, it could aim at identifying the values that are in the process of being clarified in the course of assessing the literature. A selected bibliography for the behavioral sciences, derived from the evaluation made by behavioral scientists, would concentrate on the literature marked as significant. It would then provide all salient data, especially those relating to values. Not only the leading value positions but also the processes of evaluation that govern their impact could then be continuously reassessed (Bry 1962).

As long as research in any single discipline, designed to observe, explain, and predict human behavior, could be used for this basic scientific purpose only, the literature fitted into the existing bibliographic systems; if it did not fit, new disciplines created their own visible bibliographic records, as did psychology and psychoanalysis at the beginning of the twentieth century. There has been no such direct correspondence between literature and bibliographic presentation in the multidisciplinary behavioral sciences. Since knowledge potentially evolving from the behavioral sciences might be used to modify human behavior in fundamental ways or help in the solution of the urgent problems of mankind, the need for a widely visible record of the representative works and values in the literature of the behavioral sciences is no longer only a bibliographic but also a social issue.

ILSE BRY

[*See also* BEHAVIORAL SCIENCES; KNOWLEDGE, SOCIOLOGY OF.]

BIBLIOGRAPHY

ALBERT, ETHEL M.; and KLUCKHOHN, CLYDE 1959 *A Selected Bibliography on Values, Ethics, and Esthetics in the Behavioral Sciences and Philosophy, 1920–1958.* Glencoe, Ill.: Free Press.

THE AMERICAN BEHAVIORAL SCIENTIST 1965 *The ABS Guide to Recent Publications in the Social and Behavioral Sciences.* New York: The American Behavioral Scientist. → An annotated, selective bibliography of 6,664 books and articles.

BAYNE, HELEN; and BRY, ILSE 1954 Problems and Projects in the Bibliography of Psychiatry and Psychology. *Libri* 3:363–387. → Contains 14 pages of bibliography.

BRY, ILSE 1962 To Foster Human Greatness. *Insight: Quarterly Review of Religion and Mental Health* 1, no. 2:2–15, 36. → A historical essay on the concept of genius and human greatness, with a section on values and honors.

BRY, ILSE; and AFFLERBACH, LOIS (1964) 1965 Bibliographical Challenges in the Age of the Computer. *Library Journal* 90:813–818. → First published as an editorial in the *Mental Health Book Review Index.*

BRY, ILSE; and AFFLERBACH, LOIS 1965 In Search of an Organizing Principle for the Behavioral Science Literature. *Mental Health Book Review Index* 10:i–vii.

BRY, ILSE; BAYNE, HELEN; and EBERT, MYRL 1953 Bibliography of Early Psychoanalytic Monographic Series. 2 parts. *Journal of the American Psychoanalytic Association* 1:519–525, 706–718.

BRY, ILSE; and RIFKIN, ALFRED H. 1962 Freud and the History of Ideas: Primary Sources, 1886–1910. Pages 6–36 in Jules H. Masserman (editor), *Science and Psychoanalysis.* Volume 5: Psychoanalytic Education. New York: Grune & Stratton.

Editorial. 1960 The Behavioral Sciences and Mental Health in Relation to the Organization of Knowledge, the Organization of Science, and Bibliography. *A.M.A. Archives of General Psychiatry* 2:701–706. → First published as an editorial in the *Mental Health Book Review Index.*

Editorial. 1961 Book Reviewing in the Sciences of Human Behavior as a Contribution to Scholarship by the Scientific Community. *Mental Health Book Review Index* 6:i–viii.

Editorial. 1962 The Conservation of Knowledge About Human Behavior. *Mental Health Book Review Index* 7:i–iv.

FOSKETT, D. J. 1963 *Classification and Indexing in the Social Sciences.* Washington: Butterworth.

HANDY, ROLLO; and KURTZ, PAUL 1964 *A Current Appraisal of the Behavioral Sciences.* Great Barrington, Mass.: Behavioral Research Council for Scientific Inquiry Into the Problems of Men in Society. → Contains bibliographies and lists of journals.

Journal of the History of the Behavioral Sciences. → Published since 1965.

KINNEY, MARGARET M.; FRANCK, MARGA; and BRY, ILSE 1955 The Book Review: A Hybrid in Literature and a Stepchild in Documentation. Pages 80–86 in *International Congress of Libraries and Documentation Centres, Brussels,* 1955. Volume 2*a*: Communications. The Hague: Nijhoff.

MACKENZIE, RUTH C.; and BLOOMQUIST, HAROLD 1964 The Impact of the Behavioral Sciences on the Collecting Policy of Medical School Libraries. Medical Library Association, *Bulletin* 52:220–233. → Contains a master list of journals relating to the behavioral sciences in the Harvard Medical Library.

Mental Health Book Review Index. → Published since 1956.

MENTAL HEALTH BOOK REVIEW INDEX, EDITORIAL COMMITTEE (1963) 1965 Changes in the Concept of "Scientific Literature." *Journal of the History of the Behavioral Sciences* 1:235–243. → First published as an editorial in the *Mental Health Book Review Index.*

PEARSALL, MARION 1963 *Medical Behavioral Science: A Selected Bibliography of Cultural Anthropology, Social Psychology, and Sociology in Medicine.* Lexington: Univ. of Kentucky Press.

INFORMATION THEORY

The concepts and measures of the statistical theory of selective information (information theory) have become so thoroughly enmeshed with the whole of behavioral science that delineation of the exact contribution of the theory is nearly impossible. The very verbal descriptive fabric of the behavioral sciences has become thoroughly interlaced with informational concepts: individuals or groups are described as "information sources" or "receivers"; skilled performance is described as "information processing"; memory is described as "information storage"; nerves are described as "communication channels"; the patterning of neural impulses is described as "information coding"; the brain is described as "an informational computer," etc. Indeed, the molecule, the cell, the organ, the individual, the group, the organization, and the society have all been examined from the point of view of a general systems theory which focuses upon the information-processing, rather than upon the energetic, characteristics of each system (J. G. Miller 1955). Perhaps the closest analogue to the impact of information theory upon psychology is the impact that behaviorism had upon psychology, with the subsequent redefinition of psychology as the science of behavior. In both cases questions of definition have replaced questions of possible relevance. [*See* SYSTEMS ANALYSIS, *article on* GENERAL SYSTEMS THEORY.]

Information theory is a formal mathematical theory, a branch of the theory of probability. As such, the theory is self-contained; it does not require verification by experiment (Frick 1959). Yet, formal theories often have profound influence as conceptual models and as models for experiment. The theory is indelibly flavored by the context of electrical communications and control in which it was developed. Cherry ([1957] 1961, pp. 30–65) has charted the development of the theory within the field of communications. The genesis of the modern theory of statistical communications is due primarily to Hartley (1928). Building upon earlier work, by Nyquist and Küpfmüller, Hartley showed that in order to transmit a given amount of information a communication channel must undergo an exchange between its duration and its bandwidth, or frequency range. With a narrower frequency range, the communication channel must be available for a longer duration to transmit a given amount of information. Information was identified with a arbitrary selection of symbols from a set of defined symbols. The measure of information was defined in terms of the logarithm of the number of equally likely symbols available for communication. The essence of the idea is that information is measured in terms of what *could have been* communicated under a defined set of circumstances rather than in terms of what actually *is* communicated at a particular moment. The definition is sufficiently broad to provide a general framework for the specification of a wide class of communication systems. Following Hartley, numerous distinguished contributions were made throughout the world. These included the contribution by R. A. Fisher in characterizing the efficiency and sufficiency of statistics and that of D. Gabor, who introduced the concept of the *logan* as the elementary unit of information. It was the contributions of Shannon (1948) and of Wiener (1948), however, which provided the intellectual synthesis that marked the birth of modern information theory. [*See* CYBERNETICS *and the biography of* WIENER; *see also* Frick 1959.]

Shannon provides a scheme for a general communication system.

> It consists of essentially five parts: 1. An *information source* which produces a message or a sequence of messages to be communicated to the receiving terminal. . . . 2. A *transmitter* which operates on the message in some way to produce a signal suitable for transmission over the channel. . . . 3. The *channel* is merely the medium used to transmit the signal from

transmitter to receiver. . . . During transmission, or at one of the terminals, the signal may be perturbed by noise. . . . 4. The *receiver* ordinarily performs the inverse operation of that done by the transmitter, reconstructing the message from the signal. . . . 5. The *destination* is the person (or thing) for whom the message is intended. ([1948] 1962, pp. 4–6)

This description, while initially directed toward electrical communication systems, is sufficiently general to use in the consideration of a wide class of information systems.

The measure of information. The essential idea of the Shannon–Wiener mathematical theory of communication is that communication is a statistical process which can be described only in probabilistic terms. When it is possible to predict completely each message out of a source of possible messages, by definition no information will be conveyed by the message. When any one message is as probable as any other possible message, maximum information will be conveyed by the message. From this point of view, the information of any message is associated with the reduction in the range of possible selections by the receiver of any message, i.e., with the reduction of the receiver's uncertainty. Uncertainty, choice, information, surprise value, and range of selections, therefore, all become intimately related concepts. The meaning, reasonableness, and personal importance of the message, however, are not considered within this approach to communications. The concern of the theory is to provide a measure of the amount of information for any selection or choice from defined sources of information.

The measure of the amount of information associated with a given selection can be arbitrarily defined as the logarithm of the number of equally likely alternatives. The measure can also be rigorously derived by initially defining a set of conditions which it must satisfy. Shannon employed the latter procedure, and the interested reader is referred to the original article (1948) for the statement of the conditions. Luce (1960) has also listed a set of necessary conditions which lead to the same result. The conditions are (*a*) independence of irrelevant alternatives—the amount of information transmitted by the selection of any item from a defined set of items shall be a real number which depends only upon the probability of that item, $p(i)$, and not upon the probability distribution of the other items; (*b*) continuity—the measure of information shall be a continuous (in the mathematical sense) function of $p(i)$; (*c*) additivity—if two independent selections, i and j, with probabilities $p(i)$ and $p(j)$, are made, the amount of information transmitted in the joint selection of (i, j) shall be a simple sum of the information transmitted by each of the selections; and (*d*) scale—one unit of information is associated with a binary selection between two equally likely alternatives; the unit is called the *bit*. The only measure which satisfies all of these conditions for any symbol i is the negative logarithm (to the base 2) of the probability of i, $p(i)$. And, over the ensemble of possible items, the average information of the ensemble is the average weighted logarithmic measure, H, or

$$H = -\sum_{i=1}^{n} p(i) \log_2 p(i).$$

The H measure has a number of important properties. First, $H \geqslant 0$; it is 0 if, and only if, the probability of a single i equals 1, while the probability of the remaining $(n-1)i$ is equal to 0; otherwise H is greater than 0. Information is associated with any ensemble of items whenever there is uncertainty about which item will be presented. Second, H is maximum when all of the items are equally probable. If there are n possible items, the uncertainty associated with the set of items is maximum when $p(i) = 1/n$. Third, H is maximum if all items occur independently of each other. If the occurrence of one item is related to the occurrence of another, the average information is reduced by the extent of that relatedness. This property is extremely important for the behavioral sciences, since the information measure provides a measure of the degree of relatedness between items in a set of possible items. The ratio of the uncertainty of a source to the maximum possible uncertainty with the same set of symbols is a measure of the relative transmitting efficiency of the source; Shannon has termed this the relative entropy of the source. And 1 minus the relative entropy has been defined as the *redundancy* of the source. Fourth, it is possible to encode a long sequence of items so that, on the average, H binary units per item are required to specify the sequence, even though more than H binary units per item are required to specify a short sequence. This property, called the encoding property, has recently become extremely important for electrical communications but has not been much exploited by the behavioral sciences.

History. Although Hartley's development of the theory provided both the essential definition of information and a measure for its description, it went little noticed in the behavioral sciences. The historian of science will probably note that the behavioral sciences were not ready for the idea, nor, for that matter, was communications engineering fully ready. Shannon's development, on the other hand, was enthusiastically grasped very early by a handful of psychologists, primarily those associated with the Psycho-Acoustics Laboratory at Harvard University.

George A. Miller, in a personal communication to the author of this article in January 1964, has described the intellectual ferment associated with the early developments. Noteworthy is Miller's comment that "had the group not been actively interested in other related ideas from the communication engineers, the occurrence of Shannon's paper probably would have gone unnoticed by the group." The initial enthusiasm was stirred by the realization that Shannon had provided a tool for describing discrete events that at the same time was compatible with the continuous Fourier analysis of communication systems, with which the group was already acquainted.

Dahling has provided a valuable bibliographic survey of the early spread of concepts of the theory of selective information through a number of fields, ranging from telecommunication to journalism. Information theory provides an interesting case study for the diffusion of ideas in modern science, because of its great impact and its relative recency. From his analysis Dahling concluded that "the idea was drawn from a flurry of current related activity and, as the idea developed, it gained impetus and speed of adoption from the same surrounding activity that gave rise to it" and that "the adoption of the theory was speeded by a clearly apparent need for such a theory" (1962, p. 121). Moreover, "because the idea dealt with matters of common interest, it was able to spread more rapidly between disciplines" (p. 126). The idea "spread to other disciplines in proportion to its congeniality with their methods" and "to its analogic and suggestive value" (p. 132). Experimental psychologists working in communication problems and trained in the mathematics of communication engineering became logical carriers of the theory to the behavioral sciences. The introduction of information concepts to psychology was made by several routes. A number of excellent summaries are available that trace this development within experimental psychology: Attneave (1959), Garner (1962), Luce (1960), G. A. Miller (1956), and Quastler (1955). Here we shall briefly summarize a few of the salient avenues of entry into the field of experimental psychology, although parallel developments can doubtlessly be cited in any of the behavioral sciences. Thus, the balance of this review is a highly selective examination of the role of information theory in the social sciences. It is not a *general* review.

Organization of behavior sequences. The information measure was introduced to psychology in a now classic paper by Miller and Frick (1949). Their primary concern was the description of sequences of discrete responses. Their aim was twofold: the development of a stochastic model of behaviorial sequences and the development of a quantitative measure of the organization of the sequences. The Markov model, employed by Shannon, served as their descriptive model for the generation of response sequences; the information measure served as their measure of the degree of organization of the sequences [*see* MARKOV CHAINS].

For illustrative purposes response sequences of rats and of young girls, provided earlier in a multiple-choice experiment by Hamilton, were analyzed. An index of response stereotypy was identified as 1.0 minus the ratio of the obtained uncertainty, relative to maximum possible uncertainty. Thus, the measure of the stereotypy of response sequences is formally identical with the measure of relative redundancy of communication sources. For example, two responses, left and right, are defined as the class of responses available for observation of a rat in a given experimental situation. If the sequence of the rat's responses were perfectly predictable (e.g., were all left responses or a left–right alternation sequence), there would be 0 uncertainty in specifying successive responses. Thus, an index of response stereotypy of 1 would be obtained. Conversely, if the rat responded left and right equally often and if the sequence of responses was unpredictable, there would be maximum uncertainty in specifying successive responses. An index of response stereotypy of 0 would be obtained. In Hamilton's data identical indexes of response stereotypy were obtained for both girls and rats when the distributions of single-response choices were examined and when the distributions of pairs of successive choices were examined. The responses of girls became differentiated from those of the rats only when sequences of three successive choices were analyzed. In pointing out the importance of the higher-order statistical structure of response sequences and in providing an objective measure of its patterning, Miller and Frick laid the groundwork for the mathematical modeling of complex response sequences. [*See* RESPONSE SETS.]

Language. The statistical analysis of language represents a special application of the analysis of response sequences. Indeed, interest in cryptographic secrecy systems profoundly shaped the direction of Shannon's development of information theory. The English alphabet is potentially capable of producing many more different messages than it actually does. In practice certain letters are employed more frequently than others, e.g., *e* relative to *z*; and certain sequences occur more frequently than others, e.g., *th* relative to *ht*. Shannon (1951) measured the relative redundancy of English and obtained a lower bound of about 50 per cent and an upper bound of about 75 per cent redundancy relative to a random distribution of letters. A related observation is that English text may be nearly completely reconstructed when as much as 50 per cent of the text has been deleted (Shannon 1951; Chapanis 1954). Furthermore, in most communications environments the range of possible communications is strongly restricted by situational factors. In tower–pilot communications at air force bases (e.g., Fritz & Grier 1955; Frick & Sumby 1952), it was demonstrated that the over-all redundancy may approach 95 per cent, again relative to a random distribution of letters. As a result of Shannon's work and, especially, its popularization by Miller, nonlinguists became willing to tackle the intricacies of language as a complex series of response sequences, amenable to measurement and quantitative specification. [*See* LINGUISTICS.]

A related development of information concepts in psychology was the demonstration of the important role of informational factors in the perception of speech (G. A. Miller 1951). For example, the intelligibility of words heard against a noise background is a critical function of the size of the test vocabulary (Miller et al. 1951), i.e., a critical function of stimulus information. A given word might be perceived nearly perfectly when it is embedded within a small vocabulary of possible words but might be perceived correctly only rarely when it is embedded within a large vocabulary of possible words. This result is reasonable if information is associated with what could have been presented, rather than in terms of what actually is presented.

A number of different investigators have found the Miller, Heise, and Lichten data to be a rich source for testing theories of choice behavior. For example, Garner (1962) has demonstrated that these data are consistent with the assumption that under a given signal-to-noise ratio different vocabularies may transmit the same information. Stated differently, a large vocabulary coupled with a high error rate may yield nearly the same amount of information as that transmitted by a small vocabulary and a low error rate. [*See* PERCEPTION, *article on* SPEECH PERCEPTION.]

Identification experiments. Another way that information concepts have been introduced to psychology is by the quantitative description, in informational terms, of the identification experiment (Garner & Hake 1951). In the identification experiment, one of *n* possible stimuli is presented to the subject, whose task is to identify which one of the *n* stimuli was presented. For example, the instruments of a symphony orchestra are defined as the class of objects for study, and one of the instruments is sounded at random. The listener is instructed to indicate which instrument of the defined set was sounded. When the stimuli are well ordered and associated with a common unit of measurement—weight, length, duration, frequency, etc.—identification performance may readily be described in terms of conventional statistical measures, e.g., the average error. When the stimuli are not well ordered, as in the case of the symphonic instruments or a series of photographs depicting various emotional moods, identification performance cannot readily be described in terms of such conventional statistical measures. The transmitted-information measure is ideally suited to be an appropriate nonmetric measure of relatedness between stimuli and responses. In addition, a vexing methodological problem is associated with the identification experiment for ordered stimuli. The identification experiment attempts to answer a straightforward question: how many stimuli can be correctly identified? The answer to the question, furnished by a given body of data, depends upon what criterion for errors is adopted. If a small average error is permitted, the same body of data will admit a larger number of distinguishable stimuli than if a large average error is permitted.

A resolution to this problem is suggested by Hake and Garner (1951), who demonstrated that while the proportion of errors is greater in locating a point at one of 50 possible positions than at one of ten positions, the amount of transmitted information for ten possible positions is about equal to that for 50 possible positions. In turn, the amount of transmitted information specifies an equivalent number of perfectly identified categories.

A concentrated flurry of experimental activity demonstrated limited transmitted-informational capabilities with a wide variety of stimulus variables. Although the categorical measure of information was better matched to nonmetric variables, most of the initial studies took place with well-defined stimulus variables upon continuous scales, e.g., length of line, direction, sound frequency, etc. The only apparent advantage of the information measure to these studies was that a single measure of performance could be employed across a wide set of variables. The historian will probably judge that many experimental psychologists had previously steered clear of variables with weak metric properties and, as a result, were unable to appreciate immediately the full potential of the informational technique for nonmetric variables. In any event, the number of identifiable stimulus components associated with any single stimulus variable was found to be disappointingly small—from less than four to about ten stimuli. However, experimenters quickly discovered that a large number of identifiable stimulus components could be achieved by employing a large number of different stimulus variables, as long as the number of components per variable was kept reasonably small. (This story is told in G. A. Miller 1956, by means of the engaging title "The Magical Number Seven, Plus or Minus Two"; and in Garner 1962.)

Response speed and skilled tasks. An area of active experimental interest is the relation between the speed of response and the informational characteristics of skilled tasks. Hick (1952) sparked interest in this area with his demonstration that reaction time was linearly related to the logarithm of the number of possible alternatives available to the subject. Further, he suggested that a measure of the *rate* of information transmitted, in terms of the reciprocal of the slope of the empirical function relating reaction time to stimulus information, might be achieved from a discrete-trials reaction-time experiment. This transformation provides an estimate of the rate of information transmission in humans as about five to seven bits per second (Bricker 1955). More recent findings, however, have shown that with highly overlearned tasks, such as the reading of numerals, there is little change in reaction time as a function of the information of the task (Mowbray & Rhoades 1959; Leonard 1959). In this circumstance, identification of the rate of information transmission with the reciprocal of the slope of the reaction-time functions would lead to the unreasonable conclusion that there is an infinitely high rate of information transmission. The rate of information transmitted by the human receiver has been measured directly, in a variety of tasks, by a number of investigators. (This work is summarized in Quastler 1955, pp. 305–359.) In highly overlearned tasks there is an upper limit of about 35 bits per second, which is jointly a function of the highest effective speed, the highest effective range of alternatives, and the highest effective transmission rate (*ibid.*, p. 345). For most tasks, man's information-transmission rate is far lower than 35 bits per second. Electronic channels of communication, by contrast, have capabilities of millions or billions of bits per second. Clearly, man's forte is not the rate at which he can process information. When one examines certain structural features of information processing, however, the disparity between man and machine is narrowed. The largest and most elaborate of computers cannot yet perform many pattern-recognition tasks routinely performed by children. However, the rapid development of sophisticated computer programs may radically alter this situation. As Garner suggests, we shall need to devote more emphasis to the structural, as distinguished from the metric, characteristics of information if we are to understand human information processing. [*See* LEARNING, *article on* ACQUISITION OF SKILL; REACTION TIME.]

Structure of information. The structural examination of information is based upon a multivariate extension of Shannon's analysis by McGill (1954; 1955) and by Garner and McGill (1956). This work is summarized by Garner (1962). Garner has demonstrated the power of a multivariate information analysis for dissecting the information-relevant features of complex information sources. In this development, formulas associated with multiple correlation and with the analysis of variance find their direct counterparts within multivariate information analysis. Multivariate information analysis thus achieves the status of a general statistical tool for categorical materials, regardless of the appropriateness of the specific conceptualization of behavior in the terms of source, channel, noise, receiver, designation, etc. Furthermore, the efficiency of experimental design may be evaluated from the point of view of multivariate informational analysis. [*See* MULTIVARIATE ANALYSIS; *see also* McGill 1955.]

Garner's approach to a structural analysis of an information source rests on the distinction between *internal* structure, the relations between variables composing a set of stimuli, and *external* structure, the relations between stimuli and responses. This distinction is perhaps clarified by referring to Figure 1. A total ensemble of 16 possible stimulus patterns results from the binary coding of four variables: figure shape (circle or triangle), dot location (above or below), gap location (right or left), and number of internal lines (one or two). Thus, the 16 possible patterns have a potential

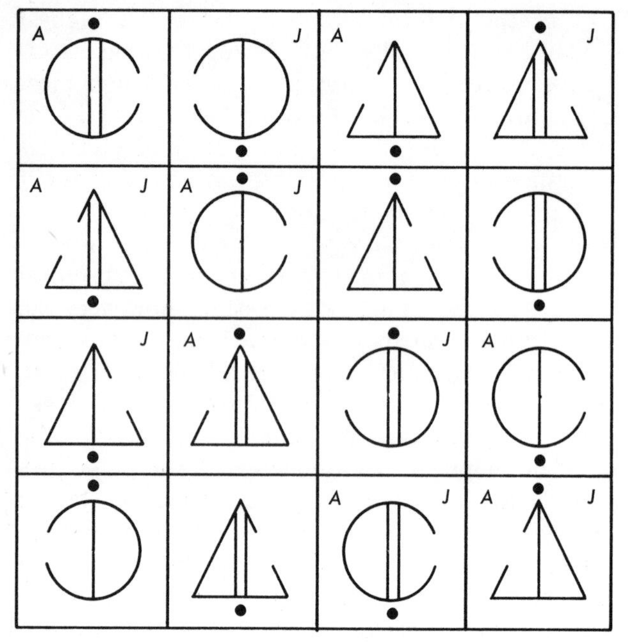

Examples of two subsets (*A* and *J*) are shown. The subset label (*A* or *J*) was omitted when the patterns were presented to subjects.

Figure 1 — An ensemble of 16 possible patterns consisting of four binary-coded variables

Source: From Whitman & Garner 1963.

information transmission of four bits per pattern. Let us now arbitrarily select a subset of eight of the possible 16 patterns. Such a subset has a potential information transmission of only three bits per pattern. According to Garner, the one bit lost in terms of external structure can appear in the form of internal structure. In the eight patterns of subset *A* of Figure 1, internal structure is represented by a simple contingency between figure shape and gap location (right gap with circles; left gap with triangles). In the eight patterns of subset *J*, internal structure is represented by a four-variable interaction among the variables. In these terms, subsets *A* and *J* represent the same amount of external structure and the same amount of internal structure but differ in the *form* of their internal structure. As a result of the differences in form of internal structure, the identification, from the 16 possible patterns, of the eight patterns of subset *A* is substantially superior to the identification of the eight patterns of subset *J*. The free recall of subsets with simple internal structure is also superior to that of subsets with complex internal structure (Whitman & Garner 1962). In the opinion of the author of this article, an extension of this method of structural analysis might reasonably be expected to provide a tool for the experimental assault upon qualitative differences in information. [*For further discussion of structural analysis, see* SYSTEMS ANALYSIS, *article on* PSYCHOLOGICAL SYSTEMS.]

The close relationship between information theory and psychology can be best summarized by the concluding remarks of the 1954 Conference on Information Theory in Psychology, organized by Henry Quastler. Although more than a decade has intervened, the remarks are nonetheless appropriate today.

> There is something frustrating and elusive about information theory. At first glance, it seems to be the answer to one's problems, whatever these problems may be. At second glance it turns out that it doesn't work out as smoothly or as easily as anticipated. Such disappointments, together with some instances of undoubtedly ill-advised use, have caused a certain amount of irritation. So nowadays one is not safe in using information theory without loudly proclaiming that he knows what he is doing and that he is quite aware that this method is not going to alleviate all worries. Even then, he is bound to get his quota of stern warnings against unfounded assumptions he has allegedly made.
>
> It seems that these warnings have reached a point of diminishing returns. Most of us who still use information theory are quite aware of the fact that this method is difficult, full of pitfalls, and definitely limited. We are hopeful, of course—nobody would work in a difficult field without expecting results—but always ready for a sober evaluation of the domain of our method.
>
> It has become very clear that information theory is one thing, information measures another. The two are historically linked, but can very well be disassociated. Information theory is defined by concepts and problems. It deals in a very particular way with amounts of variation, and with operations which have effect on such amounts. Information theory needs some measure of variation—but it doesn't have to be *H*; neither is the applicability of *H* and related measures restricted to information theory. (Quastler 1955, pp. 2–3)

Although a biophysicist by training, Quastler was acutely sensitive to psychological problems, as witnessed by the perspective of the quotation cited above. His death was a serious setback to the further definition of the role of information theory within psychology.

The historian of psychology will undoubtedly note the evangelistic endeavors in the early 1950s to remake psychology in the image of information theory. He will also note the flickering of that evangelical spirit as the concepts became more and more absorbed into the fabric of psychology. It is this author's guess that future historians will note that the development of information theory within psychology followed Garner's lead in highlighting the structural, rather than the metric, features of information measurement.

IRWIN POLLACK

[*Other relevant material may be found in* CYBERNETICS; MATHEMATICS; MODELS, MATHEMATICAL; PROBABILITY; SIMULATION; *and in the biography of* WIENER.]

BIBLIOGRAPHY

ATTNEAVE, FRED 1959 *Applications of Information Theory to Psychology: A Summary of Basic Concepts, Methods, and Results.* New York: Holt.

BRICKER, PETER D. 1955 The Identification of Redundant Stimulus Patterns. *Journal of Experimental Psychology* 49:73–81.

BROADBENT, DONALD E. 1958 *Perception and Communication.* Oxford: Pergamon.

BROSS, IRWIN D. J. 1966 Algebra and Illusion. *Science* 152:1330 only. → An interesting comment on the "fruitfulness" of applying formal models to science.

CALIFORNIA, UNIVERSITY OF, LOS ANGELES, WESTERN DATA PROCESSING CENTER 1961 *Contributions to Scientific Research in Management: The Proceedings of a Scientific Program.* Los Angeles: The University. → See especially the article by Jacob Marshak, "Remarks on the Economics of Information."

CHAPANIS, ALPHONSE 1954 The Reconstruction of Abbreviated Printed Messages. *Journal of Experimental Psychology* 48:496–510.

CHERRY, COLIN (1957) 1961 *On Human Communication: A Review, a Survey, and a Criticism.* New York: Wiley. → A paperback edition was published in 1963.

DAHLING, RANDALL L. 1962 Shannon's Information Theory: The Spread of an Idea. Pages 119–139 in Stanford University, Institute for Communication Research, *Studies of Innovation and of Communication to the Public,* by Elihu Katz et al. Stanford, Calif.: The Institute.

FRICK, F. C. 1959 Information Theory. Volume 2, pages 611–636 in Sigmund Koch (editor), *Psychology: A Study of a Science.* New York: McGraw-Hill.

FRICK, F. C.; and SUMBY, W. H. 1952 Control Tower Language. *Journal of the Acoustical Society of America* 24:595–596.

FRITZ, L.; and GRIER, GEORGE W. JR. 1955 Pragmatic Communication: A Study of Information Flow in Air Traffic Control. Pages 232–243 in Henry Quastler (editor), *Information Theory in Psychology.* Glencoe, Ill.: Free Press.

GARNER, WENDELL R. 1962 *Uncertainty and Structure as Psychological Concepts.* New York: Wiley.

GARNER, WENDELL R.; and HAKE, HAROLD W. 1951 The Amount of Information in Absolute Judgments. *Psychological Review* 58:446–459.

GARNER, WENDELL R.; and MCGILL, WILLIAM J. 1956 The Relation Between Information and Variance Analyses. *Psychometrika* 21:219–228.

GILBERT, E. N. 1966 Information Theory After 18 Years. *Science* 152:320–326. → An overview from the point of view of the mathematical statistician.

HAKE, HAROLD W.; and GARNER, WENDELL R. 1951 The Effect of Presenting Various Numbers of Discrete Steps on Scale Reading Accuracy. *Journal of Experimental Psychology* 42:358–366.

HARTLEY, R. V. L. 1928 Transmission of Information. *Bell System Technical Journal* 7:535–563.

HICK, W. E. 1952 On the Rate of Gain of Information. *Quarterly Journal of Experimental Psychology* 4:11–26.

KULLBACK, SOLOMON 1959 *Information Theory and Statistics.* New York: Wiley. → Considers a development of statistical theory along information lines.

LEONARD, J. ALFRED 1959 Tactical Choice Reactions: I. *Quarterly Journal of Experimental Psychology* 11:76–83.

LUCE, R. DUNCAN 1960 The Theory of Selective Information and Some of Its Behavioral Applications. Pages 1–119 in R. Duncan Luce (editor), *Developments in Mathematical Psychology.* Glencoe, Ill.: Free Press.

MCGILL, WILLIAM J. 1954 Multivariate Information Transmission. *Psychometrika* 19:97–116.

MCGILL, WILLIAM J. 1955 Isomorphism in Statistical Analysis. Pages 56–62 in Henry Quastler (editor), *Information Theory in Psychology.* Glencoe, Ill.: Free Press.

MILLER, GEORGE A. 1951 *Language and Communication.* New York: McGraw-Hill. → A paperback edition was published in 1963.

MILLER, GEORGE A. 1953 What Is Information Measurement? *American Psychologist* 8:3–11.

MILLER, GEORGE A. 1956 The Magical Number Seven, Plus or Minus Two: Some Limits on Our Capacity for Processing Information. *Psychological Review* 63:81–97.

MILLER, GEORGE A.; and FRICK, FREDERICK C. 1949 Statistical Behavioristics and Sequences of Responses. *Psychological Review* 56:311–324.

MILLER, GEORGE A.; HEISE, GEORGE A.; and LICHTEN, WILLIAM 1951 The Intelligibility of Speech as a Function of the Context of the Test Materials. *Journal of Experimental Psychology* 41:329–335.

MILLER, JAMES G. 1955 Toward a General Theory for the Behavioral Sciences. *American Psychologist* 10:513–531.

MOWBRAY, G. H.; and RHOADES, M. V. 1959 On the Reduction of Choice Reaction Times With Practice. *Quarterly Journal of Experimental Psychology* 11:16–23.

QUASTLER, HENRY (editor) 1955 *Information Theory in Psychology: Problems and Methods.* Glencoe, Ill.: Free Press.

SHANNON, CLAUDE E. (1948) 1962 The Mathematical Theory of Communication. Pages 3–91 in Claude E. Shannon and Warren Weaver, *The Mathematical Theory of Communication.* Urbana: Univ. of Illinois Press. → First published in Volume 27 of the *Bell System Technical Journal.*

SHANNON, CLAUDE E. 1951 Prediction and Entropy of Printed English. *Bell System Technical Journal* 30:50–64.

WHITMAN, JAMES R.; and GARNER, WENDELL R. 1962 Free Recall Learning of Visual Figures as a Function of Form of Internal Structure. *Journal of Experimental Psychology* 64:558–564.

WHITMAN, JAMES R.; and GARNER, WENDELL R. 1963 Concept Learning as a Function of Form of Internal Structure. *Journal of Verbal Learning and Verbal Behavior* 2:195–202.

WIENER, NORBERT (1948) 1962 *Cybernetics: Or, Control and Communication in the Animal and the Machine.* 2d ed. Cambridge, Mass.: M.I.T. Press.

INHERITANCE TAXES

See TAXATION, *article on* DEATH AND GIFT TAXES.

INITIATION

See RITUAL *and the biography of* GENNEP.

INNIS, HAROLD ADAMS

Harold Innis (1894–1952) was a Canadian economic historian whose study of history became the basis for new insights into the nature of economic society and of the social process. Writing a sketch of Canadian economic history as an introductory chapter to his doctoral thesis, *A History of the Canadian Pacific Railway* (1923), Innis became aware of the paucity of the materials for such a history and the poverty of the concepts so far employed. With vast industry he devoted himself to the accumulation of the materials. Not content with books and documents, he traveled all over Canada to get the feel of the economic life about which he wrote. (Typical of such activity was his toilsome and dangerous journey down the Mackenzie River in 1924.)

Innis' industry was matched by his imagination; his contribution to the materials was less important than his development of a new concept, a new approach. The key was the "staple product," together with the recognition that Canadian economic development had to be seen as an extension of European economic history, or, in this century, an extension of the economic history of the United States. C. R. Fay in his article "The Toronto School of Economic History" said of Innis' focus on the character of the staple product that "the emphasis is on the commodity itself: its significance for policy; the tying in of one activity with another; the way in which a basic commodity sets the general pace, creates new activities and is itself strengthened and perhaps dethroned by its own creation" (1934, p. 171). Pursuing the staple product approach, Innis published *The Fur Trade in Canada* (1930), *Settlement and the Mining Frontier* (1936), *The Cod Fisheries* (1940).

Newsprint was to have been the next staple to be studied; but he became more interested in the newspaper than in newsprint, and more interested in the communication of ideas than in the trade in commodities. *Empire and Communications* (1950), the substance of his Beit Lectures delivered at Oxford in 1948, was the first full-dress presentation of his work on communication. There followed two volumes of essays, *The Bias of Communication* (1951) and *Changing Concepts of Time* (1952), but his magnum opus was incomplete when he died. His interest in communication was stimulated by reading the works of Arnold Toynbee, Oswald Spengler, and A. L. Kroeber and by discussions with his colleague Charles Cochrane, author of *Christianity and Classical Culture,* published in 1940. Further stimulation came through the contemplation of the similarity of the problems of government, communication, and maintenance of individual initiative in the Northwest Company and the Roman Empire.

Education. Innis was born on a farm near Woodstock, Ontario, and received his schooling in a one-room public school near Norwich, then at Otterville High School, Woodstock Collegiate Institute, McMaster University, and, after a period of active service in France in the course of which he was severely wounded, at the University of Chicago. At Chicago he was a pupil of John Bates Clark, Frank H. Knight, Harry A. Millis, Harold G. Moulton, and Jacob Viner; his thesis was written under the direction of Chester Wright; and he was heavily influenced by the writings of Thorstein Veblen.

Professional career. In 1920 he joined the staff of the department of political economy in the University of Toronto, where he served until his death; in 1937 he had become head of the department and in 1947, dean of the school of graduate studies. His influence in the Canadian world of scholarship was very great. He gave encouragement and support to his colleagues across the country, and he knew them all through his travels. Recognizing the importance of organization, he played a key role in reactivating the Canadian Political Science Association in 1929 and in founding its journal, *The Canadian Journal of Economics and Political Science,* in 1935. He assisted in planning the "Canadian Frontiers of Settlement" series edited by W. A. Mackintosh, to which he contributed the volume on mining; and he played a major role as Canadian editor of the series on *Relations of Canada and the United States,* edited by J. T. Shotwell. He was one of three who took the lead in establishing the Canadian Social Science Research Council in 1940, and he helped his colleagues in the humanities to establish a similar council in 1944. Colleagues who had come under his influence and pupils who had worked under him as undergraduates or as graduate students came to permeate Canadian universities. Recognition of his leadership is evidenced by his election as president of the Canadian Political Science Association in 1937 and president of the Royal Society of Canada in 1946. That his influence was felt beyond the bounds of Canada is indicated by his election as president of the Economic History Association in 1942 and president of the American Economic Association in 1951.

Government service. Innis distrusted governments but served on three royal commissions: the Nova Scotia Royal Commission of Economic Inquiry, 1934; the Manitoba Royal Commission on Adult Education, 1946; and the Dominion Royal Commission on Transportation, 1948–1950. While his direct participation in the making of public policy was limited, he was deeply concerned and not without influence. But he was suspicious of scholars who play too large a part in public affairs; he was worried lest they lose their independence and their habit of continued questioning. He was worried by their undue concern with the present, for his own concern was not with months and years but generations; and he was worried by their readiness to grasp at solutions, for he believed that an economist who is certain of the solution of any problem is certain to be wrong. Finally, he found their solutions generally involved planning and regimentation. Perhaps it was his Baptist upbringing that left the agnostic Innis with a residue of tough individualism and a strong distrust of the state. Or was it perhaps the austere life of the farm?

V. W. BLADEN

WORKS BY INNIS

1923 *A History of the Canadian Pacific Railway.* London: King.

(1930) 1956 *The Fur Trade in Canada: An Introduction to Canadian Economic History.* Rev. ed. Univ. of Toronto Press.

1936 *Settlement and the Mining Frontier.* Canadian Frontiers of Settlement, Vol. 9. Toronto: Macmillan.

(1940) 1954 *The Cod Fisheries: The History of an International Economy.* 2d rev. ed. The Relations of Canada and the United States Series. Univ. of Toronto Press.

1950 *Empire and Communications.* Oxford: Clarendon.

1951 *The Bias of Communication.* Univ. of Toronto Press.

1952 *Changing Concepts of Time.* Univ. of Toronto Press.

1956 *Essays in Canadian Economic History.* Edited by Mary Q. Innis. Univ. of Toronto Press.

WORKS ABOUT INNIS

BLADEN, V. W. 1953 H. A. Innis. *American Economic Review* 43:1–15. → Tributes paid to Innis by V. W. Bladen, W. T. Easterbrook, and J. H. Willits at the 65th annual meeting of the American Economic Association.

BRADY, ALEXANDER 1953 Harold Adams Innis, 1894–1952 (obituary). *Canadian Journal of Economics and Political Science* 19:87–96.

CREIGHTON, DONALD 1957 *Harold Adams Innis: Portrait of a Scholar.* Univ. of Toronto Press.

FAY, CHARLES R. 1934 The Toronto School of Economic History. *Economic History: A Supplement to the Economic Journal* 3:168–171.

WARD, JANE (compiler) 1953 The Published Works of H. A. Innis. *Canadian Journal of Economics and Political Science* 19:233–244.

INNOVATION

Innovation is here defined as the process by which new products and techniques are introduced into the economic system. Successful innovation results in the capability of doing something that could not be done before, or at least not so well, or so economically. In Schumpeter's terms (1912), innovation results in the establishment of a new production function—a change in the set of possibilities that defines what can be produced and how.

In economic theory a sharp conceptual line is drawn between changes in the quantity of capital or labor used with already known techniques and practices, and changes to new ways of using capital and labor. Of course, changes in the inputs of the various factors of production, for example, increases in the amount of capital per worker, generally involve some changes in technique used, if not the utilization of a previously unknown way of doing things. Cutting with a power saw is not exactly the same process as cutting with a handsaw. Changes from one well-established technique to another that are the routine and obvious consequence of changing factor supplies or costs (such as switching from a coal furnace to a gas furnace because of lowered gas prices, or installing a long-available automatic machine in response to rising labor costs) would not be considered innovations. By contrast, the discovery and use of a new energy source, or design and use of a machine based on a new principle would be innovations, since they result in the establishment of a new capability.

However, it obviously is impossible to draw a fine line between changes in technique that are innovations and those that are not. Many of the changes in technique stimulated by the steadily rising cost of labor relative to capital that we have experienced in the United States for at least the past century have involved changes to ways of doing things quite different from those used before. The saving of labor often has required the designing of new machinery. While the degree to which the change in design or technique was more or less routine has varied from case to case, the design or use of anything that has not been produced or applied before is at least slightly risky and requires some imagination. Generally the term "innovation" is reserved to denote a change which requires a significant amount of imagination, represents a relatively sharp break with established ways of doing things, and thus essentially creates a new capability. But these qualifiers are not precise. Innovation clearly is a matter of degree.

Factors determining rate and direction

Invention and innovation. It is useful to distinguish between the conception of a new product or means of production and the practical implementation of that conception; in much of the economic literature the term "innovation" is reserved for the second of these two stages (see Ruttan 1959). In this article we shall view the process of innovation more broadly as involving the invention and development of new products and processes as well as their introduction to the economy. However, even defining innovation narrowly, analysis of the determinants of innovation must take invention into consideration.

Schumpeter has stressed that often innovation can occur without the presence of anything that we would identify as a technical invention. Thus, the opening up and utilization of a new source of raw materials is an innovation; it introduces a new capability to the economic system. This is so whether it is the result of an invention that enabled a previously uneconomic ore source to be tapped economically or of the initiative of an imaginative entrepreneur who seized a long-available opportunity that others had neglected. Further, even when a new conception is involved, the underlying invention need not be technical in the sense of a product or machine; rather it may be a new managerial concept (like statistical quality control or time–motion analysis) or an organizational concept (like the self-service supermarket). However, innovations based on technological advances have constituted a very large share of the innovations we have experienced, and the rate and direction of innovation obviously is affected by the rate and direction of the invention and development of technically new products and processes.

Social scientists have only begun to understand the determinants of technical invention, but it is clear that at least two variables play an important role in influencing what kinds of inventions are made: the state of technical knowledge and the perceived payoffs from successful inventions in different fields (see Nelson 1959).

In recent years there has been a tendency to view technical knowledge and formal scientific knowledge as being inseparable; certainly such inventions as the transistor and nylon were in large part the result of closely preceding scientific research and probably would have been impossible without the knowledge provided by modern science. However, it is clear that a large number of inventions have not been dependent for their conception and successful development upon closely preceding advances in formal science (Schmookler 1962; Gilfillan 1935). Thus, while the design of the gas refrigerator rests on the principle that expanding gases absorb heat, this was known long before the refrigerator was developed; and the development of the automatic cotton picker seems to have required no scientific concepts or data that were not known more than a century ago. It also appears that even when a particular design is closely dependent on recent advances in science, there often is an alternative design not resting on these advances that would accomplish roughly the same objective. Thus, while there certainly are exceptions, the role of formal science in influencing efforts to invent new products and processes seems to be more that of a reference book used to find solutions to problems than that of a spur to specific inventive efforts.

On the other hand, the data suggest that perceived needs have a strong effect on the kinds of problems focused on by inventors and organizations engaged in inventing. In particular, as the size of an industry grows relative to other industries, and as the amount of new equipment purchased by that industry increases, inventors appear to be drawn by the expanding opportunities and potential payoffs to work on problems related to that industry (Schmookler 1962). Less clearly, it also appears that changes in the relative scarcity of different factors tend to stimulate inventors to try to economize on the more scarce factor (Habakkuk 1962). Changes in both relative size of industries and relative scarcity of factors seem to stimulate reasonably rapid inventive response. Thus, as a first approximation, it seems fruitful to view conditions of perceived return as determining what problems inventors try to solve, and the state of scientific and other technical knowledge as determining how they go about solving them.

In recent years a growing share of the patented inventions made in the United States has been made in corporate R & D laboratories; the relative role of the private, free-lance inventor clearly is much smaller today than in 1900. However, despite many predictions to the contrary, many of the most significant technical inventions still come from private inventors or small companies, although this differs from field to field (see Jewkes et al. 1958; Schmookler 1959).

From invention to first practical use. Inventions, of course, have no impact upon the economic system unless they are brought into practice. The stock of unexploited inventions is one part of the set of possibilities for innovation open to potential entrepreneurs—individuals who are in a position to try to introduce something new to the economic system [*see* ENTREPRENEURSHIP].

It is sometimes convenient to conceive of the decision to try to introduce a new product or apply a new process as essentially occurring after the technical development is complete; this is the primary reason for the sharp conceptual distinction between invention and innovation that occurs in some of the literature. However, the use of the corporate R & D laboratory suggests that today at least (and probably a century ago also) a large part of the development work on a process or product (if not the original conception) occurs within the firm which subsequently tries to rise or market it (see the case studies in Jewkes et al. 1958). Further, it is clear that the early versions of new products and processes often have serious technical difficulties. Generally a considerable amount of development work remains to be done after a product or process is first introduced. The studies of learning curves by Hirsch (1952) bring this out clearly. Thus, in most cases development and innovation are tightly linked decisions, and the image of the entrepreneur as the chooser among an autonomously supplied set of complete, unexploited inventions is misleading.

Of course the fact that something has been invented does not mean that it will be, or should be, applied, even if all the technical development is complete. Whether it is, or should be, depends on how well it stands up in competition with existing products and processes, at existing conditions of supply and demand. The use of atomic energy for the production of power is economic in parts of Europe where the demand for power is great and the costs of mineral fuels are high, but not, at present, in the United States. And, when demand is not expanding, it is not economic to introduce a new process that requires new equipment until the old equipment has deteriorated to the point where the total costs (including the costs of buying the new equipment) of the new process are less than the variable costs of using the old. Thus, the time to bring even a potentially economic invention into use depends strongly on economic conditions, and very often there is a considerable lag between invention and first practical use (see Gilfillan 1935).

At the present time it is not clear what is the effect of market structure—the average size of firms and the degree of competition—upon the speed with which firms respond to new technical possibilities (for a theoretical discussion see Fellner 1951; Schmookler 1959). Mansfield's studies (1963) suggest that large firms tend to be the innovative leaders when the innovations are expensive to adopt and require large-scale operations to be economic, but perhaps not otherwise.

From early use to general use. Just as there is a lag between invention and first use, there also is a lag between early use and widespread use. If new productive capacity is required, it takes time for it to be expanded and labor hired. If the product replaces older products, it takes time for the older products to depreciate to the point where a switchover is economic. And, most important, it takes time for the potential consumers to learn about and appreciate the merits of the innovation.

Several studies have shown that the growth path of a new product or process can be approximated by a logistic curve: the growth is slow at first, then becomes quite rapid, and finally slows down as market equilibrium is reached (see Rogers 1962). Griliches (1957) and Mansfield (1961) have found that the speed with which equilibrium is reached is a function of the advantages of the new product over the old and the cost of purchasing it. Many sociological studies have identified other variables that determine the speed of diffusion and have begun to come to grips with the decision mechanisms involved [*for a review of the literature see* Rogers 1962; *see also* DIFFUSION, *article on* THE DIFFUSION OF INNOVATIONS].

The economic effects

Innovation and potential output. The most important economic effect of innovation is to increase the capability of the economic system to provide wanted goods and services—its potential output. In this article we shall call the effects of innovation upon the potential output of an economy *technical progress.*

It is useful, but not precise, to distinguish between innovations that create new or substantially improved final goods and services and innovations that increase the output of established goods and services which a given amount of labor and capital can produce. Perhaps the most dramatic impact of innovation has been in the creation of new and potentially better final goods and services. The improved standard of living that we have achieved since 1900 is in considerable part due to such innovations as the automobile, radio, and antibiotics. Although less dramatic, the role of innovations in increasing the productivity of capital and labor in production of existing goods and services may have been even more important. These innovations have been organizational as well as technological; they have included improvements in job-scheduling techniques, factory and warehouse layout, and mechanisms of labor–management relations, as well as new machinery and materials. Compared with 1900, the American economy is capable of producing not only a wider and more satisfactory range of final products and services but also much more of all kinds of products.

Unfortunately, given the present state of economic analysis, there is no practical way of measuring the contribution to improved well-being of innovation which results in really new goods and services. However, it is possible to get some qualitative feel for the role of innovation in increasing productivity.

While only a few studies have attempted to measure carefully the productivity advances that have resulted from specific innovations, the results of these studies are quite impressive. For example, Enos' study (1962) of the effects of various technological developments in catalytic cracking suggests productivity increases of several hundred per cent. Griliches' study (1958) of the effects of the introduction of hybrid corn also shows very great increases in productivity. In addition, the numerous histories of technology (for example, Habakkuk 1962) provide strong qualitative evidence of the tremendous impact of various innovations upon productivity.

While case studies can provide a qualitative feel for the over-all contribution of innovation, it is very risky to generalize from such a small sample. To assess the over-all contribution of innovation, an aggregative approach is needed.

There are a number of studies which have attempted to quantify the contribution of innovation and of other factors in our over-all economic growth (for example, Solow 1957; Denison 1962; Nelson 1964). These studies have tried to relate the growth of real Gross National Product (GNP) to such variables as growth of man-hours worked, growth of the stock of plant and equipment, rising educational attainments, and changing composition of output and employment—as well as to improved technology. These studies have all tended to show that growth of man-hours worked and of capital of unchanged quality together account for about half of the growth we have experienced, and that since 1900 the output a given quantity of labor and capital can produce has more than doubled. But the relative contribution of the other factors is extremely sensitive to the particular assumptions of the model and to the techniques of estimation. While the case studies of innovation mentioned above suggest that innovation has been an extremely important factor, the aggregate growth models are unable to specify, save under very restrictive assumptions, how much of the over-all increase in productivity has been due to innovation and how much is due to rising educational attainments and other factors. [*See* AGRICULTURE, *article on* PRODUCTIVITY AND TECHNOLOGY; CAPITAL, HUMAN.]

When the interaction among the various factors which jointly contribute to growth is considered, it is easy to understand why it is so difficult to isolate the importance of any one of them. It is clear that the contribution of innovation to the improved ability of the economic system to meet the material wants of society cannot be considered in isolation from the role of other factors. New capital equipment and highly trained and educated manpower were often required to achieve the benefits of new technology. But on the other hand, technological innovation certainly has played a role in determining the kinds and costs of capital equipment that could be built and the type of technological information and patterns of technological thinking that were imparted to the students who became the nation's trained manpower. Further, if technological advances had been less rapid it would have been impossible to have achieved the growth of the capital stock we have experienced without sharply declining rates of profit on new physical investment; thus the rate of growth of the capital stock probably would have been slower.

Because of interactions such as these it is impossible to determine precisely, given the present state of our economic understanding, the over-all contribution to economic growth that innovation has played. But clearly that contribution has been large.

Innovation and effective demand. Increased potential output can be used to meet more fully the private and public wants of society, but this need not occur automatically. If increased potential output is to be realized, effective aggregate demand for goods and services must grow in pace with the increased ability to supply them. If aggregate demand grows too slowly (or too rapidly), depression (or inflation) is the result.

There are many determinants of the rate of growth of aggregate demand; the rate of innovation is one of them. Indeed Schumpeter (1939) has placed innovation at center stage in his theory of the determinants of fluctuations in the rate of economic activity, as well as in the leading role in his theory of long-run economic progress. While the quantitative effect is difficult to measure, it is clear that rapid innovation raises the profitability of new equipment and hence spurs business investment and that retardation of innovation reduces the profitability of new investment and hence shifts the demand curve for investment downward (see Fellner 1956). If private savings are not particularly sensitive to changes in the rate of return these savings can earn, and if government fiscal and monetary policies are not particularly responsive to the state of over-all demand–supply balance in the economic system, then fluctuations in the rate of technological progress, by stimulating fluctuations in business investment, can cause business cycles. Thus Schumpeter associates the boom in the mid-nineteenth century with railroad and steel innovations and the boom of the 1920s with innovations in the automobile, chemical, and electrical industries. Conversely, periods of depression, such as the 1870s and the 1930s, can be blamed on a falling off of investment opportunities associated with a lack of major innovation. While it is probable that the Schumpeterian theory overstresses one-way causation (it is clear that there is a feedback from demand to innovation) and ignores the effectiveness of modern fiscal policies, Schumpeter's analysis does have considerable plausibility.

The implications appear paradoxical. Productivity grows at a faster rate when technological advance is rapid than when it is slow; hence, demand must grow more rapidly if it is to keep pace with a probably growing labor force plus the growth of productivity. However, an economy with rapid innovation may not require as expansionary a fiscal and monetary policy to keep employment high as an economy with a slower rate of technological progress and slower growth of productivity; for an economy with little innovation may not be able to sustain a high investment rate.

However, given modern fiscal and monetary policies, there is no reason why we must be dependent upon rapid technological progress and high investment demand to keep demand growing in line with potential output, or why fluctuations in innovation must cause severe business cycles. Changes in taxes and public spending, together with changes in government monetary operations, can compensate for large fluctuations in investment demand. The relationship between innovation and aggregate demand, stressed so strongly by Schumpeter and probably of major importance in the pre-World War II world, is not of major significance, save as a guide for fiscal and monetary policy in a world which has learned from Keynes and taken his lessons seriously.

Innovation and economic structure. Beneath the changes in aggregative economic activity and performance we have experienced, there have been dramatic shifts in the composition of GNP and in the allocation of the nation's human and material resources. These changes in composition have been essential aspects of the process of economic growth and, in particular, of the way in which technological change affects the economic system. These shifts have permitted the society to gain maximum benefits from new technological advances. At the same time, however, the necessity of making these shifts has imposed serious social costs.

The changing composition of output and employment that the United States has experienced since 1900 has been the result of interaction between changing patterns of demand and changing relative costs. While even without technological advance there would have been a shift in the composition of output and employment, it is difficult to avoid the judgment that in the absence of technological change the shift in the composition of output and employment would have been significantly smaller. Technological change certainly has played a major role both in shifting demand patterns—by changing the spectrum of available products and services, and changing relative costs—by creating new and more productive techniques (see Terleckyj 1957).

The shifting of the allocation of resources is an essential part of the process by which society takes maximum benefit from the new opportunities presented by technological advance. If an economy has freedom to reallocate its resources, it has a choice between taking the benefits of the technological advance primarily in the form of increased output by the initiating industry, or by shifting labor from that industry so as to increase output in other industries. In general, when new or improved products have been developed, society has chosen to shift labor and resources into their production and away from production of close substitutes. When technological advance has led to increased efficiency in producing existing products, the result in general has been lower prices and increased output of these products. In these cases where price has been quite sensitive to cost reduction and demand quite sensitive to changes in price, employment has increased. In the cases where price has not been particularly sensitive to cost reductions or demand not particularly sensitive to price reductions, labor has been released. There are many examples of both cases and both Kendrick's (1961) and Salter's (1960) data show that instances of the former have been about as frequent as instances of the latter. Where the industry is young and its products are just being introduced to the economy (as automobiles during the 1920s), rapid technological change tends to spur increases in employment. When the industries and their products were well established (as agriculture during the 1950s and 1960s), more often than not rapid technological change tends to cause cutbacks in employment.

In addition to causing changes in the composition of output and employment, innovation may change the balance between the rates of return to the different factors of production—particularly between labor and capital—by changing their relative marginal productivities (see Hicks 1932). There is a considerable body of economic thought relating to the effect of innovation on the relative returns to, and relative shares in national income of, labor and capital. While it is possible for an innovation to increase the marginal productivity of both labor and capital in the same proportion, it also is possible for the effects of innovation to be unbalanced: to raise the marginal productivity of capital more than the marginal productivity of labor and thus stimulate a substitution of capital for labor (labor-saving innovation) or vice versa (capital-saving innovation). It even is possible for an innovation to reduce absolutely the marginal productivity of one factor or another.

At the present time it is not possible to judge whether on balance innovation has been capital-saving, labor-saving, or neutral. In fact, the shares of capital and labor in the United States in 1960 were not drastically different from what they were in 1929, and probably not much different from 1900. But, of course, innovation is not the only factor which affects relative shares, and while neutral technological change is consistent with the data, other explanations are consistent as well. For example, it is possible that innovation has tended to be labor-saving, but labor's share did not fall because the rising capital–labor ratio we have experienced has sharply increased the relative returns to labor (in technical language—the aggregate elasticity of substitution is less than one). Indeed, several recent studies suggest that this may be the correct explanation (see Brown & De Cani 1963). But at present we cannot hold this conclusion with any real confidence.

RICHARD R. NELSON

[*See also* INCOME DISTRIBUTION, *article on* FUNCTIONAL SHARE; PATENTS; PRODUCTIVITY; RESEARCH AND DEVELOPMENT, *article on* INDUSTRIAL RESEARCH AND DEVELOPMENT; *and the biography of* SCHUMPETER.]

BIBLIOGRAPHY

BLAUG, MARK 1963 A Survey of the Theory of Process-innovations. *Economica* New Series 30:13–32.

BROWN, MURRAY; and DE CANI, JOHN S. 1963 Technological Change and the Distribution of Income. *International Economic Review* 4:289–309.

DENISON, EDWARD F. 1962 *The Sources of Economic Growth in the United States and the Alternatives Before Us.* New York: Committee for Economic Development.

ENOS, JOHN L. 1962 Invention and Innovation in the Petroleum Refining Industry. Pages 299–322 in Universities–National Bureau Committee for Economic Research, *The Rate and Direction of Inventive Activity.* Princeton Univ. Press.

FELLNER, WILLIAM J. 1951 The Influence of Market Structure Upon Technological Progress. *Quarterly Journal of Economics* 65:556–577.

FELLNER, WILLIAM J. 1956 *Trends and Cycles in Economic Activity.* New York: Holt.

GILFILLAN, S. COLUM 1935 *The Sociology of Invention: An Essay in the Social Causes of Technic Invention and Some of Its Social Results.* Chicago: Follet.

GRILICHES, ZVI 1957 Hybrid Corn: An Exploration in the Economics of Technological Change. *Econometrica* 25:501–522.

GRILICHES, ZVI 1958 Research Costs and Social Returns: Hybrid Corn and Related Innovations. *Journal of Political Economy* 66:419–431.

HABAKKUK, H. J. 1962 *American and British Technology in the Nineteenth Century.* Cambridge Univ. Press.

HICKS, JOHN R. (1932) 1964 *The Theory of Wages.* New York: St. Martins.

HIRSCH, W. Z. 1952 Manufacturing Progress Functions. *Review of Economics and Statistics* 34, no. 2:143–155.

JEWKES, JOHN; SAWERS, DAVID; and STILLERMAN, RICHARD 1958 *The Sources of Invention.* London: Macmillan; New York: St. Martins.

KENDRICK, JOHN W. 1961 *Productivity Trends in the United States.* National Bureau of Economic Research, General Series, No. 71. Princeton Univ. Press.

MACLAURIN, WILLIAM R. 1949 *Invention and Innovation in the Radio Industry.* New York: Macmillan.

MANSFIELD, EDWIN 1961 Technical Change and the Rate of Imitation. *Econometrica* 29:741–766.

MANSFIELD, EDWIN 1963 Size of Firm, Market Structure, and Innovation. *Journal of Political Economy* 71:556–576.

NELSON, RICHARD R. 1959 The Economics of Invention: A Survey of the Literature. *Journal of Business* 32: 101–127.

NELSON, RICHARD R. 1964 Aggregate Production Functions and Medium-range Growth Projections. *American Economic Review* 54:575–606.

ROGERS, EVERETT M. 1962 *Diffusion of Innovations.* New York: Free Press.

RUTTAN, VERNON W. 1959 Usher and Schumpeter on Invention, Innovation, and Technological Change. *Quarterly Journal of Economics* 73:596–606.

SALTER, W. E. G. 1960 *Productivity and Technical Change.* Cambridge Univ. Press.

SCHMOOKLER, JACOB 1959 Technological Progress and the Modern American Corporation. Pages 141–165 in

Edward S. Mason (editor), *The Corporation in Modern Society*. Cambridge, Mass.: Harvard Univ. Press.
SCHMOOKLER, JACOB 1962 Changes in Industry and in the State of Knowledge as Determinants of Industrial Invention. Pages 195–232 in Universities–National Bureau Committee for Economic Research, *The Rate and Direction of Inventive Activity*. Princeton Univ. Press.
SCHUMPETER, JOSEPH A. (1912) 1934 *The Theory of Economic Development: An Inquiry Into Profits, Capital, Credit, Interest, and the Business Cycle*. Harvard Economic Studies, Vol. 46. Cambridge, Mass.: Harvard Univ. Press. → First published as *Theorie der Wirtschaftlichen Entwicklung*. An abridged edition was published in 1964 by McGraw-Hill.
SCHUMPETER, JOSEPH A. 1939 *Business Cycles: A Theoretical, Historical, and Statistical Analysis of the Capitalist Process*. 2 vols. New York and London: McGraw-Hill.
SOLOW, ROBERT M. 1957 Technical Change and the Aggregate Production Function. *Review of Economics and Statistics* 39:312–320.
STRASSMAN, WOLFGANG P. 1959 *Risk and Technological Innovation: American Manufacturing Methods During the Nineteenth Century*. Ithaca, N.Y.: Cornell Univ. Press.
TERLECKYJ, NESTOR E. 1957 Factors Underlying Productivity Advance: Some Empirical Observations. American Statistical Association, Business and Economic Statistics Section, *Proceedings* [1957]:300–309. → Includes one page of discussion.
UNIVERSITIES–NATIONAL BUREAU COMMITTEE FOR ECONOMIC RESEARCH 1962 *The Rate and Direction of Inventive Activity: Economic and Social Factors*. Edited by Richard R. Nelson. Princeton Univ. Press.

INPUT–OUTPUT ANALYSIS

The input–output method is an adaptation of the neoclassical theory of general equilibrium [*see* ECONOMIC EQUILIBRIUM] to the empirical study of the quantitative interdependence between interrelated economic activities. It was originally developed to analyze and measure the connections between the various producing and consuming sectors within a national economy, but it has also been applied to the study of smaller economic systems, such as metropolitan areas or even large integrated individual enterprises, and to the analysis of international economic relationships.

In all instances the approach is basically the same: The interdependence of the individual sectors of the given system is described by a set of linear equations. The specific structural characteristics of the system are thus determined by the numerical magnitude of the coefficients of these equations. These coefficients must be determined empirically; in the analysis of the structural characteristics of an entire national economy, they are usually derived from a so-called statistical input–output table.

Applications. Application of the input–output method in empirical research requires the availability of basic statistical information. By 1963, input–output tables had been compiled for more than forty countries. The principal economic applications, as distinct from engineering and business-management applications, have been made in such fields as economic projections of demand, output, employment, and investment for the individual sectors of entire countries and of smaller economic regions (for example, metropolitan areas); study of technological change and its effect on productivity; analysis of the effect of wage, profit, and tax changes on prices; and study of international and interregional economic relationships, utilization of natural resources, and developmental planning.

Some of these applications require construction of special purpose input–output models. A great variety of special models is used, for instance, in the analysis of interregional relationships and in the study of problems of developmental planning.

Input–output tables

An input–output table describes the flow of goods and services between all the individual sectors of a national economy over a stated period of time—say, a year. An example of an input–output table depicting a three-sector economy is shown in Table 1. The three sectors are agriculture, whose total annual output amounted to 100 bushels of wheat; manufacturing, which produced 50 yards of cloth; and households, which supplied 300 man-years of labor. The nine entries inside the main body of the table show the intersectoral flows. Of the 100 bushels of wheat turned out by agriculture, 25 bushels were used up within the agricultural sector itself, 20 were delivered to and absorbed, as one of its inputs, by manufacturing, and 55 were taken by the household sector. The second and the third rows of the table describe in the same way the allocation of outputs of the two other sectors.

The figures entered in each column of the main body of the table thus describe the input structure

Table 1 — Example of an input–output table (in physical units)

Into / From	Sector 1: Agriculture	Sector 2: Manufacturing	Sector 3: Households	Total output
Sector 1: Agriculture	25	20	55	100 bushels of wheat
Sector 2: Manufacturing	14	6	30	50 yards of cloth
Sector 3: Households	80	180	40	300 man-years of labor

of the corresponding sector. In producing 100 bushels of wheat, agriculture absorbed 25 bushels of its own products, 14 yards of manufactured goods, and 80 man-years of labor received from the households. In producing 50 yards of cloth, manufacturing absorbed 20 bushels of wheat, 6 yards of its own products, and 180 man-years of labor. In their turn, the households used their income, which they received for supplying 300 man-years of labor, to pay for 55 bushels of wheat, 30 yards of cloth, and 40 man-years of direct services of labor, which they consumed.

All entries in this table are supposed to represent quantities, or at least physical indexes of quantities, of specific goods or services. A less aggregative, more detailed input–output table describing the same national economy in terms of 50, 100, or even 1,000 different sectors would permit a more specific qualitative identification of the individual entries. In a larger table, manufacturing would be represented not by one but by many distinct industrial sectors; its output—and consequently also the inputs of the other sectors—would be described in terms of yards of cotton cloth and tons of paper products, or possibly yards of percale, yards of heavy cotton cloth, tons of newsprint, and tons of writing paper.

Input–output tables and income accounts. Although in principle the intersectoral flows, as represented in an input–output table, can be thought of as being measured in physical units, in practice most input–output tables are constructed in value terms. Table 2 represents a translation of Table 1 into value terms on the assumption that the price of wheat is $2 per bushel, the price of cloth is $5 per yard, and the price of services supplied by the household sector is $1 per man-year. Thus, the values of the total outputs of agriculture, manufacturing, and households are shown in Table 2 as $200 (= 100 × $2), $250 (= 50 × $5), and $300 (= 300 × $1), respectively. The last row shows the combined value of all outputs absorbed by each

Table 2 — Example of an input–output table (in dollars)

From \ Into	*Sector 1: Agriculture*	*Sector 2: Manufacturing*	*Sector 3: Households*	*Total output*
Sector 1: Agriculture	50	40	110	200
Sector 2: Manufacturing	70	30	150	250
Sector 3: Households	80	180	40	300
Total input	200	250	300	

of the three sectors. Such column totals could not have been shown on Table 1, since the physical quantities of different inputs absorbed by each sector cannot be meaningfully added.

The input–output table expressed in value terms can be interpreted as a system of national accounts. The $300 showing the value of services rendered by households during the year obviously represents the annual national income. It equals the total of the income payments (shown in the third row) received by households for services rendered to each sector; it also equals the total value of goods and services (shown in the third column) purchased by households from themselves and from the other sectors. To the extent that the column entries (showing the input structure of each productive sector) cover current expenditures but not purchases made on capital account, the capital expenditures—being paid out of the net income—should be entered in the households' column.

All figures in Table 2, except the column sums shown in the bottom row, can also be interpreted as physical quantities of the goods or services to which they refer. This requires only that the physical unit in which one measures the entries in each row be redefined as the amount of output of the particular sector that can be purchased for $1 at prices that prevailed during the interval of time for which the table was constructed.

Input coefficients. Let the national economy be subdivided into $n + 1$ sectors. Sectors $1, \cdots, n$ are industries—that is, producing sectors—and sector $n + 1$ is the final demand sector, represented in input–output Tables 1 and 2 by households. For purposes of mathematical manipulation, the physical output of sector i is usually represented by x_i, and the symbol x_{ij} stands for the amount of the product of sector i absorbed as an input by sector j. The quantity of the product of sector i delivered to the final demand sector, $x_{i,n+1}$, is usually identified in short as y_i.

The quantity of the output of sector i absorbed by sector j per unit of j's total output is represented by the symbol a_{ij} and is called the *input coefficient* of sector i into sector j. Thus,

$$(1) \qquad a_{ij} = \frac{x_{ij}}{x_j}.$$

A complete set of the input coefficients of all sectors of a given economy arranged in the form of a rectangular table, corresponding to the input–output table of the same economy, is called the *structural matrix* of that economy. Table 3 presents the structural matrix of the economy whose flow

Table 3 — Structural matrix corresponding to the input–output table of Table 1

Into / From	Sector 1: Agriculture	Sector 2: Manufacturing	Sector 3: Households
Sector 1: Agriculture	0.25	0.40	0.183
Sector 2: Manufacturing	0.14	0.12	0.100
Sector 3: Households	0.80	3.60	0.133

matrix is shown in Table 1. The flow matrix constitutes the usual, although not necessarily the only possible, source of empirical information on the input structure of the various sectors of an economy. The entries in Table 3 are computed, according to equations (1), from the figures presented in Table 1—for example, $a_{11} = 25/100 = 0.25$, and $a_{12} = 20/50 = 0.40$.

In practice, the structural matrices are usually computed from input–output tables described in value terms, such as Table 2. In any case, the input coefficients must be interpreted, for analytical purposes described below, as ratios of two quantities measured in physical units. To emphasize this fact, we derived the structural matrix in this example from Table 1, not Table 2.

Theory of static input–output systems

The balance between the total output and the combined input uses of the product of each sector, as shown in tables 1 and 2, can be described by the following set of n equations:

$$
\begin{array}{rcccl}
(x_1 - x_{11}) & - x_{12} & - \cdots & - x_{1n} & = y_1 \\
- x_{21} & + (x_2 - x_{22}) & - \cdots & - x_{2n} & = y_2 \\
\vdots & \vdots & & \vdots & \vdots \\
- x_{n1} & - x_{n2} & - \cdots & + (x_n - x_{nn}) & = y_n .
\end{array} \qquad (2)
$$

A substitution of equations (1) into (2) yields n general equilibrium relationships between the total outputs, $x_1, x_2, \cdots, x_n$, of the producing sectors and the final bill of goods, $y_1, y_2, \cdots, y_n$, absorbed by households, government, and other final users:

$$
\begin{array}{rcccl}
(1 - a_{11})x_1 & - a_{12}\, x_2 & - \cdots & - a_{1n}\, x_n & = y_1 \\
- a_{21}\, x_1 & + (1 - a_{22})x_2 & - \cdots & - a_{2n}\, x_n & = y_2 \\
\vdots & \vdots & & \vdots & \vdots \\
- a_{n1}\, x_1 & - a_{n2}\, x_2 & - \cdots & + (1 - a_{nn})x_n & = y_n .
\end{array} \qquad (3)
$$

If the final demands, $y_1, y_2, \cdots, y_n$, that is, the quantities of the different goods absorbed by households and any other sector whose outputs are not represented by the variables appearing on the left-hand side of equations (3), are given, the system can be solved for the total outputs, $x_1, x_2, \cdots, x_n$.

The general solution of these equilibrium equations for the unknown x's in terms of the given y's can be presented in the following form:

$$
\begin{array}{l}
x_1 = A_{11}y_1 + A_{12}y_2 + \cdots + A_{1n}y_n \\
x_2 = A_{21}y_1 + A_{22}y_2 + \cdots + A_{2n}y_n \\
\vdots \qquad \vdots \qquad \vdots \qquad \vdots \\
x_n = A_{n1}y_1 + A_{n2}y_2 + \cdots + A_{nn}y_n .
\end{array} \qquad (4)
$$

The constant A_{ij} indicates by how much x_i would increase if y_j were increased by one unit. An increase in y_j would affect sector i directly (and also indirectly) if $i = j$, but even if $i \neq j$, sector i is affected indirectly, since it has to provide additional inputs to all other sectors that must contribute directly or indirectly to producing the additional y_j. From the computational point of view, this means that the magnitude of each coefficient A_{ij} in the solution (4) depends, in general, on all the input coefficients appearing on the left-hand side of the system of equilibrium equations, (3). In mathematical language, the matrix

$$
\begin{bmatrix}
A_{11} & A_{12} & \cdots & A_{1n} \\
A_{21} & A_{22} & \cdots & A_{2n} \\
\vdots & \vdots & & \vdots \\
A_{n1} & A_{n2} & \cdots & A_{nn}
\end{bmatrix}
$$

is the inverse of the matrix

$$
\begin{bmatrix}
(1 - a_{11}) & - a_{12} & \cdots & - a_{1n} \\
- a_{21} & (1 - a_{22}) & \cdots & - a_{2n} \\
\vdots & \vdots & & \vdots \\
- a_{n1} & - a_{n2} & \cdots & (1 - a_{nn})
\end{bmatrix} .
$$

The computation involved in finding the solution of (3) is called the *inversion of the coefficient matrix.*

The inverse of the matrix

$$
\begin{bmatrix}
(1-0.25) & -0.40 \\
-0.14 & (1-0.12)
\end{bmatrix}
$$

based on Table 3 is

$$
\begin{bmatrix}
1.4570 & 0.6623 \\
0.2318 & 1.2417
\end{bmatrix} .
$$

(Each element of the inverse has been rounded to four decimal places.) When inserted into (4), this yields two equations—namely,

$$
\begin{array}{l}
x_1 = 1.4570y_1 + 0.6623y_2 , \\
x_2 = 0.2318y_1 + 1.2417y_2 ,
\end{array} \qquad (5)
$$

which permit us to determine the total outputs, x_1 and x_2, of agriculture and manufacturing corresponding to any given combination of the deliveries of their respective products, y_1 and y_2, to the exogenous household sector. For example, setting

$y_1 = 55$ and $y_2 = 30$, we find that $x_1 = 100$ and $x_2 = 50$, which agrees with the figures in Table 1.

Only if all the A_{ij} are nonnegative will there necessarily exist a set of *positive* total outputs for *any* given set of final deliveries. A sufficient condition for the nonnegativity of the A_{ij} is that in the structural matrix

$$\begin{bmatrix} a_{11} & a_{12} & \cdots & a_{1n} \\ a_{21} & a_{22} & \cdots & a_{2n} \\ \vdots & \vdots & & \vdots \\ a_{n1} & a_{n2} & \cdots & a_{nn} \end{bmatrix}$$

the sum of the coefficients in each column (or in each row) be not larger than one and that at least one of these column (or row) sums be smaller than one. A national economy whose structural matrix does not satisfy this condition will be unable to sustain itself—that is, the combined input requirements of all sectors in such an economy would exceed the combined productive capabilities of the sectors.

When the structural matrix of a national economy is derived from a set of empirically observed value flows, the condition stated above is generally found to be satisfied.

In applying this criterion to a given structural matrix, it is useful to keep in mind that by doubling the size of the physical unit used in measuring the output of a particular sector, one can double the magnitude of all the technical input coefficients that make up the corresponding row and reduce to one-half their previous size all entries in the corresponding column.

In an *open* input–output system, households are usually treated as an exogenous sector—that is, total output of households, x_{n+1}, which is total employment, usually does not appear as an unknown variable on the left-hand side of system (3) and on the right-hand side of the solution (4). After the outputs of the endogenous sectors have been determined, total employment can be computed from the following equation:

$$x_{n+1} = a_{n+1,1}x_1 + a_{n+1,2}x_2 + \cdots + a_{n+1,n}x_n + y_{n+1}. \tag{6}$$

The technical coefficients, $a_{n+1,1}, a_{n+1,2}, \cdots, a_{n+1,n}$, are the inputs of labor absorbed by various industries (sectors) per unit of their respective outputs; y_{n+1} is the total amount of labor directly absorbed by households and other exogenous sectors. The employment equation for the three-sector system whose structural matrix is shown in Table 3 is

$$x_3 = 0.80x_1 + 3.60x_2 + y_3. \tag{7}$$

Households are not always treated as an exogenous sector. In dealing with problems of income generation in its relation to employment, the quantities of consumer goods and services absorbed by households can be considered (in a Keynesian manner) to be structurally dependent on the total level of employment, just as the quantities of coke and ore absorbed by blast furnaces are considered to be structurally related to the amount of pig iron produced by them. With households shifted to the left side of equations (2) and (4), the exogenous final demand appearing on the right side will contain only such items as government purchases, exports, and, in any case, additions to or reductions in stocks of goods—that is, real investment or disinvestment.

When all sectors and all purchases are considered to be endogenous, the input–output system is called *closed.* A static system cannot be truly closed since endogenous explanation of investment or disinvestment requires consideration of structural relationships between inputs and outputs that occur during different periods of time (see "Theory of dynamic input–output systems," below).

Exports and imports. In an input–output table of a country or a region that trades across its borders, exports can be entered as positive components and imports as negative components of final demand. If the economy described in Table 1 ceased to be self-sufficient and started, say, to import 20 bushels of wheat and to export 8 yards of cloth, while letting households consume the same amounts of both products as before, a new balance between all inputs and outputs would be established, which is described in Table 4.

The input coefficients of the endogenous sectors, and consequently also the structural matrix of the system and its inverse, remain the same as they were before. To form the new column of final demand, we have to add to the quantity of each good absorbed by households the amount that was exported less the amount that was imported. Defining E_i, $i = 1, \cdots, n$, as net exports (exports minus imports) of good i, and redefining $x_{i,n+1}$, $i = 1, \cdots, n$, as final demand for good i by households only, we have

$$y_i = x_{i,n+1} + E_i, \qquad i = 1, \cdots, n. \tag{8}$$

The sectoral outputs can then be derived (see "Theory of static input–output systems," above) from the general solution (4). For our numerical example, we can use equations (5) directly. The total labor requirement of the economy—300 man-years—remains in this particular case unchanged after the economy enters foreign trade, because the total direct and indirect labor content of the 20

Table 4 — Input–output table of the economy described in Table 1 with foreign trade added (in physical units)

From \ Into	Sector 1: Agriculture	Sector 2: Manufacturing	FINAL DEMAND: Sector 3: Households	Exports (+) or Imports (−)	Total	Total output
Sector 1: Agriculture	19.04	22.12	55	−20	35	76.16 bushels of wheat
Sector 2: Manufacturing	10.66	6.64	30	+8	38	55.30 yards of cloth
Sector 3: Households	60.93	199.07	40		40	300 man-years of labor

bushels of imported wheat happens to be equal to the labor content of the 8 yards of exported cloth.

If the imports of good i (that is, the negative E_i) happen to exceed the final domestic consumption of that good, the corresponding "net" final demand, y_i, will turn out to be negative. As y_i diminishes, the total output of all sectors and in particular the total output of sector i must, *ceteris paribus*, diminish. For some value of y_i, the output of sector i will be reduced to zero, which means that the entire direct and indirect demand for that particular commodity will be covered by imports. The industry will then be eliminated from the endogenous part of the input–output table. The imports of such goods are called noncompeting, particularly when, as in the case of coffee and certain minerals, even a large increase in domestic demand does not call forth domestic production of the good. The magnitude of domestic demand for a good that can be satisfied without domestic production of the good can be computed in the same way that the total demand for labor is computed from equation (6).

Prices. Prices in an open static input–output system are determined from a set of equations that state that the price that each productive sector receives must equal its total payments per unit of output for inputs purchased from itself and from the other industries, plus a "value added" per unit of output, which essentially represents payments made to the exogenous sectors. Defining p_i as the price received by industry i and V_i as the value added by industry i per unit of output, these equations are

$$(9)\quad \begin{aligned} (1-a_{11})p_1 \quad &- a_{21}\,p_2 - \cdots &- a_{n1}\,p_n &= V_1 \\ -a_{12}\,p_1 + (1-a_{22})p_2 &- \cdots &- a_{n2}\,p_n &= V_2 \\ \vdots \qquad\quad & \vdots & \vdots \quad & \quad\vdots \\ -a_{1n}\,p_1 \quad &- a_{2n}\,p_2 - \cdots &+ (1-a_{nn})p_n &= V_n. \end{aligned}$$

Each equation describes the balance between the price received and payments made by each endogenous sector per unit of its product; V_i represents the payments made by sector i, per unit of its product, to all exogenous (that is, final demand) sectors. The V_i usually consist of wages, interest on capital and entrepreneurial revenues credited to households, taxes paid to the government, and so on.

The solution of the price equations (9) permits the determination of prices of all products from given values added by each sector. The solution can be written

$$(10)\quad \begin{aligned} p_1 &= A_{11}V_1 + A_{21}V_2 + \cdots + A_{n1}V_n \\ p_2 &= A_{12}V_1 + A_{22}V_2 + \cdots + A_{n2}V_n \\ &\vdots \\ p_n &= A_{1n}V_1 + A_{2n}V_2 + \cdots + A_{nn}V_n. \end{aligned}$$

The constant, A_{ij}, measures the dependence of the price of the product of sector j on the value added by sector i.

The coefficients a_{ij} appearing in each row of the output equations (3) make up the corresponding column of coefficients appearing in the price equations (9); the coefficients A_{ij} appearing in each row of the output solution (4) make up the corresponding column of coefficients in the price solution (10).

Only if all the A_{ij} in the price solution are nonnegative will there necessarily exist *positive* prices enabling each sector to balance exactly its input–output accounts in value terms for *any* given set of positive values added. Since A_{ij} in the price solution equals A_{ji} in the output solution, this condition is the same as that needed to assure positive outputs for any given set of final demands.

Inserting into (10) the inverse computed for the example used above, we have:

$$(11)\quad \begin{aligned} p_1 &= 1.4570V_1 + 0.2318V_2, \\ p_2 &= 0.6623V_1 + 1.2417V_2. \end{aligned}$$

From tables 2 and 3 we can see that in our example the values added (that is, the wages) per unit of output by agriculture and manufacturing amounted to \$0.80 and \$3.60. According to equations (11), this yields $p_1 = \$2$ and $p_2 = \$5$, which are the prices of agricultural and manufactured products used in deriving from Table 1 the value figures presented in Table 2.

The internal consistency of the price and quantity relationships within an open input–output system is confirmed by the following identity derived from equations (4) and (9):

$$(12)\quad x_1V_1 + x_2V_2 + \cdots + x_nV_n \equiv y_1p_1 + y_2p_2 + \cdots + y_np_n.$$

On the left-hand side is the sum of the values added paid out by the endogenous sectors to the exogenous sectors of the system; on the right-hand side is the sum of the values (quantities times prices) of products delivered by all endogenous sectors to the final (exogenous) demand sector. This identity confirms, in other words, the accounting identity between the national income received and the national income spent, as shown in Table 2.

Theory of dynamic input–output systems

Dynamic input–output theory grows out of the static theory through consideration of intersectoral dependences involving lags or rates of change of variables over time. Structural relations between stocks and flows of goods constitute the theoretical basis for the input–output approach to empirical analysis of the accumulation process and of developmental planning.

The stock of goods produced by sector i that sector j must hold *per unit* of its full capacity output is called the capital coefficient of good i in sector j and is usually designated by b_{ij}. A column of capital coefficients indicating the stocks of buildings, machinery, inventories of raw materials and spare parts, and other supplies used by a particular sector describes what may be called that sector's real capital structure. The matrix

$$\begin{bmatrix} b_{11} & b_{12} & \cdots & b_{1n} \\ b_{21} & b_{22} & \cdots & b_{2n} \\ \vdots & \vdots & & \vdots \\ b_{n1} & b_{n2} & \cdots & b_{nn} \end{bmatrix}$$

describes the real capital structure of a national economy as a whole.

The current inputs and capital stocks required to produce the output of a particular industry might have to be utilized during the period in which the output is produced, or they might have to be made available and used, at least in part, one or more periods before that. An analytically general and at the same time realistic description of dynamic input–output relationships can be given if separate variables are used to designate the flows of inputs and of outputs absorbed or produced by the same industry in different years. The balance between the output and the available capacity of sector i in a particular year t can, for example, be described by a linear differential equation involving structural interrelationships between the inputs and the outputs of the various sectors and the *rates of change* of the inputs and outputs. The equation is

$$(13)\quad \begin{aligned} x_i(t) - a_{i1}x_1(t) - a_{i2}x_2(t) - \cdots - a_{in}x_n(t) \\ - b_{i1}\dot{x}_1(t) - b_{i2}\dot{x}_2(t) - \cdots - b_{in}\dot{x}_n(t) \\ = y_i(t), \end{aligned}$$

where $x_i(t)$ is the output and $\dot{x}_i(t)$ the rate of change of output of sector i at time t. If the time path of all final demands and the levels of all outputs at an initial point of time are assumed to be given, a system of n such linear differential equations, one for each sector, can be solved for all the n outputs. The solution gives the level of each output, $x_i(t)$, at any point of time—that is, for any t.

Although this approach to the study of dynamic input–output relationships offers certain theoretical advantages, most empirical work in the field is conducted in terms of discrete period analysis based on systems of difference equations of the following kind:

$$(14)\quad \begin{aligned} x_i^{(t)} - a_{i1}x_1^{(t)} - a_{i2}x_2^{(t)} - \cdots - a_{in}x_n^{(t)} \\ - b_{i1}(x_1^{(t+1)} - x_1^{(t)}) - b_{i2}(x_2^{(t+1)} - x_2^{(t)}) \\ - \cdots - b_{in}(x_n^{(t+1)} - x_n^{(t)}) = y_i^{(t)}. \end{aligned}$$

(Superscripts indicate the time period to which the variables refer.) The first $n + 1$ terms of this equation are identical to the left-hand side of the corresponding equations in the static system (3). The next n terms represent the deliveries from sector i to itself and to all other sectors in response to needs for additional productive capacities, which in turn depend on the differences between current and future outputs. These changes in outputs multiplied by the appropriate capital coefficients, i.e., productive stock required per unit of additional output, give the magnitude of the deliveries on the capital account.

In a static formulation investment in additional productive capacity is treated as a component of the given final demand, but in a dynamic analysis investment must be explained and cannot be considered as having been fixed beforehand. Hence the final demand for the product of industry i in period t, $y_i^{(t)}$ now comprises deliveries to households, government, and so on, but no additions to the stock of productive capital.

Equation (14) is a basic building block that can be used to construct a system describing intertemporal input–output relationships between the different sectors of a particular economy over an interval of time containing any number of years. The set of six equations (15) spans the intersectoral relationships within a three-sector economy, of which only two are endogenous, over a period of three years.

$$
(15)\qquad
\begin{aligned}
&(1 - a_{11} + b_{11})x_1^{(1)} - (a_{12} - b_{12})x_2^{(1)} - b_{11}x_1^{(2)} - b_{12}x_2^{(2)} = y_1^{(1)}\\
&(-a_{21} + b_{21})x_1^{(1)} + (1 - a_{22} + b_{22})x_2^{(1)} - b_{21}x_1^{(2)} - b_{22}x_2^{(2)} = y_2^{(1)}\\
&(1 - a_{11} + b_{11})x_1^{(2)} - (a_{12} - b_{12})x_2^{(2)} - b_{11}x_1^{(3)} - b_{12}x_2^{(3)} = y_1^{(2)}\\
&(-a_{21} + b_{21})x_1^{(2)} + (1 - a_{22} + b_{22})x_2^{(2)} - b_{21}x_1^{(3)} - b_{22}x_2^{(3)} = y_2^{(2)}\\
&(1 - a_{11} + b_{11})x_1^{(3)} - (a_{12} - b_{12})x_2^{(3)} - b_{11}x_1^{(4)} - b_{12}x_2^{(4)} = y_1^{(3)}\\
&(-a_{21} + b_{21})x_1^{(3)} + (1 - a_{22} + b_{22})x_2^{(3)} - b_{21}x_1^{(4)} - b_{22}x_2^{(4)} = y_2^{(3)}.
\end{aligned}
$$

Even if the final deliveries of both goods in each of the three years—that is, all the y's—are considered given, the six equations would still contain eight unknowns. In the last two equations, which describe the input–output balance of both industries in the third year, the amounts allocated to investment are seen to depend on the output levels of the next, that is, the fourth year. Two of the x's must also be given before one can proceed to solve the system of six equations for the remaining six unknowns. Thus, for example, if the outputs of both sectors in the first year, i.e., $x_1^{(1)}$ and $x_2^{(1)}$, are given, the system can be solved for the outputs of the second, third, and fourth years as functions of the six y's, that is, as functions of the annual deliveries of both goods over the period of the first three years.

Instead of being anchored in the first year and solved for the next three years, the system can be used in reverse; that is, after having fixed the output of both endogenous sectors in the last (fourth) year, the system can be solved so as to display the dependence of production on the final consumption levels over the period of the first three years.

The numerical example of a three-sector economy presented above can now be extended to demonstrate the solution of a dynamic input–output system. The flow coefficients shown in Table 3 must first be supplemented by a corresponding matrix of capital coefficients. Let it be

$$
\begin{bmatrix} 0.20 & 0.05 \\ 0.01 & 0.07 \end{bmatrix}.
$$

The entries in the first column show that 0.20 units of agricultural goods and 0.01 units of manufactured goods would have to be added to the capital stocks held by agriculture if the productive capacity of that sector were to be stepped up so as to enable it to increase its annual production by one unit. The two figures in the second column supply analogous information on the capital structure of manufacturing.

With the appropriate number inserted for all the a's and b's, system (15) takes on the form shown in (16).

$$
(16)\qquad
\begin{aligned}
&(1 - 0.25 + 0.20)x_1^{(1)} - (0.40 - 0.05)x_2^{(1)} - 0.20x_1^{(2)} - 0.05x_2^{(2)} = y_1^{(1)}\\
&(-0.14 + 0.01)x_1^{(1)} + (1 - 0.12 + 0.07)x_2^{(1)} - 0.01x_1^{(2)} - 0.07x_2^{(2)} = y_2^{(1)}\\
&(1 - 0.25 + 0.20)x_1^{(2)} - (0.40 - 0.05)x_2^{(2)} - 0.20x_1^{(3)} - 0.05x_2^{(3)} = y_1^{(2)}\\
&(-0.14 + 0.01)x_1^{(2)} + (1 - 0.12 + 0.07)x_2^{(2)} - 0.01x_1^{(3)} - 0.07x_2^{(3)} = y_2^{(2)}\\
&(1 - 0.25 + 0.20)x_1^{(3)} - (0.40 - 0.05)x_2^{(3)} = y_1^{(3)} + 0.20x_1^{(4)} + 0.05x_2^{(4)}\\
&(-0.14 + 0.01)x_1^{(3)} + (1 - 0.12 + 0.07)x_2^{(3)} = y_2^{(3)} + 0.01x_1^{(4)} + 0.07x_2^{(4)}.
\end{aligned}
$$

The terms containing $x_1^{(4)}$ and $x_2^{(4)}$ are transferred to the right-hand side in the last two equations, because in the general solution shown below these outputs will be considered given.

For purposes of computation, the fourth year's total outputs of both sectors were assumed to equal those entered in the last column of Table 1, that is, $x_1^{(4)} = 100$ bushels of wheat, and $x_2^{(4)} = 50$ yards of cloth. The solution for the remaining unknown outputs is given in equations (17).

$$
(17)\qquad
\begin{aligned}
x_1^{(1)} &= 1.6773 + 1.1088y_1^{(1)} + 0.4077y_2^{(1)} + 0.2631y_1^{(2)} + 0.1850y_2^{(2)} + 0.0644y_1^{(3)} + 0.0510y_2^{(3)}\\
x_2^{(1)} &= 0.4355 + 0.1517y_1^{(1)} + 1.1080y_2^{(1)} + 0.0589y_1^{(2)} + 0.1112y_2^{(2)} + 0.0159y_1^{(3)} + 0.0172y_2^{(3)}\\
x_1^{(2)} &= 6.7499 + 1.1088y_1^{(2)} + 0.4077y_2^{(2)} + 0.2631y_1^{(3)} + 0.1850y_2^{(3)}\\
x_2^{(2)} &= 1.8264 + 0.1517y_1^{(2)} + 1.1080y_2^{(2)} + 0.0589y_1^{(3)} + 0.1112y_2^{(3)}\\
x_1^{(3)} &= 26.773 + 1.1088y_1^{(3)} + 0.4077y_2^{(3)}\\
x_2^{(3)} &= 8.405 + 0.1517y_1^{(3)} + 1.1080y_2^{(3)}.
\end{aligned}
$$

Equations (17) represent a general numerical solution of the dynamic input–output system (16) in the same sense in which the inversion of the flow coefficient matrix incorporated in (5) yields a general solution of the original static system. These six equations describe explicitly the dependence of the total outputs of both industries in the first, second, and third years on the levels of final deliveries of both products in the first, second, and third years. To compute the sequence of annual outputs corresponding to any given sequence of annual deliveries to final demand, one has only to assign appropriate numerical magnitudes to all the y's on the right-hand side of each equation, perform the necessary multiplications, and sum up the results for each line.

As a simple check on the internal consistency of this general solution, the amounts of 55 bushels of wheat and 30 yards of cloth actually allocated to households in Table 1 can be substituted, respectively, for y_1 and y_2 in each of the six equations. After the performance of appropriate multiplications and additions the result would show that in this particular case the total output of wheat would be maintained at a constant level of 100 bushels and the total annual output of manufactured products at a constant level of 50 yards of cloth throughout the entire period. Since from the first year on nothing would have been added to, or subtracted from, its productive stocks, the economy would in this particular case maintain itself without expansion or contraction in either sector.

The same analytical procedure can be used to construct and solve an open dynamic input–output system incorporating structural change. Both the analytical approach and the numerical manipulations remain essentially the same; only the magnitude of the a's and b's inserted in each equation would have to be distinguished by appropriate time subscripts, thus permitting the numerical values of these flow and capital coefficients to change from year to year.

Since no outputs can be negative, only those sequences and combinations of final deliveries that turn out to require nonnegative total outputs in all sectors for all years can in fact be realized within the framework of a particular dynamic structure. The presence of many negative constants in the general solution of the type presented above indicates how narrow the range of alternative developmental paths open to a particular economy might actually be.

The major deficiency of the simple input–output approach to the description of dynamic processes presented here is its inability to handle situations in which one or more industries operate over significantly long periods of time under conditions of excess capacity. Stocks of fixed capital invested in one sector cannot as a rule be dismantled and shifted to use in another sector. Thus idle capacities—that is, excess stocks—are bound to appear whenever the rate of output in a particular industry goes down from one year to another.

To take account of idle stocks within the framework of a dynamic input–output system, the artificial concept of capacity-holding or stock-holding activity has to be introduced. For example, whenever the output of the manufacturing sector goes down from one year to the next by, say, one hundred units, the dummy activity of "holding idle manufacturing capacity" is assumed to increase by the same amount. Since the capital coefficients of that new activity are by definition identical to those of the manufacturing industry itself, the total stocks held by the manufacturing sector remain unchanged despite the fact that its annual output has been reduced.

The introduction of this new analytical device transforms the simple dynamic input–output scheme described above into a much more complex linear programming model [*see* PROGRAMMING].

A linear programming formulation can also be appropriately used in the analysis of dynamic (and also static) input–output systems in which two or more alternative techniques of production, each described by a different column of input coefficients, are available for some sectors or in which exogenously fixed supplies of several different primary factors of production impose limitations on the attainable combinations of total outputs.

Any linear programming solution of a dynamic input–output system will contain as a rule as many nonzero variables as there are equations in the system; the objective function essentially determines which variables should be reduced to zero and thus be eliminated from the set of balance equations so as to make the number of remaining variables equal to the number of equations. The simpler nonmaximizing types of solutions reduce the number of unknowns through deliberate decisions based on direct empirical evidence or pragmatic assumptions.

Classification, aggregation, and computation

The greater is the number of sectors included in an input–output table, the more detailed can be the statement of the final results in analytical applications. The majority of input–output tables now in use contain from 10 to 100 sectors; however, tables with several hundred sectors have been constructed and used. As better statistical information becomes available, the trend toward larger, more detailed tables becomes more pronounced.

The classification of industries in input–output analysis is guided by consideration of technological homogeneity, and the classification of households by structural similarity of expenditure patterns. The problem of *aggregation* arises when the size of an input–output matrix is reduced through combination of some of its columns and of the corresponding rows. The relationship between the properties of the aggregated and of the nonaggregated matrix depends upon the position within the latter of the input columns that are consolidated. Under certain ideal conditions, the consolidated inverse of the original matrix is identical to the inverse of the consolidated matrix. When these conditions are not fully but approximately satisfied, the forementioned identity is of course only approximately realized. [*See* AGGREGATION.]

Most applications of the input–output method require numerical solutions of large systems of linear equations, inversions of large matrices containing up to several hundred rows and columns, and computationally very similar solutions of large linear programming problems.

An example of the special computational procedures is the iterative procedure used to invert the matrix $(\boldsymbol{I} - \boldsymbol{A})$, where $\boldsymbol{A}$ is the structural matrix of coefficients a_{ij} and $\boldsymbol{I}$ is the identity matrix, that is,

$$\boldsymbol{I} = \begin{bmatrix} 1 & 0 & \cdots & 0 \\ 0 & 1 & \cdots & 0 \\ \vdots & \vdots & & \vdots \\ 0 & 0 & \cdots & 1 \end{bmatrix}.$$

The inverse of $(\boldsymbol{I} - \boldsymbol{A})$, denoted by $(\boldsymbol{I} - \boldsymbol{A})^{-1}$, can be written as the sum of an infinite series of increasing powers of $\boldsymbol{A}$, namely,

$$(\boldsymbol{I} - \boldsymbol{A})^{-1} = \boldsymbol{I} + \boldsymbol{A} + \boldsymbol{A}^2 + \boldsymbol{A}^3 + \cdots.$$

This series is convergent if the structural matrix $\boldsymbol{A}$ satisfies the conditions stated in the section "Theory of static input–output systems"—that is, if the national economy described by $\boldsymbol{A}$ is capable of being self-sustaining. A matrix of this kind also possesses another property that is very useful in numerical input–output computations: small variations (caused, for example, by observational errors) in the magnitude of its elements can cause only small changes in any element of $(\boldsymbol{I} - \boldsymbol{A})^{-1}$.

WASSILY LEONTIEF

[*The input–output method is used widely in the development and empirical application of many areas of economics. To gain an appreciation and understanding of its uses, the reader should consult* ECONOMIC GROWTH, *article on* MATHEMATICAL THEORY; INTERNATIONAL TRADE, *article on* MATHEMATICAL THEORY; SPATIAL ECONOMICS, *article on* THE GENERAL EQUILIBRIUM APPROACH. *For a general discussion of production relations, which are the major ingredients of input–output analysis, see* PRODUCTION.]

BIBLIOGRAPHY

ALMON, CLOPPER JR. 1966 *The American Economy to 1975: An Interindustry Forecast.* New York: Harper.

ARTLE, ROLAND 1959 *Studies in the Structure of the Stockholm Economy: Towards a Framework for Projecting Metropolitan Community Development.* Stockholm School of Economics, Business Research Institute.

BELGIUM, INSTITUT NATIONAL DE STATISTIQUE 1964–1965 *Tableau "entrées-sorties" de la Belgique en 1959.* 7 vols. Brussels: The Institute.

BERMAN, BARBARA R.; CHINITZ, BENJAMIN; and HOOVER, EDGAR M. 1960 *Projection of a Metropolis: Technical Supplement to the New York Metropolitan Region Study.* Cambridge, Mass.: Harvard Univ. Press.

BRUNO, MICHAEL 1962 *Interdependence, Resource Use and Structural Change in Israel.* Jerusalem: Bank of Israel.

CARTER, A. P. 1967 Changes in the Structure of the American Economy: 1947–1958–1962. *Review of Economics and Statistics* 49: May.

CHENERY, HOLLIS B.; and CLARK, PAUL G. 1959 *Interindustry Economics.* New York: Wiley.

CONFERENCE ON INTER-INDUSTRIAL RELATIONS, DRIEBERGEN, NETHERLANDS, *1950* 1953 *Input–Output Relations: Proceedings.* Edited by the Netherlands Economic Institute. Leiden (Netherlands): Kroese. → This conference, held in September 1950, was the first international conference on the subject.

CONFERENCE ON RESEARCH IN INCOME AND WEALTH 1955 *Input–Output Analysis: An Appraisal.* Studies in Income and Wealth, Vol. 18. Princeton Univ. Press.

CORNFIELD, JEROME; EVANS, W. DUANE; and HOFFENBERG, MARVIN 1947 Full Employment Patterns, 1950. *Monthly Labor Review* 64:163–190, 420–432.

FRANCE, INSTITUT NATIONAL DE LA STATISTIQUE ET DES ÉTUDES ÉCONOMIQUES 1966 *Méthodes de la comptabilité nationale—cadres et définitions de la base 1959.* Paris: The Institute. → Contains interindustry relations tables for 1959.

FRANCE, INSTITUT NATIONAL DE LA STATISTIQUE ET DES ÉTUDES ÉCONOMIQUES, *Études de comptabilité nationale* [1965]: No. 8. → A special number of "Études et conjoncture." Devoted to the discussion of input–output tables and their applications by the French government in economic planning.

GREAT BRITAIN, CENTRAL STATISTICAL OFFICE 1961 *Input–Output Tables for the United Kingdom, 1954.* London: H.M. Stationery Office.

HATANAKA, MICHIO 1960 *The Workability of Input–Output Analysis.* Ludwigshafen am Rhein (Germany): Fachverlag für Wirtschaftstheorie und Ökonometrie.

HIRSCH, WERNER Z. 1959 Interindustry Relations of a Metropolitan Area. *Review of Economics and Statistics* 41:360–369.

HOGLUND, BENGT; and WERIN, LARS 1964 *The Production System of the Swedish Economy: An Input–Output Study.* Stockholm: Almqvist & Wiksell.

IFO-INSTITUT FÜR WIRTSCHAFTSFORSCHUNG 1964 *Input–Output Tabellen für die westdeutsche Volkswirtschaft mit vorläufigen Ergebnissen für 1961.* 2 vols. Munich: The Institute.

INTERNATIONAL CONFERENCE ON INPUT–OUTPUT TECHNIQUES, GENEVA, *1961* 1963 *Structural Interdependence and Economic Development: Proceedings.* Edited by Tibor Barna. New York: St. Martins. → This conference, held under the auspices of the United Nations, was the third international conference on the subject.

ITALY, ISTITUTO CENTRALE DI STATISTICA 1965 *Primi studi sulle interdipendenze settoriali dell' economia italiana.* Note e relazioni, No. 27. Rome: The Institute. → Contains an input–output table of Italy for the year 1959.

JAPAN, GYŌSEI KANRICHŌ, TŌKEI KIJUNKYOKU 1963 *Report on the Compilation of Japan's Interindustry Relations Table for 1960.* Tokyo: The Agency. → In Japanese, with an English summary.

JAPAN, KEIZAI KIKAKUCHŌ 1965 *Medium Term Economic Plan 1964–1968.* Tokyo: The Agency. → Contains input–output tables for Japan for 1950, 1960, and projections to 1968.

JOHANSEN, LEIF 1960 *A Multi-sectoral Study of Economic Growth.* Amsterdam: North Holland Publishing.

KOSSOV, V. V. 1964 *Mezhotraslevoi balans* (Interindustry Balance). Akademiia Nauk SSSR, Tsentral'nyi Ekonomiko–matematicheskii Institut. Moscow: Nauka. → A textbook for input–output analysis.

LEONTIEF, WASSILY (1941) 1951 *The Structure of the American Economy; 1919–1939: An Empirical Application of Equilibrium Analysis.* 2d ed. New York: Oxford Univ. Press.

LEONTIEF, WASSILY 1966 *Input–Output Economics.* New York: Oxford Univ. Press. → Contains 11 essays by the author published over a period of 20 years.

LEONTIEF, WASSILY et al. 1953 *Studies in the Structure of the American Economy.* New York: Oxford Univ. Press.

MANNE, A. S. et al. 1965 A Consistency Model of India's Fourth Plan. *Sankhyā: The Indian Journal of Statistics* Series B [1965]:57–144. → Also published by the MIT Center for International Studies and the Planning Unit of the Indian Statistical Institute. Contains an interindustry transactions matrix of India for the fiscal year 1960–1961 and projections for the year 1970–1971.

MIERNYK, WILLIAM H. 1965 *The Elements of Input–Output Analysis.* New York: Random House. → A presentation of the essentials of input–output analysis in nonmathematical terms.

MIERNYK, WILLIAM H. et al. 1965 *The Impact of Space and Space Related Activities on a Local Economy: A Case Study of Boulder, Colorado.* Part 1: The Input–Output Analysis. Springfield, Va.: U.S. Department of Commerce, Clearinghouse for Federal Scientific and Technical Information.

MORGENSTERN, OSKAR (editor) 1954 *Economic Activity Analysis.* New York: Wiley.

NETHERLANDS (KINGDOM) CENTRAAL BUREAU VOOR DE STATISTIEK 1963 *Input–Output Tables for the Netherlands.* Statistical Studies, No. 16. Zeist (Netherlands): Haan. → Contains input–output tables of the Netherlands for 1948–1957.

PARETTI, DI V. et al. 1960 *Struttura e prospettive dell' economia energetica italiana.* Turin (Italy): Einaudi.

PISA, UNIVERSITÀ, FACOLTÀ DI ECONOMIA E COMMERCIO 1956 *The Structural Interdependence of the Economy: Proceedings of an International Conference on Input–Output Analysis, Varenna 27 June–10 July 1954.* Edited by Tibor Barna. New York: Wiley. → This conference, held at Varenna, Italy, in June 1954, was the second international conference on the subject.

RESEARCH PROJECT ON THE STRUCTURE OF THE AMERICAN ECONOMY 1953 *Studies in the Structure of the American Economy: Theoretical and Empirical Explorations in Input–Output Analysis,* by Wassily Leontief et al. New York: Oxford Univ. Press.

RILEY, VERA; and ALLEN, ROBERT L. 1955 *Interindustry Economic Studies.* Baltimore: Johns Hopkins Press. → An annotated bibliography.

SCIENTIFIC CONFERENCE ON STATISTICAL PROBLEMS, BUDAPEST, *1961* 1962 *Input–Output Tables: Their Compilation and Use.* Edited by Otto Lukács. Budapest: Akadémiai Kiadó. → Contains a description of the application of input–output analysis for planning purposes in the Soviet Union and other socialist countries.

STATISTICAL OFFICE OF THE EUROPEAN ECONOMIC COMMUNITIES 1965 *Tableaux "entrées-sorties" pour les pays de la Communauté Économique Européenne (seconde version).* Brussels: The Office. → Contains 1959 input–output tables for Belgium, France, Germany (Federal Republic including West Berlin), Italy, and the Netherlands.

STONE, RICHARD 1961 *Input–Output and National Accounts.* Paris: Organization for European Economic Co-operation.

TASKIER, CHARLOTTE E. 1961 *Input–Output Bibliography: 1955–1960.* New York: United Nations. → An annotated bibliography.

TASKIER, CHARLOTTE E. 1964 *Input–Output Bibliography, 1960–1963.* New York: United Nations.

THEIL, HENRI 1966 *Applied Economic Forecasting.* Chicago: Rand McNally. → Discusses input–output methods and the results of economic predictions based on input–output tables of the Netherlands.

TILANUS, CHRISTIAAN B. 1965 *Input–Output Experiments: The Netherlands 1948–1961.* Rotterdam: Universitaire Pers.

U.S. BUREAU OF LABOR STATISTICS 1966 *Projections 1970: Interindustry Relationships—Potential Demand —Employment.* Bulletin 1536. Washington: Government Printing Office.

U.S. CONGRESS, JOINT ECONOMIC COMMITTEE 1966 *New Directions in the Soviet Economy: Studies Prepared for the Subcommittee on Foreign Economic Policy.* Part II-A: Economic Performance. 89th Congress, 2d Session. Washington: Government Printing Office. → See especially "The 1959 Soviet Input–Output Table," by V. G. Treml.

U.S. DEPARTMENT OF COMMERCE, OFFICE OF BUSINESS ECONOMICS 1965 The Transaction Table of the 1958 Input–Output Study and Revised Direct and Total Requirements Data. *Survey of Current Business* 45, no. 9:33–49, 56.

WONNACOTT, RONALD J. 1961 *Canadian–American Dependence: An Interindustry Analysis of Production and Prices.* Amsterdam: North-Holland Publishing.

YAMADA, ISAMU 1961 *Theory and Application of Interindustry Analysis.* Tokyo: Kinokuniya.

INSANITY

See MENTAL DISORDERS.

INSECURITY

See ANXIETY; INFANCY, *article on* THE EFFECTS OF EARLY EXPERIENCE.

INSTALLMENT CREDIT

Installment credit is the most important form of consumer credit, which is the short-term and medium-term portion of individual debt. Consumer credit accounts for about 30 per cent of total household debt in the United States, with mortgage debt amounting to most of the rest, and for about 10 per cent of the total private debt in the country. Consumer credit is, excepting real estate mortgage credit, the credit granted to consumers for household, family, and other personal reasons. Noninstallment credit includes all single-payment loans, charge accounts, and service credits. Installment credit (or hire purchase, as it is known in Great Britain) is composed of loans to finance automobiles and other durable consumer goods, repair and modernization loans, and certain other personal loans. Installment loans are repayable at regular intervals over a specific period of time. Contracts frequently provide that the goods purchased shall not become the legal property of the purchaser until every installment has been paid.

The demand for consumer credit arises in countries where there is the need to finance automobiles, refrigerators, laundry equipment, and other such products. In all the wealthy countries in the world, the greatest single use of installment credit is for the purchase of automobiles. In the United States, since the 1920s, except for a short period after World War II, from 60 to 70 per cent of the automobiles have been purchased with installment credit. [*See* CONSUMERS, *article on* CONSUMER ASSETS.] Other exceptionally large expenditures, such as tax payments, insurance premiums, travel expenses, Christmas expenses, and unpaid bills are also financed by installment credit. Single-payment credit is used to meet more transitory financial requirements or arises as the result of sellers offering delayed payment terms for customer convenience.

The major lenders of consumer credit are financial institutions such as commercial banks, sales finance companies, credit unions, and consumer finance companies. Retail outlets such as department stores, furniture stores, and appliance and automobile dealers also extend substantial amounts of consumer credit. Commercial banks are by far the largest issuer, owning about 50 per cent of all the consumer credit financed by financial institutions and over 40 per cent of all consumer credit.

The volume of consumer credit in a country depends on the employment and income conditions, the types of goods produced, and the level of competition in the sale of these goods. Installment credit is feasible only where a large part of the population receives its income in regular periodic amounts, such as weekly or monthly payments of wages and salaries. At the same time, these incomes must be large enough for the population to afford rather expensive consumer goods. Postwar Europe, including the United Kingdom, has experienced a rapid growth in consumer credit as incomes have risen. Single-payment credit requires the ability to forecast the future availability of funds to repay the loan. Much of this type of consumer credit is offered to attract customers to specific stores or products.

History. Individual or consumer credit is an old institution. Ever since markets existed where

Table 1 — Consumer credit and disposable personal income (in billions of dollars)*

	TOTAL CONSUMER CREDIT	INSTALLMENT CREDIT		NONINSTALLMENT CREDIT	DISPOSABLE PERSONAL INCOME
		Total	*Automobile*		
1945	5.7	2.5	0.5	3.2	150.2
1946	8.4	4.2	1.0	4.2	160.0
1947	11.6	6.7	1.9	4.9	169.8
1948	14.4	9.0	3.0	5.5	189.1
1949	17.4	11.6	4.6	5.8	188.6
1950	21.5	14.7	6.1	6.8	206.9
1951	22.7	15.3	6.0	7.4	226.6
1952	27.5	19.4	7.7	8.1	238.3
1953	31.4	23.0	9.8	8.4	252.6
1954	32.5	23.6	9.8	8.9	257.4
1955	38.8	28.9	13.5	9.9	275.3
1956	42.3	31.7	14.4	10.6	293.2
1957	45.0	33.9	15.3	11.1	308.5
1958	45.1	33.6	14.2	11.5	318.8
1959	51.5	39.2	16.4	12.3	337.3
1960	56.0	42.8	17.7	13.2	350.0
1961	57.7	43.5	17.2	14.2	364.4
1962	63.2	48.0	19.5	15.1	385.3
1963	70.5	54.2	22.4	16.3	404.6
1964	78.4	60.5	25.2	17.9	436.6
1965	87.9	68.6	28.9	19.3	469.1

* Details may not add to totals because of rounding.

Source: U.S. President, *Economic Report. . . .*

products were sold, there has been financing of consumers. Until the nineteenth century, however, much of this credit was on a personal basis: debt was not institutionalized, and repayment agreements were often not formally written down. Installment loans for the purchase of consumer durable goods, such as furniture, appeared in the nineteenth century in the United States. Serious attention to installment credit first arose after World War I. The introduction of the mass-produced passenger automobile was facilitated by the very rapid expansion of consumer credit in the 1920s.

The rapid growth of consumer credit in the United States since the 1920s has aroused great public interest and discussion. The development is regarded by some as unsound from the viewpoint of the economy and unwise from the viewpoint of the borrower. Others feel that installment credit is necessary for the distribution of new durable goods among broad groups of the population, permitting the development of industry on an efficient and highly productive basis. During the depression of the early 1930s, consumer credit proved to be a sound asset. However, some observers continue to feel that installment credit does contribute to economic instability and ought to be regulated.

Between 1947 and 1965 consumer credit grew at a faster rate than individual mortgage credit in the United States. In 1947 consumer credit amounted to $11,600 million; in 1965 it amounted to $87,900 million. The rate of increase in consumer credit has been 10 per cent per year, or about double the rate of growth of income (see Table 1). Installment credit constitutes about 75 per cent of consumer credit; noninstallment loans, about 25 per cent. About 40 per cent of installment credit is automobile loans. Personal loans and loans to purchase consumer durables account about equally for the balance.

Table 2 — Consumer credit outstanding, by type, 1947 and 1965 (end of years)

	1947		*1965*		*1965*
	Billions of dollars	Per cent of total	Billions of dollars	Per cent of total	AS A MULTIPLE OF 1947*
Total	11.6	100.0	87.9	100.0	7.5
Noninstallment	4.9	42.3	19.3	21.6	3.8
Installment	6.7	57.7	68.6	78.4	10.1
Automobile paper	1.9	16.6	28.8	32.8	14.8
Other consumer goods paper	2.2	18.5	17.7	20.2	7.9
Repair and modernization loans	.7	6.2	3.7	4.2	5.1
Personal loans	1.9	16.4	18.4	21.2	9.6

* Multiples computed from unrounded figures.

Source: *Federal Reserve Bulletin.*

Table 3 — Growth of consumer credit and of installment debt repayments relative to disposable income

	Consumer credit as percentage of disposable income	Installment debt repayments as percentage of disposable income
1947	6.8	6.0
1948	7.6	7.0
1949	9.2	8.2
1950	10.3	8.9
1951	10.0	10.1
1952	11.5	10.7
1953	12.4	11.0
1954	12.6	11.8
1955	14.2	12.3
1956	14.5	12.7
1957	14.6	12.9
1958	14.2	12.7
1959	15.3	12.6
1960	16.0	13.1
1961	15.8	13.1
1962	16.4	13.2
1963	17.4	13.7
1964	17.8	14.0
1965	18.3	14.3

Source: U.S. President, *Economic Report. . . .*

Throughout the postwar period installment credit has increased relative to noninstallment loans (see Table 2). The initial spurt after World War II probably reflects the end of the wartime period of short supply of automobiles and consumer durables. Easily available credit and the widening variety of uses for personal loans help to explain the growth since then.

Not only has consumer credit been growing more rapidly than income, but consumer debt repayments as a percentage of disposable income have also been rising (see Table 3). These trends have caused some observers to question how long this can continue and to express alarm over the long-run and cyclical effects of the growth in debt. Many fear that consumers may become overextended.

Cyclical implications. Since consumer credit accounts for a significant share of purchases of consumer durables, variations in the rate of growth of consumer credit may not only intensify the business cycle but may, in fact, act to create it. Throughout the postwar period, consumer credit has exhibited a strong growth trend. The change in consumer credit outstanding, however, displays a lagging cyclical pattern. Net extensions increase most rapidly after income rises sharply and decline after a downturn has begun. This suggests that consumers borrow heavily to purchase durable goods during a cyclical upswing in anticipation of future growth in income. The additional spending, however, acting through the multiplier and accelerator, tends to amplify the boom.

During recessions, when income prospects are less certain, new borrowing declines. Repayments of debt granted during the expansion, however, must be met. Borrowers may be forced to reduce the proportion of their disposable income spent for consumption, thus aggravating the decline. Difficulties will be compounded if, at the peak, the level of indebtedness is pressing against the ability of borrowers to meet scheduled repayments. In this instance a decline in income, even of modest proportions, could produce widespread defaults. If the solvency of creditors is threatened, they may refuse to grant additional loans, and spending will be further reduced. Thus, consumer credit can add to the forces causing business cycles. [*See* BUSINESS CYCLES.]

Variations in the rate of growth of consumer credit may also create a business cycle. Since repayments represent a drain, or leakage, from currently available income, new installment loans at least equal to repayments are required to supply consumers with purchasing power. If new borrowing declines or repayments rise for any length of time, sales of consumer durables will fall. In 1961, for example, new installment loans on automobiles fell $1,600 million from the 1960 level of $16,000 million, and repayments rose negligibly to $16,500 million. The fact that repayments were slightly larger than new lending helps to explain the reduction in automobile sales from 556,000 monthly in 1960 to 462,000 monthly in 1961. If additional net purchases financed on credit are required to sustain a boom, extensions must always exceed repayments.

In the postwar period the cyclical swings in the change in consumer credit outstanding have followed the business cycle. For this reason, consumer credit variations have probably delayed recoveries and added to inflationary pressures later on during expansions. The fluctuations, however, do not appear to have been a major independent influence in creating business cycles.

Trend implications. The fact that installment credit has been growing more rapidly than income and that installment debt repayments as a percentage of disposable income (see Table 3) have been rising suggests that families may have been borrowing larger and larger amounts relative to their incomes. If this were to continue, the burden of the debt would eventually become intolerable, and its growth would stop. When this happens, some authorities maintain, sales of consumer durables will decline, and the prosperity, which has been financed in part by installment credit, will end.

Alain Enthoven has presented (1957–1964) a model which shows that the growth of installment credit can be explained primarily by the increase in the proportion of households using installment debt rather than by a rise in the average indebtedness of households that already have some debt outstanding. According to this model, if the number of families using installment credit suddenly rises, and total debt initially is small, and the debt–income ratio (average propensity to incur debt) for each family remains constant, the installment credit–income ratio will asymptotically approach a stable limit from below. As the number of families using installment credit increases, the limiting debt–income ratio will rise.

Other models have been suggested that relate the number of families borrowing to the level of income in the economy, and the amount of borrowing per family to the income level in that family. These models suggest that the ratio of consumer credit to income will rise as income levels rise.

There is no consensus on how high the debt–income ratio may go before the burden of the debt becomes intolerable. There is fairly general agreement, however, that very serious problems are not likely to arise as long as income remains high and growing. In analyzing the total burden of household debt, not only consumer credit but also mortgage debt, security credit, and other household debt must be considered. As suggested above, the burden depends on the distribution of the debt and the financial resources that borrowers could marshal to repay their debt if their incomes should falter.

Individual debt has increased relative to disposable income each year since 1955 and has risen relative to discretionary income in eight of the nine years from 1956 to 1964 (see Table 4). Although

Table 4 — Total household debt relative to disposable and discretionary income and liquid assets [a]

	TOTAL HOUSEHOLD DEBT	TOTAL HOUSEHOLD DEBT AS A PERCENTAGE OF		
	(In billions of dollars)	Disposable income	Discretionary income	Liquid assets
1955	136.0	49.6	139.9	59.4
1956	150.6	51.4	143.4	62.8
1957	161.9	52.4	148.0	64.5
1958	173.6	54.6	158.7	65.7
1959	193.7	57.5	162.5	70.6
1960	209.3	59.8	173.5	69.8
1961	224.6	61.6	177.1	70.5
1962	244.0	63.4	179.0	69.9
1963	266.8	66.3	190.6	69.6
1964	291.3	67.5	186.1	72.5
1965	319.0	68.6	b	b

a. Household debt includes mortgage debt. Liquid assets includes currency plus demand deposits, time and savings accounts, savings bonds and other federal government security holdings.

b. Not available.

Sources: Federal Reserve Bulletin; U.S. President, Economic Report. . . .

the ratio of debt to liquid assets for households leveled off in 1960, the most recent figure indicates a sharp jump. While these figures tend to show that the burden of the debt has become greater, the discretionary income of households has increased, indicating their debt capacity may have risen substantially over the period. Basic expenditures, such as food, now account for about 20 per cent of current household expenditures, down from 28 per cent in 1947. Also a considerable portion of borrowing results in the substitution of durable goods and housing for services and in a consequent reduction in other relatively fixed expenses. Consumers borrow to buy homes, cars, and washing machines rather than pay rent, subway and taxi fares, and laundry bills.

These figures, however, are aggregated and may present a misleading picture. They do not show the distribution of debt by income class and liquid asset holdings. If liquid assets are owned primarily by debt-free consumers, it would be incorrect to assume that all liquid assets could serve as a backstop for debt repayments. Ideally one would like to know the total debt—mortgage plus consumer credit—owed by families relative to their incomes and wealth, but this information is not available. (Some data on the distribution of households owing *installment* debt is provided in the 1964 volume of Michigan, University of . . . *Survey of Consumer Finances.*)

In 1964, 47 per cent of American families owed installment debt (see Table 5). Most families in debt owed relatively small amounts; almost one-half owed less than $500, and only 6 per cent owed $2,000 or more. The distribution of families according to installment credit repayments as a percentage of income has not changed greatly in the last ten years. In 1964, about one family in ten was committed to debt repayments greater than 20 per cent of income. Twelve per cent of all families with incomes below $3,000 and 17 per cent of all families in the $3,000–$4,999 income bracket were obligated for annual repayments of at least 20 per cent of income. Only 8 per cent of the families made debt repayments between 20 and 39 per cent of their incomes, and only 2 per cent were obligated to make repayments in excess of 40 per cent of their incomes. Most families with relatively high debt repayment–income ratios also had relatively low incomes (below $5,000). Perhaps some of these families had suffered a temporary reduction in income. From these figures, relatively few families appear to have excessive debt. If there is a problem, it would seem to be with a few borrowers rather than with most.

Table 5 — Number of spending units and percentage having installment debt, selected years, 1950–1964

	Percentage of spending units having installment debts	Number of spending units (in millions)
1950	24	52.5
1952	38	53.0
1956	45	55.0
1957	47	56.1
1958	48	56.9
1959	48	56.8
1960	48	57.1
1961	48	58.0
1962	46	58.8
1963	50	61.2
1964	47*	61.1

* Family units.

Source: Michigan, University of . . . Survey of Consumer Finances.

Throughout the postwar period debt–income and debt repayment–income ratios have been rising. Although the cyclical movements in installment credit have tended to reinforce the business cycle, variations in consumer credit have not played a major independent role in creating a business cycle. Until recent years most of the growth in installment credit could be explained by the widening of its use rather than a deepening of the intensity with which individual families use it. This distribution of installment debt indicates that some borrowers may be overcommitted, but this is not a widespread occurrence. There is no consensus on how high the debt–income ratios may go before the burden of making repayments is likely to create widespread defaults. As long as income is rising, serious problems are not likely to be encountered. The existence of debt, however, does make recovery from a recession slower and more difficult than it otherwise would be.

Consumer credit regulation. On three occasions the federal government has undertaken to regulate the terms of consumer installment lending in order to curb the volume of this type of borrowing. Federal selective control of consumer credit was first imposed during World War II by Regulation W of the Board of Governors of the Federal Reserve System as the result of an executive order of the president in 1941 based on war-emergency legislation. The major purpose of Regulation W was to dampen the demand for consumer durable goods containing strategic materials needed for defense, and then, war production. Prior to this time, however, theoretical recommendations for the adoption of installment credit controls were based on arguments for moderating peacetime business fluctuations rather than on "emergency" considerations. The conflict that still exists about whether this type of control should have emergency or permanent status really stems from the fact that it was proposed to accomplish one set of objectives and was adopted to accomplish others of an emergency nature. Nevertheless, the executive order of August 9, 1941, was drawn broadly enough to include more objectives than the transfer of resources to defense industries:

> The public interest requires control of the use of instalment credit for financing and refinancing purchases of consumers' durable goods . . . in order (a) to facilitate the transfer of productive resources to defense industries, (b) to assist in curbing unwarranted price advances and profiteering which tend to result when the supply of such goods is curtailed without corresponding curtailment of demand, (c) to assist in restraining general inflationary tendencies, to support or supplement taxation imposed to restrain such tendencies and to promote the accumulation of savings available for financing the defense program, (d) to aid in creating a backlog of demand for consumers' durable goods, and (e) to restrain the development of a consumer debt structure that would repress effective demand for goods and services in the post-defense period. . . . (Code of Federal Regulations . . . [1943] 1965)

The regulation established minimum down payments and maximum maturities for installment sales of consumer durable goods and for installment loans used to purchase consumer durables. This phase of the regulation lasted until November 1, 1947, when controls were terminated.

In the early postwar period the general upward movement of prices, accompanied by increases in consumer credit, caused growing concern about this segment of the economy. In a special session in 1948 Congress enacted a measure authorizing credit regulation until June 1949. By 1950 the economy had started into the expansionary phase of a business cycle. The demand for consumer durables increased and by early 1950 had reached the limit of productive capacity. This produced an inflationary situation, which was aggravated by the start of the Korean conflict in June 1950. The president accordingly urged reinstatement of Regulation W, and in September 1950 controls were re-established. Regulation lapsed May 7, 1952. In April 1966 the House Committee on Banking and Currency urged that the president be given stand-by authority over consumer credit as a part of the Defense Production Act extension bill.

During each instance of consumer installment credit regulation the Board of Governors of the Federal Reserve was authorized to regulate the maximum maturities and minimum down payments required for borrowers purchasing different types of commodities.

Effect of changing maturities. A shortening of contract maturities increases the required monthly repayment. Since repayments will take a larger share of income, some potential borrowers will refrain from buying. This will reduce the amount of consumer credit extended and lower the demand for consumer durables. A lengthening of contracts, on the other hand, is intended to induce consumers to make additional purchases.

Although the change in the monthly repayments will have an immediate impact on the number of borrowers, there is also a secondary reaction for those who obtain credit. Increased monthly repayments reduce the discretionary income of the borrower, so that less remains to be spent on other goods. Rising repayments, therefore, also tend to curtail consumer spending, but this effect is of uncertain magnitude and is likely to have a considerable lag.

Effect of changing down payments. Theoretically an increase in the minimum down payment will eliminate potential borrowers whose liquid asset holdings are not sufficient to meet the minimum requirements. This will tend to reduce the amount of consumer credit extended and lower demand for consumer durables. A reduction in minimum down payments, on the other hand, is intended to encourage greater borrowing and spending.

In practice, since automobile credit transactions usually involve trade-ins that fulfill all or part of the down payment requirement, the impact of changes in the minimum down payment is likely to be small unless the down payment is large relative to the purchase price. This may so restrict effective operation of changes in minimum down payments that the desired result can be achieved more effectively through variations in maximum maturities. When Regulation W was in force, automobile down payments were set at one-third the purchase price and remained there throughout the period of regulation. Since many household durable goods have relatively low purchase prices, any change in down payment requirements must be fairly drastic to be effective. For these reasons, variations in the maturity of installment credit loans are likely to be a more effective regulator of the volume of installment credit than are changes in minimum down payments.

Regulation and monetary policy. Although their ultimate desire is to dampen cyclical fluctuations in the production and sale of consumer durables, proponents of selective credit controls generally establish their case by maintaining that monetary policies and variations in interest rates will have little or no influence on the demand and supply of consumer installment credit. Borrowers are believed to be concerned primarily with minimum down payments and monthly repayments, so that demand tends to be interest inelastic. Lenders, on the other hand, are only slightly affected by variations in interest rates. Since rates charged borrowers are always much greater than the cost of obtaining funds in the money market and since the federal income tax absorbs almost half of the interest payments by corporations (since they are a deductible expense), rising interest rates do not make sales and consumer finance companies reluctant to grant loans. Although banks may restrain other types of credit during periods of tight money, they are not likely to curtail installment lending because of its profitability. Competition from sales finance companies is likely to make banks adopt liberal installment lending policies, even during periods of tight money. The record-breaking increase in installment credit in 1955, when interest rates were rising, is often cited as proof that installment lending is not sensitive to general monetary policies.

Opponents of credit controls argue that consumer installment credit deserves special consideration only if expansion in installment credit makes it impossible for the Federal Reserve to limit expansion in total bank credit and the money supply during periods of boom. Since 1951 the average rate of increase of the money supply has been slightly less than 3.5 per cent per year. Since the economy historically has grown about 3.5 per cent per year and since the money supply needs to grow secularly at about the same rate, the performance since 1951 indicates that the Federal Reserve has been quite successful in keeping the expansion in bank credit and the money supply within a desirable range. The annual increases in the money supply and bank credit, moreover, were greatest during periods of recession—as would be desired. Opponents claim that 1955 is a poor example for showing that the Federal Reserve could not regulate installment lending because the Federal Reserve did not tighten monetary policies significantly until mid-fall.

Although installment credit continued to rise during this period of tight money, there is evidence the growth was less than otherwise would have occurred. In 1956 a number of banks reported the imposition of ceilings on the volume of installment loans. Despite high profitability they were unwilling to expand consumer credit at the expense of other types of credit for fear that it might involve a sacrifice of existing borrower relationships in other loan areas. Longer maturities were discouraged, and stricter credit standards were imposed on borrowers. Drawing on what would otherwise have been idle balances does not seem to have constituted a major source of financing for installment credit. The immediate goal of monetary policies is to make over-all credit expansion less than it otherwise would be. In this respect, monetary policies appear successful in influencing all types of credit. If the evidence suggests that the Federal Reserve can limit the expansion in total bank credit, then the case for direct regulation of installment borrowing must rest on specific imperfections in the money and capital markets that result in an "incorrect" allocation among the numerous claimants of a "correct" amount of credit. Most economists, however, would agree that government controls to influence the allocation of resources during periods of peacetime are contrary to the basic notion of economic freedom.

Instability of durable goods production. One of the major obstacles to the Federal Reserve's efforts to stabilize aggregate demand is its inability to influence the production and sale of automobiles and other consumer durables. General monetary policies cannot protect against sharp independent shifts in consumption, such as occurred when the United States became involved in the Korean conflict. Historically, variations in installment credit and production of durables may have intensified the business cycle. As the economy approaches full employment, increases in installment credit are likely to come at the expense of credit for investment, with the result that capital formation and economic growth will suffer. It is argued that consumer credit controls wisely used would smooth the production of durable goods and prevent overexpansion in one period at the expense of the next. Greater economic stability and economic growth could be achieved. Selective controls over consumer credit, moreover, would make it unnecessary to adopt a policy of active restraint in periods of overbuying of consumer durables while other sectors of the economy were still operating below capacity.

Opposition to consumer controls. Many economists are opposed to the use of selective consumer credit controls. In their view, the goal of monetary and fiscal policies should be to prevent undue fluctuations in total aggregate demand, not to stabilize each component of the total. Variations in the components—for example, consumer durables—reflect changes in the demand and supply of particular commodities and are a sign of progress. They show the adaptation of production to the changing tastes of the public and are to be welcomed. Destabilizing effects occur only when an expansion in the sale of consumer durables does not represent a reduction in spending on other types of goods and services. In this case, the net addition to aggregate demand will create a higher level of income and consumption among those producing durable goods. This secondary reaction, or multiplier effect, may intensify or even cause a business cycle. The problem, therefore, is a general excess or deficiency of aggregate demand. Total aggregate demand, however, may be stabilized more effectively by general monetary and fiscal policies than by operating on the narrow base of consumer installment credit.

Even if installment credit controls were available, they would be exceedingly difficult to apply, for the regulatory authorities would be forced to make judgments on whether particular sectors of the economy were growing too slowly or too rapidly. The 1955 boom in automobile sales was the immediate cause of interest in credit controls. Yet the expansion of automobile production and the subsequent decline did not have the secondary repercussions that were so widely feared. Few cases calling for regulation, however, are likely to be as clear as the one in 1955 appeared to be at that time.

Controls to protect against loan losses. During a sustained boom, the profitability of lending is likely to be high, and some financial institutions may lower their lending standards and liquidity to accommodate a greater volume of loans. The reduced quality of credit is likely to be concealed by the exuberance of the expansion. If a cyclical downturn occurs, however, large loan losses may occur, which would weaken financial institutions and would have undesirable repercussions on the money supply and on confidence in financial institutions. Consumer credit regulations could help to prevent undesirable growth of this type of credit or a possible lowering of standards of lending in the consumer credit field.

Although economists have not emphasized this aspect of consumer credit controls, it has been very influential with lenders who fear the consequences of reduced down payments and longer periods of repayment. Most economists maintain that this fear is entirely hypothetical and is not based on historical experience. Consumer credit, they point out, has produced few, if any, bank failures and has never been responsible for a loss of confidence in banks.

Despite a general easing of terms throughout the postwar period, it is interesting to note that loan-loss data show no significant trend. For sales finance companies, the loss experience has improved recently; for consumer finance companies, it has deteriorated slightly. A study by the Federal Reserve ([U.S.] Board of Governors . . . 1957) indicated that if the worst loan-loss experience encountered in 1938 were to occur again, losses to companies in the industry would amount to 17 per cent of their reserves and net worth in 1955. With income after taxes amounting to 10 per cent of net worth per year, possible losses could largely be absorbed in the general operations of a business. Losses, actual and potential, therefore, do not appear great enough to jeopardize the solvency of consumer credit institutions as a group.

Need for additional tools. Many proponents of installment credit controls argue that the greater the number of tools available to the regulatory authorities, the more likely they are to be successful in smoothing or eliminating business cycles. Consumer credit control may not be the best tool, but it is effective in the sense that the regulations can be reasonably well enforced and that changes in terms appear to affect the sales of particular goods. Those opposed to consumer credit regulation maintain that business cycles could be countered by more effective and wiser use of the existing tools than has been the case in the past. Business cycles will not be eliminated by giving the regulatory authorities additional tools.

Shifts in consumption. It is usually assumed that if the consumer cannot buy durable goods because of a high down payment or a short maturity, he will save the funds he would have spent rather than spend them elsewhere. If he shifts some of his buying from consumer durables to other goods and services, the installment credit regulation will be responsible for a change in consumption patterns rather than a reduction in aggregate demand equal to reduced purchases on durables. If both durable and nondurable goods production is initially at capacity, a tightening of consumer credit regulations could cause inflationary pressures in nondurables. Most economists opposed to consumer credit regulation believe shifts in consumption patterns could be considerable. As before, the question of installment credit controls really hinges on whether there is excess demand for all goods and services or merely for consumer durables.

Evasion. One of the most effective arguments against installment credit regulations is that they would be impossible to enforce. Both sellers and buyers would have incentives to evade the regulations. Sellers of durable goods often extend credit and retain the paper rather than sell it to a financial institution. Except in times of national emergency, stores are likely to be more interested in achieving a high level of sales than in enforcing credit regulations. In 1950 about 150,000 establishments were covered by credit regulations. Unless the regulatory authorities are prepared to hire thousands of investigators to police stores and lending agencies, the likelihood of compliance is low.

Borrowers could avoid the regulations by shifting from "purpose" to "nonpurpose" loans. Since the minimum down payment and maximum maturity would vary for different types of goods, a borrower could skirt the requirements by borrowing without any specific purpose against his general credit or by alleging a purpose for which the minimum down payment is lower or maturity greater. Although this would probably be impossible whenever the loan is large, such as for a new car, it could be significant for sales of used cars and other consumer durables.

Dealers could avoid minimum down payment requirements by starting with unrealistically high prices and then giving an overallowance for trade-ins. This, of course, could be avoided by imposing maximum loans-to-value ratios based on dealers costs. However, the number of commodities involved is so large, the availability of list prices so limited, and the practices of manufacturers in setting suggested retail prices so varied, that it would be very difficult to determine reasonable maximum loan-value ratios for each commodity and make them widely known to sales finance companies, banks, and dealers to facilitate compliance.

At the moment no clear consensus exists on the need for, or the usefulness of, consumer credit controls in achieving economic stability. It is generally agreed that such controls must remain subordinate to general monetary and fiscal policies. The real question to be answered is whether fluctuations in the production of consumer durables have been sufficiently destabilizing to warrant special regulation. Those in favor of regulations tend to assume that greater stability in all components of aggregate demand is desirable. Overextension of consumer credit, however, is unlikely to have caused any of the postwar recessions. Several proponents believe the same objectives would be achieved as effectively by selective excise taxes or more active fiscal policies but see little hope in this direction because of congressional delays in revising tax laws. Others have urged passage of legislation to improve the short-run effectiveness of fiscal policy.

To be effective, consumer credit controls would require the support of the public. Since there is no clear agreement on the objectives to be sought and since few would agree that consumer credit should be regulated to control the allocation of resources in peacetime or periods of limited involvement in hostilities, the public is unlikely to support consumer credit regulation. Even if rationing of credit by individual lenders is defective, many would consider it extremely dangerous to have the central bank assume this function.

In 1957, after an extensive study by the Federal Reserve System ([U.S.] Board of Governors . . . 1957), President Eisenhower concluded that the evidence did not justify a request for authority to reimpose controls. The Federal Reserve concurred in this decision. In explaining the decision, five points were made: First, fluctuations in consumer installment credit, though tending to accentuate swings in business conditions, have accounted for a fairly small proportion of changes in total credit. Second, losses involved, even in recessions, have not been large enough to affect seriously the financial position of lending institutions. Third, the relatively rapid growth in this type of credit largely reflects the growing proportion of middle-income people using it. Fourth, existing instruments of policy can hold changes in total bank credit and the money supply within reasonable limits. Fifth, the large 1955 expansion reflected a concatenation of special factors not likely to be repeated.

In 1960 the Joint Economic Committee (U.S. Congress . . . 1960), after extensive study of the problems involved in maintaining full employment, rapid economic growth, and stable prices, concluded that the Federal Reserve should be given stand-by authority to regulate consumer credit. In 1961 the Commission on Money and Credit reported no clear consensus among its members on the desirability of permanent consumer credit controls. In 1966 Congress granted the president stand-by authority to control consumer credit. The desirability of installment credit regulation remains a topic of active debate.

ELI SHAPIRO

BIBLIOGRAPHY

ARTIS, M. J. 1963 Monetary Policy and Financial Intermediaries: The Hire Purchase Finance Houses. Oxford, University of, Institute of Economics and Statistics, *Bulletin* 25:11–46.

BERNSTEIN, BLANCHE 1940 *The Pattern of Consumer Debt, 1935–1936: A Statistical Analysis.* New York: National Bureau of Economic Research.

CHAPMAN, JOHN M. 1940 *Commercial Banks and Consumer Instalment Credit.* New York: National Bureau of Economic Research.

CHIANG, ALPHA C. 1961 The Short-run Effects of Instalment Credit Control. *Canadian Journal of Economics and Political Science* 27:357–366.

Code of Federal Regulations, Cumulative Supplement. 2,1. (1943) 1965 Pages 144–145 in Paul W. McCracken, James C. T. Mao, and Cedric Fricke, *Consumer Instalment Credit and Public Policy.* Ann Arbor: Univ. of Michigan, Graduate School of Business, Bureau of Business Research.

COMMISSION ON MONEY AND CREDIT 1961 *Money and Credit: Their Influence on Jobs, Prices, and Growth; Report.* Englewood Cliffs, N.J.: Prentice-Hall.

COPPOCK, JOSEPH D. 1940 *Government Agencies of Consumer Instalment Credit.* New York: National Bureau of Economic Research.

COTTLE, S. 1960 The Earnings Performance of the Consumer Finance Industry. *Journal of Finance* 15:387–406.

COX, REAVIS 1948 *The Economics of Instalment Buying.* New York: Ronald.

COX, REAVIS 1965 *Consumers' Credit and Wealth: A Study in Consumer Credit.* Washington: National Foundation for Consumer Credit.

DAUER, ERNST A. 1944 *Comparative Operating Experience of Consumer Instalment Financing Agencies and Commercial Banks, 1929–1941.* New York: National Bureau of Economic Research.

DURAND, DAVID 1941 *Risk Elements in Consumer Instalment Financing.* New York: National Bureau of Economic Research.

EINZIG, PAUL 1956 The Dynamics of Hire–Purchase Credit. *Economic Journal* 66:17–24.

ENTHOVEN, ALAIN C. 1957–1964 Growth of Instalment Credit and the Future of Prosperity. *American Economic Review* 47:913–929; 54:417–423.

Federal Reserve Bulletin. → Published since 1915 by the [U.S.] Board of Governors of the Federal Reserve System.

FISHER, JANET A. 1963 Consumer Durable Goods Expenditures, With Major Emphasis on the Role of Assets, Credit, and Intentions. *Journal of the American Statistical Association* 58:648–657.

FOUSEK, PETER G. 1958 Prerequisites for the Growth of Consumer Instalment Credit. *Journal of Finance* 13: 163–175.

GREAT BRITAIN, COMMITTEE ON THE WORKING OF THE MONETARY SYSTEM 1959 *Report.* Papers by Command, Cmnd. 827. London: H.M. Stationery Office.

GREAT BRITAIN, COMMITTEE ON THE WORKING OF THE MONETARY SYSTEM 1960 *Principal Memoranda of Evidence.* 3 vols. London: H.M. Stationery Office.

HABERLER, GOTTFRIED 1942 *Consumer Instalment Credit and Economic Fluctuations.* New York: National Bureau of Economic Research.

HARRIS, RALPH; NAYLOR, MARGOT; and SELDON, ARTHUR (1958) 1961 *Hire Purchase in a Free Society.* 3d ed. London: Hutchinson.

HOLTHAUSEN, DUNCAN McC. 1940 *The Volume of Consumer Instalment Credit, 1929–1938.* New York: National Bureau of Economic Research.

HUNTER, H. MANNING 1966 A Behavioral Model of the Long-run Growth of Aggregate Consumer Credit in the United States. *Review of Economics and Statistics* 48:690–695.

JUNG, ALLEN F. 1962 Charges for Appliance and Automobile Instalment Credit in Major Cities. *Journal of Business* 35:386–391.

JUSTER, F. T.; and SHAY, ROBERT P. 1964 *Consumer Sensitivity to Finance Rates.* New York: National Bureau of Economic Research.

KISSELGOFF, AVRAM L. 1952 *Factors Affecting the Demand for Consumer Instalment Sales Credit.* National Bureau of Economic Research, Technical Paper No. 7. New York: The Bureau.

LEE, MAW L. 1962 An Analysis of Instalment Borrowing by Durable Goods Buyers. *Econometrica* 30:770–787.

MCCRACKEN, PAUL W.; MAO, JAMES C. T.; and FRICKE, CEDRIC 1965 *Consumer Instalment Credit and Public Policy.* Ann Arbor: Univ. of Michigan, Graduate School of Business, Bureau of Business Research.

MICHIGAN, UNIVERSITY OF, SURVEY RESEARCH CENTER *Survey of Consumer Finances.* → Published since 1945/1946.

MORS, WALLACE P. 1965 *Consumer Credit Finance Charges: Rate Information and Quotation.* New York: National Bureau of Economic Research.

NATIONAL CONSUMER FINANCE ASSOCIATION 1962 *The Consumer Finance Industry.* Englewood Cliffs, N.J.: Prentice-Hall.

NUGENT, ROLF 1939 *Consumer Credit and Economic Stability.* New York: Russell Sage Foundation.

PLUMMER, WILBUR C.; and YOUNG, RALPH A. 1940 *Sales Finance Companies and Their Credit Practices.* New York: National Bureau of Economic Research.

SAULNIER, RAYMOND J. 1940 *Industrial Banking Companies and Their Credit Practices.* New York: National Bureau of Economic Research.

SHAY, ROBERT P. 1963 *New-automobile Finance Rates, 1924–1962.* New York: National Bureau of Economic Research.

SMITH, PAUL F. 1964 *Consumer Credit Costs, 1949–1959.* Princeton Univ. Press.

[U.S.] BOARD OF GOVERNORS OF THE FEDERAL RESERVE SYSTEM 1957 *Consumer Installment Credit.* 4 parts in 3 vols. Washington: Government Printing Office.

U.S. CONGRESS, SENATE, COMMITTEE ON BANKING AND CURRENCY 1947 *Consumer Credit Control: Hearings. . . .* Washington: Government Printing Office.

U.S. CONGRESS, JOINT ECONOMIC COMMITTEE 1960 *Employment, Growth and Price Levels Report.* 86th Congress, 2d Session. Washington: Government Printing Office.

U.S. FEDERAL RESERVE BOARD *Consumer Credit.* → A monthly mimeographed release.

U.S. PRESIDENT *Economic Report of the President.* Washington: Government Printing Office. → Published annually since 1947.

YOUNG, RALPH A. 1940 *Personal Finance Companies and Their Credit Practices.* New York: National Bureau of Economic Research.

ZUPNICK, ELLIOT 1962 Consumer Credit and Monetary Policy in the United States and the United Kingdom. *Journal of Finance* 17:342–354.

INSTINCT

Reference to the concept of instinct is to be found in most of the major writings on social psychology and on behavior in general. However, the nature of such reference has not always been acceptance or approval. The career of the term "instinct" in the history of psychology has been a checkered one. Like the phoenix, instinct has been "consigned to the flames" only to rise again. Like Proteus, it has survived by repeatedly adopting new forms.

Instinct in common usage. Instinct has led a less troubled existence in common usage, and it is here that one might find reasons for both its vicissitudes and its persistence in academic psychology. In common speech, instinct and instinctive occur in a variety of situations and with a variety of meanings. We say that someone acts instinctively if his act is done without thought or deliberation but rather on impulse. We speak of knowing, believing, or feeling something instinctively and thereby mean that we cannot recall having learned or having been told about it but rather that the knowledge, belief, or feeling just arose within us. We say of someone that he has an instinct for, say, mathematics or stage direction, meaning that he is by nature good at these things. We speak of maternal or creative instincts when referring to behavior that seems to be the expression of a deep and perhaps characteristically human urge. We describe someone as acting out of an instinct of revenge, meaning that revenge was his motive. We speak of blind instinct when someone cannot say why he acted in a certain way or what the purpose of his action was. We might say that someone was obeying the herd instinct if he followed the crowd instead of his own judgment. We might claim to have found our way home by instinct, meaning that we did not arrive home by accident, or by the conscious use of a map or memory, but were guided in some unconscious way.

This list of how instinct and instinctive are used every day in reference to human thought and action is by no means exhaustive, and many more differences and shades of meaning could be added if we were to extend the list to the behavior of animals. But it should be clear already that there is no one meaning common to all these usages. There is continuity between the several meanings in the sense that no usage is completely unrelated to at least one of the others. We have what Wittgenstein referred to as "family resemblances" between words, "a complicated network of similarities overlapping and criss-crossing: sometimes overall similarities, sometimes similarities of detail" ([1953] 1964, p. 32). In spite of the range of meanings that instinct and instinctive have in everyday language, usage seldom leads to misunderstanding; context and custom usually furnish whatever is necessary to convey the meaning that is intended on a particular occasion.

Concepts of instinct

Science and philosophy traditionally aim at a greater degree of precision or rigor than is characteristic of the statements of ordinary language. A scientist or philosopher might object that many of the uses of instinct are loose and vague, that underlying the varieties of use there must be a single concept of which instinct is the name, but of which the ordinary man is only dimly aware. The inconsistency of ordinary language will be avoided by making the underlying concept explicit and by defining instinct in terms of it. We find frequent reference in psychological writing to *the* concept of instinct and numerous attempts to define instinct in a precise way.

However, the variability of the definitions that scholars have proposed for instinct is almost as great as the variety of its uses in ordinary language. Any new theory of, or outlook on, behavior is likely to incorporate a concept, category, or distinction that is matched by at least one of the uses of instinct in ordinary language. Scholars have tended to settle on the ordinary language use or uses that suit their purposes, and they define instinct accordingly. Hence the persistence of the word in psychology. But there has also been a tendency to assume, albeit tacitly, that an explicit definition of instinct in terms of one of its meanings somehow incorporates its other meanings as well; at least the other meanings tend to be retained regardless of the definition—hence, in part, the difficulties that psychologists encounter in using the term. To assume that all, or most, of the many meanings of instinct can be gathered into one precise concept in fact leads to the reverse of precision, to the blurring of distinctions, to the confounding of questions, and hence to misunderstanding and confusion. A detailed analysis of the several kinds of uses to which instinct has been put—demarcation of the several kinds of facts, concepts, questions, and explanations with which instinct has been associated—would be a move in the direction of greater precision. Until such analysis has been made it is unlikely that questions about the relations between the different meanings of instinct and the possibility of their being reduced to one concept can be profitably discussed. In what follows, some examples will be used to illustrate the hybrid character of the instinct concepts and the controversies to which these concepts have led.

Darwin's concept. Most modern theories of instinct are derived from Darwin as much as from anyone else. However, Darwin was well aware of the ambiguity of instinct; he declined to give an unequivocal definition of instinct on the grounds that "several distinct mental actions are commonly embraced by the term . . ." ([1859] 1964, p. 184). And he used instinct in a number of ways: to refer to what impels a behavior pattern such as bird migration, to a disposition like courage or obstinacy in a dog, to feelings such as sympathy in man, and to stereotyped and species-characteristic behavior patterns such as hive building in the bee.

Nevertheless, some of Darwin's discussion of instinct, in particular some of the inferences he drew from facts that he cited, indicates that he tended at times to think of instinct as a single concept that united a number of distinct notions. For instance, it was essential to his argument that instincts be hereditary, but he assumed that being hereditary implies, and is implied by, development without the mediation of experience. Now if instinct is defined in terms of both inheritance and independence of experience, it follows that one can be inferred from the other if we know that we are dealing with a phenomenon to which this notion of instinct is applicable. The connection is a logical one—true by definition. But how are we to know that we are dealing with a phenomenon to which this definition applies, unless we already know, as a matter of fact, that this phenomenon is both hereditary and independent of experience? For it is at least conceivable that something could be inherited and yet depend on some sort of experience for its development and that something could develop independently of experience, in the sense in which this is usually understood, and yet not be inherited. Intelligence has a hereditary basis but also requires experience for its development. Whether or not a particular pattern of behavior is both inherited and independent of experience cannot be decided by inference from evidence in favor of only one of these possibilities; the question can be decided only on the basis of observation.

In fact, in compiling material for the *Origin of Species*, Darwin had little detailed information about how behavior patterns and dispositions develop in individual animals, and he apparently made little effort to obtain it. Such information would not have been as obviously relevant to his argument—that behavior has evolved by natural selection—as the kinds of facts he did document: evidence for the evolution of behavior, the inheritance of behavior, and the adaptiveness of behavior. A restricted and precise scientific concept could have been formulated on the basis of these facts, but ideas about ontogeny and subjective content (absence of reason, foresight, and so on) traditionally associated with instinct adhered to Darwin's use of the term and, hence, were part of the concept he passed on to those who followed him.

In the *Descent of Man* (1871) Darwin employed instinct mainly in the sense of natural urge or compulsion to action. An instinct in this sense was a unitary or autonomous entity of which there are a specific number in each kind of animal. Such an instinct has three main aspects: the nature of the impulse, the behavior it impels, and the goal toward which the impulse, and hence the behavior, is directed. In fact it is by its goal more than anything else that such an instinct is identified; whether a behavior, such as a pecking movement, belongs to a particular instinct will be judged not on the basis of form alone (stereotyped or not) but rather on whether it is the kind of behavior that in the circumstances will tend to bring about acquisition of the goal of the instinct—the building of a nest, the securing of food, the defeat of a rival, and so on. Unfortunately there can often be more than one version of what the goals of behavior are, and it is a questionable assumption that a classification of behavior patterns according to the goals they serve corresponds to a set of internal unitary driving systems. These are difficulties which adherents of this concept of instinct had to contend with. However, if one assumes the existence of a certain number of distinct natural impulses in an animal the possibility arises that there can be interactions between them. In social behavior, Darwin said, we often see the simultaneous arousal of incompatible tendencies—for example, self-preservation instincts and parental instincts—and so we are led to the notion of conflict between instincts and to the notion that instincts can differ in strength and that one can overcome another [*see* CONFLICT, *article on* PSYCHOLOGICAL ASPECTS]. Darwin examined the long-maintained idea that the strength of an instinct is determined by its tendency to promote the attainment of pleasure or the avoidance of pain; he agreed that there are some instincts to which this idea applies, but that in the case of others, "it is probable that instincts are presently followed from the mere force of inheritance, without the stimulus of either pleasure or pain" ([1871] 1948, p. 477). As this discussion suggests, Darwin anticipated most of the questions and confusions associated with the term "instinct" in the writings of students of behavior who succeeded him.

Freud's concept. Instinct in Freud's writings refers to a natural impulse or innate driving force.

Freud made much use of the notion of conflict, in particular, conflicts between instinct and experientially acquired features of mental life. He assumed the existence of two broad categories of instinct in man, aggression and sex, each of which was to be considered as consisting of, or differentiating into, a number of subinstincts [*see* AGGRESSION, *article on* PSYCHOLOGICAL ASPECTS].

According to Freud (1900), the goals of overt behavior are not always sufficient to reveal its instinctive basis, since the social, convention-ridden life of man involves suppression or distortion of many of the natural expressions of instinct. Only the techniques of psychoanalysis, such as the analysis of word associations and dreams, can reveal the true inner dynamics of human behavior—the ways in which the instincts and their conflicts express themselves. Freud's concept of instinct was derived from clinical observations but was an "armchair" concept in that it contained little direct empirical reference, and no attempt was made to subject it to direct empirical analysis. It also contained contradictory elements that led to some inconsistency in its use. Freud wrote at times as though instinct were a kind of blind energy, at least analogous with the energy of physics, the dynamics of which follow quasi-mechanical laws; at other times he wrote as though instinct were something that could have intention and could employ strategies.

A good part of Freud's later thinking about instinct was devoted to developing theories of how instinctive pressures are transformed and integrated through experience into socially compatible patterns of thought and action. Subsequently, some psychoanalysts such as Karen Horney and her colleagues (e.g., Horney 1937), placed even greater emphasis on the role of society and culture in the shaping of the structure and dynamics of the mind. They did not deny the existence of instincts as biologically grounded forces affecting behavior, but they took the position that the available facts allot a greater contribution to social forces in the generation of psychological conflicts, psychoses, and so forth, than was allowed by the speculative notions of classical Freudian theory about the functioning of instincts [*see* HORNEY].

McDougall's concept. Perhaps the most influential champion of instinct in psychology was William McDougall, whose *Introduction to Social Psychology* (1908) was one of the first textbooks of social psychology. In it he employed a concept of instinct as a base for an extremely persuasive comprehensive theory of behavior, a theory that was credited with the dual achievement of bringing a new and elegant synthesis to the subject matter of psychology and of giving psychology the status of a natural science based on biological principles. The biological principles were those of Darwinism. The core of McDougall's thinking about instinct was the conception, given widespread currency by Darwin and his followers, of instincts as hereditary and unitary behavior systems driven by internal goal-directed impulsions. To this McDougall grafted the traditional (particularly Kantian) conception of the tripartite division of mind into faculties of knowing, feeling, and willing. He defined instinct as "an inherited or innate psycho-physical disposition which determines its possessor to perceive, and to pay attention to, objects of a certain class, to experience an emotional excitement of a particular quality upon perceiving such an object, and to act in regard to it in a particular manner, or, at least, to experience an impulse to such action" (McDougall 1908, p. 25 in the 1936 edition). Conveniently at hand was the three-part division of neurophysiological systems, and McDougall took what to him was the obvious step of locating the cognitive aspect (knowing) of instinct in sensory pathways, the affective aspect (feeling) in associative pathways, and the conative aspect (willing) in motor pathways. The connections between the three parts of an instinct were thus thought of as neural, but McDougall insisted that the dynamics of instinct are not purely mechanical, after the manner of reflexes. He insisted that an instinct is a psychophysical system, by which he meant that mental phenomena—the awareness of feeling, emotion, and impulse—play an essential and active role in determining instinctive action.

According to McDougall, instincts are capable of modification during the life of an individual within limits that differ from species to species, man having wider limits than other animals. But the possibility of modification through experience pertains only to cognition and conation (1908, p. 29 in the 1936 edition). Hence identification of the distinct primary emotions is the one valid method of discovering what, and how many, instincts there are. According to McDougall, such an analysis of instincts is necessary before one can make significant progress in understanding the nature of complex derived or secondary patterns of behavior or mental phenomena. He presented a list of what he considered to be the primary emotions and hence the principal instincts in man. He attempted to justify his list on Darwinian principles by reference to the probable adaptive significance, and hence evolutionary basis, of each instinct.

McDougall's success established a fashion for

instinct and other Darwinian ideas in psychology. Lists of instincts multiplied in psychological writings, and the concept took root in such fields as economics (e.g., Veblen 1914) and the study of wars (e.g., Trotter 1916). However, as the lists multiplied, so did their variety. Different writers based their lists on different criteria: primary emotions, purposive behavior patterns, the number of species-characteristic behavior patterns, and so on. Even those who adhered to McDougall's argument and based their analyses only on primary emotions were rarely in agreement. Introspection, or whatever other means of judgment were used, yielded different lists for different people, and there was no recognized way of deciding who was right and who was wrong. [*See* TROTTER; VEBLEN.]

In part McDougall's own practice encouraged the indiscriminate and vague use of instinct against which he had argued in the introduction to his book. For, according to his theory, with the exception of reflexes all behavior is instinctive or has an instinctive base. Also, his concept of instinct appeared to provide a bridge between at least two kinds of explanation of behavior: explanation in terms of causes and effects and explanation in terms of intentions and actions. But the age-old question about the relations between these two kinds of explanation was not solved by talk about psychophysical processes. McDougall's own concept was, in fact, vague—a composite of largely unanalyzed ideas that were not really fitted together. Furthermore, the concept and the theory of which it was a part were speculations whose connections with facts were left, to a large extent, indeterminate and hence were difficult to pin down for empirical test. At least so it appeared to those who led what became known as the "anti-instinct revolt."

The anti-instinct revolt. The first significant shot in the anti-instinct revolt was fired by Dunlap in a paper that appeared in 1919. According to Dunlap, McDougall's theory was vitiated because it contained the notion of subjective purposiveness and hence involved recourse to unobservable phenomena. On the premise that science deals only with what is publicly observable and with concepts defined solely in terms of what is publicly observable, McDougall's theory was judged to be unscientific. Other critics attacked the use of the idea of inborn behavior patterns; they cited evidence that encouraged the view that all but the simplest reflexes are molded by experience. By and large, instinct theories proved no match for new and rival movements, such as behaviorism, that toughmindedly insisted on the priority of hard facts and on the value of experimental methods.

However, while discarding instinct as a scientific term, the behaviorists retained some of the ideas that had been connoted by it. For instance, the concept of primary biological need persisted in drive-reduction theories of learning, and concepts of impulses or subjective purposiveness covertly continued despite efforts to bring "operational" purity to the theoretical language of psychology (Taylor 1964). Nevertheless, the opponents of instinct, no less than its champions, seemed to have assumed that its many facets rose or fell together, that to affirm or question independence of experience, or subjective purposiveness, was to affirm or question instinct in all its senses. In fact, behaviorists, with perhaps a few exceptions, did not apply their methods to a number of questions and facts with which the instinct theorists had concerned themselves; for example, the adaptive significance of species-characteristic behavior patterns, spontaneity in behavior, the relation of behavioral similarities and differences to questions about evolutionary relationships.

Instinct in ethology

A resurgence of concern with biological aspects of behavior brought about the most recent rejuvenation of instinct. Beginning in the late 1930s the ethologists, led by Konrad Lorenz and Nikolaas Tinbergen, accused both the proponents and opponents of instinct of failure to pay sufficient attention to large classes of facts about animal behavior. Ethologists proceeded to develop ideas about instinctive behavior that purportedly were based on, and took account of, such facts. The aim was to make instinct an objective concept and the study of instinct an objective science.

The background of ethology was classical zoology (comparative morphology and evolution) and amateur natural history. The facts from which ethologists started were the contents of detailed inventories of species-characteristic behavior patterns, observations of the sequential patterning and frequency distributions of occurrences of such patterns, the taxonomic distribution of variations of behavior patterns, and the biological functions of species-characteristic behavior patterns.

Lorenz and Tinbergen. According to Lorenz, ethology was founded on the discovery of a "distinct and particulate physiological process . . . a certain type of innate genetically determined behaviour patterns" (1950, p. 221). This type of behavior pattern was referred to as an "instinctive activity" (*Instinkthandlung*). It was characterized as (*a*) stereotyped, (*b*) possessed by all members of at least one sex of a species, (*c*) innate in the sense of genetical inheritance, (*d*) innate in the sense of being unlearned, (*e*) endogenously controlled—once set in motion it is completed without further mediation by peripheral stimuli, and (*f*) the goal and terminus of a variable sequence of "appetitive" behavior. In an early paper Lorenz (1937, p. 329) also included the idea of being craved (*Angestrebtwerden*) in his definition of the instinctive activity. To explain the timing of attempts to perform an instinctive activity, Lorenz postulated that spontaneous endogenous generation and accumulation of "energy," specific to each kind of instinctive activity, initiates and drives the appropriate appetitive behavior until "discharged" in performance of the instinctive activity. Performance of the activity is precipitated, or "released," by an encounter with some specific external stimulus that engages an "innate release mechanism."

Here again we encounter a concept of instinct that groups together a number of distinct characteristics. Was this grouping a matter of definition or a matter of fact? There is no doubt that there are stereotyped, environment-resistant, species-characteristic behavior patterns that terminate variable chains of searching activities; and interspecies comparison of variations in the forms of such behavior patterns indicates that they do reflect genetic affinity. But that Lorenz had at his disposal the kinds of facts about ontogeny that could justify the use of the term "unlearned," and the kinds of facts about physiological control that could justify descriptions such as "spontaneous," "endogenous," and "independent of peripheral stimulation" for even one instinctive activity, is disputable. On the other hand, the facts of neurophysiology disqualify the energy model from being anything more than a picturesque way of describing certain facts about behavior.

Other ethologists became dissatisfied with the unphysiological character of Lorenz' energy model and also with the atomistic character of his picture of instinctive activities and their control. Tinbergen (1951), for example, observed that the behavior patterns serving any one of the primary biological functions, such as nutrition or reproduction, tend to be carried out in a sequence in which more and more specific types of appetitive behavior succeed one another, only the final one of which terminates in performance of a stereotyped "end act." Transition from one type of appetitive behavior to the next is effected by an animal's encountering a particular releasing stimulus. At each stage of the sequence, with the exception of the last, there are usually several alternative types of appetitive behavior that can follow; which type occurs on any occasion will depend upon which of the several kinds of possible releasing stimuli is encountered. Thus a hunting predator might begin its search for prey with behavior that is not specific to the capture of only one type of prey; it then switches to the appropriate one of a set of prey-catching patterns as soon as it sees or smells a particular type of prey. The prey-catching behavior will, in turn, vary according to the avoiding measures taken by the prey and be switched to the stereotyped pattern specific for killing the prey once the prey is caught. Underlying such a sequence, Tinbergen pictured a mechanism consisting of a hierarchically arranged system of nervous centers and innate releasing mechanisms that channel the flow of "motivational impulses" of which the behavior is the expression. According to Tinbergen's scheme, there is a hierarchical system corresponding to each of the primary biological functions, and he referred to each such system as an instinct. Activation of the reproductive instinct, then, would mean production of motivational impulses from the highest part of the reproductive hierarchy and the expression of these impulses in courting, territorial fighting, copulation, nest building, parental behavior, and so on, depending at any time on the level of the hierarchy at which the impulses were accumulating and the releasing stimuli available. Incidentally, Tinbergen did not believe that there were grounds for postulating a "social instinct."

Tinbergen's theory, like McDougall's, related the behavior of an animal to a small number of distinct systems which were inborn and hence the product of natural selection. But Tinbergen avoided the inclusion of subjective phenomena by accounting for the purposive aspects of behavior with a purely mechanical or quasi-mechanical model. Nevertheless, the empirical status of this model was as questionable as McDougall's, although for different reasons. In spite of the quasi-physiological terms used to describe the model, many of its key properties were known not to have any close correspondence with physiological reality. In fact, the structure of the hierarchical scheme was based on a classification of overt patterns according to their functional characteristics—the biological ends they promote—and analysis of these classes into temporal and sequential patterns. The only solid evidence in support of the theory, then, was contained in the overt patterns it purportedly accounted for, and it was begging a crucial question to assume a simple correspondence between this evidence and the underlying physiology. But the description of overt behavior was not entirely anterior to the theory; for instance, the idea that instinct involves the generation of energy and the consumption of this energy in performance of a fixed action pattern diverted attention from evidence that the goals of certain patterns are not "end acts" or their "releasers" but specific stimulus situations *per se*.

Evaluation. The instinct theories of Lorenz and Tinbergen were of positive value in that they revived interest in questions and facts about the survival value, the taxonomic relevance, and the temporal and sequential patterning of animal behavior. But they suffered the same type of fate as their predecessors, and for the same sort of reason: they overreached themselves. Unsympathetic critics (e.g., Lehrman 1953; Schneirla 1956) accused them of adducing unobservable entities, of failure to distinguish and pay sufficient attention to the facts of overt behavior, physiology, and ontogeny and even to phyletic differences. In later writings ethologists tried to meet these objections by reformulating their ideas in terms of operationally defined concepts. For instance, "action specific energy" or "motivational impulses" were replaced by "specific action potentiality" or "tendency"—terms that were supposed to refer only to probabilities of occurrence, judged on the basis of observation, of behavior patterns (see Beer 1963–1964).

However, if one limits oneself, in talking about a particular subject matter, to concepts defined solely in terms of that subject matter, one places considerable restriction on the kinds of things that can be said about it. One can make generalizations about, and describe relationships between, items of the subject matter, but one cannot explain such generalizations or relationships by referring them to a wider field of knowledge. That the restrictions of operationism are uncongenial to at least some ethologists is evident from inconsistencies in their use of certain terms. "Tendency," for instance, is defined as "probability of occurrence," but that a particular probability of occurrence is such-and-such is sometimes explained as due to the strength of the relevant tendency. For tendency to convey anything here, it must refer to something other than probability; it will be covertly doing the sort of work that action specific energy was doing in the instinct theory. The same kind of problem is encountered in the way the concept of conflict is used. Alongside, and sometimes confused with, the operational definition of conflict as equality of probabilities of incompatible responses, are two uses that preserve patterns of explanation of older conceptions, conflict in the sense of simultaneous arousal of internal mechanisms underlying incompatible responses and conflict applied to opposition of selection pressures. Some of the ingredients of the instinct theories of ethology thus persist, although they are often disguised in forms that stand in the way of both consistent operationism and explicit presentation of explanatory hypotheses in forms that could be subjected to testing.

Thorpe. Recently an attempt to reformulate an ethological concept of instinct has been made by Thorpe (1956). According to Thorpe, the central notion of this concept is that of "internal drive"; in addition, instincts are characterized as consisting of (*a*) an inherited system of coordination, (*b*) more or less rigid inherited action patterns, and (*c*) more or less rigid releasing mechanisms. He explains "inherited" in terms of current ideas about genetic coding and eschews "preformationism" by saying that what is encoded in the genes is a set of instructions that determines what an organism takes from its environment in the way of materials and stimulation to build up an instinctive mechanism. Following Lorenz (1961; see also 1965) he maintains that "we are justified in saying that the behaviour pattern is innate in the sense that the complexity which it displays arises primarily from the instructions in the germ cell and not from instructions which are contributed by the environment" (Thorpe [1956] 1963, p. 17). Both Thorpe and Lorenz consider this formulation a valuable refinement of the concept of innateness. Allusion to the concept of "information" of cybernetics gives an air of mathematical precision, even though the exact meaning to be given to "instructions" is anybody's guess. But it is difficult to see how this concept of "innate" adds a useful tool either to thinking about the inheritance of behavior or to thinking about the development of behavior. Indeed, the concept promises to perpetuate the confusion between these two classes of problems that has vitiated much of the past discussion of "nature versus nurture." [*See* CYBERNETICS *and* INFORMATION THEORY.]

Thorpe is aware that ambiguity has attended use of the word "innate." However, he places the ambiguity not between inherited and unlearned but between "(1) inherited or genetically fixed and therefore characteristic of the species; (2) internally co-ordinated; [and] (3) internally motivated" (*ibid.*, p. 15). Instinct, according to Thorpe, is innate in each of these senses. There is space here only for a remark about the third one.

According to Thorpe, "there is within the drive itself some inherent directiveness, some extremely restrictive purposive influence, perhaps identical (with) . . . expectancy and insight . . ." (p. 49), and purpose here is to be understood as "a striving after a future goal retained as some kind of image or idea" (p. 3). This thesis represents yet another attempt to build a bridge between the two apparently contradictory patterns of explanation of behavior: in terms of intentions or motives on the one hand and causes and mechanisms on the other (e.g., McDougall). Thorpe is probably right in his belief that the relation between these patterns of explanation poses one of the central problems for students of behavior. We seem to find it impossible to exclude from our descriptions of behavior categories of behavior identified by goals that, in some sense, are goals for (entertained by) the animal (consider fleeing, for example), and yet, as scientists we seem to be committed to the attempt to reduce such description to language devoid of teleological or subjective reference. Unfortunately, Thorpe's discussion of the problem does not solve it. If a solution is to be found, it will probably not come before the several concepts and questions involved have been clearly sorted out and their logic mapped. Thorpe, however, trades on the ambiguities of terms like "drive," "motivation," and "purpose" with the result that all the difficulties are preserved. At least so it has appeared to his tough-minded readers on the western side of the Atlantic.

Instinct in comparative psychology

By and large, the American psychologists who study animals other than humans reflect the legacy of behaviorism or the patterns of thought of which behaviorism was an expression: they tend to be pragmatic, positivistic, operational, and hostile to theories of instinct. However, their attitudes on theories of instinct have not all been the same, and as we have noted, the drive theorists preserve one of the connotations of instinct, albeit under different names.

Lashley (e.g., 1938) was one comparative psychologist for whom instinct had considerable attraction and who perceived that the anti-instinct revolt directed most of its attack on only one aspect of what was a composite notion. Lashley thought that there was still a place for a concept of instinct, but true to the spirit of positivism, his approach was essentially objective and experimental.

Lashley distinguished species-characteristic behavior patterns that are reactions to specific stimuli from variable, searching types of behavior that could be considered reactions to the absence of some form of stimulus situation. The former he chose to refer to as instinctive activities and the latter as "reactions to a deficit." Instinctive activities were, furthermore, to be distinguished from reflexes by being "determined by the pattern of organization of the stimulus" rather than by the effect of stimuli of a particular modality on receptor endings at a particular locus. Explanation of variations in the "excitability of the sensorimotor mechanism and of reaction to a deficit" he referred to as "the problem of the activation of the instinct."

Parallels between Lashley and Lorenz are evident here, even though they arrived at their ideas independently and by quite different routes. There are equally striking contrasts. Whereas Lorenz made his categories the basis of an over-all theory of behavior, Lashley aimed at sorting out a particular problem and describing it in terms that would suggest the kinds of physiological approaches that might throw light on it. For Lashley the study of instinct comprised problems of sensory organization, the integration of sensory input and motor output, the growth processes that effect the establishment of the sensorimotor mechanisms, and the roles of factors like hormone secretion in the activation of the sensorimotor mechanisms. He developed no theory and postulated the existence of no unobservable entities; he did not suggest that what might be found to be true for one instinct would necessarily hold true for others. His category of instinctive activities was intended to be a pragmatic one.

The question of the innateness of instinctive activities was one that Lashley passed over with little comment, even though he was aware of the difficulties it posed and of the fact that the use of instinct would inevitably be associated with the notion of innateness in one or both of its senses. Beach went so far as to say, "When all the criteria which supposedly differentiate instinctive from acquired responses are critically evaluated, the only one which seems universally applicable is that instincts are unlearned" (1955, p. 405). Beach, in this paper, was renewing the attack on the use of instinct in psychology and including Lashley's use of the term. According to Beach, it is generally assumed by psychologists who think in terms of instinct that behavior can be assorted into two mutually exclusive and collectively exhaustive categories: learned behavior on the one hand, inherited and/or unlearned behavior on the other. Even those psychologists who, like Z. Y. Kuo, reject instinct seem to accept the dichotomy between inherited and acquired elements of behavior, in maintaining that inherited elements are few and simple and the rest learned. Beach argued that such a dichotomy is indefensible. If the dichotomy is taken to be between learning and heredity, there is abundant evidence to show, for instance, that learning has a hereditary basis and, hence, that mutual exclusion does not obtain. If the dichotomy is taken to be between learning and its absence, we have one category that is defined by exclusion from another that is poorly understood—logically a dubious state of affairs, to say the least. Moreover, inheritance and learning are only two of many kinds of influences that can contribute to the ontogeny of behavior. Beach's message was that the psychologist should resist the temptation of his armchair and should try to settle questions about the genetics and ontogeny of behavior in the only way that they can be, by appropriate observations and appropriate experiments: "When [such] methods have been applied to the various types of behaviour which today are called 'instinctive' the concept of instinct will disappear, to be replaced by scientifically valid and useful explanations" (1955, p. 409).

Lehrman (1953), Schneirla (e.g., 1956), and Hebb (1953) have been as tough-mindedly insistent as Beach that understanding of how behavior develops in different animals will be advanced only by investigation unrestricted by a priori ideas about how many different kinds of processes there are. Lehrman, for instance, summed up his position as follows: "Any instinct theory which regards 'instinct' as immanent, preformed, inherited, or based on specific neural structures is bound to divert the investigation of behavior development from fundamental analysis and the study of developmental problems. Any such theory of 'instinct' inevitably tends to short-circuit the scientist's investigation of intraorganic and organism–environment developmental relationships which underlie the development of 'instinctive' behavior" (1953, p. 359).

In spite of continuities that exist between past and present thinking, instinct is seldom used with any of its older theoretical connotations in the writings of present-day ethologists and comparative psychologists. If it occurs at all, it is usually as a loose but often convenient label for a rather ill-defined class of species-characteristic and stereotyped behavior patterns about which questions of causation, ontogeny, and so forth remain, for the most part, open.

The ambition to arrive at an over-all theory of animal behavior no doubt persists and perhaps will some day be realized in a synthesis that will not involve confusions between facts and questions of different sorts. It may be that a concept of instinct will have a place in future syntheses. But unless history is to repeat itself yet again, such a concept would do well to pay heed to the lessons to be learned from its forerunners: they thrived on blurred distinctions, but to their ultimate undoing.

C. G. Beer

[*Directly related are the entries* Ethology; Evolution; Genetics, *article on* genetics and behavior; Imprinting. *Other relevant material may be found in* Communication, animal; Drives; Emotion; Motivation; Nervous system; Psychoanalysis; Psychology, *article on* comparative psychology; Sexual behavior, *article on* animal sexual behavior; Sympathy and empathy; *and in the biographies of* Darwin; Lashley; McDougall.]

BIBLIOGRAPHY

Beach, Frank A. 1955 The Descent of Instinct. *Psychological Review* 62:401–410.

Beer, C. G. 1963–1964 Ethology: The Zoologist's Approach to Behaviour. *Tuatara* 11:170–177; 12:16–39.

Darwin, Charles (1859) 1964 *On the Origin of Species.* Cambridge, Mass.: Harvard Univ. Press.

Darwin, Charles (1871) 1948 *The Descent of Man and Selection in Relation to Sex.* In Charles Darwin, *The Origin of Species* and *The Descent of Man.* New York: Modern Library.

Dunlap, Knight 1919 Are There Any Instincts? *Journal of Abnormal Psychology* 14:307–311.

Freud, Sigmund (1888–1938) 1959 *Collected Papers.* 5 vols. Authorized translation under the supervision of Joan Riviere. Vol. 5 edited by James Strachey. International Psycho-analytic Library, Nos. 7–10, 34. New York: Basic Books; London: Hogarth. → A 10-volume paperback edition was published in 1963 by Collier.

Freud, Sigmund (1900) 1953 The Interpretation of Dreams. Volumes 4–5 of *The Standard Edition of the Complete Psychological Works of Sigmund Freud.* London: Hogarth; New York: Macmillan. → First published as *Die Traumdeutung.*

Hebb, D. O. 1953 Heredity and Environment in Mammalian Behaviour. *British Journal of Animal Behaviour* 1:43–47.

Horney, Karen 1937 *The Neurotic Personality of Our Time.* New York: Norton.

Lashley, K. S. 1938 The Experimental Analysis of Instinctive Behavior. *Psychological Review* 45:445–471.

Lehrman, Daniel S. 1953 A Critique of Konrad Lorenz's Theory of Instinctive Behavior. *Quarterly Review of Biology* 28:337–363.

Lorenz, Konrad Z. 1937 Über die Bildung des Instinktbegriffes. *Naturwissenschaften* 25:289–300, 307–318, 324–331.

Lorenz, Konrad Z. 1950 The Comparative Method in Studying Innate Behaviour Patterns. Pages 221–268 in Society for Experimental Biology, *Physiological Mechanisms in Animal Behaviour.* Symposium No. 4. New York: Academic Press.

Lorenz, Konrad Z. 1961 Phylogenetische Anpassung und adaptive Modifikazion des Verhaltens. *Zeitschrift für Tierpsychologie* 18:139–187.

Lorenz, Konrad Z. 1965 *Evolution and Modification of Behavior.* Univ. of Chicago Press.

McDougall, William (1908) 1950 *An Introduction to Social Psychology.* 30th ed. London: Methuen. → A paperback edition was published in 1960 by Barnes and Noble.

SCHNEIRLA, T. C. 1956 Interrelationships of the "Innate" and the "Acquired" in Instinctive Behavior. Pages 387–452 in *L'instinct dans le comportement des animaux et de l'homme*, by M. Autuori et al. Paris: Masson.

TAYLOR, CHARLES 1964 *The Explanation of Behaviour.* New York: Humanities Press.

THORPE, WILLIAM H. (1956) 1963 *Learning and Instinct in Animals.* 2d ed., rev. & enl. Cambridge, Mass.: Harvard Univ. Press.

TINBERGEN, NIKOLAAS 1951 *The Study of Instinct.* Oxford: Clarendon.

TROTTER, WILFRED (1916) 1953 *Instincts of the Herd in Peace and War: 1916–1919.* Edited by R. W. Chapman. New York: Macmillan. → First published as *Instincts of the Herd in Peace and War.*

VEBLEN, THORSTEIN 1914 *The Instinct of Workmanship and the State of the Industrial Arts.* New York: Macmillan.

WHEELER, WILLIAM M. (1920–1921) 1939 On Instincts. Pages 37–70 in William M. Wheeler, *Essays in Philosophical Biology.* Cambridge, Mass.: Harvard Univ. Press. → First published in the *Journal of Abnormal Psychology.*

WILM, EMIL C. 1925 *The Theories of Instinct.* New Haven: Yale Univ. Press.

WITTGENSTEIN, LUDWIG (1953) 1964 *Philosophical Investigations; Philosophische Untersuchungen.* New York: Macmillan. → The title and the text are in both German and English.

INSTITUTIONAL SCHOOL
See under ECONOMIC THOUGHT.

INSTITUTIONS
See SOCIAL INSTITUTIONS.

INSTRUMENTAL LEARNING
See under LEARNING.

INSURANCE
See AGING, *article on* ECONOMIC ASPECTS; FINANCIAL INTERMEDIARIES; LIFE TABLES; MEDICAL CARE, *article on* ECONOMIC ASPECTS; PLANNING, SOCIAL, *article on* WELFARE PLANNING; UNEMPLOYMENT INSURANCE; WORKMEN'S COMPENSATION.

INTEGRATION

I
CULTURAL INTEGRATION

The idea that the diverse parts of any culture normally cohere in some determinate fashion has proven useful in the past in at least five contexts. (1) As an aid to description, the assumption of cultural integration has provided an economical way of summarizing large bodies of cultural data and has facilitated the portrayal of cultures in ideal-typical terms. (2) It has been used to help explain the particular ways in which members of a society accept, reject, or modify items which have diffused from other cultures. (3) Administrators and reformers have been guided by the concept in their efforts to find innovations and modes of introducing change which "fit" most comfortably into existing cultures. (4) The breakdown of cultural integration has been hypothesized as a causative factor in accounting for such phenomena as ennui, suicide, crime, and cultural lability. (5) Philosophers of culture have invoked the ideal of cultural integration as a criterion to be used in the evaluation of cultures.

Although cultural integration has been the subject of few sustained theoretical analyses and even fewer empirical studies, recent developments in modern society and in social theory alike have increased the salience of the concept. The cultural dislocations caused by the accelerated pace of change in our times; the increasing number of roles affected by contradictory cultural standards; greater awareness of cultural contradictions in consequence of higher education, mass communications, and more intimate interaction among people with diverse cultural orientations; and anxiety about such inconsistencies resulting from the importance of rationality in a culture increasingly subjected to universalistic standards—these are some of the sociological factors which appear to have promoted concern about the coherence of culture patterns. In addition, the world-wide modernization of traditional societies has stimulated numerous discussions concerning the integration of traditional and modern culture patterns (e.g., Redfield 1950; Almond 1960; Chicago, University of . . . 1963; Levine 1965).

The practical interest in the subject that stems from such considerations is matched by its significance from the point of view of current social theory. The nine distinguished scholars who signed the 1951 statement on the general theory of action assert that "the internal coherence of a body of cultural patterns is always a crucial problem for the student of culture" (Parsons & Shils 1951, p. 21). Much of the scientific excitement over this concept derives from the fact that so "crucial" an aspect of culture is to a large extent covert, unknown to the bearers of cultures themselves, and must be uncovered through the most imaginative efforts of scientific curiosity. Theoretically, the concept is related to contemporary efforts to deal in a more precise manner with the differential properties of culture systems and social systems and with their interpenetrations.

Indeed, one of the chief rewards of using the terms "culture" and "social structure" as analytic concepts rather than as global categories has been an increasingly differentiated understanding of the forms and dynamics of integration at the collective level. Consistent with the vagueness of those omnibus categories, earlier social scientists used the term integration in a fairly diffuse sense (e.g., Durkheim 1897; Sumner 1906; Benedict 1934). Sorokin's insistence on the distinction between systems integrated on the basis of functional interdependence and systems integrated in terms of logical and meaningful coherence (1937–1941) may be identified as the bench mark of a new orientation, even though the distinction as formulated by Sorokin crosscuts the dichotomy of culture and social structure. Most subsequent discussions of cultural integration have either repeated this distinction (Cohen 1948; Geertz 1957), elaborated and refined it (Landecker 1951; Parsons & Shils 1951), or else have dealt with cultural integration in the special sense of a phenomenon *sui generis* (Kluckhohn 1941; Redfield 1941; Kroeber 1948; Eggan 1955; Parsons 1959).

In addition to this movement from ambiguity to specificity in using the concept of cultural integration, social scientists also raised a number of provocative questions about the sources, forms, limits, and consequences of cultural integration, and in at least a few cases (Linton 1936; Sorokin 1937–1941; Redfield 1941; Kluckhohn 1941; Opler 1945) have circumspectly related the concept to bodies of reliable data. In so doing, they have transformed the character of the concept from an assumed principle to an analytic variable and from an evaluative to a nonevaluative category.

Cultural integration—structural variable

The related assumptions that sociocultural systems are characterized by an inner coherence and unity that is essential to their nature and that this integrity is a salutary and valuable property draw on intellectual traditions that are more than two centuries old. Vico and Montesquieu were early modern proponents of the view that the beliefs, purposes, laws, and customs of a society constitute a meaningfully interrelated complex of traits, not a haphazard assortment. Burke and de Maistre stressed the idea that a society is like an organism, the parts of which are in a natural balance that should not be disrupted by arbitrary innovations derived from abstract reasoning. Rousseau, Herder, and Chaadaev espoused the romantic conception that societies are integrated through their embodiment of distinctive principles, that their "mission" is to realize these unique principles and avoid extraneous influences which interfere with that realization. Such perspectives were incorporated into historical studies through the work of men like Burckhardt, Dilthey, and Lamprecht, for whom the task of scholarship was to discern the characteristic configurations of historical periods which reflect a distinctive harmony, world view, or collective spirit (*Volksseele*)—a mission revived in this century by the efforts of scholars like Spengler, Jaeger, and Basham.

Largely because of anthropological work in the 1930s and after, such extreme views of both the extent and the value of cultural integration have been substantially rejected. The rejection of the view of cultures as totally integrated organic unities—which in any case was probably never adhered to by more than a small minority of serious scholars—may be traced in two stages. Despite Malinowski's implication that all living cultures are fully integrated—"the significance of culture consists in the relation between its elements, and the existence of accidental or fortuitous culture complexes is not admitted" (1931, p. 625—those cultural anthropologists who were concerned with the problem developed the view that integration is not a vital principle to be assumed fully operative in all cultures but is rather a formal property which varies on a continuum from high to low. Ruth Benedict, who has at times been accused of "mystically" imputing such a principle to cultures, stated explicitly that "lack of integration seems to be as characteristic of certain cultures as extreme integration is of others" (1934, p. 223). Cultural integration came to be visualized as an emergent property—not an essential attribute, but the outgrowth of a continuing process of mutual selection and adjustment of elements into a *more or less* coherent pattern. "It is not," stated Kroeber, "a growth of parts unfolding from a germ in accord with a pre-existing harmonious master plan. Such an unfolding has often been assumed, insinuated, or asserted . . . but it remains wholly undemonstrated, and history shows it to be at least partly untrue" (1948, p. 287).

Using cultural integration as a structural variable, students began to analyze the limits of the extent to which *any* culture could be called integrated. As other investigators came upon data which diverged from her interpretation of Zuñi culture, Benedict's own cases of "extreme integration" were rendered suspect. Following to a large extent in Benedict's footsteps, Kluckhohn nevertheless observed that most cultures are "permeated by apparent contradictions" (Kluckhohn & Kelly 1945). And Malinowski himself, despite alleged assumptions of the complete integration of cultures, provided eloquent documentation of the clash of normative principles in primitive society (1926). Observations of this sort were paralleled by two main lines of argument against the theoretical possibility of a perfectly integrated human culture. Since change of some sort due to invention, diffusion, or environmental alteration is always going on, no culture can ever have all its elements in a condition of complete mutual adjustment (Linton 1936, p. 357). Even if change were not inevitable, moreover, culture is "borne" only by being institutionalized in social systems and internalized in personalities, and the "structural imperatives" of these systems of action are such as to require more kinds of culture than can be included in any single consistently integrated pattern (Parsons 1951).

Yet, however much scientific estimates of culture's capacity for integration get revised downward, the consensus is that the study of culture can never again be reduced to the collecting of pebbles. Redfield has stated the case with characteristic elegance: "There is no society the conventional life of which may be described realistically in terms of a series of accounts of customs and beliefs taken one by one so that each is completely reported without reference to any one of the other" (1941, p. 132). And Opler confessed that ". . . in a good many years of intensive field work I have never found 'isolated segments of behavior logically unrelated to the remainder of the culture' " (1946, p. 44). Surveying this whole development, Kluckhohn concluded that "the greatest advance in contemporary anthropological theory is probably the increasing recognition that there is something more to culture than artifacts, linguistic texts, and lists of atomized traits" ([1951] 1959, p. 89).

The current view, then, is that integration is a quality of culture that is never perfect but never absent—a structural property that varies from relatively high to relatively low and that can be related empirically and theoretically to other cultural and sociological variables. The increased realism and flexibility with which the concept is now handled has produced a more subtle conception of cultural integration as an ideological category. By the 1930s two traditions in social science converged to create what might be called the pathos of cultural integrity. A number of anthropologists, impressed by the aesthetic coherence of some of the primitive cultures they had encountered, came to view cultural integration as a touchstone of human excellence and euphoria. Edward Sapir maintained that the only culture worthy of the name is that which is "inherently harmonious, balanced, self-satisfactory . . . the expression of a richly varied and yet somehow unified and consistent attitude toward life . . ." (1924, p. 410). Others saw cultural integrity as the primary source of individual morale and vitality, of social cohesion, and of a profound outlook on life. A number of sociologists, on the other hand, took their point of departure from the ills of modern society and traced them back to cultural disorganization. The concept of culture conflict became the key to the sociological understanding of crime (Sellin 1938). Sociologists and others depicted contemporary American culture as one shot through with crippling contradictions (Bain 1935; Horney 1937; Lynd 1939). Ralph Linton proclaimed:

> . . . what the modern world needs far more than improved production methods or even a more equitable distribution of their results is a series of mutually consistent ideas and values in which all its members can participate. Perhaps something of the sort can be developed in time to prevent the collapse which otherwise seems inevitable. If not, another "dark age" is in order. . . . (1936, p. 287)

Such strong views of the virtues of extreme cultural integration and the dangers of malintegration have been tempered by a number of considerations. (1) A very high degree of cultural integration may counteract other values which are important in some societies, such as creativity and novelty, or cultural pluralism. (2) While the integral growth of complex cultures is of great value, it can only be attained at the expense of the development of individual personality. As civilization advances, the conflict between "objective culture" and "subjective culture" becomes increasingly tragic (Simmel 1911). (3) As Linton himself came to stress in later years when dealing with the problems of developing areas, less tightly integrated cultures have greater adaptability; when a new culture element is introduced, ". . . the closer the integration, the more extensive and immediate the dislocations" ([1952] 1956, p. 86). (4) Cultures are after all not very fragile entities. Their power of persistence has impressed most observers, and they have a regenerative capacity which enables them to resolve contradictions and create new forms of order. What is experienced by a participant or observer as the disorganization and impending doom of a culture may well be simply a phase of adjustment in the process of cultural reintegration (Redfield 1941; Kroeber 1948). (5) No less significant than these substantive insights into the nature of culture has been the increasing sophistication of our method of coping with such normative problems. In accord with the level of complexity on which contemporary social science proceeds, one would no longer maintain that cultural integration as such is inherently valuable or not, but rather ask: What kind of integration of what kinds of contents has what kinds of consequences for whom?

To state the normative problem in this fashion is to return to the scientific problem of analyzing and measuring cultural integration. Contemporary approaches are marked by a great diversity with respect to the forms, processes, and consequences of cultural integration. There is further diversity with respect to the kinds of cultural contents which are referred to in the study of integration. Since the relationship among the diverse phenomena referred to by these varying notions of cultural integration is problematic, a more differentiated treatment of the concept henceforth is indicated. It is symptomatic of the gap between cultural theory and the theory of social structure that, whereas the latter has available a rich and complex conceptual framework, analysis of cultural structure still proceeds—with the notable exception of linguistics—at a level not far from common sense. In one of the most clearly reasoned classifications of types of collective integration (Landecker 1952), nine forms of social integration are distinguished, but only three forms of cultural integration. The following classification of the dimensions of cultural integration is offered as a contribution toward closing that gap.

All the scholars whose work will be reviewed here agree on two points: that culture consists of symbols and that cultural integration has reference to the relationships among these symbols. They differ with respect to (1) the kinds of symbols that are studied—the problem of the *contents* of culture; (2) the groups whose cultures are studied—the problem of the *levels* of cultural integration; and (3) the nature of the relationship between symbols—the problem of the *forms* of cultural integration. We begin with the last of these, since that is where most of the issues lie.

The forms of cultural integration

Configurational or thematic integration. The first type of cultural integration is that made prominent by the work of Ruth Benedict (1934). It refers to an identity of meaning within a diversity of cultural items: their conformity to a common pattern, their embodiment of a common theme. It is integration through similarity. It is illustrated by the extent to which, among the Zuñi, marriage customs, dance forms, attitudes toward death, and other aspects of culture all tend to reflect a characteristic interest in sobriety, moderation, and ceremoniousness. The existence of this dimension of integration has been related to the imperative of *selectivity:* man's genetic heritage is insufficient to orient him in this world and the potentialities for behavior are innumerable. Therefore, some segment of the total arc of possibilities must be selected in order to provide direction in behavior and meaning in the environment. Students using this approach differ as to whether this principle of selectivity is to be conceived of as a structure (Kluckhohn's "configuration"), a dynamic postulate (Opler's "theme"), or a kind of cognitive disposition (Sorokin's "culture mentality"). They also disagree about whether the canons of choice are unconscious: Kluckhohn used the term configuration to refer specifically to structural regularities that are unconscious and defines the integrating principle of a culture as its "single dominant master configuration" (1943, p. 218), whereas Opler implicitly rejects the premise of the covertness of basic orienting themes in culture as an unnecessary restriction (1945, p. 198). An obvious method of measuring the extent of this type of integration in a culture would be to count the proportion of items which embody its posited integrating principle—a vast undertaking and one that has been attempted only once in this century. Sorokin sought to measure the extent to which various periods in the history of Western civilization were integrated in terms of the "identity of the fundamental principles and values that permeate all (their) parts" ([1937–1941] 1962, vol. 4, p. 11) by devising numerical indices to represent the extent to which the various departments of culture—painting, architecture, music, literature, philosophy, etc.—were informed by one or another kind of basic cultural mentality.

Opler recommends counting unformalized expressions of a theme as well as formalized ones, a task requiring "close observation, accounts of personal experiences, and autobiographical materials," and also observation of "the intensity of the reaction and the character of the sanctions invoked . . ." when the terms of a theme are violated (1945, p. 201).

With respect to the consequences of configurational integration, it is evident that a very high degree of conformity of the elements of culture to a particular pattern imposes serious restrictions on the freedom of individuals who are inclined toward alternative patterns; there is little scope for the realization of variant and deviant patterns. While, moreover, it has been suggested that cultures which do not subordinate all their parts to a ruling principle give "an impression of extreme poverty" (Benedict 1934, p. 196), the point has also been made that the predominance of a single theme in a culture may have highly disruptive consequences and is to be regarded as socially pathological (Opler 1945, p. 199).

Connective integration. A second type of cultural integration concerns the extent to which the diverse parts of culture are directly connected with one another. In describing this phenomenon of the mutual association of different cultural elements, anthropologists have used terms like "connotative interdependence" (Redfield 1941, p. 352), "systemic pattern" (Kroeber 1948, p. 312), and "assemblage" (Opler 1959, p. 962); and for cultural traits which are discrete and not associated with others, the term "separates" (Redfield 1941, p. 138). The distinction between this type of integration and that discussed in the first category may be readily illustrated: while, following Weber (1904–1905), one may say that modern Western culture is highly integrated in that its various branches—music, law, science, etc.—are all characterized by a dominant "rationalistic" culture orientation, there has been relatively little association between the worlds of music, law, and science in modern Western culture. Conversely, while there is a close association between military symbols (carrying rifles, martial chants) and devotional symbols (hymns, pious poetry) on the occasion of Ethiopian Orthodox holidays, these two sets of symbols represent directly opposed themes or configurations in Ethiopian Christian culture. In one attempt to study integration in the sense of interconnection, Redfield sought to measure this dimension of cultural organization in four Yucatecan communities by observing the number of "separates" in each. His study supported the hypothesis that connective integration is promoted by isolation and cultural homogeneity. In the relatively isolated tribal community, he found that pagan and Christian complexes were closely interwoven: ". . . the bee cult is under the care of the Virgin; the patronage of certain saints over certain animals is more explicit . . ." (Redfield 1941, p. 139); whereas in the less isolated peasant village, he found a greater compartmentalization of ideas—for example, ". . . the care of the hives and the cult of the bee deities remain pagan in nature . . . no saint enters into the conceptions . . ." (*ibid.*, p. 136).

The consequences of a high degree of cultural interconnection, Redfield proposed, are the greater efficacy of culture as a design for living, greater durability in style of life, and greater depth of the world view; whereas in the less organized culture of the town, the presumably related characteristics were found to be uncertainty, self-consciousness, restlessness and, frequently, distress. The existence of this form of integration may thus be seen as a response to man's need for *coherence*. On the other hand, it seems to be clear that any sort of cultural excellence above the most primitive sort requires the presence of cultural specialists. The extent to which cultural specialization requires compartmentalization and segregation is an important question for the theory of culture, one which has not yet received the attention it deserves.

Logical integration. A third dimension of integration concerns the extent to which cultural items tend to contradict one another. This perspective defines integration not as identity or as interlocking diversity but in terms of logical consistency —a criterion that primarily affects existential beliefs and systems of norms. This type of integration is by definition a response to man's need for *rationality*. While this need may not be very fully developed in relatively undifferentiated societies— the existence of such rationalized bodies of culture as philosophical systems or legal codes requires the presence of cultural specialists working under special conditions—the discomfort psychologists have come to refer to as "cognitive dissonance" (Festinger 1957) is presumably endemic in human nature. Students of logical integration have stressed the importance of distinguishing between what appears to an outsider as a logical contradiction and what is "felt as such" by those who live in the culture (Landecker 1951), or inconsistencies which ". . . present a dilemma with regard to attitude or overt behavior" (Redfield 1941, p. 137). A negative index of the logical integration of culture would thus be the number of experienced "incompatibles," a variable also examined in Redfield's study of Yucatan. Adapting Linton's terms to the study of this phenomenon, Landecker has proposed that cultural integration be measured by (1) the number of inconsistencies among "universals" and (2) the number of inconsistencies among "specialties with societal reference." Following a line of thought of some prominence in modern sociology, he has also hypothesized that one consequence of consistency among cultural standards is a high degree of "normative integration": ". . . the higher the degree of (logical) integration among the standards of a culture is, the higher the degree of behavioral conformity to these standards will be" (1952, p. 398).

Adaptive or functional integration. The "strain of consistency" among folkways which Sumner is famous for emphasizing is not the consistency of pure logic: whatever the contradictions in a culture from the point of view of pure reason, the folkways are "true" and can make anything seem right. Sumner stresses rather the adaptive character of culture —traits are ways of satisfying needs—and finds that ". . . they all answer their several purposes with less friction and antagonism when they co-operate and support each other" (1906, sec. 5 in 1940 edition). The functional integration of culture is an outgrowth of the desire for *efficiency*. As Sorokin has pointed out, Pareto's concept of "logical" action really refers not to logical consistency but to functional effectiveness ([1947] 1962, p. 340).

Although it is due to his view of culture as "essentially an instrumental apparatus" that Malinowski in his theoretical writing stresses that culture ". . . is an integral in which the various elements are interdependent" and rejects the notion that any culture traits can be a nonfunctional survival (1944, p. 150), students of functional integration generally have stressed the imperfections and dislocations in the organization of culture from this point of view. They tend to see changes chronically originating in the technological sector which then upset whatever functional equilibrium had previously been obtained. Because of what Sumner calls the strain of improvement toward better adaptation of means to ends and because instrumental techniques are the foundation on which the whole elaborate superstructure of culture is founded, ". . . societies are thus constantly trapped into accepting elements which are highly disruptive" (Linton 1936, p. 356). The result is a lack of integration, a "culture lag," which frequently becomes cumulative and so dysfunctional that sometimes revolution or war is the only way to overcome it (Ogburn 1957).

Stylistic integration. A fifth type of integration is that which emerges from the mutual adaptation of parts of experience felt so intensely that their contrasts and organization produce an emotionally gratifying whole. Its locus is those characteristic modes of behavior and manners of expression we term styles. This type of integration springs not from the rational impulse for logical consistency nor from the practical impulse for instrumental effectiveness—though these may be fused with it—but from the aesthetic impulse for authentic expression of experience in satisfying form. Spontaneity and creativity are the essence of this form of integration; ". . . where compulsion or physical or physiological necessity reign, there is no room for style" (Kroeber 1957, p. 150). While stylistic integration is usually associated primarily with the fine arts, styles have also been identified in such diverse spheres as social thought (Mannheim 1927), political and economic behavior (Riesman 1950), and science and philosophy (Kroeber 1948; 1957), not to mention the commonly appreciated activities of eating and dressing.

While the concept "style of life" has long been familiar to social scientists from the work of Max Weber, their investigation of stylistic integration is still in the earliest stages; they have much to learn about methods of studying style from scholars in the humanities, for whom it has naturally been a central concept. Kroeber is one of the few social scientists to have dealt at length with the problem of style outside the fine arts. His work supports the idea of applying the term "style" not only to the most diverse branches of culture but also to total cultures—not in the Spenglerian sense of considering a whole culture as a sort of expanded style but in that its several styles ". . . will tend to accommodate somewhat to one another; so that the whole may come . . . to possess a fairly high degree of congruence" (Kroeber 1957, p. 152). Such a total-culture style is what Sapir presumably had in mind in his conception of "genuine culture," illustrated by his thumbnail characterization of French culture as marked by "the qualities of clarity, lucid systematization, balance, care in choice of means, and good taste" and also "overmechanization, emotional timidity or shallowness . . . [and] exaggeration of manner at the expense of content"; it was its lack of such a cultural style that made Sapir so critical of American culture (Sapir 1924, p. 407).

Some of Kroeber's most stimulating work concerns the temporal dimension of stylistic integration: he argued (1944) that style patterns have specific potentialities that are realized in climactic spurts of creativity and are then exhausted, leading to their abandonment and the generation of new styles, and that periods of societal breakdown and reconstitution are accompanied by losses of style. One of the chief consequences of the attainment of a style pattern is thus the provision of a matrix of creative potentialities, and stylistic integration is the cultural substratum for the flowering of men of genius. [*See* STYLE.]

Regulative integration. Common to all the approaches which have just been described is a conception of cultural integration in terms of coherence and harmony. Whether this harmony is defined as identity of pattern, connotative interdependence, logical consistency, functional appropriateness, or stylistic congruence, the point of departure is an assumption that the parts of culture tend for various reasons to be related in a harmonious way. The one-sidedness of this view becomes apparent if one considers the forms of integration in social systems; for in addition to the types of social integration based on conformity to norms, spontaneous interaction, and functional interdependence, sociologists have long recognized the importance of "integrative mechanisms" which deal directly with real or threatened eruptions of social conflict. Accordingly, any classification of forms of cultural integration which omits phenomena specifically related to the manifestation and control of cultural conflict must be considered incomplete.

Examples of three different approaches to the problem of regulative integration may be found in recent literature. (1) As observed above, Opler regards the uninhibited expression of a single theme in any culture as a disequilibrating factor. He defines integration in cultural structure in terms of the equilibrium that is achieved or approximated in most cultures by virtue of the existence of "limiting factors"—circumstances and counterthemes which control the number, force, and variety of a theme's expressions (Opler 1945, p. 201). Thus, the theme of male superiority in Chiricahua culture is balanced by such factors as uxorilocal residence; so, while it is true that Chiricahua women may not use the sweat lodge, the sweat lodge is not considered a crucial element of their ceremonialism and, moreover, women *may* obtain supernatural power like men and become shamans. Regulative integration appears as a kind of balance of power among various cultural items. (2) A second type of regulation of divergent cultural patterns is through hierarchical organization. Talcott Parsons has presented highly suggestive analyses of this dimension of cultural structure in two contexts: the hierarchical arrangement of various value-orientations in a culture and the hierarchical ordering of the various types of cultural systems (1953; 1959; 1961). (3) A third example is what might be called the "moral division of labor" (Durkheim 1897; Levine 1965). Cultural conflict is avoided by relegating divergent patterns to different segments of the population, with the implicit support by each segment of the values of the other, though overtly these may be in complete conflict. Matza's work on youth subcultures has uncovered the interesting mechanisms of "conventional versions" (1961) and "subterranean convergence" (1964), through which deviant subcultural patterns are kept from total conflict with the dominant patterns.

Integration and the content of culture

If careful comparison of the approaches of different students of cultural integration leads to awareness of a variety of forms or dimensions of cultural integration, a survey of recent work in the field quickly reveals that our perception of what it is that becomes integrated has become no less differentiated. One aspect of this differentiation concerns the diversity of concrete cultures; another concerns the differentiation of analytically distinguishable systems within concrete cultures.

Just as a principal accomplishment of anthropologists working in the 1920s was to replace the generic study of culture by the study of particular cultures, so has the generation of social scientists working in the middle of this century rendered obsolete the concept of an undifferentiated particular culture and demanded the discrimination of various subcultures within any whole culture. Sociologists have identified and described in detail a number of persisting and coherent subcultures in the United States—including those borne by social classes (Warner 1949), ethnic groups (Glazer & Moynihan 1963), age groups (Matza 1961), and many others. Political scientists have found important differences between the subcultures of elites and masses in various nations (Pye & Verba 1965). Anthropologists who have moved from the study of relatively small, isolated societies to more complex societies have found it necessary to distinguish between segmental cultures and national cultures (Steward 1955) or between little traditions and great traditions (Redfield 1956). The call has been sounded for students of cultural integration in complex societies to take explicit account of such internal differentiation in making their analyses (Aberle 1950).

A fivefold schema, based on that proposed by Landecker, would seem adequate to handle the kinds of problems posed by that requirement. ". . . the first and most obvious structural distinction relevant to a complex group is that between the group as a whole and a smaller group within it. It will be terminologically convenient to call the larger group, when seen as a whole, the 'compound-group,' and to call the smaller group . . . the 'subgroup'" (Landecker 1952, p. 394). The proposed distinction is relative: the same group may be viewed now as a compound-group, now as a subgroup that exists within a much larger group. This distinction generates five questions concerning the cultural integration of complex groups:

(1) Intrinsic subgroup (cultural) integration—the extent to which the subgroup culture is internally integrated;

(2) Extrinsic subgroup integration, horizontal—the extent to which one subgroup culture is integrated with another;

(3) Extrinsic subgroup integration, vertical—

the extent to which a subgroup culture is integrated with the compound-group culture;

(4) Compound-group integration, horizontal—the extent to which culture at the compound-group level is integrated; and

(5) Compound-group integration, vertical—the extent to which the total compound-group culture, including its subgroup cultures, is integrated.

This classification would of course be crosscut by that outlined in the preceding section on the forms of integration.

Another type of differentiation to which students of culture have become increasingly sensitive concerns the different kinds of symbol systems within a given subculture. While this area of cultural theory exists in a state of flux, one of the more prominent classifications divides culture into belief systems, normative systems, and systems of expressive symbolism; these in turn have been further subdivided. The analysis of cultural integration from this perspective focuses on the internal coherence of a particular symbol system and its relations with other analytic systems of action. Two categories of problems emerge at once: (1) intrasystemic problems—the degree of integration among the parts of a particular symbol system, say, the empirical beliefs or the expressive symbols of a given subculture; and (2) intersystemic problems—the degree of integration among two or more types of symbol system. The latter category would include such classical problems as Weber's concern about the relationship between ultimate ideas about reality and practical ethics in the world religions and Mannheim's concern about the relationship between empirical beliefs and systems of value orientations. Beyond this, there are the many problems having to do with the integration of symbol systems with the other dimensions of action, social systems, and personalities; but at this point the study of cultural integration itself dissolves as a boundary-maintaining system and becomes fused with such complex pursuits as the psychology of knowledge, cultural psychology, and the sociology of culture.

It may simply be noted here that earlier theories which treated cultural integration as epiphenomenal—reducing it to a function of the rationalization of class interests or the projection of psychological impulses—have given way to a growing awareness that the emergent properties of cultural systems themselves include integrative problems of a distinct order.

DONALD N. LEVINE

[*Directly related are the entries* CONFLICT; CULTURE; SOCIAL STRUCTURE. *Other relevant material may be found in the biographies of* BENEDICT; KROEBER; REDFIELD; SAPIR; SOROKIN.]

BIBLIOGRAPHY

ABERLE, DAVID F. 1950 Shared Values in Complex Societies. *American Sociological Review* 15:495–502.

ALMOND, GABRIEL A. 1960 Introduction: A Functional Approach to Comparative Politics. Pages 3–64 in Gabriel A. Almond and James S. Coleman (editors), *The Politics of the Developing Areas.* Princeton Univ. Press.

BAIN, READ 1935 Our Schizoid Culture. *Sociology and Social Research* 19:266–276.

BENEDICT, RUTH 1934 *Patterns of Culture.* Boston: Houghton Mifflin. → A paperback edition was published in 1961.

CHICAGO, UNIVERSITY OF, COMMITTEE FOR THE COMPARATIVE STUDY OF NEW NATIONS 1963 *Old Societies and New States: The Quest for Modernity in Asia and Africa.* Edited by Clifford Geertz. New York: Free Press.

COHEN, ALBERT K. 1948 On the Place of "Themes" and Kindred Concepts in Social Theory. *American Anthropologist* New Series 50:436–443.

DURKHEIM, ÉMILE (1897) 1951 *Suicide: A Study in Sociology.* Glencoe, Ill.: Free Press. → First published in French.

EGGAN, FRED (1955) 1962 Social Anthropology: Methods and Results. Pages 485–551 in *Social Anthropology of North American Tribes.* 2d ed., enl. Univ. of Chicago Press.

FESTINGER, LEON 1957 *A Theory of Cognitive Dissonance.* Evanston, Ill.: Row, Peterson.

GEERTZ, CLIFFORD 1957 Ritual and Social Change: A Javanese Example. *American Anthropologist* New Series 59:32–54.

GLAZER, NATHAN; and MOYNIHAN, DANIEL P. 1963 *Beyond the Melting Pot: The Negroes, Puerto Ricans, Jews, Italians, and the Irish of New York City.* Cambridge, Mass.: M.I.T. Press.

HORNEY, KAREN 1937 *The Neurotic Personality of Our Time.* New York: Norton.

KLUCKHOHN, CLYDE (1941) 1960 Patterning as Exemplified in Navaho Culture. Pages 109–130 in *Language, Culture and Personality: Essays in Memory of Edward Sapir.* Salt Lake City: Univ. of Utah Press.

KLUCKHOHN, CLYDE 1943 Covert Culture and Administrative Problems. *American Anthropologist* New Series 45:213–227.

KLUCKHOHN, CLYDE (1951) 1959 The Study of Culture. Pages 86–101 in Daniel Lerner and Harold D. Lasswell (editors), *The Policy Sciences: Recent Developments in Scope and Method.* Stanford Univ. Press.

KLUCKHOHN, CLYDE; and KELLY, W. H. 1945 The Concept of Culture. Pages 78–105 in *The Science of Man in the World Crisis.* Edited by Ralph Linton. New York: Columbia Univ. Press.

KROEBER, ALFRED L. 1944 *Configurations of Culture Growth.* Berkeley: Univ. of California Press.

KROEBER, ALFRED L. 1948 *Anthropology: Race, Language, Culture, Psychology, Prehistory.* New York: Harcourt. → First published in 1923 as *Anthropology.*

KROEBER, ALFRED L. 1957 *Style and Civilizations.* Ithaca, N.Y.: Cornell Univ. Press.

LANDECKER, WERNER S. 1951 Types of Integration and Their Measurement. *American Journal of Sociology* 56:332–340.

LANDECKER, WERNER S. 1952 Integration and Group Structure: An Area for Research. *Social Forces* 30: 394–400.

LEVINE, DONALD N. 1965 *Wax and Gold: Tradition and Innovation in Ethiopian Culture.* Univ. of Chicago Press.

LINTON, RALPH 1936 *The Study of Man: An Introduction.* New York: Appleton.

LINTON, RALPH (1952) 1956 Cultural and Personality Factors Affecting Economic Growth. Pages 73–88 in Bert F. Hoselitz (editor), *The Progress of Underdeveloped Areas.* Univ. of Chicago Press.

LYND, ROBERT S. 1939 *Knowledge for What? The Place of Social Science in American Culture.* Princeton Univ. Press.

MALINOWSKI, BRONISLAW (1926) 1961 *Crime and Custom in Savage Society.* London: Routledge.

MALINOWSKI, BRONISLAW 1931 Culture. Volume 4, pages 621–646 in *Encyclopaedia of the Social Sciences.* New York: Macmillan.

MALINOWSKI, BRONISLAW 1944 *A Scientific Theory of Culture, and Other Essays.* Chapel Hill: Univ. of North Carolina Press.

MANNHEIM, KARL (1927) 1953 Conservative Thought. Pages 74–164 in Karl Mannheim, *Essays on Sociology and Social Psychology.* Edited by Paul Kecskemeti. London: Routledge. → First published in German.

MATZA, DAVID 1961 Subterranean Traditions of Youth. American Academy of Political and Social Science, *Annals* 338:102–118.

MATZA, DAVID 1964 *Delinquency and Drift.* New York: Wiley.

OGBURN, WILLIAM F. 1957 Cultural Lag as Theory. *Sociology and Social Research* 41:167–174.

OPLER, MORRIS E. 1945 Themes as Dynamic Forces in Culture. *American Journal of Sociology* 51:198–206.

OPLER, MORRIS E. 1946 Rejoinder. *American Journal of Sociology* 52:43–44.

OPLER, MORRIS E. 1959 Component, Assemblage, and Theme in Cultural Integration and Differentiation. *American Anthropologist* New Series 61:955–964.

PARSONS, TALCOTT 1951 *The Social System.* Glencoe, Ill.: Free Press.

PARSONS, TALCOTT 1953 A Revised Analytical Approach to the Theory of Social Stratification. Pages 92–128 in Reinhard Bendix and Seymour M. Lipset (editors), *Class, Status and Power: A Reader in Social Stratification.* Glencoe, Ill.: Free Press.

PARSONS, TALCOTT 1959 An Approach to the Sociology of Knowledge. Volume 4, pages 25–49 in World Congress of Sociology, Fourth, Milan and Stresa, 1959, *Transactions.* Louvain (Belgium): International Sociological Association.

PARSONS, TALCOTT (1961) 1965 The Dimensions of Cultural Variation. Pages 964–971 in Talcott Parsons et al. (editors), *Theories of Society: Foundations of Modern Sociological Theory.* New York: Free Press.

PARSONS, TALCOTT; and SHILS, EDWARD A. (editors) 1951 *Toward a General Theory of Action.* Cambridge, Mass.: Harvard Univ. Press. → A paperback edition was published in 1962 by Harper.

PYE, LUCIAN W.; and VERBA, SIDNEY (editors) 1965 *Political Culture and Political Development.* Princeton Univ. Press.

REDFIELD, ROBERT 1941 *The Folk Culture of Yucatan.* Univ. of Chicago Press.

REDFIELD, ROBERT 1950 *A Village That Chose Progress: Chan Kom Revisited.* Univ. of Chicago Press. → A paperback edition was published in 1962.

REDFIELD, ROBERT 1956 *Peasant Society and Culture: An Anthropological Approach to Civilization.* Univ. of Chicago Press. → A paperback edition, bound together with *The Little Community,* was published in 1961 by Cambridge Univ. Press.

RIESMAN, DAVID 1950 *The Lonely Crowd: A Study of the Changing American Character.* New Haven: Yale Univ. Press. → An abridged paperback edition was published in 1960.

SAPIR, EDWARD (1924) 1949 Culture, Genuine and Spurious. Pages 308–331 in Edward Sapir, *Selected Writings in Language, Culture, and Personality.* Berkeley: Univ. of California Press. → First published in Volume 29 of the *American Journal of Sociology.*

SELLIN, THORSTEN 1938 *Culture Conflict and Crime.* New York: Social Science Research Council.

SIMMEL, GEORG 1911 Der Begriff und die Tragödie der Kultur. Pages 245–277 in Georg Simmel, *Philosophische Kultur.* Potsdam (Germany): Kiepenheuer.

SOROKIN, PITIRIM A. (1937–1941) 1962 *Social and Cultural Dynamics.* 4 vols. Englewood Cliffs, N.J.: Bedminster. → Volume 1: *Fluctuation of Forms of Art.* Volume 2: *Fluctuation of Systems of Truth, Ethics, and Law.* Volume 3: *Fluctuation of Social Relationships, War, and Revolution.* Volume 4: *Basic Problems, Principles, and Methods.*

SOROKIN, PITIRIM A. (1947) 1962 *Society, Culture, and Personality; Their Structure and Dynamics: A System of General Sociology.* New York: Cooper.

STEWARD, JULIAN H. 1955 *Theory of Culture Change: The Methodology of Multilinear Evolution.* Urbana: Univ. of Illinois Press.

SUMNER, WILLIAM G. (1906) 1959 *Folkways: A Study of the Sociological Importance of Usages, Manners, Customs, Mores, and Morals.* New York: Dover. → A paperback edition was published in 1960 by New American Library.

WARNER, W. LLOYD (1949) 1960 *Social Class in America: A Manual of Procedure for the Measurement of Social Status.* New York: Harper.

WEBER, MAX (1904–1905) 1930 *The Protestant Ethic and the Spirit of Capitalism.* Translated by Talcott Parsons, with a foreword by R. H. Tawney. London: Allen & Unwin; New York: Scribner. → First published in German. A paperback edition was published in 1958 by Scribner.

WHITE, LESLIE 1949 *The Science of Culture: A Study of Man and Civilization.* New York: Farrar, Straus. → A paperback edition was published in 1958 by Grove.

II
SOCIAL INTEGRATION

The fitting together of the parts of a social system to constitute a whole has long been a matter of both practical and scientific interest. Historically, the often disruptive effects of the industrial revolution have directed attention to the practical problems of maintaining social integration or achieving reintegration. Both societies and communities have tried to ward off fragmentation or to recapture effective unity once fragmentation has occurred. Scientifically, there are both definitional and theoretical challenges. Is social integration one-dimensional, or is it a phenomenon having a number of facets? What are the useful criteria for judging whether it is present or absent? No questions are more basic, since to deal with social units at all is to be able to distinguish units from nonunits, and this requires some notion of integration. Once the problem of conceptualization is settled, there are the far-reaching theoretical problems of the causes of high and low degrees of integration and of their effects on a great variety of other social phenomena.

Social integration is problematic at many levels, from the small group to the society. Although analytically each level may be treated separately, in real life the same group is usually a matter of concern on two levels. On a lower level it is a whole whose parts require integration, but at the next higher level it is a part that is more or less well integrated into some larger whole. Communities, for instance, have their own problems of integration, but they constitute elements in the integrative problem of their society. This article will treat only large social systems, such as cities, whole societies, and international communities; integration in small social systems is treated elsewhere [*see* COHESION, SOCIAL].

Types of integration. The tendency in recent sociology has been to differentiate types of integration rather than to make the concept unidimensional. As Landecker points out in a seminal article (1951), it is useful in the early stages of exploration to determine the relation to one another of different facets of a phenomenon and thus to discover the degree to which it is unified. He distinguishes the following four types of integration: *cultural,* or the consistency among cultural standards; *normative*, or the consistency between cultural standards and the conduct of persons; *communicative,* or the extent to which the network of communication permeates the social system; and *functional,* or the degree to which there is mutual interdependence among the units of a system of division of labor. Here the last three types of integration will be regarded as subsumed by social integration. Since the distinction between cultural systems and social systems was not widely made before 1951 (Parsons & Shils 1951; Parsons 1951), analyses before that date that deal with the integration of sociocultural systems as wholes will also be discussed.

Durkheim's contributions. The great pioneer in the study of social integration was Durkheim (1893). Picking up two ideas that go far back in the history of social thought, he presented two contrasting types, the first of which is a combination of cultural and normative integration and the second of which is functional integration.

What he called "mechanical solidarity" is the integration of parts through common values and beliefs. These values and beliefs constitute a collective conscience that enables persons and groups to cooperate successfully. In positing this conscience, Durkheim took for granted, without clear proof, both the congruence of the cultural standards and their effective internalization in persons. Since the members of the society express the collective conscience in the same way, just as the molecules in a solid express its fundamental property, he thought the term "mechanical solidarity" appropriate.

In contrast to mechanical solidarity, Durkheim distinguished "organic solidarity," which is integration through interdependence: the parts of the whole reciprocate services as do the parts of an organism. Durkheim believed that the central contribution of his treatise was the demonstration that the division of labor, which is usually considered only an economic fact, is also a moral fact. Duties spring from the necessary cooperation of specialists—not just the duties specified in a contract, but the legitimate expectations with respect to means, quality of performance, and the like.

Although Durkheim was interested in the integration of the social system, he used two elements of the cultural system—the amount of repressive law and the amount of restitutive law—as indexes of the relative importance of the two types of integration. His theory is that to the degree that the system is one in which persons act alike, there is repressive law; to the degree that it is a system of reciprocating differences, there is restitutive law. He concluded that organic solidarity is becoming proportionately more important as civilization advances, since restitutive law is increasing while repressive law is decreasing.

Sorokin's approach. A very different distinction between two types of integration in the sociocultural system is that of Sorokin (1937–1941). Although his emphasis is mainly on cultural integration, one of his types—the "causal–functional" —is concerned with the operative interdependence of cultural elements in the ongoing social system; thus it includes both cultural and functional integration, according to Landecker's usage of these terms. The causal–functional type recalls Sumner's "strain of consistency" among folkways (1906, p. 5). Sorokin did not carry his analysis of this type far, since he believed it inferior to the second type of integration, the "logico–meaningful." Later analysts among sociologists have preferred to think of functional integration as occurring among roles, groups, or institutions in the social system rather than among elements of culture. Sorokin's logico–meaningful type of integration is purely cultural, since it refers to the degree to which cultural elements reflect a central theme or principle. This type of integration was extensively explored through history by Sorokin and became one of the facets of the work of other students of cultural integration.

Later theoretical approaches

Subsequent to Sorokin's work, the separation of normative and functional integration from cultural integration became clearer, and a concern for communicative integration appeared. Analyses related to each of these three will be taken up in turn.

Normative integration. A central motif of Parsons' work (1937; 1951; 1960) has been the analysis of normative integration. According to his theory, such integration is achieved when the focal elements in the cultural system—the society's common values—are institutionalized in structural elements of the social system. This occurs at three levels. Most general in application are norms that apply to categories of persons, such as men and women. Less general are the normative controls of collectivities, such as business enterprises and schools. Finally, there are structured roles within collectivities, for example, mother, father, teacher, pupil. Sanctions exist at each of the three levels, as well as the specifications of correct conduct.

There is evidence, however, that normative integration of large systems is not supported exclusively by the normative integration of their subsystems. One of the findings of a study of the German Wehrmacht in World War II by Shils and Janowitz (1948) was that a prime factor in the adherence to national military norms was the social cohesion of basic units like squads. Grodzins (1956, p. 29) found evidence of the same influence of small groups in the patriotism of Englishmen. This sense of fellowship is different from any of the types of integration discussed in this article, since it depends upon person-to-person relations [*see* COHESION, SOCIAL].

Because so little research has been done on normative integration, there is little theory that relates it to other aspects of the social system. Folk wisdom has long assumed that external opposition tends to increase the adherence to societal norms because of fears for the society's survival. This proposition seems to be true, however, only above a certain level of integration already achieved; if the parts of the whole are weakly involved in a collective conscience, outside opposition may destroy the collectivity rather than strengthen it. With respect to internal factors, most students assume that normative integration tends to vary inversely with the size of the society, because of the greater difficulties of adequate internalization of societal norms in complex societies. However, because of the inadequacy of measuring devices, there is no proof that this is true. Again, although leadership is widely believed to make a difference, there are no data on its relationship to normative integration, except for studies of very small groups [*see* LEADERSHIP].

There is an equal paucity of theory about the effect of different levels of normative integration on other phenomena. Many believe that a high degree of it is a "good thing": that it promotes social stability, gives meaning to life, and ensures the survival of the system. Others are more skeptical, pointing out that deviance from norms is sometimes creative and that too firm a moral order may lead to lack of adaptability under changing circumstances. Ryan and Straus (1954), for instance, claim that the loose structure of Sinhalese society, with much tolerance of normative deviation, is not a handicap to its integration.

Functional integration. Since the time of Durkheim, the development of the concept of functional integration has been entangled with the discussion of functionalism in anthropology and sociology. If it is assumed, as has been done by some anthropologists, that the specialized parts of society that survive in the course of evolution are making a positive contribution to the social system, then functional integration is not problematic; it is there by the very nature of the processes of social selection. Since each part is contributing to the welfare of the same whole, all the parts are making reciprocal contributions to one another. However, most sociologists do not take this position. Merton (1949), for instance, holds that each part probably contributes a net balance of functional consequences to the whole; but the dysfunctional consequences obscured by the net positive balance may render the relationship between particular parts anything but beneficial. Thus a chemical plant that brings prosperity to a community by the wages it pays may so pollute the air as seriously to endanger the health of patients in a nearby hospital. In such a case functional integration is weak.

Even the assumption of a net balance of functional consequences is not a necessary one. According to those who take an extremely nominalist view of society, the parts may or may not complement one another; there is no truly organic whole, and functional integration is therefore not essential. Much the same skepticism about the universality of functional integration is evidenced by conflict theorists like Dahrendorf (1957), for whom functional integration would have to be empirically proven to exist in each instance. Whether such proof is essential or not, empirical research using the concept of functional integration cannot be done without having clear criteria for measuring it. As Landecker points out (1951, p. 338) at least two criteria are involved: the degree of specialization and the degree of interdependence. Little work has been done on measuring either.

Most writers have assumed that social integration is equivalent to equilibrium—if not static, then moving. Gouldner (1959) challenges this assumption, at least for functional integration. He states that parts have some tendency toward functional *autonomy* and that therefore the system's inclination toward integration creates tension. According to this view, equilibrium thus requires the insulation as well as the integration of parts; if a system has insufficient insulating mechanisms, increasing integration may lead to strife among parts and thus to disequilibrium. Gouldner (1960) makes a more fundamental point about the reciprocal relations that functional integration presupposes: that the contribution of any two parts to each other is often far from equal and that, because of superior power, one may be exploiting the other. He regards this situation as unstable, however, because he believes a norm of reciprocity tends to develop, requiring something like a fair exchange. Following Gouldner's argument, one can infer that functional integration requires adherence to this norm of reciprocity and hence is related to, if not dependent on, normative integration.

Parsons approaches the same conclusion in a different way (1960). In an essay on Durkheim he approves the distinction between mechanical and organic solidarity and hence between normative and functional integration as a fruitful one, but he states that they are connected at a higher level in a manner that Durkheim did not appreciate. Parsons suggests that mechanical solidarity is the expression of common values through the collectivity that is called government. Organic solidarity, on the other hand, derives from the economy—from its norms of property, contract, market relations, and the like. Thus organic solidarity is ultimately dependent on common values, just as is mechanical solidarity. Here Parsons seems to be subsuming functional integration under normative integration by asserting that interdependence is not integrative unless there are norms that control its operation. He does not, however, subordinate organic solidarity to mechanical solidarity, since they are at the same level of institutionalization. He coins the term "diffuse solidarity" to express attachment to common values and to represent the higher category in which they both are subsumed. What the social structure is that realizes diffuse solidarity is not clear from Parsons' account.

Parsons' reshaping of Durkheim's scheme makes it more consistent with Durkheim's own later work (1912), where there is every indication that he no longer believed that mechanical solidarity was becoming proportionately weaker and organic solidarity stronger. Actually, Durkheim had great difficulty in supporting this proposition when, in the preface to the second edition of *The Division of Labor in Society*, he tried to indicate how organic solidarity was bound to develop through occupational groups.

Although there is a rich literature on functional analysis, there is little work on the concept of functional integration and even less on its relations to other variables. Human ecologists have been interested in a general way in the causes of high degrees of functional integration and in its effects, but they have not yet provided a satisfactory way of measuring it so that research can proceed. Most of the variables that are thought to conduce to functional integration are not passive conditions but rather rational and purposive actions, such as conducting and applying manpower studies, and regional planning.

Theories about the effects of functional integration are few. One theory—which is almost tautological, since the result is implied in the definition—is that an increase in functional integration will lessen inefficiency and waste. There is little or no theory about the effects of functional integration other than its economic consequences.

Communicative integration. Among those who have been interested in communicative integration are the sociologists Wirth and Shils and the political scientist Deutsch. Wirth shows the importance of the mass media in achieving consensus in modern democracies. However, he sees communicative means as only one causal factor in that consensus.

> Consensus is supported and maintained not merely by the ties of interdependence and by a common cultural base, by a set of institutions embodying the settled traditions of the people, and the norms and standards that they imply and impose, not merely by the living together and dealing with one another, but also, and not least important, by the continuing currents of mass communication, which in turn rest for their meaningfulness and effectiveness upon the pre-existence of some form of a society, which hold that society together and mobilize it for continuous concerted action. (1948, p. 10)

Shils carries the idea a step further, arguing that through the mass media the center and the periphery of modern societies are more closely attached to each other than ever before. He believes that the mutual sense of responsibility thus engendered—which he calls "civility"—represents a new level of consensus: "The mass society is not the most peaceful or 'orderly' society that has ever existed; but it is the most consensual" (1962, p. 53). To Shils the connection between the periphery and the center largely consists in the attachment of the masses to the central institutional and value system of the society. The communicative factor is thus seen as closely associated with the normative factor.

Deutsch (1953), more consistently than any other social scientist, employs the communication model pioneered by electrical engineers and psychologists [*see* INFORMATION THEORY]. Although he does not explicitly use the term "communicative integration," his treatment of the concept of nationalism clearly implies it. According to Deutsch, the formation of a "community" by the people of a nation depends on the degree to which they are *assimilated* (have a common language and a common culture for fidelity in communication) and are *mobilized* (reached by the mass media and thus capable of national participation). These are concepts that can be applied to collectivities other than nations.

Deutsch's analysis is persuasive because, if it can be accepted, the communication model might serve to bring together the rather disparate concepts of normative and functional integration. However, the difficulty is that there is much evidence that communication alone is not sufficient to achieve social integration. Units in the same communicative net that understand each other very well do not always cooperate; bitter political battles within a culturally homogeneous and highly educated country would otherwise not occur. It appears that communicative integration may be a necessary, but is not a sufficient, condition of social integration.

If Deutsch's concepts of assimilation and mobilization are accepted as defining communicative integration, the immediate causes of high degrees of integration are fairly obvious—a common and rich set of symbols and access by all to the mass media. The conditions under which these immediate causes are produced, however, have not been adequately studied, although Deutsch has set forth a number of hypotheses. On the side of the effects of communicative integration, Deutsch is chiefly concerned with the greater efficacy of the policy-forming process that a high degree of integration makes possible. But it must be stressed that communicative integration is only the *capability* of acting together, not the actuality.

Connections between subtypes. In addition to the causes and effects of integration of the three types dealt with, there is the question of how these three, together with cultural integration, affect one another. Landecker (1952) poses this as an important research problem and offers some interesting hypotheses. One of them is that low communicative integration is associated with low normative integration, at least in modern cities. It is known that anomie is associated with crime, and it can be argued that anomie is a symptom of low communicative integration. But the last connection needs to be demonstrated by research.

The question can be raised whether all the phenomena that deserve inclusion under the concept of social integration can be allocated to one or another of the types. What of the legislative and judicial bodies of modern societies? Are not their activities conflict-resolving and therefore integrative? To the extent that judges merely apply existing law, they are helping to ensure that conduct conforms to cultural standards. But legislatures are creating new law, and to a degree judges also perform a creative role. This function does not fall explicitly under any of Landecker's types as defined. It seems more closely related to normative integration than to the others, because new standards are being created to bring conduct into line with the ultimate values of the society (Angell 1958). But it could be argued that there can be similar problem solving both in the network of communication, as when desegregation breaks down communicative barriers, and in the functional integration of the system, as when new balancing mechanisms are worked out. Perhaps the best way to incorporate such phenomena in an integrative schema is to recognize a dynamic aspect of each type of integration that copes with changed conditions in a systematic way.

Empirical studies of social integration

The amount of thought that has gone into the verbal definition and refinement of concepts of social integration is altogether disproportionate to the amount of empirical research that has been devoted to testing hypotheses. This may be because potential investigators see the integration of large social systems as too global a phenomenon to be amenable to research; but a more likely reason is that a prerequisite type of research—the discovery of the best operational definition for a given concept—has rarely been attempted. It is not at all obvious how a concept like functional integration should be operationalized. Until the various operational definitions have been compared on the basis of their congruence to the intuitive idea, the most effective definition cannot be chosen, nor can the concept be standardized. It is perhaps significant that there have been only two ambitious empirical studies of social integration and that both of them have wrestled with this problem as a preliminary to the testing of hypotheses.

Angell (1951) studied the integration of American cities from the normative standpoint; his aims were to compare the degree of normative integration of 42 cities and to discover the causes of the differences. A measure of integration was derived by combining an index of the rate of crime (reversed) with a positive index of the devotion of the citizens to the community (using community fund figures), and it was validated by testing its covariance with a number of other indicators of normative integration, such as suicides, illegitimate births, and deaths from venereal disease. The integration scores for each city were then correlated with other data. Two causal factors were discovered, unrelated to each other, that in combination yielded a coefficient of −.79 with normative integration. These factors were the heterogeneity of the population in terms of racial stock and national background, and the rate of in- and out-migration of the population. Sample surveys conducted later in four of the cities confirmed the results and pointed to three other factors of probable significance for normative integration—the structure of community leadership, the amount of emphasis given to the community in the schools, and the amount of such emphasis in the churches.

The ambitious study of integration by Deutsch and his associates (1957) focuses on communicative integration, although it has overtones of both normative and functional integration. In this study Deutsch's general approach to integration that was developed at the national level (1953) is carried to the international level. Thus he seeks to throw light on the causes of that high degree of integration among states that brings them into a so-called "security community," where the resort to large-scale physical force becomes unthinkable. Historical evidence on ten cases of the formation of security communities in the North Atlantic area is carefully analyzed.

Deutsch et al. define integration as ". . . the attainment, within a territory, of a 'sense of community' and of institutions and practices strong enough and widespread enough to assure, for a 'long' time, dependable expectations of 'peaceful change' among its population" (1957, p. 5). The research itself fleshes out the skeletal concept in terms of such indicators as mutual sympathy and loyalties; "we-feeling," trust and mutual consideration; partial identification in terms of self-images and interests; mutually successful predictions of behavior; and cooperative action in accordance with such predictions. All of these concepts are reminiscent of the indicators of integration in small groups and clearly stem from an outlook based in communication theory.

Although Deutsch did not set up specific hypotheses about causal factors, his findings suggest that the data were looked at in terms of communicative integration. The causal factors are grouped into the precedent conditions on the one hand and the characteristics of the movement toward integration on the other. Two prior conditions for integration are emphasized. The first is the compatibility of major values relevant to political decision making. This does not mean that all important values must be similar; those that may be different, such as religious values, may have been made compatible by being "depoliticized." Nevertheless, there is an element of normative integration here as well as of communicative integration. The other important condition is the capacity of the governments concerned to respond to one another's needs, messages, and actions quickly, adequately, and without resort to violence (there is a hint of functional integration here, since the needs are said to be differentiated). This capacity depends upon the existence of habits and institutions that insure that messages will be understood and given weight in the decision-making process. The reasoning here appears to be somewhat circular, since integration itself would create such habits and institutions. Finally, in discussing the dynamics of a movement toward political integration, the authors stress the importance of intellectuals and the bridges they build, of the mobility of populations, and of the feeling of a shared way of life.

Future prospects

One must conclude that the states of conceptualization, of operationalization, and of research-validated theory on social integration are all unsatisfactory. Although the concept has here been subdivided into three types—normative, functional, and communicative—and these treated separately, there is little consensus among scholars that this is the best way to proceed.

Of the three types, the concept of normative integration is best defined, thanks largely to the work of Parsons, but even it is somewhat unclear. The concept of functional integration is rudimentary, since no one is certain what slice of reality it represents; there is merely a belief that the division of labor is an integrative phenomenon. As for communicative integration, the meaning of the concept is quite clear—the interconnection of all parts of the system by serviceable channels over which understandable messages flow—but the question remains whether this is not a means to, rather than a kind of, integration. It is small wonder that the connections between such ill-defined subtypes are themselves unclear. The only tentative move toward an ordering is Parsons' suggestion of diffuse solidarity as equivalent to social integration (since it subsumes mechanical and organic solidarity and presumably would subsume communicative integration too).

Perhaps the key weakness in research on integration is the failure of most scholars to express their criteria clearly and to specify the operations for judging the degree of their fulfillment. Hypotheses regarding the causes or the effects of any sort of integration cannot be tested until this is done. Hence the paucity of research results on which theory can be built.

Social integration, then, remains a central concept in the minds of many, but it is a concept that so far has borne little fruit. Time will tell which of two alternatives is to be the destiny of the concept. Either it will fall into disuse because social scientists find the idea too broad and encompassing for a scientific concept, or it will enlist scientific devotees who will shape it and make it useful in the development of sound theory.

ROBERT COOLEY ANGELL

[*Directly related are the entries* COOPERATION; SYSTEMS ANALYSIS, *article on* SOCIAL SYSTEMS. *Other relevant material may be found in* ECOLOGY, *article on* HUMAN ECOLOGY; FUNCTIONAL ANALYSIS; PLANNING, SOCIAL, *article on* REGIONAL AND URBAN PLANNING; *and in the biographies of* DURKHEIM; SOROKIN; SUMNER.]

BIBLIOGRAPHY

ANGELL, ROBERT C. 1951 The Moral Integration of American Cities. *American Journal of Sociology* 57, no. 1, part 2:1–140.

ANGELL, ROBERT C. 1958 *Free Society and Moral Crisis.* Ann Arbor: Univ. of Michigan Press. → A paperback edition was published in 1965.

DAHRENDORF, RALF (1957) 1959 *Class and Class Conflict in Industrial Society.* Rev. & enl. ed. Stanford (Calif.) Univ. Press. → First published as *Soziale Klassen und Klassen-Konflikt in der industriellen Gesellschaft.*

DEUTSCH, KARL W. 1953 *Nationalism and Social Communication: An Inquiry Into the Foundations of Nationality.* Cambridge, Mass.: M.I.T. Press; New York: Wiley.

DEUTSCH, KARL W. et al. 1957 *Political Community and the North Atlantic Area: International Organization in the Light of Historical Experience.* Princeton Univ. Press.

DURKHEIM, ÉMILE (1893) 1960 *The Division of Labor in Society.* Glencoe, Ill.: Free Press. → First published as *De la division du travail social.*

DURKHEIM, ÉMILE (1912) 1954 *The Elementary Forms of the Religious Life.* London: Allen & Unwin; New York: Macmillan. → First published as *Les formes élémentaires de la vie religieuse, le système totémique en Australie.* A paperback edition was published in 1961 by Collier.

GOULDNER, ALVIN W. 1959 Reciprocity and Autonomy in Functional Theory. Pages 241–270 in Llewellyn Gross (editor), *Symposium on Sociological Theory.* Evanston, Ill.: Row, Peterson.

GOULDNER, ALVIN W. 1960 The Norm of Reciprocity: A Preliminary Statement. *American Sociological Review* 25:161–178.

GRODZINS, MORTON 1956 *The Loyal and the Disloyal: Social Boundaries of Patriotism and Treason.* Univ. of Chicago Press.

LANDECKER, WERNER S. 1951 Types of Integration and Their Measurement. *American Journal of Sociology* 56:332–340.

LANDECKER, WERNER S. 1952 Integration and Group Structure: An Area for Research. *Social Forces* 30: 394–400.

MERTON, ROBERT K. (1949) 1957 *Social Theory and Social Structure.* Rev. & enl. ed. Glencoe, Ill.: Free Press. → See especially pages 21–81 on "Manifest and Latent Functions."

PARSONS, TALCOTT 1937 *The Structure of Social Action: A Study in Social Theory With Special Reference to a Group of Recent European Writers.* New York: McGraw-Hill.

PARSONS, TALCOTT 1951 *The Social System.* Glencoe, Ill.: Free Press.

PARSONS, TALCOTT 1960 Durkheim's Contribution to the Theory of Integration of Social Systems. Pages 118–153 in Kurt Wolff (editor), *Émile Durkheim, 1858–1917: A Collection of Essays With Translations and a Bibliography.* Columbus: Ohio State Univ. Press.

PARSONS, TALCOTT; and SHILS, EDWARD A. (editors) 1951 *Toward a General Theory of Action.* Cambridge, Mass.: Harvard Univ. Press. → A paperback edition was published in 1962 by Harper.

RYAN, BRYCE F.; and STRAUS, MURRAY A. 1954 The Integration of Sinhalese Society. Washington State College, Pullman, *Research Studies* 22:179–227.

SHILS, EDWARD 1962 The Theory of Mass Society. *Diogenes* 39:45–66.

SHILS, EDWARD; and JANOWITZ, MORRIS 1948 Cohesion and Disintegration in the Wehrmacht in World War II. *Public Opinion Quarterly* 12:280–315.

SOROKIN, PITIRIM A. (1937–1941) 1962 *Social and Cultural Dynamics.* 4 vols. Englewood Cliffs, N.J.: Bedminster Press. → Volume 1: *Fluctuation of Forms of Art.* Volume 2: *Fluctuation of Systems of Truth, Ethics, and Law.* Volume 3: *Fluctuation of Social Relationships, War, and Revolution.* Volume 4: *Basic Problems, Principles, and Methods.*

SUMNER, WILLIAM G. (1906) 1959 *Folkways: A Study of the Sociological Importance of Usages, Manners, Customs, Mores, and Morals.* New York: Dover.

WIRTH, LOUIS 1948 Consensus and Mass Communication. *American Sociological Review* 13:1–15.

INTELLECTUAL DEVELOPMENT

Intellectual development refers here to the changes that occur, as a result of growth and experience, in a person's capacities for thinking, reasoning, relating, judging, conceptualizing, etc. In particular it concerns such changes in children.

There are a number of different approaches to the study of intellectual development in children. As in the history of most branches of scientific knowledge, the study began with observation and description. For many years descriptive accounts of children's thinking, reasoning, and other intellectual capacities were thoroughly mixed with descriptions of their social and emotional development and of their verbal and motor skills. Moreover, there was at first a tendency to attribute to the child mental processes that were simply miniature versions of adult thought patterns. Such early observers as Darwin (1877) were careful and deliberate, but their records often revealed the limitations of studying only one child, and the biases of the observer.

Predictably, the early, unsystematic observation of one child at a time was eventually replaced by systematic efforts to measure children's behavior and capacities in standardized and objective ways. The growth of the mental testing movement in the first 40 years of the twentieth century testifies to the enthusiasm that was generated by the possibility of applying the precision of quantitative measurement to the task of comparing individual children and calibrating the changes that take place over the early years of life. Although observation had been supplemented by measurement, the primary purpose of these efforts remained descriptive, and the generalizations achieved were themselves only descriptions of trends and improvements that occurred consistently with increasing age.

Still more recently, since about 1950, there has been an increasing movement toward the laboratory study of the ways in which patterns of development themselves change as age changes. This recent work has been not so much concerned with the effects of age itself as with the development in children of certain functional relationships between experience and performance that have been demonstrated in human adults and have been found lacking in most infrahuman species. The emphasis is on the application of laboratory controls and experimental manipulations to the study of cognitive development. The aim is to control the stimulus conditions under which behavior is observed and to explain *why* intellect develops, as well as describing how and when it develops.

Such an approach does not obviate the need for study of the child's understanding as it changes with age. Rather, it relies on developmental descriptions of intellectual processes and products for clues as to when a certain level of understanding or specific intellectual accomplishment is likely to be achieved, and what repertoire of cognitive processes constitutes the means available for such an accomplishment at that age. Even the correlation of processes with products over ages, however, leaves the detailed cause–effect analysis still to be performed.

Although the present article is not primarily concerned with age changes per se, it should be noted that the description of age changes in intellectual functioning continues to thrive in two lines of research. One is the continued development and refinement of standardized tests of intelligence in order to predict an individual's future intellectual achievement and to select, train, and guide children whenever a test-derived forecast can aid in making decisions on their behalf [*see* INTELLIGENCE AND INTELLIGENCE TESTING].

The second line of research is that of Jean Piaget and his associates on cognitive development. This large body of work has been concerned with the ontogenetic unfolding and evolution of cognitive capacities in the child, and like the work of Heinz Werner (1926), it has an organic quality and a complexity that are quite different from the empirical, item-analysis tradition of the test developers.

Both of these lines of research are *structural* in emphasis, i.e., they are primarily concerned with identifying the component parts or capacities of the intellect and with the organization and arrangement of these parts. The test developers are concerned with objective measurement of capacities in quantitative terms governed by a sophisticated statistics and a well-worked-out theory of measurement. The genetic epistemologists, on the other hand, have followed Piaget's lead in attempting to describe the step-by-step development of the child's understanding of his world as it progresses toward a formal, abstract, and logical comprehension of operations and relations in that world. Recent investigators stimulated by Piaget's work have begun the task of isolating the conditions necessary for cognitive change and the explication of processes as well as products. [*See* DEVELOPMENTAL PSYCHOLOGY, *especially the article on* A THEORY OF DEVELOPMENT.]

In contrast, a *functional* emphasis, i.e., a concern with dynamics, processes, and interrelationships, is found in the descriptions of cognitive development and in the explorations of dynamic mechanisms in cognitive change that have largely been undertaken by American behaviorists and behavior analysts and by Soviet pedagogists. These lines of research are more concerned with the *processes* of learning and thinking than with the *structure* of understanding. It is to the contributions of these functionalists that the present article is primarily devoted. It will be necessary first to summarize the most important age changes that have been described from infancy to adolescence. Consideration is then given to cognition, seen as the elaboration and selective generalization of simpler forms of learning and conditioning. Concepts such as mediation, learning set, and expectancy are discussed in relation to experimental studies of discrimination learning and discrimination reversal, concept formation, and the perceptual constancies. Curiosity and exploratory motivation are treated in relation to orienting responses and observing behavior. Research on acquired distinctiveness, equivalence, and relevance of cues is presented as evidence for the importance of a general class of intervening responses, and the major role of language in this connection is stressed. Finally, consideration is given to individual differences in cognitive style, including discussion of such variables as field dependency, rigidity, reflectivity, and creativity.

Overview of age changes

Infancy. Very little behavior in infancy possesses that degree of orderliness and abstractness which would qualify it as intellectual or cognitive. There are evident, however, the beginnings of systematic relations with the environment that imply understanding on a primitive level. Beyond the specific and identifiable reflexes, newborn behavior is usually described as massive, diffuse, and all-or-none in its occurrence. Recent investigations of neonatal behavior have shown that such descriptions mask at least seven reliably discriminable states of arousal, ranging from deep, unresponsive sleep to intense crying or sucking that is equally unresponsive to external stimulation. Reactivity to external stimuli is greatest at intermediate values on the arousal dimension. [*See* DRIVES, *article on* PHYSIOLOGICAL DRIVES.]

Beyond the neonatal period (birth to ten days) there are three kinds of behavior in infants that appear to mark the beginnings of cognitive development: the development of simple stimulus equivalences, expectations, and persistent exploratory behavior.

Stimulus equivalence. Stimulus equivalence means perceptual recognition of the same object, person, or event under variable appearances due to changes in distance, illumination, context, angle of regard, and the like. While there have been no formal psychophysical investigations of perceptual constancies in infants, studies of attention and recognition of familiar people and objects have indicated that considerable equivalence learning takes place in early infancy (Rheingold et al. 1959). Infants also show selective attention, indicating some kind of differential sensitivity to faces and patterned stimuli (R. L. Fantz, quoted in Gibson 1963). [*See* PERCEPTION, *article on* PERCEPTUAL CONSTANCY.]

Expectations. If certain events occur in a brief, invariant sequence with considerable frequency and regularity in the infant's environment, he is capable of displaying anticipatory responses that constitute for many psychologists sufficient evidence of expectancy. For example, it is commonly observed that quieting and sucking responses at first occur primarily in response to tactile stimulation of the mouth or cheek and general handling. Very soon, however, they begin to occur in response to vocalization by the mother and to other sights and sounds accompanying her approach. Another example is the eye blink, which at first occurs in response to tactile stimulation only and later occurs whenever a figure grows rapidly in size ("looms"), as if it were approaching the face at high speed. The acquisition of such simple preparatory responses as these does not require a cognitive interpretation and is explained satisfactorily by either classical or operant conditioning theories. But motoric anticipation does seem to provide a promising basis from which the child may develop more abstract capacities to anticipate the outcomes of his actions and to interpret signals of events.

Exploratory behavior. One of the most persistent and ubiquitous observations of infants of many species is their exploratory behavior, from which curiosity, both as a cognitive and as a motivational variable, is inferred. Persistent handling, mouthing, smelling, and visual scanning seem to occur in the first year or nine months in proportion to the familiarity of the stimuli, and in the first half of the second year in proportion to the relative novelty of the stimuli. It has been suggested that this apparent reversal merely reflects an increase with experience in the degree of variation required to make a stimulus relatively novel. In any case, the behavior is persistent and repetitive, and only toward the end of infancy is there evidence for selective matching of the child's exploratory behavior to the nature of the object being explored. Before 18 months the repertoire of exploratory movements is small and undifferentiated. [*See* STIMULATION DRIVES.]

The toddler. Intellectual development in the second and third years is dominated by the acquisition of communicative and referential language. Although it is not until age five or six that language becomes available as a conceptual system for the mediation of thinking, reasoning, and problem solving, the child of $1\frac{1}{2}$ to 2 years begins to respond to verbal stimuli and to make verbal responses that are selectively appropriate to his immediate environment.

Communicative language. Acquisition of communicative language means the child's learning to respond to simple instructions and demands made by others and his growing ability to verbalize his own need states and wishes with sufficient accuracy and clarity that others can respond appropriately. Most of this learning is acquired as part of training in daily routines, such as feeding, dressing, sleeping, and elimination. Not only are verbal demands made that require the child to discriminate the appropriate occasions and circumstances for each of these activities, but also he is expected to report with some accuracy on his internal need states, such as hunger, fatigue, pain, and need to eliminate. Because of the deliberate simplicity of the verbal demands made on him, the consistency with which they are made, and the immediacy of feedback from the child's compliance (or noncompliance), this learning proceeds rapidly but remains at a concrete level. Similarly, the primacy and strength of the needs that the child is asked to verbalize and the usual promptness of their satisfaction ensure the accuracy, but limit the subtlety, of his verbal self-report. Typically, all that is required of him is a "Yes" or "No" answer or a choice of simple responses.

Referential language. Referential language consists of a collection of names for objects and events that enables the establishment of a simple representational system. The child of three can name common objects and actions and can pick objects out of an array by name. The development of this capacity is said to proceed from control of behavior by the gross motoric aspects of speech toward control by the semantic aspects of speech. This accomplishment in the third year depends, according to Luriia (1961), on establishing verbal control of the child's attentional and orienting behavior. [*See* ATTENTION; LANGUAGE, *article on* LANGUAGE DEVELOPMENT; LEARNING, *article on* VERBAL LEARNING.]

Unverbalized comprehension. Progress in unverbalized comprehension during the second and third years is less noticeable than is linguistic development. The child can interpret the social significance of an increased range of gestures and facial expressions, which by association come to signal more primary rewards and threats. He engages in considerable testing of the social consequences of his own behavior, reading these secondary cues in place of verbal feedback. Thus he is able to explore the socially imposed limitations of his own autonomy, interpreting the behavior of others so as to stop short of provoking severe threat or punishment. [*See* PERCEPTION, *article on* SOCIAL PERCEPTION.]

In the laboratory the child of less than three years cannot readily solve even simple discrimination and concept formation problems. His attention is diffusely focused and highly distractable. His representational system is concrete, egocentric, lacking in temporal perspective, and generally inflexible. His learning seems to proceed by simple associations, and despite his capacity for speech, the child rarely uses language to organize information or to direct his own behavior.

Preschool. The child from three to five years makes intellectual progress primarily in establishing a frame of reference for his own identity within the family, internalizing a set of societal standards or behavior, copying a set of assumptions and beliefs about good and bad conduct, and assuming prescribed age and sex roles. The basic process of family socialization that began formally in the first year is substantially completed by the beginning of the sixth year in most Western cultures. During the preschool years the child gains considerable understanding of himself as one person in a world of people. He begins to be able to take the viewpoint of others and perceive the reciprocity of interpersonal encounters. [*See* IDENTITY, PSYCHOSOCIAL; SOCIALIZATION.]

Objectivity and planning. While the process of socialization discussed above is not a pure instance of cognitive development, it furnishes evidence for, and practice with, a new relativity and objectivity in the child's thought. His representational system is well enough developed so that he can deal with hypothetical cause and effect in situations that he has never experienced concretely. His play and fantasy give evidence of a high degree of realism, internal logic, and continuity. In simple situations he can reason backward from a desired state of affairs to the existing circumstances, and thus can increase the likelihood that his first actions will move him in the desired direction by simple but intelligent planning.

Discrimination learning. Dimensions of meaning other than the evaluative become available to the child. He can discriminate actions and events on such dimensions as fair–unfair, masculine–feminine, certain–uncertain, near–far in time, active–passive, and fast–slow. Simultaneous discrimination learning and simple concept learning are within his capacities, but successive discriminations and multivariate concepts remain difficult or impossible for him to learn. He can readily learn to make comparisons among stimuli on the basis of size, shape, color, texture, weight, material, speed, warmth, hardness, or numerosity, and in simple situations he can transfer these discriminations to new stimuli with some success. [*See* LEARNING, *article on* DISCRIMINATION LEARNING.]

Language and verbal behavior. Language gains are extensive in the period from three to six years, but the progress appears more in pronunciation, grammar, and vocabulary than as an aid to abstraction and generalization. Language structure gains some independence of the words used, so that the child can shape sentences containing proper negation, tense, voice, person, number, and sometimes mood. For the first time, word order and invariant prefixes and suffixes seem to be acquired more as general rules than as rigid fragments of rote-learned verbal associations.

In spite of these demonstrated relationships between language and learning, there is good evidence that semantic verbal mediation as an aid to problem solving is neither typically nor fully available at this age. Studies indicate that while the child of five may sometimes solve the problem, his performance lacks that degree of reliance upon verbal mediation which characterizes the performance of a seven- or eight-year-old. Presumably for this reason, the younger child's learning is not as rapid, flexible, consistent, and free of irrelevant responses as is that of the older, mediating child (see Kendler 1963). One might make such comparisons at any age, however, and it is likely that in general a curvilinear relationship will usually be found between reliance on verbal mediators and task difficulty, with the most mediation occurring on problems of intermediate difficulty.

Middle childhood. Between the ages of six and eleven the child's capacity for thought and reasoning shows its most significant growth. To an undetermined degree this growth is stimulated by the beginning of formal scholastic instruction and the acquisition of reading and writing skills. But educators and psychologists generally agree that the maturation of intellectual capacities at about age six provides a readiness for formal learning and instruction. It has been claimed that there is a discontinuity in cognitive functioning at about age six, before which learning is basically a process of simple association and primary generalization. Before six, thinking is said to be a matter of recognition, literal recall, and direct transfer of training. After six, learning is said to be more focused and systematic, more abstract and selective, and much more flexibly applicable to a variety of contexts and contents. Thinking is more rapid, orderly, and precise. It is characterized by more insightful induction of generalities and more parsimonious application of general principles to a much greater range of content (White 1965).

Verbal mediation. Recent research indicates that the discontinuity in cognitive functioning is not so much an abrupt change at a specific time as it is a reflection of an underlying dichotomy between verbal and nonverbal approaches to problem solving. Thus, there may be a gradual shift over several years from reliance on nonverbal solutions to reliance on verbally mediated ones. Again, task difficulty relative to his present level will often determine whether a child in transition will attempt a verbal approach.

After this transition, language is employed to mediate all kinds of learning and problem solving, whether the child has a set to employ verbal mediation or not. Symbolic notation and graphic analogues become useful tools for problem solving and supplement the process of verbal reasoning. The child's knowledge about the world becomes coded, hierarchically organized, and interconnected. Intact chains and clusters of associations or meanings can be applied to new problems at different levels of generality, in sharp contrast with the chaotic array of fragmentary facts and associations that characterized the knowledge of the younger child. Moreover, by age 11 the child learns to discriminate levels of abstraction and generality, relevance and importance of new information, regularities and patterns in sequential events, and intermediate degrees of likelihood between certainty and indeterminacy.

Role-taking and communication. There is a corresponding growth during middle childhood in role-taking and communications skills. The growing abstractness and relativity of the child's understanding is applied to many new social situations, producing a complementary growth in his ability to understand and take into account the viewpoints of others in the course of his social interaction with them.

He understands concepts like fairness and sharing, although he applies them rigidly and indiscriminately. His perspective is broader and his experiences, now that they are codable, are consequently more readily available for use in making decisions. Not only is the child's knowledge coded and ordered by means of verbal labels so that it can be selectively retrieved from memory, but also by middle childhood the child can use language to guide and monitor his own behavior through complex and contingently branching alternate plans from the definition of a problem through its solution.

Later childhood. Beyond age 10 to 11, development is more quantitative than qualitative. Existing capacities are refined and extended to new material. In particular the child's ability to view problems in a variety of social contexts, to comprehend the variable sources of other people's behavior, expands rapidly during adolescence. The capacity to see the world as another sees it and to act on the basis of a more sophisticated interpersonal relativity reaches full development only in late adolescence and young adulthood. There is, however, little evidence that the major personal reorientation that takes place during adolescence in many cultures has any necessary structural implications for cognitive development.

Processes and mechanisms of cognitive change

Perception. Research on children's perception concerns itself mostly with psychophysical determination of absolute and differential thresholds, susceptibility to illusions and aftereffects, perceptual constancies, scaling of preferences, and capacities of blind and deaf children. (For a recent review of new research in perceptual development, see Pick et al. 1966.)

Constancies and concepts. There is a considerable body of literature on the development of the perceptual constancies in children (see Wohlwill 1960) and the field determination of perceptual experience as a function of age (Piaget et al. 1958). Because experience and knowledge are highly relevant to illusion susceptibility and the perceptual constancies, it is unfortunate that these relationships have not been more thoroughly explored, especially in the literature available in English. The perceptual constancies, for example, may be regarded as prototypic instances of concept formation. To the extent that an object is recognizably itself, regardless of distance, angle of regard, illumination, and other variable conditions of viewing, its successive appearances may be formally analyzed as different instances of a single concept. [*See* PERCEPTION, *articles on* PERCEPTUAL DEVELOPMENT, PERCEPTUAL CONSTANCY, *and* ILLUSIONS AND AFTEREFFECTS.]

The capacity to understand spoken language is another perceptual bridge to conceptual thought. Just as the child without clear intent or formal training comes to recognize the same object consistently through all its different appearances, so he comes to comprehend spoken language despite the many distortions and irrelevant variations that occur with different speakers and on different occasions.

For example, spectrographic analysis of speech indicates that certain critical features of phonemes must remain constant in order for an utterance to be accurately perceived, while certain aspects of pitch, vowel quality, and timing can vary widely without diminishing intelligibility. We infer that the child learns to select a small number of relevant cues from the complex of speech sounds that he hears. The major unsolved problem in speech perception, then, is the mechanism by which the hearer can come to tolerate such a wide range of irrelevant variation while remaining so selectively tuned to the critical features. This problem too is primarily one of concept formation. [*See* PERCEPTION, *article on* SPEECH PERCEPTION.]

The young child's experience with sequentially invariant routines can serve to induce perceptual equivalences that also resemble concepts. Whether the process is viewed as the classical conditioning of a terminal response to cues located earlier and earlier in the sequence, or whether it is viewed as the establishment of expectancies through chained anticipatory responses, the successive cues in such a routine all come to elicit a similar response pattern and are equivalent at least in the sense that any one of them will elicit the same response once the sequence is learned.

The common observation of sequential generalization in infants with respect to the mother supports this notion. At first only the touch of the nipple may elicit cessation of crying and reaching for contact. With repetition, however, earlier events in the nursing sequence, such as being picked up and held in a certain way, the sound of the mother's voice, and the sound of the mother's approaching footsteps or the opening of a door come to elicit the same response or an anticipatory portion of it. Typically the acquisition of such sequential equivalences of stimuli is analyzed according to a model of classical conditioning or operant chaining, but to the extent that a number of quite different cues come to have the same significance for the child, one could defend the view that concept formation of a primitive sort is taking place and that equivalence and expectancy may be the earliest examples of conceptual learning.

The perceptual capacities of the infant that involve possibly innate predispositions to differentiate and respond to a limited number of critical features of his environment have just come under study. Work on releaser stimuli, imprinting, and critical periods in infrahuman animals has helped to accelerate this mapping of prepotent discriminations in humans. Two outstanding examples are the work of Fantz on attention to patterned stimuli in the first six months of life and that of Gibson on avoidance of depth in the second half-year of life (see Gibson 1963). [*See* IMPRINTING; PERCEPTION, *article on* DEPTH PERCEPTION.]

Exploration and recognition. A quite different research tradition in perceptual development is the Soviet literature on exploratory behavior and the recognition of objects, forms, patterns, and auditory pitch. Most of this work is untranslated, but a general summary has been provided by Pick (1963). The work is derived from a "motor-copy" theory of perceptual recognition, whereby incoming stimuli are matched against an image of the standard stimulus that is somehow stored in the memory of the organism. The most interesting feature of this approach is its experimental analysis of the image during initial training of children. An image is said to be formed and effectively stored to the extent that the child engages in voluntary scanning, handling, vocalizing, or other exploratory activity that provides him with feedback from this activity. The feedback must be isomorphic with critical features of the object being explored in order for a useful image to be formed. Thus the proprioceptive feedback from thorough, active exploration of relevant aspects of a stimulus *is* the stored image against which the feedback from subsequent exploration of new stimuli can be compared to determine equivalence or difference.

The significance of this approach is that at least potentially it provides a mechanism for the abstract coding and storage of knowledge that is neither symbolic nor verbal, unlike most models currently under investigation by Western psychologists, and is thus applicable to "preverbal" children. In implicit support of the motor-copy notion, there is good evidence that stereometric, three-dimensional objects which the preschool child can handle as well as look at produce more rapid and generalizable learning than do two-dimensional pattern stimuli or pictures, at which the child can only look.

Reading. Traditionally the borderline between perception and cognition has been obscure, and the same general assumptions and procedures have characterized some research in both areas. An outstanding recent example of the perceptual approach to cognitive development is the work of E. J. Gibson (1963) on children's perception of letter-like forms, or graphemes. In Gibson's work the child has to select the match of a standard artificial grapheme from an array containing a copy of the standard and a number of systematically constructed variants of the standard that are more or less difficult to discriminate from it. The transformations used to generate the array of variants are based on a prior analysis of critical and noncritical variations in letters of the alphabet. Examples of critical variations are line-to-curve transformations (e.g., D vs. O), break-to-close transformations (e.g., C vs. O), rotations and reversals (e.g., N vs. Z or W vs. M). Noncritical transformations included slants or tilts, with resulting compression, foreshortening, and other perspective distortions.

The results indicated that there are few errors and little improvement with age for break-to-close transformations; for the other transformations that were selected as critical for reading the Western alphabet, there were many errors at age four (nonreaders) but very few by age seven (readers). Discrimination on the basis of perspective transformations, which are not only noncritical for reading but actually represent variations which the child must learn to ignore in reading, showed the most errors of all, with little improvement from age four to age eight. [*See* LEARNING, *article on* DISCRIMINATION LEARNING; READING DISABILITIES.]

These results, of course, have implications far beyond the development of grapheme perception and the process of learning to read. They confirm the prediction that as a child learns to discriminate perceptually on the basis of some differences and not others, he also acquires a general tendency to look at certain kinds of differences among any set of stimuli and to ignore others. The generality of such attentional sets and their ready application by the child to new stimulus materials are indeed impressive.

Observing and orienting responses. Just as the Soviet motor-copy theory of perceptual recognition demands the reproduction of critical features of the stimulus through relevant exploratory behavior, so a selective attention model of learning set formation requires that attention be viewed as a discriminative response that systematically selects certain features of a stimulus and makes them *available* for conditioning to a final response by selective reinforcement. (For a discussion of this approach, see Cantor 1965.)

General support for this point of view is provided in studies of learning under experimentally produced conditions of distraction or delay, where it can be demonstrated that distracting attention from the task interferes with learning more for younger than for older children, more in the early than in the later trials of the session, and more when the task is complex or ambiguous than when it is not.

While there are very few published studies wherein the observing responses of children have been directly manipulated or even systematically measured during learning, there is support from the literature on animal and human adult learning for the claim that relevant deployment of attention, as indicated by selective observing behavior, is itself a learnable response set that has considerable generality and power. It is not known, however, to what extent improvements with age in problem-solving ability can be directly traced to development of the capacity to attend to the most likely relevant cues at the outset of a problem, based on cumulative experience with similar problems.

The notion that attention can be adequately conceptualized as a set of centrally controlled, conditionable, voluntary, and discriminable observing responses is receiving continued emphasis in the research literature on learning in infrahuman organisms. At the level of overt behavior, activity such as vicarious trial and error in the rat, and reliance on the depth cue of motion-produced parallax in cats and chickens, provides evidence of the voluntary nature of important information intake processes. Similarly, physiological phenomena, such as the centrally mediated suppression of peripheral sensory activity ("peripheral gating"), are evidence of cortical control over the selection of cues, the acquisition of which should have massive effects on learning abilities. Additional evidence for the importance of observing behavior in children comes from experiments where stimulus presentation is deliberately designed to produce either interfering or facilitating effects with respect to relevant attending responses. Typically, corresponding effects on efficiency of learning are obtained. For example, in children's discrimination learning, it appears to matter whether the locus of response is in the stimulus, immediately adjacent to it, or spatially removed from it. Similarly, reinforcement is most effective when its locus is closest to that of the stimulus and response and when a minimum of distracting consummatory behavior is elicited by delivery of reinforcement. [*See* ATTENTION.]

These effects of relevant attending responses are most pronounced in the early stages of problem solving or learning and when the task is relatively difficult for the child. With the increasing familiarity and mastery that come with repetition and experience, the explicitly overt orienting and observing responses become attenuated and streamlined. Once a particular problem has been solved a number of times in different contexts, the elements require and elicit much less extensive and deliberate investigation, and the full-blown pattern of exploratory responses can then be elicited only by novel stimuli, unexpected outcomes, or arousal originating in some extrinsically motivating event, such as startle or threat. These phenomena of inhibition and disinhibition of investigatory behavior are discernible both as a function of chronological age and as a result of practice over relatively short intervals.

Just as spatial proximity of stimulus, response, and reinforcement facilitates learning by minimizing the occurrence of competing attending responses, so proximity in time contributes to learning efficiency by preventing distraction. Delay of response and delay of reinforcement are detrimental to learning, apparently as a result of the competition of irrelevant objects and events for the child's attention during the delay interval, unless that interval is filled with relevant observing, labeling, or rehearsing behavior. If a child can be induced by pretraining, instructions, or the demands of the task to engage in some form of relevant thought during these delays, there is good evidence that the delay-produced deficit is replaced by an advantage in both acquisition and retention.

Distinct from the cortically controlled, "voluntary" observing responses are involuntary, autonomic orienting reactions that occur whenever attention is focused on a particular stimulus. These orienting reactions have been investigated most extensively by Soviet psychologists and physiologists, primarily by means of classical conditioning techniques. This work is important to cognitive development because of the significance of bringing attentional processes under experimental control and because much of this research has employed children as subjects. The catalogue of orienting reactions developed by Sokolov (1958) and others includes changes in the state of the sense organs, changes in the musculature that directs sense organs, changes in the skeletal–postural musculature, and changes in the central nervous system. Specifically, the pattern of orienting reactions that might be aroused by any attention-getting stimulus includes pupillary dilation; photochemical changes in the retina (which act to lower the absolute intensity threshold for light); turning of eyes, head, trunk, or whole body toward the source of stimulation; erection of the ears and sniffing in lower mammals; interruption of ongoing activity (especially proprioceptive behavior such as nonnutritive sucking); increase in general body tonus and rate of electromyographically recorded efferent impulses; desynchronization of slow-wave patterns in the electroencephalogram; constriction of blood vessels in the extremities, accompanied by dilation of those in the head; galvanic skin response (GSR); acceleration of heart rate; and momentary deceleration of respiration, followed by acceleration. Nearly all of these responses are subject to classical conditioning, and some are susceptible to operant control as well. To the extent that these attentional indicators are elicited in response to relevant cues with proper timing and sequence, they can facilitate the "higher mental processes," such as conditional discrimination, concept formation, and rule-following behavior in complex tasks. [*See* NERVOUS SYSTEM; SENSES.]

Semantic conditioning. Research on semantic conditioning (Razran 1961) suggests that the significance of a familiar stimulus to an individual child can sometimes be mapped in terms of the pattern of selective generalization of responses conditioned to that stimulus. Although the techniques employed are different, this work is directly comparable with American work on primary and secondary stimulus generalization in children. A typical procedure might begin by conditioning vasodilation or GSR by pairing presentations of the word "house" with mild electric shock or a loud noise of sudden onset and brief duration. Once conditioning is established, a test series of words is presented, including "house" but also, for example, "mouse" and "building." A response to the former would be regarded as evidence for morphological (primary) generalization and is characteristic of young children. A response to the latter would constitute evidence for semantic (mediated or secondary) generalization and is characteristic of older children and adults.

Learning sets and transfer of training. Developmental studies of children's learning have increasingly been concerned with the effects of certain kinds of pretraining experiences on subsequent learning and transfer test performances. To the extent that the task does not change substantially from pretraining to test, the experiment measures only recall or savings, and would not ordinarily be of much interest to the student of cognitive development. To the extent, however, that the pretraining establishes a general set, strategy, expectation, or principle that can be effectively transferred to a new set of materials, or be selectively applied to an entirely new task, then one could argue that the facilitating or interfering effects are germane to cognitive development. Similarly, a simple performance set or warm-up effect can be demonstrated in children as young as five years and can be experimentally differentiated from a discrimination learning set (learning to learn), of which children at this age are also capable (Cantor 1965). The extensive investigations of object discrimination learning sets in primates have been approximately replicated with positive results, using children as young as three years.

Studies comparing normal children with both retarded and gifted children of different ages have shown that with mental age (MA) held constant, learning sets are formed with increasing speed and precision as intelligence increases (as chronological age, or CA, decreases). (In these studies, intelligence is defined as synonymous with IQ.) Conversely, holding intelligence (MA/CA) constant, performance improves with increasing MA and CA. Pretraining of an appropriate attentional set facilitates performance in both normal and retarded children, while pretraining of an irrelevant attentional set produces interference when performance is compared with a control group receiving no pretraining. There is considerable evidence that learning difficulties in mentally retarded children can in large part be traced to a deficiency in acquiring a set to respond to relevant cues, and it has been proposed by a number of investigators that the key acquisition in a discrimination learning set is a general tendency to pay selective attention to relevant and informative cues. Zeaman and House (1963) demonstrated that the first improvement over a chance performance came on much later trials for retarded children than for normals of the same MA, though the rate of improvement once they started to improve was the same for the two groups. [*See* LEARNING, *article on* TRANSFER; MENTAL RETARDATION.]

Concept formation. The more generalized and abstract capacities and sets of which children are capable have been investigated most frequently either in the context of laboratory experiments on strategies of problem-solving and rule-following behavior or in a context of applied research on individual differences, curriculum development, and the acceleration of cognitive growth. Concept formation should be used as a rather inclusive generic term, denoting the most abstract and generalized aspects of grouping, ordering, and interrelating items of information. To the extent that a rule or principle abstracted from one experience or task or set of materials can be applied successfully to many others, it can be argued that a higher-order conceptual set has been established.

As early as 1941 Long and Welch demonstrated that young children could establish identity concepts more readily than relational concepts. Kuenne (1946) showed that while both school-age and preschool children could learn relational concepts, the range and scope of application to new stimuli was much greater among the older children. Heidbreder (1948) has established a general order of difficulty in concept formation; with some exceptions, such perceptually concrete features as object quality and shape are more readily learned as a basis for grouping than are derived attributes such as number.

More recently, developmental studies of groupings of common objects have demonstrated preference hierarchies for certain bases of classification (Bruner & Olver 1963; 1966). Between ages 5 and 11, the capacity to impose a superordinate conceptual structure on collections of terms develops, indicating an attempt by the child to achieve simplicity, economy, and parsimony of groupings without sacrificing specificity, discriminability, and reproducibility of the members of a grouping on the basis of its definition. The bases of ordering terms begin with simple, functional groupings, equivalences by assertion, centration of associations to a single instance, chaining, and other asymmetrical combinations. With increasing age these groupings proceed toward greater abstractness, balance, and generality. [*See* CONCEPT FORMATION.]

Other types of concept formation tasks, such as the Vygotsky blocks and the Wisconsin Card Sorting Test, have been used with children, but ordinarily in a context of clinical diagnosis or assessment of differential intellectual abilities and cognitive styles. Similarly, there is an extensive literature on the application of concepts, techniques, and materials originating in child psychology laboratories to training programs and curricula designed to foster more rapid conceptual growth (e.g., see Lovell 1961). Action research studies of real life environments have similarly taken as their point of departure the laboratory studies of the effects of stimulus enrichment and deprivation on learning and problem solving. Such efforts are typically aimed at defining, and in some cases improving, the potential stimulation toward abstract and conceptual thinking that is available in the child's natural environment. [*See* MONTESSORI.]

Language and verbal mediation. Perhaps the single most critical instrument of intellectual development is the acquisition of language, together with the capacity to use it as a working abstract representation of real objects, actions, and events. It would be difficult to overrate the significance of the development of working language, and more research has been focused on its relationship to complex learning and thinking than on all other aspects of cognitive growth combined. At the earliest and simplest level, words act as demands, first made on the child by others, then made by the child on his environment as well. The ontogenetic origins of language, like its historical and cultural origins, are still subject to considerable debate, but there is general agreement that the emotional and expressive verbal behavior related to the child's primary needs is the most primitive. The naming of objects is the next skill that emerges from the language of demands, as the child begins to use nouns to communicate his wants more specifically than is possible by the use of negative and affirmative or pleasure and distress indicators only. Naming things also appears to be the first significant step in the child's use of language to help solve problems of a conceptual nature.

A major unsolved problem is, of course, how language as verbal behavior is learned. The conditioning approach has been taken in Soviet investigations of what Pavlov called the "second signaling system." Starting with the assumption that perceptual responses to a real object are unconditioned, they have demonstrated that even in young children, successive presentations of a real object, immediately preceded by the sound of its name, result in the capacity of the name alone to evoke the "image" of the object by a process of ordinary classical conditioning. The next step was to demonstrate that second- and third-order conditioning could be established in children by using words as the conditioned stimuli to elicit verbal responses which in turn denoted the original object. Although many of the ordinary phenomena of classical conditioning, such as extinction, recovery, external inhibition, external disinhibition, and "irradiation" (generalization), can be demonstrated in this context, the power, generality, specificity, and flexibility of words as conditioning stimuli led Soviet psychologists to propose special laws for conditioning in the second signaling system, laws unique to the human organism.

There is, however, a growing tendency in the United States among psycholinguists to believe that linguistic competence is not the product of simple learning processes compounded and practiced over a number of years. Chomsky (1963), for example, believes that associative learning will not suffice to account for the acquisition of the *structure* of language, a structure that he contends is present in all languages and is apparent in the speech of surprisingly young children. While children doubtless imitate the expansions and corrections of their fragmentary speech that are provided by adults, there is evidence that even rudimentary exposure to grammatical language is often as effective as more structured kinds of linguistic training in eliciting grammatical speech. One wonders whether this reorientation may not require the assumption of a genetically determined and species-specific predisposition to structure speech. Such a predisposition would govern the structure and the motivation, while the environment would provide the idiomatic content of a particular language. The psychological model for such a process would resemble that of imprinting rather than that of classical conditioning or imitative operant learning. [*See* LANGUAGE, *article on* LANGUAGE DEVELOPMENT; LEARNING, *article on* VERBAL LEARNING.]

From the behavioristic point of view, one unique aspect of words is the fact that they serve as both stimuli and responses. That is, the child can learn to manufacture verbal stimuli for himself almost as early as he can learn to respond to them as external events. Thus, there has been considerable research on how the child comes to use words, not only as abstract representations of objects not present but also as the basis for conditional self-instructions for the monitoring and guiding of complex sequences of goal-oriented, instrumental behavior.

By about the age of four the child is able to group objects, in part on the basis of their names. Investigators such as Spiker (1963) have shown that cues can acquire distinctiveness or similarity, depending upon the distinctiveness or similarity of the names attached to them and the strength of that attachment. The possession of similar-sounding names facilitates the grouping of disparate objects into the same class and interferes with learning to discriminate them into separate classes. Conversely, the acquisition of distinctive names for objects facilitates their discrimination and interferes with equivalence learning, to the extent that the names have a distinctive sound and are learned sufficiently thoroughly that they are not misapplied to their referents. By age six or seven, the child begins to use language not just to code stimuli but to mediate new learning and thinking.

Mediation theory. Mediation theory, specifically verbal mediation theory, has developed in the United States within the body of stimulus–response behaviorism. The key concept of mediation theory is the intervening response and the distinctive feedback that regularly result from its occurrence. Any response will qualify as such a mediator if it can be conditioned either classically or instrumentally to an initial stimulus and if it produces reliable proprioceptive stimulation to which a final motor response can, in turn, be conditioned. The original prototype of the intervening response was Hull's fractional anticipatory goal response (r_G). Such responses were said to produce feedback stimulation that strengthened running behavior in the rat by virtue of the fact that r_G was selectively conditioned to external stimuli along the previously reinforced route to the goal box. The notion was adopted and generalized by Osgood (1953) to suggest that if verbal or autonomic responses were conditioned to any stimulus, the proprioceptive feedback from these responses could serve to define the meaning of the stimulus in an associational context. If the *name* of an object is the initial stimulus, the same mediating chain of intervening response and feedback will operate in the absence of the object itself, leading to the same behavior as when the object itself was present as the initial stimulus. When the intervening response is a verbal mediator (either overt or covert), the response-produced stimulation functions in the same way as the response, and the possibility of self-instruction is literally realized.

The general intervening response model can encompass not only the effects of mediation on verbal learning and verbal behavior but phenomena such as acquired distinctiveness or equivalence of cues, relational learning, and inferential learning as well. Broadly interpreted as a feedback model, it is also applicable to semantic conditioning, selective observing behavior, learning sets for relevance of cues, and even a motor-copy theory of perceptual recognition. In addition, it provides the child with a degree of abstract and flexible control over his own behavior that is compatible with behavioristic determinism yet consonant with the rather high degree of purpose, insight, and intelligence that is commonly inferred from observation of children's voluntary behavior. And it does so by means of a rather simple mechanism that would have been branded as unacceptably teleological by many of the behaviorists of the 1940s. Intervening response and feedback models, especially as applied to verbal processes, are among the most promising for contemporary research and future understanding of cognitive development. These models are theoretically neutral with respect to the problem of language acquisition but delineate two tasks that are prerequisites for language to facilitate thinking: the production of relevant verbal behavior and the use of the resulting feedback to control conceptual behavior. Finally, they are compatible with the internal logic of computer-based models for the simulation of human cognitive processes. [*See* SIMULATION, *article on* INDIVIDUAL BEHAVIOR.]

Thus language serves to keep the child on the track of his own intentions, preventing irrelevant detours, ordering his responses in proper sequence, and informing him whether his behavior is bringing him closer to the desired conclusion. In the course of verbalizing a plan for solving a problem and developing self-instructions for monitoring progress toward solution, the child is increasingly able to codify whole sets of information-processing rules and strategies with sufficient generality to give him positive transfer from one problem to the next, even when the content is radically different. Not only can he develop a repertoire of learning sets that facilitate solutions to new problems when they are logically similar to those previously mastered, but he can also label these sets, strategies, or problem-solving routines themselves. Thus they can be called upon when appropriate, much as a computer stores and identifies subroutines to be called whenever the program or its output requires them (see Miller et al. 1960).

Individual differences

Beyond the study of stages and mechanisms of cognitive development, and beyond the testing of general intellectual potential by standard means, there is a considerable body of research on qualitative and stylistic differences in cognitive functioning among individuals. It has long been recognized that certain aspects of personality and temperament can both influence and be influenced by cognitive capacities, but systematic and objective research into the structure of cognitive styles and their influence on thinking and subsidiary processes is fairly recent. The same is true of motivational factors inherent in cognitive activity. General personality variables that have been shown to be correlated with cognitive performances include achievement motivation, authoritarianism, manifest anxiety level, somatotype, and "ego control," to name but a few. Typically, such research has shown how a well-organized characterological predisposition can have specific biasing effects on thinking, reasoning, and problem solving. In most cases such effects have not been studied developmentally, and although there is considerable speculation, little hard knowledge is available on the ontogenesis of such traits. Other stylistic variables have emerged directly from research on perceptual, learning, and cognitive processes themselves rather than from personality theory. Such variables as field articulation (Witkin et al. 1954; 1962), reflection-impulsivity (Kagan et al. 1964), and creativity (Getzels & Jackson 1962; Wallach & Kogan 1965; Guilford 1956) are beginning to receive the research attention they deserve.

As is the case in personality research, the naming of syndromes and the demonstration by correlational means that certain clusters of traits tend to inhere in the same individuals do not explain the development and causation of such patterns. Nor do they suffice to demonstrate that similar patterns often characterize parents and their children, attributing the perpetuation of styles to genetic factors, imitative learning, or selective reinforcement. While such effects undoubtedly do occur, more functional study of the genesis of cognitive styles in individuals is sorely needed. One successful example is the work on origins of need for achievement in early independence training of children. Another is the quasi-psychoanalytic account of the development of intolerance for ambiguity as an aspect of the authoritarian personality. [*See* ACHIEVEMENT MOTIVATION; PERSONALITY, POLITICAL, *article on* CONSERVATISM AND RADICALISM.]

Without excessive oversimplification, it is possible to regroup cognitive style variables into two general classifications: one dealing with the precision, accuracy, stability, and independence of cognitive processes; the other dealing with their fluency, spontaneity, and openness. For example, under precision one might include rigidity, reflectivity, field articulation and independence, ego overcontrol, and intolerance of ambiguity, among others. Under fluency one could group flexibility, originality, creativity, impulsivity, field-dependency, and ego undercontrol. Depending upon the variables included, these two classifications would be either independent or negatively related. The number of orthogonal (independent) syndromes to be defined appears to be strikingly limited, and the relations among a plethora of proposed variables, clusters, and factors have yet to be satisfactorily resolved.

Even when such a resolution is achieved, the resulting syndromes need careful developmental study. Two variables whose origins and incidence in children have been investigated are creativity and reflectivity. Research on creativity has been carried on independently in a number of research centers with different orientations, objectives, and methods. The current status may be summarized as follows: A loose cluster of variables called creativity can be reliably distinguished from intelligence by a number of objective means. A tendency to produce novel, clever, unusually organized, original, or simply uncommon responses in a variety of tasks, while it is often a consistent trait in the individual, does not predict general intellectual accomplishment as well as intelligence test scores do. As a stylistic variable it seems to develop most commonly in a generally flexible, stimulating, casual, nonconforming, and permissive home environment, but no particular set of experiences has been identified as the major causal determinant. It does not correlate with social and emotional adjustment any more highly than it does with intelligence. [*See* CREATIVITY, *article on* PSYCHOLOGICAL ASPECTS.]

Reflection–impulsivity. The style variable of reflection–impulsivity has been investigated by Kagan and his collaborators (Kagan et al. 1963; 1964) and is a likely candidate to account for a good deal of individual variability in perceptual, conceptual, and motor tasks involving speed and accuracy. It is of interest to students of intellectual development because it has been investigated extensively in children, as well as in adults, and because it correlates consistently with an extensive cluster of performance measures. A number of different tasks have been developed to serve as the criterion measure of reflection, or analytic style, as it has sometimes been called, but all of them have three features in common: (1) The tasks contain some degree of ambiguity or response uncertainty, such that no response is obviously correct at the outset. Thus it is possible that in assessing how people tackle a cognitive task they are in fact measuring some mixture of preference and ability. (2) The criterion tasks require a certain amount of perceptual analysis of detailed, often minute stimulus differences. They require careful, orderly comparisons among and between stimuli in order to yield a highly reflective score, but they are in no sense tests of sensory acuity. (3) Either directly or indirectly they take account of the speed of response as well as the nature of response, the faster performances generally being classified as impulsive.

Performances at the reflective, analytic end of this style dimension are in general precise, relatively slow, systematic, logical, objective, and somewhat literal-minded. Reflective adults in the Fels Institute longitudinal sample displayed, as young children, less physical activity, motility, and restlessness; longer attention spans; and less distractibility than did those adults who scored at the impulsive and global end of the distribution. The impulsive, nonanalytic syndrome, conversely, is characterized by fast, relatively inaccurate, and inconsistent, though perhaps more imaginative, performance in perceptual–cognitive tasks. One recent study (Kagan 1965) has given some indication of a relationship between impulsivity and reading difficulties in the primary grades. There is, moreover, evidence of sufficient stability of this characteristic from as early as the second year of life to warrant consideration of the possible contribution of genetic determinants. A developmental trend of declining impulsivity and increasing reflectivity with age has also been noted. Like other promising style variables, reflectivity possesses both a developmental and a differential component and will require both kinds of analysis if we are fully to understand its epigenesis and its role as a modifier of individual intellectual development.

JOHN C. WRIGHT

[*Directly related are the entries* DEVELOPMENTAL PSYCHOLOGY; INTELLIGENCE AND INTELLIGENCE TESTING; LANGUAGE, *article on* LANGUAGE DEVELOPMENT; MORAL DEVELOPMENT; PERCEPTION, *article on* PERCEPTUAL DEVELOPMENT; SENSORY AND MOTOR DEVELOPMENT. *Other relevant material may be found in* ADOLESCENCE; EDUCATIONAL PSYCHOLOGY; INFANCY; LEARNING, *articles on* CLASSICAL CONDITIONING, INSTRUMENTAL LEARNING, DISCRIMINATION LEARNING, VERBAL LEARNING, LEARNING IN CHILDREN, TRANSFER; PROBLEM SOLVING; REASONING AND LOGIC; *and in the biography of* MONTESSORI.]

BIBLIOGRAPHY

BRUNER, JEROME S.; and OLVER, ROSE R. 1963 Development of Equivalence Transformations in Children. Society for Research in Child Development, *Monographs* 28, no. 2:125–141.

BRUNER, JEROME S.; and OLVER, ROSE R. (editors) 1966 *Studies in Cognitive Growth.* New York: Wiley.

CANTOR, JOAN 1965 Transfer of Stimulus Pretraining to Motor Paired-associate and Discrimination Learning Tasks. Volume 2, pages 19–58 in *Advances in Child Development and Behavior.* Edited by Lewis P. Lipsitt and Charles C. Spiker. New York: Academic Press.

CHOMSKY, NOAM 1963 Formal Properties of Grammars. Volume 2, pages 323–418 in R. Duncan Luce, Robert R. Bush, and Eugene Galanter (editors), *Handbook of Mathematical Psychology.* New York: Wiley.

DARWIN, CHARLES 1877 A Biographical Sketch of an Infant. *Mind* 2:285–294.

FALKNER, FRANK (editor) 1966 Human Development. Unpublished manuscript. → See especially the article on cognitive development.

GETZELS, JACOB W.; and JACKSON, PHILIP W. 1962 *Creativity and Intelligence.* New York: Wiley.

GIBSON, ELEANOR J. 1963 Perceptual Development. Pages 144–195 in National Society for the Study of Education, *Child Psychology.* 62d Yearbook, Part 1. Edited by Harold W. Stevenson. Univ. of Chicago Press.

GUILFORD, J. P. 1956 The Structure of Intellect. *Psychological Bulletin* 53:267–293.

HEIDBREDER, EDNA 1948 The Attainment of Concepts: VI. Exploratory Experiments on Conceptualization at Perceptual Levels. *Journal of Psychology* 26:193–216.

KAGAN, JEROME S. 1965 Reflection–Impulsivity and Reading Ability in Primary Grade Children. *Child Development* 36:609–628.

KAGAN, JEROME S.; MOSS, HOWARD; and SIGEL, IRVING 1963 Psychological Significance of Styles of Conceptualization. Society for Research in Child Development, *Monographs* 28, no. 2:73–112.

KAGAN, JEROME S. et al. 1964 Information Processing in the Child: Significance of Analytic and Reflective Attitudes. *Psychological Monographs* 78, no. 1.

KENDLER, TRACY S. 1963 Development of Mediating Responses in Children. Society for Research in Child Development, *Monographs* 28, no. 2:33–48.

KUENNE, MARGARET R. 1946 Experimental Investigation of the Relation of Language to Transposition Behavior in Young Children. *Journal of Experimental Psychology* 36:471–490.

LONG, LOUIS; and WELCH, LIVINGSTON 1941 Reasoning Ability in Young Children. *Journal of Psychology* 12: 21–44.

LOVELL, KENNETH 1961 *The Growth of Basic Mathematical and Scientific Concepts in Children.* New York: Philosophical Library.

LURIIA, ALEKSANDR R. 1961 *The Role of Speech in the Regulation of Normal and Abnormal Behavior.* New York: Pergamon; Liveright.

MILLER, GEORGE A.; GALANTER, E.; and PRIBRAM, K. H. 1960 *Plans and the Structure of Behavior.* New York: Holt.

MONTESSORI, MARIA (1909) 1964 *The Montessori Method: Scientific Pedagogy as Applied to Child Education in "The Children's Houses."* Cambridge, Mass.: Bentley. → First published as *Il metodo della pedagogia scientifica.*

OSGOOD, CHARLES E. (1953) 1959 *Method and Theory in Experimental Psychology.* New York: Oxford Univ. Press.

PIAGET, JEAN; VINH-BANG; and MATALON, B. 1958 Note on the Law of the Temporal Maximum of Some Optico-Geometric Illusions. *American Journal of Psychology* 71:277–282.

PICK, HERBERT L. JR. 1963 Some Soviet Research on Learning and Perception in Children. Society for Research in Child Development, *Monographs* 28, no. 2: 185–190.

PICK, HERBERT L. JR.; PICK, ANNE; and KLEIN, ROBERT 1966 Perceptual Integration in Children. Unpublished manuscript.

RAZRAN, GREGORY 1961 The Observable Unconscious and the Inferable Conscious in Current Soviet Psychophysiology: Interoceptive Conditioning, Semantic Conditioning, and the Orienting Reflex. *Psychological Review* 68:81–147.

RHEINGOLD, HARRIET L.; GEWIRTZ, JACOB L.; and ROSS, HELEN W. 1959 Social Conditioning of Vocalizations in the Infant. *Journal of Comparative and Physiological Psychology* 52:68–73.

SOKOLOV, EVGENII N. (1958) 1963 *Perception and the Conditioned Reflex.* New York: Macmillan. → First published as *Vospriiatie i uslovnyi refleks.*

SPIKER, CHARLES C. 1963 Verbal Factors in the Discrimination Learning of Children. Society for Research in Child Development, *Monographs* 28, no. 2:53–69.

WALLACH, MICHAEL A.; and KOGAN, NATHAN 1965 *Modes of Thinking in Young Children.* New York: Holt.

WERNER, HEINZ (1926) 1957 *Comparative Psychology of Mental Development.* Rev. ed. New York: International Universities Press. → First translated from German in 1940. The revised edition was first published in 1948.

WHITE, SHELDON H. 1965 Evidence for a Hierarchical Arrangement of Learning Processes. Volume 2, pages 187–220 in *Advances in Child Development and Behavior.* Edited by Lewis P. Lipsitt and Charles C. Spiker. New York: Academic Press.

WITKIN, HERMAN A. et al. 1954 *Personality Through Perception.* New York: Harper.

WITKIN, HERMAN A. et al. 1962 *Psychological Differentiation: Studies of Development.* New York: Wiley.

WOHLWILL, JOACHIM F. 1960 Developmental Studies of Perception. *Psychological Bulletin* 57:249–288.

ZEAMAN, DAVID; and HOUSE, BETTY J. 1963 The Role of Attention in Retardate Discrimination Learning. Pages 159–223 in Norman R. Ellis (editor), *Handbook of Mental Deficiency.* New York: McGraw-Hill.

INTELLECTUAL HISTORY

See under HISTORY.

INTELLECTUALS

Intellectuals are the aggregate of persons in any society who employ in their communication and expression, with relatively higher frequency than most other members of their society, symbols of general scope and abstract reference, concerning man, society, nature, and the cosmos. The high frequency of their use of such symbols may be a function of their own subjective propensity or of the obligations of an occupational role, the performance of which entails such use. These two major motivations of intellectual actions can exist in the same person, and they can be present in the same action. They can also exist relatively independently of each other. Intellectual propensities or interests vary in intensity among persons performing intellectual roles and are sometimes also found among those who practice nonintellectual occupations.

Intellectual interests arise from the need to perceive, experience, and express—in words, colors, shapes, or sounds—a general significance in particular, concrete events. They arise from the need to be in cognitive, moral, and appreciative contact with the most general or "essential" features of man, society, nature, and the cosmos. This need is deeply, indeed constitutively, rooted in human beings, albeit unequally distributed among individuals. It underlies the production (creation) and consumption (reception) of works of science, scholarship, philosophy, theology, literature, and art. However, the objectified products of scientific, scholarly, philosophical, theological, literary, and artistic actions are not solely the result of the spontaneous expression of these propensities. The expressive, cognitive, and moral propensities which seek coherent, objective form are aroused, nurtured, heightened, and focused by traditions (which are manifested in the models exemplified by great works and creative personalities) and by the explicit teaching and the culture of the social circles and institutions in which the various intellectual activities are practiced. These propensities are sustained, too, by the institutionalization of expectations of intellectual production, reproduction, and consumption.

Intellectual activities are institutionalized because many individuals who do not have strong or intense intellectual interests of their own need the results of such interests, either to satisfy the necessities of their own mental and physical constitution or because they believe intellectual products to be necessary for the effective functioning of institutions and of society as a whole. Even the most rudimentary and relatively undifferentiated societies have a place for the intellectual functions which are expressed in art and interpretative speculation, even if they do not provide many specialized roles in which these activities are carried on. More differentiated societies require and provide for more specialized intellectual roles which help to locate the individual, his group, and the society in the universe; to interpret, explain, and attempt to control the occurrence of evil; to legitimate authority and define its responsibilities; to interpret the society's past experiences; to instruct the youth in the traditions and skills of the society; to facilitate and guide the aesthetic and religious experiences of various sectors of the society; and to offer assistance in the control of nature.

The propensities or needs which give rise to functional intellectual roles also impel intellectual creativity. They do so because they are operative in the consumption (reception) of intellectual products. Those who do not themselves have the powers or capacities to reach out directly and productively toward the general and abstract level of existence still need, if only intermittently, to be in contact with, and to participate in, the symbolic objectifications which are created or disclosed by the more creative; they also need the skills which are developed in conjunction with the development of the powers involved in productive or reproductive intellectual action. In other words, they are the consumers of intellectual products (e.g., laity, readers, audiences, patients, clients).

Intellectual objectifications are received or consumed not only because of a pressing need for contact with the "essential" but also because many of the tasks undertaken in certain societies call for the performance of certain functional roles which require intellectual skill and reward such performances. The more complex the structure and the larger the scale of the undertaking, the more likely it is to involve a component of intellectual action.

Large-scale engineering projects, irrigation schemes, military operations, and administrative and judicial organizations tend to utilize generalized knowledge. Even where the empirical element (i.e., the experience of the practitioner) dominates, the large scale of such operations evokes in those responsible for their execution a sense of need for some more general principles to govern their actions. These general principles are not merely theoretical legitimations of the undertaking but are integral to the executive actions through which the projects are realized. The techniques and skills in these executive actions rest on or involve the performance of intellectual actions.

Persons are recruited to intellectual or intellectual–executive roles not solely, or even primarily, because of their deep personal propensity to perform the intellectual actions entailed in such roles. Some of those who enter these roles do so above all because they offer the opportunity of experiencing the gratification of intellectual action as such; others do so more because they are encouraged by parents, teachers, and the prevailing opinion of their class and culture, as well as by the prospective rewards of money and prestige. Once it is perceived that there are intellectual actions capable of incorporation into them, the roles are created, and recruitment into them is economically, politically, and culturally facilitated and rewarded. In the present century the closer associations between scientific research and industrial and military technology, between scientific research and health, and between scientific research and agricultural technology have come about because research workers, politicians, military men, farmers, and civil servants came to believe that the tasks set by "interests" (anticipations of advantage) and aspirations confronted by existing and prospective situations could be dealt with by persons trained in science and technology. The same is true of the utilization of statistics and economic and sociological analysis, in private and public economic life. The custodians of the established order and the authoritative institutions through which their needs are satisfied provide the resources which permit technological–intellectual roles to be established, set tasks for the incumbents of the roles, present opportunities, and offer incentives for the performance of intellectual work. These intellectual–executive roles are not, however, wholly the creation of the "powers"—that is, those who have executive authority and financial resources. The very notion that such roles are possible arises from the perception of the existence of intellectual actions by those who hope to benefit by them and from the desires of the performers of these actions to bring their intellectual production to fruition in the actions of those who have no intellectual interests.

The intellectual stratum

Every society has its intellectuals. Primitive societies—despite their undifferentiatedness, which is a function of poverty, of the thinness of their intellectual traditions, and of the feebleness of their technology—also have their intellectuals or at least their protointellectuals. Frontier societies too, despite the special criteria by which their members are recruited, also produce intellectuals. In the great European and Oriental empires of antiquity and the Middle Ages the magnitude of the tasks undertaken by their political elites, the precipitation of "revelations" in their written literature, and the surplus wealth resulting from their large size and relatively advanced technologies required, and provided for, substantial numbers of intellectuals.

Still, prior to modern societies, poverty, the empirical character of technology, the restricted role and aspirations of government, and the rudimentariness of educational institutions kept the intellectual stratum relatively small and internally relatively undifferentiated. The intellectual class acquired a pervasive importance first in modern Western societies and then in societies outside the West when they began to assimilate Western beliefs and to establish institutions resembling those of the West.

The tasks set by the aspirations and demands of those sections of modern society which care to influence the exercise of authority generate an elaborate system of differentiated and professionalized intellectual roles. The numerous conflicts of activated demands, the vastly increased "legal initiative" of the population, and the wider and deeper ramifications of the concerns of the state require trained lawyers and judges. The modern idea of the responsibilities of the state generates a civil service which requires persons who have studied law, economics, statistics, and administration or whose intellectual powers have been cultivated by exercise in intellectual activities not directly connected with administration, such as mathematics, classics, or literature. Religious institutions now, as in the past, require clergymen and theologians; even though they now make up a significantly smaller proportion of the intellectual stratum than they did before the development of modern societies, they still form a large bloc among the intellectuals. The extension of political interest and activity—from a small group of wealthy and traditionally ascendant families, first to the wider reaches of the property-owning classes and then to the citizenry at large—as well as the greater efficacy of the state in modern society have magnified the amount and organization of political contention. Party politics, whether in democratic or in one-party states, require journalists, political analysts, and leader-writers.

The great increase in the scale of organization of the units of economic life and the emergence of an intimacy between technology and scientific research such as never existed before the last part of the nineteenth century have between them increased the demand for research workers, scientifically qualified technologists, statisticians, economists, and, increasingly, managers with technological and other intellectual disciplines. The industrialization of warfare has also increased the demand for scientific research workers and technologists; new conceptions and resources for military administration and policy have created a demand for intellectual practices such as strategic studies, intelligence analysis, and manpower studies, each of which has become a subprofession in its own right.

Humanitarianism and democracy have led to a new emphasis on the protection and improvement of health, which requires physicians, physiologists, biochemists, surgeons, public health specialists, and the like. The need to feed a larger and more urbanized population, with greater purchasing power and more differentiated tastes, has caused governments and individual agriculturalists to summon the assistance of geneticists, soil chemists, botanists, economists, agricultural-extension officials, statisticians, and other experts. The increasingly widespread demand for enlightenment throughout society—for a share of the cultural inheritance as well as for the improved status and economic rewards afforded by education—has created a corresponding demand for teachers, librarians, editors, and journalists.

None or few of these numerous intellectual–practical roles (engendered by practical needs and not by intellectual propensities) would have been possible, nor could they continue, without the simultaneous or prior exercise of purely intellectual propensities. Intellectual–practical needs could not have been met, nor for that matter could some of the needs have been conceived of as needs, without the accomplishments of men impelled primarily by their intellectual propensities. Furthermore, the provision of personnel for these intellectual–practical roles would be impossible without a system of institutions in which intellectual propensities are relatively free and dominant (that is, universities and institutions of advanced technological training and research) and without the recruitment of persons with predominantly intellectual propensities.

Some of these intellectual–practical roles have a high intellectual component. The superior judiciary, higher technological roles, the higher civil service, the editorial, and the analytical-journalistic roles, even when they are directly engaged in executive performance, require the mastery and practice of complex patterns of symbols of wide generality. Those at lower levels of authority and with narrower ranges of responsibility also require some measure of intellectual expertise. Thus, many of these roles can be entered, according to custom or formal requirement, only after passage through a course of disciplined or organized intellectual study. (In the case of the lower levels of these fields—for example, the ordinary lawyer, the general medical practitioner, the middle and lower ranks of civil servants, the ordinary engineer, the routine local-newspaper reporter—the intellectual training through which they must pass often contains considerable intellectual elements which do not enter into their practice.) Thus, the training of large numbers of persons for the wide variety of intellectual–practical roles generates a system of predominantly intellectual roles in teaching and research.

Alongside these intellectual roles, which are an integral part of the political, administrative, legal, and economic spheres of a complex modern society, there are other intellectual roles which constitute the cultural system and which are largely the product of intellectual propensities as such, shaped by intellectual traditions and the resources made available out of respect for their intrinsically intellectual character.

The institutions of intellectual life

Except in small societies and in societies which, although large, have a small stratum of intellectuals, the intellectuals seldom, if ever, possess an inclusive sense of identity. In contemporary large-scale societies the specialization of education and practice, the consequent tendencies toward segregation along professional lines, and the wide extension of secondary and higher education have made for vague external boundaries of the intellectual stratum. Even in small intellectual strata, differences in religious and political beliefs and in ethnic and class connections have caused rifts in the solidarity which might otherwise have prevailed in situations where a common participation in high culture offered a criterion for an inclusive self-identification.

Nonetheless, the intellectual stratum of any society possesses a structure; it is more than the statistical aggregate of all those who perform intellectual actions. Even though the intellectual stratum ordinarily does not have, in the present century, an entirely common culture, it increasingly tends to pass through a common institutional system: the academic or university system. The highly specialized and particularized intellectual–practical cultures nurtured outside the universities would not be what they are without the link between them and the more general and abstract culture of the university system. Within this source of the more specialized and segregated intellectual–practical professions, there is more of a common culture and more of a coherent and integral corporate structure than in the intellectual stratum as a whole. Thus, from the university system comes a certain measure of institutional interconnectedness of the whole intellectual stratum.

The structure of the intellectual system of any society is defined by four main factors: (1) the sources of financial support of the performers of intellectual actions; (2) the modes of administration of intellectual actions; (3) the patterns of demand for intellectual objects and intellectual–practical performances; and (4) the relationships between past and present intellectual accomplishments (i.e., the relationship of tradition and creativity in the various fields of intellectual action).

Sources of financial support. The forms of financial support of productive and reproductive intellectual actions are: (a) income gained from inherited wealth; (b) income gained from the practice of nonintellectual occupations; (c) patronage; (d) income from the sale of the products of the individual's own intellectual actions; (e) income received as salary (or from other types of payment) for services performed, usually within corporate intellectual bodies; and (f) income for services performed in intellectual–practical (executive) occupations.

In most literate societies intellectual life is sustained by combinations of several or all of these modes of support. In Europe prior to the eighteenth century, intellectual life was characteristically sustained by income from inherited wealth and from patronage and to a lesser extent by income derived from payment for intellectual services (e.g., teaching) and intellectual–practical services (e.g., administration). Support from the sale of intellectual products (books, plays, poems, paintings, sculpture, and music) appeared for the first time during the Italian Renaissance—and then only in connection with the sale of paintings and sculpture produced on commission. Prior to the development of inexpensive printing and the expansion of literacy, the free-lance intellectual who lived from the sale of his intellectual products was extremely rare and was confined to painting and sculpture. Prior to the growth of universities and organized research institutions, support from salary for intellectual work (research, writing, and teaching) was likewise rare; it was confined mainly to court intellectuals (historians, astronomers, and astrologers).

In advanced modern societies and in the modern sector of underdeveloped societies intellectuals are supported predominantly through employment in corporate intellectual bodies (universities and research institutions) and to a lesser extent through employment in intellectual–practical occupations in, for example, the civil service, military organizations, churches, newspapers, and research departments of industrial enterprises. Free-lance intellectuals living from the sale of their products, although much larger in number than in the eighteenth and nineteenth centuries, still constitute a relatively small proportion of the total intellectual stratum. (The proportion of free-lance intellectuals was probably greatest in the eighteenth and nineteenth centuries, before the great expansion of universities and corporately organized research.) In underdeveloped countries, where most of the population is still illiterate, the free-lance intellectual who lives from the sale of his intellectual products is a rarity.

The proportion of productive intellectuals who live or have lived on income derived from nonintellectual occupations (e.g., professional soldiers, merchants, bankers, clerks, laborers) has always been small, although certain very distinguished figures are to be included in this category (e.g., Thucydides, Ibn Khaldūn, George Grote, Edward Hyde, H. C. Lea, Chateaubriand, and T. S. Eliot for part of his career).

Administration of intellectual actions. The trend toward the increasing envelopment of intellectual life within corporate intellectual institutions is in part a function of a change in the interests of an increasingly large proportion of the intellectual stratum—that is, a change from predominantly literary, philosophical, and theological concerns to scientific and scholarly interests. This trend is also a function of changes in techniques of scientific and scholarly research. As long as scholarship was confined to a relatively small number of books and manuscripts and as long as scientific research could be done with relatively simple and inexpensive instruments, these interests could be pursued independently and with the financial resources made available through inherited wealth or from income earned in other occupations. However, once scholarship began to require the use of very large libraries, well-ordered museums, widely dispersed manuscripts, and the "finds" of large archeological inquiries, and as the number of scholars who could not provide these from their earned and unearned income increased, the conduct of scholarly research required that much larger sums of money be found if research was to proceed on the scale that came to be thought desirable in the nineteenth century. Research in the biological, medical, and physical sciences underwent similar experiences. The demand for greater precision and reliability of observations imposed the need for more expensive equipment which could not be provided by a *rentier* or an amateur scientist from his private income. The greater numbers of persons seeking scientific education, as well as the newly created association of research and education, required larger laboratories with larger masses of equipment. There was no alternative to a denser, more encompassing organization of scientific activity.

These changes in the techniques of scholarship and science coincided with the growth of national wealth and a new development in the attitudes of governments toward university education and toward the scholarly and scientific studies pursued within them. Governments responded munificently to these changes, as did wealthy private persons and the foundations established by them (particularly in the United States). The combination of the increased number of students to be looked after, of buildings, books, and equipment to be procured and cared for, and of scientists and scholars (who were also teachers) to be paid made more organization and control inevitable.

Patterns of demand. As long as rulers were concerned only with their own glory and that of the state, intellectual performance could be left to those with intellectual propensities and the culture necessary to express them. The works of genius could only be the product of those with strong and intensive intellectual propensities. Patronage, court employment, official sinecures, and ecclesiastical livings could suffice for those whose inherited wealth was too meager to maintain them and who could not gain a livelihood through their activities as university teachers, painters and sculptors on commission, theatrical managers, soldiers, and diplomats. Genius and the glory which it brought were what counted—alongside of flattery—and numbers were not especially significant.

When, however, intellectual performance came to be associated with the strength of the state and its internal order and, later, with the physical and mental well-being of the large mass of the people, random and irregular patronage was not able to meet the new demand. The numbers of intellectuals demanded were too great, and the results of the predominant modes of recruitment, which depended on strong and intense intellectual propensity and the accidents of inheritance and patronage, were too uncertain. This vastly increased demand entailed an organized pattern of training and a certification of accomplishment. Intellectual accomplishment in reception and reproduction had to be standardized so that the users in the "practical" sphere—in commerce and industry, education, the civil service, and the judiciary—would be assured that their recruits were reliable.

However, in those spheres of intellectual life which did not obviously contribute to the strength and order of the state and the physical well-being of society and in which the product of intellectual activity was an artifact which could be judged by its consumer, intellectual propensity could still be relied upon. There was no need for certification; the product—a novel, a poem, a painting, or a statue—carried its own certification, in the response of its consumer or recipient, who was assisted increasingly by critics without official status. Self-recruitment could therefore dominate. The arts thus remained the sector of intellectual life in which a free-lance structure could persist. This is at least the way in which things have happened in countries which, in principle or in fact, permitted freedom of intellectual production.

Where the glory of the state required organized and costly parks and buildings, architectural education and practice and schools of painting and sculpture underwent the process of organization and control which the provision of personnel for the intellectual–practical skills (for the civil service, education, law, and so forth) had established. Painting and sculpture have not, however, been subject to the same degree of organization as architecture, partly because of the continuing private demand for paintings and sculptures. This has freed painters and sculptors from the degree of subjection to authority to which engineers and architects, as performers of intellectual–practical activities, have had to submit.

In some states, however, the arts have not been regarded primarily as sources of glory for rulers and of private satisfaction for individual citizens; rather, intellectual activity in the arts has been, and is, regarded as a factor in public order and in the strength and fame of the state. As a result, artistic activities have been subjected to processes of organization and control so that output can be guaranteed or certified. However, since in this sphere quantity is recognized to be less important than quality, more attention is paid to distribution than to production of works of art. Censorship through the control of access to a public audience is the mode of organization found appropriate when intellectual actions, including artistic action, are seen as factors in the maintenance of public order and the security of rulers. But even in countries which take this view, the free-lance principle of support is allowed to predominate within the limits set by censorship, since the belief still prevails that works of art are to a much greater extent the products of intellectual propensity than are the works accomplished in the intellectual–practical professions (the same is true of pure science).

Tradition and creativity. All intellectual actions, however great the genius of their performers, are shaped within a context of tradition. The relationships between intellectual actions and tradition vary in the degree of compellingness and immediacy. In the pattern of scientific work, it is the latest manifestation of the tradition which serves as the point of departure for any particular work of research. The remoter points in the stream of tradition are respected for having set the path for subsequent work, and particular figures are respected not only for their specific accomplishments but for the general tone or ethos which infused their work and which inspires subsequent research workers even at a distance of several centuries. But it is the latest point reached by the tradition which is decisive for the research scientist; it is the latest work which offers both authority and challenge. There is little choice of the tradition to which a research worker must submit; once his problem is chosen, the tradition which he confronts can no longer be chosen. It is *there!*

This is why scientific research must rest on such a disciplined mastery of what has been accomplished in "the literature." This is the reason, too, why training and certification can be standardized. This relationship to tradition lends itself readily to class instruction, textbooks, and examinations.

In contrast, certain fields of intellectual activity, such as philosophy, literature, and painting, have no such inevitable subjection to the immediate past. They are freer to turn wholly against it—although very few do—and to choose more usefully or more selectively from the wide variety of traditions and models which have been effective in the course of the development of their respective subjects. Whereas a scientist who rejects much of a current tradition must confront it and respond to it, a writer or painter need not do so. Although most writers and painters do in fact use the currently received tradition as their platform, they need not do so, and they may do so as selectively as they wish. Their divergence from the current pattern is noted, but they will not be censured for it. At least there is no binding consensus that they should do justice to the tradition of the last moment. There is no *necessary* orthodoxy in literature and art such as there is in science. Thus, whereas it is not a defect in a scientist or scholar to be "academic"—indeed, it is the precondition of his originality—there is no comparable obligation on the part of a literary man or a painter to be academic.

The traditions which govern the life of the intellectual stratum may be divided into the substantive traditions of the special fields of intellectual activity, such as the traditions of psychology, physics, or literature, and their subordinate or technical traditions, such as those concerned with the study of vision, low-temperature physics, or the short story. These traditions contain the results of past accomplishments. The merit of any intellectual performance is assessed by the degree to which it has mastered the inherited tradition and gone beyond it. (The transcendence of tradition as an element in accomplishment is a modern conception; prior to the formation of the romantic conception of genius the merit of an intellectual work was considered to lie in the degree to which it approximated the model offered by tradition. This assessment was in fact an assessment of originality as well as of conformity. It was a creative conformity.)

Intellectual traditions and social authority

Training in intellectual work has two goals: the mastery of both the articulated and promulgated substance and the techniques offered by tradition, and the development of tacit expertise which is the assimilation of the unarticulated spirit of what the tradition offers so that one can transcend and transform traditions while still adhering to them.

Assessment of degree of success in the attainment of these two goals, which stand in such a paradoxical relationship within the larger paradox of tradition and creativity, is one major task of the institutional system of intellectual life, along with the tasks of recruiting, training, facilitating production, and communicating results. The assessment of persons and works is necessary for maintaining traditions of the highest achievement in a given field of intellectual work and for fostering innovation which is not arbitrary and which respects the substance of the tradition even when rejecting it. Among the chief institutions of assessment are examining bodies, appointments committees, the editorial staffs of periodicals, publishing houses, patronage (grants) and prize-awarding bodies, the reviewing sections of periodicals and newspapers, and the selection committees of museums.

In fields of intellectual action in which the insistence on the observance of the latest tradition as a precondition for its transcendence and transformation is great, the institutions of assessment are highly integrated, functioning as a single system, both nationally and internationally. The institutions of assessment themselves, especially at the peaks of the hierarchy, maintain a universally acknowledged standard. The decisions at the peak are acknowledged as valid by a practically world-wide consensus of those who have themselves passed successfully through the machinery of recruitment, training, and assessment. The mediocrities are relegated to the lesser institutions, and failures drop to the bottom or are forced to leave the field. Within each field in which everyone is nominally equal, there is in fact an aristocracy, which is largely an aristocracy of contemporaneous accomplishment but which is also, in small part at least, an aristocracy of particularistic institutional affiliation. (Persons at institutions which are acknowledged to be the richest in accomplishment are, simply by virtue of that fact, carried along and accorded some measure of precedence.) As a result of the operation of the institutions of assessment, certain works and the persons who have produced these works are promoted to the center of attention of those who work on the same or related subjects. Their accomplishments constitute and present the highest and most immediate form of the tradition which must be universally acknowledged and confronted.

The situation is somewhat different in those fields of intellectual action in which there is more self-recruitment, in which training is more a matter of self-discipline than of ordered institutional pressure, and in which the relevant traditions may be more freely chosen. In such fields there is a less far-reaching and less compelling consensus. Although each field has a dominant tradition, each also comprises divergent traditions which have their adherents within and across national boundaries. These diverse traditions have their own institutions of assessment (publishing houses, bookshops, magazines, museums, and galleries) and their own informal circles (friendships and acquaintanceships centered on salons, cafes, etc.), which nurture the particular tradition and make their assessments in its light. The traditions which are asserted in these acts of assessment are the vital substance of the life of the intellectual stratum. They comprise the standards and rules which guide the striving for accomplishment, and the substantive beliefs and symbols which constitute the heritage of valid accomplishment.

It should be emphasized that these traditions are not maintained simply by the authoritativeness of the institutions of assessment and of the body of accomplishment on behalf of which they act. The vitality of these traditions is sustained by the passionate propensity of the "natural" intellectual to be in contact with symbols of general scope. They are traditions which are, so to speak, given by the nature of intellectual work. They are the immanent traditions of intellectual performance, the accepted body of rules of procedure, standards of judgment, criteria for the selection of subject matters and problems, modes of presentation, canons for the assessment of excellence, and models of previous accomplishment and prospective emulation. Every field of intellectual performance, more than any other craft or profession possessing a long and acknowledged accumulation of accomplishments, has such a cultural tradition, which is always being added to and modified, although at varying rates. Without the tradition which is called scientific method in each particular field of science and scholarship and which is called technique in the fields of literary creation and the plastic and other arts, even the greatest and most creative geniuses could not be effective. Colleges and universities, scientific, scholarly, and artistic journals, museums, galleries—in short the whole system of intellectual institutions—function to select those who are qualified to work within these traditions and to train those who are selected in their appreciation, application, and development. Even the most creative and rapidly developing domains of intellectual performance could disregard these traditions only with very great loss.

Secondary traditions have prevailed for a very long time in the intellectual strata of most societies with a written corpus of intellectual works and with specialized intellectuals. These secondary traditions are in a sense marginal to actual intellectual work, but their relation to intense intellectual action is not wholly accidental. The vital substantive and technical traditions of intellectual work seem to entail a measure of tension between themselves and the laity. Although this tension is not constitutive of intellectual work, it seems to be a necessary by-product. The values inherent in these vital traditions are remote from the practical routines of daily life, from the pleasures of the ordinary man, and from the obligations, compromises, and corruptions of those who exercise commanding authority in church, state, economy, and army. Thus, the very intensity and concentration of commitment required by the vital traditions of intellectual life dispose intellectuals to feel some sense of a distance separating the intellectual from the routine and practical.

Intellectual action arose out of religious preoccupations. In the early history of the human race it tended in its concern with the ultimate, or at least with what lies beyond the immediate concrete experience, to operate with religious symbols. Intellectual action of the most intense kind continues to share with genuine religious experience the fascination with the sacred, or the ultimate ground of thought and experience, and the aspiration to enter into intimate contact with it. In secular intellectual work this concern involves the search for the truth, for the principles embedded in events and actions and for the establishment of a relationship between the empirical self and the "essential," whether the relationship be cognitive, appreciative, or expressive. It is therefore no stretching of the term "religion" to say that science and philosophy, even though they are not religious in a conventional sense, are as concerned with the sacred as religion itself.

Thus, it may be said that a tradition of awesome respect and of *serious* striving for contact with the sacred underlies the vital intellectual traditions and the actions which carry them forward. This is perhaps the first, the most comprehensive, and the most important of all the traditions of the intellectuals. In the great religious cultures of Islam, Buddhism, Taoism, and Hinduism, prior to the emergence of a differentiated modern intellectual stratum, the care of the sacred through the mastery, interpretation, and exposition of sacred writings, as well as the cultivation of the appropriate mental states or qualities, were the prime interests of intellectuals. (In China a class of Confucian intellectuals in the civil service produced its own tradition, more civil and aesthetic than religious in the conventional sense.) In the West, too, in antiquity, a substantial number of the philosophical intellectuals bore this tradition of concern with the sacred, and on the higher reaches even those who cut themselves off from the tribal and territorial religions continued to be impelled by such considerations (e.g., Pythagoras, Euclid, Ptolemy, Aristotle, Plato, Socrates, Lucretius, Seneca). Although religious orientations attract a diminishing share of the creative capacities of the elite of the intellectual stratum in modern times, they still remain a major preoccupation of a substantial fraction of the educated classes and of the most creative minds.

With this striving for contact with the ultimately important comes the self-esteem which always accompanies the performance of important activities. Anyone who tries to understand the traditions of the central part of the intellectual stratum and their relations with the authorities who rule the other spheres of society at any given time must bear in mind the crucial significance of the self-regard which comes from preoccupation and contact with the most vital facts of human and cosmic existence, as well as the implied attitude of derogation toward those who act in more mundane or more routine capacities. Naturally this sentiment is not shared equally by all intellectuals. Not all are equally involved in these "vital facts" and therefore not all have the same sense of the dignity of their activities.

When intellectuals ceased to be primarily religious intellectuals or when they ceased to share the prevailing religious orthodoxy, the very act of separation, even where gradual and undeliberate, set up a tension between the intellectuals and the religious authority of their society. Moreover, where the religious authority had close ties with the civil authority, as was often the case, tension between the deviant intellectuals and the civil authorities was aggravated. Ecclesiastical authority became an object of the distrust of some of the most intense and creative intellectuals, and insofar as the civil authorities associated themselves with the religious powers, they too shared in that skepticism. This attitude has not by any means been universal, nor has the distrust always been aggressive. Confucian civil servants, disdainful of Taoism or Buddhism, did not become rebels against their sovereigns as long as they themselves were treated respectfully. In the West, where the separation of religious and other intellectual activities has become most pronounced, a more general feeling of distance from authority has been engendered and has become one of the strongest of the secondary traditions of the intellectuals. It happened first in the West and then, in the present century, in Africa and Asia among intellectuals who have come under the influence of Western traditions.

This attitude is not an integral part of intellectual work, except in political philosophy and the fields related to it, but it has nonetheless found very wide acceptance among those who do intellectual work. It is, moreover, the matrix from which a number of other important secondary traditions have grown. The tension between the intellectuals and the authorities stems from the intellectuals' urge to locate and acknowledge an authority which is the bearer of the highest good, whether it be science, order, progress, or some other value, and to resist or condemn actual authority as a betrayer of the highest values. In other words, this tension comes from the vital tradition of the intellectual stratum which propels it toward the discovery and expression of what is "ultimately" true and thus "sacred." Practically all of the more concrete traditions in the light and shadows of which intellectuals have lived embody this tension. These secondary traditions which, however diverse in their age and origin, have played a great part in forming the relations of the modern intellectuals to authority are: the tradition of scientism; the romantic tradition; the apocalyptic tradition; the populistic tradition; and the anti-intellectual tradition of order.

All of these traditions are in conflict with other traditions of deference toward ecclesiastical and temporal authorities and the expectation of a career in their service. Even in those modern cultures in which a tradition of acceptance of legitimate civil and ecclesiastic authorities by the intellectual stratum is strongest, as in modern Britain and modern Germany, it has by no means had the field to itself. More recently, antiauthoritarian secondary traditions have found a widespread and enthusiastic reception in Asia, where devotion to the prevailing religious values and service to temporal authority have always had a powerful hold.

Scientism. The tradition of scientism denies the validity of tradition as such. It insists on the testing of everything which is received and on its rejection if it does not correspond with the "facts of experience." It is the tradition which demands the avoidance of every extraneous impediment to the precise perception of reality, regardless of whether that impediment comes from tradition, institutional authority, or internal passion or impulse. It is critical of the arbitrary and the irrational. In its emphasis on the indispensability of first-hand and direct experience, it sets itself in opposition to everything which comes between the mind of the knowing individual and "reality." It is easy to see how social convention and the traditional authority associated with institutions would fall prey to the ravages of this powerfully persuasive tradition, which tends to corrode competing traditions.

Romanticism. The romantic tradition appears at first sight to be in irreconcilable opposition to the tradition of scientism. At certain points, such as the estimation of the value of impulse and passion, there is a real and unbridgeable antagonism. In many important respects, however, they share fundamental features. Romanticism starts with the appreciation of the spontaneous manifestations of the essence of concrete individuality. Hence, it values originality, that is, the novel, that which is produced by the genius of the individual (or the folk) in contrast with the stereotyped and tradition-bound actions of the philistine. Since ratiocination and detachment obstruct spontaneous expression, they are thought to be life-destroying. Institutions, which have rules and which prescribe the conduct of the indivdual members by conventions and commands, are likewise viewed as life-destroying. The bourgeois family, mercantile activity, the market—indeed, civil society in general, with its curb on enthusiasm and its sober acceptance of obligation—are repugnant to the romantic tradition; all are regarded as the enemies of spontaneity and genuineness, since they impose a role on the individual and do not permit him to be himself. They also kill what is really "living" in the folk, that is, the spontaneous and undeliberate. Civil society is thought to have no place for the intellectual, who thus becomes afflicted with a sense of his moral solitude within it; moral solitude is viewed as the "natural condition" of the spontaneous individuality in a society of philistines living a routine existence. The affinities of the romantic tradition to the revolutionary criticism of the established order and to the bohemian refusal to have more part in that order than is absolutely necessary are obvious. The romantic tradition is one of the most explosively antiauthoritarian, and even anticivil, powers of modern intellectual life.

Revolution. The revolutionary tradition, which has found so many of its leading recipients and exponents in the intellectual stratum, has drawn much from scientism and romanticism, but essentially it rests on one, much older tradition, namely the *apocalyptic*, or millenarian, tradition. The belief that the evil world as we know it, so full of temptation and corruption, will come to an end one day and will be replaced by a purer and better world originates in the apocalyptic outlook of the prophets of the Old Testament. It is promulgated in the Christian idea of the kingdom of God, which the earlier Christians expected in their own time, and it persists into the present; the revolutionary tradition itself is hidden by the efforts of the church but recurrently appears on the surface of history in the teaching and action of heretical sects. The apocalyptic tradition received a powerful impetus from Manicheanism. In the Donatists, the Bogomils, the Albigensians and Waldensians, the Hussites and Lollards, the Anabaptists, and the Fifth Monarchy Men, this tradition has lived on. It has come down to our own times in a transmuted form. Although the apocalyptic outlook still exists in its religious form among numerous Christian, quasi-Christian, and non-Christian sects in Europe, America, Asia, and Africa, its intellectually most important recipients are the modern revolutionary movements, especially the Marxian movements. (Marxian writers of the early part of this century acknowledged the Anabaptists, the Fifth Monarchy Men, the Levellers, and the Diggers as their forerunners, and although the Bolsheviks have been less willing to admit Russian sectarianism as an antecedent, it is probable that the Russian sectarian image of the world and its cataclysmic future made it easier for the Marxian conception of society and its historical destiny to find acceptance in Russia.) The disposition to distinguish sharply between good and evil and to refuse to permit any admixture, the insistence that justice be done though the heavens fall, the obstinate refusal to compromise or to tolerate compromise—all the features of doctrinaire politics, or the politics of the ideal—which are common to many modern intellectuals, must be attributed in some measure at least to the revolutionary tradition.

Populism. Another tradition which has moved nearly all intellectuals in the nineteenth and twentieth centuries is the *populistic tradition.* Populism, which is partly an offspring of the romantic tradition, is a belief in the creativity and the superior moral worth of the ordinary people, of the uneducated and unintellectual; it perceives virtue in their actual qualities or in their potentialities. In the simplicity and wisdom of the ways of the ordinary people, the populist tradition alleges that it has discerned virtues which are morally superior to those found in the educated and in the higher social classes. Even where, as in Marxism, the actual state of the lower classes is not esteemed, they are alleged to be fitted by destiny to become the salvationary nucleus of their whole society. Elements of the populistic disposition are manifested in romanticism, with its distrust of the rational and calculating elements in bourgeois society; in revolutionism, with its hatred of the upper classes as the agents of wicked authority; and in the apocalyptic attitude, which sees the last coming first and which alleges that official learning (religious and secular) has falsified the truths which the Last Judgment and the leap into freedom will validate. German historical and philological scholarship in the nineteenth century, imbued with the romantic hatred of the rational, the economic, and the analytic spirit, which it castigated as the source and product of the whole rationalistic trend of western European culture, discovered in the nameless masses, the folk, the fountain of linguistic and cultural creativity. French socialism went a step further, and Marxism elevated this essentially romantic outlook into a systematic, "scientific" theory.

In all countries peripheral to the most creative centers of Western culture at the height of its hegemony over the modern mind, intellectuals were both fascinated and rendered uneasy by the culture of western Europe. Not only in early nineteenth-century Germany, but in Russia of the 1850s, in the middlewestern United States in the late nineteenth and early twentieth centuries, in Brazil (in the doctrine of "Indianismo"), in the resentful and embittered aesthetic "left" and romantic "right" of the Weimar Republic, in India since the ascendancy of Gandhi, and in the emerging intellectual strata of the new countries of Africa, populistic tendencies have been massively at work.

In the newly sovereign countries of Asia and Africa the intellectuals have been educated either in foreign countries or in institutions within their own countries modeled after those at the center of the culture they have sought to emulate. In all these countries the intellectuals have developed anxiety about whether they have not allowed themselves to be corrupted by excessive permeation with the admired foreign culture. To identify themselves with "the people"—that is, to praise the culture of the ordinary man as richer, truer, wiser, and more relevant than the foreign culture in which they had themselves been educated—has been a way out of this distress. In most cases this development is a protest against the "official" culture, the culture of the higher civil servants and of the universities. As such, it has fused easily with the other traditions hostile to civil institutions and civil authority.

Order. Closely connected with the traditions discussed above and yet apparently a negation of them is the anti-intellectual tradition of order. Here, order is understood as a perfect integration of society under a powerful authority, in accordance with which each individual has a prefixed status and role. Best known in the West in the form of French positivism (as in the work of Saint-Simon and Comte), the anti-intellectual tradition has its roots in antiquity and in the belief that excessive intellectual analysis and discussion can disrupt the foundations of social order. Evidence of an ambivalence in the traditional antiauthoritarianism of intellectuals is afforded by Plato's attitude toward poets, the burning of the books by the repentant Confucian Li Ssu at the origin of the Ch'in dynasty, Hobbes's analysis of the role of intellectuals in bringing about the English civil war, Taine's interpretation of the significance of the *philosophes* in bringing on the French Revolution of 1789, and the ideas of Joseph de Maistre and of the French "right" since his time. It should be noted that this anti-intellectual tradition of order is also usually hostile to civil authority, which it regards as ineffectual wherever such authority permits some measure of intellectual freedom. It is not antagonistic toward all intellectuals but only toward those who are "critical" and whose criticism is an instigation to the disruption of "order."

Since these secondary traditions are all hostile to civil authority, they are not supported by the type of institutional system which is directed to the meeting of those "needs" (for intellectual–practical services) which authority regards as legitimate. The continuance of these secondary traditions rests in part, therefore, on their attractiveness to persons of strongly intellectual propensities. They also depend on dissensual institutions; for example, political and religious sects often develop their own sets of intellectual institutions—schools, publishing houses, bookshops, periodicals, and circles. These secondary traditions depend, too, on a continuing self-renewal at the peripheries of such central cultural institutions as universities, research institutions, and the more civil political parties. They are maintained there by dissidents from the prevailing outlook among the elders, as well as by the more sensitive, less routinizable sectors of the oncoming generation. Student "movements" are important sources of recruits.

However, the life of these secondary traditions depends, above all, on the literature which the great figures of these traditions have created. Much of this literature forms part of the intellectual tradition which the more highly organized intellectual institutions cultivate as part of their task of training recruits for intellectual and intellectual–practical actions. However, since the secondary traditions themselves are not cultivated by the organized intellectual institutions, the transmission of these traditions and their institutions of assessment tends to be fragmentary and discontinuous. The intellectual institutional system of the secondary traditions resembles the institutional system which provides those intellectual products for which there is no institutionalized "demand." This structural affinity is supported by the greater responsiveness to these secondary traditions among those who produce literary and artistic works. Bohemia is thus the common hearth of literary and artistic production and consumption and of the reception and cultivation of the secondary traditions.

Nonetheless, the intellectual stratum lives in society, even though professional necessities and tastes tend to segregate intellectuals in terms of places of work and centers of conviviality. Although the intellectual stratum in modern societies is mainly of middle-class origin and in earlier societies was largely of upper-class origin, it is not self-reproducing. Intellectuals grow up in families and in schools in which they come to share the wider and less intellectual culture of their society. Moreover, given the strong attraction which authority has for intellectuals, their awareness of an authority which rules their society gives them some sense of affinity with the rest of that society. Intellectuals are usually patriots, and the frequent "antipatriotism" of some sectors of the intellectual stratum is, in fact, merely an inverted manifestation of their patriotism. More than most of their fellow countrymen, they feel the falling away of their country from perfection.

The functions of intellectuals

The most obvious function of intellectual action is the production of intellectual works which are added to the tradition or stock of intellectual works —the "high culture"—available to their society. Intellectuals also carry on, elaborate, and modify the tradition of beliefs about various sectors of the universe; they transmit to the next generations of intellectuals those fundamental dispositions, tastes, and modes of apprehending reality which cannot be readily articulated and codified and which cannot be transmitted except by prolonged and intimate interaction.

Creating and diffusing high culture. The creation and development of this high culture is the primary function of the intellectuals whose productiveness stems from an inner intellectual propensity. Their propensities are directed toward intellectual tasks set largely by intellectual traditions but also by the conditions of their society. Primary intellectual production has its own autonomy: it works on what is offered by its traditions, seeking to improve, refine, correct, and transform these traditions in the form of new works. Where creativity and originality are emphatically acknowledged and prized and where innovation is admitted and accepted, this function is perceived as a primary obligation of intellectuals. Even in traditional societies, in which individual creativity has not been seen as having positive value, the labor of powerful minds and irrepressible individualities on what has been received from the past has modified that heritage and has adapted it to meet new tasks and to overcome hitherto unmastered, or perhaps even unnoticed, obstacles. In this process of elaboration, divergent potentialities of the system of cultural values have been made explicit, and conflicting positions have been established. Each generation of intellectuals performs this elaborating function for its own and the next succeeding generations.

Only a very small proportion of the works produced in a society within a given generation represents significantly novel and valuable additions to the cultural stock. Many are reproductive of earlier innovations, and many are done at a low level of proficiency. (The hierarchies of individual intellectuals and of intellectual institutions correspond to hierarchies of originality and individuality of intellectual works.) Most of the productive intellectuals of any generation are also reproductive, although in unequal degrees. The most original of them therefore perform a twofold function in the creation and extension of high culture. First and most important, they create new and valuable works as such; second, they guide, by providing models for emulation, the large substratum of reproductive intellectuals, who in turn diffuse, in modified form, the patterns of procedure and belief of the most creative workers in their respective fields.

The relationship between the productive and the reproductive is not, however, simply a matter of diffusion. In some fields the reproductive stratum often tends to be more attached to past models of creative intellectual works than to the newly created ones. This is particularly true where there is a highly institutionalized system of transmission of intellectual traditions, as a result of which many persons with relatively feeble intellectual propensities of their own acquire a quite considerable obsolescent intellectual culture. Even where there is not an active attack on creative innovations, the sheer persistence of this attachment to past patterns restricts the speed of diffusion of the new beliefs. In other fields, where training is less organized and the institutions which do the training are less authoritative in their assessments and their control over promotion (as in literature), innovations are likely to find a speedier reproduction among some intellectuals and a less enduring resistance among other intellectuals. In such fields, however, the dissensus between the devotees and the opponents of tradition is greater.

In fields of scientific research the unification of the intranational system leaves only the lower fringes of the reproductive stratum (e.g., school science) untouched by important innovations. In other fields that are less compellingly consensual in the assessment of accomplishments, more obdurate resistance and even aggressively dissensual counterattacks against creative innovations are almost endemic in the nature of the things in question.

Providing national and cross-national models. The primary intellectual function of the production of new additions to the high culture of a society is performed not only for other intellectuals of that society but for the intellectuals of other societies as well. Just as there is a roughly defined hierarchy of intellectuals for each category of intellectual action and to a lesser extent for much of the intellectual stratum as a whole, so there is a hierarchy, even more roughly delineated, among the intellectuals of different societies. When similar genres of intellectual action are performed in different societies, there is a tendency toward a universalization of standards of assessment of intellectual accomplishments. In the Middle Ages and in early modern times the Indian intellectuals performed this function for southeast Asia. The intellectuals of republican and imperial Rome looked up to, and learned from, Greek intellectuals. For a time Chinese intellectuals performed this function for Japan. In modern times the British intellectuals of Oxford, Cambridge, and the London School of Economics have provided the model for intellectuals of India and Africa. Nineteenth-century German academic intellectuals provided a world-wide model, just as in the nineteenth and twentieth centuries French artistic and literary intellectuals have provided models of development for aesthetically sensitive intellectuals all over the civilized world. In the eighteenth century the intellectuals of the French Enlightenment inspired their confreres in Spain, Italy, Prussia, and Russia. Positions in the hierarchy shift. Centers lose their pre-eminence; new centers emerge either to share pre-eminence with the older centers or to displace them.

The function of providing a model for primary intellectual production within and among societies implies the attribution of universal validity to the criterion of superior quality of accomplishment. The pattern of action of a certain group of intellectuals comes to be regarded as exemplary, because it is thought to correspond more closely to certain ideal requirements of truth, beauty, or virtue. Such standards are never the objects of complete consensus, least of all in the fields of expressive intellectual action. But they are often accepted over very extensive areas of the world at any given time; this is the situation of scientific knowledge in the world today.

Developing common cultures. The hierarchies of creative intellectuals, of metropolitan and provincial intellectuals, have a parallel in the hierarchy of high and common cultures. The term "common culture" refers to the moral unity of a society. Since most societies are too large, in terms of territory and population, to be united through kinship connection and firsthand experience, the development of a common culture ordinarily depends on reproductive intellectual institutions such as schools, churches, and newspapers. Through these intellectual institutions ordinary persons become aware of each other's existence as members of the same society. A sense of identity and of membership in a society is formed thereby, and content is given to the symbolism of the national society. Moreover, through these reproductive intellectual institutions children and adults enter into some degree of contact with the custodians and exponents of the beliefs espoused by the central institutional system. By means of preaching, teaching, and writing, reproductive intellectuals infuse into those sections of the population which are intellectual neither by propensity nor by role beliefs which they would otherwise lack. By the provision of such techniques as reading, writing, and calculation they enable the laity to enter into a wider universe. The creation of nations out of tribal, village, and regional cultures in early modern times in Europe and in contemporary Asia and Africa is the work of teachers, authors, agitators, and journalists, just as the formation of the American nation out of diverse ethnic groups is the achievement of teachers, clergymen, and journalists.

The establishment of relatively unitary societies in modern times has not been a product only of the transmission and reception of a minimal common culture; it has owed much to "practical" power-exercising actions. The legitimation of a reigning authority results, to some extent, from the effectiveness of the incumbent authority in maintaining order, in showing strength, and in dispensing a semblance of justice. But these practical activities, especially at the peaks of the hierarchies which performed them, have had intellectual components and have often been done by intellectuals, even by productive intellectuals (e.g., John Locke at the Board of Trade, Isaac Newton at the Mint). Thus, the apparently nonintellectual exercise of power has proceeded through institutions which were not infrequently manned by intellectuals. The legitimacy of authority is, moreover, a matter of beliefs; beliefs about authority, even in societies less educated than the advanced societies of the present day, are far from resting entirely on firsthand experience and observation of the efficacy of authority. Much of what is believed beyond firsthand experience is in the form of received traditions into which have entered and accumulated, alongside of other elements, the beliefs promulgated by productive intellectuals over extended periods in the past.

Influencing social change. By providing models and standards and through the presentation of symbols to be appreciated, productive and reproductive intellectuals elicit, guide, and form the expressive dispositions within a society. However, this is not to say that the expressive life of a society is under the exclusive dominion of its intellectuals. Indeed, the situation has never existed (and in fact could never exist) in which the expressive life of a society—its aesthetic tastes, its artistic creations, or the ultimately aesthetic grounds of its ethical judgments—fell entirely within the traditions espoused by the intellectuals of the society. Societies vary in the extent to which the expressive actions and orientations are consensual with what is taught and represented by the dominant "primary-productive" intellectuals. In modern societies there is certainly too much diversity in expressive intellectual practices and too much dissensus in beliefs about these practices among expressive intellectual producers for such a consensus of producers, reproducers, and recipients to exist. Nonetheless, despite these variations it is true that much of the expressive life of a society, even what is most vulgar and tasteless, echoes some of the expressive practices and beliefs of intellectuals.

Thus, the degree of intellectual consensus in a society can never be great, not only because of the dissensus among the primary producers but because of temporal stratification and other types of dissensus in the intellectual attachments of the reproductive intellectuals. The quite different social situations of the recipients of high culture, the extreme discrepancies in educational preparation and receptive capacity, class attachments and resentments, regional attachments and resistances, generational antagonisms, and the continuation of autonomous cultural traditions in the mass of the society all work against the possibility of a far-reaching intellectual consensus in society. Nevertheless, some consensus does exist, and some common cultures exist in countries which have been sovereign and have therefore had their own autonomous central institutional and cultural systems for a long time. In the creation of this common culture, an important part is played by the intellectual works of generation after generation of primary-productive intellectuals.

The process of elaborating and developing further the potentialities inherent in a system of beliefs entails some degree of rejecton of the inherited tradition. In all societies, even those in which the intellectual elite are notable for their conservatism, the diverse paths of creativity and the tradition of antitraditionality impel a partial rejection of the prevailing system of cultural values. The range of rejection of the inherited varies greatly; it can never be complete and all-embracing. Even where the rejecting intellectuals allege that they are "nihilistic" with respect to everything that is inherited, complete repudiation without physical self-annihilation is impossible. The act of rejection practically always is an act of observance and development of an alternative stream of tradition, sometimes one which has been buried for a long time. Without a genius and his works, acts of rejection among reproductive intellectuals cannot create a new tradition or revive a forgotten one. The power of recent and present creativity is too great to resist.

The inherent potentialities of any high intellectual tradition for divergent interpretations are potentialities of conflict within the intellectual stratum, both in the intellectual elite and at the lower levels of creativity and productivity. In the domains of scientific and scholarly research the modes of conflict, which in the course of time produce changes in the content and shape of consensus, are subjected to quite strict regulation. The criteria and the institutions of assessment of the contending alternatives are, on the whole, quite firmly established and clearly defined.

It is quite different in the fields of expressive intellectual action. In the middle ground, between scientific research and expressive activity, stands the mode of contention over contemporaneous, or contemporaneously relevant, social, political, and moral phenomena. Here criteria other than the intellectual enter. Attachments to particular patterns of distribution of wealth, income, or deference, to particular modes of organization of authority, and to particular incumbents or classes of incumbents of authoritative roles, play an important part in intellectual contention. These particular attachments are often generalized and subjected to intellectual discipline, but the particularistic elements remain. Through this fusion of particular attachments (and antagonisms) with intellectual traditions, some intellectuals are enabled to influence the movement of the social structure, changes in incumbents of authoritative roles, changes in allocations, etc.

Playing political roles. The affirmation or rejection of the legitimacy of authority is a major preoccupation of every form of intellectual life. It could not be otherwise, since intellectual life could not exist without the authority of tradition—an inherited corpus of works and standards for the production of works of high quality—or without creativity which challenges the authority of tradition. Authority, furthermore, engages the minds of intellectuals, especially those active in primary intellectual production. Involvement in primary intellectual production is a pursuit of the "essential," the "ultimately right," and the sacred, and political authority claims a similar involvement on behalf of its legitimacy. What is more, the political elite wants intellectuals. It needs their approbation and their services. However, it is less ready to share the highest authority with them and less eager to hear their criticism of how the nonintellectual ruler conducts himself in office. This is where the conflict centers. Despite the long-standing and recurrent mutual distrust between intellectuals (especially those who share the high and general intellectual culture) and politicians, numerous intellectuals, including some who have been among the greatest of primary producers, have affirmed, accepted, and served the ruling authorities.

Intellectuals attached to the high culture of their institutional systems have played a great historical role on the higher levels of state administration and the judiciary, especially in China, in British and independent India, in the Ottoman Empire, and in modern Europe. (In contrast, in private economic organizations the employment of intellectuals in administrative capacities has for a very long time been uncommon to the point of rarity; neither have intellectuals ever shown any inclination to become business enterprisers. It is only since the nineteenth century that business firms—first in Germany, then in America, and later in other industrialized countries—have taken to the large-scale employment of scientists in research departments and to a much smaller extent in executive capacities. However, the increased importance attributed to industrial research has changed the situation in industry quite markedly in the present century and especially since World War II.) Sovereigns have often considered a high standard of education, either humanistic or technical–legal, confirmed by diplomas and examinations, necessary for the satisfactory functioning of the state. Without the general acceptance of the appropriateness of appointing persons with high intellectual training and culture to administrative posts, the intellectual institutional system as we know it, in which the universities occupy a central place, would never have developed as it has.

Equal in antiquity to the role of the highly educated in state administration is the role of the intellectual as personal agent, counselor, tutor, or friend of the sovereign. Plato's experience in Syracuse, Aristotle's relations with Alexander III, Alcuin's with Charlemagne, Clarendon's with Charles I, Hobbes's with Charles II prior to the Restoration, Milton's with Cromwell, Lord Keynes with the Treasury during and after World War II, the "brain trust" under Franklin Roosevelt, and the circle around President Kennedy represent only a few of numerous instances throughout history in which intellectuals have been drawn into the entourage of rulers and have had their advice and aid sought and their approval valued. On the other hand, there have been many states and periods in which this has not been so. The court of Wilhelm II, for example, drew relatively little on the educated classes of the time; important events in Chinese history can be explained by the intellectuals' reactions to the rulers' refusals to draw them into the most intimate and influential circle of counselors. American history from the time of the Jacksonian revolution until the "New Liberalism" of Woodrow Wilson was characterized by the separation of intellectuals from the higher executive and the legislative branches of government.

Intellectuals as the heads of states and governments have been more characteristic of democratic than of monarchical regimes. Intellectuals have emerged occasionally in monarchies at the pinnacles of authority, through sheer accident or at least through no deliberate process of selection. Aśoka, Marcus Aurelius, and Ikhnaton are a few such men. In the liberal–democratic party politics of the nineteenth and twentieth centuries there have been numerous impressive instances of productive intellectuals who have been able, by their own efforts and a widespread appreciation for their gifts of civil politics, to play a notable role in the exercise of great political authority: e.g., Benjamin Disraeli, William Gladstone, François Guizot, Woodrow Wilson, Jawaharlal Nehru, Thomas Masaryk, Luigi Einaudi, Amintore Fanfani, Harold Wilson, and Ludwig Erhard. This has not been entirely accidental. For one thing, liberal and constitutional politics in great modern states and democratic and "progressive" nationalist movements in colonial territories have to a large extent been "intellectuals' politics"—that is, politics vaguely impelled by ideals precipitated into programs.

Indeed, in modern times, first in the West and then, in the nineteenth and twentieth centuries, at the peripheries of Western civilization and in the Orient, the major political vocation of the intellectuals has lain in the enunciation and pursuit of the ideal. Modern liberal and constitutional politics have largely been the creation of intellectuals with bourgeois affinities and sympathies who live in societies dominated by military and land-owning aristocracies. This effort has been one major form of the pursuit of the ideal.

Another form of the pursuit of the ideal has been the promulgation and inspiration of ideological politics, that is, revolutionary politics working outside the boundaries of constitutional traditions. Prior to the origins of modern ideological politics, which came into the open with the Reformation, conspiracies, putsches, and the subversion of existing regimes, although they were common and often involved intellectuals, did not manifest any particular affinity between intellectuals and ideological revolutionism. In modern times, however, with the emergence of ideologically dominated political activities as a constitutive part of public life, such an affinity has emerged and is constantly being reinforced by the secondary traditions of the culture of the intellectuals. Its bearers are young persons not yet assimilated into intellectual–practical occupations, bohemian free-lance intellectuals, the educated in underdeveloped countries (the economic and administrative systems of which were not capable of absorbing them), and, occasionally, already well established persons with unusually sensitive moral consciences.

By no means have all intellectuals been equally attracted by ideological politics. Moderation and devotion to the rules of civil politics, quiet and apolitical concentration on specialized intellectual tasks, cynical antipolitical passivity, and faithful acceptance of, and service to, the existing order are all to be found in substantial proportions among modern intellectuals, just as among intellectuals in antiquity. Nonetheless, the function of modern intellectuals in supplying the doctrines and some of the leaders of revolutionary ideological movements is to be considered one of their most important accomplishments.

EDWARD SHILS

[*See also* ACADEMIC FREEDOM; CENSORSHIP; CREATIVITY, *article on* SOCIAL ASPECTS; FINE ARTS; IDEOLOGY; KNOWLEDGE, SOCIOLOGY OF; LITERATURE; ORGANIZATIONS, *article on* ORGANIZATIONAL INTELLIGENCE; PROFESSIONS; RELIGIOUS SPECIALISTS; SCIENCE; UNIVERSITIES.]

BIBLIOGRAPHY

ARON, RAYMOND (1955) 1957 *The Opium of the Intellectuals.* Garden City, N.Y.: Doubleday. → First published in French. A paperback edition was published in 1962 by Norton.

BENDA, HARRY J. (1960) 1962 Non-Western Intelligentsias as Political Elites. Pages 235–251 in John H. Kautsky (editor), *Political Change in Underdeveloped Countries: Nationalism and Communism.* New York: Wiley.

BODIN, LOUIS (1962) 1964 *Les intellectuels.* 2d ed. Paris: Presses Universitaires de France.

COLEMAN, JAMES S. (editor) 1965 *Education and Political Development.* Princeton Univ. Press.

COSER, LEWIS A. 1965 *Men of Ideas: A Sociologist's View.* New York: Free Press.

CROZIER, MICHEL 1964 The Cultural Revolution: Notes on the Changes in the Intellectual Climate of France. *Dædalus* 93:514–542.

GEIGER, THEODOR (1944) 1949 *Aufgaben und Stellung der Intelligenz in der Gesellschaft.* Stuttgart (Germany): Enke. → First published in Swedish as *Intelligensen.*

HUSZAR, GEORGE B. (editor) 1960 *The Intellectuals: A Controversial Portrait.* Glencoe, Ill.: Free Press.

KAUTSKY, JOHN H. (editor) 1962 *Political Change in Underdeveloped Countries: Nationalism and Communism.* New York: Wiley.

LASCH, CHRISTOPHER 1965 *The New Radicalism in America, 1889–1963: The Intellectual as a Social Type.* New York: Knopf.

LIPSET, SEYMOUR M. 1960 *Political Man: The Social Bases of Politics.* Garden City, N.Y.: Doubleday. → A paperback edition was published in 1963. See especially pages 332–371 in the 1963 edition, "American Intellectuals: Their Politics and Status."

MANNHEIM, KARL (1929–1931) 1954 *Ideology and Utopia: An Introduction to the Sociology of Knowledge.* New York: Harcourt; London: Routledge. → A paperback edition was published in 1955 by Harcourt. Parts 2–4 are a translation of *Ideologie und Utopie* (1929); Part 5 is a translation of the article "Wissenssoziologie" (1931).

MANNHEIM, KARL (1935) 1940 *Man and Society in an Age of Reconstruction: Studies in Modern Social Structure.* New York: Harcourt. → First published as *Mensch und Gesellschaft im Zeitalter des Umbaus.*

MANNHEIM, KARL 1956 *Essays on the Sociology of Culture.* Oxford Univ. Press. → Published posthumously.

MICHELS, ROBERT (1911) 1959 *Political Parties: A Sociological Study of the Oligarchical Tendencies of Modern Democracy.* New York: Dover. → First published as *Zur Soziologie des Parteiwesens in der modernen Demokratie.* A paperback edition was published in 1962 by Collier.

MICHELS, ROBERT 1932 Intellectuals. Volume 8, pages 118–126 in *Encyclopaedia of the Social Sciences.* New York: Macmillan.

PIPES, RICHARD (editor) (1960) 1961 *The Russian Intelligentsia.* New York: Columbia Univ. Press. → First published as the Summer 1960 issue of *Dædalus.*

PYE, LUCIEN W. (editor) 1963 *Communications and Political Development.* Princeton Univ. Press.

SHILS, EDWARD 1955 The Intellectuals: 1. Great Britain. *Encounter* 4, no. 4:5–16.

SHILS, EDWARD 1958 Ideology and Civility: On the Politics of the Intellectual. *Sewanee Review* 66:450–480.

SHILS, EDWARD 1960 The Traditions of Intellectual Life: Their Conditions of Existence and Growth in Contemporary Societies. *International Journal of Comparative Sociology* 1:177–194.

SHILS, EDWARD 1961 *The Intellectual Between Tradition and Modernity: The Indian Situation.* Comparative Studies in Society and History, Supplement 1. The Hague: Mouton.

SHILS, EDWARD 1962 The Intellectuals in the Political Development of the New States. Pages 195–234 in John H. Kautsky (editor), *Political Change in Underdeveloped Countries: Nationalism and Communism.* New York: Wiley.

SOUVANI, N. V.; and DANDEKAR, KUMUDINI (editors) 1961 *Changing India: Essays in Honour of Professor D. G. Gadgil.* New York: Taplinger. → See especially the article by Edward Shils, "Metropolis and Province in the Intellectual Community."

WEBER, MAX (1921) 1958 *The Religion of India: The Sociology of Hinduism and Buddhism.* Translated and edited by Hans H. Gerth and Don Martindale. Glencoe, Ill.: Free Press. → First published as *Hinduismus und Buddhismus*, Volume 2 of *Gesammelte Aufsätze zur Religionssoziologie.*

WEBER, MAX (1922) 1951 *The Religion of China: Confucianism and Taoism.* Glencoe, Ill.: Free Press. → First published as "Konfuzianismus und Taoismus" in Volume 1 of Weber's *Gesammelte Aufsätze zur Religionssoziologie.*

WILENSKY, HAROLD L. 1956 *Intellectuals in Labor Unions: Organizational Pressures on Professional Roles.* Glencoe, Ill.: Free Press.

ZNANIECKI, FLORIAN 1940 *The Social Role of the Man of Knowledge.* New York: Columbia Univ. Press.

INTELLIGENCE, POLITICAL AND MILITARY

Political and military intelligence refers primarily to evaluated information about the capabilities and intentions of foreign governments, about foreign areas in which a government may maintain a strategic interest, or about international relations in general. Because information in some form is required at every level of rational decision making, there are endless categories of specialized, functional information, such as economic, scientific, or biographic intelligence. Information may range from low-level "combat" or "tactical" to high-level "strategic" or "national" intelligence.

Intelligence is often used as a synonym for espionage, which is but one of many methods of collecting intelligence data. Intelligence may also be confused with counterintelligence, a police and security function that is closely allied with and may be productive of intelligence information but is a separate function. Still further confusion results from the designation "intelligence operations," which refers to activities that constitute political intervention or subversion.

From the beginnings of national foreign policies, political and military intelligence has been indispensable to statesmen, diplomats, and soldiers. A body of evaluated information labeled strategic intelligence or national intelligence has come to be routinely required in the highest councils of modern governments in the process of setting national objectives, in policy making and planning, in choosing and applying policy instruments toward attaining objectives, and for evaluating results. With the increasing complexity of world politics and advancing technologies, intelligence organizations have expanded enormously in size and have become professionalized and increasingly concerned with every field of economic, political, and social inquiry.

Few topics, however, have to be discussed with such extraordinarily limited access to and comprehension of essential facts. In all periods of history, intelligence organization, process, and product have been guarded government secrets. Those legitimately possessing facts about intelligence are sworn to secrecy. Intelligence analysts and operators are routinely organized in small compartments. Only a very few leaders are ever afforded a broad perspective of the process and substance of intelligence work. Although some intelligence records are maintained, they are highly secret; other records are systematically destroyed. The United States Central Intelligence Agency, for example, neither confirms nor denies published reports, never explains its organization or identifies its personnel except at the highest echelons, and never publicly discusses its budget, methods of operation, or sources of information. Much that is public information is a result of intelligence failures, inadvertent disclosures, or speculation. While a growing volume of popular literature exists regarding various phases of intelligence work, particularly espionage, systematic studies of intelligence are comparatively meager, considering the importance of the intelligence function and the fact that tens of thousands of individuals—many of them social scientists—are engaged in it. More is known about the United States intelligence system than any other because of the difficulty of maintaining secrecy in the American milieu. Even so, much of this information cannot be documented by the usual scholarly standards.

History

The need for knowledge of the external environment for planning and decision has been recognized since the beginnings of explicit political systems; indeed, it has always been a condition of rational political survival. Decision makers of the dynastic empires of the ancient world as well as the various governmental forms of the Middle Ages maintained intelligence systems. The medieval church utilized a complex secret intelligence apparatus for five centuries. During the twelfth and thirteenth centuries the Mongols maintained an aggressive espionage system. But not until the advent of the great national states after the Treaty of Westphalia in 1648 did state intelligence bureaus begin to take modern form. During this period foreign ministers and cabinet secretaries began to devote major efforts to the acquisition by every feasible means of all knowledge of other states relevant to promoting national, particularly military, power. As Italian city-states and the larger country systems of the north began to maintain professional diplomats, create standing armies, and build colonial empires, rational foreign policies required a substantial body of political and military information.

With the French Revolution and Napoleonic wars came the period of explicitly national foreign policies, supported by citizen armies which went to war loyal to nationalistic objectives. The nature of war and military organization changed from limited class participation to involvement of the entire citizenry. Mass loyalty, morale, and degrees of identification with national policies and power became a direct object of concern to political and military leaders. Thus, the scope of the intelligence function broadened.

The creation of a systematically organized intelligence service along modern lines is widely credited to Frederick the Great. Under him, and later under Bismarck, the Prussians developed intelligence as an essential military staff function. By the late nineteenth century it had been adopted, after the Prussian model, by most other European nations. Balance-of-power politics, further advances in military technology, and the competitive war plans of the Continental powers required an increasing amount of the kind of information which sovereign nations were at greatest pains to conceal. Intelligence bureaus blossomed in Europe, and their heavy investment in espionage efforts provoked great counterintelligence activity. By the eve of World War I, Europe was covered by a complex network of espionage and counterespionage. Much of this was military rather than political intelligence activity. Most European nations developed a single military intelligence agency, which became the principal foreign intelligence arm. Even so, the available evidence suggests that leaders of the Great Powers entered the war with inefficient intelligence bureaus that supplied them with inadequate information. Not a single strategic action in the war was decisively influenced by any of the military espionage services (Rowan 1931, vol. 5, p. 595).

The political and military experiences of World War I and, more importantly, the advances in technology, particularly radio and aircraft—facilitating both information gathering and reporting—led to the growth and proliferation of intelligence agencies between the two world wars. Activity was further stimulated in the interwar years by the advent of dictatorships in Russia, Italy, Germany, and Japan, each with expansionist aims. These in turn produced defensive and counterintelligence organizations in the representative democracies.

World War II saw the creation of numerous intelligence services, military and political, and their expansion to unprecedented size and scope of operations. This was particularly so in the United States, which, in its previous isolation, had never developed large, permanent, professionalized intelligence services. With an advancing technology and particularly the advent of blitzkrieg tactics and strategic air warfare, intelligence agencies played a more crucial role than ever before. But generalizations are hazardous with regard to their over-all performance, so large was the size and so broad the scope of intelligence functions. Suffice it to say, there were great intelligence failures as well as successes on both sides in World War II. Significant techniques for intelligence analysis and prediction were developed, and social scientists in great numbers, particularly on the Allied side, were involved in these developments (Daugherty & Janowitz 1958; Jones 1947; Pettee 1946).

The major trends and patterns in world politics after World War II, particularly the rise of the United States and the Soviet Union to competitive positions of unprecedented power and great conflict and the onset of the cold war, stimulated an enormous expansion of the role and scope of intelligence activities. In the setting of nuclear power and intercontinental missiles, political and military intelligence became major government industries. Intelligence agencies came to be seen as a vital "first line of defense." Intelligence organizations grew to be larger than foreign offices, and intelligence professionals began to compete for power and influence with diplomats and soldiers.

Intelligence activities

These developments have created major problems of organization, doctrine, and interdepartmental definition of mission. Only in the United

States have such issues been extensively discussed in public, but any nation with a large-scale intelligence system is confronted with similar problems. The following treatment will emphasize the intelligence systems of the United States and the U.S.S.R., which are the world's two largest, and about which, in the context of cold war, the most authentic information has come to light. Most other nations have been more successful in maintaining the secrecy that traditionally covers intelligence activities.

In postwar planning for United States intelligence, some advocated a single centralized agency responsible for gathering and evaluating all foreign intelligence required by the government. Others, particularly the existing armed services intelligence units, feared that a central agency would fail to serve their specialized needs. In a compromise, the Central Intelligence Agency (CIA) was created by the National Security Act of 1947 (61 Stat. 495) to preside over a confederated "intelligence community" of various functional units and to perform those functions best done centrally, including foreign espionage and clandestine political action. The director of central intelligence is both head of CIA and the principal intelligence adviser to the president and the National Security Council, which provides the government's intelligence operating directives. The "community" is composed of intelligence units in the Department of Defense, which operates the centralized Defense Intelligence Agency (DIA) serving the secretary of defense and joint chiefs of staff, and the National Security Agency (NSA), charged with code making and breaking and overseas electronic surveillance and communications intelligence; separate intelligence units in the Army, Navy, and Air Force; the Bureau of Intelligence and Research in the Department of State; an intelligence section of the Atomic Energy Commission; and the Federal Bureau of Investigation, which has no overseas intelligence role but, in its domestic counterintelligence functions, cooperates with the intelligence community. The United States Intelligence Board, with representatives of each of these units, excepting the separate armed services, and with the CIA director as chairman, serves as a board of directors for the community and gives final approval to "national intelligence estimates" submitted to the National Security Council, over which the president of the United States presides (Ransom 1958, chapters 3 and 6).

The Soviet Union maintains a central intelligence organization in many ways resembling that of the United States but distinctly different in important respects. The similarity is that major intelligence functions are unified under the leadership of the Komitet Gosudarstvennoi Bezopastnosti (KGB), the State Security Committee. Large-scale military intelligence operations are also performed within the Defense Ministry's main Intelligence Directorate, which has a foreign intelligence unit commonly known as Glavnoe Razvedyvatel'noe Upravlenie (GRU).

The major difference between the Russian and American systems is that KGB combines positive foreign intelligence with domestic counterintelligence and internal security functions. The precise relationship between KGB and GRU has not been made clear, but they are potential competitors for influence and power, and the chief of KGB patently outranks the head of GRU, which is but a section of the military general staff. The two agencies were combined in 1947 under single leadership for a brief period and again separated. KGB's overseas operations emphasize political operations, while GRU concentrates on more technical military intelligence.

Unlike the United States and the Soviet Union, Great Britain has no central intelligence agency, nor is there very much detailed authenticatable information about the British intelligence services. Britain maintains various functional intelligence units, the most important of which are three: (1) The Secret Intelligence Service, in popular usage termed the "British Secret Service" or "MI-6." The latter label derives from its origins as the espionage section of military intelligence in World War I, but today it is a civilian agency under general Foreign Office and Cabinet policy controls. The Government barely acknowledges the existence of this service, its director's name (the anonymous "C" in government usage) is never published, and no details of its organization, personnel, or activities are intentionally revealed, even to Parliament. The Secret Service is the government's principal arm for secret foreign operations, including espionage and covert political intervention. (2) The Security Service, which is commonly referred to as "MI-5" but which is today also a civilian force of largely secret counterintelligence agents, concerned primarily with domestic internal security. Its director-general is also an anonymous figure who reports to the prime minister through the Home Secretary, with additional supervision provided by the permanent head of the British Civil Service. (3) A Defence Intelligence Staff is located in the Ministry of Defence, where formerly separate Army, Navy, and Air Force intelligence units have been increasingly centralized in recent years. In 1965 separate service intelligence directors were eliminated and replaced by an integrated, all-service military intelligence staff within the Defence Ministry.

The British intelligence system is coordinated and supervised in the upper echelons of government by a Defence subcommittee of the Cabinet. Here are represented the major functional subdivisions of the intelligence community. Chairmanship is normally held by a Foreign Office representative. Ultimate responsibility for the system is the prime minister's.

Even less precise information is available on the political and military intelligence organizations of other major nations, such as France, Italy, China, Japan, and Canada. Each is known to have its functional intelligence organizations at various levels, but none operates a single central intelligence agency.

The intelligence process. The intelligence process is traditionally described as various procedural "steps" in a cycle, outlined here in simplified form. First comes collection, the procuring of all data believed to be pertinent to requirements previously set. These are normally termed "raw" intelligence. Second is evaluation and production, sorting and assessing the reliability of the information, drawing inferences from its analysis, and the interpretation of such inferences with reference to questions posed by planners, policy makers, and operators. Finally comes the communication of findings in the most suitable form to appropriate consumers.

Requirements are set on the basis of various functional categories, which Kent has described as "basic descriptive," "current reportorial," and "speculative–evaluative" (Kent 1949, pp. 11–65). The basic descriptive ("storage") requirement is that of maintaining an up-to-date encyclopedic survey of all the world's geographic and political areas or simply having available any fact which a decision maker may call for at some future date, such as "What is the adequacy of the water supply at Addis Ababa?" The current reportorial mission is that of supplying the policy maker or operator with the best possible daily digest of information pertinent to his role. The speculative–evaluative assignment is the most difficult of all tasks, since it involves forecasting the future, providing forewarning of events, and predicting the intentions of foreign decision makers.

While it is possible to identify "steps" in the process and to categorize requirements, the process in reality is immensely complex and highly interrelated because of the scale and scope of contemporary intelligence requirements and activities. The consequent problem can be illustrated by a military example.

At the lowest level of military intelligence there is the manageable job of setting requirements, analyzing results, and taking decisions while observing reactions to them. When a low-level military commander directs a soldier to observe and report to him directly certain types of information, the commander knows the capability of his collector and can set requirements accordingly. The commander in this case is also the interpreter of the information supplied and the decision maker. But upon ascending to higher levels, to battalion, division, army, and finally to the highest general staff councils or responsible political leadership, major problems result from the hierarchical distance of collector, analyst, and decision maker. At the highest level of the intelligence organization the sources of information are far more varied and inclusive than at the lowest level. Here more can be known of foreign capabilities and intentions. Yet at these upper levels a division of labor among evaluators, analysts, interpreters, and communicators is required, producing formidable problems of communication among specialists and ultimately between specialists and decision makers.

Sources of intelligence. Although sources of modern intelligence are boundless, there are two standard categories: overt and covert.

The overt, nonsecret sources are those theoretically available to any scholar. By far the greatest amount of effort and allocation of resources go toward the undramatic, painstaking search for relevant data from open sources, and the problem ultimately becomes one of efficient management of a mountainous mass of data. This has called for improved systems and machinery for documentation, indexing, and retrieval of essential information. Among the features of modern systems are specialized microphotography, facsimile-printing machines, punch cards, and translation computers capable, for example, of rendering Russian texts into rough English at 30,000 words per hour. As a result, the physical scientist and technician have come to the fore in recent years to challenge the once dominant role of the social scientist as intelligence collector and analyst.

While the classical spy in his covert activity normally contributes but a tiny percentage of the massive amount of information gathered, great advantage has been taken of advancing technology in seeking information which sovereign governments try to conceal. Modern espionage methods have included high-altitude aerial photography, the use of infrared sensing devices to penetrate camouflage, electronic recording devices and radar, and many new techniques for automated espionage in the space age. Such techniques become identifiable as espionage when they violate sovereign territorial integrity.

Wartime espionage has been seen in international law to be but one of several forms of belligerency, practiced outside of any obligation of a belligerent to respect the territory or government of an enemy nation. Espionage in peacetime is, however, without status in an international law that imposes a duty upon states to respect the territorial integrity of other states. Each state has the right to define espionage according to its lights (Stanger 1962). The problem of cold-war espionage has not been resolved by international lawyers, who must develop new concepts for an age in which technology challenges traditional concepts of sovereignty.

The final step in the intelligence process is dissemination. A continuing problem exists as to who is to be privy to the various types of intelligence reports. Levels of privilege exist. Too narrow a circle of dissemination can be self-defeating. Prior to the 1941 Japanese surprise attack on Pearl Harbor, American officers, attempting to keep from the Japanese the information that the United States had broken their secret code, were equally successful in withholding crucial information from their own decision makers (Wohlstetter 1962, p. 394 and *passim*). The costs of too much secrecy in disseminating intelligence information may be greater than the risks of fuller distribution.

Political problems

Principal doctrinal issues concern the role of the intelligence professional and intelligence information in policy making and the closely related issue of proper organization. A broader issue is that of responsible political control of a secret intelligence system. Briefly stated, prevailing United States doctrines are based upon the premises that if a policy maker has all the facts the correct decision is likely to follow, that intelligence and policy functions are best organized in separate compartments, and that a high degree of secrecy is required for all intelligence activities. Major observers on these issues include George S. Pettee, Sherman Kent, Willmoore Kendall, Roger Hilsman, and Allen Dulles.

Pettee saw intelligence as a specialized, large-scale task of analysis, essentially distinct from policy making. He saw, however, the need to keep policy makers and intelligence analysts in continuous liaison for mutual guidance. He favored decentralizing intelligence functions, with each government department serving its own informational needs but with a central agency supplying strategic intelligence for top decision makers (Pettee 1946, *passim*).

Kent saw two basic categories of foreign policy. For positive policy, decision makers need information on the nature of a foreign nation's society, its ideology, power, and vulnerabilities, and its probable reaction to various contingencies. For defensive policy, information is needed on the capabilities and intentions of other nations. For either, a nation needs a body of information which cannot be adequately developed by the same individuals who plan or decide policy. Kent's main point is that intelligence is a staff or service function and that analysts ought not to be involved directly in setting national objectives, determining plans and policy, or conducting operations (1949, pp. 180–206).

Kendall disagreed with prevailing doctrine, characterized by a wartime conception, a compulsive concern with prediction, and an overly bureaucratic definition of the intelligence role, which had intelligence analysts communicating with other bureaucrats and not sufficiently with responsible decision makers (1949, pp. 547–552). He criticized intelligence analysts for their "crassly empirical" conception of social science research and for assigning too little weight to theory, to analysis of basic policy objectives and alternatives, and to contingent predictions.

After a survey of producers and consumers of strategic intelligence in Washington, D.C., Hilsman (1956, pp. 37–122) reported a common acceptance of a "report the facts only" doctrine among policy makers and operators, intelligence administrators, and intelligence analysts. Policy making and intelligence production were seen to call for sharply separate skills, with the proper role of the intelligence officer that of inducing facts without bias in a separate organizational compartment. Hilsman saw in this an unwise subordination of intelligence to policy, with the intelligence system producing vast amounts of information of little relevance to the real problems. Other consequences are the inability of intelligence personnel to comprehend the conceptual frameworks of policy makers, failure to explore adequately in advance the possible results of alternative policies, and suppression of or inattention to information that challenges or conflicts with an existing policy framework.

More recently there has been little systematic, openly available academic writing on intelligence doctrine. Ransom, although emphasizing organization, questioned the adequacy of a narrowly empirical intelligence doctrine (1958, pp. 210–215). Wasserman, analyzing the failures of intelligence prediction, suggested that intelligence failures may be avoided by proper interaction between policy and intelligence functions. He attributed major failures in intelligence predictions to inadequate understanding of the conceptual frameworks of foreign states (1960, pp. 166–169).

Dulles expressed an early view that intelligence and policy functions should be sharply separated (1947, pp. 525–528). Writing in 1963, Dulles again stressed the forewarning and current reportorial functions of intelligence. His rationale for the existence of a separate, central agency was that information ought to be collected, processed, and interpreted by an agency "which has no responsibility for policy" (1963, p. 51).

The issue of control of secret agencies confronts both constitutional democracies and dictatorships. A secret agency of any government, claiming to possess secret knowledge and skilled in the techniques of acquiring, communicating, and using information secretly, is a source of potential power. Secret knowledge is secret power. A democratic society is confronted with the problem that some intelligence activities require maximum secrecy and that its missions may be spoiled by publicity, whereas democratic government requires publicity. Totalitarian regimes, with ability to control the formal media of communications and to suppress opposition groups and with a highly centralized hierarchy of authority, have fewer problems of disclosure and control than do democracies. But dictatorships have their problems. Not only may disclosures come from defection of loyalty to the regime, but interpretation of information is in continual danger of distortion by ideological dogma. From earliest times the intelligence apparatus has sometimes served as a vehicle for internal political conspiracy. Power that is invisible is a potential threat to constituted authority, whatever the form of government (Ransom 1963, chapter 7).

In establishing the United States Central Intelligence Agency in 1947, Congress delegated the responsibility for secrecy to a director of central intelligence and stipulated that the agency's budget, plans, and programs should not be subjected to the normal Congressional reviews. Congress has established special appropriations and armed services subcommittees in the Senate and House of Representatives for periodic surveillance of central intelligence, but these committees have functioned sporadically. In addition, a presidentially appointed Board of Consultants on Foreign Intelligence Activities has been in existence since 1956, composed of private citizens with distinguished public service who conduct periodic inspections of intelligence activities.

To meet the problem of surveillance and invisible power, two basic reforms in U.S. intelligence organization have been proposed. One is the creation of a joint Congressional committee on central intelligence, equipped with a permanent professional staff and charged with maintaining routine legislative surveillance over intelligence activities. Such a proposal reached a vote in the Senate in 1956 but was defeated 59 to 27; it has remained routinely before Congress.

The other proposed reform involves a reorganization of the intelligence system and reassignment of its multiple functions. Such reform is based upon the argument that it is unwise to combine under one roof the functions of intelligence collection, its analysis and interpretation, and the conduct of clandestine political action in foreign areas.

Research needs

Current and potential research activities are inhibited and hampered by secrecy. Social scientists have written in considerable volume on the role of intelligence in psychological warfare activities during World War II (Daugherty & Janowitz 1958, chapter 7). Contemporary intelligence is too crucial a variable in foreign-policy decision making to permit it to remain relatively unexplored by social scientists. Studies falling into three categories may prove fruitful. Some examples follow.

First, further research is needed on information as a variable in the foreign-policy decision process; on the international law of espionage and other secret intelligence activities, including the impact of man's exploration of space on the traditional legal status of espionage; conceptual studies of the role and control of secret intelligence activities in a disarmed or disarming world; philosophical inquiries into moral problems in the use of secret operations as instruments of policy; and studies dealing more generally with the problem of secrecy in various governmental forms, particularly democratic societies.

Second, historical studies are needed on the organization and role of political and military intelligence from earliest times; case studies that attempt to identify the function of intelligence information, its perception and use in historically significant political decisions of the past; and comparative studies of the evolution of intelligence services and their relationship to national political development.

Finally, useful technical studies could deal with

automation in the collection, processing, and communication of information, including information storage and retrieval systems and machine translation of documents; with information and its communication in military and diplomatic command and control; and with man's capability in space as it pertains to intelligence collection and communication.

The relationship of knowledge and action is of fundamental importance to the understanding of human behavior. Thus the institutions, doctrines, and practices by which man tries to integrate external information with foreign-policy action ought, in spite of formidable barriers to the collection of data, to provoke the continuing interest of social scientists.

HARRY HOWE RANSOM

[*See also* DIPLOMACY; FOREIGN POLICY; ORGANIZATIONS, *article on* ORGANIZATIONAL INTELLIGENCE. *Guides to other relevant material may be found under* INTERNATIONAL RELATIONS; MILITARY; WAR.]

BIBLIOGRAPHY

BLACKSTOCK, PAUL W. 1964 *The Strategy of Subversion.* Chicago: Quadrangle Books. → A scholarly, descriptive analysis of the interrelationship of intelligence and political warfare.

DALLIN, DAVID J. 1955 *Soviet Espionage.* New Haven: Yale Univ. Press. → The most scholarly of many books on Soviet espionage.

DAUGHERTY, WILLIAM E.; and JANOWITZ, MORRIS (compilers) 1958 *A Psychological Warfare Casebook.* Baltimore: Johns Hopkins Press. → Chapter 7 contains selections by social scientists on the role of intelligence in psychological warfare, with principal reference to World War II.

DULLES, ALLEN W. 1947 Memorandum Respecting . . . Central Intelligence Agency . . . April 25, 1947. Part 1, pages 525–528 in U.S. Congress, Senate, Committee on Armed Services, *National Defense Establishment: . . . Hearings Before the Committee. . . .* Washington: Government Printing Office. → Reprinted in Ransom 1958, pages 217–224.

DULLES, ALLEN W. 1963 *The Craft of Intelligence.* New York: Harper. → A general survey of modern intelligence, counterintelligence, and political warfare, with emphasis on the U.S. Central Intelligence Agency, of which Allen Dulles was director, 1953–1962.

HILSMAN, ROGER 1956 *Strategic Intelligence and National Decisions.* Glencoe Ill.: Free Press. → An analysis and critical survey of intelligence doctrines in the United States, based upon interviews with officials.

JONES, R. V. 1947 Scientific Intelligence. *Journal of the Royal United Service Institution* 92:352–369. → An incisive account of the work of physical scientists in World War II intelligence.

KENDALL, WILLMOORE 1949 The Function of Intelligence. *World Politics* 1:542–552. → A critical review of Kent 1949.

KENT, SHERMAN 1949 *Strategic Intelligence for American World Policy.* Princeton Univ. Press. → An influential treatise on the role and functions of the American intelligence services.

KNORR, KLAUS 1964*a* *Foreign Intelligence and the Social Sciences.* Center of International Studies, Research Monograph No. 17. Princeton Univ. Press.

KNORR, KLAUS 1964*b* Failures in National Intelligence Estimates: The Case of the Cuban Missiles. *World Politics* 16:455–467.

MILLIKAN, MAX F. 1959 Inquiry and Policy: The Relation of Knowledge to Action. Pages 158–180 in Daniel Lerner (editor), *The Human Meaning of the Social Sciences.* New York: Meridian.

PETTEE, GEORGE S. 1946 *The Future of American Secret Intelligence.* Washington: Infantry Journal. → A pioneering book on modern intelligence based on the lessons of World War II.

RANSOM, HARRY HOWE 1958 *Central Intelligence and National Security.* Cambridge, Mass.: Harvard Univ. Press. → A detailed study of the organization of the intelligence community of the United States; contains a bibliography.

RANSOM, HARRY HOWE 1963 *Can American Democracy Survive Cold War?* Garden City, N.Y.: Doubleday. → Intelligence failures in the Korean conflict and the problems of control of secret intelligence in the American democratic framework are dealt with in Chapters 6 and 7.

ROWAN, RICHARD W. 1931 Espionage. Volume 5, pages 594–596 in *Encyclopaedia of the Social Sciences.* New York: Macmillan. → A concise history by a leading authority.

ROWAN, RICHARD W. 1937 *The Story of Secret Service.* Garden City, N.Y.: Doubleday. → The best general survey of espionage in all major periods of world history to the mid-1930s.

STANGER, ROLAND J. (editor) 1962 *Essays on Espionage and International Law.* Columbus: Ohio State Univ. Press. → Contains commentaries by Quincy Wright, Julius Stone, Richard A. Falk, and Roland J. Stanger.

WASSERMAN, BENNO 1960 The Failure of Intelligence Prediction. *Political Studies* 8:156–169. → A conceptual analysis of the deficiencies in modern intelligence doctrines.

WOHLSTETTER, ROBERTA 1962 *Pearl Harbor: Warning and Decision.* Stanford Univ. Press. → A detailed and authoritative analysis of the reasons for the surprise attack on Pearl Harbor on December 7, 1941.

INTELLIGENCE AND INTELLIGENCE TESTING

The term "intelligence," like much of the vocabulary of psychology, is drawn from the vocabulary of everyday speech. In a general way, everyone knows what intelligence or intelligent behavior is. We think of behavior as intelligent to the extent that it is efficient and adaptive in handling a situation that the individual faces and to the extent that it meets the demands of the situation, in its novelty, complexity, and abstractness. But psychologists have had little success in reaching a definition in verbal terms that is much more precise and satisfactory than the common-sense understanding of the term held by the layman. Different writers have emphasized different aspects of intelligent behavior—one has emphasized its dependence on ability to learn, another its close relationship to abstract thinking, another its dependence on judgment and reasoning, and yet another its concern with perception and formulation of relationships ("Intelligence . . ." 1921). These are in large part supplementary rather than contradictory emphases, each sensibly pointing to a different aspect of intelligent behavior. But the attempt to formulate *the* definition of intelligence has not carried us very far beyond our general lay understanding of the concept.

In light of the difficulties inherent in attempting a precise verbal formulation, it is not surprising that much of the energy of psychologists has been expended in the development of operations for measuring intellectual ability or abilities and in the attempt to clarify the concept inductively from a study of the data resulting from the application of these measurement operations. Test tasks have been developed based upon common-sense notions of the types of performances that call for intelligent behavior. These have included apprehension of relationships among words, numbers, and spatial patterns, reasoning tasks, span of immediate memory, general information about one's environment, and judgment as to the appropriate action in problematic situations. Various assortments of these tests have been administered to groups of subjects, and from the pattern of relationships among them, the investigators have attempted to infer the underlying structure and nature of intellect. The statistical techniques used have mainly been those of correlational analysis and factor analysis. Correlational analysis traditionally means the examination of partial and multiple correlation coefficients. Factor analysis examines the matrix of correlations among a set of tests with the objective of determining a simpler set of primary variables that could account parsimoniously for the given correlation matrix. [*See* FACTOR ANALYSIS; MULTIVARIATE ANALYSIS, *articles on* CORRELATION.]

Early research was interpreted by Charles Spearman (1927) as indicating that the communality, or common variance, among tests involving a wide variety of cognitive performances could be accounted for by one single and underlying general factor (g) running through all the tests, supplemented by a different specific (s) factor for each test. Intelligence was equated with this general factor that accounted for the correlations among the several tests. The general factor was spoken of by Spearman at times as a kind of general "mental energy," the specific factors representing the different "engines" through which this energy expressed itself. Spearman also felt that the common theme represented by g could be described as the ability to educe relationships [*see* SPEARMAN].

As additional evidence accumulated, it became apparent that Spearman's original formulation was an oversimplification and that it was necessary to postulate additional factors. Typically, these are "group factors," involving some but not all of the tests. Some workers in the field of intelligence testing (e.g., Thurstone 1938; Guilford 1959) have attached primary importance to an array of group factors dealing with more limited aspects of cognitive functioning—factors of verbal ability, numerical ability, spatial visualizing, reasoning, etc.—and they have minimized and even undertaken to dispense with the notion of a g or general intellective factor. However, the fact remains that the correlations among different types of cognitive tests are predominantly positive. To represent this fact, most formulations based entirely upon group factors have had to recognize that these factors were themselves not independent but related; thus a general factor was reintroduced in the form of a "second-order factor" expressing the relationship between the group factors themselves. It is this nucleus of relationship between a wide variety of tasks that provides the psychometric basis for a concept of "general intelligence" and the justification for using a single score to express individual differences along such a dimension [*see* THURSTONE].

Major types of tests

The Binet tests. Stimulated by a concern for pupils who seemed unable to progress in school and responding to the request of the French Minister of Public Instruction, Binet, with the assistance of Simon, prepared a series of tasks in 1905 to be used for the appraisal of the intellectual abilities of pupils. The original series of tasks was revised, expanded, and organized by age levels in 1908, and a further revision appeared in 1911. Binet's work provided the basis for a number of modified versions in other languages and countries, perhaps the best known and most widely used of which has been the Stanford–Binet Intelligence Scale developed at Stanford University by Lewis M. Terman. An original edition was published by Terman in 1916 (Terman 1916), and revisions appeared in 1937 (Terman & Merrill 1937) and 1960 (Terman & Merrill 1960) [*see* BINET; TERMAN].

The Stanford–Binet is an individual intelligence test administered to one examinee at a time by a trained examiner in a face-to-face interview situation. The test is organized by age levels, the most recent editions having items extending from those for age two to those suitable for superior adults. The six subtests for a given age level present varied types of tasks, but in general the tasks are characterized as being quite verbal and quite abstract.

The IQ concept. Test performance on the Binet is expressed in terms of an age scale, a basal age being established at the age level at which the examinee passes all tests; additional months of credit are given for tests passed above the basal level. The resulting "mental age" serves as a unit in terms of which the level of the individual's performance is expressed. However, it soon became apparent that, in addition to level of performance, it would be desirable to have an index that would relate that level to the performance typical of the individual's age group. For this purpose the intelligence quotient, or IQ, first suggested by Wilhelm Stern, was universally adopted. The IQ may be expressed as

$$100\left(\frac{\text{Mental Age (MA)}}{\text{Chronological Age (CA)}}\right).$$

The IQ had certain properties which made it very appealing as an index of relative performance on a mental test and which thus fixed it firmly in the vocabulary of both the psychological profession and the general public:

(1) By definition and by the process of test development, the average IQ is substantially the same at all age levels, having a value of approximately 100.

(2) The variability of IQ's around this average also is about the same at all age levels (standard deviation of about 16 for recent revisions of the Stanford–Binet).

(3) As a result of (1) and (2) and of the fairly high consistency in an individual's performance from year to year, IQ's of most individuals of school age or above show rather small (and unsystematic) shifts from one testing to another a year or even several years later.

The relative stability of IQ values and the apparently random nature of many of the shifts have given rise in some quarters to the practice of speaking and thinking about the IQ as if it were an individual constant, determined unequivocally by the individual's genetic constitution. This is untrue. Any test performance, as will be elaborated more fully later, is a current achievement resulting from the interaction of genetic constitution with the whole social history of the individual.

In popular speech, the term "IQ test" has become a substitute for "intelligence test," and what was originally merely the unit of measure in which relative performance was expressed has come to have a type of substantive existence. This development appears unfortunate, because the mensurational soundness of the original IQ ratio, 100(MA/CA), can be questioned. In particular, the variability of the MA/CA ratio has been found to differ significantly from one age to another, so that the same IQ does not have truly comparable meaning at different ages (Pinneau 1961). Furthermore, the basic age unit becomes essentially meaningless after adolescence, and it has been necessary to develop completely artificial age levels for items and to use an arbitrary chronological age base for computing the ratio after the age of about 13 or 14. Test makers have become increasingly conscious of these problems, and consequently, for most recently developed tests results are expressed as a percentile rank in a group or as a standard score; even when the scores have numerical values similar to IQ's (i.e., mean of 100 and standard deviation of 15 or 16), they are not based upon age as a unit of measure.

The Wechsler tests. A second series of tests very widely used for individual administration in the United States is that prepared by David Wechsler. At first designed (Wechsler 1939) to provide tests with content appropriate for adults rather than children—the original clientele for the Binet tests—the Wechsler series has now been developed to include tests for children of school age. The Wechsler Adult Intelligence Scale (Wechsler 1955) and the Wechsler Intelligence Scale for Children (Wechsler 1949) differ from tests in the Binet tradition in several respects. The total test is made up of distinct subtests, each administered as a unit. In addition to a total test IQ, two separate subtotal IQ's are reported—one for the verbal subtests and one for the performance subtests. The results are expressed as standard scores without using age as a frame of reference.

Group tests. The Binet and Wechsler tests were designed to be administered to one examinee at a time in a face-to-face situation by an examiner trained in the techniques of presenting the tasks and evaluating the examinee's responses. Individually administered tests are widely used in clinical work, for example, with pupils who are experiencing special difficulties in school, delinquents appearing in court, emotionally disturbed clients coming for counseling services, or institutionalized psychotics. For routine use in education, in military personnel selection, and in industry, group tests of intellectual ability have found a larger role. Group tests had their first large-scale use in the United States at the time of World War I (Yerkes 1921), when they were used to help in the screening and classification of military personnel. Since then, many series of group tests have been produced for use in schools, in industry, and in the military establishment. It is estimated that millions of these tests are administered annually (Hawes 1964, pp. 53–55), with the greatest concentration of testing being in the United States. [*See* YERKES.]

Group tests of mental ability present, in varying combinations, tasks involving word meanings, verbal relationships, arithmetical reasoning, form classification, spatial relationships, and other abstract symbolic material. They differ from measures of school achievement in being somewhat less directly related to school instruction. However, in many cases the resemblance in content between tests designed to function as intelligence or scholastic aptitude tests and those designed to serve as achievement measures is marked. The statistical overlap between the two categories of tests, especially when the aptitude test is based primarily upon verbal and numerical symbolism, is also substantial. Correlations between the two categories of tests run in the .70s and .80s, and Kelley's early estimate (1927, chapter 8) that fully 90 per cent of the non-chance variance of each category of test is shared by the other seems as sound now as when it was originally made [*see* APTITUDE TESTING].

Nonverbal and culture-free tests. Individual tests of the Binet type, as well as the bulk of group tests, present tasks that depend heavily upon the use of words and upon grasping relationships among words. Because these tests are obviously inappropriate for those who do not speak the language in which the test is written, because they appear quite closely tied to school achievement, and because they would appear to penalize those whose intellectual talents are most developed in some medium other than the verbal, a number of tests have been developed that do not use verbal symbolism. These tests tend to make use of concrete materials (i.e., blocks, form-boards, paper cutouts) or of pictures and geometric diagrams and tend to call for analysis and discrimination of relationships between these forms or objects. The mental functions measured by the nonverbal tests are somewhat different from those measured by the verbal tests, as shown by the patterning of subtest correlations. The nonverbal tests are somewhat less accurate predictors of academic performance and consequently tend to be used less in educational situations.

One problem that has been of continuing concern to research workers in the field of intelligence measurement is the development of tests that may appropriately be used with individuals of different social classes within a given society and that may appropriately be used cross-culturally in a number of different societies. Since practically all tests have been prepared by individuals who are members of the middle-class European–American culture, there is a feeling that the test content, and even perhaps the intellectual processes called for, may be biased in favor of the cultural content and values of such a group.

A number of efforts have been made to prepare tests, typically nonverbal, that are based upon content that is "culture-free" or at least "culture-fair." Perhaps the most widely used of these tests is the Progressive Matrices test prepared by Raven (1958). The content of the test's items contains material that is nonlinguistic and nonrepresentational; in this sense it does not depend upon the culture of any particular group. However, one can hardly contend that the materials are entirely culture-free. The very use of graphic representation, the orientation toward problem-solving in this type of puzzle situation, and the habits of abstraction and classification that are called for with these materials—any or all of these factors may be foreign to certain cultures. (It may be remarked in passing that many nonverbal tasks are most readily solved by verbalizing the relationships—at least for word-minded individuals.) The Progressive Matrices test has been widely used in different countries and cultures. However, those who have tried to use it with primitive groups have had serious questions as to its appropriateness for them.

There have also been attempts to develop tests that are "fair" to different classes in American society. Reacting critically to the content of available intelligence tests, Davis and Eells (1952–1953) prepared the Davis–Eells Games, a test that uses only oral language and presents problem situations designed to be familiar to the lower-class child. The test has been quite extensively studied in the United States since it appeared in 1951. Unfortunately, although the test is somewhat less academically oriented than conventional group intelligence tests and as a result shows lower correlation with school success, it continues to show about the same relationship to socioeconomic indices as do the more conventional tests. There is little indication that underprivileged groups perform better on this test, or on any of the other nonverbal tests that have been developed so far, than they do on the conventional verbal and school-related measures. To the extent that poor test performance is a function of cultural deprivation, this effect appears to be far-reaching and to include almost all test-taking performances rather than merely verbal or school-oriented ones.

Tests for infants and preschoolers. Initially, tests of intellectual ability were developed for school-age children. In the army testing program and, subsequently, in the Wechsler Adult Intelligence Scale, these were extended upward for adults. There have also been efforts to extend objective testing procedures downward to permit the appraisal of intelligence in preschool children and even infants. With infants a "test" in the conventional sense is obviously impossible, but observation of the infant's responses to a standard set of stimuli can be made. For example, one can observe whether the infant follows with his eyes a point of light that is moved back and forth transversely or whether he grasps a pellet that is placed upon the table before him and by what type of opposition of thumb and fingers or palm and fingers he does this. Data gathered by Gesell (see Yale University 1940) and others indicate that certain patterns of behavior typically appear at certain ages, to be replaced by more mature patterns at later ages. Status with respect to this developmental sequence has been thought to provide in the infant an index of something analogous to intelligence. However, as data have accumulated (e.g., Wittenborn et al. 1956), it has become clear that there is very little relationship between any appraisals of the infant during the first year of life and his status on the intelligence tests at school age. Whether this reflects the changing nature of the tasks through which intelligence manifests itself or the basic instability of growth patterns during infancy and childhood is difficult to determine, but to date it does not appear that, except in cases of extreme deficiency, observations during infancy give any substantial basis for predicting intellectual performances during school age and in adulthood.

Tests developed for the preschool years have fared somewhat better, and as a matter of fact the Stanford–Binet itself extends down to the two-year level. Other tests have been developed for children ranging from one year to five years of age. These tend to involve perceptual and motor tasks somewhat more heavily than do the typical school-age tests, but they also depend somewhat more heavily than do infant tests upon verbal comprehension by the child. Tests at these ages permit somewhat better forecasts of school-age development (Honzik et al. 1948), although the stability is much less than is true for a comparable time period with school children and with adolescents. Again, this is probably due in part to changes in the tests, in part to the negativism and distractibility that make young children difficult to test reliably, and in part to the cumulative impact of changing school, family, and community environments upon intellectual growth as the individual moves out of his family into the wider environment of the school and the community.

Evaluation

Kinds of intelligence. In recent years conventional tests of intelligence have come under some criticism because, it is alleged, they do not appraise the "creativity" of the individual. It is asserted that conventional tests require the individual to select or produce a predetermined "right" answer, so that there is little leeway for individual originality or inventiveness. The examinee is required to reproduce the thought process of the test maker, or at least to come out with the same answer. This is, of course, true. However, if the thought processes of the test maker are sufficiently ingenious, subtle, and various from item to item, it may still call for a good deal of flexibility and ingenuity on the part of the examinee to reproduce them.

Some recent test construction has emphasized the measurement of "divergent thinking" as opposed to the "convergent thinking" that is considered to characterize conventional tests. In measures of divergent thinking the individual receives credit for the number, the variety, and the originality of his productions in response to an intellectual task. One representative task is "List as many different uses as you can for a brick." Fluency is evidenced by the number of responses given, flexibility by the number of different categories of response (i.e., building material, weight, tool, etc.) represented in the list, and originality by the rarity or unusualness of the responses.

There is clearly some overlap between performance on convergent and divergent tests. However, the correlation is fairly low, especially within the abler and better educated groups. Although the overlap among different divergent measures is rather modest, the correlations seem to justify speaking of a divergent thinking factor that has some degree of generality (Thorndike 1963). Studies of the correlates of divergent thinking are still incomplete, but it appears that those students high on divergent thinking make a different and generally less favorable impression upon conventional teachers in conventional schools than do those who excel in convergent thinking, and they present generally somewhat different and more tempestuous personality patterns.

The relationship of divergent thinking, as measured by tests, to creativity in the sense of producing socially valued products remains largely to be explored. [*See* CREATIVITY, *article on* PSYCHOLOGICAL ASPECTS.]

Early work on cognitive test development emphasized the single factor of general intellectual ability. However, test theory has increasingly emphasized the multiplicity of factors involved in cognitive performances. For example, basing his work partly on a priori analyses and partly on data from factor analytic studies, Guilford (1957) developed an elaborate three-dimensional "structure of intellect," in which 72 cells represent different facets of intellectual functioning. There has been a corresponding trend in practical test development toward the development of test batteries composed of a number of tests, each designed to measure a distinct cognitive ability, e.g., verbal, numerical, spatial visualizing, mechanical, inductive reasoning, etc. Although the tests of specific abilities typically show positive intercorrelations, thus providing support for the concept of an underlying general intellectual factor, there is enough that is specific to each test so that the battery can be considered to give a usefully differentiated map of the individual's cognitive development.

If one is to make any practical interpretation or use of intelligence test results, it is important to know something about their stability and their correlates. There are so many specific facts involved, depending upon the specific test in question, age or educational group referred to, and definition of the correlative variable, that it is hard to present a summary that will be both brief and accurate. However, an attempt will be made to capture the main trends of the evidence.

Stability over time. As indicated earlier, observations of behavior during infancy permit no better than a chance forecast of intelligence as measured in later years. A core of stability develops during the preschool years, and the relationship between successive tests with a constant time interval (e.g., one year, five years) increases as a person progresses through the elementary school years. By the time of adolescence, the relative standing of the typical individual on measures of intelligence has stabilized, and subsequent changes in his standing in his group arise in large part from random errors of measurement. Relative position is maintained with a good deal of consistency throughout adult life, although patterns of increment or decrement do to some extent reflect amount of schooling and other types of opportunities and advantages.

Age and sex differences. The determination of age trends in intelligence is complicated by the difficulty, both practical and theoretical, of identifying comparable groups at different ages. Within this limitation, data suggest that performance on measures of intelligence increases at a rapid and apparently fairly uniform rate during childhood, slows down during adolescence, reaches a maximum, and subsequently declines. However, the age at which a maximum is reached and the rate of subsequent decline is a function both of the nature of the test task and of the life history of the individual. Tests that depend in large measure upon the accumulation of experience (i.e., vocabulary or general information) continue to show increments in performance through the twenties and perhaps longer, and show a decline only with the approach of senescence. On the other hand, performance on tests that depend upon speed, flexibility, and adaptation to novel and unfamiliar tasks appears to reach a maximum during the teens and declines shortly thereafter. However, the time and rate of decline is a function of educational level and pattern of life experience, being slower for those who continue their schooling and who live and work in situations where traffic in ideas and abstractions is a part of their daily living.

Some sex differences appear with respect to specific types of test tasks. Girls generally have been found to do better on tasks with a substantial verbal component, and boys have been found to do better on quantitative and concrete types of tasks. In general, however, sex differences are of modest size and appear to reflect in considerable part cultural demands and expectations rather than inherent differences.

Socioeconomic differences. In Western cultures there has been consistently a relationship between socioeconomic status and average level of intelligence test performance. Thus, in the standardization population for the 1937 edition of the Stanford–Binet (McNemar 1942) the following mean IQ's were found for children whose fathers fell in the indicated occupational levels: professional,

116; semiprofessional and managerial, 112; clerical, skilled trades, and retail business, 107; semiskilled, minor clerical, and minor business, 105; slightly skilled, 98; day laborers, 96. This trend is found for all types of tests, although there is some evidence, far from unanimous or unequivocal, that differences are less marked for cross-cultural tests such as the Progressive Matrices. The presence of these differences is unquestioned; their source is a matter of some disagreement and debate. The issue of genetic as opposed to cultural causation is considered later in this article.

Many studies attest to an occupational hierarchy of intellectual performance, with the professional groups at the top and rough unskilled laboring groups at the bottom (Stewart 1947). However, the range within any given occupation is typically large, with a substantial per cent of overlapping even between occupations well separated in the occupational scale.

With respect to relationships to success within a given occupation, the results are less clear. The definition of "success" itself is often a problem, and results vary with the type of job. The most promising results have been found for clerical, skilled, and supervisory occupations (Ghiselli & Brown 1948). However, it must be admitted that even for these groups relationships tend to be quite modest. Test results appear to be more predictive of ability to enter and survive in an occupation than they are of degrees of success above the survival level.

Whatever is said about socioeconomic differences may be repeated with respect to Negro–white differences in the United States. The caste differences are of a size comparable to those between middle-class and lower-class groups, and racial differences have been inevitably and inextricably bound up with class differences.

Academic success. It is practically guaranteed by the nature of their content and the procedures by which test items are selected that intelligence tests will show substantial correlations with academic achievement. When that achievement itself is measured by objective tests the correlation is quite high, reflecting the similarity of processes called for and in some cases actual communality of test content. When achievement is represented by teachers' appraisals of their pupils, the correlations tend to be lower, reflecting in some measure the diverse considerations that enter into teacher appraisals. The relationships are most marked in the public schools, in which the whole range of intellectual talent is represented, and become progressively less marked as one proceeds up the educational ladder to the more and more screened and intellectually homogeneous groups of college and graduate or professional schools.

Other success criteria. There have been vast numbers of studies relating measured intelligence to all sorts of other indicators of adjustment in or failure to adjust to life. Intelligence has been studied in delinquents, criminals, psychopaths, addicts, and others within the range of social problems and ills. However, for many of these socially deviating groups there is an association between deviancy and low socioeconomic status. Thus, the results for many of the studies have been confounded by the coexistent low socioeconomic status and low educational level. What interpretation to give to the relationships that are found is far from clear.

Causation of differences in intelligence

The existence of individual and especially group differences in measured intellect raises insistently the question of the causation of the differences that are found. To what extent should differences be attributed to hereditary differences transmitted through the genes and to what extent should they be attributed to differences in the physical and social environment subsequent to conception and birth?

The effort to clarify this issue, or to provide evidence in support of either a genetic or an environmentalist point of view, generated a great volume and variety of research, especially in the period just prior to World War II; much of it was suggestive but none of it really definitive. There have been many correlational studies of siblings, fraternal twins, and identical twins (Erlenmeyer-Kimling & Jarvik 1963), and these have shown correlations ranging from about .50 for siblings to about .90 for identical twins. (The correlations between identical twins are substantially as high as those between two testings of the same individual.) Data have been laboriously assembled on identical twins reared in separate homes, and those persons have been found to be less alike than identical twins reared together but more alike than fraternal twins growing up together in the same family.

Studies of foster children have been complicated by the possibility of selective placement, so that correlations between foster siblings and between adopted children and their foster parents have been difficult to interpret clearly. A further complication has been the equivocality of test results for very young children. The average level of performance of foster children, typically placed in average or above-average homes, has been found at least equal to that of the general population, even though these children's own mothers performed well below average when tested as adults. However, the intelligence of individual foster children appears to bear little relationship to measures of the foster home in which they are placed, while appreciable correlations do appear between the IQ of the foster child and that of his own mother, from whom he has been separated almost from birth (Skodak & Skeels 1949). [*See* GENETICS, *article on* GENETICS AND BEHAVIOR.]

A number of patterns of investigation have been developed involving changed environment. Children from orphanages have been retested after a period of residence in a foster home. Negroes from the South have been compared with those migrating to New York City. Both Negro and Puerto Rican children in New York City have been studied in an attempt to relate length of residence in New York to level of test performance. Many of these studies show higher test performance associated with exposure to the presumably more stimulating environment and suggest that a greater increment is associated with early and extended exposure to the improved environment (Jones 1946).

Thus, at the present time there would be little dissent from the proposition that measured intelligence is a function of the environment to which the individual or group has been exposed and that some part of the difference between individuals and between groups is attributable to such environmental differences. It is when one attempts to ascertain how much, that conflict is generated and uncertainty arises. This attempt appears to be extraordinarily difficult, for the following reasons, among others:

(1) It is difficult to identify the relevant and crucial aspects of environmental influence. The important aspects are only crudely represented by gross indicators of socioeconomic status. Consequently, it is almost impossible to state when two environments are "equal," or to express in quantitative terms the amount of difference between two environments.

(2) The effects of genetic and environmental factors are almost certainly interactive rather than summational. What is a stimulating environment for one genetic constitution may be an overpowering one for another, and the gains one may expect to accrue from a particular type of environmental stimulation are almost certainly a function of the genetic materials to which that environment is applied.

(3) For intelligence test performance, as for any other attribute of the individual, one faces the somewhat paradoxical situation that the more nearly optimum the surroundings are for each individual's development, the less the differences between individuals can be attributed to environmental factors. Thus any estimate of the per cent of variance attributable to environmental factors is always specific to a given time and place and the range of environmental opportunities (and of genetic constitutions) that characterize that specific population. If the democratic ideal of equal educational and other opportunities for everyone were achieved, environmental differences would recede into the background as a cause of differences among individuals and groups.

In recent years the interest of psychologists and educators seems to have shifted away from attempts to estimate the relative role of nature and nurture in intellectual development; it seems to be focused more on the attempt to analyze more incisively what the crucial elements in an environment are that foster optimum intellectual development. At least for the short haul, this seems to be a more productive enterprise.

ROBERT L. THORNDIKE

[*Directly related are the entries* ACHIEVEMENT TESTING; APTITUDE TESTING; INTELLECTUAL DEVELOPMENT. *Other relevant material may be found in* COUNSELING PSYCHOLOGY; DEVELOPMENTAL PSYCHOLOGY, *article on* A THEORY OF DEVELOPMENT; EDUCATIONAL PSYCHOLOGY; PSYCHOMETRICS; *and in the biographies of* BINET; TERMAN.]

BIBLIOGRAPHY

BINET, ALFRED 1911 Nouvelles recherches sur la mesure du niveau intellectuel chez les enfants d'école. *Année psychologique* 17:145–201.

BINET, ALFRED; and SIMON, TH. 1908 Le développement de l'intelligence chez les enfants. *Année psychologique* 14:1–94.

CATTELL, PSYCHE 1940 *The Measurement of Intelligence of Infants and Young Children.* New York: Psychological Corp.

DAVIS, ALLISON; and EELLS, KENNETH 1952–1953 *Davis–Eells Games: Davis–Eells Test of General Intelligence or Problem-solving Ability.* Tarrytown-on-Hudson, N.Y.: World Book.

ERLENMEYER-KIMLING, L.; and JARVIK, LISSY F. 1963 Genetics and Intelligence: A Review. *Science* 142: 1477–1479.

GHISELLI, EDWIN E.; and BROWN, CLARENCE W. 1948 The Effectiveness of Intelligence Tests in the Selection of Workers. *Journal of Applied Psychology* 32:575–580.

GUILFORD, JOY P. 1957 A Revised Structure of Intellect. University of Southern California, *Reports From the Psychological Laboratory* No. 19.

GUILFORD, JOY P. 1959 Three Faces of Intellect. *American Psychologist* 14:469–479.

HAWES, GENE R. 1964 *Educational Testing for the Millions.* New York: McGraw-Hill.

HONZIK, MARJORIE P.; MACFARLANE, JEAN W.; and ALLEN, LUCILLE 1948 The Stability of Mental Test Performance Between Two and Eighteen Years. *Journal of Experimental Education* 17:309–324.

Intelligence and Its Measurement: A Symposium. 1921 *Journal of Educational Psychology* 12:123–147, 195–216.

JONES, HAROLD E. (1946) 1954 The Environment and Mental Development. Pages 631–696 in Leonard Carmichael (editor), *Manual of Child Psychology.* 2d ed. New York: Wiley.

KELLEY, TRUMAN L. 1927 *Interpretation of Educational Measurements.* Yonkers-on-Hudson, N.Y.: World Book.

MCNEMAR, QUINN 1942 *The Revision of the Stanford–Binet Scale.* Boston: Houghton Mifflin.

PINNEAU, SAMUEL R. 1961 *Changes in Intelligence Quotient: Infancy to Maturity.* Boston: Houghton Mifflin.

RAVEN, J. C. 1958 *Guide to Using the Coloured Progressive Matrices (1947): Sets A, Ab, B.* London: Lewis.

SKODAK, MARIE; and SKEELS, HAROLD M. 1949 A Final Follow-up Study of One Hundred Adopted Children. *Journal of Genetic Psychology* 75:85–125.

SPEARMAN, CHARLES E. 1927 *The Abilities of Man: Their Nature and Measurement.* London: Macmillan.

STEWART, NAOMI 1947 A.G.C.T. Scores of Army Personnel Grouped by Occupations. *Occupations* 26:5–41.

TERMAN, LEWIS M. 1916 *The Measurement of Intelligence.* Boston: Houghton Mifflin.

TERMAN, LEWIS M.; and MERRILL, MAUD A. (1937) 1960 *Measuring Intelligence: A Guide to the Administration of the New Revised Stanford–Binet Tests of Intelligence.* Boston: Houghton Mifflin.

TERMAN, LEWIS M.; and MERRILL, MAUDE A. 1960 *Stanford–Binet Intelligence Scales: Manual for the Third Revision, Form L-M.* Boston: Houghton Mifflin.

THORNDIKE, ROBERT L. 1963 Some Methodological Issues in the Study of Creativity. Pages 40–54 in Invitational Conference on Testing Problems, 1962, *Proceedings.* Princeton, N.J.: Educational Testing Service.

THURSTONE, LOUIS L. 1938 Primary Mental Abilities. *Psychometric Monographs* No. 1.

WECHSLER, DAVID 1939 *The Measurement of Adult Intelligence.* Baltimore: Williams & Wilkins.

WECHSLER, DAVID 1949 *Wechsler Intelligence Scale for Children.* New York: Psychological Corp.

WECHSLER, DAVID 1955 *Wechsler Adult Intelligence Scale* (WAIS). New York: Psychological Corp.

WITTENBORN, JOHN R. et al. 1956 A Study of Adoptive Children. II: The Predictive Validity of the Yale Developmental Examination of Infant Behavior. *Psychological Monographs* 70, no. 2:59–92.

WOODWORTH, ROBERT S. 1941 *Heredity and Environment: A Critical Survey of Recently Published Material on Twins and Foster Children.* New York: Social Science Research Council.

YALE UNIVERSITY, CLINIC OF CHILD DEVELOPMENT 1940 *The First Five Years of Life: A Guide to the Study of the Preschool Child.* New York: Harper. → Contains "Early Mental Growth" by Arnold Gesell and "The Study of the Individual Child" by Arnold Gesell and Catherine S. Amatruda.

YERKES, ROBERT M. (editor) 1921 Psychological Examining in the United States Army. Volume 15 of National Academy of Sciences, *Memoirs.* Washington: Government Printing Office.

INTERACTION

I
SOCIAL INTERACTION

It is almost pure tautology to say that human "social" phenomena are cases of the *interaction* between two or more human beings conceived as "persons," "organisms," "selves," or "actors." Hence, it may be thought that what is meant and implied by the concept of interaction and its theoretical context is the sheerest common sense. However, this is not so. This theoretical complex has had a long, complicated history, and the outlines of its place in modern social science, which is our concern here, have emerged only gradually.

On reflection this should not be too surprising. After all, science is not common sense, and its most basic theoretical ideas and frames of reference require development through complex intellectual processes which involve not only interpretations of observation but also theoretical and partly philosophical conceptualization. Perhaps this process has been particularly difficult in the case of human social action, because the subject matter is so close to immediate experience that isolating a scientifically usable scheme from the matrix of common sense is particularly difficult. In any case, for the limited purposes of this article it seems useful to begin by sketching the historical background of the problem.

Early history of the concept

From one point of view modern philosophy "got off on the wrong foot" for clarifying the nature of human interaction, while, from another viewpoint, it appears that indirectly this was fruitful over the long run. In any case, I think there is general agreement that of all the areas in which modern philosophy originated, the most relevant to the present discussion is the problem of knowledge.

The Cartesian schema. The focal early statement of this problem was Descartes's *Discourse on Method.* This work is justly considered the basic philosophical charter of modern science, having posed the problem of the philosophical basis of empirical knowledge of the external world with the greatest clarity. This clarity, however, was bought at the price of assumptions and predilections which proved restrictive in two directions, both of which are central to our problem.

The first was the treatment of the significant "external world" as the *physical* world. This was natural, in that, among other things, the science of the time, which had recently made very striking advances, was overwhelmingly physical science. Consequently, the object of knowledge for Descartes was not conceived as "knowing" or "acting" (since physical objects do not act). Thus, his formulation blocked concern with the interplay between entities which are *both* subject and object at the same time and, hence, with the analytical distinction between these aspects of social actors.

The second was the treatment of the problem solely as one of *knowledge*. Presumably it was in order to facilitate this that Descartes treated his subject as a given—e.g., in the famous formula *Cogito ergo sum*—rather than analyzing it as a structured identity. In this respect the Cartesian analysis did not venture beyond asserting the existence of the "thinker" and the fact of his cognitive relation to objects in the external world.

Of course we can now say, almost at the level of common sense, that Descartes dealt with a limiting case of social action. First, he excluded the "inter-" in our formula of interaction by assuming that there was no "action" on one side of the relation, i.e., that the object only came to be known and that "being known" was in no way a stimulus for the object to intervene in and possibly change the relation to the knower. Second, he excluded analysis of the complex nature of the "entity which" knows, which is part of the basic relational system of the subject–object relation. We would now hold that empirical cognition is an activity or "function" of persons, an understanding of which entails analyzing the structures and processes of personalities by virtue of which a variety of factors become so organized as to facilitate the "attainment of knowledge" as a goal output of personality systems. Furthermore, the recognition of complexity *in* the units on both sides of the relationship obviously entails complicating the conceptualization of the relational pattern between them. Here Descartes considered the relation merely one of the flow of "information" from object to subject, resulting in consequent "understanding," or knowledge, with little specificity about how far and in what ways such understanding involved processes other than the simple input of information.

Differentiation of the Cartesian object. The Cartesian schema may be regarded as the primary reference point for a process of differentiation. Because it formulated a relational scheme, its differentiation necessarily cut across all of its components, involving both subject and object *and* the character of the relation between them. Since we are concerned with science, it is easier to understand the differentiation on the object side, which entailed the first step away from the more purely physicalist predilection of Descartes.

The human object came to be regarded not merely as a "knower" but also as a physical organism "behaving" (to use a later term) in an environment and actuated by "wants"—or, as Hobbes said, "passions"—which accounted for its action. This differentiation appeared even in Descartes's own century, the seventeenth, notably in the writings of Hobbes and Locke. This development marked the beginning of utilitarianism, established the theoretical groundwork of both the discipline of economics and a major branch of psychology, and had important side effects upon law, political science, and sociology.

The utilitarian differentiation. The Cartesian pattern was maintained in the assumption that the individual's wants were given. Even though these wants were also assumed to be plural, the problem of how, specifically, they were patterned and organized was not dealt with. However, the analytical concern was now no longer confined to knowing the external world but included "rationally" manipulating it through goal-directed activities. The early modern social scientist, then, is conceived of as an observer of objects who are at the same time actors striving to satisfy their wants through action. Moreover, only in a limiting case does the observer confine his observation to single individuals; generally he observes an interacting plurality. Economic exchange, through barter or the more elaborate market systems, became a prototype of such interaction, but the men of Hobbes's state of nature, seeking to "destroy or subdue one another," were also conceived of as interacting in this sense. Clearly, trying to satisfy wants or seeking to destroy others involves action in a sense not attributable, for example, to celestial bodies. Such wants or passions are easily distinguished from the activities—to use a term later made much of by Alfred Marshall—intended to implement them. Problems of the nature of the interaction systems generated by action conceived within this framework and of the conditions on which such systems can "function" become very important here. The nature and significance of "self-interest," in the classic modern sense, and the basis of normative order in social systems become very problematic in this frame of reference.

Thus, the "utilitarian" frame of reference can be

said to have emerged from the Cartesian problem-statement through the inclusion in the schema of a class of objects which are not physical and which interact in a sense in which neither knowers nor physical objects do. Although this conception emerges by differentiation on the object side of the Cartesian scheme, it implicitly raises the question about the position of the observer. Very clearly, knowledge of the *situation*, of the wants and activities of others in the interaction system, itself becomes a factor in want satisfaction. The utilitarian actor, considered as an observer, is a Cartesian "knower," but he is more than that. Thus, introducing this additional element into the total scheme presents exceedingly important problems.

Idealistic differentiation of subject. As noted, Descartes left the structure of his subject unanalyzed: the "I" which thinks, and therefore exists, is *given*. Very broadly, the idealistic movement was an attempt to analyze the content of this given entity. Most crucially in Kant, it took the content of knowledge as its primary reference point. Contrary to the views of the British empiricists, knowledge was considered to be patterned and organized according to the Kantian schemata of intuition and the categories of understanding and not derivable from the "intrinsic" properties of the object world itself as they impinged on the subject in the form of "sense impresssions," or in Locke's term, "ideas."

As for Descartes, the idealists' reference here was the scientific understanding of the physical world. However, it had now been greatly "relativized"—in a special sense—because the major structure of empirical knowledge was attributed not only to the "nature" of the objects known but also to the "categories" in terms of which they are known. These categories could not be located in the objects of cognition, nor could they be treated basically as variant properties of the individual personalities of the knowers. In more modern terms, they constitute a *cultural* frame of reference which partly governs the whole action system so far as it is dependent on empirical knowledge. This raises a problem parallel to the utilitarian one concerning actors who are not only knowers.

It is fair to say that such a differentiation of the Cartesian subject, parallel to the utilitarian differentiation of the Cartesian object, was a principal consequence of Kant's analysis. Thus "pure reason" concerned essentially the epistemological grounding of physical science, whereas "practical reason" regarded the other, especially noncognitive, concerns of human "actors." Utilitarianism treated wants only as given and analyzed activities overwhelmingly by projecting a Cartesian rational knower into the role of the actor—hence the formula of rational self-interest. Kant took practical needs, which he considered predominantly *moral*, as essentially given, and he heavily discounted the possibilities of solving intellectually the underlying problems. Here he came close to the view that the moral imperative is existentially given.

Hegelianism. The Hegelian movement attempted to fuse the cultural component of Kant's empirical epistemology, especially the "categories," with the sphere of practical reason, thereby developing a unified idealistic metaphysics built about the key concept of the "objective spirit" (*objectiver Geist*). It then conceived of the whole of history as the "unfolding" of the world spirit, human action being essentially an "acting out" or implementation of the spirit's "ideal" content.

Perhaps the primary disposition of the Cartesian phase of this broad intellectual development was to derive as much as possible from the inherent nature of objects; the conception of the "mind" as a *tabula rasa* which is only a recipient of sense impressions just carried this to an extreme. By contrast, idealism tended to attribute as much as possible to the creative activity of mind. On the one hand, this emphasized the importance in action of individual human agents as distinguished from the circumstances of their situations. But on the other hand, the problem of a cultural system, *transcending* (in the strict Kantian sense) the individual actor was necessarily extremely prominent.

Marxism. As the massive development of economics and, later, of psychology into firm disciplines led in the nineteenth century to the establishment of a strong intellectual tradition which positively institutionalized recognition of the wants-activities differentiation within human objects of scientific observations, so the idealistic conception of an "unfolding" *Geist* could not satisfy for long. It required a parallel to the utilitarian differentiation between wants and activities. Such theoretical formulation emerged most clearly with the conceptions of Marx, who set a world of "material" factors over against the "ideal" factors of the Hegelian tradition. The famous aphorism about "setting Hegel on his head" makes clear, I think, that on broader grounds Marx intended to stay within the idealistic framework. The Marxian category of "material" was therefore in no way identical with that of "physical," which had figured in Descartes and even Kant. It concerned, above all, those aspects of the human condition which are *conditional* to the attainment of human goals. The old primacy problem, which is inherent in the use of dichotomous conceptualization, came, in this case, to focus on whether primacy lay in the "ideal" realm or in the conditions necessary for their implementation. Marx's materialism consisted essentially in his confronting the "utopians" with the necessity to be "realistic" in taking account of such conditions. Importantly, his "material" system was not simply an "unfolding spirit" but a social system, in present terms an interaction system, however inadequately analyzed.

Modern developments

There are two limiting boundaries of the "action" aspect of the human condition: the biological, conceived of in terms of heredity and environment; and the cultural, conceived of as a symbolically defined system of order with normative primacy, to which men are *obligated* to conform on pain of this-worldly—or otherworldly—sanctions. Both major trends of social thought have been under pressure toward a reductionism grounded at one of these two boundaries. The utilitarian tradition has tended to be biologized, and the Kantian tradition to be "Hegelianized"—if one may take Hegelianism as the relative extreme of idealistic reductionism. At the same time, considerations similar to those that gave rise to the Marxian revolt against Hegelianism stimulated movements from both traditions that have brought conceptual definiteness and clarity into the middle ground between these two extremes.

Freud and personality theory. On the utilitarian side, the development of biological science in the latter half of the nineteenth century and the florescence of varieties of "social Darwinism" acutely posed the problem of how the essential components of human social action could be treated in a manner that would be realistic about the continuity between "human nature" and the organic world. Here the most important single figure was Freud, who, as a physician, started with the conception of man as organism but, as a psychiatrist, became primarily concerned with man's behavior, not the internal state of his organs. Furthermore, the clinical method developed by Freud stressed the emotions and wishes and goals, rather than cognitive matters.

Freud started as an "instinctivist," in the familiar hereditarist sense. Although, of course, he never abandoned emphasizing the importance of instinctual needs, he developed the concept of instinct itself from the more conventional idea of a hereditarily given pattern of behavior "triggered" by environmental stimuli to that of a highly generalized motivational system involving a complex relation between basic instinctual energy and the mechanisms of its goal specification and its control. The erotic complex, the focus of the "pleasure principle," became a complex system which was by no means given and which was complexly integrated (or malintegrated, as the case might be) with the noninstinctual components of personality.

Relatively early, Freud gained the insight that the expression of instinctual need was regulated by the society's moral standards—often, but in no simple sense always, in conflict with instinctual needs—and that these standards were *introjected* into the personality itself, becoming components of its structure. The final form of this conception crystallized about the famous idea of the superego. Later this basic mode of conceptualization was extended to the social environment, conceived of as an environment much in the Cartesian–Durkheimian sense. The famous "reality principle" came to focus on "object relations," which for Freud meant relations to other persons, especially the parents, considered as agents of socialization. But these human objects were not only "adapted to" in the sense true for physical objects; they were also introjected—or, as we now usually say, internalized—to form part of the personality structure, particularly of the ego, in Freud's sense.

Thus, Freud brought the distinctive properties of the social, as distinguished from the physical, environment of the action of the individual to the forefront of analytical consideration in two connections: that of normative standards and that of the more empirical aspects of the social object world. Indeed, it can be shown that even the id, the third of Freud's primary structural subsystems of personality, is not purely "instinctual" but is organized about the "precipitates of lost objects," especially those salient in the earliest phases of a person's socialization experience (Parsons 1958).

Durkheim and the content of culture. Whereas Freud, from a biological starting point, arrived at the recognition of the distinctive properties of social systems, Durkheim began with the conviction that clear distinctions between social and personal systems were essential; in his famous phrase, society was a reality *sui generis*. In order to ground this, however, he had to escape the toils of utilitarianism. He chose to do this by harking back to the Cartesian frame of reference, including its cognitive primacy. Durkheim's basic difference from Descartes was his insistence on exploring the distinctive category he called *social facts*, the facts of the social environment of the actor of reference. However, Durkheim also recognized a strong need to consider the actor as something more than a "thinker." Furthermore, since the relevant environment was social, insofar as it included a plurality of individual actors they were all units of the same character as the original actor of reference and were conceived of as *interacting* with him.

From this start Durkheim came to converge with Freud at three essential points. The first was Durkheim's primary starting position, his analysis of the distinctiveness of the *social* object world. If we combine this analysis with that of Freud, we can confidently speak of its distinctiveness vis-à-vis not only the physical world in the narrower sense but also the organic world. The second was the idea that an essential aspect of the social environment is that it imposes normative requirements on the individual and sanctions him for compliance and noncompliance. The third was that the structure of this social environment, particularly its normative component, comes to be internalized in the personality of the individual. Otherwise, the *moral authority* of "society" as an agency of the control of the individual's action—as an agency of constraint, in Durkheim's sense—could not be understood. Although Durkheim did not develop a technical theory of the personality of the individual as a system, clearly the structure of his theoretical scheme articulates very directly with the type of personality theory Freud developed and even demands such articulation for theoretical closure.

Durkheim's treatment of the normative components of social systems, however, went well beyond Freud, in a direction that brought him close to Kant. Since concern with the social system was primary for him (rather than residual, as for Freud), he was aware of the conception that normative components are part of a cultural system and in that sense transcend the individual. Durkheim developed this theme particularly well with his conception of "collective representations" and spelled it out in his analysis of religion in *The Elementary Forms of the Religious Life* (1912). He made it quite clear, as Freud did not, that systems of "representations"—no longer just a Cartesian mode of expression—were basically *symbolic*. In so doing, he took a most important step toward conceiving of the content of culture as consisting of codified symbolic systems and toward a general understanding of their articulation both with social systems and personalities.

Durkheim and Marx. Although this late development of Durkheim's work brought him into direct contact with the idealistic movement, he was no more an idealist than Marx. It is interesting to compare them in this connection. Marx represents, of course, a particularly notable reaction against the Hegelian extreme, and indeed his conception of social systems is closer to Durkheim's than has generally been believed. It can, however, be said that Marx was particularly ambiguous about the status of the normative components of social order. This ambiguity resulted from his scheme's being incompletely differentiated in two main respects. First, the ideological–evaluative aspect was not clearly differentiated from the scientific aspect. For instance, with reference to "capitalism," the moral condemnation of its normative structure tended to underrate its empirical importance in an analytical sense, suggesting that it merely cloaked exploitative interests. Second, Marxian thought shared with Hegelian and other postidealistic theories a commitment to *historicism*. This position denied the possibility, for the sociocultural field, of generalized analytical theory. Marxian theory is a theory of the development of a succession of dynamically linked *particular* socioeconomic systems, not an analytical theory of society in general. Marx does not use Ricardian economic theory as economic theory in the general sense but as the theory of capitalist process within one historical economic system.

Durkheim was not caught in these difficulties. He assumed, as a good Cartesian, that if social facts were facts, the general methodology of science, including general analytical theory, applied to them. And dealing with the problem of the "ideal" factors from a rather pre-Hegelian, Kantian viewpoint, he did not worry about the alleged dilemma of whether ideal or material factors determined human action "in the last analysis."

Max Weber and the individual actor. If Durkheim avoided the ideal–material dilemma, Max Weber, starting from reference points within the German idealistic tradition, worked his way out of it, in a manner converging directly with Durkheim's position. His crucial reference was the "motives of individuals"; only through understanding (*Verstehen*) of the *meanings* of motives of actual and typical individuals could the motives be used to explain empirical courses of action—in relation, of course, to the conditions of the action situation. These motives of individuals were by no means the same as the wants of the utilitarians, precisely because, instead of being taken as given, their structure was a matter of major interest. Indeed, cultural meaning systems constituted a primary focus of Weber's interest, as developed most clearly in his studies in the sociology of religion.

At the same time, Weber's position is by no means a Hegelian idealism or a post-Hegelian "gestaltism" in the manner of Dilthey. In these latter cases the principal relation of a meaning complex (*Sinnzusammenhang*) to material reality is simply that of "unfolding." Weber, however, made the crucial contribution of breaking down the rigid alternative of using *either* ideal *or* material *systems* as empirically closed, in that he developed a way of analyzing the complex interdependences between them. This is how Weber could become eminent *both* as a "sociologist of culture," e.g., of religion, and as a sociologist of economic and political phenomena (particularly the latter), with his analysis of the social significance of law providing the most important link between them (cf. Parsons 1965). Thus, he managed to emphasize the complete reality of the "material" interests of persons and groups, while avoiding the faulty assumption of the Marxian model that these interests constitute a closed system which can be broken through only by a total revolutionary transformation. In regard to the individual actor, Weber, rather than having to arrive at a conception of internalization—as did the utilitarians, as well as Freud and Durkheim—quite naturally took it for granted, on the basis of his general theoretical position.

This orientation can be detailed only through the systematic analysis of interaction. Unit-by-unit social systems must be analyzed as engaged in detailed interchanges with each other, interchanges which constitute performances or sanctions according to which unit, the "sender" or the "receiver," is the point of reference. Weber, more than any other figure emerging predominantly from the idealistic tradition, laid the groundwork and demonstrated the use of the more generalized schema toward which the movements of thought we are considering had been evolving. The relations of the authority of office to the use of power and of property to markets and exchange were primary focuses of the vast range of his empirical studies. Power and economic resources, of course, constitute particularly salient sanctions and resources in the more-differentiated interaction systems, and Weber's work may serve us as a kind of charter for analyzing them in social-system rather than purely economic or political terms.

A paradigm of social interaction. The broad outline of the present conceptions of interaction has emerged from the above movements. Its focus is a social system generated by and composed of the interaction of units which are "behaving organisms," personalities, or various levels of collectivity. Acting units, however, are always involved in cultural systems, which express, symbolize, order, and control human orientations through patterned meaning systems consisting of both codes of meaning and specific combinations of symbols in particular contexts. At a minimum, an interaction system in this sense involves four analytically distinguishable aspects or components: (1) a set of "units" which interact with each other; (2) a set of rules or other "code" factors, the terms of which structure both the orientations of the units and the interaction itself; (3) an ordered or patterned system or process of the interaction itself; and (4) an environment in which the system operates and with which systematic interchanges take place. It can be seen that the various intellectual movements reviewed contributed one or another special emphasis or combination of components to this paradigm but that only at a late stage did anything like the complete paradigm emerge.

Pragmatism and the nature of the self. Before a fuller exposition of the paradigm is attempted, two further movements, which contributed less to its main outlines than those already reviewed but which have nevertheless been very influential, should receive brief attention. The first of these is primarily American and may be considered an aspect of the pragmatist movement. In a sense, James and Peirce cut through the structured rigidity of the European thought of their time to bring the whole self–object system into a new flux. Particularly in view of the "scientistic" trends in American thought, pragmatism raised questions about the self which were particularly important. James introduced a distinctively un-Cartesian pluralism into the concept: besides the *I*, which thought, there were an *I*, a *me*, and various other possible *selves*.

Symbolic interaction—Cooley and Mead. One branch of the pragmatist movement made a special contribution to social interaction theory, namely, that associated with Charles Horton Cooley and George Herbert Mead, which eventuated in a special kind of social psychology. It was Cooley who first took seriously the truly indeterminate character of the self as a structure independent of others. This led to the idea that the self developed in the process of interaction with others. As Mead said, to Cooley the "other" belonged in the same field as the self and was just as immediately given (Mead 1930).

Cooley, however, despite some arresting insights about the "looking-glass" features of the self, adhered to a semi-idealistic, subjectivist concept of "mind" which, though no longer individualistic in the Cartesian or the utilitarian sense, achieved only a truncated conception of interaction systems.

Mead, however, took the essential step of treating the individual as being both subject and object at the same time and in the same interpersonal system. Furthermore, he was far clearer than Cooley in showing that the personality of the individual emerges from the process we now call socialization precisely through the interplay between these subjective and objective aspects. This is not (as the idealists would have it) a process of the "unfolding" of the mind, individual or collective, but vitally includes the internalization of *objects*.

Mead also contributed a most important conception in his idea of the *generalized other*. Through symbolic interaction the individual learns to use and develop generalized codes that can interrelate a conception of the particular other with generalized categories and collectivities. This is the foundation, in the process of socialization, of the internalization of cultural, as well as social, systems, which in turn can come to be differentiated from each other. Mead took much longer steps than Cooley toward opening sociology and social psychology to the substitution of more technical research procedures for reliance on interpretative insight alone.

This was social psychology, in that it demonstrated and analyzed the intimacy of the relation between personality and social system by showing (in a way related to but different from Freud's) that the personality cannot be understood independently of its articulation, including its genetic involvement, with social interaction. Moreover, particularly in Mead, who was a kind of symbolic behaviorist, there was an even fuller awareness than in Freud of the evolutionary continuity of phenomena between the human levels of action and those of organic life more generally. Mead also surpassed Freud in beginning the exploration of truly symbolic processes and in building a bridge between behavior theory and linguistics. There was certainly impressive convergence between this version of "symbolic-interaction" theory and the ideas of both Freud and Durkheim on the internalization of social objects.

The existentialist tradition. German, or, more broadly, continental European, thought has for a considerable period involved a strand of thinking which has recently gained prominence in analyzing interaction in a manner playing into a basic, if still relatively unclear, synthesis with the American tradition of social psychology. Perhaps it is most conveniently traced back to the Kantian phase in the development of idealism. Kant's sphere of "practical reason" was specifically unstructured, in any sense comparable to that of either the phenomenal or the physical world. It was the world of will, individuality, and what may be considered socially unorganized meanings. It is perhaps particularly important here that this tradition experienced great difficulty in making the crucial discrimination between the biological–environmental and the cultural–cosmological reference poles of action systems. It has tended to merge the two in speaking of the "deeper" human needs of motivations.

In the early phase, perhaps Schelling was the interpreter of the Kantian tradition who veered furthest in this direction. Later, various more or less definitely "existentialist" orientations, but particularly those of Kierkegaard and Nietzsche, seem to be most prominent. A rough continuum among three distinct emphases evidently characterizes the more modern and more sociologically oriented phase.

Weber is at one end, self-consciously analyzing the interdependence of "intended meanings" and situation, interaction and sanctions, and being less concerned with the "fate" of subjective fantasies and hopes themselves than with the nature of the interaction systems generated by the complex modes of their implementation (and the failure thereof).

Perhaps Georg Simmel, who has had a very important impact on American social science, can be placed in the middle. Simmel attempted to confine "phenomenal" determinacy to the "forms" of interaction, and he devoted his immense intuitive talents to the interpretative understanding of the meanings individual actors and types of action injected into interaction, thereby creating, in a broad and rather loose sense, the determinate framework of such interaction. Significantly, Simmel's influence came into American social science via the University of Chicago, which was also the home of Mead. Simmel's "forms of social relationship" were not explanatory categories so much as a frame of reference for interpretive essays (see Naegele 1958).

The third movement, that furthest from Weber, is grounded philosophically in the phenomenological tradition of Husserl and, in part, Heidegger and has affiliations with existentialism. Less immediately, it is also certainly linked with the post-Hegelian historicism that was Weber's major critical foil. It focuses primarily on the most intimate experiences and feelings of the individual and from that vantage point mounts a relativizing criticism upon the more conventionalized and supposedly "superficial" structures of social life. At least certain elements in the movement stress individualism to the borders of a philosophical anarchy, running strongly counter to traditional sociological emphases on the grounding of basic order in social life.

Perhaps the most prominent writer in American sociology today strongly influenced by both a Meadian symbolic interactionism and a phenomenological viewpoint is Erving Goffman. Goffman's most distinctive line of thought is a stress on the discrepancies between the self-image which the actor presents to others in the interactive process and his underlying private attitudes and preoccupations (Goffman 1956).

Empirical approaches. Since World War II there has been an important movement in the United States in favor of the empirical study of interaction, especially in small-group research. Three aspects of this may be mentioned. The so-called "group-dynamics" tradition was founded by the social psychologist Kurt Lewin (1939–1947; Lewin et al. 1944; Benne et al. 1950). It has been relatively eclectic, with an emphasis on the malleability of human goals through interaction. This environmentalism has been associated with a strong "action" orientation, i.e., toward changing behavior in desired directions through group participation experience.

The second movement has been the experimental and laboratory study of interaction in small groups by Bales and his associates (cf. Bales 1950). This group has concentrated on technical observational and analytical methods and theoretically has strongly emphasized the concept of social system at this level, as well as that of larger systems; in this respect it may be said to be in the theory-of-action tradition.

The third type of work is that of Homans, which took its departure from the study of informal organization in industry by Elton Mayo and his associates (cf. Homans 1950). In his latest work, Homans (1961) has, broadly in what above has been called a utilitarian framework, attempted to derive the main features of what he terms "elementary social behavior" from experimental psychology of Skinner's type and from certain postulates of the theory of economic exchange.

Interaction and the social system

The remainder of this article will attempt a systematic outline of both the components of an interaction system and some major aspects of the interaction process itself. I shall try to show that the principal emphases of the historical theories outlined above figure somewhere in a more generalized and theoretically comprehensive scheme. This more comprehensive scheme is a "theory of action," in the sense long used by the author and also, in substance, by very many others, although their terminology may differ.

The concept of interaction is the first-order step beyond the action concept itself toward formulating the concept of social system. In speaking of action, we assume meaningful motivations and goal directedness. Motives, goals, and the like are expressed in, and hence must be interpreted as embodying, cultural-level symbolic form. There are infrastructures of all action systems which are not symbolically structured, but there is no *system* of action, in the present sense, which does not involve cultural symbolization—pre-eminently, of course, through language.

The concept of a dyadic interaction is convenient for clarifying certain fundamentals of interaction phenomena generally. But since it is a limiting case, general inferences from it should be made with care. This is true in the same sense that, although the unicellular organism is convenient for studying certain fundamentals of all organic life, alone it can scarcely provide adequate evidence for a theory of organic evolution.

The crucial reference points for analyzing interaction are two: (1) that each actor is *both* acting agent and object of orientation *both* to himself and to the others; and (2) that, as acting agent, he orients to himself and to others and, as object, has meaning to himself and to others, in *all* of the primary modes or aspects. The actor is knower and object of cognition, utilizer of instrumental means and himself a means, emotionally attached to others and an object of attachment, evaluator and object of evalution, interpreter of symbols and himself a symbol.

From these premises derives the fundamental proposition of the *double* contingency of interaction. Not only, as for isolated behaving units, animal or human, is a goal outcome contingent on successful cognition and manipulation of environmental objects by the actors, but since the most important objects involved in interaction act too, it is also contingent on *their* action or intervention in the course of events. The theory of games is perhaps the most sophisticated analysis of the implications of such double contingency. Of course, the contingency factor multiplies with each addition to the number of interacting units (for my own earlier formulations, see Parsons & Shils 1951).

Double contingency and more-complex contingencies have a crucial set of consequences. On the one hand, as analyzed pre-eminently by Hobbes, in an interaction system the possibilities of instability far exceed those to which isolated actors are exposed in relation to environments containing only nonactors, e.g., physical objects, as the significant objects. On the other hand, if the autonomy possessed by each acting unit relative to its environment is *integrated* with that of the others with which it interacts, the interaction system as a whole can gain vastly in autonomy, or freedom of action. Moreover, under certain conditions this enhanced autonomy of the system can be shared by the units within the system. In this situation a unit within the "organized" interaction system has greater freedom to act autonomously than does a unit which has the same capacities but which is isolated in relation to its physical environment, in the manner of Robinson Crusoe. This is the analytical basis of the "institutionalized individualism" which Durkheim so clearly demonstrated to be a product of the division of labor, in his sense.

Conditions of integration. The most important *single* condition of the integration of an interaction system is a *shared basis of normative order*. Because it must operate to control the disruptive potentialities (for the system of reference) of the autonomy of units, as well as to guide autonomous action into channels which, through mutual reinforcement, enhance the potential for autonomy of both the system as a whole and its member units, such a basis of order *must* be normative. It must guide action by establishing some distinctions between desirable and undesirable lines of action which can serve to stabilize interaction in these fundamental senses. Whether the stabilized system is "static" or "dynamically changing" in one or more of many senses is another issue. The theory of games can be said to have proved that a complex interaction system with no rules, but in which each unit is supposed only to be "rationally pursuing its self-interest," *cannot* be stable in the above sense. This is a critical point for understanding the place of "rationality" in social behavior.

The concept of a shared basis of normative order is basically the same as that of a *common culture* or a "symbolic system." The prototype of such an order is language. A language involves a *code*, consisting of the generalized norms which define "correct" speech or writing, as the basis for using symbols to formulate and transmit messages. Although there is considerable minor deviation, the massive fact is that *all* speakers of a language "observe" the norms of the code—"conform" to them, if you will—on penalty of not being understood.

Language, to be sure, is not a primary normative constituent of *social* systems in the sense true of the law in complex systems, but it is a primary normative constituent of distinct *cultural* systems. However, the point I wish to make here is that *all* culture is a matter of normative control, or the "guidance" of action. This is one sense in which the dyad is clearly a limiting case of interaction. However isolated a dyad may be in other respects, it can *never* generate the ramified common culture which makes *meaningful* and stable interaction possible. A dyad always presupposes a culture shared in a wider system. Furthermore, such a culture is always the product of a "historical" process long transcending the duration of a particular dyadic relationship.

As Durkheim made clear, for actors in interaction this common normative culture has a double significance. On the one hand, for each actor it constitutes a primary part of the situation or environment of his action. Its existence and the ways in which it guides the actions of system members are social facts of which the actor must take account. These facts include the probabilities of the imposition of sanctions contingent on action relative to the norms: rewards for conformity and negative sanctions for nonconformity. On the other hand, the normative culture becomes, in the paradigmatic cases, internalized in the personalities of individual actors—and institutionalized in collectivities—and thereby comes to control action, in part, by *moral* authority. To this extent conformity is voluntary, and hence internal sanctions come into play.

The phenomenon that cultural norms are internalized to personalities and institutionalized in collectivities is a case of the *interpenetration* of subsystems of action, in this case social system, cultural system, and personality. Since these subsystems are defined analytically, not concretely, it is understandable that the concrete boundary of any one subsystem may include within it spheres or zones which require an especially intimate integration with part of one or more other subsystems. Here the critical proposition is that institutionalized normative culture is an essential part of *all* stable systems of social interaction. Therefore, the social system and the culture must be integrated in specific ways in the area of their interpenetration.

The dyadic paradigm of interaction also constitutes a special limiting case in regard to the way in which an interaction system constitutes a collectivity. This point deserves special emphasis. Treatment of the dyad as the typical rather than the limiting case tends to perpetuate the utilitarian view of interaction and to underplay both solidarity and the role of normative culture in favor of the "wants" of individuals—or any other version of individual "interests." Any given dyadic relation, as well as any given "individual," should be seen in the context of a wider social system interpenetrating with a broader, shared culture.

Role pluralism and personality. Relative stability of a significant level of integration over time implies both a common normative culture and rather definite criteria of membership status. Members share with each other a level of solidarity not applying, in the relevant collectivity reference, to the relations between members and nonmembers. Solidarity involves some special quality and level of presumptive mutual trust and loyalty to the collective interest, on occasion involving the sacrifice of unit interests. In principle a collectivity is capable of "action in concert," in the sense of taking collective action toward goals defined in social process as those of the collectivity and resisting centrifugal forces which might reduce the collective involvements of member actors to pure self-interest. Indeed, the possibility of such action provides the primary basis for the boundaries between a social system and its environment, consisting of other social systems or other types of systems.

Dyadic interaction systems may constitute collectivities and be solidary in significant degree, but they are always subsystems of more-extensive social systems. One reason for this is the necessity of a common culture; thus, for example, the interaction possible without a common language is very limited indeed. A second reason involves the relation of the interaction system to the personalities of its members. A dyad, as a matter of empirical fact, never constitutes an independent society; a member of a dyad never interacts *only* with the particular role partner of that dyad. Hence, his *whole* personality, so far as it is engaged in social interaction, is never engaged only in a single dyadic interaction. Thus, although marriage is a particularly important dyadic relation, it is typical in *all* known societies that married couples have children and that the role of spouse is differentiated from that of parent; moreover, the nuclear family always constitutes a more inclusive collectivity in which each member plays *plural* roles.

The phenomenon of *role pluralism* is a central feature of all human societies, and this is more important the more highly differentiated the society. Therefore, the interactive spheres of different individuals, although overlapping and interpenetrating, are not identical. Any given individual participates in a considerable number of specific interaction systems, the more important and enduring of which are the stable collectivities in which he is a member. Thus, the unit of collectivity membership is not *the individual* in general but the *person in role.*

Two consequences follow from this. First, parallel to the interpenetration between social and cultural systems noted above, there must be interpenetration between social systems and personalities. Concretely, just as normative culture is internalized in personalities as well as institutionalized, there must be institutionalized expectations about the particular role in the particular collectivity which are also internalized in the personalities of incumbents. Typically, of course, internalized expectations of reciprocity shade in varying degrees into alienation and propensities for deviance.

Second, however, the specifications of normative culture to the different collectivities in which the individual participates and the expectations about behavior in the individual's various roles must be integrated with each other *at the level of the personality.* One-to-one matching between the specific structures of particular personalities and the behavioral requirements of socially organized roles is precluded by, together, the pluralistic differentiation of subcollectivities in the social system and the plural role participations of individual persons. The sociological reason for this, which combines with genetic, psychological, and other kinds of reasons, is that no two persons have the same combination of role involvements—a circumstance greatly accentuated in societies where a substantial proportion of role involvements are nonascriptive —and, hence, role involvements are entered as a matter of, in some sense, voluntary choice. (Positing such a correspondence between the bases of social system and of personality integration has been a major fallacy in many theories of "culture and personality" and "national character.")

Here we encounter again Durkheim's analysis of the double relations between actor and normative culture. From the perspective of the social system the personalities of its participating members are at the same time, in different respects, *both part of the social system*, through interpenetration, *and part of its environment.* The zone of interpenetration is that of the expectations about role performance, since they are both institutionalized in the social system and internalized in individual personalities. Here it is particularly important that where the roles of role partners are differentiated, expectations are, not for identical, but for *different yet complementary*, performances. For instance, husband and wife, in their differentiated roles in the family, are generally expected to act, not alike, but differently, each having a distinct proper sex role. The differences between roles, as well as their common solidarity, are legitimized by the values shared between them.

Organism and environment. The personality of the individual, as an analytically defined action system, is one major parameter, linked to the living organism, the two being, in our terminology, ascribed to each other. They must nevertheless be distinguished analytically because the structure and mechanisms of the organism are physical, while those of the personality are psychocultural and learned. As with the personality and social system, there can be no one-to-one correspondence between the properties of an organism and the personality's internalized content of normative culture and social role expectations. In certain contexts, this is very well known; thus, no expert contends that, in any but a "programmed" sense, there is specific anatomical or physiological structure distinguishing the speakers of a given language from those of another.

The organism is the link between action systems and the physical world. *All* concrete action is, in one aspect, the "behavior of organisms," but only in one aspect. Thus, all linguistic communication involves the speech organs, the auditory apparatus, and the brain (or alternative mechanisms, as in the case of writing and reading). Since organisms are always located in particular places at given times, all social systems have their ecological aspect, i.e., there is location, movement, and distribution of organisms and activities in space. Clearly, an individual's own body and the bodies of others are crucial objects of orientation to him in a wide variety of ways.

It seems to follow that the organism should be included in the physical environment of action systems, and hence of social systems. In the light of our traditions of thought, the physical environment is clearly the least problematic of the environments of interaction systems. However, the old difficulties over the sense in which the individual as a whole (including his organic aspects) should be included in the concept of social system can be resolved with the same logic that has been used in relating social systems to the cultural and psychological systems of action.

First, there is a category of objects which are *only* physical, whether they be "natural" objects or artifacts. These cannot and do not interact in human social systems, animals being a marginal case. In this sense, human organisms not only are physical but also interpenetrate with the other action systems. They are environmental objects and also, through interpenetration, parts of the action (and interaction) system.

This dual relation to interaction, however, does not apply equally to all aspects of the human organism. The concept "behavioral organism" designates the components of the organism for which interpenetration with personality, social system, and culture is most important. Some (for instance, H. A. Murray) have used the concept "vegetative organism" to designate aspects, such as most of the metabolic processes and mechanisms, that are minimally involved in action. One should not, however, assume that the line is empirically fixed; action phenomena may shift (through stress or psychotherapy, for instance) to involve rather directly organic processes that ordinarily are insulated from them.

Certainly, the involvement of the organism in interaction comprises all the modes of orientation and modalities of objects. The organism is perhaps particularly important as an instrumentality, but Freud's concept of primary narcissism rightly considers the child's love of his own body an authentic case of love. Similarly, there is an organic aspect interpenetrating with the nonorganic aspects in every subsystem of the orientation of actors. There has been considerable research, for example, on the organic "bases" of the emotions, starting with the well-known work of Cannon (1915).

Interaction as process

We may conclude with a brief outline of interaction as process. First, we presume that whatever the intermediate stages in the course of evolution from simple animal behavior to human social interaction, the latter is couched primarily at symbolic–cultural levels, although it certainly has various "subcultural" underpinnings. The action process, then, can be analyzed into two phases: what happens *within* the acting unit (e.g., a person in role or a collectivity) and what happens *between* such units. It seems to be generally acceptable terminology to refer to the former process as "decision" and to the latter as "communication."

In decision processes, information communicated to the deciding unit (this is the interaction case, but environmental information may also be relevant) is "processed" in the light of the "dispositions," goals, sentiments, etc., of the unit. An *act* is then performed, which typically consists of a communication to other units in the system. Whether the communication is verbal or not is an open question, as it may consist, for example, in a gesture of the sort Mead analyzed so clearly. This communication then becomes an input to the receiving units, including the promulgator, who may be, in terms of a stock phrase for this type of situation, "appalled by what he just said."

Every output of communication involves crossing a boundary, as does its receipt as input. Its meaning must be interpreted and introduced into a combinatorial process, along with other inputs and with aspects of the internal structures and processes of the unit, whether a personality or a collectivity. This interpretive and combinatorial process constitutes "decision," from which emerges new communicative output.

The output must also undergo a process that involves an indefinite number of stages before the communication reaches the target unit, units, or categories of units. In a variety of ways this process involves media of communication, which expose the communication to a variety of influences, such as modifications or distortions or maintenance of its "message" by special measures. Such influences are, of course, the outcome of decisions made by units through which the communication passes.

Generalized media of interaction. Of the many aspects of the communication process in interaction, one may be singled out for special comment, namely, the role of *generalized* media. I have already mentioned language a number of times as the prototypical medium. At the cultural level it is clearly the fundamental matrix of the whole system of media. Large-scale social systems, however, contain more specialized media (if you will, specialized "languages"), such as money, power, and influence (see Parsons 1963*a*; 1963*b*). Such media, like language, *control* behavior in the processes of interaction. They do so, however, by *symbolic* means, i.e., by presenting the actor, not with an intrinsically important object, such as a food object, but with a symbolic "representation" of such an object. Symbols can arouse the expectation that a meal will be served; hence they prepare the communication's recipient for the experience of food-gratification and, within important limits, even substitute for the experience. The working of money in this regard is the best-understood example of a social system medium. It has, as the classical economists put it, no "value in use," but only "value in exchange." Possession of money symbolically concretizes expectations of access to gratifying objects of utility, but money is not itself such an object.

There are various other such media in human interaction. Freud's "erotic pleasure" certainly constitutes one, as do the phenomena referred to by such terms as "affect" and "social acceptance," and what W. I. Thomas called the "wishes" for response and recognition. The demonstration that such media are deeply needed by persons at a psychological level is excellent evidence of the phenomena of internalization discussed above and, more generally, of interpenetration.

TALCOTT PARSONS

[*Directly related are the entries* GROUPS, *article on* THE STUDY OF GROUPS; INTEGRATION; NORMS; SYSTEMS ANALYSIS. *Other relevant material may be found in* LANGUAGE, *article on* LANGUAGE AND CULTURE; PERSONALITY; SELF CONCEPT; SOCIALIZATION; UTILITARIANISM; *and in the biographies of* CANNON; COOLEY; DESCARTES; DURKHEIM; FREUD; HEGEL; HOBBES; HUSSERL; JAMES; KANT; LEWIN; LOCKE; MARSHALL; MARX; MAYO; MEAD; PEIRCE; SIMMEL; THOMAS; WEBER, MAX.]

BIBLIOGRAPHY

BALES, ROBERT F. 1950 *Interaction Process Analysis: A Method for the Study of Small Groups.* Reading, Mass.: Addison-Wesley.

BENNE, KENNETH D.; BRADFORD, LELAND I.; and LIPPITT, RONALD 1950 *Social Action.* New York: B'nai B'rith Anti-Defamation League.

CANNON, WALTER B. (1915) 1953 *Bodily Changes in Pain, Hunger, Fear and Rage: An Account of Recent Researches Into the Function of Emotional Excitement.* 2d ed. Boston: Branford.

COOLEY, CHARLES H. (1902) 1956 *Human Nature and the Social Order.* Rev. ed. In Charles H. Cooley, *Two Major Works:* Social Organization *and* Human Nature and the Social Order. Glencoe, Ill.: Free Press. → Each title reprinted with individual title page and pagination. Separate paperback editions were published in 1964 by Schocken.

DURKHEIM, ÉMILE (1893) 1960 *The Division of Labor in Society.* Glencoe, Ill.: Free Press. → First published as *De la division du travail social.*

DURKHEIM, ÉMILE (1895) 1958 *The Rules of Sociological Method.* 8th ed. Edited by George E. G. Catlin. Glencoe, Ill.: Free Press. → First published as *Les règles de la méthode sociologique.*

DURKHEIM, ÉMILE (1912) 1954 *The Elementary Forms of the Religious Life.* London: Allen & Unwin; New York: Macmillan. → First published as *Les formes élémentaires de la vie religieuse, le système totémique en Australie.*

GOFFMAN, ERVING (1956) 1959 *The Presentation of Self in Everyday Life.* Garden City, N.Y.: Doubleday.

HOMANS, GEORGE C. 1950 *The Human Group.* New York: Harcourt.

HOMANS, GEORGE C. 1961 *Social Behavior: Its Elementary Forms.* New York: Harcourt.

LEWIN, KURT (1939–1947) 1963 *Field Theory in Social Science: Selected Theoretical Papers.* Edited by Dorwin Cartwright. London: Tavistock.

LEWIN, KURT et al. 1944 *Authority and Frustration.* Iowa City: Univ. of Iowa Press.

MEAD, GEORGE H. (1930) 1964 Cooley's Contribution to American Social Thought. Pages 293–307 in George H. Mead, *George Herbert Mead on Social Psychology.* Rev. ed. Edited by Anselm Strauss. Univ. of Chicago Press.

Mead, George H. (1934) 1963 *Mind, Self and Society From the Standpoint of a Social Behaviorist.* Edited by Charles W. Morris. Univ. of Chicago Press. → Published posthumously.

Mead, George H. 1938 *The Philosophy of the Act.* Univ. of Chicago Press. → This volume consists almost entirely of papers unpublished during Mead's lifetime.

Naegele, Kasper D. 1958 Attachment and Alienation: Complementary Aspects of the Work of Durkheim and Simmel. *American Journal of Sociology* 63:580–589.

Parsons, Talcott (1958) 1964 Social Structure and the Development of Personality: Freud's Contribution to the Integration of Psychology and Sociology. Pages 78–111 in Talcott Parsons, *Social Structure and Personality.* New York: Free Press.

Parsons, Talcott 1963*a* On the Concept of Influence. *Public Opinion Quarterly* 27:37–62. → A comment by J. S. Coleman appears on pages 63–82; a communication by R. A. Bauer appears on pages 83–86; and a rejoinder by Talcott Parsons appears on pages 87–92.

Parsons, Talcott 1963*b* On the Concept of Political Power. American Philosophical Society, *Proceedings* 107:232–262.

Parsons, Talcott 1965 Evaluation and Objectivity in Social Science: An Interpretation of Weber's Contribution. *International Social Science Journal* 17:46–63.

Parsons, Talcott; and Shils, Edward A. (editors) 1951 *Toward a General Theory of Action.* Cambridge, Mass.: Harvard Univ. Press. → A paperback edition was published in 1962 by Harper.

Simmel, Georg (1902–1917) 1950 *The Sociology of Georg Simmel.* Edited and translated by Kurt H. Wolff. Glencoe, Ill.: Free Press.

Simmel, Georg (1908) 1955 *Conflict; The Web of Group Affiliations.* Glencoe, Ill.: Free Press. → These essays appeared originally as "Der Streit" and "Die Kreuzung sozialer Kreise" in Georg Simmel's *Soziologie.*

Simmel, Georg *Georg Simmel, 1858–1918: A Collection of Essays.* Edited by Kurt H. Wolff. Columbus: Ohio State Univ. Press, 1959.

Tiryakian, Edward A. 1962 *Sociologism and Existentialism: Two Perspectives on the Individual and Society.* Englewood Cliffs, N.J.: Prentice-Hall.

Weber, Max (1922) 1957 *The Theory of Social and Economic Organization.* Edited by Talcott Parsons. Glencoe, Ill.: Free Press. → First published as Part 1 of *Wirtschaft und Gesellschaft.*

II
SYMBOLIC INTERACTION

The term "symbolic interaction" refers to the process by which individuals relate to their own minds or the minds of others; the process, that is, in which individuals take account of their own or their fellows' motives, needs, desires, means and ends, knowledge, and the like. This process was first labeled symbolic interaction by Blumer (1937). Among sociologists it is often called social interaction.

The more distinctive problems of modern social psychology concern symbolic interaction—its rise, general characteristics, persistence, or dissolution. The more distinctive problems of modern sociology concern the occurrence, maintenance, or dissolution of special forms of symbolic interaction. Crowds, communities, friendships, economies, concerts, and cotillions are instances of such forms.

In the definition of "symbolic interaction," the word "mind" is employed in the sense first clarified by C. S. Peirce, William James, John Dewey, and G. H. Mead (Morris 1932). It denotes instrumental activities that animals direct toward their environments. These instrumental activities, sometimes referred to as action or as psychological activities, relate the organism's requirements to the conditions and resources in the environment that are relevant for meeting those requirements. What usually are considered to be the units or aspects of purely psychological events—for example, attitudes, beliefs, motivation, perception, thought, or choice—are here interpreted as ingredients or aspects of instrumental activity. In his capacity as a minded organism, the individual is called an "actor." Groups or other collectivities can also be conceived of as actors, to the extent that they make decisions and relate to their own instrumental processes and to those of other collectivities.

One additional property distinguishes mind from other organic functions, such as respiration, ingestion, or excretion, that mediate between an animal and its outer environment. An activity is instrumental only if the probability of its appearance is affected by the relevance to the organism's needs of that activity's prior occurrence in similar situations. The term "learning" refers to changes in such probabilities. Situations are similar when they resemble one another in the requirements made by the organism and in the conditions afforded by the environment for meeting those requirements.

When individuals take account of one another's minds, they observe, and adapt to, the existence of these instrumental processes as such. This means that they take into account something of the specifically instrumental character of one another's behavior. It would be possible to perceive simply the physical patterns embodied in another man's grimace or stride, but some perception of the place of those patterns in an instrumental process is involved in judging the grimace to be friendly or the stride to be hurried or determined.

The conception of symbolic interaction does not require that the individuals concerned reflect upon what they do. Mice and men learn to distinguish among the properties of their environment—among colors, sounds, and distances—and in this sense they are conscious, or aware, of those properties. They may not, however, be aware of their awareness; they may not know what they know. Similarly, it is conceivable, and probably common, for a man to be aware of his own mind or the minds of others without the existence of this knowledge becoming the object of his attention. Indeed, an individual often cannot say just why he has the impressions of others that he has or reaches the conclusions he does. It is proper to say that men aware of their own minds are "self-conscious," but some other term, perhaps "reflective self-consciousness," is needed to indicate the further step of knowing that one is self-conscious. That further step, or the even more complex stage of knowing that one knows what one knows, is a possible but not necessary development of symbolic interaction.

Emergence of the concept. Symbolic interaction was first put forward as a distinct and important type of relationship in order to interpret some of men's oldest observations. Since ancient times it has been thought that men's behavior and experience differ from that of other animals, whether in degree or in kind. Specifically, men are often capable of rational activity—of identifying objectives in the environment and locating means by which those objectives may be attained. In the course of rational activity, men typically exercise control over their own behavior, exhibit reflective self-consciousness, and display an orientation to the past and future, as well as to the present. They experience themselves as deciding to act as they do. They employ some manner of signs or symbols, and they apply some normative standards in guiding their own behavior or that of others. They relate to the world in terms of its significance for their developing activities. In addition, sequences of human behavior are sometimes directed toward objectives which can be attained only in the far-distant future. On occasion, as in efforts toward achieving moral perfection, the objective may be conceived of as unobtainable yet men may feel obligated to approximate its attainment as best they can. Taken together, these several abilities especially conspicuous in man are said to constitute his "human nature."

A major step in explaining human nature was taken in the seventeenth and eighteenth centuries, when several British philosophers, and especially John Locke and David Hume, proposed that it consisted, not of innate abilities, but of skills acquired in the course of men's interacting with their fellows. Speculations about the exact process by which human nature emerged in interaction continued in Europe and the United States throughout the nineteenth century (Hughes 1958). It was, however, not until the two decades after World War I that a sociologist, Charles H. Cooley (1909), and a philosopher, George Herbert Mead (1934), provided a detailed and explicit account of the origins of human nature as aspects of the rise of symbolic interaction.

Mead and other writers who shared his outlook paid particular attention to views of behavior or of organized social life that precluded an interpretation of human nature's origin in symbolic interaction. In Mead's time instinctivism and behaviorism were the most conspicuous views of behavior that were obviously incompatible with Mead's position. Instinctivism rooted human nature in biological inheritance. The behaviorism of Mead's day sought, in physicalistic descriptions of the environment, properties which could be thought to determine conduct, quite apart from the relevance of those properties for the individual's particular needs or his present lines of behavior. Mass, velocity, and extent are instances of these properties. These behavioristic accounts often accorded full ontological status only to such properties. Believing that behaviorism was inadequate to explain the rise of human nature, Mead and other writers sought to endow symbolic interaction with equal ontological status.

Writers who shared Mead's position also objected to certain conceptions of organized social life, particularly the cultural determinism prevalent in the literature of their time. This determinism conceived of men as so completely immured within society, so thoroughly shaped as mere parts of society, that the role of novelty, fluidity, and change in social relations was completely obscured. By contrast, interpretations of social life as symbolic interaction conceived of actors as constantly establishing and re-establishing their mutual relations, modifying or abandoning them as the occasion demanded. Thus, social life was viewed as a process by which actors collectively solved problems, the nature and persistence of their solutions varying with the problems they defined.

Varieties of interaction

Symbolic or social interaction is conceived of as developing from prior relations that men have in their capacities as physical bodies, as organisms, and as actors. When people affect one another as physical bodies, we can speak of physical interaction. Two men hurrying around a corner from opposite directions, colliding, and falling to the ground provide a case in point. When individuals affect one another in their capacity as living organisms, we speak of ecological or biological interaction. In this capacity each individual, by using resources relevant for sustaining life and by otherwise modifying those resources, affects the life of the others. When men acting as minded individuals, that is, as actors, behave toward their fellows as they might toward any other objects in the environment, we may speak of "behavioral" interaction. No requirement is then made that the actors take the minds of others into account.

Current notions and explanations of symbolic interaction depend on the assumption that men influence each other as physical bodies and that they cluster together and affect each other because of their status as living organisms. Explanations of symbolic interaction rest even more explicitly on the pre-existence of behavioral interaction, that is, on assumptions like the following: that minds and accompanying gestures already exist for men to observe; that patterned dependencies among actors exist ready to be discriminated; and that individuals come to identify the existence and significance of each other's minds in the course of efforts to increase the amount and dependability of resources available to them. In short, both empirical observations and current theories require our treating behavioral interaction as a necessary condition for the rise and persistence of symbolic interaction.

We find symbolic interaction not only emerging over the long course of human evolution but also appearing, and then either persisting or dissolving, in men's daily encounters. The principal occasions on which one may witness its ebb and flow are those when previously unrelated individuals establish contacts with one another's minds or when existing patterns of symbolic interaction are subjected to strain. On such occasions appear events like those recorded in Table 1. The last three columns of Table 1 concern events which might be labeled symbolic interaction. The first column clearly refers to behavioral interaction.

The classification in Table 1 reflects the incompleteness and inaccuracy of our knowledge. Its categories are gross, recording little of the detailed understanding now available on each broad topic. However, the table does display key topics and suggests the essential unity among them.

The columns in Table 1 represent types of interaction presently known to occur, each having at least the characteristics that are minimal for behavioral interaction. Reading from left to right, we find that each column adds some characteristic to that minimum. In column IV we reach elements of what we are calling symbolic or social interaction. These elements are fully present in column V. Column VI treats a subclass of symbolic interaction. The type of relation represented in each column is assumed to be among the prerequisites for relations specified in columns further to the right. The reciprocal action described in any column can regress to types of interaction further to the left.

Row *A* in Table 1 records perceptions that individuals have of others and themselves. These perceptions concern characteristics of individuals as sources of influence. Row *A*1 and row *A*2 record coordinations required when actors relate to the conditions in row *A*. These coordinations involve some modification of each participant's behavior. There are no reasonably standardized labels for rows *A*1 and *A*2 of the first three columns. This is so because the very nature of the processes is poorly understood and is the subject of controversy. Some investigators would be satisfied were "self-stimulation" inserted in row *A*1 of column I and "interpersonal stimulation" in row *A*2 of the same column. Others would find this quite inappropriate. Concepts appropriate for columns II and III are even less certain.

On the other hand, there is considerable agree-

Table 1 — Some varieties of interaction

	Social stimulation (I)	*Circular reaction* (II)	*Conversation of gestures* (III)	*Interpretive interaction* (IV)	*Symbolic interaction* (V)	*Communication* (VI)
A. Each actor acts toward himself and others as loci of:	stimuli	cues	gestures	signs	selves	identity
1. Directed toward his own behavior, this action is:				insight		
a. It results in some degree of:				self-control		
2. Directed toward others' behavior, this action is:				empathy		
a. It results in some degree of:				social influence		
B. Actors so engaged may yet have difficulties in coordinating their relations as:	objects	actors	coparticipants in several types of act	coparticipants in a division of labor (i.e., a role system)	coparticipants in several role systems	
1. The difficulties may be resolved if they pay attention to and routinize their use of the wider context provided by:	cues	gestures	signs	selves	identity	

ment regarding the concepts recorded for rows *A*1 and *A*2 in column IV. Indeed, the same concepts are often employed to designate the contents of these rows in columns V and VI as well. Occasionally, more specific terms are used. Thus, "search for identity" might be inserted in row *A*1 of column VI, "role taking" in row *A*1 of column V, and "role playing" in row *A*2 of that column. However, firmer empirical knowledge about the processes involved must precede agreement on appropriate concepts and labels.

As row *B* indicates, difficulties may arise when actors try to coordinate their efforts. When that happens, actors have a greater chance of success if they know something of the conditions under which the behavior of their fellows occurs. Thus, they are likely to deal more effectively with one another as sources of stimuli if they are forewarned of those stimuli. Cues are stimuli which, an actor discovers, precede the appearance of other stimuli. Column by column, row *B*1 indicates progressively broader contexts of conditions, which, if perceived, make more dependable and effective an actor's dealings with conditions specified in row *A*.

We now may notice that the figure's successive columns are linked, in that the broader context developed in row *B*1 of any column (e.g., an understanding of cues in order to cope with related stimuli) becomes itself the focus of attention in the column immediately to the right. It is essential to offer a brief justification for saying that the conditions given in row *B*1 are a context for and an aid to coping with those given in row *A*.

The relation between cues and stimuli has already been mentioned. What of that between gestures and cues? A gesture is an overt behavior that occurs in the early stages of a particular act. It can serve, therefore, as a cue to later stages. It differs from other cues in being relevant to instrumental activity as the special kind of stimulus with which one seeks to cope. A sign is an overt behavior that occurs in the early stages of a *class* of acts. It can serve, therefore, as a cue to a mind, but it differs from other gestures by referring to qualities common to many acts instead of characteristics peculiar to any one of them. "Self" refers to signs representing classes of acts in which a given actor engages. These classes of acts are identified as *his*. Each of an actor's selves provides a context for understanding and forecasting his more specific and immediate activities. "Actor's identity" refers to signs representing the more persistent and general categories of action that he employs in all situations. Knowledge of his identity enables a more adequate interpretation and forecasting of the selves he will exhibit in particular situations.

Row *B* refers to events that are of great psychological and sociological importance but that are not well understood. In columns I to V of that row are specified relationships between participants in some joint action. The establishment and maintenance of each variety of joint action is a problem to participants. Our present information is too slight for any confident description of the problems appropriate to any single column. One can say with confidence only that the succession of problems from left to right across Table 1 should involve participants in increasingly complex relations with one another.

Social scientists still need to learn many things concerning each of these relationships. For example, little is known about the steps by which infants and young children come to identify each type of problem and to participate with others in its solution. Moreover, we have still to identify the steps that socialized actors must take to maintain each type of relationship once it is established. We have yet to discover more than the rudiments of the "grammar" of cues, gestures, signs, selves, and identities. We know but little of the means by which actors make valid interpretations of those phenomena. We presently are unable to specify in any detail the potentialities and limitations for collective undertakings of each variety of interaction.

Relations between types of interaction. Although detailed knowledge of the different types of interaction has been slow to accumulate, many of the general processes by which one type of interaction changes into another have long been familiar to social scientists. Four of these processes—elementary collective behavior, socialization, institutionalization, and social control—can be at least partly described in terms of the relationships outlined in Table 1. Thus, elementary collective behavior is a change from the types of interaction in column V or VI to those in columns I to IV and back again. Socialization is a process in which an actor is trained to engage in any or all types of symbolic interaction or communication. Similarly, institutionalization takes place to some degree in any situation in which actors jointly define some relationships as legitimate and as necessary for their continued interaction. Finally, social control clearly involves change from one type of interaction to another, since it is a process in which actors encourage others to engage in, or prevent others from engaging in, some relationship because it meets or violates an institutionalized standard. Three of these four processes probably occur in most movements between columns. Thus, there probably are rudiments of socialization and of institutionalization in any move across these columns from left to right. Similarly, there are at least some rudiments of social control being exercised in all shifts, whether to the right or left. Collective behavior differs from the other three in referring to a sequence of changes in type of interaction from certain columns to others, in particular from column V or VI to columns I to IV and back again.

Sequences of stages in socialization like those proposed by Mead (1934), Freud and his followers (Fenichel 1945), or Newcomb (1961) distinguish successive steps in the movement from behavioral to symbolic interaction. Thus, Mead offers progressive discriminations in a cognitive sequence. From solo play to participation in simple games to relations with a generalized other, his sequence marks the steps toward interaction that is more fully symbolic. These steps progress from relations with a single other person to relations with several other persons and, finally, to adaptations to more-abstract social structures. In Freud's work we find stages of growing dependence on others as minded individuals, beginning with a recognition of one's dependence on their actions and ending with the commitment to support actively the social norms that facilitate, govern, and rationalize continued social interaction with them. In Newcomb's studies appear the steps through which experienced social participants establish intimate contacts with one another, from (*a*) first impressions of one another's overt behavior to (*b*) a classification of each other in terms of such common social roles as age, sex, and social class, thence to (*c*) a mutual reconnaissance of ideologies (e.g., those connected with politics or religion) that guide men's relations as comembers of the larger society, and, finally, to (*d*) reciprocal investigations of more idiosyncratic attitudes and dispositions relevant to the subjects' possible relations as friends and intimates.

Many of these developmental schemes are guided by the image of a complete or perfected social situation. In such perfected situations, we are told, the full range of skills that distinguish symbolic interaction are employed. Cooley's vision of the primary group (1909) belongs here, as does the psychoanalysts' picture of mature love (Abraham 1925; Fromm 1947). In each case, experience with the perfected social situation is advanced as the necessary condition for training and reinforcing individuals in symbolic interaction. Each writer reminds us that fully symbolic interaction is rarely achieved, always tends to revert to behavioral or biological interaction, and must be reachieved over and over again. Indeed, it is the effort to achieve some essential stability of symbolic interaction that forces men to act in support of social relations—to distinguish and legitimize their joint actions, in contrast with activities that support only their personal interests. This is the origin of social systems.

GUY E. SWANSON

[*Directly related are the entries* COMMUNICATION; GROUPS, *article on* THE STUDY OF GROUPS; LEARNING THEORY; SEMANTICS AND SEMIOTICS. *Other relevant material may be found in* COLLECTIVE BEHAVIOR; LANGUAGE; SOCIAL CONTROL; SOCIAL INSTITUTIONS; SOCIALIZATION; *and in the biographies of* COOLEY; DEWEY; FREUD; HUME; JAMES; LOCKE; MEAD; PEIRCE.]

BIBLIOGRAPHY

ABRAHAM, KARL (1925) 1953 Character-formation on the Genital Level of Libido-development. Pages 407–417 in Karl Abraham, *Selected Papers*. Volume 1: Selected Papers on Psychoanalysis. New York: Basic Books. → First published in German in Volume 7 of the *International Journal of Psycho-analysis*.

BLUMER, HERBERT 1937 Social Psychology. Pages 144–198 in Emerson P. Schmidt (editor), *Man and Society*. New York: Prentice-Hall.

COOLEY, CHARLES H. (1909) 1956 *Social Organization: A Study of the Larger Mind*. In Charles H. Cooley, *Two Major Works:* Social Organization *and* Human Nature and the Social Order. Glencoe, Ill.: Free Press. → Each title reprinted with individual title page and pagination. Separate paperback editions were published in 1964 by Schocken.

FENICHEL, OTTO 1945 *The Psychoanalytic Theory of Neurosis*. New York: Norton. → See especially pages 463–540.

FROMM, ERICH 1947 *Man For Himself: An Inquiry Into the Psychology of Ethics*. New York: Holt.

HUGHES, H. STUART 1958 *Consciousness and Society: The Reorientation of European Social Thought, 1890–1930*. New York: Knopf.

MEAD, GEORGE H. (1934) 1963 *Mind, Self and Society From the Standpoint of a Social Behaviorist*. Edited by Charles W. Morris. Univ. of Chicago Press. → Published posthumously.

MORRIS, CHARLES W. 1932 *Six Theories of Mind*. Univ. of Chicago Press.

NEWCOMB, THEODORE M. 1961 *The Acquaintance Process*. New York: Holt.

III
DRAMATISM

Dramatism is a method of analysis and a corresponding critique of terminology designed to show that the most direct route to the study of human relations and human motives is via a methodical inquiry into cycles or clusters of terms and their functions.

The dramatistic approach is implicit in the key term "act." "Act" is thus a terministic center from which many related considerations can be shown to "radiate," as though it were a "god-term" from which a whole universe of terms is derived. The dramatistic study of language comes to a focus in a philosophy of language (and of "symbolicity" in general); the latter provides the basis for a general conception of man and of human relations. The present article will consider primarily the dramatistic concern with the resources, limitations, and paradoxes of terminology, particularly in connection with the imputing of motives.

The dramatistic approach to action

Dramatism centers in observations of this sort: for there to be an *act*, there must be an *agent*. Similarly, there must be a *scene* in which the agent acts. To act in a scene, the agent must employ some means, or *agency*. And it can be called an act in the full sense of the term only if it involves a *purpose* (that is, if a support happens to give way and one falls, such motion on the agent's part is not an act, but an accident). These five terms (act, scene, agent, agency, purpose) have been labeled the dramatistic pentad; the aim of calling attention to them in this way is to show how the functions which they designate operate in the imputing of motives (Burke [1945–1950] 1962, Introduction). The pattern is incipiently a hexad when viewed in connection with the different but complementary analysis of *attitude* (as an ambiguous term for *incipient* action) undertaken by George Herbert Mead (1938) and by I. A. Richards (1959).

Later we shall consider the question whether the key terms of dramatism are literal or metaphorical. In the meantime, other important things about the terms themselves should be noted.

Obviously, for instance, the concept of scene can be widened or narrowed (conceived of in terms of varying "scope" or circumference). Thus, an agent's behavior ("act") might be thought of as taking place against a polytheistic background; or the over-all scene may be thought of as grounded in one god; or the circumference of the situation can be narrowed to naturalistic limits, as in Darwinism; or it can be localized in such terms as "Western civilization," "Elizabethanism," "capitalism," "D day," "10 Downing Street," "on this train ride," and so on, endlessly. Any change of the circumference in terms of which an act is viewed implies a corresponding change in one's view of the quality of the act's motivation. Such a loose yet compelling correspondence between act and scene is called a "scene–act ratio" (Burke [1945–1950] 1962, pp. 1–7).

All the terms are capable of similar relationships. A "purpose–agency ratio," for instance, would concern the logic of "means selecting," the relation of means to ends (as the Supreme Court might decide that an emergency measure is constitutional because it was taken in an emergency situation). An "agent–act ratio" would reflect the correspondence between a man's character and the character of his behavior (as, in a drama, the principles of formal consistency require that each member of the dramatis personae act in character, though such correspondences in art can have a perfection not often found in life). In actual practice, such ratios are used sometimes to explain an act and sometimes to *justify* it (*ibid.*, pp. 15–20). Such correlations are not strict, but analogical. Thus, by "scene–act ratio" is meant a proposition such as: Though agent and act are necessarily different in many of their attributes, some notable element of one is implicitly or analogously present in the other.

David Hume's *An Inquiry Concerning Human Understanding* (first published in 1748) throws a serviceable light upon the dramatistic "ratios." His treatise begins with the observation that "moral philosophy, or the science of human nature, may be treated after two different manners." One of these "considers man chiefly as born for action." The other would "consider man in the light of a reasonable rather than an active being, and endeavor to form his understanding more than cultivate his manners" ([1748] 1952, p. 451). Here, in essence, is the distinction between a dramatistic approach in terms of *action* and an approach in terms of *knowledge*. For, as a "reasonable being," Hume says, man "receives from science" his proper food and nourishment. But man "is a sociable, no less than a reasonable being. . . . Man is also an active being; and from that disposition, as well as from the various necessities of human life, must submit to business and occupation" (*ibid.*, p. 452).

Insofar as men's actions are to be interpreted in terms of the circumstances in which they are acting, their behavior would fall under the heading of a "scene–act ratio." But insofar as their acts reveal their different characters, their behavior would fall under the heading of an "agent–act ratio." For instance, in a time of great crisis, such as a shipwreck, the conduct of all persons involved in that crisis could be expected to manifest in some way the motivating influence of the crisis. Yet, within such a "scene–act ratio" there would be a range of "agent–act ratios," insofar as one man was "proved" to be cowardly, another bold, another resourceful, and so on.

Talcott Parsons, in one of his earlier works, has analytically unfolded, for sociological purposes, much the same set of terministic functions that is here being called dramatistic (owing to their nature as implied in the idea of an "act"). Thus, in dealing with "the unit of action systems," Parsons writes:

> An "act" involves logically the following: (1) It implies an agent, an "actor." (2) For purposes of definition the act must have an "end," a future state of affairs toward which the process of action is oriented. (3) It must be initiated in a "situation" of which the trends of development differ in one or more important respects from the state of affairs to which the action is oriented, the end. This situation is in turn analyzable into two elements: those over which the actor has no control, that is which he cannot alter, or prevent from being altered, in conformity with his end, and those over which he has such control. The former may be termed the "conditions" of action, the latter the "means." Finally (4) there is inherent in the conception of this unit, in its analytical uses, a certain mode of relationship between these elements. That is, in the choice of alternative means to the end, in so far as the situation allows alternatives, there is a "normative orientation" of actions. (1937, p. 44)

Aristotle, from whom Aquinas got his definition of God as "pure act," gives us much the same lineup when enumerating the circumstances about which we may be ignorant, with corresponding inability to act voluntarily:

> A man may be ignorant, then, of who he is, what he is doing, what or whom he is acting on, and sometimes also what (e.g. what instrument) he is doing it with, and to what end (e.g. he may think his act will conduce to some one's safety), and how he is doing it (e.g. whether gently or violently). (*Nichomachean Ethics* 1111a5)

This pattern became fixed in the medieval questions: *quis* (agent), *quid* (act), *ubi* (scene defined as place), *quibus auxiliis* (agency), *cur* (purpose), *quo modo* (manner, "attitude"), *quando* (scene defined temporally).

The nature of symbolic action

Within the practically limitless range of scenes (or motivating situations) in terms of which human action can be defined and studied, there is one over-all dramatistic distinction as regards the widening or narrowing of circumference. This is the distinction between "action" and "sheer motion." "Action," is a term for the kind of behavior possible to a typically symbol-using animal (such as man) in contrast with the extrasymbolic or nonsymbolic operations of nature.

Whatever terministic paradoxes we may encounter en route (and the dramatistic view of terminology leads one to expect them on the grounds that language is primarily a species of action, or expression of attitudes, rather than an instrument of definition), there is the self-evident distinction between symbol and *symbolized* (in the sense that the *word* "tree" is categorically distinguishable from the *thing* tree). Whatever may be the ultimate confusions that result from man's intrinsic involvement with "symbolicity" as a necessary part of his nature, one can at least *begin* with this sufficiently clear distinction between a "thing" and its name.

The distinction is generalized in dramatism as one between "sheer motion" and "action." It involves an empirical shift of circumference in the sense that although man's ability to speak depends upon the existence of speechless nature, the existence of speechless nature does not depend upon man's ability to speak. The relation between these two distinct terministic realms can be summed up in three propositions:

(1) There can be no action without motion—that is, even the "symbolic action" of pure thought requires corresponding motions of the brain.

(2) There can be motion without action. (For instance, the motions of the tides, of sunlight, of growth and decay.)

(3) Action is not reducible to terms of motion. For instance, the "essence" or "meaning" of a sentence is not reducible to its sheer physical existence as sounds in the air or marks on the page, although material motions of some sort are necessary for the production, transmission, and reception of the sentence. As has been said by Talcott Parsons:

> Certainly the situation of action includes parts of what is called in common-sense terms the physical environment and the biological organism . . . these elements of the situation of action are capable of analysis in terms of the physical and biological sciences, and the phenomena in question are subject to analysis in terms of the units in use in those sciences. Thus a bridge may, with perfect truth, be said to consist of atoms of iron, a small amount of carbon, etc., and their constituent electrons, protons, neutrons and the like. Must the student of action, then, become a physicist, chemist, biologist in order to understand his subject? In a sense this is true, but for purposes of the theory of action it is not necessary or desirable to carry such analyses as far as science in general is capable of doing. A limit is set by the frame of reference with which the student of action is working. That is, he is interested in phenomena with an aspect not reducible to action terms only in so far as they impinge on the schema of action in a relevant way—in the role of conditions or means. . . . For the purposes of the theory of action the smallest conceivable concrete unit is the unit act, and while it is in turn analyzable into the elements to which reference has been made—end, means, conditions and guiding norms—further analysis of the phenomena of which these are

in turn aspects is relevant to the theory of action only in so far as the units arrived at can be referred to as constituting such elements of a unit act or a system of them. (1937, pp. 47–48)

Is dramatism merely metaphorical? Although such prototypically dramatistic usages as "all the world's a stage" are clearly metaphors, the situation looks quite otherwise when approached from another point of view. For instance, a physical scientist's relation to the materials involved in the study of motion differs in quality from his relation to his colleagues. He would never think of "petitioning" the objects of his experiment or "arguing with them," as he would with persons whom he asks to collaborate with him or to judge the results of his experiment. Implicit in these two relations is the distinction between the sheer motion of things and the actions of persons.

In this sense, man is defined literally as an animal characterized by his special aptitude for "symbolic action," which is itself a literal term. And from there on, drama is employed, not as a metaphor but as a fixed form that helps us discover what the implications of the terms "act" and "person" *really are*. Once we choose a generalized term for what people do, it is certainly as literal to say that "people act" as it is to say that they "but move like mere things."

Dramatism and the social system. Strictly speaking, then, dramatism is a theory of terminology. In this respect a nomenclature could be called dramatistic only if it were specifically designed to talk, at one remove, about the cycle of terms implicit in the idea of an act. But in a wider sense any study of human relations in terms of "action" could to that extent be called dramatistic. A major difficulty in delimiting the field of reference derives from the fact that common-sense vocabularies of motives are spontaneously personalistic, hence innately given to drama-laden terms. And the turn from the naïve to the speculative is marked by such "action words" as *tao, karma, dike, hodos, islām* (to designate a submissive *attitude*), all of which are clearly dramatistic when contrasted with the terminological ideals proper to the natural sciences (Burke [1945–1950] 1962, p. 15).

The dramatistic nature of the Bible is proclaimed in the verb (*bara*) of the opening sentence that designates God's creative act; and the series of fiats that follows identifies such action with the principle of symbolicity ("the Word"). Both Plato's philosophy of the Good as ultimate motive and Aristotle's potentiality–actuality pair would obviously belong here, as would the strategic accountancy of active and passive in Spinoza's *Ethics* (Burke [1945–1950] 1962, pp. 146–152). The modern sociological concern with "values" as motives does not differ in principle from Aristotle's list of persuasive "topics" in his *Rhetoric*. One need not look very closely at Lucretius' atomism to discern the personality in those willful particles. Contemporary theories of role-taking would obviously fall within this looser usage, as indicated on its face by the term itself. Rhetorical studies of political exhortation meet the same test, as do typical news reports of people's actions, predicaments, and expressions. Most historiography would be similarly classed, insofar as its modes of systematization and generalization can be called a scientifically documented species of storytelling. And humanistic criticism (of either ethical or aesthetic sorts) usually embodies, in the broad sense, a dramatistic attitude toward questions of personality. Shifts in the locus and scope of a terminology's circumference allow for countless subdivisions, ranging from words like "transaction," "exchange," "competition," and "cooperation," or the maneuvers studied in the obviously dramalike situations of game theories, down to the endless individual verbs designed to narrate specifically what some one person did, or said, or thought at some one time. Thus Duncan (1962) has explicitly applied a dramatistic nomenclature to hierarchy and the sociology of comedy. Similarly, Goffman (1956) has characterized his study of "impression management" as "dramaturgical."

Does dramatism have a scientific use? If the dramatistic nature of terms for human motives is made obvious in Burke's pentad (act, scene, agent, agency, purpose), is this element radically eliminated if we but introduce a *synonym* for each of those terms? Have we, for instance, effectively dodged the dramatistic "logic" if instead of "act" we say "response," instead of "scene" we say "situation" or "stimulus," instead of "agent" we say "subject" or "the specimen under observation in this case," instead of "agency" we say "implementation," and instead of "purpose" we use some term like "target"? Or to what extent has reduction *wholly* taken place when the dramatistic grammar of "active," "passive," and "reflexive" gets for its analogues, in the realm of sheer motion, "effectors," "receptors" (output, input), and "feedback," respectively? Might we have here but a *truncated* terminology of action, rather than a terminology intrinsically nondramatistic? Such issues are not resolved by a dramatistic perspective; but they are systematically brought up for consideration.

A dramatistic analysis of nomenclature can

make clear the paradoxical ways in which even systematically generated "theories of action" can culminate in kinds of observation best described by analogy with mechanistic models. The resultant of many disparate acts cannot itself be considered an act in the same purposive sense that characterizes each one of such acts (just as the movement of the stock market in its totality is not "personal" in the sense of the myriad decisions made by each of the variously minded traders). Thus, a systematic analysis of interactions among a society of agents whose individual acts variously reinforce and counter one another may best be carried out in terms of concepts of "equilibrium" and "disequilibrium" borrowed from the terminology of mechanics.

In this regard it should also be noted that although equilibrium theories are usually interpreted as intrinsically adapted only to an upholding of the *status quo*, according to the dramatistic perspective this need not be the case. A work such as Albert Mathiez's *The French Revolution* (1922–1927) could be viewed as the expression of an *anima naturaliter dramatistica* in that it traces step by step an ironic development whereby a succession of unintentionally wrong moves led to unwanted results. If one viewed this whole disorderly sequence as itself a species of order, then each of the stages in its advance could be interpreted as if "designed" to stabilize, in constantly changing circumstances, the underlying pattern of conditions favorable to the eventual outcome (namely, the kind of equilibrium that could be maintained only by a series of progressive developments leading into, through, and beyond the Terror).

Though a drama is a mode of symbolic action so designed that an audience might be induced to "act symbolically" in sympathy with it, insofar as the drama serves this function it may be studied as a "perfect mechanism" composed of parts moving in mutual adjustment to one another like clockwork. The paradox is not unlike that which happened in metaphysics when a mystical view of the world as a manifestation of God's purposes prepared the way for mechanistic views, since the perfect representation of such a "design" seemed to be a machine in perfect order.

This brings up the further consideration that mechanical models might best be analyzed, not as downright antidramatistic, but as fragments of the dramatistic. For whatever humanist critics might say about the "dehumanizing" effects of the machine, it is a characteristically *human* invention, conceived by the perfecting of some human aptitudes and the elimination of others (thus in effect being not inhuman, but man's powerful "caricature" of himself—a kind of mighty homunculus).

If, on the other hand, it is held that a dramatistic nomenclature is to be avoided in any form as categorically inappropriate to a science of social relations, then a systematic study of symbolic action could at least be of use in helping to reveal any hitherto undetected traces of dramatistic thinking that might still survive. For otherwise the old Adam of human symbolicity, whereby man still persists in thinking of himself as a *personal agent capable of acting*, may lurk in a symbol system undetected (a tendency revealed in the fact that the distinction between "action" and "sheer motion" so readily gets lost, as with a term like *kinesis* in Aristotle or the shift between the mechanistic connotations of "equilibrium" and the histrionic connotations of "equilibrist"). Similarly, since pragmatist terminologies lay great stress upon "agencies" (means) and since all machines have a kind of built-in purpose, any nomenclature conceived along the lines of pragmatist instrumentalism offers a halfway house between teleology and sheer aimless motion.

At one point dramatism as a critique of terminology is necessarily at odds with dramatism as applied for specifically scientific purposes. This has been made clear in an article by Wrong (1961), who charges that although "modern sociology after all originated as a protest against the partial views of man contained in such doctrines as utilitarianism, classical economics, social Darwinism, and vulgar Marxism," it risks contributing to "the creation of yet another reified abstraction in socialized man, the status-seeker of our contemporary sociologists" (p. 190). He grants that "such an image of man is . . . valuable for limited purposes," but only "so long as it is not taken for the whole truth" (p. 190). He offers various corrections, among them a stress upon "role-playing," and upon "forces in man that are resistant to socialization," such as certain "biological" and "psychological" factors—even though some sociologists might promptly see "the specter of 'biological determinism' " (p. 191) and others might complain that already there is "too much 'psychologism' in contemporary sociology" (p. 192).

Viewed from the standpoint of dramatism as a critique of terminology, Wrong's article suggests two notable problems. Insofar as any science has a nomenclature especially adapted to its particular field of study, the extension of its *special* terms to provide a definition of man *in general* would necessarily oversociologize, overbiologize, overpsychologize, or overphysicize, etc., its subject; or the definition would have to be corrected by the addition of elements from other specialized nomenclatures (thereby producing a kind of amalgam that would lie outside the strict methodic confines of any specialized scientific discipline). A dramatistic view of this situation suggests that an over-all definition of man would be not strictly "scientific," but philosophical.

Similarly, the dramatistic concept of a scene–act ratio aims to admonish against an overly positivistic view of descriptive terms, or "empirical data," as regards an account of the conditions that men are thought to confront at a given time in history. For insofar as such a grammatical function does figure in our thoughts about motives and purpose, in the choice and scope of the terms that are used for characterizing a given situation dramatism would discern implicit corresponding attitudes and programs of action. If the principle of the scene–act ratio always figures in some form, it follows that one could not possibly select descriptive terms in which policies of some sort are not more or less clearly inherent. In the selection of terms for describing a scene, one automatically prescribes the range of acts that will seem reasonable, implicit, or necessary in that situation.

Dramatistic analyses of order

Following a lead from Bergson (1907, especially chapter 4), dramatism is devoted to a stress upon the all-importance of the negative as a specifically linguistic invention. But whereas Bergson's fertile chapter on "the idea of nothing" centers in the propositional negative ("It is not"), the dramatistic emphasis focuses attention upon the "moralistic" or "hortatory" negative ("Thou shalt not"). Burke (1961, pp. 183–196) has applied this principle of negativity to a cycle of terms implicit in the idea of "order," in keeping with the fact that "order," being a polar term, implies a corresponding idea of "disorder," while these terms in turn involve ideas of "obedience" or "disobedience" to the "authority" implicit in "order" (with further terministic radiations, such as the attitude of "humility" that leads to the act of obedience or the attitude of "pride" that leads to the act of disobedience, these in turn involving ideas of guidance or temptation, reward or punishment, and so on).

On the side of order, or control, there are the variants of faith and reason (faith to the extent that one accepts a given command, proscription, or statement as authoritative; reason to the extent that one's acceptance is contingent upon such proofs as are established by a methodic weighing of doubts and rebuttals). On the side of disorder there are the temptations of the senses and the imagination. The senses can function as temptations to the extent that the prescribed order does not wholly gratify our impulses (whether they are natural or a by-product of the very order that requires their control). Similarly, the imagination falls on the side of disorder insofar as it encourages interests inimical to the given order, though it is serviceable to order if used as a deterrent by picturing the risks of disorder—or, in other words, if it is kept "under the control of reason."

Midway between the two slopes of order and disorder (technically the realm where one can say yes or no to a thou-shalt-not) there is an area of indeterminacy often called the will. Ontologically, action is treated as a function of the will. But logologically the situation is reversed: the idea of the will is viewed as derivable from the idea of an act.

From ideas of the will there follow in turn ideas of grace, or an intrinsic ability to make proper choices (though such an aptitude can be impaired by various factors), and sacrifice (insofar as any choices involve the "mortification" of some desires). The dramatistic perspective thus rounds out the pattern in accordance with the notion that insofar as a given order involves sacrifices of some sort, the sacrificial principle is intrinsic to the nature of order. Hence, since substitution is a prime resource available to symbol systems, the sacrificial principle comes to ultimate fulfillment in vicarious sacrifice, which is variously rationalized, and can be viewed accordingly as a way to some kind of ultimate rewards.

By tracing and analyzing such terms, a dramatistic analysis shows how the negativistic principle of guilt implicit in the nature of order combines with the principles of thoroughness (or "perfection") and substitution that are characteristic of symbol systems in such a way that the sacrificial principle of victimage (the "scapegoat") is intrinsic to human congregation. The intricate line of exposition might be summed up thus: If order, then guilt; if guilt, then need for redemption; but any such "payment" is victimage. Or: If action, then drama; if drama, then conflict; if conflict. then victimage.

Adapting theology ("words about God") to secular, empirical purposes ("words about words"), dramatistic analysis stresses the perennial vitality of the scapegoat principle, explaining why it fits so disastrously well into the "logologic" of man's symbolic resources. It aims to show why, just as the two primary and sometimes conflicting functions of religion (solace and control) worked together in the doctrines of Christianity, we should expect to find their analogues in any society. Dramatism, as so conceived, asks not how the sacrificial motives revealed in the institutions of magic and religion might be eliminated in a scientific culture, but what new forms they take (Burke [1945–1950] 1962, pp. 406–408).

This view of vicarious victimage extends the range of those manifestations far beyond the areas ordinarily so labeled. Besides extreme instances like Hitlerite genocide, or the symbolic "cleansings" sought in wars, uprisings, and heated political campaigns, victimage would include psychogenic illness, social exclusiveness (the malaise of the "hierarchal psychosis"), "beatnik" art, rabid partisanship in sports, the excessive pollution of air and streams, the "bulldozer mentality" that rips into natural conditions without qualms, the many enterprises that keep men busy destroying in the name of progress or profit the ecological balance on which, in the last analysis, our eventual well-being depends, and so on.

The strongly terministic, or logological, emphasis of dramatism would view the scapegoat principle not primarily as a survival from earlier eras, but as a device natural to language here and now. Aristotle, in the third book of his *Rhetoric* (chapter 10), particularly stresses the stylistic importance of antithesis as a means of persuasion (as when a policy is recommended in terms of what it is *against*). In this spirit dramatism would look upon the scapegoat (or the principle of vicarious victimage) as but a special case of antithesis, combined with another major resource of symbol systems, namely, substitution.

In the polemics of politics, the use of the scapegoat to establish identification in terms of an enemy shared in common is also said to have the notable rhetorical advantage that the candidate who presents himself as a spokesman for "us" can prod his audience to consider local ills primarily in terms of alien figures viewed as the outstanding causes of those ills. In accord with this emphasis, when analyzing the rhetorical tactics of *Mein Kampf*, Burke (1922–1961) lays particular stress upon Hitler's use of such deflections to provide a "noneconomic interpretation of economic ills."

While recognizing the amenities of property and holding that "mine-ownness" or "our-ownness" in some form or other is an inevitable aspect of human congregation, dramatistic analysis also contends that property in any form sets the conditions for conflict (and hence culminates in some sort of victimage). It is pointed out that the recent great advances in the development of technological power require a corresponding extension in the realm of negativity (the "thou-shalt-nots" of control). Thus, the strikingly "positive" nature of such resources (as described in terms of "sheer motion") is viewed dramatistically as deceptive; for they may seem too simply like "promises," whereas in being *powers* they are *properties*, and all properties are *problems*, since powers are bones of contention (Burke 1960).

A dramatistic view of human motives thus culminates in the ironic admonition that perversions of the sacrificial principle (purgation by scapegoat, congregation by segregation) are the constant temptation of human societies, whose orders are built by a kind of animal exceptionally adept in the ways of symbolic action (Burke [1941] 1957, pp. 87–113).

KENNETH BURKE

[*See also* ETHICS, *article on* ETHICAL SYSTEMS AND SOCIAL STRUCTURES; HISTORIOGRAPHY, *article on* THE RHETORIC OF HISTORY; LITERATURE; RELIGION; ROLE; SEMANTICS AND SEMIOTICS; SYSTEMS ANALYSIS, *article on* SOCIAL SYSTEMS; *and the biographies of* ARISTOTLE; HUME; MEAD.]

BIBLIOGRAPHY

BENNE, KENNETH D. 1964 From Polarization to Paradox. Pages 216–247 in Leland P. Bradford, Jack R. Gibb, and Kenneth D. Benne (editors), *T-Group Theory and Laboratory Method: Innovation in Re-education*. New York: Wiley.

BERGSON, HENRI (1907) 1944 *Creative Evolution*. New York: Modern Library. → First published in French.

BURKE, KENNETH (1922–1961) 1964 *Perspectives by Incongruity* and *Terms for Order*. Edited by Stanley Edgar Hyman. Bloomington: Indiana Univ. Press. → Two representative collections of readings from Burke's works. Each collection is also available separately in paperback from the same publisher.

BURKE, KENNETH (1937) 1959 *Attitudes Toward History*. 2d ed., rev. Los Altos, Calif.: Hermes.

BURKE, KENNETH (1941) 1957 *The Philosophy of Literary Form: Studies in Symbolic Action*. Rev. ed., abridged by the author. New York: Vintage. → The Louisiana State University Press reprinted the unabridged edition in 1967.

BURKE, KENNETH (1945–1950) 1962 *A Grammar of Motives* and *A Rhetoric of Motives*. Cleveland: World.

BURKE, KENNETH 1955 Linguistic Approach to Problems of Education. Pages 259–303 in National Society for the Study of Education, Committee on Modern Philosophies and Education, *Modern Philosophies and Education*. Edited by Nelson B. Henry. National Society for the Study of Education Yearbook 54, Part 1. Univ. of Chicago Press.

BURKE, KENNETH 1960 Motion, Action, Words. *Teachers College Record* 62:244–249.

BURKE, KENNETH 1961 *The Rhetoric of Religion: Studies in Logology.* Boston: Beacon.

BURKE, KENNETH 1966 *Language as Symbolic Action: Essays on Life, Literature, and Method.* Berkeley: Univ. of California Press.

DUNCAN, HUGH D. 1962 *Communication and Social Order.* Totowa, N.J.: Bedminster Press.

GOFFMAN, ERVING (1956) 1959 *The Presentation of Self in Everyday Life.* Garden City, N.Y.: Doubleday.

HUME, DAVID (1748) 1952 An Inquiry Concerning Human Understanding. Pages 451–509 in *Great Books of the Western World.* Volume 35: Locke, Berkeley, Hume. Chicago: Benton.

MATHIEZ, ALBERT (1922–1927) 1962 *The French Revolution.* New York: Russell. → First published in French in three volumes. A paperback edition was published in 1964 by Grosset and Dunlap.

MEAD, GEORGE HERBERT 1938 *The Philosophy of the Act.* Univ. of Chicago Press. → Consists almost entirely of unpublished papers which Mead left at his death in 1931.

PARSONS, TALCOTT 1937 *The Structure of Social Action: A Study in Social Theory With Special Reference to a Group of Recent European Writers.* New York: McGraw-Hill.

RICHARDS, IVOR A. (1959) 1961 *Principles of Literary Criticism.* New York: Harcourt.

RUECKERT, WILLIAM H. 1963 *Kenneth Burke and the Drama of Human Relations.* Minneapolis: Univ. of Minnesota Press.

WRONG, DENNIS H. 1961 The Oversocialized Conception of Man in Modern Sociology. *American Sociological Review* 26:183–193.

IV
SOCIAL EXCHANGE

Most gratifications of human beings have their source in the actions of other human beings. To experience excitement in sexual pleasure or contentment in love, to enjoy intellectual stimulation or relaxing diversion, to achieve professional recognition or a happy family life, to satisfy the lust for power or the need for acceptance—to attain any of these ends requires that one induce others to behave in certain ways. The fact that many rewards men seek can be obtained only in social interaction is what underlies the conceptualization of interaction as social exchange.

Basic assumptions. The basic assumptions of the theory of social exchange are that men enter into new social associations because they expect doing so to be rewarding and that they continue relations with old associates and expand their interaction with them because they actually find doing so to be rewarding. Associating with another person may be intrinsically rewarding, as in love and in sociability, or it may bring rewards that are extrinsic to the association itself, such as advice from a colleague and help from a neighbor. In either case, the desire to satisfy some want is assumed to underlie the association. As Simmel (1908, p. 6) put it: "Social association refers to the widely varying forms that are generated as the diverse interests of individuals prompt them to develop social units in which they realize these interests, be they sensual or ideal, lasting or fleeting, conscious or unconscious, causally impelling or teleologically inducing." To be sure, not all needs or interests are satisfied directly in social interaction, as hunger illustrates, and not all social interaction is primarily governed by an interest in rewards, since irrational forces and moral values also influence it. But many aspects of social life do reflect an interest in profiting from social interaction, and these are the focus of the theory of social exchange. Far from being confined to strictly rational conduct oriented toward material gain, however, the theory is intended to encompass all striving for rewarding social experiences, including the desire to further humanitarian ideals or spiritual values as well as the pursuit of personal advantage and emotional satisfaction.

The conception of social interaction as an exchange process follows logically from the assumption that men seek to obtain rewards in their social associations. If a man is attracted to others because he expects associating with them to be rewarding to himself, he will wish to associate with them in order to realize the anticipated rewards. Likewise, for them to engage in social interaction with him, they must also have an interest in doing so. But their interest in associating with him depends, according to the assumption, on their expectation that interacting with him will be rewarding to them. To implement his desire to associate with them, therefore, he must demonstrate to them that associating with him would benefit them. In brief, to reap the rewards expected from attractive potential associates, a man must impress them as a desirable associate by implicitly conveying the promise that social interaction with him will be rewarding for them too.

A person who derives benefits from associates is under obligation to reciprocate by supplying benefits to them in turn. People often go out of their way to do favors not only for friends but also for mere acquaintances and even for strangers, and they thereby create social obligations. The individual who fails to discharge his obligations and reciprocate in some form for benefits received robs others of incentives to continue to befriend him. Besides, such an individual is likely to be accused of ingratitude. This very accusation indicates that reciprocation for favors freely given is expected, and it serves as a social sanction to discourage men from forgetting their obligations. Gratitude, as Simmel ([1902–1917] 1950, p. 387) noted, "establishes the bond of interaction, of the reciprocity of service and return service, even when they are not guaranteed by external coercion."

When obligations for benefits received are discharged by providing benefits in return, both parties profit from the association, and their exchange of rewarding experiences fortifies the social bond between them. A man who helps others earns their gratitude and appreciation, and he puts them into his debt, which promises to bring him further rewards in the future. These advantageous consequences of doing favors are undoubtedly a major reason why men frequently go to great trouble to help others and enjoy doing so. Giving is, indeed, more blessed than receiving, for having social credit is preferable to being socially indebted. To be sure, there are men who selflessly work for others without thought of reward and even without expecting gratitude, but these are virtually saints, and saints are rare. Other men also act unselfishly sometimes, but they require a more direct incentive for doing so, if it is only the social acknowledgment that they are unselfish. Such social approval is, of course, a very significant reward men seek in social interaction.

Defining social exchange. Exchange is not restricted to economic markets: social exchange is ubiquitous. Neighbors exchange help with chores; discussants, ideas; children, toys; friends, social support; politicians, concessions. The novice must meet the demands of the group to find acceptance in it. Colleagues exchange advice, and if the superior competence of one prevents the rest from reciprocating in kind for his advice, they discharge their obligation by paying their respect to his abilities and thus raising his status. Even the lover whose only apparent concern is to please his girl seeks to win her affection in return for his devotion. Groups and organized collectivities, too, are engaged in social exchange. For example, the medical profession receives exclusive license to practice medicine in return for assuming the obligation to meet the health needs of the community, or a political party makes concessions in its program to an interest group in return for support at the election booth.

Homans (1961, p. 13) developed the first systematic theory that focuses on social behavior "as an exchange of activity, tangible or intangible, and more or less rewarding or costly, between at least two persons." Of special concern to Homans are the psychological processes that motivate men to engage in exchange, and the psychological reductionism of the theory has been criticized by other sociologists. Homans was, however, by no means the first to call attention to social exchange. Anthropologists had earlier discussed the significance and pervasiveness of the exchange of gifts and services in simpler societies. For instance, Mauss (1925) had presented a general analysis of gift exchange in such societies. But anthropologists were not the first to observe this phenomenon either.

Given the ubiquity of social exchange, it is perhaps not surprising that social philosophers have discussed it ever since antiquity. Aristotle's *Nicomachean Ethics* (1162a34–1163a24) deals extensively with social exchange, which he distinguishes from economic exchange by saying that it "is not based on stated terms, but the gift or other service is given as to a friend, although the giver expects to receive an equivalent or greater return, as though it had not been a free gift but a loan." Many writers of the intervening centuries, such as La Rochefoucauld (1664), Mandeville (1714), and Adam Smith (1759), have been intrigued by the exchange nexus observable in much of social life. More recently, a conception of exchange is implicit in Whyte's discussion of the obligations of a gang leader (1943); it is explicit in Blau's analysis of consultation in a group of government officials (1955); and it is an underlying element in Thibaut and Kelley's theory of dyads and triads (1959).

The pervasiveness of social exchange makes it tempting to explore the fruitfulness of the concept by trying to apply it to all social conduct. But the concept of exchange loses its distinctive meaning and becomes tautological if all behavior in interpersonal relations is subsumed under it. Although much of social conduct is oriented toward expected returns from others—indeed, more than we usually think—not all of it is.

The concept of exchange can be delimited with the aid of some illustrations of why a man gives money to others. First, he may do so because they stand in front of him with guns in a holdup. While this could be viewed as an exchange of his money for his life, it seems preferable to exclude the results of physical coercion from the definition of the term "exchange." Second, a man may donate money to charity because his conscience demands that he help the poor and without expecting gratitude in any form from them. While this could be viewed as an exchange of his money for the internal approval of his superego, here again it seems preferable to exclude conformity with internalized norms from what is meant by the term "exchange." Third, an uncontrollable impulse may compel a man to squander his money; such behavior motivated by irrational drives does not entail any exchange either. Finally, a man may give alms to beggars because he enjoys receiving their expressions of deferential gratitude and discontinue giving them money if they fail to react with such expressions. This last case illustrates social exchange, whereas the others delineate the boundaries of the concept. In brief, the concept of exchange refers to voluntary social actions that are contingent on rewarding reactions from others and that cease when these expected reactions are not forthcoming.

Social and economic exchange. The very term "social exchange" is designed to indicate that social interaction outside the economic sphere has important similarities with economic transactions. Above all, the expectation that benefits rendered will yield returns characterizes not only economic transactions but also social ones in which gifts and services appear to be freely bestowed. Moreover, the economic principle of eventually declining marginal utility applies to social exchange as well. Advice from an expert colleague is worth much to a man who needs help with a problem, but once the problem has been clarified, additional counsel is no longer as valuable. No matter how much two friends enjoy one another's company, after a certain amount of time together they will become less eager to continue their association. The more a man concentrates on obtaining a given social reward rather than others, the more the significance of the alternatives forgone will impinge upon his consciousness, making this reward relatively less significant. All of these examples manifest the marginal principle in social life.

There are, however, also important differences between social and strictly economic exchange. The most basic difference is that the obligations incurred in social transactions are not clearly specified in advance. In economic transactions the exact obligations of both parties are simultaneously agreed upon: a given product is sold for a certain price. Both commodities may change hands at the time the agreement is reached, or a contract is made that stipulates precisely the obligations either party has to discharge in the future. In social exchange, by contrast, one party supplies benefits to another, and although there is a general expectation of reciprocation, the exact nature of the return is left unspecified. Indeed, it must remain unspecified, since any attempt to specify it in advance destroys the social meaning of the transaction by transforming it into a merely economic one. Doing a favor has an entirely different social significance from making a bargain. If a man does a service for another and then indicates what the return for this service should be, he reveals that he does not want to consider the service a favor but prefers to make it part of a bargain; he thereby insists on keeping the relationship businesslike and refuses to enter a more sociable association. If the recipient immediately states what return he will make, he reveals the same disinclination to enter a sociable relation.

Social exchange, therefore, entails supplying benefits that create diffuse future obligations. The nature of the return is invariably not stipulated in advance, cannot be bargained about, and must be left to the discretion of the one who makes it. Thus, if a person gives a dinner party, he expects his guests to reciprocate in the future. But he can hardly bargain with them about the kind of party to which they should invite him, though he expects them not simply to ask him for a quick lunch if he has given a formal dinner for them. Generally, a man expects some expressions of gratitude and appreciation for favors he has done for others, but he can neither bargain with them over how to reciprocate nor force them to reciprocate at all. Any attempt to assure repayment for one's generosity discloses that it was really not generosity in the first place. The distinctive significance of social obligations requires that they remain unspecific, and the fact that social, as distinguished from economic, commodities have no exact price facilitates meeting this requirement.

Since the recipient is the one who decides when and how to reciprocate for a favor, or whether to reciprocate at all, social exchange requires trusting others, whereas the immediate transfer of goods or the formal contract that can be enforced obviates such trust in economic exchange. Typically, however, social exchange relations evolve in a slow process, starting with minor transactions in which little trust is required because little risk is involved and in which both partners can prove their trustworthiness, enabling them to expand their relation and engage in major transactions. Thus, the process of social exchange leads to the trust required for it in a self-generating fashion. Indeed, creating trust seems to be a major function of social exchange, and special mechanisms exist that prolong the period of being under obligation and thereby strengthen bonds of indebtedness and trust. In the ceremonial gift exchange of the *kula* among the Trobriand Islanders, for example, returns for gifts received at one expedition can be made only at the next, many months later, and hasty reciprocation is generally condemned (Malinowski 1922, pp. 210–211 in 1961 edition). In our society, similarly, it is considered improper to reciprocate for a gift or return an invitation too quickly. The condemnation of posthaste reciprocation stimulates the growth of trust by constraining exchange partners to remain under obligation to each other for extended periods.

Social benefits are also less detachable from the source that supplies them than are economic commodities. At one extreme is the diffuse social support derived in a love relationship, the significance of which depends entirely on the person who supplies it. At the other extreme are such economic goods as shares in a corporation or money, the value of which is completely independent of the supplier. Most social benefits are intermediate between these extremes, having a value that is extrinsic to the exchange relations in which they are supplied but having this value modified by the significance of these relations. A man who consults a colleague is interested in good advice, whatever its source, but his personal relation with the consultant makes it more or less easy for him to ask for assistance and to understand the advice he receives. (Although in the economic sphere the services of the friendly corner grocer may be preferable to those of the impersonal supermarket, such personal relations generally encroach less on economic than on social exchange.)

Economic exchange may be considered a special case of the general phenomenon of exchange, with social exchange being the excluded residual category. When goods and services are given a price in terms of a single medium of exchange, economic transactions are institutionalized. Their price defines the value of commodities independent of any particular exchange relations, making this value separable from that of other benefits accruing in these relations, and it permits exact specification of the obligations incurred in economic transactions. Economic institutions, such as the impersonal market, are designed to exclude other considerations than price from exchange decisions. Many social benefits have no price, either because they are never traded on an economic market, as is the case with social support, or because they are not so traded in this instance, as exemplified by the advice from a friend in contrast with that from a professional consultant. These are the benefits that enter into social exchange, which means that their supply is not contingent on stipulated returns, though there is a general expectation of reciprocation. The fact that the return is at the discretion of the one who makes it gives social exchange its fundamental significance for developing bonds of trust and friendship, and mechanisms such as the social norms prohibiting bargaining and hasty reciprocation tend to protect this discretion. The most important benefits involved in social exchange, furthermore, do not have any material value on which a price can be put at all, as exemplified by social approval and respect.

Exchange and power. A paradox of social exchange is that it serves not only to establish bonds of friendship between peers but also to create status differences between men. The *kula* exchange described by Malinowski (1922, p. 92 in 1961 edition), for instance, "provides every man . . . with a few friends near at hand, and with some friendly allies in the far-away, dangerous, foreign districts." The potlatch of the Kwakiutl, on the other hand, is a system of giving away valuables in which "status in associations and clans, and rank of every kind, are determined by the war of property," as Mauss ([1925] 1954, p. 35) noted. An important function of gift exchange in simple societies is, in the words of Lévi-Strauss (1957, p. 85), "to surpass a rival in generosity, to crush him if possible under future obligations which it is hoped he cannot meet, thus taking from him privileges, titles, rank, authority, and prestige." In modern society, too, supplying benefits to others serves sometimes as an expression of friendship for them and at other times as a means for establishing superiority over them.

A person who gives others valuable gifts or renders them important services makes an implicit claim to superior status by obligating them. A benefactor is not a peer but a superior on whom others depend. If they return benefits that adequately discharge their obligations, they deny his claim to superiority; and if their returns are excessive, they make a counterclaim to superiority over him. Continuing mutual exchange strengthens bonds between equals. But if they fail to reciprocate with benefits that are as important to him as his are to them, they validate his claim to superior status. In simple societies the resulting differentiation of status seems to be rooted in the institutionalized significance of one-sided benefactions, while in modern societies it is typically due to unilateral dependence on a supplier of needs.

The recurrent unilateral supply of important benefits is a basic source of power. A man with resources at his disposal that enable him to meet other men's needs can attain power over them provided that four conditions are met, as suggested in a somewhat different formulation by Emerson

(1962). First, they must not have resources that the benefactor needs, otherwise they can obtain what they want from him in direct exchange. Second, they must not be able to obtain the benefits he has to offer from an alternative source, which would make them independent of him. Third, they must be unable or unwilling to take what they want from him by force. Fourth, they must not undergo a change in values that enables them to do without the benefits they originally needed. If these four conditions are met, they have no choice but to comply with his wishes and submit to his power in order to obtain the needed benefits. The four alternatives to compliance are assumed to be exhaustive; in their absence, the supply of important services inevitably generates power.

Under specifiable conditions, then, exchange processes give rise to a differentiation of power. A man who commands services others cannot do without, who is independent of any services at their command, and whose services they can neither obtain elsewhere nor take from him by force can attain power over them by making the satisfaction of their needs contingent on their compliance with his directives. By acceding to his wishes, they reciprocate for the benefits he supplies. The exchange balance is restored as unilateral services are compensated by an imbalance of power. The man who recurrently supplies needed services to others makes them dependent on and obligated to him, and their accumulated obligations constrain them to comply with his wishes lest he cease to supply further services. Their indebtedness to him takes the form of a pool of willing compliance on which he can draw at his discretion whenever it is to his interest to impose his will upon them.

The compliance of men with another's wishes and his consequent power, with which they repay him for services received, may appear to be no different from other social rewards that enter into exchange transactions. Yet there is a basic distinction between the differentiation of power and mutual social exchange, just as there is a basic distinction between social and economic exchange. The distinguishing criterion lies in the answer to the question, Who has discretion over the repayment? In economic exchange, neither party can exercise discretion over making the return, since the exact conditions of repayment are specified when the initial transaction takes place. In mutual social exchange, the nature and timing of the return are decided on by the one who makes it, that is, the recipient of the original benefit. In power relations, on the other hand, the return is made on the demand of the one to whom it is owed, that is, the supplier of the original benefit. Accumulated obligations and unilateral dependence transfer the power of discretion over the return from the debtor to the creditor and transform an exchange relation between peers into a power relation between superior and subordinate.

Secondary exchange. The study of complex social structures must take into account the social forces that emerge in them and that are not observable in face-to-face interaction. To be sure, the concept of exchange itself refers to emergent properties of social relations that cannot be reduced to the psychological processes that motivate individual behavior. Exchange theory is concerned with the interaction processes that emerge as individuals seek rewards in social relations, whatever the psychological forces that lead each to want certain rewards. The differentiation of power in a collectivity gives rise to still other social processes in the complex structure, and these may be conceived of as constituting a secondary exchange that becomes superimposed upon the primary one characteristic of interpersonal relations.

Power makes it possible to enforce demands, and these demands are judged by those subject to the power in terms of social norms of fairness. The fair exchange of power by a ruler or ruling group elicits social approval, whereas unfair demands that are experienced as exploitative or oppressive evoke social disapproval. Thus, a secondary exchange—of fairness in the exercise of power in return for social approval by subordinates—emerges as power becomes differentiated in a collectivity. The social forces set into motion by this secondary exchange lead to legitimation and organization, on the one hand, and to opposition and change, on the other.

Collective approval of power legitimates that power. If men profit from the way they are governed by those in power and consider the demands made on them to be fully justified by the advantages the leadership provides, common feelings of loyalty are likely to develop as they communicate to each other their appreciation of the leadership. Their joint obligations to the leadership tend to find expression in social norms that make compliance with its directives mandatory. The collectivity of subordinates repays those in power for the benefits derived from their leadership by enforcing the leaders' directives as part of the enforcement of the collectivity's own social norms, that is, by legitimating the leadership's authority. For the distinctive characteristic of legitimate authority is that a superior's commands are obeyed, not because of his sanctioning power but because of the normative pressure exercised among the subordinates themselves, particularly once these normative constraints have become institutionalized. Authority, in turn, promotes organization.

Collective disapproval of power engenders opposition. Men who share the feeling of being exploited and oppressed by the excessive demands of those in power are inclined to communicate their grievances to each other. A wish to retaliate by striking down the oppressors is often kindled in these discussions, in which men receive social support for their aggressive feelings. An opposition ideology may be adopted that further justifies and reinforces the hostility against existing powers. It is out of such shared discontent that opposition movements develop: for example, that men band together to organize a union against their employer or a radical party against their government. Such opposition is an important catalyst of basic social change.

A prime determinant of social conduct is the institutionalized system of values in a society: the distinctive values that define the in-group's identity, the common standards of morality and of achievement, the values that legitimate governing authority and organization, and the ideologies that sometimes foster opposition to those in power. Guided by these values, men often set aside immediate self-interest and considerations of exchange; for instance, the professional's standards may require him to help clients, disregarding the return he receives from them.

However, social values and norms largely set broad limits on conduct without prescribing it in detail. Within these limits, men are free to pursue their interest in social rewards, and considerations of exchange do apply. While social norms prohibit lying and cheating in order to get advice from another, they permit inducing him to give advice by expressing genuine respect or by any other means not specifically proscribed. Both common values and exchange principles influence social conduct, and neither may be neglected in studying it. Of particular importance in the analysis of social life is the modifying influence social values have on the rewards in which men are interested. Patriotic or opposition ideals often inspire men to make great material sacrifices, for these values make furthering the common cause more rewarding for them than material gain.

Exchange theory is most directly concerned with face-to-face relations, and thus it must be complemented by other theoretical principles that focus on complex structures with institutionalized values. However, even in the study of complex structures, exchange theory has something to contribute.

PETER M. BLAU

[*Directly related are the entries* CONFLICT; COOPERATION; DUTY; EXCHANGE AND DISPLAY; FRIENDSHIP. *Other relevant material may be found in* COALITIONS; GROUPS; POWER; SOCIOMETRY; *and in the biographies of* MAUSS *and* SIMMEL.]

BIBLIOGRAPHY

BLAU, PETER M. (1955) 1963 *The Dynamics of Bureaucracy: A Study of Interpersonal Relations in Two Government Agencies.* Rev. ed. Univ. of Chicago Press.

BLAU, PETER M. 1964 *Exchange and Power in Social Life.* New York: Wiley.

BOULDING, KENNETH E. 1962 *Conflict and Defense: A General Theory.* A publication of the Center for Research in Conflict Resolution at the University of Michigan. New York: Harper.

EMERSON, RICHARD M. 1962 Power–Dependence Relations. *American Sociological Review* 27:31–41.

GOULDNER, ALVIN W. 1960 The Norm of Reciprocity: A Preliminary Statement. *American Sociological Review* 25:161–178.

HOMANS, GEORGE C. 1958 Social Behavior as Exchange. *American Journal of Sociology* 63:597–606.

HOMANS, GEORGE C. 1961 *Social Behavior: Its Elementary Forms.* New York: Harcourt.

LA ROCHEFOUCAULD, FRANÇOIS (1664) 1940 *The Maxims.* Oxford Univ. Press. → First published as *Réflexions . . . et maximes morales.*

LÉVI-STRAUSS, CLAUDE (1957) 1964 The Principle of Reciprocity. Pages 84–94 in Lewis A. Coser and Bernard Rosenberg (editors), *Sociological Theory.* New York: Macmillan.

MALINOWSKI, BRONISLAW (1922) 1960 *Argonauts of the Western Pacific: An Account of Native Enterprise and Adventure in the Archipelagoes of Melanesian New Guinea.* London School of Economics and Political Science Studies, No. 65. London: Routledge; New York: Dutton. → A paperback edition was published in 1961 by Dutton.

MANDEVILLE, BERNARD (1714) 1957 *The Fable of the Bees: Or Private Vices, Publick Benefits.* Edited by F. B. Kaye. Oxford: Clarendon. → A reprint of the 1924 edition. The introduction and notes include a life, a bibliography, a critical and historical evaluation, and an annoted bibliography of secondary works.

MAUSS, MARCEL (1925) 1954 *The Gift: Forms and Functions of Exchange in Archaic Societies.* Glencoe, Ill.: Free Press. → First published as *Essai sur le don: Forme et raison de l'échange dans les sociétés archaïques.*

SIMMEL, GEORG (1902–1917) 1950 *The Sociology of Georg Simmel.* Edited and translated by Kurt H. Wolff. Glencoe, Ill.: Free Press.

SIMMEL, GEORG (1908) 1958 *Soziologie.* Berlin: Duncker & Humblot. → The translation of the extract in the text was provided by Peter M. Blau.

SMITH, ADAM (1759) 1892 *The Theory of Moral Sentiments.* London: Bell.

THIBAUT, JOHN W.; and KELLEY, HAROLD H. 1959 *The Social Psychology of Groups.* New York: Wiley.
WHYTE, WILLIAM F. (1943) 1961 *Street Corner Society: The Social Structure of an Italian Slum.* 2d ed., enl. Univ. of Chicago Press.

V
INTERACTION AND PERSONALITY

The functioning of modern society depends a great deal on the success of human encounters. Summit meetings, labor–management negotiations, biracial conferences, indeed the success of virtually every area of public life ultimately rests on the effectiveness of people working together. Private life is no less subject to this requirement. Marital crises, parent–child misunderstandings, and the appallingly high proportion of homicides committed by close relatives of the victim—all of these attest to the excruciating difficulty of achieving satisfying and productive relations between people.

Why does a civilization that copes so successfully with the physical world make so little progress toward understanding the factors that lead to successful human relationships? This inability has always been at the center of religious and philosophical discussions. Recently, social scientists have applied their experimental methods to this problem. Psychotherapists, especially Harry Stack Sullivan, have given increased attention to the problem through the recognition of the centrality of interpersonal relations in the development of personality. Some of the new trends in psychotherapy concentrate on the small group and the family as the therapeutic unit. These techniques are based on a recognition of the importance of interactional factors and on the assumption that an individual's personality can be understood better by seeing him in interaction with others. [*See* MENTAL DISORDERS, TREATMENT OF, *article on* GROUP PSYCHOTHERAPY; *and the biography of* SULLIVAN.] In this essay the basic concern is with the relations between behavior at the social or group level and the personalities of the participants in this social interaction.

The problem

Before exploring the empirical work that has been done in the field, it will be useful to develop a more precise statement of the problem. Intuitively, it seems that it should be possible to predict, at least to some degree, the nature of social interaction from a knowledge of participating personalities. Experience suggests that two highly combative, unyielding people, for example, seem not to fare as well as a more flexible pair and that the effect of two personalities on each other is greater in the case of people who must live close together for a long period of time and whose decisions affect each other, such as men in a submerged submarine or persons in a space capsule going to the moon, than it is for two people who associate little and have stereotyped, structured relations with each other, such as a bus driver and a passenger or a theater ticket seller and a customer.

The outcome of an interaction requires not only a knowledge of the properties of the elements (personalities) but also of the laws that relate them (laws of human interaction). To understand social interaction more fully, consideration must also be given to influences other than personality. Factors such as social role and cultural norms affect social interaction. There is considerable variability, too, in the consistency of individual behavior. There are times when the same behaviors are elicited by virtually any other human being. Some severe neurotics, for example, will feel anxious or suspicious in the presence of any other person. These feelings exist regardless of roles, personalities, or setting. This type of reaction is found more often in pathological personalities, but it is not uncommon in the general population.

Sometimes identical behaviors are elicited by the external individual characteristics of others, such as their social role or ethnic group membership. For example, a person's reaction may be the same to all authority figures, or all women, or all short people, or all unknown people, or all Negroes, or all popular people. Some external property of the observed individual causes the reaction regardless of the behavior of that individual. There also are consistent reactions toward social groupings, such as crowds, cocktail parties, or a group composed only of old men. The personality of the individual members of the social group does not influence the response.

Often people respond in the same way toward all persons who are domineering, or very affectionate, or withdrawn, or indecisive, or ingratiating, regardless of the remainder of the personality. These reactions are sometimes combined with the above category ("subgroups") to elicit, for example, a reaction to indecisive women specifically or to aggressive Jews as opposed to aggressive people in general. This category differs from the above in that the person is reacting to personality attributes rather than to external characteristics.

Sometimes, too, people react to other people as unique individuals. This is a reality-oriented reaction and is associated with mental health. The reaction is to a person as he really is, recognizing both his similarities to and differences from other people and groups.

The role of personality factors. These considerations of social interaction make clear that the personalities of the group members account for only a part of the behavior observed in social interaction but a very significant part. There is evidence that as a social interaction increases in time, personality factors play a more important role in determining the course of the relationship. For a complete understanding of social interaction, situational and personality factors must be taken account of simultaneously. Predictions based only on situational factors seem doomed to a limited success and usually result in abstract statements, such as "people have a general tendency to conform to group norms." Specification of the applicability of this generalization requires further work with situational factors, such as the types of decisions to which people conform; individual factors, such as the status differences among the conformers; and personality traits, such as rebellion and the need to be accepted.

Similarly, attempts to explain social interaction in terms of personality factors only also appear inadequate. The limited success of attempting to predict the outcome of a marriage based on the complementarity of needs attests to the necessity for considering situational factors as well as personality factors in order to understand social interaction.

Thus, the precise statement of the problem of this essay is the following:

Which characteristics of social interaction are predictable—and to what degree and under what circumstances—from a knowledge of the personalities of the interacting individuals and of the laws governing the interaction of personalities?

Approaches. Investigators of the relation between personality and social interaction have used several approaches. At times they have studied the personality of one individual; at other times two or more; and, at still other times, the personalities of all of the members of a group. Sometimes, too, the entire group is studied as if it were a single, individual personality.

Combinations of personalities

The predictability of social phenomena from a knowledge of the individual personalities is directly tested by establishing a group and predicting the subsequent interaction of its members.

Means and variability. Approaches to studying the results of group composition may be distinguished by the various assumptions that are made about interaction by the investigators. Some of the earliest work assumed that social interaction was predictable from mean scores on a trait or from the variability of that trait among the group members. Results of the following type were obtained:

High group *means* on the personality characteristics of adventuresomeness, vigor, dominance, purposefulness, orderliness, willed application, and freedom from anxiety are associated with high performance on tasks requiring vigorous coordinated action and with a preference for such tasks over discussion.

High *variances* on personality measures of tough- versus tender-mindedness, "bohemian aggressiveness," and paranoid suspiciousness are associated with the group's dislike for a task requiring the resolving of opinion and attitude differences, with the group's slowness in ranking attitude preferences, and with a feeling by its members that other members hinder progress (Cattell & Stice 1954).

Similarities and differences. Another set of experiments was based on the assumption that social interaction is predictable from a knowledge of the similarities of, or differences between, personality traits of the interactors.

Defense mechanisms. Differences in defense-mechanism preference of two persons in interaction were used as a basis for investigation (Cohen 1956). Three pairs of subjects were used: one pair manifested projection (the tendency to attribute to someone else the impulses which the subject finds unacceptable in himself), another pair had similar defenses other than projection, and a third pair had defenses that were dissimilar. The members of each pair were asked to read some short stories which would arouse their common area of disturbance, to make individual judgments about the motives of the actors in the stories, and to arrive at a common decision about the motives through discussion.

The pairs of subjects who used projection perceived their own interaction as more hostile than did pairs of subjects who utilized other defenses. This severe negative effect was obtained only when projectors were paired with each other. When projectors interacted with persons using other defenses, their perceptions of hostility were no different from those of any other pairs having dissimilar defenses. The interaction that was perceived as next most hostile was that of two regressors, followed by that of two persons using reaction formation, while the least hostility was felt by two interacting users of denial or repression. [*See* DEFENSE MECHANISMS.]

Authoritarianism. Another experimenter explored similarity or differences in authoritarianism of group members as a determinant of interaction. It was hypothesized that leaders emerging in groups made up entirely of authoritarian members would, for example, be generally less effective than would leaders emerging from groups made up entirely of equalitarian members. The hypotheses were supported by the data, although not always to a statistically significant degree (Haythorn 1953).

Interpersonal needs. In another investigation, similarity of interpersonal needs, that is, needs that can be satisfied only through the attainment of a satisfactory relation with other people, was used as the basis for composing ten-person groups for purposes of learning about human relations. Groups were composed along the dimensions of the Fundamental Interpersonal Relations Orientation (FIRO) theory of interpersonal behavior (Schutz 1958). The groups were divided into those with (*a*) strong attempts to control others—high expressed control, (*b*) strong desire to be controlled by others—high wanting to be controlled, (*c*) strong desire to receive affection—high wanted affection, and (*d*) strong preference for initiating behavior in areas such as control and affection. The scores of each group were randomly distributed on the other uncontrolled scales. After one week the group members could accurately identify their own characteristic from observing themselves interacting. It was easiest for them to identify a positive common group trait, such as expressing control, and most difficult to identify the common group trait when it was a covert desire, such as wanting affection. The type of interaction exhibited by each group was unique and quite consistent with the prediction based on their composition. The highly controlling group ejected their leader in the third meeting, while the group that was high in wanting to be controlled became highly dependent on their leader. The group high in initiating behavior spent their time talking about authority, competition, and feelings of adequacy and proceeded to compete with each other and with the leader. The group high in wanting affection spent much of their time discussing the problems of expressing feelings and crying. Thus, personality data obtained from a paper-and-pencil test did predict several aspects of group behavior.

Compatibility and complementarity. More complex assumptions about interaction underlie another study aimed at predicting the behavior of pairs that were composed on the basis of compatibility and complementarity.

Defense mechanisms. Building upon the study of defense preferences reported above, predictions were made, based on clinical knowledge, about the result of each combination of defense mechanisms —denial, isolation, projection, regression, turning-against-self, and intellectualizing. For example, for two isolators it was reasoned that each of the isolators wants to handle feelings by intellectualizing or rationalizing and expects that the other will deal with an anxiety situation in the same way so that threatening feelings need not be considered. Since each agrees with this means of handling the problem, their interaction would be expected to be positive (Waxler 1960).

It was found, as predicted, that pairs of two regressors were least satisfied, while the regressor–isolator pairs liked each other and were most satisfied. The satisfaction and liking ratings were not related to an individual's defense mechanism but, instead, were related to the combination of such mechanisms in the pair.

Interpersonal needs. Another approach centers on the concept of compatibility of interpersonal needs (Schutz 1958).

The types of compatibility proposed may be understood best by considering the diagonals of the diagram shown in Figure 1. The horizontal axis represents the behavior a person expresses toward others; the vertical axis, the behavior the persons wants from others. This schema is used separately for each interpersonal area proposed in the theory—inclusion (need for human contact), control (need for influence), and affection (need for love). The high-interchange quadrant represents interactions of those who prefer a great deal

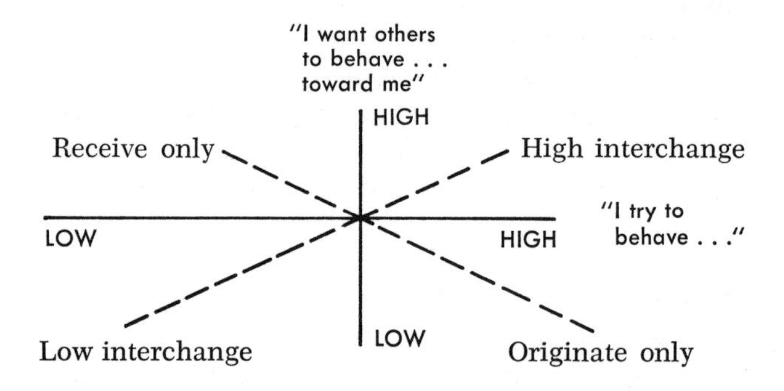

Figure 1 — Schema for deriving compatibility

Source: Schutz 1958.

of exchange of the "commodity" (contact, influence, love) relevant to the interpersonal area. The low-interchange quadrant represents those people who neither initiate nor want to receive these commodities. In order to be compatible, two people should be similar with respect to the interchange variable. Compatibility based on similarity along this diagonal is called *interchange compatibility*.

The other diagonal extends from a point representing those who desire only to initiate or originate behavior to a point representing those who wish only to receive it. For example, for control the lower right quadrant represents someone who likes to give orders and not take them, while the upper left represents someone who does not like to give orders but who likes to be told what to do. On this diagonal, two people should complement each other, that is, be equidistant from the center in opposite directions, in order to be compatible. Compatibility based on complementarity along this diagonal is called *originator compatibility*.

Conflict arises when there is disagreement regarding who shall originate relations and who shall receive them. For each need area (inclusion, control, affection) there are two types of conflict: between two originators—*competitive originator incompatibility*—and between two receivers—*apathetic originator incompatibility*.

In the inclusion area, competitive conflict is between two persons, each of whom wants to "select his own company." Each wants to join only the activities he wishes but not to have others join him. The apathetic conflict is between two persons, both of whom want to be included but neither of whom will act to join the other.

In the control area the competitive conflict is between two persons, each of whom wants to be dominant and to run the activities but does not want to be told what to do. The apathetic conflict in this area is between two submissive people, each of whom wants to be told what to do but neither of whom will take the initiative for doing it. This situation arises with a boss who cannot make decisions and an employee with no initiative.

In the affection area the competitive conflict is between two persons who desire to originate close relations but not to receive them. One example of this would be the Don Juan, for whom pursuit is an end in itself and reciprocation is threatening. The apathetic conflict is between two people who want to be liked but do not want to initiate warm feelings. An example would be two co-workers secretly fond of each other but neither ever initiating a personal relation.

Interchange compatibility highlights a different aspect of the relation. Whereas the situations covered by originator compatibility refer to need satisfactions by a specific person, interchange compatibility refers to the general context or "atmosphere" in which a relationship exists. On the interchange axis, two individuals' scores should be similar for maximum compatibility.

In the area of inclusion, high interchange means high interaction with others; low interchange, to being separated from other people and being alone. Conflict arises because one person likes to be with people and the other person prefers to be alone.

In the area of control, high interchange means a preference to be both controlled by others and to control their actions; low interchange, to neither influencing nor being influenced by others. Conflict arises because one person wants a highly structured relation and the other person wants a free and spontaneous one.

In the area of affection, high interchange means reciprocal preferences for close personal relations with people; low interchange, a reciprocal preference for maintaining affectional distance. Conflict arises when one person wants an atmosphere of personal warmth and closeness and the other person prefers a more impersonal task-oriented atmosphere.

These indices of compatibility have been applied to several experimental situations, including selection of roommates and sociometric selection of naval personnel and task groups. Results seem to be fairly consistent: use of compatibility scores increases the predictability from a chance level of 50 per cent to about 70 per cent (Schutz & Gross 1959).

By use of this theory of compatibility, success was achieved in predicting the ability of an experimenter to condition a subject by considering the interpersonal compatibility of the two. When subject and experimenter were incompatible the conditioning proceeded more slowly than when subject and experimenter were compatible. Then, in an ingenious experimental maneuver, each experimenter asked his subject to continue with the conditioning procedure while the experimenter left the room. The subjects from the incompatible pairs immediately improved their performances to the point where they equaled the compatible subjects, thus confirming the hypothesis that it was the presence of the experimenter that led to the depressed rate of conditioning (Sapolsky 1960).

Another set of investigations was based on Winch's hypothesis (Winch 1958), which asserts that marital success is a function of the husband's and wife's need complementarity, particularly in the areas of dominance–submission and nurturance–succorance. Unfortunately, to date the results of this method of investigation are not encouraging.

Larger groups. Two attempts have been made to expand the compatibility concept to groups of more than two members. An experiment using groups of college students illustrates one method of arranging five-membered groups to be compatible or incompatible. Four groups of college students equated for intelligence were composed according to a pattern of interchange compatibility based on high-affection scores. Four other groups were established on the basis of interchange compatibility reflecting low affection and four followed an incompatible pattern.

High-affection compatible groups contained one member who was predicted on the basis of his test scores to be a "focal person," another who was predicted to be a "main supporting member," and three members who were predicted to be less intelligent and less assertive. All of the subjects in these groups had a liking for close, intimate relationships. The subjects in the compatible groups with low-affection scores were selected to play similar roles, except that they were all persons who liked to keep others at a distance. In the incompatible groups there were two focal person–follower pairs, one pair had high-affection scores, and the other had low-affection scores; there was one neutral person. It was predicted that the two subgroups would clash and that, therefore, energy which would ordinarily be devoted to productive work would be diverted into interpersonal problem solving; hence, these groups would be less productive.

Each of the 12 groups met 14 times in a laboratory over a period of six weeks, during which time each group was given a sequence of several types of tasks to perform.

The difference in productivity between the "compatibles" and the "incompatibles" was highly significant. Both types of compatible groups clearly outperformed the incompatibles, and there was virtually no difference in productivity between the high-affection compatibles and the low-affection compatibles (Schutz 1958).

Organizational structure. Another attempt to devise a theory for compatibility of groups larger than two arose out of the desire to assess compatibility within an organization. Although no rigorous empirical work has yet been done to test this method, it has already revealed the necessity of considering factors other than personality.

To measure the compatibility of people working together within a complex structure, by summing the degree of compatibility of each dyad within the organization, is an unsatisfactory method of assessing the compatibility of a large group since:

(1) The over-all compatibility of an organization is often more dependent on some dyads than on others. For example, how well the boss gets along with a key department head is often far more pivotal for organizational compatibility than is the compatibility of two subordinates doing a routine job.

(2) Compatibility between people who must work together closely to produce something is more important than compatibility between two whose jobs do not require their interaction.

These two considerations suggest a method for extending the concept of compatibility to organizations. The organization must first be analyzed in terms of the acual working groups, that is, a chart should be drawn indicating who must actually work with whom in order to accomplish a certain task. Within these groupings the importance of each dyadic relationship must be assessed.

The best way to determine the functional pattern of the organization is to do it subjectively, that is, to have as many people as possible who are acquainted with the organization make such an analysis. A consensus of informed judgments is usually possible.

Likewise, the best means of weighting the importance of any given dyad to the functioning of the organization is to obtain a subjective judgment, that is, to get a consensus of all knowledgeable people. It may be possible in some organizations to approximate the weighting by making it proportional to the dyad's status level within the organization; the higher up in the hierarchy, the more important to the organization's functioning is the dyadic compatibility, but it would be inaccurate to assume this for all situations. Experience, so far, indicates only that the number of distinguishably different levels of importance are usually small, of the order of three or four within an organization.

After the functional groups and weightings are determined, all dyadic compatibilities between relevant pairs are computed and weighted. The organizational compatibility can be represented by the sum of these weighted compatibilities divided by the sum of the weights—in other words, the mean compatibility over the organization.

This method is very new but gives promise of extending the notion of compatibility to groups larger than two.

Personality as internalized interaction

One of the most interesting theoretical developments in the area of personality and social interaction concerns the use of social interaction as a model for theorizing about personality. This position reverses the usual analogy that a larger social unit is like an individual organism and asserts that the individual can be treated as a small group of interacting people.

This assertion is not an attempt merely to establish an analogy, but it is a contention that the same laws hold for both the individual and the group levels and that the substitution of corresponding variables from these levels will result in correspondingly valid hypotheses. A parallel can be made between a person and a group, since it is often assumed that an individual has a group "within" him. In the course of an infant's development many initially ambiguous figures in his environment are gradually brought into focus and differentiated. These figures are then introjected to various degrees and exert a differential influence on the behavior of the developing child and, later, on the behavior of the adult. [*See* DEVELOPMENTAL PSYCHOLOGY; IDENTITY, PSYCHOSOCIAL; PERCEPTION, *article on* PERCEPTUAL DEVELOPMENT.]

The individual, therefore, may be conceptualized as a group in which he is struggling to become the leader. This group is composed of all those people whom he has incorporated into his own ego—his introjections. Just as some leaders seem to be dominated by one group member, so may an individual be influenced by a particular introjection; just as external forces influence group behavior, so do an individual's external personal relations affect the interaction of his introjections; just as a group at times acts as if it were torn by dissension, so does an individual's behavior at times reflect internal conflict; just as groups vary in cohesiveness, so do individuals vary in their integration; just as groups become immobilized and unproductive, so do people.

An individual arriving at a decision may be regarded as symbolically working out the interaction of the group within himself to reach a decision. The group equivalent of individual behavior is a group decision or a topic that a group chooses to discuss, as opposed to idiosyncratic topics. Group decision behavior is analogous to ego functioning.

Berne (1961) states that the individual personality consists of parts called the Parent, the Adult, and the Child. Fairbairn (1952) emphasizes the importance of internalized objects as a conceptual framework for understanding individual personality. Schutz (1961*a*) evolves his point of view through the vehicle of psychoanalytic ego psychology, especially as developed by Hartmann (1939). Hartmann discusses ego development in terms of three sets of factors: inherited ego characteristics, influences of instinctual drives, and influences of outer reality. Schutz transforms this into corresponding terms for small groups, and Bennis (1964), in a review of organization theory, expresses organization problems in much the same terms.

There seems to be general agreement that each social unit must deal with an environment, or outer reality, with its own internal emotional forces or interpersonal needs and with those factors involved in task behavior, such as intellect and other abilities. The following integration is suggested.

Outer reality. It is necessary for each social unit to establish and maintain sufficient contact and interaction with outside groups and individuals to avoid isolation of the unit, but it is not necessary to engage in so much contact that the unit loses its identity.

It is also necessary to establish and maintain sufficient control over outer reality so that the group can function satisfactorily without outside interference, and yet it is not necessary to assume so much control that the group is forced to undertake more responsibility than it can handle.

There is, furthermore, a need to establish and maintain sufficient closeness and intimacy with outside reality so that the group can feel the pleasures of friendship and affection, and yet there is no need to experience so much intimacy with outside reality that the actions of the group become distorted and detrimental to group objectives.

Interpersonal needs. The group's existence is greatly dependent upon everyone's feeling that he is part of the group. The desire for inclusion becomes a motivation for efficiency in activities, such as notifying members of meetings. However, group members must also be allowed to maintain some degree of distance from other group members and some degree of individuality.

It is necessary for members to influence other members to some extent in order to make decisions and to establish behavior patterns leading to a restriction of the amount of control some members have over others. The institutional procedures of majority rule and consenus are often used to balance control relations.

People must relate to each other with sufficient warmth and closeness so that group processes may occur. If there is not enough freedom to express feelings among members, then productivity suffers because of the tie-up of energy in the suppression of hostile impulses. However, excessive intimacy and closeness may have the effect of detracting from the main purposes of the group and of personalizing task issues to an undesirable extent. Hence, it is necessary to balance the degree of closeness in groups.

Task behavior. In the area of the task behavior the precise functions of the group are not as clear, but they do include at least the following: (*a*) establishment and clarification of the hierarchy of group goals and values; (*b*) recognition and integration of the various modes of problem solving existing within the group; and (*c*) development and utilization of the full potential of each group member.

Examples and extensions. These descriptions of group functions are directly transferable to individual personalities and organizations. Specification of these areas of concern originated in ego psychology and, through the use of the analogy to small groups, generated the above theoretical structure. The value of the approach is also felt in the other direction—suggestions for personality theory derived from the analogy to small-group theory. Two illustrations will develop this point.

In Redl's (1942) analysis of group leadership he distinguishes ten types of "central persons," that is, a person around whom a group forms as a result of his eliciting common feelings from group members. These types suggest ten ways in which individual personalities are integrated, that is, ten kinds of ego integration. For example, one of the ways groups are formed, according to Redl, is through the use of the central person as an object of love. Another mode of group formation uses the central person as the object of aggression. Perhaps these two processes occurring within one individual may be distinguishable by strong feelings of self-love on the one hand and of self-hate on the other. For example, a person in whom the self-hate self concept exists at an unconscious level is analogous to a group organized around a central person on the basis of the members' commonly shared feelings of aggression toward that person.

Another type of group formation centers around a common-conflict solver, a person who acts in such a way as to resolve enervating conflicts in other group members. Where there is a great deal of conflict within an individual, he may select an introjection that is not a source of conflict in order to orient his own ego, thereby allowing him to solve this problem. One might wonder, however, about the stability of such an individual; for groups this formation is a very volatile one, the leadership pattern being dependent on the immediate conflict only. Possibly, a useful classification of pathological conditions may be made on the basis of inadequate types of ego integration.

This parallel leads to lines of research in which the group, conceptualized as one individual, becomes the basic tool. Attempts can be made to reproduce in the group various kinds of ego-integration patterns found in individuals and to examine their consequences. Since it is ordinarily easier to see phenomena in a group than within an individual, experimental personality research can be expedited with the use of the small group.

Another application of this point of view has been made by certain psychotherapists, although their theoretical basis may be somewhat different. The gestalt therapists and those in sociodrama make use of the multifaceted personality. For example, the therapist may say (in an appropriate situation), "Imagine someone inside your head saying to you, 'You are a mature adult,' and someone else inside your head saying, 'You are an immature child.' Make them have a discussion or argument with each other until one wins. Act out each part." In this way the therapist is helping the patient to understand the nature of a conflict. He is doing it by utilizing the concept that a personality is made up of introjected people. Often the patient will visualize his father, or himself at an earlier time, or mother, or boss, or some other significant figure in his past as one of the people in his head. The internal conflict he is presently experiencing can then be understood as a struggle between parts of "others" that he has internalized.

There is ample promise that progress is being made toward predicting social interaction from a knowledge of the personality of the interactors and the laws of human interaction. The notion that the laws of group behavior and the laws governing the individual personality are similar or perhaps even the same is an exciting one and seems likely to lead to some fruitful investigations. In short, the apparently ineffable relations that exist between men are slowly being identified and measured.

WILLIAM C. SCHUTZ

[*Other relevant material may be found in* CONFLICT, *article on* SOCIAL ASPECTS; GROUPS; IDENTITY, PSYCHOSOCIAL; ORGANIZATIONS; SELF CONCEPT; SOCIALIZATION; *and the biographies of* COOLEY *and* MEAD.]

BIBLIOGRAPHY

BENNIS, W. 1964 The Decline of Bureaucracy and Organizations of the Future. Unpublished manuscript.

→ Paper presented at the annual meeting of the American Psychological Association.

BERNE, ERIC 1961 *Transactional Analysis in Psychotherapy.* New York: Grove.

CATTELL, RAYMOND; and STICE, GLEN F. 1954 Four Formulae for Selecting Leaders on the Basis of Personality. *Human Relations* 7:493–507.

COHEN, ARTHUR R. 1956 Experimental Effects of Ego Defense Preference on Interpersonal Relations. *Journal of Abnormal and Social Psychology* 52:19–27.

FAIRBAIRN, WILLIAM R. (1952) 1954 *An Object–Relations Theory of the Personality.* New York: Basic Books. → First published as *Psychoanalytic Studies of the Personality.*

HARE, ALEXANDER P. 1962 *Handbook of Small Group Research.* New York: Free Press.

HARTMANN, HEINZ (1939) 1958 *Ego Psychology and the Problem of Adaptation.* Translated by David Rapaport. New York: International Universities Press. → First published as *Ich-Psychologie und Anpassungsproblem.*

HAYTHORN, WILLIAM 1953 The Influence of Individual Members on the Characteristics of Small Groups. *Journal of Abnormal and Social Psychology* 48:276–284.

KERCKHOFF, ALAN; and DAVIS, KEITH 1962 Value Consensus and Need Complementarity in Mate Selection. *American Sociological Review* 27:295–303.

PERLS, FREDERICK; HEFFERLINE, RALPH; and GOODMAN, PAUL (1951) 1962 *Gestalt Therapy.* New York: Julian.

REDL, FRITZ 1942 Group Emotion and Leadership. *Psychiatry* 5:573–596.

SAPOLSKY, ALLAN 1960 Effect of Interpersonal Relationships Upon Verbal Conditioning. *Journal of Abnormal and Social Psychology* 60:241–246.

SCHUTZ, WILLIAM C. 1958 *FIRO: A Three-dimensional Theory of Interpersonal Behavior.* New York: Holt.

SCHUTZ, WILLIAM C. 1961*a* The Ego, FIRO Theory and the Leader as Completer. Pages 48–65 in Luigi Petrullo and Bernard Bass (editors), *Leadership and Interpersonal Behavior.* New York: Holt.

SCHUTZ, WILLIAM C. 1958 *FIRO: A Three-dimensional Journal of Abnormal and Social Psychology* 62:275–281.

SCHUTZ, WILLIAM C. 1964 Organizational Compatibility. Unpublished manuscript.

SCHUTZ, WILLIAM C.; and GROSS, EUGEN F. 1959 The FIRO Theory of Interpersonal Behavior: Empirical Tests and Applications to Business Administration. Pages 161–172 in California, University of, Los Angeles, Western Data Processing Center, *Contributions to Scientific Research in Management.* Berkeley: Univ. of California Press.

WAXLER, N. 1960 Defense Mechanisms and Interpersonal Behavior. Ph.D. dissertation, Harvard Univ.

WINCH, ROBERT F. 1958 *Mate-selection: A Study of Complementary Needs.* New York: Harper.

VI
INTERACTION PROCESS ANALYSIS

Interaction process analysis is an observational method for the study of the social and emotional behavior of individuals in small groups—their approach to problem solving, their roles and status structure, and changes in these over time. The method is sometimes treated as a type of content analysis, because, like content analysis, it is employed to estimate the relative strength of various underlying determinants of overt behavior. It is distinguished from content analysis, however, in that the observer abstracts from the content, in the ordinary sense of "what is talked about," and focuses attention instead upon the form of the behavior and the changing patterns of action and reaction among individuals by which the content is communicated.

The term "interaction process analysis" was introduced into the literature as the title of a book by the present author (Bales 1950). It was presented as a generic designation for a number of similar methods. Some of these methods were then being used in experimental studies of groups, particularly studies by researchers in group dynamics; others were being used in studies of counseling and therapy, particularly research in nondirective therapy, and in studies of classroom groups. Earlier methods for the study of child play and for the study of discussion groups had appeared as much as twenty and thirty years previously. Theoretically, therefore, there is justification for using "interaction process analysis" as a generic term, but in practice it has been closely associated with the particular method and set of categories advanced by the present author.

The method to be described here was the first to be self-consciously developed as a general-purpose descriptive and diagnostic procedure designed to produce theoretically relevant measures for all sorts of small groups, thus encouraging the development of empirical norms. The method has been used by a number of different investigators, and norms as well as a number of useful empirical generalizations have resulted. Table 1 shows the categories with information on the distribution of rates in a sample of 21 widely different types of situations (representing many times that number of groups) observed by different investigators.

In a survey of the usage of the method, Bales and Hare (1965) describe the setting, type of group, and other details, and report the total summary profile for each of 21 different studies. The profiles of acts initiated are reported in percentage rates in each category, usually on large numbers of acts. The 21 studies give indications of the ways in which the rates in each category are likely to vary over many situations and investigators. However, the results reported in Table 1 should be used as norms only with caution, since the sample may not represent the appropriate range of variability for many diagnostic purposes. Table 1 represents variability due to different observers, situations, organizational settings, sizes of group, tasks, gross

Table 1 — List of categories used in interaction process analyses, showing distribution of rates obtained in each category in a sample of 21 studies by different investigators*

Category of act initiated	Median rate	Range of lowest 7 rates	Range of middle 7 rates	Range of highest 7 rates
		Low	*Medium*	*High*
1. Shows solidarity	2.3	0.1–1.9	2.0–3.3	3.4–9.5
2. Shows tension release	6.2	0.5–5.3	5.4–7.4	7.5–30.4
3. Agrees	9.5	0.9–7.9	8.0–13.6	13.7–21.5
4. Gives suggestion	3.7	0.0–2.9	3.0–7.0	7.1–25.2
5. Gives opinion	22.8	3.5–19.8	19.9–27.2	27.3–33.4
6. Gives orientation	29.0	13.6–21.0	21.1–33.7	33.8–56.9
7. Asks for orientation	5.1	1.8–3.9	4.0–7.2	7.3–12.9
8. Asks for opinion	2.2	0.5–1.9	2.0–3.9	4.0–9.3
9. Asks for suggestion	0.4	0.0–0.2	0.3–0.9	1.0–2.2
10. Disagrees	4.4	0.6–3.0	3.1–5.3	5.4–14.3
11. Shows tension	2.2	0.2–1.7	1.8–3.0	3.1–15.5
12. Shows antagonism	1.6	0.0–0.5	0.6–2.4	2.5–9.2

* The rates for a given category across the total sample of 21 studies are rank-ordered and divided into the lowest seven, the middle seven, and the highest seven. Cutting points are established so that the range shown contains all seven rates, but no gap is left between thirds of the distribution. The labels "Low," "Medium," and "High" are added for use in connection with Table 2.

Source: Bales & Hare 1965.

differences between groups because of age, sex, general physical condition of members (such as whether or not intoxicated), and the like.

Procedure

The observer studies the list of categories and definitions until he is thoroughly familiar with them, not only singly, but as an ordered scheme. Prior to the interaction he assigns and memorizes an identification number for each of the participants. In observing he keeps his eyes on the group as much as possible. He divides the ongoing behavior, nonverbal as well as verbal, into separate acts, each of which is recorded by entering the identification number of the person speaking, followed by the identification number of the person spoken to, under the category which best describes the act. The criterion as to how much behavior constitutes an act is pragmatic—enough to allow the observer to make a classification. A single act is essentially equivalent to a single simple sentence. Tone of voice, facial expression, bodily movement, and cues of all kinds, nonverbal as well as verbal, are used in making the classification and in determining to whom the act is directed. The group as a whole is recognized as a recipient of communication, as well as specific other individuals. But the group as a whole is not recognized as an actor. Acts performed in unison (notably laughing) are recorded by a single score but later credited back to individual actors. The observer scores continuously, usually at a rate of ten to twenty scores per minute. Comparable methods differ from each other not only as to the list of categories but also on all these points of procedure. The issues have been discussed in several standard works on methods (see *Research Methods in Social Relations* 1951; Festinger & Katz 1953; Lindzey 1954).

Interaction process analysis is designed for on-the-spot concurrent recording of the behavior, but it may be applied to a sound recording or a written transcript of interaction. The method was developed and is most easily applied with the aid of a laboratory observation room, connected to the group meeting room by one-way mirrors, with sound monitoring, tape recording, and a paper-moving device called an interaction recorder to enable the observer to keep scores in time sequence. None of these aids is strictly necessary, however. Hare (1957) has applied the method to observation of the leadership behavior of boys on a playground; he used nothing more elaborate than a pencil and a pad of scoring forms. For a field study Strodtbeck (1951) used a pickup truck with a portable sound recorder. Husband-and-wife couples sat in the front seat and talked. The sound recordings were translated, where necessary, by local assistants, Strodtbeck added notations of sighs, laughs, and the like, and the interaction scoring was done by a third person from the written transcript. In an experimental study of jury deliberations Strodtbeck and Mann (1956) noted a few words of content as well as who-to-whom and nonverbal signs at the time of interaction, and the scoring was done later from these notes plus the sound recording. Some researchers may prefer a two-step method like this for the sake of higher reliability or to ease the training problem, but many successful studies have been made using on-the-spot scoring. Learning the method may require one or two months. Through training, correlation between two observers of rates in a given category over a series of sessions may be as high as .90 for some pairs of observers on the categories of higher frequency, but the same observers may find it difficult to obtain correlations higher than .60 for the categories of lower frequency.

Frame of reference

In order to present the correlates of measures to be obtained from interaction process analysis it is helpful to make reference to a three-dimensional "property space" (for which see Barton 1955) that has turned up repeatedly in factor analyses of interpersonal behavior, perceptions, and ratings persons make of each other in small groups. The space was first recognized as rather general by Carter (1954) and Couch (1960), who factor-analyzed data of their own and reviewed a series of other factor analytic studies. The work of Borgatta, Cottrell, and Meyer (1956) and Borgatta (1960) has been particularly notable in carrying on this inquiry. Hare (1962) has presented a review of the relevant studies, to which should be added the work of Leary (1957), who constructed an interpersonal diagnostic system around two of the dimensions. It has not yet been shown that the different property or factor spaces cited are all indicators of the same fundamental evaluative tendencies of persons as they view other persons and actions, but the assumption is plausible. A factor analysis by Couch (1960), which employed an exceptionally large number of measures from a study conducted with the present author, turned up as the three most important factors the same three found most important in previous studies. Couch's factor loadings form the factual basis for the description and interpretation employed here. The types of variables included overt social interaction (the present categories), personality tests, interpersonal perceptions and ratings, value statements, and observer's ratings.

Dimensions of social evaluation. Let us suppose that there are at least three fundamental *dimensions of social evaluation* involved as one person views another in a group setting. The first is concerned with the degree of power, dominance, ascendance, or individual prominence of the person as perceived by the evaluator. In ordinary language this dimension is often referred to as if it were vertical in physical space: a person is said to move "upward" in the group as his power, dominance, or prominence increases and "downward" as his power decreases.

The second dimension is concerned with the pleasant or unpleasant quality of feeling aroused by the person. If the feeling aroused in the evaluator is pleasant, one of acceptance and liking, the evaluation may be called "positive." If it is unpleasant, one of rejection and disliking, it may be called "negative." For purposes of visualization one may think of this dimension as horizontal, with positive to the right-hand side and negative to the left-hand side.

The third dimension is concerned with the value of the other person in the performance of group tasks and the achievement of group goals—that is, those tasks and goals given by acceptance of whatever authority the group recognizes. A spatial metaphor is often used to refer to this dimension: the direction toward achievement of group goals is said to be "forward"; the direction away from achievement is said to be "backward." The person who moves forward may be said to conform to the values given by acceptance of the authority that is effective within the group, while the person who moves backward may be said to deviate.

The spatial metaphors should not be taken too seriously—they are suggested here as an aid to visualization and memory. It may be, of course, that the spatial metaphors continue to be used because they provide an effective, though primitive, way of remembering a complicated set of relationships. It is not easy to find a better model for a three-dimensional set of relationships than the physical space that surrounds us. If the reader wishes to think in terms of the theory, he is urged to adopt the physical space model. He may then think of the directions in relation to his head as the center of the space.

According to this theory, then, persons judge or evaluate each other according to their significance in relation to power, affection, and contribution to group tasks. The dimensions of social evaluation must be understood broadly as correlated clusters of more concrete attitudes of persons toward others, not as single well-defined attitudes. But so far as they can be thought of as variables, the factor studies suggest that we ought to think of the dimensions as *unrelated* to each other—as uncorrelated ("orthogonal" in the language of factor analysis). If the variables were actually uncorrelated, individuals would be found about equally distributed in all positions described by all combinations of the directions. Thus, the factor analytic findings imply that the possession of a position of power by a person in a small group should not lead us to expect that the possessor will be either positively or negatively evaluated (liked or disliked), or that he will be either conforming or deviant with regard

Table 2 — Key for interpretation of high and low rates on the interaction profile[a]

Interaction category	INTERACTION INITIATED: Directional components[b] indicated if the rate of initiating is:		INTERACTION RECEIVED: Directional components[b] indicated if the rate of receiving is:	
1. Shows solidarity	Low = DF	High = UB	Low = NF	High = PB
2. Shows tension release	Low = U	High = D	Low = DPF	High = UNB
3. Agrees	Low = NB	High = PF	Low = UB	High = DF
4. Gives suggestion	Low = 0	High = 0	Low = DN	High = UP
5. Gives opinion	Low = DPB	High = UNF	Low = DNB	High = UPF
6. Gives orientation	Low = U	High = D	Low = N	High = P
7. Asks for orientation	Low = DN	High = UP	Low = UPF	High = DNB
8. Asks for opinion	Low = N	High = P	Low = UP	High = DN
9. Asks for suggestion	Low = 0	High = 0	Low = B	High = F
10. Disagrees	Low = P	High = N	Low = DPB	High = UNF
11. Shows tension	Low = UF	High = DB	Low = PB	High = NF
12. Shows antagonism	Low = DP	High = UN	Low = DPB	High = UNF

a. High and low rates of interaction in all categories of interaction initiated and received by an individual may be combined to predict the attitudes other members may have toward that individual, that is, where they place him in the three-dimensional evaluative space. The combination is performed by addition of the directional components.

b. A directional component is an indicator of a direction of movement in the three-dimensional evaluative space. The dimensions and directions are:

Dimension I	Dimension II	Dimension III
U = Upward	P = Positive	F = Forward
D = Downward	N = Negative	B = Backward

No movement in any direction is indicated by 0. Directional components are considered to be algebraically additive as they are in three-dimensional physical space. U and D are of opposite sign and cancel each other. The same is true of P and N, and again of F and B. Thus, $U + U = 2U$, but $U + D = 0$, and similarly for the other dimensions. The prediction of actual movement is obtained by summing all components to a single resultant direction. A resultant direction may name one, two, or three components, such as: U, UP, UPF. Thus $U + P + F = UPF$. A number of personality and role traits related to each resultant direction are known.

Source: The directional components indicated are based on factor loadings reported in Couch 1960. Unfortunately, the components shown for categories 1 and 2 are not characteristic, since in the source study jokes were scored in category 1 instead of 2.

to the task-oriented common values of the group. We should not expect that the task-oriented conformist is necessarily well liked, nor that the socially–emotionally oriented deviant is necessarily disliked. Knowing the person's position on any one dimension we should not expect to be able to predict his position on either of the other two dimensions.

The conception of three independent dimensions or scales along which any person or any act within the group may be given a position by the social evaluation of group members is, if truly sound and typical, a useful basis for classifying not only positions within the group but also directions of motivational movement, types of values, types of acts, types of roles—in fact anything which may be considered an object of social-psychological evaluation. Properly understood, such a dimensional space is an appropriate starting point for a classification of the functional problems of small groups (the a priori base from which the interaction categories of the present system were originally derived). The classes of functional problems as originally presented (Bales 1950) were four in number: adaptive, integrative, instrumental, and expressive. Unfortunately, their relations to each other were not very clear. The empirical results of factor analysis now suggest that the adaptive direction may be identified as the downward direction of yielding power or submitting. Its opposite is upward or dominating. The integrative direction may be identified as the positive direction. Its opposite is disintegrative or negative. Finally, the instrumental and expressive directions turn out to be the two opposite directions of the *same* dimension, here called forward and backward.

Thus, to move upward rather than downward in the social evaluation of another person or the group means to acquire the connotation in the minds of others of overcoming by possession of power rather than of *adapting* because of lack of power. To move positively rather than negatively means to acquire the connotation of promoting feelings of social acceptance and *integration* rather than feelings of antagonism and rejection. To move forward rather than backward means to acquire the connotation of contributing *instrumentally* to the achievement of group goals rather than of encouraging deviance by the *expression* of fantasies, tensions, or feelings in such a way as to hamper achievement.

Status and leadership. Is "higher social status" the primitive meaning of "upward"? Probably what most sociologists mean by "higher status" is not simply "upward" but a combination of "upward," "positive," and "forward," in the present dimensional system. High status of an individual in the small group, as in the large, is probably best thought of as an additive combination of high evaluation on several components, not necessarily correlated with each other. In the present case, the components are uncorrelated with each other over a population of many individuals in many groups. Leadership, like high status, is a complex direction. Apparently what most group members mean when they rate a member high on leadership is that he combines the components of "upward," "positive," and "forward" movement. The traits which make for each of the components are uncorrelated over a population of many individuals in many groups. Hence, "great men" who combine them are rare. They must be simultaneously high on "activity," "likeability," and "taskability," to use the language of an earlier formulation (Bales 1958).

The interaction profile

An interaction profile is an array of the rates of activity in each category. The profile of acts initiated by an individual is obtained by calculating the percentage of his total acts falling in each of the categories. The profile of acts received by an individual may be obtained as well as the profile of acts initiated. Individuals may be compared to each other or to general norms (the norms given in Table 1 are not completely appropriate for the examination of individual profiles, and especially not for acts received, but they are the best available). Comparison with these norms, or with some more appropriate set, can be translated into judgments of the individual as high, medium, or low on each category. These judgments in turn can be used as diagnostic indicators for placement of the individual on the three dimensions described above. Table 2 shows the placements most consistent with empirical evidence so far.

The interaction matrix

An interaction matrix is a tabulation of the number of acts addressed by each individual in a group to each other individual, and to the group as a whole, with appropriate subtotals and totals, as shown in Table 3. The symbol $\sum I$ is used to indicate the subtotal of acts addressed to specific individuals by a given actor. The symbol $\sum O$ is used to indicate the subtotal of acts he addresses to the group as a whole rather than to specific individuals. The symbol $\sum R$ is used to indicate the subtotal of acts he receives from all others. Finally, the term "total participation" is used to designate the sum of these three subtotals—that is, the total number of acts initiated plus the total number of acts received by that individual. The internal cells of the matrix show the number of acts each individual addresses specifically to each other individual.

The matrix is most easily examined if ordered according to rank of the individuals on total participation, as in Table 3. In most groups the amount initiated by a given actor to a specific other person tends to be of the same order of magnitude as the amount the other addresses to the actor. This can be seen in Table 3. But more exactly, it is generally true that the lower of the two participators addresses a little more to the higher participator than the higher participator addresses to him. It is generally true that persons in uncontested higher power positions address a relatively large part of their total participation to the group as a whole ($\sum O$) rather than to specific individuals. For the highest participator in many groups the amount addressed to the group as a whole ($\sum O$) exceeds the sum addressed to all individuals specifically ($\sum I$). This is the case in Table 3. For the lowest participators, on the contrary, the amount ad-

Table 3 — Aggregate who-to-whom matrix for 18 sessions of six-man groups (individuals ordered according to rank on total participation*)

Initiator \ Receiver	1	2	3	4	5	6	ΣI	ΣO	Total participation $\Sigma I + \Sigma O + \Sigma R$
1		1,238	961	545	445	317	3,506	5,661	14,370
2	1,748		443	310	175	102	2,778	1,211	6,302
3	1,371	415		305	125	69	2,285	742	4,971
4	952	310	282		83	49	1,676	676	3,660
5	662	224	144	83		28	1,141	443	2,456
6	470	126	114	65	44		819	373	1,757
ΣR	5,203	2,313	1,944	1,308	872	565	12,205	9,106	33,516

* Individuals ranked for each matrix before aggregation of matrices.

Source: Adapted from Bales 1953.

dressed to the group as a whole tends to fall short of the amount addressed to specific individuals, as Table 3 also shows. When, for a given individual, the amount addressed to the group as a whole exceeds the amount addressed to specific individuals, it may be inferred that he is at least trying to move "upward." Conversely, when the amount he addresses to specific individuals exceeds the amount he addresses to the group as a whole, it may be inferred that he is tending to move "downward." The ratio of the two amounts can be used to give a more refined measure.

An act addressed to the group as a whole may be taken as a bid for power; an act received in return which does not require an answer or an argument may be taken as an agreement or vote of confidence. The actual power position of a given person in the group may be roughly estimated, then, by counting the number of other persons who will regularly respond to his bids for power with agreement, thus leaving him free to continue further bids for power by speaking to the group as a whole, instead of arguing with each of them specifically. The person who is successful in this way will build up a high total participation. For most individuals there is no better indicator of relative power or position in the upward–downward evaluation of the group than his total participation compared to that of others.

Phase movements

Under certain conditions of organization, and when there is a clear-cut but complex task of group decision to be arrived at within a given session, groups tend to move through an orbit of directional movement over the course of the session (Bales & Strodtbeck 1951). They may start with preliminary pleasantries that average toward the positive side. As they begin with the task proper they move downward with high rates of giving orientation, then forward and upward as rates of orientation fall and rates of giving opinion and suggestion rise. The movement tends toward the negative side as giving opinion rises accompanied by disagreement. (Actually, rates of agreement as well as disagreement tend to rise, but on the average the negative movement is at first stronger.) Some groups, especially those which begin with low status consensus, may hang in this phase indefinitely. Others, particularly if their status problems are not severe, pass through the crisis, and begin to swing back toward the positive side as agreement is reached. The average movement swings upward and backward as the group begins a period of joking and laughing. As the laughter grows and spreads, the movement swings backward, downward, and positive, completing the orbit at about the same place as the starting position, on the positive side.

Somewhat similar cycles can be described for longer time spans for groups (Heinicke & Bales 1953). It seems probable that a similar orbital model could be useful for examining successful as compared to unsuccessful episodes in child socialization, as well as other social processes which have a basic phasic character. This remains to be seen. It also seems likely that the conceptualization of evaluative space as a theory will have many applications in which actual observation of interaction may play only a minor part. It should be noted that estimates of position in the space may be made from many bases other than interaction.

ROBERT F. BALES

[*Directly related are the entries* GROUPS, *article on* ROLE STRUCTURE; LEADERSHIP. *Other relevant material may be found in* SOCIOMETRY.]

BIBLIOGRAPHY

BALES, ROBERT F. (1950) 1951 *Interaction Process Analysis: A Method for the Study of Small Groups.* Reading, Mass.: Addison-Wesley.

BALES, ROBERT F. 1953 The Equilibrium Problem in Small Groups. Pages 111–161 in Talcott Parsons, Robert F. Bales, and Edward A. Shils, *Working Papers in the Theory of Action.* Glencoe, Ill.: Free Press.

BALES, ROBERT F. 1958 Task Roles and Social Roles in Problem-solving Groups. Pages 437–447 in Society for the Psychological Study of Social Issues, *Readings in Social Psychology.* 3d ed. Edited by Eleanor E. Maccoby, Theodore M. Newcomb, and Eugene L. Hartley. New York: Holt.

BALES, ROBERT F.; and HARE, A. PAUL 1965 Diagnostic Use of the Interaction Profile. *Journal of Social Psychology* 67:239–258.

BALES, ROBERT F.; and STRODTBECK, FRED L. 1951 Phases in Group Problem-solving. *Journal of Abnormal and Social Psychology* 46:485–495.

BARTON, ALLEN H. 1955 The Concept of Property Space in Social Research. Pages 40–54 in Paul F. Lazarsfeld and Morris Rosenberg (editors), *The Language of Social Research.* Glencoe, Ill.: Free Press.

BORGATTA, EDGAR F. 1960 The Stability of Interpersonal Judgments in Independent Situations. *Journal of Abnormal and Social Psychology* 60:188–194.

BORGATTA, EDGAR F.; COTTRELL, LEONARD S.; and MEYER, HENRY J. 1956 On the Dimensions of Group Behavior. *Sociometry* 19:223–240.

CARTER, LAUNOR F. 1954 Evaluating the Performance of Individuals as Members of Small Groups. *Personnel Psychology* 7:477–484.

COUCH, ARTHUR S. 1960 Psychological Determinants of Interpersonal Behavior. Ph.D. dissertation, Harvard Univ.

FESTINGER, LEON; and KATZ, DANIEL (editors) (1953) 1965 *Research Methods in the Behavioral Sciences.* New York: Holt.

HARE, A. PAUL 1957 Situational Differences in Leader Behavior. *Journal of Abnormal and Social Psychology* 55:132–135.
HARE, A. PAUL 1962 *Handbook of Small Group Research.* New York: Free Press.
HEINICKE, CHRISTOPHER; and BALES, ROBERT F. 1953 Developmental Trends in the Structure of Small Groups. *Sociometry* 16:7–38.
LEARY, TIMOTHY 1957 *Interpersonal Diagnosis of Personality: A Functional Theory and Methodology for Personality Evaluation.* New York: Ronald Press.
LINDZEY, GARDNER (editor) (1954) 1959 *Handbook of Social Psychology.* 2 vols. Cambridge, Mass.: Addison-Wesley. → Volume 1: *Theory and Method.* Volume 2: *Special Fields and Applications.*
Research Methods in Social Relations. Rev. ed. By Claire Selltiz et al. (1951) 1964 New York: Holt.
STRODTBECK, FRED L. 1951 Husband–Wife Interaction Over Revealed Differences. *American Sociological Review* 16:468–473.
STRODTBECK, FRED L.; and MANN, RICHARD D. 1956 Sex Role Differentiation in Jury Deliberations. *Sociometry* 19:3–11.

INTERACTION, STATISTICAL

See EXPERIMENTAL DESIGN *and* LINEAR HYPOTHESES.

INTEREST

Interest is one of the forms of income from property, the other forms being dividends, rents, and profits. Interest usually originates in the payment for a loan of money over a period of time—although it can also arise from loans in kind. Interest is essentially measured by the difference between the amount that the borrower repays and the amount that he originally received from the lender (which is called the principal).

The term *interest* sometimes has the broader connotation of all income from property. This is the case when we speak of "the interest charge on capital," which denotes the alternative income that can be earned on a given quantity of money capital. It is, however, with the narrower sense of the term that this article will almost exclusively be concerned.

Etymologically, *interest* stems from the Medieval Latin word *interesse*, although the meaning of *interesse* was sharply distinguished by the medieval canonists from what is now denoted by *interest.* In particular, the canonists used *interesse* to refer to the compensation made by a debtor to his creditor for damages caused to the creditor as a result of default or delay in the repayment of a loan; as such the compensation evolved from the *quod interest* of Roman law, which was the payment for damages arising from the nonfulfillment of any contractual obligation. The canonists considered *interesse* to be conceptually distinct from the payment for the use of a loan, which they (and Roman law) denoted by the term *usura* (Noonan 1957, pp. 105–106). Since canon law permitted *interesse* but forbade *usura*, the reason for the evolvement of the modern term *interest* is clear.

In the case of a loan repaid in one lump sum, the total amount of interest that is due depends on the principal, P, on the percentage rate of interest per unit of time, r, on the number of time units over which the loan is outstanding, h, and on the number of time units after which the interest obligation is added to the debt of the borrower, m. If this obligation is added only once, when the loan matures (that is, if $h = m$), the interest is said to be simple. The total amount to be repaid at maturity, S, is then

$$S = P(1 + mr). \tag{1}$$

Correspondingly, the total interest payment is

$$S - P = P(1 + mr) - P = mrP. \tag{2}$$

If, in addition, the time unit with respect to which the rate of interest is measured is the same as that of the duration of the loan, then $h = m = 1$, and formulas (1) and (2) are further simplified.

If the interest obligation is added more than once, interest is said to be compounded. In this case h is usually a multiple of m, so that h/m represents the number of times that interest is compounded over the duration of the loan. The total amount to be repaid at the maturity of the loan in this case is

$$S = P(1 + mr)^{h/m}. \tag{3}$$

The shorter is the period after which interest is compounded (that is, the smaller m is), the larger is the amount payable, S. In the limiting case, one can conceive of compounding being carried out continuously over time, in which case the amount payable is derived from formula (3) by letting m approach zero, thus obtaining

$$S = Pe^{rh}, \tag{4}$$

where e is the transcendental number 2.71828 ⋯ The variable r in this case is frequently called "the force of interest."

In order to compare the rates of interest effectively paid on loans with different arrangements for compounding, it is necessary to express the loans in a standardized form. This form is usually that of a loan granted at a rate of interest of i per year, compounded once a year. The standardized rate of interest, i, corresponding to any single-repayment loan extending for h years, is then determined by solving for i in

$$(5) \qquad S/P = (1+i)^h,$$

where S, P, and h are the actual terms of the loan. Alternatively—and frequently more conveniently—the standardized rate is the force of interest, ρ, as solved from

$$(6) \qquad S/P = e^{\rho h}.$$

Loans need not be made in the form of money but can be made in the form of a commodity (for example, wheat, in ancient times). The rate of interest on such loans is frequently called "the own-rate of interest"—a term originated by Keynes (1936, p. 223; see also Lerner 1953, pp. 354–356). Because the anticipated price movements of various commodities differ, their own-rates need not be equal to each other or to the rate of interest on money loans. If, however, there is perfect arbitrage, then in equilibrium we must have approximately $r_n = r_c + s_c$, where r_n is the rate of interest on money loans, r_c is the own-rate of interest on the loan of any commodity, and s_c is the anticipated rate of increase (net of carrying charges) in the money price of that commodity. For if (say) the right-hand side of the foregoing equation were to exceed the left-hand side, a profit could be made by borrowing money, using the proceeds to purchase wheat to be lent out at its own-rate, and subsequently selling the wheat received in repayment of the loan. Such arbitrage transactions would raise r_n and lower r_c and s_c until the foregoing equality was established.

If the formula is applied to commodities in general—so that s_c represents the anticipated increase in the general price level—it becomes an expression of Irving Fisher's celebrated distinction between the money rate and the real rate of interest. The real rate is the rate of interest as measured in terms of commodities and accordingly is approximated by $r_n - s_c$ (Fisher 1930, chapters 2 and 19). The logic behind this relationship explains the fact that money rates of interest tend to be high in periods of inflation. It also explains the appearance in inflationary economies of so-called linked or escalated bonds—that is, bonds whose principal and/or interest payments are proportionately adjusted in accordance with some price index (Brown 1955, pp. 200–203; Finch 1956; Robson 1960).

Since they are alternatives to one another, the different forms of property income must be quantitatively related. In a world of certainty and perfect markets, the ratio of the dividends paid by a stock (including net appreciation in the value of the stock) to the original price of the stock, the ratio of the rent of an asset (net of depreciation and other operating costs) to the original price of the asset, and the ratio of the profits of a firm to the amount invested in it all have a common value, equal to the rate of interest. This equality reflects the fact that in such a world the individual is indifferent about the form in which he receives his income from property.

Conversely, the preferences that individuals in the real world have for particular forms of property income reflect the differing degrees of risk and uncertainty attached to these various forms, the individual's own attitudes toward the risk and uncertainty, the differing degree of knowledge that individuals have of market conditions, differing anticipations of future price conditions, and the like. Of the four forms of property income, interest usually involves the least risk and the least necessity for acquiring detailed knowledge of market conditions. Assuming that the individual has an aversion both to risk and to the effort involved in acquiring information, we should on the average expect the rate of interest to be lower than the rates of return implicit in other forms of property income.

Historical aspects of the interest rate

Credit arrangements go back to prehistoric times and may even have antedated the emergence of a money economy. Similarly, there is ethnological evidence of the existence of credit in kind in primitive communities having no trace of a medium of exchange.

In prehistoric agricultural communities, loans of seed—to be repaid by a greater quantity of seed at harvest time—were undoubtedly a recognized type of arrangement. However, to the extent that repayment was not required in the case of harvest failure, such arrangements were not pure loans but had at least some aspects of what we would today call a partnership or, more generally, an equity investment. Such mixed arrangements complicate any attempt to compare modern credit arrangements with those of earlier periods. In any event, it seems possible that the natural productivity of agriculture suggested the concept of interest on loans to men in prehistoric—and then in historic—times.

Loans bearing interest are described in contracts from the Sumerian civilization (beginning about 3000 B.C.), and mentions of such loans are numerous in the descriptions of credit agreements that have come down to us from the Babylonian empire (beginning about 1900 B.C.). In the Sumerian period the customary annual rates of interest on loans of barley and silver were, respectively, $33\frac{1}{3}$ per cent and 20 per cent. These rates were later established as the legal maxima by the Code of Hammurabi (c. 1800 B.C.) as part of its general tendency to regulate prices, terms of contracts, and other aspects of economic life (Heichelheim [1938] 1958, vol. 1, pp. 55, 111–112, 134–136; Einzig 1949, p. 372; Homer 1963, chapters 1–2).

An even greater development of the credit system characterized the Greek city-states of the seventh century B.C. and onward. Particularly popular were "bottomry loans," in which the money advanced by a lender was secured by the hull of a ship or by its cargo on a specific voyage. In the case of shipwreck the debt was usually canceled; if the voyage was successful the borrower paid from 22 to 100 per cent interest, depending on the length and hazardousness of the voyage. In contrast, loans secured by real estate and loans to cities frequently bore interest of 8 to 10 per cent. Similar rates prevailed during the Roman era, which was characterized by legal maximum rates, first of 8.5 per cent per year and subsequently of 12 per cent.

Most loans in ancient times were granted for what would today be considered a short period: a year or a part of a year. Since there were no business firms in the modern sense of the term, the loans were necessarily to persons or partnerships. From this, however, we should not infer that these loans were predominantly for consumption purposes. It should also be noted that the Greeks and Romans looked down upon the earning of income from interest. According to certain authorities, this contrasts with the view of the peoples of the ancient Oriental civilizations, who (it is claimed) accepted interest as a normal feature of economic life (Heichelheim [1938] 1958, vol. 1, pp. 104–105, 219).

The absolute prohibition of interest was an outstanding feature of ancient Hebrew economic legislation, as incorporated in the well-known Biblical passages "If thou lend money to any of my people that is poor by thee, thou shalt not be to him as an usurer" (Exodus 22.25) and "Thou shalt not lend upon usury to thy brother" (Deuteronomy 23.19). The rabbis of the Mishnah (200 B.C.–A.D. 200) applied this proscription to commercial transactions as well. At the same time they accepted its effective evasion in certain instances by means of the legal fiction of considering the lender to be a partner entitled to profits from the enterprise financed by his funds (Mishnah: Baba Metzia v, 4).

In the Middle Ages the prohibition of interest (or, as it was then called, usury) was a central feature of canon law. But since the church did not prohibit income from property as a category, here too there rapidly developed legal fictions by which the prohibited interest from loans was converted into other—and permissible—forms of income from property. For some scholars this process represents an evasion and a vitiation of the canon law; for others it reflects the deliberate attempt of the church authorities to accommodate themselves to the business needs of the community and accordingly to place the main emphasis of the prohibition of usury on loans made for consumption purposes (Pirenne [1933] 1936, p. 146; Knight [1921–1935] 1951, p. 256; Noonan 1957, pp. 169–170, 190–195).

An important aspect of the Reformation in the sixteenth century was the movement to abolish the legal prohibition of interest. The outstanding theological protagonist of this movement was Calvin. Toward the end of Henry VIII's reign in England, a law was enacted (1545) legalizing interest but limiting it to a legal maximum of 10 per cent. In the first half of the nineteenth century, Roman Catholic authorities also publicly decreed that the interest permitted by law could be taken by everyone (Nelson 1949, chapter 3; Noonan 1957, chapter 19).

With due allowance for the scarcity and imperfections of the data, there seems to have been a decline in interest rates in Europe from the medieval period to the Renaissance. The minimum interest rates on loans secured by land in the Spanish Netherlands from the twelfth century through the fifteenth century ranged from 8 to 10 per cent, as compared with corresponding rates of 6 to 8 per cent in the Dutch Republic during the sixteenth and seventeenth centuries. At the beginning of the eighteenth century in England, long-term government-bond yields were from 6 to 8 per cent, declining to 3 per cent in the midyears of the century and rising erratically toward the end of the century to 5 to 6 per cent. These last rates continued during the Napoleonic wars at the beginning of the nineteenth century. Subsequently, the rate fell again to somewhat above 3 per cent and declined even further toward the end of the century. Corresponding yields during the twentieth century have generally been higher and in 1955–1965 have again reached 6 per cent. Thus, there may have been a slight downward secular trend in long-term interest rates in England over the past two hundred years, although it remains to be seen if this trend has not been reversed in the period since World War II (Homer 1963, pp. 137–138, 193, 411, 504–506).

In any event, there does seem to have been a downward trend during the past fifty to one hundred years in the share of interest in the national income of developed countries. Thus, in the United States this share fell from 5.7 per cent in 1899–1908 to 4.0 per cent in 1954–1960. More generally, the data from the United Kingdom, France, Germany, and the United States all show a marked decline over this period in the share of property income (including that of unincorporated enterprises) in total national income. Kuznets attributes this finding in part to the fact that over the same period the ratio of total wealth to national income (the capital–output ratio) has moved downward in these countries; he also conjectures that the decline was reinforced by a secular downward trend in the yield on capital.

Similarly, Kuznets shows that in 1958 the share of income from assets (excluding those of unincorporated enterprises) in total national income was slightly higher in underdeveloped countries (20.6 per cent) than in developed countries (18.4 per cent). He attributes this finding to the much higher yield on capital in the underdeveloped countries, which more than offsets their lower proportion of corporate assets. Correspondingly, the extent to which the share of property income in the underdeveloped countries exceeds that of the developed ones is much greater when account is taken of all such income—including that of unincorporated enterprises. This finding, as well as that mentioned in the preceding paragraph, would, of course, be modified if we were to take account of the capital invested in the form of education in human beings and accordingly of that part of wages and salaries which reflects the return on this capital (Kuznets 1966, tables 4.2, 4.3, and 8.1 and accompanying text). [*See* CAPITAL, HUMAN; INCOME DISTRIBUTION, *article on* FUNCTIONAL SHARE.]

Studies of the business cycle in the United States have shown that the rate of interest (as measured by the yield on railroad bonds) more or less conforms, with a lag, to the level of general economic activity. Similarly, it conforms, with a lag, to the movements of the price level—a fact (referred to generally by Keynes as the "Gibson paradox") that raises certain theoretical questions discussed below, under "Interest in a money economy," in the section "Theories of interest" (Keynes 1930, vol. 2, pp. 198 ff.; Macaulay 1938, chapter 6; Burns & Mitchell 1946, p. 501; Burns 1961, p. 28; Cagan 1966).

Theories of interest

Interest in a barter economy. From the definition of the interest rate as the price paid for the use of a loan for one unit of time, it seems natural to analyze the determination of this rate in terms of the demand for and supply of loans. Although there are many theories that have not been explicitly formulated in terms of this "loanable-funds approach" to interest, they can nevertheless be examined from this viewpoint.

Investment and the demand for loans. For simplicity, let us define "households" as those economic units that engage solely in the sale of the services of factors of production and in the consumption of goods and services, and let us define "businesses" as the locus of all production and investment activity. Then in an economy in which money exists only as an abstract unit of account (and for the present purpose such an economy is equivalent to a barter economy) any savings that a household makes will be lent out. Correspondingly, the supply of loans by households to the business sector must equal the total amount that households save. (Consumption loans will be discussed later.) Similarly, under the assumption of a perfect capital market, the net investment of the business sector can be considered as being equal to its total demand for new loans (that is, net of refundings) from the household sector, for in such a market it can make no difference either to businesses or to households whether investment is financed by means of loans, stock issues, or undistributed corporate profits.

The basic fact that lies behind businesses' demand for loans is the productivity of capital [*see* CAPITAL; INVESTMENT]. By this is meant the fact that an investment project can yield over time a stream of returns that exceeds the total costs of carrying it out. In particular, if a project is planned for n years, and if $S_1, S_2, \cdots, S_n$ represents its expected stream of net returns or, in more technical terms, of quasi rents (that is, the expected receipts in each year from the sale of the output of the project *less* the corresponding current operating expenses in the form of wages, costs of raw materials, and the like—exclusive of depreciation), then the productivity of the capital invested in the project is reflected in the fact that $S_1 + S_2 \cdots + S_n$ (where S_n also includes the possible scrap value) is greater than the cost of the plant and equipment, V, involved in the project.

More precisely, the marginal productivity of capital—which for our purposes can be taken as synonymous with Keynes's marginal efficiency of capital—is defined as that rate which equalizes the present value of the stream of quasi rents with the cost of plant and equipment. It is that rate, ρ, which satisfies the equation

$$\frac{S_1}{1+\rho} + \frac{S_2}{(1+\rho)^2} + \cdots + \frac{S_n}{(1+\rho)^n} - V = 0,$$

where it has been assumed that net positive receipts occur at the end of each period, whereas the total payment for plant and equipment is made at the beginning of the first period. In a world of certainty and a perfect capital market, potential investors will carry out any project whose marginal rate of return, ρ, exceeds or equals the interest rate, r, which is assumed to remain constant over the economic horizon and which measures the actual or imputed marginal cost of the funds invested in the project. Correspondingly, investors will not carry out any project whose rate of return is less than r. Thus, under these assumptions, the rate of interest serves as the rationing device that allocates scarce capital funds in an optimal manner among competing investments projects. From this it also follows that the lower the rate of interest, the larger the number of investment projects that it pays to carry out.

This relationship is frequently described by means of a negatively sloped curve relating increasing volumes of investment to a declining rate of interest. It should be emphasized that the concept of investment basic to this curve is that of *gross* investment. The firm's decision about a particular investment project can in no way be affected by whether this project represents "replacement" or "new capital"; nor, in a perfect capital market, can it be affected by the accounting distinction between funds made available from depreciation allowances and those made available from new loans. For our purposes, however, it will be more convenient to deal with the derivative concept "*net* investment," defined as gross investment less depreciation. As a first approximation (whose accuracy increases the shorter the life of the project) the calculation of this depreciation can be assumed to be unaffected by the rate of interest. Correspondingly, the net-investment curve is obtained from the gross-investment curve by simply shifting the latter to the left by an amount equal to depreciation.

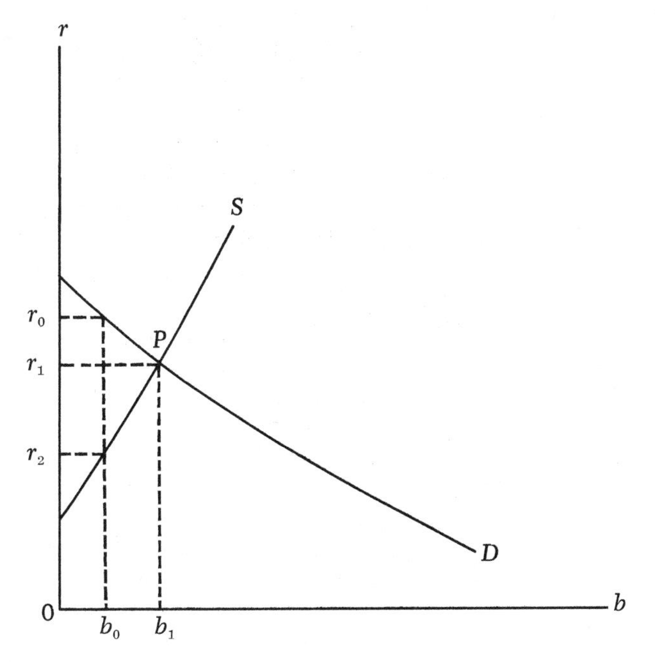

Figure 1

This, then, is the explanation of the negative slope of the demand curve for loans, D, in Figure 1, which under our present assumptions is identical with the net-investment curve. The vertical axis in this diagram represents the (real) rate of interest and the horizontal axis the real volume of new loans made during the specified period of time (say, a year) to which the analysis refers. By construction, any rate of interest on this curve (say, r_0) corresponding to a given volume of loans (say, b_0) equals the marginal productivity of capital after net investments of the designated volume have been carried out. In other words, if the stock of capital (and hence real volume of loans) in the economy at the beginning of the year in question is B_0, then r_0 measures the marginal productivity of a stock of capital of $B_0 + b_0$ units.

Another property of the demand curve that has been frequently assumed in the literature is that in the absence of uncertainty the demand for loans approaches infinity as the rate of interest approaches zero, for in such circumstances it would pay to carry out any investment project that would yield a perpetual stream of net income. Thus, at a zero rate of interest it would pay to level the Alps or to build a canal across the United States—if such activities would enable us to anticipate with certainty net savings in transportation costs through all future time.

It is clear from the foregoing presentation that b has the dimensions of a stock and is thus not affected by changes in the unit of time used to measure the period specified in the analysis. In other words, at the rate of interest r_0, firms will desire to contract b_0 units of new loans during the year—whether the year is called a year or 12 months or 52 weeks. Alternatively, however, b can be interpreted (as it frequently is) as the average rate at which new loans are contracted during the year. Under such an interpretation, b clearly has the dimensions of a flow and is accordingly affected by the time unit used to measure the year. In this case the firms' total stock of borrowing at the end of the year (at the rate of interest r_0) is represented by $B_0 + \int_0^T b_0\,dt = B_0 + b_0T$, where T is the length of the year as measured in the stipulated time units and where b_0T thus has the dimensions of a stock. Clearly, b_0T in the preceding expression is equal, in both dimensions and magnitude, to the b_0 of the interpretation given at the beginning of this paragraph (Patinkin [1956] 1965, pp. 515–523).

Savings and the supply of loans. The supply side of the loan market as described above represents the savings behavior of households [*see* CONSUMPTION FUNCTION]. In the analysis of this behavior by, for example, Marshall and Cassel, it was pointed out that an individual who saved in order to assure himself a given level of income in the future (say, after retirement) would have to accumulate a smaller capital sum the higher the rate of interest; correspondingly, such an individual would respond to a rise in interest rates by saving less. More generally—and more precisely—a rise in interest rates generates a wealth effect which, in the case of a lender, tends to offset the substitution effect. The rise makes current consumption more expensive relative to future consumption (by decreasing the present value of the cost of a unit of future consumption). Hence, it generates a substitution effect that decreases current consumption and thereby increases current saving. At the same time, it makes lenders better off by virtue of the higher interest they can earn and thus generates a wealth effect that tends to increase current consumption. If the wealth effect were to predominate (as is implicitly assumed by Marshall and Cassel in the case mentioned above), the individual's savings curve would, in the relevant region, be negatively sloped with respect to the interest rate.

It is, however, unlikely that such a negative slope could characterize the savings curve of the economy as a whole. To every lender in a closed economy there corresponds a borrower for whom the wealth effect works in the opposite direction. Hence, in the absence of distribution effects, these wealth effects will cancel out, leaving the aggregate savings curve to reflect solely the uniformly positive influence of the substitution effects. Correspondingly, the supply curve of loans, S, in Figure 1 has been drawn with a positive slope (Bailey 1957; Bear 1961).

In the standard Fisher case of an individual with a two-period horizon, the individual is in an optimum position when he adjusts his current consumption (and hence his savings) so as to equalize his marginal rate of substitution of future (C_2) for present (C_1) consumption with $1 + r$. In the case of an individual with a horizon of n periods, the planned stream of future consumption $C_2, C_3, \cdots, C_n$ (where C_t represents consumption at the beginning of period t) can be considered as a single, composite good. The quantity of this good, C_F, is defined as equal to the constant level of per-period consumption over the future which has the same present value as $C_2, C_3, \cdots, C_n$; that is,

$$\sum_{t=2}^{n} \frac{C_F}{(1+r)^{t-1}} = C_F \sum_{t=2}^{n} \frac{1}{(1+r)^{t-1}} = \sum_{t=2}^{n} \frac{C_t}{(1+r)^{t-1}}.$$

It can then be shown that the optimum marginal rate of substitution of future (C_F) for present (C_1) consumption in this case is

$$\frac{r}{1-\left(\frac{1}{1+r}\right)^{n-1}}.$$

For large values of n, this marginal rate can thus be approximated by r. That is, the individual in his optimum position can be induced to give up one dollar of present consumption by compensating him with a constant stream of future consumption of (approximately) r dollars per period (Leontief 1958; Liviatan 1966). In this sense, then, the rate of interest (say, r_2) on curve S corresponding to any volume of new loans made during the year (say, b_0) equals the marginal time preference of the individuals in the economy after they have carried out the savings that provide these loans.

The equilibrium rate of interest. The equilibrium rate of interest for the year in question is determined in Figure 1 (interpreted as above in terms of either a stock or a flow) by the intersection of the demand and supply curves for loans at point P, corresponding to the rate of interest of r_1. As already indicated, for the barter economy now being discussed these curves can also be interpreted as respectively representing the *net* investment and savings curves of neoclassical interest theory. Correspondingly, by construction of these curves the equilibrium rate measures at one and the same time the marginal productivity of capital and the marginal rate of substitution between future and present consumption. (This analysis could just as well be carried out in terms of *gross* investment and saving—the curves in Figure 1 could be made to represent these magnitudes by simply shifting them to the right by an amount equal to depreciation allowances; hence they would continue to intersect at the rate of interest r_1.)

The foregoing analysis can be recast in terms of the demand and supply for the total stock of loans to be outstanding at the end of the year in question. Clearly, the amount of this stock demanded at the rate of interest r_1 is $B_0 + b_1$, where, as before, B_0 represents the stock at the beginning of the year. Similarly, the stock supplied at the end of the year is also $B_0 + b_1$. Thus, this approach yields the same equilibrium rate of interest, r_1, as the preceding one and in this sense is equivalent to it.

On the other hand, the elasticity (although not the slope) of the curves in Figure 1 at each point would be less if they referred to the total stock outstanding. This elasticity is the percentage change in the total stock of loans (say) demanded following a unit percentage decrease in the rate of interest; the same absolute increase in the amount demanded is a much smaller percentage of the total stock of bonds outstanding than of the net accretion during a year. Conversely, a one per cent increase in this net accretion will require a much smaller fall in the rate of interest insisted upon by debtors than will a one per cent increase in the total stock of bonds held.

Consumption loans can be incorporated into the analysis of Figure 1 either by adding them to the demand side or by deducting them from the supply side—in which case S would represent the net supply of loans by households to the business sector. From either viewpoint, in a modern economy the relative influence of such loans on the over-all demand-and-supply situation—and hence on the equilibrium rate of interest—is a minor one. Correspondingly, it is a much better approximation of the truth to say that interest must be paid on consumption loans because the potential lender has the alternative of lending money at interest on productive loans than to say that the demand for consumption loans is the reason for the existence of interest.

It should also be emphasized that "impatience" or "time preference"—in the sense that an individual with a two-period horizon systematically prefers (say) ten units of consumption goods today and four tomorrow to the alternative combination of four units today and ten tomorrow—is not a necessary condition for the existence of interest. For the major manifestation of time preference in this sense—in an economy in which all individuals have a finite horizon and anticipate a constant stream of income payments—is that (strictly) positive savings will be forthcoming only at a (strictly) positive rate of interest. Conversely, absence of time preference manifests itself in the fact that if the rate of interest is zero, then savings are also zero (Boulding [1941], pp. 746–752 in 1948 edition; Friedman 1957, p. 12). Thus, the fact that individuals in such an economy insist on receiving interest in order to save is no evidence of a systematic preference for present goods over future ones. More generally, the fact that an individual will, at the margin, insist on receiving more than one unit of future goods to compensate him for forgoing one unit of present goods is not necessarily the *cause* of the existence of interest but its *effect:* the individual insists on receiving more because he has the alternative of obtaining more by lending out at interest the money that would be released from current consumption by saving.

Whether b in Figure 1 is interpreted as the net accretion to the stock of loans over the year or as the average rate of flow of new loans during the year, the equilibrium determined there is that of the short run. (Alternatively, in terms that derive from the second of the two interpretations, it is a "flow equilibrium.") The stock of capital (and hence the stock of outstanding loans) at the beginning of the subsequent year will increase, shifting both the demand and supply curves that could be drawn in Figure 1 for that year. In particular, if technology and the quantities of other factors of production are kept constant, the law of diminishing returns will cause a leftward shift of the investment curve and hence of D. At the same time, the increased capital will generate an increased stream of income, thus increasing the amount of savings forthcoming at any rate of interest and thereby shifting S to the right. The new equilibrium situation generated by these shifts is represented by the intersection at Q of the dashed curves D' and S' in Figure 2. For the same reason as before, point Q also represents a position of short-run equilibrium, so the curves will shift once again.

The stationary state. A question that has frequently been raised in the literature is whether the shifts just discussed can ultimately bring the economy to a position of long-run equilibrium (or "stock equilibrium," in the alternative terminology described above) in which no further capital accumulation will take place—and whether in this classical "stationary state" the rate of interest can be positive [*see* CAPITAL].

A situation in which both these conditions are met is illustrated in Figure 2 by the intersection of D'' and S'' at point R on the vertical axis. At this point the marginal productivity of the existing stock of capital equals the prevailing rate of interest r_L, so firms have no inducement either to augment or to reduce this stock—and with it the stock of their outstanding loans from households. (The possibility of corresponding reductions in both of these stocks at rates of interest above r_L is represented by the extension of D'' to the left of the vertical axis.) Similarly, households have no inducement either to make new (net) loans to firms or to insist on the redemption of part of their outstanding loans in order to consume the proceeds.

A necessary condition for the existence of a stationary state with a positive rate of interest is that the individuals of this state (assumed to be of a given, finite life expectancy and to anticipate a constant stream of income) have a preference for present as against future consumption; for, as noted above, in the absence of such a preference these individuals would have zero savings only at a zero rate of interest—that is, their savings curve would always start at the origin of Figure 2 (cf. Pigou 1935, chapter 10).

Growth models. We must now note that—as Frank Knight has particularly emphasized ([1921–1935] 1951, pp. 262–264; 1936, pp. 614–619, 626–630; 1944)—the concept of the stationary state has no relevance to the real world, which historically has been characterized by continuous growth in total capital and (as noted above, in "Historical aspects of the interest rate") relative stability of the rate of interest. These developments can in part be interpreted as reflecting the absence in the real world of the two basic assumptions that underlie the theory of the stationary state—namely, constancy in the quantity of other factors of production (that is, labor) and constancy of the state of technology. Indeed, a major concern of economic theory in recent years has been to analyze

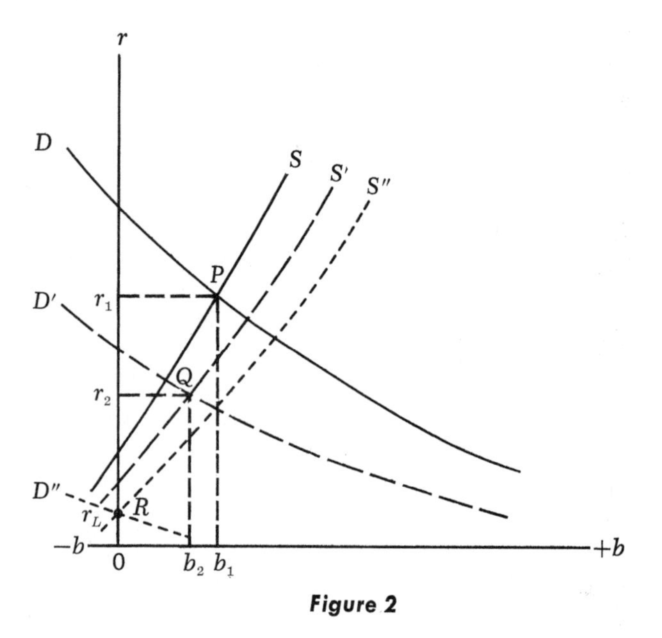

Figure 2

the growth patterns of economies in which one or both of these assumptions do not hold.

One case of a growing economy that has been particularly studied is that of a one-good, two-factor (capital and labor), perfect-competition economy with a given constant-returns-to-scale technology in which the labor supply is expanding at a constant, exogenously determined rate of n per cent per year (Solow 1956; Swan 1956). Assume for simplicity that the individuals in this economy save a constant proportion, s, of their incomes. Represent this behavior in some initial position by the vertical line S^* in Figure 3, where for convenience savings are measured as a percentage of the total existing stock of capital in that position. Similarly, let I^* represent the investment curve of the economy, also measured as a percentage of initial capital. The intersection of these curves at point A—corresponding to the rate of interest r^*—then represents the equilibrium position of the economy.

It is clear, however, that this is only a short-run equilibrium, for the percentage rate of growth of capital (I/K) at point A equals m, which is less than the corresponding rate of growth of labor, n. Hence total output, total income, and (by assumption) total savings must all increase at some common rate greater than m and less than n; therefore, S/K must increase, shifting S^* to the right. Similarly, the fact that the ratio of labor to capital is increasing means (assuming that we are in the region of diminishing returns) that the marginal productivity of capital is increasing accordingly, so that I^* also shifts to the right. Furthermore, if we assume that the rate of interest throughout this adjustment process equals the marginal productivity of capital, then the investment curve must shift farther to the right than the savings curve, thus intersecting the latter at a higher rate of interest.

This process could continue indefinitely without the system's ever reaching a position of long-run equilibrium. However, under certain assumptions about the nature of the production function, such a position will be reached. In this case the rightward shifts of the vertical savings curve in Figure 3 continue until the curve reaches S^{**} at point n on the abscissa, where it is intersected at a higher rate of interest, say r^{**}, by an investment curve (I^{**}) that has also shifted to the right during the adjustment process. The point of intersection, B, between S^{**} and I^{**} represents a situation in which capital and labor—and hence total output, income, savings, and investment—are all expanding at the common rate n. Correspondingly, there will be no further shifts in the savings and investment curves of Figure 3. Point B thus represents a long-run moving equilibrium in which the labor–capital ratio and hence (by virtue of the properties of a constant-returns-to-scale production function) the rate of interest and the real wage rate remain constant. Clearly, per-capita income and consumption also remain constant in this moving equilibrium.

The same argument holds, *mutatis mutandis*, if the initial equilibrium position in Figure 3 corresponds to a rate of capital accumulation v greater than n. In this case output (income) will increase at a rate less than v, so that S/K shifts to the left. Similarly, the increasing ratio of capital to labor will shift the investment curve to the left, and the equilibrium rate of interest will fall. Once again, long-run moving equilibrium will be reached only if the investment curve ultimately intersects the savings curve in the vertical position S^{**}, corresponding to a rate of growth of total output of n per cent per year.

As might be expected, a special case of this long-run equilibrium is the classical stationary state represented in Figure 2, above. This can be represented in Figure 3 by setting the rate of growth of labor, n, equal to zero and drawing S^{**} accordingly to coincide with the vertical axis.

Returning to the nonstationary case depicted in Figure 3, let us assume that the long-run equilibrium position B is disturbed by an exogenous decrease in the savings ratio s that shifts the savings curve to S^*. The initial effect of this decrease is to shift the economy to short-run equilibrium position C. Here the forces described above will again come into operation, shifting the savings and investment curves to the right and thus generating the path of short-run equilibrium positions—say, CD—by which the economy is brought to the new long-run equilibrium position—say, D. Labor, capital, and hence total output at D are once again growing at the rate n. On the other hand, the decrease in the savings ratio has caused an increase (from r^{**} to r^{***}) in the long-run equilibrium rate of interest and (because of the constant-returns-to-scale assumption) a decrease in the real wage rate. Both of these changes reflect the fact that along path CD labor is expanding more rapidly than capital, so the labor–capital ratio is higher at D than at B. Similarly, along path CD output is expanding at a lower rate than labor, so per-capita output is less at D than at B.

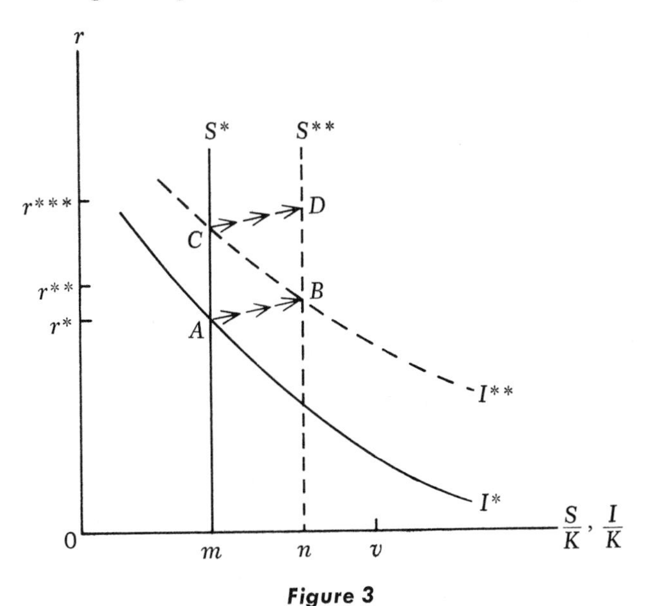

Figure 3

In brief, a decrease in the savings ratio in this model will decrease the long-run equilibrium ratio of capital to labor, with corresponding consequences for factor prices. The savings ratio, however, will not affect the equilibrium growth rate of the economy, which is uniquely determined by the exogenously given rate of growth of the labor supply.

It should be emphasized that the fact that per-capita income is less at D than at B does not imply that per-capita consumption is also less at D than at B. The lower level of income might be offset by the lower savings ratio (higher consumption ratio) that by assumption prevails at D. This suggests that among long-run equilibrium positions with alternative savings ratios there exists one specific ratio that maximizes per-capita consumption. It can be shown that such a maximum is achieved when the savings ratio is such as to bring the economy to a long-run equilibrium capital–labor ratio that generates a marginal productivity of capital equal to the equilibrium rate of growth, n. The mathematical demonstration is straightforward: Per-capita consumption equals

$$\frac{F(K, L)}{L} - \frac{S}{L},$$

where L is the quantity of labor and $Y = F(K,L)$ is the production function. By the assumption of constant returns to scale, this expression can be rewritten in terms of the capital–labor ratio, K/L, as

$$F\left(\frac{K}{L}, 1\right) - \frac{S}{K} \cdot \frac{K}{L},$$

where the second term has been multiplied and divided by K. Since only positions of long-run equilibrium are being considered, S/K can be replaced by the constant n. Maximizing the resulting expression by differentiating it with respect to K/L and setting the result equal to zero then yields

$$F_1\left(\frac{K}{L}, 1\right) - n = 0,$$

where $F_1(K/L, 1)$ is the partial derivative of $F(K/L, 1)$ with respect to its first argument and thus represents the marginal productivity of capital. The value of K/L that satisfies this equation is, thus, the capital–labor ratio that maximizes long-run per-capita consumption.

An economy satisfying this equality between the marginal productivity of capital and the rate of growth is said to be growing in accordance with the "golden rule of accumulation." Under the assumption of perfect competition (in which case the marginal productivity of capital equals the rate of interest) this rule can be stated alternatively in terms of the equality between the long-run equilibrium rate of interest and the growth rate. This in turn implies that if point B in Figure 3 is on the golden-rule path, then it satisfies the relation

$$\frac{S}{K} = \frac{I}{K} = n = r^{**},$$

so that

$$S = I = r^{**} K.$$

That is, in a competitive economy growing in accordance with the "golden rule," total savings or investment during any period equals total income from capital. It should be noted that this is a macroeconomic relationship and does not imply that all income from capital is saved (Phelps 1965; Marty 1964).

The foregoing graphical analysis can be generalized to the case in which the savings ratio is an increasing function, $s = s(r)$, of the rate of interest, so that the savings function (expressed again as a percentage of the stock of capital) has the form

$$\frac{S}{K} = s(r)\frac{Y}{K}.$$

Such a function could be represented in Figure 3 by a positively sloped curve that would shift during the adjustment process in a manner analogous to that in which the vertical savings curve shifts.

The analysis can also be readily generalized to the case of technological change which is entirely labor augmenting (Harrod-neutral). In this case n can be considered as the rate of growth of the "effective quantity" of labor, where this rate equals the sum of the natural rate of increase of the labor force (say, n') and the rate of increase in labor efficiency per unit of labor (say, n''). The argument proceeds exactly as before, with the sole difference that the position of long-run equilibrium (in which savings, investment, capital, and output are once again all growing at the rate n) is characterized by an increase of n'' per cent per period in per-capita consumption.

Much attention has been given in the recent literature to more complicated growth models with more general kinds of technological changes or with more than one good, or both. These models are described elsewhere [*see* ECONOMIC GROWTH, *article on* MATHEMATICAL THEORY].

Interest in a money economy. An economy in which money exists as a medium of exchange is not characterized by the identity that holds in a barter economy between planned investment and the demand for loans, on the one hand, and between planned savings and the supply of loans, on the other. In a money economy, firms can plan to finance investment in plant and equipment—and households can plan to supply loans—by reducing their money balances. Similarly, the supply of loans can be affected by changes in the quantity of money in the system. Another noteworthy difference between a barter economy and a money economy is that in a money economy the wealth of households includes the real value of their money holdings (or, more generally, of their net financial assets); correspondingly, an increase in wealth in this form will increase consumption and thus (*inter alia*) affect the rate of interest. This is a manifestation of what has been called the real-balance effect.

The stock of money that individuals want to hold is positively dependent on their total wealth (or income) and inversely dependent on the rate of interest, which measures the individual's opportunity cost of holding a unit of money instead of an income-yielding asset. Although the analysis of this dependence of money holdings on interest has its antecedents in the writings of the neoclassical economists, these economists did not really integrate the relationship into their expositions of the quantity theory of money, and into their analyses of the velocity of circulation in particular. This was indeed one of Keynes's major contributions. [*See* LIQUIDITY PREFERENCE; MONEY, *article on* QUANTITY THEORY.]

In any event, individuals will not be willing to hold the existing stock of money in the economy unless the value they attribute to the liquidity service provided by this stock at the margin equals the rate of interest that could alternatively be earned by making a loan (or, in more familiar Keynesian terms, by holding a bond). It follows that when the system as a whole is in equilibrium, the rate of interest must at one and the same time equal the "threefold margin" of liquidity services, productivity of capital, and time preference (Robertson [1924–1940], pp. 16–17 in the 1940 edition). Indeed, the money balances of a firm can be considered as part of its working capital—just like any other inventory that it holds—and must accordingly yield a corresponding marginal productivity.

The two major problems in the theory of interest that (by definition) are specific to a money economy are the effects of changes in the quantity of money and the effects of shifts in liquidity preference. These problems will now be discussed, first under the neoclassical assumptions of price flexibility and a constant full-employment level of income and then under the Keynesian assumptions of price rigidity and unemployment. For simplicity, it will be assumed that the economy's reaction to these monetary changes is rapid enough to make it possible to study them within the framework of short-run equilibrium analysis (on the rest of this section, see Patinkin [1956] 1965).

A major theme of classical and neoclassical interest theory was that an increase in the quantity of money (generated by gold discoveries or by a government deficit) in the first instance increases the supply of loans and thus depresses the rate of interest. This is reflected by the shift from S to S''' in Figure 4. At the same time, classical and neoclassical economists argued that the increased quantity of money also raises prices and thus causes the real supply of loans to decrease once again. Ultimately—after prices have increased in the same proportion, restoring the real value of the public's money holdings—the supply curve returns to its original position, S, so that the rate of interest is once again r_1. Thus, the ultimate invariance of the rate of interest with respect to changes in the quantity of money (that is, the "neutrality of money") was an integral part of classical quantity-theory reasoning.

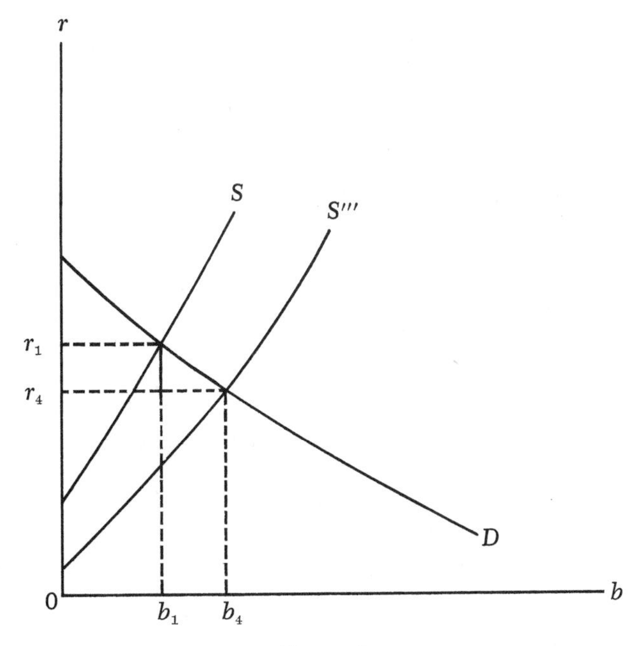

Figure 4

The details of the process just described were set out by classical and neoclassical economists in various ways. Among the best known expositions is that of Wicksell, who referred to the rate of interest actually prevailing as the "money" or "market" rate—as distinct from the "real" or "natural" rate, which equates planned savings with investment (r_1 in Figure 4). By definition, the natural rate is also the rate equating the aggregate demand for commodities with the corresponding supply. The mechanism by which the money rate becomes equated with the natural rate was called by Wicksell the "cumulative process." The basic component of this process is the fact that the rising price level generated by the excess demand for commodities increases the demand for hand-to-hand currency, which the public satisfies by converting their bank deposits into cash. The resulting internal drain on bank reserves forces the banks to raise their lending rate until it is once again equal to the natural rate. Wicksell used the lag with which the market rate adjusts itself to the natural rate to explain the fact (noted above, at the end of the section "Historical aspects of the interest rate") that empirically the interest rate and the price level have tended to move together (Wicksell [1898] 1936, pp. 107, 167–168; [1906] 1935, vol. 2, pp. 205–207; Cagan 1965, pp. 252–259).

It should be emphasized that the invariance of the equilibrium rate of interest holds even under the Keynesian assumption that the real demand for money also depends on the rate of interest. After prices have risen in the same proportion as the quantity of money, individuals will be willing to hold this increased nominal quantity—which will then represent an unchanged real quantity—at a correspondingly unchanged rate of interest.

However, classical and neoclassical economists did recognize that under certain circumstances monetary changes could have real consequences. Thus, they sometimes argued that—as a result, say, of the lag of wages behind prices—the inflationary process generated by an increase in the money supply could change the distribution of real income in favor of profit recipients and against wage earners. The profit recipients' presumed lower propensity to consume would then bring about a decrease in the total real consumption of the economy and hence an increase in its total real savings. Because of these "forced savings" (as they came to be called) the savings curve would not return to its original position even if prices were to increase in the same proportion as the quantity of money. In such cases these economists readily recognized that the monetary expansion was not neutral: it would increase the stock of capital in the economy and thus permanently depress the rate of interest.

Similarly, an increase in the quantity of money generated by an open-market purchase of bonds (instead of by the gold discoveries or the government deficit assumed until now) will also have a depressing effect on the equilibrium rate of interest. In the first instance, such a purchase merely replaces bonds by an equivalent amount of money in the public's portfolio and hence leaves undisturbed total wealth, the aggregate demand for commodities, and the initial equilibrium in the commodity market. But by simultaneously increasing the demand for bonds and supply of money, it disturbs the equilibrium in both these markets and causes the rate of interest to decline. This decline reacts back on the commodity market, stimulating aggregate demand there and eventually causing prices to rise. It follows that if the reduction in the rate of interest stimulates investment relatively more than consumption, government open-market policy will have a long-run effect on the growth path of the economy.

Exactly the same reasoning can be applied to show that an increased supply of loans financed by a decrease in the desire to hold money balances (in Keynesian terms, by a decrease in liquidity preference) will also depress the equilibrium interest rate. The possibility of such an effect was not recognized by the neoclassical economists. This is another manifestation of the fact, which we have already noted, that although in their quantity-theory discussions these economists adverted to the holding of bonds and other productive assets as an alternative to holding money, they did not fully integrate this possibility into their thinking.

The initial impact of both the foregoing changes is again illustrated by means of the shift from S to S''' in Figure 4. The resulting decline in the interest rate generates an excess demand in the commodity market and hence an increase in the price level. This, in turn, reduces the real supply of loans and causes S''' to begin to shift to the left again. But in this case, unlike the case of an increase in the quantity of money generated by a government deficit, the supply curve cannot return to its original position. In that position the rate of interest would be the same as it originally was, but prices would be higher. Since the nominal value of the public's net financial assets is not affected by the open-market purchase or the shift in liquidity preference, this would imply the existence of a negative real-balance effect, which would preclude equilibrium in the commodity market. Thus equilibrium will be reached at a rate of interest below r_1 but above r_4.

The extent of the depressing effect on the equilibrium interest rate in both of the preceding cases clearly depends on the strength of the real-balance effect, which empirically has been shown to be fairly weak. Indeed, in an economy in which the net financial assets of the public were zero—and in which, accordingly, there was a unique rate of interest at which full-employment equilibrium in the commodity market could obtain—the equilibrium rate would be unaffected. Such an economy is one in which there is no government debt and in which the money supply is created entirely by the banking system in the process of extending loans to the private sector (the so-called "pure inside-money economy").

Under the Keynesian assumptions of price rigidity and unemployment, the rate of interest would be affected in all of the cases discussed above. For example, if the quantity of money was increased while prices remained unchanged or rose only slightly, then the economy would be brought to a new position in which the interest rate was lower—and hence the levels of aggregate demand and employment were higher—than before the monetary expansion. It should be noted that the decline in the rate of interest in this case is of the same nature as the short-run decline specified in the neoclassical analysis described in the last section.

Once we depart from the analytical framework of an economy with a given productive capacity and turn to growth models, there are additional reasons for the nonneutrality of money. For example, it will generally be true that a growing economy whose money supply is continuously expanded at a rate that stabilizes the price level will have a different growth path than one in which the quantity of money is kept constant and the price level declines over time. In general terms, the reason for this difference is that the declining price level increases the rate of return obtained by holding money balances (by virtue of the increase in their purchasing power that it generates), and thus increases the attractiveness of holding savings in this form. Hence, even if the over-all savings ratio, s, should remain constant, the amount of savings (at any given level of output) that will take the form of physical capital goods will decrease; that is, the *physical* savings ratio will decrease. Thus, the effects of a declining price level can be analyzed in Figure 3 (which refers only to *physical* savings) in terms of a leftward shift of the (physical) savings curve from S^{**} to S^{*}; just as in the earlier analysis of such a shift, the long-run equilibrium rate of interest will then rise, and the long-run real wage rate will fall. More generally, the lower the rate of increase of the money supply, the greater the rate of decrease of prices and the smaller the long-run-equilibrium capital/labor ratio, hence the higher the corresponding marginal productivity of capital and the rate of interest. This result, however, need not obtain if the over-all savings ratio is not constant, but instead depends directly on the respective rates of return of the various assets, including the rate of return on money balances (i.e., the rate of decrease of prices) (Gurley & Shaw 1960; Enthoven 1960; Patinkin [1956] 1965, pp. 360–364; Tobin 1965; Stein 1966).

General equilibrium analysis. Although the analysis of the determination of the equilibrium interest rate was presented above in terms of the demand and supply curves for loans (the so-called loanable-funds approach), it is clear from the discussion that these curves also reflect the forces at work in the markets for money and commodities, respectively. Correspondingly—and in a completely equivalent manner—it would be possible to present a "liquidity-preference approach" that would depict the equilibrium rate of interest as occurring at the intersection of the demand and supply curves for money—and in which these curves would in turn reflect the forces at work in the markets for loans and commodities.

Thus, no substantive meaning can be attached to the choice of the particular market in which one carries out the analysis of the rate of interest. This choice does not alter the basic fact that the rate of interest influences behavior in all the markets of the economy and that accordingly its equilibrium value (like that of any other price) is determined by the necessity for all these markets to be in equilibrium. This fundamental point can best be brought home by actually carrying out the analysis within a general-equilibrium framework in which all these markets are considered simultaneously (Hicks 1939, chapter 12; Patinkin [1956] 1965, pp. 258–260, 330–334, 375–381).

A meaningful question, however, is the nature of the forces that have affected the equilibrium rate of interest over the course of time. The classical and neoclassical view has been that the major forces are changes in tastes, which affect the desire to save, and changes in factor proportions and technology, which affect the productivity of capital. On the other hand, this view attributes only minor importance to changes in the quantity of money and (by inference) to shifts in liquidity preference. It is in this sense that in the classical scheme interest is a "real" phenomenon. In contrast, the Keynesian view attaches much more importance to the monetary factors mentioned above and in this sense treats interest as a "monetary phenomenon."

The emphasis placed on monetary factors seems to have diminished in the more recent expositions of the Keynesian theory (Robinson 1951, especially pp. 93 and 110). This might be interpreted as reflecting the fact that the Keynesian monetary theory of interest had its genesis in the great depression of the 1930s, when "excess savings" and extensive unemployment of plant and equipment discouraged thinking in terms of the scarcity and marginal productivity of capital. Conversely, the renewed emphasis on these traditional, real factors in recent years can be interpreted as a reflection of the widespread "capital shortage" of the post-World War II boom period in developed countries—and, even more so, of the key role played by the volume of capital formation and its productivity in the development plans of underdeveloped countries.

Interest differentials. The discussion thus far has been presented in terms of a single interest rate. Actually, however, there is a whole array of interest rates in the market. The major source of differentials in interest rates is the varying degree of risk associated with different loans. Two types of risk have received particular attention in the literature: the risk of default and the risk of illiquidity. "Illiquidity" refers to the risk that the lender may have to sell the bond under unfavorable circumstances before its maturity. This, indeed, is the basis of the Keynesian explanation of the fact that individuals hold money even though they have the alternative of holding interest-bearing bonds (Tobin 1958). In any event, the actual rate of interest on any particular bond can be viewed as being composed of the "pure" rate of interest that would be paid on a riskless loan plus an appropriate risk premium.

Insofar as the risk of default is concerned, a study of corporate bonds of different quality classes in the United States for the period 1900–1943 showed that the bonds that were rated highest by investment agencies (for example, Moody's) yielded on the average 5.1 per cent, whereas those rated lowest (and whose default rate was eight times as great) yielded 9.5 per cent. It has been claimed that an important reason why this risk premium has been so large (4.4 per cent) is the legal and traditional limitations on large institutional investors, which have prevented them from buying the larger quantity of high-yield, low-quality bonds appropriate to a rationally diversified portfolio (Hickman 1958, pp. 10–17).

The risks of illiquidity have been analyzed particularly in connection with the tendency of the interest rate in most periods to increase with the duration of the loan. The formal analysis of this "term structure of interest rates" distinguishes between the long-term rate (say, the annual rate of interest, R, on a loan granted for n years), the forward short-term rate (the rate of interest r_t at which a one-year loan to be given in year t can now be contracted), and the spot short-term rate (the existing rate for a one-year loan). In equilibrium, $(1+R)^n = (1+r_1)(1+r_2)\cdots(1+r_n)$, for unless this equality obtains, individuals will find it advantageous to shift from long-term loans to an arrangement of refinancing by means of forward contracts for a series of short-term loans.

As can be inferred from the discussion above, a basic contention of liquidity-preference theory is that in order to induce lenders to make long-term loans—which in principle is equivalent to making forward contracts for short-term loans—the forward rate for year t must exceed the actually expected spot rate for that year by a "liquidity premium" that will compensate the lender for the risks involved in tying up his funds. This implies that if the short-term rate is expected to remain unchanged in the future, then the current short-term rate will be lower than the current long-term rate (Hicks 1939, chapter 11).

Although the empirical evidence is not unequivocal, it does on balance seem to support the foregoing theory. It might also be noted that the yield on short-term government securities in the United States during the past forty years has typically been lower than the yield on corresponding long-term securities. Again, the history of business cycles in the United States during the past century has shown that the short-term rate has tended to rise relative to the long-term rate near the peak of the cycle. This can be interpreted in terms of the preceding equation as reflecting the market's opinion that the short-term rates at such a time are abnormally high and are due to fall. A corresponding interpretation holds, *mutatis mutandis*, for the symmetrical finding that the short-term rate falls relative to the long-term rate near the trough of the cycle (see Kessel 1965 and references there cited).

To return to the discussion of a single rate of interest, it should be emphasized that neoclassical and Keynesian economics, although they differ in their analyses of the equilibrating mechanism, are at one in equating the rate of interest with the value of the productive services of capital as determined by the market. However, as Knight emphasized many years ago in his fundamental and incisive critique of "productivity ethics," this does not constitute an ethical legitimation of the resulting income distribution and of its interest component in particular. Among other things, this distribution can be no more "just" than the distribution of the wealth that generates the interest income (Knight [1921–1935] 1951, pp. 41–75 and 255).

In the Marxist theory of labor value, interest has a negative ethical connotation; it is one of the forms of "surplus value" that stem from the exploitation of labor in a capitalist economy. Because of this ideological connotation, interest costs were largely ignored in the economic planning of the U.S.S.R. in the 1930s and after. In more recent years, however, widespread agreement has developed among Soviet economists and practitioners on the theoretical necessity of making some sort of interest charge on capital (although usually under a different name) in order to make an optimal choice among alternative investment projects. There also seems to be increasing evidence of the actual use of such a charge by the planning authorities (Kaplan 1952; Nove 1961, pp. 209–217, 228–231; Bergson 1964, chapter 11, especially p. 252; Barkai 1967).

DON PATINKIN

BIBLIOGRAPHY

BAILEY, MARTIN J. 1957 Saving and the Rate of Interest. *Journal of Political Economy* 65:279–305.

BARKAI, HAIM 1967 A "Recoupment Period" Model of Investment and Pricing in a Socialist Economy. Pages 183–202 in D. C. Hague (editor), *Price Formations in Various Economies*. New York: St. Martins. → A discussion appears on pages 262–268.

BEAR, DONALD V. T. 1961 The Relationship of Saving to the Rate of Interest, Real Income, and Expected Future Prices. *Review of Economics and Statistics* 43:27–35.

BERGSON, ABRAM 1964 *The Economics of Soviet Planning*. New Haven: Yale Univ. Press.

BOULDING, KENNETH E. (1941) 1966 *Economic Analysis*. 4th ed., 2 vols. New York: Harper.

BROWN, ARTHUR J. 1955 *The Great Inflation: 1939–1951*. Oxford Univ. Press.

BURNS, ARTHUR F. 1961 New Facts on Business Cycles. Pages 13–44 in Geoffrey H. Moore (editor), *Business*

Cycle Indicators. Volume 1: Contributions to the Analysis of Current Business Conditions. Princeton Univ. Press.

BURNS, ARTHUR F.; and MITCHELL, WESLEY C. 1946 *Measuring Business Cycles.* National Bureau of Economic Research, Studies in Business Cycles, No. 2. New York: The Bureau.

CAGAN, PHILLIP 1965 *Determinants and Effects of Changes in the Stock of Money, 1875–1960.* New York: National Bureau of Economic Research.

CAGAN, PHILLIP 1966 Changes in the Cyclical Behavior of Interest Rates. *Review of Economics and Statistics* 48, no. 3:219–250.

CONARD, JOSEPH W. 1959 *An Introduction to the Theory of Interest.* Berkeley: Univ. of California Press.

EINZIG, PAUL 1949 *Primitive Money in Its Ethnological, Historical and Economic Aspects.* London: Eyre & Spottiswoode.

ENTHOVEN, ALAIN C. 1960 A Neo-classical Model of Money, Debt, and Economic Growth. Pages 301–359 in John G. Gurley and Edward S. Shaw, *Money in a Theory of Finance.* Washington: Brookings Institution. → A mathematical appendix to the volume.

FINCH, DAVID 1956 Purchasing Power Guarantees for Deferred Payments. International Monetary Fund, *Staff Papers* 5:1–22.

FISHER, IRVING (1930) 1961 *The Theory of Interest.* New York: Kelley. → A revision of the author's *The Rate of Interest* (1907).

FRIEDMAN, MILTON 1957 *A Theory of the Consumption Function.* National Bureau of Economic Research, General Series, No. 63. Princeton Univ. Press.

GURLEY, JOHN G.; and SHAW, EDWARD S. 1960 *Money in a Theory of Finance.* With a mathematical appendix by Alain C. Enthoven. Washington: Brookings Institution.

HEICHELHEIM, FRITZ M. (1938) 1958–1964 *An Ancient Economic History: From the Palaeolithic Age to the Migrations of the Germanic, Slavic and Arabic Nations.* Rev. English ed. 2 vols. Leiden (Netherlands): Sijthoff. → First published in German.

HICKMAN, W. BRADDOCK 1958 *Corporate Bond Quality and Investor Experience.* Princeton Univ. Press.

HICKS, JOHN R. (1939) 1946 *Value and Capital: An Inquiry Into Some Fundamental Principles of Economic Theory.* 2d ed. Oxford: Clarendon.

HOMER, SIDNEY 1963 *A History of Interest Rates.* New Brunswick, N.J.: Rutgers Univ. Press.

KAPLAN, NORMAN 1952 Investment Alternatives in Soviet Economic Theory. *Journal of Political Economy* 60:133–144.

KESSEL, REUBEN A. 1965 *Cyclical Behavior of the Term Structure of Interest Rates.* National Bureau of Economic Research, Occasional Paper No. 91. New York: The Bureau.

KEYNES, JOHN MAYNARD (1930) 1958–1960 *A Treatise on Money.* 2 vols. London: Macmillan. → Volume 1: *The Pure Theory of Money.* Volume 2: *The Applied Theory of Money.*

KEYNES, JOHN MAYNARD 1936 *The General Theory of Employment, Interest and Money.* London: Macmillan. → A paperback edition was published in 1965 by Harcourt.

KNIGHT, FRANK H. (1921–1935) 1951 *The Ethics of Competition, and Other Essays.* New York: Kelley.

KNIGHT, FRANK H. 1936 The Quantity of Capital and the Rate of Interest. *Journal of Political Economy* 44:433–463, 612–642.

KNIGHT, FRANK H. 1944 Diminishing Returns From Investment. *Journal of Political Economy* 52:26–47.

KUZNETS, SIMON S. 1966 *Modern Economic Growth: Rate, Structure, and Spread.* New Haven: Yale Univ. Press.

LEONTIEF, WASSILY 1958 Theoretical Note on Time-preference, Productivity of Capital, Stagnation and Economic Growth. *American Economic Review* 48: 105–111.

LERNER, ABBA P. 1953 *Essays in Economic Analysis.* London: Macmillan.

LIVIATAN, NISSAN 1966 Multiperiod Future Consumption as an Aggregate. *American Economic Review* 56:828–840.

MACAULAY, FREDERICK R. 1938 *Some Theoretical Problems Suggested by the Movements of Interest Rates, Bond Yields and Stock Prices in the United States Since 1856.* New York: National Bureau of Economic Research.

MARTY, ALVIN L. 1964 The Neoclassical Theorem. *American Economic Review* 54:1026–1029.

NELSON, BENJAMIN N. 1949 *The Idea of Usury: From Tribal Brotherhood to Universal Otherhood.* Princeton Univ. Press.

NOONAN, JOHN T. 1957 *The Scholastic Analysis of Usury.* Cambridge, Mass.: Harvard Univ. Press.

NOVE, ALEC 1961 *The Soviet Economy: An Introduction.* New York: Praeger.

PATINKIN, DON (1956) 1965 *Money, Interest, and Prices: An Integration of Monetary and Value Theory.* 2d ed. New York: Harper.

PHELPS, EDMUND S. 1965 Second Essay on the Golden Rule of Accumulation. *American Economic Review* 55:793–814.

PIGOU, ARTHUR C. 1935 *The Economics of Stationary States.* London: Macmillan.

PIRENNE, HENRI (1933) 1936 *Economic and Social History of Medieval Europe.* London: Routledge. → A paperback edition was published in 1956 by Harcourt. A new, revised French edition with a critical bibliography by H. van Werveke was published in 1963 by Presses Universitaires de France.

ROBERTSON, DENNIS HOLME (1924–1940) 1956 *Essays in Monetary Theory.* London: Staples. → First published in book form in 1940.

ROBINSON, JOAN 1951 The Rate of Interest. *Econometrica* 19:92–111.

ROBSON, PETER 1960 Index-linked Bonds. *Review of Economic Studies* 28:57–68.

SOLOW, ROBERT M. 1956 A Contribution to the Theory of Economic Growth. *Quarterly Journal of Economics* 70:65–94.

STEIN, JEROME L. 1966 Money and Capacity Growth. *Journal of Political Economy* 74:451–465.

SWAN, T. W. 1956 Economic Growth and Capital Accumulation. *Economic Record* 32:334–361.

TOBIN, JAMES 1958 Liquidity Preference as Behavior Towards Risk. *Review of Economic Studies* 25:65–86.

TOBIN, JAMES 1965 Money and Economic Growth. *Econometrica* 33:671–684.

WICKSELL, KNUT (1898) 1936 *Interest and Prices: A Study of the Causes Regulating the Value of Money.* London: Macmillan. → First published as *Geldzins und Güterpreise.*

WICKSELL, KNUT (1906) 1935 *Lectures on Political Economy.* Volume 2: Money. New York: Macmillan. → First published in Swedish.

INTEREST, CONFLICT OF

See CONFLICT OF INTEREST.

INTEREST GROUPS

Interaction between the polity and organized interests has taken place in all periods of history. Estates, guilds, trading companies, and the like are the more immediate antecedents of the modern interest group, which may be defined as a voluntary association of individuals who band together for the defense of an "interest." The definition of an interest as a "*conscious* desire to have public policy, or the authoritative allocation of values, move in a particular general or specific direction" (LaPalombara 1964, p. 16) may be controversial, but it usefully limits the concept by excluding the numerous groups whose members share certain attitudes but are not concerned with public policy. Once it is determined that only those organizations which have a stake in the political process belong to the interest group universe, the term may be used interchangeably with "pressure groups," "organized interests," "lobbies," "political groups," or "power groups."

Groups represent the interest of the sections into which a society divides; with advanced specialization groups will be more numerous and specialized. Invariably management, labor, and agriculture will appear as federated organizations on the markets where their interests are at stake. They are not only recognized by international organizations but occasionally form groupings across national borders, for example, the International Confederation of Free Trade Unions or the Council of European Federations of Industry. Within almost every country there is also a web of more specialized trade associations, trade unions, and farmers' organizations extending in a vertical as well as a horizontal direction. In Western societies the organizations of the professions, such as medicine or law, are usually among the oldest interest groups.

In addition to sectional interests, the promotion of causes also gives rise to the formation of political interest groups. The Anti-Corn Law League, the Anti-Saloon League, societies devoted to the purification of air or of manners, movements for penal reform or for civil liberties, peacemongers or warmongers—in every society there is an inexhaustible supply of causes which find their spokesmen, who form organizations and mount campaigns.

Functions of interest groups

To manage the flow of influence between government and the governed is the main function of interest groups in a wide variety of contemporary political systems. The mere fact that groups participate in the political competition of a given system and seek to obtain and maintain power does not distinguish them from other social structures such as parties. In the past the dividing line between parties and interest groups was often drawn by pointing to a difference in functions. Groups were expected to convey to the political apparatus the total claims of a supposedly homogeneous clientele, while parties were to select, aggregate, and thereby transform the raw demands of an electorate. This is no longer true. Most modern interest groups, and especially the elaborate structures which many of them form for effective action, are so complex that they are compelled to sift claims and establish preferences. Indeed, the legitimization of their activities may depend on it.

This does not mean that all differences between parties and groups have disappeared. Except in extraordinary circumstances interest groups do not seek responsibility for direct management of government. When their officers or members win elective office (which is considered improper only in some countries), the formal responsibility of the groups to which they belong is not involved. On the other hand, if the role of groups in recruiting decision makers for the system is less conspicuous than that of parties, their influence in the selection process is often considerable and can be decisive. [*See* POLITICAL RECRUITMENT AND CAREERS.]

What is most distinctive about a great many interest groups is the place which they hold in society. The interests which they represent link their membership with community values. Hence, groups are likely to reflect more accurately than do other bodies the concerns of the society in which they operate. In fully developed as well as in developing countries, certain critical conflicts will, for a variety of reasons, never enter the party–political realm. Yet any conflict that has been taken into the public domain will invariably affect group activities. Where the formal system of representation proves inadequate, interest groups represent community values more realistically than do parties.

In the nexus between economic, social, and political power (Neumann 1957) interest groups translate economic power into social power and share with parties the function of transforming social power into political decisions. Groups which defend noneconomic interests play a similar role in the broad context of social and cultural change.

Historically it has been the task of organized interests in many systems to function as agents of innovation. In the modern service state, however, where public authorities—possibly in conjunction with political parties—have become an important source of innovation, interest groups are more likely to defend the *status quo* and an established position. The struggle over values in which groups engage and the claims they lay to scarce resources sometimes prevent, sometimes promote, change. They may destroy an existing consensus as well as prepare for a new one. Their part in providing a balance between stability and change within a governmental system remains important.

Groups not only articulate the demands of their potential or actual membership, they also serve as an outlet for the social energies of their members. Both the compulsory mass organizations of totalitarian states and the voluntary associations of representative regimes facilitate identification of the individual with the political system.

Compared with the intermittence of party activities and the sometimes abstract generalities of party propaganda, group campaigns appear concrete and continuous. Thus the socialization of the citizen by interest groups often proves more effective and lasting. Where they provide a framework for the social life of their members, groups fulfill, or at least supplement, the functions of political parties, e.g., the large labor and Catholic parties of western Europe, which had, in their turn, replaced the network of traditional social relations.

The organizational structure of a group determines whether its rank and file, in fact, is able to overcome isolation and possibly achieve identification with political authority. Group leadership, no less than party leadership, provides an opportunity for acquiring and exercising political skills and, possibly, an avenue to social promotion. In many of the new nations the task of training the citizenry in the art of rational political calculations falls to the groups at least as much as to parties.

Activities

Groups must come to terms with their environment by meeting conflicting claims and provoking favorable government decisions. Success or failure will be related directly to the assets which a group can command. The most crucial of these assets is a group's position in society, which may, but need not, depend on such variables as leadership capability, wealth, and size and cohesion of the membership. Most important is an assessment of the opinion which competitors, the public, and decision makers have formed about the group. Hence, many of the publicity campaigns in which modern interest groups engage are designed to create a legitimizing image.

The less confident a group is that it can secure benefits or ward off threats through other channels, the more energy it will devote to public relations activities. Typically, promotional or attitude groups which require little immediate administrative consideration, such as an association for the abolition of the death penalty, will give major emphasis to the molding of public opinion. Others are more effective in cultivating discreet relationships. But even for groups pursuing similar ends in different societies, e.g., business organizations, the amount of publicity and of secretiveness will vary from one political culture to another.

Similarly, the style of appeal which groups address to their own membership or to the general public does not depend solely on the nature of the interests involved; more frequently the temper that pervades all political behavior in a society will determine whether an impassioned or a factual, a radical or a moderate, an ideological or a pragmatic approach is in order.

The structure and activities of interest groups must be adjusted to the distribution of effective power within the political system. Hence, where there is power there will be pressure, although pressure—the continuation of bargaining by other means (Wootton 1963, p. 7)—denotes only one form of group influence. Conversely, the high or low density of group activity can serve as a gauge of the flow of influence in a given system and at various periods.

At least in representative regimes the relationship between interest groups and the party system is of critical importance to the process of transforming power. In their formative stage, many parties have to rely on the support of groups in order to make their appeal to the electorate effective, indeed to insure survival and growth. Once a party is established in the political process, the relationship becomes more interdependent. Interlocking leadership and membership, a common policy orientation expressed in party platforms, and the groups' action programs may lead to a frank participation of the groups in the electoral process through subsidies and the nomination of candidates. Yet, the nonpartisan stance which many political regimes forced upon interest groups in the nineteenth century is usually not entirely abandoned. Very few groups consider a complete identification with a single political party compatible with their mission. On the other hand, political organizations which appeal to an audience representing a single interest are parties in name only, even if temporarily they win seats in parliament.

Conjectures about the respective strength or weakness of parties and pressure groups abound. The thesis that where party organization is decentralized and party discipline feeble, interest groups will be vigorous and successful can be substantiated in some countries but is contrary to fact in most. The characteristics of the legislative process and of the administrative process, social stratification, and public attitudes toward authority are among the many factors that affect the distribution of power and function between parties and interest groups.

The decline of ideological conflict, especially in the parties of western Europe, and the waning of meaningful opposition in European parliaments appear to have made organized interests preeminent over parties and to have created a situation long prevalent in the United States. What has happened, in fact, is that in a highly organized pluralist state the parliamentary representative is no longer inclined to defend individual and local interests but instead feels called upon to express the views of the large modern pressure groups. Interest groups are indeed participating in the parliamentary stage of decision making, but the importance of political parties for the defense of organized interests has increased rather than diminished.

In many systems the major group effort has shifted to the bureaucracy. The expansion of governmental activities and the dispersion of governmental powers in the modern state, the delegation of rule making to the civil service, and the technical difficulties of rational rule application all invite intimate collaboration between groups and administration. Not all groups can count on being consulted. But those groups to which the bureaucracy turns regularly for expert advice are deemed to possess information which is indispensable for the proper discharge of administrative functions. Groups are expected to exercise enough control over their members to insure the acceptance of government regulation or, alternatively, to warn the bureaucracy about obstacles in the way of policy implementation.

Most modern interest groups boast staffs whose qualifications supplement the training and knowledge of the public administrator. Moreover, group officials may have been selected because they share with their counterparts in the bureaucracy social background, education, and, frequently, an affinity of views. Where the administrators of functionally specialized agencies and group executives feel responsible to an identical clientele, the symbiosis of officialdom and private interests is bound to grow. Where, as in the modern welfare state, bureaucracy and large economic interests emerge as the best organized forces in the nation, both groups and officials can hope to draw increased strength from mutual support.

Under such conditions it is formalistic to insist that, except in a rare corporatist regime, the advice offered by even the most powerful interest group does not bind the official. Legally this may be so, and the defense of public interest against particularistic demands remains a condition of survival for pluralistic democracy.

But civil servants and group officials interact in a political "subsystem"; in some countries, among them the United States, the chairmen or the staff members of parliamentary committees also participate. These subsystems function with such regularity that they generally become the source of important official decision making. The advice offered by the groups is easily incorporated in the decisions, and organized interests assume a direct and sometimes acknowledged responsibility for the formation of public policy and occasionally even for its execution.

Collaboration between bureaucracy and groups may be based on either formal or informal contacts. The degree to which it becomes institutionalized is usually of secondary importance. In many regimes advisory committees and councils, on which interest groups of all kinds are statutorily represented, may be counted by the hundreds and be concerned with a wide range of activities. They may give a voice to interests which have failed to win regular access to administration. However, for the major groups, such committees only buttress the informal and useful contacts which they have long enjoyed.

In some countries indispensable collaboration has turned into "colonization" of the bureaucracy by the groups. These interest groups are in a position to veto the appointment (or the promotion) of civil servants to administrative positions of importance to the groups. A ministry might thus in fact become the fief of organized interests. Although open exercise of such a veto right is still generally frowned upon, subtle influences, possibly exercised through parliamentary channels, sometimes yield the same results.

Even in totalitarian regimes contact between administration and agencies representing special interests is an everyday occurrence. However, existing political controls are designed to keep the interaction between bureaucracy and interests from resulting in decentralized policy determination.

The group activities that have been described are considered typical in a wide variety of regimes at different stages of development. Normally, interest groups make demands on an existing political system and will therefore move within the rules set by that system. This does not preclude an occasional show of violence. But when interest groups proceed to challenge the existing order, anomic activities become frequent and the function of the group changes. Disgruntled ex-servicemen may storm the parliamentary building; small businessmen or property owners, threatened by bankruptcy or foreclosures, may assault tax inspectors and court officials. The representatives they elect may correctly believe that their mandate is absolute obstruction rather than reformatory legislation. But such movements transcend their role as interest groups and become revolutionary. It is nonetheless true that certain revolutionary organizations may try to appear, at least for a time, as pressure groups.

Structures

Highly structured, bureaucratized interest organizations often exist in the same society as functionally diffuse movements, with a minimum of interaction between the membership of both. When modern interest groups began to form, most of them wished to acquire an image different from that of guilds and feudal corporations. Hence they laid emphasis on the purely voluntary association and a subjectively experienced community of views providing common ground for their adherents. Moreover, police regulations often restricted their activities to single localities.

The multiplication of services which the membership expects at present from interest groups has contributed more than anything else to organizational expansion. There is, of course, a connection between the services a group provides and its operation as a pressure group. But in general, far more effort is expended on assisting the membership than on influencing the environment in which the group moves.

In all modern and in many developing societies, interest groups organize a more numerous clientele than do political parties. A well-filled treasury, specialized and general publications, and a highly trained staff are among the usual assets, at least of those groups which represent sectional interests of the population. Other organizations, such as cause groups or civic groups, might decide that the prestige which they too wish to acquire depends on factors other than an impressive hierarchical structure.

The heterogeneity of any pluralistic society, and particularly the divisions in its social structure, are reflected in the multiplicity of groups. Ideological differences, or divergent interests clothed in ideological terms, frequently lead to further fragmentation (e.g., of labor unions, of youth organizations, etc.). When they are threatened by a dissipation of power, groups may enter into federations, coalitions, or broad fronts of either permanent or ephemeral design. Everywhere the number of units interacting in the realm of interest representation lends special characteristics to the entire system.

The bureaucratization of decision making within groups and the attendant stultification of internal group life pose a number of special problems. If groups have the function of furthering the socialization of the individual, there must be room for an active participation of the members in group processes. Actually, such participation is often minimal. The fact that in modern society the most active citizens belong to several groups rather than to a single interest group has been considered a significant modifier of group activities (especially by Truman 1951, pp. 159–164 and *passim*). But the possible effects of multiple membership are nullified where the membership has little or no leverage in determining group policies. Oligarchic tendencies in interest groups are not checked by popular suffrage, and the opposition of parliamentary representatives, which party leadership frequently encounters, is absent from groups.

Only detailed research probing intragroup conflict, leadership recruitment and turnover, and membership involvement and cohesion can determine whether the democratic structure which most interest groups exhibit corresponds to actual power distribution. Group tyranny over the individual, never envisaged by the European pluralists, can be as oppressive as that of other authoritarian structures. Behind the façade of collective group life the individual may remain isolated and unable to alter the way in which the leadership perceives his interests and values.

The realities of group structures assume particular importance where membership is, in fact if not in law, compulsory for those engaged in a given activity. When this happens, the recoil from contract to status, generally observed in modern society, is accelerated, and interest groups will invariably be instrumental in such a development. Then the state might encourage the organizational completeness of the groups and sanction it by awarding to them quasi-fiscal powers. This creates for the modern interest groups duties and privileges similar to those of the *Zwangsverband* (Max Weber) in patriarchical and patrimonial societies. Among the advantages which public authorities derive at present from such a use of a trade association, a lawyers' "guild," or a growers' federation is the promise of decentralized, efficient rule enforcement. In a representative system, such arrangements are most frequent in a war economy; but they have often outlasted the emergency. It is likely that they provide increased security for both the administration and the administered, but in the process interest groups must lose the characteristics of the voluntary association.

Legitimacy

With the exception of the old Whig theory, there was no place for interest groups in any of the classical theories of democracy. Rousseau considered all forms of interest representation as a manifestation of the *volontés particulières* inimical to the general will. Madison denounced "faction . . . actuated by some common impulse of passion, or of interest" as a threat "to the permanent and aggregate interests of the community" (Hamilton et al. [1787–1788] 1961, "Federalist Paper No. 10," p. 57). The liberal and radical traditions in both Great Britain and the United States were equally unsympathetic to "special interests": the investigations by the Temporary National Economic Committee during the New Deal and the voluminous reports by the House Committee on Lobbying Activities reflect such continuing hostility.

However, animosity toward interest groups is in no way confined to concepts which have an atomistic or individualistic bias. The theories of the *Obrigkeitsstaat* too, as they emerged in early modern times, have never sanctioned interest group activities. Totalitarian regimes and many of the emerging nations deny to groups any right to autonomous action and often do so in Rousseauist or Jacobin terms. This does not prevent some of their constitutions from affirming the right of citizens to unite in vocational or other interest groups (cf. the "public organizations" enumerated in article 126 of the Soviet constitution). A different and new development has taken place in eastern Europe, where in the 1960s the extent of legitimate group action and its impact on political decisions have become the subject of searching discussions.

In the pluralistic democracies of the West, the groups are regarded as a nonpathological and ubiquitous phenomenon. But although the heterogeneous pluralistic society refuses to suppress interest group representation or to press it into the mold of governmental directives (the *Gleichschaltung* of the authoritarian state), it nevertheless suffers constant tension between particularistic group demands and the public interest. In concrete decisions, according to the democratic ethos, the public interest will be found and elaborated not in overcoming the fragmenting effects of group activities but in giving their spokesmen a full hearing (Herring 1936 *passim;* Fraenkel 1964). Groups derive their legitimacy from an assumed compatibility of their claims with community values. They will therefore formulate their demands in such a manner as to correspond to commonly held concepts of justice. But they must adhere to the limits which preservation of the common good sets for the defense of special interests, not only in their programs and policy statements but in actual practice. The notion of the public interest may remain as controversial as that of natural law, fraught as it is with epistemological and ontological difficulties. [*See* PUBLIC INTEREST.] It is nonetheless true that, at least in all Western democracies, discussions concerned with the legitimacy of group activities do weigh the effect of group pressures on the commonweal.

Whether groups contribute to the operation of the political system or undermine it cannot be determined in the abstract. Not only the nature of their claims and the means by which they assert them are important but so is the total relationship between organized interests and governmental organs. Some authors speak of a "new feudalism" whenever governmental functions are parceled out to economic organizations which then appropriate them and use them as their private property (Morgenthau 1960). At that point authoritative decisions merely sanction a determination of policy that has been reached in a subsystem. The pluralistic objectives which are the very reason for the legitimization of group action in a democratic society are, in fact, endangered when certain groups succeed in destroying the position of the government as an umpire between conflicting claims.

Both the recognition that interest groups are indispensable for the functioning of a modern democracy and the distrust that they might abuse the power derived from the exercise of legitimate functions have led in many countries to statutory or constitutional enactments. They try either to police group activities or to integrate them directly into the decision-making process.

Legislation dealing with lobbying by interest groups has, however, encountered similar and perennial difficulties everywhere. It has tended to treat symptoms rather than cause. An uncertain diagnosis of the evils to combat has led to uncertainties about available and potentially successful remedies. Nowhere has it been easy to distinguish between the legitimate exercise of the right to petition and of the freedom of association on the one hand, and corrupt practices, deception, or coercion on the other. [*See* LOBBYING.]

In the United States, more than half of the states have imposed criminal sanctions or civil penalties on certain lobbying activities. The Federal Regulation of Lobbying Act of 1946 attempts to draw conclusions from more than a century of experience with state regulation. The underlying principle of this legislation is its insistence on disclosure, a belief that if group activities are open to public scrutiny they can have no ill effect on the democratic process. This legitimizes all group behavior which does not fall under the terms of the law. Moreover, American courts have construed the legislation quite narrowly, so as to protect fundamental rights. Altogether, the American example has not been deemed successful enough to warrant direct imitation in other countries. Legislation concerning election expenses, business concentration, etc., frequently aims in similar fashion at disclosure of dealings between groups, legislature, and administration. [*See also* POLITICAL FINANCING.] Even if it were possible to enact strict standards for an operational code for interest groups, legislation of this nature would still remain unsatisfactory; it would not adequately insure to public authorities the latitude needed to deal with a coalition of organized interests.

Functional representation is a more ambitious attempt to give to groups a legitimate place in the constitutional framework. The economic councils that existed in the Weimar Republic and that have survived in the French Fifth Republic seek to institutionalize the advisory role of the major interest groups. This orderly and seemingly rational scheme of interest representation has disappointed the expectations of its promoters, and not only because of the difficulty of deciding how such institutions should be constituted. Economic councils are generally unable to monopolize the flow of expert advice, of predictions and warnings, between groups and governments. The influence which organized interests bring to bear on public policy has continued to utilize other, long-established channels, circumventing the open debates and the balloting in the councils. Proposals to make the decisions of economic councils binding rather than advisory involve more than the mere legitimization of interest group activities; such schemes would give constitutional sanction to a corporatist structure which so far exists only *de facto* in certain of the subsystems of representative democracy. By seeking to assure to the groups a high and official place in the decision-making process these proposals invariably neglect and misconstrue the roles of both political parties and groups in the governmental process.

Problems of analysis and research

Scholarly investigations of interest groups have often been prompted by the same impulse of demystification which has motivated muckraking descriptions of lobbying. The desire to see politics in the round, to understand better the evident discrepancies between constitutional structure and political reality, and to analyze the values and beliefs underlying political conduct has drawn attention to the study of interest groups.

Interest groups are by no means an American invention; their growth was equally luxuriant in imperial Germany, in republican France, and elsewhere. But it was easier to discover them in a political system where party programs remained inconsequential and where a tight net of nonparty groups surrounds and penetrates the parties at all times. When after World War II pressure group studies also became the research vogue in Europe, and soon thereafter in most parts of the world, they acknowledged their debt to the earlier American findings. But they also inherited much of the confusion which had characterized previous group analysis.

For all its impressive descriptive wealth, American research has in the past provided little systematic reflection on the general role which interest groups play in political and social change. If any theoretial insights have emerged from the empirical studies, they are far from coherent and often accommodate conflicting concepts of representative government (Eldersveld 1958). Even exercises in group taxonomy, indispensable for systematic and especially for comparative studies, have not been too successful. Classification according to the interests which the groups represent (especially the frequent distinction between the defenders of sectional interests and the promoters of causes) often prove too simplistic even for the description of single systems. The division into institutional, nonassociational, associational, and anomic groups, which Almond and Coleman have developed for comparative purposes (1960, pp. 33–45), is useful but seems to broaden the group universe unduly.

The complex relationship between the so-called group theory of politics, an American version of analytical pluralism, and empirical group studies, is discussed elsewhere [*see* POLITICAL GROUP ANALYSIS]. The question whether or not an updated and refined group approach, supported by empirical research, can serve as a general theory of the political process has been debated hotly, albeit inconclusively. Demands for better definitions, for a more elaborate conceptual framework, and for more systematic observations have come from all sides; but as yet there have been no appreciable results, even while monographic and comparative studies have added much to the realistic knowledge of politics in many countries.

The studies which Jean Meynaud (1962) has

devoted to the French and other interest group systems excel by their combination of descriptive analysis and methodological and theoretical considerations. The writer not only warns against a mechanistic view of the political process which may result from all too exclusive a preoccupation with interest groups, he also points to the difficulties still in the way of satisfactory group research.

Frequently these difficulties result from insufficient evidence. Some case studies have been successful in isolating group influences among the multiple factors that determine policy. Such studies have also described, although never measured exactly, the intensity and the scope of pressures applied in a particular situation. Yet generalizations about the actual effectiveness of pressures remain hazardous. Not only sociological but also political analysis calls for a precise understanding of internal group processes. Formal group structure may hide more than it reveals about actual power relationships. Yet any probing beneath the surface will in general be impeded by the impossibility of penetrating inside the groups with a scholarly and replicable research design. In the past, institutional economists have sometimes investigated, if only marginally, the positive or negative role which interest groups have played in innovation. Now that political scientists also wish to scrutinize this question, they are often hampered by a lack of historical evidence.

For these and other reasons, probabilistic statements abound in both one-country and multicountry group research; comparisons of group impact have been less rigorous than is desirable. However, even at present the dimension which group research has added to the study of politics permits testing the validity of some hypotheses about political organization and behavior in different political cultures.

HENRY W. EHRMANN

[*Directly related are the entries* PARTIES, POLITICAL; PLURALISM; POLITICAL GROUP ANALYSIS; VOLUNTARY ASSOCIATIONS. *Other relevant material may be found in* ORGANIZATIONS; POLITICAL PARTICIPATION; POLITICAL PROCESS; REPRESENTATION; SOCIAL MOVEMENTS.]

BIBLIOGRAPHY

ALMOND, GABRIEL A.; and COLEMAN, JAMES S. (editors) 1960 *The Politics of the Developing Areas.* Princeton Univ. Press.

AMERICAN ACADEMY OF POLITICAL AND SOCIAL SCIENCE 1958 *Unofficial Government: Pressure Groups and Lobbies.* Edited by Donald C. Blaisdell. Annals, Vol. 319. Philadelphia: The Academy.

BENTLEY, ARTHUR F. (1908) 1949 *The Process of Government: A Study of Social Pressures.* Introduction by H. T. Davis. Bloomington, Ind.: Principia Press.

BLAISDELL, DONALD C. 1957 *American Democracy Under Pressure.* New York: Ronald Press.

BREITLING, RUPERT 1960 Die zentralen Begriffe der Verbandsforschung. *Politische Vierteljahresschrift* 1:47–73.

ECKSTEIN, HARRY H. 1960 *Pressure Group Politics: The Case of the British Medical Association.* London: Allen & Unwin; Stanford Univ. Press.

EHRMANN, HENRY W. 1957 *Organized Business in France.* Princeton Univ. Press.

ELDERSVELD, SAMUEL J. 1958 American Interest Groups: A Survey of Research and Some Implications for Theory and Method. Pages 173–196 in International Political Science Association, *Interest Groups on Four Continents.* Edited by Henry W. Ehrmann. Univ. of Pittsburgh Press.

FINER, SAMUEL E. 1958 *Anonymous Empire: A Study of the Lobby in Great Britain.* London: Pall Mall.

FRAENKEL, ERNST 1964 *Deutschland und die westlichen Demokratien.* Stuttgart (Germany): Kohlhammer. → See especially pages 32–47.

HAMILTON, ALEXANDER; MADISON, JAMES; and JAY, JOHN (1787–1788) 1961 *The Federalist.* Edited with introduction and notes by Jacob E. Cooke. Middletown, Conn.: Wesleyan Univ. Press.

HERRING, E. PENDLETON 1929 *Group Representation Before Congress.* Baltimore: Johns Hopkins Press.

HERRING, E. PENDLETON 1936 *Public Administration and the Public Interest.* New York: McGraw-Hill.

INTERNATIONAL POLITICAL SCIENCE ASSOCIATION 1958 *Interest Groups on Four Continents.* Edited by Henry W. Ehrmann. Univ. of Pittsburgh Press.

KAISER, JOSEPH H. 1956 *Die Repräsentation organisierter Interessen.* Berlin: Duncker & Humblot.

KEY, VALDIMER O. (1942) 1964 *Politics, Parties, and Pressure Groups.* 5th ed. New York: Crowell.

LAPALOMBARA, JOSEPH G. 1964 *Interest Groups in Italian Politics.* Princeton Univ. Press.

MACKENZIE, WILLIAM J. M. 1955 Pressure Groups: The Conceptual Framework. *Political Studies* 3:247–255.

MEYNAUD, JEAN 1962 *Nouvelles études sur les groupes de pression en France.* Paris: Colin.

MORGENTHAU, HANS J. (1960) 1964 *The Purpose of American Politics.* New York: Random House. → See especially pages 274–292 on "The New Feudalism: The Paradox of Thwarted Government."

NEUMANN, FRANZ L. 1957 *The Democratic and the Authoritarian State: Essays in Political and Legal Theory.* Edited by Herbert Marcuse. Glencoe, Ill.: Free Press. → See especially pages 3–21 on "Approaches to the Study of Political Power."

POTTER, ALLEN M. 1961 *Organized Groups in British National Politics.* London: Faber.

TRUMAN, DAVID B. (1951) 1962 *The Governmental Process: Political Interests and Public Opinion.* New York: Knopf.

WOOTTON, GRAHAM 1963 *The Politics of Influence: British Ex-servicemen, Cabinet Decisions and Cultural Change, 1917–1957.* Cambridge, Mass.: Harvard Univ. Press.

INTEREST TESTING

See VOCATIONAL INTEREST TESTING.

INTERGROUP RELATIONS

See GROUPS; PREJUDICE; RACE RELATIONS.

INTERNAL TRADE

In most countries internal trade ranks second or third among types of industries generating the national product, but it has been a stepchild of economic analysis. Early classical economists considered productive activity to consist of form-changing only. Marx added consideration of the labor input into transport, warehousing, and other physical handling. But, in the Soviet Union, as consumer goods have become more plentiful and varied, retailing has come to include display of goods, salesclerk time to provide information, and even some competitive advertising (Goldman 1963, pp. 191–200). Non-Marxian economic theory has long recognized that consumer satisfaction (and hence production) is enhanced by trade among specialists at various steps in commodity production and by the service of distribution that puts finished goods in a certain place at the time that users want them. But in the development of price and output theory, economists have dealt primarily with the structure and performance of the raw-material and manufacturing industries (or with transport and electric power) and have treated these as if manufacturers sold finished products directly to consumers or, alternatively, as if the distributive trades were analytically neutral. Except in an occasional empirical study (e.g., Adelman 1959, pp. 109–149, 248–274), the distributive trades have been neglected in their roles as buyers from, or as potential entrants into, supplying industries (whereby they influence significantly the performance of earlier-stage markets), or as resellers that affect the information provided about, and consumers' choices among, goods made by rival manufacturers. This lack of economic analysis and the general confusion about the economic function of the distributive trades have contributed in no small part to the question asked in the book *Does Distribution Cost Too Much?* (see Twentieth Century Fund 1939), which is answered affirmatively there and elsewhere.

Trade as part of production. Transactions between autonomous ownership units make possible and are augmented by specialization in commodity production. A primitive household producing all that it consumes does not engage in trade. But once some goods are supplied by others there is trade, even though the maker of the goods is himself the seller to consumers. Long before recorded history, when a locality produced a surplus of a commodity traders distributed the goods elsewhere. The industrial revolution greatly enhanced specialization by, and transfers among, establishments, firms, and localities involved in the various vertical steps from raw material to finished consumer goods production. While such transfers can occur between establishments in common ownership (even within the government, say), trade ordinarily connotes exchanges between autonomous units whose activities are coordinated through market transactions. Indeed, internal trade differs from international trade only in that the latter involves transactions beyond the boundaries of a sovereign political authority, which ordinarily imposes restraints on trade that inhibit geographic specialization in production or, alternatively, the geographic mobility of labor and capital.

In the broad usage, including transportation, warehousing, and advertising, internal trade accounted for about 40 per cent of the value of goods as bought by all final buyers in the United States in 1947 (Cox et al. 1965, p. 148). Of the total value of all articles supplied to households, internal trade accounted for almost 43 per cent (*ibid.*, p. 145). Nearly 12 of these 43 percentage points were accounted for by trading activities of the nondistributive industries, chiefly those producing commodities. The remaining 31 points were attributed to the distributive industries—3 of these points represented value added by transportation and storage, almost 2 were added by advertising, and the residual of almost 27 per cent was provided by the wholesale and retail industries (adapted from Cox et al. 1965, p. 145). Because this is an estimate of "value added," it excludes the distributive trades' purchases of supplies, power, fuel, transportation, and advertising, and, for this reason, is much lower than the composite wholesale–retail gross margins cited below. Were comparable data for other countries available, they probably would reflect the degree of specialization in commodity production among ownership units and the comparative efficiency of such productive activities and of trading.

The economic function of the distribution to consumers of goods in final physical form consists of providing the satisfaction of "place and time utility" —to which one can add "information utility." Manufacturers perform part of these services by packaging goods, receiving orders, and shipping or arranging transportation. Some would include manufacturers' advertising and sales personnel costs (Twentieth Century Fund 1939, pp. 6, 7); but much of this activity is directed to persuading consumers to buy manufacturer *A*'s brand rather than *B*'s on grounds other than clear-cut superiority—the form of rivalry elected because the structure of some manufacturing industries lessens or estops price competition [*see* OLIGOPOLY]. Further analysis will be directed, therefore, primarily to the wholesaling and retailing of finished goods to households and other small-scale purchasers.

Because commodity production is more specialized geographically than are the locations of consumers, commodities must be assembled from many areas and a stock held in the locality of consumption. This is the function of wholesaling, whether done by a manufacturer's branch, an autonomous enterprise, or a purchasing–warehousing operation owned by one or by many retailers. Making the goods available at the specific place and time consumers prefer and providing some information are the functions of retailing. Only then is production in the economic sense complete.

The "price" of the distributive service. Symmetrical with the distributive trades' product is the "price" of the distributive services, which is defined as the gross margin between invoice cost of the good landed at the wholesaler's or retailer's establishment and the resale price. This margin is usually expressed as a percentage of the latter.

When analyzing economic performance of a distributive trade, the article-by-article gross margins are not as important as is the margin obtained on a group of articles or even for a type of outlet as a whole. Most costs of wholesaling and of retailing are both common and joint among the goods handled, although there is some opportunity in the long run to alter what is handled. But the selling in the same space and by the same personnel of items that have similar purchasing characteristics from the consumers' point of view, although they may differ widely in consumer use, means that selling one food is facilitated by simultaneously offering other foods and other household articles that consumers' behavior indicates they prefer to buy in the same outlet. Consequently, the intensity and elasticity of demand for the service of various retailers reflect primarily consumer preferences among composites of prices, locations, and qualities of service offered by retailers of families of articles.

The gross margin is a weighted average of margins on the various articles in the group. For example, the storewide gross margins of large-chain food retailers (including purchasing and warehousing operations) averaged about 15 per cent in early 1942, but the average margins for individual dry-grocery articles in the United States (as found by the Office of Price Administration 1943) ranged from about 7 to more than 20 per cent. Such differences must reflect the net outcome of rivalry among food stores, each of which seeks, as a multiproduct firm, to adjust margins on various articles so as to maximize the return on its investment in retailing (Holdren 1960). But the social performance consists of the efficiency and price of the distributive service for families of articles or for the whole outlet.

Distribution as a share of gross output. Distribution does cost much or, it is equally correct to say, produces much. "Trade and commerce," identified as primarily wholesale and retail trade but explicitly excluding transportation, contributes between 6 and 20 per cent of the gross product of most nations (circa 1958). The percentages are positively but not highly correlated with per capita output (United Nations 1963, pp. 491–497; *Yearbook of National Accounts Statistics* 1962, pp. 314–317). The chief exceptions to this correlation are the high shares of trade in total output in most Mediterranean countries and the low shares reported for communist countries, of which more later. But using the percentage of the labor force employed in retailing to indicate distribution's share, the correlation with per capita gross product is high in western Europe (Jefferys & Knee 1962, p. 13). A similar indication is the higher general level of retail margins in the United States than in Great Britain (Hall et al. 1961, p. 50).

In the Western countries the share of wholesale and retail distribution in total economic activity has risen generally with historical advances in output per capita. This can be deduced from the small increase in sales per person engaged in these activities from 1910 to 1950 in the United States and Great Britain (Hall et al. 1961, p. 10) compared to the known much sharper rise over this period in productivity in commodity production. A similar inference can be drawn from the advance in the ratio of employment in distribution to employment in commodity production over recent decades in western Europe (Jefferys & Knee 1962, p. 10) and over an eighty-year period in the United States (Barger 1955, p. 8), and from the substantial rise from 1869 to 1909 in distributive margins for most commodity lines in the United States, followed by a very slow upward creep to 1948 (*ibid.*, pp. 8, 38, 57, 60, 70, 77, and 81). This is consistent with the increase from 1929 to 1958 of distribution's share of the gross national product of the United States—with government activity omitted (Cox et al. 1965, p. 53).

Productivity in distribution. There is no fully satisfactory measure of the output of the distributive trades. The physical volume of goods sold at retail, weighted by distributive margins in various lines of trade, is affected by differences in the quality of distributive service among times, places, and types of outlets. (These defects do not affect the significance of distributive margins themselves insofar as differences in quality of service affect costs.) Retail sales per person engaged are the only data available for most comparisons and, after adjustment for price level, can be quite useful. Both measures show similar changes in output per person engaged in the United States from 1910 to about 1950 (cf. Barger 1955, p. 38, with Hall et al. 1961, p. 10).

Economies of scale. Economies of size are quite limited for the individual retail outlet but not for the firm. Measured by sales per person engaged in food and in shoe retailing in Britain and the United States, efficiency is substantially higher for moderate-sized shops than for small ones but very little higher, and in some cases lower, for large stores (Hall et al. 1961, pp. 66–70). Gain from large size is limited by the added costs of advertising, or the lower gross margin, needed to attract more customers to one location.

A firm of more than very small size usually engages in multisite operations, but neither British nor United States data show clearly higher sales per person engaged (except for food stores) in shops of a given size for chains above about ten outlets (Hall et al. 1961, pp. 66–70; and as computed from U.S. Bureau of the Census 1957). U.S. food chains report ratios of operating expenses to sales for the composite of their purchasing, warehousing, and retailing (Earle & Sheehan 1966, pp. 14–15) that vary inversely with firms' sales volumes. But these differences are related to the fact that the smaller chains buy to a large extent through wholesalers and therefore pay somewhat higher prices for goods that are delivered to their stores.

The observed success of large-chain retailers stems primarily from lower invoice cost of goods, which is achieved through skill in purchasing combined with volume enough in each locality to turn wholesaling into a logistics-type warehousing operation. An important phase of purchasing is specification-buying, or even own-manufacturing, of goods to be resold under a chain's own brands. Chains have also gone far in rationalizing the retailing step but they clearly did not initiate important innovations at that step. In Britain, Canada, and the United States giant chains have no clear advantage over those of moderate size in the distribution (but do at times in procurement) of food and of low-priced clothing, furniture, and hardware, when providing qualities of articles and of distributive service consumers expect at the prices charged. Offsetting changes in organization and practices of the few-store chains and of single-outlet retailers have slowed down large-chain growth, as will be seen below.

Historical changes in productivity. In substantial degree the historical rise in distribution's share of gross output reflects the lesser advance in productivity in distribution than in commodity production. In the United States output per worker in commodity production in 1949 was over five times the 1869 level but in distribution less than twice (Barger 1955, p. 38). In western Europe sales per person engaged in distribution rose sharply between the 1930s and the late 1950s, but the ratio of employment in distribution to that in commodity production rose nevertheless (Jefferys & Knee 1962, pp. 10, 45).

As real incomes rise in advanced countries distributive margins tend to account for a higher percentage of the retail value of consumer goods. In addition to the much less rapid advance of productivity in distribution than in commodity production, there is the fact that at higher income levels a larger proportion of consumer demand is for goods for which retail margins are relatively wide (Barger 1955, p. 131). Hence distributive margins for most types of goods rose historically in the United States (the only country for which long-period estimates are available), particularly prior to World War I (*ibid.*, pp. 81, 84, 92). For the same reason, distributive margins were substantially higher in the United States than in Britain in 1948–1950 (Hall et al. 1961, p. 26), except in food distribution where innovation in the former country had reduced labor input sharply.

In Great Britain and the United States post-World War II margins ranged from a low of about 20 per cent for food up to more than 40 per cent for furniture and jewelry (Hall et al. 1961; Barger 1955, p. 81). Even with food declining in relative importance, the composite distributive margin for all goods sold at retail in the United States rose substantially prior to World War I (Barger 1955, p. 92). After that date, innovations in distributive organization and methods, chiefly in food distribution, and the lower quality of retail service provided by the burgeoning mass distributors, slowed down the advance of the composite margin on all goods.

The very low distributive costs, of about 7 per cent of retail prices, reported for the Soviet Union do not reflect corresponding efficiency. By including in retail sales a turnover tax of about 40 per cent of retail prices, the denominator in computing distribution costs as a per cent of retail sales volume is enlarged correspondingly. (General retail sales taxes are not included in reported retail sales volume in the United States, for example.) After eliminating the Soviet turnover tax and making other adjustments so that the data are more comparable with those for the United States, the Soviet percentage is doubled but even then remains far lower. The very low quality of retail service and high proportion of all consumer goods that consists of food (the lowest-margin category in the United States) in communist countries vitiates comparison of over-all distributive costs and margins between them and advanced capitalist countries. Recently, the added variety of consumer goods and the lessening of rationing by queues, plus higher quality of retail service, have led to an upward trend in distribution costs in the Soviet Union (Goldman 1963, pp. 84–167).

For reasons cited in the preceding paragraphs, available data do not permit precise comparisons of the efficiency of finished good distribution among commodity lines, among nations, or for a given nation at different dates. But much of value can be concluded for free enterprise economies from the developments in and characteristics of distributive trade markets and of consumer behavior.

Current performance of distributive markets. While productivity has advanced more rapidly in commodity production than in distribution, a fundamental innovation in organization, often called "mass distribution," has altered the size of retail outlets, influenced even more the size of the firm and the degree of vertical integration, and worked toward lower gross margins. Starting in the United States in the last century, primarily in food but extending progressively to apparel, "hard goods," and selling by mail, the innovation spread to Canada decades ago, then, after a considerable interval, to Britain and Australia, but not to western Europe until after 1945. It has not yet been adopted widely in other countries.

The innovators saw the operating-cost savings made possible by high-turnover retailing, usually with sales for cash only and often with reduced service, both in retail stores and by mail (Adelman 1959, pp. 25–50; Emmet & Jeuck 1950, particularly chapters 3, 8, 21).

Preconditions for these cost savings, particularly of self-service, were prepackaging by manufacturers and consumer purchase by description, usually by brand, because of conviction of quality fostered by advertising and not refuted by experience. Success led to the adding of stores to which the word "chain" or "multiple" was applied. Firms attained substantial volume and, aided by developments in transportation, communication, and record-keeping, integrated from retailing into the warehousing function and began to buy from primary sources. Distribution changed from a three-stage movement —from a wholesale stock to a retail stock to consumers—to a flow movement with inventories minimized at all stages. Little room was left for the traditional general line wholesaler.

In the United States the food chains' (11 or more stores) share of sales rose from approximately zero in 1869 to more than 40 per cent in 1962, bringing a sharp reduction in the weighted average of chains' and independents' distributive spread for food (Barger 1955, p. 92). This fact, together with the relatively narrower margins of chain and mail-order sellers of lower-price apparel and some "hard goods," contributed to the relative stability of the composite distributive spread for all consumer goods since 1910. A quite similar growth of chains' shares, but probably not in cost savings, has occurred in Great Britain and a major start has been made in western Europe since 1945 (Jefferys & Knee 1962, pp. 49–71).

Belatedly, by adopting analogous organization and methods, many independent retailers and wholesalers are now able to at least come close to matching the chains' costs and prices. Many retailers have cooperatively integrated into wholesale warehousing or have joined "voluntary" groups that contract to purchase from a sponsoring wholesaler. They can therefore buy the goods landed at their establishments at prices comparable, or nearly so, to those paid by chains (Jefferys & Knee 1962, pp. 76–83; Heflebower 1957, p. 276). These arrangements enable retailers to get the advantages of large-scale buying by specification, and of group merchandising of the owned or associated wholesaler brands. So that they will have the necessary scale a group of small food chains in the United States own a cooperative buying–merchandising enterprise. Numerous independent retailers have adopted the chains' retailing method of rapid turnover achieved by low prices and lesser service. Reorganization of the wholesaler–independent retailer arrangement and changed practices in retailing have slowed down but not everywhere checked the growth of the chains' share of retail volume. The revived independent retailer performance and rivalry among the chain food stores have held the latter's net profits (after corporate income taxes) to about 1 per cent of sales in the United States and to 10 per cent of equity (Earle & Sheehan 1966, pp. 9, 19), a modest earning rate for this generally highly prosperous postwar period.

Monopolistic competition. The typical local retail market tends to be strongly but not perfectly competitive in the short run [*see* COMPETITION]. Much of the imperfection stems from the small size of markets geographically, for, despite the fact that the efficient scale of retailer outlets is not large absolutely, often it is large compared to the volume of trade that can be attracted to one site without sharply rising costs. The very few outlets handling similar families of articles in a shopping center are not fully restrained by the possibility of entry of an additional seller, for the capacity added would tend to force down margins and make entry uninviting even though the capital required is quite small. But established stores in a shopping center often experiment with handling added product lines—a form of entry. Finally, where consumers can easily shift from one shopping locality to another, a ceiling on prices in each center is imposed.

On the other side of the market, consumers choose between the gain, in the form of better (in their opinion) combinations of distributive service and price, from added search, and the cost of that search, which consists chiefly of time expended (Stigler 1961, pp. 218–224). Once a shop has been found to be optimal however, repeated purchases involve zero search costs. Consumers also tend to be passive and to respond only to the attention-getting devices of sellers, of which store display has proved very effective. Furthermore, the marginal cost of search tends to be correlated positively with level of consumers' incomes because of the time required to acquire information about the added types and varied character of the goods bought out of the higher income. At the same time, the marginal satisfaction from making better purchases falls, *ceteris paribus*. Consumers do not perform with the expertness of a purchasing agent who specializes in buying a few articles for a large enterprise. But this does not demonstrate that consumers' performance is suboptimal, given their preferences. [*See* CONSUMER SOVEREIGNTY.]

Closely related to retail distribution cost and performance is the degree of excess capacity. One observes underutilized space and personnel at some hours, days, or seasons, but at other times there are crowded stores and slow service. Despite some planned variations in number of employees, cost per unit of sales usually falls sharply when stores are crowded and rises when they are not. But quality of service moves in the opposite direction so that neither the recorded costs nor the "capacity" for service are fully comparable between the two types of occasions. Stores have had but little success with inducements to shop during slack hours or days. Clearly, consumers will accept inferior retailing service rather than change when possible their times of shopping sufficiently to even out the quality of service and make fuller use of the more fixed inputs in store operation.

What emerges is a picture of retailing as monopolistically competitive, in part because of differences in retailers' location and combination of service, variety of goods offered, and hours of service. Equally important are differences in consumers' preferences as to combination of service and price and in outlay of time and other costs they are willing to incur in order to identify the preferred combination. Consequently, each seller has a small amount of "built-in" monopoly. No alternative arrangement could bring perfect competition, nor would consumers' welfare necessarily be improved thereby—except by some means of lessening the cost of valid information to them (Chamberlin [1933] 1950, pp. 213, 214; Lewis 1949, pp. 150–156).

The competitive character of the scene just portrayed rests on the autonomy of each shop, but it could be quite different where chain organizations do business at hundreds or even thousands of local shopping points. In the United States the largest two firms (chain store) accounted for 42 per cent of food sales, on the average, in 133 cities in 1958, and the largest four accounted for 58 per cent (Mueller & Garoian 1961, p. 9). Introduce the additional fact that some of these chains meet each other, but also one or more other chains and numerous independents in each of the various metropolitan areas, and the potentiality of reduced competition, at least in the form of low margins, is amplified. Thus far, such developments do not appear to have lessened price competition or to have increased profit rates. Restraining forces on monopoly include the difficulties of "agreeing" on the margins for each of hundreds of articles, the effectiveness of nonprice competition in shifting consumers' custom, and the limited advantage of large chains over smaller ones and even over independents who have integrated themselves into wholesaling.

Effects on monopoly tendencies in supplying industries. A final phase of evaluating the performance of the distributive trades is whether they lessen or augment monopoly in the supplying industries. One purpose of manufacturers' sales programs for most consumer goods is to limit the retailer to physical handling and order taking. This is achieved to varying degrees for "convenience goods" bought frequently in small amounts, and it has occurred fully for cigarettes sold by dispensing machines. For "specialty goods," or those bought infrequently, of high unit value and beyond the consumers' capacity to judge by inspection, the manufacturer frequently makes the retailer of a brand *de facto* his exclusive agent (in a submarket), and the retailer builds his enterprise around his supplier's product line (e.g., Pashigian 1961, pp. 11–51). There may be *de facto* "full-line forcing," which compels retailers to pass back to the manufacturer any monopoly gains that arise from consumers' preferences for the supplier's goods (Burstein 1960).

For many goods, however, differentiation sets in motion dynamic counterdevelopments that pave the way for varying degrees of entry by large distributive enterprises into the supplying industries. For new goods, and these have become a substantial portion of consumers' purchases in advanced countries, the techniques of persuading consumers to buy also inform them about the functional properties of a good and about its added reliability as quality is improved. At some point, consumers become more willing to break away from the manufacturer–retailer channel on which they had come to rely and to buy essentially the same product with a little-known label if offered at a substantial price saving. The firms in the best position to start this process of entry by an unknown, usually termed "private," brand are the mass distributors (Heflebower 1957, pp. 278–285). They already have numerous retail outlets and a staff to purchase on a specification basis. If they are unable to buy a good that has reached this stage in the dynamic process, or more standard goods, at a very narrow small margin above manufacturing (not total) cost, they have the ability to overcome the entry barriers to manufacturing (Adelman 1959, pp. 248–274; Emmet & Jeuck 1950, pp. 374–470). Whether gains from such steps are retained for long or are passed on to consumers depends on the extent of retail price competition, which in the United States has been generally effective. But the processes just portrayed have not evolved for automobiles, tobacco items, or most proprietary drugs—for reasons that have not been studied thoroughly.

Efficiency in trade and economic development. Internal trade is more highly developed and more responsive to innovative influences in the growing, advanced countries than in those at an earlier stage of development. With regard to the consumer goods entering the markets of the latter, most evidence indicates that trade takes a much larger share of the retail price than in advanced countries. But there is debate as to whether this represents comparative inefficiency or the small volume, expensive transport, and slow turnover for goods, and the limited mobility of consumers, rather than monopoly. In very low income economies most distribution (except wholesaling of imported goods) is a form of self-employment.

There can be little debate about trade as a precondition to transfer from production for use to production for sale and the accompanying growth of efficiency. Availability of manufactured goods has a demonstration effect that stimulates production for sale or work for money wages. But during transition, the development of the efficient size of outlet and rapid turnover, with lower margins, comes only slowly indigenously. Speeding a reorganization of distribution often would do more to augment the real income of urban consumers than would probable improvements in commodity production. Where outside entrepreneurship and capital have been discouraged, distributive efficiency has lagged and there, as in some Western countries, the optimal distribution of resource use among commodity production, transportation, and internal trade has been slow in coming.

R. B. HEFLEBOWER

BIBLIOGRAPHY

ADELMAN, MORRIS A. 1959 *A & P: A Study in Price–Cost Behavior and Public Policy.* Cambridge, Mass.: Harvard Univ. Press.

BARGER, HAROLD 1955 *Distribution's Place in the American Economy Since 1869.* Princeton Univ. Press.

BURSTEIN, MEYER L. 1960 A Theory of Full-line Forcing. *Northwestern University Law Review* 55:62–95.

CHAMBERLIN, EDWARD H. (1933) 1950 *The Theory of Monopolistic Competition.* 6th ed. Cambridge, Mass.: Harvard Univ. Press.

COX, REAVIS; GOODMAN, CHARLES S.; and FICHANDLER, THOMAS C. 1965 *Distribution in a High Level Economy.* Englewood Cliffs, N.J.: Prentice-Hall.

EARLE, WENDELL; and SHEEHAN, JOHN 1966 Operating Results of Food Chains, 1965–1966. Unpublished manuscript, Cornell Univ.

EMMET, BORIS; and JEUCK, JOHN E. 1950 *Catalogs and Counters: A History of Sears, Roebuck and Company.* Univ. of Chicago Press.

GOLDMAN, MARSHALL I. 1963 *Soviet Marketing: Distribution in a Controlled Economy.* New York: Free Press.

HALL, MARGARET; KNAPP, JOHN; and WINSTON, CHRISTOPHER 1961 *Distribution in Great Britain and North America: A Study in Structure and Productivity.* Oxford Univ. Press.

HEFLEBOWER, RICHARD B. 1957 Mass Distribution: A Phase of Bilateral Oligopoly or of Competition? *American Economic Review* 47, no. 2:274–285.

HOLDREN, BOB R. 1960 *The Structure of a Retail Market and the Market Behavior of Retail Units.* Englewood Cliffs, N.J.: Prentice-Hall.

JEFFERYS, JAMES B.; and KNEE, DEREK 1962 *Retailing in Europe: Present Structure and Future Trends.* New York: St. Martins; London: Macmillan.

LEWIS, W. ARTHUR 1949 *Overhead Costs: Some Essays in Economic Analysis.* London: Allen & Unwin.

MUELLER, WILLARD F.; and GAROIAN, LEON 1961 *Changes in Market Structure of Grocery Retailing.* Madison: Univ. of Wisconsin Press.

PASHIGIAN, B. PETER 1961 *The Distribution of Automobiles: An Economic Analysis of the Franchise System.* Englewood Cliffs, N.J.: Prentice-Hall.

SMITH, HENRY (1937) 1948 *Retail Distribution: A Critical Analysis.* 2d ed. Oxford Univ. Press.

STIGLER, GEORGE J. 1961 The Economics of Information. *Journal of Political Economy* 69:213–225.

TWENTIETH CENTURY FUND, COMMITTEE ON DISTRIBUTION 1939 *Does Distribution Cost Too Much? A Review of the Costs Involved in Current Marketing Methods and a Program for Improvement,* by Paul W. Stewart and J. Frederic Dewhurst. New York: The Fund.

UNITED NATIONS 1963 *Statistical Yearbook, 1962.* New York: United Nations.

U.S. BUREAU OF THE CENSUS 1957 *1954 Census of Business.* Volume 1: Retail Trade. Washington: Government Printing Office. → See especially Table 3A.

U.S. OFFICE OF PRICE ADMINISTRATION 1943 Food and Food Products. United States, *Federal Register* 8, no. 135:9388–9417.

Yearbook of National Accounts Statistics. → Published since 1957 by the United Nations. See especially the 1962 volume.

INTERNAL WARFARE

The articles under this heading deal with the organization, strategy, tactics, and social and political implications of civil war and guerrilla warfare. Broader aspects of these topics are covered in CIVIL DISOBEDIENCE; CONFLICT; REVOLUTION; SOCIAL MOVEMENTS. *Guides to additional related subjects can be found under* INTERNATIONAL RELATIONS *and* WAR.

I
CIVIL WAR

Civil war is conflict within a society resulting from an attempt to seize or maintain power and symbols of legitimacy by extralegal means. It is civil because civilians are engaged in it. It is war because violence is applied by both sides. Civil war is intrasocietal and may take place within a group, some parts of which either desire to maintain or wish to initiate separate ethnic and/or political identity or wish to change the government.

There are two basic types of civil war. The first is the *spontaneous type:* without any previous planning or even actual leadership, a street crowd can take on the characteristics of a mob and on impulse initiate events leading to the overthrow of the government in power. Subsequently, a political vacuum is created, providing opportunities for the seizure of power. This type of civil war defies systematic classification and is prone to occur in societies having no tradition of stable political institutions within which political changes could take place. This situation usually coincides with the weakening of the power structure to such an extent that the crowds on the streets can perceive its weakness.

It is, however, the second type of civil war—the *planned* one—that has been responsible for the majority of intrasocietal conflicts and has been of most interest to social scientists. In these cases a conscious division of labor and planning takes place. Planned civil war is a case of pathology in politics, upon which anatomical probing can be done with some precision.

Development of planned civil war. Two conditions appear to be prerequisites for the initiation of planned civil war. The first is an absence of effective formal and informal channels for settling political grievances or a sense of futility or fear of reprisals in claiming such grievances. Second is the assumption or conviction that there is no recourse other than violence for securing redress. Given these factors, a systematic building of the apparatus for subversion may begin. The ultimate objective is, of course, to seize power by violence, but unlike the spontaneous civil war, this approach is carefully calculated.

For long-range and planned civil war, it is necessary to build the structure of a resistance movement. This structure is the prerequisite for the emergence of sabotage and guerrilla groups systematically engaged in rendering violence. In an industrialized country, from one to two years is required for centrally controlled sabotage and guerrilla units to emerge from the resistance structure.

The second phase is the direct application of violence, occurring systematically but at varying intervals, against the physical resources and morale of the enemy.

The final phase is an insurrection in which the conflict explodes into open, coordinated uprisings in various parts of the country, preferably in cities. With this action the insurgents hope that the rest of the country will follow, that the power structure in existence will be overthrown, and that they will be able to assume the symbols of legitimacy and claim their political objectives openly. In this event, the result is an accomplished revolution.

The contemporary American term for this type of operation is "unconventional warfare" (Zawodny 1962). The term encompasses tactics and strategies of resistance movements, counterresistance measures, guerrilla, sabotage, and evasion activities, and related psychological warfare.

The stages of organizational development of a resistance movement resulting in civil war may also be described in terms of the escalation of violence. In the initial stage, while the structure of the resistance movement is being erected, the appliction of violence will be sporadic, uncoordinated, and nonselective.

In the intermediate stage, when the structure has solidified and covers the country with its order-giving, message-receiving network, the sabotage, underground, and guerrilla units apply terror at intervals, selectively hitting the brain and nervous system of the enemy power structure—the elite, the communication centers, transportation centers, the most sensitive industries, etc. Such actions are usually regulated and planned in terms of their frequency, intensity, and territorial coverage.

The third step in the escalation of violence in civil war consists of probes on the part of the resistance movement to obtain control of either the capital or strategic parts of the country in order to establish some sort of legitimate "government" which would act openly on behalf of the organization. This stage is critical because it compels the resistance to emerge on the streets and to fight until it wins or is destroyed. At this point the insurgents act in large units, and street fighting is conducted according to the rules of infantry tactics. The insurgents' objective is a series of uprisings, spreading like brushfire, intended to destroy the enemy's formal power structure and machinery of violence throughout the whole territory. The time intervals between the phases and the length of each phase will depend not only upon the relative power ratio of the factions engaged in conflict but, above all, upon the cultural values, lore, and conditioning of the groups involved in the struggle.

The difference between civil disorder and civil war can be discerned by any of the following phenomena, which indicate a state of civil war: The insurgents control an area continuously without an attempt to disappear after clashing with the government forces; the insurgents act in units of approximately battalion size; they control the country during the night; they compel the legal government to invoke martial law; they are able to create and maintain a government of their own in the contested territory.

Organizational structures. It must be recognized that a clandestine organization is a social structure within which there is some division of labor. Five basic factors affect this structure. (1) A primary consideration is the density of population and the manner in which it is clustered. Organization of an urban underground will differ markedly from that of an agricultural country. (2) Topographical features are extremely important. (3) The ethnic composition must be taken into account. There is a propensity for ethnic groups to cluster and to treat other ethnic groups with suspicion, especially when under stress. (4) The local customs, lore, traditions, and social mores all affect the organization. For example, in some cultures women are encouraged to join fighting units, while in others this is not true. (5) Finally, and obviously, the quality and rate of influx of members greatly affect the group.

It can be assumed that the basic structural elements are: (*a*) the civil leadership of the resistance movement, who preferably should live abroad for security reasons; (*b*) the military headquarters, which, if possible, should also be abroad for the same reasons; (*c*) intelligence; (*d*) communication; (*e*) propaganda; (*f*) cadres in reserve and training; (*g*) logistic support; (*h*) fighting arms (guerrilla and sabotage units); and (*i*) services (units providing false documents, medical care, evasion assistance, etc.).

The most important problem in the formation of such an organization is the degree to which centralization should be imposed upon the structure. The issue here is that of control *versus* security. The more highly centralized and closely knit an organization is, the more easily it can be controlled by the underground leadership. However, when penetrated by the enemy, it is much more easily destroyed. The more loosely tied the organizational network, the more difficult it is for the enemy to penetrate it and arrest its development. On the other hand, it is then quite difficult to control and, consequently, might be conducive to the proliferation of various splinters in which ambitious politicians, playing the roles of local Robin Hoods, create their own resistance units, quite often keeping the membership under false pretenses; or the units can be misused for other private purposes under the guise of patriotic duty. There is a visible reluctance on the part of political leaders to surrender their private armies to a unified political leadership in these instances. In fact, one gauge of the stage of preparation for a nationwide revolution is the degree of cohesion among the various factions of the resistance organization. The greater the cohesion and centralization of leadership, the greater the possibility that unified action is approaching.

Techniques of violence in civil war. Guerrilla and sabotage units, the armed forces of resistance movements, which are usually organized along military lines, bring violence directly to the enemy. The techniques of guerrilla and sabotage units may range from inciting and assisting riots to selective or nonselective assassination, massacres, all forms of terror, sabotage on all levels of civilian activity and all phases of production, and the support of industrial strikes and slowdowns.

There are also nonviolent techniques aimed at separating the enemy in power from the population. This can be done by applying psychological warfare in both directions, that is, molding the hostile attitudes in the population, and creating self-doubts by disrupting images within the ranks of the enemy.

One of the most important contributions of sabotage and guerrilla units to the ultimate success of a civil war is that they catalyze the application of nonselective counterterror by the enemy. The dynamics of this process are quite simple. Even in the beginning phase of organizational development, during which nonselective terror is spontaneously applied by initial and rudimentary elements of resistance movements, the government delegates its security organs to restore order and prevent repetition of terrorist acts. As a rule the security organs (usually police in conjunction with counterinsurgency military units) apply pressure to the population from which, obviously, the logistic support and manpower for guerrilla and sabotage units come. Such pressure can be applied by controlling the movements of population or through other nonviolent means, including supervised hamlets and resettlement. What occurs more often, however, is counterterror in which the counterinsurgency forces, frustrated as they usually are with their inability to pin down guerrillas and saboteurs, in one way or another vent their frustration through violence on the population. If and when counterterror commences, the long-range result is that the population recoils against the counterinsurgency forces, and either from the fear of repression, or for revenge, joins and augments the guerrilla forces. Thus begins a chain reaction ultimately working to the benefit of those who initiated the terror—the guerrillas.

The impact upon the participants. Mass participation in violence has a conditioning effect upon the participants and also upon the operational values of the society. Some of these effects are of particular interest to social scientists.

It can be speculated that inevitably some experiences will leave permanent scars on the personalities of participants. On the other hand, it is possible to argue that for some an opportunity for direct expression of hostility would have a therapeutic effect.

In terms of group behavior, it is recognized that a profound reorientation of the operational values of a society takes place during strife. What was previously respectable and in conformity with social mores possibly would not be in time of war. For example, an honest fulfillment of a working contract in a factory situation is expected under normal conditions. However, during civil strife it will be a newly created social virtue to slow down and to sabotage production in all possible ways. What normally would be dishonest acquires the attribute of a social virtue, if not a duty.

To this can be added an inferred expectation that when conflict has broken out, both sides are beyond the stage of accommodation in a peaceful fashion. This means that there is a mutual expectation of violence and that violence has become an expected *modus operandi*. From this attitude it is only one step to a common approval of violence as a technique of social problem solving. Under normal circumstances violence is controlled by ethical and moral norms of society. However, during civil strife such norms are, as a rule, greatly modified, resulting in common expectation of violence. Moreover, in this type of violence the original causes are quite often forgotten and the struggles become merely an opportunity for waging personal vendettas.

In terms of political analysis, two developments appear to be the traditional aftermath of civil war. First, when the insurgents are victorious and their position has become legitimate, there is already a nucleus of a counterrevolutionary force within their own ranks, potentially ready to trigger the aspirations and develop the structures of a new countermovement. There are two explanations for this paradox: (*a*) With victory comes the elaboration of the political, social, and economic program of the new elite, which obviously cannot satisfy all the latent aspirations of all the revolutionaries; and (*b*) violence has become a part of the operational code of the participants. Quite often after a successful revolution, new revolutionaries are immediately ready to repeat the whole experience. The postrevolutionary difficulties of the Ben Bella government in Algeria in 1963 and of Castro's regime in 1961 illustrate this point.

The second development (and this is particularly conspicuous when the revolutionary government has placed itself in a position of dependency upon strong supporters from abroad) is that even if the revolution is successful, the revolutionary leadership is apt to be eliminated by the foreign government which had been supporting the insurgents. In such a situation, the real purpose of the civil war and the intent of its supporters are likely to be distorted. A rule of political survival can be postulated: No revolutionary government or government-in-exile should permit itself to become politically dependent. An example is the unenviable position of the Polish government-in-exile after World War II, when the American and British governments withdrew recognition to placate the Soviet Union and disregarded the Polish leadership's choices in decisions which determined the political makeup of Poland, her frontiers, and national fate.

Further research in intrasocietal violence

Civil strife and the application of unconventional warfare has increased markedly since World War II: at least 12 countries have changed their ruling elite through civil war. In 1964 there were active resistance movements in at least 11 countries—Angola, Cambodia, Congo, Cuba, Cyprus, Guatemala, Laos, New Guinea, Republic of South Africa, Vietnam, and Yemen. In at least ten other countries one could discern symptoms of presently dormant underground movements waiting for an opportunity to initiate violence. There are two explanations for this phenomenon. Not only is there accelerated striving toward national identity in the twentieth century and resentment toward the last vestiges of colonialism, but there is also the plain fact that extralegal violence and its techniques are "cheap" in strictly economic terms. Under combat conditions the U.S. soldier uses 37 pounds of supplies per day (consisting of 6 pounds of equipment, 5 pounds of fuel and oil, 20 pounds of ammunition, and 6 pounds of miscellaneous supplies). However, for the monetary equivalent of this day's supply, volunteers, guerrillas, and saboteurs in underdeveloped countries can maintain whole units for a month.

Because civil war has become a common instrument for the allocation of political power and values, more research is needed in order to understand its dynamics. Specifically, there is not enough knowledge about catalysts, organizational development and behavior, symptoms of emergence and escalation, methods for discernment, and manipulation of the stages of formation, to name several factors.

So far the bulk of the literature on subjects related to civil war deals mainly with historical treatment of events or descriptions of personal experiences of participants. It is expected, however, that analytical works will appear in the years to come.

Revolutionary organizations are basically groups in frustration and conflict, and they could serve as laboratories for systematic inquiry into the general nature and propensity of man to apply violence in solving his problems. It is suggested that a research institute under academic auspices be established for the sole purpose of analyzing the political and organizational behavior of resistance movements, guerrillas, and subversive organizations. The focus should be on selected cultural groups in frustration and under stress. Data could be tabulated and stored in a manner permitting efficient access. Such an institute should be staffed by an interdisciplinary team of social scientists. The range of investigation could include: (1) integration of the available body of theories and empirically validated hypotheses in the social sciences bearing upon behavior of groups in frustration which apply violence; (2) development of methods and techniques for discerning the sources of tensions in other cultures from a distance; (3) psychological barriers to communication; (4) escalation of conflict on various levels; (5) decision making under stress; (6) controlling factors in human motivation with regard to cooperation; (7) the integrative process of group behavior under stress.

There is already a considerable body of research in some areas of human behavior. What is needed now is a systematic and sustained effort in collating the data to fill the gaps in knowledge and to draw conclusions concerning human behavior under specific conditions of intrasocietal and intersocietal strife. Such work would not only expand our knowledge of political behavior but would also provide empirically certified data for making policies relating to violence as an instrument of social and political change.

J. K. ZAWODNY

BIBLIOGRAPHY

AMERICAN ACADEMY OF POLITICAL AND SOCIAL SCIENCE 1962 *Unconventional Warfare.* Edited by J. K. Zawodny. Annals, Vol. 341. Philadelphia: The Academy.

BRINTON, CLARENCE CRANE (1938) 1952 *The Anatomy of Revolution.* Rev. ed. Englewood Cliffs, N.J.: Prentice-Hall.

CANETTI, ELIAS (1960) 1962 *Crowds and Power.* New York: Viking. → First published as *Masse und Macht.*

CLUTTERBUCK, RICHARD L. 1966 *The Long, Long War: Counterinsurgency in Malaya and Vietnam.* New York: Praeger.

GUTHRIE, EDWIN R. (1938) 1962 *The Psychology of Human Conflict: The Clash of Motives Within the Individual.* Gloucester, Mass.: Smith.

HOPPER, REX D. 1950 The Revolutionary Process: A Frame of Reference for the Study of Revolutionary Movements. *Social Forces* 28:270–279.

KOMOROWSKI, TADEUSZ (1950) 1951 *The Secret Army.* New York: Macmillan; London: Gollancz.

TRINQUIER, ROGER (1961) 1964 *Modern Warfare: A French View of Counterinsurgency.* New York: Praeger. → First published in French.

ZAWODNY, J. K. 1962 Unconventional Warfare. *American Scholar* 31:384–394.

ZAWODNY, J. K. 1966 *Men and International Relations: Contributions of the Social Sciences to the Study of Conflict and Integration.* 2 vols. San Francisco: Chandler.

II
GUERRILLA WARFARE

The term *guerrilla*, which means literally "small war," was originally used to define the resistance activities of armed Spanish civilians who harried the French occupation army during the Peninsular War of 1808–1814. It has come into common English usage to describe all nonregular militarylike combat that has accompanied partisan activities in civil wars, revolutionary wars, and popular resistance to foreign invasion and occupation. A guerrilla force is usually viewed as an irregular tactical adjunct or supporting arm of the professional army.

In modern times, the objectives of guerrilla warfare have been more political than military. Since the end of World War II, there have been at least ten revolutionary wars using guerrilla warfare as the principal means of violence. In most cases the revolutionary leaders have ascended to national power. Where the revolutionary wars were lost militarily, the conflict nevertheless often had the effect of influencing, if not directly initiating, political and social changes, and in several cases national independence ultimately resulted. The principles of revolutionary war and guerrilla warfare have become so enmeshed in recent times that the two seem inseparable. The most adequate descriptive term would seem to be "revolutionary guerrilla warfare." It is revolutionary in that it is used as a means of acquiring national power for the purpose of altering or completely changing the social and political structure of a nation. It is guerrilla warfare in that its participating advocates of change are indigenous civilians waging a small war utilizing principles learned from guerrilla history. The following is a brief description of the basic historical characteristics of guerrilla warfare, with emphasis on modern revolutionary manifestations. (The term "ruling power" is used below to denote the military or political governmental body that the guerrillas seek to dislodge.)

Military–political characteristics

The strategic objectives of the guerrillas are to reduce the military and political strength of the ruling power while increasing their own until the guerrilla force can be organized and trained as a regular army capable of defeating the ruling-power army on the open battlefield or causing the ruling power to collapse or otherwise surrender to revolutionary guerrilla demands, thus producing guerrilla national victory by political default.

The main tactical strength of the guerrilla fighter lies in his intimate knowledge of the local terrain and populace. Guerrilla tactics are adapted to the local social conditions, capabilities of the participating guerrillas, terrain, and strength of the ruling-power forces earmarked for attack. Guerrilla tactics consist of raids, ambushes, and sabotage. The primary targets of attack are isolated police and army outposts and units, national and military communications, transportation, and supplies, and sources of ruling-power economic revenue.

Guerrillas usually attack only when they are numerically superior, hold the tactical advantage, or are otherwise assured of success. They traditionally avoid pitched battles not of their own choosing, rapidly concentrate for an attack, rapidly disperse after an attack, and avoid concentrating in large numbers for long periods of time. They avoid providing the enemy with a target for the utilization of superior technological weaponry such as artillery, tanks, and air power. Guerrillas attack when and where the enemy is most vulnerable, planning attacks so that many occur at the same time at widely different locations, creating the impression of numerical strength greater than actual strength. The guerrilla seeks to create a special psychological effect within the ranks of the ruling power and the populace: he wants to be perceived as being everywhere yet nowhere.

Guerrillas constantly strive to maintain the offensive and seek to force the enemy to be on the defensive. Guerrilla attacks (particularly when they involve the destruction of national sources of economic revenue or disruption of lines of communication, transportation, and supply) create a paralyzing effect, restricting the mobility of the ruling-power forces and reducing their numerical superiority by causing the diversion of many troops to static protection duties and the concentration of a large proportion of the remaining forces at the places under attack. All of these tactics considerably reduce the ruling power's administrative control, thus demonstrating to the populace its inability to maintain law and order. These tactics provide the guerrillas with the time, space, and conditions necessary for them to implant their own political and economic apparatus, further insuring guerrilla strength and control of population and national resources.

Geopolitical characteristics

The types of geographic environment in which revolutionary guerrilla wars take place usually contain thick forests, mountain ranges, swamps, jungles, deserts, or a combination of these. Such areas are usually characterized by inadequate roads and by poor or absolutely no communications between the sparsely settled population clusters and the center of the ruling power. Far removed from ruling-power control, such areas provide ideal natural settings for establishment and maintenance of guerrilla base areas, sometimes referred to as redoubts or base camps.

A base area is usually located in a near-impenetrable region containing adequate natural concealment from air or ground observation and surprise attack. It is ideally suited to guerrilla foot and pack-animal mobility and insures tactical advantage in ambush or other combat operations. It provides natural obstacles to the effective utilization of the superior technological mobility and armament of the ruling power. Adequate roads would make security for a base area nearly impossible, since a ruling power can utilize modern motorized transport to encircle and disrupt the base or destroy it completely.

Base areas are essential, particularly in the early stages of revolutionary guerrilla development. Strategically, they serve as centers for the development of political and combat guerrilla elements. Without secure base areas, guerrillas are little more than armed stragglers with little or no means of control and coordination of political and military activities.

Most base areas are within the country in which the conflict is occurring, though several—often those containing the principal revolutionary guerrilla leaders, clandestine radio stations, and large hospitals—are located across the geopolitical boundaries of a contiguous country. Such locations are often referred to as friendly sanctuaries or safe havens and have had significant influence on the success of several revolutionary guerrilla wars since 1945. Neighboring foreign ruling powers separated from the countries under contention by natural land-mass borders have allowed and logistically supported such activities either when they favored the political objectives of the guerrillas or when they were obligated to another foreign ruling power that was not adjacent to the country but favored the political objectives of the guerrillas.

Such external support to guerrillas is unheralded and often publicly denied by the supporting foreign ruling power and by the revolutionary guerrillas. Both recognize the international political significance of maintaining that the conflict is indigenous. Indigenous ruling powers, faced with the knowledge that the guerrillas are being supported and given safe sanctuary by a neighboring country, are usually reluctant to violate the border sovereignty of the offending country for fear of escalating the conflict and for a host of other political and economic reasons.

When there is no contiguous land-mass border, or when the ruling power adjacent to the country does not favor the political objectives of the guerrillas, external logistical support can reach the guerrillas if there is a sea access to the country that is not adequately controlled by the ruling power. Although air supply to anti-Axis guerrilla groups was perfected by the Allied Powers during World War II, since 1945 there have been relatively few cases of external support being delivered by this method. It is difficult to keep air supply secret. The full impact of modern guerrilla operations is seldom realized until external support is attained —first logistical, then political.

Generally, external support on a large scale is not rendered until the guerrillas have established a strong political and military organization and have displayed other indications of eventual victory. This is also true when foreign powers have trained and indoctrinated indigenous groups and have returned them to their native countries to initiate a revolutionary guerrilla movement. Once the guerrillas have established a strong political organization and have wide popular support, terrain factors increasingly decline in importance, and population density becomes decisive.

Sociopolitical characteristics

Revolutionary guerrillas must establish not only physical base areas but political mass bases as well. A political mass base is a sociopolitical condition resulting when the guerrillas successfully gain the support or neutralization of the majority of the populace in given areas. While the modern guerrilla relies heavily on political and logistical support from the international foreign community, he relies most importantly, as did his historical predecessors, on the indigenous populace. Effective control of the local population is the indispensable condition of success, and guerrillas cannot operate, or even exist, for long without the active support of an enthusiastic minority, plus at least the political apathy of a significant portion of the majority. Operationally, the guerrillas carry out overt and covert actions on the basis of timely intelligence information from agents within the populace. The populace further aids the guerrillas by providing food, shelter, medical supplies and care, guides, laborers, and recruits. Most significantly, the population under guerrilla control denies the ruling-power forces information concerning the activities and locations of the guerrillas. Guerrilla operations are fought by few but depend on many. Men, women, and children of all ages participate in a variety of roles, such as fighters, couriers, intelligence agents, and food providers. In fact, guerrilla wars, and particularly revolutionary guerrilla wars, are frequently referred to as "people's wars," although, of course, never by the opposing ruling power.

The nature of guerrilla conflict, with its inherent sociopolitical subtleties, has thus far precluded the systematic application of modern social science methodology. Generally, however, available data imply that, at the outset of many modern guerrilla wars, the populace may be found to be divided into three distinct opinion groups: a minority (perhaps 20 per cent) are disposed to favor the guerrillas; a majority (perhaps 60 per cent) are completely neutral; and another minority (again 20 per cent) are actively opposed to the objectives of the guerrillas. Both the guerrillas and the ruling power compete for the support of the 60 per cent. The guerrillas' efforts are facilitated by the fact that the bulk of the population will refrain from participating actively on either side and will remain passively neutral until confident of the eventual outcome. The political apathy of the majority favors the guerrillas because the ruling power cannot enact adequate defensive or offensive measures without intelligence provided by the segment of the populace that is aware of guerrilla movements. The guerrilla force increases its support percentage and keeps the majority passively apathetic by the advocacy of an acceptable political doctrine or the identification with a popular "cause," by the use of terrorism, and by demonstrations of military victories. And these functions are all amplified and reinforced by an extensive propaganda program.

Guerrilla wars have often occurred in nations in which societal grievances are manifested by a desire for social and political change, resulting in conflict and disorganization. These grievances are often considered primary causes of revolutionary wars. The severity of conditions causing the grievances can be actual or imagined. Societal grievances can be nationalistic, e.g., foreign occupation, exploitation, or influence; political, e.g., a corrupt ruling power or a nonrepresentative political system; economic, e.g., inequitable distribution of privilege, revenue, or other sources of wealth; social, e.g., sectarian, racial, or class discrimination; or psychological, e.g., injustices and oppression. When a combination of these conditions exists, the populace often welcomes agents of change.

Guerrilla leadership often professes the desire and potential ability to remedy societal grievances and attempts to unite all of the dissatisfied elements of the populace under the guerrilla political banner in an effort to rally the support and the sympathy, as well as the neutrality, of the civil populace.

Guerrilla methods

Specific and common acts of terrorism by guerrilla, as well as ruling-power, forces are murder (assassination), kidnaping, and property destruction. Although there have been a few cases in history in which guerrillas have attempted to garner popular support or neutrality primarily by pure nonselective terrorism, guerrillas have generally attempted to keep this tactic at a minimum. Terrorism is an obvious indication of weakness, and it has proved to have short-term effectiveness. In the long run its use usually alienates essential popular support.

Guerrilla terrorism is generally "selective," that is, the targets are representatives of the ruling power, such as local government officials, uncooperative and influential village chiefs, town mayors, local police and other security forces, school teachers, and ruling-power informers. The populace itself is not immune to experiencing terrorism. Complete villages are sometimes burned to the ground. Psychologically, and in this case practically, selective violence is patterned to influence the perceivers of the violence. The assassination of one individual is intended to influence many. The burning of one village is intended to influence the attitudes and behavior of the populations of many villages.

However, guerrillas usually will not implement terrorism—selective or nonselective—until they have established a firm foothold within the population. Also, guerrillas will attempt to justify, through various psychological operations techniques, the necessity of any particular act of terrorism.

In guerrilla warfare, favorable political propaganda is at least as important as success in combat and the destruction of enemy resources. The goal of the guerrillas' psychological operations program is to solidify public and international opinion in favor of their objectives. Although specific guerrilla units are responsible for carrying out a psychological operations program, all guerrilla personnel are imbued with the importance of creating a favorable public image.

Revolutionary guerrilla leadership directs its appeals to four target audiences: rank-and-file guerrilla personnel, local populace, ruling-power personnel, and the international community. All ancient and modern means of transmission are utilized. Face-to-face communications, e.g., rumors, mobile drama groups, and lectures; and propaganda-of-the-deed, e.g., battle victories, civic action, and exemplary behavior in dealing with the populace, are the most frequent methods. Communications media ranging from clandestine radio stations to the printed word are widely used.

The combination of a natural inclination by many Western nations to favor the underdog and improved international mass communications tends to favor the guerrilla. Modern guerrillas go to great pains to prepare interesting, readable, and selected factual news releases for foreign news representatives and agencies. Such releases contain information regarding guerrilla victories, ruling-power misdeeds, and an outline of guerrilla objectives. Propaganda themes will vary according to local situations, but, in general, guerrilla themes promote the ideas that the revolutionary guerrilla cause is a just one—consequently, guerrilla victory is inevitable—and that the enemy ruling power is morally and legally unqualified to rule and has been doing so against the wishes of the majority of the populace. The continual objective of the revolutionary guerrilla is to separate the populace and the international community of nations from the ruling power morally, physically, and politically. While nonparticipant guerrilla historians have often neglected to give proper attention and analysis to the importance of psychological operations, successful guerrillas have not. [*See* PSYCHOLOGICAL WARFARE.]

In this age of potentially devastating nuclear weaponry, with the accompanying reluctance on the part of nations to release such destructive power, guerrilla and other forms of internal war may become the only forms of political violence that are internationally tolerable. Guerrilla warfare, traditionally considered to be of minor significance and useful primarily as a tactical adjunct to regular warfare, may become an entity in itself. Regular war, and even nuclear war, may indeed become a by-product of guerrilla warfare.

A perusal of a modern geopolitical map and mass media coverage readily indicates many areas of the world in which geopolitical and sociopolitical conditions exist for the application of violence by means of revolutionary guerrilla and other forms of internal war. Revolutionary guerrilla warfare, when induced or applied by revolution-inclined world powers, can become both the strategy and the tactics of political violence as a means of social and political change.

Little systematic knowledge exists about the organization, tactics, methodology, participants, escalation potential, and sociopolitical interaction dynamics of revolutionary guerrilla wars. The clandestine, subtle, and varied nature of internal war seems to defy scientific inquiry. With a few exceptions, the available literature is general, and it is often emotional and biased. The greatest confusion lies in the area of definitional terms and semantics.

The current and potential significance of the subject will require a greater use of social scientific intellectual resources. With few exceptions, social scientists have traditionally viewed guerrilla warfare as a strictly military phenomenon. The first step, then, is an acceptance by the international community of social scientists that internal wars are worthy of scientific inquiry. The second step is the application of social scientific research methodology to this laboratory of violence. The third step is to make the findings of this research available—through publications and university curricula—to the academic community and to those who frame and implement policy.

FRANKLIN MARK OSANKA

BIBLIOGRAPHY

ALMOND, GABRIEL 1947 The Resistance and the Political Parties of Western Europe. *Political Science Quarterly* 62:27–61.

AMERICAN ACADEMY OF POLITICAL AND SOCIAL SCIENCE 1962 *Unconventional Warfare.* Edited by J. K. Zawodny. Annals, Vol. 341. Philadelphia: The Academy.

BARBER, WILLARD F.; and RONNING, C. N. NEALE 1966 *Internal Security and Military Power: Counterinsurgency and Civic Action in Latin America.* Columbus: Ohio State Univ. Press.

BAYO, ALBERTO 1963 *150 Questions for a Guerrilla.* Boulder, Colo.: Panther.

CALLWELL, CHARLES E. (1896) 1906 *Small Wars: Their Principles and Practice.* 3d ed. London: H.M. Stationery Office.

CLUTTERBUCK, RICHARD L. 1966 *The Long, Long War: Counterinsurgency in Malaya and Vietnam.* New York: Praeger.

CROZIER, BRIAN 1960 *The Rebels: A Study of Post-war Insurrections.* Boston: Beacon.

DACH BERN, H. VON 1965 *Total Resistance.* Boulder, Colo.: Panther.

ECKSTEIN, HARRY (editor) 1964 *Internal War: Problems and Approaches.* New York: Free Press.

GRIVAS, GEORGE (1963) 1965 *General Grivas on Guerrilla Warfare.* New York: Praeger. → First published in Greek.

GUEVARA, ERNESTO "CHE" (1961) 1962 La guerra de guerrillas. Pages 336–375 in Franklin M. Osanka (editor), *Modern Guerrilla Warfare: Fighting Communist Guerrilla Movements, 1941–1961.* New York: Free Press.

HEILBRUNN, OTTO 1962 *Partisan Warfare.* New York: Praeger.

INTERNATIONAL CONFERENCE ON THE HISTORY OF THE RESISTANCE MOVEMENTS, SECOND, MILAN, *1961* 1964 *European Resistance Movements, 1939–45: Proceedings.* Edited by J. de Launay. New York: Macmillan.

JANOS, ANDREW C. 1963 Unconventional Warfare: Framework and Analysis. *World Politics* 15:636–646.

JOHNSON, CHALMERS A. 1962 Civilian Loyalties and Guerrilla Conflict. *World Politics* 14:646–661.

LAWRENCE, T. E. 1920 The Evolution of a Revolt. *Army Quarterly* (London) 1:55–69.

LAWRENCE, T. E. (1926) 1947 *Seven Pillars of Wisdom.* Garden City, N.Y.: Doubleday. → A paperback edition was published in 1962 by Dell.

LENIN, V. I. (1906) 1962 Partisan Warfare. Pages 65–79 in Franklin M. Osanka (editor), *Modern Guerrilla Warfare: Fighting Communist Guerrilla Movements, 1941–1961.* New York: Free Press. → First published in Russian in *Proletar'.*

LEVY, BERT (1941) 1964 *Guerrilla Warfare.* Boulder, Colo.: Panther.

MALINOWSKI, WLADYSLAW R. 1944 The Pattern of Underground Resistance. American Academy of Political and Social Science, *Annals* 232:126–133.

MAO, TSÊ-TUNG 1954–1962 *Selected Works.* 5 vols. New York: International Publishers. → See especially Volume 2.

MIKSCHE, FERDINAND O. (1950) 1951 *Secret Forces: The Technique of Underground Movements.* London: Faber.

OSANKA, FRANKLIN M. (compiler) 1962*a* Guerrilla War: A Paperback Bibliography. *Marine Corps Gazette* 46, no. 2:14–15.

OSANKA, FRANKLIN M. (editor) 1962*b* *Modern Guerrilla Warfare: Fighting Communist Guerrilla Movements, 1941–1961.* New York: Free Press. → Contains an extensive research bibliography on pages 475–508.

OSANKA, FRANKLIN M. 1964*a* Historical Procedures of Recruiting Guerrillas. *Australian Army Journal* no. 185:8–14.

OSANKA, FRANKLIN M. 1964*b* Population Control Techniques of Communist Insurgents: A Sociological Analysis. *Australian Army Journal* no. 175:11–19.

ROSENAU, JAMES N. (editor) 1964 *International Aspects of Civil Strife.* Princeton Univ. Press.

VO NGUYEN GIAP (1961) 1962 *People's War, People's Army: The Viet Công Insurrection Manual for Undeveloped Countries.* New York: Praeger.

WARMBRUNN, WERNER 1963 *The Dutch Under German Occupation, 1940–1945.* Stanford Univ. Press.

WRIGHT, GORDON 1962 Reflections on the French Resistance (1940–1944). *Political Science Quarterly* 77:336–349.

INTERNATIONAL COMMODITY AGREEMENTS

See COMMODITY AGREEMENTS, INTERNATIONAL.

INTERNATIONAL CONFLICT RESOLUTION

International conflict resolution is concerned with processes of removing tensions between states or maintaining them at levels consistent with continued peaceful pursuit by states of their goals (individual or collective). A full description of the processes of conflict resolution within a community would entail a full description of the numerous and complex kinds and degrees of the divisive and common concerns among its members. This statement acknowledges, on the one hand, that conflict and even war are by no means an abnormal part of international life (Stone 1954; Wright 1942; Boasson 1950; Singer 1949; Boulding 1962; International Sociological Association 1957). It has been calculated that only 270 years of the 3,500 years known to history have been free of wars. On the other hand, we should not go so far as to identify "international politics" wholly with "oppositional" relations of groups (Wright 1955, p. 131). Charles Boasson correctly says that such identification does not sufficiently take into account the role of accommodation and renunciation, the influence of norms of legal and ethical judgment, and the impact of the appeal to justice (Boasson 1963, pp. 77–78; Stone 1965). The cooperative aspect is stressed by Ernst Haas, who re-explored the prospects of contemporary international "functionalism" in the face of varied and changing types of national societies and the future international environment [*see* INTERNATIONAL INTEGRATION; Haas 1964], and by John Burton, who offered the thesis that the use of power is steadily yielding place to cooperative measures even in oppositional relations between states pursuing only their own, independent, "nonaligned," interests in regional and functional arrangements (1965).

The study of international conflict resolution cannot be reduced to a detailed study of decision making, even if we could obtain all the information, perceptions, interpretations, and alternative choices available to decision makers (Snyder et al. 1954; and for a more diffuse project for guiding decision makers, see McDougal 1953). Decisions *are* often deeply relevant to conflict, but such decisions are only part of the context and content of a conflict and its resolution. Detailed decision-making studies have two serious drawbacks: they entail endless and often fruitless piling up of detail, and they may lose sight of important factors by concentrating on *reported* or *knowable decisions.* The full constellation of circumstances that constitutes an international conflict is operative even if decision makers do not act and are not aware of all the circumstances. To count such inaction and unawareness as being themselves decisions would, of course, only fictionalize the whole approach (Boasson 1963, pp. 22–35, 75–77).

It is an undoubted gain that since World War I the study of international conflict and its resolution has moved out of the general monopoly of the historian (Boasson 1963, pp. 43–49) and away from the specialized, technical concerns of the international lawyer and publicist (Stone 1954, introduction; Stone 1956; Boasson 1963, pp. 50–59). There is now a *Journal of Conflict Resolution*, and teaching and research in this area are widespread, especially in the United States. Notable experiments in methodology are also proceeding. A project of the Carnegie Endowment for International Peace sought to identify conflicts and the phases through which they pass, with relation to rise and fall of tension and violent or nonviolent resolution. At the important Center for Research in Conflict Resolution at the University of Michigan, Kenneth Boulding has essayed a systematic study of conflict as a general social process and of international conflict within this framework (1962, pp. 227–276, 304–343). Robert North at Stanford University is seeking, with the aid of computers, to identify, from the myriad of factors constituting the constellation of circumstances of past international crises, those factors that are generally significant in interpreting and handling such crises. Relevant work has also been done by biologists on animal conflicts and by psychologists and sociologists on individual and group behavior (e.g., Freud 1915–1933; West 1949; Scott 1958). These approaches, whatever they may add to knowledge, have scarcely revolutionized the handling of international conflict. But awareness of intractability even to specialized research may in itself promote patience and restraint on action that would be a positive factor in conflict resolution.

The purpose of this article is to identify and describe some of the approaches to resolution of conflict between states that have become institutionalized, or at any rate nominate. Specifically, this encompases the wide range of approaches between war and international sanctions, at one extreme, and mere negotiation, at the other, and includes good offices, mediation, commissions of enquiry, and arbitration [*see* ADJUDICATION].

In municipal society we naturally think of process of law as a mandatory frame for handling major disputes. And despite the comparative weakness of international law, conflict resolution cannot neglect this. Yet, the international legal frame is not only weaker; it seems to rest on a base diametrically opposed to the municipal. There subjection to binding third-party judgment is considered normal, while international law starts from the point that a state is not, save by its own consent, subject to any third-party decision (or even the less peremptory "good offices" or mediation). Though each state remains its own judge, this gives it no competence over another state; for every other state also enjoys the same prerogative. It takes two to make a quarrel; and it also takes both disputants to confer international competence.

A simple corollary to this is that each disputant is also at liberty to give effect to its own determination of its own rights. Although this liberty has been restrained by various international instruments such as the Kellogg–Briand Pact and the League of Nations Covenant (now replaced by the United Nations Charter), the *extent* of the restraints remains debated and problematical. The inhibitions on the major use of force between states are today not primarily legal but factual and psychological, springing from the distribution of economic and technological power and from the universal implications of the resort to nuclear weapons. Bargaining and positional maneuvering take place within an essentially military arena, whatever the final, correct legal interpretation. The contemporary problems connected with the resort to force by major powers, which face us *as a matter of fact*, are largely a continuation of those that faced the pre-1914 world *as a matter of both law and fact* (Stone 1958; 1961).

Good offices and mediation

Good offices and mediation are special forms of negotiation in which a third party plays a role (Nicolson 1954; Forgac 1937; Stone 1954, pp. 68–72). It is indicative of the comparatively recent growth and primitive nature of international arrangements for conflict resolution that even good offices is so highly valued as a method. For its import is only to restore communication and negotiation between disputants and perhaps induce some restraint in that communication; there is no obligation of the parties to go further. Its most famous success occurred when President Theodore Roosevelt's approach to the belligerents helped to end the Russo–Japanese War in 1905; and its most abject failure, when President Franklin D. Roosevelt's efforts in 1939 to stop the outbreak of World War II were unavailing. The central negative feature of good offices is that its function does not extend even to expressing opinions on the merits, much less to any decision making. These functions are extremely modest, each party maintaining (as the Palestine and Kashmir and other contemporary cases have painfully shown) both the right of final decision and that of deciding whether negotiation (with or without mediation) is to proceed at all. Such legal rules as exist for both good offices and mediation are mainly concerned with legitimizing these mild, third-party intrusions into other states' quarrels.

It was still thought necessary in the first Hague Peace Conference, in 1899, to declare that the offer of such services was not an "unfriendly act." And after two generations of struggle for more effective and peremptory procedures through the League of Nations and the United Nations, these tentative prenegotiation procedures still play an important role in conflict resolution.

Mediation differs from good offices mainly in the degree of noncoercive initiative permitted to the third party. The mediator, once he is invited to act, is free not only to transmit but also to initiate suggestions for solution (Wehberg 1958). However, the terms "good offices" and "mediation" are sometimes loosely used, without consistent distinction, especially in the United Nations; and the term "conciliation" (which has no *technical* meaning) also is often used interchangeably with "mediation" (Stone 1965, p. 71).

Fact finding. Success in any of these procedures being manifest in agreement, not decision, the merits of the dispute as to fact or law may never emerge at all. It is notorious that disputants see facts their own way, and this is especially true of states, which are often better able to conceal the evidence than are individuals. State resistance to third-party intrusion has always extended with particular jealousy to third-party fact finding, even when this is merely advisory. Not surprisingly, therefore, institutionalization of procedures of international fact finding is almost as recent as that of international adjudication.

International commissions of enquiry were provided for by the Hague Convention of 1899, which established a legal frame within which a commission could, by agreement of the parties, be appointed to find facts on a particular dispute. Such commissions proved useful in several instances, mostly naval incidents, of which the best known was the Anglo–Russian dispute concerning the Dogger Bank incident during the Russo–Japanese War. Both the League of Nations and the United Nations adapted this kind of technique to their own organizational arrangements, the former exploiting it particularly well as a means of procrastination and persuasion.

Alongside the scarcely inhibited powers of the United Nations Security Council to make binding decisions in conflicts involving threats to the peace or breaches of the peace, these traditional procedures seem puny and timid. The League of Nations and its successor, by collectivizing even the mild, traditional procedures, greatly developed and strengthened them (Conwell-Evans 1929; Walters 1952; Stone 1954, pp. 165–176). The United Nations, however, has been much hampered in these efforts by the steady voting alignments in the present bipolar political situation (Stone 1958, pp. 165–183; Morgenthau 1946; Claude 1958).

Peoples in crisis have always built stereotypes of themselves and their adversaries and molded the issues to the stereotypes. This, however, is greatly intensified today, when stereotyped attitudes are spread, often deliberately and with the blessing of state authorities, through all the channels of mass communication in advance of the particular crisis. These stereotypes stand ever ready to determine what version of each future dispute shall receive national credence, so that even when the conflict-initiating state has itself invited the impartial inquiry, the "facts," as rationally found, often labor in vain to penetrate the national version. Thus, as the need for processes of really impartial fact finding increases, the difficulties of even this modest objective increase even more. Numerous specific conflicts illustrate these difficulties, but they appear most significantly in the problem of fact finding by an international organ acceptable to the two major antagonists as part of the inspection system in a world nuclear-disarmament plan. Each side has been stereotyped for the other as headed by cliques bent on world domination by treachery or force. The issues for the impartial organ involve survival for each side, and there is a lack of third parties who, on such issues, stand sufficiently above the suspicion that they are sympathetic to or intimidated by one side or the other to be trusted by both. Successful establishment of an organ with such functions would be a sign that the survival crisis is over and not just a first step toward meeting it.

"Internationalist" effort since World War I has not always respected these realities. Impatience with the weak diplomatic methods caused blueprints for more "modern" machinery to be created. Under the League of Nations the response to the ambitious General Act for Pacific Settlement of 1928 was poor. But the response of United Nations members to the proposed revision of this Act in 1949 was even more discouraging. Indeed, though each Part of the Act may be accepted separately, even Part I, on conciliation, has not been accepted by a single communist state or by any new Asian state. Disappointment of hopes for stronger measures has stimulated some interest in the possibilities of improving mediation techniques. The matter has, for example, been among the projects of the Institut de Droit International and the United Nations Educational, Scientific and Cultural Organization (Rolin 1959; Jessup 1956; Efremov 1927; Hill 1932; Revel 1931; Jackson 1952; "Techniques of Mediation . . ." 1958; Douglas 1957).

The discussion has centered on the degree to which the mediation process could benefit from (1) being stylized and (2) permitting the mediator to make tentative, nonbinding kinds of third-party findings. Unfortunately, it has not been possible to escape the fact that mediation is valued by states precisely because of its informal, nonstylized nature, treating each case as unique, and because it affords means of catharsis and of frank exchange through the mediator. Reforms, which raise fears that concessions or admissions in the course of this exchange may be used against one party if the conciliation finally fails, frustrate the whole function of mediation.

Another question of wide sociological interest concerns the difficulty of expanding knowledge of such informal procedures. How far and in what detail should reports of conciliation procedures be made available for juristic, political, and sociological study? The problem is that the needs of efficient handling of the *particular* dispute are at odds with those of the accumulation and transmission of knowledge and experience for understanding interstate conflicts *generally*. As with "secret diplomacy," the data for full scholarly evaluation may be rendered unavailable by the preconditions of success in the activity to be evaluated.

Arbitration

Even in modern times, when the binding force of arbitral decision is normally assured by the inclusion of at least one independent member in the tribunal, the parties to a dispute still maintain a quadruple control over the arbitral process (Ralston 1929; Johnson 1953; Stone 1954, pp. 73–105; Carlston 1946; Hudson 1944; United Nations . . . 1949). They control, first, the preliminary decision as to whether a dispute is to be submitted. They control, second, the selection of the arbitrators. They can control, third, the rules to be applied. Finally, even after the award, they have a certain indirect control over its effect, since under international law an award is null if induced by fraud or made without jurisdiction or based on "essential error" leading to "manifest injustice." Since no tribunal has jurisdiction to determine a claim of nullity, the effect is that the claimant can block further clarification.

The International Law Commission, through its Draft Convention on Arbitral Procedure of 1953, proposed to mitigate these weaknesses by designating organs or persons, such as the International Court or its president, to act in certain of these and other situations. This has received regrettably small support from United Nations members. In any case, however, as the Netherlands government pointed out, states would remain free, even under the draft, not to enter at all into agreements to arbitrate. The effect of depriving them of escapes by tightening up the law might merely reduce the number and range of submissions. No mere verbal prescriptions can alter the fact that the disputant's freedom not to submit is the master control, as it is also the master blockage to proposals for general submission.

While these weaknesses dampen intemperate hopes of assuring peace by general arbitration, they should not lead us to underrate the actual, if modest, role of arbitration in conflict resolution. Between the Jay Treaty of 1794 (providing for third-party settlement of Anglo–American disputes in the aftermath of the War of Independence) and the end of the nineteenth century there were 238 individual formal arbitrations. In addition, since 1794 more than sixty standing (though temporary) tribunals have disposed of great categories of claims that were referred to them by the pairs of states concerned. This kind of settlement is, in effect, comparable to the business of regular municipal courts (Stone 1954, pp. 86, 97, bibliography). Arbitration has made a great contribution to the quieting of claims after great wars and as an ancillary to the modern growth of international administration.

The Permanent Court of Arbitration—consisting of a regular framework within which states desiring to arbitrate could select arbitrators from a standing panel, with related permanent registry services—was established by the first Hague conference, and well over twenty of its tribunals have functioned (François 1955; Stone 1954). It is true that despite its name this was neither permanent nor a court, and more than sixty years after its establishment and after more than a century and a half of modern arbitration, chronic weaknesses still persist and only a handful of persons fully experienced in dispute handling has ever emerged.

Without pinning excessive hopes on general compulsory arbitration as a recipe against war, we can distinguish at least four kinds of legal submission by states that must be far more developed and generalized before any hopes can materialize.

(1) *Ad-hoc submission of particular existing conflicts of known and determinate range.* The essence of distinguishing these as a class is that they are cases (for example, those concerning compensation to be paid for the requisition by a state of foreign ships) where both sides know pretty well the factual and legal limits within which their rights will be put at stake by subjection to third-party decision.

(2) *Ad-hoc submission of existing conflicts of indeterminate but noncritical range.* Interests at stake in a conflict, though factually or legally indeterminate, may still be seen by a state as noncritical to its safety or prosperity. The very fact that a dispute has fully matured usually allows at least the outer limits of risk to be seen. The Anglo–American dispute surrounding the *Alabama* case, arising from British recognition of the belligerency of the Confederate states in the American Civil War and submitted to arbitration by the Treaty of Washington in 1871, is a good example. During the Civil War itself, the dispute became almost a *casus belli;* afterward, submission by the parties still imported a vastly greater abnegation of state liberty of action than is involved under category (1) above, because of the uncertainties touching law and facts and, therefore, the range of liability. But the outer range was clear enough to settle this *cause célèbre*, and the case is a major landmark in international arbitration.

(3) *General submission of carefully delimited classes of future minor conflicts.* Submission of a class of *future* disputes is a distinct phase, with its own subphases. The element of futurity always affects the limits of commitment, for a state cannot know in advance the precise range of its exposure on disputes that have not yet arisen. Submission here can still be restrained at various levels, however, by careful delimitation of the class of disputes involved. The commonest examples are compromissory clauses attached to and covering the range of commercial treaties, treaties of consular rights, and technical treaties of many kinds.

(4) *Submission of future conflicts without close delimitation but with reservation of indeterminate classes of conflicts, the range of the reservation being self-determined by each party in each conflict.* When, under pressure of internationalist sentiment, states have seemed to overcome their resistance to broad submissions, the resulting submissory clauses, when closely examined, revealed other limiting devices. The most famous of these, popular before World War I, was the overriding reservation known as the "vital interests, honor, and independence" clause. This formulation served to pay lip service to the pressure of opinion, while giving little away in a legal, political, or otherwise substantial sense. Its mood was natural enough in treaties like the one that established the Anglo–French Entente Cordiale. It was a model also, however, for more sober peaceful settlement undertakings, such as the United States–United Kingdom treaty of 1908. The reservation tended, in overcompensation for the extent of submission, to be drawn so widely as to be virtually subjective in application. By tragic irony, excessive zeal resulted in illusory gains and actual backsliding.

Third-party decision making *could* become determinative for war prevention *only if* states were prepared to expose in advance even the gravest interest that would be affected by future conflicts. It is such a postulated (rather than experienced) phase of international arbitration that is taken as an ideal model by most of those who press for "the rule of law among nations" as an achievable alternative to "the balance of terror." Much of this undue sanguineness arises from failure to make distinctions such as those just sketched.

In fact, it is difficult to find even unsuccessful modern instances of such submission of future conflicts unqualified as to the interests at stake. The arbitration provisions of the Locarno treaties after World War I, as part of an attempt to prevent a renewal of Franco–German struggles on France's eastern frontiers by a regional security system guaranteed by neighboring states, contained no vital-interests reservation, but they still excluded nonjusticiable disputes from the obligation to arbitrate (Stone 1954, pp. 79–81). And the United Kingdom in 1939 showed considerable agitation when it realized that its advance submission to the jurisdiction of the Permanent Court of International Justice might have been made in terms broad enough to challenge positions concerning belligerent naval rights that Britain regarded as basic. The submission was withdrawn and suitably replaced at the earliest opportunity.

Justiciability and conflict resolution

A good deal of fruitless controversy in the vast literature produced since World War I arises from the ambiguity of the word "justiciable," especially when we take it out of its historical–international context. It is often understood, for example, to refer merely to the question whether, *assuming the parties are willing* to accept binding third-party decision, a tribunal could offer some kind of solution. This really makes the problem of justiciability disappear altogether. For the hard core of that problem lies not in the difficulty of getting a third party to propose some solution or other, but in getting the states in conflict to invite him to do so and in his then finding a solution that will settle the real issues about which they are in conflict (Stone 1961, pp. 18–21). What is involved here transcends the concerns of the technical lawyer; for, of course, the so-called nonjusticiable problems tend to be the very ones that threaten to provoke wars.

The chronic and festering East–West conflict concerning Berlin after World War II, for example, could no doubt be reduced to a series of legal questions eminently suitable for adjudication by the International Court. Some of these would be: What is the extent of any obligation of the Soviet Union to permit traffic of German personnel and goods between the Federal Republic of Germany and West Berlin under the Jessup–Malik talks of 1949? What limits, if any, are there to the Soviet obligation to permit Allied military rail, motor, or air communications between West Germany and West Berlin? And there would also be many legal subquestions. Yet, when all such questions had been answered by a tribunal, the resolution of the conflict would not necessarily have been advanced. For the concerns that have brought about and maintain this conflict really have little to do with such questions (Stone 1954, pp. 146–152; Bloomfield 1958; Wengler 1956; Boasson 1950). The reasons why this and the numerous similar contemporary conflicts endanger peace are for the most part the very reasons they are said to be nonjusticiable.

The problem of justiciability shows itself, first, in the case of a simple refusal of the parties in conflict to submit to any third-party determination. Before such submission, the question has no technical legal import, and justiciability is then a mere policy issue between those favoring and those opposing submission.

The question whether a dispute is justiciable may also arise as a technical legal question. This happens in cases where there has been an apparently relevant submission of a class of future conflicts, the class being delimited in the instrument of submission to exclude conflicts that are "nonjusticiable" (sometimes called "political") or to include only those that are "justiciable" (sometimes called "legal"). There is, moreover, no magic in these literal words. The distinction in the General Act of 1928 is in terms of "legal" and "nonlegal"; and when states agree under the "optional clause" of article 36(2) of the Statute of the International Court of Justice to submit to the court the categories of disputes there enumerated, the whole enumeration is qualified by the problematic words, "legal disputes concerning." There is, moreover, a view that some treaty obligations, for instance to join another party in war, are *in their nature* political, or nonjusticiable, in the sense that each party must determine for itself whether the obligation has matured.

Clearly, under the older "vital interests, honor, and independence" reservations formula, the determination of whether the issue was justiciable was subjective to each party in conflict. This probably remains so whenever the question of justiciability in the present sense arises, unless a state's submission or the constitution of a standing tribunal to which the matter is submitted makes the contrary clear (Stone 1958, p. 32). The effect is to allow the state concerned, if it chooses to be arbitrary (and face any moral disapproval entailed), to escape altogether its obligation to submit to arbitration. Indeed, advocates of extended arbitration have used this as a point of cogent logical attack upon the notion that there are disputes that can be nonjusticiable. Unfortunately, the basic weaknesses of the international legal order, from which this notion continues to draw its force, are such hard empirical facts that, although they can be exposed, they cannot be removed by logic.

The term "nonjusticiable" (and its synonyms such as "political"), as used above, refers to the gravity of the interests involved in a conflict, which the states concerned regard as preventing their submission to adjustment by third parties. It can also mean that the applicable legal rules are unjust and should be changed (Clark & Sohn 1958, art. 36; Stone 1956, pp. 165–177) or that no applicable rules can be found (*non liquet*) (Lauterpacht 1930; Stone 1954, pp. 152–164).

Unilateral settlement procedures

Experience has belied the wishful view that the veto in the United Nations Security Council was merely an ephemeral exception to a general movement toward giving the power of making binding majority decisions to organs concerned with conflict resolution (Stone 1954, pp. 185–186). Indeed, in the contemporary period, marked as it is by conflicts of both the old, bilateral and the new, bloc-ideological types and by dispersed but deep tensions of the thermonuclear balance of terror, the veto may have won a new and resurgent role in the handling of conflict. Disdain for the weak negotiatory procedures discussed earlier and denunciations of the veto in the Security Council have certainly faded. And there has come at least a grudging recognition of the value of predesigned, agreed methods of processing conflicts, even when each party remains legally free to the end to veto any emergent decision. For it is increasingly evident that where a strong state is convinced that its vital interests are involved, the legal veto is unlikely to be decisive, since that state will, in any case, have a *de facto* veto.

Related to this is also the increased awareness that to press on with hopelessly blocked negotiations is not necessarily better than ending them.

Repeated confrontation of irreconcilable antagonisms can itself maintain or even increase tension, so that mutual withdrawal may be a positive step toward relaxation. Furthermore, persistence in hopeless negotiation at such a stage may deter or discourage exploration of "weaker" but more promising recourses. It is with the fading out, rather than the reinvigoration, of East–West disarmament negotiations that certain limited advances have come to be made by parallel unilateral steps. The United States and the Soviet Union took carefully synchronized, yet not mutually dependent, measures to reduce their armed forces and stockpiles of nuclear materials. In relation to this, as well as other contemporary conflicts, approaches through unilateral de-escalation, or "graduated and reciprocated initiatives in tension reduction," are in important part applications of the general principle here under discussion (Osgood 1965).

Such parallel but studiously independent action leaves each party free to reverse its unilateral stance at any moment without formality or embarrassment. It permits a kind of prenatal veto, allowing each side to abort, if it wishes, the design behind the parallel action; and it may be the assurance of this "veto" that makes the states concerned willing to go further in fact than in law. Negotiators about commitments for the future must bring into speculative assessment contingencies in which the obligations contemplated would conceivably be dangerous. Such contingencies, contemplation of which would have produced an impasse in negotiation, *may in fact, however, never occur*. Therefore, when both parties turn from negotiation to act unilaterally and without commitment on matters and in ways that they failed to agree about in negotiation, the objective of the negotiations may in fact be furthered by the very recognition of their failure. Unilateralism, in certain situations, has its virtues for conflict resolution.

It is perhaps not too fanciful to carry this line of analysis somewhat further. Amid dreams of somehow replacing the "balance of terror" by "the rule of law among nations," the cluster of problems to which the "hot line" agreement is directed is a nightmarish intrusion. For those who proposed or implemented the idea of the "hot line," however, the assurance of adequate channels of communication right up to the last moment of possibly catastrophic crisis is, in the existing world, a critical pillar supporting in a diffuse way all the potential means of conflict resolution. The "hot line" does not ensure negotiation, much less agreement, on substantive conflict issues, but failure to assure the means of communication in crisis may certainly bar even the possibility of negotiation. Still more important is the tempering effect of the assurance that channels will remain open during intervening postures and when there is a growth of tensions. Insofar as there is reality in the notion that the nuclear giants have a common interest in survival, the "hot line" will allow this interest to operate at the moment of greatest need. Although neither of the great nuclear powers could have agreed to bind itself legally to give the other notice of an imminent danger of war, the "hot line" allows them to move together in that direction.

Coercive procedures short of war

The nominate coercive procedures, short of war, are severance of diplomatic relations, retortion, reprisal, embargo, boycott, and pacific blockade, most of which are affected by the problems surrounding prohibition of the use or threat of force [*see* SANCTIONS, INTERNATIONAL]. Along with war, these are methods of settling disputes only in the sense that in a society where common conviction is lacking and machinery of law enforcement is weak, self-help by the aggrieved party may be the only means of "settling" them. They hover disconsolately on the Stygian waters which divide the imperfectly held terrain of international law from the uncontrolled terrain of extralegal anarchy, and in which the customarily licensed choice between war and peace still holds some sway. The United States "quarantine" of Cuba in 1962 made clear that whatever the correct answer to the legal problematics, coercive methods short of war still have their role to play.

Indeed, tolerance of certain limited coercive measures may have special significance for an age that can neither banish international conflict nor afford solutions by nuclear war. There is need to rethink the whole question of coercions short of war, juxtaposing them not with an image of a world wishfully postulated as free of *all* force, but with the harsh actuality of international conflict that still takes place within an essentially military arena.

JULIUS STONE

[*See also* ADJUDICATION, *article on* INTERNATIONAL ADJUDICATION; CONFLICT; INTERNATIONAL INTEGRATION; INTERNATIONAL LAW; INTERNATIONAL ORGANIZATION; PEACE; WAR.]

BIBLIOGRAPHY

BLOOMFIELD, LINCOLN 1958 Law, Politics and International Disputes. *International Conciliation* Whole no. 516.

BOASSON, CHARLES 1950 *Sociological Aspects of Law and International Adjustment*. Amsterdam: North-Holland Publishing.

BOASSON, CHARLES 1963 *Approaches to the Study of International Relations.* Assen (Netherlands): Van Gorcum.

BOULDING, KENNETH E. 1962 *Conflict and Defense: A General Theory.* A publication of the Center for Research in Conflict Resolution at the University of Michigan. New York: Harper.

BURTON, JOHN W. 1965 *International Relations: A General Theory.* Cambridge Univ. Press.

CARLSTON, KENNETH S. 1946 *The Process of International Arbitration.* New York: Columbia Univ. Press.

CLARK, GRENVILLE; and SOHN, LOUIS B. (1958) 1960 *World Peace Through World Law.* 2d ed., rev. Cambridge, Mass.: Harvard Univ. Press.

CLAUDE, INIS L. JR. 1958 Multilateralism: Diplomatic and Otherwise. *International Organization* 12:43–52.

CONWELL-EVANS, THOMAS P. 1929 *The League Council in Action: A Study of the Methods Employed by the Council of the League of Nations to Prevent War and to Settle International Disputes.* Oxford Univ. Press.

DOUGLAS, ANN 1957 The Peaceful Settlement of Industrial and Intergroup Disputes. *Journal of Conflict Resolution* 1:69–81.

EFREMOV, IVAN 1927 La conciliation internationale. The Hague, Academy of International Law, *Recueil des cours* 18:1–148.

FORGAC, ALBERT A. (1937) 1950 *Essai sur la diplomatie nouvelle.* New ed., rev. Paris: Pedone.

FRANÇOIS, J. P. A. 1955 La Cour Permanente d'Arbitrage: Son origine, sa jurisprudence, son avenir. The Hague, Academy of International Law, *Recueil des cours* 87:457–553.

FREUD, SIGMUND (1915–1933) 1939 *Civilization, War and Death.* Selections from three works by Sigmund Freud, edited by John Rickman. London: Hogarth. → The three works are "Thoughts for the Times on War and Death"; "Civilization and Its Discontents"; and "Why War?"

HAAS, ERNST B. 1964 *Beyond the Nation-state: Functionalism and International Organization.* Stanford Univ. Press.

HAGUE, PERMANENT COURT OF ARBITRATION 1916–1932 *The Hague Court Reports.* 2 vols. Edited by James Brown Scott. New York: Oxford Univ. Press.

HAGUE, PERMANENT COURT OF ARBITRATION 1934 *Analyses des sentences rendues . . . : 1899–1934.* The Hague: Bureau International de la Cour Permanente d'Arbitrage.

HETTE, JEAN G. P. 1934 *L'évolution de la conciliation internationale.* Paris: Muller.

HILL, NORMAN L. 1932 International Commissions of Inquiry and Conciliation. *International Conciliation* Whole no. 278.

HUDSON, MANLEY O. 1944 *International Tribunals: Past and Future.* Washington: Brookings Institution.

INTERNATIONAL SOCIOLOGICAL ASSOCIATION 1957 *The Nature of Conflict: Studies on the Sociological Aspects of International Tensions.* Paris: UNESCO.

JACKSON, ELMORE 1952 *Meeting of Minds: A Way to Peace Through Mediation.* New York: McGraw-Hill.

JESSUP, PHILIP C. 1956 Parliamentary Diplomacy: An Examination of the Legal Quality of the Rules of Procedure of Organs of the United Nations. The Hague, Academy of International Law, *Recueil des cours* 89:181–320.

JOHNSON, D. H. 1953 The Constitution of an Arbitral Tribunal. *British Year Book of International Law* 30: 152–177.

LAUTERPACHT, H. 1930 La théorie des différends non justifiables en droit international. The Hague, Academy of International Law, *Recueil des cours* 34:493–654.

McDOUGAL, MYRES S. 1953 International Law, Power and Policy: A Contemporary Conception. The Hague, Academy of International Law, *Recueil des cours* 82: 133–259.

MOORE, JOHN B. 1898 *History and Digest of the International Arbitrations to Which the United States Has Been a Party.* 6 vols. Washington: Government Printing Office.

MOORE, JOHN B. (editor) 1929–1933 *International Adjudications: Ancient and Modern.* 6 vols. New York: Oxford Univ. Press.

MORGENTHAU, HANS J. 1946 Diplomacy. *Yale Law Journal* 55:1067–1080.

MYERS, DENYS P. (1911) 1915 *Arbitration Engagements Now Existing in Treaties, Treaty Provisions and National Constitutions.* World Peace Foundation Pamphlet Series, Vol. 5, no. 5, part 3. Boston: The Foundation. → First published as *List of Arbitration Treaties.*

NICOLSON, HAROLD 1954 *The Evolution of the Diplomatic Method.* London: Constable.

OSGOOD, CHARLES E. 1965 *Perspective in Foreign Policy.* Urbana, Ill.: Privately published.

RALSTON, JACKSON H. 1929 *International Arbitration: From Athens to Locarno.* Stanford Univ. Press; Oxford Univ. Press.

REVEL, G. 1931 Rôle et caractère des commissions de conciliation. *Revue générale de droit international public* 38:564–607.

ROLIN, HENRI 1959 La conciliation internationale (Trentième Commission) rapport définitif. Institute of International Law, *Annuaire de l'Institut de Droit International* 48, no. 1:5–130.

SCOTT, JOHN P. 1958 *Aggression.* Univ. of Chicago Press.

SINGER, KURT 1949 *The Idea of Conflict.* Melbourne Univ. Press.

SNYDER, RICHARD C.; BRUCK, H. W.; and SAPIN, BURTON 1954 *Decision-making as an Approach to the Study of International Politics.* Princeton Univ., Organizational Behavior Section.

STONE, JULIUS (1954) 1959 *Legal Controls of International Conflict: A Treatise on the Dynamics of Disputes- and War-law.* Rev. ed. New York: Rinehart. → Includes a supplement for 1953–1958.

STONE, JULIUS 1956 Problems Confronting Sociological Enquiries Concerning International Law. The Hague, Academy of International Law, *Recueil des cours* 89: 61–180.

STONE, JULIUS 1958 *Aggression and World Order: A Critique of United Nations Theories of Aggression.* Berkeley: Univ. of California Press.

STONE, JULIUS 1961 *Quest for Survival: The Role of Law and Foreign Policy.* Cambridge, Mass.: Harvard Univ. Press.

STONE, JULIUS 1965 *Human Law and Human Justice.* Stanford Univ. Press.

STONE, JULIUS 1966 *Social Dimensions of Law and Justice.* Stanford Univ. Press.

Techniques of Mediation and Conciliation. 1958 *International Social Science Bulletin* 10:507–628. → Contains an essay entitled "Mediation and Conciliation in International Law," by Elmore Jackson.

UNITED NATIONS, SECRETARIAT 1949 *Systematic Survey of Treaties for the Pacific Settlement of International Disputes: 1928–1948.* Lake Success, N.Y.: United Nations.

VISSCHER, CHARLES DE (1953) 1957 *Theory and Reality in Public International Law.* Princeton Univ. Press. → First published in French.

WALTERS, FRANCIS P. (1952) 1960 *A History of the League of Nations.* Oxford Univ. Press.

WEHBERG, HANS 1958 Die Vergleichskommissionen im modernen Völkerrecht. *Zeitschrift für ausländisches öffentliches Recht und Völkerrecht* 19:551–593.

WENGLER, WILHELM 1956 *Der Begriff des Politischen im internationalen Recht.* Tübingen (Germany): Mohr.

WEST, RANYARD 1949 A Plea for a Rational Approach to the Problem of War and Peace. *University of Chicago Law Review* 16:390–396.

WRIGHT, QUINCY (1942) 1965 *A Study of War.* 2d ed. Univ. of Chicago Press.

WRIGHT, QUINCY 1955 *The Study of International Relations.* New York: Appleton.

INTERNATIONAL CRIMES

"A crime is any act or omission prohibited by public law for the protection of the public, and made punishable by the state in a judicial proceeding in its own name. It is a public wrong, as distinguished from a mere private wrong or civil injury to an individual" (Clark & Marshall [1900] 1952, p. 1). This is an authoritative definition of crime as a concept in municipal law. In any municipal law system, even a very primitive one, there is a substantial body of criminal law wherein are defined many crimes, and provision is made for legal machinery to try and to punish criminals.

Although international law in the modern sense has been in existence for over three hundred years, the states of the world have not developed a very extensive body of international criminal law. Very few crimes are defined by positive international law, and there is no permanent legal machinery for the trial of persons accused of international crimes. Still, the concept of international criminal law has been firmly established. In order to discuss the specific details of that law let us first indicate the place of international criminal law in general international law.

International law is that law which states and other international entities (e.g., international organizations, nonsovereign parties to international conflicts) create to govern their mutual relations. It is a body of law made, interpreted, enforced, and changed by its subjects rather than by a higher authority. Accordingly, the definition of international crimes and the application of sanctions against transgressors result from the interaction of states in this decentralized law-making process. No theoretical criminal code or judicial machinery which does not receive the acceptance of a working majority of states is in any sense binding international law.

International crimes must be distinguished from international delicts generally. As a corollary of their rights as sovereigns, states bear responsibility for their own acts and for acts committed within their jurisdiction which violate international law and are injurious to the rights of other states and their nationals. That this responsibility is a corporate responsibility of the state qua state was the position taken in the traditional doctrine. International crimes are those international delicts for which individuals, as distinct from states, are directly responsible under international law.

International crimes must also be distinguished from international torts. Crimes are illegal transgressions against the rights of the *public*, or the common good, and the criminal must be punished in the name of the public; torts, on the other hand, are violations of *private* rights for which the law provides a remedy. There are a great many international torts, or "denials of justice," recognized by international law. Injured individuals seek remedies for such torts through the diplomatic intercession of the state to which they owe allegiance, notably through international reclamations. But an international crime is a transgression against the whole international legal order and must be punished on behalf of that order. One important result of this distinction is that whereas remedies for international torts may be sought only by a state having personal jurisdiction over the claimant (or, as in the UN Reparations Case, by an international organization for its own personnel), any and all states have a right and duty to apprehend, try, and punish international criminals.

Finally, the punishment of international criminals must be distinguished from other sanctions of international law. It is notorious that international law is comparatively lacking in sanctions. Traditionally the principal sanction was self-help, coercion exercised both to uphold a state's rights and to deter and punish unlawful behavior. Under the right of self-help, measures that would ordinarily be illegal were justified by the need to oppose antecedent delictual conduct, either by repelling it (self-defense) or deterring and punishing it (reprisals). The right of self-help with armed force is much reduced in the modern regime with respect to recourse to force, *jus ad bellum*, and it is questionable whether armed reprisals are permissible. But in the law governing hostilities, *jus in bello*, reprisals are still permitted and they are generally considered to be the principal sanction for the law of war. International criminal law as a sanction seeks to punish the specific individuals who are guilty rather than, as is the case in most recourse to self-help, persons who only have the same nationality as the perpetrators of international delinquencies. This distinction would also be of importance in cases of enforcement of the law by the United Nations or other international organizations.

History of international criminal law

The history of international criminal law is the history of the evolution of the status of the individual in international law. The classical doctrine held that only states were "subjects" of international law, that only they were international persons possessing rights and duties directly under the law. Individuals were deemed to be "objects" of international law, which reached them only through the intermediary of states. Until individuals were recognized as possessing a degree of international personality, responsibility for their internationally delictual conduct could be attributed only to the state to which they owed allegiance. This view predominated with few exceptions until after World War I.

Piracy. The best known international crime in earlier times was piracy. In 1820, for example, Justice Story asserted:

> The common law, too, recognizes and punishes piracy as an offense, not against its own municipal code, but as an offense against the law of nations (which is part of the common law), as an offense against the universal law of society, a pirate being deemed an enemy of the human race. . . . The general practice of all nations in punishing all persons, whether natives or foreigners, who have committed this offense against any persons whatsoever, with whom they are in amity, is a conclusive proof that the offence is supposed to depend, not upon the particular provisions of any municipal code, but upon the law of nations, both for its definition and punishment. (*United States* v. *Smith* 5 Wheaton 153 in Bishop [1953] 1962, p. 266)

Thus all states had jurisdiction over pirates for the reason that such persons had committed an offense against international law. Piracy has recently been defined in the 1958 Geneva Convention on the High Seas, and it remains an international crime. According to the convention, piracy consists of any of the following acts:

> (1) Any illegal acts of violence, detention or any act of depredation committed for private ends by the crew or the passengers of a private ship or a private aircraft, and directed:
>
> (*a*) On the high seas, against another ship or aircraft, or against persons or property on board such ship or aircraft;
>
> (*b*) Against a ship, aircraft, persons or property in a place outside the jurisdiction of any state;
>
> (2) Any act of voluntary participation in the operation of a ship or of an aircraft with knowledge of the facts making it a pirate ship or aircraft;
>
> (3) Any act of inciting or of intentionally facilitating an act described in subparagraph (1) or subparagraph (2) of this article. (Bishop [1953] 1962, p. 466.)

Other crimes. The recognition of other international crimes in the pre-World War I period was not so clear-cut and emphatic. In the late eighteenth and nineteenth centuries, the slave trade was increasingly recognized as immoral and was prohibited by municipal law in many states; gradually, in a number of international agreements, it became recognized as an international crime punishable by any state. Violation of diplomatic immunity was held to be an international crime, although punishment for such violations was usually accomplished through the municipal courts of the state in which they occurred. Counterfeiting of foreign moneys or securities was considered a crime which a state must punish. Finally, individual responsibility for violations of the law of war was well established by the eighteenth century.

Three major developments after World War I greatly increased prospects for international criminal law. First, the Versailles Treaty introduced the concept of individual responsibility for war crimes and for what would today be called crimes against the peace. Even though the German kaiser escaped trial and justice was not done in the trials in municipal German courts of accused war criminals, the concept of war crimes was strengthened and broadened. Second, the German–Polish Convention relating to Upper Silesia gave major impetus to a trend toward attributing international law rights and duties directly to individuals (although the system thereby created was not in itself concerned with international crimes). Third, the League of Nations system gave birth to functional organizations which defined as international crimes engaging in white slavery, illegal narcotic and drug trade, and customs violations. In addition to these developments, the interwar period saw a marked increase in research and writing about international criminal law. One major aspect of this literature was its concern for the suppression of political terrorism which affronted the whole international legal order, such as the assassination of notables in Marseilles in 1934.

Of course, the tragic events of World War II produced a major breakthrough in this field. From the many war crimes trials, national as well as international, came an enormous body of case law. In the wake of these trials and a vast accompanying body of national executive decrees and legislation, the international law-making process produced conventions such as the Genocide Convention, the Human Rights Convention, the Geneva Conventions of 1949 and 1958, all of which contain provisions relevant to a growing but still fledgling international criminal law.

The law of Nuremberg

Virtually all of the war crimes trials after World War II have been based on the precedent set by the International Military Tribunal in its judgment of October 1, 1946. The jurisdiction of the tribunal was established by the London Agreement of August 8, 1945, and the charter annexed to that agreement. Authority for the agreement, in turn, was based upon the right of *debellatra*, that is, the right of the victorious Allies to deal with the defeated Axis powers. References to war crimes trials as "victor's justice" generally connote opprobrium, but it should be emphasized that in the absence of a higher international authority, it is, generally speaking, only when there is a victor that there can be a war crimes trial.

The indictment brought against Hermann Göring and other Nazi leaders included four counts. The first charged participation of all the accused in "a common plan or conspiracy" to commit the crimes covered by the remaining counts. Count two, "crimes against peace," charged them with having "participated in the planning, preparation, initiation and waging of wars of aggression, which were also wars in violation of international treaties, agreements and assurances. . . ." Count three, "war crimes," charged them with war crimes as defined in the charter, i.e., numerous violations of the law of war. Count four, "crimes against humanity," charged them with "violations of international conventions, of internal penal laws and of the general principles of criminal law as derived from the criminal law of all civilized nations. . . ." All but three of the accused who lived through the trial were found guilty on enough counts (usually all) to warrant the death sentence, with the exception of Rudolf Hess, who received life imprisonment (International Military Tribunal 1947–1949, vol. 1, "Indictment," pp. 27 ff., "Judgment," pp. 171 ff.).

It is fair to say that the evidence of the acts with which the accused were charged was overwhelming. If what the accused had done engendered individual criminal responsibility under international law, they were clearly criminals. But the defense objected, first, on the grounds that only states were responsible for alleged international delictual behavior and that individuals acting for a sovereign state are immune from international legal prosecution. In a ruling which goes to the heart of international criminal law, the judgment of the court found that "crimes against international law are committed by men, not by abstract entities, and only by punishing individuals who commit such crimes can the provisions of international law be enforced" (International Military Tribunal 1947–1949, vol. 1, p. 223). In this connection the court followed the provisions of the London Charter, which precluded the plea of superior orders as a bar to prosecution but admitted it as a justification to be considered "in mitigation of punishment" (International Military Tribunal 1947–1949, vol. 1, p. 223).

The second fundamental objection of the defense was that the acts set forth in the indictment were not crimes when performed and that the charges constituted ex post facto laws violative of the principle "Nullum crimen sine lege, nulla poena sine lege." Aside from the opinion of the court that this principle is not absolute, it was held that all transgressions mentioned in all of the counts were in fact recognized as crimes under positive international law at all relevant times. Although the court did not so distinguish the counts, it is necessary to analyze each one somewhat differently, insofar as the contention that they were known to be crimes by the accused is concerned (International Military Tribunal 1947–1949, vol. 1, p. 219).

It is apparent in retrospect that the count of conspiracy was primarily the work of the Englishmen and Americans participating in the trial and that it may have been overstressed. It probably does not materially alter the interpretations of the other counts except to underscore the deliberate character of the criminal acts done. The validity of count two, "crimes against peace," depends upon the contention that after 1918, when recourse to force was neither legal nor illegal but a legally neuter prerogative of all sovereign states, the international legal order developed a prescription against aggressive recourse to force. On the basis of the total fabric of international agreements directed to this end, the court found that such a prescription had been established and was well known to the accused. Count three, "war crimes," is unexceptional. As we have said, the right to punish such crimes had been recognized for a century and a half or more. Finally, count four, "crimes against humanity," is in turn somewhat different, since it really is based on the higher law concept that some things are recognized as crimes by all men and all legal systems. Failure to specify these crimes in positive international law does not prevent justified punishment for their commission.

There were many criticisms of the Nuremberg

trials of major war criminals, their counterparts the Tokyo trials, and hundreds of lesser trials held by other war crimes tribunals as well as by regularly constituted municipal courts (see the excellent series by the UN War Crimes Commission 1947–1949, which has a summary in vol. 15). But the lasting contribution of these trials to international criminal law will depend upon the acceptance, rejection, or alteration of the principles they established. In this regard, the postwar period has seen a mixture of favorable, unfavorable, and innocuous developments. On the positive side we may cite:

(1) The reaffirmation by the UN General Assembly of the principles of Nuremberg by a resolution of November 21, 1947, and, at the request of the Assembly, the preparation by the UN International Law Commission of a Draft Code of Offenses Against the Peace and Security of Mankind in 1954 based largely on the Nuremberg Judgment.

(2) The adoption by the General Assembly on December 9, 1948, of the Convention on Genocide, which entered into force January 12, 1951 (see below).

(3) The adoption by a conference in Geneva on August 12, 1949, and subsequent ratification by many states of the Convention for the Amelioration of the Condition of the Wounded and Sick in Armed Forces in the Field, of the Convention for Amelioration of the Conditions of Wounded, Sick and Shipwrecked Members of Armed Forces at Sea, and of the Convention Relative to the Treatment of Prisoners of War, all of which prohibit a number of the practices covered in counts three and four at Nuremberg, particularly in a common article III setting minimal standards of conduct, even for conflicts not of an international character.

(4) Continuation by the government of the German Federal Republic of municipal war crimes proceedings against persons within its jurisdiction.

(5) The trial and execution of Adolf Eichmann for his participation in the crime of genocide against Jews and others during World War II on the basis not of a victorious belligerent or a state having territorial jurisdiction, but of universal jurisdiction, as well as of the character of the crimes in question and their specific character as being designed to exterminate the Jewish people. Although the irregular recovery of Eichmann from Argentina by Israeli agents and some aspects of the trial have been criticized, it nevertheless constitutes an important precedent for international criminal law.

On the negative or inconclusive side we may list the following developments:

(1) Abandonment of indictments prepared for war crimes trials in the Korean War, because the absence of a "victor," the presence of large numbers of UN personnel in communist prison camps, and the resultant necessity for prisoner exchanges made prosecution of war crimes trials impossible.

(2) Prosecution of spurious "war crimes trials" by totalitarian states, notably by the communists in Korea and, with respect to their own nationals, by the Castro government in Cuba.

(3) Failure of efforts initiated by the General Assembly to create an international criminal court which would obviate the problem of victor's justice and of abuse of the concept of international criminal proceedings. The draft statute for such a court, prepared by the Committee on International Criminal Jurisdiction, was never voted upon, because the debate became interminably tied up with the question of the definition of aggression.

The Genocide Convention

Genocide is a term first used during World War II. Of all the crimes defined at Nuremberg it is the most dreadful and universally condemned. The Genocide Convention of December 9, 1948, confirms that ". . . genocide, whether committed in time of peace or in time of war, is a crime under international law which the parties to the Convention undertake to prevent and punish." Article II of the convention defines genocide as

> . . . any of the following acts committed with intent to destroy, in whole or in part, a national, ethnic, racial, or religious group as such: (a) Killing members of the group; (b) Causing serious bodily or mental harm to members of the group; (c) Deliberately inflicting on the group conditions of life calculated to bring about its physical destruction in whole or in part; (d) Imposing measures intended to prevent births within the group; (e) Forcibly transferring children of the group to another group. (Bishop [1953] 1962, p. 476)

Conspiracy, incitement, and complicity as regards genocide are also punishable under the convention. Parties to the convention are obliged to enact implementing legislation to assure punishment of persons guilty of this crime. Article VI provides that "persons charged with genocide or any of the other acts enumerated . . . shall be tried by a competent tribunal of the state in the territory of which the act was committed, or by such international penal tribunal as may have jurisdiction with respect to those contracting parties which shall have accepted its jurisdiction" (Bishop [1953] 1962, p. 476). Genocide is not considered a "political crime" for purposes of extradition (art. VII), and the parties agree to extradition of those accused of genocide in accordance with their own laws and treaties in force.

As of February 28, 1965, 67 nations had become signatories of the convention. However, no action has ever been taken under it.

Literature on international crimes

Publicists who are noted as authorities on international criminal law as such have been and remain rare. Among the pioneers who developed the field in the interwar period were Donnedieu de Vabres (whose "Le procès de Nuremberg devant les principes modernes du droit pénal international" [1947] summarizes the work of a career capped by service as a judge at Nuremberg), Pella (1930), and Sottile (1938). The post-World War II period saw an outburst of research and writing connected with all of the crimes punished at Nuremberg. Authoritative analysis of the war crimes trials is to be found in such works as those of Oppenheim ([1905–1906] 1948–1952), Bishop (1953), Stone (1954), McDougal and Feliciano (1961), Friedmann (1964), and Dahm (1958–1961). These also contain valuable assessments of the other subjects germane to international criminal law, such as human rights, genocide, and so on.

However, the apparent conviction that war crimes trials will not often be possible in contemporary conflicts has produced declining interest in this subject. It is notable that whereas the war-crimes literature in English is voluminous, English-language works on international criminal law as such are extremely rare. The subject seems to have attracted primarily Europeans and Latin Americans. Aronéanu (1961), Graven (1950), and Drost (1959), as well as García Mora (1962) and Quintano Ripollés (1952–1955), have been particularly concerned with crimes against humanity in the broad sense. But there are very few publicists like Glaser (1954) who have devoted themselves to the study of international criminal law as a comprehensive field within public international law (as distinct from comparative criminal law, about which a great deal is written).

One initiative worthy of note is that of García Mora (1962). He extends the concept of individual responsibility for crimes against the peace into the area of indirect aggression, which is of such significance in modern conflict.

International criminal law may develop in several directions. Friedmann calls attention to the "evolution of a new category of crime, which may be broadly defined as 'economic crimes,' variously defined in communist and western states, notably in West Germany" (see Friedmann 1964, p. 169). Closely related is the problem of extraterritoriality of antitrust law in an interdependent world (note particularly the pioneering work of Kronstein [1962] on this subject). Obviously, it will be difficult to gain the same kind of consensus on this category of offenses that exists in principle with respect to war crimes. Another subject requiring more attention is that of extradition, which assumes the near universality of certain offenses.

Finally, international lawyers have only begun to probe the possibilities of an international criminal law to sanction possible future disarmament and arms control agreements. If such agreements materialize, adhering states will undoubtedly be obliged to develop, to a hitherto unaccomplished degree, the concepts of the world public order and of the impermissibility of offenses against it (see especially McDougal & Feliciano 1961).

WILLIAM V. O'BRIEN

[*See also* HUMAN RIGHTS; INTERNATIONAL LAW. *Other relevant material may be found in* CRIMINAL LAW; POLITICAL JUSTICE.]

BIBLIOGRAPHY

ARONÉANU, EUGÈNE 1961 *Le crime contre l'humanité.* Paris: Dalloz.

BISHOP, WILLIAM W. (editor) (1953) 1962 *International Law Cases and Materials.* 2d ed. Boston: Little.

CLARK, WILLIAM L.; and MARSHALL, WILLIAM L. (1900) 1952 *A Treatise on the Law of Crimes.* 5th ed. Chicago: Callaghan.

DAHM, GEORG 1958–1961 *Völkerrecht.* 3 vols. Stuttgart (Germany): Kohlhammer.

DONNEDIEU DE VABRES, HENRI F. 1947 Le procès de Nuremberg devant les principes modernes du droit pénal international. The Hague, Academy of International Law, *Recueil des cours* 70:481–580.

DROST, PIETER N. 1959 *The Crime of State: Penal Protection for Fundamental Freedoms of Persons and Peoples.* 2 vols. Leiden (Netherlands): Sythoff. → Volume 1: *Humanicide: International Governmental Crime Against Individual Human Rights.* Volume 2: *Genocide: United Nations Legislation on International Criminal Law.*

FRIEDMANN, WOLFGANG G. 1964 *The Changing Structure of International Law.* New York: Columbia Univ. Press.

GARCÍA MORA, MANUEL R. 1962 *International Responsibility for Hostile Acts of Private Persons Against Foreign States.* The Hague: Nijhoff.

GLASER, STEFAN 1954 *Introduction à l'étude du droit international pénal.* Brussels: Bruylant.

GRAVEN, JEAN 1950 Les crimes contre l'humanité. The Hague, Academy of International Law, *Recueil des cours* 76:429–606.

INTERNATIONAL MILITARY TRIBUNAL 1947–1949 *Trial of the Major War Criminals Before the International Military Tribunal.* 42 vols. Nuremberg (Germany): The Tribunal.

KRONSTEIN, HEINRICH D. 1962 *Recht und wirtschaftliche Macht: Ausgewählte Schriften.* Karlsruhe (Germany): Müller. → Contains contributions in English and German.

MCDOUGAL, MYRES S.; and FELICIANO, FLORENTINO P. 1961 *Law and Minimum World Public Order: The Legal Regulation of International Coercion.* New Haven: Yale Univ. Press.

O'Brien, William V. 1960 Legitimate Military Necessity in Nuclear War. *World Polity: A Yearbook of Studies in International Law and Organization* 2:35–120.

Oppenheim, Lassa F. L. (1905–1906) 1948–1952 *International Law: A Treatise.* 2 vols. 7th ed. London and New York: Longmans. → Volume 1: *Peace.* Volume 2: *Disputes, War and Neutrality.* Edited by Hersch Lauterpacht.

Pella, Vespasian V. 1930 La répression des crimes contre la personalité de l'état. The Hague, Academy of International Law, *Recueil des cours* 33:673–830.

Quintano Ripollés, Antonio 1952–1955 *Tratado de derecho penal internacional e internacional penal.* 2 vols. Madrid. Consejo Superior de Investigaciones Cientificas, Instituto "Francisco de Vitoria."

Sottile, Antoine 1938 Le terrorisme international. The Hague, Academy of International Law, *Recueil des cours* 65:87–184.

Stone, Julius (1954) 1959 *Legal Controls of International Conflict: A Treatise on the Dynamics of Disputes- and War-law.* Rev. New York: Rinehart. → Includes a supplement for 1953–1958.

UN War Crimes Commission 1947–1949 *Law Reports of Trials of War Criminals.* 15 vols. London: H.M. Stationery Office.

INTERNATIONAL CULTURAL COOPERATION

In general usage, the term international cultural cooperation refers to both public and private and to both national and international efforts to promote the transmission of knowledge, skills, arts, and information across national boundaries. It includes such activities as exchanges of students and scholars, technical assistance programs, and informational programs through mass media. However, the meaning of the term has been undergoing significant changes since the 1940s and there are signs that it will acquire a more precise meaning in the immediate future.

In its earlier phases international cultural cooperation was principally the concern of individuals or such voluntary organizations as religious bodies, educational institutions, foundations, and business groups. Although national cultural resources were sometimes marshaled for the development of colonial territories, most national governments did not undertake the systematic promotion of cultural activities across national boundaries until comparatively recently.

Governmentally sponsored cultural activities remained for many years a kind of optional adjunct to the governmental conduct of foreign relations and even until World War II were recognized to be of importance for the attainment of foreign policy objectives by only a few countries, notably France, Germany, and the United Kingdom. Today, the cultural dimension is recognized in some degree by virtually all countries to be an essential element in the conduct of foreign relations. At the same time, this dimension has become central to the work of most international organizations, whether for the stimulation of a sense of community or for providing varieties of technical assistance to newly developing countries.

Strictly speaking, the term international cultural cooperation should be limited to activities of international organizations, such as the United Nations, the Organization of American States, or the European Community organizations. National efforts using cultural resources as instruments of foreign policy are not really international in the modern use of the term.

The recent impetus to international cultural cooperation is the result of several factors in the contemporary international scene: (1) the positive role assigned by member states to the United Nations in the maintenance of peace and in the development of conditions essential to a peaceful community; (2) a widely held belief that increasing cultural cooperation can contribute to international understanding and the development of the peaceful world community; (3) the reality of interdependence among all nations in their development and in their need for access to the cultural, intellectual, and technological resources of the world; and (4) a recognition that while postwar tensions and ideological conflicts cannot be resolved by resort to modern weapons, they may at least be mitigated by promotion of international understanding and advancement of human welfare through cultural cooperation among nations.

In the organized promotion of international cultural cooperation, the United Nations Educational, Scientific and Cultural Organization clearly was given the central role among the United Nations agencies. Its focus was initially upon the general advancement of knowledge and promotion of international understanding by encouraging communication and cooperation in education, science, culture, and the mass media. The rapid emergence of new states in former colonial territories led, however, to increasing focus upon cultural cooperation as a means of dealing with developmental problems. These called for assistance in strengthening the basic resources of education, science, the mass media, and the humanities. But from the start UNESCO assistance required coordination with the technical assistance coming from other United Nations agencies and especially the World Health Organization, the International Labour Organisation, the International Bank for Reconstruction and Development, the Food and Agriculture Organization, the United Nations itself, and the UN regional commissions in Africa, Asia, and Latin America. The Expanded Program of Technical Assistance for Economic Development and the related work of the Special Fund became a composite effort of the United Nations agencies to promote international cultural cooperation in the widest sense of that term: that is, marshaling world resources of knowledge, skill, education, science, and the arts in a world community effort to speed the development process in new countries. This is in cost and quantity the most important part of present-day international cultural cooperation.

Regional organizations, such as the Organization of American States and the Organization for Economic Cooperation and Development, have developed cultural cooperation programs of considerable importance, both to promote understanding and to provide developmental assistance.

International cultural cooperation is still overshadowed by natural cultural activities in support of foreign policy objectives (student exchanges, technical assistance, information programs, etc.). These activities may complement international cultural activities insofar as national policy is consistent with policies of the international agencies.

A large segment of cultural cooperation across national boundaries lies outside the domain of international organizations and national governments. It is carried on by national and international nongovernmental agencies, including foundations, business, welfare, religious, and professional agencies. They place a substantial emphasis on assistance to newly developing countries and in this way help reduce the need for national and international governmental activities.

The literature on cultural cooperation has rapidly increased, especially during the postwar period. Official documentation of international organizations and national governments has focused on policy questions, organization, administration, and financing, and to some extent upon evaluation of effectiveness. Lengthy committee discussions and debates in national legislatures, especially the U.S. Congress, and in the United Nations agencies have revealed growing interest and recognition that a new dimension is developing in international relations. Scholarly writings have been partially historical and descriptive and partially analytical and have sought to test the significance of this new dimension. Among the principal concerns of social scientists have been:

(1) Techniques for evaluation of the impact of cultural cooperation activities.

(2) Definition of goals toward which cultural cooperation can contribute.

(3) Evaluations of types of cultural cooperation, including exchanges of scholars and students, information, propaganda, communications, and technical assistance.

(4) Evaluations of specific cultural cooperation programs and experiences.

(5) Governmental and international organization policy in relation to cultural cooperation.

(6) Institutional facilities for cultural cooperation within the world community, including the role of universities.

(7) Communication *between* cultures and between nations, often with special reference to cross-cultural education.

WALTER H. C. LAVES

[*See also* INTERNATIONAL ORGANIZATION; TECHNICAL ASSISTANCE.]

BIBLIOGRAPHY

AMERICAN ASSEMBLY 1963 *Cultural Affairs and Foreign Relations.* Englewood Cliffs, N.J.: Prentice-Hall.

BARGHOORN, FREDERICK C. 1960 *The Soviet Cultural Offensive: The Role of Cultural Diplomacy in Soviet Foreign Policy.* Princeton Univ. Press.

BEARDSLEY, SEYMOUR W.; and EDGELL, ALVIN G. 1956 *Human Relations in International Affairs: A Guide to Significant Interpretation and Research.* Washington: Public Affairs Press.

BENNETT, JOHN W.; PASSIN, HERBERT; and MCKNIGHT, ROBERT K. 1958 *In Search of Identity: The Japanese Overseas Scholar in America and Japan.* Minneapolis: Univ. of Minnesota Press.

BUCHANAN, WILLIAM; and CANTRIL, HADLEY 1953 *How Nations See Each Other: A Study in Public Opinion.* Urbana: Univ. of Illinois Press.

BUREAU OF SOCIAL SCIENCE RESEARCH, WASHINGTON, D.C. 1956 *International Communication and Political Opinion: A Guide to the Literature,* by Bruce L. Smith and Chitra M. Smith. Princeton Univ. Press.

CURTI, MERLE E. (1955) 1962 *Probing Our Past.* Gloucester, Mass.: Smith.

DOKA, CARL 1956 *Kulturelle Aussenpolitik.* Zurich: Berichthaus.

DUBOIS, CORA A. 1956 *Foreign Students and Higher Education in the United States.* Washington: American Council on Education.

Evaluation Methods Employed by Certain Non-governmental Organizations Approved for Consultative Arrangements With UNESCO. 1956 *International Social Science Bulletin* 8:667–670.

FRANKEL, CHARLES 1966 *The Neglected Aspect of Foreign Affairs: American Educational and Cultural Policy Abroad.* Washington: Brookings Institution.

HAYES, SAMUEL P. 1959 *Measuring the Results of Development Projects: A Manual for the Use of Field Workers.* Paris: UNESCO.

INTERNATIONAL BANK FOR RECONSTRUCTION AND DEVELOPMENT *Annual Report.* → Published since 1945–1946.

JOHNSON, WALTER; and COLLIGAN, F. J. 1965 *The Fulbright Program: A History.* Univ. of Chicago Press.

KLINEBERG, OTTO 1955 Introduction: The Problem of Evaluation. *International Social Science Bulletin* 7: 346–352.

LAVES, WALTER H. C.; and THOMSON, CHARLES A. 1957 *UNESCO: Purpose, Progress, Prospects*. Bloomington: Indiana Univ. Press.

MCMURRY, RUTH E.; and LEE, MUNA 1947 *The Cultural Approach: Another Way in International Relations*. Chapel Hill: Univ. of North Carolina Press.

NATIONAL PLANNING ASSOCIATION 1956 *Technical Co-operation in Latin America: Recommendations for the Future*. Washington: The Association.

SELLTIZ, CLAIRE et al. 1963 *Attitudes and Social Relations of Foreign Students in the United States*. Minneapolis: Univ. of Minnesota Press. → Contains many references to studies sponsored by the Social Science Research Council Committee on Cross-cultural Education.

SHUSTER, GEORGE N. 1963 *UNESCO: Assessment and Promise*. New York: Harper.

Study Abroad. → Published since 1948 by UNESCO.

THOMSON, CHARLES A.; and LAVES, WALTER H. C. 1963 *Cultural Relations and U.S. Foreign Policy*. Bloomington: Indiana Univ. Press.

Toward a National Effort in International Educational and Cultural Affairs. 1961 Appendix in U.S. Advisory Commission on Educational Exchange, 87th Congress, 1st Session, *26th Semi-annual Report*. Washington: Government Printing Office.

Two Meetings on the Study of Evaluation Techniques, Montreal 31 May–2 June 1956; Paris 1–3 August 1956. *International Social Science Bulletin* 8:746–748.

UNITED NATIONS 1960 *Five-year Perspective: 1960–64*. New York: United Nations. → Consolidated report on the appraisals of the scope, trends, and costs of the programs of the United Nations, ILO, UNESCO, WHO, and IAEA in the economic, social, and human rights fields.

UNESCO PROGRAM COMMISSION 1954 *Report on Cultural Agreements*. Document 8C/PRG/11. Paris: UNESCO.

USEEM, JOHN; and USEEM, RUTH H. 1955 *The Western-educated Man in India: A Study of His Social Roles and Influence*. New York: Dryden Press.

WATSON, JEANNE; and LIPPITT, RONALD 1955 *Learning Across Cultures: A Study of Germans Visiting America*. Ann Arbor: Univ. of Michigan, Research Center for Group Dynamics.

WEIDNER, EDWARD W. 1962 *The World Role of Universities*. New York: McGraw-Hill.

INTERNATIONAL INTEGRATION

I
REGIONAL INTEGRATION

The term "integration" refers to a process whereby the quality of relations among autonomous social units (kinship groups, tribes, cities, trade unions, trade associations, political parties) changes in such a way as to erode the autonomy of each and make it part of a larger aggregate. In specifically political discussions the term is reserved for the analysis of such changes among more or less "sovereign" political units, and in the study of international relations the term is confined to the analysis of cumulatively changing relations among states, resulting in their acceptance of some new central authority. Historically, such authority has most commonly been imposed by military force—by a conquering group upon the vanquished. In order to distinguish "integration" from the forcible establishment of empires we must specify that the erosion of local autonomy may be based on deliberate and voluntary decisions by actors or result from unintended consequences of such decisions, but it may never rest on force.

Specifically, "regional" integration refers to that process among two or more states on a geographically confined scale, at a level below that of global integration, which sums up such world-wide phenomena as international law, the United Nations, and world trade or population movements. So defined, "regional integration" is an identifiable process in ancient Greece, eighteenth-century and nineteenth-century North America, and nineteenth-century Germany, to cite some obvious instances. Regional integration since 1945 has been an observable phenomenon in both eastern and western Europe, in the "Atlantic area," the Middle East, Africa, Latin America, and in the Western Hemisphere as a whole. At the same time, "regional disintegration" has been apparent in the weakening of ties among the heirs of former colonial empires, the British Commonwealth, and the French Community.

"Integration" is sometimes also used to specify the *result* of a process of erosion of autonomy—the condition which obtains at the termination of the process; but we shall confine the meaning to the process. The term is important as an analytical tool in the hands of scholars and observers generalizing about the ideas and motives of political actors who are likely to describe their actions with such terms as "unification," "federation," "*rapprochement*," "establishing peaceful relations," or "bringing prosperity to all." Integration, therefore, is also an objective concept for summing up and projecting the possibly subjective aims of political actors.

Regional integration as a concept

Considered as an analytical concept, regional integration sums up a number of separate but related concerns appropriate to the study and—within limits—prediction of regional integration processes under way in various places. It groups behavioral and institutional forces describable by the term "spill-over," which in turn draws on the notion of "functionalism" and "functional integration." Regional integration concepts also rely on certain tendencies inherent in bureaucratic organizations. In particular they rely on the tendency of international organizations to expand along functional lines, with the help of functional legal ideas responding to new perceptions of need by the actors.

Specifically, the term "spill-over" describes the accretion of new powers and tasks to a central institutional structure, based on changing demands and expectations on the part of such political actors as interest groups, political parties, and bureaucracies. It refers to the specific process which originates in one functional context, initially separate from other political concerns, and then expands into related activities as it becomes clear to the chief political actors that the achievement of the initial aims cannot take place without such expansion. Demands and expectations for further centralized spheres of activity develop from perceptions of inadequate performance on the part of existing institutions. The inadequacy of the performance is attributed to an insufficient grant of powers or timid policy on the part of the central authorities; hence the claim for new central powers to achieve better performance is a direct outgrowth of the earlier institutional system and the realignment of group expectations produced through it.

By means of the spill-over concept we can analyze broad movements of integration without having to posit identity of aims or perfect agreement among the actors. Integration may proceed merely on the basis of a series of parallel and mutually complementary realignments of expectations and demands, with each actor merely seeking "to get the most out of" the initially centralized functional context. Application of the concept thus permits the projection of integrative trends without having to assume profound consensus among the states.

The extent to which the actors perceive the probable results of their demands on the over-all system is a crucial component of the concept. One type of "learning" is conducive to the progressive adoption of behavior patterns further reinforcing spill-over tendencies; but another type of "learning" may well stop the trend dead in its tracks: there is nothing inevitable in it. One type of "learning" rests on the reasoning associated with the concept of "unintended consequences." Actors striving for the better achievement of some aims dear to them will commit themselves to modes of behavior which have the unintended result of strengthening certain central institutions, or result in the creation of such institutions. The aims motivating the actors are —to them—manifest and overt, but the logic of events transforms the consciously expected results into something not wholly anticipated in terms of dependence on new central authorities.

Now two things can happen: the actor, having learned that unintended consequences can follow from his initial desires, may consciously make the unintended a manifest desire and thereby deliberately contribute to the process of centralization; but he may also draw the conclusion from the trend of spill-over events that his initial aims were to blame for the unintended and unwanted consequences, thereby compelling a reformulation of initial aims. The second case would produce an adaptation with disintegrative results. In that event the chain of events associated with the spill-over concept would come to a halt. There is little ground for believing that this outcome is less likely than integrative consequences. The positive spill-over concept summarizes adaptive tendencies of extreme fragility—tendencies which have been reversed in many well-known historical situations.

Regional integration as a process

Federations. The history of regional integration is as old as recorded efforts to achieve the peaceful unification of sovereign entities, efforts which have in the past been described under such rubrics as "federation," "leagues," and "alliances." The literature devoted to these experiences in the past has stressed the political component in the aims of the actors and has tended to assume the need for a pre-existing political consensus for the continuation of integration. Furthermore, emphasis was put on the analysis and description of the constitutions of such entities; the grant of power to central authorities was taken as the measure of political consensus among the integrating units. Hence, the usual conclusion older writers developed was that the mere convergence of military and security aims was an insufficiently permanent demand, preventing leagues and alliances from acquiring the constitutions necessary for integration and therefore disappearing once an immediate military danger was averted. In the analysis of federations stress was put on the question of whether ultimate sovereignty lies with the central or the local governments, whether the "will" to be a nation was stronger than the desire to be locally autonomous. Relatively little effort was devoted to analyzing the patterns of interaction summed up under the spill-over concept. The presumption in favor of the primacy of actors' political aims militated against raising the question of whether political consensus can emerge from functional preoccupations.

Communities. Since the end of World War II the emphasis has been reversed. Scholars (and many actors), impressed with the constantly increasing powers of governments to deal with almost all facets of life—particularly economic welfare—began to be interested in exploring the connection between patterns of commercial, social, and technical transactions and the growth of common or converging aims among important actors. Questions of social structure, demography, migration, economic development, and psychological distance were added to the earlier concern with military and armaments questions in dealing with regional integration. Specific proposals for regional integration were advanced in western Europe (such as the Schuman and Pléven plans in 1950) seeking to build eventual political federation on a substructure of closer ties and common practical concerns generated by institutional steps merging certain vital sectors of the national economies and the defense establishments. In addition, several common and centrally determined plans arose as an unintended consequence of institutional and programmatic patterns in the fields of defense and economic welfare. The initial tasks and powers of many agencies (for example, the Organization for European Economic Cooperation, OEEC; the North Atlantic Treaty Organization, NATO; the Organization of American States, OAS; and the United Nations Economic Commission for Latin America, ECLA) proved insufficient and gave rise to unplanned growth in functionally restricted fields. Concomitantly, a new body of law developed, regulating, for the states concerned, the new types of functional transactions.

Since the institutional forms associated with this development defied traditional constitutional classifications and tended to change *de facto* with the accretion of new tasks, the discussion of "federation" as the technique for regional integration gave way to the terms "community" and "community formation." With the failure of two frontal attempts to establish a united western Europe by means of political federation (Council of Europe during the years 1949–1951; European Political Community, 1952–1954) the notion of "community" has gained wide currency, especially in connection with ambitious efforts to use the mechanism of economic integration and the establishment of "common markets" as the functional trigger for the spill-over process. Such efforts at community formation have spread from western Europe to Latin America (Latin American Free Trade Association since 1961; Central American Common Market since 1960) to independent Africa with discussions for an African common market (since 1962), and to regional economic planning in eastern Europe (Council for Mutual Economic Assistance, CEMA, since 1956).

European economic integration. The most dramatic illustration of the community building process is the functional and geographic expansion of the scope of western European economic integration. The initial step was the creation of a common market for coal and steel in 1952, eliminating not only trade barriers among the "Continental Six" (Belgium, France, Italy, Luxembourg, Netherlands, West Germany) but also involving common policies on the rules of competition, subsidies, cartels, and investments. Expectations built up among the actors participating in the coal–steel nexus resulted in demands which simply could not be carried out by the existing central mechanism, the European Coal and Steel Community. Demands which spilled over from this sector thus infected the field of economics generally, resulting by 1958 in the establishment of the European Economic Community and Euratom, the latter owing its origin in part to the inability of the Coal and Steel Community to resolve a major European fuel crisis. New economic pressures and relationships which were generated by the union of the "Continental Six" spilled over geographically and led Britain, Denmark, Norway, and Ireland to seek membership in the Common Market in 1962.

The actors in regional integration. The initial steps of economic integration influence four distinct types of actors, who seek to adjust to the change by making demands which, in turn, tend to reinforce integration.

(1) Expanding group expectations emerge among industrialists, dealers, and trade unions in the initially merged economic sectors. A desire to bring as yet unintegrated but closely related economic sectors under the central rules becomes manifest, as well as a desire to develop means of political control over these larger issues. And in the process of reformulating expectations and demands, the interest groups in question approach one another across national boundaries by forming new associations while their erstwhile ties with national friends deteriorate.

(2) Among political parties a similar phenomenon takes place. Here the spill-over makes itself felt by the desire to control the new central administrative organs, agencies of a pronounced technocratic character—whether these be federal or intergovernmental in legal competence. But, in

addition, the larger field of legislative action opens up opportunities for the realization of party programs heretofore stymied in the *immobilisme* of tightly partitioned national economies. This is as true for the welfare-state-minded socialists as it is for free-trade-oriented liberals. Both think they stand to gain from the new dispensation.

(3) Furthermore, the process asserts itself in the relations among civil servants, national government offices, central banks, and technical advisers. A commitment to the realization of agreed-upon economic goals permits of no indefinite sabotaging of collective decisions. Momentary crises and obstacles tend to yield only if the bureaucrats agree to new central control devices. Commitment to one set of joint measures leads inexorably to later commitments for additional joint measures in order to carry out the first set. National bureaucracies thus tend to interpenetrate one another in the peculiar European institutional context in which integration is carried on.

(4) Finally, integration is advanced by the inability of governments and private actors outside the system of states undergoing integration to remain aloof from the process. In making the decision to join the union they then expose themselves to the spill-over tendencies implicit in the relations among interest groups, political parties, and civil servants, thus confirming and accelerating the trend initiated by the original governmental decision to join.

Patterns of regional integration. As the summary of the evolution of the concept and the process has shown, the actual pattern of regional integration can be divided according to (1) the subject matter singled out for joint action, (2) the nature of the participating states, and (3) the kind of central institutions which they set up. By correlating items in each of these types with actual situations we can then say something about the success of specific integration efforts.

(1) *Subject matter.* Regional efforts at integration may proceed along a directly political front by seeking to work out joint foreign policies for the associated states (OAS, Council of Europe, Arab League, certain African groupings). Alternatively, they may stress one or several functional tasks, most commonly in the fields of customs unions, economic unions, economic development and finance, joint technological and scientific research, transportation, and telecommunications. Less commonly, the functional emphasis is placed on joint defense, military planning, and rearmament policies, sometimes through the creation of single commands and procurement systems (NATO, Western European Union, Warsaw Pact). More rarely still, the common task involves regional legal systems for the protection of human rights (Council of Europe, OAS).

(2) *Nature of participating states.* Much hinges on whether the participants in regional integration are mutually homogeneous or not. Organizations grouping states of dramatically different power, economic development, and political institutions rarely function harmoniously (OAS, CEMA). Organizations grouping states with political systems, political parties, interest groups, and social institutions which differ from member to member find it difficult to make common policy on anything but the most trivial functional concerns (Arab League, OAS, UN Economic Commission for Europe).

(3) *Institutions.* Regional organizations range from the minimal traditional intergovernmental conference to the extreme of a federation with limited purposes. The intergovernmental arrangement predominates (NATO; OEEC; Organization for Economic Cooperation and Development, OECD; OAS; Arab League; CEMA; UN regional economic commissions). Decisions are made by instructed national delegates, usually on the basis of unanimity, aided by a central secretariat with minimal powers and many commissions of technical experts, recruited nationally and regionally. Truly federal institutions existed for some purposes in east Africa and functioned in the unsuccessful West Indian Federation until 1962. The European communities, however, feature "supranational" institutions, a hybrid of federal and intergovernmental techniques of making decisions and allocating power. These "supranational" techniques, which are also found in many other intergovernmental organizations, militate against the autonomy of functional concerns because they demand the participation of so many public and private decision-making units.

Supranationality. The institutional characteristics of supranationality are unique in three ways. First, they involve the simultaneous presence of instructed high-ranking governmental representatives, uninstructed or permissively instructed experts recruited from the national bureaucracies, experts representing the major interest groups, and the "European" staff of experts and high-ranking officials who, on behalf of the communities, make proposals and seek to arrange compromises among clashing demands. Second, a parliamentary and quasi-legislative factor is introduced through the debates and resolutions of transnational political parties active in the European parliament. Finally, the existence of an independent European judiciary with complete jurisdiction over economic integration matters automatically removes the possibility of seeking national legal remedies against unpopular central decisions (European Communities' Court, European Court of Human Rights).

Decisions filtered through this process rarely reflect the untrammeled wishes of any one party, whether it be a powerful national ministry or a marginal interest group. Every decision is a compromise between politicians, industrialists, farmers, trade unionists, and bureaucrats. The parties redefine their conflict and work out a solution at a higher level, which almost invariably implies the expansion of the mandate or task of an international or national governmental agency. In terms of method, this upgrading of the parties' common interests relies heavily on the services of an institutionalized mediator—whether a single person or a board of experts—with an autonomous range of powers. In terms of results, this mode of accommodation maximizes integration: policies made pursuant to an initial task and grant of power can be realized only if the task itself is expanded, as reflected in the compromises between the states interested in the task.

Factors maximizing integration. Certain kinds of organizational tasks are by nature expansive while others are easily confined. The ideal task for maximizing the spill-over tendency must be closely related to welfare, highly specific in terms of initial requirements, and yet broad enough so that the initial requirements cannot be achieved without the grant of new powers.

Specificity of task is essential, with respect to such assignments as creating a common market for narrowly defined products, unifying railway rates, removing restrictive practices in certain branches of industry, removing import quotas by fixed percentage points during fixed periods, and the like. Functional specificity, however, may be so trivial as to remain outside the stream of human expectations and actions vital for integration. This would seem to be the case with the standardization of railway rolling stock, for example, or the installation of uniform road signs. The task, in short, must be both specific and economically important in the sense of containing the potential for spilling over from one vital area of welfare policy into others.

Expectations of rewards entertained by crucial national elites must be regionally complementary. Hence, organizations grouping states of widely differing power and economic potential rarely provide an ideal setting for the continuation of integration. A frontal attack on political unity seldom succeeds, and the functional concentration on defense and armaments displays less tendency toward spill-over than the creation of common markets. Concentration on cultural programs and the implementation of values relating to the protection of human rights have so far resulted in little active integration.

Hence it can be concluded that for organizations to expand their task they must first be based on specific expectations of the participating elites. While these need not share a profound consensus on ends or means, their objectives must nevertheless be parallel or converging. They may achieve their agreement on the basis of differing paths of reasoning, and their desire to work together may be purely tactical or motivated by sheer expediency. However, their values must be sufficiently congruent to make possible cooperation in joint institutions for purely instrumental motives. Elites lacking even this rudimentary sharing of values will prove to be unprepossessing partners in a cooperative enterprise.

Furthermore, rigid elite structures are unlikely to attain a sufficient degree of instrumental receptivity to the aspirations of others. An elite which recruits its members from large segments of society, which is both rationally and bureaucratically organized, and which eschews firm ideological commitments is most likely to prove receptive to the stimuli associated with the spill-over concept. Totalitarian elites do not qualify for such a role any more than do oligarchical cliques in traditional societies. Members of open elites may permit themselves to be co-opted into international and supranational administrative bodies and thereby commit their followers to active participation in spill-over tendencies while not feeling that they are betraying their beliefs or their followers. Members of closed elites are unlikely to possess this kind of adaptive ability.

The elites best equipped for participating in changing social situations in which the spill-over process may be manifest are the kinds produced by societies with considerable social mobility, technical and professional education, industrial–managerial values, and a high degree of tolerance for technocratic–bureaucratic efficiency. While active industrialism need not be a precondition, the desire to industrialize probably must be; even though high standards of consumption need not exist, the will to create such standards should prevail; and although democracy in the formal sense need not prevail, toleration for dissident groups and a desire to placate them must be present.

Regional integration in action

This characterization of tasks and elite skills suggests that regions marked by homogeneously distributed pluralistic–democratic elites are likely to integrate rapidly if there is some instrumental attachment to a shared aim. It suggests also that homogeneously distributed totalitarian elites with a sharp common purpose, or at least, elites agreeing internationally on some well-defined ideological program, are equally equipped to advance integration. On the other hand, regional associations characterized by a heterogeneous distribution of elites in member states and by very sporadically shared aims have great difficulty achieving a central programmatic and institutional consensus going beyond the minimum common denominator of preserving the territorial and functional *status quo;* such groupings are likely to stress sovereignty, nonintervention, equality, and intergovernmental cooperation for the achievement of these minimal tasks. Only a sudden realization of common danger is likely to break through this minimalism and then trigger a supranational integration process. This theme will now be illustrated.

Western Europe. By the end of the 1960s the six countries of the European communities may achieve economic and *de facto* political union with respect to all functions concerning economic and social welfare. In the process they will absorb such smaller regional groupings in Europe as Benelux, WEU, the Scandinavian system, and the European Free Trade Association (EFTA). Because of size and industrial potential the EEC countries will continue to attract the members of EFTA (Austria, Denmark, Norway, Portugal, Sweden, Switzerland, United Kingdom) so that an integrated European economy will emerge. The extent to which common markets and economic union *must* force over-all political union is less clear. Efforts are being made to reserve joint political and military decisions to a confederal structure, which would be superimposed over the existing supranational institutions. Military and foreign policy integration among western European states has been the result of NATO aims and programs, not specifically European ones. The future of political unification, therefore, is closely connected with the pattern of Atlantic integration.

North Atlantic area. Military integration and foreign policy coordination in NATO evolved gradually in response to military weakness during the Korean crisis (1950–1953); such integration had not been intended by the chief architects of NATO in 1948. Since 1953, however, integration has proceeded largely in areas where costs were great and savings for welfare purposes could be achieved only through joint and centrally planned action. Until the question of developing a multinational nuclear force for the alliance came to the fore in the early 1960s, military integration had not proceeded far beyond the initial creation of joint commands, procurement systems, air defense arrangements, and intergovernmental political consultation machinery. Changes in eastern Europe, nuclear deterrents and the European aim of assuring speedy *collective* control over their use, served to confuse the common aim of the member states and caused disintegration in NATO. In the areas of trade, investment, and the coordination of foreign economic policies, OECD provides the vehicle for North Atlantic integration, a vehicle which has not acquired supranational features. Integration here, as elsewhere, is very much a function of a sense of danger and common purpose triggered by the integration of rival regional blocs in world politics.

Eastern Europe. After the death of Stalin in 1953 and the evidence of unrest in communist eastern Europe (especially the Hungarian revolution in 1956), a deliberate policy of joint economic planning was initiated through CEMA, based on the doctrine of a "socialist division of labor" and a "world socialist economy." This resulted in the growth of a planned regional economy featuring national economic specialization. Tied to a political process of consultation among "fraternal" Communist parties and to a military process of joint planning similar to NATO's, an integrated European communist realm based on polycentric authority is taking shape.

Middle East. Efforts to forge all-Arab unity on the basis of the purely intergovernmental Arab League failed because of the irreconcilable aims of the nationally based revolutionary and the traditional elites. Member states consistently intervened in each other's affairs rather than making a joint policy. Integration, therefore, proceeds on the basis of partial unions and federations among ideologically kindred revolutionary regimes stressing similar programs of drastic economic and social modernization.

Africa. In principle all new African states share a commitment to the values of pan-Africanism, the unity of the "African personality," and the need to pool resources for speedy economic modernization. As in the Middle East, however, the elite and party structures are regionally heterogeneous, so a variety of unstable groupings have arisen. One of the dividing issues is whether association with the EEC will advance modernization or open the door to "neocolonialism." Hence the states stress sovereignty and nonintervention more consistently than joint action through the Organization of African Unity.

Western Hemisphere. The same is true of the OAS, which unites a very heterogeneous collection of states and elites. They have agreed on joint action only in the face of obvious common military danger from one of their own number. The possibility remains that multilaterally administered economic development and technical assistance programs will trigger a supranational institutional development. The same is true of joint antisubversion policies and the protection of human rights.

Latin American economic unions. Two economic groupings with unstable membership are functioning—the Latin American Free Trade Association (LAFTA) and the Central American Common Market. Both are based on the underlying common doctrine that industrialization can develop more rapidly on the basis of regional markets, specialization agreements among new industries, and joint investment planning; both are reacting, in part, to an economic threat perceived by their elites as posed by the EEC and the United States. Political union is not overtly demanded and the cohesive sentiment flows from a shared "underdog" mentality which may not readily lend itself to a marked spill-over tendency. LAFTA is likely to grow in proportion to the lack of growth of OAS programs and powers, and vice versa.

Other areas. Efforts at regional integration in Asia have been superficial and sporadic. Economic unification among southeast Asian countries, following the same argument as Latin America, has been delayed by territorial disputes. In Asia regional common markets and joint economic planning are discussed but are not being implemented, in large part because of the heterogeneity of elites and the unequal industrial potential of the prospective member states. Efforts at regional integration in the former British West Indies at first developed along the lines of joint functional programs, to be followed by political federation. However, the more rapid development of local national sentiment in Jamaica and Trinidad and speedy local economic development reduced expectations of future rewards, thus dooming the federation. The same process also defeated the proposed federation of Tanganyika, Kenya, and Uganda.

ERNST B. HAAS

[*See also* FEDERALISM; INTERNATIONAL ORGANIZATION; INTERNATIONAL POLITICS; INTERNATIONAL RELATIONS; PAN MOVEMENTS.]

BIBLIOGRAPHY

BRZEZINSKI, ZBIGNIEW K. (1960) 1961 *The Soviet Bloc: Unity and Conflict.* Rev. ed. New York: Praeger.

BUSEY, JAMES L. 1961 Central American Union: The Latest Attempt. *Western Political Quarterly* 14:49–63.

CERNY, KARL H.; and BRIEFS, HENRY W. (editors) 1965 *NATO in Quest of Cohesion.* New York: Praeger.

DEUTSCH, KARL W. 1953 *Political Community at the International Level: Problems of Definition and Measurement.* Princeton Univ. Press.

DEUTSCH, KARL W. et al. 1957 *Political Community and the North Atlantic Area: International Organization in the Light of Historical Experience.* Princeton Univ. Press.

DIEBOLD, WILLIAM 1959 *The Schuman Plan: A Study in Economic Cooperation, 1950–1959.* New York: Praeger.

DREIER, JOHN C. 1962 *The Organization of American States and the Hemisphere Crisis.* New York: Harper.

ETZIONI, AMITAI 1965 *Political Unification.* New York: Holt.

FENWICK, CHARLES G. 1963 *The Organization of American States: The Inter-American Regional System.* Washington: Pan American Union.

FRIEDMANN, WOLFGANG G. 1964 *The Changing Structure of International Law.* New York: Columbia Univ. Press.

HAAS, ERNST B. 1958 *The Uniting of Europe: Political, Social, and Economic Forces, 1950–1957.* Stanford Univ. Press.

HAAS, ERNST B.; and SCHMITTER, PHILIPPE C. 1964 Economics and Differential Patterns of Political Integration: Projections About Unity in Latin America. *International Organization* 18:705–737.

JENSEN, FINN; and INGO, WALTER 1965 *The Common Market: Economic Integration in Europe.* Philadelphia: Lippincott.

KORBONSKI, ANDRZEJ 1964 COMECON. *International Conciliation* No. 549.

LAWSON, RUTH C. (editor) 1962 *International Regional Organizations: Constitutional Foundations.* New York: Praeger.

LEGUM, COLIN 1962 *Pan-Africanism: A Short Political Guide.* New York: Praeger.

LICHTHEIM, GEORGE 1963 *The New Europe: Today and Tomorrow.* New York: Praeger.

LINDBERG, LEON N. 1963 *The Political Dynamics of European Economic Integration.* Stanford Univ. Press.

MACDONALD, ROBERT W. 1965 *The League of Arab States.* Princeton Univ. Press.

MACMAHON, ARTHUR W. (editor) (1955) 1962 *Federalism: Mature and Emergent.* New York: Russell.

POLITICAL AND ECONOMIC PLANNING 1959 *European Organisations.* London: Allen & Unwin.

ROBERTSON, ARTHUR H. (1956) 1961 *The Council of Europe: Its Structure, Functions and Achievements.* 2d ed. New York: Praeger.

SCHEINGOLD, STUART A. 1965 *The Rule of Law in European Integration.* New Haven: Yale Univ. Press.

URQUIDI, VICTOR L. (1960) 1962 *Free Trade and Economic Integration in Latin America: The Evolution of a Common Market Policy.* Berkeley: Univ. of California Press. → First published as *Trayectoria del mercado común latinoamericano.*

WIONCZEK, MIGUEL S. 1965 Latin American Free Trade Association. *International Conciliation* No. 551.

WRIGHTMAN, DAVID 1963 *Toward Economic Cooperation in Asia.* New Haven: Yale Univ. Press.

II
GLOBAL INTEGRATION

Political integration may be defined as a cumulative process of change in the nature of relations among more or less sovereign political units, such as states, during which these units voluntarily accept some kind of new central authority. This process requires at least four constituent elements: (*a*) the political units involved must permit the establishment of central institutions which promulgate policies; (*b*) the functions of this central authority may not be trivial or vague but must be important and specific; (*c*) the functions, or tasks, performed by the central institutions should be inherently "expansive"; (*d*) the political units must remain committed to the common enterprise because they perceive ensuing benefits.

The disintegration or diminution of local autonomies may be the consequence of deliberate choice by the decision makers of the units or it may be the unintended consequence of policies which initially had no foreseeable connection with resulting processes of integration. In either case, integration refers to a process which is voluntary and hence endows the new central authority not only with power but also with legitimacy. Imposition of a central authority by military conquest—historically, the main force which induced autonomous political units to submit to a new central authority—thus cannot be viewed as an example of integration as defined here.

Global integration, in contrast to regional integration or the integration of structures of authority within a state, refers to processes of integration during which functions are delegated to a new central authority whose decisions are accepted as legitimate by the component members of world society. What constitutes the members of a world society, or world society itself, is a question that can be investigated historically. Different historical periods are characterized by different types of world society, and the attributes of the members of these world societies may also differ quite radically in terms of size, number, absolute and relative power, internal cohesion, value systems, objectives, and so forth. The members of the world society may be nation-states (as is generally the case today), empires, principalities, city-states, or any other forms of political organization endowed with the authority to deal with external affairs.

The boundaries of a world society are determined by the frequency of interaction among its members. As a consequence, several "world" societies may have existed simultaneously because one world society—whose members interacted frequently—was not aware of the existence of other world societies or because it deliberately chose to keep interaction with its environs to a minimum. In some cases, such as the Inca world of A.D. 1200–1530, the outer limits of such world societies can be determined fairly accurately; in other cases, such as the ancient empires of the Middle East or the empires that bordered the Mediterranean, the difficulties of delimitation are greater.

Contemporary world society is a global society and, in fact, is about to transcend its global confines and extend into outer space. The attributes of this contemporary global world society and the nature of its component members can be usefully described and summarized by the term "international system." That is, the contemporary international system may be regarded as one of many possible ways in which the members of a world society can interact. An international system in turn may be defined as a pattern of relations among the major units of world politics (states) that is characterized by the absolute and relative power of these units and by the conflicting and converging objectives pursued by these units. The resulting patterns of power and purpose are thus the consequence of the physical and psychological–motivational forces that operate within and among the major units.

Processes relevant to integration

Interaction. It is important, both historically and analytically, to distinguish between processes of interaction among the members of a world society and processes of integration. Clearly, there can be no processes of global integration if there are no processes of global interaction; at the same time, frequent interaction can take place without diminution of the autonomy of the members that could lead to the establishment of a new central authority. The frequency of interaction and the range of different types of interaction among the members of the contemporary international system are probably higher and more extensive than in any other period of history. This is in large part the consequence of technological developments in the fields of communications and transport which have "shrunk" the world, allowing social interaction to take place with relative speed and economy.

Interdependence. The consequences of this increased interaction on relationships of interdependence are somewhat ambivalent. On the one hand, interdependence, when perceived, at times has been resisted and measures have been taken to counteract it. In recent history some states, or groups of states, have deliberately sought to reduce their dependence on other states of the international system—say, in matters of military security, the exchange of raw materials or finished commodities, etc.—so as to preserve for themselves a higher degree of political maneuverability or to deny advantages to an actual or potential opponent. Restrictions on international travel and on the free flow of labor across international borders, and restrictive immigration or emigration policies, are other examples of curtailing social interaction with the expected consequence of reducing some type of interdependence.

Furthermore, it can by no means be taken for granted that increasing interaction, even if coupled with interdependence, must necessarily lead to ensuing processes of integration. For example, in examining historical developments, the closer one gets to the modern age and its increasing opportunities for interaction, the fewer the historical examples of full-fledged successful integration of two or more previously sovereign units. For both psychological and practical reasons the modern nation-state has become the most important source of authority and the central arbitrator for groups and individuals with conflicting interpretations of what constitutes the public good and how to share its benefits equitably. With the development of modern nationalism in the late eighteenth and in the nineteenth century, the nation-state emerged as the most important large-scale sociopolitical organization that could command the overriding loyalty of groups and individuals and provide the psychological satisfactions of identifying with and serving a common cause. Although international causes, such as communism, international socialism, and Zionism produced rival value systems, the nation-state remained by and large the central authority endowed with the legitimate exercise of sovereign power. (In recent years this phenomenon is poignantly illustrated by the centrifugal tendencies which have affected both cold war camps and which have taken as their focal point a reorientation of public policy around the authority of the nation-state. It is further illustrated by the ardent nationalism displayed by the ruling elites of the developing nations of Africa and Asia.) These essentially psychological dimensions were buttressed by developments which delegated to the modern social-service state extensive functions for regulating economic life and for providing social welfare services. As a result the modern nation-state became, and in a large measure has remained, the central authority and major institutional structure for the effective conduct of both external and internal affairs. [*See* NATION.]

Interpenetration. Notwithstanding these qualifying factors, the contemporary international system is generally regarded as being so highly interdependent that some analysts have suggested the term "penetration" as most applicable for describing the relationships of mutual influence among the members of the system. James Rosenau, for example, has proposed the concept of a new kind of political system, the penetrated system, to comprehend the fusion of national and international systems. He argues that national societies have become so penetrated by their external environment that they are no longer the only source of legitimacy or even of the employment of coercive techniques and that, consequently, national political systems now permeate, as well as depend on, each other and that their functioning now embraces actors who are not formally members of the system (1966, pp. 63–65).

Perhaps the most striking manifestation of the phenomenon of penetration is that many of the national units in the contemporary international system find it more and more difficult, if not meaningless, to distinguish between foreign policy and domestic policy. This holds true not only for the developing new nations that are going through the slow processes of modernization and the building of a viable nationhood but also for the industrialized nations of the Northern Hemisphere whose reallocations of resources and values are strongly affected by international factors. The occupation regimes of Germany and Japan in the postwar period, United States involvement in South Vietnam, United Nations operations in the Congo, foreign aid grants which require the recipient states to adhere to a specified program of utilization—these are just a few examples of where the allocation of values in a national unit is strongly affected by the prevailing patterns of power and purpose in the international system. Not only are domestic allocations of values strongly affected by the international environment, but national decision makers have begun to recognize that in a large number of issues external events have a direct impact on the allocation of values which traditionally took place largely within the domain of essentially national institutional structures.

Nowhere is the phenomenon of interpenetration more clearly visible and institutionalized than in the operations of regional international organizations which are endowed with some measure of supranational authority, that is, in functional contexts such as the European Common Market, where interpenetration has in fact led to processes of integration.

Another example of interpenetration is a result of the changing nature of the nation-state. As John Herz (1959) has cogently argued, the previously existing "hard shell" of physical, legal, and psychological boundaries which national systems have traditionally maintained vis-à-vis their external environment is becoming increasingly "permeated," primarily because of developments in modern weapons technology and the application of economic and psychological warfare. Indeed, one cannot think of a more fundamental, or unavoidable, type of interdependence or interpenetration than that which results from the possibility that a nuclear exchange between members of the system may abolish the system itself.

All these examples—and they are by no means exhaustive—go beyond the mere fact that there is an increasing interdependence among national actors in the system; rather, they are examples of a process of interpenetration in which the traditional political, economic, legal, and psychological boundaries separating the nation-state from the environing international factors are becoming increasingly tenuous.

Global integration and the UN

Measured against the magnitude of the tasks that evolve from the conditions of the international system, and in spite of the interpenetrative attributes of present-day world politics, existing global integrative structures cannot be regarded as anything more than inadequate and minimal. International law and the functioning global organizations that are effectively operating bodies and approximate the precepts of integration, such as the Universal Postal Union (UPU), the International Labour Organisation (ILO), and some of the other UN specialized agencies, do not greatly influence the major political concerns that preoccupy the members of the international system. Although not entirely noncontroversial, the essentially technical and rather specialized nature of the tasks performed by these functional organizations preserves a certain "autonomy of functional contexts" that does not lend itself to extensive "spillover" into more controversial, political areas. [*See* INTERNATIONAL INTEGRATION, *article on* FUNCTIONALISM AND FUNCTIONAL INTEGRATION.]

Some of the most important functions for a stable but dynamic world order, such as providing a central and authoritative machinery for channeling forces of change in ways that avoid a violent disruption of world society, are denied anything but a loosely structured organizational construct on the global level. Some of the functions that were explicitly or implicitly assigned to the UN, such as collective security, peaceful change, and pacific settlement tasks, have resulted in neither patterns of expectations nor patterns of behavior that portend an integrated international system with a corresponding accretion of power for a central authority. It is nonetheless useful to consider these functions, if only to highlight the strictures against global integration that prevail in the contemporary system and to point out the effect of global functional efforts on processes of regional integration.

Collective security. The hope that global integrative trends would lead to a world society whose members would resolve their conflicts with a minimum of violence is at the heart of the more ambitious proposals for an integrated international system. A key attribute of a highly integrated international system would thus be a central authority endowed with a monopoly of the legitimate use of physical force. The concept of collective security, as embodied in the UN Charter, does not correspond precisely with the idea that a central global authority *should* possess this kind of authority over the use of force. It is, however, sufficiently similar in its intended effect—i.e., that a collective response can stifle an aggressor—and, moreover, supplies a concrete historical example of attempts to regulate the use of force among the members of the international system by a global organization. [*See* COLLECTIVE SECURITY.]

Four major factors of the international system made it extremely difficult for the UN to operate effectively in the functional area of collective security.

(*a*) The anticipated harmony of interests among the "Big Five," the permanent members of the Security Council, evaporated rapidly. The developing polarization of conflict, perceived interests, and ideology between the Soviet bloc and the Western powers shattered the concert envisaged by the framers of the Charter. In addition, the global dimensions of the postwar international system made the cold war blocs evaluate most conflicts arising in the system in the light of their possible repercussions on the East–West balance of power.

(*b*) The polarization of perceived interests between the cold war blocs was coupled with a polarization of capabilities. Up to the late 1950s, power in the international system was not diffused but concentrated in two power blocs—more specifically, in the alliance superpowers, the United States and the Soviet Union.

(*c*) The very nature of the state system posed vexing problems for UN collective security functions. The possibility of making rather clear distinctions between domestic and international issues is an important premise for collective security responses because they are triggered most unambiguously when transgression involves the violation of territorial integrity. For reasons already noted, this condition could not be met in many parts of the world. Particularly in conflicts between colonial powers and their colonies, and among some of the new states, it was often difficult to distinguish between internal and external dimensions of a conflict. Moreover, the outcome of an essentially domestic power struggle was often assessed by the cold war antagonists in a global context because it could affect the cold war balance of power.

(*d*) Finally, the UN itself became a forum which the superpowers exploited for their national policies and in which they sought to gain the support of the membership for cold war issues. The UN was thus prevented from securing the flexibility of alignment against an aggressor which is required for collective security functions.

In light of these strictures, it is not surprising that the success of the UN in this task area was minimal. However, "collective security" functions were performed in the international system by structures other than the UN. For example, the restraints imposed on each other by the two cold war military blocs and the gradually developing nuclear "balance of terror" undoubtedly contributed substantially to the stability of the international system. This is one of the most striking ironies of the postwar international order: factors that stabilized the system at the same time prevented global collective security functions. The polarization of power and purpose—undoubtedly a stabilizing influence because of the resulting deterrence effect—was antithetical to a collective security arrangement which ideally requires diffusion of power, albeit with centralized *ad hoc* management in the event of aggression.

Peaceful change and pacific settlement. In contrast to collective security functions, peaceful change operations require that the global institution concern itself with (*a*) the merits of the dispute (that is, make a value judgment about the need and type of changes in the international system); (*b*) the internal political attributes of the disputants; and (*c*) the forces of unrest, before they escalate to the point of aggression. In short, a peaceful change operation entails a management of ends and projects that requires a positive attitude toward change, substantive evaluation of aspirations, and concern with the internal disposition of states.

The operational assumptions of pacific settlement functions are a hybrid between those of collective security and peaceful change. Instead of sanctions (as for collective security operations), pacific settlement relies chiefly on methods of mediation, conciliation, and inquiry. Pacific settlement is not as much concerned with the intrinsic merit of the dispute as peaceful change is (in fact, it implicitly encourages compromise), but neither does it envisage a purely instrumental response as the means of management of collective security. [*See* INTERNATIONAL CONFLICT RESOLUTION.]

UN "balancing." With the impasse experienced by the UN in the task area of collective security, the organization gradually turned to alternative functions which in some ways are akin to the operational assumptions of peaceful change and pacific settlement. This was accomplished through the processes of "balancing" (cf. Haas 1955; 1956). The concept of balancing describes and rests upon an intricate negotiating process in the UN during which the Afro–Asian members, as neutral mediators, traded their support on cold war security issues in which the superpowers were interested against the superpowers' support on colonial, social, and economic issues in which the mediators were interested. In particular, the superpowers sought to enlist the symbol of the UN for their cold war projects by supporting the neutrals' projects of colonial emancipation, human rights, and economic development.

Clearly, in its balancing operations the UN became involved in functional contexts that called for declarations and commitments as to what the world ought to be like and how the organization could aid in its transformation; that is, the UN had to take a stance on the substantive merits of a grievance and, as a corollary, had to become concerned to some extent with the internal political conditions of the member states. To have done otherwise would have meant abdication of the organization's relevance not only in the task area of collective security but also in the area of peaceful change and pacific settlement.

What is particularly striking is that the UN's limited success in the peaceful change area (for example, Palestine, the former Italian colonies, the Togo trust territories, West Irian, and the general issue area of colonial emancipation) was made possible not so much in spite of, but because of, cold war tensions. For example, the shift of influence from the Council to the Assembly and the blurring of functions between the two bodies was in good part an outgrowth of the collective security impasse resulting from the use of the veto in the Council. This provided the growing number of smaller powers with the parliamentary lever to exert a stronger influence over UN functions than their actual power would have justified. Their role as mediators in the cold war conflict and UN influence in the creation of new states further enhanced their advantage in a setting of multilateral diplomacy, cross-functional balancing, and egalitarian voting procedures. The basis for these permissive conditions was that both cold war camps, in competing for the allegiance or at least neutrality of the new states, were committed to advocating and supporting forces of change, modernization, and economic development.

On the whole, all the obstacles that hampered UN collective security functions—polarization of power and purpose in the earlier phase of the postwar world, heterogeneous membership of the international system, north–south polarization of economic development and industrial capacity—were precisely the factors that allowed the UN to fulfill important, if limited, functions in the area of peaceful change and pacific settlement.

The processes of balancing in the UN had a twofold implication for international integration. First, although balancing operations did not lead to processes of global integration, they reflected and underscored a high degree of interdependence among the members of the international system. This, in turn, had a significant effect on bargaining processes among the members of the Western alliance in the context of the North Atlantic Treaty Organization (NATO) and the European Common Market: that is, global balancing had an impact on regional integration (cf. Haas 1956; 1961). As noted, bipolarity of power and the nuclear standoff between East and West prevented institutionalized global collective security but stabilized the international system. Nuclear bipolarity, however, also produced fissures in the Western alliance by eroding previously more complementary security interests among the Western powers. The ensuing tensions within the alliance were sharpened by differing policies on the pace of colonial emancipation and by the conflicts which developed between the United States and some western European allies because of economic regionalism and nationalism in western Europe. It is here that global balancing had an important effect on regional integrative ventures. To the extent that the differences among the Western allies could not be fully adjusted on the level of Western regional organizations but had to be further compromised at the global UN level in order to obtain a united Western voting posture, the world organization contributed to the adjustment of interests not only among, but also within, regional groups.

Second, processes of balancing not only reflected the shifting patterns of power and purpose in the international system but to some extent aided in systemic transformations by providing for them an institutional setting which made them clearly visible. When the major alignments in the system shifted from the postwar bipolar pattern to a tripolar one after the Bandung Conference and to a multipolar pattern thereafter with the admission of a large number of African nations, the UN forum served as an institutional structure where these shifts became clearly manifest and could be utilized by all parties concerned for cross-functional balancing. Even though these processes resulted in only minimal global integrative trends, they played an important role by symbolizing the interdependence among the members of the international system.

WOLFRAM F. HANRIEDER

[*See also* ALLIANCES; COLLECTIVE SECURITY; DIPLOMACY; INTERNATIONAL POLITICS; SYSTEMS ANALYSIS, *article on* INTERNATIONAL SYSTEMS. *Other relevant material may be found under* INTERNATIONAL RELATIONS.]

BIBLIOGRAPHY

CLAUDE, INIS L. (1956) 1964 *Swords Into Plowshares: The Problems and Progress of International Organization*. 3d ed. New York: Random House.

CLAUDE, INIS L. 1961 The Management of Power in the Changing United Nations. *International Organization* 15:219–235.

CLAUDE, INIS L. (1962) 1964 *Power and International Relations*. New York: Random House.

DEUTSCH, KARL W. 1953 *Political Community at the International Level: Problems of Definition and Measurement*. Foreign Policy Analysis Series, No. 2. Princeton Univ. Press.

DEUTSCH, KARL W. et al. 1957 *Political Community and the North Atlantic Area: International Organization in the Light of Historical Experience*. Princeton Univ. Press.

HAAS, ERNST B. 1955 Types of Collective Security: An Examination of Operational Concepts. *American Political Science Review* 49:40–62.

HAAS, ERNST B. 1956 Regionalism, Functionalism, and Universal International Organization. *World Politics* 8:238–263.

HAAS, ERNST B. 1961 International Integration: The European and the Universal Process. *International Organization* 15:366–392.

HAAS, ERNST B. 1962 Dynamic Environment and Static System: Revolutionary Regimes in the United Nations. Pages 267–309 in Morton A. Kaplan (editor), *The Revolution in World Politics*. New York: Wiley.

HAAS, ERNST B. 1964 *Beyond the Nation-state: Functionalism and International Organization*. Stanford Univ. Press.

HERZ, JOHN H. 1959 *International Politics in the Atomic Age*. New York: Columbia Univ. Press. → A paperback edition was published in 1962.

JACOB, PHILIP E.; and TOSCANO, J. V. (editors) 1964 *The Integration of Political Communities*. Philadelphia: Lippincott.

JENKS, C. WILFRED 1958 *The Common Law of Mankind*. New York: Praeger.

LINDBERG, LEON N. 1963 *The Political Dynamics of European Economic Integration.* Stanford Univ. Press.

MANGONE, GERARD J. 1951 *The Idea and Practice of World Government.* New York: Columbia Univ. Press.

MITRANY, DAVID (1943) 1966 *A Working Peace System: An Argument for the Functional Development of International Organizations.* 4th ed. Chicago: Quadrangle Books. → The 1966 edition includes material added between 1948 and 1965.

ROSENAU, JAMES N. 1966 Pre-theories and Theories of Foreign Policy. Pages 27–92 in R. Barry Farrell (editor), *Approaches to Comparative and International Politics.* Evanston, Ill.: Northwestern Univ. Press.

III
FUNCTIONALISM AND FUNCTIONAL INTEGRATION

Functionalism in its different meanings is a much discussed topic [*see* FUNCTIONAL ANALYSIS]. This article, however, will deal only with the specialized meaning that the term has in international organization, tracing its origins and influence in international affairs, and emphasizing its contributions to the study of international integration.

Functionalism in international organization

Starting in the late nineteenth century, a number of scholars took the proliferation of international organizations—like the Universal Postal Union and the International Telegraphic Union—as an indication of a growing sense of world community and as a guarantee for future international stability. Paul S. Reinsch, Leonard Woolf, G. D. H. Cole, Pitman Potter, and others (see Martin 1950; Engle 1957) have all expanded on these basic points. But it was David Mitrany who best formulated the doctrine and the theory of functionalism in international organization. His essay *A Working Peace System* (1943) summarized the main arguments of the functionalists and by its very title drew attention to their major claim: functionalism is the road to a lasting peace. This claim has been the main target—and a very easy one—of the attacks on the functionalists. However, a close examination of the doctrine reveals that it may have other, more useful ideas to offer to the student of international relations.

The functionalist doctrine. The functionalist believes that contemporary nationalism rests on factors which cut across national lines, i.e., that there is a movement away from a demand for national rights and toward a demand for services (Mitrany 1943, p. 17. It must be remembered that Mitrany was writing during World War II and was predicting the shape of the postwar world by projecting the domestic trend toward welfare statism into the international arena). The functionalist maintains that social and economic maladjustments are the basic causes of war and that social and economic welfare is the precondition of peace. The real task of our common society is the conquest of poverty, ignorance, and disease; our social interdependence is all-pervasive and all-embracing.

The existing state system, according to the functionalist, contributes to international tensions and conflicts because it is institutionally inadequate. It cannot deal with basic global problems because it arbitrarily divides global society into national units based on territory, and not on the problem to be solved. International institutions based on *function* rather than on *territory* would be appropriate for the solution of such problems. Establishing such institutions is possible, he argues, because social activities can be separated into political and nonpolitical ("technical") ones. The particular activity (or function) will determine the form of the agency in any given case.

Furthermore, the experience gained in one area can be transferred to other areas so that a successful institutional device can serve as a model for devices in many different settings. Successful experience will spread and accumulate, forming part of the foundation for an international society. (This idea serves as the basis for the "spill-over" concept discussed below.)

The existing state system, in the functionalist canon, promotes the subjective allegiances which send men to war. International bodies that focus attention on areas of common interest may, on the other hand, foster international loyalty among people at large and counteract harmful nationalistic attitudes. Similarly, the leaders of national states—politicians, diplomats, and soldiers—are blinded by their narrow view of their national interests and do not have the proper perspective to encourage international cooperation. Experts working for international organizations will develop international loyalties and will help to create a peaceful international community.

Finally, the most basic premise of the functionalists, albeit not explicity stated, is that human beings are fundamentally rational, that they see the advantages of harmony over conflict in social relations, and that they can control their destiny through the evolutionary steps that will lead to a peaceful world.

The functionalist program emerges quite simply and clearly from the above premises. In selected areas of life, "comprehensive and solid" authorities will be created. Some of these already exist, but many more must be added, until a "web of international activities and agencies" will "overlay political divisions" (Mitrany 1943, pp. 10–11). Ultimately, international government, consisting of the sum of these agencies, will be coextensive with all international activities. Coordination among these various organizations will also emerge functionally. First there will be ties between individual bodies, based on common needs and problems. When these prove inadequate, groups of agencies will start to work together. Later, general international planning agencies will emerge, covering broad ranges of activities. Finally, a general political authority will emerge, out of the necessity for over-all coordination. (However, this last step is left rather vague and is not considered of immediate importance.)

The functionalists do recognize that difficulties may arise in the course of implementing their program, but they claim that such difficulties are merely mechanical and can be mechanically solved as they arise.

Criticism. Among the more sophisticated critics of functionalism is Inis Claude ([1956] 1964, chapter 16), who rejects most of the functionalist premises. War, he states, is not a product of economic and social conditions; rather, to quote Kelsen: "the unsatisfactory situation of world economy is the consequence of war" (1944, p. 16).

Furthermore, Claude rejects the notion of the "separability" of the economic and social strata of life from the political, and even if they could be separated, he believes that states would insist on putting off welfare matters until they had solved the political issues that divide them.

As for transferring cooperative experience from one sphere to another and accumulating cooperative spirit, here again Claude is pessimistic, believing that functional development is bounded by political issues and will expand only until halted by some crisis. "The problem of the recurrent setback, the interruption and disruption by war of the projects of functionalism for the eventual elimination of war, poses a critical dilemma" (Claude [1956] 1964, p. 354).

Claude also challenges the functionalists' reliance on human rationality, particularly the rational transfer of loyalties from national to international agencies. New institutions do not necessarily create new loyalties. Finally, Claude notes that the functionalist program for building the foundation of peace is a long-range one, and he is not sure that all that time is available (presumably before another world war erupts).

Most of this criticism is, of course, directed at the programmatic features of functionalism, challenging the proposition that this is the road to peace. In other words, Claude is engaging in an ideological debate (other critics do the same, only not as well). The empirical evidence he presents is not much better than the original evidence presented by the functionalists. However, regardless of the validity of these assertions and counterassertions, functionalism must also be examined from two other points of view: (*a*) as a phenomenon in international politics and (*b*) as a theoretical contribution to the study of international organization.

Functionalism in operation. Functionalists advocate building on existing foundations—extending the network of international agencies and increasing their powers. As already noted, this practical approach is one of the chief attractions of functionalism, for functional international organizations have existed for well over one hundred years, and their number has steadily increased. Accurate figures are hard to obtain because they depend on one's definition of a functional international organization. However, a general picture of governmental and nongovernmental organizations can be found in the *Yearbook of International Organizations* (see also Reuter 1956; Angell 1965).

In the nineteenth century, as a result of the rapid technological progress and the exploitation of new sources of energy, the range of international relations was greatly widened and nations found more and more common interests, which led to the creation of numerous international organizations, both private and governmental (Mangone 1954). From the functionalist's point of view, the most significant of these institutions were the "public unions" or "administrative unions." These generally started as treaties signed by states to protect specific interests. The treaties led to the establishment of international bureaus or secretariats which coordinated the activities of the members and handled administrative matters. Periodic meetings were held at which representatives of the member states set broad policies, generally making decisions by unanimous vote only.

These organizations emerged primarily in the fields of communications, transport, and commerce, and to a lesser extent in the areas of health and social welfare. Thus they represented primarily the economic and social interests of nations and were comparatively untouched by issues of war and peace. Several of these public unions have survived both world wars and are still functioning—some as specialized agencies of the United Nations but others as independent organizations. It is easy to see why the functionalists lay so much emphasis on separating economic from political issues and on increasing the number of such organizations: these are the ones that have continued to function and, within their limited spheres of competence, have achieved considerable success.

The founders of the League of Nations, although at first reluctant, did finally incorporate articles 23–25 into the Covenant (Walters 1952, vol. 1, p. 59). These articles suggest at least an awareness of functionalist concerns. Article 23 sketches areas of social concern; article 24 provides for administrative coordination of existing international bureaus, and even for the financing of such bodies if placed under the direction of the League; and article 25 is devoted to encouraging international health and prevention of disease. (Since a whole article is devoted to matters of health, it is quite clear that this was considered, at the time, a most important functional area.)

As the League started to operate, these "functional" aspects of its work assumed increasing importance. It set up technical committees, organized conferences, started technical assistance, and conducted studies in social and economic problem areas (Asher et al. 1957). In fact, most retrospective appraisals of the League single out this area of activity as its most notable achievement. For example: "In retrospect, the successes scored by its functional agencies seem to be the main redeeming features of the record of the League . . ." (Claude [1956] 1964, p. 357; see also Goodspeed 1959, pp. 76–77).

Although the League recognized the autonomy of some international public unions, such as the International Labour Organisation (ILO), it was basically committed to centralizing all its activities. The Council, therefore, was in charge of coordinating, supervising, and controlling even economic and social matters. The political pressures that were thus brought into the functional field were of some concern to the League, and a special committee was established to recommend improvements. The Bruce Report (League of Nations 1939) recommended the creation of a special body of governmental representatives *and experts* to replace the Council as the supervisory agency of the League's technical activities. In other words, this was a functionalist solution.

During and after World War II there was a growing awareness of the need for international social and economic collaboration. The United Nations Charter specifically provided for specialized agencies and for coordinating welfare activities through the Economic and Social Council (articles 55–72). It may be an exaggeration to call the whole United Nations system "a full fledged experiment in the application of the functional theory to international affairs" (Claude [1956] 1964, pp. 357–358), but there is no doubt that functionalist ideas were influential in creating the machinery for dealing with social and economic problems (Asher et al. 1957, pp. 420–639).

Since the drafting of the charter, the functional program of the United Nations has expanded considerably, and there has been an increase in the number of functional agencies outside the United Nations system (Jessup & Taubenfeld 1959, pp. 85–116, 117–134). True, in many fields the international organizations concerned have quite narrow, limited functions of an essentially administrative nature, and the important policies and decisions are made by the member states individually. Nevertheless, in several cases "supranational" political power has been given to the organizations, and in the case of the European Economic Community and its predecessors, the road seems to be leading to political integration.

In the discussion thus far it has not been made clear whether these functional phenomena were directly related to the work of the functionalists. Clearly, David Mitrany, Gunnar Myrdal, James Avery Joyce, and others used these international developments to illustrate their claims, but it is far from certain that these men, in turn, influenced the events. All one can say is that functionalist ideas influenced a considerable number of international civil servants and even some national leaders, both before and after World War II.

Important individuals like Albert Thomas of the ILO, Lord Boyd Orr of the Food and Agriculture Organization (FAO), Brock Chisolm of the World Health Organization (WHO), and Aake Ording of the United Nations International Children's Emergency Fund (UNICEF) often expressed views that would have pleased any functionalist (Schuman 1952). These men all occupied important positions during the formative years of their organizations and undoubtedly helped to create an atmosphere favorable to functionalism. In the European context, Jean Monnet, Walter Hallstein, and others have also expressed views that show their sympathy with functionalist ideas.

To conclude, the significance of functionalism in operation is that both international organizations and their leaders reflect many of its views and assumptions, and follow policies that agree with its programs.

Theoretical contributions. The fact that functionalist ideas were derived from international phenomena, and in turn influenced some policy makers and international institutions, draws attention to the contributions that functionalism can make to the study of international relations. It shows the importance of certain aspects of international relations that would otherwise be neglected and raises important questions about the nature of international political processes. In so doing, moreover, it enables students to use concepts and techniques from other areas of political science and from other social sciences to examine international relations.

The study of functional international organizations has traditionally occupied few scholars, and the topic has been allocated few pages in most books on international organization; general works on international relations barely mention them. Although this situation still prevails, there are signs of change, and credit is due to the functionalists and their emphasis on the role of such organizations (see, e.g., Alexandrowicz 1962).

The questions that arise out of the functionalist emphasis apply to several aspects of international relations. For example, do institutions precede functions or vice versa? Mitrany argued that only when the need for an organization is clear will that organization emerge. On the other hand it is obvious that as organizations grow, they subsume new functions and occasionally even create them. Clearly the relationship is worth investigating. Another example: What kind of constitution should an international organization have? Mitrany claimed that nothing could be worse than a written one. Yet most international bodies do in fact have some founding document—be it a covenant, a charter, or a treaty. Is this a factor in their difficulties? Should such agencies have unwritten constitutions? No constitutions? The connections here to international public law are obvious and important. A final example: Mitrany has been criticized for suggesting the Tennessee Valley Authority as a model for international public authorities. Much of the criticism may be valid, but the critics do not systematically examine why the analogy is faulty. The groundwork for such examinations is only now being laid, but clearly much can be learned by comparing national and international functional agencies (Alger 1963).

In addition to the institutions themselves, functionalism draws attention to the parts played by interest groups in international politics. Here, too, traditional scholarship was deficient, concentrating merely on governments and, at best, mentioning the *domestic* influence of pressure groups on foreign offices and diplomats. Very occasionally someone would refer to international nongovernmental organizations, only to dismiss them as mildly interesting but unimportant. There is, however, some evidence that the role of nongovernmental bodies is by no means insignificant, and their influence may occasionally even exceed that of governments (Meynaud 1961; Bock 1966).

Functionalists are often accused of having an idealized and therefore "unrealistic" view of human nature when they suggest that international institutions will develop international loyalties in their officials and help to overcome divisive national loyalties. This criticism oversimplifies the true position of the functionalists who also claim that officials may act to promote *international* interests even though their reasons are *nationalistic.* This argument can, of course, be empirically tested. Careful investigation will be able to determine the effects that working for an international organization has on the individuals concerned. At present, information of this kind is practically nonexistent. (But see some recent contributions in Kelman 1965.) In fact, little is systematically known about international civil servants, their backgrounds, their attitudes, etc. Even less is known about government representatives and interest group officials who act in the international arena. By drawing attention to these questions, functionalism opens another area for investigation.

Functionalism has also had a definite impact on the study of international law since 1945. The work of scholars like Philip C. Jessup and Howard J. Taubenfeld (1959), C. Wilfred Jenks (1958), and Wolfgang Friedmann (1964) clearly bears the mark of functionalist ideas. Friedmann, for example, notes with approval that "a functional approach to international organization correlates the development of international law and organization with political and social realities and tendencies of international life" (p. 276). A further reflection of this influence is the growth of international legal studies devoted to functional concerns, e.g., trade, conservation of resources, and social welfare. [*See* INTERNATIONAL LAW.]

But perhaps the major contribution of functionalism has been to the study of international integration. It is precisely in these terms that Haas (1964) examines it and finds it, on the whole, quite useful. The concepts of separability, transferability, and spill-over, which play such an important role in all discussions of international integration, originate in the ideas of the functionalists; and, of course, at the heart of the doctrine of functionalism lies the notion of integrating the nation-state system into a world community to achieve lasting peace.

Functional international integration

The concept of functional international integration, which refers to the integration of "technical" or "noncontroversial" activities of nations, forms a part of the broader concept of international integration. [*See* INTERNATIONAL INTEGRATION, *articles on* GLOBAL INTEGRATION *and* REGIONAL INTEGRATION.] Since the concept is of recent origin and since little work has been done on it, it might be useful to trace its origins before discussing its characteristics and potentialities.

Interest in "world community," "world government," the "commonwealth of man," or "one world" is, of course, quite old (see the survey in Schuman 1952); but only since the end of World War II have social scientists made serious efforts to study the phenomena described by these labels, largely because only since then have there been enough such phenomena to make empirical study worthwhile. [*See* PEACE.]

The growing interdependence of the nations of the world as a result of the enormous rate of technological change has been the subject of much comment. However, this interdependence has by no means been a one-way street leading to internationalism or a sense of world community. There has been an increase in world trade and international communication, which has brought developed countries into closer commercial relationships; at the same time poorer countries have been encouraged to multiply their international trade and financial contacts (Kindelberger 1965). But the same technological advances have also enabled national governments to increase their powers and activities and have made nationalism more popular and intractable than before. This process has been furthered by the growing discrepancy between rich countries and poor, by the fact that most developed countries devote a smaller part of their resources to foreign trade than they did in the past, and by the decline of large-scale international migrations which were quite common before 1914 (Deutsch et al. 1957, pp. 22–25). Similarly, the development of nuclear weapons has had a mixed effect, on the one hand creating the interdependence of "a community of fear" and encouraging negotiations and cooperation, and on the other hand increasing the tempo of the arms race and whetting the appetite of individual nations to acquire nuclear weapons of their own. Yet, important as the problem of interdependence is, it has not had as great an impact on scholarly interest as have the post-1945 developments in Europe. The evolution of a European economic community and the beginnings of political unification have presented economists and political scientists with data and have led them to develop the concept, or rather concepts, of "international integration." (Scholars are still far from agreeing on a definition of the term.)

Two other developments have contributed to the interest in integration and have broadened its subject matter. First, the emergence of a large number of new nations, many of them without unified political traditions or "sense of community," has led scholars to study "national integration." Second, the combination of technological advances and rapid urbanization has created problems inside many industrial countries; local or metropolitan governments are incapable of providing for the needs of people and larger units have not yet emerged; scholars, therefore, have begun to talk about "community formation" and "regional integration."

International integration, political as well as economic, has been defined variously as a *process*, a *condition*, or both. Arguments can be made for all three positions, but, from my point of view, defining integration as a process is the most useful. This has led me to accept the definition of Leon Lindberg, according to which political integration is "the process whereby nations forgo the desire and ability to conduct foreign and key domestic policies independently of each other, seeking instead to make *joint decisions* or to *delegate* the decision making process to new central organs" (1963, p. 5). Lindberg goes on to suggest that this process requires four conditions: (1) the development of central institutions and policies; (2) the assignment to these institutions of important specific tasks; (3) an inherently expansive nature to these tasks; and (4) the continued commitment of member states, i.e., they must continue to see their interests as consistent with the enterprise. (For different approaches see Jacob & Toscano 1964, pp. 1–11; Deutsch et al. 1957, p. 5; North et al. 1960.)

Note that this definition does not deal with the result of the process. Thus, no point is postulated at which integration is complete. For that matter, no special predetermined line of evolution is established; the process of integration may go on for any length of time and *may* result in a new political entity, but it does not have to.

As already indicated, most of the scholarly work on integration by economists and political scientists has concerned the European community, although some very recent studies have dealt with Africa (Nye 1965) and Latin America (Wionczek 1966). The emphasis has naturally been on *regional* phenomena, and very little attention has been paid either to global or to functional phenomena.

Economic integration. A possible exception to the emphasis upon regional phenomena can be found in the work of some economists. There is probably consensus among economists to regard economic integration as a process *and* a condition: a process encompassing measures to abolish discrimination between economic units belonging to different national states and a condition in which various forms of discrimination between national economies are absent (Balassa 1961, p. 1). As such, economic integration can take various forms, from free trade area to customs union to common market to economic union to complete economic integration, and it also describes the steps leading to the attainment of each of these forms. [*See* INTERNATIONAL INTEGRATION, *article on* ECONOMIC UNIONS.]

As to the means and objectives of economic integration, two extreme views may be contrasted: the "liberalist" and the "dirigist." The liberalist approach, also called "functional" (but not to be confused with our usage of the word), involves gradually eliminating impediments to commodity movements and eventually establishing "a larger market in which the laws of supply and demand can be effective without regional administrative intervention" (Sannwald & Stohler [1958] 1959, p. 84). The advocates of this approach (e.g., Maurice Allais, Wilhelm Röpke, and M. A. Heilperin) equate integration with trade liberalization and oppose the establishment of supranational institutions or, indeed, any form of political unification. Proponents of the dirigist or "institutional" approach (e.g., André Philip, Maurice Bye) say that integration should be established through positive administrative measures and maintained through continuous administrative action. They propose creating a supranational authority with the delegated functions of coordinating economic policies. (Obviously it is the dirigists who are closer in approach to the functionalists.)

By and large, however, economists agree on the way in which to study integration and tend to concentrate on such subjects as commodity and factors movements, size and growth of markets, economies of scale, and external economies. They acknowledge that political aspects are "of great consequence" but "leave it for the political scientist to determine the political implications of such developments" (Balassa 1961, pp. 6–7).

When political scientists do look at the work of the economists—and far too few have done so—they are not quite sure of its contributions. Haas and Schmitter seem to feel that "sophisticated economic analysis" and "pure economic theory" are not especially helpful, because the political actors do not see things the way economists do. On the other hand, they admit that economic analysis could indicate "the limits of the politically possible" if only economists could agree on welfare gains and losses in particular cases. Furthermore, they argue for viewing economic union as a prelude to political integration, even though the chief actors may not see it that way in the beginning (Haas & Schmitter 1964, pp. 707–709).

Global and functional integration. Clearly, the relationship between economic and political integration needs further exploration. I believe that the study of economic integration can certainly contribute to the study of international *political* integration along several important lines.

First, political scientists can use the concepts and techniques evolved by economists to study global integration, even though most of the economists' studies have been regional and European in scope. The universal process of economic integration, though much less advanced than the regional one, is nevertheless measurable in the same terms. And while the political elements that are absent from the economic formulation will not be discovered by this approach, it is fair to assume that precisely these elements are least developed on the global level. In brief, this approach could supply data on what might be called the "infrastructure" of the integration process.

Second, economic integration can be viewed as an important instance of functional integration, i.e., the integration of "technical" or "noncontroversial" activities of nations. Since almost all the empirical data on global integration concerns precisely such activities, this concept needs further elaboration. (Functional integration can, of course, also play an important role in the study of domestic integrative attempts—national, regional, or even local.)

Separability. The terms *technical* and *noncontroversial* have been used, rather than *nonpolitical*, to avoid the pitfall which trapped the functionalists. In their desire to promote international agencies they insisted that political and nonpolitical (i.e., social, economic, scientific, technological, etc.) activities can be separated and that the latter can be dealt with while the former remain in abeyance. Critics were quick to point out that such separability is a myth, since all the nonpolitical activities mentioned have definite political implications, and that as soon as nations feel their impact, they will intervene politically and destroy or at least change the nature of the organization, if indeed they don't create it as a political instrument in the first place.

This criticism is well taken, but to go further and argue that there is, therefore, no meaningful difference among international activities along these lines is totally unjustified. Every international activity may well have its political implications, but so long as the actors perceive it as *primarily* technical, noncontroversial, or unimportant to their major political concerns, it can be placed in a separate category for purposes of analysis and comparison. From this point of view, the idea of separability does come into play, and we can talk of the "autonomy of functional contexts" (Haas 1961), of functional international organizations, and of functional international integration.

There is some historical evidence that functional approaches were dominant in the early stages of most cases of international integration (Deutsch et al. 1957, p. 87). These approaches were the intermediate ground in those integrative attempts which led to the establishment of a new political entity as well as in those that led to more pluralism. In either instance, leaders found functional steps congenial and useful to advocate. Such steps do not visibly encroach on national sovereignty; they do not imply automatic political unification; and they generally do have immediate, visible, beneficial effects. Thus, "practical" men can support them. On the other hand, eventual expansion of integration into other fields, extending even to full-fledged political unity, is *not* excluded, so "idealists" can also rally round. Finally, functional activities are, by definition, specialized, and interest only limited segments of the population; national leaders, therefore, do not perceive them as threatening their domestic reputation. Consequently, functional international organizations meet with very little political opposition in most nations.

Spill-over. The major importance of functional integration, however, lies in the unintended consequences that such efforts have for the international integrative process. According to some observers, an "expansive logic" operates. Jean Monnet is represented as feeling that "the very disequilibrium produced by the integration of one sector and the nonintegration of the surrounding ones, the pressures from the central institutions and from the new community-wide political processes, will result in an ascending spiral of integration" (Hoffmann 1963, p. 530).

This idea of the expansive logic of functional integration is closely related to the "spill-over" concept evolved to explain the progress of integration in the face of the separate and autonomous policies that constitute each stage of the whole integrative process. The spill-over describes the way the powers and tasks of an institution expand because its existing powers and tasks are inadequate to meet the demands and expectations of the political actors involved. These expanded tasks then lead to further actions and new expectations and still further expansion. The concept helps us to analyze integration efforts without having to assume that all the participants share the same view of the desired end product. Spill-over is a significant concept because it draws attention to the different patterns of growth of institutional authority and of the decision-making process in international bodies.

Functional integration proceeds through the progressive delegation of the decision-making power. At first the decisions may be made in individual capitals on the basis of recommendations from an international nongovernmental group; then they are made jointly by representatives of nations in an international conference; and finally they are made by the international agency itself, thus contributing, almost casually, to international integration.

Another unintended consequence of the functional integrative process is the emergence of a new type of international actor: the functional specialist. He may be an international civil servant or a national specialist, but in either case preliminary studies show that he begins to feel a sense of community and develops a special interest in maintaining the system. His increasing decision-making power, of course, reinforces these feelings and allows him, if he is one of the more capable members of the organization, to initiate creative personal action to further the integrative process.

In conclusion, it should be obvious that functional international organizations are important agents in functional integration and should be studied from that point of view. There is no need to prejudge the case by implying that all such organizations inevitably lead to world peace and greater international unity. Quite the contrary: many of them may lead to conflict and disunity. However, it is clear that either result can be assessed in terms of the integrative process; and it is, therefore, important to find out which organization contributes how much under what circumstances and for what reasons to international integration or disintegration. This kind of research should rank high on the agenda of needed work in international organization and could lead to important contributions to international relations theory.

P. G. Bock

[*See also* International organization; Peace. *Other relevant material may be found under* Integration; International relations.]

BIBLIOGRAPHY

ALEXANDROWICZ, CHARLES H. 1962 *World Economic Agencies: Law and Practice.* New York: Praeger.

ALGER, CHADWICK F. 1963 Comparison of Intranational and International Politics. *American Political Science Review* 57:406–419.

ALKER, H. R.; and RUSSETT, B. M. 1964 *World Politics in the General Assembly.* New Haven: Yale Univ. Press.

ANGELL, ROBERT C. 1965 An Analysis of Trends in International Organizations. Peace Research Society, *Papers* 3:185–195.

ASHER, ROBERT E. et al. 1957 *The United Nations and Promotion of the General Welfare.* Washington: Brookings Institution. → An authoritative, scholarly analysis of policy and administration.

BALASSA, BELA A. (1961) 1962 *The Theory of Economic Integration.* London: Allen & Unwin.

BOCK, PETER GIDON 1966 A Study in International Regulation: The Case of Whaling. Ph.D. dissertation, New York Univ.

CLAUDE, INIS L. (1956) 1964 *Swords Into Plowshares: The Problems and Progress of International Organization.* 3d ed. New York: Random House.

DEUTSCH, KARL W. et al. 1957 *Political Community and the North Atlantic Area: International Organization in the Light of Historical Experience.* Princeton Univ. Press.

ENGLE, HAROLD E. 1957 A Critical Study of the Functionalist Approach to International Organization. Ph.D. dissertation, Columbia Univ.

FRIEDMANN, WOLFGANG G. 1964 *The Changing Structure of International Law.* New York: Columbia Univ. Press.

GOODSPEED, STEPHEN S. 1959 *The Nature and Function of International Organization.* New York: Oxford Univ. Press.

HAAS, ERNST B. 1961 International Integration: The European and the Universal Process. *International Organization* 15:366–392.

HAAS, ERNST B. 1964 *Beyond the Nation-state: Functionalism and International Organization.* Stanford Univ. Press.

HAAS, ERNST B.; and SCHMITTER, PHILIPPE C. 1964 Economics and Differential Patterns of Political Integration: Projections About Unity in Latin America. *International Organization* 18:705–737.

HOFFMANN, STANLEY 1963 Discord in Community: The North Atlantic Area as a Partial International System. *International Organization* 17:521–549.

JACOB, PHILIP E.; and TOSCANO, J. V. (editors) 1964 *The Integration of Political Communities.* Philadelphia: Lippincott.

JENKS, C. WILFRED 1958 *The Common Law of Mankind.* New York: Praeger.

JESSUP, PHILIP C.; and TAUBENFELD, HOWARD J. 1959 *Controls for Outer Space and the Antarctic Analogy.* New York: Columbia Univ. Press.

KELMAN, HERBERT C. (editor) 1965 *International Behavior: A Social-psychological Analysis.* New York: Holt.

KELSEN, HANS 1944 *Peace Through Law.* Chapel Hill: Univ. of North Carolina Press.

KIHL, YOUNG WHAN 1963 A Study of Functionalism in International Organization, With Special Reference to the Cases of the Universal Postal Union and the International Telecommunication Union. Ph.D. dissertation, New York Univ.

KINDELBERGER, CHARLES P. 1965 Trends in International Economics. American Academy of Political and Social Science, *Annals* 358:170–179.

KITZINGER, UWE W. (1961) 1963 *The Politics and Economics of European Integration: Britain, Europe and the United States.* Rev. ed. New York: Praeger. → See especially Chapter 3. Previous editions were published under the title *The Challenge of the Common Market.*

LEAGUE OF NATIONS 1939 *The Development of International Co-operation in Economic and Social Affairs: Report of the Special Committee.* Geneva: The League.

LINDBERG, LEON N. 1963 *The Political Dynamics of European Economic Integration.* Stanford Univ. Press.

MANGONE, GERARD J. 1954 *A Short History of International Organization.* New York. McGraw-Hill.

MARTIN, CURTIS W. 1950 The History and Theory of the Functional Approach to International Organization. Ph.D. dissertation, Harvard Univ.

MEYNAUD, JEAN 1961 *Les groupes de pression internationaux.* Lausanne (Switzerland): Études de Science Politique.

MITRANY, DAVID (1943) 1966 *A Working Peace System.* 4th ed. Chicago: Quadrangle. → The 1966 edition includes additional material dated 1948–1965.

NORTH, ROBERT C.; KOCH, HOWARD E.; and ZINNES, DINA A. 1960 The Integrative Functions of Conflict. *Journal of Conflict Resolution* 4:355–374.

NYE, J. S. 1965 Patterns and Catalysts in Regional Integration. *International Organization* 19:870–884.

REUTER, PAUL (1956) 1958 *International Institutions.* New York: Rinehart; London: Allen & Unwin. → First published in French.

SANNWALD, ROLF; and STOHLER, JACQUES (1958) 1959 *Economic Integration: Theoretical Assumptions and Consequences of European Unification.* Princeton Univ. Press. → First published in German.

SCHUMAN, FREDERICK L. 1952 *The Commonwealth of Man: An Inquiry Into Power Politics and World Government.* New York: Knopf.

SEWELL, JAMES P. 1966 *Functionalism and World Politics: A Study Based on United Nations Programs Financing Economic Development.* Princeton Univ. Press. → Compares the operational impact of the IBRD, IFC, IDA, and the UN Special Fund in a "functionalist" context.

WALTERS, FRANCIS P. (1952) 1960 *A History of the League of Nations.* Oxford Univ. Press.

WEINER, MYRON 1965 Political Integration and Political Development. American Academy of Political and Social Science, *Annals* 358:52–64.

WIONCZEK, MIGUEL S. (editor) 1966 *Latin American Economic Integration: Experiences and Prospects.* New York: Praeger.

Yearbook of International Organizations. → Published since 1948. Brussels: Union of International Associations.

IV
ECONOMIC UNIONS

The partial integration of the economies of a group of countries can take a number of characteristic forms. A *preferential tariff system* is composed of a group of countries charging lower tariffs on products imported from each other than are charged on products imported from the rest of the world. A *free trade area* is composed of a set of countries with no tariffs on trade among themselves but with no common tariff against the outside world. A free trade area requires customs points at internal borders since, in their absence, goods destined for any member would enter the area through the member country with the lowest rate of tariff on that good. A *customs union* has free trade between member countries plus a common external tariff. A customs union does not require customs points to regulate the movement within the area of goods imported from outside the area. A *common market* is a customs union with additional provisions to ensure the free movement of factors of production between member countries. An *economic union* is a common market with some provision for common monetary, fiscal, and other governmental policies, while *complete economic integration* implies a single economic policy over all the participating countries.

Historically, economic policies to foster the freer movement of factors and goods have usually been associated with political objectives. The United States provided one of the earliest experiments in economic union, and this was combined with political union. In this case the union became inward-looking, erecting a tariff barrier against the outside world and fostering local industrial development; imports as a percentage of national product declined steadily from quite a high level at the outset to a level of less than 3 per cent in the 1960s. The political unification of Germany was also associated first with a customs union, the Zollverein, and later with a high-tariff policy introduced by Bismarck in the 1870s which fostered domestic industries at the expense of imported goods and coincided, as in the United States, with an era of rapid industrial development. In the 1930s, under the impact of the great depression, Britain abandoned her 100-year-old policy of free trade and adopted the imperial preference system. Under this system member countries of the commonwealth and empire adopted tariffs on most imports but set their rates substantially lower on goods originating in other member countries than on goods from nonmembers.

After World War II, economic unions of various kinds became popular, undoubtedly in reaction to the inadequacies of the old nation-state. The West Indies common market was originally linked to the political drive to establish the West Indies Federation. Plans are also proceeding to group Argentina, Brazil, Chile, Paraguay, Peru, Uruguay, and Mexico into the Latin American Free Trade Association and to unite El Salvador, Guatemala, Honduras, and Nicaragua into the Central American Common Market. The movement toward economic integration that has aroused most interest is the one that developed in western Europe shortly after the war. The Netherlands, Belgium, and Luxembourg first formed a customs union, then a full economic union. Subsequently, these three Benelux countries plus France, Germany, and Italy formed the European Common Market. In 1960 the "outer seven" countries of Austria, Denmark, Great Britain, Norway, Portugal, Sweden, and Switzerland formed the European Free Trade Association.

The early stages of the European Common Market (ECM) were very successful. A schedule was drawn up for the phased elimination of tariff on manufactured goods; subsequently the timetable was adhered to and sometimes accelerated. In the contexts of fully employed economies these tariff reductions have generally caused less economic dislocation than many had feared at the outset. Extending the Common Market to cover the agricultural sector has, however, proved to be very difficult. The central authorities of most countries are committed to a much more comprehensive and complex set of interventions in the agricultural sector than in manufacturing. Arrangements for establishing a single agricultural market and a common agricultural policy were not agreed on at the outset, but a timetable was set up for the various stages of negotiations on this subject. It subsequently proved impossible to adhere strictly to this schedule for delayed agreement.

There can be little doubt that the drive toward the ECM was motivated mainly by those whose ultimate aim was the political union of Europe and who saw economic union as a means to this political end rather than as a means to more specific economic goals, such as improving the efficiency of resource allocation, increasing the degree of competition, or raising the rate of growth. The Common Market negotiations were successful because there was a climate of opinion in favor of some supranational development in Europe. As time has passed and the ravages of World War II have become more remote to memory, the climate has swung back to a more nationalistic outlook. This change has been particularly marked in France, and it has undoubtedly made more difficult the skillful handling of the two largest problems confronting the Common Market in recent times: the as yet unsuccessful attempts to agree on terms for the entry of Great Britain into the market and the extreme difficulties encountered in finding a solution to the agricultural problem.

Analysis of economic welfare effects

In spite of the obvious political motivation behind the European and other common markets, evidenced by the lack of interest of member countries in attempts to quantify the potential economic gains, economists have been interested in discovering and quantifying the sources of potential economic gains and losses arising out of such unions. And the discussion of such issues among economists has been given considerable practical importance by the fact that politicians in those countries which want to stay out of the European and other economic unions because they disapprove of the political objectives have been forced to ask themselves if their countries can afford the economic cost of doing so.

A theoretical study begins with a classification of tariff systems. A nondiscriminating tariff system charges a single *ad valorem* rate on all commodities. A discriminating tariff system discriminates between commodities when different rates are charged on different commodities and discriminates between countries when different rates are charged on a single commodity, the rate varying with the country of origin. All of the forms of partial economic integration distinguished at the outset of this article involve the introduction of geographically discriminating tariff systems.

In the past, statesmen have often taken differing attitudes to preferential tariff systems and customs unions, condemning the former and praising the latter. From the economists' point of view there is no fundamental distinction between the two. The critical factor in both cases is the introduction of a geographically discriminating tariff system, and what matters is that the rate of tariff on goods coming from other member countries is made lower than the rate on goods coming from outside countries; the situation when the tariff on members is zero is only a special case.

Static considerations. It has become customary to divide the effects of unions into static and dynamic ones. Static effects concern resource allocation, the location of consumption, and the terms of trade. We shall consider each of these in turn.

Resource allocation. The effects of a customs union on resource allocation have been divided by Viner (1950) into trade-creating and trade-diverting effects. If two or more of the member countries have an industry producing some commodity under tariff protection, then, with the abolition of tariffs on trade between union members, the lowest-cost source of supply within the union will capture the union market and will drive out the higher-cost sources of supply. This change represents a shift toward lower-cost sources of production, and it creates trade between union members where previously protected industries had each satisfied its own national market. Such a change is called a *trade-creating* one. If, however, one of the union countries has a tariff-protected industry producing some commodity, X, while at least one other union country does not have such a protected industry, then *trade diversion* is likely to occur. Before the union, the nonproducing country would be buying from the cheapest possible foreign source, since its tariff system would not distort the real structure of the relative prices of one good imported from alternative sources. The customs union does, however, distort these relative prices. If the protected industry's price without tariff is less than the price of the same good bought from the outside world including tariff, then the nonproducing union country will switch from buying from the outside world to buying from its union partner. This causes a shift of resources from lower-cost to higher-cost sources of production and diverts one of the partners' trade from nonunion sources of supply. Both trade-creating and trade-diverting effects can occur if the formation of the union leaves unchanged the average level of tariffs on goods from third countries. If the formation of the union is the occasion of increasing tariffs against nonunion countries, then the trade-diverting element will be reinforced.

Consumption patterns. Customs unions also affect the pattern of consumption by changing the structure of relative prices of goods. Even if production were totally unaffected by the union, there would tend to be a reallocation of world consumption. The union has the effect of lowering the relative prices of goods imported from other union countries vis-à-vis the prices both of domestically produced goods and of goods imported from the outside world. This will usually cause each union country to consume more of the goods produced by its partners and less of goods produced both domestically and by nonunion countries. The welfare effects of these consumption changes are most easily appreciated intuitively by considering the two sets of changes in relative prices separately. The union brings relative prices into conformity with the real terms of trade existing between union countries and, *ceteris paribus*, this tends to raise welfare, but it creates a divergence between the relative prices of goods imported from other union countries on the one hand and from the outside world on the other. *Ceteris paribus*, this tends to lower welfare.

Terms of trade. The third main effect of a union on welfare is through the terms of trade. Generally, the trade-diverting effects of the union will mean that union countries are reducing their demands for goods from nonunion countries, and this will usually tend to turn the terms of trade in the union's favor. If the tariffs levied by the union countries against the rest of the world were at or above the optimum level before the union was formed, this "favorable" change in the terms of trade will tend to lower union welfare.

All three static effects can either raise or lower welfare, so there can be no general qualitative prediction about the direction of the welfare changes caused by customs unions. Some generalizations about factors pushing the balance toward gain or loss have been put forward. The most important are that unions are more likely to bring gain in each of the following circumstances: (1) the larger the area covered by the union, because the larger the area, the larger is the volume of trade creation likely to be relative to the volume of trade diversion; (2) the higher the level of preunion tariffs between union members, because the higher the level, the more nearly self-sufficient the members will have been and the larger the number of protected industries that may be subject to trade creation; (3) the further apart the unit costs in the different union countries of any commodity subject to trade creation, because the further apart the costs, the greater the gain per unit of trade created; (4) the lower the level of preunion and postunion tariffs against the outside world, because the lower the level, the smaller the number of commodities subject to trade diversion; (5) the closer together the unit costs of union and nonunion members for any commodity subject to trade diversion, because the smaller will be the loss per unit of trade diversion; (6) the lower the outside world's own general level of tariffs, because the lower this is, the smaller the distorting effect on the relative prices of union and nonunion members' goods as seen in markets both within and without the union.

Quantification of gains. Several notable attempts have been made to quantify the possible welfare effects of customs unions or of other tariff cuts on a similar scale. The most important are those of P. J. Verdoorn (1960), H. G. Johnson (1958), and J. Wemelsfelder (1960). All of these have come up with the answer that the potential gains from resource reallocation are extremely small—probably a once-for-all gain on the order of the magnitude of 1 per cent of a country's national income. This gain, which is equivalent to that brought about by no more than a few months of economic growth, seems hardly worth making a vast effort to attain or taking any substantial risks to obtain. Clearly, the whole case of free trade versus modest tariffs on the order of 10 per cent or 20 per cent *ad valorem* needs to be rethought in the light of these figures.

A simple calculation, using no more than one or two well-known facts, shows that the results of the detailed studies mentioned above are unlikely to have underestimated the order of magnitude of the static gains. Typical tariff levels of European countries prior to the formation of the Common Market were on the order of 20 per cent. This meant that the *maximum level* of inefficiency of a protected domestic industry was 20 per cent. The *average level* was likely to have been closer to 10 per cent than to 20 per cent. The percentage of a country's resources that are engaged in producing goods inefficiently under tariff protection is more difficult to estimate, but the upper limit can be taken as the percentage of resources in those industries which are unable to cover existing costs without tariff protection. This could hardly have exceeded 10 per cent of total resources in the countries of western Europe and is likely to have been much less in many. Taking these rough orders of magnitudes, we have 10 per cent of a country's resources producing goods on average 10 per cent less efficiently than they could have been produced abroad. Eliminating this inefficiency should raise the over-all productivity of a country's resources by 1 per cent, thus raising national income by the same figure.

Dynamic considerations. With the publication of the above estimates the supporters of economic unions shifted their case from static arguments, which were the ones mainly relied on until then, to dynamic arguments. The main dynamic considerations are economies of scale, the effects on market structures, and the effects on the underlying growth rate.

Economies of scale. Let us consider the industries in a particular member country that are efficient enough to survive the formation of the union. If, in the preunion situation, their domestic and export market was not large enough to allow all significant economies of scale to have been exhausted, then the enlargement of the market consequent to the formation of a union will allow further scale economies to be realized, and the reduction in real unit costs of production will contribute to a once-for-all rise in living standards. The rise may, of course, be spread over several years, while the economies are realized through time, but it is not a source of permanent change in the rate of growth.

Effect on market structures. If the unified market contributes to wider competition and breaks down monopoly positions in the formerly protected markets of individual member countries, then the formation of the union may lead to welfare gains. If, on the other hand, the climate of the union is conducive to the formation of monopolies and restrictive practice agreements, welfare may be lowered. It is also believed by many that the chill winds of international competition will force more efficient behavior on people who were formerly sheltered behind high national tariff walls and were willing to earn only modest profits in return for quite unadventurous business behavior.

Effect on long-term growth rates. The possible effect of a union on long-term growth rates is more difficult to determine. If larger firms have more funds to devote to research and development than have the smaller firms that satisfy separate national markets, this could be an important source of dynamic gain. If the union fosters a more competitive spirit which in turn leads to a more active search for innovations, this could also be important. On the other hand, it is possible that some member areas could suffer seriously if the union accentuates regional inequalities by reinforcing the advantages of already well advanced areas. The way in which this could happen is outlined in the works of Myrdal (1956) and Perroux (1955) that are discussed briefly later in this article.

Quantitative importance of dynamic gains. Empirical knowledge of the quantitative importance of the dynamic factors is sketchy. Various economists have given widely different guesses on the unexploited economies of scale existing in the various countries of western Europe. Bela Balassa (1961) has reviewed much of the evidence and has made a good case for the existence of unexploited economies in the Common Market countries, thus supporting the belief that an increase in the size of the market consequent on the formation of the ECM would lead to some reduction in real costs of production. We have virtually no knowledge, however, of how significant this would be in quantitative terms. As in the case of resource reallocation, the gains could be trivial. If, say, 20 per cent of a country's productive units found their real costs falling by 5 per cent, the gain could be in the order of a once-for-all rise in national income of 1 per cent. For the gains to be substantial, either costs would have to fall dramatically, or a very large proportion of the country's total productive activities would have to be involved.

Empirical evidence is very sketchy on the second effect of unions: that on the degree of competition. Persons favorable to the European Common Market have suggested that, while not being hostile to bigness per se, the market authorities are trying to encourage competition. Persons hostile to the market have argued that the actions of the authorities will in the end encourage the growth of more effective monopolies than were likely when a single central policy could not affect behavior in all six member countries. The fact that both views are still argued vigorously shows that sufficient evidence has not yet been accumulated to allow us to take a final stand on the important case study of the effect of the European Common Market on encouraging or discouraging various market forms.

It has also been argued that, while not actually changing market forms, the Common Market will increase the degree of effective competition within any existing form. For example, many people in Great Britain have put great stress on the beneficial effects of continental European competition in forcing a more progressive attitude on management and labor. Others believe, however, that the adaptation of labor and management will not occur fast enough and that as a result of the sudden introduction of competition from the Continent, Britain would be turned into a permanently depressed area. It is argued that these unfavorable trends would be accentuated by the near certainty that Britain would go into the Common Market with an overvalued exchange rate due to misplaced feelings of national pride. This might reduplicate the situation of the 1920s, when Britain, following a return to the gold standard at an overvalued exchange rate, experienced a severe local depression, with over 10 per cent unemployment, from 1925 to 1930. Those holding this view argue that to take even a small chance of a large loss in order to get a fairly large chance of a small gain is a gamble that should appeal to very few.

There remains the third possible source of gain: the effect of the union on the long-term growth rate of the participating countries taken as a whole. Here we have very little evidence as yet, and about all that can be said is that the work of Lamfalussy (1961) shows that the rapid growth in "the six" cannot, with any reasonable degree of probability, be ascribed to developments in the Common Market to date.

There is also concern about the effects of the union on differential growth rates in various developed and backward areas of the union. The work of Myrdal (1956) and Perroux (1955) suggests that unions may accentuate regional inequalities as already established centers of growth attract the most mobile and most productive factors from the underdeveloped areas. This theory is in contradiction to the classical theory of resource allocation, but it can be developed as a fully consistent theory based on certain dynamic postulates. The choice between the two must thus be made on empirical grounds. Borts and Stein (1964) have produced evidence from the United States that regional inequalities tend to lessen as growth proceeds. This evidence is in favor of the classical theory, but a final verdict must await further studies. In the meantime the outcome is critical to underdeveloped economies on the fringe of the Common Market that must decide whether or not to make a determined effort to enter the organization.

The general state of empirical knowledge on all possible effects of unions, other than the reallocation of resources according to comparative advantage, is most unsatisfactory. The knowledge existing at the time of writing was reviewed to this effect by Lipsey (1960). In spite of a great deal of discussion and argument on qualitative issues, we remain profoundly ignorant on most of the important questions which are capable of being quantified. This lack of knowledge was dramatically illustrated by a poll of British economists taken by the London *Observer* at a time of British negotiations for entry into the Common Market. The opinions of highly reputable economists ran the entire gamut from "total disaster" to "enormous gains" ("The *Observer* . . ." 1962). Such divergent views could not be held by large numbers in the face of any solid body of evidence. The significance of some of the views expressed has been discussed in another context by Hutchison (1964).

The political implications of economic union have already been mentioned, and there can be no doubt that many supporters of customs unions and common markets see them as a first step toward political union. Some economists (for example, Meade 1953) argue that the practical problems of a common market will force greater harmony of policies on the central authorities, irrespective of their own desires. These economists thus see a high degree of economic and political integration as the inevitable result of economic union. This possibility explains the hostile attitude to economic union on the part of many who might be favorably inclined to its more limited economic objectives.

There is general agreement that some economic and social policies will have to be harmonized; minimum wage laws and corporate income taxes are two examples. It is accepted, however, and American experience seems to confirm this, that quite substantial differences in some tax rates and in some social policies can be sustained within the framework of a closely integrated common market.

To what extent independent monetary and fiscal policies can be operated is still conjectural. Clearly the high degree of economic interdependence fostered by a union, together with a fixed exchange rate policy, reduces the freedom of one country to operate a full employment policy independent of its partners. Within a union there is no way to insulate the balance of payments of one country from the effects of an inflation of that country's aggregate demand by exchange depreciation or tax and quota policies to reduce imports. Clearly some degree of autonomy must be abandoned. Just how much and whether it is a modest or an exorbitant price to pay for the advantage of union are some of the most important unsolved problems facing policy makers today.

RICHARD G. LIPSEY

[*See also* INTERNATIONAL TRADE; INTERNATIONAL TRADE CONTROLS.]

BIBLIOGRAPHY

BALASSA, BELA A. (1961) 1962 *The Theory of Economic Integration.* London: Allen & Unwin.

BORTS, GEORGE H.; and STEIN, JEROME L. 1964 *Economic Growth in a Free Market.* New York: Columbia Univ. Press.

HUTCHISON, T. W. 1964 *"Positive" Economics and Policy Objectives.* London: Allen & Unwin.

JOHNSON, HARRY G. 1958 The Gains From Freer Trade With Europe: An Estimate. *Manchester School of Economics and Social Studies* 26:247–255.

LAMFALUSSY, ALEXANDER 1961 Europe's Progress: Due to Common Market? *Lloyd's Bank Review* Second Series, No. 62:1–16.

LIPSEY, R. G. 1960 The Theory of Customs Unions: A General Survey. *Economic Journal* 70:496–513.

MEADE, JAMES E. 1953 *Problems of Economic Union.* Univ. of Chicago Press.

MYRDAL, GUNNAR (1956) 1957 *Rich Lands and Poor: The Road to World Prosperity.* Rev. ed. New York: Harper. → First published as *Development and Underdevelopment.*

The *Observer* Poll of Economists' Views on the Common Market. 1962 *Observer* Oct. 14, 1962.

PERROUX, FRANÇOIS 1955 Note sur la notion de "pôle de croissance." *Économie appliquée* 8:307–320.

SCITOVSKY, TIBOR (1958) 1962 *Economic Theory and Western European Integration.* Stanford Univ. Press; London: Allen & Unwin.

VERDOORN, PETRUS J. 1960 The Intra-block Trade of Benelux. Pages 291–329 in International Economic Association, *Economic Consequences of the Size of Nations.* Edited by E. A. G. Robinson. New York: St. Martins.

VINER, JACOB 1950 *The Customs Union Issue.* Studies in the Administration of International Law and Organization, No. 10. New York: Carnegie Endowment for International Peace.

WEMELSFELDER, J. 1960 The Short-term Effect of the Lowering of Import Duties in Germany. *Economic Journal* 70:94–103.

INTERNATIONAL LAW

The article under this heading deals with the nature, scope, and study of international law. Major areas of the field are discussed in ADJUDICATION, *article on* INTERNATIONAL ADJUDICATION; CONFLICT OF LAWS; INTERNATIONAL LEGISLATION. *Various international legal problems are analyzed in* DIPLOMACY; DISARMAMENT; HUMAN RIGHTS; INTERNATIONAL CONFLICT RESOLUTION; INTERNATIONAL CRIMES; SANCTIONS, INTERNATIONAL; SPACE, OUTER, *article on* POLITICAL AND LEGAL ASPECTS. *Especially relevant to the development of the field are the biographies of* GROTIUS; KELSEN; MOORE, JOHN BASSETT; SUÁREZ; VATTEL. *Related material can be found under* INTERNATIONAL ORGANIZATION; INTERNATIONAL RELATIONS; PUBLIC LAW; *and in the detailed guide under* LAW.

Two fields of jurisprudence claim the title "international law." Private international law, also known as conflict of laws, consists of the principles by which national courts decide which of two or more national systems of law should apply to a transaction marked by international elements of place, participation, or subject matter. Apart from treaty, these principles rest solely upon national authority, and the title "international" for this field is therefore in dispute, though the transnational features of the claims involved provide some justification for it. What is more commonly and undisputedly understood by international law is public international law, and it is with this alone that the present article is concerned.

Scope and development

The traditional definition of public international law presents it, in the much quoted words of Brierly ([1928] 1963, p. 1), as "the body of rules and principles of action which are binding upon civilized states in their relations with one another." There are, unhappily, ambiguities in this hallowed description that rob it of the accuracy expected of definition. It begs essential questions. In what sense, for example, is what we call international law binding upon states? What is the meaning and relevance of "civilized"?

We move nearer to the facts when we describe international law as the complex of rules, principles, standards, and procedures more or less observed by governments in their business with one another. Governments habitually assert that they are scrupulously observing internationally approved norms of official conduct in such business. They even acknowledge a legal obligation so to act. But they also reserve the right to determine for themselves what the rules are. Their submission to impartial adjudication is either by special agreement or, if made in advance, subject to such exceptions as "political disputes" and "domestic jurisdiction." General also is the tacit reservation of self-preservation as defined by the interested state party, whereas in national systems this plea is subject to judicial scrutiny and limited by the rights of others. We have not yet reached in the international sphere that basic rule of modern legal systems which requires universal submission to impartial determination of what the law is in any given situation.

Such reservations narrow the scope and limit the efficacy of international law. When all these qualifications have been made, however, it remains true that the norms grouped under that title do play a part in shaping the policies and determining the conduct of governments and do serve importantly in the resolution of international conflict. They are invoked in the assertion of title to territory and in support of the authority of states therein, while on the other hand they define responsibilities for injuries to alien persons and enterprises within the national jurisdiction. These norms stipulate the freedom of the high seas and set limits to the maritime jurisdiction of states. They define rights and duties in the air and are being extended to outer space. They regulate diplomatic and consular interchange and the conclusion and effect of treaties. Historically, they have limited the scope and moderated the savagery of war, though the conditions of a nuclear age call for drastic revision of what used to be the most highly elaborated portion of international law.

In our time, more than ever, it is useful for even the most powerful state to make out a broadly respected legal case for any important international action it may wish to take. The "parliamentary diplomacy" that has become so familiar in the multifarious activities of the United Nations and in incessant *ad hoc* conferences requires constant justification of national policies, and the support of a strong majority reduces the material and other costs of performance. The appeal to law is accordingly a commonplace of international political debate. As for international arbitral and judicial proceedings, these depend for their present limited success, as well as for their promise of increasing efficacy as a substitute for war, upon exhaustive argumentation and reasoned decision couched in international legal terms. The resulting "case law" clarifies and enriches the fund of principles available for the rational disposal of disputes among nations.

References to law binding upon governments abound in the ancient, medieval, and modern literature of East and West alike. Until a relatively recent time these references were essentially exhortations, more or less elaborate and more or less direct, to personal sovereigns, urging them to obey laws imposed by God or nature or the consensus of mankind upon all human beings regardless of rank and position. Their special object was to persuade the sovereign that, vast as his authority might be, he was still subject to *jus divinum*, *jus naturae*, and *jus gentium* (a mixture never clearly analyzed) both in his treatment of those under his own rule and in his dealings with other sovereigns and their peoples. Sovereignty, though the highest human authority, was represented as a divine trust, to be administered under a supreme law.

In the Western world these invocations of divine and natural law and law of nations took on increasing precision and system with the Renaissance. The emergence of independent and powerful nation-states, with their violent rivalries in Europe and their arrogant claims to newly discovered lands and seas, sharpened the need for legal demarcation of rights and duties. More or less coherent essays and treatises, with dominant emphasis on the just occasions and lawful conduct of war, were written by such jurists and theologians as Pierino Belli (1563), Balthazar Ayala (1582), Francisco de Vitoria (1557), Francisco Suárez (1612–1621), and Hugo Grotius (1625). Gradually, in spite of Samuel von Pufendorf's dogma (1688, book 2, chapter 3, § 23) that natural law is alone binding on the state, the authority of customary practice embodying general consensus became dominant in the mixture. In England, Richard Zouche (1650) made this his chief source. In Neuchâtel, Emer de Vattel did his confused best to keep a foot upon the natural-law foundation; but it was his treatment of such practical matters as maritime rights and duties, the privileges of rulers and their diplomatic agents, contraband, and the general relations of belligerents and neutrals (1758) that won for his work the unrivaled respect that it enjoyed for most of a century. His German contemporary Johann Jakob Moser established (1777–1780) the pure strain of positivism that set the tone for the literature of the subject in the nineteenth century.

Positivism, the doctrine that law is necessarily man-made and that the consent of states, expressed in the form of customary practice or treaty, is the sole basis of international law, has since that time continued to be the prevalent theory underlying the actual conduct of states. It has been reinforced of late by the energetic adherence of the Soviet Union and by the explosive emergence of new states insisting upon independence and the right to question norms established before they became recognized members of the "family of nations."

Both in the classrooms and in learned treatises, positivism has recently come under heavy attack. Natural law, which has never ceased to have its champions, is recruiting new believers, while the sociological analysis of law-making processes in all their complexity de-emphasizes the role of consent in the international order, as it has de-emphasized the role of command in the national sphere (Hart 1961, chapters 5 and 10). The jurist who approaches his subject from a general study of social processes is likely to regard law as a crystallization of a culture, a communal way of life, deriving its authority from all the factors that hold a community together.

Main schools of thought

The range of contemporary thought upon international law may be indicated by a brief notice of two contrasting doctrines and some intervening positions.

We begin with the doctrine that asserts the primacy of international law. National law is a subordinate, delegated order, the validity of its content being determined by the international order. State sovereignty is merely the competence assigned by international law to the state. Like the law of the state, the law of the international community is a coercive order, and its rules do not depend for their validity upon the consent of the state to which they are being applied. They are derived from a basic norm, which has been variously stated as *pacta sunt servanda*, agreements are to be kept (Anzilotti 1923, chapter 2), "States ought to behave as they have customarily behaved" (Kelsen 1945, p. 369), and "The will of the international community must be obeyed" (Lauterpacht 1933, p. 421). Since the legal orders of the states belonging to the international community are derivatives of the international order, their authority has its ultimate source in this basic norm.

The works produced under the banner of international primacy have had the merit of bringing into sharp relief the contradictions inherent in traditional theories of international law, and the best of them present an admirably coherent image of a supranational order at a stage of development at which it could do for a world community what national legal orders do for the best-governed states of our time. Yet, though the doctrine does little more than draw out the logical implications of daily official utterances on the legal aspects of international relations, the image projected is remote from present realities and prospects. One index of this remoteness is the summary rejection of the doctrine by Soviet jurists, for whom state sovereignty is the greatest of the commandments and who insist that national and international law are necessarily separate orders, each with specific character, the former being an order of subordination, the latter an order of coordination among equal subjects (V. I. Lisovskii 1961, pp. 7–8).

At the other end of the scale we find a school that conceives of law as a process that determines how the collective power of a community is in fact applied. Its so-called rules are neither commands nor derivatives of any a priori universal principle or postulate and do not dictate specific decisions. They are principles developed in the life of a community, reflecting its prevalent demands, identifications, and expectations. Their function is to direct the attention of decision makers to factors that should be taken into account (McDougal & Feliciano 1961, pp. 62–63, 96, and *passim*). The duty of the administrator, legislator, or judge in the national or international order is, then, to examine claims in all their relevant aspects and to make the decision that will go furthest to promote the values of the community which he serves.

This doctrine is criticized on the ground that it unduly reduces the compulsory character of law and endows it with a degree of flexibility that is incompatible with its stabilizing function. It appears to favor a government of men, not of law. The familiar dichotomy is of course false, except insofar as it contrasts the extremes of fixed prescription and personal caprice. Adherents of the "policy-sciences" school rightly observe that no verbal formula can dispense with or escape interpretation varying with time, circumstance, and personality; and they maintain that their approach goes furthest toward decision in full cognizance of community interests and consequences. Perhaps a more substantial objection is that, as a model for decision makers, what they offer amounts to a counsel of perfection. In its insistence upon recondite analysis of contending claims, the doctrine would seem to demand qualities and qualifications that no present mode of selection calls for in the responsible actor.

Between the two schools of thought just sketched stand others, differing among themselves in detail, but united in rejecting, on the one hand, the Olympian view that attributes primacy to the international order and, on the other hand, a suspected trend toward identification of law and behavior. Explicit or implicit here is the dualism, unquestioned until recent times, that separates national and international orders into distinct systems deriving their authority from different sources. The more recent writers in this category start from a re-examination of the relative roles of law and power in the relations of states, make allowance for the transforming effect of environmental change, admit that the legal rule may be a passing balance of shifting interests, but at the same time emphasize its temporarily imperative intent and stabilizing function. The reality of international society or community, which is taken for granted in most theory, is here questioned, and the characterization of the international order as a legal system is accordingly held dubious (de Visscher 1953). "Law in the making" would be a more accurate, yet sufficiently optimistic, description of norms operating in a milieu where subjectively determined national interests still enjoy marked priority over collective values. Insofar as sociological refinement of the tools used by decision makers and their advisers would lead to a more enlightened calculus of interests, the need is admitted. The tendency, however, is to look to a revolution in morals, rather than in legal theory, as the necessary condition of an effective world order.

The Soviet approach. The practical value of theory, in the field of international law as elsewhere, may be measured in terms of the light thrown upon paths of potential development. From this point of view, current Soviet theory, taken at its face value, appears full of promise for the legal integration of a world community. It asserts the development, under Soviet leadership, of a new law of nations implementing the central principle of "peaceful coexistence," which is presented as a Soviet invention. This principle, as elaborated in the program of the Communist party of the U.S.S.R., has five premises or components, namely (1) renunciation of war as an instrument of settling differences between states and the substitution of pacific means; (2) equality, understanding, and trust among states, with full consideration of one another's interests; (3) nonintervention in internal affairs and recognition of each people's right to decide for itself all questions concerning it; (4) strict respect for the sovereignty and territorial integrity of all countries; (5) the development of economic and cultural cooperation on the basis of full equality and mutual advantage (Akademiia Nauk 1951, pp. 11–15; Tunkin 1963, pp. 26–37).

If we add to these, as the same program does, the corollary principle of general and complete disarmament "under strict international control" as the efficient way of securing peaceful coexistence, we have before us on paper the outline of a world order that might well satisfy the most devout idealist.

The program is not, however, generally accepted at its face value. In its insistence upon state sovereignty, implemented in practice as this has been by Soviet opposition to every proposal suggestive of world government, it manifests an insuperable inner contradiction. Since, moreover, it is accompanied by the firm declaration of continued class struggle on an international scale, it is regarded in influential Western quarters not as a manifesto of peace but as a covenant of conflict by all means short, at best, of war. Armed violence is indeed by no means excluded, since international continuance of the class struggle is assured by the avowed policy of encouraging "wars of liberation," and this holds out the disturbing prospect of unlimited incitement to rebellion. Yet, despite such skepticism, the slogan of "peaceful coexistence" has had sufficient appeal to add another item to the crowded agenda of the United Nations. The General Assembly's sixth (legal) committee has been given the ambitious task of working out an agreed statement of the "International Law of Peaceful Relations." Unless the aim is merely a declaration of vague general principles, this would seem to call for a total codification of the law of peace, an enterprise already assigned to the International Law Commission.

A common law of mankind?

Recent developments in the theory and practice of international relations have led some observers to the conclusion that international law has entered a stage of transition—from a system governing states as units engaged in increasingly complex interchange to the common law of a world community (Jenks 1958). The theory dominant in the nineteenth century that made states the sole persons or subjects of international law came under attack by eminent publicists after 1918. Their assertion of rights and duties lodged directly in the individual by the international order was substantiated by the joint Allied tribunals, which in 1946 found enemy officials personally responsible for crimes against humanity. The trend continued in the more recent multilateral declarations and conventions designed to secure the international protection of human rights, even between governments and their own nationals. The simultaneous multiplication of international agencies devoted to the promotion of individual welfare throughout the world pointed in the same direction. The economic sphere witnessed a concurrent growth of common national patterns in the regulation of world-wide private business and a broad movement toward the unification of private law to facilitate the interchange of personnel, goods, and services. More and more, law was becoming transnational (Jessup 1948; 1956). Theory and practice alike seemed to be breaking through the hard crust of the state with a practical assertion of the belief that the purpose of social, economic, and political institutions is, after all, not the grandeur of groups but a better life for individual human beings.

Multifarious as these unifying activities have become, however, it is important not to exaggerate their total effect or to underestimate the resistance that still guards the sanctuary of state sovereignty in East and West alike. Given the existing conflict of ideologies and political objectives, any rapid advance to a common law of mankind interpreted by supranational courts and commissions and enforced by supranational agencies is a remote prospect. Not even the fear of imminent nuclear extinction has sufficed to launch the revolution in the ideas and aims of leaders and of peoples that must precede the organization of a universal legal order backed by a monopoly of force.

The development of international law must then in all probability proceed along conventional lines, the resulting norms depending as hitherto upon the good will of governments and their perception of advantage, rather than upon any powerful supranational enforcement agency.

The "progressive development and codification" called for by article 13 of the United Nations Charter is necessarily a slow and arduous enterprise. Yet there are some encouraging proofs of progress, particularly in the law of the sea, diplomatic and consular intercourse, and outer space. Putting the premium they do on sovereignty, Soviet jurists emphasize the state's consent as the necessary basis of rules binding upon it. Because consent is more clearly expressed by participation in treaties than in the obscure and debatable growth of rules by usage, they regard treaties as the one efficient method of developing international law and have begun not merely to express but to prove some interest in codification by multilateral convention. Their position here has, in spite of the suspicious posture of representatives of the U.S.S.R. in the early work of the United Nations International Law Commission, found favor among the newly independent nations, to whom codification offers the opportunity of active participation in the law-making process.

There remains the vital question of submission to international adjudication. No single step could carry us further toward the rule of law on a world scale than the general establishment of compulsory jurisdiction. This must await a marked reduction in that distrust of the West that underlies the Soviet argument that no impartial adjudication is possible between the sharply opposed systems of communism and capitalism. It must also await the withdrawal by certain Western powers of their unlimited reservation of domestic jurisdiction.

PERCY E. CORBETT

BIBLIOGRAPHY

AKADEMIIA NAUK SSSR, INSTITUT GOSUDARSTVA I PRAVA (1951) 1960 *International Law: A Textbook for Use in Law Schools.* Moscow: Foreign Languages Publishing House. → First published as *Mezhdunarodnoe pravo.*

ANZILOTTI, DIONISIO (1923) 1955 *Corso di diritto internazionale.* 4th ed. Padua (Italy): Casa Editrice Dott. Antonio Milani.

AYALA, BALTHAZAR (1582) 1912 *De jure et officiis belliciis et disciplina militari.* 2 vols. Washington: Carnegie Institution of Washington.

BELLI, PIERINO (1563) 1936 *De re militari et bello tractatus.* 2 vols. Oxford: Clarendon.

BRIERLY, JAMES L. (1928) 1963 *The Law of Nations: An Introduction to the International Law of Peace.* 6th ed. Oxford: Clarendon.

FRANCISCO DE VITORIA (1557) 1917 *De Indis et de iure belli relectiones.* Edited by Ernest Nys. Washington: Carnegie Institution of Washington.

GROTIUS, HUGO (1625) 1962 *The Law of War and Peace: De jure belli ac pacis.* Translated by Francis W. Kelsey, with an introduction by James Brown Scott. Indianapolis, Ind.: Bobbs-Merrill.

HART, HERBERT L. A. 1961 *The Concept of Law.* Oxford: Clarendon.

JENKS, C. WILFRED 1958 *The Common Law of Mankind.* New York: Praeger.

JESSUP, PHILIP C. 1948 *A Modern Law of Nations: An Introduction.* New York: Macmillan.

JESSUP, PHILIP C. 1956 *Transnational Law.* New Haven: Yale Univ. Press.

KELSEN, HANS (1945) 1961 *General Theory of Law and State.* New York: Russell.

LAUTERPACHT, HERSCH 1933 *The Function of Law in the International Community.* Oxford: Clarendon.

LISOVSKII, VADIM I. 1961 *Mezhdunarodnoe pravo i IV sessiia general'noi assamblei OON* (International Law and the Fourth Session of the General Assembly of the United Nations). Moscow: Gosudarstvennoe Izdatel'stvo Iuridicheskoi Literatury.

McDOUGAL, MYRES S.; and BURKE, WILLIAM T. 1962 *The Public Order of the Oceans: A Contemporary International Law of the Sea.* New Haven: Yale Univ. Press.

McDOUGAL, MYRES S.; and FELICIANO, FLORENTINO P. 1961 *Law and Minimum World Public Order: The Legal Regulation of International Coercion.* New Haven: Yale Univ. Press.

MOSER, JOHANN J. 1777–1780 *Versuch des neuesten europäischen Völkerrechts im Friedens- und Kriegszeiten.* 10 vols. in 12. Frankfurt-am-Main (Germany): Varrentrapp & Wenner.

NUSSBAUM, ARTHUR (1947) 1954 *A Concise History of the Law of Nations.* Rev. ed. New York: Macmillan.

PUFENDORF, SAMUEL VON (1688) 1934 *De jure naturae et gentium libri octo.* 2 vols. Oxford: Clarendon.

SUÁREZ, FRANCISCO (1612–1621) 1944 *Selections from Three Works of Francisco Suárez. De legibus, ac Deo legislatore, 1612. Defensio fidei catholicae, et apostolicae adversus anglicanae sectae errores, 1613. De triplici virtute theologica, fide, spe, et charitate, 1621.* 2 vols. Oxford: Clarendon.

TUNKIN, G. I. 1963 Printsip mirnogo sosushchestvovaniia: General'naiia liniia vneshnepoliticheskoi deiatel'nosti KPSS i Sovetskogo Gosudarstva (The Principle of Peaceful Coexistence: The General Line of the CPSS and the Soviet Government's Activity). *Sovetskoe gosudarstvo i pravo* 33, no. 7:26–37.

VATTEL, EMER DE (1758) 1916 *Le droit des gens: Ou, principes de la loi naturelle appliqués à la conduite et aux affaires des nations et des souverains.* 3 vols. Washington: Carnegie Institution of Washington.

VISSCHER, CHARLES DE (1953) 1957 *Theory and Reality in Public International Law.* Princeton Univ. Press.

ZOUCHE, RICHARD (1650) 1911 *Iuris et iudicii fecialis, sive, iuris inter gentes, et quaestionum de eodem explicatio, qua quae ad pacem & bellum inter diversos principes . . .* 2 vols. Washington: Carnegie Institution of Washington. → Volume 1 is a reproduction of the first edition. Volume 2 is an English translation.

INTERNATIONAL LEGISLATION

The term "international legislation" is used by writers on international law principally to refer to treaties and conventions which have a large number of parties and which purport to lay down rules of law of general application (Hudson 1931–1950, vol. 1, pp. xiii–xix; McNair 1961, pp. 729–739). The term has also been employed by certain authorities to include treaties which, although adhered to by few states, have established regimes or international settlements that are considered to be "objectively valid," even vis-à-vis states that are not parties to the treaty ("Law of Treaties" 1960, pp. 87–95; McNair 1961, pp. 259, 749–750). Both categories of treaties are also characterized as "law-making treaties," an expression which is often used synonymously with international legislation (McNair 1961, pp. 749–752).

Apart from multilateral treaties, "international legislation" may be appropriately applied to enactments of international organizations which formulate rules of conduct that are legally binding on states under the authority granted by the constituent instruments of the organizations. On occasion, the term "international legislation" has also been extended to include declarations of legal principles which have been adopted by a large number of states in an international organ, such as the General Assembly of the United Nations or a governing body of a specialized agency (Friedmann 1964, pp. 139 ff.).

"International legislation" and its near equivalent, "law-making treaty," are not generally regarded as precise legal terms but rather as convenient designations for instruments which contain legal norms applicable to a large number of states. Some international lawyers object to the use of both expressions on the ground that they suggest a misleading analogy to domestic legislation and create the illusion of a "statute-substitute" in international law (Jennings 1964, p. 388; Fitzmaurice 1958, p. 158). This objection, insofar as it relates to multilateral treaties, rests primarily on the position that treaties, whether or not they prescribe general rules, create obligations only for the parties to the treaty based on their express consent and consequently that it is misleading to treat such treaties, even if they are adhered to by most states, as analogous to domestic legislation. With respect to nontreaty declarations such as those adopted by the General Assembly of the United Nations, the objection to the term "legislation" derives from the premise that the General Assembly has not been granted authority or competence to adopt rules binding on states (save for internal organizational regulations such as procedural and financial rules).

These objections to the use of the expression "international legislation" are essentially semantic; they are largely due to the misleading connotation of the word "legislation" when it is used to describe international instruments which differ in important respects from the normal statutory legislation of national states. The semantic difficulty can be met in some degree by defining "international legislation" so as to make quite clear its special meaning in the international context. However, beyond the semantic question there are more substantial problems regarding the law-making effects of treaties and declarations that cannot be settled simply by definition.

In analyzing these problems of international law-making, international lawyers customarily begin wth the most widely accepted formulation of the "sources" of international law, that found in article 38, paragraph 1 of the Statute of the International Court of Justice to which all members of the United Nations and several nonmember states have adhered. That paragraph declares that:

> The Court, whose function is to decide in accordance with international law such disputes as are submitted to it, shall apply:
> (a) international conventions, whether general or particular, establishing rules expressly recognized by the contesting States;
> (b) international custom, as evidence of a general practice accepted as law;
> (c) the general principles of law recognized by civilized nations;
> (d) subject to the provisions of Article 59, judicial decisions and the teachings of the most highly qualified publicists of the various nations, as subsidiary means for the determination of rules of law.

It will be noted that this article makes no distinction between "law-making" and other treaties; all international conventions, whether general or particular, establishing rules expressly recognized by the contesting states, are to be applied by the court in deciding cases between them. In that sense, all treaties which lay down rules of conduct (whatever their subject matter or number of parties) are "legislative" for the parties. However, there is an evident difference between treaties to which only two or a few states have adhered and which concern questions of exclusive interest to them and those to which a large number of states have adhered (or are expected to do so) and which concern matters of general interest to states as a whole.

In this latter group are found the numerous multilateral conventions concluded under the auspices of the United Nations and its related agencies, such as those dealing with the law of the sea, with diplomatic and consular immunities, with telecommunications, narcotics control, labor standards, civil aviation, suppression of slave traffic, and genocide. The fact that these treaties have or are intended to have a wide application and are designed to serve the common interests of the whole community of states provides the basis for designating them as "legislation" and "law-making." In contrast, the treaties with limited participation and interest are sometimes referred to as treaty-contracts (Starke 1947, pp. 42–43). The distinction between the two categories is not a rigid one, and there are a number of treaties which do not easily fit into one or another of the two categories (for example, the various agreements governing trade in and prices of certain primary commodities).

Nonetheless, the utility of the distinction is generally recognized, even if it may be debated whether "legislation" is an appropriate term to apply. The International Law Commission of the United Nations, an organ composed of eminent jurists representative of various legal systems, suggested in 1962 use of the category "the general multilateral treaty," which the commission has defined as a multilateral treaty to which all or a very large number of states may become parties and which "concerns norms of general international law or deals with matters of general interest to States as a whole" (International Law Commission 1962).

The following discussion will deal, therefore, with those agreements of greater importance in the creation of norms of international law—general multilateral treaties and enactments of international organizations.

General multilateral treaties

Participation and universality. Governments and jurists generally agree that "international legislation" should be universal in application and therefore open in principle to adherence by all national states (International Law Commission 1962). Notwithstanding the agreement on this objective, its implementation has given rise to considerable controversy of a political character as to the principle and procedure for determining what entities are eligible to become parties. The controversies stem principally from the fact that there are sharp divergencies of view among governments on whether certain territorial communities should be regarded as "states"; these differences in their most acute form arise from the East–West conflict and concern especially such areas as East Germany, North Korea, and mainland China (Schwelb 1964, pp. 653–660). In most cases the issue has revolved around proposals that treaties be open to "all states" as against a provision that would define the eligible states as those which are members of the United Nations or one of its specialized agencies or which are invited by the General Assembly (Schwelb 1964, p. 654). The recent practice of the United Nations and of conferences held under its auspices has left it to the General Assembly or a similar political body to decide whether an entity wishing to become a party is a "state" for treaty purposes. Those opposed to this practice contend that it results in discrimination against territorial entities which meet the traditional legal criteria of statehood but which are excluded for political reasons by a number of governments.

It has been suggested by some international lawyers that in the case of a general multilateral treaty every state may become a party to the treaty unless otherwise provided by the treaty itself or by the established rules of an international organization (International Law Commission 1962). Thus, where a general multilateral treaty is silent concerning the states to which it is open, it would be presumed that every state may become a party. However, this rule would not settle the question of who determines whether a doubtful entity (that is, one which many governments do not consider to be a state) is or is not to be considered a state within the meaning of this rule. The secretary-general of the United Nations, who as a rule is the depositary of the general multilateral treaties concluded under the auspices of the United Nations or one of its related agencies, has expressed the view that as depositary he could not decide a controversy as to whether a particular entity (which is not a member of the United Nations or one of its specialized agencies) should be regarded as a state and he would have to refer this question to the General Assembly (United Nations General Assembly 1963, Record of 1258th meeting). Another procedure for dealing with this controversial problem was adopted in the Nuclear Test Ban Treaty of 1963, which provided that three governments—the U.S.S.R., the United Kingdom, and the United States—were depositaries. This enabled governments of territories (such as East Germany), recognized as states by one of the depositaries but not by the others, to accede to the treaty (Schwelb 1964, pp. 654–658).

Effects on nonparties. While the important features of widespread adherence and general interest in the subject matter of general multilateral treaties are often considered as sufficient to designate them as legislation, some authorities place emphasis on a third aspect—namely that some of these multilateral treaties have legal effects for all states whether or not they are parties to them. Obviously, if such treaties can be said to express rules binding on all states, they may then be characterized as "legislative" in a more direct sense than if they applied only to states which had bound themselves contractually. However, the conclusion that some treaties have "objective" legal effects for nonparties is not on its face compatible with the generally accepted principle that a treaty can only create law as between the parties to it (Roxburgh 1917, pp. 19 ff.). International lawyers have therefore considered it necessary to look outside the treaty itself to find a doctrinal basis for the application of treaty provisions to nonparties.

A generally accepted view is that treaty provisions can be considered a law for nonparties if the rules in question have become part of international customary law (International Law Commission 1964, pp. 182–183). Although this conclusion appears to be little more than a tautology—since it only asserts that customary law is law—it has considerable significance, in theory and practice, for the development of international law, reflecting as it does international experience rich in examples of treaties that have been treated as sources of general international law. Such treaties fall into three separate (though often overlapping) categories: first, the treaties which purport to restate and thus codify existing rules of customary law; second, the treaties which lay down new rules of general application of interest to states as a whole; third, the treaties which establish certain specific territorial or institutional arrangements. Each of these categories involves somewhat different considerations relevant to their consequences for all states, but especially for those states which are not parties.

Codifications of customary law. In the case of multilateral conventions which purport to codify existing customary law, the rules will often have a high degree of persuasive authority even before the treaty has received the required number of ratifications for its entry into force. Such authority arises from the fact that the rules in a treaty of this kind will usually have been formulated by a body of experts (such as the International Law Commission) on the basis of state practice and precedent and then adopted at an international conference by at least a two-thirds majority of the states of the world. Even if states fail to commit themselves formally to the treaty, the rules represent so authoritative an expression of existing law that they will probably be invoked and applied by nonparties as well as by parties in the course of events ("Law of Treaties" 1962, p. 83; Lachs 1957, pp. 317–319). Examples of recent codifying treaties which are widely accepted as authoritative formulations of general international law are the 1958 Geneva Conventions on the Régime of the High Seas and on the Continental Shelf, the Vienna Convention of 1961 on Diplomatic Intercourse and Immunities, and the Vienna Convention of 1963 on Consular Intercourse and Immunities.

Prescriptions of new norms. The situation is somewhat different when a multilateral treaty prescribes new general norms; for even if a large number of states have concluded the treaty, the rules in question cannot be regarded as expressing existing law, and therefore only states that have become parties will be bound by them. There is, however, a possibility that with the passage of time states that are not parties will follow the treaty rules in practice and will in due course come to accept them as declaratory of existing law ("Law of Treaties" 1960, pp. 72–107). The most commonly cited example of this phenomenon is the Hague Convention of 1907 on Land Warfare in regard to which the Nuremberg International Military Tribunal in 1945 stated that the rules laid down in the convention constituted "an advance over the then [1907] existing international law" but that by 1939 the rules laid down "were regarded as being declaratory of the laws and customs of war" (International Military Tribunal 1946). In a case of this kind, most international lawyers are careful to avoid stating that it is the treaty itself that creates law for states which are not parties to it and to emphasize that one must look to actual practice of other states to determine whether the rules of the treaty have come to be accepted by states generally as law (International Law Commission 1964, p. 183). In doing so, they seek to maintain the traditional distinction between treaty and custom as sources of international law while recognizing that states may by their conduct manifest acceptance of treaty rules as general law without formal adherence to the treaty. Although this process of "grafting an international custom on to the provisions of a treaty" ("Law of Treaties" 1964, pp. 61–62) involves more uncertainty as to the position of states than it expresses adherence to the treaty, it provides a means for governments to accept new law on the basis of concrete situations without formal commitments, which *in abstracto* may appear unduly restrictive. This consideration may be especially important when parliamentary ratification is required or when domestic political attitudes are involved; the process of tacit acceptance through conduct in such cases might prove a more feasible political means of adhering to the new rules than would ratification or accession.

Territorial and institutional arrangements. A third group of treaties which may have the effect of imposing rules on nonparties are those that establish territorial or institutional arrangements. In the view of some authorities (but not all), such treaties are considered to have created "objective regimes" valid *erga omnes* (Lachs 1957, pp. 313–315; McNair 1961, chapter 14). The treaties within this category include those which provide freedom of navigation of certain international rivers or waterways, treaties for the neutralization or demilitarization of particular territories, and international agreements for mandates or trusteeship of particular territories. Some examples, among many, are the Berlin Act of 1885 (relating to navigation on the Congo and Niger rivers), the Suez Canal Convention of 1888, the Vienna Agreements of 1815 regarding the neutralization of Switzerland, the 1959 Treaty on Antarctica, the Montreux Convention of 1936, and the mandate agreement for South-West Africa. Treaties of cession or boundary are also sometimes included in this category (for example, the Vienna settlement of 1815 relating to the free zones at the frontiers of Switzerland). Of a somewhat different character—because they do not concern a particular territory—are the treaties establishing a general international organization; the principal example is the charter of the United Nations which has been held to have created "an entity possessing objective international personality" and not merely personality recognized by the members (International Court of Justice, p. 185 in the 1949 volume).

While international lawyers generally recognize that treaties of this kind may result in the creation of rights and obligations for third states (i.e., not parties to the treaty), a number reject the principle of "objective regimes," maintaining that the cases in which nonparties are regarded as having obligations and rights in respect to certain territorial or institutional regimes must result either from the development of a customary rule grafted on the treaty or from the assent of the nonparty to the regime established by the treaty (International Law Commission 1964, vol. 2, pp. 181–185). Some who object to the doctrine of objective regimes contend that it arose mainly in connection with the Concert of Europe in the nineteenth century and implies the imposition of a regime by more powerful states on weaker countries without their consent.

In terms of practical application the difference between the two doctrinal views may be of little consequence in many cases, because in regard to a regime which has been maintained for a substantial period of time custom as well as treaty can usually be advanced as the basis for its validity *erga omnes*. In some cases, however, it may be difficult to justify the objective status of the regime on the basis of custom or consent of nonparties. For example, there have been situations in which a nonparty has invoked a treaty establishing a regime of free navigation before it would have been reasonable to speak of any custom (Roxburgh 1917, pp. 49–50), and there have been several cases where international tribunals have indicated that they regarded the treaty rather than custom as the source of the international regime (S.S. "Wimbledon," 1923, P.C.I.J., Series A, No. 1, p. 22; League of Nations . . . 1920, p. 18). Moreover, treaties involving neutralization (such as the 1955 Austrian treaty) are widely regarded as establishing a status *erga omnes* which all states are expected to respect (Lachs 1957, pp. 315–316); a similar position is taken by many in regard to a treaty of demilitarization such as the 1959 Antarctica Treaty.

In point of fact the legal situations created by treaties of this kind tend to receive widespread recognition soon after they have entered into force, so it would seem somewhat artificial to describe their effect on nonparties as the result of custom. Nor can one reasonably say in these cases that nonparties have assented to the regime in question. A more realistic view is that these regimes of neutralization and demilitarization receive general recognition from the time of the treaty largely because a large number of states, including those which are not parties to the treaty, acknowledge the competence of the treaty states to establish the regime in question and consider they have an obligation to refrain from violating its status ("Law of Treaties" 1964). In regard to international waterways, the rights and obligations of third parties may be based on the fact that the territorial state has dedicated the canal to international use and that third parties have relied on such dedication (Baxter 1964, pp. 182–184). Nevertheless, it remains difficult for many governments and jurists to accept the doctrinal principle of objective regimes because of its apparent "legislative" character and its connotation that states may be bound without their clear consent. They find it more acceptable to base the acceptance of such regimes (in cases where custom cannot be implied) on the consent of the third states to the regime (constituting, in effect, a supplementary agreement), a theory which gives effect to the right of a state to regard itself as free of obligations imposed by a treaty which it has not clearly accepted (International Law Commission 1964, vol. 2, pp. 181–184).

The charter of the United Nations requires special mention in this connection. Based on the necessity of maintaining peace on a global basis and not merely among its members, the charter includes among its major principles a paragraph stating that "The Organization shall ensure that states which are not Members of the United Nations act in accordance with these principles so far as may be necessary for the maintenance of international peace and security" (United Nations Charter 1945, art. 2, par. 6). Jurists have expressed divergent views as to whether this provision validly creates legal obligations for nonmembers, and various theories have been suggested as the basis for the extension of certain charter obligations to the nonparties (see for example Kelsen 1950, pp. 90, 109–110; Ross 1950, p. 40; Jessup 1948, p. 168; Guggenheim 1953–1954, vol. 1, p. 92; Falk 1965, pp. 75–76, 100–101). Notwithstanding these theoretical differences, the organs of the United Nations have accepted the validity of article 2, paragraph 6, and have accordingly considered themselves competent to adopt measures involving nonmembers so far as such action was considered necessary for international peace, and at least to that extent it can be said that the obligations of the charter may be regarded as applicable to nonmembers.

Reservations. A significant limitation on the law-making effect of multilateral treaties for the parties themselves arises from the practice of states to make reservations to such treaties. Such reservations normally take the form of declarations made at the time of signature—ratification or accession; a state, while accepting a treaty in general, excludes from its acceptance certain provisions by which it does not wish to be bound (Wilcox 1935, p. 55).

The practice of making reservations to multilateral treaties has increased considerably along with the great increase in the number, variety, and scope of such treaties (Bishop 1961, pp. 253–256). Some jurists have deplored the growing use of reservations on the ground that they tend to impair the integrity of negotiated multilateral agreements and weaken the contribution of treaties to general international law ("Law of Treaties" 1962, p. 83). On the other hand, the right to make reservations has been regarded by many scholars and governments as a positive factor in promoting the participation in treaties by an increased number of states even though such participation may involve less than complete conformity to the treaty (Bishop 1961, pp. 336–338; Schachter 1960).

While these conflicting policy considerations are clear in general terms, the concrete juridical, procedural, and political problems raised by reservations have been highly complex and have given rise to an extensive scholarly literature and a series of varying pronouncements by governments and international bodies.

The principal issue has centered upon the permissibility and effect of a reservation where the treaty in question is silent as to its receivability and the procedure for determining its effect. (Many multilateral treaties have clauses which permit reservations to certain articles; some treaties also stipulate procedures under which a reservation submitted by a state may be accepted.) One school of thought considered that a reservation implies the refusal of the "offer" constituting the treaty and the making of a fresh offer; consequently, the reservation can only be effective if it is accepted by all the parties to the treaty (Oppenheim [1905] 1955, pp. 913–914). This position, often described as the traditional view, resulted in a "unanimity rule" under which an objection to a reservation by even a single party meant that the reserving state could not become a party to the treaty unless it withdrew its reservation (McNair 1961, pp. 158–161).

However, several states have never followed this doctrine, and in 1951 the International Court of Justice in an advisory opinion relating to the Convention on Genocide concluded that the unanimity principle was not a rule of law even though the principle might be applicable in some circumstances (International Court of Justice, pp. 15–30 in the 1951 volume). In the view of the majority of the court, the absence of a treaty clause permitting a reservation does not preclude a state from making a reservation, at least with respect to a general humanitarian treaty such as that on genocide. A state making a reservation that has been objected to by one or more parties to the convention but not by others can nonetheless be regarded as a party to the convention "if the reservation is compatible with the object and purpose of the Convention" (p. 29). The court went on to say that in such circumstances the reserving state would not be a party vis-à-vis a state which objected to the reservation. The position taken by the majority of the court in regard to the Convention on Genocide conformed to the practice followed for many years in Latin American treaty relations (Inter-American Council of Jurists . . . 1959, pp. 29–30). Subsequently, discussions in the General Assembly of the United Nations revealed widespread approval of this practice among governments from various parts of the world.

The attitude of most states did not go as far as to countenance an unlimited unilateral right to make any kind of reservation whatsoever; it was generally maintained—in keeping with the opinion of the International Court—that a reservation would have to be consistent with the essential object and purpose of the treaty. However, for most multilateral treaties the determination of the acceptability of the reservation was to be left to each state concerned, and the acceptance of a reservation by a party to the treaty would mean that the reserving state becomes a party to the treaty in relation to the accepting state. On the other hand, a state which considers the reservation to be incompatible with the object and purpose of the treaty may object to it and in doing so would prevent the treaty from coming into force between it and the reserving state, irrespective of what other states may do.

These principles were adopted by the International Law Commission in its reports on the law of treaties in 1962 and 1966, and it seems safe to predict that they will be followed in state practice relating to many general multilateral treaties. The commission, however, did specify certain exceptions. One such exception holds that in case of a treaty which is a constituent instrument of an international organization the effect of a reservation to which objection has been made is to be determined by decision of the competent organ of the organization unless the treaty itself provides otherwise (International Law Commission 1962). Another exception relates to a treaty concluded between a limited group of states; in that case the acceptance of all the parties is required if it appears from the purpose of the treaty that the application of the treaty in its entirety between all the parties is an essential condition of the consent of each one to be bound by the treaty (International Law Commission 1966, art. 17 of Draft Articles on the Law of Treaties).

Termination and denunciation. Many general multilateral treaties contain provisions for termination—for example, by fixing their duration, stating a condition which is to bring about termination, or providing for a right to denounce or withdraw from the treaty ("Law of Treaties" 1957, p. 45). The texts of several law-making treaties provide for termination when the number of parties falls below a specified minimum.

It is not unusual, however, for general multilateral treaties to lack any provision regarding termination or denunciation (recent examples are the charter of the United Nations, the four Geneva conventions on the law of the sea and the two Vienna conventions on diplomatic relations and on consular relations). In these cases, it is often a matter of controversy whether the treaty is terminable only by common agreement of the parties or whether individual parties have an implied right to denounce or withdraw in certain circumstances. Most authorities take the position that, in general, an individual party may denounce or withdraw from a treaty only if the treaty provides for such denunciation or withdrawal or if it is otherwise established that the parties intended to admit the possibility of denunciation or withdrawal (International Law Commission 1966). Thus a right of denunciation or withdrawal may be inferred under certain conditions from the treaty as a whole or from the character of the treaty. It has been suggested that in the case of treaties of alliance and commercial treaties there is usually a probability that the parties do not intend commitments binding for all time ("Law of Treaties" 1957, pp. 38–39; McNair 1961, pp. 501–505). On the other hand, with regard to a law-making treaty there may be a presumption that the parties intended to exclude a unilateral right of termination or withdrawal without agreement of the other parties when the treaty is silent on this point. Thus the character of the treaty would be relevant in deciding whether it meant to imply a unilateral right of denunciation or withdrawal, and there is no reason to exclude other elements which may throw light on the intention of the parties, such as the *travaux préparatoires* of the treaty and the subsequent conduct of the parties (International Law Commission 1962).

When a party has violated the treaty in a serious or "material" respect, it is generally agreed that the other parties may terminate or suspend the performance of their obligations ("Law of Treaties" 1935, pp. 1081–1083). Some authorities have questioned whether the right of suspension should be admissible in the case of law-making treaties; on the other hand it appears inequitable to many that a state which has breached its treaty obligations should be allowed to enforce it against the injured party. Consequently, most authorities would grant to a state affected by the breach the right to suspend the treaty in whole or in part as between itself and the state guilty of the violation. If the breach by one state radically changes the position of all the parties with respect to further performance of their obligations, the others would be entitled to terminate or suspend the treaty (International Law Commission 1962; 1966).

Many authorities hold that the right to terminate a treaty or to withdraw from it may also be exercised under the principle of *rebus sic stantibus*, according to which a treaty may cease to be binding where a fundamental change of circumstances has occurred with regard to a fact or situation that existed at the time the treaty was entered into (Oppenheim [1905] 1955, pp. 938–944; McNair 1961, pp. 681–691; "Law of Treaties" 1935, pp. 1096–1126). While there are doubts as to how far this principle can be regarded as an accepted rule of international law and as to its effect on the security of treaties, it is widely felt that the principle is necessary to give a party to a treaty relief from outmoded and burdensome provisions (International Law Commission 1963). Moreover, there is considerable evidence that the principle is widely accepted in international law (Rousseau 1953, pp. 59–61; "Law of Treaties" 1957, pp. 56–60).

In formulating the doctrine of changed circumstances, international lawyers often lay stress on the requirement that changes of circumstances can be invoked as a ground for terminating the treaty only if their effect is to alter a fact or situation that constitutes an essential basis of the consent of the parties. It is commonly said that the change must be a fundamental one, the effect of which is to transform in an important respect the scope of the obligations undertaken in the treaty. Whether or not these broadly stated limitations would be effective in preventing arbitrary reliance on *rebus sic stantibus* depends largely on whether procedures are available and are used for determinations by the other parties to the treaty (or by arbitral or judicial tribunals) as to the validity of the attempted termination and the measures that might be taken if the termination is found to be invalid.

Enactments of international organizations

Although the term "international legislation" is mainly applied to multilateral treaties, it may also be used appropriately to include those rules and declarations of international organizations which are binding on states or other entities subject to the authority of the organization. Such enactments comprise two broad categories: (1) rules and regulations dealing with the structure, procedure, and functions of the organization; and (2) rules which impose obligations on or confer rights to states.

The first category, often referred to as "internal law," typically includes rules of procedure, financial rules, regulations governing personnel, terms of reference of organs, and regulations applicable to administration of premises. Authority to issue such rules is often stipulated in the constitutional instrument of the organization; in the absence of such express authorization, the competence to issue such internal rules is regarded as an inherent power or as implied by the constitutional authority (Jessup 1956, pp. 185–319; Cahier 1963).

The second category which comprises enactments binding on states derives from authority granted in the constituent instrument of the organization or in a separate treaty conferring such legislative authority on the international body. In several organizations, unanimous approval of the members is required for the rules to be binding, as for example in the Central Commission for the Navigation of the Rhine and the Organization for Economic Cooperation and Development (OECD). Some international organizations are authorized to enact regulations by majority decisions, but the dissenting states are not bound if they reject the regulation or make reservations; this is referred to as a "contracting-out" procedure. Examples include the "annexes" adopted by the International Civil Aviation Organization, the International Sanitary Regulations adopted by the World Health Assembly, and rules on meteorology adopted by the World Meteorological Congress. The organs of the three European communities—common market, coal and steel, and atomic energy—are empowered to adopt, in some cases by majority decision, rules unconditionally binding on all member states whether or not they dissent (Pescatore 1958, pp. 51 ff.). In some circumstances these international enactments are given effect in the municipal legal systems and are directly binding on individuals (Stein 1965).

Finally, mention should be made of certain declarations of legal principles which have been adopted by the General Assembly of the United Nations; examples are the Declaration of Legal Principles Governing the Activities of States in the Use and Exploration of Outer Space (United Nations, *Yearbook* for 1963, p. 101), the Declaration on the Granting of Independence to Colonial Countries and Peoples (United Nations, *Yearbook* for 1960, pp. 49–50), and the Declaration of Principles on Permanent Sovereignty Over Natural Wealth and Resources (United Nations, *Yearbook* for 1962, pp. 503–504). These declarations are to be distinguished from those declarations (such as the Universal Declaration of Human Rights) which are expressed as standards for achievement and are clearly no more than recommendations.

Whether the declarations that purport to state principles of law (*lex lata*) should be considered obligatory per se (in the technical sense a "source of law") or as evidence of legal rules or as recommendations has given rise to varying views among scholars and governments. A widely held view is that since the General Assembly lacks competence under the charter to adopt binding rules of conduct for states (except, as indicated above, in regard to internal procedures and administration), the declarations—whatever their wording—must in law be treated as recommendatory (Johnson 1955–1956). On the other hand, a number of authorities have maintained that the declarations adopted by almost all the states of the world containing legal principles accepted by them will generally be regarded as authoritative or at least as highly persuasive evidence that the principles in question will be applied as "law" (Friedmann 1964, pp. 139–141; Schachter 1964, pp. 95–98).

In some cases, as for example the declarations relating to activities in outer space and to sovereignty over natural resources, the principles set forth can be viewed as formulations of general international law; in other instances, as for example the declaration on independence of colonial territories, they may be considered as embodying an authentic interpretation of the charter adopted by its parties (Schachter 1963, pp. 186–188). Some writers place emphasis on the condition that the declarations should reflect general or even unanimous support in order to be treated as authoritative law (Lachs 1961). Yet even a unanimous declaration of legal principles may prove to be honored only in the breach and to be no more than a "dead-letter" rule. Realistically, therefore, the test of whether a given declaration has legislative effect can only be found in the future behavior of governments as shown by their practice and claims.

It may be possible, however, to characterize a declaration at the time of its adoption as an authoritative statement of law on the basis of various factors—in particular if it has received general support of governments (including all major groupings) and if the principles conform to prior authoritative precedents or are adopted in circumstances which indicate that governments are likely to observe them as obligatory rules. There is, in short, no single conceptual touchstone for determining the future legal effect of a declaration adopted by the General Assembly but, in view of the likelihood that some such declarations will be regarded as highly persuasive evidence of the legal rules they embody, it is not inappropriate to include them within the broad spectrum of international legislation.

OSCAR SCHACHTER

[*See also* ADJUDICATION, *article on* INTERNATIONAL ADJUDICATION; INTERNATIONAL LAW. *Other relevant material may be found under* INTERNATIONAL ORGANIZATION; LAW; LEGISLATION.]

BIBLIOGRAPHY

BAXTER, RICHARD R. 1964 *The Law of International Waterways, With Particular Regard to Interoceanic Canals.* Cambridge, Mass.: Harvard Univ. Press.

BISHOP, WILLIAM W. 1961 Reservations to Treaties. The Hague, Academy of International Law, *Recueil des cours* 103:245–341.

CAHIER, PHILIPPE 1963 Le droit interne des organisations internationales. *Revue générale de droit international public* 67:563–602.

FALK, RICHARD A. 1965 *The Authority of the United Nations Over Non-members.* Princeton University, Center of International Studies, Research Monograph No. 18. Princeton Univ., Woodrow Wilson School of Public and International Affairs.

FITZMAURICE, GERALD G. 1958 Some Problems Regarding the Formal Sources of International Law. Pages 153–176 in *Symbolae Verzijl: Présentées au professeur J. H. W. Verzijl . . .* The Hague: Nijhoff.

FRIEDMANN, WOLFGANG G. 1964 *The Changing Structure of International Law.* New York: Columbia Univ. Press.

GUGGENHEIM, PAUL 1953–1954 *Traité de droit international public: Avec mention de la pratique internationale et suisse.* 2 vols. Geneva: Georg.

HIGGINS, ROSALYN 1963 *The Development of International Law Through the Political Organs of the United Nations.* London: Oxford Univ. Press.

HUDSON, MANLEY O. (editor) 1931–1950 *International Legislation: A Collection of the Texts of Multipartite International Instruments of General Interest Beginning With the Covenant of the League of Nations.* 9 vols. Washington: Carnegie Endowment for International Peace.

INTER-AMERICAN COUNCIL OF JURISTS, FOURTH MEETING, SANTIAGO, CHILE, *1959* 1959 *Final Act.* Washington: Organization of American States, General Secretariat; Pan American Union.

INTERNATIONAL COURT OF JUSTICE, THE HAGUE *Reports of Judgments, Advisory Opinions and Orders.* Leiden (Netherlands): Sijthoff. → Published since 1947. See especially the 1949 and 1951 volumes.

INTERNATIONAL LAW COMMISSION 1962 Report of the Commission to the General Assembly on Its Fourteenth Session. United Nations, International Law Commission, *Yearbook* 2:157–195.

INTERNATIONAL LAW COMMISSION 1963 Report of the Commission to the General Assembly on Its Fifteenth Session. United Nations, International Law Commission, *Yearbook* 2:187–300.

INTERNATIONAL LAW COMMISSION 1964 Report of the Commission to the General Assembly on Its Sixteenth Session. United Nations, International Law Commission, *Yearbook* 2:173–227.

INTERNATIONAL LAW COMMISSION 1966 Report of the Commission to the General Assembly on Its Eighteenth Session. United Nations, International Law Commission, *Yearbook* 2.

INTERNATIONAL MILITARY TRIBUNAL 1946 *Jugement rendu par le Tribunal Militaire International au cours de ses audiences tenues les 30 septembre et 1er octobre 1946 dans le procès des grands criminels de guerre.* Paris: Imprimeries des Journaux Officiels.

JENNINGS, R. Y. 1964 Recent Developments in the International Law Commission: Its Relation to the Sources of International Law. *International and Comparative Law Quarterly* 13:385–397.

JESSUP, PHILIP C. 1948 *A Modern Law of Nations: An Introduction.* New York: Macmillan.

JESSUP, PHILIP C. 1956 Parliamentary Diplomacy: An Examination of the Legal Quality of the Rules of Procedure of Organs of the United Nations. The Hague, Academy of International Law, *Recueil des cours* 89:181–320.

JOHNSON, D. H. 1955–1956 The Effect of Resolutions of the General Assembly of the United Nations. *British Year Book of International Law* 32:97–122.

KELSEN, HANS (1950) 1951 *The Law of the United Nations: A Critical Analysis of Its Fundamental Problems.* With Supplement. London: Stevens; New York: Praeger.

LACHS, MANFRED 1957 Le développement et les fonctions des traités multilatéraux. The Hague, Academy of International Law, *Recueil des cours* 92:229–341.

LACHS, MANFRED 1961 The Law in and of the United Nations: Some Reflections on the Principle of Self-determination. *Indian Journal of International Law* 1:429–442.

Law of Treaties. 1935 *American Journal of International Law* 29 (Supplement):653–1226.

Law of Treaties. 1957 United Nations, International Law Commission, *Yearbook* [1957], 2:16–70. → Second Report, by Sir Gerald Fitzmaurice.

Law of Treaties. 1960 United Nations, International Law Commission, *Yearbook* [1960], 2:69–107. → Fifth Report, by Sir Gerald Fitzmaurice.

Law of Treaties. 1962 United Nations, International Law Commission, *Yearbook* [1962], 2:27–83. → First Report, by Sir Humphrey Waldock.

Law of Treaties. 1964 United Nations, International Law Commission, *Yearbook* [1964], 2:5–65. → Third Report, by Sir Humphrey Waldock.

LEAGUE OF NATIONS, INTERNATIONAL COMMITTEE OF JURISTS 1920 Aaland Islands Question. League of Nations, *Official Journal* Special Supplement no. 3.

McDOUGAL, MYRES S.; LASSWELL, HAROLD D.; and VLASIO, IVAN A. 1963 *Law and Public Order in Space.* New Haven, Conn.: Yale Univ. Press.

McNair, Arnold D. 1961 *The Law of Treaties.* Oxford: Clarendon.

Oppenheim, Lassa F. L. (1905) 1955 *International Law: A Treatise.* 8th ed., Volume 1: Peace. London and New York: Longmans.

Pescatore, Pierre 1958 Les aspects fonctionnels de la Communauté Économique Européenne, notamment les sources du droit. Pages 51–73 in Commission Droit et Vie des Affaires, *Les aspects juridiques du marché commun.* Liège (Belgium), Université de, Faculté de Droit.

Rosenne, Shabtai 1955 United Nations Treaty Practice. The Hague, Academy of International Law, *Recueil des cours* 86:275–444.

Ross, Alf 1950 *Constitution of the United Nations: Analysis of Structure and Function.* New York: Holt.

Rousseau, Charles E. (1953) 1965 *Droit international public.* 3d ed. Paris: Dalloz.

Roxburgh, Ronald F. 1917 *International Conventions and Third States: A Monograph.* London and New York: Longmans.

Schachter, Oscar 1960 Editorial Comment: The Question of Treaty Reservations at the 1959 General Assembly. *American Journal of International Law* 54:372–379.

Schachter, Oscar 1963 The Relations of Law, Politics and Action in the United Nations. The Hague, Academy of International Law, *Recueil des cours* 109:165–256.

Schachter, Oscar 1964 The Prospects for a Regime in Outer Space and International Organization. Pages 95–102 in McGill Conference on the Law of Outer Space, First, Montreal, 1963, *Law and Politics in Space.* Edited by Maxwell Cohen. Montreal: McGill Univ. Press.

Schwelb, Egon 1964 The Nuclear Test Ban Treaty and International Law. *American Journal of International Law* 58:642–670.

Skubiszewski, Krzysztof 1964 Forms of Participation of International Organizations in the Lawmaking Processes. *International Organization* 18:790–805.

Starke, Joseph G. (1947) 1963 *An Introduction to International Law.* 5th ed. London: Butterworth.

Stein, Eric 1965 Toward Supremacy of Treaty-constitution by Judicial Fiat: On the Margin of the *Costa* Case. *Michigan Law Review* 63:491–518.

United Nations Charter 1945 *Charter of the United Nations and Statute of the International Court of Justice.* New York: United Nations.

United Nations *Yearbook.* → Published since 1946/1947. See especially the 1960, 1962, and 1963 volumes.

Wilcox, Francis O. 1935 *The Ratification of International Conventions: A Study of the Relationship of the Ratification Process to the Development of International Legislation.* London: Allen & Unwin.